F. ☑ **W9-COU-325**

(H) 215-6780434

STRATEGIC MANAGEMENT

**Text and Cases on
Business Policy**

LaRue T. Hosmer
University of Michigan

STRATEGIC MANAGEMENT

Text and Cases on Business Policy

Prentice-Hall, Inc., Englewood Cliffs, New Jersey 07632

Library of Congress Cataloging in Publication Data

HOSMER, LARUE T.
   Strategic management.

     1. Industrial management.   2. Industrial management—
Case studies. I. Title.
HD31.H6537   658   81-8830
ISBN 0-13-851063-6   AACR2

Printed in the United States of America
10 9 8 7 6 5 4

ISBN 0-13-851063-6

Prentice-Hall International, Inc., *London*
Prentice-Hall of Australia Pty. Limited, *Sydney*
Prentice-Hall of Canada, Ltd., *Toronto*
Prentice-Hall of India Private Limited, *New Delhi*
Prentice-Hall of Japan, Inc., *Tokyo*
Prentice-Hall of Southeast Asia Pte. Ltd., *Singapore*
Whitehall Books Limited, *Wellington, New Zealand*

CONTENTS

PREFACE

Business policy, as taught at most graduate schools and many undergraduate programs, is a very broad topic. It starts with the selection of an overall direction or strategy for the firm, chosen relative to the environmental trends, organizational resources, and managerial values; it continues with the integration of the functional and technical areas of marketing, production, finance, information technology, and organizational development into that direction or strategy; and it concludes with the development of the hierarchical structure and the design of the managerial systems to implement that direction or strategy. Industry analysis, market analysis, trend analysis, ratio analysis, and resource evaluation are needed just for strategy formulation, and a knowledge of organizational structures and information systems, planning systems, control systems, and motivation systems, together with an understanding of leadership styles and communication methods, are required for strategy implementation. The topic may have become too broad for existing methods of instruction.

Business policy courses, also as taught at most graduate schools and many undergraduate programs, seem popular with the students. They appear to like the last-term opportunity to apply prior learning to complex problems; they appear to like the practical aspects of case instructions; they even appear to like, despite frequent complaints, the heavy work load that is traditional in the policy area. I am not certain that instructors in many business policy courses are equally pleased with the outcome. As the subject matter has broadened, from strategy as a general concept of goals and objectives to strategy as a specific process for planning at the functional, divisional, and corporate levels, and as the orientation has shifted from primary emphasis on formulation to equal emphasis on formulation and implementation, the traditional reliance upon unstructured case analysis has seemed less satisfactory. It is difficult to cover all of the topics that are subsumed in the phrase "duties and responsibilities of the general manager," which many of us use to describe the contents of business policy classes, without adding more course structure, more explanatory text, and more focused cases. That is the reason for this book: to provide the structure, text, and cases needed for the broader range of concepts in modern business policy courses. There are eight elements in this approach to a modern business policy course that I should like to discuss with potential participants, both instructors and students:

1. *Formal structure.* The book is divided into fourteen sections, and the intent is that each section should add a further level of complexity, and understanding, to the strategic planning process. There is a formal progression from an introduction to the concept of strategy as the long-term method of competition for a business firm through the process of strategy formulation at different types of business organizations (smaller companies, product divisions of larger firms, single-industry corporations, and multiple-industry conglomerates), and then to the application of strategy as a long-term concept of performance to nonprofit and public institutions.

   The second half of the book also follows a formal structure, from the need for strategy implementation to the design of the organizational structure and managerial systems as the means of that implementation, and finally to the problems that can be encountered in planning techniques, leadership styles, and communication methods in attempting to link the formulation and implementation processes. The intent is to provide an integrated description of the general management task.

2. *Explicit text.* The text introducing each of the sections in the book is short, but hopefully explicit. There are definitions of the numerous concepts required in strategy formulation and implementation, and graphic illustrations of the relationships among those concepts. The intent is that students can use the concepts in class discussions, with a clear understanding of the terms, and they can apply the concepts in case analysis, with a basic knowledge of the methods. My experience has been that an explicit introductory text greatly helps the learning process since the class discussion is more naturally focused, and needs less external direction by the instructor.

3. *Graduated cases.* The cases included in each section of the book increase in the expected level of difficulty, and vary in the anticipated direction of discussion. The first case in each series is termed "introductory" in the table of contents, but a more apt term would probably be "instructional"; it is designed to show the application of the concepts described in the text, and to illustrate some of the problems of that application. The second case in each series is termed "discussion"; it is designed to generate class discussions on the limits of the approach, and the assumptions of the theory. The last case is termed "complex," and hopefully it is exactly what the name implies: a difficult problem in general management with no obvious answers or easy solutions. All cases in the book have been written to sustain a class discussion easily, with multiple problems that extend throughout the organization. All cases in the book have been derived from actual situations at existing firms; some of the cases have been disguised, at the request of the managers or owners, but none have been fabricated.

4. *Diversified examples.* The cases in each series, used as examples for the application of the theoretical concepts in strategy formulation and implementation, have been drawn from a diversified list of industries, and include both manufacturing and service firms. The intent here has been to bring business policy away from its traditional manufacturing orientation, and to look at a wide range of general management situations in the types of companies that employ so many of the graduates of our programs in business administration: accounting firms, brokerage houses, banks, railroads, trucking companies, consumer products, basic industries, nonprofit institutions, and governmental agencies. My experience has been that the diverse types of firms generate student interest, and reduce the need for continued pressure for preparation by the instructor.

5. *Implementation and formulation.* The book has been divided into seven sections on strategy formulation, four sections on strategy implementation, and the remainder on general or introductory topics. Strategy implementation, of course, refers to the definition of the various tasks required by the selected strategy of the firm, and to the design of the organizational structure and the managerial systems needed to coordinate and integrate the performance of those tasks. The intent has been to create a *balanced emphasis* between formulation and implementation. My belief is that the implementation portion of business policy will become increasingly important in future years, with growing recognition that the "strategy + structure = performance" equation is the distinctive province of our area.

   This strategy and structure continuum has been stressed in the book, with the inclusion of *sequential* or *follow-up cases* that require students to design the structure and systems for companies that have previously been studied in the formulation sections. These sequential cases can be short, since information about the company and the industry has been conveyed previously, but they also can be very instructive, as students will select different structures and systems depending upon their original choice for the strategy.

6. *Ethical content.* Short cases have been included in nearly each section of the book to illustrate problems in managerial ethics and social responsibility. These can be used at the option of the instructor as an adjunct to the regular class assignments. My opinion is that some discussion of managerial ethics and corporate responsibilities is essential in every program in business administration. My experience is that these short cases provide a lively discussion for 10 to 15 minutes at the end of a class session, and provide a meaningful method for including these important topics in the program curriculum.

7. *Focused conclusion.* The book is designed to conclude with the selection of a major case from the section on Strategic Management and Leadership; these cases combine the prior learning, and require a change in the corporate strategy, and a redesign of the organizational structure and managerial systems, to effect a change in the overall performance of the organization. In addition, these cases hopefully demonstrate that objective analysis alone is not sufficient, and that the general manager must add more subjective decisions on action timing, personnel selection, and leadership methods.

8. *Improved communication.* Finally, the book includes a section on the importance of communication in the general management process, and suggestions for the im-

provement of written and oral reports. My experience has been that these suggestions definitely improve the quality of student reports.

9. *Teaching guide.* The teaching guide will be complete. I think that all of us who teach by the case method have experienced the frustrations and trials of attempting to use new cases without adequate assistance or instructional guidance from the author. Obviously, we can all do the required analysis, but I feel that it is critical for the writer to explain the pedagogical objectives of each case, to suggest alternative assignments (especially for group reports that can enrich the class discussion), to detail the expected course of the class discussion, to complete the quantitative analysis, to prepare the pro forma statements, and to explain the final outcome. This material will be available to faculty members who select the book for use in a policy course.

I should like to conclude with the acknowledgment that, while my intent has been to provide a book with a structure, text, and cases adapted to the broader range of concepts in modern business policy courses, many of the ideas are not my own. I have benefited from my associations with colleagues such as William Hall, James Reece, Brian Talbot, C. K. Prahalad, Cynthia Montgomery, and Aneel Karnani at the University of Michigan, and with friends such as Steven Brandt, Henry Riggs, and Kirk Hanson at Stanford University, where I spent a very pleasant year on a visiting appointment. I thank them all.

LaRue T. Hosmer

STRATEGIC MANAGEMENT

**Text and Cases on
Business Policy**

Chapter 1

INTRODUCTION TO STRATEGIC MANAGEMENT

Strategic management is concerned with the definition of the major goals and objectives for an organization, and the design of the functional policies and plans and the organizational structure and systems to achieve those goals and objectives, all in response to changing environmental conditions, institutional resources, and individual motives and values. It is the study generally of leadership in business organizations, and specifically of the functions and responsibilities of the general manager of the firm, whose task is to combine and direct the efforts and activities of the other members of the company toward the successful completion of a stated mission or purpose.

Strategy may be considered either as the present product–market–process position of the company, or as the future growth plans for the firm, but the most meaningful definition is probably the method of competition to be followed by the business. There are different methods of competition (alternative strategies) that are possible within each industry, and the function of strategic management is to first select the method (strategy formulation) with the greatest probability of success, given the specific opportunities and risks within the environment and the specific strengths and weaknesses within the corporation, and then to coordinate the efforts and activities of the functional and technical specialists necessary to carry out this method of competition (strategy implementation) through explicit statements of the corporate objectives, policies, programs, and plans, and through consistent design of the organizational structure and systems. Strategy formulation and implementation are both required in strategic management; the first portion, formulation, can be presented in outline format as shown on the top of the next page.

The selected strategy, or method of competition chosen for the business, is then expressed through explicit statements about the goals, policies, programs, and actions for each of the functional areas of marketing management, market research, production management, financial management, product development, informa-

1

Environmental characteristics
and trends

Economic

Technological

Social/political

Competitive

Organizational mission or charter	Specific opportunities and risks within the industry	
		Selected strategy, or method of com- petition
Corporate perform- ance and position	Range of strategic alternatives open to the firm	
↑	↑	
Managerial values and attitudes	Specific strengths and weak- nesses within the company	

↑

Money

Equipment

People

Market position

Organizational resources, or
assets and skills

---

tion services, and personnel services. These functional objectives, policies, programs, and actions define the tasks or jobs that are essential for strategic success,
and the organizational structure and systems are then designed to coordinate and
assist in the performance of these tasks. This view of strategic implementation can
also be expressed in outline form, as shown at the top of page 3.

Strategic management cannot, in practice, be separated into the twin halves of
formulation and implementation since the selected method of competition, or formulated strategy, can only be expressed in terms of the implementing objectives,
policies, programs, and actions and since the strategic alternatives can only be considered in terms of the information provided and the performance recorded by the
existing structure and systems. Strategic management is not a divided process; it is
the simultaneous consideration of the formulation and implementation of strategy,
and this consideration is essential for the success of the company due to the continual process of change in the environment and in the organization which must be
reflected in the method of competition for the firm.

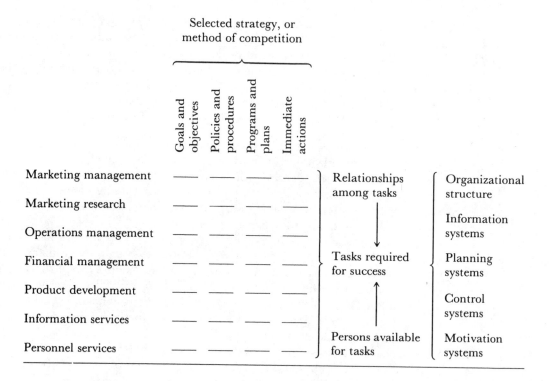

Selected strategy, or method of competition

	Goals and objectives	Policies and procedures	Programs and plans	Immediate actions		
Marketing management	—	—	—	—	Relationships among tasks	Organizational structure
Marketing research	—	—	—	—		
Operations management	—	—	—	—		Information systems
Financial management	—	—	—	—	Tasks required for success	Planning systems
Product development	—	—	—	—		Control systems
Information services	—	—	—	—		
Personnel services	—	—	—	—	Persons available for tasks	Motivation systems

Strategic management, then, consists of the simultaneous and continual formulation and implementation of the method of competition for a business firm; it coordinates the marketing, production, finance, and product development functions of the company, and directs this coordinated effort toward the achievement of specific goals and objectives, the establishment of a defined product–market–process position, and the development of a planned program of growth and change. Strategic management, in short, plans the long-term competitive posture of the firm, and designs the general character of the organization. It answers two essential questions: "What sort of business are we in?" and "What sort of company should we have?"

Organizational Mission or Charter. The first step in strategy formulation is to examine the organizational mission or charter which provides a very general statement of the philosophy of the firm and the direction of its efforts. This statement, which may be an explicit and written listing of corporate goals and products (charter), or an implicit and nebulous understanding of managerial intentions (mission), usually serves to establish the basic purpose of the organization and to indicate the general product–market–process position of the firm. The product–market–process description, which combines the product characteristics, the customer needs, the market segments, the marketing methods, and the production process, summarizes the line of business that the company is pursuing, and specifies the common linkage that unites all the company's products or services. As a combined statement of the purpose and position of the company, the organizational mission or charter sets, to some extent, the boundaries of the business, and limits the possible alternatives to be considered in designing the strategy, or method of competition, for the firm; it is a statement that is important for strategic planning since it provides a base for the course and character of the company that is known to all the management of the organization. In reviewing, revising, or preparing a statement of this nature, there are three basic considerations for the general manager of the firm:

1. Profit maximization is not an adequate description of the purpose of most business firms. As organizations of individuals, companies usually have multiple corporate objectives that express individual and social as well as economic concerns; a corporate charter should recognize these concerns and include such factors as sales growth, investment return, market share, employment stability, professional reputation, and personal opportunity.
2. Existing products are not an adequate description of the position of most business firms. As organizations of functions, companies usually have marketing, manufacturing, and engineering responsibilities that extend beyond the simple provision of a product line; a corporate charter should recognize these activities, and include such factors as customer needs, buyer behavior, market segments, pricing levels, distribution channels, promotional methods, production processes, and product development.
3. Written charters are poorly expressed at many business firms since they are often prepared to be innocuous and general, with a statement of the objectives of the firm that is too idealistic to be useful, and a description of the business of the corporation that is too broad to be understandable. The written charter of a firm should provide multiple corporate objectives, with some sense of the priority among those objectives, and should describe the products, markets, and processes, with some level of detail, in order to define the goals and activities of the firm. A written charter of this nature, combining explicit statements of the purpose and position of the firm, is difficult to prepare, but exceedingly valuable for long-range planning and strategic management.

Managerial Values and Attitudes. The second step in strategic management is to consider the values and attitudes of the managerial personnel whose participation and cooperation is essential for the success of the firm. Individuals make up organizations, and each individual has a set of ambitions, beliefs, and moral standards that is at least partially unique; it is important for the general manager to understand these personal aspirations and individual attitudes toward risk, reward, and social responsibility by the members of the firm since this understanding provides another version of the purpose of the organization, which can then be compared to the existing mission or charter. Discrepancies between the mission or charter of the firm and the values and attitudes of the executives should be resolved by the general manager as a condition for effective strategic planning since there needs to be a considerable area of agreement upon the purpose of the organization for effective operations.

1. The recognition of individual values and attitudes is not an exact science, with established methods for quantitative measurement; instead, it is an indefinite area where reliance has to be placed upon some degree of managerial empathy and personal understanding.
2. The resolution of conflicting values and attitudes is not a simple task, with all individuals and groups acting on the basis of economic rationality; instead, it is an illogical area where reliance again has to be placed upon some degree of managerial patience and personal effort. The resolution of conflicts between individual ambitions, group goals, and the organizational mission or purpose is difficult, but exceedingly useful for long-range planning and strategic management.

Corporate Performance and Position. The last of the three preliminary steps in strategy formulation is the review of the past performance and the present position of the firm, and the comparison of this performance and position with the mission or charter of the organization and the ambitions and goals of the management. Discrepancies, of course, would indicate the need for change; this change could be either in the purpose of the organization and the goals of the executives, or in the strategy, or method of competition of the business, which eventually would lead to a change in the performance and position of the firm. The examination of the past performance and present position of the firm indicates how well the company is doing relative to the mission and goals established for it; this examination should consider all the major functional areas:

1. *Marketing.* The examination of the performance and position of the marketing function of the firm should consider the market share and the industry position of the major products of the company, and the recent trends in these standings.
2. *Operations.* The examination of the performance and position of the production function of the firm should consider the cost per unit, relative to estimated industry costs, and the productive capacity in units for the major products of the company, and the recent trends in these figures.
3. *Development.* The examination of the performance and position of the research and development function of the firm should consider the percentage of successful products, together with some measure of that success and some estimate of the costs of that development, and the recent trends in these statistics.
4. *Finance.* The financial position summarizes, to a very considerable extent, the past performance of the marketing, production, and development functions of the firm, and also facilitates the comparison, in very explicit quantitative terms, of the performance and position of the company with the mission of the organization and the ambitions of the members, so that this examination should include liquidity ratios (current ratio and acid test), profitability ratios (return on sales and return on assets), utilization ratios (receivable turnover and inventory turnover, both in days), debt ratios (total debt to net worth, and number of times debt interest or total debt payments are earned), and equity ratios (price/earnings ratio and dividend yield), together with recent trends in these financial ratios. The examination of the financial functions should also include cash flow

analysis to indicate the source and application of funds over the past time periods, and the preparation of pro forma balance sheets and income statements to indicate the expected position of the company in future time periods.

Environmental Characteristics and Trends. The first of the major steps in strategy formulation is the examination of the organizational environment in order to identify the opportunities and risks for the strategy of the firm. Detailed and accurate environmental analysis is important since the strategy of each company must fit the industry within which it operates, but it is also difficult since the general manager of the company has to understand not only the existing economic, technological, social, political, and competitive characteristics of the industry, but also the trends that may change these characteristics in the future. Economic, technological, social, political, and competitive trends are seldom clear until they have had a jarring impact upon an organization, yet they must be anticipated in strategy formulation since the selected strategy defines the future method of competition of the business and the long-term growth plans of the firm. Anticipation requires forecasting, but it must be remembered that all forecasts, ranging on a scale of complexity from personal intuition to expert consensus to quantitative methodologies, are based upon past events and prior relationships, and therefore will be wrong, in varying degrees, in predicting future conditions. The general manager must review the forecasts, select the most probable set of future conditions, and state these conditions as assumptions, or premises for strategic planning, in each of the major environmental areas:

1. *Economic assumptions.* The economic characteristics and trends that should be considered would include the growth of the national income, the state of the business cycle, and the rate of monetary inflation for the general economy, and the availability of raw materials, trained employees, and debt or equity capital for the specific industry.
2. *Technological assumptions.* The technical characteristics and trends that should be examined would include the development of new products, the availability of new materials, and the design of new processes, both within the given industry and within potentially competitive industries.
3. *Social assumptions.* The social factors that should be reviewed would include demographic changes in such areas as population growth, educational level, and income distribution, and public concerns, resulting in informal requests to management, on such topics as environmental deterioration, consumer protection, and minority employment.
4. *Political assumptions.* The political factors that should be surveyed would include changing patterns in urban services, state programs, and federal expenditures, and the public concerns that have led to governmental actions and formal requirements upon management.
5. *Competitive assumptions.* The competitive characteristics and trends that should be studied would include both new competitors and new strategies or new pro-

grams by existing competitors; the ease of entry within an industry, and the ease of changing established industry practices, should be reviewed.

Specific Opportunities and Risks. The usual environmental analysis results in a listing of very general characteristics and trends, expressed as assumptions about the future conditions within a given sector of the economy; these general characteristics and trends of the industry should be converted to very specific opportunities and risks for the firm by stating the implications and potential effects upon the strategy, or method of competition, of the company.

1. Key assumptions are the fundamental economic, technical, and competitive conditions, both existing and anticipated, that will definitely affect the future operations of the firm; these essential characteristics of the environment are not just what is happening in the industry, they are what is happening in the industry that is vital to the planned success of the company.

Organizational Resources. The second of the major steps in strategy formulation is the examination of the organizational resources, or assets and skills, in order to identify the potential scope and existing limits upon the strategy of the firm. Accurate resource analysis is important since the strategy or method of competition of each company must fit the capabilities of the organization. However, this is also difficult since the general manager has to evaluate the financial, physical, managerial, and positional assets of the firm, and only the first of these resources can be accurately expressed in financial or quantitative terms:

1. *Financial resources.* The balance sheet of a company lists the current assets and liabilities in dollar terms, and accurately reflects the current financial position of the firm, but the potential sources of additional debt or equity capital are not stated, and must be estimated.
2. *Physical resources.* The balance sheet of a company also lists the fixed assets, both buildings and equipment, in dollar terms, but these amounts reflect the accounting convention of original cost less depreciation at an annual rate, and not the current value for use in a given strategy of the firm, which must be estimated.
3. *Managerial resources.* The balance sheet of a company lists no value, of course, for the human competences, which, in many cases, are the most valuable assets of the firm. These human competences include the technical skills and abilities of the functional and staff specialists, and the innovation and leadership capacities of the corporate management; these cannot be valued in dollar terms, but must be recognized as essential for the success of a given strategy for the firm.
4. *Positional resources.* The last of the organizational resources, which also does not appear on the balance sheet but is again a valuable asset of the firm, is the company's position within a market and reputation within an industry. These positional resources also cannot be valued in dollar terms, but must be recognized as important for the success of a given strategy for the firm.

Specific Strengths and Weaknesses. The usual organizational analysis results in a listing of very general assets and skills that might be applicable to many firms in many industries; these general resources should be converted to very specific strengths and weaknesses of the firm by evaluating them relative to the characteristics of the environment, the capabilities of the competition, and the requirement of the strategy, or method of competition, of the company.

1. Key resources are the essential financial, physical, managerial, and positional assets of the firm, both existing and obtainable, that will definitely affect the future success of the firm; these distinctive competences are not just what the company can do, they are what the company can do particularly well, and they are vital to the selected strategy of the firm.

Range of Strategic Alternatives. The third of the major steps in strategy formulation is the identification of the range of strategic alternatives that are open to the firm. The examination of the characteristics and trends of the environment produces a series of specific opportunities and risks for the future of the company, and the analysis of resources and skills of the organization defines a set of specific strengths and weaknesses which serve as boundaries or constraints upon those opportunities. Within these boundaries, there exists a range of strategic alternatives, or different methods of competition, that goes beyond the standard industry traditions or the accepted company conventions; it is the function of the general manager to identify these alternatives, listing for each the opportunities and risks foreseen, and the assets and skills required.

1. The identification of strategic alternatives is a creative process. Imagination, innovation, and perception are necessary to formulate the full range of long-term plans for competing within an industry; the tools and techniques of business administration are of limited value here, since they have been developed primarily to evaluate or improve existing alternatives, not to create new ones.

Selection from the Strategic Alternatives. The last of the major steps in strategy formulation is the selection of the proper strategy, or method of competition, from the range of alternatives that are open to the firm at any given point in time. The selection of the strategy is an iterative process: each alternative, representing specific opportunities and risks within the environment, is compared to the organizational resources, consisting of specific strengths and weaknesses of the firm, and the resultant match is measured along the dimensions of the organizational mission or purpose and the individual values and attitudes. The proper strategy should be internally consistent with the organizational assets and skills and externally consistent with the environmental characteristics and trends; it should provide a competitive advantage, and promise the maximum probability of achieving the organizational mission or purpose and satisfying the managerial values and attitudes, at an accepted or acknowledged level of risk.

1. The actual strategy of a company may be the result of design, chance, or hope; the probability of success is maximized, and the risk of loss is minimized, when the strategy, or long-term competitive plan, has been consciously designed and deliberately selected from among evaluated alternatives.

2. The selected strategy is basically a rational approach to the future; it defines the long-term competitive position of the company within the industry, and it details the requirements for the future success of the business.
3. The selected strategy establishes the character of the business, and provides the cohesiveness and unity of purpose among diverse functional and technical specialists that are essential for success.
4. The evaluation of strategic alternatives is a judgmental process. Strategic alternatives must be tested for consistency with the company's external environment and internal resources along the dimensions of the organizational mission or purpose and the managerial values and attitudes. This test is difficult since the external environment and the internal resources include a multiplicity of factors, most of which are changing, with uncertain estimates for the future, many of which are subjective, expressed in qualitative terms, some of which cannot be measured. And the organizational mission or purpose and the managerial values and attitudes are often not clearly stated, and can seldom be expressed on a unidimensional scale. The result is that subjective judgments are necessary to evaluate the full potential of each strategic alternative, in addition to the applicable tools and techniques of quantitative analysis.
5. The evaluation of strategic alternatives is, in the final analysis, a matter of individual choice. Leadership in business organizations probably can be defined as the choice among these alternatives.

Functional Objectives. The selected strategy must be translated into a precise series of statements on objectives, policies, programs, and actions for each functional area and technical department within the organization, or the long-term competitive plans for the business will remain an unachieved expression of intentions and hopes. The first step in this translation is to define specific and realistic objectives for each of the units within the organization. These objectives are the results that are expected in marketing, production, finance, product development, and the various staff units; they are statements of where the functional and technical units are expected to be at a specific time in the future. These goals give members of the units the sense of direction and purpose that is necessary to coordinate the efforts of the functional and technical specialists, and they permit evaluation of the performance of the departments. Functional objectives, in short, serve as targets for achievement and standards for control.

1. Functional objectives are usually expressed in quantitative terms. The primary areas of responsibility of each organizational unit have to be defined, a scale of measurement for each area of responsibility has to be devised, and then a goal or target can be established on each scale. Quantitative objectives are clear and precise, but it must be remembered that they are limited, and many important concepts cannot be stated in numerical terms. If qualitative objectives are used, they have to be carefully expressed to avoid misunderstanding and confusion.
2. Functional objectives are often the subject of negotiations between the general manager of the firm and the head of the functional or technical department involved since the achievement of the objectives is dependent not only upon the

activity and ability of the department, but also upon the policies prescribed and the resources allocated by the central administration.

Functional Policies. The second step in the translation of the selected strategy into a series of statements on the objectives, policies, programs, and actions for each of the functional and technical departments within the organization is the design of the functional policies and standard procedures. Policies and procedures serve as parameters for the decisions and actions of people within an organization; they are the guides to be followed to achieve the stated objectives in marketing, production, finance, product development, and the various staff units. The objective specifies the target or results that are expected; the policies specify the manner by which these results are to be accomplished. (Objective: achieve 20% market share for product A. Policies: price is to be 1.8 times the direct variable costs of product A; distribution is to be through exclusive company representatives, and promotion is to be by industry trade journals.) Policies may be either positive (allow company representatives 22.5% discount off the list price) or negative (do not cut the list price to increase market share; do not engage in price fixing or market allocation with competitors). Policies and procedures are general statements which convey the intentions and instructions of the central management, and serve as guidelines so that the managerial decisions and actions throughout the organization can be consistent with the selected strategy. If a meaningful difference exists, functional policies serve as guidelines for decision and standard procedures serve as guidelines for action, but both are intended to describe the customary or accepted method of reacting to certain recurring, similar situations. In short, policies and procedures together state the expected guidelines for both decisions and actions within an organization, and consequently they serve to coordinate the efforts of the functional and technical specialists within that organization.

1. Functional policies may be expressed with either quantitative or qualitative terms. Obviously, the quantitative terms are clear, but they also tend to become fairly rigid rules and regulations, and they do not then permit a range of discretionary actions on the part of the functional or technical manager directly involved with the situation. "Sell at 1.8 times the direct variable cost" is a clear quantitative policy, but it precludes the marketing flexibility and prompt reaction to competitive pressure of "don't sell below full cost."
2. Functional policies probably should be expressed in written form, since copies of the documents can be made available to everyone concerned with the operational or technical unit, and this availability tends to eliminate misunderstandings and confusion. However, written policies and procedures can become codified into a quasi-legal system for the firm, and not kept current. Published policies and procedures should be reviewed periodically, and changed to remain consistent with changes in the corporate strategy.

Functional Programs. The third step in the translation of the selected strategy into a series of statements on the objectives, policies, programs, and actions for each of the functional and technical departments within the organization, for the purpose of coordinating the activities of these departments, is the design of the functional programs and the development of the budgetary plans. Functional programs involve the description of the specific activities proposed by each organizational unit to achieve the stated objectives within the policy guidelines, while the budgetary plans concern the estimated expenditures for these activities, expressed on a monthly or quarterly pro forma accounting statement. To give an example, an advertising program might be established as part of the marketing department's effort to achieve an objective of 20% market share for a specific product, and this advertising program might operate under the twin policies, or directions from the corporate management, to concentrate on the stimulation of secondary demand through trade journals rather than primary demand through consumer magazines and television, and to limit expenditures to an annual rate approximating 5% of the projected sales of the product. The advertising program would then detail the magazines and the issues selected, and the message and format of the ads. The advertising budget would report the cost of these ads, together with the managerial and clerical expenses and the allocated overhead of the program, on a pro forma accounting statement.

1. Functional and technical programs often tend to continue unaltered despite modifications or outright changes in the selected strategy; this resistance to change is caused by the loyalty and adherence to established activities that can build up within organizational units. The functional programs should be reviewed periodically, and redirected to remain consistent with changes in the corporate strategy.
2. Functional and technical budgetary plans can be expressed in fixed terms (the amounts to be spent during the accounting period), in variable terms (the amounts to be spent at various levels of sales or production), or in discretionary terms (the amounts to be spent, if needed in the opinion of the executive in charge of the program). These plans are also usually divided into operating budgets (expenditures for program activities that will be deducted from income in the current accounting period) and capital budgets (expenditures for new plant and equipment or product/process development that will be capitalized and deducted through depreciation or amortization over future accounting periods). Finally, program budgets also tend to continue unaltered despite modifications or changes in the selected strategy; this is due to the natural inclination to start budgetary planning at the current expense level. The functional and technical budgets should be reviewed periodically, and revised to remain consistent with changes in the corporate strategy.

Functional Actions. The fourth, and last step in the translation of the selected strategy into a series of statements on the objectives, policies, programs, and actions for each of the functional and technical departments within the organization is the decision to take appropriate actions to start on the new strategy. Functional actions can be defined as the sequence of activities on a plan or program to achieve specific goals and objectives within given policies and procedures; they are what has to be done next to implement the corporate strategy.

The major portion of this chapter has been concerned with the managerial process of formulating and implementing the corporate strategy for a business firm, or the long-term method of competition to be followed by that company. The important consideration in strategic management, however, is not the formulation and implementation process, but the impact of that process upon the members of the organization. Unless all members of the organization, including the senior executives, the functional and technical specialists, the supervisory personnel, production workers, office employees, and maintenance crew, are able to work together easily and, hopefully, enthusiastically, with coordinated activities and cooperative actions, the corporate performance will be ineffective and the competitive position of the firm will decline. For effective performance and improved position, all members of the organization must understand the selected strategy, and guide their decisions and actions in line with that strategy.

Complete understanding and acceptance of the corporate strategy is difficult to achieve. Each member of an organization can have three views or impressions of the strategy of that organization. The first view can be termed the "proper" strategy for the organization. Each member, depending upon his or her position within that organization, is able to gauge the current performance and position of the firm, and has some understanding of the environmental opportunities and risks and the organizational strengths and weaknesses. Each member, therefore, has a concept of what the organization *ought* to be doing.

The second view of the corporate strategy by the individual members of the organization can be termed the "present" strategy. Each member, again depending upon his or her position within the firm, has some contact with the goals and objectives, policies and procedures, programs and plans, and current actions of many of the functional and technical departments, all of which are, or should be, based upon the selected strategy of the company. Each member, therefore, has a concept of what the organization presently *is* doing.

The last view of the corporate strategy by the individual members of the organization can be termed the "personal" strategy. Each member within the organization is affected by the organizational structure, and by the planning, control, and motivational systems. The relationships imposed by the structure and the behavior encouraged by the systems give each person a concept of what he or she *should be* doing for individual self-interest. The derivation of these three individual concepts or perceptions of the organizational strategy is shown in schematic form on the following page.

The three perceptions of the organizational strategy by the individual members of the organization must be consistent for improved corporate performance and competitive position. Members of an organization who believe that what the firm ought to be doing, what the firm is doing, and what it is in their best interest to do are not approximate or parallel but identical will base their decisions and actions in line with that strategy. Coordinated decisions and cooperative actions in line with

Organizational
mission or charter

Corporate perform-
ance and position

Managerial values
and attitudes

Opportunities and
risks within the
industry

Range of strategic
alternatives open to
the firm

Strengths and
weaknesses within
the company

Individual perception
of the "proper" orga-
nizational strategy

Departmental goals
and objectives

Departmental policies
and procedures

Departmental pro-
grams and plans

Departmental
immediate actions

Individual perception
of the "present" orga-
nizational strategy

Corporate organiza-
tional structure

Corporate planning
system

Corporate control
system

Corporate motiva-
tional system

Individual perception
of the "personal" or-
ganizational strategy

Individual sense of di-
rection and purpose,
resulting in improved
corporate perform-
ance and competitive
position

---

a rationally selected strategy will result, over time, in improved corporate performance and competitive position.

Identical perception of the strategy of the organization by all the members of the
organization is probably an impossibility, but an impossibility which can be approached. The approach requires a consistent selection of the strategy from the
current performance and position of the firm relative to the environmental opportunities and risks and the organizational strengths and weaknesses; a consistent
statement of the strategy in the functional and technical goals and objectives, policies and procedures, and programs and plans; and a consistent design of the organi-

zational structure and the planning, control, and motivational systems. This consistent analytical and developmental approach is the responsibility of the general management; well done, it provides the members of the organization with a sense of direction and purpose. This is a managerial process worthy of study, and it is the subject matter of this book.

Cambridge Computer Corporation

The Cambridge Computer Corporation (CamComp) was started in November 1967 to manufacture low-cost computer terminals with built-in computation and storage capabilities that could record, manipulate, and verify data prior to transmission to the central processor. The intentions of the founders of the new company were to provide equipment that would spread data-processing tasks through an organization rather than centralize them in a single staff unit; that would make computerized data available to all members of the organization rather than limit it to systems analysts, programmers, and recipients of the printed output; and that would reduce the cost of data preparation, transmission, and utilization. The trend of developments in the data-processing industry in 1967 was in the direction of bigger, faster, and more expensive central computers for batch processing; Cambridge Computer Corporation was formed to reverse this trend, and to supply smaller, slower, and less expensive decentralized facilities for continuous data processing.

The founders of the company, Dr. Edward Benson and Dr. Joseph Siegal, were scientists who had developed a decentralized management planning system for the Air Force while working at a government-sponsored research institute in Lexington, Massachusetts. The basis of the Air Force system was a telephone network connecting standard terminals at each participant's desk to a large central processing unit. Data were entered as received (real-time) at each station and not held for batch processing, and information was available (on-line) at each station without the need for special program design. This interactive planning system was the first on-line, real-time use of a computer for management functions; it enabled nontechnical personnel to use the computer to get information needed for planning and control, but problems developed in the reliability of the data recording, the cost of the data transmission, and the capacity of the data processing. It was felt that these problems were not flaws in the design of the system, but were inherent faults of the equipment that was then available, and that these faults had been magnified by the number of persons participating. That is, data were entered by the operator at each terminal, but the combined typographical and format errors of all the operators made much of the resultant output misleading; the terminals were connected to the central computer by permanent telephone lines, but the combined charges for all the wires made the continuous service exceedingly expensive; and the routine computations were performed on the central processor, but the combined usage of all the participants overloaded the machine. Drs. Benson and Siegal felt that a new terminal was needed that would permit the verification of data as they were recorded in standard formats, the transmission of the data in batches at lower costs, and the manipulation of these data locally in smaller processors. Dr. Siegal developed this concept of the terminal, and Dr. Benson saw the commercial application.

> Although the basic prototype system was developed for use in military command, its philosophy and concepts were more applicable to management planning and information systems in industrial organizations. That is why they started the company. (Statement of an industry executive)

Drs. Benson and Siegal started the company with four other scientists who had worked on the Air Force project at the research institute; together they managed to raise $106,000 from their personal savings, and to prepare a report on the financial potential of decentralized data processing that convinced the partners of Dillon Read and Company, a large and prestigious investment banking firm in New York City, to invest somewhat over $300,000. With the initial capitalization, and with additional personnel hired from the universities, research centers, and electronic firms in the Boston area, the company started the full design of the new equipment for decentralized data processing.

The basic piece of equipment that was developed by Cambridge Computer was not complex; it was based upon established technology and proven components, but it combined this technology and these components in a new and very different package. The complete unit consisted of a computer terminal with a standard typewriter keyboard for data input; a video screen for data viewing and verification; a microprocessor, or small computer with wired software programs for simple data manipulation and storage; two magnetic tape drives, one for data input and one for data output; a communication channel for data transmission to the central processor; and a printing robot for hard copies of the data output. The finished unit was small, and would fit easily on the top of a desk.

The features of the new data-processing unit were the standard typewriter keyboard so that any experienced typist or hunt-and-peck executive could operate the machine, the video screen which displayed the data as they were entered so that corrections could easily be made, the microprocessor so that calculations could be performed locally, the wired software so that systems analysts and programmers were not needed, and the use of ordinary cassette tape decks for input and output storage so that large data banks could be assembled inexpensively for each machine, or sent easily between machines. The use of cassette tapes rather than the much more expensive computer tapes was one of the distinctive concepts of the design. Computer tapes are highly accurate, but they are designed to work with precision equipment in environments where dust, humidity, and temperature are all carefully controlled. When they are moved out of antiseptic conditions or used on less precise equipment, the accuracy declines rapidly, and misreading or misrecording of single bits of information occurs. Cassette tape is much less precise, and subject to the same environmental contaminants, so that normally it cannot be used in data processing, but Cambridge Computer devised a process to record each individual bit of information five times and to read this information with a majority logic test. The probabilities are over 1 in 10 million that three or more of the five characters would not be either recorded or read erroneously, even under conditions of dust, dirt, and humidity, so the cassette tapes provided a very simple, inexpensive, and nearly error-free means of data storage and transmission.

The founders of Cambridge Computer felt that this combination of components, consisting of the microprocessor, keyboard, video display, two tape drives, one communication channel, and one printing robot, would be useful in recording data, transmitting data, storing data, or manipulating data, since all these functions could be performed locally, at the point where the information either originated or was needed, and since they could be done interactively by the person who was familiar with the information. This was decentralized data processing, and company advertising brochures gave the following examples of the four major functions of the decentralized data-processing terminals.

Data Recording. Data recording, or data entry for subsequent processing by a central computer, was the most elementary function foreseen for the new equipment, but also one of the most useful. Many people thought of the Cambridge Computer terminal as a replacement for the keypunch or teleprocessor, especially since the input tape cassette could provide coded headings and a standard format for the data input, while the video screen offered a quick and simple means of visual verification. For example, in recording accounts payable invoices, a clerk would select an input tape cassette containing the names and billing addresses of suppliers and the standard format of entries in the accounts payable journal. When the operator typed the identification number of the supplier, the machine would search and retrieve the needed information from the tape, and display it on the screen:

        Supplier name and address
        Order number: ____
        Order date: ____
        Delivery date: ____
        Current date: ____
        Invoice code: ____
        Invoice date: ____
        Invoice amounts: ____

The operator then typed in the required information, verified it visually, and recorded it on the output tape. This "fill in the blanks" capability was the second of the distinctive

features of the design, since it enabled inexperienced personnel to produce nearly error-free data entry in the required format. This capability was confirmed by a keypunch and data entry service bureau in San Francisco that tested four trial models of the machine in a training program for minority groups:

> The ease of rapidly changing from one format to another allows us to guarantee 100% accuracy despite a wide range of source documents and a lack of operator experience with the forms. In a given day our operators are faced with credit application forms, prescription billing slips, program coding sheets, hospital charge amounts, freight waybills, and a variety of accounting documents from several large manufacturing firms. However, from a single CamTape cartridge an operator can automatically call in any one of over 200 formats, and from a Cam-Tape deck (an auxiliary device with 32 cassettes mounted in banks) she can choose from over 6,400 forms. This format capability allows an easy, fast transition from coding sheets to prescription forms to credit card applications. If the operator senses she has made an error, a quick glance at the screen indicates the character in question and she then merely retypes the correct character, and goes on with her work. (Statement of a customer quoted in company advertising brochure entitled "CamComp Vitalizes Data Center")

Data Transmission. Data entered by the operators at each machine, after verification, were recorded on the output tape cassette; this cassette could be mailed to the central processing unit, or the data could be transmitted by a telephone recorder in a single batch at the close of each working day. Batch telephone service greatly reduced data transmission costs, and provided rapid turnaround since the process data could be returned through the same system, with hard-copy reports prepared by the printing robot attached, as an optional feature, to most machines. This rapid turnaround capability was the third of the distinctive features of the machine; it permitted on-line type service at greatly reduced data transmission costs. This feature was demonstrated at another test location for the equipment, a data-processing firm in Chicago which provided bookkeeping services for automobile dealers in the Midwest:

> We had to rely on the mail to collect data until we installed CamComp terminals at each of our dealer locations. Now, an operator for each dealer keys in all the information on sales, repair jobs, expenses and invoices during the day, and records it on CamTape. Whatever she has to record, she can find the format for it on the master tape, so that it is recorded correctly, and she can check it visually, so that it is recorded accurately; the system has virtually eliminated input errors. Then, we call the terminal at night, since it can operate in an unattended mode, receive the data, process it, and send it back. Transmission time averages five minutes per dealer. Next morning, the operator starts the machine, and it makes hard copy reports from the incoming tape. Turnaround time has been reduced from nine days with mail to less than 12 hours with CamComp. (Statement of a customer quoted in company advertising brochure entitled "CamComp Helps Automotive Dealers")

Data Storage. Data entry and transmission were not the only functions of the new terminals designed for decentralized data processing; Cambridge Computer believed that the storage and computation capabilities of the equipment, although limited, were adequate to replace much of the routine paper work presently required in business. The data storage methodology, on inexpensive magnetic tape cassettes, has already been described; the application of this methodology was the fourth distinctive feature of the machine since the ready availability of information on input cassettes at each machine, and the easy transfer of output cassettes between machines, eliminated much of the paper preparation, sorting, sending, and filing that was necessary to store and transmit the detailed information needed in industrial and commercial operations. As an example of this data access capability, the company described possible uses in the receiving, inspection, and stocking of incoming goods:

> *Receiving.* Delivered goods at the receiving dock are generally checked by comparison with paper copies of the purchase order to confirm that the proper type and quantity of each item has been delivered, and then additional paper work is generated to notify purchasing, accounts payable and the stock room that the material has been received. A CamComp terminal would store purchase order information on CamTape, from which it could be retrieved easily by the order number for comparison with the incoming goods. Then, the information could be transferred to an output CamTape for purchasing and accounts receivable, recording all the receipts for the day, while a hard-copy travel card could be prepared on the printing robot to be sent with the goods to inspection and inventory.

> *Inspection.* All received goods requiring inspection would be forwarded, together with the travel card prepared by the CamComp terminal at the receiving dock, to an inspection station. Here, another CamComp terminal could be used to retrieve information on the proper inspection procedures for each part, the critical dimensions and allowable tolerances, and then to prepare CamTapes for purchasing and accounts payable, and a travel card for inventory, on the acceptability of the material.

> *Inventory.* All received and inspected goods would be sent to the stockroom with hard copies of the travel cards prepared by the CamComp terminals at the

receiving dock and the inspection station. The stock clerk would add the material received to the perpetual inventory record on CamTape on his CamComp terminal, and note the storage location on an output CamTape. Parts and material disbursed from inventory would be deducted from the master CamTape perpetual inventory record, with a second CamTape prepared for cost accounting, listing the parts disbursements by job number for transmission at the close of each day. Weekly, a copy of the master CamTape perpetual inventory record could be sent to purchasing for automatic reordering of items below the minimum order quantity. (Statement in company advertising brochure entitled "Systems of the 70's")

Data Manipulation. The microprocessor in each terminal, with prewired software substituting for the more common computer program storage, could perform simple numerative processes such as addition, subtraction, multiplication, and division, and display the output in a predetermined format selected from the master input tape. This was felt to be the fifth distinctive feature of the machine, since it permitted calculations to be performed as part of the data entry process, without requiring on-line connections to the central computer or continual use of this central unit. Company advertising described a number of applications of this numerative capability:

Engineering. Engineers are faced with a constant need for computation, yet slide rules are inaccurate and slow, centralized computers are inaccessible and time sharing is too expensive. The answer is a personalized computer that is fast, accurate, and inexpensive; the answer is Cam-Comp.

Sales. Customers require rapid quotations on their requirements, often with a specific bid on the cost of a total contract. These estimates must be made at the district sales offices, away from the

data-processing capability of the central headquarters. The CamComp terminal provides this capability locally; standard prices per unit can be stored on the input CamTape, multiplied within the machine by the units required, subtotaled by each class of product, the applicable discount subtracted, and finally added for the total bid. The CamComp printing robot will prepare a hard copy of this bid for submission to the customer; the output CamTape will record the estimate for the company files. (Statement in company advertising brochure entitled "Systems of the 70's")

Data Utilization. The combined capabilities of the Cambridge Computer terminal in data recording, transmission, storage, and computation made the new data-processing units useful in managerial decisions requiring prompt and easy access to current information. This combined capability in data utilization for management was felt to be the sixth, and most important feature of the machine since the units were small enough and inexpensive enough to be put on every desk where decisions were made throughout an organization, and simple enough to be operated by all the decision makers. The company believed that the terminals could be used in each production department to collect direct labor, material, and overhead expenses for cost accounting, and to record job status and machine availability for production control; in each sales branch to provide a file of customer order patterns and seasonal fluctuations for sales forecasts, and expected order completion dates and delivery route mileages for truck scheduling; in each engineering section to control drafting records and part numbers; in each personnel office for payroll information and job requirements; and in the general and financial offices for immediate access to all the production, sales, engineering, and personnel data. At each station, either a secretary, foreman, salesman, engineer, or executive could rapidly search and retrieve needed information from the files, and compare cost records, labor standards, production schedules, inventory amounts, or customer orders with the existing situation to make prompt and informed decisions. Company advertising made the following statement about the new system:

Purchasing. All decision making is left to the purchasing agent. The CamComp terminal is simply a tool which helps control the massive flow of paperwork associated with the purchasing operations. It files and reports data, and it frees the purchasing agent to do the job he was hired for—make decisions which save his company money.

Production. Most of the data collection and feedback equipment that has been tested on the factory floor to date has been unsuccessful for several reasons. It has been too complex for nontechnical personnel, too expensive for operational usage, and too delicate for the factory environment. CamComp offers an excellent solution for factory data collection: it is easy to use, it is inexpensive, and it is designed to work in a factory environment.

General. CamComp has created data stations and computers that everyone can use, and that can be placed in any environment, and that you can afford to put on every desk where data originates or is used. With this new technology you can build systems that parallel—rather than divert—the channels through which information must flow to make decisions and keep records.

These new systems are something that people can touch, see, and work with to handle the problems that are on their desks. These new systems distribute computer logic to those places where it is needed, instead of trying to funnel everything through the central computer room. Data is processed as it is gathered through the use of logically programmed CamComp terminals, freeing the central processing unit for the big jobs it was designed to do. (Statement in company ad-

vertising brochure entitled "Systems of the 70's")

The normal method of electronic data recording, storage, and manipulation at the time of the case was sequential batch processing on large and expensive central computers: data were gathered from various locations within a company, wherever it was generated, then sorted, classified, coded, formatted, and keypunched by a corporate staff unit, and finally run on the central computer in specific programs, or batches. The output of each program was printed for distribution to interested or involved managerial personnel throughout the firm. This was centralized data processing.

The major advantage of centralized data processing was the existence of the central data base, which included all the marketing, manufacturing, and financial transactions of the firm, and which could be compounded, combined, or compared in different ways to analyze the operations of the firm. The disadvantages were the need to bring all the data together at one location for processing, the need to design special computer programs for analysis, and the need to use printed output for distribution. All these requirements took time, and tended to delay or eliminate the use of computerized data in management. Cambridge Computer, as has been described, wanted to change this centralized batch processing to decentralized continuous processing; this was a major change for the computer industry:

Present-day data management systems are orientated to the giant central processing unit in the computer room; this orientation has precluded using computer logic for everyday data search, comparison and processing. The CamComp terminal, consisting of an input keyboard, viewing screen, microprocessor, magnetic tape storage, and output channel and printer, is capable of performing many of the routine batch processing and computation tasks that currently overburden the central computer, and can distribute data to the people who actually need and use it. (Statement in company advertising brochure entitled "Systems of the 70's")

These people were going to change the standard method of data processing in the United States; they were going to put a small data management station on every desk, just like an electric typewriter, and virtually eliminate the need for large central computers. (Statement of an industry executive)

There was a consequence, neither unintended nor unforeseen, for this decision by Cambridge Computer to decentralize data processing: the company would have to compete directly with the International Business Machines Corporation, which held a predominate position in data processing, and which was committed, with an investment estimated at $27 billion, to the design, manufacture, and sales of large central computers.

In 1970, the data-processing industry was dependent upon the large central computer, and the design, manufacture, and sale of these mainframe processing units was dominated by IBM, since that company was responsible for the installation of approximately 70% of all mainframe computers sold in the United States, and 85% of all those sold abroad. Hundreds, and even thousands, of other companies produced peripheral equipment, such as input/output terminals, optical scanners, drum or disk memories, high-speed printers, magnetic tape drives, etc., or developed software programs for general or specific applications, but the characteristics of all the auxiliary hardware and software were determined by the design of the mainframe units, which meant that they were dependent upon the designs of IBM. The traditional strategy for others in the data-processing industry, whether large or small, was to carve out a niche under the IBM fortress, and to avoid direct, head-on competition. Cambridge Com-

puter decided to alter this traditional stance of dependence and subservience, and planned to compete directly with IBM.

You couldn't compete with IBM on central processors; RCA and General Electric proved that. But you probably could compete with them on a totally new approach to data processing. Cambridge Computer had this new approach. If they had been successful, there wouldn't be enough money in the vaults of the State Street Bank and Trust [a large and prestigious Boston banking firm] to buy 10 shares of their stock. (Statement of an industry executive)

You have to be audacious to win big in the data-processing business, and those bastards were certainly audacious. They didn't want to compete with IBM; they wanted to defeat IBM. (Statement of an industry executive)

Cambridge Computer discovered a big, shining, gaping hole in the computer market structure, and they were running hard to get through that hole and grab the business before the rest of the industry realized what was going on. (Statement of an industry executive)

The IBM approach to data processing was dead; all Benson and Siegal planned to do was to bury it. (Statement of an industry executive)

To compete with IBM, the Cambridge Computer Corporation developed a new and very different strategy that was based on the use of metal-oxide-semiconductor integrated circuitry. To understand this strategy, and particularly to understand the subsequent corporate policies in marketing, production, finance, and product development, it is necessary to review very briefly this microelectronic technology and its application to computer design.

Essentially, a computer is a very simple, logical device, capable of performing only the most elementary operations. Its logic is based on the binary number system, with only two allowable integers, 0 and 1 (the decimal system has 10 allowable integers, 0 through 9). The binary system is required since the computer circuitry is basically a two-state design, on or off. Data are represented in the electronic system of a digital computer by a pattern of two-state electrical impulses; these, however, can represent any possible number by the addition of place values; these place values are on the radix of 2, for each place is exactly twice that of the preceding place (in the decimal system, each place is exactly 10 times that of the preceding place). Sample binary place values are 128, 64, 32, 16, 8, 4, 2, 1, and 0; sixty in the binary system can be represented by 0111 1000 (32 + 16 + 8 + 4 + 0 + 0 + 0).

To avoid the long strings of zeros and ones in the binary system representations of large numbers, a binary-coded-decimal system has been developed. The four position in the place values 8, 4, 2, and 1 can provide the binary equivalents of the decimal digits 1 through 9, and decimal place values can be added to each group of four binary digits; that is, six in the binary-coded-decimal system is 0110 (0 + 4 + 2 + 0), and sixty is 0110 0000. The actual system used for computation is a binary-coded-hexadecimal system, with a base of 15, since that is the total of the four numbers in the place values 8, 4, 2, and 1; the hexadecimal system further reduces the number of zeros and ones needed to represent large numbers.

Despite the use of decimal or hexadecimal codes, all computations and comparisons are performed on the binary system, 0 and 1, and therefore all computer circuitry is based on two-stage devices, on or off. The history of computer development is basically the development of more efficient and reliable and inexpensive two-stage devices. The earliest digital computers, which were used during the 1940s to develop firing tables for naval guns to check the analog units mounted on shipboard for gunnery control, used thousands of electrical on–off relays; the power require-

ments were substantial, the heat generation was immense, and the noise, as the electromechanical relays clicked on and off, was reported to be awesome. This computer was more a large calculator; it performed extensive calculations as the input of discrete integers was indexed forward for each of 27 variables. Computers developed after World War II for scientific use, particularly in physics and astronomy with a need for large computation capability but low data storage, substituted radio tubes for the electromechanical relays; these greatly reduced the power requirements, since the radio tubes could amplify the binary signals, or pulses, but heat generation remained a problem. Second-generation computers, introduced about 1952 for business rather than scientific use, particularly in accounting and finance, with the consequent need for large data storage capacities and relatively slow data computation, made use of transistors in place of the radio tubes to eliminate the heat problem and permit the closer packing of the vastly more complicated components.

Transistors are crystal semiconductors, generally silicon or germanium, with an electrical property, or ability to transmit electrical energy, determined by their electrical state. That is, each transistor is an electronic on–off switch with no moving parts and very minimal heat generation; they are termed "semiconductors" since they conduct low-voltage impulses only in one direction and only when activated. Transistors were so small, approximately 1/10 in. square and 1/100 in. thick, and required so little current for operation that 50 or 100 could be mounted on a printed circuit board, or piece of insulating material with the necessary electrical connections lithographed in copper or aluminum. This substantially reduced the hand wiring required, and consequently the cost of computer manufacture; however, the increased size of the computers designed for business use during the 1960s meant that large numbers of transistors, mounted on numerous circuit boards which were still interconnected by hand wiring, were needed for both computation and storage. Further miniaturization was needed.

Integrated circuits were the next major development in computer circuitry; it was discovered that 10 or more transistors could be formed as a single unit, together with all the necessary connections to form an integrated electronic circuit, by a photoengraving process. By 1965, 25 transistors were being placed on a single silicon or germanium chip, still $1/10$ in. square and $1/100$ in. thick, together with the wiring for the control and transmission circuits. This integrated circuit, or chip, was made by first designing the logic, or interrelationships of the transistors, and then drawing the transistors and interconnections as a series of layers, or composite, on a scale 500 times the finished size. Each layer of the composite was then photographed and the negatives were reproduced and mounted side by side in rows to form a mural with perhaps 250 negatives; this mural was then photographed again and reduced in size to form a glass plate approximately 2 in. square, with each individual negative the finished $1/10$ in. by $1/10$ in. size. This plate, or mask, could be placed over a crystal wafer of silicon or germanium, about 3 in. in diameter and $1/100$ in. thick, and 250 integrated circuits, each consisting of 10 to 25 transistors and the necessary control and transmission circuits, could be photoengraved at the same time. This process was repeated for each layer of the composite; after each photoengraving stage, boron or indium was deposited on the engraved spots for the transistors, and then the crystal wafer was heated in a diffusion furnace to fuse the impurity with the silicon or germanium to form the transistors. The microcircuits for each layer were also etched photoelectrolytically with a hydrogen fluoride acid; the crystal was then washed and placed in an aluminum sulfide solution, and the current flow for the photoengraving process was reversed to deposit the metallic electrical connections on the freshly etched surface. After each layer of the integrated circuit was completed, the crystal was coated with silicon oxide for the isolation of the active elements and the insulation of the interconnections; after the total process was completed, the crystal wafer, consisting of 250 integrated circuits, was separated into individual circuit chips by scratching the surface between the circuit patterns and breaking the wafer.

The manufacturing process for integrated circuits was awesomely complex; it required totally clean rooms to eliminate environmental contamination, precision processing equipment to maintain the close tolerances, a trained staff to supervise the intricate operations, and expensive testing instruments to evaluate the final products, but hundreds of chips could be manufactured at one time with minimal labor, and integrated circuits, each consisting of 10 to 25 transistors and the required interconnections, could be mass-produced at greatly reduced costs. Integrated circuits made possible the development of the third generation of computers in 1968, with greatly increased memory and computation capabilities.

Cambridge Computer could have used the existing integrated-circuit technology for their decentralized data-processing terminals in 1968. The circuits could have been purchased easily from a number of different suppliers. However, there was a new technology which appeared to be even more promising for lower costs, termed "metal-oxide-semiconductor (MOS) large-scale integrated (LSI) circuitry."

Most integrated circuitry, at the date of the case, was etched on standard silicon or germanium semiconductor chips, and contained 10 to 25 transistors and the related wiring. It was possible to increase the active-element packing density approximately 40 times, mounting 400 to 1,000 transistors and interconnections on a single chip, by using silicon or germanium oxide as the basic crystal structure. A wafer of silicon or germanium could be heated to 1100° centigrade in a diffusion furnace to convert the metal to a metal oxide; the metal oxide could then be photoengraved by the normal process to form the integrated circuit, but the superior insulation and isolation properties of the oxide permitted tighter packing of the elements, and a consequent reduction of costs per element.

The metal-oxide-semiconductor (MOS) technology made possible the use of large-scale integrated (LSI) circuitry, with 40 times as many transistors per chip, and manufacturing costs per transistor reduced by a factor of at least 10 and perhaps by as much as 25. Transistors costing $1/25$ as much as those commercially available were attractive to the company, particularly since additional cost savings were possible through simplified chassis design and easier subassembly connections. There was a problem with the MOS technology, for the integrated devices operated much more slowly than conventional integrated circuits, acting in thousandths of a second rather than in the typical billionth of a second, but this was not considered to be decisive for Cambridge Computer since their decentralized data-processing system was designed to interface with much slower human requests for information, and to batch data for tape transmission to the faster central computers.

The management of Cambridge Computer decided to adopt the new, and unproven, MOS technology sine the potential reduction in costs opened up new and very large markets, and made possible mass marketing and mass production methods that could change the entire data-processing industry. Drs. Benson and Siegal knew, at the time that they decided on this admittedly risky course of action, that a prior effort to use MOS/LSI circuitry by the Victor Comptometer Corporation had ended in failure, but they believed that their company had the research competence and the financial resources necessary to succeed. Cambridge Computer spent ap-

proximately $10 million between the formation of the company in 1968 and the start of full-scale production in 1970, and they did succeed: they designed effective, inexpensive, and reliable metal oxide semiconductors for large-scale integrated circuitry that could be used in the CamComp terminals. This success made possible the subsequent use of mass marketing and mass production techniques:

> As for CamComp's plans to use MOS, the idea at first had all the attractiveness of the bubonic plague. CamComp's hopes to utilize metal oxide semiconductor devices in its systems immediately conjured up memories of Victor Comptometer's highly publicized flop in attempting to use MOS in one of its electronic calculators. The semiconductor industry simply couldn't come up with the devices for Victor in 1967, and the widespread feeling in 1968 was that Cambridge Computer couldn't do it either.
>
> But Cambridge Computer did do it.
>
> Nearly all of the leading sesmiconductor houses in the country, possibly fearing they could be left behind as Cambridge Computer led the drive into production of the new technology, made heavy and costly commitments in developing custom MOS devices for CamComp. In addition, CamComp built its own microelectronic facilities at great expense. By demonstrating its own commitment to MOS, CamComp certainly proved to any doubtful semiconductor house that it was serious about the new development. (Statement of an investment analyst)

To summarize, in the late winter of 1969, Cambridge Computer planned to compete directly against IBM with their concept of decentralized data processing, their invention of a terminal with data recording, transmission, storage, and computation capabilities, their technology of metal-oxide-semiconductor large-scale integrated circuitry, and their intention to mass-market and mass-produce their product. This was a strategy that differed considerably from others in the data-processing industry and it was, to a great extent, a reflection of the personal qualities of Dr. Benson, the president of the firm and one of its major founders:

> Benson is an aggressive guy. He is intelligent, witty, articulate, and able to express complicated scientific and financial matters concisely and simply. But his principal characteristic is that he likes to win, and win big. (Statement of an industry executive)
>
> Benson was ready to take risks, and Cambridge Computer was a very risky endeavor; they adopted a brash sink-or-swim philosophy, and then began swimming like hell. (Statement of an industry executive)
>
> Cambridge Computer represented one of the most imaginative and daring—and unorthodox—business endeavors in the history of electronic data processing. (Statement of an industry executive)

The strategy that was adopted for the Cambridge Computer Corporation was aggressive, brash, and imaginative. The objectives of the strategy were to make the company a major factor in the data-processing industry, a primary competitor of IBM, and a very profitable investment for the founders and initial stockholders, within a limited number of years. The management of the firm intended to achieve these objectives by setting very specific policies in market selection, pricing, distribution, advertising, service and repair, production, finance, product development, and personnel; these policies will be described in the balance of the case.

Market Selection. Cambridge Computer perceived its market as consisting of two distinct segments. The first segment was composed of the large-scale users of existing data-processing machines, who would either adopt the CamComp terminal for low-cost data entry and verification in prepared formats, or the CamComp concept of decentralized desktop stations for data storage and computation; either way, there would be a very consid-

erable sales potential from established users of information technology:

> In 1972, 90% of U.S. computer users expect to use remote terminal devices, vs. only 20% currently [1969]. Behind this fast growth is the increasing need for fast access to information. However, our respondents—a cross section from industry, education, and government—pointed out that price could be the market-limiting factor. Over 80% considered 30% reductions in the price of terminal devices a necessity, and more than 40% thought that a cut of 50% would be necessary before they substantially upped their use of terminals. (Statement of investment analyst)

The second market segment consisted of smaller firms who had previously shied away from electronic data processing because of the high initial cost:

> Historically, the computer industry has been dominated by a few manufacturers producing limited quantities of highly specialized and highly priced equipment. To date, the companies providing the most costly marketing and most extensive service have been the most successful, followed by those who have emphasized equipment performance in terms of speed, power and sophistication. The result has been the proliferation of elaborate data processing systems which have markets limited not by service or performance, but by price. Cambridge Computer is opening new markets by adding a price competitive posture to an industry dominated by high-priced products. Primarily Cambridge Computer offers its customers low-priced, reliable data processing systems. (Statement in Cambridge Computer Corporation, *Annual Report for 1969*, p. 14)

Pricing. The management of Cambridge Computer agreed that price was an essential factor in expanding the market for their new terminals, both for use as input/output devices with existing central computers, and as decentralized data-processing stations in situations where information technology had previously been considered uneconomic. To expand their potential markets quickly, and to interest potential customers easily in the new machines, the company announced a "rental only" sales policy at $39.00 per month. This was a reduction of approximately 65% from the existing rental or lease charges for simple input/output terminals, without the additional data storage and computation capabilities of the CamComp unit, and it was based on the company's development of the inexpensive metal-oxide-semiconductor large-scale integrated circuitry, and on their plans for savings from mass marketing and mass production of the new machines. The announcement astonished the data-processing industry:

> If they'd announced for $110 a month instead of $39, they still would have been competitive. (Statement of an industry executive)
>
> We couldn't believe it. Our executives called an all-day conference just to study this thing. We concluded that either Cambridge Computer was crazy or we were. We hoped that they were. (Statement of an industry executive)
>
> Pour 270 francs par mois le dialogue avec un ordinateur à la portée de tous. Cinq fois moins cher à l'achat. (Statement in *France-Soir*, quoted in Cambridge Computer Corporation, *Annual Report for 1969*, back cover)

Distribution. The low price that was announced by Cambridge Computer was based, at least partially, upon expectations of considerable savings that could be generated through the low-key, nontraditional sales effort that was planned. Most of the other companies in the data-processing industry employed large numbers of well-trained and well-paid sales representatives who developed close contacts with their customers, performing systems analyses of the decision process and information needs for each client before recommending the data-processing equip-

ment and software programs that would meet the perceived requirements. This meant a lengthy cycle of visits to each customer, and brought heavy analysis and developmental cost for each sale; together the sales calls, systems analysis, and program development pushed the personal selling expenses of the data-processing industry to an estimated 20% of the net revenues.

The management of Cambridge Computer believed that their terminal, which was standard, with prewired software programs for routine computations, could be sold without customer analysis and program development costs. They also felt that the distinctive features of the terminal design, the large number of possible applications, and the low level of the rental charges would sell the machines without the need for the traditional personal sales effort. They planned, instead, to market the new data-processing units with advertisements in trade magazines and business publications, and with promotions and demonstrations at industry shows, and felt that this approach would result in a definite cost savings:

> In another cost-cutting gambit, CamComp's sales staff was small in size. Marketing was handled through attention-grabbing advertisements in specialty and general interest publications, as well as by roadshows at selected trade get-togethers. (Statement of an industry executive)

Cambridge Computer planned to change the entire marketing structure of the industry, starting with the person they deal with in each company. You realize that data-processing equipment is a mystery to most of the people who actually buy it. The treasurer of a company may know what is meant by a "byte," but he probably does not know whether he needs a 40K or 100K byte storage for his main core, and he certainly has no knowledge about multiplexor channels, solid-state logic technology, or intersystem capability. Most businessmen are the captives of their EDP consultants or of their staff specialists in systems analysis and program design, and they have to rely on those people for hardware selection, which is sort of a joint effort between the sales force of the equipment manufacturer and the technical staff of the company. But this cooperative effort, which seems so good in theory, has ended in disaster any number of times, and there have been countless "work-out" situations, where the problems had to be worked out in use, at tremendous cost in computer time, programmer effort, employee irritation and customer resentment. The result was that management personnel wanted simple systems that they could understand. Cambridge Computer was going to provide those simple systems, and they were going to sell them by bringing a unit to your office, setting it on your desk, and letting you play with it. The system might not be any good, but they could still sell a million units since they would be selling them to the right people in the right way. Also, they could cut costs since they didn't have to hire technically trained salesmen; any novice with a smile and an M.B.A. could do it. (Statement of an industry executive)

The marketing of the CamComp terminals will be principally by participation in business shows, advertising in newspapers, magazines and trade journals, and by demonstration. The Company anticipates that if the CamComp system is favorably received, the Company will require facilities in a number of cities to serve as demonstration and distribution centers. (Statement in the *Prospectus* of the Cambridge Computer Corporation, March 12, 1969, p. 9)

The management of the company planned, after sales became established, to substitute office machinery dealers in at least 40 cities throughout the country for the small centralized sales force. They believed that potential customers would learn of the new data-processing terminals either through descriptions in the extensive advertising program or by

recommendations from the existing equipment users, and ask for a demonstration. The local dealer would provide the demonstration, take the subsequent orders, and supply the machines from stock. No other data-processing equipment manufacturer sold through office machinery dealers since they were generally considered to lack the technical competence necessary to perform the usual information analysis and program design for each customer. The Cambridge Computer terminal, however, was standard, and fitted into the existing information system of each customer without additional programming, so it was felt that the dealer could demonstrate the unit easily, almost as simply as an electric calculator or typewriter. It was expected that this method of distribution would substantially reduce sales expenses since each dealer required only a discount of approximately 10%:

Selling costs in the data processing and computer field typically have been high, and represent a significant portion of the sales price. The Company expects to sell through a network of local dealers, which should reduce selling costs. Should the Company incur costs which are typical in the industry, such costs might have serious adverse effects upon the Company. (Statement in the *Prospectus* of the Cambridge Computer Corporation, March 12, 1969, p. 10)

Advertising. The reliance of Cambridge Computer upon local dealers for equipment demonstrations and sales required supporting advertisements to convince potential customers to ask for a demonstration. Basically, the company was relying upon "pull" marketing rather than upon the traditional "push," and they budgeted substantial sums for the necessary publicity. During 1969, while the product was still under development, they spent $2,000,000 in both general business publications such as the *Wall Street Journal* and the *Harvard Business Review,* and in specialized trade magazines such as *Datamation, Data Management, Computerworld,* and the *Electronic News.* An equivalent amount was allocated to continue the advertising program in 1970:

> Well, Cambridge Computer blitzed with an advertising campaign the likes of which the data-processing industry had never seen before, and CamComp quickly became the most talked about company in the industry. (Statement of an industry executive)

Service and Repair. The use by Cambridge Computer of local dealers also permitted the company to change the traditional methods of service and repair of electronic data-processing equipment. Other companies in the industry maintained large numbers of highly trained and highly paid servicemen to repair electronic equipment for their customers in the field. Cambridge Computer planned to offer a replacement rather than a repair service; extra machines would be stocked by the dealer in each area, and terminals which failed in use would be replaced and brought back to the dealer's location where company personnel, on a planned travel schedule, would test and repair the units at their convenience by replacing stock subassemblies and circuit boards. It was expected that this method of repair would substantially reduce the service expense since the repair work would be simpler and better scheduled.

> The company plans to service CamComp terminals by replacing any machine which becomes inoperative. Under this program, two standby terminals will be provided to the local dealer for each 50 units sold or leased. (Statement in the *Prospectus* of the Cambridge Computer Corporation, dated March 12, 1969, p. 10)
>
> As far as maintenance is concerned, the company plans a departure from conventional arrangements in which hordes of high-priced field service personnel are kept at the ready or on the go. Customers

ordering volume lots will get two extra machines with each 50 installed for use as immediate replacements in case of breakdowns. Otherwise, failed sections will be replaced with stock subassemblies and circuit boards from the dealer network. At present, management estimates that only 7% of monthly rental income need be allocated to cover all servicing and associated overhead under this setup. By industry standards, this is a phenomenally low level. (Statement of an industry executive)

Production. Cambridge Computer planned to keep total costs low and to reduce fixed investments by purchasing most of the electronic components from suppliers within the United States, by arranging for the subassembly of these components on circuit boards abroad, in Hong Kong, Japan, and Korea, and by performing only the final assembly of the data-processing terminal at their own plant in Cambridge, Massachusetts. Unlike most other manufacturers of data-processing equipment, who built various models of both central processing units and peripheral equipment in batches, Cambridge Computer intended to mass produce standard terminals on a production line:

> Benson wants to do for the computer industry what Henry Ford did for automobiles: he wants to be the first to provide mass production. (Statement of an industry executive)

Component manufacture was the first problem in mass production of the new data-processing terminals. Metal oxide semiconductors (MOS) were, as described previously in the section of the case on technology, an inexpensive form of integrated circuitry, but also a relatively new advance in microelectronics. Since the technology was new, no manufacturer was prepared to produce MOS circuitry in volume, and few were willing to make the investment required to produce the new large-scale integrated circuits at all:

There was a certain Alphonse and Gaston aspect to the situation; there was no mass outlet for MOS circuitry since there were few MOS chips to be had at any price; likewise, MOS chips were unavailable commercially because sizeable markets were lacking. It remained for Cambridge Computer to recognize the opportunity, and get things going. (Statement of an industry executive)

The company broke the deadlock on MOS circuitry by financing the development of the production methodology in their own labs, and then making the results of this development available to the electronics industry generally. They designed the logic for their standard chips, drew the subsequent circuits to scale, photographed the drawings and reduced the negatives to form the masks for the photoengraving process, and then gave the masks to the suppliers. This development of the manufacturing process was expensive, both in the research effort for design and in the capital investment for equipment, but it was also successful. The assets of the company for microelectronic processing expanded from less than $10,000 in October 1968 to over $1,400,000 in October 1969. (Source: Cambridge Computer Corporation, *Annual Report for 1969*.). But numerous suppliers became interested:

Volume was the key. The company planned to buy so much MOS componentry that even slim profit margins would mean big money for suppliers. . . . The company was the biggest commercial outlet for MOS. Its initial annual requirements were estimated at 2.5 million circuits, worth upwards of $12.5 million. This represented quite a bonanza for the semiconductor industry whose total sales volume was only $5 million just a few years ago. Thus, it was not at all surprising that when the company snapped its fingers, semiconductor suppliers started to look for a hoop to jump through. (Statement of a financial analyst)

The company planned to keep the costs of electronic components as low as possible by sharing the developmental charges for each circuit with suppliers and by purchasing each resultant chip in substantial volume. Non-electronic parts were also designed in-house, and the designs were then fabricated locally, by nearly captive suppliers, to keep these expenses down:

Once Cambridge Computer got rolling, it planned to take a leaf from the automakers' book and bankroll some of its subcontractors. Something of a start had been made along these lines as the company developed captive capacities to make motors, power supplies, keyboards, and related items. It was planned to run those operations as semiautonomous subsidiaries as soon as the company got over the hump. (Statement of a financial analyst)

Subassembly of the MOS chips on printed-circuit boards was to be performed abroad, in areas with low labor charges, such as Hong Kong, Korea, and Japan, and the final assembly of the circuit boards and other electronic and mechanical components was to be automated to further reduce costs. Automation was possible since the company planned a monthly output of 5,000 to 6,000 machines:

Even though every single part for the CamComp terminal was to be coming in at the lowest possible price, production costs could still put the project over the proposed rental rate if due care were not exercised. With this in mind, and with the thought that savings of only a few dollars apiece on each of 60,000 or 70,000 terminals per year would be worthwhile, Cambridge Computer planned on automating everywhere savings could be realized. Eventually, 80% of assembly operations were handled this way. (Statement of a financial analyst)

Finance. The design of the new data-processing terminals, the development of the new MOS technology, and the promotion of the new decentralized information and decision system concept all required substantial amounts of money. Cambridge Computer deliberately expensed all of these developmental and promotional charges, so that the income statements for the first two years showed large deficits (Exhibit 1).

Exhibit 1 *Income statement for Cambridge Computer Corporation, 1968 and 1969*

	1968	1969
Net sales and interest income	$ 102,000	$ 1,067,100
Operating expenses	118,300	1,110,200
Product development and marketing expenses	909,300	5,886,900
General and administrative expenses	382,900	3,541,600
	$1,356,300	$10,538,700
Net profit or (loss) for the year	(1,254,300)	(9,471,600)

Source: Annual Report for 1969, p. 3.

The total deficit for the first two years was $10,725,900. These losses were expected; Drs. Benson and Siegal had planned to operate at a loss for the first few years, concentrating on product, process, and market development and they had raised sufficient funds to carry the company through this period. At year end 1968, Cambridge Computer still had a 1.7:1 current ratio, and cash and marketable securities of over $4 million (Exhibit 2).

Exhibit 2 *Balance sheet for Cambridge Computer Corporation at year end, 1969*

Cash	$ 621,800	
Short-term investments at cost or market	3,449,600	
Accounts receivable less reserve	218,600	
Inventories, at lower of cost or market	1,025,600	
Deposits and prepaid expenses	211,600	$5,527,300
Fixed asset, less depreciation	1,944,900	
Other assets, principally lease deposits	302,500	2,247,400
		$7,774,700
Notes payable to banks	100,000	
Accounts payable to suppliers	2,842,700	
Accrued expenses	286,000	$3,228,700
Common stock, at $1.00 stated value	3,145,200	
Amount in excess of stated value	12,126,700	
Retained earnings (deficit)	(10,725,900)	4,546,000
		$7,774,700

Source: Annual Report for 1969, p. 5.

The equity, which totaled $15,271,900, had been raised through a series of private and public placements:

Initial fund, provided by the founders and the members of Dillon Read and Company	$ 807,300
Private placement, arranged through Shields and Company	1,130,000
Private placement, arranged through Herzfeld and Stern	2,225,300
Public issuance, underwritten by Shields and Company, with 800,000 shares sold at $15/share less expenses	11,109,300
	$15,271,900

In addition to the funds already committed to the company at the end of 1969, an issuance of $25,000,000 of 6¼% 20-year convertible subordinated debentures was arranged early in 1970 to yield approximately $24,000,000 to Cambridge Computer. These debentures were convertible at $30 per share, and contained a sinking-fund requirement of $1,250,000 per year after 1975; they were sold to raise the funds required to finance the start of production and sales under the "rental only" policy. Additional funds were available, if needed, through a major line of credit arranged with Boston and New York banks.

Cambridge Computer Corporation was able to raise over $40,000,000 in equity and near-equity (convertible subordinated debentures). There were a number of reasons for this generous response from the financial community; one of the major reasons was that 1968 was a period of national prosperity and of investor interest in venture capital opportunities:

> In 1968 and 1969, that segment of America that deals in and buys stocks and bonds and is sometimes referred to as the financial community was on the lookout for speculative deals and stocks that had

the potential of becoming high flyers. The more speculative the proposal, the more attractive a situation could look. Warnings that there might never be dividends, that the competition was fierce, that there was no patent protection ... all these seemed to lull investors into a sense of security since the warnings only proved that the company was aware of all the potential pitfalls. (Statement of a financial analyst)

A second reason for the ability of Cambridge Computer to raise large sums of money from the financial community was the financial and technical competence of Dr. Benson:

> While Benson had earned high marks as a scientist and manager at MITRE (the government-sponsored research institute in Lexington, Massachusetts) and, before that, as a member of the faculty at Tufts University for about eight years, it became abundantly clear when he started Cambridge Computer that he had at last found his true calling; he was a born hustler of venture capital. Members of prestigious Wall Street institutions—houses that tended to look upon new computer companies with the same skepticism with which they viewed uranium mining ventures—were impressed enough by Benson and his company that they backed his venture and helped raise additional funds for CamComp. (Statement of a financial analyst)

The last reason for the availability of capital to finance the design of the new terminals, the development of the new technology, and the promotion of the new data-processing system was the appeal of the product that Cambridge Computer had devised: the data-processing industry was large, profitable, and expanding rapidly; and the thought of participating in that industry through a small and easily understood desktop terminal was attractive to many investors:

> Dr. Benson raised a lot of money for Cambridge Computer, and to some ex-

tent he was the right man at the right time. But he also had the right product. People who had owned IBM or Xerox stock in the early 1960s had generally made a lot of money; others were looking for the same type of investment in the 1970s. Cambridge Computer certainly seemed to offer the same appreciation potential with their product. (Statement of an industry executive)

The combination of the product, the technology, and the promotion raised the price of the stock from $0.50 per share at the founding, in November 1967, to $3.00 per share at the first private placement in August 1968, to $15.00 per share at the time of the public issuance in April 1969, and then to $64.00 on the over-the-counter market in January 1970. The management of the company felt, in view of the recent debenture sale that brought in $24,000,000, the high stock price that made future equity financing attractive, and the large line of credit available from Boston and New York banks, that financing the future growth of the company would not be a problem.

Product Development. Cambridge Computer had a substantial technological lead in the development of metal-oxide-semiconductor (MOS) large-scale integrated (LSI) circuitry. They planned to use this circuitry in the design of such diverse products as small computers for the control of industrial processes, large computers for centralized data processing, data banks for attachment to existing computers, optical character readers, digital wrist watches, portable televisions, and pocket calculators:

> Your students may think that the company is spreading out too thinly, but they have to realize that all of these products, from large computers to small TV's, are based on the MOS/LSI technology which gives CamComp a cost advantage of about 10:1 over their competitors. You

have to realize that each of the MOS/LSI chips contains circuitry equivalent to 100 radios; they intend to use that low-cost circuitry in all sorts of new products. (Statement of an industry executive)

Cambridge Computer began moving into new product areas at a fast pace. Two 16-bit small computers, scheduled for delivery in the spring of 1970, were announced at startlingly low rates—$99 a month with 4K memory and $199 a month with 8K memory. In addition, CamComp was working on two more computers, a cut-rate model that was to sell for $2,000 and a high-performance model that would round out the top of the line. Then, they were working on a family of OCR devices that would revolutionize the optical character reading industry and a semiconductor memory based on a chip with a 10,000-bit read/write memory. (Statement of an industry executive)

Personnel. Cambridge Computer grew rapidly during the period of development, from 12 employees in November 1967, to 100 in October 1968, to 570 in October 1969, to 1,300 in January 1970. These employees, as is often true in a company that is growing rapidly with numerous opportunities for promotion, were enthusiastic about the products and potential of the company, but also seemed to have a special spirit that was often noted by industry observers.

> CamComp's employees were deeply committed to the company, and displayed a remarkable esprit de corps. One Wall Street newsletter described the phenomenon like this: "The personnel of Cam-Comp, from secretaries to president, exude vitality, excitement." From the free soft drinks, coffee, popcorn, and potato chips to the one month's vacation and liberal stock options, CamComp's benevolence and paternalism toward its employees fired them with an enthusiasm seldom, if ever, found among any com-

pany's rank-and-file employees. (Statement of a financial analyst)

Present Situation. At the date of the case, January 1970, Cambridge Computer had finished the design of the new terminals, completed the development of the MOS/LSI circuitry, and concluded the initial promotion of the decentralized data-processing concept. They were about to start the phase of mass manufacture and mass marketing of their products. The following statements will confirm the company's position in the important areas of product characteristics, technological innovations, marketing, production, and finance at this time:

1. *Product characteristics.* The new CamComp terminals were not only designed, but also produced and installed, for over 200 units had been tested at various locations throughout the country:

   Cambridge Computer really makes a sweet computer terminal. (Statement of an industry executive quoted in the *Wall Street Journal,* April 30, 1970, p. 1)

   We're very satisfied; we've found the CamComp system to be very reliable. (Statement of a New England Telephone and Telegraph executive, quoted in the *Wall Street Journal,* April 30, 1970, p. 1)

   Customers like the idea of data entry, transmission, storage, and computation combined in one decentralized system so the information can be used for current decisions. (Statement of an industry executive)

2. *Technological innovations.* The metal-oxide-semiconductor (MOS) large-scale integrated (LSI) circuitry was not only developed, it was in use in the various CamComp products:

   These people really have something; there is no question of that. What they have is a cost and reliability advantage over everyone else in the data-processing industry due to their development of the MOS/LSI technology. (Statement of an industry executive)

3. *Marketing.* Cambridge Computer priced the new terminals low, in comparison with existing equipment, to sell customers; provided demonstration, first through a small central sales force and then by a network of dispersed local dealers, to convince customers; and promoted the concept of decentralized data processing, by extensive ads in general business and specialty trade magazines, to attract customers. This marketing plan was successful; the company had received, by January 1970, letters of intent representing potential orders for 30,000 to 100,000 machines:

   Their first approach of using the media and sending demonstration teams around the country worked immensely well. Under this approach, they developed 30,000 solid letters-of-intent. And more than 50% of these were from Fortune 500 companies. (Statement of an industry executive)

   The success of the Cambridge Computer marketing plan was attested to by the large numbers of letters of intent that poured into the company files; there were over 20,000, each of which sought to reserve from 1 to 100 machines.... Unlike orders for large machines, which typically dribble in one at a time, bookings for these terminals could be very big deals, in bunches of 100 or more. (Statement of a financial analyst)

4. *Production.* Cambridge Computer started full-scale manufacturing of the new terminals in January 1970, when 600 units were produced. This was very considerably below the original target of 5,000 to 6,000 units, but it was felt that this was a respectable number for the start of the year, and that it provided a knowledge and experience base for the mass production to be achieved about the middle of the year:

   CamComp employees and stockholders were jubilant over the terminals that were being shipped from their Massachusetts plant. (Statement of a financial analyst)

5. *Finance.* Cambridge Computer had, after the sale of the convertible subordinated debentures in January 1970, cash and marketable securities in excess of $28,000,-000; financing was not thought to be a problem:

For the first time in their short history, the company was not worried about money. (Statement of a financial analyst)

The position of Cambridge Computer Corporation in January 1970, as viewed by the management, can probably best be summarized in a quotation from the *Annual Report for 1969*, and the opinion of the financial community can be seen in a final quotation from the report of a major brokerage firm.

At the end of Cambridge Computer's second fiscal year, your Company shared top billing with IBM as one of the most influential companies in the data processing industry. This route from concept and design to production and delivery was marked by several noteworthy milestones:
    Cambridge Computer moved, in March 1969, to its present headquarters building in Cambridge, Massachusetts.
    Cambridge Computer employment increased from approximately 150 to more than 600 people.
    Cambridge Computer developed an outstanding capability in large-scale integrated (LSI) metal-oxide-semiconductor (MOS) technology.
    Cambridge Computer established a manufacturing and assembly operation, with over 120,000 square feet, for the production of CamComp products.
    Cambridge Computer announced two small general-purpose computers.
    The Directors and Officers join me in expressing our appreciation to our stockholders for their help in making this fiscal year one of growth and achievement.
    Together we enter the decade of the seventies with CamComp an important name in data processing. My goal is that together we can leave the decade with

CamComp the important name. (Cambridge Computer Corporation, *Annual Report for 1969*, pp. 1ff.)

Meaningful earnings projections are difficult to make in the case of a pioneer operation like Cambridge Computer. But if the company can keep to its ambitious schedule through early next year, as we think probable, it will be virtually home free with R&D and preliminary marketing introductions behind it. We consider per-share earnings of $6 to $8 well within reach by the mid-1970s.
    The risks involved in a commitment in Cambridge Computer are, as we have noted, considerable. The company is launching a radically new EDP product line, built around a commercially unproven technology. The cost of this temerity is appallingly high. And even if production and delivery schedules are made on the dot, the quarterly earnings reports will probably continue to be written in red ink until well into the early 1970s. Meanwhile, the book value is only about $3.50 per share.
    For all these problems, however, we think the game is well worth the candle. Seldom is there such a clear-cut and attractive opportunity to get in on the ground floor of an outfit like Cambridge Computer. We're fully aware of the double-edged leverage in the situation, but are inclined to view it favorably in light of our analysis of the company's prospects for technological and marketing success. If nothing else, management's track record of having shepherded the company past the rocks and shoals of MOS technology to a spot within sight of the marketplace's far shore speaks volumes for its capacities to map out a goal and harness technical talent to reach it. Moreover, the company's executives have proven themselves infinitely resourceful at raising required funds in a difficult money market. In view of the company's immense potential, we advise purchase of its shares by risk-oriented accounts. (Report by a brokerage firm)

Class Assignment. The class assignment is divided into five parts:

1. Describe the strategy, or mixture of goals and objectives and the major financial policies and plans for achieving those goals and objectives, designed by Drs. Benson and Siegal for the Cambridge Computer Corporation.
2. Design at least two alternative strategies, or mixtures of other goals and objectives and the consistent functional policies and plans needed for the achievement of those other goals and objectives, for the Cambridge Computer Corporation.

    Note: It is suggested that a matrix be prepared to compare the existing strategy and the two alternative strategies by very specific definitions of the corporate objectives, product characteristics, market segments, marketing policies, production policies, financial policies, R&D policies, and personnel policies (see accompanying table).

3. Evaluate the existing strategy, designed by Drs. Benson and Siegal, and the alternative strategies conceived by you, in light of the characteristics and trends of the data-processing industry, the strengths and weaknesses of the Cambridge Computer Corporation, and the values and attitudes toward risk of the management of the company, all at the date of the case, January 1970.
4. Based upon your evaluation, select the proper strategy for the Cambridge Computer Corporation. What is your estimate of the probability of the future success of the firm, given the existing strategy and the existing conditions of the industry, the company, and the management, in January 1970?
5. Define, in your own terms, the concepts of "strategy," "objectives," and "policies."

	Current strategy	Alternative A strategy	Alternative B strategy
Corporate objectives			
Product characteristics			
Product uses			
Market segments			
Marketing policies			
Production policies			
Financial policies			
R&D policies			
Personnel policies			

Chapter 2

STRATEGIC DESIGN IN SMALLER BUSINESS FIRMS

Strategic design was defined, in Chapter 1, as the long-term method of competition to be followed by a company. There are different methods of competition (alternative strategies) that are possible within each industry, and the function of the general manager of the company is to select the method (strategy formulation) with the greatest probability of success, given the specific opportunities and risks within the environment and the specific strengths and weaknesses within the corporation. This process of strategic management was shown in outline format as repeated here at the top of the following page.

Strategic design differs between smaller firms and large corporations. The smaller firm operates in only one industry, unlike larger companies, which often have diversified across numerous industries. The smaller firm generally has a low market share, unlike larger companies, which can use a high market share to dominate an industry. The smaller firm may appear to have room for growth within a given industry, due to their low share of the existing market, but this growth potential is often severely limited by a lack of promotional, productive, or financial resources. Small companies are commonly defined by a ceiling on sales (e.g., under $20,000,000 revenues) or by an upper limit on personnel (e.g., fewer than 500 employees), but probably an equally valid though less precise definition would center on the lack of relevant resources (market advantages, production facilities, or financial assets). Most smaller companies never seem to have the resources necessary to take advantage of the opportunities that exist within their environment. In very simple terms, small companies never seem to have quite enough money or people.

Because of the importance of resources in the selection of the strategy, or the long-term method of competition, for a smaller business firm, the primary emphasis in strategic design for these companies has to be placed upon an analysis of the corporate performance and position and, deriving from this analysis, an understanding of the organizational resources, or strengths and weaknesses. In basic terms, organi-

Environmental characteristics
and trends

Economic

Technological

Social/political

Competitive

↓

Organizational mission or charter	Specific opportunities and risks within the industry	
↓	↓	Selected strategy, or method of com- petition
Corporate perform- ance and position	Range of strategic alternatives open to the firm	
↑	↑	
Managerial values and attitudes	Specific strengths and weak- nesses within the company	

↑

Money

Equipment

People

Market position

Organizational resources, or
assets and skills

---

zational resources, assets, and skills are not what the company has, but what the company can do, and particularly what the company can do better than their competitors in the same industry. Consequently, the evaluation of the organizational resources has to be dependent upon an analysis of the prior performance and current position of the firm. Of course, despite this emphasis upon corporate performance and organizational resources in the design of the strategy for a smaller business firm, the other elements of organizational mission, managerial values, and environmental characteristics should not be forgotten. In a small company particularly, the ambitions, intentions, assumptions, and ethical standards of the owners and managers, and the gradual trends or sudden changes in the economic/technical/competitive environment are often determinant in strategy selection. But environmental trends and changes are difficult to forecast, and individual ambitions and assumptions are awkward to understand; a good starting place is the competitive position and performance of the firm. This analysis of the competitive position and performance can be divided for purpose of explanation and review into the three primary functional areas of marketing, production, and finance.

EVALUATION OF THE MARKETING PERFORMANCE AND POSITION OF THE FIRM

Marketing can be described, quite simply, as the process of adapting the characteristics of a product or service to fit the needs and wants of customers in a specific market segment, and then combining the price level, distribution methods, and advertising or promotional expenditures into a consistent marketing plan, adjusted to the features of the product, the desires of the customers, and their motives and methods for purchase. This summarization of the marketing function can be portrayed graphically as follows:

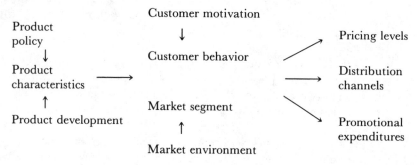

Not all of these components of the marketing function are subject to company control. Demand variables, such as the demographic, economic, social, political, and competitive factors in the market environment, and the psychological, social, and rational patterns in customer motivation, are autonomous. Semi-demand variables, which include market segmentation and customer behavior, are only partially under the control of the company, while the decision variables, which are the product characteristics and the pricing, distribution, and promotional policies, are totally under company control. The essential responsibility of marketing management is the design of an integrated marketing plan that relates the demand and semi-demand variables of the market and consumer to the decision variables of the firm to generate an optimal sales response. An evaluation of the performance of the marketing management requires consideration of the interrelationships of these demand, semi-demand, and decision variables in a logical sequence.

Product Characteristics. A product is a physical or symbolic good or service expected to yield satisfactions and benefits to the buyer. The first step in the evaluation of the marketing function is the identification of the specific tangible and intangible product features that provide these satisfactions and benefits. Tangible product features include esthetic (appearance, style, etc.), use (convenience, preparation, etc.), and performance (effectiveness, reliability, etc.) characteristics. Intangible product features include gratification (personal reactions to the product related to appearance, health, etc.) and status (interpersonal and social reactions to the product related to acceptance, esteem, etc.) characteristics. Differentiation of a product, of course, refers to the tangible and intangible product features that distinguish it from the competition. Differentiation of a product is often important in the marketing performance of a business firm.

Product Development. The features of a product are not irrevocably set; they may be changed to differentiate the product from the competition, or modified to adapt the product to trends within the market. Under modern conditions of competition, feature changes and modifications are increasingly important; they are also increasingly expensive and uncertain. The design life cycle, of course, refers to a fairly predictable maturation of a product, without feature change or modification, through the stages of introduction, growth, popularity, saturation, and decline. Identification of the stages of the life cycle is often important in the evaluation of the marketing performance of a business firm.

Product Policy. Product policy includes the classification of a company's products into types, the grouping of types into product lines, and the selection of lines for the product mix of the firm. Product types are the basic modular units of the company's design, generally produced with similar components, and usually offering similar tangible and intangible features. Product lines are the composite of product types, generally produced with interchangeable components and often offering only slightly different tangible and intangible features. Product mix is the composite of the product lines offered by a company. Identification of the total product mix is usually important in the evaluation of the marketing performance of a business firm.

Market Environment. The market environment includes the demographic, economic, social, political, and competitive factors that influence the primary demand for a product or service. Demographic demand factors include such trends as the increasing population numbers, changing age groups, and existing social, religious, or ethnic classes. Economic demand factors include the rising national, personal, and disposable incomes, and increasing costs for services, repair, or construction. Social demand factors are the increasing leisure time, geographic mobility, and ethnic or racial consciousness, while political demand factors include increasing welfare payments, urban services, aerospace expenditures, etc. Competitive demand factors refer to the promotion, distribution, and sale of similar or substitute product lines. Identification of the relevant factors in the market environment is critical in the evaluation of the marketing performance of a business firm.

Market Segmentation. Market segmentation refers to the division of the primary national market into secondary groupings of customers with identical socioeconomic, geographic, or behavioral characteristics who tend to respond similarly to product features or marketing methods. To be useful, these market segments should be measurable, accessible, and substantial. An integrated marketing plan should specifically identify the market segments expected for each product line by such group characteristics as the socioeconomic factors (groupings by age, sex, income, occupation, education, family life cycle, etc.), the geographic factors (groupings by region of the country, density of the population, type of the climate, etc.), and the behavioral factors (groupings by usage rate, buyer motive, brand loyalty, channel allegiance, price sensitivity, etc.). Specification of the relevant factors in market segmentation is essential in the evaluation of the marketing performance of a business firm.

Customer Motivation. Customer motivation refers to the reasons for purchase of a specific product by a member of a given market segment. Various theories from the academic disciplines have been adapted to marketing applications to help explain these subjective factors in the decisions and attitudes of buyers. An integrated marketing plan should consider the reasons expected for purchase of each product line as interpreted by economic theory (explains purchasing decisions as the result of rational and conscious economic calculations, through maximization of the utility function; the purchase is rational and thoughtful), psychological theory (explains purchasing decisions as a learned response to marketing stimuli, such as product features or promotional policies; the purchase is habitual rather than thoughtful), psychoanalytical theory (explains purchasing decisions as a response to symbolic as well as economic and functional product features; the purchase is controlled by unconscious hopes, fears, and duties rather than by conscious thought processes), and social–psychological theory (explains purchasing decisions as the result of the individual conforming to the norms, beliefs, and values of the various groups, organizations, and subcultures to which he/she belongs; the purchase is for social approval). An understanding of the applicable theories in customer motivation is useful in the evaluation of the marketing performance of the firm.

Customer Behavior. Customer behavior refers to the stages of the buying decision, the participants in that decision, and the process of purchase that together help to identify the objective factors in the actions and attitudes of customers within a specific market segment, as influenced by the subjective factors of the customer motivation. The stages in the buying decision include the felt need, prepurchase comparisons, purchase choice, produce use, and postuse reactions. Participants in the buying decision include, for consumer products, the family members and friends who may influence the purchase or use of the product, and for industrial products, the technical, operational, or financial personnel who may advise on the purchase or use of the product. The process of buying includes the normal time, place, and frequency of purchase, the method of delivery, and the terms of payment. An understanding of these sequential elements in customer behavior is useful in the evaluation of the marketing performance of the firm.

Pricing Decisions. The selection of the price level is the first of the three decision variables that relate the marketing play to the product characteristics, market segment, and customer motivation and behavior. Pricing is important, since the level selected limits or expands the potential market, and limits or expands the operating margin. There are two major methods for this selection of the price level for a product line. Theoretical pricing models have been developed for firms that know their demand and cost functions; these models use mathematical programs to maximize profits within market and financial parameters. Pragmatic pricing methods have traditionally been used by firms that do not know their demand and cost functions; these methods include markups over cost at a standard percentage, target returns on investment at a standard volume, competitive pricing at industry levels, etc. An understanding of the methods of price-level determination, and the relevance of each method to the product characteristics, market segment, and customer behavior, is critical in the evaluation of the marketing performance of the firm.

Distribution Decisions. The selection of the distribution method is the second of the three decision variables that relate the marketing plan to the product characteristics, market segment, and customer behavior. Distribution is important, since the channel selected initiates and maintains the contact between the producer and the user for the transfer of both goods and information. Types of distribution channels range from direct contact between the producer and the ultimate users (direct sales), to one, two, or three intermediaries (wholesalers, jobbers, and retailers). Activities of the distribution channels vary from selling only to include transportation, storage, delivery, installation, and repair of goods, and supervision of credit. An understanding of the benefits, costs, and problems of the various types of distributors, and the relevance of that type to the product characteristics, market segment, and customer behavior, is important in the evaluation of the marketing performance of the firm.

Promotional Decisions. The selection of the promotional program is the last of the decision variables that relate the marketing plan to the product characteristics, market segment, and customer behavior. Advertising is important, for it provides a contact between the producer and the user for an explanation of the product features (tangible and intangible) and a description of the marketing plan (relative price and available locations). The content of the promotional program includes decisions on expenditures, media, and message. An understanding of the content of the promotional program, and the relationship of that content to the product characteristics, market segment, and customer behavior, is essential in the evaluation of the marketing performance of the firm.

EVALUATION OF THE PRODUCTION PERFORMANCE AND POSITION OF THE FIRM

The term "production" has traditionally been associated with the factory, and with the planning, scheduling, and control of large-scale manufacturing processes, but the same concepts and techniques that are used in manufacturing firms are certainly applicable in service organizations, financial institutions, retail stores, and distribution companies. Production should be considered, in its broadest context, as the design of a system to produce a given good or service, and the management of that system for optimal performance. The productive system, of course, utilizes the physical facilities of the firm to maximize the total output for a given mixture of inputs. The view of production can be shown in outline form as follows:

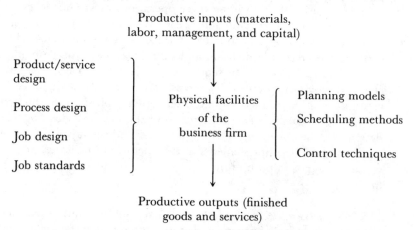

Productive inputs (materials, labor, management, and capital)

Product/service design

Process design

Job design

Job standards

Physical facilities of the business firm

Planning models

Scheduling methods

Control techniques

Productive outputs (finished goods and services)

The management of the productive process, therefore, involves combining the product, process, and job designs with the establishment of job standards to define effective physical facilities, and the planning, scheduling, and control of those facilities for efficient usage of the inputs. Production management is important in the overall performance and position of the firm, and the evaluation of this function involves consideration of each of the system's elements, in sequence.

Product/Service Design. The design of the product or service is the first step in the development of an effective productive system. This operational design is in addition to the engineering design that earlier has determined the performance and appearance of the product; the operational design is concerned with the efficient production of the item or service, and involves standardization and simplification. Standardization can be defined as the reduction of product or service variations to gain uniformity and interchangeability, while simplification is the reduction of product or service complexities to gain easier operational methods, and includes substitution of materials, relaxation of tolerances, and combination of operations. Both standardization and simplification are often illustrated by examples from mechanical engineering and machinery manufacturing, but the concepts are equally applicable in service, financial, distribution, and retail operations. Consideration of possible improvements in the standardization or simplification of the product or service design is important in the evaluation of the productive performance of the firm.

Process Design. The design of the process to meet product or service specifications is the second step in the development of an effective productive system. Process design includes the selection of operations, facilities, and sequences. The selection of operations is based upon the design characteristics of the product or service, and involves the translation of the engineering specifications into process requirements. The selection of facilities is then based upon this list of process requirements, for the operations necessary to manufacture each part of a product or to provide each portion of a service are translated into the process equipment or machinery capable of performing these operations at various levels of demand. The operations required to manufacture each part and assembly of a product or to provide each element and portion of a service can be sequenced in different ways, depending on the standardization and simplification of the design and the expected volume of the demand. The sequence of operations governs the flow of material or clients through the productive process. There are two basic flows that are possible: continuous (line production) and intermittent (job-shop production), with combinations between these two extremes, and the material flow, or selected sequence, determines the placement of the equipment and the layout of the process. Investigation of possible improvements in the operations, facilities, and sequences of the process design is important in the evaluation of the productive performance of the firm.

Job Design. Despite recent advances in automation and process technology, manual work remains an important element in most manufacturing and service industries. Therefore, job design remains an important consideration in the development of an effective productive system. Job design may be divided into determination of the work content, recommendations for the work methods, and design of the work environment. Work content is not consciously designed; it is the direct result of prior decisions on product or service design and process planning. It is what the workers must do to accomplish a given task or operation. Work methods, on the other hand, are consciously designed; they are the direct results of efforts to improve the performance of the work content through changes in the workplace arrangement or the process equipment controls. Work methods are what the workers should do to accomplish a given task or operation in the most economical fashion. Work environment is the setting in which the work methods are performed. It includes temperature, humidity, noise, lighting, etc., all of which can have a marked effect on productivity and quality levels. Examination of possible improvements in the work methods and work environment is important both for the evaluation of the productive performance of the firm, and for the recognition of the employment responsibilities and the individual obligations of the company.

Job Standards. A job standard is the amount of time it should take an average worker to perform a specific job after the essential work content has been defined and after the optimal work methods and work environment have been established. Job standards are used for production planning, scheduling, and control, and for product costing and wage incentives. They are normally set by time study in which either a stopwatch or synthetic times are used, and despite the inaccuracies and skepticisms associated with time study, job standards are important in the evaluation of the productive performance of the firm.

Production Planning Models. Production planning involves the adjustment of the designed capacity of the physical facilities to meet variations in aggregate product

or service demand. These adjustments may be made by changes in the employment level, in overtime or undertime payments, in order backlogs or inventory
buildup, or by make-buy decisions. The objective of production planning is to
minimize the total costs of meeting expected but uncertain demand under the restrictions of a given productive system. Decisions on how to minimize these planning costs can be made by expressing the relationships between variables and constraints within the system through such techniques as linear cost models, quadratic
cost functions, queuing networks, or computer simulations. An understanding of
the potential of production planning models is important in the evaluation of the
productive performance of the firm.

Production Scheduling Techniques. Production scheduling involves the adjustment of the designed capacity of the physical facilities to meet variations in individual product or service demand. The objective of production scheduling is to minimize the total costs of meeting existing and known demand under the restrictions of
a given productive system. Decisions on how to minimize these scheduling costs
can be made by expressing the relationships between variables and constraints
within the system through such methods as linear programming, integer programming, or dynamic programming. An understanding of the potential of production
scheduling techniques is important in the evaluation of the productive performance
of the firm.

Production Control Methods. Production control involves the supervision of the
output of the physical facilities to adjust for variations in individual effort or machine performance. Supervision is performed by recording the output in product
units, machine times, or quality tolerances, and comparing these measurements
with accepted standards. The objective of production control is to maintain performance at the anticipated quantity, cost, and quality standards. The methods
that are employed use computerized data processing and statistical sampling since
the amount of data produced and information needed in even a small system is
enormous. An understanding of the methods of production control is important in
the evaluation of the productive performance of the firm.

EVALUATION OF THE FINANCIAL PERFORMANCE AND POSITION
OF THE FIRM

Financial management is concerned with the effective utilization of the assets, both
current (short-term) and fixed (long-term), of a business organization, and with the
means of providing funds to support those assets through the use of current liabilities, intermediate loans, and capital debt or equity. Financial decisions are those
that eventually affect the ability of the firm to support the investments in new products, markets, processes, or capacities that are needed for growth, and the objective
of financial management is to maximize this financial capability by combining the
uses of capital with the sources, structure, and cost of capital, in a consistent financial program. The view of financial management can be portrayed in schematic
form as shown at the top of the next page.

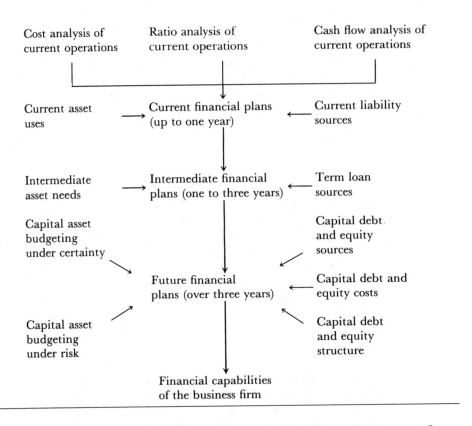

Financial management, in short, combines administration of the current financial position with planning for the intermediate and future financial conditions of a company to provide funds to support the operations and investments of that firm. It is the means of "meeting the payroll" now and "paying the bills" in the future for a continuing business organization; it is the method of providing the financial capabilities needed for the growth of an active business firm.

Financial management, to a very real extent, summarizes the performance of the other functional areas of the firm. A business firm is an economic entity, and the accounting data, which are condensed into the financial statements, reflect the competitive performance of the total entity. Consequently, an understanding of the financial statements is essential in the evaluation of the performance and position of the firm. This understanding can be developed through cost analysis, ratio analysis, and cash flow analysis:

Cost Analysis of Current Operations. The analysis of the costs of the existing operations is the first step in the evaluation of the financial position of the firm since a knowledge of costs is essential for financial planning and control. Costs may be of different types, and may be accumulated and allocated by different systems:

1. *Types of costs.* Costs are generally divided between direct versus indirect types and between fixed versus semifixed versus variable classes. Direct costs can be

identified with specific departments, products, or processes, while indirect costs cannot be easily identified for allocation, and have a general applicability. Fixed costs remain constant over a range of production rates, while semi-fixed costs vary in a discontinuous fashion or step function with production, and variable costs vary directly with the production rate.

2. *Types of cost accumulation systems.* Costs may be accumulated by the job, by the product, by the process, or by the area of responsibility. Job costing collects expenses for each individual product or service as it moves through the productive system; this method is used where goods or services are individually produced and heterogeneous. Product costing collects expenses for each group of similar products or services as they move through the productive system; this method is used where goods and services are mass-produced but still heterogeneous. Process costing collects expenses for a time period, with no attempt to separate those costs by individual products or groups of products; it is used when goods and services are mass-produced and homogeneous. Finally, area costing collects expenses for a physical space, with no attempt to separate those costs by individual products or groups of products; it is used for overhead costs that are recorded by each area, or center, responsible for their incurrence.

3. *Types of cost allocation systems.* Costs may be allocated to products, processes, or services through direct costing, standard costing, or full costing systems. Direct costing charges the variable production costs of direct labor, direct material, and direct overhead, with no allocation of fixed expenses, or indirect overhead, to the product, process, or service. Direct costs are those that vary directly with the rate of production; at the close of each accounting period, the actual costs that have not been allocated are charged to the period as general overhead expenses. Standard costing charges the estimated production costs of standard labor, standard material, and standard overhead, based upon an allocation at various predetermined levels of production, to the product, process, or service. Standard costs are those that should have been incurred at a given level of production; at the close of each accounting period, the actual costs are reconciled with the standard costs through variance analysis. Full costing charges the actual production costs of direct labor, direct material, and complete overhead, based upon an allocation at an existing percentage of direct labor, to the product, process, or service. Full costs are those which were incurred at a given level of production; at the close of each accounting period, the actual costs should have been completely allocated to the specific units of production.

4. *Cost-decision analysis.* Many financial decisions involve alternative courses of action, with different costs attached to each alternative. For each decision, it must be established which costs are relevant, and which are marginal or incremental. Relevant costs are the "out-of-pocket" expenditures which require an allocation of current resources to the alternative under study, while sunk costs represent a resource previously allocated, and thus should be irrelevant to the decision. Marginal costs are those expenses added by producing one additional unit of the good or service, while incremental costs are those added by producing a predetermined number of additional units; both marginal and incremental costs are often relevant to a financial decision.

Ratio Analysis of Current Operations. The analysis of the ratios of the existing operations is the second step in the evaluation of the financial position of the firm since these ratios, which relate two or more pieces of financial data, permit comparisons with past, present, or future ratios for the same firm, for similar firms, or for industry averages. The financial ratios for a single year are interesting; these same ratios, compared across prior years or compared with industry averages, are vital for understanding the operations and problems of a firm. Six types of financial ratios are commonly computed from balance sheet and income statement data:

1. *Liquidity ratios,* which show the company's ability to meet short-term debts, are used to indicate the credit strength and financial risk of the firm. Liquidity ratios commonly used include the current ratio and the acid-test ratio:

$$\text{current ratio} = \frac{\text{current assets}}{\text{current liabilities}}$$

$$\text{acid-test ratio} = \frac{\text{current assets} - \text{inventory}}{\text{current liabilities}}$$

2. *Profitability ratios,* which show the company's profitability in relation to either sales or investments, are used to indicate the operational efficiency of the firm. Commonly used profitability ratios include the return on sales, the return on assets, and the return on equity:

$$\text{return on sales} = \frac{\text{profits after tax}}{\text{total sales}}$$

$$\text{return on assets} = \frac{\text{profits after tax}}{\text{total assets}}$$

$$\text{return on equity} = \frac{\text{profits after tax}}{\text{total equity (assets} - \text{debt)}}$$

3. *Utilization ratios,* which show the company's ability to use short-term assets, are used to indicate the financial efficiency of the firm. Commonly used utilization ratios include the receivables in days, the inventory in days, and the payables in days:

$$\text{receivables in days} = \frac{\text{accounts receivable}}{\text{annual sales} \div 360 \text{ days}}$$

$$\text{inventory in days} = \frac{\text{total inventory}}{\text{annual cost of goods sold} \div 360 \text{ days}}$$

$$\text{payables in days} = \frac{\text{accounts payable}}{\text{annual purchases} \div 360 \text{ days}}$$

4. *Debt ratios,* which show the proportion of debt in the company's capital structure, are used to indicate the credit strength and financial risk of the firm. Commonly used debt ratios include the debt/equity ratio and the long-term debt percentage:

$$\text{debt/equity ratio} = \frac{\text{total debt (current liability + long-term debt)}}{\text{total equity (assets − debt)}}$$

$$\text{long-term debt \%} = \frac{\text{long-term debt}}{\text{total capitalization (assets − current liabilities)}}$$

5. *Coverage ratios,* which show the company's ability to meet the fixed financial charges of the long-term debt in the capital structure, are also used to indicate the credit strength and financial risk of the firm. Commonly used coverage ratios include the number of times debt interest is earned, and the number of times debt payments, both interest and principle, are earned:

$$\text{debt interest earned} = \frac{\text{company profits before interest and taxes}}{\text{annual debt interest payments}}$$

$$\text{debt interest earned} = \frac{\text{company profits before interest and taxes}}{\text{annual debt (interest and principal) payments}}$$

6. *Expense ratios,* which show the company's various expense categories in relation to sales, are used to compare the firm's performance with past time periods and with industry averages. Expense ratios are commonly calculated for all the major expense categories, such as material cost, labor cost, selling expense, professional (legal and accounting) services, etc.:

$$\text{expense ratios} = \frac{\text{expense category}}{\text{annual sales}}$$

Cash Flow Analysis of Current Operations. The analysis of the cash flow of the existing operations is the third step in the evaluation of the financial position of the firm since a source and application of funds statement summarizes the major changes in the financial condition of a company over a given accounting period.

1. Preparation of a source and application of funds statement is basically a comparison of balance sheets for the beginning and end of a given accounting period. Changes within the individual accounts represent either a commitment or reduction of resources; these changes may be a result of explicit managerial decisions or unrecognized environmental conditions, but result in either an application or source of funds. An application of funds is an increase in an asset account, or a decrease in a liability or equity account, over the accounting

period. A source of funds is a decrease in an asset account, or an increase in a liability or equity account, over the period.

2. Adjustment of a source and application of funds statement is performed to either eliminate or explain balance sheet changes brought about by accounting conventions that do not truly represent a commitment or reduction of resources. Changes in the net property account should be reconciled with the depreciation reported for the period to indicate the full investment, inclusive of write-offs of property. Change in the retained earnings account should be reconciled with the net profits after tax reported for the period, inclusive of write-offs of capitalized expenses or payments of dividends.

This section has reviewed the major factors involved in an evaluation of the marketing, production, and financial functions within a business firm. Marketing, production, and finance do not include the sum of all activities with a firm, for they neglect product development, process engineering, market research, labor relations, data processing, and general management, but they do include many of the essential tasks that govern the competitive performance and position of the organization. To a certain extent, evaluation of the secondary activities can be derived from a study of the three primary functions. That is, competent product development can be assumed from sales revenue growth and new product introductions, and concerned labor relations can be projected from production volume, quality, and cost performance. In summary, it is necessary to consider the full range of managerial activities, but to concentrate on the marketing, production, and financial functions in evaluating the performance and position of a firm.

An accounting of the resources of the company can be derived from a study of the performance and position of the firm. Resources are capabilities; they are the tasks that the company can do well, and particularly, they are the tasks that the company can do better than their competitors within a given industry. Financial and physical assets are resources also, but only for their potential conversion into improved or expanded managerial performance. That is, the secure financial position of a corporation, with large cash resources and extensive borrowing capacity, is valuable in strategic terms for its eventual conversion into new products, new processes, new markets, or new capacities that, if the managerial tasks are well performed, will lead to an even stronger financial position. Timing, of course, is important. The conversion does not have to be immediate, and the same secure financial position can be used to wait out a period of industry overcapacity. Direction is also important, and the same financial resources can be used to change industries, or to achieve product differentiation and market diversification.

Direction and timing are almost synonyms for strategic design. They are the critical components in strategy selection, for the general manager must decide upon the direction in which the competitive posture of the firm is to move, and the timing of that move. Direction and timing are particularly important in smaller business firms, owing to their usual lack of a dominant market position, and their typical shortage of competitive resources. Smaller firms must make optimal use of what they have.

The process of strategic design in a smaller business firm starts, as described previously, with an evaluation of the corporate performance and position. This analysis should not be limited to the most recent accounting statements, and should not be expressed solely in terms of profits (or losses) as a percentage of sales or assets; instead, the past performance and current position of the firm should be critically reviewed in all the major functional areas to determine the future competitive potential of the business. Remember that history is filled with accounts of companies that appeared to be performing poorly while developing the new products, markets, or processes that provided this future competitive potential; while nearly every stockholder and creditor of smaller companies can give examples of firms that apparently were very successful, but that permitted their competitive positions to totally deteriorate. The evaluation of the performance and position and potential of a company should be thorough, and explicit.

The past performance, current position, and future potential of a company, particularly in smaller businesses, should be compared not against accepted standards, such as 10% annual growth or a 15% return on equity, but against the charter or mission of the organization and the values and attitudes of the managers. The central question is not whether the company is performing well, but whether the company has the potential to achieve the goals stated by the founders, or to fulfill the ambitions of the managers and others associated with the organization. Once again, remember that high annual profits, personal salaries, and capital gains are not necessarily the objectives of everyone associated with a business enterprise. It is necessary to consider what the people involved want from an organization, and this is normally stated in the mission or charter, or expressed in their values and attitudes.

After comparing the performance, position, and potential of a company against the goals and ambitions of the owners, managers, and employees, it is often obvious that there is a gap. The company has not performed, and does not appear to have the potential to perform, as well as expected by those involved. It is this gap that should be filled by the strategic manager, either by a new direction (strategy formulation or design), or by a new effort along the existing direction (strategy implementation or administration).

Strategy formulation or design for the small single-product business firm, the subject of this chapter, is primarily a selection of the product–market position. The smaller company normally cannot expect to dominate an entire market against existing competitors, many of which will be considerably larger, with much greater financial and managerial resources, but the management of the smaller company can search for a segment of the total market, in which competition is not intensive, and then concentrate their efforts and activities in that segment. Strategic design for the smaller company is primarily product–market positioning, using product characteristics, both tangible and intangible, to match customer needs, motives, and behavior patterns in a specific segment of the market. To find this segment, it is useful to divide the primary market into secondary groupings of customers with identical socioeconomic, geographic, or behavioral characteristics (for consumer products) or with similar economic and technical needs (for industrial products), and then to identify the competitive products or services that are offered to these segments. This analysis can be visually portrayed in a simple matrix:

	Product characteristics	Market segment A	Market segment B	Market segment C
Segment characteristics	✕			
Product 1				
Product 2				
Product 3				

Strategic design, in the most basic terms, is a search for a competitive advantage. For the smaller company, with limited resources, this competitive advantage most often is a product–market position, or market "niche," with limited competition, adequate margins, and an opportunity for growth. For each small company, there is a range of possible product–market positions; the function of the general manager of the firm is to select the position that most closely fits the limited resources of the company. Strategic planning for a smaller firm is, therefore, product–market oriented and resource based. The intent of the planning process is to improve the performance, position, and potential of the company; the following cases illustrate this strategic planning process in smaller business firms.

Concord Fashion Clothing Corporation

Martin and Arnold Pozniak were two brothers who had taken over the management of the Concord Fashion Clothing Corporation in 1970, following the death of their uncle, and who were in the process of taking over the ownership of the firm by paying their aunt for her stock. The two brothers were ambitious, and felt that their uncle had been overly conservative and had neglected many good opportunities for expansion and growth over the years since he had founded the company in 1948 to produce medium-priced women's dresses for sale to the smaller department stores and clothing chains in New England. Martin and Arnold planned to expand the size of the company rapidly, by modernizing the production facilities and by adding new products. In 1974, sales had expanded to $3,158,000, from only $1,470,000 in 1970, but in February 1975 the two brothers were looking with dismay at the audited financial records, which showed the first loss in the company's history (Exhibit 1).

Exhibit 1 *Income statements for Concord Fashion Clothing Corporation, 1970–1974*

	1970	1971	1972	1973	1974
Contract dress sales	$1,470,600	$1,587,200	$1,920,300	$2,361,700	$2,266,300
Houseware sales	—	264,700	441,500	480,100	474,200
Toy and novelty sales	—	16,500	31,900	46,300	55,800
Sleepware sales	—	—	371,000	408,400	361,700
Total company sales	1,470,600	1,868,400	2,764,700	3,296,500	3,158,000
Material cost	612,300	761,400	1,141,800	1,397,700	1,389,500
Labor cost	470,600	614,700	931,700	1,190,000	1,174,700
Manufacturing overhead	160,900	168,300	309,600	379,100	397,900
Total direct costs	1,243,800	1,544,400	2,383,100	2,966,800	2,962,100
Gross profit	226,800	324,000	381,600	329,700	195,900
Selling and promotional expenses	51,700	69,800	124,400	141,700	132,600
Administrative expenses	64,200	75,400	84,100	93,600	89,700
Interest expenses	3,400	41,200	52,700	58,300	66,700
Total indirect expenses	119,300	186,400	261,200	293,600	289,000
Pretax profit or (loss)	107,500	137,600	120,400	36,100	(91,100)
Federal and state taxes	− 55,900	− 71,400	− 62,600	− 10,700	+ 38,700
Net profit or (loss)	51,600	66,200	57,800	25,400	(52,400)

Source: Company records.

The two brothers were also concerned by a substantial deterioration in the financial position of the firm, which had been partially caused by provisions in the purchase agreement, partially by expenditures for new equipment and a corporate acquisition, and partially by the operating loss. The balance sheets for the years 1970–1974 are shown in Exhibit 2.

The purchase agreement was designed to provide a firm value for the stock which would be accepted by the Internal Revenue Service, and to permit payment for this stock primarily from the cash flow of the company. $500,000 in subordinated debentures ("subordinated" is a term that is used when debentures or bonds are legally recognized to be junior to all other debt, and thus are considered to be equity or "near equity" by the banks and other creditors) were issued to Mrs. I. R. Kapsky, the widow of the founder, in exchange for her stock, worth $60,000 at par value, which was returned to the company treasury. These debentures were to be repaid at the rate of $12,500 per quarter, plus interest at 8% annually; in each year in which the full payments were made, the two brothers were each permitted to purchase 5% of the stock from the company treasury at par value. The intent of the purchase agreement was that over 10 years Mrs. Kapsky would receive full payment of $500,000 plus interest from the company, and the two brothers would own the 6,000 shares of her stock, with a personal investment of only $30,000 each.

The financial transactions connected with the purchase of the company by Martin and

Exhibit 2 *Balance sheets for Concord Fashion Clothing Corporation, 1970–1974*

	1970	1971	1972	1973	1974
Cash	$ 21,700	$ 19,700	$ 14,900	$ 21,900	$ 5,200
Accounts receivable	116,100	134,500	240,500	299,900	353,700
Inventory	98,600	125,700	221,800	317,800	387,900
Net current assets	236,400	279,900	477,200	639,600	746,800
Machinery and equipment (net)	207,300	214,300	267,800	237,700	223,900
Land and building (net)	140,700	135,200	148,300	141,500	136,500
Prepaid expenses	11,900	9,700	12,700	17,600	16,300
Goodwill	—	—	10,000	10,000	10,000
Net fixed assets	359,900	359,200	438,800	406,800	386,700
Total assets	596,300	639,100	916,000	1,046,400	1,113,500
Accounts payable	12,200	17,300	94,500	146,400	213,200
Bank loans—current	42,500	59,000	169,900	300,100	208,400
Taxes due	11,100	7,700	14,000	8,500	2,100
Accrued expenses	3,100	5,500	14,200	16,600	21,400
Net current liabilities	68,900	89,500	292,600	471,600	445,100
Bank loan—term	—	—	60,000	30,000	
Bank loan—secured	—	—	—	—	240,000
Subordinated debentures	—	450,000	400,000	350,000	300,000
Net long-term debt	—	450,000	460,000	380,000	540,000
Common stock	87,500	33,500	39,500	45,500	51,500
Retained earnings	439,900	66,100	123,900	149,300	96,900
Net equity	527,400	99,600	163,400	194,800	148,400
Total liabilities and equity	596,300	639,100	916,000	1,046,400	1,113,500

Source: Company records.

Arnold Pozniak in 1970 are not central to the problems of the company in 1974, but in order that the purchase agreement may be quickly understood, and the balance sheets rapidly analyzed, the accounting transactions that occurred in 1971 are explained in detail at the top of page 53.

It had always been expected that the two brothers would eventually own the company. Their uncle and aunt, Mr. and Mrs. Kapsky, had only one child, a daughter who had married a physician and lived in Ann Arbor, Michigan, and neither she nor her husband had any interest in managing the company, although she was a member of the board of directors, and was paid to attend the quarterly board meetings. Mr. Kapsky had died more suddenly than expected, so that neither brother had had an opportunity to participate in the management of the firm,

Long-Term Debt

1. $500,000 of 8% subordinated debentures were issued to Mrs. I. R. Kapsky in exchange for 6,000 shares of $10.00 par value stock, at the negotiated price of $83.33 per share (approximately 10 times earnings and close to the book value of the company in 1971) — $500,000

2. $50,000 was repaid on the debentures by the Concord Fashion Clothing Corporation during 1971, at the stated rate of $12,500 per quarter — − 50,000

3. $450,000 of 8% subordinated debentures was reported on the December 31, 1971, balance sheet — $450,000

Common Stock

1. 8,750 shares of $10.00 par value common stock were reported on the December 31, 1970, balance sheet (prior to the purchase) — $ 87,500

2. 6,000 shares of $10.00 par value common stock were returned to the company treasury by Mrs. I. R. Kapsky during 1971, at par — − 60,000

3. 600 shares of $10.00 par value common stock were purchased by Martin and Arnold Pozniak during 1971, at par — + 6,000

4. 3,350 shares of $10.00 par value common stock were reported on the December 31, 1971, balance sheet, at par — $ 33,500

Retained Earnings

1. $439,900 retained earnings were reported on the December 31, 1970, balance sheet — $439,900

2. $440,000 was charged to retained earnings for the issuance of the 8% subordinated debentures ($500,000 total amount less $60,000 charged to common stock account) — − 440,000

3. $66,200 after-tax profits for 1971 were added to the retained earnings account — + 66,200

4. $66,100 retained earnings were reported on the December 31, 1971, balance sheet — $ 66,100

but both had worked at the company during summer vacations and had performed many of the skilled jobs, such as cutting the cloth to fit the patterns and repairing the sewing machines, and had done all of the manual jobs, such as packing the dresses for shipment and sweeping the factory floors, so that they both felt that they knew the production process reasonably well, and Arnold had been a salesman for his uncle one summer, so that he thought that he knew the marketing problems. Both brothers were confident that they would have no difficulties in running the company, partially as a result of their experience, and partially as a result of their education. Martin had a law degree from Boston University, and had worked for a law firm in Manchester (largest city in New Hampshire, and 21 miles south of Concord) for five years, while Arnold was a recent graduate of the University of Vermont, where he had majored in sociology, but had also taken a number of courses in business administration. Martin planned to remain active in his law firm, although he was listed as the president of the Concord Fashion Clothing Corporation, and he expected to leave the day-to-day management of the company in the hands of his younger brother, Arnold, and another uncle, Gordon Wirtz, who was the brother of Mrs. Kapsky and the owner of the balance of the common stock, 2,750 shares.

The Concord Fashion Clothing Corporation was basically a contract dress manufacturer that existed to provide a service to many of the smaller department stores and local dress shops in northern New England. These small retailers often found it difficult to buy from the large dress manufacturers in New York City since they did not have the sales volume, purchasing power, or market prestige of the regional chains and Boston-based stores. Numerous instances existed of the local companies being charged substantially higher prices for the same merchandise, despite the explicit provisions of antitrust legislation, or having popular merchandise delayed in shipment in favor of the larger buyers. Price level and style availability are important in women's clothing sales, so many of the small retailers would attend the shows and sales in New York City, but would place orders for "equivalent" merchandise with Concord Fashions.

Mr. Kapsky had started the company in Concord, New Hampshire, since this location was central to his market, and his customers in Vermont, New Hampshire, and Maine could easily visit the factory to negotiate prices, place orders, press for deliveries, pick up shipments, or just visit with "I. R.," who had a reputation as an outgoing, though opinionated individual who was always willing to discuss fashion trends, economic prospects, or merchandising methods. In 1948, at the start of the company, Concord was also a low-wage area since two ancient textile mills had recently moved to the South, and the locomotive repair shops of the Boston and Maine and the Concord had recently closed. (Steam locomotives required service every 100 miles, and therefore Concord had been the natural repair center since it was located 100 miles north of Boston, 100 miles east of Portland, and 100 miles south of Woodsville, the major railway junction in Vermont; diesel engines require service only every 5,000 miles, so the regional repair shops were closed as the new diesels replaced the steam locomotives.) By 1970, the advantage of the low wage rates had nearly disappeared as small electronic firms and machinery manufacturers moved north from Boston, but the advantage of the central location had been greatly strengthened as Concord became the hub of three routes in the interstate highway system.

Mr. Kapsky, in 1956, had purchased an old stone warehouse from the Concord and Claremont railroad, and had converted it for use as a clothing factory, wholesale showroom, and general office. It was located near a park on the river, but with easy access from city streets and with ample parking for customers and workers. The company purchased cloth from the large dealers in Boston and from the small textile mills that remained in New England, cut the cloth to patterns for the various styles and sizes of dresses, and then sewed, finished, pressed, and packaged the dresses for shipment. Lots as small as 10 dresses in one style would be processed, but the typical order was for 75, in different sizes and colors, and often it was possible to combine orders from different customers so that the run could be 300 to 500 units.

> When our uncle ran the company, it was just a job shop. He would produce any dress for any customer; all he needed were the patterns, or an "equivalent" dress he could take apart to make the patterns; one or two of the older workers here could even draw the patterns from a picture in *Vogue* or *Harper's Bazaar*. My uncle would figure the price himself, and since he had a tough foreman who made certain that there was no unnecessary waste or idle time in the shop, he seldom lost money. But he didn't make much money either. He worked hard all of his life, and he wound up with a nice house and $500,-000. Martin and I want to do a lot better than that. (Statement of Mr. Arnold Pozniak)

In 1971, the first year that they managed the company, the two brothers added two new products. The first, reported in the income statement as "household items," consisted of a line of matched barbecue aprons and gloves that were bright and colorful, and often either decorated with pictures of hot dogs, hamburgers, or martinis, or lettered with expressions of gently amusing intent; these were sold through hardward stores, department stores, and gift stores. The second new product was a line of stuffed animals and dolls, together with clothing for both, that was manufactured from waste cloth and sold through toy stores and hobby shops.

> The barbecue aprons and gloves fitted right into our production process, and helped us get volume. The sales rep, Paul Cummings, had handled a line made in Mississippi, but he came to us since we could do a little better on the commission, given the freight savings and given that we wanted to get into the business.
>
> I added the toy line since I always felt that it was wasteful to throw away the scraps of cloth that are left over after the cutting operation. I designed a bear, a dog and a cat, and a "Raggedy Ann"-type doll, and the same clothing items, shorts, vest, and a hat, fit them all. I look after the sales. The stuffed toys are going to be a big item with us—we've doubled sales each year since we started—if I can just spend enough time calling on the trade to get distribution. (Statement of Mr. Arnold Pozniak)

The company also added about $28,000 of new machinery and equipment in 1971, primarily in partially automated sewing machines to finish the seams in the dresses, aprons, and toys after the cut fabric had been "tacked" or partially stitched on a manual machine, and they placed an order for a $67,000 computerized cutting system to reduce waste and increase production in shearing cloth to the patterns; $18,000 in building alterations were required to install the cutting system, which came complete with material-handling facilities.

Cutting and sewing cloth is a volume business; the more cloth you cut and sew, the more money you make. So we added some new, high-speed sewing machines to increase capacity. The big change, though, was in cutting. My uncle used to manually lay out the cloth and then arrange the patterns; we've been able to automate that entire process. We still cut with electric shears, just as he did, but eventually we'll put in a pantograph and automate the cutting also. (Statement of Mr. Arnold Pozniak)

In 1972, another new product was added to the company's line: flannel sleeping garments for children. The brothers heard of a small clothing company with this product line that was for sale in northern New York from one of their textile suppliers; they arranged to buy the business as a going concern, with accounts receivable, inventory, 15 flannel sewing machines (flannel requires a special feeding attachment during sewing to prevent stretching and malforming the cloth), and a long-standing relationship with a wholesaler in Albany, for $60,000. They moved the machines to Concord, and continued manufacturing for the Albany wholesaler while soliciting business from local department stores and children's wear retailers.

> It was too good a deal to pass up; we bought almost $400,000 in annual sales volume for just $60,000, and all the machinery, inventory and accounts receivable. We even got a few thousand dollars in cash. We plan to keep looking for other deals like this. You'd be surprised at the business you can find if you just keep your eyes open. (Statement of Mr. Arnold Pozniak)

In 1975, following the loss that was reported for fiscal 1974, a member of the faculty at the Graduate School of Business Administration at the University of Michigan was asked by the daughter of Mrs. I. R. Kapsky, who had sold the company to the two brothers, to visit the firm, talk with the managers, and make some recommendations or suggestions to avoid losses in the future. The daughter knew the faculty member since they were neighbors in Ann Arbor, the site of the University of Michigan, and she knew that her friend had once worked in New Hampshire, and often visited the state for both business and personal reasons. On the next trip, the faculty member made an appointment, drove to Concord, met with the brothers, and received the following comments and explanations during that meeting:

We're certainly willing to talk to you since our cousin asked you to come over to see us, and since we like her and she's on our Board. But she really doesn't have a thing to worry about; we're going to keep right on making those payments to her mother, right on time.

The problem is that 1974 was just about the worst year in the clothing business since the depression. Nobody was buying styled garments, so there just wasn't much business for our contract dresses. And the business that was there was at cut-throat prices; the buyers were just talking price, not what you had done for them last week or last month or last year. 1975 will be a lot better, and we've got a deal going. We're going to cut dresses, skirts, and slacks from patterns, baste the seams, do some of the detail work such as button holes, but not finish the garments. Instead, we will fold the cut and basted fabrics, package them in envelopes that have a color picture of the finished garment on the outside, mark them for size, and sell them to K-Mart. This merchandising company came to us, since we have the capacity; all we have to do is put in an automatic presser on the second floor, and set up a packaging line. The buyer at K-Mart is really excited, and we have a guarantee of at least $500,000 worth of business.

We do have some problems; we'll be frank about them. We're the same as any other company, and there are some things that we probably could do better. For example, Paul Cummings, the sales rep who handles our household line of barbecue aprons, is talking about going back to his old company. He is just trying to hold us up for more money. I wish that those people had more loyalty, but they don't. What do you think we ought to do; you're the expert from the university. I think that we ought to tell him to go right back to his old company, and find somebody else. There are plenty of good sales reps around. (Statement of Mr. Martin Pozniak)

We've got a problem with pricing the contract dresses. We keep getting price increases on the fabric we buy, and you may think that we can just pass those price increases on to our customers, but we can't. We have contracts with our customers, and even where we don't, their buyers will fight price increases all the way. We know our material cost, and that's all you really need to know in this business since your labor is generally 75 to 80% of the material—it takes so much labor to cut up and finish so much cloth—but how do we get our customers to pay the increases. We're in the middle, and inflation is hard on the small company in the middle.

Another problem is our shop foreman, Jean Bouttilier. He's older, and he's just not doing as well as he used to; there's too much wasted cloth and wasted time in the shop now. The whole shop used to be French [many persons of French Canadian ancestry had emigrated to northern New England during the early part of the twentieth century], and my uncle, who spoke Polish and German as a boy, learned French just to be able to talk to the workers. But, now we hire anyone, and there aren't many of the old women left. The morale is poor, and Jean doesn't help at all since he is from the old school, and just yells at the workers. That used to work, when jobs were scarce, but it certainly doesn't work today. How do you motivate people now? Maybe we ought to put in a piece rate system, just like they have in the union shops in New York. (Statement of Mr. Arnold Pozniak)

One last problem, as long as we're being really frank in talking to you, is that we're worried about Gordon [Gordon Wirtz, brother of Mrs. I. R. Kapsky, and a person who had helped his brother-in-law start the company in 1948 with a personal investment of $27,500]. Gordon is the treasurer of the company, but he doesn't do much. He even tried to prevent us from buying that flannel nightwear business. I think that he is upset because we didn't offer to buy his stock, but we can't afford to do that. Instead, we have kept him on as treasurer, at a good salary, but he's got to start helping. How do you get a guy to cooperate?

But, these are all people problems; they're not marketing or production or financial problems. So tell our cousin not to worry. The contract dress business is coming back, and we'll have that deal with K-Mart, which will boost the volume, and Arnold is going to spend his time pushing the stuffed animals and dolls, which can't help but do well. Finally, there is a bowling alley nearby that we can buy, which would smooth out our sales, and we would not have to push so much on the contract dresses. So you can see that there is nothing for our cousin to worry about; tell her that when you get back to Ann Arbor. (Statement of Mr. Martin Pozniak)

Class Assignment. Members of the class should consider the following questions:

1. Do you agree with the optimistic assessment of the two brothers that Mrs. Kapsky and her daughter have "nothing to worry about"?
2. If you do not agree, consider the problems facing this company; list five problems in your order of importance.
3. How should these problems have been avoided; list five specific suggestions for changes in management practices over the past four years, again in your order of importance.
4. What would you do now if you were the consultant from Ann Arbor? Make specific suggestions for improvement.

Advanced Hydraulic Technologies, Inc.

Advanced Hydraulic Technologies, Inc., or Ad-Tech as it was known from the trademark embossed on all products, was founded in February 1964 to manufacture and market a new fitting or connector for hydraulic sys-

This case was prepared from an earlier version written by Professor Henry E. Riggs of the Graduate School of Business Administration at Stanford University, and is used with his permission and with the permission of the Board of Trustees of Leland Stanford Junior University.

tems. Hydraulic systems are used to convey fluids under pressure either to utilize the fluid (as, for example, in the fuel-injection system for a diesel engine) or to utilize the pressure for mechanical actions (as in the hydraulic brake system on an automobile, or for the power transmission system on the front-end loader of a tractor). Each hydraulic system normally consists of a fluid reservoir, a rotary pump, a control valve, an actuating device such as a fuel injector or a hydraulic cylinder, and the pipes, tubing, or hoses to tie the components together. Each component has entry and exit ports, and each port has either tapered threads or straight threads with a flared internal shelf. Each piece of pipe, tubing, or hose has a fitting with a matching thread, either tapered or straight with a flared end. The tapered threads are coated with a sealing compound and then turned together tightly to prevent leaks; the straight threads use an elastic "O"-ring that fits between the flared end of the fitting and the internal shelf of the port to prevent leaks.

Charles Altlan, the founder of Ad-Tech, felt that there were two major problems with the existing connectors for hydraulic systems. First, the connectors were an item on which the major manufacturers and users of hydraulic equipment had never been able to agree on common standards, and therefore the threads in the entry and exit ports of hydraulic components could either be tapered in 14 different sizes (⅛- to 3-in. internal diameters) or straight with three different flares (37° SAE, 37° MS, or 45° MS) and 12 different sizes (1/16- to 2-in. internal diameters). Since the components in a system could be connected with gray iron pipe or plastic tubing (both for low pressure only) or by thin-wall tubing, thick-wall tubing, standard hose, and high-pressure hose, and since it was necessary theoretically to be able to connect each type and size of pipe, tubing, or hose to each type and size of the entry and exit ports, the total number of potential fittings was immense. This total number was even larger than the use of simple permutations might suggest, for it was often necessary to redirect or divide a hydraulic line, and therefore elbows (two connectors with a 45° or 90° bend), tees (three connectors at 90° angles), or crosses (four connectors at 90° angles) were needed. Further, connectors could be made in plastic (low pressure), brass (medium pressure), and steel (high pressure) and the threads could be either external or internal. Mr. Graham estimated that 60,000 com-

binations were reasonable (a ⅛-in. tapered thread port to a 2-in. hydraulic hose was not considered to be a "reasonable" combination), and that 1,800 combinations were commonly used. To reduce the problems caused by the lack of standardization, most manufacturers and users of hydraulic equipment stocked "converters," which were short, straight fittings with different threads on each end, such as tapered external threads to straight internal threads with 37° SAE flare, but the use of converters increased the cost and complexity of the system.

The second problem that Mr. Altlan felt was inherent in the existing connectors for hydraulic systems was caused by the need to turn each fitting on threads to obtain a tight seal. Each connector with internal threads was made in two sections with a union joint that permitted rotary motion between the two sections; the section that contained the internal threads could be turned without turning the section attached to the pipe, tubing, or hose. The union joint became leakproof as it was turned tightly on the matching fitting with a flared end that compressed the internal "O"-ring. However, as the union joint became leakproof, it also became rigid, and further tightening on the threads would transmit torsional forces through the pipes, tubes, and hoses of the system, and those torsional forces could create minor leaks in other fittings and connectors. Also, it was very difficult in many hydraulic systems, where the components, fittings, and tubing had been mounted either inside a control panel or inside the structure of the machinery, to turn the fittings on the threads to obtain a tight seal. Theoretically, designers were to leave adequate clearances to turn a wrench 90° around each fitting, but in practice these tolerances were often narrowed or neglected, and it became very difficult to assemble many hydraulic systems, and particularly difficult to disassemble them for maintenance and repair.

Mr. Altlan had developed, during 1965

while he was struggling to complete a very complex hydraulic system for the National Aeronautics and Space Administration, a hydraulic fitting that snapped onto a connector block rather than turning on threads onto a connecting fitting (see the accompanying illustration). Each connector block had a machined slot, an internal flared shelf, and an "O"-ring; each fitting had two machined wings that fitted precisely into the slot in the connector block, and an external flared end that would compress the "O"-ring and provide a tight seal. In use, the connector block was threaded into the entry or exit port on one of the components of a hydraulic system, and the new fitting was mounted, through the

normal means of swaging, pressing, or threading, onto a section of pipe, tubing, or hose, and then the two parts were snapped together. Final assembly was much easier, and torsional forces were not transmitted through the system, since no turning was required to connect the parts and obtain a tight seal. Also, because of the modular nature of the parts, a large number of combination fittings in elbows, tees, and crosses could be assembled from a limited number of snap-on fittings and connector blocks.

Pleased with the performance of the new connectors, and impressed with their potential in the $570,000,000 hydraulic fittings market within the United States, Mr. Altlan

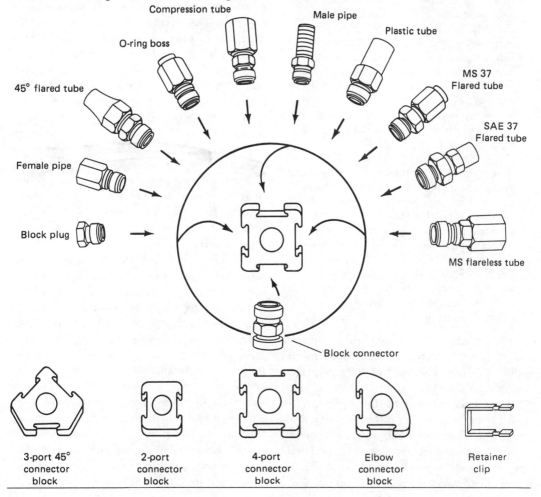

Compression tube

O-ring boss

Male pipe

Plastic tube

45° flared tube

MS 37
Flared tube

SAE 37
Flared tube

Female pipe

Block plug

MS flareless tube

Block connector

3-port 45°
connector
block

2-port
connector
block

4-port
connector
block

Elbow
connector
block

Retainer
clip

redirected his company from subcontract assembly of complex hydraulic systems to proprietary manufacture and sale of snap-on hydraulic fittings and connectors.

The Ad-Tech fitting is another example of the "spin-off" effect that you get from government expenditures for aerospace research. Charlie had a contract to build a hydraulically operated robot to test space suits for the National Aeronautics and Space Administration. He found he could not connect the hydraulics.

The robot, of course, had to be man-sized, and had to be capable of mimicking most human movements. The intent was to put a space suit on the robot, and then have it make repetitive movements until something wore out. It was a good idea, and an essential test, but like many ideas in the space program, some of the important details had been left out. In this case, the designer had shown all of the cylinders and valves on the blueprints, but none of the connections. There was no room, inside the robot, to turn a wrench in order to tighten the threaded pipe fittings.

Charlie had a fixed-fee contract to assemble the robot, and no way to connect the components. But he is an ingenious guy, and he thought up the idea of the snap-on fitting. He had a local machine shop make the parts, and he put together a mass of piping and a tangle of hoses inside that robot, and everything worked and nothing leaked. Everybody told him it was the greatest invention since canned beer. He started his company the next week. (Statement of Hobart Ryerson)

In February 1965, when the company started to actively market the new hydraulic fitting, the firm consisted of a three-person product development group and a small machine shop that were both financed partially from savings which Mr. Altlan had accumulated from previous jobs in project engineering and subcontract assembly, and partially through a stock issuance of 70,000 shares which had been sold at $1.00 per share

to a group of local investors. Mr. Altlan spent the first few months after the stock issuance visiting potential customers to determine the future acceptance of his new product, while the other members of the product development group manufactured sample fittings and requested bids from local machine shops for volume production of the various parts.

As a result of his market research, during which many potential customers had expressed a willingness to try the new hydraulic fittings, Mr. Altlan decided to market the product line through local distributors. He recognized that these distributors, who normally carried a large number of products for sale to customers within a given geographic area, such as northern California, could be expected to have only a limited familiarity with each line, and would probably devote only a small portion of their efforts to developing sales for new products, but he also thought that the customers he had contacted appeared to be willing to try the new fitting, and would need little missionary selling. The distributors might be little more than order-takers when contacting customers, but they would stock parts for prompt delivery, and they would assume the credit risk for final payment, both of which were important for a small company starting in a new industry.

In mid-1965, Mr. Altlan began shifting his sales effort toward OEMs, the original equipment manufacturers, who would use the hydraulic fittings in their own products. By September 1965, in view of his increasing preoccupation with missionary sales, he hired a sales manager, whose responsibility was to improve the distributor organization and increase its geographic coverage. This individual was in his mid-fifties, and had had experience in a wide variety of enterprises ranging from investment banking in Arizona to cattle ranching in Colorado; at the time he was hired he was working as an independent sales consultant in San Francisco.

The new sales manager's stated objective upon accepting the job with Ad-Tech was "to set up an improved distributor system in terms of coverage and quality." He used trade directories to eliminate distributors who handled competitive lines, and then investigated potential candidates by driving around the warehouse to check for orderly stocking and active employees, by talking to the distributor's customers to check for general reputation and sales call frequency, and by visiting the distributor's bank to check on financial reliability. He would then interview the distributor, and depending upon his evaluation of the warehouse operations, the sales performance, the financial standing, and the managerial competence, he would offer the Ad-Tech product line. By early 1966, forty-seven distributors had been added, and sales of $300,000 had been made to these distributors to provide each with a basic inventory of the snap-on fittings, with the understanding that all unsold items could be returned for a full refund. In addition, the sales manager had attempted to motivate the distributors and their sales people by direct mail ads to local manufacturers and by special sales contests for the distributors, but these promotions had been limited due to the continual shortage of funds within Ad-Tech.

During the fall of 1965, Mr. Altlan had also hired an operations manager to coordinate the activities of the company between the suppliers and the distributors. As a result of office misdirections and personal misunderstandings, incorrect items had often been ordered, customer shipments had commonly been late, and product quality had recently been deteriorating. The verbal assignment to the operations manager had been "to set up a larger supply organization, a better inventory system, and improved inquiry-responding and order-filling procedures." The operations manager fulfilled these functions; however, he disagreed strongly with the sales manager's policy of shipping inventory items to the distributors on a cash refund basis, and he also objected to Mr. Altlan's method of selling trial units to original equipment manufacturers on no-charge terms, since both of these practices confused the order forecasting and inventory control procedures he had established. In the spring of 1966, these disagreements became heated, and Mr. Altlan asked that person to leave the company.

At this time, April 1966, corporate financing had again become a problem, owing to the continued expenses of product design and market development. The investment group which had originally purchased 70,000 shares at $1.00 per share offered to purchase an additional 50,000 shares at $5.00 each if Mr. Altlan would agree to place his 35,000 shares in a voting trust, to be controlled by members of the investment group, and if he would assent to hiring a more compatible operations manager. Hobart Ryerson, a member of the second-year class at the Stanford Business School, heard of this opportunity, and asked to be considered. He had been looking for a "growth situation" in which he could invest his management talent and some of his inherited savings, and it was agreed that he could purchase an additional 12,000 shares, while his father bought 7,000 shares, at $7.00 each, and that he would join the company as operations manager in June, after graduation.

As part of the provisions of the new financing agreement, a member of the investment group who was also a partner in a Palo Alto consulting firm was asked to provide part-time managerial assistance. This consultant undertook a study of the company's problems, and decided to deal first with what he considered to be Ad-Tech's most critical area: internal coordination. He convinced Charles Altlan that the most effective way to handle the day-to-day operating decisions was in discussion groups made up of the firm's members; in this way each could contribute personal opinions, each would hear alternative points of view, and each should understand the final decision. Two committees were established: the Policy Committee, consisting of the consultant, Charles Altlan and Hobart Ryerson, which was to discuss all general management questions, and the Operating Committee, consisting of Charles Altlan, Hobart Ryerson, and the sales manager, which was to consider problems in marketing, purchasing, and inventory supply. Although neither committee had authority to enforce its decisions when Altlan, the president, disagreed with the consensus of the other members, the two committees did appear to add needed stability to the relationships amongst the members of the firm.

The consultant also strongly recommended that the company deemphasize the local distributors, and concentrate on getting manufacturers representatives to handle the new product line. He felt that these representatives normally carried only five to six noncompeting product lines, as opposed to the hundreds of lines handled by the typical distributor, so that each representative should have more knowledge about the technical features of the product, and could spend more time developing special applications in the market. Representatives are paid on commission, so that there is no fixed sales expense for the company, but they generally insist upon an exclusive agreement for a given area so that they receive the commissions on all sales in the territory, whether made by the representative individually, by the company directly, or by one of the distributors indirectly. They like to carry lines that are clearly related in order to get the maximum benefit from their knowledge of a particular field and their acquaintance with engineers and purchasing agents in a specific company. The consultant felt that the manufacturer's representatives would provide a more concentrated sales effort than had been made by the local distributors, and that this effort would approach the effectiveness of a direct sales force, without the fixed expense. By the fall of 1966, Charles Altlan had signed up six

representatives, and was actively looking for others.

Ad-Tech, burdened with the high costs of new product design (modular hydraulic valves for both manual and electrical operation, and modular hydraulic manifolds for the distribution of fluid under pressure had been added to the product line during 1966) and the continued expenses for new market development (representatives or distributors had been obtained for all sections of the country, also during 1966), reported a loss of $159,427 for the fiscal year ending February 28, 1967, and a further loss of $139,425 for the six months ending August 31, 1967. Income statements for these periods are given in Exhibit 1, and the balance sheet for the end of the second period is shown in Exhibit 2.

Despite these losses, and despite the tenuous financial position which resulted from the deficits, Hobart Ryerson remained optimistic about the future of the Ad-Tech company. He based this optimism on the distinctive nature of the product line, the secure protection of the patent application, and the substantial savings realized by the larger customers.

An Ad-Tech system costs about 20 to 25% more than a standard hydraulic system, but the snap-on fittings provide very real savings for our customers in assembly time and leak detection, and very real savings for their customers in replacement time and maintenance costs. We've been working with International Harvester [a large manufacturer of farm machinery and commercial trucks] for months, and they finally built three of their trucks with our fittings on the brake system, the steering system and the fuel system. These trucks were reported to be the first units assembled by International Harvester that did not leak. After all the fittings were put on by the regular assembly workers, the standard leak detection tests were performed individually on each fitting. No leaks were found. Generally, 5%

Exhibit 1 *Income statements of Ad-Tech, Inc., for the fiscal year ending February 28, 1967, and for the six-month period ending August 31, 1967*

	12 months ending 2/28/67	6 months ending 8/31/67
Net sales (less returned merchandise)	$132,314	$ 19,214
Cost of goods sold, estimated at 38%	50,377	7,301
Gross margin	$ 81,937	$ 11,913
Administrative salaries	$ 36,640	$ 28,800
Shop and packaging wages	32,469	14,235
General and clerical wages	17,769	9,181
Engineering salaries and wages	16,330	15,893
Payroll taxes	3,872	2,558
Total employment expenses	$107,080	$ 70,667
Travel and entertainment	$ 21,950	$ 18,940
Catalogs, advertising, and promotion	39,790	15,677
Commissions	2,100	2,933
Total marketing expenses	$ 63,840	$ 37,550
Rentals for building and equipment	$ 8,803	$ 4,665
Supplies	9,110	7,014
Utilities	2,630	1,604
Postage and shipping	5,657	3,507
Insurance	4,489	2,724
Telephone	4,725	3,820
Legal, accounting, and advisory	10,694	6,572
Interest	2,100	1,050
Provision for bad debts	4,000	2,000
Miscellaneous	5,428	3,194
Total plant and office expenses	$ 57,636	$ 36,150
Depreciation on machinery and equipment	$ 4,048	$ 2,591
Amortization of patents and tools	8,760	4,380
Total noncash expenses	$ 12,808	$ 6,971
Net loss from operations	($159,427)	($139,425)

Source: Company records; prepared without audit.

of their fittings would leak, and those fittings would have to be pulled out and replaced, at considerable time and expense.

Let me give you another example. Cummins Engine has always been troubled by leaks caused by high frequency vibrations on the fuel injection system of their diesel engines. Each of the six fuel injection points requires a fitting, and a line to the fuel pump. We made a special manifold, and they used our fittings in the manifold and at the fuel injection points. They had a test engine running with this system, and a vice president took one look and said, "What are

Exhibit 2 *Balance sheets of Ad-Tech, Inc., August 31, 1967*

Cash	$ 3,743.67	Accounts payable	$ 25,879.18
Notes receivable	1,676.11	Contracts payable	546.00
Accounts receivable (net)	6,178.91	Notes payable—bank	35,000.00
Inventories	182,751.19	Notes payable—other	13,398.46
Prepayments and deposits	5,688.55	Accrued payroll and commissions	784.55
Total current assets	$200,038.43	Total current liabilities	$ 75,608.19
Property and equipment	$ 47,768.49	Capital stock	$201,200.00
less depreciation	−14,902.48	Capital surplus	518,850.00
		Retained earnings (deficit)	(398,640.95)
Net property and equipment	$ 32,866.01	Current profit (loss)	(139,425.45)
		Total owner's equity	$181,983.45
Development and patents	$ 44,471.57		
less amortization	−19,784.22		
Net development and patents	$ 24,687.35		
Total assets	$257,591.79	Total liabilities and equity	$257,591.79

Source: Company records; prepared without audit.

those fittings? They don't leak." That will lead to large orders.

Both International Harvester and Cummins have been very receptive to us because we offer a special advantage. If they need a special manifold, we can design it, produce it and deliver it in three days; their regular supplier might take three months.

We've been calling on Ford, General Motors, and Chrysler; there are 50 places under the hood of a car where snap-on fittings can be used. Detroit is no pushover, because of the magnitude of the changeover problem, but a 9 million-car year could put us into the really big time.

We made some valves, connectors, and fittings from magnesium in order to reduce the weight of the hydraulic controls for the aerospace program. Lockheed has just finished testing its first rocket equipped with these new parts; we reduced the weight of the control system by 20 pounds, which resulted in a 400-pound savings in fuel.

We've also made some special valves for Collins Radio to use in a new automated plant. The first sample was approved last month, and Collins has already placed an order for 150 more valves to be delivered in three weeks. Once they start using our valves, they'll use our connectors and fittings all through the plant. Texas Instruments and the other microelectronic manufacturing firms with comparable automated processes can use the same valve concept, which will get them started using our connectors and fittings.

Disney Productions promises to be one of our major customers; they have already purchased about $40,000 worth of valves and fittings. They asked us to develop a 1/32-in. (internal diameter) system for use in the moving figures in Disneyland. Pneumatically operated figures have jerky movement since you can't control the flow of air as well as you can the flow of liquids, but to use hydraulics they had to find 1/32-in. valves, tubing and connectors to fit inside the figures, and these very small parts were not available on the market. The people at Disneyland have been pleased with the performance of the Ad-Tech fittings since they have not been troubled with leaks; you can't have oil leaking from the representations of famous people, and expect those representations to be realistic.

We have so many customers that are past the testing stage, and are now in the approval stage, that we expect sales to break open almost any month. We are forecasting OEM sales alone to be $800,-000 in the next 12 months. (Statement of Hobart Ryerson)

Mr. Ryerson developed a forecast of OEM sales, by customer, for the 12-month period October 1967 to September 1968, based upon reports from the sales representatives and area distributors. This forecast is shown in Exhibit 3, and was to be presented to the board of directors at their next quarterly meeting. Mr. Ryerson also prepared a pro forma income statement for the same 12-month period that anticipated total sales both to OEM accounts and to area distributors of $1,056,000, and profits before taxes of approximately $293,000; this income statement is reproduced in Exhibit 4.

Hobart Ryerson was confident that the OEM sales would develop as planned, owing to the inherent advantages of the product design and the invested effort in the market development, and he was certain that the required parts could be purchased at the listed costs, despite the substantial increase in expected volume, because of the ready availability of contract machine shops in the Bay area of northern California, but he was concerned about continuing problems in the managerial and financial areas. He ascribed many of the managerial problems to Mr. Altlan's desire to be involved in all of the activities and decisions within the company.

Charlie is very competent in the technical design of both products and processes, but he does spend a great deal of his time

pursuing areas of the business which theoretically he has turned over to his colleagues. I was told, at the time that I was hired, that I was to be in charge of planning, budgeting, financing, personnel and inside sales—just about everything that comes along—while Charlie was to look after technical sales and product development. But, he wants to know everything that's going on, and if he disagrees with what you're doing, you'll hear about it, in detail. (Statement of Hobart Ryerson)

During 1966 and the early part of 1967, regular weekly meetings of the Policy Committee, consisting of Charles Altlan, Hobart Ryerson, and the local consultant, had been held to discuss problems and plan responses, but the consultant had decided to phase out of active involvement with the company in the spring of 1967, and the regular planning sessions had been discontinued.

I'm in the dark around here. I don't know what's going on half the time. If we have a plan, Charlie will modify it without bothering to tell me, and he'll have a new program all worked out while everybody else is still trying to operate on the original concept.

Charlie sees past, present and future as one. He has an enormous number of things going on in his brain, but he'll get fixed on one idea, and then you can't change him. For example, he wants to manufacture parts in the back room since he says that we already have our fixed costs so that all we'll add are the variable costs for material and labor. I feel that we would have to buy more machinery and hire somebody to manage the shop, but his answer is to buy the machinery and hire the manager. Here we have a classic problem of make versus buy, but he doesn't want to analyze, he just wants to act.

On the other hand, he has a brilliant ability to analyze technical problems, and to provide ingenious solutions. He can go back into the shop for five minutes, and

Exhibit 3 *Anticipated OEM sales, by customer, for Ad-Tech, Inc., for the period September 1967–August 1968*

	1st quarter, Sept.–Nov.	2nd quarter, Dec.–Feb.	3rd quarter, Mar.–May	4th quarter, June–Aug.
Disney Productions	$10,000	$ 15,000	$ 15,000	$ 15,000
Freightliner, Inc.	2,000	7,500	18,000	24,000
Bostrom Air-Ride Mfg.	3,500	12,500	15,000	15,000
Stanley Door Company	3,000	9,000	9,000	9,000
Onan Electric Company	7,000	27,000	30,000	30,000
Lindsay Water Softener	—	33,000	60,000	60,000
Bruner Water Softener	—	—	6,000	15,000
International Harvester	—	20,000	40,000	60,000
Ritter Dental Chair Co.	3,000	11,000	15,000	15,000
McCormick Corp.	3,000	—	6,000	15,000
Holex Company	—	1,000	5,000	10,000
Numatics Corp.	—	—	20,000	30,000
Tronics, Incorporated	2,500	—	2,500	2,500
Fisher Electro-Static	—	—	12,000	12,000
Ransburg Spray Paint Co.	—	—	2,000	6,000
Cummins Engine Company	—	—	5,000	25,000
	$34,000	$136,000	$264,500	$358,500

Notes: Disney Productions is reported to have specified Ad-Tech valves and fittings as standard for all hydraulic equipment at the Orlando, Florida, project.

Freightliner is a truck manufacturer owned by Consolidated Freightways; management has given approval to engineering and purchasing for conversion to Ad-Tech fittings.

Bostrom manufactures "air-ride" seats for trucks and construction equipment; Ad-Tech fittings have been designed into the system.

Stanley Door Company makes air-operated doors for factories, garages, and service stations; management has given approval for the use of Ad-Tech fittings.

Onan Electric Company is a leading manufacturer of power generator sets; engineering approval has been received for Ad-Tech fittings and tubing on the fuel lines.

Lindsay and Bruner are manufacturers of water-softening appliances, and leaks have been a continual problem for both. Ad-Tech fittings have been approved for use.

International Harvester expects to finish testing three trucks with Ad-Tech fittings in September; volume, when approved, will reach $2,000 per day at the San Leandro plant.

Ritter company has designed Ad-Tech manifolds and fittings into a new dental chair; the company anticipates sales of 2,500 chairs per year and $100 fittings per chair.

McCormick and Holex make productive equipment for the microelectronics industry; Ad-Tech manifolds and fittings are much easier to assemble in the cramped control panels.

Numatics Corp. has been testing Ad-Tech fittings for 2 years; they have advised us that we can expect volume orders starting in the 3rd quarter.

Fisher and Ransburg both make electrostatic paint spraying equipment, and simple disassembly for cleaning is critical. Tests have been concluded and orders are expected.

Source: Company records.

Exhibit 4 *Anticipated sales revenues (OEM and repair), production costs, and overhead expenses for Ad-Tech, Inc., September 1967–August 1968*

	1st quarter, Sept.–Nov.	2nd quarter, Dec.–Feb.	3rd quarter, Mar.–May	4th quarter, June–Aug.
Brass fitting sales	$18,000	$ 55,000	$120,000	$210,000
Steel fitting sales	2,000	8,000	15,000	20,000
Plastic fitting sales	18,000	70,000	170,000	350,000
Total sales revenues	38,000	133,000	305,000	580,000
Brass purchased cost	6,840	20,900	45,600	79,800
Steel purchased cost	840	3,360	6,300	8,400
Plastic purchased cost	3,600	14,000	34,000	70,000
Total purchased costs	11,280	38,260	85,900	158,200
Shop wages	18,000	19,000	19,500	20,000
Shop materials	1,400	1,650	1,750	2,000
Shop supervision	—	—	2,000	3,800
Payroll taxes and benefits	1,985	2,461	2,879	3,288
Supplies and small tools	2,500	2,750	2,950	3,300
Allocated expenses	4,500	4,800	5,350	6,100
Total shop costs	28,385	30,661	34,429	38,488
Contribution to expenses	(1,665)	64,079	184,671	383,812
Marketing salaries	4,800	7,800	7,800	7,800
Payroll taxes and benefits	504	804	744	744
Commissions to sales reps.	2,900	9,400	20,700	53,400
Travel and entertainment	4,000	8,000	6,000	6,000
Advertising and promotion	2,600	3,500	4,500	5,000
Supplies and postage	985	1,250	1,350	1,550
Allocated expenses	2,250	2,400	2,550	2,700
Total marketing expenses	18,039	33,154	43,644	77,194
Administrative salaries	13,400	16,000	20,000	21,000
Payroll taxes and benefits	1,310	1,520	1,840	1,920
Supplies and postage	765	775	930	1,080
Professional services	6,000	4,500	3,500	3,000
Travel and entertainment	1,000	3,000	2,500	2,250
Allocated expenses	6,000	6,500	7,500	7,500
Total administrative expenses	28,475	32,295	36,270	36,750
Engineering salaries	3,600	3,900	4,000	4,200
Payroll taxes and benefits	420	435	440	450
Materials and supplies	1,800	1,850	1,975	2,075
Allocated expenses	1,500	1,650	1,800	1,900
Total engineering expenses	7,320	7,835	8,215	8,625
Profit (loss) before tax	(55,499)	(8,205)	96,542	261,243

Note: Brass, steel, and plastic "fitting" sales include valves, connectors, and fittings. Brass, steel, and plastic "purchased" costs include material and subcontract machining.
Source: Company records.

cut the cost of an operation by 50%, or improve the performance of a product by an equal amount. For example, on the valve for Collins Radio which we quoted at $50.00, our production costs turned out to be $35.00, until Charlie walked in there for exactly twenty minutes, and he reduced the cost by $12.50. In another 30 minutes the next week, he took $5.00 more out of it. He has the basic feeling that there is nothing in hydraulics that he cannot do better, and he's usually right. (Statement of Hobart Ryerson)

Hobart Ryerson felt that the managerial problems of the company would be solved not with altered procedures or changed assignments, but with increased personnel, and he was prepared to recommend to the board of directors that a production expediter and a chief executive be hired during the fall of 1967.

We need people who can free the company from Charlie's direct day-to-day influence, and free Charlie for the work that he does best: technical problem solving.

Basically, we need a production expediter; he has to be a competent engineer, he has to be able to work with the outside suppliers, and he has to know the local companies. He is the most important person needed now.

We also need a chief executive, preferably one with a knowledge of the fittings industry, but certainly with some experience in hydraulic components and fluid power. He should be on the sales side; the type of man who can go into General Motors, sit down with a vice president and say, "OK, buster, let's talk turkey."

He would complement me. Although I came up from the sales side, I prefer to handle finance and general management. He could handle OEM sales, and bring in Charlie whenever he needed technical assistance. A new chief executive and an engineering expediter are all the company needs now, in the way of increased management. Then there would be two strong people on the Policy Committee, in addition to Charlie and myself, to work out our plans and procedures. And, Charlie could spend his time on R&D, which is where he really wants to be anyway. (Statement of Hobart Ryerson)

Hobart Ryerson was also concerned about the financial position of the company. The high costs of product development, coupled with the heavy selling expenses required to introduce a new product concept to the market, had depleted much of the original capital. Hobart felt that he had trimmed expenses as much as was possible, through cancellation of a consulting contract and termination of all data-processing services, and he thought that he had raised as much money as was possible, by the sale of 27,000 shares of common stock, at $8.50 per share, to a small mutual fund based in San Francisco, but he believed that an additional investment, probably in the range of $250,000 to $350,000, would be needed to carry the company until a positive cash flow could be derived from the large potential orders.

It's almost impossible to adequately forecast cash needs, because it depends completely on whether we start generating big sales tomorrow, in six months, or in one year. We might not need additional capital at all. For example, if we got an order from GM on the Buick account tomorrow, we could start shipping in 30 days, we could get 60-day terms from our suppliers, and we could arrange 30-day payments from Buick. The margins are good enough on our products so that we can have a self-financing business, if the orders come soon enough. (Statement of Hobart Ryerson)

The management of Ad-Tech, Inc., felt that there were a number of financial alternatives available to the company at the date of the case (early September 1967). Preliminary merger talks with two venture capital firms had already taken place. One, a new and very aggressive venture capital company in the Detroit area, selling over-the-counter at $3.50 to $3.75 per share, had proposed an exchange of stock with Ad-Tech on a share-for-share basis. That price appeared to be favorable, and Hobart Ryerson felt that the Detroit office might be of considerable assistance in selling to the automotive industry, but neither he nor Charles Altlan knew much about the partners or the practices of the acquiring firm.

Another venture capital firm, located in the Northwest, had suggested purchasing newly issued common stock for $0.75 per share to obtain 50% ownership in Ad-Tech. Hobart thought that this price was much too low, but he expected it to be raised as soon as that firm completed a more detailed study of the market potential for the snap-on hydraulic fittings. The company in the Northwest insisted upon naming one of their partners as president of Ad-Tech.

> The price is low, but we'd be in stronger hands because they would put in the management that's necessary, yet the old stockholders would still have a chance to participate. That is not such a bad idea. (Statement of Hobart Ryerson)

Finally, a very successful executive in the Palo Alto area had approached Ad-Tech and offered to buy a 51% interest in the company, if Charles Altlan were willing to step down as President and become vice president of engineering, with an employment contract for five years. This proposal was highly complex, particularly in regards to continued employment after the five-year period, but again Hobart Ryerson was not entirely averse to the concept of a new chief executive for Ad-Tech.

> We don't really need a buyer; we need a manager with money. I know that there are untapped sources of funds in San Francisco, but the right person is going to be harder to find. This company needs a good chief executive. I'm not the chief executive type; I work best at general management on a lower level. We have to put in a man to run the company. Charlie could then run R&D, with his own tool room, his own design staff, his own expense account. I could look after finance, and supervise the production expediter. (Statement of Hobart Ryerson)

Class Assignment. As a prior classmate and current personal friend of Hobart Ryerson, assume that you have been asked to advise him on the future strategy of Ad-Tech, Inc.

1. Based upon the information presented in the cases, evaluate the past performance, current position, and future potential of the company. List five past decisions that have led to the present situation. List five current problems as of the date of the case (September 1967) that need to be resolved.
2. Strategic design was defined in the text of Chapter 2 as the search for a competitive advantage. For the smaller firm, with limited resources, this competitive advantage is often the selection of a market segment, or niche, with limited competition, adequate margins, and an opportunity for growth. Divide the total market for the Ad-Tech line of "snap-on" hydraulic fittings into at least eight segments, and identify specific characteristics, customer motives, and patterns of buyer behavior for each segment. For each segment, compare the advantages of Ad-Tech fittings with "standard" hydraulic fittings.
3. Strategic design was also defined in the text of Chapter 2 as the match between the potential of the market, the resources of the company, and the ambitions of the managers and owners. What are the assets and skills of this company? What are the attitudes and goals of these managers?

4. What strategy would you recommend to Hobart Ryerson? Express your recommendations in concise, explicit terms.

5. Define, in your own terms, the concepts "managerial values and attitudes," "environmental opportunities and risks," and "organizational strengths and weaknesses." Be prepared to illustrate each definition with examples from the Ad-Tech case.

Black Hills Bottling Company

The Black Hills Bottling Company was founded in 1936 by Adolf Freidenrich to manufacture and market carbonated soft drinks within a 4,000-square-mile area of southwestern South Dakota. Members of the family claim that at the time Mr. Freidenrich had a choice between Coca-Cola, Pepsi Cola, and Royal Crown, and that he selected the latter since he thought that the gold crown trademark would be very impressive on his company letterhead, business cards, and delivery trucks. It was the wrong choice, for the sales of the Royal Crown soft drinks did not expand as rapidly as those of the other two brands, and in 1977 George Freidenrich, the grandson of the founder and a recent graduate of the M.B.A. program at the Wharton School in Philadelphia, was faced with a decision on the continuation of the company.

The soft-drink industry within the United States operates on two levels, with large national firms that develop and promote branded flavors, and much smaller local companies that purchase the syrups for these flavors under a franchising agreement, combine the syrups with sugar and carbonated water, package the mixtures in bottles and cans, and distribute the finished soft drinks through retail stores, restaurants, and vending machines, within a specific territory. The national franchising companies are large, and have historically been very successful, with a continual growth in revenues and a substantial return on sales and equity (Exhibit 1).

Four of the five major soft-drink franchisers increased their market share over the period 1971–1976, generally at the expense of the smaller firms, such as Crush International, Cott Beverages, and Howard Johnson's, and at the expense of Royal Crown. The total market share for all Royal Crown beverages dropped 13% over the five-year period, as seen in Exhibit 2.

It was reported in the late 1970s that the soft-drink industry was becoming more mature and more competitive, with a decreasing rate of increase in consumption, probably caused by a small but important change in the percentage of the U.S. population in the 5- to 21-year age bracket, who collectively consume over 50% of all soft drinks (Exhibit 3).

The reactions of the major soft-drink franchising firms to the increasing competition and decreasing consumption varied. The three largest firms diversified, in markedly different degrees and directions, and two of those firms expanded both foreign production and sales; the two smaller companies, Seven-Up and Dr. Pepper, continued to market only soft drinks, primarily in the North American area (Exhibit 4).

Exhibit 1 *Total revenues, net income, and net equity (000,000's omitted) for the five largest soft-drink franchising firms, 1968–1976*

	1968	1970	1972	1974	1976
Coca-Cola					
Sales revenues	$1,185	$1,606	$1,876	$2,522	$3,022
Net income (after taxes)	110	146	190	195	284
Net equity	497	654	834	1,021	1,356
Pepsico					
Sales revenues	848	1,122	1,400	2,321	2,727
Net income (after taxes)	46	56	71	87	136
Net equity	264	331	440	557	753
Royal Crown					
Sales revenues	83	116	191	223	282
Net income (after taxes)	5	6	11	8	17
Net equity	24	31	58	69	88
Seven-Up					
Sales revenues	75	100	132	191	233
Net income	5	9	12	16	24
Net equity	16	28	48	54	96
Dr. Pepper					
Sales revenues	41	57	82	128	151
Net income	4	5	8	10	15
Net equity	15	19	31	43	52

Source: Standard and Poor's Stock Reports, and Standard and Poor's Beverage Industry Survey, July 1978.

The large soft-drink franchising firms were diversifying their product lines and expanding their market areas in 1977, but most of the local bottlers, who purchased flavored syrups and marketing rights from the franchising firms, did not have those strategic options. Bottlers in large metropolitan areas remained very profitable; some, such as the Coca-Cola Bottling Companies of New York, Miami, and Los Angeles, had sales that averaged well over $100,000,000 annually and very secure financial positions. Franchised bottlers in some of the smaller cities and rural areas were less successful, and there was a continual pattern of consolidation on this level of the soft-drink industry as the small companies were purchased by larger neighbors, or simply went out of business. There was a steady decline from 1950 to 1977 in the number of independent bottlers (Exhibit 5).

In South Dakota, the number of independent bottlers had declined from 11 to 3 firms over the period 1960–1977. The Black Hills Bottling Company was the smallest, by far, of these three, for the other two companies operated on a statewide basis, while the Black Hills firm was limited to the southwestern portion of the state. It was located in Rapid City, and served a franchised territory that extended 75 miles from the plant site; this area had been delineated in 1936, at the founding of the company, by the distance that a small truck could travel over rural roads, make deliveries to numerous small stores, and still return to the plant after an 8-

Exhibit 2   *Market share percentages for the five largest soft-drink franchising firms, 1971–1976*

	1971	1972	1973	1974	1975	1976	% change 1971–1976
Coca-Cola	27.1	26.8	26.7	26.5	26.2	26.5	− 2.2
Sprite	1.8	1.9	2.1	2.4	2.6	2.9	61.1
Tab	1.7	2.0	2.2	2.2	2.6	2.8	64.7
Fresca	1.3	1.2	1.0	0.9	0.8	0.9	− 30.7
Others (7)	2.1	2.4	2.6	2.7	3.1	3.0	57.8
Total	34.0	34.3	34.6	34.7	35.3	36.1	6.2
Pepsi Cola	17.4	17.5	17.4	17.5	17.4	17.6	1.1
Diet Pepsi	1.3	1.4	1.4	1.5	1.7	1.9	46.1
Mountain Dew	0.9	0.8	0.9	1.0	1.3	1.5	66.6
Teem	0.4	0.3	0.3	0.3	0.3	0.3	− 25.0
Others (3)	0.4	0.4	0.4	0.4	0.5	0.8	100.0
Total	20.4	20.4	20.4	20.7	21.1	22.1	11.2
Royal Crown	3.9	3.9	3.9	3.4	3.4	3.3	− 15.4
Diet Rite	1.0	1.0	0.9	0.8	0.8	0.8	− 20.0
Nehi Flavors	1.2	1.2	1.2	1.2	1.2	1.2	0.0
Total	6.1	6.1	6.0	5.4	5.4	5.3	− 13.1
Seven-Up	6.9	6.9	7.1	7.0	6.6	6.3	− 8.7
Sugar-Free	0.2	0.2	0.3	0.6	1.0	1.2	500.0
Howdy Flavors	—	0.1	—	—	—	—	0.0
Total	7.1	7.2	7.4	7.6	7.6	7.5	5.6
Dr. Pepper	3.7	4.3	4.7	4.8	4.9	5.0	35.1
Sugar Free	0.2	0.3	0.3	0.4	0.6	0.8	400.0
Total	3.9	4.6	5.0	5.2	5.5	5.8	48.7
Five companies	71.5	72.6	73.4	73.6	74.9	76.8	7.4

Source: Standard and Poor's Beverage Industry Survey, July 1978.

Exhibit 3 *Total shipments and growth index in the soft-drink industry, and percentage of U.S. population in the 5- to 21-year age bracket, 1971–1976*

	1971	1972	1973	1974	1975	1976
Industry shipments (millions of cases)	3,950	4,200	4,500	5,600	4,700	4,850
Index of industry shipments (1971 = 100)	100	106	114	116	118	122
Population percentage in 5- to 21-year age bracket	32.9	32.6	32.2	31.8	31.3	31.0

Source: Standard and Poor's Beverage Industry Survey, July 1978, p. B-65, and the Statistical Abstract of the United States, 1977.

to 10-hour shift. The assigned territory had never been changed, and in 1977 it covered approximately 3,800 square miles and contained a population of slightly less than 122,000 persons.

The Black Hills Bottling Company had been moderately profitable for a number of years, partially because the industry in the early days was not capital-intensive, so that the break-even volume was low and could easily be obtained, even in a small market area with a limited population base, but primarily because within this small and somewhat isolated market area the company competed with only two other bottlers, who had the advantage of the better-known brands, but who also had the onus of out-of-state ownership. Mr. Freidenrich had been born in

Exhibit 4 *Product diversification and international operations of the three largest soft-drink franchising firms, 1977*

	Coca-Cola, Inc.	Pepsi Corp.	Royal Crown, Inc.
Soft-drink segment	75% of sales, 85% of earnings*	40% of sales, 46% of earnings	58% of sales, 54% of earnings
Product diversification	Minute Maid (orange juice) Snow Crop (fruit juice) Food Division (coffee) Taylor Wine Company Hi C (artificial juice) Aqua Chem (water purification)	FritoLay (snacks) Pizza Hut (fast foods) Taco Bell (fast foods) N.A. Van Line (moving) Wilson (sporting goods)	Arby's (fast foods) Adams (fruit juice) Home Products (furniture and building materials)
Vertical integration	Sugar plantation in southern Africa Orange groves in central Florida	—	—
Foreign-operation segment	44% of sales	28% of sales	7% of sales*
Foreign markets	Western Europe Israel Pacific	Russia Eastern Europe Near East	South America*

Source: Annual reports for the respective companies, supplemented by industry estimates (*).

Exhibit 5 *Numbers of independent soft-drink bottlers within the United States, 1950–1977*

	1950	1960	1965	1970	1973	1975	1977
Number of independent bottlers	6,600	4,500	3,900	3,150	2,700	2,400	2,309

Source: Company records.

Rapid City, from parents who had emigrated to the area from southern Germany in 1904, and he had lived and worked here, as a carpenter and contractor, until he started the company in 1936. In addition to being well known, he was an intelligent and friendly man who found it easy to obtain the contracts for exclusive sale of soft drinks to school cafeterias and county fairs. Profits, however, reached a peak in 1965 and began to decline in subsequent years, despite continually rising sales (Exhibit 6).

In 1977, Mr. Freidenrich, concerned by the declining profits and recognizing his approaching retirement, asked his grandson to return and assist in the management of the firm. The grandson, George Freidenrich, was 30 years old, a graduate in industrial engineering of the University of South Dakota, a veteran of three years' service in the navy, and a recent recipient of the M.B.A. degree from the Wharton School of the University of Pennsylvania. He was working for a bank in New York City when he decided to return to South Dakota.

In retrospect, I guess you can always rationalize your actions. I enjoyed the work at the bank, and I was doing well there, and I even enjoyed New York City; it is not as bad as it has been depicted. But, grandpa needed some help, and he is a very unusual man: very honest and straightforward—a little rigid, perhaps, like the old time settlers out here often

Exhibit 6 *Income statements for the Black Hills Bottling Company, 1960–1977*

	1960	1965	1970	1975	1977
Sales revenues	$781,600	$907,000	$1,269,400	$1,697,200	$1,803,000
Direct materials	261,100	301,100	455,700	631,400	694,700
Direct labor	79,700	88,000	133,300	186,700	203,900
Total direct costs	340,800	389,100	589,000	818,000	898,600
Gross margin	440,800	517,900	680,400	879,100	905,100
Bottling overhead	131,300	142,400	170,000	205,400	210,300
Delivery expense	181,300	224,000	350,400	578,700	580,000
Administrative expense	45,300	57,100	77,400	88,300	89,200
Total fixed costs	357,900	423,500	597,800	872,400	879,500
Gross profit (before taxes)	82,900	94,400	82,600	6,700	25,600
Income taxes	36,500	44,200	48,700	1,300	5,100
Net profit (after taxes)	46,400	50,200	33,900	5,400	20,500

Source: Company records.

Exhibit 7 *Estimated market share of the Black Hills Bottling Company, 1960–1977*

	1960	1965	1970	1975	1977
Population in market area	143,300	134,400	128,800	123,500	122,000
National per capita consumption of 10-oz units	213	259	362	439	454
Estimated consumption in area, 10-oz units (thousands)	30,523	34,809	46,626	54,216	55,388
Company production, 10-oz units (thousands)	15,322	16,813	20,469	16,969	15,287
Estimated company market share (%)	50.2	48.3	43.9	31.3	27.6

Note: All soft-drink industry data are reported on the basis of 10-oz containers. This was the original bottle size, and its use for reporting purposes is now an industry tradition. Production, sales, and costs for reporting companies are converted to 10-oz equivalents in order to avoid the complexity introduced by the current variety in container sizes.
Source: Company records.

were—but also kind and intelligent. So I came to help him. And I came to help the state. There are very substantial coal reserves here, and the power companies in the Midwest will strip mine the whole place if we don't stop them. Finally, I came to help myself; this company was successful for the past 40 years, and it can be successful for the next 40 years, if we can adapt to the industry changes. (Statement of George Freidenrich)

George Freidenrich told his grandfather he wanted to spend the first few months getting as much data as possible on the soft-drink industry, and analyzing the competitive position of the company. He found, of course, that much of the specific area information he wanted was not available, but he did obtain considerable data from the Soft Drink Bottlers Association on a national level, and was able to apply it locally.

He quickly found that the probable market share of the Black Hills Bottling Company had been declining since 1960, from 50.2% to 27.6% (Exhibit 7).

George Freidenrich felt that the declining market share within the area was partially a result of the extensive advertising campaigns conducted since 1965 by Coca-Cola and Pepsi Cola, which raised their market shares nationally, at the expense of Royal Crown and the other small franchising companies. However, he felt that the primary cause of the declining market share was an inability by Black Hills Bottling to service the large chain stores, which on a national level accounted for 42.6% of all sales of packaged soft drinks, but within South Dakota represented only 13.0% of the sales by the Black Hills Bottling Company (Exhibit 8).

The very low percentage of sales through the large chain stores was due to a problem in packaging. Customers at the chain food stores preferred steel or aluminum cans to glass bottles, but Black Hills did not have the equipment to package soft drinks in cans. Managers and clerks at the chain stores liked the 32-oz bottles, rather than the smaller 12-oz and 16-oz sizes, due to the ease of handling and stocking, but Black Hills could not fill the large-size containers on its existing equipment. The company was limited to 10-oz, 12-oz, and 16-oz bottles, in both returnable and nonreturnable types, but recognized that no one—customers, managers, or clerks —at the chain food stores liked the returnable bottles.

Exhibit 8 *Distribution channels (percent) of the Black Hills Bottling Company, compared to national averages for the distribution of soft drinks, 1977*

	Company distribution	National distribution
Take-home market		
Chain food stores	13.0	42.6
Local food stores	28.4	11.8
Liquor and convenience stores	14.6	9.6
Other retail stores	2.0	4.1
	58.0	68.1
On-premises A market		
Vending machines at factories	4.2	5.3
Vending machines at gas stations	9.3	5.2
Vending machines at retail stores	4.7	3.3
Vending machines at other locations	2.2	1.7
	20.4	15.5
On-premises B market		
Bottle sales at restaurants	9.1	5.5
Bottle sales at bars and taverns	6.3	5.2
Bottle sales at amusement locations	4.0	4.7
Bottle sales at other locations	2.2	1.0
	21.6	16.4

Source: Company records.

Most returnable bottles are sold through vending machines at offices, factories or gas stations, or through bottle sales at restaurants or bowling alleys, for on-premises consumption, because the drink is a little bit cheaper, and therefore the profit is a little bit greater for the sales location. Our sales of returnable bottles in retail locations for the take-home market is minimal. (Statement of George Freidenrich)

Black Hills Bottling Company had originally produced only returnable bottles, but had added the nonreturnable types in the 1960s in response to consumer demand. Changes in consumer demand, and the availability of a wide variety of container types, had occurred rapidly over the past 10 to 15 years in the soft-drink industry (Exhibit 9).

Part of the problem facing the Black Hills Bottling Company was the decreasing market share and declining unit sales caused by the company's inability either to supply the most popular soft-drink containers or to distribute through the most popular retail outlets. Another part of the problem was a cost structure that was higher than the industry average. George Freidenrich obtained, from the National Soft Drink Bottlers Association, a statement of average costs for the 224 reporting members, expressed in the industry convention of costs per case of 10-oz returnable bottles. (Production for each company is converted to 10-oz bottle equivalents, and this total, in 24-bottle cases, is divided into the labor and overhead costs; variable costs for the material are reported at purchase prices, plus freight-in.) George Freidenrich compared the industry costs with those for the Black Hills company (Exhibit 10).

George Freidenrich had the following comments on the comparison of company and industry costs:

The price of sugar is determined by a stochastic process with political and international constraints. The prices are wild, they went from $12.00 per hundredweight in 1973, to $60.00 cwt in 1974, to $24.00 cwt in 1975, down to $9.80 cwt in 1976, and now they're at $22.00. There isn't much we can do; we change our retail price to reflect the cost of sugar, but you have to balance maintaining margins and maintaining sales. Larger companies do more forecasting and hedging, but we just don't have the volume.

The cost of returnable bottles is hard to estimate since it depends upon the trippage. Trippage can be defined as the number of times a returnable bottle makes the cycle of filling, distribution, sale and return for refill. Trippage nationally averages 10 cycles, but that average is helped immeasureably by the South, where it is just traditional to bring the Coca-Cola bottles back to the store. Here our trippage averages 7 cycles, but that is slowly going down; low trippage can be improved by increases in the deposit amount, but that is a two-edged sword, for it can lead to decreased

sales by making the returnables seem much less attractive to the customer.

Our direct labor costs for mixing and filling reflect the speed of our bottling line, which runs at 100 units (10-oz bottles) per minute. Bottling lines are available that run at 1,200 units, and the modern canning lines run twice as fast. The average for the industry is now 600 units per minute.

The direct labor costs for sorting and washing are fairly standard. The washing (hot caustic soda) and inspection (light refraction) process is simple and has been automated, but someone has to pick the returnable bottles out of the cases and set them upright on the line. That has not been automated, and it is one of the reasons no one really likes returnable bottles.

Bottling overhead involves process supervision, indirect labor, machine maintenance and general cleaning, and is partially a fixed cost and partially a function of volume. We produced 636,958 equivalent cases last year, but the average for the reporting companies was just under 3,000,000.

Delivery expense is for the truck and

Exhibit 9 *Percentage of container types in the soft-drink industry, 1960–1977*

	1960	1965	1970	1975	1977
Returnable bottles					
10-oz	84.0	59.8	31.3	20.3	18.2
16-oz	8.0	7.4	19.6	14.3	15.3
32-oz	—	—	—	1.7	3.0
	92.0	67.2	40.9	36.3	36.5
Nonreturnable bottles					
12-oz	—	8.9	17.6	12.4	8.6
16-oz	—	4.2	10.7	14.4	15.2
32-oz	—	—	—	1.1	4.7
	—	13.1	28.3	27.9	28.5
Nonreturnable cans					
12-oz	4.0	19.7	29.6	31.6	31.3
16-oz	—	—	2.3	4.2	3.7
	4.0	19.7	31.9	35.8	35.0

Source: Company records.

Exhibit 10 *Comparison of company and industry costs per equivalent case (24 units) of 10-oz bottles*

	Company	Industry	Explanation
Flavoring	$0.250	$0.250	Known cost from franchising companies, regardless of quantity
Sweetener	0.332	0.306	Uncertain cost due to fluctuations in price of sugar; larger companies are better able to hedge; etc.
CO_2 and citric acid	0.026	0.026	Known cost from suppliers due to near-commodity nature of product
10-oz returnable bottles	0.412	0.287	Uncertain cost due to variations in trippage; 10 trips nationally, but 7 locally on returnable bottles
Crown (bottle cap)	0.070	0.070	Known cost from suppliers due to standard nature of item
Material cost	$1.090	$0.939	
Direct labor mix and fill	0.243	0.180	Labor cost varies with speed and automation of bottling line and wage rates in area
Direct labor sort and wash	0.077	0.082	Labor cost varies with wage rates in area; no fully automatic washing lines for returnable bottles are available
Labor cost	$0.320	$0.262	
Bottling overhead	0.330	0.250	Industry average overhead cost/case reflects higher production volumes
Delivery expense	0.911	0.869	Industry average delivery cost/case reflects smaller metropolitan areas
Administrative expense	0.140	0.285	Company administrative cost/case reflects deliberate cost cutting efforts
Total costs	$2.791	$2.605	
Profit margin	0.040	0.226	
Wholesale price	$2.831	$2.831	Franchising companies "encourage" consistent wholesale pricing
Retail discount	0.969	0.969	25.5% retail discount is considered to be standard in the industry
Consumer price	$3.800	$3.800	Retail prices vary only slightly by region

Source: Company records; industry and company costs have been disguised to avoid revealing proprietary information.

driver, and is partially a fixed cost and partially a function of load volume, market dispersion and traffic conditions. We have good traffic conditions, and only limited delays, but our distribution points are spread out over eight counties. (Statement of George Freidenrich)

George Freidenrich began to look at investments to either reduce unit costs or to increase total sales, and one of the first alternatives that was available was the replacement of the existing bottling line, which had been installed in 1962 and was now considered to be both slow (100 units per minute vs. 600-unit industry average) and costly ($0.243 direct labor charges vs. $0.180 industry average). Using information obtained from the equipment manufacturers and the bottlers association, he prepared cost comparisons (Exhibit 11).

George Freidenrich explained some of the costs in the comparison of new bottling equipment to the case writer in the following terms:

The investment figures are for new machines, delivered, installed and tested for full volume operation. We could buy used equipment, at about 20 to 25% off, but the used equipment that is available now won't handle the large 32-oz bottles, or the metric liter and half-liter sizes.

The fixed overhead costs are technically for one shift, but all bottling plants have to run an occasional second shift during the hot days in the summer or just before the holidays in the winter. It is traditional that the supervisor, the two leadsmen and the mechanic divide the total time amongst themselves, and interchange responsibilities. We're running a second shift two weeks out of every six now (636,985 unit cases sold in 1977 vs. 480,000 annual one shift production rate) without increases in our fixed overhead, but some of our skilled people must be getting a little tired of their varying hours and unpaid overtime.

The semifixed overhead will vary with the type of machinery we install; our present bottling line is fully depreciated and completely paid off, so that we don't have any interest or depreciation expenses now. We will have increases in property taxes and fire insurance, based upon the cost of the new equipment, and the electric rate will be based upon the highest demand during the month, and not on our actual usage, so that will vary with the equipment. The cooling units and liquid pumps use a lot of electric power in the larger size machines.

Variable overhead is primarily indirect labor, for stocking the filled cases in the warehouse and in the delivery trucks. Since we don't carry much inventory, much of our production in the more popular flavors goes directly from the bottling line to the delivery truck.

Direct labor is for people on the line, unpacking and feeding empty bottles, etc. We can hire direct and indirect labor for a second shift fairly easily since the jobs are not skilled and since people in this area seem glad to get some additional work at night on an occasional basis. (Statement of George Freidenrich)

George Freidenrich also considered adding a canning line since he knew that most of the large chain stores in the area would be willing to handle the products of the Black Hills Bottling Company in cans, and he also recognized that many of the local food stores and convenience stores would prefer cans to the current returnable bottles. Canning lines were available at speeds of 250, 400, and 600 12-oz cans per minute. Again, comparative costs for these investment alternatives were prepared on the basis of the industry standard 10-oz units (1 case of 12-oz cans = 1.2 cases of 10-oz standard units, and a production rate of 250 cans per minute = 300 units per minute) (Exhibit 12).

Again, George Freidenrich explained some of the costs he had projected in his comparison of the three different canning lines:

The required investment figures are for used canning lines; new ones aren't made any more for much less than 1,000 cans or 1,200 units per minute. But the used equipment would be reconditioned and guaranteed by the manufacturer, so that we should have no trouble.

The fixed costs would be exactly the same for either the bottling lines or the canning lines, for the superintendent, the warehouse leadsmen, and the maintenance mechanic could interchange between the lines easily. We would never be large enough to run both lines simultaneously, so that we would have to allocate the fixed costs on some basis, such as standard units produced or dollar volume sold.

The categories in the semifixed over-head are the same for the canning lines as for the bottling lines, but the amounts, of course, differ. For the variable overhead, product insurance is product liability insurance, and maintenance parts are the replacement materials, particularly seals and gaskets, that are used to repair the equipment. (Statement of George Freidenrich)

George Freidenrich also investigated the alternatives that were available to the Black Hills Bottling Company in shipment and delivery. Delivery costs for soft drinks are high, partially due to the heavy nature of the product (a filled case of standard 10-oz returnable bottles weighs 26 pounds), and partially due to the competitive nature of the industry. While the primary demand for soft drinks is

Exhibit 11 *Comparison of projected costs per equivalent case (24 units) of 10-oz bottles for bottling lines running from 100 to 500 units per minute*

	100 units	200 units	300 units	400 units	500 units
Required investment	—	$158,000	$213,000	$243,000	$271,000
Cases at full (one shift) production	480,000	960,000	1,440,000	1,920,000	2,400,000
Fixed overhead costs					
Supervision	$ 24,000	$ 24,000	$ 24,000	$ 24,000	$ 24,000
Warehouse leadsmen	28,000	28,000	28,000	28,000	28,000
Maintenance mechanic	13,500	13,500	13,500	13,500	13,500
Cleaning worker	12,500	12,500	12,500	12,500	12,500
Payroll taxes and benefits	17,200	17,200	17,200	17,200	17,200
Building maintenance	3,100	3,100	3,100	3,100	3,100
Building taxes	3,200	3,200	3,200	3,200	3,200
	$101,500	$101,500	$101,500	$101,500	$101,500
Semifixed overhead					
Electric power	$11,400	$17,200	$25,800	$ 34,400	$ 42,900
Equipment taxes	8,700	15,300	20,400	23,000	25,500
Equipment depreciation	—	19,700	26,600	30,400	33,800
Equipment insurance	3,400	7,300	9,800	11,200	12,500
Equipment interest	—	6,300	8,500	9,700	10,800
	$23,500	$65,800	$91,100	$108,700	$125,500
Variable overhead					
Indirect labor	$0.073	$0.070	$0.067	$0.064	$0.062
Product insurance	0.028	0.028	0.028	0.028	0.028
Maintenance parts	0.033	0.033	0.033	0.033	0.033
	$0.134	$0.131	$0.128	$0.125	$0.123

Exhibit 11 (*continued*)

	100 units	200 units	300 units	400 units	500 units
Direct labor costs, bottling-line workers	$0.243	$0.224	$0.208	$0.198	$0.190
Cost at full (one shift) production					
Fixed overhead	$101,500	$101,500	$101,500	$101,500	$101,500
Semifixed overhead	23,500	65,800	91,100	108,700	125,500
Variable overhead	64,300	125,800	184,300	240,000	295,200
Direct labor costs	116,600	215,000	299,500	380,200	456,000
	$305,900	$501,800	$668,500	$820,700	$967,400
Cost at full (one shift) production per case of 24 units	$0.637	$0.523	$0.464	$0.427	$0.403
Cost at the current (636,985 case) production					
Fixed overhead	$101,500	$101,500	$101,500	$101,500	$101,500
Semifixed overhead	23,500	65,800	91,100	108,700	125,500
Variable overhead	85,400	83,500	81,500	79,600	78,300
Direct labor costs	154,800	142,700	132,500	126,123	121,000
	$365,200	$393,500	$406,600	$415,900	$426,300
Cost at the current (636,985 case) production per case of 24 units	$0.573	$0.617	$0.638	$0.652	$0.669

Notes: All costs are expressed in terms of the 10-oz bottle since larger sizes fill at a rate proportional to these standard units; e.g., the 32-oz bottle would take 3.2 times as long to fill as the 10-oz, and the production rate per minute would be reduced accordingly.

Depreciation charges are based upon an estimated eight-year life and a straight-line rate. Interest charges are based upon an expected 8% loan with the amount declining from the required investment to zero over the term of the loan.

Source: Company records; projected costs have been disguised to avoid revealing proprietary information.

stimulated by the national and regional advertising conducted by the large franchising companies, secondary demand is generated by the personal selling and extensive distribution of the local bottlers, and the local bottlers rely upon their truck drivers to perform both functions. Each driver is assigned a number of routes, and each is expected to service the retail stores, vending machines, and on-premises distributors on those routes, replenishing depleted inventories, improving display locations, installing promotional materials, maintaining good will, and encouraging increased consumption. These driver/salesmen are well paid, and they utilize expensive vehicles (2½-ton trucks with specialized racks to simplify handling of the cases) to service a large number of geographically dispersed distribution points in an inherently inefficient manner (the truck must be loaded at the start of the day with the driver's estimate of the expected sales for the various drink flavors, container types, and serving sizes for a specific route; during the day some of the products will run out, requiring a return to the customer the next day, while others will be left

Exhibit 12 *Comparison of projected costs per equivalent case (24 units) of 10-oz bottles for canning lines running at 300, 480, and 720 standard units per minute.*

	300 units	480 units	720 units
Required investment	$187,200	$269,500	$359,200
Cases per year at full (one-shift) production	1,440,000	2,304,000	3,456,000
Fixed overhead costs: same as bottling lines	$101,500	$101,500	$101,500
Semifixed overhead			
Electric power	$26,700	$ 42,600	$ 63,900
Equipment taxes	18,200	25,600	33,400
Equipment depreciation	23,400	33,700	44,900
Equipment insurance	8,600	12,100	15,800
Equipment interest	7,500	10,800	14,400
	$84,400	$124,800	$172,400
Variable overhead per case			
Indirect labor	$0.065	$0.061	$0.056
Product insurance	0.028	0.028	0.028
Maintenance parts	0.042	0.042	0.042
	$0.135	$0.131	$0.126
Direct labor costs per case, canning-line workers	$0.070	$0.060	$0.050
Costs at full (one-shift) production			
Fixed overhead	$101,500	$101,500	$101,500
Semifixed overhead	84,400	124,800	172,400
Variable overhead	194,400	301,800	435,500
Direct labor costs	100,800	138,200	172,800
	$486,100	$666,300	$882,800
Costs at full (one-shift) production per case of 24 standard units	$0.337	$0.289	$0.255

Source: Company records; projected costs have been disguised to avoid revealing proprietary information.

over, and have to be brought back to the plant). The result is a high cost per case for shipment from the bottler to the retail location. George Freidenrich compared company costs to industry averages, and felt that the variances were due to understandable differences in the size of the market territory and the nature of the traffic conditions. He also investigated a new method of soft-drink delivery termed bulk shipment, which utilized large over-the-road tractor trailers, with a 32,-000-lb load capacity, to deliver 200 to 400 cases per stop to very large retail stores. The cases were often palletized on movable carts, and the carts were moved from the shipping dock to the sales floor to minimize handling. He recognized that bulk shipment costs were very low for soft drinks, but he also felt that this method of delivery was probably not applicable in their existing market territory (Exhibit 13).

The products of the Black Hills Bottling Company were distributed, as described previously, through chain and independent retail

Exhibit 13 *Comparison of company and industry costs per equivalent cost (24 units) of 10-oz bottles for delivery by standard truck and by tractor trailer*

	Company 2½-ton delivery truck	Industry 2½-ton delivery truck	Industry 16-ton trailer truck
Investment per vehicle	$12,700	$12,700	$34,500
Truck depreciation, registration, and insurance/day	$ 30.40	$ 31.00	$ 63.70
Truck gas, oil, and repairs/day: $0.22/mile gasoline delivery, $0.28/mile diesel trailer	24.20	10.30	19.60
Driver/salesman (including benefits): $8.50/hour for company, $11.00/hour for industry	71.25	88.00	88.00
Total costs per day	$125.85	$129.30	$171.30
Cases delivered per day	138	148	1,185
Cost per case for delivery	$ 0.911	$ 0.869	$ 0.145

Source: Company records; company and industry costs have been disguised to avoid revealing proprietary information.

stores, vending machines, and on-premises locations. The standard industry discount was 25.5% to both the retail stores and the restaurants, taverns, and recreational facilities, although George Freidenrich suspected that the bottlers in many areas went above that figure to the large chain stores to obtain volume orders. The combined rental charges and depreciation costs on vending machines were widely believed within the industry to average the same 25.5% amount, although actual amounts varied by location and volume, etc.; rental charges for vending machines were payments to the owner of the gas station or motel, etc., for permission to install the unit.

The new development in soft-drink distribution was the "pop shop," a factory outlet that was generally owned by a local bottling company, and used to sell nonbranded or private branded soft drinks, generally in 12-oz or 16-oz returnable bottles, at a substantial price discount that averaged 28%. The Soft Drink Bottlers Association did not approve of discount sales, and therefore did not report on expected volume or average costs of the pop shops, but George Freidenrich had heard at

an industry convention that sales averaged 35,000 to 50,000 equivalent cases per year, and he was able to estimate monthly costs of operating an outlet of this nature fairly easily (Exhibit 14).

As George Freidenrich continued to look at the alternatives that were open to the Black Hills Bottling Company, he realized that it would be possible to expand the market territory served by the company. No other bottler operated under a Royal Crown franchise in South Dakota, so that it was technically possible to serve the entire state, either by direct shipment from Rapid City, or by setting up a small warehouse or local bottling plant in one of the three other major cities in the state: Pierre (central trading area), Aberdeen (northeastern trading area), and Sioux Falls (southeastern trading area). The Coca-Cola and Pepsi Cola bottlers were both state-wide organizations, and operated bottling lines in each of those areas and in Rapid City, which was considered to be the center for the western trading area, and each firm operated at least one canning line, and shipped the cans by bulk delivery trailer truck to the bottling

Exhibit 14 *Estimated monthly costs for operating a pop shop or factory-owned outlet for soft-drink sales*

	Monthly costs
Rent, at small shopping center or street store with provision (truck dock) for trailer delivery	$ 600
Heat, light, power, and insurance	200
Store manager, responsible for 60-hour week	900
Store clerk, employed for 30-hour week	360
Total pop-shop costs, per month	$2,060

Source: Company records.

plants which served as central warehouses and distribution points for their respective trading areas.

There were 14 natural trading areas in the western plains states that were reasonably close to Rapid City, South Dakota, and potential markets for expansion of the Black Hills Bottling Company. Population statistics and competitive firms for these areas are given in Exhibit 15, and the geographic locations are shown on a map in Exhibit 16.

As explained previously, the Black Hills Bottling Company could expand into the other trading areas in South Dakota without infringing on the franchised rights or assigned territory of any other Royal Crown bottler. It would be necessary to obtain permission for this expansion from the Royal Crown Corporation, but George Freidenrich thought that this permission would be readily given. Expansion outside the state would be more difficult since there were existing Royal Crown bottlers to the west in Casper, Wyoming, to the south in Scotts Bluff, Nebraska, and to the southwest, in Denver, Colorado. Black Hills could not market their products in those areas unless they first arranged to purchase either the franchising rights or the ongoing operations of the other bottlers. The purchase of territorial rights or complete companies was common in the soft-drink industry, where the process of consolidation was well advanced, but all purchase prices were reputed to be individually nego-

tiated, and there were no industry standards on price/earnings or price/asset ratios.

I have been over to visit the Royal Crown bottler in Casper, Wyoming. That company must be losing money; they have an old and slow bottling line—even older and slower than our own—and they operate a fleet of ancient trucks. The owner is one of those irritating small-town business people, narrow minded and self-centered, although he probably thinks of himself as a shrewd trader. He refuses to talk about sales volume or financial position, and just keeps saying, "You know this industry; make me an offer." They have only 12 trucks, so their sales can't be much more than $1,000,000, but they distribute to some extent in both Sheridan and Laramie, so they do have a good market base, with about 240,000 population, although probably a low market share. I'm guessing that $75,000 would buy the marketing rights, if we let him keep whatever he could make by liquidating the trucks and equipment, which can't be worth much more than an additional $75,000. He can't be losing too much money, or he would not keep the company going, but if the losses are small, I don't see why he will not let us see his financial statements. He may be brighter than I think he is.

The bottling firm in Scotts Bluff, Nebraska is owned by the widow of the founder, Mrs. Hamlin Truscott. She has to be one of the nicest old ladies I've ever met.

Exhibit 15 *Population in 1975, population change 1965–1975, and soft-drink competition in the trading areas of the western plains states*

Area	Population, 1975	Population change, 1965–1975 (%)	Per capita income	Bottling lines	Canning lines
Rapid City, South Dakota	121,810	−11	$4,620	Coca-Cola Pepsi Cola Royal Crown	—
Pierre, South Dakota	77,385	−23	4,420	Coca-Cola Pepsi Cola	Coca-Cola
Aberdeen, South Dakota	177,360	− 4	4,670	Coca-Cola Pepsi Cola	—
Sioux Falls, South Dakota	265,565	− 3	4,810	Coca-Cola Pepsi Cola	Coca-Cola Pepsi Cola
Sheridan, Wyoming	65,035	−14	4,190	Pepsi Cola	—
Casper, Wyoming	135,900	−11	4,430	Coca-Cola Pepsi Cola Royal Crown	Coca-Cola
Laramie, Wyoming	38,130	−12	4,360	Pepsi Cola	Pepsi Cola
Cheyenne, Wyoming	152,700	− 3	5,240	Coca-Cola Pepsi Cola	Coca-Cola Pepsi Cola
Scotts Bluff, Nebraska	81,930	−11	5,060	Royal Crown	—
North Platte, Nebraska	76,820	− 6	4,610	Coca-Cola Pepsi Cola	Coca-Cola Pepsi Cola
Bismarck, North Dakota	154,010	−14	4,500	Coca-Cola Pepsi Cola	Pepsi Cola
Greeley, Colorado	111,200	+19	5,680	Pepsi Cola	Pepsi Cola
Fort Collins, Colorado	118,660	+51	5,620	Coca-Cola Pepsi Cola	Coca-Cola
Denver, Colorado	680,790	+36	5,920	Coca-Cola Pepsi Cola Royal Crown Independents	Coca-Cola Pepsi Cola Royal Crown

Source: Company records.

When you go down to see her, she serves tea and cookies, and homemade cake, and there is a little pitcher of milk for the tea, and also a little pitcher of bourbon. Hamlin, her husband, liked "strong" tea, she told me. I've seen the tax returns for that company, and while they were un-audited they were prepared by a reliable local accounting office. They show sales of about $2,000,000 and profits after tax of $27,000, but the bottling line is not much better than our own, and the trucks are well maintained, but small. They have a warehouse in Cheyenne, which gives them a good population base, and they must have a much better market share than the fellow in Casper. The trucks and equipment and real estate are probably worth about $150,000. I don't know what we should offer for her com-

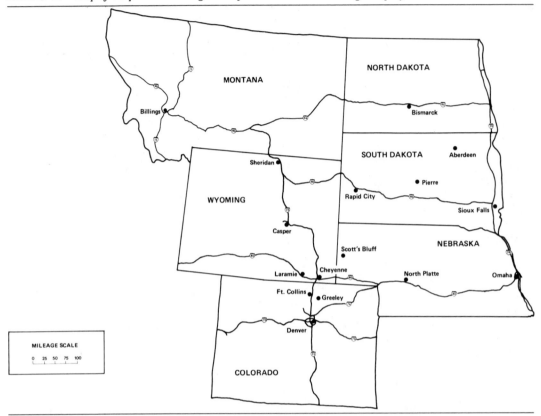

pany. I would feel better if she asked an attorney or a banker to be her business advisor, but she relies on the minister of her church, who says a short prayer before every meeting and then helps himself to the "strong" tea. I had a course on mergers and acquisitions at Wharton, but they never taught us about Mrs. Truscott.

The Royal Crown bottler in Denver is big and successful. They have a modern bottling line and a new canning line, both of which run at over 1,000 units per minute, and bulk distribution equipment. We certainly can't even think of buying that company, but we have to recognize its existence. I've met the owner at industry conventions, and he feels that eventually the entire western plains area, western Nebraska, eastern Colorado, east-

ern Wyoming, and all of the Dakotas will be served from Denver since he thinks that the economies of scale of mass production will offset the additional costs of truck transportation. The real problem is that he may be right. I know that he has been in touch with the fellow in Casper, Wyoming, for that person told me once that he had a "standing offer from Denver," but I don't know if he has tried to negotiate with Mrs. Truscott. He may be just waiting for the three of us to fold up, so that he can pick up the pieces for nothing. (Statement of George Freidenrich)

The last alternative considered by George Freidenrich was the expansion of the product line to include company brands and private brands. The Royal Crown company insisted

Exhibit 17 *Contribution margins for various container types and sizes for "name"-brand soft drinks*

	Returnable			Nonreturnable		
	10-oz	16-oz	32-oz	12 (cans)	16-oz	32-oz
Bottles/case	24	24	12	24	24	12
Retail price	$3.800	$5.840	$5.740	$6.760	$6.760	$6.600
Retail discount	0.969	1.483	1.463	1.724	1.724	1.683
Bottler's price	2.831	4.357	4.277	5.036	5.036	4.917
Flavoring	0.250	0.400	0.400	0.300	0.400	0.400
Sweetener	0.306	0.489	0.489	0.367	0.489	0.489
CO_2 and citric acid	0.026	0.042	0.042	0.031	0.042	0.042
Container	0.287	0.384	0.322	2.198	1.035	0.902
Crown	0.070	0.070	0.104	—	0.070	0.104
Shipping cartons	—	—	—	0.110	0.110	0.110
Total material	0.939	1.385	1.357	3.006	2.146	2.047
Filling labor	0.180	0.250	0.230	0.050	0.250	0.230
Washing labor	0.082	0.082	0.082	—	—	—
Total labor	0.262	0.332	0.280	0.050	0.250	0.230
Contribution/case	$1.650	$2.640	$2.640	$1.980	$2.640	$2.640
Ounces/case	240	384	384	288	384	384
Contribution/100 oz	$0.687	$0.687	$0.687	$0.687	$0.687	$0.687

Note: Cost of the returnable containers assumes 10 trips per bottle. Cost of the crown assumes resealable cap for 32-oz bottles.
Source: Company records; industry costs have been disguised to avoid revealing proprietary information.

that their franchised bottlers not handle other "name" brands, such as Coca-Cola, Pepsi Cola, Seven-Up, or Dr. Pepper, but they had no objection to a company brand, such as Black Hills Cola, or a private brand supplied to one of the large retail chains. Company brands and private brands were termed "off" brands in the soft drink industry, and they normally produced a considerably smaller contribution (sales price minus direct material and labor costs) since they were generally sold at a much lower retail sales price.

The pricing policy for the "name" brands usually involved a standard contribution per ounce for all flavor varieties and container sizes of soft drinks (Exhibit 17).

The "off" brands were somewhat less expensive to bottle, owing to the reduced cost of the flavoring (purchased from chemical companies rather than from franchising firms) and the reduced use of the sweetener (20% less sugar or saccharine), and they generated a reduced margin (Exhibit 18). The 12-oz cans of "off" brands were often considered to be a loss-leader, to convince customers of potential savings, since the most common price comparison is between six-packs of 12-oz cans, and on an industry-wide basis both the re-

Exhibit 18 *Contribution margins for various container types and sizes for "off"-brand soft drinks*

	Returnable			Nonreturnable		
	10-oz	16-oz	32-oz	12 (cans)	16-oz	32-oz
Retail price	$2.800	$4.230	$4.120	$4.800	$5.140	$4.980
Retail discount	0.716	1.076	1.045	0.864	1.310	1.265
Bottler's price	2.084	3.154	3.075	3.936	3.830	3.715
Flavoring	0.125	0.200	0.200	0.150	0.200	0.200
Sweetener	0.245	0.392	0.392	0.294	0.392	0.392
Other material	0.383	0.496	0.468	2.239	1.257	1.158
Total material	0.753	1.088	1.060	2.683	1.849	1.750
Total labor	0.242	0.332	0.280	0.050	0.250	0.230
Contribution/case	$1.089	$1.734	$1.735	$1.203	$1.734	$1.735
Ounces/case	240	384	384	288	384	384
Contribution/100 oz	$0.452	$0.452	$0.452	$0.417	$0.452	$0.452

Source: Company records; industry costs have been disguised to avoid revealing proprietary information.

tailer's discount and the bottler's margin were narrowed on these containers.

In addition to offering "off" brands, George Freidenrich recognized that it would be possible to expand the product line of the Black Hills Company by adding other beverages, particularly fruit punch or beer, to the existing soft drinks. The markets for these other beverages were not small; on a national basis the amount of beer consumed was 61.5% of the volume of soft drinks, and the ratio of fruit drinks was 17.5% (Exhibit 19).

George Freidenrich found that he could purchase the dry mixture for noncarbonated fruit drinks (lemonade, orangeade, fruit punch, or iced tea) at approximately the same cost as the flavoring for the franchised flavors for soft drinks ($0.250 per case of standard 10-oz units). He could purchase beer in pressurized bulk containers, ready for canning or bottling, from a small brewery in Minnesota, at $0.550 per gallon delivered, with both federal and state excise taxes paid; this price was equivalent to $0.430 per 100 fluid oz. At the time, regional beer (nonnational brands, or *not* Budweiser, Millers, Schlitz, Pabst, Coor's, etc.) was selling in the South Dakota area at $7.16 per case for 12-oz cans, and at $7.29 per

Exhibit 19 *National per capita consumption of soft drinks, fruit drinks, beer, wines, and alcoholic spirits, 1975*

	Soft drinks	Fruit drinks	Beer	Wine	Alcoholic spirits
Per capita consumption in gallons (128 fluid oz)	35.4	6.2	21.8	1.8	1.9

Source: Company records.

case of 16-oz nonreturnable bottles; these prices, with the usual retail discount of 25.5%, resulted in a contribution to the bottler of $0.602 per 100 oz.

Finally, George Freidenrich commissioned a market research study in the four major trading areas of the state, conducted by an advertising agency in Sioux Falls, South Dakota. The research study was divided into two projects. First, shoppers at representative grocery stores were asked nondirective questions regarding their recognition of the terms Royal Crown, Diet Rite (1-calorie version of Royal Crown cola), and Nehi (alternative fruit flavors produced by Royal Crown), and then the respondents who correctly identified each brand were asked about their verbal associations ("What do you think about when you hear the name Royal Crown?"). The various responses were classified into standard terms, such as "high quality" or "youthful

image," and reported in order of frequency.

In the second project, family groups at shopping centers were shown a proposed advertisement introducing a "Black Hills Pop Shop" and stressing the reduced prices, company brands, returnable bottles, and central locations, and were then asked if they found the new ad "believable" and the new service "needed." People who responded either positively or negatively were then asked about their verbal associations with the picture of the new Pop Shop. The responses for both parts of the market research study are given in Exhibit 20.

George Freidenrich had a number of concluding statements that he asked the case writer to include in the material presented to the students:

> Vermont and Oregon have both passed legislation which has outlawed the nonreturnable beverage container, and equiva-

Exhibit 20 *Quantified responses to market research studies conducted for the Black Hills Bottling Company, 1977*

	Rapid City	Pierre	Aberdeen	Sioux Falls
Recognition of Royal Crown	99% positive	92% positive	95% positive	96% positive
Associations with Royal Crown	Good quality	Youthful	Youthful	Active
	Healthful	Sweet taste	Good quality	Youthful
	Youthful	Medium quality	Active	Good quality
Recognition of Diet Rite	65% positive	18% positive	23% positive	31% positive
Associations with Diet Rite	Good quality	Low quality	Middle aged	Middle aged
	Middle aged	Bitter taste	Sweet taste	Medium quality
	Healthful	Middle aged	Youthful	Sweet taste
Recognition of Nehi flavors	43% positive	7% positive	11% positive	11% positive
Associations with Nehi flavors	Good quality	Medium quality	Middle aged	Middle aged
	Money saving	Middle aged	Medium quality	Medium quality
	Youthful	Sweet taste	Money saving	Sweet taste
Believe "Pop Shop" ads	74%	78%	68%	81%
Need "Pop Shop" service	63%	54%	58%	67%
Negative associations	Poor quality	Unkempt store	Low quality	Low quality
	Unkempt store	Loose bottles	Bitter taste	Long drive
	Loose bottles	Long drive	Long drive	Loose bottles
Positive associations	Good quality	Money savings	Good parent	Good parent
	Money savings	Sweet taste	Money savings	Good quality
	Good parent	Long drive	Good quality	Long drive

Source: Company records.

lent laws are being considered in Michigan, Wisconsin, and Maine. But, I don't think that is likely to happen in South Dakota for a long time, if ever. Environmental concerns are not as strong here as economic problems—we have a declining population due to a lack of job opportunities and low economic growth. You'll also find that no one is really worried about roadside litter—the state is just too big, with too small a population base, to have a litter problem. I'd love to have a returnable bottle law passed—it would save our company—but make certain that your students understand that we could not force it through the legislature, which tends here in South Dakota to be tough, independent, and honest.

I have asked the buyers for the statewide grocery chains about handling Royal Crown and Diet Riet. Their response is very simple. They say they will try it, in cans and maybe 32-oz bottles, and if it sells they will keep on handling it for us. If it doesn't sell, we can forget about them. I also asked them about a contract to produce private brands—two of the statewide chains now have private brands at reduced prices produced by one of the other bottlers—and they all said the same thing; if we can do "considerably" better on the retail discount for the 12-oz cans, they would be interested.

I have asked the Royal Crown company about some help. They say that if we move into the three other trading areas, and become a state-wide distributor, they will provide a cooperative advertising allowance ($0.12 per case) for a three-year period, and low-cost loans (6% interest) for three-year repayment. I'm not certain that we need the loans; the financial position of this company is excellent since grandpa has never paid dividends and never paid himself a high salary. [Exhibit 21 lists the major assets and liabilities of the Black Hills Bottling Company.]

When I was in the M.B.A. program at Wharton, I felt that many of the cases never included enough information. This case will probably have too much information, and will seem too long with too many exhibits, but after reading it, the students will know exactly what I know about the soft-drink industry in South Dakota, and I have to decide about the future of this company within the next few weeks. I probably will call on a consultant to help structure all the information, and make certain that we recognize all the choices. I wish that the case was finished, so that I could hear what your students would have to say. (Statement of George Freidenrich)

Class Assignment. As a consultant employed by Mr. Freidenrich, structure the strategic alternatives open to the Black Hills Bottling Company in a logical sequence (by increasing investment or increasing change, etc.) or in a decision diagram. Concentrate on the major alternatives (six to eight, perhaps), and compute the investment required and estimate the probable sales and income for each alternative.

1. Which alternative strategy would you recommend for the Black Hills Bottling Company, and why?
2. If the alternative you selected represents a major change in the operations of the company, be prepared to defend your decision. Specifically, be able to identify the organizational resources.
3. Consider the general problem of identifying and evaluating resources within a given organization. The text defines resources as "capabilities; they are the tasks that the company can do well, and particularly, they are the tasks that the company can do better than their competitors within the industry. Financial and physical assets are resources also, but only for their potential conversion into improved or expanded managerial performance." Do you agree with this definition?
4. If the alternative you selected does not

Exhibit 21 *Balance sheet for the Black Hills Bottling Company, December 31, 1977*

Cash	$ 45,100	Accounts payable	$ 23,600
Marketable securities	70,000	Wages accrued	13,400
Accounts receivable	109,600	Employment taxes due	3,100
Inventory flavorings and sweeteners	113,500	Property taxes due	000
Inventory bottles and caps	86,200	Income taxes due	1,300
Prepaid expenses	43,600		41,400
	470,100		
Bottling equipment	$ 92,300	Common stock, no par value	$ 93,700
less accumulated depreciation	92,300	Retained earnings	447,600
	000		541,300
Land and buildings	$ 74,100		
less accumulated depreciation	32,400		
	41,700		
Delivery trucks	$265,700		
less accumulated depreciation	197,700		
	68,000		
Office furniture and equipment	$ 12,400		
less accumulated depreciation	9,500		
	2,900		
Total assets	$582,700	Total liabilities and equity	$582,700

Source: Company records.

have the highest return on investment, be prepared again to defend your decision. Specifically, be able to identify and evaluate the environmental risks.

5. Consider the general problem of identifying and evaluating risks over a lengthy time span, with inadequate information. How should these risks be reflected in marketing, production, and financial policies and plans?

Forestry Equipment Company

The Forestry Equipment Company was founded in 1955 to produce a new machine that would permit the recovery and sale of the waste products at a sawmill. When a round log is cut into square lumber, the outer portions of the wood, termed slabs and edgings, are surplus. In the nineteenth and early twentieth centuries, when sawmilling was a major industry in the United States, these slabs and edgings were burned in a boiler to produce steam power for the mill; with the extension of electrical service to rural areas in the 1930s and 1940s, it became cheaper to purchase power, and the slabs and edgings became a complete waste product, which had to be disposed of through open-air burning or dumping. Since the slabs and edgings represented 20 to 25% of the content of the logs, by weight, this disposal represented a considerable problem and expense for the mills.

Many persons, particularly those associated with the various conservation groups, had suggested that the slabs and edgings might be chipped, or reduced into pieces about ⅝ in. × 1 in. × 1 in. through a mechanical knife action, and then sold for use as pulpwood, in the production of paper. The problem, however, was that the bark was still on the slabs and edgings, and the bark did not dissolve in the pulping process, but remained as gritty black specks in the finished paper, which obviously detracted from the quality. The Pinchot League, an organization dedicated to the preservation of the American forests, had sponsored a contest in the early 1950s for the design of a machine to debark the slabs and edgings, but this sawmill waste is in the form of long, awkward strips of wood, with knots and root swells, that are costly to handle and difficult to debark, and no successful machines were produced.

The founder of the Forestry Equipment Company had the idea of debarking the logs before they were sawn; this would obviously reduce the handling required for the individual slabs and edgings, and would also reduce many of the mechanical problems involved in the bark removal. The prototype machine was finished in the fall of 1955, and ran successfully at a sawmill in northern Maine through the winter. However, sales were not as quick to develop as had been anticipated; only 12 machines, at an average price of $12,500, were sold during 1956, and while sales increased in 1957 and 1958, the company by 1958 was just barely above break-even:

	1956	1957	1958
Company sales	$158,000	$324,000	$575,000
Company profits	(22,000)	(3,000)	14,000

There were a number of reasons for the disappointing growth in sales. There were 18,000 sawmills east of the Mississippi, many of which were interested in the machine as a solution to the disposal of the waste slabs and edgings and as a source of additional revenue through the sale of the pulp chips, but many of these sawmills did not have adequate cash or credit to purchase the debarkers. Also, each sawmill required a contract from a paper company to purchase the chips, but the paper companies were very hesitant to sign these contracts since they had to install expensive truck and railcar unloading equipment to handle the wood chips. (Until 1956, all pulpwood was delivered to paper mills in the form of logs cut 5 ft in length, to be debarked in large drums and then chipped at the mill.) Pulpmills in Georgia and Alabama, where there was a shortage of pulpwood, were the only ones to install the chip unloading and handling equipment up to 1958, and over 100 log debarkers were sold in those two states, but two small companies started in that area to build competitive (and copied) equipment.

In 1959 one of the major paper companies in the United States, with pulpmills at three locations in the New England area, decided to conserve their own forest resources by purchasing chips from local sawmills; chip unloading and handling equipment was to be installed at all three pulpmills, and 120 log debarkers were to be purchased for lease to the sawmills. The action would prove the validity of the log barking and slab chipping concept in the eastern United States and would lead to increased sales as other paper companies followed their example. This sale of 120 machines would ensure the success of the Forestry Equipment Company; since the firm was already operating at break-even, the contribution would flow directly through to retained earnings, and provide the financial basis for expansion into other sawmill and pulpmill equipment.

There was just one problem: the vice-president of woodlands for the paper company wanted a guarantee that he would receive a personal payment of 5% of the purchase price, in cash, in return for placing the order with the Forestry Equipment Company.

Class Assignment. What action should the founder and general manager of the Forestry Equipment Company take in regard to the potential order for 120 log debarkers?

Northern Steel Fabricators, Inc.

Northern Steel Fabricators, Inc., was started in 1974 in Roscommon, Michigan, to cut, bend, and weld steel plate into machine parts on a contract basis. Mr. Jessie Thompson, the founder of the company, had worked for 23 years as an industrial engineer and estimator in the plant maintenance department of Chrysler Corporation, but was laid off during the severe slump in auto sales that occurred during 1974.

> My supervisor at Chrysler said that it was just a "furlough" and that I would be called back as soon as car sales picked up, but I knew that he was just telling me a story; all the older engineers in the plant design and maintenance departments were being let go. I knew that we could either use up our savings gradually, waiting for the call back from Chrysler, or use them up in a hurry, investing in a small company. Certainly, no one else was going to hire a 53-year-old automotive engineer, so we decided to go for broke, and start the business. (Statement of Jessie Thompson)

Mr. Thompson and his wife owned a summer cottage on a lake near Roscommon, so they knew the area and had a house in which they could live inexpensively while starting the company. They were able to rent an abandoned service station on the outskirts of the town, a large cement block building with four bays and an office, and they then purchased three electric welders and arranged to lease a shear (to cut steel plate), a brake (to bend steel plate) and four winders (to form steel wire) from a used machinery dealer in Detroit.

> We started this company on a shoestring because we didn't have much money. What we did have was my knowledge of estimating the material and labor cost of steel parts, and my experience in the automobile business. I knew the parts that they used, the prices that they paid for them, and the people who bought them. (Statement of Jessie Thompson)

Mr. Thompson planned to make steel parts used in the production process, such as wire baskets, parts bins, assembly fixtures, and test stands. The company was successful almost immediately.

When we started, I would go down to Detroit and get an order, and then come back to make the parts. Unlike most salesmen, I could estimate the cost right in the buyer's office, and they liked that, and because we were so small and flexible we could accept rush orders, and they appreciated that. (Statement of Jessie Thompson)

The company started with just three employees: Mr. Thompson, who was both salesman and foreman; Mrs. Thompson, who was the secretary and bookkeeper; and one shop worker. In three years, the company had grown to eight shop workers, and annual sales of $200,000.

> The company is a comfortable size right now; it's about all that my wife and I can handle. As we've grown, we've had to borrow quite a bit of money to cover our accounts receivable and inventory; there's no problem there since the banks like loans on good current assets such as receivables to Ford and General Motors. And the company is profitable enough so that we have been paying the loans off on schedule. In about three years we will be free of debt, and then maybe we'll hire a full-time salesman and start to grow. But there is a problem that may keep us from growing, and that is the welding smoke. We can't afford the equipment to eliminate the smoke, and it must be a health hazard. (Statement of Jessie Thompson)

Electric welding involves using a high-voltage direct current that melts and fuses the wire of the electrode into the metal of the pieces to be joined. The electrode wire is an alloy steel coated with a thick flux, which is a deoxidizing agent that burns during welding to create a protective vapor about the arc and a protective coating over the weld. The burning flux, however, generates a thick brown smoke that is very noticeable in welding shops, and can be irritating to the eyes and lungs.

> Most shops that do a lot of welding have a high roof, and that seems to dissipate the smoke. But, we have a low roof in the service bays of this old garage, and the smoke hangs in the air continually. It coats the windows and the walls, and cannot be good for our lungs. (Statement of Jessie Thompson)

Mr. Thompson had investigated three alternative means of eliminating the problem of the welding smoke; none of them seemed satisfactory given the financial conditions of the company and the competetive conditions of the industry.

> One way, of course, is just to increase the ventilation. This is fine during the summer, when we just open the garage doors and put in a couple of big fans. But during the winter, the temperatures here get down below zero, and we just could not afford the heating costs.
>
> Large companies, if they don't have a high roof in the welding area, use electronic precipitators, which hang from the ceiling and trap the smoke particles by giving them a negative charge and then collecting them on a positive plate. You wash off the positive plate every now and again. But a good precipitator for the amount of welding we do would cost $43,000, and we don't have the money.
>
> Finally, we could go to shielded arc welding, in which you blow helium or argon gas around the electrode wire to get the protective vapor, and you don't use any flux, but it would cost us about $12,000 for these industrial gases each year, and our profits only run about $10,000. (Statement of Jessie Thompson)

Mr. Thompson was concerned about the possible hazard to the health of his workers due to the heavy concentration of welding smoke in the shop, but he was also concerned about the future of his company.

> If any of the OSHA (Occupational Safety and Health Act) inspectors came by in the winter, they would probably close us

down. But they never do come by in the winter, because the driving can be so bad up here then; they only come by in the summer and the fall when they have no problem with the driving and we have no problem with the smoke. The men aren't going to complain either; there just aren't any other jobs in the county that pay as well as working here. I don't think that we should keep on doing something that may be wrong just because we won't get caught. What should we do? (Statement of Jessie Thompson)

Class Assignment. Make a specific recommendation to Mr. and Mrs. Thompson relative to the possible health hazard caused by the welding smoke in the shop of Northern Steel Fabricators, Inc.

Chapter 3

STRATEGIC DESIGN IN PRODUCT DIVISIONS OF LARGER FIRMS

Strategic design in smaller firms is primarily a process of evaluating the past performance of the company relative to the organizational objectives and managerial ambitions, developing a range of strategic alternatives to fill whatever gap might exist between performance and intent, and then selecting the optimal alternative through consideration of the organizational strengths and weaknesses and the environmental opportunities and risks. This managerial process has been described previously in schematic form, and is repeated one more time for emphasis and understanding on the top of the following page.

Strategic design in larger firms, and particularly in the product divisions of larger firms that are responsible for a single product or product line, differs from the planning process employed for smaller companies. Smaller companies are usually short of resources. They tend not to have the financial assets, physical facilities, technical skills, or market positions of the larger corporations, and consequently they often try to conserve their limited resources, and to utilize them most effectively, by avoiding direct competition with other companies. Strategic design for smaller firms, therefore, often consists of attempts to find a market niche with limited competition, through product differentiation and market segmentation. This has created a "product–market" orientation for strategic design in smaller firms, with emphasis upon the "what product in what market" series of decisions. The entrepreneur in a smaller company considers alternative product–market positions, matching very specific product characteristics with very explicit market segments, and then selects from among those alternatives by comparing each strategic option with the limited resources. Strategic planning in a smaller company is product–market oriented and resource based.

Larger companies have resources. Their financial, physical, and technical assets are limited, of course, but they are generally available to support the approved strategy of one of their product divisions. Each product division is normally responsible for a single product or product line, so that there is a surface similarity to

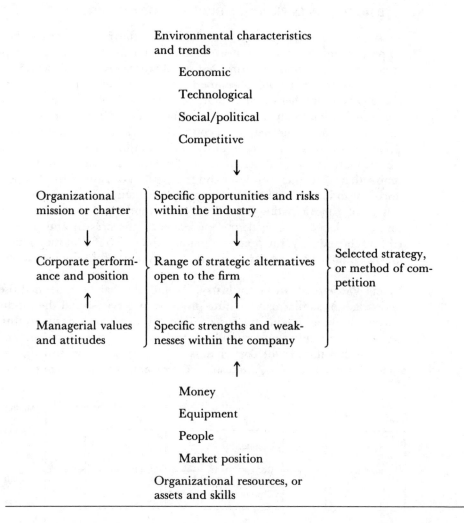

Environmental characteristics
and trends

Economic

Technological

Social/political

Competitive

↓

Organizational mission or charter	Specific opportunities and risks within the industry	
↓	↓	Selected strategy, or method of competition
Corporate perform- ance and position	Range of strategic alternatives open to the firm	
↑	↑	
Managerial values and attitudes	Specific strengths and weak- nesses within the company	

↑

Money

Equipment

People

Market position

Organizational resources, or
assets and skills

the smaller company, but the product divisions have access to these greater re-sources, and consequently they often try to apply these available resources, and uti-lize them most effectively, by planning for direct competition with other firms. The markets for larger companies, by definition, are larger and less subject to segmenta-tion, and the products are more general, and less susceptible to differentia-tion. Strategic design for the product divisions of larger companies, therefore, is less oriented toward a "product–market" position, or niche, and more toward a "prod-uct–process" posture, with low competitive costs. The manager in the product di-vision of a large company considers alternative investments in process technology and productive capacity, and then selects from among those alternatives by com-paring each strategic option with the relevant opportunities and risks within the environment. Strategic planning in the product division of a larger company is product–process oriented and environmentally based.

The environment for the product division of a larger company is essentially the industry in which that division operates. This industry is more than the market for the products of that division; it is the market for similar or substitute products or services, and the producing firms that supply those products or services. An industry basically defines a group of competing firms that can affect the performance and position of one another by changes in product design, market demarcation, pricing level, distribution method, and advertising effort. The level or degree of competition and the pattern or method of competition within the industry determines the opportunities and risks for each of the participating firms.

Each industry has a different level of competition, and a different pattern of competition. Together, this level and this pattern constitute the competitive structure of the industry; an understanding of this structure is critical to the design of the strategy of a participating firm. This understanding of the competitive structure can be developed by considering, in sequence, the present and potential participants in the industry, the present and potential economics of the industry, and the present equilibrium and potential disequilibriums within the industry.

Present Participants in the Industry. An industry has been defined previously as the market for similar or substitute products or services, and the producing firms that supply those products or services, but it is necessary to expand this definition somewhat for a fuller understanding, and to include the suppliers and distributors. The full number of participants within an industry, and the relationships among those participants, are displayed schematically, as shown.

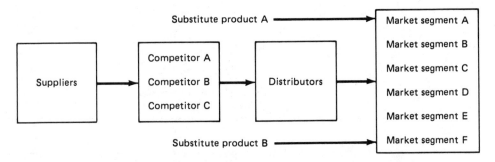

It is possible to express the relationships between the present participants within an industry in quantitative terms; this use of the quantitative methodologies for industry analysis is termed econometrics. The development of an econometric model for strategic design is probably not necessary, and may not be feasible, but it certainly is useful to consider the number, relative size, and comparative power of each of the major groups of participants:

1. *Number and relative size of the producing firms.* The pattern of the producing firms may range from concentration, or dominance by a few large corporations, to dispersion, or participation by a number of equally sized competitors. Dominance by a few large companies usually results in oligopolistic competition, with administered prices and reduced rivalries in product designs, distribution

methods, and promotional efforts. The reduced competition in prices, products, channels, and advertising comes about as a result of the power of the large firms to retaliate for unexpected moves.

2. *Number and relative size of the supplying firms.* The pattern of the supplying firms may also range from concentration to dispersion, and a comparison of these patterns for the producing versus the supplying segments of the industry indicates the relative power of these two groups. Power is a difficult concept to define, and an almost impossible quantity to measure, but it is an easy idea to understand. Power essentially is the ability of one economic unit to impose conditions of purchase or sale upon others; in an industry structured with many suppliers and few producers, the terms and conditions of purchase will normally be established by the producers. There are exceptions, of course, for unusual conditions such as a shortage of raw materials or a lack of transport capacity, but in general terms economic power accrues to the larger business units.

3. *Number and relative size of the distributing firms.* Distributing firms (brokers, wholesalers, and retailers) do not necessarily exist within an industry; it is possible for producing firms to sell directly to the final consumers or users. However, when specialized distribution companies are present in the industry structure, the same analysis of relative size and comparative power should be made of the distributors as was done previously for the suppliers. Economic power in distribution is derived from the size of the company and the ability of the distributor to influence the buying decision of the final customer through a personal relationship, convenient location, or needed service.

4. *Number and relative size of the market segments.* The market segments within an industry are obviously related to the product or service characteristics offered by the producing firms. Products with minimal differences in features, such as commodities and basic materials, are generally sold to a single large segment of the industry. Products with inherent differences in features, such as technical goods and services, are sold to a wide range of market segments, based upon customer wants and perceived needs; while products with contrived differences, primarily in the personal goods and services, are sold to a more limited number of market segments, based upon price and perceived value. The number of market segments, the relative size of each of the consuming units (individual consumer, group of consumers, business firm, or public institution) within each market segment, and the annual purchased volume of each of the consuming units together determine the relative power of the consumers versus the distributors and producers. Individual consumers normally have very limited economic power within an industry structure, and their interests are often protected by organized groups or governmental regulations.

5. *Number and relative size of the producers of substitute products.* Very few products are unique in their ability to satisfy all customer wants in all market segments of a given industry. Products from producing firms in other industries can often satisfy some of the customer needs (for example, products from the aluminum and lumber industries can satisfy some of the customer needs in the steel industry), so that the manufacturers of these substitute products have to be included in the

analysis of the present participants within an industry for they can change the relative power positions of the suppliers, producers, distributors, and consumers.

Potential Participants in the Industry. The present participants within an industry are, as described previously, the suppliers, producers, distributors, and consumers of a similar product or service, and the manufacturers of substitute products and services. Most industries, however, are not static, and these current participants may occasionally be joined by new entrants, either from adjacent industries with substitute products or allied production processes and marketing methods, or from nearby geographic areas with similar products and identical processes and markets. Local and regional companies in the United States in many industries were surprised by the advent of national competitors in the early 1900s, and these same national firms were often dismayed by the start of international competition in the 1960s; neither group had considered the possibility of added participants within an apparently static industry. In order to consider the possibility of new entrants, it is necessary to evaluate the attractiveness of the industry, based upon rates of growth and indices of profitability, and the barriers to entry:

1. *Rates of growth.* The growth rate of an industry can be measured by increases in unit shipments and sales revenues of all the producing firms within that industry, with some recognition of changes in the market share of the producing firms over time. Industries with high growth rates tend to attract new participants.
2. *Indices of profitability.* The profitability of an industry can be measured by average returns on sales, equities, or assets of all the producing firms within the industry, with some recognition of changes in the distribution of these returns over time. Industries with substantial returns tend to attract new participants.
3. *Barriers to entry.* It may be difficult for new participants to enter an industry, despite the attractiveness of high growth rates and substantial returns. In some cases, very large capital investments may be required to obtain the technological capabilities, production facilities, distribution channels, or market acceptance needed to effectively compete within the industry. In other instances capital expenditures may not be enough; an effective competitive position can be blocked by current patents, restrictive licenses, or proprietary technologies.
4. *Barriers to exit.* Barriers to exit obviously do not affect new participants within an industry, but they often maintain existing competitors in the industry structure. Physical facilities that were designed to produce a specific product or service are generally expensive to modify for a different product or service, and they may be costly to liquidate or to sell. Union agreements, managerial relations, and the emotional attachment to a company's history and tradition are important noneconomic factors that also make it difficult for a participant to leave an industry.

Present Economics of the Industry. The "economics" of an industry can refer, in very simple terms, to the pattern of sales revenues, fixed costs, and variable costs that is typical for the firms within that industry. Just as each industry has a recognizable pattern of participants, each industry also has an understandable pattern of revenues and costs and consequent margins. These patterns can be examined through the mechanics of break-even analysis and value-added observations for the major participants within the industry.

1. *Break-even analysis.* The break-even point is the sales volume in units for a specific product or service at which the total costs, both variable and fixed, are equal to the total revenues. This relationship between sales revenues, unit costs, and production volume can be expressed either algebraically or graphically (see the accompanying illustration).

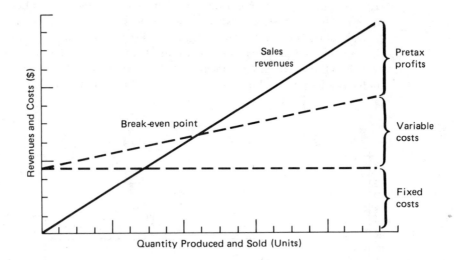

Break-even analysis is more properly cost–volume analysis. Increases in volume, above the break-even point, bring increases in unit margins since the fixed costs can be allocated over a larger number of units; conversely, these volume increases bring continued decreases in average unit costs. The decreases in average unit costs are the "economies of scale," which have an immediate strategic impact: companies with large production volumes tend to have low-cost positions within the industry.

Break-even or cost–volume analysis is usually performed for the total organization, with the assumption that the major variable costs are derived from the productive process. This assumption, depending upon the requirements of the industry and the strategy of the company, may not be warranted; it is often useful to consider separately the cost–volume relationships in the purchasing, production, engineering, distribution, and promotional activities of the firm, if the fixed and variable costs can be properly collected and allocated by function. Economies of scale can be found in product development and marketing management, as well as in production processing.

2. *Value-added analysis.* The term "value-added" refers to the margin between purchased material costs and final sales revenues for a specific product or product line as those materials and products are transferred between the partici-

pating firms within an industry; obviously, the sales revenues/unit for one firm become the purchased costs/unit for the next firm in the industry structure. The value added, or margin between sales revenues and material costs for each firm, includes both an amount for the variable costs of purchasing, processing, distributing, and promoting the product or product line, and an allowance for fixed costs and profit. The value-added figure, therefore, reflects both the relative complexity and cost of the supplying, processing, wholesaling, and retailing activities, and the comparative power of the participating firms. Firms with the greater power, or the ability to impose conditions of purchase or sale upon other economic units within the industry, will tend to have the higher value-added margins. If the material costs and sales prices are known, or can be estimated, for each of the supplying, processing, and distributing stages within an industry, the value-added margins can be computed, and displayed graphically, as shown here, for all the participants in the industry structure. This analysis will assist in understanding the relative complexity of the activities and the comparative power of the firms.

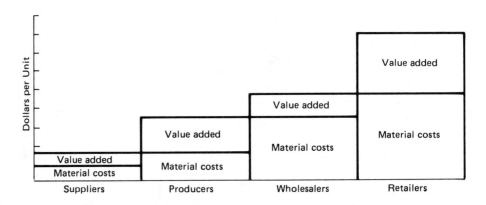

Potential Economics of the Industry. The pattern of sales revenues, fixed expenses, and variable costs that together establish the break-even point for each of the participants within an industry is not static. Break-even analysis shows the relationship of revenues and costs with changes in current volume, but it is also necessary to consider potential changes in this relationship imposed by cumulative volume (experience), improved technology, or continued inflation.

1. *Cumulative volume.* It has been claimed by one of the larger consulting firms that costs per unit for most products and services will decrease over time with increases in the cumulative volume. Specifically, it has been stated that unit costs can be expected to decline 15 to 20% each time the cumulative production volume is doubled. This cumulative volume is not the annual production rate; instead, it is the total production in units since the start of processing for a specific product or service. The decrease of unit costs at a given percentage for each doubling of cumulative volume results in an exponential relationship termed the "experience" curve, shown in the illustration on page 103.

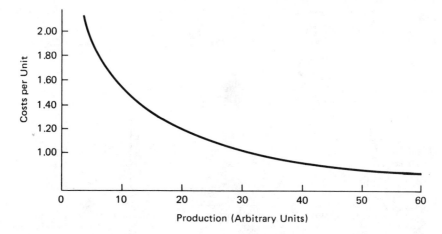

The decline in average costs per unit associated with increases in cumulative volume has been demonstrated for numerous products and services, such as electronic circuits, mechanical watches, and organic chemicals. It is felt that this decline is a result of the incremental improvements in product standards, process methods, and job performances that can be expected to come with increasing experience. Acceptance of the experience curve concept leads to a major strategic precept: gain market share quickly, for the implication of the experience-curve theory is that the firm with the largest cumulative volume will have an important cost advantage over all other participants within the industry.

2. *Improved technology.* Average costs per unit can be reduced by the incremental changes in product, process, and performance brought about by increased experience, or by the abrupt changes brought about by improved technology. New product designs and new process methods can lower average unit costs precipitously. The implication of potential improvements in technology is that the firm with the most modern plant may have an important cost advantage over all other participants within the industry.

3. *Continued inflation.* Average costs per unit can be reduced, relative to the other participants in the industry, by the use of assets that were originally purchased at a much lower point on the inflationary curve. Costs of equipment and prices for construction increase at a compound rate during a period of inflation; this results in substantially greater charges for depreciation and interest. The implication of continued inflation, unfortunately, is that the firm with the oldest plant may have an important cost advantage.

Present Equilibrium within the Industry. The classical definition of economic equilibrium is the stable situation that exists when the demand for a given product or service is balanced with the supply of that product or service at a specific price. At this point, theoretically, the incremental costs of production (cost of producing one more unit) are equal to the incremental revenues from sales (income derived from selling one more unit) for each of the participants within the industry. This position of economic equilibrium is shown here in the very familiar total demand and supply charts for the industry, and the equally familiar marginal cost and revenue curves for the company.

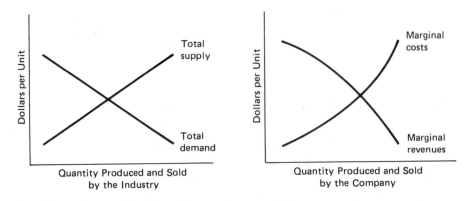

The marginal revenues for the company decline with the quantity produced and sold by the industry for, theoretically, in a perfectly competitive market, the industry price would decline with the total quantity sold. The marginal costs for the company increase with the quantity produced and sold by the industry for, again theoretically, in a perfectly competitive economy, the industry costs for the factors of production (material, labor, capital, and management) would increase with the total quantity produced. There are, of course, some obvious problems in applying these theoretical constructs: marginal costs and marginal revenues are often not known, and company sales are generally the result of other variables than price. Product quality, brand reputation, and promotional image are also important. However, the economic concepts do describe a common competitive condition in which, despite variations in demand caused by seasonal or cyclical swings in the market, and despite changes in cost brought about by advances in product or process technology, the price is adjusted on an industry-wide basis, and only minimal changes occur in the competitive positions of the participants. Relative market shares, held reasonably constant over time, are a more certain, and more obvious, indication of an industry in economic equilibrium than are total supply and demand intersections, or marginal cost and revenue curves. There are two economic and political factors that help to explain the relatively constant market shares of an industry in equilibrium.

1. *Competitive reaction.* In a mature market, with a product or service in the advanced stages of the life cycle, there often can be only limited expansion of the overall demand, so that sales growth by one competitor has to be at the expense of the other participants within the industry. The competitive actions of one participant in product improvement, distribution expansion, promotional effort, or price reduction tend to provoke equivalent competitive reactions; these anticipated reactions often deter the initial competitive change, and thus tend to maintain relative equilibrium in the competitive structure of the industry.

2. *Governmental regulation.* In a mature industry, particularly in the service area, governmental regulation may restrict the industry participants (television and

radio), the market areas (railroads and airlines), and the price levels (electrical utilities and telephone companies). Other companies, generally in manufacturing, are subsidized by governmental grants (shipping), protected by governmental quotas (steel), and constrained by governmental agencies (Department of Labor) and laws (Occupational Safety and Health Act). All of these governmental actions and regulations tend to maintain relative equilibrium in the competitive structure of an industry by penalizing or preventing change.

Potential Disequilibrium within the Industry. Most industries can be said to operate in a continual state of irritable equilibrium, or industrial discontent. Minor changes are initiated by the industry participants in product designs, process improvements, market demarcations, distribution channels, promotional expenditures, and pricing levels at a fairly constant rate. These changes, if rationally designed, may provide a momentary competitive advantage to the initiator, but that advantage is usually quickly removed or reduced by competitive reaction so that the market shares of the industry participants remain reasonably constant. Major changes that result in obvious disequilibriums in the economics of the industry, and substantial changes in the market shares of the participants, come about from new entrants, advanced technologies, or innovative strategies.

1. *New entrants.* Additional competitors can alter the competitive structure of an industry, despite the large capital investments that may be required to obtain the technical capabilities, production facilities, distribution channels, or consumer acceptances needed to effectively compete, by expanding either geographically (from an adjacent area) or technologically (from a substitute product or similar process). New entrants to an industry, with adequate resources and a determined approach, can change the relative market shares of the competitors.
2. *Advanced technologies.* Existing competitors can alter the competitive structure of an industry, despite the uncertainties inherent in advanced technologies, by initiating new product designs or new processing methods. Advanced designs provide a competitive advantage in product characteristics; advanced methods provide a competitive advantage in product margins. Major advances in products or processes are not common, but when successfully developed they can be used to change the relative market shares of the participants within an industry.
3. *Innovative strategies.* Existing competitors can also alter the competitive structure of an industry, despite the problems inherent in major organizational changes, by instituting new strategies. These new strategies involve more than minor changes in pricing, distribution, or promotion; they introduce a totally different method of competition that may be based upon a new integration of the product line, a new segmentation of the market, a new emphasis upon marketing, or a new concentration upon production. Innovative strategies are not common, but when rationally developed they can change the relative market shares of the participants within an industry.

Analysis of the present and potential participants in an industry, the present and potential economics of the industry, and the present equilibrium and potential disequilibrium within that industry provides the background for strategic planning in the product division of a larger company. Product divisions of larger companies are generally responsible for only a single product or product line so that there is a surface similarity to smaller firms, but their annual sales are often very much larger than those of a small company, and consequently they are less able to find a market niche without competition. Product divisions usually must meet competition, not avoid it, and they often search for a competitive advantage by combining capacity expansions and technical improvements to find a low-cost production process. Strategic planning for the product division of a larger company is primarily product–process positioning, matching existing demand and competitive conditions to productive capacity, experience, and technology to establish the low-cost position. To find this position, it is useful to specify the alternative technologies and different capacities that are possible, and then to identify the competitive products or services that are produced by these methods. This analysis can be portrayed in a simple matrix:

	Product characteristics	Production process A	Production process B	Production process C
Process characteristics				
Product 1				
Product 2				
Product 3				

Strategic design, in the most basic terms, is a search for a competitive advantage. For the product division of a larger company, with adequate resources, this competitive advantage often takes the form of a product–process position with lower costs, and consequently higher margins, than the other participants in the industry. For each product division of a large company there is a range of possible product–process positions; the function of the general manager of the division is to select the position that most clearly fits the competitive conditions of the industry. Strategic planning for the product division of a larger company is, therefore, product–process oriented and industry based. The intent of the planning process, of course, is to improve the performance, position, and potential of the division; the following cases illustrate this strategic planning process in the product divisions of larger companies.

The Domestic Automobile Industry in 1974

The domestic automobile industry within the United States was dominated by three large companies in 1974: Chrysler, Ford, and General Motors. Their sales of passenger cars had represented 81.8% of the total market over the prior year (Exhibit 1).

The three dominant firms were large, well-financed, profitable, and growing, as shown by the sales revenues, variable costs, fixed expenses, financial ratios, and growth indexes (Exhibit 2).

The balance of this case consists of exhibits that provide historical data on the operations of the three major domestic car producers plus a fourth, much smaller firm, American Motors (Exhibits 3, 4, 5, and 6); on the sales trends of domestic passenger cars by make (Exhibit 7), by body style (Exhibit 8), by body size (Exhibit 9), and on the prices and specifications of representative domestic cars (Exhibit 10). Historical data are also provided on the sales trends of imported passenger cars by manufacturer (Exhibit 11) and on the prices of specifications of representative imported cars (Exhibit 12). Finally, comparative manufacturing rates, contribution rates, income statements, and balance sheets are given for the four U.S. auto companies (Exhibits 13 to 16).

Class Assignment. The text states: "Each industry has a different level of competition, and a different pattern of competition. Together, this level and this pattern constitute the competitive structure of the industry; an understanding of this structure is critical to the design of the strategy of a participating firm." Examine the competitive structure of the domestic automobile industry, the present and the potential economics of that industry, and the present equilibrium and potential disequilibriums within that industry:

1. Present participants in the domestic automobile industry. Identify the number and relative size of the producing firms, the supplying firms, the distributing firms, the market segments, etc. The text states that "power is a different concept to define and an almost impossible quantity to measure, but it is an easy idea to understand." Where is the economic power in this industry?

2. Potential participants in the domestic automobile industry. Identify the number and relative size of potential participants, and particularly evaluate the attractiveness of the industry through consideration of rates of growth, indices of profitability, barriers to entry, and barriers to exit.

3. Present economics of the industry. The text states that the "economics of an industry refers, in very simple terms, to the pattern of sales revenues, fixed costs, and variable costs that is typical for the firms within that industry." Compute the break-even point, and understand the cost–volume relationships, for each of the four domestic automobile producers.

4. Potential economics of the industry. Consider the potential changes that may occur in the cost–volume relationships of the domestic automobile industry through the actions of cumulative volume, improved technology, and continued inflation.

5. Present equilibrium of the industry. Would you define the domestic automobile industry in 1974 as being in equilibrium or disequilibrium, and why? Consider what may happen, after 1974, in terms of competitive reactions, governmental regulations, new entrants, advanced technologies, and innovative strategies. Which of the four companies were most vulnerable to these changes, and why? Why didn't the management of those firms understand what could happen to the industry, and to their companies?

Exhibit 1 *Passenger car sales (units) within the United States by all imports, American Motors, Chrysler, Ford, and General Motors, 1973*

	All imports	American Motors	Chrysler	Ford Motor	General Motors
Car sales	1,716,081	356,472	1,576,743	2,494,961	5,252,734
Market share	15.0%	3.1%	13.8%	21.9%	46.1%

Source: Ward's Automotive Yearbook, 1974, p. 24, for domestic sales and p. 47 for import sales.

Exhibit 2 *Simplified income statements, financial ratios, and growth indexes for Chrysler, Ford, and General Motors, 1973*

	Chrysler	Ford Motor	General Motors
Sales revenues (thousands)	$11,774,372	$23,015,100	$35,798,289
Miscellaneous income	11,659	253,600	400,177
Total revenues	11,786,031	23,268,600	36,198,466
Cost of goods sold (thousands)	10,417,751	19,069,300	28,114,074
Selling and administrative expenses	484,804	1,047,400	1,328,086
Pension and bonus expenses	218,582	396,400	112,823
Depreciation and amortization	180,489	948,200	1,983,874
Interest expenses	32,171	174,700	147,506
Total expenses	11,333,797	21,636,000	31,685,363
Profit before taxes	452,234	1,632,600	4,513,103
Federal and foreign taxes	197,089	726,100	2,115,000
Profit after taxes	255,145	906,500	2,398,103
Current assets/current liabilities	1.55	1.37	2.04
Long-term debt/total equity	0.35	0.15	0.06
Profit after taxes/total revenues	2.17%	3.94%	6.70%
Profit after taxes/total assets	4.18%	7.00%	11.82%
Profit after taxes/total equity	9.36%	14.15%	19.08%
Five-year growth in total dollar sales	166.72%	156.97%	147.66%
Five-year growth in total vehicle sales	140.27%	125.68%	121.40%

Source: Moody's Industrial Handbook, 1974.

Exhibit 3 *Simplified income statements (000's omitted), car production (units), and financial ratios for American Motors, Inc., 1969–1973*

	1969	1970	1971	1972	1973
Sales revenues	$737,448	$1,089,787	$1,232,558	$1,403,803	$1,739,025
Miscellaneous income	7,013	8,429	7,865	9,182	17,915
Total revenues	744,461	1,098,216	1,240,423	1,412,985	1,756,940
Cost of goods	626,914	998,474	1,068,385	1,205,909	1,475,424
Selling and administration	87,390	121,942	124,998	137,277	164,550
Pension and bonus expenses	10,650	15,386	16,521	17,654	20,927
Depreciation and amortization	10,335	12,709	13,774	14,217	13,798
Interest expenses	2,194	5,946	5,568	6,371	6,614
Total expenses	737,483	1,154,457	1,229,246	1,381,428	1,681,314
Profit before taxes	6,978	(56,241)	11,177	31,557	75,626
Federal and foreign taxes	2,050	—	5,650	15,100	31,100
Tax adjustments prior years	—	—	+ 4,650	+13,700	+14,450
Profit after taxes	4,928	(56,241)	10,177	30,157	85,976
U.S. car sales	242,810	276,349	235,597	279,395	356,472
U.S. Jeep sales	n.a.	n.a.	92,951	106,841	131,870
U.S. bus sales	n.a.	n.a.	18,653	26,272	34,120
Total vehicle sales	338,791	372,720	347,201	412,508	522,462
Earnings per share	$0.26	($2.22)	$0.20	$1.19	$3.17
Dividends per share	—	—	—	—	—
Current assets/current liabilities	1.71	1.29	1.39	1.64	1.66
Long-term debt/total equity	0.17	0.22	0.20	0.28	0.19
Profit/total revenues	0.68%	def.	0.45%	1.17%	2.56%
Profit/total assets	1.28%	def.	1.95%	2.86%	6.25%
Profit/total equity	2.42%	def.	4.76%	6.74%	12.96%
Five-year growth in dollar sales	100.00%	147.51%	166.62%	188.56%	235.87%
Five-year growth in vehicle sales	100.00%	110.01%	102.48%	121.75%	154.21%

Source: Moody's Industrial Handbook, 1974, p. 7.

Exhibit 4 *Simplified income statements (000's omitted), car production (units), and financial ratios for Chrysler Corporation, 1969–1973*

	1969	1970	1971	1972	1973
Sales revenues	$7,052,184	$6,999,675	$7,999,339	$9,759,129	$11,774,372
Miscellaneous income	16,975	2,270	− 1,166	21,771	11,659
Total revenues	7,069,159	7,001,945	7,998,173	9,780,900	11,786,031
Cost of goods	6,133,926	6,275,819	7,073,083	8,512,153	10,417,751
Selling and administration expenses	431,707	386,042	384,204	435,072	484,804
Pension and bonus expenses	114,577	121,406	151,585	194,302	218,582
Depreciation and amortization	170,306	176,758	176,212	173,314	180,489
Interest expenses	31,703	75,440	70,533	56,427	32,171
Total expenses	6,882,219	7,035,465	7,855,614	9,371,268	11,333,797
Profit before taxes	189,940	(33,520)	142,566	409,632	452,234
Federal and foreign taxes	86,300	—	58,300	223,100	193,700
Tax adjustments prior years	− 4,669	+ 25,917	− 597	+ 33,923	− 3,389
Profit after taxes	98,971	(7,603)	83,659	220,455	255,145
U.S. car sales*	1,391,814	1,274,080	1,314,535	1,367,411	1,576,743
U.S. truck sales	225,911	240,522	207,025	326,666	375,293
Canada car sales	n.a.	n.a.	232,099	264,950	258,823
Canada truck sales	n.a.	n.a.	18,652	27,540	24,155
Foreign car sales	n.a.	n.a.	912,936	1,056,454	1,219,817
Foreign truck sales	n.a.	n.a.	inc.	inc.	inc.
Total vehicle sales*	2,446,605	2,459,336	2,685,247	3,045,021	3,445,831
Earnings per share	$2.06	($0.15)	$1.64	$4.21	$4.69
Dividends per share	2.00	0.60	0.60	0.90	1.30
Current assets/current liabilities	1.32	1.40	1.46	1.49	1.55
Long-term debt/total equity	0.28	0.37	0.36	0.32	0.35
Profit/total revenues	1.40%	def.	1.05%	2.26%	2.17%
Profit/total assets	2.11%	def.	1.67%	4.01%	4.18%
Profit/total equity	4.71%	def.	3.69%	8.86%	9.36%
Five-year growth in dollar sales	100.00%	99.00%	113.14%	138.36%	166.72%
Five-year growth in vehicle sales	100.00%	100.52%	109.75%	124.37%	140.27%

Source: Moody's Industrial Handbook, 1974, p. 947, supplemented by industry estimates (*).

Exhibit 5 *Simplified income statements (000's omitted), car production (units), and financial ratios for Ford Motor Company, 1969–1973*

	1969	1970	1971	1972	1973
Sales revenues	$14,775,600	$14,979,900	$16,433,000	$20,194,400	$23,015,100
Miscellaneous income	67,800	81,200	139,400	178,300	253,600
Total revenues	14,823,400	15,061,100	16,572,400	20,372,700	23,268,600
Cost of goods	12,162,000	12,453,000	13,179,500	16,280,200	19,069,300
Selling and administration expenses	903,800	910,500	879,300	1,006,900	1,047,400
Pension and bonus expenses	194,600	188,000	283,200	376,100	396,400
Depreciation and amortization	385,200	413,600	823,600	913,300	948,200
Interest expenses	62,700	89,800	114,400	133,600	174,700
Total expenses	13,708,300	14,054,900	15,280,000	18,710,100	21,636,000
Profit before taxes	1,115,100	1,006,200	1,292,400	1,662,600	1,632,600
Federal and foreign taxes	554,400	504,500	624,200	773,300	702,000
Tax adjustments prior years	− 14,200	+ 14,000	− 11,500	− 19,300	− 24,100
Profit after taxes	546,500	515,700	656,700	870,000	906,500
U.S. car sales*	2,161,719	2,016,187	2,175,947	2,400,805	2,494,961
U.S. truck sales*	745,825	718,754	716,462	924,459	1,026,459
Canada car sales*	182,956	164,527	178,491	208,812	233,144
Canada truck sales*	69,552	64,267	66,061	75,996	96,780
Foreign car sales*	875,311	973,812	1,001,711	1,066,652	1,165,639
Foreign truck sales*	198,175	202,175	240,260	278,330	303,761
Total vehicle sales*	4,233,538	4,139,721	4,379,417	4,955,054	5,320,744
Earnings per share	$5.03	$4.77	$6.18	$8.52	$9.13
Dividends per share	2.40	2.40	2.50	2.67	3.20
Current assets/current liabilities	1.37	1.33	1.39	1.44	1.37
Long-term debt/total equity	0.06	0.08	0.14	0.16	0.15
Profit/total revenues	3.70%	3.44%	4.00%	4.31%	3.94%
Profit/total assets	5.94%	5.21%	6.25%	7.48%	7.00%
Profit/total equity	10.47%	94.43%	11.84%	14.59%	14.15%
Five-year growth in dollar sales	100.00%	101.60%	111.79%	137.43%	156.97%
Five-year growth in vehicle sales	100.00%	97.78%	103.44%	117.04%	125.68%

Source: *Moody's Industrial Handbook,* 1974, p. 1024, supplemented by industry estimates (*).

Exhibit 6 *Simplified income statements (000's omitted), car production (units), and financial ratios for General Motors Corporation, 1969–1973*

	1969	1970	1971	1972	1973
Sales revenues	$24,295,141	$18,752,353	$28,263,918	$30,435,231	$35,798,289
Miscellaneous income	218,330	186,122	201,624	259,649	400,177
Total revenues	24,513,471	18,938,475	28,465,542	30,694,880	36,198,466
Cost of goods	18,106,500	15,595,575	21,620,860	23,336,855	28,114,074
Selling and administration expenses	1,120,095	1,006,965	1,106,779	1,162,537	1,328,086
Bonus expenses	110,000	—	90,000	101,358	112,823
Depreciation and amortization	1,657,544	1,498,788	1,790,668	1,786,654	1,983,874
Interest expenses	65,336	58,661	137,423	84,870	146,505
Total expenses	21,049,475	18,159,989	24,745,730	26,472,274	31,684,363
Profits before taxes	3,453,996	778,486	3,719,812	4,222,606	4,513,103
Federal and foreign taxes	1,743,301	169,399	1,580,703	2,059,799	1,870,000
Tax adjustments prior years	—	—	− 203,400	—	− 245,000
Profit after taxes	1,710,695	609,087	1,935,709	2,162,807	2,398,103
U.S. car sales*	4,420,272	2,979,240	4,854,117	4,775,124	5,253,174
U.S. truck sales	834,380	613,824	910,021	962,316	1,261,089
Canada car sales	501,134	290,927	508,665	459,128	579,808
Canada truck sales	inc.	inc.	inc.	inc.	inc.
Foreign car sales	1,398,740	1,426,502	1,503,422	1,509,957	1,591,729
Foreign truck sales	inc.	inc.	inc.	inc.	inc.
Total vehicle sales*	7,154,526	5,310,493	7,776,225	7,785,525	8,685,800
Earnings per share	$5.95	$2.09	$6.72	$7.51	$8.34
Dividends per share	4.30	3.40	3.40	4.45	5.25
Current assets/current liabilities	2.30	1.93	1.76	2.12	2.04
Long-term debt/total equity	0.03	0.03	0.06	0.09	0.06
Profit/total revenues	7.04%	3.25%	6.85%	7.10%	6.70%
Profit/total assets	11.54%	4.30%	10.61%	11.84%	11.82%
Profit/total equity	16.73%	6.18%	17.91%	18.51%	19.08%
Five-year growth in dollar sales	100.00%	77.25%	116.12%	125.12%	147.66%
Five-year growth in vehicle sales	100.00%	74.22%	108.68%	108.81%	121.40%

Source: Moody's Industrial Handbook, 1974, p. 1066, supplemented by industry estimates (*).

Exhibit 7 *Sales trends (units, 000's omitted) of domestic passenger cars within the United States, 1960–1973*

	1960	1965	1969	1970	1971	1972	1973
American Motors	486	346	243	276	236	279	356
Plymouth	483	679	651	699	637	613	743
Dodge	412	548	496	406	474	534	593
DeSoto	19	—	—	—	—	—	—
Chrysler	104	240	245	169	203	220	221
	1,018	1,467	1,392	1,274	1,314	1,367	1,557
Ford	1,509	2,164	1,743	1,647	1,761	1,868	1,909
Mercury	360	355	354	310	343	428	453
Lincoln	21	45	65	59	72	105	133
	1,890	2,564	2,162	2,016	2,176	2,401	2,495
Chevrolet	1,874	2,588	1,999	1,504	2,321	2,299	2,334
Pontiac	450	861	772	422	729	703	867
Oldsmobile	403	651	668	440	775	807	918
Buick	308	654	714	460	752	689	826
Cadillac	159	197	267	153	277	277	308
	3,194	4,951	4,420	2,979	4,854	4,755	5,253
Studebaker	106	—	—	—	—	—	—
Checker	7	6	5	4	5	5	6
Total U.S.	7,421	9,334	8,224	6,550	8,583	8,828	9,667

Source: Automotive Facts and Figures, 1974, p. 10, and Automotive Facts and Figures, 1965, p. 11.

Exhibit 8 *Sales trends (percent) of body styles for domestic passenger cars within the United States, 1960–1973*

	1960	1965	1969	1970	1971	1972	1973
2-dr sedan	16.4	7.9	6.1	10.9	14.5	12.1	12.2
2-dr hardtop	11.9	33.8	45.0	41.6	35.7	34.8	35.8
2-dr hatchback	—	—	—	1.1	3.1	4.6	6.1
2-dr wagon	—	—	—	—	0.6	1.6	3.1
2-dr convertible	4.7	5.7	2.7	1.7	1.1	0.8	0.5
	33.0	47.4	53.8	55.3	55.0	53.9	57.7
4-dr sedan	40.2	30.8	22.5	21.4	21.4	21.2	21.0
4-dr hardtop	11.4	11.0	13.5	13.6	13.3	13.4	11.1
4-dr wagon	15.4	10.8	10.2	9.7	10.3	11.5	10.2
	67.0	52.6	46.2	44.7	45.0	46.1	42.3

Source: Wards Automotive Yearbook, 1974, p. 98, and 1965, p. 39.

Exhibit 9 *Sales trends (percent) of body sizes for domestic passenger cars within the United States, 1969–1973*

	1969	1970	1971	1972	1973
Subcompact	—	1.7	7.4	8.2	9.4
Compact	9.6	13.7	11.6	12.6	14.1
Intermediate	22.8	20.8	18.1	19.3	19.2
Standard	26.3	22.8	21.1	19.4	16.1
Medium	17.0	13.9	15.4	15.1	13.2
Luxury	2.9	2.3	2.7	2.6	2.6
Low-priced speciality	7.3	8.0	5.8	4.8	6.4
High-priced speciality	3.0	2.3	2.8	3.3	3.8
Foreign (three major producers)	7.5	10.1	9.9	8.9	8.6
Miscellaneous	3.6	4.4	5.2	5.8	6.6
	100.0	100.0	100.0	100.0	100.0

Source: Standard and Poor's Industrial Surveys, October 1978, p. A-141.

Exhibit 10 *Prices, specifications, and unit sales of representative domestic passenger cars within the United States, 1973*

	Factory price	Wheel-base (in.)	Curb weight (lb.)	Standard engine	Engine hp	1974 sales
American						
Gremlin 2-dr coupe	$ 2,798	96	2,739	L-6	100	76,347
Hornet 4-dr sedan	3,124	108	2,893	L-6	100	51,503
Matador 4-dr sedan	3,301	118	3,536	L-6	100	41,145
Javelin 2-dr sports	3,599	110	2,929	V-8	150	31,286
Buick						
Century 2-dr sedan	3,907	116	4,126	V-8	150	94,306
Electra 4-dr sedan	6,214	127	4,767	V-8	230	177,772
Cadillac						
Deville 4-dr sedan	8,814	130	5,174	V-8	205	216,243
Eldorado 4-dr sedan	9,948	126	5,105	V-8	210	51,451
Chevrolet						
Vega 2-dr coupe	2,799	97	2,466	L-4	75	324,551
Nova 2-dr coupe	3,218	111	3,254	L-6	100	106,437
Malibu 2-dr coupe	3,420	112	3,683	L-6	100	229,486
Impala 4-dr sedan	4,561	121	4,389	V-8	145	549,489
Monte Carlo 4-dr sedan	4,262	116	4,281	V-8	145	212,745
Corvette 2-dr sports	6,810	98	3,390	V-8	195	25,521
Chrysler						
Newport 4-dr sedan	4,937	124	4,630	V-8	185	128,361
New Yorker 2-dr coupe	6,334	124	4,670	V-8	230	14,407

Exhibit 10 (*continued*)

	Factory price	Wheel-base (in.)	Curb weight (lb.)	Standard engine	Engine hp	1974 sales
Dodge						
Dart 2-dr coupe	$ 3,269	111	3,315	L-6	95	65,516
Coronet 4-dr sedan	3,661	115	3,610	L-6	105	83,197
Polara 4-dr sedan	4,631	122	4,540	V-8	185	65,204
Ford						
Pinto 2-dr coupe	2,919	94	2,443	L-4	80	341,470
Maverick 2-dr sedan	3,061	103	2,901	L-6	86	115,438
Mustang 2-dr coupe	3,529	96	2,743	V-6	105	134,867
Gran Torino 4-dr sedan	4,234	118	4,092	V-8	140	154,924
Thunderbird 2-dr sports	7,701	120	5,033	V-8	220	87,269
Lincoln						
Continental 2-dr coupe	9,656	127	5,366	V-8	215	58,636
Mark IV 2-dr coupe	11,082	120	5,377	V-8	220	69,437
Mercury						
Comet 2-dr coupe	3,147	103	2,874	L-6	84	94,008
Montego 2-dr sedan	4,092	118	3,977	V-8	140	53,112
Cougar 2-dr coupe	5,153	114	4,275	V-8	162	57,438
Marquis 4-dr sedan	5,016	121	4,993	V-8	170	80,007
Oldsmobile						
Cutlass 2-dr coupe	3,756	112	3,984	V-8	180	135,158
Ninety-Eight 4-dr sedan	6,104	127	4,830	V-8	210	116,624
Plymouth						
Duster 2-dr coupe	3,243	108	3,055	L-6	95	223,840
Duster 2-dr sports	3,979	108	3,156	V-8	148	13,862
Barracuda 2-dr coupe	3,973	108	3,290	V-8	150	19,281
Sebring 2-dr sedan	4,280	117	3,615	L-6	120	89,959
Fury 2-dr sedan	4,565	122	4,351	V-8	180	128,991
Pontiac						
Ventura 2-dr coupe	3,317	111	3,291	L-6	100	96,502
Firebird 2-dr coupe	3,726	108	3,390	L-6	100	43,613
Grand Prix 4-dr sedan	4,625	124	4,584	V-8	175	153,889

Note: All models are not included; consequently, totals per company will not add to annual sales figures of Exhibits 3 to 6.
Source: Ward's Automotive Yearbook, 1975, pp. 100, 216–220.

Exhibit 11 *Sales trends (units, 000's omitted) of imported passenger cars within the United States, 1963–1973*

	1963	1965	1967	1969	1971	1972	1973
Volkswagen	278	371	455	566	532	492	481
Toyota	1	6	38	130	309	312	326
Datsun	5	18	45	87	252	269	319
Capri (Ford)	—	—	—	—	56	92	113
Opel (Buick)	—	17	52	94	89	69	68
British Leyland	56	57	58	69	66	69	66
Volvo	14	18	34	36	48	58	61
Fiat	—	—	16	21	27	58	58
Porsche-Audi	4	5	7	5	17	20	24
Mercedes-Benz	11	12	21	26	35	42	42
Honda	—	—	—	—	9	21	39
Subaru	—	—	—	—	14	24	38
Colt (Dodge)	—	—	—	—	28	34	36
Saab	4	6	11	11	13	14	17
B.M.W.	—	—	—	15	20	21	14
Renault	24	13	21	20	19	14	9
Peugeot	3	3	4	4	6	5	4
Pantera	—	—	—	—	—	1	1
	400	526	742	997	1,540	1,550	1,716

Note: British Leyland includes M.G., Triumph, Jaguar, Rover, Austin, Austin-Healy, and Morris.
Source: Ward's Automotive Yearbook, 1974, p. 47.

Exhibit 12 *Prices, specifications, and unit sales of representative imported passenger cars within the United States, 1973*

	P.O.E. price	Wheelbase (in.)	Curb weight (lb.)	Standard engine	Engine hp	1974 sales
Volkswagen						
Beetle sedan	$ 2,895	94.5	1,973	4 cyl.	46	⎫
Super Beetle	3,370	95.3	2,072	4 cyl.	46	} 372,376
Kharmann Ghia	3,975	94.5	2,094	4 cyl.	46	⎭
Dasher sedan	4,295	97.2	2,108	4 cyl.	89	32,711
Stationwagen	4,440	94.5	3,042	4 cyl.	109	31,039
Panel truck	4,800	94.5	2,744	4 cyl.	109	44,476
Toyota						
Corolla 2-dr sedan	2,711	91.9	1,815	4 cyl.	65	116,905
Corona 2-dr sedan	3,679	98.4	2,310	4 cyl.	97	61,305
½-ton truck	3,330	101.6	2,489	4 cyl.	97	37,466
Celica 2-dr coupe	3,949	95.5	2,425	4 cyl.	97	59,601
Mark II 4-dr sedan	4,570	101.6	2,820	6 cyl.	138	25,269
Datsun						
210 2-dr sedan	2,849	92.1	1,915	4 cyl.	75	15,133
510 2-dr sedan	3,469	92.1	1,960	4 cyl.	75	30,680
610 4-dr sedan	4,029	98.4	2,430	4 cyl.	100	162,615
280 2-dr coupe	6,284	90.7	2,499	6 cyl.	139	46,282
Porsche-Audi						
100 (Fox) sedan	4,450	105.3	2,172	4 cyl.	91	31,065
914 2-dr coupe	6,300	96.8	2,139	4 cyl.	91	17,933
911 2-dr convertible	13,475	89.4	2,425	6 cyl.	143	5,838
Ford Motor Co.						
Capri (Mercury) sedan	3,980	100.8	2,374	4 cyl.	114	113,069
Pantera 2-dr coupe	11,475	98.4	3,200	8 cyl.	266	1,831
General Motors						
Opel (Buick) coupe	3,899	95.7	2,152	4 cyl.	75	57,018
Opel (Buick) station	4,085	95.7	2,185	4 cyl.	75	11,382
Fiat						
128 sedan	2,741	96.4	1,980	4 cyl.	66	22,916
124 sedan	3,958	95.3	2,265	4 cyl.	78	27,341
124 (Spider) coupe	4,687	95.3	2,370	4 cyl.	92	8,190
Saab						
99 LE sedan	5,198	97.4	2,500	4 cyl.	110	8,921
99 EMS sedan	5,872	94.4	2,672	4 cyl.	110	8,512
Peugeot						
304 sedan	4,810	108.0	2,860	4 cyl.	82	2,172
504 sedan	5,610	114.0	3,105	4 cyl.	82	2,002

Note: All manufacturers and all models are not included; consequently, totals per company will not add to annual import figures of Exhibits 1 and 2.
Source: Ward's Automotive Yearbook, 1975, pp. 24 to 48.

Exhibit 13 *Comparative manufacturing rates (units, 000's omitted) for U.S. automotive companies, 1974*

	AMC		Chrysler		Ford		GM	
U.S. car production	AMC	352.1	Ply.	602.6	Ford	1,717.0	Chev.	1,903.9
	Jeep	134.9	Dodge	464.0	Mer.	400.7	Pont.	502.1
			Chry.	96.6	Lin.	87.6	Olds.	548.7
			Imper.	13.4			Buick	400.3
							Cad.	230.6
		487.0		1,176.6		2,205.3		3,585.5
U.S. truck production		40.8		362.0		892.7	Chev.	867.9
							GMC	219.3
		40.8		362.0		892.7		1,087.2
Foreign car production		—		1,169.2		1,626.7		1,303.2
Foreign truck production		—		129.2		534.3		714.1
Total U.S. and foreign prod.		527.8		2,837.0		5,259.0		6,690.0

Note: The pattern of manufacturing rates for 1974, by company, may appear inconsistent with the pattern of vehicle sales for 1969–1973, by company, as reported in Exhibits 3 to 6 due to inventory adjustments between manufacturing and sales, and to export/import shipments between foreign and U.S. Further, 1974 was considered to be a "depression" year in the U.S. auto industry because of the oil embargo.

Source: Industry consultant; some figures have been disguised at the request of the source.

Exhibit 14 *Comparative contribution rates (000's omitted) for U.S. automotive companies, 1974*

	AMC	Chrysler	Ford	GM
U.S. car sales	$1,592,500	$3,894,500	$7,872,900	$12,943,600
Direct labor cost	313,000	898,700	2,250,900	2,943,400
Direct material cost	948,800	2,188,200	3,134,100	5,760,800
Direct factory cost	77,700	279,200	752,900	1,052,400
Total direct costs	1,339,500	3,366,100	6,137,900	9,756,600
U.S. car contribution	253,000	528,400	1,735,000	3,186,900
U.S. truck sales	362,200	2,693,300	6,713,100	8,643,200
Direct labor cost	60,500	521,300	1,821,300	1,902,900
Direct material cost	183,500	1,269,300	2,535,900	3,734,200
Direct factory cost	15,000	162,000	609,200	682,300
Total direct costs	259,000	1,952,600	4,966,400	6,319,400
U.S. truck contribution	103,200	740,700	1,746,700	2,323,800
Foreign car sales	—	3,437,400	4,652,400	3,740,100
Direct labor cost	—	847,700	1,144,600	867,200
Direct material cost	—	2,051,200	2,377,500	1,994,300
Direct factory cost	—	201,800	296,500	231,900
Total direct costs	—	3,100,700	3,818,600	3,093,400
Foreign car contribution	—	336,700	833,800	646,700
Foreign truck sales	—	541,200	2,289,000	3,652,900
Direct labor cost	—	124,600	518,900	808,100
Direct material cost	—	301,500	1,077,800	1,858,300
Direct factory cost	—	29,600	134,300	216,100
Total direct costs	—	455,700	1,731,000	2,882,500
Foreign truck contribution	—	85,500	558,000	770,400

Source: Industry consultant; some figures have been disguised at the request of the source.

Exhibit 15 *Comparative income statements (000's omitted) for U.S. automotive companies, 1974*

	AMC	Chrysler	Ford	GM
Automotive sales	$1,954,700	$10,566,400	$21,527,400	$28,979,000
Direct labor costs	373,500	2,392,300	5,735,700	6,521,600
Direct material costs	1,132,300	5,810,200	9,125,300	13,347,600
Direct factory costs	92,700	672,600	1,792,900	2,182,700
Total direct costs	1,598,500	8,875,100	16,653,900	22,051,900
Nonautomotive sales	45,200	405,000	2,093,200	2,569,700
Total direct costs	37,300	358,200	1,722,300	2,071,900
Nonautomotive margin	7,900	46,800	370,900	497,800
Automotive gross margin	356,200	1,691,300	4,873,500	6,927,900
Nonautomotive margin	7,900	46,800	370,900	497,800
Total gross margin	364,100	1,738,100	5,244,400	7,425,700
Factory overhead (fixed)	61,700	448,600	1,195,300	1,455,400
Depreciation of plant and equipment	15,900	184,500	530,800	846,600
Amortization of tools and dies	23,800	139,500	392,700	858,400
Total manufacturing overhead	101,400	772,600	2,118,800	3,160,400
Engineering expenses	38,100	241,200	814,900	1,069,500
Selling expenses	39,300	117,000	245,700	304,100
Advertising expenses	43,100	113,000	213,000	247,900
Administrative expenses	91,700	273,100	573,300	653,400
Total management overhead	212,200	744,300	1,846,900	2,274,900
Pensions for employees	24,700	256,400	385,300	364,200
Interest on debt	6,800	107,300	281,500	70,100
Total financial overhead	31,500	363,700	666,800	434,300
Total gross margin	364,100	1,738,100	5,244,400	7,425,700
Total fixed overhead	345,100	1,880,600	4,632,500	5,869,600
Total manufacturing profit (loss)	19,000	(142,500)	611,900	1,556,100
Income from operations	19,000	(142,500)	611,900	1,556,100
Income from unconsolidated subs.	22,500	14,900	58,400	114,400
Income (expenses) from miscellaneous	—	(8,500)	(82,900)	6,700
Income (loss) total	41,500	(136,100)	587,400	1,677,200
Income credit (taxes)	(14,000)	86,400	(201,500)	(727,100)
Income (due) minority in subsidiaries	—	(2,400)	(25,000)	—
Reported net income (loss)	27,500	(52,100)	360,900	950,100

Source: Industry consultant; some figures have been disguised at the request of the source.

Exhibit 16 *Comparative balance sheets (000's omitted) for U.S. automotive companies, 1974*

	AMC	Chrysler	Ford	GM
Cash	$ 75,800	$ 138,000	$ 234,200	$ 400,600
Marketable securities	—	129,700	371,700	937,700
Accounts receivable	104,800	707,100	1,457,100	3,000,800
Inventory	298,600	2,452,900	4,253,000	6,404,700
Prepaid expenses	6,700	111,400	303,800	900,900
Prepaid income taxes	27,200	47,500	221,400	119,300
Refundable income taxes	—	110,600	—	—
Total current assets	513,100	3,697,200	6,841,200	11,764,000
Investments unconsolidated subsidiaries	75,400	847,000	1,140,100	1,416,900
Investments other firms	18,900	78,400	229,100	134,700
Investments common stock	—	—	—	86,700
Total investments	94,300	925,400	1,369,200	1,638,300
Total plant and equipment	371,400*	3,646,300	9,476,400	16,808,500
Accumulated depreciation	160,800*	2,167,500	4,834,500	10,593,000
Net plant and equipment	210,600	1,478,800	4,641,900	6,215,500
Special tools and dies	80,000*	810,000*	1,580,000*	2,760,000*
Accumulated amortization	45,000*	226,500*	537,900*	1,942,100*
Net tools and dies	35,000*	583,500	1,042,100	817,900
Goodwill, less amortization	10,300	47,900	279,200	32,500
Total assets	863,300	6,732,800	14,173,600	20,296,900
Accounts payable	278,300	1,282,500	3,932,300	3,600,400
Accrued expenses	68,500	611,100	—	2,144,600
Short-term debt	—	619,500	1,219,300	—
Payments due on long-term debt	900	183,900	61,500	—
Payments due on income taxes	8,400	12,300	127,800	357,800
Total current liability	356,100	2,709,300	5,340,900	6,102,800
Long-term debt	78,900	995,300	1,476,700	876,600
Long-term liabilities	31,200	113,000	396,500	430,400
Deferred income taxes	14,100	104,100	376,000	—
Deferred investment credits	—	22,800	128,100	189,100
Deferred employment benefits	—	75,900	48,400	11,400
Total long-term liability	124,200	1,311,200	2,425,700	1,507,500
International operations research	—	35,500	26,200	141,700
Minority interest subsidiaries	—	16,200	139,500	185,500
Total miscellaneous liabilities	—	51,700	165,700	326,200

Exhibit 16   (*continued*)

	AMC	Chrysler	Ford	GM
Capital stock—preferred	—	—	—	283,600
Capital stock—common	48,900	370,500	234,000	479,400
Capital surplus	128,500	644,900	361,900	766,900
Earned surplus	205,500	1,645,300	5,645,400	11,000,700
Total liabilities	382,900	2,608,800	6,241,300	12,530,600
Total debt and equity	863,300	6,732,800	14,173,600	20,296,900

Note: * indicates estimated figure.
Source: Annual Report for the respective companies.

Bricklin Vehicle Corporation

In August 1974, after three years of product planning, production engineering, and financial skimping, the first Bricklin automobile rolled off the assembly line in St. John, New Brunswick. Malcolm Bricklin, founder and president of the firm, was absolutely certain that this new vehicle, designed for safety, performance, and style, and his new company, 1/10,000 the size of General Motors, could both compete directly with the Big Three auto makers in Detroit.

> I assume that the auto people in Detroit just laughed when they heard that Bricklin was going to build a new car in an old wood-working factory in New Brunswick, but I'm not certain that they kept on laughing when they saw the car. It was well designed and well made, and I think that it proved that you can compete with the Big Boys, if you have imagination, innovation, and aggressiveness. Malcolm Bricklin had all three of those qualities. (Statement of an industry executive)

Malcolm Bricklin was born in Philadelphia in 1939, the son of the owner of a successful building supply company. Malcolm started his first company in 1958, also in the building supply business, at age 19 after dropping out of college. He selected Florida for the location, to take advantage of the building boom in that state, and he directed the sales toward the smaller builders, carpenters, and homeowners, since he felt that the larger contractors were already well served by the existing lumberyards and wholesale distributors. His store was named *The Handyman,* and it remained open until 9:00 at night to provide service to his customers, many of whom worked up to 5:00 in the afternoon and were unable to buy from his competitors. The concept was successful, and within a few years the single store had expanded to 174 franchises. Malcolm had always expressed a desire to be a millionaire, and at age 25 he realized his ambition by selling his store and his interests in the franchised operations for exactly $1,000,000 after taxes.

Malcolm Bricklin's next business venture introduced him to the realm of motorized transportation. The Italian firm of Innocenti, manufacturers of the Lambretta motor scooter, had overestimated demand during a recent upswing in sales in the American market, and in 1965 had an inventory of 30,000 imported motor scooters and U.S. sales of only 2,000 units per year. Bricklin purchased the inventory, rented an office in the Time-Life Building in New York City, hired a chauffered Rolls-Royce, conducted a whirlwind sales campaign, and sold all 30,000 in just 60 days. Among his best customers were police departments, whom he convinced to try the scooter for patrol duties in urban areas, and scooter rental agencies, which he established to provide low-cost transportation in the suburbs.

In order to continue supplying the scooter rental agencies, Bricklin obtained the distributorship for the Rabbit, a scooter manufactured by Fuji Heavy Industries, a large Japanese firm. After two years, however, the Japanese company decided to stop manufacturing the Rabbit, in order to concentrate more fully on automobiles. Bricklin flew to Japan to argue personally for continued motor scooter sales, but when he was shown the Subaru, the new car manufactured by Fuji, he soon forgot about renting scooters and began to think about importing cars. The Subaru came in two basic models: the 1000 was a standard import size vehicle powered by a conventional four-cylinder engine, while the 360 was a micro car, powered by a two-cylinder engine that weighed less than 1,000 pounds, carried four people, got well over 35 miles to the gallon of gasoline, and could be sold in the United States for approximately $1,500. By way of contrast, the Volkswagen Beetle at this time cost $2,170 delivered in the United States. Since the Fuji weighed less than 1000 pounds, it was exempt from federal exhaust emission regulations, and could be imported into the United States without engineering modifications.

Bricklin formed Subaru of America in 1968, investing $900,000, to start importing the 360. He established dealerships, and was approaching the break-even volume when a consumer magazine published an article calling the 360 unsafe. As a result, many banks refused to continue supplying credit for dealer inventories and retail sales, which in effect stopped the company. During the fight for survival of Subaru of America, Bricklin convinced Fuji to modify the larger 1000 model to meet American exhaust emission standards so that it could be imported and sold in the United States. To get rid of the 360s that were left in stock, Bricklin formed FasTrack International Speedways, Inc. Race courses were constructed, the tops were cut off the 360s, roll bars were fitted, and the public was charged $1.00 per lap to drive in a manner generally considered unsafe on the public highways.

In 1971, Bricklin sold his interests in Subaru of America, and retired to an expensive home near Scottsdale, Arizona. At this time he was 32 years old, wealthy, successful, independent, and determined to build a new sports car.

> I think that the challenge went out of Subaru when he was blocked from importing the 360. He always wanted to do something different from the other guys, and the 360 was different. I think that he wanted to prove that Detroit was wrong. So, if he couldn't import an inexpensive minicar, due to safety restrictions, he decided that he would build an expensive sports car that would stress safety and performance. He was competitive, and he was certain that he could compete with Detroit. (Statement of an industry executive)

Bricklin the man comes across as a very self-assured, perhaps even cocky individual. And "individual" is an apt description of Bricklin, both the man and his car. From his dress (Levis, a cowboy hat, open-necked shirt with strands of Indian jewelry) to his office in Scottsdale, Arizona (furnished in ghost-town motif complete with nineteenth-century saddles for bar stools, a live cactus garden, and rattlesnakes, skinned thankfully), he's the antithesis of the typical white-shirted, ultra-conservative Detroit auto executive. (*Road and Track,* August 1974, p. 96)

Malcolm Bricklin formed the Bricklin Vehicle Corporation in 1971, with research and development offices in Scottsdale, Arizona, and hired 10 car stylists and automotive engineers to design his version of a safe, reliable, high-performance sports car.

I think that he told them that the car was to look like a Lamborghini (hand-made Italian sports car selling for over $25,000), have gullwing doors, be able to sustain a 25-mph crash with no damage, use an American motor and drive train (transmission gears, universal joints, and differential axle), and sell for $5,000. Although the basic vehicle configuration was a sports car, the motivating concept was safety, and therefore the designation was SV-1 for Safety Vehicle One. A safe high-performance car was an approach that no other auto company had ever attempted. That, I think, is what appealed to Bricklin. (Statement of an industry executive)

The first full-scale clay model was constructed in 11 weeks, instead of the nine months normally required by Detroit automakers, and in two years the prototype car, hand-made at a shop in Livonia, Michigan, was ready for testing. This car had a number of unusual features. The body panels were molded sheet acrylic over fiberglass, a tough combination that was completely rustproof and that was substantially impact-resistant. A sledgehammer blow resulted only in scuffing, and since the color was in the pigmented outer layer of acrylic plastic rather than in a thin coating of paint, scuffs and scratches could be removed by simple polishing and buffing. The body panels were mounted on a tubular box steel frame, which was approximately twice as heavy as the frame on comparable American cars, and the front and rear bumpers were attached to this frame by a hydraulic shock-absorbing system that definitely reduced damage to the car or injury to the occupants in the event of a collision. The car was equipped with an American Motors V-8 engine that developed 220 hp at 4,400 rpm and a four-speed manual transmission that produced a top speed of 112 mph, and an acceleration from 0 to 60 mph in 7 seconds. Members of the automotive industry who were permitted to see, and eventually to test drive either the prototype or one of the early production models were generally enthusiastic about both the style and the performance of the vehicle.

Bricklin considers his car a combination safety–sports car and puts a lot of stock in the use of production-line American mechanical components. It's too early yet to know how well Bricklin's safety concept will withstand impacts, but the high box-section perimeter frame and the encircling rollcage structure should provide occupants with considerable passive safety and the massive bumper system is claimed to have better-than-legal impact resistance. The color impregnated acrylic body panels are resistant to dents and surface scratches, so the Bricklin should also be more immune to parking-lot damage of the body panels than most cars. If the shape isn't the most original—Corvette, Datsun 280Z, and above all Mercedes-Benz C111 influences are quite apparent—it is eye-catching and distinctive. The gullwing doors, of course, are the Bricklin's real claim to fame and they're more than a styling gimmick: they can be opened with as little as 11 in. of side clearance, greatly reducing the risk involved in opening a door into traffic and making it easier to get out when the parking space is tight. The impregnated fiberglass also makes parking in tight spaces more practical! The basic interior design is nice, too. There's a complete VDO instrument package, including tachometer and trip odometer, a padded and tilting steering wheel, an AM/FM radio with integral digital clock, roll-down side windows (something not normally found on gull-wing doors) and a comprehensive heating and air-conditioning system. The seats are reasonably comfortable, although the seatbacks don't recline because (Bricklin says) in the interests of achieving the safest possible seat a one-piece design was judged necessary. However, the seatback is raked more than in most U.S. cars and the soft suedelike material (in tan regardless of the exterior color) holds the body snugly and comfortably. The hatchback makes a lot of sense too: the carpeted rear compartment holds a lot of cargo and access to it is good.

The use of U.S. components for the major mechanical parts of the Bricklin is the other important selling point. Malcolm Bricklin himself has endured the inconvenience of getting an exotic import serviced, and the Bricklin will attract those who wish to avoid this (or just the expensive service of not-so-exotic but high-quality imports) by virtue of its American engine, transmission, driveline, and suspension. (*Road and Track*, April 1975, p. 67)

Publicity releases and advertising brochures prepared by the Bricklin Vehicle Corporation emphasized the safety aspects of the new sports car.

> The Bricklin is the first production car that is truly worthy of being called a safety vehicle. It contains revolutionary new safety features and engineering designs not found in most mass-produced automobiles.
>
> The Bricklin passenger compartment is protected at bumper height by a body frame made of tubular box steel which, combined with a steel roll cage that surrounds the passengers, provides greater accident protection than is found in standard auto design. Add to this a unique bumper system which recedes into the car in the event of a front or rear collision, and by so doing is capable of absorbing impacts in excess of those required by federal safety standards. The fuel tank is protected on five sides by steel partitions rather than simply strapped to the body frame and fully exposed. (Statement in Bricklin advertising brochure, 1975)

The reactions of the members of the automotive press, after production started and the new vehicle became available for evaluation and test drives, concentrated much more on performance and style than on safety, and stressed potential customer reactions more than design features.

> This is an exciting car. Sure it is probably imperfect by almost any standards—what car isn't—but it's an exciting, sexy car with a lot of charisma. Pop the Bricklin's gullwing doors open and a crowd will gather. Drive on down the street and even a Corvette owner will take a second look. People will pull up alongside at a traffic light, admire the SV-1 and then ask "what is it and where the heck did you get it?"
>
> It's a comfortable car—the seats fit the human body nicely, a pleasant contrast to those found in some cars. Headroom is minimal but adequate. Speedometer and tachometer are a tad small for easy reading, but they get the job done. Incidentally, those vertical gizmos just behind the seats are the hydraulic cylinders that open and close the doors. Reaching brake, throttle, or headlight dimmer switch is no problem, even for a 5 ft 9 in. chap with the seat all the way back. But if you are a lady wearing a form of skirt, you can expect to have your modesty challenged by the knee-high door sills.
>
> So what is it like to drive? Fun. Noisy but fun. The ride is firm almost to the point of being harsh, but cornering is superb and the Bricklin sticks to the road like it was on rails—you don't get something for nothing. Acceleration—contrary to what you might expect from the defiant proclamations of the exhaust sys-

tem—is a bit on the anemic side. And the exhaust and wind noise, even at 50 mph, are enough to discourage casual conversation. However, it is still one of those cars that makes you want to let it run just to see how fast it will go and how it will handle at top speed.

Visibility out the front and to the sides is adequate at best. The front corner posts interfere with one's view around a turn, and the rear pillars block the three-quarter rear view. Visibility directly aft is even worse. The hatch-back rear window limits the view through the inside mirror to a narrow slice of pavement directly behind the rear bumper—only by resting your chin on the steering wheel can you see anything useful in that mirror. The outside rear-view mirrors help, but even here the view could be improved and both, instead of the left mirror only, should be adjustable from the driver's seat.

Except for the mediocre visibility, the SV-1 does give one the impression that it really is what it claims to be—a safety car. And at the same time a fun-to-drive sports car. We personally wish it well. (*Automation*, June 1975, p. 49)

The final specifications for the car, after development was completed and production had started, were listed in company advertising brochures as follows:

List price, delivered East Coast, with standard equipment (gullwing doors, air conditioning, AM/FM stereo, alloy wheels, power steering and power brakes): $7,490.

Size: Curb weight of 3555 lb; wheelbase of 96 in., overall length of 178 in., width of 67.6 in., and height of 49 in.

Engine: Overhead V-8, with a 103.6 mm bore × 87.4 mm stroke and 5896-cc displacement at 85:1 compression ratio generating 220 Bhp at 4400 rpm (97 equivalent mph).

Brakes, wheels, and steering: Vacuum-assisted brake system with 10.9-in. discs on the front wheels and 10.0-in. × 1.75-in. drums on the rear; wheels are 15-in. × 7-in. cast alloy, with Goodrich FR60-15 radial tires; recirculating ball steering with 3.2 turns lock to lock, and a 32.8-ft turning circle.

Acceleration: 0 to 30 mph in 4.0 seconds; 0 to 40 in 5.5 seconds; 0 to 50 in 7.3 seconds; 0 to 60 in 9.9 seconds; 0 to 70 in 12.8 seconds; and 0 to 80 in 16.9 seconds. Top speed: 112 mph.

Despite the top speed, which was listed at 112 mph, despite the speedometer reading, which went to 160 mph, and despite the enthusiastic reports by one of the automotive reporters, who claimed to have reached 148 mph in a test drive, Malcolm Bricklin continued to emphasize the safety aspects of the car.

We're setting precedent with the safest and most advanced production car ever built. None of our safety features is an add-on. Eventually, Detroit will see fit to invest in retooling. Public demand for accident protection will necessitate it. (Statement of Mr. Bricklin, quoted in *Advertising Age,* July 1, 1974, p. 3)

If the claims of its manufacturers are true, the Bricklin, which is being billed as the safest car ever built, may be what the insurance industry has long been asking Detroit to turn out. The Bricklin ... is the first independently produced automobile to invade the U.S. market in 28 years.

The Bricklin took three years ... to produce, and will sell for $7,400. Its creator, Malcolm Bricklin, says that "We have received indications from various insurance companies that if the car passes their demonstration tests, as it has passed ours, it can be insured at lower rates, hopefully considerably lower rates." (*Journal of Commerce,* June 27, 1974, p. 11)

There were a number of unusual features to the design of the Bricklin SV-1 that directly reflected the attitudes and opinions of Malcolm Bricklin. There was no ashtray since

Bricklin did not smoke, and wanted to discourage smoking among both his employees and customers. There was no spare tire or tire-changing tools, since Bricklin felt that the steel-belted radials were impervious to punctures and blowouts. There was an air conditioner and an AM/FM stereo installed as standard equipment on all cars since Bricklin was certain that customers would want both features. In addition to those three specific examples, it seemed obvious that the general car design reflected the personal taste and product concepts of Malcolm Bricklin.

> I run this the way I see it. No market research. I know the guy we're building this car for. He's the guy who wants a beautiful car, but doesn't know a thing about cars.... He's me. (Statement of Mr. Bricklin, quoted in *Road and Track*, April 1974, p. 70)

The price of the production model of the SV-1, at $7,490, was somewhat higher than the list price for the Datsun 280Z, at $6,284, or the Chevrolet Corvette, at $6,810, but it should be remembered that the Bricklin came equipped with many standard features that were considered options on other cars, so that exact comparisons were difficult. The SV-1 was positioned to compete against the Datsun and Chevrolet sports cars, both of which were popular in 1974, with Datsun 280Z sales of 46,000 cars, and Chevrolet Corvette sales of 25,000 cars.

Distribution was initially planned only for the 12 northeastern states, with the intention to gradually expand westward as the factory production increased and additional cars became available. The company solicited franchises only from established car dealers since it was felt that their sales experience, repair facilities, and financing ability would be critical for the early sales of the Bricklin.

> We're looking for well-capitalized, well-established dealers initially in the following states: New York, New Jersey, Pennsylvania, Massachusetts, Maryland, Dela-

ware, New Hampshire, Maine, Vermont, Virginia, and Rhode Island. (Company advertisement, quoted in *Advertising Age,* September 10, 1973, p. 1)

Bricklin Vehicle Corporation offered a dealer discount of 16 to 18%, depending upon the volume, which was standard in the car industry. Franchises were sold for $8,800, which included both the franchise fee of $4,000 and payment of $4,800 for a shipment of basic repair parts, special tools, and promotional literature. At the start of production, in August 1974, 235 dealers had purchased a franchise from Bricklin, and were prepared to sell and service the SV-1 car.

Paid promotion was planned to be minimal. It was thought that adequate publicity would be generated by the introduction of the first new American-made car in 28 years (since the advent of the short-lived and poorly designed Tucker, following World War II), so that consumer advertising would not be needed. Also, it was felt that Malcolm Bricklin could provide whatever promotion was needed, without the professional services of advertising agencies or public relations consultants.

> Mr. Bricklin comes across like a promoter—a 35-year-old, fast talking, good looking, self-made millionaire from Philadelphia with a taste for western clothes and bead necklaces. Friend and foe alike agree that he may be one of the few men who could successfully sell the idea of starting a car company when, as he openly admits, "there seem to be too many automobiles already." (*Wall Street Journal,* December 30, 1974, p. 1)

Malcolm Bricklin was one of the real strengths of the company. Your students may think of him as a con-man, because who except a "con-man" would start a new company to compete with Ford and G.M., and be able to talk others into helping him do it. But that opinion is selling Malcolm Bricklin short. He was an imaginative man, who thought of different ways of doing things, and he was a zestful man, who enjoyed what he was doing. Publicity thrives on the combination of innovation and zest. He did not go out looking for publicity; publicists came looking for him. (Statement of an industry observer)

Production facilities were established in New Brunswick. The original plan of the Bricklin Vehicle Corporation had been to build the car in western Pennsylvania or central Ohio so that the assembly plant would be close to the suppliers of the major automotive parts. However, the premier of New Brunswick, in eastern Canada, offered substantial financial support in exchange for the increased employment and economic development that a large-scale manufacturing operation was certain to generate. New Brunswick, in 1974, had over 10% unemployment, and a depressed economy that was dependent upon farming, forestry, and fishing. It was estimated that the Bricklin plants would generate 700 direct manufacturing jobs, and perhaps 2,100 supporting retail and service positions, within the province. It was understood in Canada that this financial support of a new automotive company was risky, but it was also felt that the potential rewards in the form of jobs and economic development far outweighed the risk.

> Sure, it's a high risk venture. It's time someone in Canada took a chance. We Canadians are very conservative. The last time we took a real risk, it was the Canadian Pacific Railway, and it worked. (Statement of Mr. Richard Hatfield, Premier of New Brunswick, quoted in *Motor Trend,* November 1974, p. 43)

The manufacturing operations in New Brunswick were very simple, in comparison to the complex and highly automated procedures found in most U.S. car companies. A plant to fabricate the acrylic and fiberglass body panels was built at Minto, a small town near Fredericton, the capital of the province, while a nonautomated assembly line was set

up in an abandoned brush and broom factory at St. John, the largest city in the Maritime Provinces. No other manufacturing or machining was needed: the V-8 engine was purchased from American Motors; the transmission, drive shaft, universal joints, and differential axle came from Chrysler; the shock absorbers and power steering were to be supplied by General Motors; and the suspension system was a Ford product. Fasteners, gauges, seating, and carpets were to be purchased in Canada, while the steel frame was to be formed and welded in New Brunswick. The labor force, both for assembling the cars in St. John and for fabricating the body panels in Minto, were nonunionized, and averaged $2.50 per hour less in wages than their unionized counterparts in Detroit.

The assembly plant at St. John was designed to produce 1,000 cars per month on a single-shift basis, and it was thought that the addition of a second shift and the use of more automated equipment could bring the capacity to 2,500 cars per month. For comparison, the Chevrolet Vega assembly plant at Lordstown, Ohio, which is the most fully automated factory in the industry, produces 2,500 cars per day. The plan was to start the St. John plant at 12 cars per day, or 240 cars per month on a 20-working-day month, and gradually increase the rate to the designed capacity as the operations became established and the work force became trained. Expected costs and revenues of the assembly plant are given in Exhibit 1.

Malcolm Bricklin admitted that he lacked experience in manufacturing, but he hired purchasing agents and production managers from the major automobile firms to supervise the assembly of the SV-1.

> Bricklin confesses his ignorance of auto manufacturing. "But I didn't know anything about hardware or importing cars, either," he says. He has an aggressive, entrepreneurial drive that has helped him hire a dozen experienced auto men to

Exhibit 1 *Expected revenues and costs of automotive production at the Bricklin Vehicle Company (Canada) Ltd.*

	Costs per car	12,000 cars per year	30,000 cars per year
Revenues, at $7,490—18% dealer discount	$6,040/car	$72,480,000	$181,200,000
Direct labor, at local rates	1,000/car	12,000,000	30,000,000
Direct material, at delivered cost	2,800/car	33,600,000	84,000,000
Direct factory overhead	400/car	4,800,000	12,000,000
Total direct costs	4,200/car	50,400,000	126,000,000
Contribution to fixed expenses	1,840/car	22,080,000	55,200,000
Fixed factory overhead		1,800,000	2,400,000
Depreciation on plant and equipment (10 years)		600,000	900,000
Amortization on tools and dies (5 years)		300,000	450,000
Total manufacturing overhead		2,700,000	3,750,000
Engineering expenses (Note A)		1,200,000	1,800,000
Selling expenses (Note B)		2,400,000	3,600,000
Advertising expense (Note B)			
Administrative expenses (Note C)		1,200,000	1,800,000
Total managerial overhead		4,800,000	7,200,000
Interest expenses, at 8% rate		800,000	1,200,000
Royalty payments to New Brunswick (Note D)	$25/car	300,000	750,000
License payments to General Vehicle Corp.	$150/car	1,800,000	4,500,000
Total financial overhead		2,900,000	6,450,000
Profit after fixed expenses but before taxes		11,600,000	37,800,000

Note A: Engineering function, for both product design and process design, was to be performed by Bricklin Vehicle Corporation (Michigan) in Livonia, Michigan, and was to be charged at a standard rate.

Note B: Marketing function, for both dealer contacts and consumer advertising, was to be performed by Bricklin Vehicle Corporation (Northeast) in New Jersey, and was to be charged at a standard rate.

Note C: General management function was to be performed by General Vehicle Corporation in Arizona, and was to be charged at a standard rate.

Note D: Royalty payments to the Province of New Brunswick and license payments to the General Vehicle Corporation were to be payable only after the Bricklin Vehicle Corporation (Canada) was operating profitably.

Source: Industry consultant; some figures have been disguised at the request of the consultant.

mastermind his new venture. They include Jack R. Hennessy and Edward Jones, respected production men at Ford Canada; former Ford stylist Herbert Grasse; Chrysler parts and service executive Douglas Berhhart; Charles Luce, former Lear Sigler quality control manager; and Jack Reese, former U.S. sales manager for Mercedes and Renault. (*Business Week,* April 27, 1974, p. 44)

Three companies were involved in the development and manufacture of the SV-1. General Vehicle Corporation included the financial, legal, and research functions, was located in Scottsdale, Arizona, and was 100%

owned by Malcolm Bricklin. A subsidiary, Bricklin Vehicle Corporation, was responsible for product development, process engineering, and parts purchasing, was located in Livonia, Michigan, and was reported to be 80% owned by General Vehicle Corporation and 20% owned by the management and engineering personnel. Bricklin of Canada was 51% owned by the Province of New Brunswick and 49% by General Vehicle Corporation; it was responsible for fabricating the acrylic and fiberglass body panels and for assembling the cars in the two plants at Minto and St. John, New Brunswick, as described previously. When production started, it was planned to establish a fourth company, Bricklin Northeast, to coordinate the distribution and sales of the car in the selected market area of the 12 northeastern states.

Financing of the three companies involved in the SV-1 venture emphasized debt rather than equity capital. Malcolm Bricklin supplied the initial capital with a personal investment of $500,000, and advanced additional funds in the form of subordinated debentures and unsecured notes. The primary financing for the General Vehicle Corporation came from the First Pennsylvania Banking and Trust Company of Philadelphia, whose chairman, Mr. John Bunting, believed in the concept of the new car and in the ability of Malcolm Bricklin.

> "He's a promoter genius," says John R. Bunting, chairman of First Pennsylvania Banking and Trust Company. "There are only a few people—maybe five—in this whole world who could do what he's done." ... First Pennsylvania's Bunting, a maverick who has turned a sleepy bank into a deposit and profit leader, admits the venture is risky. Insiders say the bank demanded a hefty interest rate, plus special fees and such "kickers" as progress-tied fund disbursals. (*Business Week*, April 27, 1974, p. 44)

Major financing for Bricklin of Canada came from the province of New Brunswick, which supplied $500,000 in equity and guaranteed all loans from Canadian banks, in exchange for 51% of the common stock and the promise of 700 manufacturing jobs in the area. In addition, the province was to receive a royalty of $25 per car produced.

> Premier Hatfield has always admitted Bricklin is a "very high-risk venture." But he says the 700 potential jobs justify the $5 million public investment, and he's confident the car will be a booming success. (*Financial Post*, August 3, 1974, p. 3)

Balance sheets for the three companies (General Vehicle Corporation, Bricklin Vehicle Corporation, and Bricklin of Canada, Ltd.) in 1974, at the start of production, are shown in Exhibits 2, 3, and 4.

The three Bricklin companies were unstructured, without organization charts, job descriptions, or personnel departments. Malcolm Bricklin believed in "free-form" organizations, in which individual managers searched for and found their own areas of responsibility. Managerial and technical employees were almost entirely hired from the staffs of the Big Three automobile companies in either Detroit or Windsor, Ontario.

> Bricklin has put together a top management team. In New Brunswick there are eight executives who gave up positions with the big three auto-makers to "help produce a completely new car." (*Financial Post*, August 3, 1974, p. 3)

The first two production model cars were driven off the assembly line at St. John, New Brunswick, at the end of June 1974, and both vehicles were then taken to New York City for the formal introduction of the Bricklin SV-1.

> The Bricklin SV-1 safety sportster made its debut for the automotive press and the beautiful people here last week. One conclusion is that the introduction was far less conventional than is the car itself. Malcolm Bricklin, with his entrepreneurial genius flowering and his adrena-

Exhibit 2 *Comparative balance sheets for General Vehicle, Inc., December 1973–July 1974*

	Dec. 1973	Apr. 1974	July 1974
Cash	$ 373,516	$ (42,988)	$ 32,127
Accounts receivable—intercompany	138,134	601,484	—
Inventory	—	—	—
Miscellaneous current assets	—	—	6,285
	511,650	558,496	38,412
Office furniture and equipment	68,605	95,603	115,426
Test machinery and equipment	—	—	23,061
Land and test track in Arizona	554,636	554,636	554,636
Investment in Bricklin of Michigan	450,000	450,000	250,000
Investment in Bricklin of Canada	1,000,000	1,000,000	1,200,000
Capitalized preoperating expenses	1,445,009	1,445,009	1,445,009
Capitalized product development	567,066	1,625,181	2,339,349
Miscellaneous fixed assets	52,795	65,623	106,073
	4,138,111	5,236,052	6,033,554
Total current and fixed assets	4,649,761	5,794,548	6,071,966
Accounts payable—general	179,992	173,753	214,285
Accounts payable—intercompany	168,035	49,918	298,535
Loan payable—bank	257,388	2,150,000	2,500,000
Loan payable—subordinated	—	245,000	245,000
Loan payable—stockholder	100,000	100,000	—
Miscellaneous current liabilities	—	359,236	65,371
	705,345	3,077,907	3,323,191
Deposits from dealers	478,316	969,141	1,179,042
Mortgage payable on land and track	351,000	—	234,000
Notes payable—bank	1,750,000	—	—
Notes payable—affiliate	1,000,000	1,000,000	700,000
	3,579,316	1,969,141	2,113,042
Common stock	455,000	455,000	855,000
Retained earnings (deficit)	(89,900)	292,500	(219,267)
	365,100	747,500	635,733
Total liabilities and equity	4,649,761	5,794,548	6,071,966

Source: Industry consultant; some figures have been disguised at the request of the consultant.

lin pumping, plowed new ground with his sociological happening at the Four Seasons.

Legitimate working newsmen were outnumbered and all but trampled by friends, relatives, show-biz types, groupies, and hangers-on. . . .

One of the firsts for Bricklin was having the actual unveiling performed by Richard Hatfield, premier of New Brunswick, the Canadian province where the car will be assembled. Hatfield was assisted in pulling off the tarp by John Bunting, chairman of the First Pennsylvania Bank

Exhibit 3 *Comparative balance sheets for Bricklin Vehicle Company (Michigan) Inc.,*
December 1973–July 1974

	Dec. 1973	Apr. 1974	July 1974
Cash	$ 34,501	$ 22,817	$ 4,455
Deposits to vendors	22,472	38,780	9,667
Accounts receivable—general	315	7,198	7,072
Accounts receivable—intercompany	49,918	49,918	—
Inventory	571,382	664,250	—
	678,597	782,963	21,194
Office furniture and equipment	37,243	39,814	20,171
Test machinery and equipment	51,444	42,811	19,750
Miscellaneous fixed assets	4,050	4,050	4,050
	92,737	86,675	65,165
Total current and fixed assets	771,334	869,638	83,359
Accounts payable—general	97,810	161,248	74,828
Accounts payable—intercompany	138,134	224,000	—
Loan payable—subordinated	28,000	28,000	—
Loan payable—stockholder	—	49,000	—
	263,944	462,248	74,828
Notes payable—bank	300,000	200,000	—
Notes payable—General Vehicle	450,000	450,000	250,000
	750,000	650,000	250,000
Common stock	5,000	5000	6,141
Retained earnings (deficit)	(247,610)	(247,610)	(247,610)
	(242,610)	(242,610)	(241,469)

Source: Industry consultant; some figures have been disguised at the request of the consultant.

and Trust Company, chief financier of the Bricklin project. . . .

Still another "first" for Bricklin was the appearance of Sammy Cahn, singing his own song, The Most Beautiful Car in the World. (Not surprisingly, in Cahn's lyrics the car turns out to be a Bricklin.) Cahn is possibly better known for such tunes as Three Coins in the Fountain, Let It Snow, I'll Walk Alone, Be My Love, and The Most Beautiful Girl in the World. (*Automotive News,* July 1, 1974, p. 3)

The production model vehicles were well received by the automotive press, despite the songs and hoopla that seemed to be required at the introduction of the new sports car.

Malcolm Bricklin, the 35-year-old entrepreneur who set out to build a car his critics said was an impossibility, scored a personal triumph here yesterday when the Bricklin Safety Vehicle was enthusiastically received at a large press party in the Four Seasons restaurant. . . .

Clad in a safari suit and open neck casual shirt revealing a two-strand necklace of Indian beads, Mr. Bricklin fielded

Exhibit 4 *Comparative balance sheets for Bricklin Vehicle Company (Canada) Ltd., December 1973–July 1974*

	Dec. 1973	Apr. 1974	July 1974
Cash	$ 73,437	$ 394,000	$ 540,225
Deposits to vendors	—	—	44,000
Accounts receivable—intercompany	118,117	—	298,535
Inventory	—	583,041	1,907,067
Miscellaneous current assets	—	—	86,561
	191,555	977,041	1,876,388
Production machinery and equipment	1,636,847	3,575,479	6,317,807
License from General Vehicle, Inc.	1,000,000	1,000,000	1,200,000
Capitalized preoperating expenses	246,292	511,647	1,161,916
	2,883,139	5,087,126	8,476,057
Total current and fixed assets	3,075,694	6,064,167	11,552,445
Accounts payable—general	249,084	1,020,400	2,187,263
Accounts payable—intercompany	—	377,484	—
Loan payable—bank	—	500,000	500,000
Loan payable—intercompany	—	—	200,000
Miscellaneous current liabilities	8,875	16,283	151,515
	257,959	1,914,167	3,038,778
Notes payable—bank	1,316,735	2,650,000	7,013,667
Common stock	1,500,000	1,500,000	1,500,000
Retained earnings (deficit)	1,000	—	—
	1,501,000	1,500,000	1,500,000
Total liabilities and equity	3,075,694	6,064,167	11,552,445

Source: Industry consultant; some figures have been disguised at the request of the consultant.

questions about the car with apparent ease, despite admitting to being "nervous as hell."

In discussing how the car was developed, he stressed that many of the design features and safety innovations were contributions of a team of experts "we stole from the Big Three." He added that these people "made a dream come true" because they gave up the security of jobs they had held for 15 to 25 years to go with him.

"Will the Bricklin be an Edsel?" a reporter asked. Mr. Bricklin shot back: "We're not sure. What we do know is that what the Edsel was selling when it was called a failure is pretty close to five times our top projection for Bricklin production." (*Advertising Age,* July 1, 1974, p. 3)

The company planned to start full-scale production of the Bricklin SV-1 in August 1974, and there appeared to be a large number of potential buyers waiting to purchase the new sports car from dealers in the Northeast.

One Boston-area dealer took out a postcard-sized ad in the Sunday *Boston Globe* sometime after June 25 (date of the formal introduction in New York City). The ad pictured the car, suggested it would arrive soon, and invited inquiries. On Monday morning the dealer arrived in his office to the sound of ringing telephones. "By noontime we had 84 phone calls" he said somewhat astounded. By late August, that dealer had deposits on 18 cars. Sight unseen. "If this thing works out, it'll be the best thing since night baseball."

Another dealer received a check in the mail. "Some guy had seen one of the stories in a car magazine, found out we were one of the dealers, and sent us a check for $6,500. I have never heard of such a thing in all my years in the business."

Another Lincoln-Mercury dealership is sitting on 43 deposits of $500 each. The manager estimates inquiries in six weeks reached more than 500, including calls and checks from western states.

One more dealer: "I just hope and pray that they stop promoting this car and stop advertising. It just causes more problems. Bricklin goes on TV the other night (NBC's *Tomorrow* show) and the next day the phone is ringing off the hook. People just get mad when you tell them you don't even have one of the cars."

One man is not complaining. His name is Walter Crisconi and he's the owner of a well-established Oldsmobile dealership in Philadelphia. Crisconi has a Bricklin, the second car off the line (the first went for crash tests in Phoenix). The experience he says, "is the most exciting thing that's happened to me since my son was born. People have been pouring into this place from 8 a.m. until 10 at night. I've never seen anything like it," says Crisconi, who's been selling cars for 41 years. "They oooh and aaah and they push the buttons to the gull-wing doors and they go nuts! Yesterday I drove the car to my barber—it's about 10 miles from here—and two people, one guy in a Volks and another in a Mercedes, stopped

me—they literally pulled me over to the curb!"

Crisconi was one of the first dealerships to sign up with Bricklin. He expects to start delivering cars "within the next month." He has "30 or 32 bona fide orders for the car. I asked for 8 to 10 cars when I signed up with Bricklin, and that was a mistake. I'm really sorry I didn't order 20 to 25 cars a month. You've got to see this to believe it!" (*Motor Trend*, November 1974, p. 44)

In spite of the impressive demand, production got a slow start. There were problems in the parts supply: 1,700 different parts were required to build the Bricklin SV-1, ranging from simple fasteners to the complex body panels, and through standardization and repetitive use of some of the parts, more than 9,000 individual items were needed. There were problems in assembly line balancing: approximately 5,000 different tasks were required to build the car, and it was difficult to combine those tasks into jobs of equal time requirements and logical assembly sequences. There were also problems in employee training: few of the workers of New Brunswick had experience in mechanical work or were accustomed to repetitive tasks. Finally, there were delays in installing the necessary power tools and transfer equipment needed to make the assembly tasks easier and the assembly process more efficient.

I saw the plant at St. John in late August, and the major problem then was the parts shortage. If it takes 9,000 parts to build one car, and you have 8,999 parts in stock, you don't build that car. The part that is missing is never the rear view mirror or a wheel bolt that you can put on later; the missing part is always a body panel or a transmission bearing that you have to have right at the start. Their other problem was in assembly line equipment; they were putting tires onto the wheels with the same manual tire

stand that you would find in a rural garage or small gas station. But the finished cars were well made; those people in New Brunswick were careful in their work, maybe too careful for volume production. (Statement of an industry executive)

At that time (formal unveiling of the SV-1 in New York on June 25, 1974) company officials claimed production would start immediately and that the assembly plant at St. John and the body plant at Minto, near Fredericton, would be fully operational by September. It's highly unlikely, however, that the company can meet that deadline.

While several units were completed in St. John recently, the operation is moving at a crawl. Last week, for instance, several partially completed units were sitting on the St. John production line where about 100 men were putting together the 1,700 or so different components in each car. But some equipment has yet to be installed; consequently various parts are being produced by hand.

While Bricklin executives in St. John are generally optimistic that the plant will be producing 1,000 cars per month by October, some workers are pessimistic. They talk about equipment yet to be installed, parts and components for the cars that are not available, and the major task of training a production line staff. (*Financial Post,* August 3, 1974, p. 3)

Malcolm Bricklin was pleased by the market reception of the new car, concerned by the slow start of the assembly process, and overwhelmingly optimistic about the final success of his company. In an interview with *Motor Trend* magazine, granted in September and published in November 1974, he expressed this optimism in a series of statements that summarized the position of the company in the fall of that year:

The yellow Bricklin road comes to an end, of course, at the doorstep of Malcolm Bricklin. Whether or not he can build, market and sell his sports car remains to be seen—perhaps by the time you read this the answer will be at hand. But one thing is certain: by Labor Day 1974, the odds are heavily in Bricklin's favor.

The final questions we reserve for Malcolm Bricklin himself: "What's the source of the parts problem?"

"We're having parts shortages not because of the same reasons General Motors or Ford has problems. We have them because it's the first time we've done this, the first time we've had to coordinate this. American-made parts are being shipped by truck and train and they're crossing at many points along the border. We've had delays all up and down the border. But the parts problem of weeks ago is no longer a problem today."

"Is the set back in production schedule hurting you?"

"Naw, not in terms of what we will have produced by the end of the year. In current terms, we will have made 30 cars by the end of August instead of 200. Other than our own impatience, nothing is really affected by the delay."

* * *

"The most frustrating thing about this is that I can't just scream and say, 'Get those cars out faster!' Sure, we've got problems. And we're never going to not have problems. But we know we can build those cars. We're doing it right now. Now the only thing we need to know is how long does it take to build them faster?'

* * *

"Are you having money problems—like meeting payrolls—and are you going to have to pump more money into the venture?"

"Sure we will need more money. But, no, there's no problem meeting any of our bills. It hasn't come to that. The money problem is this: One, we've got to produce cars and sell them. No company including General Motors, is permitted to exist when they keep spending money while not getting any back in sales. We'll do that soon. Nothing that has happened to date is any surprise to anyone on the financial end of it."

"Are you getting heat because of the delays in production?"

"No, the only heat we give ourselves. The schedule being behind will not bother us at the end of the year. . . . It's a normal company situation. We have two sources of income (the province and a Philadelphia banking institution) and both are pretty powerful, and both have stuck with us through the worst kinds of periods."

* * *

"What about the talk that American Motors is going to supply you with just so many engines and then you're going to have to go to Ford?"

"AMC is giving us sufficient units to take us through 1974. About 3,000 [engines]. The Ford engine is being put into a prototype car right now and it requires some engineering changes. My intention is to put the Ford engine [Windsor 351] in, but I want to be careful because things change. If AMC came back to me and said, 'We'd like to sell you some more engines,' I'd want to listen to that. And they [AMC] may very well do just that."

"Have you turned off the publicity valve on the Bricklin?"

"Yes. We're now saying 'Stop.' All it can do is make people unhappy. There are too many people who want the car and are now getting very mad about it."

"There is an ugly rumor going around among skeptics of this whole Bricklin car. The skeptics say that Malcolm Bricklin will do this: He will show the world that he can make the car, he will build, say, 500 of them, and then he will sell out for a big bundle of money. What do you say to that?"

"That's a very astute observation. And based on everything I've read about myself, I would tend to believe that would fit the pattern and therefore would happen. I must tell you we've had a number of offers—the last was for $100 million. . . ."

"Was it from someone who had $100 million?"

"The person who offered didn't, but after checking, we found he was part of a group that did. We really gave it serious consideration—but I must tell you, for not more than an hour. And the reason we did was this: One, it ain't worth $100 million right now, so anybody who buys it has to be a real schmuck and people with $100 million aren't schmucks, so those two things didn't go together. Two, we think we've passed our hardest point. We are now convinced that if anything we've underestimated the potential. We know we can make a very handsome profit. A couple of other thing too. If someone bought it, I know that the first thing he'd do is change the name: and history would say, 'Bricklin didn't make it.' And that would be very aggravating." (*Motor Trend,* November 1974, p. 49)

Class Assignment. The assignment is divided into seven questions.

1. An industry consultant stated to the casewriter that "Bricklin Vehicle Corporation operated as if it were the automotive assembly division of the Province of New Brunswick." Explain the meaning of that statement.
2. Define the strategy, or the mixture of goals and objectives and the major functional policies and plans to achieve those objectives, of the Bricklin group of companies.
3. The strategy of the Bricklin group of companies was designed to compete in the automobile industry. Based upon your understanding of the competitive structure of the industry, from prior study of the case entitled "The Domestic Automobile Industry in 1974," how well did the Bricklin strategy fit the automobile industry?
4. The size of the Bricklin group of companies was much smaller than that of other firms in the automobile industry. Describe the major resources and skills

of the Bricklin Companies; specifically, what were their strengths and weaknesses?

5. The Bricklin group of companies were bankrupt by March 1975. Design an alternative strategy for entry into the automobile industry that better fits, in your opinion, the characteristics and trends of the industry and the resources and skills of the Bricklin companies.

6. Numerous people, ranging from the Prime Minister of a Canadian province, Richard Hatfield, to the president of a Philadelphia bank, John Bunting, to established executives in Detroit auto firms, joined Malcolm Bricklin in his new venture. Why?

7. It is alleged that Mr. DeLorean, previously general manager of the Chevrolet Division of General Motors, plans, in 1979, to start producing a new sports car from purchased components at an assembly plant in Ireland. Assume that you are the president of a major bank to whom Mr. DeLorean has applied for financing. What conditions and terms would you place on the loan?

Methocel Product Division at the Dow Chemical Company

The Dow Chemical Company is a large and historically successful chemical company, with corporate headquarters in Midland, Michigan, major production sites in Michigan, Texas, Louisiana, Canada, Germany, France, Italy, Yugoslavia, Brazil, Australia, and Japan, and sales throughout the world. Dow is known in the industry as "the chemical company's chemical company" since it primarily manufactures intermediate chemical products, such as caustic soda, chlorine, acetone, glycerine, phenol, and glycol, used by other chemical companies. Dow Chemical is also a major manufacturer of magnesium plate and extrusions, polyethylene plastics, epoxy resins, and polystyrene sheet and foam. Consumer products provide a very minor portion of the total sales revenues (Exhibit 1).

Dow Chemical Company has been financially very successful, with continual increases in both sales and profits. Earnings per share on the common stock have risen from $0.13 in 1950 to $3.01 in 1977 (Exhibit 2).

The after-tax earnings of the Dow Chemical Company increased 24.9 times over the 25-year period from 1950 to 1975; by comparison, the after-tax earnings of DuPont declined over that period, and the after-tax earnings of Union Carbide increased only 3.1 times (Exhibit 3).

In fairness to DuPont, it should be noted that 1975 was a recession year, and that the earnings of E. I. du Pont de Nemours and Company actually averaged $480,000,000 over the period 1971 to 1975, for an increase of 1.6 times. Despite this adjustment, however, and despite the needed adjustment for starting from a much smaller base, it is obvious that the financial performance of Dow Chemical Company has been excellent, relative to the performance of their two major

Exhibit 1 *Sales revenues (000,000's omitted) of major product divisions at the Dow Chemical Company, 1976 and 1977*

	1976 sales	1977 sales
Inorganic chemicals, such as caustic soda, chlorine, and chlorinated solvents	$ 805	$ 830
Organic chemicals, such as acetone, glycerine, phenol, and ethylene or propylene glycol	947	1,067
Metal products, such as magnesium sheet, plate, extrusions, and ingots	268	221
Functional products and services, such as petroleum production assistance and waste treatment engineering	1,075	1,168
Plastic molding materials, such as polyethylene and polystyrene pellets for injection molding	902	1,019
Plastic coatings and monomers, such as epoxy resins, styrene, and vinyl chloride monomers	736	816
Plastic products, such as polyethylene film and polystyrene sheet and foam	253	311
Health care products and services, such as diagnostic laboratories and antibiotic medicines	324	333
Agricultural products, such as insecticides and herbicides	311	337
Consumer products, such as Dow Bathroom Cleaner, Handi-Wrap and Saran Wrap plastic film, and Ziploc bags	78	85
Total sales revenues	$5,652	$6,234

Source: Annual Report for 1977, pp. 20, 21.

competitors. There are five reasons that have been advanced for this substantial gain in profits:

1. *Diversified products.* The manufacturing processes at Dow, and their resultant products, are based approximately 30% on chlorine chemistry and 70% on hydro-carbons. This diversity ensures that the company operates in two entirely different markets, and obtains raw materials from two entirely different sources, and consequently helps to protect Dow Chemical Company from some of the problems of rapid, and sometimes unexpected, techno-

Exhibit 2 *Sales revenues, after-tax profits, and earnings per share of the Dow Chemical Company, 1950–1977*

	1950	1955	1960	1965	1970	1975	1977
Corporate sales (millions)	$200	$470	$870	$1,176	$1,911	$4,888	$6,234
After-tax profits (millions)	$25	$37	$72	$115	$130	$632	$556
Earnings per share	$0.13	$0.19	$0.38	$0.63	$0.72	$3.41	$3.01
Median price per share	$0.96	$1.40	$6.30	$11.80	$10.40	$38.60	$27.10

Note: Earnings per share and median price per share have been adjusted for stock splits and stock dividends.
Source: Annual Report for respective years.

Exhibit 3 *After-tax profits for Dow Chemical Company, E. I. du Pont de Nemours and Company, and Union Carbide Corporation, 1950 and 1975*

	1950 profits	1975 profits	Change
Dow Chemical Company	$ 25,000,000	$632,000,000	24.9×
E. I. du Pont de Nemours & Co.	307,000,000	271,000,000	0.9×
Union Carbide Corporation	124,000,000	381,000,000	3.1×

Source: Annual Report of the respective companies for the respective years.

logical and environmental change. Further, the chlorine supplies are secure; the company was founded in Midland due to the large subterranean pools of brine in the area, which are now company-owned. Hydrocarbon feedstock supplies are obviously not as certain, but Dow Chemical does have long-term contracts with the owners of petroleum reserves in southwestern United States and northcentral Canada, and has developed a new refining technology that provides very substantially improved recovery of chemical feedstocks from that petroleum.

2. *Worldwide operations.* Marketing facilities and manufacturing processes at Dow have been established on a worldwide basis. Dow was the first chemical company, and one of the first U.S. corporations, to attempt to utilize their technological competence and product research overseas, with expansion into Europe in the mid-1950s, and into South America and the Pacific region during the 1960s. For the past five

years, nearly 50% of sales have been recorded outside the United States (Exhibit 4).

3. *Leveraged financing.* The rapid growth at Dow was financed by retained earnings and long-term debt. The total debt was extensive, and in many years exceeded the stockholders' equity (Exhibit 5).

4. *Productive employees.* The workers at Dow, both hourly and salaried, were reported to be committed to the company, and highly productive. Company officials felt that this was partially due to the rural locations of the major plants of the company, partially to the early traditions of the firm (it is stated that Dr. Dow, the founder, knew all of the workers by name), and partially to the open management style of the senior executives (all executives are accessible to all employees of the company). No statistics are available to support the claim of increased productivity by the Dow work force versus that of their major competitors, but the attitude of worker participa-

Exhibit 4 *Sales revenues (000,000's omitted) of the Dow Chemical Company by geographic region, 1973–1977*

	1973	1974	1975	1976	1977
United States	$1,662	$2,619	$2,724	$3,077	$3,457
Europe/Africa	828	1,389	1,273	1,503	1,618
Latin America	232	401	387	432	468
Canada	193	314	323	370	396
Pacific	152	215	181	270	295
	$3,067	$4,938	$4,888	$5,652	$6,234

Source: Annual Report for 1977, p. 30.

Exhibit 5 *Current liabilities, long-term debt, and stockholders' equity (000,000's omitted) of the Dow Chemical Company, 1950–1975*

	1950	1955	1960	1965	1970	1975
Current liabilities and long-term debt	$106	$362	$314	$705	$1,643	$3,046
Stockholders' equity	217	316	582	816	1,102	

Source: Annual Report for the respective years.

tion was prevalent during the period of growth.

When you come right down to it, a chemical company is just a power source, some input chemicals, steel pressure vessels, the piping to tie it together, and the people to make it work. We made it work in Midland. (Statement of a retired foreman at the Dow Chemical Company)

5. *Competent management.* Operating executives at other chemical companies and investment analysts at large financial institutions generally ascribe the success of the Dow Chemical Company to the quality of their management and the flexibility of their organization.

Twenty-five years ago, Dow was a medium-sized company in the north of Michigan that specialized in chlorine chemistry and that was respected for the very solid and professional nature of their product research and process engineering, but certainly no one expected them to become the profit leaders in the chemical industry. Their stock sold at ten times earnings in 1950; a respectable price/earnings ratio, but not one associated with growth.

Now they are number 1 in the industry in profits and number 3 in sales. They made exactly the right decisions at exactly the right times. They moved into petrochemicals early; they moved into international business early; they weren't afraid to borrow money since they knew it is cheaper to finance with debt than with equity; and they started the concept of aggressive expansion, by overbuilding their productive capacity and letting the market demand catch up—how do you take business

away from them if they have the high volume, low cost capacity, and you don't. And they stayed away from the apparent attractiveness of consumer products that can soak up capital.

Those decisions were either the result of good luck or good management. I think that it was good management. Tell your students, though, that this was all done without one M.B.A. in the company. They may have one or two in the Dow Center (corporate headquarters in Midland, Michigan), but those people kept quiet about their business training. Dow hired chemical engineers and taught them how to run a company; they did not hire M.B.A.'s and attempt to teach them chemical processing. (Statement of an investment analyst)

6. *Flexible organization.* The organizational structure at Dow has been deliberately kept informal, but with specific responsibility assigned for each of the major products. (*Note:* The following description and discussion of the organizational structure applies solely to the U.S. division of the company. Dow Chemical Company is divided into six regional organizations, for the United States, Canada, Europe, Africa, Asia, and South America; each of these regional units is evaluated on a profit-center basis, has a president and staff, and a unique organization to meet area conditions.)

Dow has always worked on a consensus; in the U.S. division, we use committees, and doors truly are open for discussion, but the decisions get made because there is a person responsible for those decisions. We do believe in delegation all through the company. (Statement of a senior Dow executive)

Product responsibility at the U.S. division of Dow is delegated to business managers and product managers, who work through an informal matrix organization. The basic corporate structure of Dow–U.S. is functional, with separate departments for marketing, manufacturing, and R&D (basic research, product development, and process engineering or "technical services"). Cutting across these functional chains of command are nine department managers, 31 business managers, and 65 product managers. This organizational structure is shown in chart form in Exhibit 6.

The nine departments are grouped ac-

cording to the chemical nature of their products, and follow roughly the classifications given in Exhibit 1 (inorganic chemicals, organic chemicals, metal products, functional products, etc.), but the groupings are not entirely logical, and tend to have a historical rather than a chemical derivation; e.g., magnesium, which is a metal, is currently grouped with the inorganic chemicals since it was originally a by-product of the brine processing to make caustic soda and chlorine.

The 31 business managers are each responsible for a group of products within one of the departments. Each business manager works with representatives from marketing, manufacturing, and R&D, and each has profit responsibility for the assigned products, but each lacks formal au-

Exhibit 6 Organizational structure of the U.S. Division of Dow Chemical Company

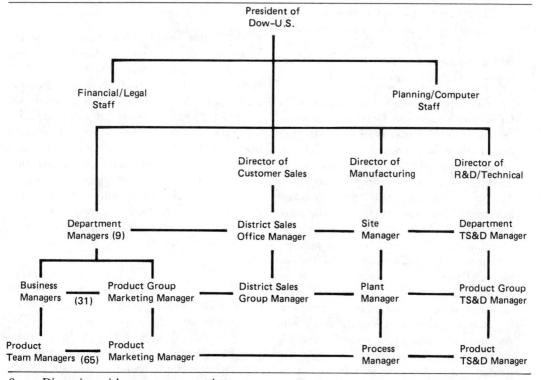

Source: Discussion with company executives.

thority over the functional representatives.

We call each product group a "business" since it is our intent that they all act like small businesses; they should set objectives and then work to achieve those objectives with the support of the corporation but independent of the hierarchy of the organization. We want flexibility and profit responsibility. But the business manager has no authority over the other members of the business group. The manager has to convince the functional people to accept or modify objectives, and then the functional people set the policies and plan the programs to achieve those objectives. The functional people have to communicate both upwards and downwards in their own departments. Capital allocations have to be approved by senior management, and policies and plans have to be approved by the functional directors, so that we do get integration. (Statement of a senior Dow executive)

The 65 product managers work within the business units and are responsible for a single product or product line. They also work with representatives from the functional departments, and have profit responsibility but no formal authority.

The 65 product managers have responsibility for 51 end products (sold for nonchemical processing by other industries or consumer use) and 14 intermediate products (sold for chemical processing by other companies or transferred for chemical processing within Dow). The product management teams (product manager and representatives from the three functional departments) are our primary planning unit. These 65 products account for 70% of our sales and, probably, 100% of our profits. These are our established, major products. One way to look at it is that the business manager looks after new products on the way up or old products on the way down, and delegates responsibility for the reliable products to the product manager. Again, the product manager has no authority over the line personnel, but must work with them to

achieve the profits that keep this company going. (Statement of a senior Dow executive) Chemical companies are hard to manage. The manufacturing processes are technically complex and completely interrelated, with the output of one process serving both as a product in the market and as an input in another process; you can't change the product, the process or the market without changing the entire company. A chemical plant really is a system, with all of the components tied together by piping and maintenance and capital, so that you can't manage just part of the system. Most chemical companies are centralized, to manage all of the system, but they have problems with market flexibility and technological change. Dow Chemical Company is centralized for functional responsibility but decentralized for profit responsibility; this works only as long as they have very good people as business managers and product managers. (Statement of an investment analyst)

Mr. Ralph Boeker was manager of the Methocel Product Team within the Organic Chemical Department from 1974 to 1977. Methocel is the Dow Chemical Company trademark for methyl cellulose, which was described to the casewriter as a "nondescript but expensive white powder that is derived from wood fiber by a highly complex and capital-intensive chemical process, and that can be used as a thickening agent or suspension aid or protective colloid to improve the properties of a wide variety of products." Some of the specific applications were described as follows:

1. *Construction.* Methocel is used as a protective colloid in gypsum (drywall) cement, plaster cements, and tile mortars to prevent liquid droplets or solid particles from coalescing (no sedimentation and no separation) and to maintain workability.

2. *Paint.* Methocel is used to thicken latex paints and to maintain the pigment in suspension throughout the paint.
3. *Pharmaceutical.* Methocel is used as a binder and film coating for medicinal tablets, and as a stabilizer for ointments and creams; since it is an inert product with a natural (woodfiber) base, it has no effect upon the patient.
4. *Cosmetics.* Methocel is also used for viscosity control, emulsification, and stabilization in hand lotions, face creams, hair dressings, shampoos, and toothpaste products; again, owing to the inert, natural nature of the product, it can be used without ill effect.
5. *Food.* Methocel is used as a binder for reconstituted potato chips, as a jell for fruit pies, and as a thickening agent for nondairy dessert toppings.
6. *Detergents.* In very low concentrations (0.005 to 1) Methocel is used for antiredeposition; to keep dirt particles in suspension during the wash cycle, and to prevent redeposition on the clothing during draining and rinsing.
7. *Agriculture.* Methocel is used for viscosity control for sprayed herbicides and insecticides to limit the size of the droplets.
8. *Ceramics.* Methocel is used as a binder for the ceramic clay prior to firing; the cellulose will burn without leaving voids or creating stresses in the final product.
9. *Tobacco.* Methocel is used as a binder for the synthetic outer leaf on cigars (made from ground tobacco that has been reconstituted by pressing into a thin sheet); the cellulose will burn without forming harmful fumes or chemical residues.
10. *Polyvinyl chloride.* Methocel is used as a protective colloid during polymerization of polyvinyl chloride (a popular thermoplastic) to improve resin porosity and particle-size distribution.

As is obvious from the previous listing, methyl cellulose is used in a variety of industries for a multitude of applications, and the manager of the product team at Dow Chemical Company that is responsible for the profitability of Methocel believes that the number of uses will continue to increase.

Methocel is a unique product with miscellaneous commercial applications. We don't know all of the uses yet. It is water soluble, yet it has no ionic charge so that it will not react with metallic salts to form insoluble precipitates. It has no taste or odor, is metabolically inert, and enzyme resistant so that it can be used in food and pharmaceutical products. It will thicken both aqueous and nonaqueous solutions, and will prevent solid particles or liquid droplets from coalescing in either solution. It will form a surface film that makes an excellent barrier to grease and oil, and it will stabilize emulsions by reducing interparticle tensions. It will serve as a binder in tobacco and paper products, and as a lubricant in rubber, concrete, and ceramic extrusions. It is a very useful product, that is sold in very small amounts, to improve the qualities of many different products. (Statement of the Methocel product manager)

In the spring of 1977, Mr. Boeker and the other members of the product management team were concerned by a number of problems, and recognized a number of opportunities, for the Methocel product line. Additional capacity was needed, but it was not clear how much capacity should be built, what process should be used, or which products should be emphasized. Mr. Boeker explained the immediate problems and the apparent opportunities in the following logical sequence, simplified for the purpose of preparing a classroom case.

1. *Uncertainty in productive capacity.* Dow had built two processing plants for methyl cellulose in the United States, one at Midland, Michigan, and one at Plaquemine, Louisiana. The productive process for

Exhibit 7 *Expected productive capacity (pounds, 000,000's omitted) of the methyl cellulose processing plants of Dow–U.S., 1978–1987*

	1978	1979	1980	1981	1982	1983	1984	1985	1986	1987
Midland	20.0	17.5	15.0	12.5	10.0	—	—	—	—	—
Plaquemine	25.0	25.0	25.0	25.0	25.0	25.0	20.0	20.0	17.5	15.0
	45.0	42.5	40.0	37.5	35.0	25.0	20.0	20.0	17.5	15.0

Note: All cost and revenue data, and all expectations of future demand and details of past demand, have been disguised at the request of the Dow Chemical Company.
Source: Company records. See Note.

Methocel was highly corrosive, and the plant at Midland was older and rapidly wearing out; it was expected to operate for only 5 more years, at a gradually declining rate. The plant at Plaquemine would run for 10 more years, but the output there would also gradually decline toward the end of that period. The actual rates of decline were not known exactly, but were estimated as shown in Exhibit 7.

2. *Uncertainty in the costs of production.* The facilities at Midland had been built over the period 1955–1962, and now consisted of four batch-processing plants, each with a capacity of 5 million pounds per year. The piping, pumping, and storage systems for all four processing plants were interconnected, so that it was not felt to be cost effective to attempt to keep the most recent of the batch plants operating in Midland after 1982 and, as stated previously, there was a distinct possibility that the plant at Midland would totally wear out and become inoperable before that date. The facilities at Plaquemine were more modern, dating from 1962–1967, but they made use of the same batch technology and suffered from the same severe corrosion and uncertain longevity. It was difficult to forecast when the Plaquemine plant would wear out, but members of the product group had selected 1987.

It was also difficult to forecast the operating costs for the two plants, partially due to uncertainty over the level of maintenance that would be required, and partially due to uncertainty over the cost of raw materials that would be needed. The operating costs were divided for the purpose of this analysis into categories of materials, labor, power, maintenance, and disposal (pollution abatement).

a. *Materials.* The basic raw materials for the Methocel process are ground cellulose fiber and toluene. Ground cellulose fiber of the required purity and quality is produced only by two small pulp mills on the south Georgia coast; in the past this material has not been subject to supply limitations or extreme price fluctuations, but neither mill has added capacity over the past four years, and the supply and demand are now very closely in balance. Toluene is a major hydrocarbon feedstock derivative; it has been subject to supply limitations and price fluctuations in the past, and those problems were expected to continue in the future. Current material costs are \$0.380/lb at Midland and \$0.360/lb at Plaquemine; the difference is due to transportation costs.

b. *Labor.* The labor costs in 1977 were \$0.315 at Midland and \$0.315 at Plaquemine. Company officials felt that their work force was well trained and efficient, and that there would be only limited labor savings in replacing

144

the existing plants with the same batch technology, although that technology had advanced far enough to permit substantial savings in material and power usage.

c. *Power.* The power costs, primarily for steam, were $0.210 at both Midland and Plaquemine. As mentioned previously, substantial savings in power usage were possible in replacing the older processing plants.

d. *Maintenance.* The repair costs are reasonably constant, regardless of the age of the plant or the technology of the process, because of the known rates of deterioration caused by the corrosive materials. Maintenance costs in 1977 were $0.115/lb at both Midland and Plaquemine.

e. *Disposal.* The waste product of the Methocel manufacturing process is dilute saltwater; this requires disposal in Midland (by concentration, so that it may be used as brine in the manufacture of chlorine and chlorinated solvents) at a cost of $0.040 per pound. In Plaquemine, the dilute saltwater may be pumped to the Mississippi River, since this runs past the plant and is within 50 miles of the Gulf of Mexico. In Texas, the dilute saltwater can be returned to the Gulf, since the plant will be built on the coastal waterway.

3. *Uncertainty in the forecast of demand.* Total demand for methyl cellulose produced by

the Dow–U.S. sector of the company was divided into three categories: U.S. sales, which represented sales to commercial users within the United States; U.S. exports, which represented shipments to the other geographic sectors (Canada, Europe, Africa, Asia, and South America) of the company; and Dow usage, which represented shipments to other product groups (inorganic, organic, functional, etc.) within the U.S. area. The U.S. exports were sold to commercial users in the other geographic areas; the Dow usage was used in production processes by the other product groups. Both U.S. exports and Dow usage shipments were invoiced at an intercompany transfer price that approximated full costs at capacity production rates.

U.S. sales had grown at approximately 10% compounded annually from 1969 to 1973, but this rate of growth had leveled off in 1974 and actually declined in 1975. This interruption, which had been unexpected, was ascribed to the business recession of 1974 and 1975, but it made future forecasting more difficult and uncertain, for it seemed no longer possible to simply extrapolate a known rate of change. U.S. exports had remained reasonably steady until 1975 when they began to decline due to the construction of a Methocel processing plant at Stade, West Germany, by the Dow–Europe sector of the company, which replaced U.S. exports to much of Europe (Exhibit 8).

Exhibit 8 *Past sales, exports, and usage of methyl cellulose (pounds, 000,000's omitted) of Dow–U.S., 1969–1977*

	1969	1970	1971	1972	1973	1974	1975	1976	1977*
Sales	19.3	21.0	22.1	25.4	26.9	26.2	22.1	26.4	28.0
Exports	10.7	11.4	13.3	12.9	13.5	14.1	9.4	7.9	9.0
Usage	0.4	0.5	0.5	0.5	0.5	0.6	0.6	0.7	0.8
	30.4	32.9	35.9	38.8	40.9	40.9	32.1	34.9	37.8

Source: Company records. (* = estimated for the full year.) (See Note in Exhibit 7.)

	1978	1979	1980	1981	1982	1983	1984	1985	1986	1987
Sales	29.0	30.0	31.0	32.0	33.5	35.0	36.5	38.5	41.0	44.0
Exports	9.5	10.0	11.0	7.0	8.5	10.0	11.5	13.0	15.0	17.5
Usage	1.0	1.0	1.0	1.0	1.5	1.5	1.5	1.5	2.0	2.9
	39.5	41.0	43.0	40.5	43.5	46.5	49.5	53.0	58.0	63.5

Source: Company records. (See Note in Exhibit 7.)

In 1977, members of the Methocel product management team in the Dow–U.S. sector of the company forecasted gradually increasing demand (approximately 5% growth per year) for U.S. sales, an equivalent increase for U.S. exports until 1981, when an additional 5-million-pound capacity was to be available at Stade, which would replace U.S. exports to all of Europe, and they anticipated generally steady Dow usage (Exhibit 9).

4. *Uncertainty in the average revenue per pound.* Methocel had originally been available only in two product types, A and E, in the lower-viscosity ranges (15 to 4,000 ubbelohde, at 2% concentration), but starting in 1970 five new product types, F, J, K, HB, and 228, in the higher-viscosity ranges (5,000 to 75,000 ubbelohde) had been gradually introduced. Types A and E were sold at $1.53/lb in 1977, and were termed Price Group I, while the new products sold at an average of $2.03/lb in 1977, and were termed Price Group II. The new products had been replacing the older materials in the market since their introduction; members of the product management

group expected that this trend would continue, but anticipated that the ratio between the Price Groups would stabilize at 50%–50% in 1981 (Exhibit 10).

5. *Uncertainty in competitive actions.* Forecasts for the sales volume of methyl cellulose, and for the distribution of those sales between the two price groups, were felt to be dependent upon the actions of the major competitors, both in the United States and abroad. No chemical company in the United States produced methyl cellulose, but both Hercules Chemical Corporation and Union Carbide Corporation manufactured hydroxyethyl cellulose (termed HEC), which competed primarily with the lower-viscosity Methocels of Price Group I. Total U.S. sales of HEC by Hercules and Union Carbide in 1977 were estimated to be 28 million pounds, primarily for volume uses as the thickening agent and protective colloid in tinted latex paints and oil well drilling muds (to lubricate the drilling bit, and to cement the side of the drilled hole). Methocel was not usable in either application (Exhibit 11).

Hydroxyethyl cellulose (HEC) was

Exhibit 10   *Past percentages of price groups of methyl cellulose for Dow–U.S. and expected future ratios for those price groups, 1972–1981*

	1972	1973	1974	1975	1976	1977	1978	1979	1980	1981
PG I	98.9	93.4	84.3	76.6	72.8	68.3	65.0	60.0	55.0	50.0
PG II	1.1	6.6	15.7	23.4	27.2	31.7	35.0	40.0	45.0	50.0

Source: Company records. (See Note in Exhibit 7.)

Exhibit 11 *Sales and applications of hydroxyethyl cellulose (HEC), and comparison of performance with Methocel, 1977*

End use of HEC	Sales (lb) of HEC	Comparison of HEC to Methocel performance
Latex paint manufactured by tint-base system	12,600,000	Methocel gels with a temperature rise and occasionally foams in mixing; both are felt to be "too risky" for paint manufacturers with a tint-base system (produce white paint base and add color tints at the retail store)
Oil-well drilling mud	10,000,000	Methocel gels with a temperature rise caused by drilling friction, and is not salt-tolerant
Construction asbestos cement	2,000,000	Methocel is equally applicable, but is somewhat higher priced
Construction tile mortar	1,000,000	Methocel is equally applicable, but is somewhat higher priced
Miscellaneous	1,500,000	Methocel competes with most miscellaneous applications, such as emulsion stabilization, etc., but does gel with temperature rise, which occasionally makes it unacceptable
Total HEC	28,000,000	

Source: Company records.

priced somewhat lower ($1.40/lb in 1977) than the equivalent Dow products in Price Group I, because of a less complex production process for HEC, and this price advantage reduced the usage of Methocel in some of the miscellaneous applications, particularly construction, where purity of the product was not a critical issue. In the tint-based latex paint and oil-well drilling mud applications, the HEC performance was clearly superior, and price was not a major factor. These were volume markets, however, at 22,600,000 lb per year, and they were expected to grow at approximately 6% per year to reach 37,000,000 lb per year in 1985; members of the product management team at Dow–U.S. occasionally considered developing a product to compete in those two large market segments.

HEC is positioned in the volume markets, where we can't compete for technical reasons; the product has a lower margin than we

might like, but currently we are just giving those markets to our competition. Sometimes giving up volume to a competitor comes back to haunt you, for they can use that volume to get a low-cost position on some of your high-margin products, if they ever develop a new process. (Statement of the Methocel product manager)

Under current production processes, hydroxyethyl cellulose (HEC) did not compete with the higher-viscosity and higher-purity products of the Methocel Price Group II products, since HEC did not meet the *Food Chemical Codex* (F.C.C.) nor the *U.S. Pharmacopeia* (U.S.P.) requirements for food and drug additives.

Although no domestic chemical company produced methyl cellulose to compete directly with Methocel, two firms in Germany (Henkel and Hoechst) and one in Japan (Shinetsu) manufactured and sold methyl cellulose that was the equivalent in both viscosity and purity of the

Dow Price Group II products. In 1977, these three companies restricted their sales efforts to Europe and Asia, but it was felt that one of the German firms might attempt to sell in the United States in the near future.

Dow–Europe built a Methocel plant at Stade, West Germany, in 1975; when it comes fully on stream, in 1981, it will create excess industry capacity in Europe. The two German firms are not going to be very happy with that situation, and I assume that they will start thinking about exporting to the United States, partially to use up their available capacity and partially to pay us back for building a plant in what they must have considered to be their private market area. I can understand their motives, but I think that it would be a financial disaster for them. They will have to buy their way in, with lower prices and improved service, and I don't think they recognize the extent of the technical services you have to offer to sell specialty chemicals in the U.S. market. But, both Henkel and Hoechst are large, well-financed firms, and they can afford to buy market share, if they want to. (Statement of a senior Dow executive)

6. *Uncertainty in the development of new products.* Beginning in 1972, Dow–U.S. had invested approximately $3,000,000 in R&D and technical services and somewhat more than $1,800,000 in fixed assets to build a small prototype plant that produced a new chemical product, hydroxyethyl methyl cellulose (HEMC), that could compete technically with both hydroxyethyl cellulose (HEC) and methyl cellulose (Metho-

cel). The new chemical had been produced, and had been sold in adequate amounts to test the market, though at a loss in the operating margin (sales revenues less direct material, labor, power, maintenance, and pollution control costs, and allocated space and depreciation expenses) because of special pricing policies and experimental production problems (Exhibit 12).

It was not possible to economically produce HEMC in the existing protoplant, but it was felt that an additional investment of $1 million in R&D and technical services and $23.8 million in fixed assets would build a 20-million-pound HEMC plant using a continuous mixing process (as opposed to the existing batch process for Methocel) that would be both cost-competitive and performance-competitive with the HEC produced by Hercules and Union Carbide. Additional processing through a unit termed the Product Modification Control (described later in this report) would be needed to make HEMC equal in technical characteristics and product performance to the Methocels of Price Group I or II.

If we ever want to compete with the HEC produced by Hercules and Union Carbide, here is the product (HEMC) and the process (continuous mixing). HEMC is somewhat cheaper to produce by the continuous process and, we think, somewhat better in performance in the two big markets (tint-based latex paints and oil-well drilling cements) than

Exhibit 12 *Sales revenues, direct costs, and operating margins (000,000's omitted) of HEMC produced by Dow–U.S., 1972*

	1972	1973	1974	1975	1976	1977	Total
Sales of HEMC	—	$0.4	$0.9	$1.5	$2.7	$2.9	$ 8.4
Costs of HEMC	$0.9	1.9	2.3	2.6	3.2	2.9	13.8
Operating margin (deficit)	(0.9)	(1.5)	(1.4)	(1.1)	(0.5)	(0.0)	(5.4)

Source: Company records. (See Note in Exhibit 7.)

Exhibit 13 *Sales revenues, direct costs, and operating margins (000,000's omitted) of developmental thickener produced by Dow–U.S., 1972–1977*

	1972	1973	1974	1975	1976	1977	Total
Sales of new thickener	—	$0.1	$0.2	$0.3	$0.3	$0.4	$1.3
Costs of new thickener	0.3	0.9	1.3	0.9	0.9	1.0	5.3
Operating margin (deficit)	(0.3)	(0.8)	(1.1)	(0.6)	(0.6)	(0.6)	(4.0)

Source: Company records. (See Note in Exhibit 7.)

HEC. (Statement of the Methocel product manager)

Also beginning in 1972, Dow–U.S. had invested $1,250,000 in R&D and technical services and $500,000 in fixed assets in an advanced cellulose thickener that could, conceivably, replace the Methocels of Price Group II for use in both foods and pharmaceuticals. Some of the raw material had been produced and sold, again at a considerable loss in the operating margin (Exhibit 13).

Company officials at Dow–U.S. were, for obvious reasons, extremely reluctant to discuss the properties, process, or performance of the new product beyond stating that it would take "a great deal of capital and a good deal of luck to come up with a new cellulose product equally as good as Methocel." When pressed, they explained that $12 to $18 million in R&D would be required, with a 75% chance (at best) of success, but with "assured" domination of the market and "considerable" expansion of the margin, if successful.

7. *Uncertainty in the development of new processes.* The continuous mixing process developed for the manufacture of hydroxyethyl methyl cellulose (HEMC) was also applicable in the manufacture of Methocel. Dow–U.S. had invested approximately $1,800,000 in R&D and technical services, $2,000,000 in fixed assets, and $4,900,000 in decreased operating margins (excess costs caused by the experimenta-

tion) in the development of the continuous mixing process for Methocel; these amounts were in addition to the funds spent for the development of HEMC. In 1977, it was felt that the continuous mixing process was proven, and that a 25-million-pound Methocel plant could be built for $45.0 million in fixed assets; this represented a 3% capital increase over replacement of the existing batch mixing plants, but the continuous process would reduce the variable costs (material, labor, power, and maintenance) by about $0.30 per pound because of higher material yield and improved labor efficiency. It was also estimated that savings in both construction capital and operating costs would increase linearly with increases in the productive capacity of continuous mixing plants; that is, a 50-million-pound Methocel plant could be built for $75.0 million in fixed assets, and would reduce the variable costs by an additional $0.068 per pound. Capital requirements and variable costs for the various process alternatives are given in Exhibit 14.

Dow–U.S. had also developed a Product Modification Control (PMOD) process that had originally been intended to make the HEMC produced in a continuous mixing process fully comparable in technical characteristics and product performance to the Methocels of Price Groups I and II. The PMOD process had never been made completely successful in this application; however, it had been tried on the

Exhibit 14 *Capital requirements and estimated operating costs for the production processes under consideration by the Methocel product management team, 1977*

	Methocel batch	Methocel continuous			HEMC	PMOD refinery
Capacity (1,000 lb)	5,000	25,000	40,000	50,000	20,000	4,000
Capital required (per pound)	$1.755	$ 1.800	$ 1.680	$ 1.500	$ 1.190	$0.900
Capital required (total)	8,775	45,000	67,200	75,000	23,800	3,600
Material cost (per pound)	0.350	0.280	0.265	0.250	0.175	Transfer price
Labor cost (per pound)	0.315	0.105	0.100	0.090	0.100	0.090
Power cost (per pound)	0.150	0.135	0.130	0.120	0.120	0.060
Maintenance (per pound)	0.115	0.110	0.106	0.102	0.110	0.030
Total variable cost	0.930	0.630	0.611	0.562	0.505	See above

Notes: Material cost and power cost for a new Methocel batch plant are somewhat less than the equivalent costs in existing plants due to advances in the batch technology.

Material cost for a new Methocel batch or continuous plant or HEMC process is assumed to be for a new installation at Plaquemine; equivalent cost at Midland would be 5.5% higher.

Disposal costs for concentrating salt water by-product are not included for a new Methocel batch or continuous plant or HEMC process since the installation is assumed to be at Plaquemine; equivalent cost at Midland would be $0.04 per pound.

Source: Company records. (See Note in Exhibit 7.)

Methocels of Price Group II, and it was found that the viscosity and consistency had been so much improved that it was possible to obtain a price premium of about 30%. In 1977, PMOD processed Methocel was selling at $2.61 per pound, and members of the product management group estimated that perhaps 10% of the U.S. sales market might wish to use this material and pay this premium; they did not believe that any of the current export sales or Dow usage would be converted to the improved product.

In 1977, Mr. Boeker found that the product management team for Methocel had invested a total of $26,150,000 over the past 6 years in both product development and process development (Exhibit 15).

Mr. Boeker also recognized that, owing to the forecasted growth in U.S. sales, exports, and usage and due to the anticipated deterioration of the existing plants, it would be necessary to make investments up to $75 million in new capacity over the coming 10-year period. However, there were uncertainties in the forecasts of demand, in the expected revenues, and in the actions of competitors, and there were two new products, one of which (HEMC) was applicable in completely new markets for latex paints and drilling cements; three new processes; four different capacities; and three different sites to be considered, all under different conditions of timing and risk. The investment decision faced by members of the Methocel product team was considered to be both complex and important.

Exhibit 15 *R&D, fixed capital, and operating margin investments (000's omitted) by the Methocel product management team, 1972–1977*

	R&D and technical services	Physical plant	Reduced margins	Total amount
New HEMC product	$3,000	$1,800	$ 5,400	$10,200
Noncellulose product	1,250	500	4,000	5,750
Continuous process	1,800	2,000	4,900	8,700
PMOD process	350	—	1,150	1,500
	5,700	3,250	15,150	26,150

Source: Company records. (See Note in Exhibit 7.)

Management of capital has to be the trademark of the Dow Chemical Company since the chemical industry has become so capital intensive. You can make mistakes in your price–volume relationships, and these won't hurt you too badly since you can change if you're wrong.

But, you can't make mistakes in your process decisions, your capacity decisions; you can't change these if you're wrong. We don't have hurdle rates for capital investments since we don't want people playing with the figures to meet a cut-off return. We want people to understand

Exhibit 16 *Graphic display of factors in Methocel investment decision, prepared by Methocel product management team, 1977*

Products	*Product developments*	*Processes*	*Process developments*
Methocel A and E Price Group I	HEC HEMC NEW (advanced)	Batch mixing	Continuous mixing PMOD
Methocel F, J, K, HB, and 228 Price Group II			

Process sites	*Market types*	*Market uses Price Group I*	*Market uses Price Group II*
Midland Plaquemine Texas Stade	U.S. sales U.S. exports Dow usage	Construction Paint Petroleum Polyvinyl chloride Ceramics	Pharmaceutical Food Cosmetics Detergents Agriculture

Market use developments	*Market demand changes (U.S.)*	*Present competition*	*Potential competition*
Oil-well cements Tint-based paint	10% compound growth, 1969–1973 2% compound decline, 1973–1976	Hercules HEC Union Carbide HEC	Henkle MC Hoechst MC Shinetsu MC

Source: Company records.

the investments, not to play with the returns. We want to manage our money intelligently. (Statement of a senior Dow executive)

Dow got into trouble—if you can call their decline in earnings from $612 million in 1976 to $555 million in 1977 "trouble"—by getting into an overcapacity, overextended condition. Their fixed costs on the interest, depreciation, maintenance, and pollution control killed them, and brought their stock price from a high of $58/share in 1976 to $24/share in 1977. Now, they've got to increase their cash flow from their competitive products, and invest that money in projects that will yield a higher rate of return. (Statement of an investment analyst)

We're not being pressured for increased cash flows and higher returns, but it is obvious that the company wants results, not promises now. (Statement of the Methocel product manager)

Members of the Methocel product management team developed a graphic display of the major factors involved in the decision process for future capacity investments; this display is shown in Exhibit 16.

Mr. Boeker identified seven major alternatives for the production of the Methocel product line; these alternatives are given below, and the resultant cash flows prepared by a computerized planning model are shown in Exhibits 17 to 24. Exhibit 25 defines the terms and explains the relationships of the planning model.

1. No additional capacity at Midland or Plaquemine; allow the Methocel plants to gradually run out, following the anticipated deterioration shown in Exhibit 7.

2. Add additional capacity at Plaquemine, using the batch process, in increments of 5 million pounds (only capacity alternative available for the batch process) at an investment of $8,775,000 for each addition. Timing of the additions would attempt to follow market demand:

	1978	1979	1980	1981	1982	1983
Additional capacity (lb)	—	5,000	—	5,000	—	5,000
Required investment	$8,775	—	$8,775	—	$8,775	—

3. Add additional capacity at Plaquemine, using the continuous process, in a single increment of 25 million pounds (smallest capacity alternative available for the continuous process), at an investment of $45 million. Timing of the addition would anticipate market demand:

	1978	1979	1980	1981	1982	1983
Additional capacity (lb)	—	—	25,000	—	—	—
Required investment	$15,000	$30,000	—	—	—	—

4. Add additional capacity at Plaquemine, using the continuous process, in a single increment of 40 million pounds, at an investment of $67.2 million. Delay the increment until 1981, in order to be able to utilize the added capacity:

	1978	1979	1980	1981	1982	1983
Additional capacity (lb)	—	—	—	40,000	—	—
Required investment	—	$22,400	$44,800	—	—	—

5. Add additional capacity at Plaquemine, using the continuous process, in a single increment of 50 million pounds, at an investment of $75 million. Delay the increment until 1981, in order to be able to utilize the added capacity:

	1978	1979	1980	1981	1982	1983
Additional capacity (lb)	—	—	—	50,000	—	—
Required investment	—	$25,000	$50,000	—	—	—

6. Build new HEMC continuous process in Texas with 20-million-pound capacity, at an investment of $23.8 million, and assume sales of 15 million pounds per year.

	1978	1979	1980	1981	1982	1983
New HEMC plant (lb)	—	—	—	20,000	—	—
Required investment	$3,966	$7,933	$11,899			

7. Build new PMOD plant at Plaquemine, with 4-million-pound capacity, at an investment of $3.6 million, and assume sales equal to 10% of Methocel per year, at a price premium of $0.58.

Class Assignment. Prepare specific, detailed recommendations for Mr. Ralph Boeker, and the members of the Methocel Product Division at Dow–U.S., and be prepared to support those recommendations. For assistance in this assignment, Exhibits 17 to 24 show the output of a financial planning model for each of the alternatives listed above, while Exhibit 25 defines the terms and explains the relationships in the computerized planning model.

Exhibit 17 *Add no additional capacity; allow the plants at Midland and Plaquemine to gradually run down*

		1978	1979	1980	1981	1982	1983	1984	1985	1986	1987
METHO CAPACITY	MM	45000.	42500.	40000.	37500.	35000.	25000.	20000.	20000.	17500.	15000.
HEMC CAPACITY	MM	0.	0.	0.	0.	0.	0.	0.	0.	0.	0.
PMOD CAPACITY		0.	0.	0.	0.	0.	0.	0.	0.	0.	0.
TOT CAPACITY		45000.	42500.	40000.	37500.	35000.	25000.	20000.	20000.	17500.	15000.
US SALES	MM	29000.	30000.	31000.	32000.	33500.	23500.	18500.	18500.	15500.	13000.
US EXPORTS	MM	9500.	10000.	4000.	4500.	1500.	1500.	0.	0.	0.	0.
DOW USAGE	MM	1000.	1000.	1000.	1000.	1500.	1500.	1500.	1500.	2000.	2000.
HEMC SALES	MM	0.	0.	0.	0.	0.	0.	0.	0.	0.	0.
TOT PRODUCTION		39500.	41000.	40000.	37500.	35000.	25000.	20000.	20000.	17500.	15000.
CAPAC UTILIZ	%	87.78	96.47	100.00	100.00	100.00	100.00	100.00	100.00	100.00	100.00
US SALES	M$	43445.	51900.	54405.	56960.	59630.	44705.	37430.	37555.	31465.	26390.
US EXPORTS	M$	11799.	12610.	10238.	5944.	1770.	1770.	1419.	1819.	2472.	2534.
DOW USAGE	M$	1180.	1180.	1140.	1180.	1770.	1770.	1419.	1819.	2472.	2534.
HEMC SALES	M$	0.	0.	0.	0.	0.	0.	0.	0.	0.	0.
TOT REVENUES		62424.	65690.	65873.	64084.	61400.	46475.	39249.	39374.	33937.	28924.
TOT VARCOST	M$	42345.	44010.	42900.	40125.	37350.	26250.	21000.	21000.	18375.	15750.
RS&A COSTS	M$	5933.	6228.	6529.	6435.	7156.	5365.	4492.	4507.	3776.	3167.
SPACE COSTS	M$	2700.	2700.	2700.	2700.	2700.	1500.	1500.	1500.	1500.	1500.
DEPRC COSTS	M$	3190.	3190.	3190.	3190.	3190.	1750.	1750.	1750.	1750.	1750.
TOT FIXCOST	M$	11823.	12118.	12419.	12725.	13046.	8615.	7742.	7757.	7026.	6417.
PROFIT BT	M$	8256.	9562.	10554.	11234.	11004.	11610.	10503.	10618.	8536.	6757.
PROFIT AT	M$	4128.	4781.	5277.	5617.	5502.	5805.	5254.	5309.	4268.	3379.
RET ON SALES	%	6.61	7.28	8.01	8.77	8.96	12.49	13.39	13.48	12.58	11.68
RET ON INVEST	%	10.65	13.18	15.93	19.02	21.36	28.01	30.22	33.90	33.56	34.25
PROFIT AT	M$	4128.	4781.	5277.	5617.	5502.	5805.	5254.	5309.	4268.	3379.
FC CHANGES	M$	3190.	3190.	3190.	3190.	3190.	1750.	1750.	1750.	1750.	1750.
WC CHANGES	M$	303.	-719.	-40.	353.	591.	3243.	1690.	-27.	1196.	1103.
AC CHANGES	M$	-1139.	-1005.	670.	1675.	1675.	6700.	3350.	3350.	1675.	1675.
TOT CASH FLOW	M$	6487.	6247.	9097.	10835.	10958.	17498.	11944.	7031.	8889.	7906.
DISCOUNTED 15% CASH FLOW		5640.	4724.	5981.	6218.	5448.	7582.	4490.	2299.	2527.	1954.
CUMULATIVE 15% CASH FLOW		5640.	10364.	16346.	22564.	28012.	35595.	40085.	42383.	44910.	46864.
FIXED CAP	M$	23010.	21820.	14630.	15440.	12650.	10500.	8750.	7000.	5250.	3500.
WORKING CAP	M$	13733.	14452.	14492.	14099.	13508.	10224.	8635.	8662.	7466.	6363.
ALLOC CAP	M$	26465.	27470.	26800.	25175.	23450.	16750.	13400.	13400.	11725.	10050.
TOTAL CAPITAL		38743.	35272.	33122.	29533.	25758.	20724.	17385.	15662.	12716.	9863.
US SALES PGI		19950.00	18000.00	17000.00	16000.00	16750.00	17500.00	18250.00	19250.00	20500.00	22000.00
US SALES PGII		10150.00	12000.00	13950.00	16000.00	16750.00	17500.00	18250.00	19250.00	20500.00	22000.00
EXPORTS PGI		6175.00	6000.00	6050.00	3500.00	4250.00	5000.00	5750.00	6500.00	7500.00	8750.00
EXPORTS PGII		3325.00	4000.00	4950.00	3500.00	4250.00	5000.00	5750.00	6500.00	7500.00	8750.00
DOW USE PGI		650.00	600.00	600.00	500.00	750.00	750.00	750.00	750.00	1000.00	1000.00
DOW USE PGII		350.00	400.00	450.00	500.00	750.00	750.00	750.00	750.00	1000.00	1000.00
HEMC SALES		15000.00	15000.00	15000.00	15000.00	15000.00	15000.00	15000.00	15000.00	15000.00	15000.00

PLANT DATA TYPE PLACE YEAR

EXECUTION TERMINATED 12:12:49 T=.065 PC=0   1.05

154

Exhibit 18 *Add capacity at Plaquemine, using the batch process, with three 5,000,000-lb additions in 1979, 1981, and 1983*

	1978	1979	1980	1981	1982	1983	1984	1985	1986	1987
METHO CAPACITY	45000.	47500.	45000.	47500.	45000.	40000.	35000.	35000.	32500.	30000.
HEMC CAPACITY	0.	0.	0.	0.	0.	0.	0.	0.	0.	0.
PMOD CAPACITY	0.	0.	0.	0.	0.	0.	0.	0.	0.	0.
TOT CAPACITY	45000.	47500.	45000.	47500.	45000.	40000.	35000.	35000.	32500.	30000.
US SALES M#	29000.	30000.	31000.	32000.	33500.	35000.	33500.	33500.	30500.	28000.
US EXPORTS M#	9500.	10000.	11000.	7000.	8500.	3500.	1500.	1500.	0.	0.
DOW USAGE M#	1000.	1000.	1000.	1000.	1500.	1500.	1500.	1500.	2000.	2000.
HEMC SALES M#	0.	0.	0.	0.	0.	0.	0.	0.	0.	0.
TOT PRODUCTION	39500.	41000.	43000.	40000.	43500.	40000.	35000.	35000.	32500.	30000.
CAPAC UTILIZ %	87.78	86.32	95.56	84.21	96.67	100.00	100.00	100.00	100.00	100.00
US SALES M$	49445.	51900.	54405.	56960.	59630.	62300.	60380.	60880.	56915.	53840.
US EXPORTS M$	11799.	12610.	14146.	8965.	11679.	4130.	0.	0.	0.	0.
DOW USAGE M$	1180.	1185.	1185.	1185.	1777.	1777.	1777.	1777.	2370.	2370.
HEMC SALES M$	0.	0.	0.	0.	0.	0.	0.	0.	0.	0.
TOT REVENUES	62424.	65695.	69736.	67110.	73086.	68207.	62157.	62657.	59285.	56210.
TOT VARCOST M$	42345.	43110.	45330.	41100.	44985.	40000.	34950.	34950.	32325.	29700.
HS&A COSTS M$	5933.	6228.	6529.	6835.	7156.	7476.	7246.	7306.	6830.	6461.
SPACE COSTS M$	2700.	3000.	3000.	3300.	3300.	2400.	2400.	2400.	2400.	2400.
DEPRC COSTS M$	3629.	3629.	4067.	4067.	4506.	3066.	3066.	3066.	3066.	3066.
TOT FIXCOST M$	12262.	12857.	13596.	14203.	14962.	12942.	12712.	12772.	12296.	11927.
PROFIT BT M$	7817.	9728.	10810.	11807.	13140.	15065.	14496.	14936.	14664.	14583.
PROFIT AT M$	3908.	4864.	5405.	5904.	6557.	7553.	7248.	7468.	7332.	7291.
RET ON SALES %	6.26	7.40	7.75	8.80	8.99	11.04	11.66	11.92	12.37	12.97
RET ON INVEST%	8.30	11.01	10.86	13.08	12.96	16.18	17.19	19.04	20.71	23.03
PROFIT AT M$	3908.	4864.	5405.	5904.	6570.	7533.	7248.	7468.	7332.	7291.
FC CHANGES M$	-5146.	3629.	-4708.	4067.	-4269.	3066.	3066.	3066.	3066.	3066.
WC CHANGES M$	308.	-720.	-889.	578.	-1315.	1073.	1331.	-110.	742.	676.
AC CHANGES M$	-1139.	-1005.	-1340.	2010.	-2345.	2345.	3350.	0.	1675.	1675.
TOT CASH FLOW	-2069.	6768.	-1532.	12559.	-1359.	14017.	14995.	10424.	12815.	12709.
DISCOUNTED 15% CASH FLOW	-1799.	5118.	-1007.	7181.	-676.	6060.	5637.	3408.	3643.	3142.
CUMULATIVE 15% CASH FLOW	-1799.	3319.	2312.	9492.	8817.	14877.	20514.	23922.	27564.	30706.
FIXED CAP M$	33346.	29718.	34425.	30358.	34626.	31560.	28494.	25428.	22361.	19295.
WORKING CAP M$	13733.	14453.	15342.	14764.	16079.	15506.	13675.	13785.	13343.	12366.
ALLOC CAP M$	26465.	27470.	28810.	26800.	29145.	26800.	23450.	23450.	21775.	20100.
TOTAL CAPITAL	47080.	44170.	49767.	45122.	50705.	46566.	42168.	39212.	35404.	31661.
US SALES PGI	18850.00	19000.00	17050.00	16000.00	16750.00	17500.00	18250.00	19250.00	20500.00	22000.00
US SALES PGII	1050.00	12000.00	13950.00	16000.00	16750.00	17500.00	18250.00	19250.00	20500.00	22000.00
EXPORTS PGI	6175.00	6000.00	6950.00	3500.00	4250.00	5000.00	5750.00	6500.00	7500.00	8750.00
EXPORTS PGII	3325.00	4000.00	4950.00	3500.00	4250.00	5000.00	5750.00	6500.00	7500.00	8750.00
DOW USE PGI	650.00	600.00	550.00	500.00	750.00	750.00	750.00	750.00	1000.00	1000.00
DOW USE PGII	350.00	400.00	450.00	500.00	750.00	750.00	750.00	750.00	1000.00	1000.00
HEMC SALES	15000.00	15000.	15000.	15000.	15000.	15000.	15000.	15000.	15000.	15000.

PLANT DATA

	TYPE	PLACE	YEAR
	1	2	1979
	1	2	1981
	1	2	1983

Exhibit 19 Add capacity at Plaquemine, using the continuous process, with a single 25,000,000-lb addition in 1980

	1978	1979	1980	1981	1982	1983	1984	1985	1986	1987
METHO CAPACITY	45000.	42500.	65000.	62500.	60000.	50000.	45000.	45000.	42500.	40000.
HEMC CAPACITY	0.	0.	0.	0.	0.	0.	0.	0.	0.	0.
PMOD CAPACITY	0.	0.	0.	0.	0.	0.	0.	0.	0.	0.
TOT CAPACITY	45000.	42500.	65000.	62500.	60000.	50000.	45000.	45000.	42500.	40000.
US SALES M#	29000.	30000.	31000.	32000.	33500.	35000.	36500.	38500.	40500.	38000.
US EXPORTS M#	9500.	10000.	11000.	7000.	8500.	10000.	7000.	5000.	0.	0.
DOW USAGE M#	1000.	1000.	1000.	1000.	1500.	1500.	1500.	1500.	2000.	2000.
HEMC SALES M#	0.	0.	0.	0.	0.	0.	0.	0.	0.	0.
TOT PRODUCTION	39500.	41000.	43000.	40000.	43500.	46500.	45000.	45000.	42500.	40000.
CAPAC UTILIZ %	87.78	96.47	66.15	64.00	72.50	93.00	100.00	100.00	100.00	100.00
US SALES M$	49445.	51900.	54405.	56960.	59630.	62300.	64970.	68530.	72215.	69140.
US EXPORTS M$	11799.	12610.	12980.	8260.	10030.	11800.	8491.	6065.	0.	0.
DOW USAGE M$	1180.	1180.	860.	860.	1290.	1290.	1290.	1290.	1720.	1720.
HEMC SALES M$	0.	0.	0.	0.	0.	0.	0.	0.	0.	0.
TOT REVENUES	62424.	65690.	68245.	66080.	70950.	75390.	74751.	75885.	73935.	70860.
TOT VARCOST M$	42345.	44010.	34650.	31500.	35175.	38325.	36750.	36750.	34125.	31500.
RS&A COSTS M$	5933.	6228.	6529.	6835.	7156.	7476.	7796.	8224.	8666.	8297.
SPACE COSTS M$	2700.	2700.	3950.	3950.	3950.	2750.	2750.	2750.	2750.	2750.
DEPRC COSTS M$	3940.	5440.	5440.	5440.	5440.	4000.	4000.	4000.	4000.	4000.
TOT FIXCOST M$	12573.	14368.	15919.	16225.	16546.	14226.	14546.	14974.	15416.	15047.
PROFIT BT M$	7506.	7312.	17676.	18355.	19229.	22839.	23455.	24161.	24394.	24313.
PROFIT AT M$	3753.	3656.	8838.	9177.	9615.	11420.	11727.	12081.	12197.	12157.
RET ON SALES %	6.01	5.57	12.95	13.89	13.55	15.15	15.69	15.92	16.50	17.16
RET ON INVEST%	7.08	4.67	12.04	13.60	15.24	19.01	20.96	23.15	25.54	28.21
PROFIT AT M$	3753.	3656.	8838.	9177.	9615.	11420.	11727.	12081.	12197.	12157.
FC CHANGES M$	-11060.	-24560.	5440.	5440.	5440.	4000.	4000.	4000.	4000.	4000.
WC CHANGES M$	308.	-719.	-562.	476.	-1071.	-977.	141.	-249.	429.	676.
AC CHANGES M$	-1139.	-1005.	-1340.	2010.	-2345.	-2010.	1005.	0.	1675.	1675.
TOT CASH FLOW M$	-8138.	-22628.	12376.	17104.	11638.	12433.	16873.	15831.	18301.	18508.
DISCOUNTED 15% CASH FLOW	-7077.	-17110.	8137.	9779.	5786.	5375.	6343.	5175.	5202.	4575.
CUMULATIVE 15% CASH FLOW	-7077.	-24187.	-16049.	-6270.	-484.	4991.	11234.	16410.	21612.	26187.
FIXED CAP M$	39260.	63820.	58380.	52940.	47500.	43500.	39500.	35500.	31500.	27500.
WORKING CAP M$	13733.	14452.	15014.	14538.	15609.	16586.	16445.	16695.	16266.	15589.
ALLOC CAP M$	26465.	27470.	28810.	26800.	29145.	31155.	30150.	30150.	28475.	26800.
TOTAL CAPITAL	52993.	78272.	73394.	67478.	63109.	60086.	55945.	52195.	47766.	43089.
US SALES PGI	18850.00	18000.00	17050.00	16000.00	16750.00	17500.00	18250.00	19250.00	20500.00	22000.00
US SALES PGII	10150.00	12000.00	13950.00	16000.00	16750.00	17500.00	18250.00	19250.00	20500.00	22000.00
EXPORTS PGI	6175.00	6000.00	6050.00	3500.00	4250.00	5000.00	5750.00	6500.00	7500.00	8750.00
EXPORTS PGII	3325.00	4000.00	4950.00	3500.00	4250.00	5000.00	5750.00	6500.00	7500.00	8750.00
DOW USE PGI	650.00	600.00	550.00	500.00	750.00	750.00	750.00	750.00	1000.00	1000.00
DOW USE PGII	350.00	400.00	450.00	500.00	750.00	750.00	750.00	750.00	1000.00	1000.00
HEMC SALES	15000.00	15000.00	15000.00	15000.00	15000.00	15000.00	15000.00	15000.00	15000.00	15000.00

PLANT DATA TYPE PLACE
            2   2
YEAR
1980

156

Exhibit 20 *Add capacity at Plaquemine, using the continuous process, with a single 40,000,000-lb addition in 1981*

	1978	1979	1980	1981	1982	1983	1984	1985	1986	1987
METHO CAPACITY	45000.	42500.	40000.	77500.	75000.	65000.	60000.	60000.	57500.	55000.
HEMC CAPACITY	0.	0.	0.	0.	0.	0.	0.	0.	0.	0.
PMOD CAPACITY	0.	0.	0.	0.	0.	0.	0.	0.	0.	0.
TOT CAPACITY	45000.	42500.	40000.	77500.	75000.	65000.	60000.	60000.	57500.	55000.
US SALES M#	23000.	30000.	31000.	32000.	33500.	35000.	36500.	38500.	41000.	44000.
US EXPORTS #	9500.	10000.	7000.	7000.	8500.	10000.	11500.	13000.	14500.	4000.
DOW USAGE M#	1000.	1000.	1000.	1000.	1590.	1500.	1500.	1500.	2000.	2000.
HEMC SALES M#	0.	0.	0.	0.	0.	0.	0.	0.	0.	0.
TOT PRODUCTION	34500.	41000.	40000.	40000.	43500.	46500.	49500.	53000.	57500.	55000.
CAPAC UTILIZ %	87.78	96.47	100.00	51.61	58.00	71.54	82.50	88.33	100.00	100.00
US SALES M$	49445.	51900.	54405.	56960.	59630.	62300.	64470.	68530.	72980.	78320.
US EXPORTS M$	11793.	12610.	19288.	5677.	6186.	10508.	13145.	15769.	17922.	11403.
DOW USAGE M$	1140.	1180.	1190.	811.	1216.	1216.	1216.	1216.	1622.	1622.
HEMC SALES M$	0.	0.	0.	0.	0.	0.	0.	0.	0.	0.
TOT REVENUES	62424.	65690.	65873.	63448.	69031.	74025.	79332.	85515.	92524.	91345.
TOT VARCOST M$	42345.	44010.	42900.	24440.	28115.	31265.	34415.	38090.	42815.	40190.
RS&A COSTS M$	5933.	6228.	6529.	6835.	7156.	7474.	7796.	8224.	8758.	9398.
SPACE COSTS M$	2700.	2700.	2700.	4300.	4300.	3100.	3100.	3100.	3100.	3100.
DEPRC COSTS M$	3190.	4310.	6550.	6550.	6550.	5110.	5110.	5110.	5110.	5110.
TOT FIXCOST M$	11823.	13238.	15779.	17685.	18006.	15686.	16006.	16434.	16968.	17608.
PROFIT AT M$	4256.	4442.	7194.	21323.	22911.	27074.	28911.	30992.	32741.	33547.
PROFIT AT M$	4128.	4221.	3597.	10661.	11455.	13537.	14455.	15496.	16371.	16773.
RET ON SALES %	6.61	6.43	5.46	16.80	16.59	14.29	14.22	18.12	17.69	18.36
RET ON INVST %	10.55	7.33	3.75	12.01	13.73	17.04	19.15	21.60	24.02	26.71
PROFIT AT M$	4128.	4221.	3597.	10661.	11455.	13537.	14455.	15496.	16371.	16773.
FC CHANGES M$	3190.	-18090.	-34250.	6550.	6550.	5110.	5110.	5110.	5110.	5110.
WC CHANGES M$	308.	-719.	-40.	533.	-1228.	-1099.	-1168.	-1360.	-1542.	-1542.
AC CHANGES M$	-1139.	-1005.	670.		-2345.	-2010.	-2010.	-2345.	-3015.	1675.
TOT CASH FLOW	6487.	-15593.	-34023.	17745.	14432.	15538.	16388.	16901.	16924.	23818.
DISCOUNTED 15% CASH FLOW	5640.	-11790.	-22371.	10146.	7175.	6718.	6161.	5525.	4811.	5887.
CUMULATIVE 15% CASH FLOW	5640.	-6150.	-28520.	-18375.	-11199.	-4482.	1679.	7204.	12015.	17902.
FIXED CAP M$	25010.	43100.	81350.	74400.	78250.	63140.	58030.	52920.	47810.	42700.
WORKING CAP M$	13733.	14452.	14442.	13959.	15187.	16845.	17453.	18813.	20355.	20096.
ALLOC CAP M$	26465.	27470.	26400.	26400.	29145.	31155.	33165.	35510.	38525.	36850.
TOTAL CAPITAL	38743.	57552.	95842.	88732.	83437.	79425.	75483.	71733.	68165.	62796.
US SALES PGI	18850.00	18000.00	17750.00	16000.00	16750.00	17750.00	18250.00	19750.00	20500.00	22000.00
US SALES PGII	10150.00	12000.00	13950.00	16000.00	16750.00	17750.00	18250.00	19250.00	20500.00	22000.00
EXPORTS PGI	6175.00	6000.00	6050.00	3500.00	4250.00	5000.00	5750.00	6500.00	7500.00	8750.00
EXPORTS PGII	3325.00	4000.00	4950.00	3500.00	4250.00	5000.00	5750.00	6500.00	7500.00	8750.00
DOW USE PGI	650.00	600.00	550.00	500.00	750.00	750.00	750.00	750.00	1000.00	1000.00
DOW USE PGII	350.00	400.00	450.00	500.00	750.00	750.00	750.00	750.00	1000.00	1000.00
HEMC SALES	15000.	15000.	15000.	15000.	15000.	15000.	15000.	15000.	15000.	15000.

PLANT DATA   TYPE 3   PLACE 2   YEAR 1981

EXECUTION TERMINATED   12:16:22   T=.07, PC=0   %.06

Exhibit 21 *Add capacity at Plaquemine, using the continuous process, with a single 50,000,000-lb addition in 1981*

	1978	1979	1980	1981	1982	1983	1984	1985	1986	1987
METHO CAPACITY	45000.	42500.	40000.	47500.	65000.	75000.	70000.	70000.	67500.	65000.
HEMC CAPACITY	0.	0.	0.	0.	0.	0.	0.	0.	0.	0.
PMOD CAPACITY	0.	0.	0.	0.	0.	0.	0.	0.	0.	0.
TOT CAPACITY	45000.	42500.	40000.	47500.	65000.	75000.	70000.	70000.	67500.	65000.
US SALES MM	27000.	30000.	31000.	32000.	33000.	35000.	36500.	38500.	41000.	44000.
US EXPORTS MM	4500.	10000.	4000.	7000.	8500.	10500.	11500.	13000.	13000.	17500.
DOW USAGE MM	1000.	1000.	1000.	1000.	1500.	1500.	1500.	1500.	2000.	2000.
HEMC SALES MM	0.	0.	0.	0.	0.	0.	0.	0.	0.	0.
TOT PRODUCTION	33500.	41000.	40000.	40000.	43000.	46500.	49500.	53000.	56000.	63500.
CAPAC UTILIZ %	87.78	96.47	100.00	45.71	51.19	62.00	70.71	75.71	85.93	97.69
US SALES M$	47445.	51900.	54405.	56960.	59630.	62390.	64970.	68530.	72980.	78320.
US EXPORTS M$	11799.	12610.	10288.	5264.	6392.	7520.	8648.	11159.	15152.	20112.
DOW USAGE M$	1140.	1140.	1140.	742.	1128.	1128.	1128.	1128.	1504.	1504.
HEMC SALES M$	0.	0.	0.	0.	0.	0.	0.	0.	0.	0.
TOT REVENUES	62424.	65690.	65873.	62976.	67150.	70948.	74746.	80817.	89636.	99936.
TOT VARCOST M$	42345.	44010.	42900.	22440.	24447.	26133.	27819.	31250.	36500.	42275.
HS&A COSTS M$	5933.	6224.	6529.	6635.	7156.	7476.	7796.	8224.	8758.	9398.
SPACE COSTS M$	2700.	2700.	2700.	4700.	4700.	3500.	3500.	3500.	3500.	3500.
DEPRC COSTS M$	3190.	4440.	6440.	6440.	6940.	5500.	5500.	5500.	5500.	5500.
TOT FIXCOST M$	11823.	13368.	16169.	18475.	13796.	14676.	16796.	17224.	17758.	18398.
PROFIT RT M$	8256.	8312.	6404.	22021.	23907.	26339.	30131.	32343.	35378.	39263.
PROFIT AT M$	4128.	4156.	3402.	11010.	11954.	14170.	15065.	16172.	17689.	19632.
RET ON SALES %	6.61	6.33	5.16	17.48	17.80	19.97	20.16	20.01	19.73	19.64
RET ON INVST%	10.65	6.92	3.30	11.52	13.35	16.70	18.79	21.27	24.41	28.35
PROFIT AT M$	4128.	4156.	3402.	11010.	11954.	14170.	15065.	16172.	17689.	19632.
FC CHANGES M$	3190.	-20560.	-4060.	6940.	6940.	5500.	5500.	5500.	5500.	5500.
WC CHANGES M$	300.	-719.	-40.	637.	-918.	-36.	-436.	-1336.	-1946.	-2266.
AC CHANGES M$	-1137.	-1005.	670.	-2345.	-2345.	-2010.	-2010.	-2345.	-3350.	-3685.
TOT CASH FLOW	6447.	-18128.	-39028.	18588.	15630.	16424.	17720.	17991.	17899.	19180.
DISCOUNTED 15% CASH FLOW	5640.	-13707.	-25662.	19629.	7771.	7773.	6662.	5881.	5088.	4741.
CUMULATIVE 15% CASH FLOW	5640.	-8067.	-33728.	-23101.	-15329.	-8656.	-1394.	4487.	9575.	14316.
FIXED CAP M$	25010.	45570.	48630.	21490.	74750.	64750.	63750.	58250.	52750.	47250.
WORKING CAP M$	13733.	14452.	14492.	13856.	14773.	16444.	16444.	17780.	19720.	21986.
ALLOC CAP M$	26465.	27470.	26300.	26300.	29145.	31165.	33165.	35510.	38860.	42545.
TOTAL CAPITAL	34743.	60022.	103122.	45545.	89523.	64659.	80194.	76030.	72470.	69236.
US SALES PGI	18850.00	18000.00	17050.00	16000.00	16750.00	17500.00	17250.00	19250.00	20500.00	22000.00
US SALES PGII	16150.00	16200.00	17050.00	16000.00	16750.00	17500.00	18250.00	19250.00	20500.00	22000.00
EXPORTS PGI	6175.00	6000.00	6950.00	3900.00	4250.00	5000.00	5750.00	6500.00	7500.00	8750.00
EXPORTS PGII	3325.00	4000.00	4950.00	3900.00	4250.00	5000.00	5750.00	6500.00	7500.00	8750.00
DOW USE PGI	600.00	600.00	550.00	500.00	750.00	750.00	750.00	750.00	1000.00	1000.00
DOW USE PGII	350.00	400.00	450.00	500.00	750.00	750.00	750.00	750.00	1000.00	1000.00
HEMC SALES	15000.	15000.	15000.	15000.	15000.	15000.	15000.	15000.	15000.	15000.

PLANT DATA   TYPE   4   PLACE   2   YEAR   1981

EXECUTION TERMINATED   13:25:05   T=.079   PC=0   3.06

158

Exhibit 22 *Build HEMC plant at Texas, with 20,000,000-lb capacity in 1981, and assume sales of 15.0 million pounds per year*

	1978	1979	1980	1981	1982	1983	1984	1985	1986	1987
METHO CAPACITY	45000.	42500.	40000.	37500.	35000.	25000.	20000.	20000.	17500.	15000.
HEMC CAPACITY	0.	0.	0.	20000.	20000.	20000.	20000.	20000.	20000.	20000.
PMOD CAPACITY	0.	0.	0.	0.	0.	0.	0.	0.	0.	0.
TOT CAPACITY	45000.	42500.	40000.	57500.	55000.	45000.	40000.	40000.	37500.	35000.
US SALES M#	29000.	30000.	31000.	32000.	33500.	23500.	18500.	18500.	15500.	13000.
US EXPORTS M#	9500.	10000.	8000.	4500.	1500.	1500.	1500.	1500.	2000.	0.
DOW USAGE M#	1000.	1000.	1000.	1000.	1500.	1500.	1500.	1500.	2000.	2000.
HEMC SALES M#	0.	0.	0.	15000.	15000.	15000.	15000.	15000.	15000.	15000.
TOT PRODUCTION	39500.	41000.	40000.	52500.	50000.	40000.	35000.	35000.	32500.	30000.
CAPAC UTILIZ %	87.78	96.47	100.00	91.30	90.91	88.89	87.50	87.50	86.67	85.71
US SALES M$	49445.	51900.	54405.	56960.	59630.	44705.	37430.	37555.	31465.	26390.
US EXPORTS M$	11799.	12610.	10288.	5944.	0.	0.	0.	0.	0.	0.
DOW USAGE M$	1180.	1180.	1180.	1180.	1770.	1770.	1819.	1819.	2472.	2534.
HEMC SALES M$	0.	0.	0.	21000.	21000.	21000.	21000.	21000.	21000.	21000.
TOT REVENUES	62424.	65690.	65873.	85084.	82400.	67475.	60249.	60374.	54937.	49924.
TOT VARCOST M$	42345.	44010.	42900.	47700.	44925.	33825.	28575.	28575.	25950.	23325.
RS&A COSTS M$	5933.	6228.	6529.	6835.	7156.	5365.	4492.	4507.	3776.	3167.
SPACE COSTS M$	2700.	2700.	2700.	4200.	4200.	3000.	3000.	3000.	3000.	3000.
DEPRC COSTS M$	3388.	3785.	4380.	4380.	4380.	2940.	2940.	2940.	2940.	2940.
TOT FIXCOST M$	12022.	12713.	13609.	15415.	15736.	11305.	10432.	10447.	9716.	9107.
PROFIT BT M$	8057.	8967.	9364.	21969.	21739.	22345.	21243.	21353.	19271.	17492.
PROFIT AT M$	4029.	4484.	4682.	10985.	10870.	11173.	10621.	10676.	9636.	8746.
RET ON SALES %	6.45	6.83	7.11	12.91	13.19	16.56	17.63	17.68	17.54	17.52
RET ON INVEST%	9.48	9.46	8.52	20.05	21.82	25.63	27.19	29.53	30.10	31.27
PROFIT AT M$	4029.	4484.	4682.	10985.	10870.	11173.	10621.	10676.	9636.	8746.
FC CHANGES M$	-579.	-4148.	-7520.	4380.	4380.	2940.	2940.	2940.	2940.	2940.
WC CHANGES M$	308.	-719.	-40.	-4227.	591.	3283.	1590.	-27.	1196.	1103.
AC CHANGES M$	-1139.	-1005.	670.	-8375.	1675.	6700.	3350.	0.	1675.	1675.
TOT CASH FLOW	2619.	-1388.	-2208.	2763.	17515.	24096.	18501.	13589.	15447.	14466.
DISCOUNTED 15% CASH FLOW	2277.	-1050.	-1452.	1580.	8708.	10417.	6955.	4442.	4391.	3575.
CUMULATIVE 15% CASH FLOW	2277.	1228.	-224.	1356.	10064.	20481.	27437.	31879.	36270.	39845.
FIXED CAP M$	28779.	32927.	40447.	36067.	31687.	28747.	25807.	22867.	19927.	16987.
WORKING CAP M$	13733.	14452.	14492.	18711.	18128.	14844.	13355.	13282.	12086.	10983.
ALLOC CAP M$	26465.	27470.	26800.	35175.	33500.	26800.	23450.	23450.	21775.	20100.
TOTAL CAPITAL	42512.	47378.	54939.	54785.	49815.	43591.	39062.	36149.	32013.	27970.
US SALES PGI	18850.00	18000.00	17050.00	16000.00	16750.00	17500.00	18250.00	19250.00	20550.00	22000.00
US SALES PGII	10150.00	12000.00	13950.00	16000.00	16750.00	17500.00	18250.00	19250.00	20550.00	22000.00
EXPORTS PGI	6175.00	6000.00	6050.00	3500.00	4250.00	5000.00	5750.00	6500.00	7500.00	8750.00
EXPORTS PGII	3325.00	4000.00	4950.00	3500.00	4250.00	5000.00	5750.00	6500.00	7500.00	8750.00
DOW USE PGI	650.00	600.00	550.00	500.00	750.00	750.00	750.00	750.00	1000.00	1000.00
DOW USE PGII	350.00	400.00	450.00	500.00	750.00	750.00	750.00	750.00	1000.00	1000.00
HEMC SALES	15000.	15000.	15000.	15000.	15000.	15000.	15000.	15000.	15000.	15000.
PLANT DATA			YEAR	1981						
		TYPE	PLACE							
		5	2							

Exhibit 23 Build HEMC plant at Texas, with 20,000,000-lb capacity in 1981, and assume sales of 10.0 million pounds per year

	1978	1979	1980	1981	1982	1983	1984	1985	1986	1987
METHO CAPACITY M#	45000.	42500.	40000.	37500.	35000.	25000.	20000.	20000.	17500.	15000.
HEMC CAPACITY M#	0.	0.	0.	20000.	20000.	20000.	20000.	20000.	20000.	20000.
PMOD CAPACITY	0.	0.	0.	0.	0.	0.	0.	0.	0.	0.
TOT CAPACITY	45000.	42500.	40000.	57500.	55000.	45000.	40000.	40000.	37500.	35000.
US SALES M#	29000.	30000.	31000.	32000.	33500.	23500.	18500.	18500.	15500.	13000.
US EXPORTS M#	9500.	10000.	8000.	4500.	0.	1500.	1500.	1500.	2000.	2000.
DOW USAGE M#	1000.	1000.	1000.	10000.	10000.	10000.	10000.	10000.	10000.	10000.
HEMC SALES M#	0.	0.	0.	0.	0.	0.	0.	0.	0.	0.
TOT PRODUCTION	39500.	41000.	40000.	47000.	45000.	35000.	30000.	30000.	27500.	25000.
CAPAC UTILIZ %	87.78	96.47	100.00	82.61	81.82	77.78	75.00	75.00	73.33	71.43
US SALES M$	49445.	51900.	54405.	56960.	59630.	44705.	37430.	37555.	31465.	26390.
US EXPORTS M$	11799.	12610.	10288.	5944.	0.	0.	0.	0.	0.	0.
DOW USAGE M$	1180.	1180.	1180.	1180.	1770.	1770.	1819.	1819.	2472.	2534.
HEMC SALES M$	0.	0.	0.	14000.	14000.	14000.	14000.	14000.	14000.	14000.
TOT REVENUES	62424.	65690.	65873.	78084.	75400.	60475.	53249.	53374.	47937.	42924.
TOT VARCOST M$	42345.	44010.	42900.	45175.	42400.	31300.	26050.	26050.	23425.	20800.
HS&A COSTS M$	5933.	6228.	6529.	6835.	7156.	5365.	4492.	4507.	3776.	3167.
SPACE COSTS M$	2700.	2700.	2700.	4200.	4200.	3000.	3000.	3000.	3000.	3000.
DEPRC COSTS M$	3388.	3785.	4380.	4380.	4380.	2940.	2940.	2940.	2940.	2940.
TOT FIXCOST M$	12022.	12713.	13609.	15415.	15736.	11305.	10432.	10447.	9716.	9107.
PROFIT BT M$	8057.	8967.	9364.	17494.	17264.	17870.	16768.	16878.	14796.	13017.
PROFIT AT M$	4029.	4484.	4682.	8747.	8632.	8935.	8384.	8439.	7398.	6509.
RET ON SALES %	6.45	6.83	7.11	11.20	11.45	14.78	15.74	15.81	15.43	15.16
RET ON INVEST%	9.48	9.46	8.52	16.43	17.88	21.25	22.34	24.38	24.28	24.63
PROFIT AT M$	4029.	4484.	4682.	8747.	8632.	8935.	8384.	8439.	7398.	6509.
FC CHANGES M$	-579.	-4148.	-7520.	-2687.	4380.	2940.	2940.	2940.	2940.	2940.
WC CHANGES M$	308.	-719.	-40.	-5025.	591.	3283.	1590.	-27.	1196.	1103.
AC CHANGES M$	-1139.	-1005.	670.	5416.	1675.	6700.	3350.	0.	1675.	1675.
TOT CASH FLOW	2619.	-1388.	-2208.	5416.	15278.	21859.	16264.	11351.	13209.	12226.
DISCOUNTED 15% CASH FLOW	2277.	-1050.	-1452.	3096.	7596.	9450.	6114.	3711.	3755.	3022.
CUMULATIVE 15% CASH FLOW	2277.	1228.	-224.	2872.	10468.	19918.	26032.	29743.	33498.	36520.
FIXED CAP M$	28779.	32927.	40447.	36067.	31687.	28747.	25807.	22867.	19927.	16987.
WORKING CAP M$	13733.	14452.	14492.	17179.	16588.	13304.	11715.	11742.	10546.	9443.
ALLOC CAP M$	26465.	27470.	26800.	31875.	30150.	23450.	20100.	20100.	18425.	16750.
TOTAL CAPITAL	42512.	47378.	54939.	53245.	48275.	42051.	37522.	34609.	30473.	26630.
US SALES PGI	18850.00	18000.00	17050.00	16000.00	16750.00	17500.00	18250.00	19250.00	20500.00	22000.00
US SALES PGII	10150.00	12000.00	13950.00	16000.00	16750.00	17500.00	18250.00	19250.00	20500.00	22000.00
EXPORTS PGI	6175.00	6000.00	5050.00	3500.00	4250.00	5000.00	5750.00	6500.00	7500.00	8750.00
EXPORTS PGII	3325.00	4000.00	4950.00	3500.00	4250.00	5000.00	5750.00	6500.00	7500.00	8750.00
DOW USE PGI	650.00	600.00	550.00	500.00	750.00	750.00	750.00	750.00	1000.00	1000.00
DOW USE PGII	350.00	400.00	450.00	500.00	750.00	750.00	750.00	750.00	1000.00	1000.00
HEMC SALES	10000.	10000.	10000.	10000.	10000.	10000.	10000.	10000.	10000.	10000.

PLANT DATA: TYPE 5, PLACE 2, YEAR 1981

160

Exhibit 24 *Build PMOD plant at Plaquemine, with a 4,000,000-lb capacity, and assume sales equal to 10% of Methocel per year*

	1978	1979	1980	1981	1982	1983	1984	1985	1986	1987
METHO CAPACITY	45000.	42500.	40000.	37500.	35000.	25000.	20000.	20000.	17500.	15000.
HEMC CAPACITY	0.	0.	0.	0.	0.	0.	0.	0.	0.	0.
PMOD CAPACITY	0.	0.	0.	4000.	4000.	4000.	4000.	4000.	4000.	4000.
TOT CAPACITY	45000.	42500.	40000.	41500.	39000.	29000.	24000.	24000.	21500.	19000.
US SALES M#	29000.	30000.	31000.	32000.	33500.	23500.	18500.	18500.	15500.	13000.
US EXPORTS M#	9500.	10000.	8000.	4500.	0.	0.	0.	0.	0.	0.
DOW USAGE M#	1000.	1000.	1000.	4199.	4849.	4999.	5149.	5349.	6000.	6000.
HEMC SALES M#	0.	0.	0.	0.	0.	0.	0.	0.	0.	0.
TOT PRODUCTION	39500.	41000.	40000.	40699.	38349.	28499.	23649.	23849.	21500.	19000.
CAPAC UTILIZ %	87.78	96.47	100.00	98.07	98.33	98.27	98.54	99.37	100.00	100.00
US SALES M$	49945.	51900.	54405.	58815.	61572.	46734.	39546.	39787.	33785.	28710.
US EXPORTS M$	11799.	12610.	10288.	5944.	0.	0.	0.	0.	0.	0.
DOW USAGE M$	1180.	1180.	1180.	4955.	5722.	5899.	6246.	6488.	7416.	7602.
HEMC SALES M$	0.	0.	0.	0.	0.	0.	0.	0.	0.	0.
TOT REVENUES M$	62424.	65690.	65873.	69715.	67294.	52633.	45792.	46276.	41201.	36312.
TOT VARCOST M$	42345.	44010.	42900.	44476.	41905.	31009.	26083.	26362.	24039.	21538.
RS&A COSTS M$	5933.	6228.	6529.	7058.	7389.	5608.	4746.	4774.	4054.	3445.
SPACE COSTS M$	2700.	2700.	2700.	2900.	2900.	1700.	1700.	1700.	1700.	1700.
DEPRC COSTS M$	3190.	3190.	3370.	3370.	3370.	1930.	1930.	1930.	1930.	1930.
TOT FIXCOST M$	11823.	12118.	12599.	13328.	13659.	9238.	8376.	8404.	7684.	7075.
PROFIT BT M$	8256.	9562.	10374.	11911.	11731.	12386.	11334.	11510.	9478.	7699.
PROFIT AT M$	4128.	4781.	5187.	5955.	5865.	6193.	5667.	5755.	4739.	3849.
RET ON SALES %	6.61	7.28	7.87	8.54	8.72	11.77	12.37	12.44	11.50	10.60
RET ON INVEST %	10.65	13.18	14.20	17.51	19.48	24.81	26.33	29.21	28.45	28.20
PROFIT AT	4128.	4781.	5187.	5956.	5865.	6193.	5667.	5755.	4739.	3849.
FC CHANGES	3190.	3190.	-230.	3370.	3370.	1930.	1930.	1930.	1930.	1930.
WC CHANGES	-308.	-719.	-40.	-845.	533.	3225.	1505.	-106.	1116.	1076.
AC CHANGES	-1139.	-1005.	670.	-468.	1574.	6599.	3249.	-134.	1574.	1675.
TOT CASH FLOW	6487.	6247.	5587.	8012.	11342.	17948.	12351.	7444.	9359.	8530.
DISCOUNTED 15% CASH FLOW	5640.	4724.	3674.	4581.	5639.	7760.	4643.	2434.	2660.	2108.
CUMULATIVE 15% CASH FLOW	5640.	10364.	14038.	18619.	24258.	32018.	36661.	39095.	41755.	43864.
FIXED CAP M$	25010.	21820.	22050.	18640.	15310.	13380.	11450.	9520.	7590.	5660.
WORKING CAP M$	13733.	14452.	14492.	15337.	14805.	11579.	10074.	10181.	9064.	7989.
ALLOC CAP M$	26465.	27470.	26800.	27268.	25694.	19094.	15845.	15979.	14405.	12730.
TOTAL CAPITAL M$	38743.	36272.	36542.	34017.	30115.	24559.	21524.	19701.	16654.	13649.
US SALES PGI	18850.00	18000.00	17050.00	16000.00	16750.00	17500.00	18250.00	19250.00	20550.00	22000.00
US SALES PGII	10150.00	12000.00	13950.00	16000.00	16750.00	17500.00	18250.00	19250.00	20550.00	22000.00
EXPORTS PGI	6175.00	6000.00	6050.00	3500.00	4250.00	5000.00	5750.00	6500.00	7500.00	8750.00
EXPORTS PGII	3325.00	4000.00	4950.00	3500.00	4250.00	5000.00	5750.00	6500.00	7500.00	8750.00
DOW USE PGI	650.00	600.00	550.00	500.00	750.00	750.00	750.00	750.00	1000.00	1000.00
DOW USE PGII	350.00	400.00	450.00	500.00	750.00	750.00	750.00	750.00	1000.00	1000.00
HEMC SALES	15000.	15000.	15000.	15000.	15000.	15000.	15000.	15000.	15000.	15000.

PLANT DATA TYPE 6 PLACE 2 YEAR 1981

Exhibit 25 *Definition of terms and explanation of relationships in the financial planning model of the Methocel Product Division*

METHO capacity	Original capacity of the two Methocel plants, at Midland and Plaquemine, both of which are expected to deteriorate over time as shown in Exhibit #7, together with additional capacity built according to the investment plan under study (size, location, and year).
HEMC capacity	Capacity of the hydroxyethyl methyl cellulose plant, if built to compete with the hydroxyethyl cellulose produced by Hercules and Union Carbide.
PMOD capacity	Capacity of the PMOD plant, if added to process the methocels of Price Group II to obtain a $0.58/lb premium in the market.
U.S. sales M#	Shipments of Methocel to customers within the continental U.S. market; input data specifies the expected shipments (1,000 lb) of Price Groups I and II, derived from Exhibits 9 and 10. In the event that company demand exceeds company capacity, it is assumed that shipments to the other Dow–U.S. product divisions will take first priority, and that U.S. sales will have the second position.
U.S. exports M#	Shipments of Methocel to customers outside the continental U.S. market, and sold by one of the other Dow regional organizations (Canada, Europe, Africa, Asia, or South America); input data specifies the expected shipments (1,000 lb) of Price Groups I and II, derived from Exhibits 9 and 10. In the event that company demand exceeds company capacity, it is assumed that U.S. exports will have third priority (i.e., will be cut back).
Dow usage M#	Shipments of Methocel to other product divisions of Dow–U.S.; input data specifies the expected shipments (1,000 lb) of Price Groups I and II, derived from Exhibits 9 and 10. In the event that company demand exceeds company capacity, it is assumed that shipments to the other Dow–U.S. product divisions will take first priority.
HEMC sales M#	Shipments of hydroxyethyl methyl cellulose to customers within the continental U.S. market; no export sales or Dow usage is expected for the HEMC material. Input data specify the expected shipments (1,000 lb) for HEMC.
PMOD sales M#	Shipments of the processed Methocels of Price Group II are not recorded separately; they are assumed to be 10% of U.S. sales, if the PMOD plant is built, and are believed to be substitutes for the other material, not additional sales.
Total production	Total production is the sum of U.S. sales, U.S. exports, Dow usage, and HEMC sales, in 1,000 lb.
Capac utiliz %	Capacity utilization refers to the utilization of the Methocel process only; it is the total Methocel capacity (as defined above) divided by the total production. In 1978, total capacity was 45,000 lb and total production was expected to be 39,500 lb, for a utilization ratio of 87.78%.
U.S. sales M$	Shipments of Methocel in Price Groups I and II to customers within the continental U.S. market in pounds times the input data on the price per pound. In 1977, the Methocels of Price Group I were selling at $1.53/lb, and Price Group II at $2.03/lb.
U.S. exports M$	Shipments of Methocel in Price Groups I and II to customers outside the continental U.S. market in pounds times the computed transfer price. Dow Chemical Company uses a cost-based transfer price for all shipments between regional organizations in the international firm, or between product divisions in a regional organization; this transfer price is the sum of the

Exhibit 25 (*continued*)

	variable production costs (material, labor, power, maintenance, and disposal) plus the allocated production costs (space and depreciation) at full capacity. In 1977, the transfer price was basically $1.08 for variable costs plus $0.06 for space costs ($2,700 ÷ 45,000 lb) plus $0.07 for depreciation ($3,190 ÷ 45,000 lb). The transfer price varies somewhat according to the production level since the variable cost differs at Midland ($1.11/lb) and at Plaquemine ($1.05/lb), and the program assigns production to the lowest-cost facility until that is at capacity.
Dow usage M$	Shipments of Methocel in Price Groups I and II to other product divisions of Dow–U.S. in pounds times the computer transfer price per pound. The computation of the transfer price is explained above.
HEMC sales M$	Shipments of hydroxyethyl methyl cellulose to customers within the continental U.S. market in pounds times the input data on the expected price per pound. In 1977, it was believed that HEMC could be sold at $1.50/lb.
PMOD sales M$	Sales of the processed Methocels of Price Group II are not reported separately; instead, they are included in the U.S. sales of Methocel, and are computed at 10% of Price Group II shipments in pounds times the input data on the expected price premium per pound. In 1977, it was believed that the processed premium would sell at a premium of $0.58/lb.
Total revenues	Total revenues represent the sum of U.S. sales, U.S. exports, Dow usage, and the PMOD premium.
Total varcosts	Total variable costs represent the sum of the material, labor, power, maintenance, and disposal costs; these costs have been described in the case for the various processing plants. Production is assigned, in the program, to the lowest-cost facility until the capacity of that facility is reached.
RS&A costs	RS&A costs are allocated expenses for research, selling, and administration; at Dow–U.S. they are allocated at 12% of U.S. sales (shipments to customers within the continental U.S. market) in dollars.
Space costs	Space costs are allocated expenses to cover local taxes for manufacturing facilities and ancillary services for manufacturing processes; the "space" refers to the area with a manufacturing complex used by a specific process. Space costs at Dow–U.S. are allocated on a complex formula that includes square footage, asset value, etc., but not facility age or production volume; the same amount is charged each year as long as the facility has even partial use. Space costs in 1977 for the present and proposed plants were as follows:

$1,200,000 for existing Midland plant
1,500,000 for existing Plaquemine plant
300,000 for proposed   5-million-pound batch plant
1,250,000 for proposed 25-million-pound continuous plant
1,600,000 for proposed 40-million-pound continuous plant
2,000,000 for proposed 50-million-pound continuous plant
1,500,000 for proposed 20-million-pound HEMC plant
200,000 for proposed   4-million-pound PMOD plant

FC changes	Fixed capital changes reflect the total cash flow resulting from depreciation (+) and new investment (−). Depreciation is at a fixed rate of 5% annually; it should be understood that Dow Chemical Company uses a variable

163

Exhibit 25   *(continued)*

	sum-of-the-digits' rate, but this has been changed for the purpose of making the various alternatives more readily comparable in this analysis.
WC changes	Working capital changes reflect the total cash flow for the Methocel Division resulting from increases (−) or decreases (+) in sales revenues, and consequently in the need for accounts receivable and inventory. Working capital is allocated to the division at 22% of total revenues.
AC changes	Allocated capital changes reflect the total cash flow for the Methocel Division resulting from increases (−) or decreases (+) in production. Allocated capital refers to the long-term funds invested by the Dow Chemical Company in company-wide research, administration, and selling facilities. It is charged to the division at $0.67 per pound of total production (the rate per pound differs for all the company's products, and is determined by a value-added concept).
U.S. sales PGI U.S. sales PGII	The last seven rows of figures, for 1978–1987, are the expected sales for each of the product categories; these are part of the input data, and are reprinted for clarity in possible sensitivity analysis.
Plant data	Plant data is a code for the investment alternative under study, and the codes translated as follows:

Type	Place	Year
1 = 5,000,000 lb batch Methocel	1 = Midland	1981
2 = 25,000,000 lb continuous Methocel	2 = Plaquemine	
3 = 40,000,000 lb continuous Methocel	3 = Texas	
4 = 50,000,000 lb continuous Methocel		
5 = 20,000,000 lb continuous HEMC		
6 = 4,000,000 lb special PMOD		

Evelyn Hollister

Evelyn Hollister was a 1974 graduate of the Massachusetts Institute of Technology, in metallurgical engineering, who worked in Detroit for the Automotive Casting Division of one of the major steel companies while her husband was attending the M.B.A. program at the University of Michigan. In the fall of 1976, Mrs. Hollister was assigned to a project team that was to investigate the cause of operating problems that had developed in the wheel castings used on the new models of one of the larger luxury cars. As part of a vehicle-weight-reduction program, the company which manufactured the car had redesigned the entire front-wheel suspension system, while the engineers at the Automotive Casting Division had developed a new wheel structure, lighter in weight, with thinner cross sections, but stronger as a result of changes in the alloy specifications. Some of the brake rotors, which are an integral part of the wheel casting, were warping, and the warped rotors would cause a chattering sound, which naturally brought customer complaints. Mrs. Hollister was part of a small group asked to investigate the cause of the problem, and to make recommendations for improvement.

> The wheel casting is part of the front-wheel assembly. It has a bearing housing that mounts on the wheel spindle, and the inner surface of the rim (rotor) is machined for the brake pads, while the outer surface is left unfinished, but is drilled for the wheel mount studs. Some of the brake rotors were warping in use, which did not directly create an unsafe condition—the brakes would still stop the car—but this did lead to chattering, and could cause uneven brake application and skids. We were told to solve the problem. (Statement of Evelyn Hollister)

The project team assigned to work on the problem of the warped brake rotors consisted of Douglas Fenner, the chief engineer of the Casting Division, Evelyn Hollister, and a laboratory technician. Douglas Fenner was a personal friend and golfing companion of the general manager of the division; both had started work for the company at about the same time, and both had similar mannerisms and appearance.

> If truth be known, "prissy" is the word that comes immediately to mind when you meet either one of them; they are both meticulous dressers, with very expensive suits and very shiny shoes, and they both have a thin-lipped, suspicious attitude. I don't like them, but that's all right; I don't suppose they like me either. (Statement of Evelyn Hollister)

The general manager told the group, at the start of the study, that he was certain that the problem was due to tensile stress in the castings, so that the early work concentrated on that aspect.

> Tensile stress is the natural place to start, since you can cure that problem with a change in the alloy specifications; if it were compressive stress, you would have to change the entire design, with all the hassle and expense of making new molds and clearing the changes with the customer. Douglas, of course, didn't like to get his little hands dirty, so the technician and I wound up doing all of the actual lab work. This involves cutting a casting in half, grinding the surfaces, using x-rays to measure the distortions in the crystal lattices of the metal, and then plotting those measurements against known curves to examine the fit. It's simple work, but time consuming and detailed. The points from our sample did not fit the curves, so that it was fairly obvious that the problem was not tensile stress. (Statement of Evelyn Hollister)

Mrs. Hollister then started work on the possibility that the warped castings were caused by compressive stress, but after about two weeks of effort she was told by one of the other metallurgists in the lab that the problem had been solved, and he showed her a copy of a report prepared by Douglas Fenner that strongly supported the tensile stress hypothesis.

> I was not surprised that I had not seen the report earlier since Douglas combines secrecy with his other abundant virtues, but I was surprised at the contents. All of the data points from our experiments had been changed to fit the curves, and some of the points which were far from where the theory would predict had been omitted. The report "proved" that tensile stress was responsible for the problem.
>
> The really shocking part came next. The report recommended a change in the alloy specifications that would certainly stop the warping, but would also greatly reduce the strength. Some of those wheel castings are going to break.
>
> I don't know what I ought to do now. These are not brakes on school

buses; these are brakes on [name of luxury car], and I don't really care what happens to the owners. There's not going to be a wholesale slaughter; there'll be a couple of bad accidents, but that will be all.

I need this job, or at the least, I need this job for another seven months until Jerry graduates from the M.B.A. program. It's not easy for women to find jobs, except for the usual secretarial work,

and it's certainly not easy for women scientists or engineers to find good, interesting jobs. I have one, and I don't want to lose it. What should I do? (Statement of Evelyn Hollister)

Class Assignment. Prepare a specific recommendation for the future actions of Mrs. Hollister.

Specialty Packaging Division of Union Pulp and Paper Corporation

The Specialty Packaging Division of Union Pulp and Paper Corporation manufactured and sold a patented form of packaging material termed plastic card stock and container board. The plastic card stock consisted of two layers of kraft cardboard (kraft is a paper-making process that yields paper and cardboard with long cellulose fibers for strength; it is commonly used for packaging, not for printing, and is usually sold unbleached, in a familiar light brown color) bound together by a layer of foamed polyurethane plastic; the plastic container board consisted of two layers of corrugated board with the same filling of foamed plastic. The plastic card stock was $\frac{5}{16}$ in. thick ($\frac{1}{16}$ in. for each layer of cardboard and $\frac{3}{16}$ in. for the foamed plastic) and was flexible enough so that it could be wound on a spindle, and then shipped in large rolls, generally 48 in. wide. The container board was $\frac{5}{8}$ in. thick ($\frac{3}{16}$ in. for each layer of corrugated board and $\frac{1}{4}$ in. for the plastic), although occasionally made in thicker form for special orders, and was not flexible enough to be wound; instead, it was shipped in sheets 48 in.

wide × 8 ft long. Both the card stock and container board were used to make folding cartons, and the inserts within those cartons, to package precision scientific and electronic equipment, such as laboratory instruments and computer frames, and to ship fragile parts such as microwave tubes and silicon circuitry. The material was even used for some consumer products, such as very expensive glassware and china, and by some moving companies, to protect art objects and paintings, etc.

Plastic container board really is the Cadillac of packaging materials. It is very strong—you could not kick a hole through it—and it is impervious to water and resilient to impacts. You can put "fragile, handle with care" stickers all over the typical package, and the trucking companies will still throw it into the truck, and the post office will still run it through their automatic stamping and sorting machines. You have to protect high-value scientific and electronic parts and equipment, during transit, and our plastic card stock and container board is ideal for the purpose, even though, compared to other materials, it is very much more expensive. In the past, it was also very much more profitable for us. (Statement of the manager of the Specialty Packing Division at Union Pulp and Paper Corporation)

Engineers at Union Pulp and Paper Corporation had developed the plastic packaging materials in the early 1950s. The chemical process was quite simple: the urethane polymer was melted and mixed with an aerosol agent, and then extruded through a nozzle as a viscous liquid that expanded as it cooled. The mechanical process was more complex, since the foamed plastic had to be sandwiched between the two layers of card stock or corrugated board, and then pressed very evenly for good adhesion and proper thickness. A process patent (that claimed innovations in the methods of manufacture rather than in the properties of the product) had been issued in 1955 for the card stock, and a second process patent had been received in 1963 for the container board. The problem facing the manager of the Specialty Packaging Division in 1978 centered on the date of the second patent; numerous smaller firms had started to make plastic card stock in 1972, when the patent protection for that process had ended, and the marketing representatives of the division had warned that those same firms planned to copy the container board process in 1980, when that patent would expire. The smaller firms tended to sell on a price basis, and in the opinion of the division manager had "ruined one market [for the card stock] and were going to ruin the other [for the container board]."

The other paper companies never got into the plastic packing material business, probably because the market was so small and the mechanics so complex. Weyerhaeuser and International Paper can do anything in paper production that we can do, and oftentimes they can do it better, but they tend not to compete where the key to success is mechanical rather than chemical; they would much rather develop a new pulping process, or an improved form of paper, than they would a different end product. They have never been good at mechanical design, and they don't like having mechanical engineers directing research chemists in a development program. And of course, they would never enter the market now, with a mature growth rate and potential price competition.

But these conditions are just right for the small, local corrugated board plants that have no chemical expertise but good mechanical skills. These companies buy card stock, liner board, and corrugating medium from other paper firms—they may even buy it from us, for all I know— and then they supply the folding box manufacturers and industrial packaging companies within a given area. They found that they could buy the polymer and the aerosol agent off the shelf from a dozen sources, get technical services and assistance from the supplier, fiddle with the mechanical process, and get into the plastic packaging material business. If truth be known, they didn't even have to fiddle very much with the mechanics; they could have purchased a case of whiskey for the maintenance man on the No. 4 line in our South Chicago plant, and gotten most of the temperature and pressure settings for nothing. These are the people you never hear about in a business school, but you certainly find them in the business world. Unfortunately, you usually find them in the offices of your customers, saying, "Why buy from Union Pulp and Paper when it is available locally, at a much better price?"

We call these local companies "garage processors," but that is not really an accurate description. They are larger than the term "garage" would indicate. They may have a sales volume of $2 to $3 million a year, and they may have invested capital of $250,000 to $500,000. They offer a specialized product line, serve a limited market area, and sell on price. We can't equal their price since they build all their own equipment, do no research or product development, and never worry about a return on capital. ROI to them is a high salary, a month's vacation in Florida, and a new Cadillac every year. We have to get a better return than that. (Statement of the manager of the Specialty Packaging Division at Union Pulp and Paper Corporation)

In 1978, the Specialty Packaging Division had sales of $10,000,000 per year in plastic card stock and $40,000,000 per year in container board. The estimated market share on a national basis was 15% for the card stock and 100% for the container board; the return on investment was 17% for card stock and 43% for container board. In 1972, the year the first process patent had expired, company sales of card stock had been $50,000,000 per year, and the return on investment had been over 50%.

The garage processors skimp on quality, so that some of the card stock business still comes to us, but not very much. There really is not much customer loyalty in the packaging materials industry, so that I assume that our sales in container board are going to deteriorate just as quickly after 1980 as our sales of card stock did after 1972. One way to look at the situation, of course, is that it was nice while it lasted, but that you have to expect price competition when markets mature and patents expire. It's easy to say that when you're not the division manager in charge of the product, and when your performance is not measured by market share, sales growth, and ROI. Unfortunately, I am the division manager, and I've got to make some hard decisions in the very near future. (Statement of the manager of the Specialty Packaging Division at Union Pulp and Paper Corporation)

Gordon Talcott had been the manager of the Specialty Packaging Division at Union Pulp and Paper Corporation since 1976, when he was promoted from the district sales office in Atlanta. He was 36 years old, with a mechanical engineering degree from Northwestern and an M.B.A. from Georgia State University, in the evening program. At the date of the case, he felt that there were three alternative strategies for the Specialty Packaging Division, none of which seemed ideal:

1. Reduce the price on the plastic container board gradually over the next two years, attempting to maintain a dominant share of the market. A summary of the financial analysis of this alternative is given in Exhibit 1, which shows a decline in the return on invested capital from 42.8% to 13.3%.

   We can make the plastic container board business much less attractive to the garage processors, so they won't spend the $200,000 needed to compete with us, but of course we would make the business much less attractive to us also. We are now selling at $7.60 per pound; we would have to bring the price down to about $5.80, which is a little bit above where they are now selling the card stock, in order to keep them out. The market is not growing, and we have 100% market share now, so that we won't pick up any volume; all that will happen is that our return on capital will come down to a barely acceptable figure. (Statement of Gordon Talcott)

2. Increase spending on R&D over the next two years, attempting to maintain technical superiority in the product or the process. $1,200,000 had been spent since 1976, under the direction of Mr. Talcott, but no major advances in product characteristics or major savings in process costs had been achieved.

   We have been attempting to mold the plastic card stock, so that we could cradle the prod-

Exhibit 1 *Financial analysis of the proposed strategy to reduce price gradually on the plastic container board to maintain a dominant share of the market*

	Current operations	Proposed operations
Sales of plastic container board (lb)	5,398,000	5,000,000
Price of plastic container board, per pound	$ 7.60	$ 5.80
	$41,024,000	$29,000,000
Direct costs for material, labor, and power	$21,218,000	$19,650,000
Allocated general and administrative expenses	4,923,000	3,480,000
Allocated plant charges, per square foot	973,000	973,000
Assigned depreciation charges	828,000	828,000
Estimated tax allowance	6,541,000	2,034,000
Total costs	$34,483,000	$26,965,000
After-tax profit on foamed plank	$ 6,541,000	$ 2,035,000
Fixed capital, at cost less depreciation	$ 5,770,000	$ 5,770,000
Plant capital, at charge per square foot	3,118,000	3,118,000
Working capital, at 22% of sales	9,925,000	6,380,000
	$17,913,000	$15,268,000
After-tax profit on depreciation/invested capital	42.8%	13.3%

ucts of our final customers; now the card stock is cut and formed by the box manufacturers to fit the different products. But we have not had much luck in molding; we get dense spots, which ruin the impact resilience, and we get thin sections, which lower the tensile strength. Plastic packaging material is used to protect expensive scientific and electronic equipment, and I don't think that we'll sell very much if we have a quality control problem. We have not had any luck at all in reducing our manufacturing costs; we already have all of the economies of scale, we are pretty far down on the experience curve, and we don't foresee any breakthrough technology in the processing methods. (Statement of Gordon Talcott)

3. Reduce the price on the plastic card stock immediately, attempting to either drive the smaller competitors out of the market, or to make certain that they would not have adequate funds to invest in the container board processing equipment, when

that patent expired in 1980. A summary of this financial analysis is given in Exhibit 2, which shows a decline in the return on invested capital from 17.6% to 11.3%.

Our return on sales goes to hell, from 12.3% to 3.6%, but our return on investment is not that bad. We have facilities for 10 million pounds of card stock in site, but this year we only ran 1.3 million pounds. We could cut the price to $4.80, which is nearly a dollar less than the garage processors are now charging, and we could pick up nearly all the business since we would be selling below their costs. They could not compete since we buy our card stock, liner board, and corrugating medium at transfer prices, not at market prices, and since our facilities are all depreciated. It is the classic big company/little company confrontation, and we have the economies of scale and we have the capital so that we can drive them out of business. There are about 30 of those small processors nationally, and some of them

Exhibit 2 *Financial analysis of the proposed strategy to reduce price immediately on the plastic card stock to protect an existing share of the container board market*

	Current operations	Proposed operations
Sales of plastic card stock (lb)	1,307,000	10,000,000
Price of plastic card stock, per pound	$ 7.60	$ 4.80
Total sales	$9,936,000	$48,000,000
Direct cost for material, labor, and power	$5,202,000	$37,700,000
Allocated general and administrative expenses	1,192,000	5,760,000
Allocated plant charges, per square foot	1,087,000	1,090,000
Assigned depreciation charges	—	—
Estimated tax allowance	1,227,000	1,730,000
Total costs	$8,708,000	$46,280,000
After-tax profit on foamed sheet	$1,228,000	$ 1,720,000
Fixed capital, at cost less depreciation	—	—
Plant capital, at charge per square foot	$4,760,000	$ 4,760,000
Working capital, at 22% of sales	2,185,000	10,560,000
Invested capital	$6,945,000	$15,320,000
After-tax profit on depreciation/invested capital	17.6%	11.3%

might survive by relying upon personal relationships with the buyers and prompt deliveries of their orders, but those that did survive would not be thinking about investing another $200,000 in container board processing equipment. There would be some squawks, but we could show that we had cut prices to increase our volume and our profits. And the dying don't squawk very loudly, or very long. (Statement of Gordon Talcott)

Class Assignment. Recommend a course of action for Mr. Talcott relative to the proper strategy for the Specialty Packaging Division of Union Pulp and Paper Corporation.

Chapter 4

STRATEGIC DESIGN IN A CHANGING ENVIRONMENT

Strategic design, as described in previous chapters, is concerned with the definition of a long-term method of competition to be followed by a business organization. There are three major factors, or more properly groups of factors, that influence the selection of this method of competition from among the range of strategic alternatives open to the firm. These factors have been discussed under the headings of the corporate performance and position, the organizational resources and skills, and the environmental characteristics and trends, and the relationships among these factors are portrayed in a schematic format at the top of the next page.

Problems exist in the identification and evaluation of the components of each of the three groups of factors. It is not easy to appraise the past performance or judge the current position of a firm in the major functions of marketing, production, and finance, and it is certainly difficult to analyze the specific strengths and weaknesses of the company in money, equipment, and people. But probably the most complex of all the factors to understand, and to use in strategic design, are the environmental characteristics and trends. These are complex since they involve the economic, technical, social, and political conditions of the future, not of the present. Companies must fit into the future environment, and consideration of the future involves forecasting problems, and substantial uncertainties.

Forecasting problems are inherently more difficult in strategic design than in operational planning because of the multitude of social, political, technical, and economic factors that are involved, and because of the extended time span that is required. Most strategic decisions, those influencing the long-term competitive position of the firm, involve changes in product or service design, market definition, operational methods, physical facilities, financial requirements, organizational structure, and managerial systems; none of these changes are accomplished easily, or quickly. Consequently, the time span for strategic planning can extend from 3 to 10 or even 15 years, depending upon the term required to obtain the governmental

Environmental characteristics
and trends

Economic

Technological

Social/political

Competitive

↓

Organizational   Specific opportunities and risks
mission or charter   within the industry

↓   ↓

Corporate perform-   Range of strategic alternatives   Selected strategy,
ance and position   open to the firm   or method of com-
                                                                            petition

↑   ↑

Managerial values   Specific strengths and weak-
and attitudes   nesses within the company

↑

Money

Equipment

People

Market position

Organizational resources, or
assets and skills

---

approval, at federal, state, and local levels, and to complete the financial arrangements and physical changes needed to implement the proposed strategy. It is
ironic, but it should be noted that the length of time required for governmental registration and physical construction has been extended recently, while the pace of
change in the national economy and the social, political, and technical areas has
been accelerating. Strategic design within organizations is increasingly necessary,
to adapt to the environmental changes, but it is also increasingly difficult since the
time span needed to implement the design has been widened, with consequent
problems in forecasting the future conditions.

The forecasting process, needed to anticipate future conditions for meaningful
strategic design in a complex and changing environment, can most easily be described as a series of three formal steps:

1. *Selection of the proper dimensions.* The environment of an organization consists of a
   multitude of economic, social, political, technical, and competitive characteris-

tics and trends; not all are equally important to the future of that organization. The first step in forecasting is to select the critical environmental elements, or dimensions, that can have a major impact upon the future performance and position of the firm. Not all the characteristics and trends of an industry, or of a society, are equally important, and not all are equally obvious. The major errors in the design of competitive strategies for business organizations that have occurred over the past 10 years have undoubtedly come about through ignoring the critical dimensions, not through mistaking an anticipated position on an accepted or acknowledged dimension, or trend. The most obvious illustration of this point is the neglect of energy and raw material availability in strategic planning at most organizations until 1973, the year of the first oil embargo. A memorable statement on the need to select the critical, rather than the obvious, dimensions in forecasting was written by Professor William Hall, a colleague at the University of Michigan: "If you don't plan for it, it will happen."

2. *Determination of a relevant scale for each dimension.* Many of the important trends within the environment are easily measurable in financial or physical terms; gross national product, consumer income, and housing starts are obvious examples. However, some equally important environmental trends cannot be measured simply; availability of energy and productivity of employees are familiar illustrations. Trends in the social and political areas are particularly difficult to measure, although critical for strategic design; public attitudes and governmental actions on environmental deterioration and corporate responsibility show the problems here. The second step in forecasting, then, is to develop a continuous scale that can be used to measure each of the selected dimensions. It is possible, in order to show the importance of a relevant scale for each dimension, to paraphrase Professor Hall: "If you can't measure it, it will be worse than you expect."

3. *Estimation of a single point or probability distribution upon the scale.* Forecasting methods, particularly those based upon quantitative rather than qualitative processes, are generally designed to estimate a single point, or a distribution of points each with a probability of occurrence, upon the known scale of a specific dimension, once that dimension and that scale have been defined. Most forecasting methods do not assist in recognizing the importance of a current trend or a future event, nor in developing means of measuring the changes over time accelerating that trend or leading to that event, but they do help greatly in estimating future conditions once the potential of a trend or event has been recognized and the method of measurement has been developed. The balance of the text of this instructional note will provide a nontechnical review of the alternative forecasting methods.

Forecasting methods can be divided into two basic types, judgmental and mathematical, and each of the types can be further divided into classes, single person vs. multiple person for the judgmental, and decision models vs. statistical models for the mathematical, with the overall relationships shown in the chart on page 174. This taxonomy is based upon earlier writings by Professor Hall (William K. Hall, "Forecasting Techniques for Use in the Corporate Planning Process," *Managerial Planning,* November/December 1972, pp. 5ff.), and is used with his permission.

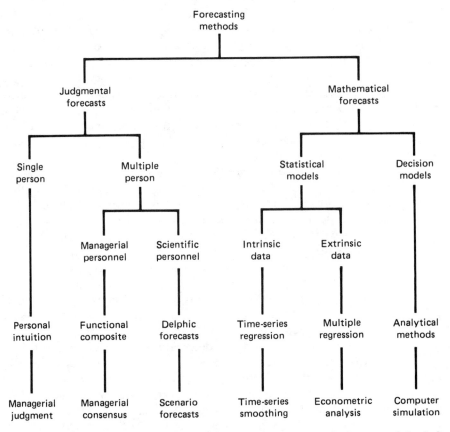

1. *Personal intuition* is by far the most common forecasting technique, and doubtless the most unscientific, but it is not necessarily the least accurate. Personal intuition is basically a statement that, "I think that X will occur." Intuition is subjective, and often not factual, but it can be imaginative, and provide a visionary anticipation of future conditions.

2. *Managerial judgment* is personal intuition carried beyond a purely subjective thought process to an evaluation of current positions, an understanding of historical trends, and a projection of future conditions. Managerial judgment can be expressed as, "I think that X will occur because. . . ." An experienced manager can include more factors, and more relationships among those factors, in a forecast than can many of the mathematical techniques, but there is no guarantee that the factors will be unbiased or that the relationships will be complete. Bias can easily be unintentional; the information received by a manager often depends upon that person's position within the organization, and the interpretation of the information often depends upon that person's function. Relationships can easily be partial; it is continually claimed that the major advantage of preparing a mathematical model of a situation is that the process forces members of the management to express relationships in an explicit, inclusive

form. Many of the "multiple person" methods of judgmental forecasts are in reality efforts to ensure the collection of unbiased data and the expression of inclusive relationships in the forecasting process, and to provide a formal structure for managerial judgment.

3. A *functional composite* is a multiple-person forecasting method that represents the combined opinions of the members of a functional or technical subgroup within an organization, such as sales personnel, production foremen, or technical staff. Their opinions are usually expressed in response to structured questions on sales volume, productive capacity, or technological feasibility, and are generally reported as a distribution, with a mean and some measure of the dispersion. The expectation is that the mean will be a useful predictor since the forecast errors of informed individuals should balance above and below an accurate estimate. The problem, however, is that the individuals, while they are informed and often have considerable experience, may have the inherent bias of a single functional group, while the information received by members of that group has obvious limitations: the very short-term nature of most customer contacts, for example. Other group forecasting methods have been developed to take advantage of the assumption that several informed persons can produce a better estimation of future conditions than can a single individual, while eliminating the biased orientation and limited information of the functional composite.

4. A *managerial consensus* is a multiple-person forecasting method that represents the combined opinions of the members of a number of functional and technical subgroups within an organization. Representatives from marketing, production, finance, engineering, and R&D, generally at the managerial rather than the operational level, and usually supported with information developed by the staffs at each of the functional groups, are brought together and asked to agree on a forecast for the firm. The discussion is unstructured, but the dimensions and the scales for the forecast have to be specified in advance. The managerial consensus has the advantages that a range of managerial viewpoints can be considered, and that the bias in information sources can be overcome, but it suffers from the personal dynamics of a large meeting since one person or one group can dominate the discussion, and obstruct a meaningful consensus.

5. The *Delphi method* was designed to remedy the interactional problems which often arise in consensus forecasts. The intention is to utilize the combined opinions of managerial or professional persons, while eliminating the problems that can be caused by a dominant personality or an obstructionist group. Persons involved in a Delphi forecast are polled individually, not at a meeting, and each responds to a series of questions, generally by selecting a value on the scale of a defined dimension. The responses for each question are statistically summarized, and then returned to the participants for possible revision. This iterative process is repeated until consensus is achieved, or until the lack of consensus is obvious. The participants are never identified, to prevent the reputation or position of one forecaster influencing the others, but dissident members of the group can record and distribute, anonymously, reasons for their differences of opinion. The Delphi method has been used to forecast technological feasibility,

and sociopolitical events where historical data are often inapplicable or misleading, but the problem is that these forecasts are limited to specifically defined dimensions, and alternative future possibilities cannot be considered.

6. The *scenario method* is used to generate alternative future possibilities, and to avoid the forecasting problems associated with predefined dimensions and established scales. Members of a scenario group are presented with a formal set of assumptions (a scenario) concerning certain aspects of the future environment, and are asked to predict the consequences of those assumptions by logical analysis. A dramatic example of a scenario would be to postulate the elimination of internal-combustion automobiles within 10 years; forecasters would be asked to predict the changes brought about in the U.S. economy and society by that event. The scenario method does force consideration of a range of future possibilities, and does limit the conservatism that seems to be inherent in most forecasting methods, but the wide-ranging nature of the process serves to detract from the precision and the reliability of the final estimates. It is often felt that closer ties to historical data and observable trends are needed, and the effective use of historical data and observable trends requires mathematical analysis.

Mathematical methods are used to generate formal, quantitative estimations of the future value of a variable that can be measured on the known scale of a given dimension. The major advantages of mathematical forecasts are the apparent precision and reliability that come from starting with historical data points; the major problem, of course, is the inability to envisage a new dimension or establish a new scale, due to the dependence on past numerical data. Mathematical forecasts from past numerical data can be divided into two generic types: statistical models and decision models. Decision models are used to predict future values of a variable that is controlled, to some extent, by organizational policies and decisions. Revenue forecasts for a company in which the future sales level is dependent both upon the state of the economy and the amount of advertising would be an example of a decision model. Statistical models generate a prediction of the future value of a variable based upon either the historical values of that variable (intrinsic models), or on the historical values of related variables (extrinsic models). Revenue forecasts for a city or town in which the past tax receipts appeared to be slowly increasing over time would be an example of an intrinsic model, while an extrinsic model would relate the tax receipts to levels of industrial activity, consumer income, housing starts, and the inflation rate.

7. *Time-series regression* is an intrinsic statistical forecasting method. The intent is to develop a simple (one independent and one dependent variable) functional relationship for the historical values of a time series, and then extrapolate that relationship to forecast future values. The functional relationship may be linear (straight), logarithmic (curved), or trigonometric (cyclical), and it may be developed either visually, on graph paper, or analytically by the "least-squares" method, on a computer. The least-squares method is linear regression, and a line is fitted to minimize the sum of the squares of the errors between the line and the historical data points; this computational method can produce both a

forecast and a "confidence interval," which expresses a range about the forecast and a probability that the actual value will occur within that range, provided that the conditions that generated the original time series remain constant.

8. *Time-series averaging* is also an intrinsic statistical forecasting method, which primarily assigns greater weight to the more recent data points in the series, through either a moving average or exponential smoothing. A moving average is simply the numerical mean of the last n data points; as each new data point is included in the calculation, the data point for the nth preceding period is omitted, so that the average remains reasonably current. Exponential smoothing provides even more weight to the current data points through the use of an exponential time relationship,

$$S_t = \alpha X_t + (1 - \alpha)^1 X_{t-1} + (1 - \alpha)^n X_{t-n}$$

Simple exponential smoothing can be extended to identify the trend and the seasonal and cyclical factors in a series, forecast each of those components, and then add the individual forecasts to provide a sophisticated prediction for time-series data.

Intrinsic statistical methods, whether simple regression or exponential smoothing, suffer from an inability to predict major changes in the series; the forecast is based entirely on historical data, and can only respond to changes after they have occurred. This, for obvious reasons, is a serious problem; time-series forecasting would have predicted the continued use of the horse for rural transportation in the 1920s, and the expanded construction of steam locomotives for passenger travel in the 1940s. Trends in the data can be observed by intrinsic statistical methods, particularly in the slowing of a growth rate, and the immediacy of those changes can be demonstrated by the use of a moving average or exponential weighting that emphasizes the recent values in a series, but the changes cannot be predicted before they occur. It is necessary to use other independent variables, related to the dependent variable in the forecast, to predict changes in a series, and the use of multiple related variables requires extrinsic statistical methods.

9. *Multiple regression* is an extrinsic statistical forecasting method, similar to time-series regression in that the intent is to develop a functional relationship between independent and dependent variables, and then extrapolate that relationship to forecast future values, but multiple related variables are used, beyond the simple chronological relationships in a time series. The multiple regression process involves selecting exogenous (outside the system) variables that have a causal connection with the variable under study, and then developing a linear relationship between those variables. Problems arise since some exogenous variables have an apparent rather than an actual relationship with the dependent variable—the length of women's skirts and the price level of common stocks is the example of apparent rather than causal connection that is most often used—and since the use of excessive numbers of exogenous variables, while apparently logical and computationally possible, is likely to offer only a marginal increase in predictive accuracy—the use of n variables can sta-

tistically explain $n - 1$ data points. Finally, of course, the independent variables selected must lead the dependent variable, or else values for all the independent variables must themselves be predicted.

The computational programs for multiple regression are, as with time-series regression, based upon a least-squares methodology. This methodology assumes a linear relationship, or a relationship which can be transformed to obtain a linear relationship through expressing the variables in logarithmic or trigonometric terms. This methodology also assumes that the values of the independent variables used in the forecast do not fall outside the ranges of those variables which were used in empirically fitting the line to the historical data. Finally, the methodology requires that none of the independent variables be controllable by decisions or policies of the organization. Despite these restrictions in the selection of the independent variables and in the application of the least-squares methodology, multiple regression is used extensively to empirically develop functional relationships between variables, and then those relationships are either extrapolated for a direct forecast, or embodied in an econometric model for an indirect forecast.

10. An *econometric model* is a system of simultaneous equations, normally developed through the use of both time-series and multiple regression, that represents the interactions between segments of the economy and areas of corporate activity. The intent of an econometric model is to compute the impact of various economic factors, such as interest rates, labor costs, material supply, consumer income, etc., upon the operations of a company; the advantage of the econometric model is that controllable variables, such as price levels and advertising expenditures, can be included in the system of equations, and forecasts including those controllable variables can be developed indirectly by sensitivity analysis rather than directly by extrapolation. Econometric analysis, in essence, combines statistical models of historical data points, and decision models of corporate policies.

11. *Analytical methods* are explanatory or decision models used to study the relationships between controllable variables and the forecast variable to be predicted. The relationship between advertising expenditures and sales volume is a common illustration of the use of an explanatory model, as is the connection of labor costs to wage rates, employment levels, productivity indexes, and bonus payments. The intent of an analytical decision model is to express the relationship of the controllable inputs to the predictable outputs through explicit mathematical functions that have been developed by logical or empirical methods.

12. *Simulation methods* are also explanatory or decision models used to study the relationships between controllable inputs and predictable outputs, but the mathematical functions are developed through experimentation on a computer-based simulation of the system. The functional relationships between variables are developed through implicit inference in simulation rather than by the explicit deductions of the analytical method.

The 12 forecasting methods differ, obviously, in their techniques, their applications, and their limitations, but they are related, and understanding those relationships makes it much easier to select the optimal method. The chart of the relationships is repeated here for emphasis.

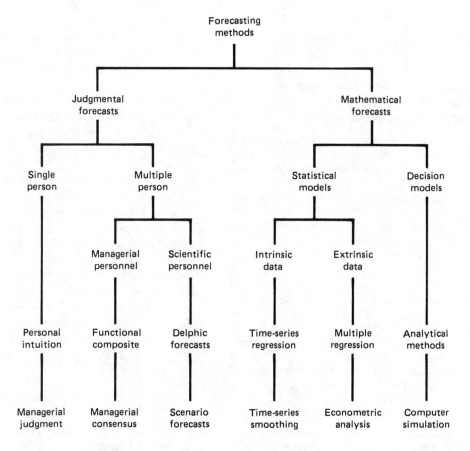

The three cases that follow illustrate the application of these forecasting methods for strategic design, not for operational planning. Operational planning is normally for a shorter time period, 1 to 3 years, and usually is concerned with expected market volume or production costs. Strategic design is for a longer time span, 3 to 10 or even 15 years, and the development of an effective long-term method of competition requires consideration of multiple dimensions in economic, social, political, technological, and competitive characteristics and trends, many of which are awkward to measure, and all of which are difficult to define. Identification, measurement, and prediction are all important for strategic design in a changing environment.

Winnebago Industries, Inc.

Winnebago Industries was founded in 1958 as a small manufacturer of recreational vehicles in Forest City, Iowa. The company grew steadily, although not spectacularly, until 1962, when four new objectives were announced by the president, Mr. John Hansen, at the time of the first public stock issuance.

> Winnebago was a small company in rural Iowa in 1962, with sales of just over $2.5 million. Most people felt that John Hansen's objectives, which he stated that spring, were just part of a personal campaign to obtain publicity and help the sale of stock. He said that he wanted Winnebago to be listed on the New York Stock Exchange, to be included in the Fortune 500, to achieve a billion dollar sales level, and to provide a huge return to the shareholders. He said that he wanted a $1,000 investment in 1962 to become a million dollar ownership in 1972. Most of us thought that he was just being boastful, and not very sophisticated in dealing with the New York financial community; instead, he meant every word. (Statement of an investment analyst)

The company became spectacularly successful after 1962, with compound sales increases that averaged 72% per year, and annual profit growth that was over 83% (Exhibit 1).

This growth in sales and profits was due partially to the aggressive nature of the Winnebago strategy, and partially to the rapid expansion of the recreational vehicle industry (Exhibit 2).

The growth in the recreational vehicle industry has been ascribed to the dramatic increases in individual income and leisure time that occurred during the 1960s, to the changed life-styles that encouraged outdoor camping and travel, and to the improved highway system that facilitated mobility (Exhibit 3).

The functional policies of Winnebago Industries, Inc., were as definite and explicit as the corporate objectives:

1. *Product policies.* Winnebago made travel trailers, camping trailers, and truck campers, but their primary emphasis was

Exhibit 1 *Simplified income statements (000's omitted) for Winnebago Industries, Inc., 1962–1972*

	1962	1964	1966	1968	1970	1972
Company sales	$2,777	$4,817	$8,371	$17,566	$44,961	$133,166
Cost of goods	2,040	3,511	6,382	13,546	35,360	93,394
Gross margin	737	1,306	1,989	4,020	9,601	34,772
Selling expenses	241	372	604	815	2,152	5,772
General and administrative	215	306	406	514	1,123	3,126
Total overhead	456	678	1,010	1,392	3,275	8,898
Pretax profits	281	628	979	2,691	6,326	25,874
Income taxes	132	302	469	1,306	3,120	12,277
After-tax profits	149	326	510	1,385	3,206	13,597

Source: Moody's Industrial Manual for the respective years.

Exhibit 2 *Sales of recreational vehicles in units (000's omitted) and in dollar volume 1962–1972*

	1962	1964	1966	1968	1970	1972
Travel trailers	38.8	58.2	85.6	114.5	139.1	253.4
Motor homes	0.7	2.8	5.6	13.3	31.8	111.6
Truck campers	16.2	33.5	52.7	78.3	94.8	104.5
Camping trailers	24.0	49.6	73.5	108.2	116.0	110.4
Dollar volume (millions)	$112.0	$199.5	$269.7	$790.2	$1,147.8	$2,428.6

Source: Industry report by investment analyst.

upon motor homes, which were the most expensive types of recreational vehicle. The intention of the company was to provide good design (external appearance and internal space) and high quality at low cost through standardized models and high-volume production.

2. *Marketing policies.* Winnebago price levels were set below the typical industry markups to offer customers more value than was available from competitors. Distribution was through a limited number of full-line, exclusive dealers who were well financed, and required to provide indoor showrooms, sales inventories, and service facilities.

3. *Production policies.* Winnebago concentrated all production at one large plant (most competitors operated geographically dispersed plants that were considerably smaller in order to save on delivery costs),

and emphasized product standardization, volume production (line concept), and backward integration (both aluminum extruding and plastic forming were performed at Forest City).

4. *Financial policies.* Winnebago financed the rapid growth with retained earnings (no dividends were paid) and very limited debt (in 1972 only $415,000 of long-term debt was outstanding, and no short-term bank loans were shown on the balance sheet).

5. *Diversification policies.* Winnebago had considered diversification into modular housing and mobile homes prior to 1972, but had made no investments nor commitments toward different products or additional markets.

The financial results (annual sales growth of 72% and annual profit increases of 83%) of

Exhibit 3 *Indices or changes in personal compensation, recreational expenditure, and highway construction, 1962–1972*

	1962	1964	1966	1968	1970	1972
Average weekly earnings in manufacturing	$ 85.6	$ 98.2	$114.3	$122.5	$133.0	$154.7
Total compensation of employees (billions)	282.6	341.6	393.8	566.0	603.9	707.1
Total expenditures for recreation (billions)	20.4	24.5	28.8	33.6	40.6	40.1
Federal funds for highway construction (billions)	2.3	4.8	4.1	3.1	3.5	3.6

Source: Statistical Abstract of the United States for the respective years.

the Winnebago strategy (long-term method of competition of the firm, or the mixture of corporate objectives and functional policies) have already been described. In 1972 it was planned to continue the aggressive and expansionistic strategy of the company until the sales level reached $1 billion.

Winnebago in 1972 had accomplished all of John Hansen's objectives, except one. It was listed on the New York Stock Exchange; it was included in the Fortune 500 (500 largest firms in the United States); and a $1,000 investment in 1962 was worth over $1 million in 1972. (A 100-share purchase for $1,250 in January 1962 represented 32,000 shares through stock splits and stock dividends in December 1972; with a stock price of $49.50, the total market value was $1,584,000.) They had not reached the $1 billion sales level, but Mr. Hansen said at the 1972 annual meeting that they expected to double their sales, and their earnings, every two years for the next ten years. I was at a security analysts meeting early the next year when John Hansen, Jr., the son of the founder and the president of the company, was asked if he believed the forecast of his father on sales growth. His reply was, "I think that we can do even better." (Statement of an investment analyst)

Class Assignment. Sales of recreational vehicles began to slow markedly in the winter of 1973, and the sales and profits of Winnebago Industries began a dramatic decline. By the end of 1973, the common stock of the company was selling at $1⅝ per share, so that the $1,000 investment in 1962 had now become worth $51,200. Put yourself in the place of the director of long-range planning for Winnebago Industries during the period 1970–1972; list 10 environmental characteristics and trends that you should have been monitoring, and develop a forecasting procedure for each of those trends.

The Future of the Brokerage Industry

The brokerage or investment banking industry (the two terms will be used synonymously in this report, even though to many people "brokerage" refers primarily to the trading of existing securities among retail customers, while "investment banking" concerns the valuation and distribution of new securities for corporate clients) underwent major changes in the early 1970s, and those changes seemed to be accelerating toward the end of that decade. Technical, social, political, economic, and competitive factors all appeared to be driving the industry toward a future that was inherently uncertain, but substantially different from the period of stable and profitable growth that had extended from the end of World War II, in 1945, to the dramatic break in the market in 1968. The purpose of this case is to describe the industry in 1978, the major changes that have occurred since 1968, and the apparent trends that may affect the structure of the industry and the conditions of competition over the next 10 years. Students are asked to forecast the impact of these trends upon the industry, and to recommend changes in the strategies of the participants.

The brokerage industry in 1978 was relatively large, with revenues of $8.8 billion; slowly growing, with an increase of revenues of 103.2% since 1968 (compared to an increase in the consumer price index of 95.9% over the same time period); marginally profitable, with a return of 3.7% on sales, 0.6% on capital, and 7.7% on equity; economically decentralized, with nearly 500 separate firms; functionally specialized, with an established division of activities among those firms; geographically concentrated with most of the operations in New York City, near Wall Street; and allegedly noncompetitive, with substantial barriers to entry and internal determinations of price.

For over 100 years, the securities industry was the only legally licensed cartel within the United States. Stocks and bonds of companies listed on the New York Stock Exchange—and those companies represented nearly 100% of the major industrial, commercial, and financial institutions within the country—could only be traded on the floor of that exchange by members of that exchange at rates set by that exchange. It was a tight little island of monopoly in a sea of competition, and the inhabitants of that island made, and only occasionally lost, very substantial personal fortunes. The first cracks in the dyke began to appear in 1968, when a few of the member firms had to declare bankruptcy because of operational problems, but now all of the barriers appear to be coming down, and many of the older firms are being swamped, and either merging or disappearing from the scene. My original thought was that it could not happen to a better bunch of people; for years they had operated as if they had a special, and often inherited right to extract a toll on all of the investments made by all of the other people within the country. But they did provide an orderly market, with liquidity for the investors and flexibility in raising funds for the corporations. I am afraid that we may lose both the liquidity and the flexibility in the future. (Statement of a brokerage industry executive)

For most of its existence, Wall Street has enjoyed a degree of insulation from outside competition almost unparalleled in American business. Although Street firms, of course, competed against one another, often vigorously, the struggle was tempered by elaborate rules of conduct and behavior engendered by the close physical proximity of the major firms, extensive family and social ties, broad reciprocal associations and collaborative endeavors such as underwriting syndicates, and the tight exclusivities embodied in the NYSE's rules. These relationships permitted the Street not only to punish any firm whose competitive aspirations became too disruptive, but also to keep unfriendly outsiders from infringing upon the presumed inalienable rights possessed by the Street to profits derived from operation of the nation's central marketplace. (*Institutional Investor,* September 1972, p. 34)

To understand the changes within the brokerage industry, the effects of which have been to dramatically increase internal competition and substantially remove the external barriers, it is necessary to understand firstly the operations of the brokerage firms, particularly in reference to their principal sources of income and major items of expense. These companies have seven different sources of income:

1. *Commission payments on the trading of securities.* Financial securities are primarily stocks and bonds, or legal evidences of ownership or debt, that may be traded on one of the two national exchanges (New York Stock Exchange and American Stock Exchange), on the various regional exchanges (Boston, Philadelphia, San Francisco, etc.), or through the over-the-counter market. There are exceptions to this rule, of course, but stocks and bonds of the larger companies are generally listed on the New York Stock Exchange, medium-sized companies on the American Stock Exchange, and smaller firms on the

over-the-counter market. Regional exchanges tend to list some of the same large and medium-sized companies that are on the national exchanges, and they offer simplified execution of orders and some cost savings for local brokerage firms, but trading on a regional basis is not extensive. In 1978, 80.3% of all trading (on a unit basis) was on the New York Stock Exchange, 10.5% on the American Stock Exchange, and only 9.2% on the regional and over-the-counter markets. The over-the-counter market is a historical term that refers to the non-Exchange sale or purchase of unlisted stocks or bonds, now generally by telegraphic requests for quotations sent to specialist brokerage firms.

Prices for the securities, whether listed on one of the formal exchanges or traded on the informal over-the-counter market, are set by a bidding procedure that does relate supply and demand, and does reflect changes in company performance, economic outlook, and investor confidence. Customers vary from middle-income individuals purchasing odd lots (less than 100 shares) to wealthy persons buying and selling in lots up to 1,000 shares, and institutions trading in blocks of 10,000 shares and more. The largest block transaction on the New York Stock Exchange in 1978 was 1,874,300 shares of the common stock of Cutler Hammer, Inc., valued at $103,086,500, but there were 10 other block trades involving more than 700,000 shares. The commissions on these trades, until 1975, varied with the number of shares in each purchase or sale, but the rates were set by the rules of the stock exchange or by an agreement among participants in the over-the-counter market. The rates were not low; in 1978 brokerage firms that traded on the New York Stock Exchange earned $3.78 billion in commissions on the combined purchases and sales of both retail and institutional customers of $199.9 billion.

2. *Capital gains on the trading of securities.* In addition to the commissions earned through executing buy and sell orders for retail and institutional customers, brokerage firms can trade in securities for their own accounts. This is partially done by firms acting as "specialists" on the trading floor of the exchange; the function of the specialist is to maintain an inventory of the assigned securities (generally one firm will specialize in the securities of approximately 10 companies), and to establish the price reflecting the relative supply and demand at any given time. Other brokerage firms wishing to buy or sell a specific security notify the specialist and offer a bid for the purchase or sale. In the event that it is not possible to match buy and sell orders, specialists are expected to buy or sell from their inventories to ensure an "orderly" market with gradual price changes rather than sudden price jumps or falls. The possible conflict of interest between the maintenance of an orderly price and the continuation of profitable operations for the specialist brokerage firm has been noted many times.

Nonspecialist brokerage firms also buy and sell securities for their own accounts, purchasing securities they believe will increase in price and selling those they believe will fall. It has been claimed that as much as 30% of the total volume of the New York Stock Exchange represents trading by brokerage firms for their own interests, and not the interests of their customers, although this is difficult to verify since much of the trading for customers is done in "street" names, or the name of the brokerage firm, to simplify bookkeeping and, perhaps, maintain secrecy. The possible conflict of interest for a brokerage firm between buying and selling securities for its own account, or for the accounts of favored street customers, and executing trades for retail clients, after advising them on those trades, has also been frequently noted.

The monetary amounts and share volumes represented by brokerage firms trading for their own accounts are not small. In 1978, it was reported that firms acting as specialists purchased 835.8 million shares and sold 875.6 million, while nonspecialists purchased 889.3 million and sold 934.6 million, all for their own accounts. Profits in this trading for all members of the New York Stock Exchange were reported at $1.54 billion.

3. *Interest on the debt of retail clients.* Retail customers are permitted to purchase securities "on margin." The margin refers to the percentage of the value of the securities that must be paid in cash (currently 65%); the balance is, in essence, borrowed from the brokerage firm. The percentage that may be borrowed is set, for the initial transaction, by the regulations of the Federal Reserve Board, while the continuing minimum figure is controlled by the rules of the New York Stock Exchange. The amounts that are borrowed are substantial: at the end of 1978 margin debt was $10.8 billion, while the purchased securities, which serve as collateral for the debt, were valued at $27.8 billion. Interest charged to the margin customers on that debt, again in 1978, amounted to $1.17 billion.

4. *Fees for the underwriting of newly issued securities.* "Underwriting" refers specifically to the guaranteeing of the full payment for new securities, issued by either business corporations or governmental units, and sold to both retail customers and financial institutions. An underwriter technically establishes a price for a new security, and pays that price to the issuer, minus commissions and fees, whether or not the new issue can be sold; however, the underwriting term has come to mean the entire process of designing the form (common stock, preferred stock, corporate bonds, convertible debentures, etc.) and terms (dividend yields, interest rates, repayment provisions, restrictive covenants, etc.) of the security, registering the issue with federal and state agencies, setting the price for the offering, arranging the syndicate for the distribution, advertising the availability of the stocks or bonds, and supervising the retail sale or private placement. In essence, an underwriter now serves as a financial consultant to the issuing company, state, or municipality, and provides advisory and supervisory service based upon his or her financial acumen and professional competence.

The underwriting function has traditionally been performed by established brokerage firms, generally based in New York City, and often with long-term relationships among the issuing companies and agencies, and an acknowledged reputation for performance with the distributing brokers and banks. Not many brokerage firms qualify as underwriters, and in 1977 ten firms dominated the new issue segment of the security industry, underwriting $25.52 billion of the $48.9 billion in new corporate equities and bonds that were distributed that year (Exhibit 1). Much of the balance of $23.4 billion represented direct offerings from the company or agency to existing security holders, or private placements from the company or agency to trust departments, mutual funds, or insurance companies, or sealed bids to the company or agency from regional brokerage firms and (for state or municipal securities only) commercial banks.

Fees on underwriting vary widely, de-

Exhibit 1 *Underwriting volume, total revenues, equity capital (000's omitted), and brokerage offices of major underwriting firms, 1977*

	Underwriting volume	Total revenues	Equity capital	Brokerage offices	Brokerage employees
Morgan Stanley	$5,240,000	$ 82,361	$ 57,700	6	1,100
Merrill Lynch	3,730,000	636,566	645,867	365	22,539
Salomon Brothers	3,540,000	92,802	161,950	11	1,431
Goldman Sachs	2,760,000	122,250	96,600	14	1,615
First Boston	2,700,000	73,427	84,164	18	1,187
Blyth East. Dillon	2,330,000	104,737	52,943	43	2,945
Lehman Brothers	1,600,000	112,671	49,100	10	1,554
Dean Witter	1,270,000	286,945	151,034	223	8,640
Kidder, Peabody	1,190,000	120,000	67,213	50	2,500
Bache Halsey Stuart	1,160,000	189,391	121,439	166	6,298

Source: Fortune, February 27, 1978, p. 90, for underwriting volume, and *Fortune,* May 22, 1978, p. 61, for balance.

pending upon the size of the issue, the state of the market, the reputation of the issuing firm, etc. Underwriting fees are usually expressed as the "spread" or the difference between the price guaranteed to the issuing corporation or agency and the price proposed to the retail or institutional investor. A spread of 2½% is not uncommon; 20% of the spread is usually reserved for the underwriting firm, with the balance allocated among the distributing syndicate in proportion to the actual sales. Many underwriters, for obvious reasons, plan to distribute a substantial portion of the new issues. Total fees paid to brokerage firms in 1978 for the underwriting and distribution of new issues amounted to $777 million.

5. *Sales of mutual funds to retail customers.* Many mutual funds are distributed through brokerage firms, and the managers of the funds pay a commission to those firms for sales to retail customers. This commission is normally higher than that earned for an equivalent dollar volume sale of listed stocks and bonds, in order to encourage placement of the funds. Despite the higher commission, sales of mutual funds have not been an important activity recently of brokerage firms, and the total income in 1978 amounted to only $59 million.

6. *Sales of futures contracts on commodities to retail customers.* A futures contract on a commodity is a commitment to either deliver or receive a specified amount of an agricultural commodity, such as wheat, soybeans, or orange juice, at a given date in the future. Swings in the price of the commodity over the term of the contract provide the possibility of a gain or loss to the purchaser, and the margin terms permitted by the commodity exchanges, much more liberal than those allowed by the national or regional stock exchanges, mean that the purchaser can leverage that gain or loss. Until 1972, most futures contracts were traded on the Chicago Commercial Exchange, and were purchased or sold only through members of the Chicago Board of Trade; by 1975 some brokerage firms were beginning to offer futures contracts to their retail customers, and in 1978 the revenues to brokerage firms for the trading of these commodity contracts was $351 million.

7. *Miscellaneous income.* The last classification

of income to brokerage firms includes such items as fees for investment advice and counsel, charges for custodial protection and service, and dividends and interest on brokerage firm investments. Miscellaneous income received by brokerage firms in 1978 amounted to $1.18 billion.

As stated previously, it is necessary to understand the operations of firms within the brokerage industry in order to forecast the final form and impact of changes taking place within that industry. The previous section explained the principal sources of income for brokerage firms, both partnerships and corporations; the next section will describe the major items of expense.

1. *Commissions paid to registered representatives.* "Registered representative" is the term used in the brokerage industry for sales personnel, who represent each firm in dealings with both retail customers and institutional clients, and who are registered with the New York Stock Exchange after having passed a series of courses and a professional examination on investment methods, terms, and policies. Nearly all of the registered representatives are paid through a straight commission, or by a minimum salary plus a commission on trades. Many representatives of the brokerage firms have been able to establish a long-term relationship with their customers, both retail and institutional, and consequently earn a high annual income based upon commissions from the trading of those customers. The potential for conflict of interest between the professional responsibility to advise a client on optimal investments and the practical need to achieve volume has often been noted. In 1978, the brokerage industry employed 42,056 registered representatives, and those people received salaries and commissions amounting to $1.62 billion, for an average income of

$38,520; the distribution about this mean for registered representatives is quite wide, and some members of this group earn over $250,000 per year.

2. *Commissions paid to nonsales personnel.* The brokerage industry has traditionally operated with an emphasis upon variable rather than fixed costs. Salaries and wages are usually low for clerical and administrative personnel, particularly in comparison to the other industries such as insurance and banking and the other institutions such as governmental units and social agencies that are normally located in the downtown sections of large metropolitan areas. Brokerage firm employees, however, usually receive a year-end bonus, provided that their firm has been profitable, of 25 to 40% of their annual income. Commissions and bonuses paid to the 102,250 nonsales personnel in the brokerage industry in 1978 amounted to $624 million, for an average payment of $6,000.

3. *Salaries and wages for clerical and administrative personnel.* The need for precise and accurate records at a brokerage house is obvious; each transaction must be recorded with numbers and prices of the securities, date of receipt or transfer, and the order for sale or purchase, and the basic journal entries have to be detailed in subsidiary ledgers by customer, by security, and by the selling or buying firm. The physical problems in counting, transferring, and safeguarding securities are also substantial. In addition, clerical and administrative persons are needed for customer correspondence, computer operations, research investigations, and interoffice communications. In 1978, salaries and wages paid to the 102,250 nonsales personnel (mostly clerical and administration since salaries and wages for the partners and officers are listed in the miscellaneous category) amounted to

$1.75 billion, for an average income of $17,170.

4. *Communication expenses.* The brokerage industry has an obvious need for prompt communication between the trading floors of the national and regional exchanges and the offices of the brokerage firms, both in New York City and other financial centers, and in local communities. Originally, this communication was based upon the telegraph system and local brokerage houses, outside the major financial centers, were termed "wire" houses; the term is still used in reference to firms that are part of a syndicate to distribute rather than underwrite new securities. The stock recorder, or "ticker," was invented in 1887 to record telegraphed stock transactions on paper tape; it was one of the first electromechanical machines, but it was slow and often ran hours behind actual trading on the busier days. The current communication is electronic, based upon the telephone system, and will instantaneously record the current price and trading volume of any security listed on the New York or American stock exchanges. The system is not inexpensive; $582 million was paid in 1978 for communication services.

5. *Occupancy expenses.* Brokerage firms are normally headquartered in the financial sections of large metropolitan areas; rental charges are expensive. Brokerage firms have also traditionally been furnished in luxurious fashion; decorating costs are high. In 1978, the brokerage industry paid $379 million for occupancy and furnishings.

6. *Promotional expenses.* Advertising expenditures have seldom been large in the brokerage industry, except for some of the retail-oriented firms such as Merrill Lynch ("Bullish on America"), E. F. Hutton ("When E. F. Hutton talks, people listen"), and Dean Witter ("You look like you just heard from Dean Wit-

ter"). Institutionally oriented firms confine their advertising to "tombstone" ads placed in financial journals that discretely list the firms participating in large public offerings or private placements. Brokerage industry expenditures for promotion in 1978 were $187 million.

7. *Interest expenses.* Brokerage firms have traditionally been heavily leveraged, and financed primarily with borrowed funds. The original partners in most of the firms were wealthy individuals, but they did not wish their private fortunes tied totally to swings of the stock market, and consequently they borrowed much of the money needed for operations. Debt-to-capital ratios for brokerage firms are far above those that would be tolerated at nonfinancial institutions. A 15:1 debt/equity ratio is permitted by the rules of the New York Stock Exchange; 11.2:1 was the debt/equity ratio of the industry in 1978 (Exhibit 2).

The balance sheet item "receivable from customers and partners" partially indicates current amounts due (within a five-day settlement period) on the purchase of securities for cash, but primarily represents loans to individuals who have purchased securities on margin. The "long position in securities" item consists of stocks and bonds held essentially in inventory for trading as a specialist on the exchange or for the benefit of the firm, and of stocks and bonds purchased for delivery at a latter day; the firm obviously expects "long" securities to rise in price. The converse liability item "short position in securities" represents stocks and bonds held in inventory that have been sold for delivery at a later date; the firm expects "short" securities to fall in price.

The primary source of financing for the brokerage industry is, as indicated above, loans from commercial banks and insurance companies, representing $25.7 bil-

Exhibit 2 *Assets, liabilities, and capital (000,000's omitted) of brokerage firms belonging to the New York Stock Exchange, 1978*

Deposits with banks	$ 984	Loans from banks	$25,766
Received from brokers and dealers	5,109	Payments to brokers and dealers	4,676
Received from customers and partners	16,070	Payments to customers and partners	7,321
Long positions in securities	29,410	Short positions in securities	6,610
Secured demand notes	248	Accrued expenses and accts. payable	5,139
Exchange memberships	108	Total liabilities	49,512
Real estate and fixed assets	306		
Miscellaneous assets	1,667	Capital and retained earnings	4,390
Total assets	$53,902	Total liabilities and capital	$53,902

Source: New York Stock Exchange Fact Book, 1979, p. 57.

lion of the total $53.9 billion in liabilities and capital. Interest payments on these loans in 1978 totaled $1.7 billion.

8. *Data processing expenses.* As described in the section on clerical and administrative salaries and wages, the brokerage industry is data-intensive. Rental contracts for computer equipment and time-sharing arrangements for computer services in 1978 cost the industry $98 million.

9. *Bad debt and transaction error expenses.* Nonpayment by customers for security purchases and improper handling by the brokerage firm of security trades (the firm is responsible for buying or selling the improper securities or the wrong amounts, if corrected by the customer within three days) cost the brokerage industry $84 million in 1978.

10. *Miscellaneous expenses.* Miscellaneous expenses include license fees, exchange assessments, professional dues, charitable contributions, and officers/partners compensation. Miscellaneous expenses in 1978 were $1.11 billion.

The relative importance of many of these classes of income and items of expense for the brokerage industry has changed over the past 18 years, as shown in Exhibit 3.

The trend in profitability of the brokerage industry has been constantly down over the past 20 years, with a decline in the average

return on revenues from 11.6% in 1960 to 3.7% in 1978, and a change in the return on assets from 2.2% to 0.6% over the same time period. The return on equity did not change so drastically, but only as the obvious consequence of an expansion in debt leverage and financial risk. There have been numerous studies of these changing industry characteristics, and an equally large number of explanations, but in general the adverse trends were thought to be the result of six interrelated factors:

1. *Expansion of the brokerage industry.* The overall size of the brokerage industry, as measured by the daily trading volume on the New York Stock Exchange and the number of representatives employed by member firms of that exchange, expanded rapidly in the early 1960s. Specifically, the trading volume went from 3.0 million shares per day in 1960 to 12.9 million in 1968, and the number of registered representatives from 27.8 thousand to 49.6 thousand. Nonsales personnel expanded even more rapidly, from 44.0 thousand in 1960 to 112.5 thousand in 1968. These changes occurred within the existing structure of the industry; few new firms were formed (Exhibit 4).

2. *Automation of the brokerage industry.* The growth in trading volume from 1960 to 1968 created more problems than opportu-

Exhibit 3 *Income and expense accounts (percent) for the brokerage industry, 1960–1978*

	1960	1965	1970	1975	1978
Commissions earned on trading securities	58.6	60.9	52.9	49.7	42.8
Capital gains on trading securities	10.2	7.3	14.3	15.4	17.5
Interest received on customer debts	10.9	11.4	9.6	7.7	13.3
Fees for underwriting new securities	8.5	7.3	12.0	13.2	8.4
Fees for selling mutual funds	2.4	2.9	2.0	0.6	0.7
Commissions earned on future contracts	inc.	inc.	1.2	3.0	4.0
Miscellaneous income	9.4	10.2	8.0	10.4	13.3
Total income in percentages	100.0	100.0	100.0	100.0	100.0
Total income (millions)	$1,047	$2,319	$3,935	$5,927	$8,832
Commissions paid to registered reps.	26.0	22.5	18.5	20.7	19.9
Commissions paid to nonsales personnel	inc.	inc.	9.0	9.8	7.6
Clerical and administrative expenses	28.4	26.3	29.1	23.1	21.6
Communication expenses	10.2	9.8	9.9	8.2	7.1
Occupancy expenses	6.3	6.8	9.1	6.5	4.6
Promotional expenses	3.7	3.7	3.6	3.0	2.3
Interest expenses	9.6	12.4	12.1	9.9	20.9
Data processing expenses	inc.	inc.	inc.	1.5	1.2
Bad debt and error expenses	inc.	inc.	inc.	1.2	1.0
Miscellaneous expenses	15.8	18.5	8.7	15.1	13.8
Total expenses in percentages	100.0	100.0	100.0	100.0	100.0
Total expenses (millions)	$794	$1,803	$3,344	$5,116	$8,148
Profit before taxes and partners distribution	$253	$516	$615	$811	$684
Federal and states taxes (estimated)	131	268	319	421	345
Profit available to partners	122	248	496	390	339
Profit as % of total revenues	11.6	10.7	7.5	6.5	3.7
Profit as % of total assets (estimated)	2.2	1.9	1.3	1.0	0.6
Profit as % of total equity	16.3	13.7	8.5	9.9	7.7

Source: New York Stock Exchange Fact Book for the respective years.

nities for member firms in the brokerage industry. They had not anticipated the tremendous expansion that occurred, and they were totally unprepared for it. The trading procedures, oriented around stock specialists on the floor of the exchange, could adapt to the increased volume, but the settlement system, which relied upon manual processing in the "back offices" of the brokerage firms, was hopelessly out-moded. Forty separate clerical operations were required to count, record, verify, and transmit the stock certificates associated with each sale, and another 28 operations were needed to record, invoice, and receive the payments associated with each purchase. Sixty-eight clerical operations were needed to complete each trade. The increase in volume from 3.8 million shares in 1962 to 4.8 million in 1964 (approximately

Exhibit 4   *Average daily trading volume on the New York Stock Exchange and other indices of change in the brokerage industry, 1950–1978*

	Average daily volume (1,000 shares)	NYSE Index (1965 = 50) year end	Median div. yield at year end (%)	Median P/E ratio at year end	Number of member firms	Number of registered reps.
1950	1,980	12.01	6.7	n.a.	620	11,409
1955	2,578	23.71	4.6	n.a.	642	17,829
1960	3,042	30.94	4.2	19.1	667	27,896
1961	4,085	38.39	3.3	22.9	681	30,628
1962	3,818	33.81	3.8	17.9	672	31,435
1963	4,567	39.92	3.6	18.5	670	31,941
1964	4,888	45.65	3.3	18.8	656	32,921
1965	6,176	50.00	3.2	18.1	651	33,805
1966	7,538	43.72	4.1	13.6	649	38,514
1967	10,080	53.88	3.2	16.8	647	42,423
1968	12,971	58.90	2.6	16.3	646	49,644
1969	11,403	51.53	3.6	14.0	622	52,466
1970	11,564	50.23	3.7	16.4	572	50,787
1971	15,381	56.43	3.2	16.2	577	52,635
1972	16,487	64.48	3.0	15.2	558	39,970
1973	16,084	51.82	5.0	9.9	523	36,310
1974	13,904	36.13	7.5	6.2	508	33,399
1975	18,551	47.61	5.0	11.3	494	35,682
1976	21,186	57.08	4.0	10.4	481	36,467
1977	20,928	52.50	4.5	9.3	473	39,034
1978	28,591	53.62	4.8	8.5	498	42,050

Source: New York Stock Exchange Fact Book for the respective years.

19,200 trades per day, with an average of 250 shares per trade) caused extensive overtime for the employees and disruption in the back offices, but volume had never increased on the New York Stock Exchange for more than three years in a row since the founding of the Exchange in 1792, and a slackening in the pace, a "breathing spell," was confidentially expected in 1965. A report prepared that year by a consultant to the New York Stock Exchange entitled "The Exchange Community in 1975: A Report on Its Po-tential, Problems and Prospects" warned that trading days with 7.5 million shares might occur at the end of the coming 10-year period, and suggested that member firms begin to plan for that eventuality, but no one expected that precise volume to be reached in two years, and certainly no one expected the 12.9 million shares per day average of 1968. The unanticipated volume created chaos. Losses in the error accounts of member firms (payments to customers for errors in trading) went from a nominal $8.7 million in 1964 to $107.7

million in 1968. Fails to deliver (failure of a brokerage firm to deliver securities purchased by another brokerage firm within the 5-day settlement period) were a random occurrence and minimal problem prior to 1965; in December 1968 the total value of undelivered securities was $4.1 billion. Aged fails to delivery (failure of a brokerage firm to deliver securities purchased by another brokerage firm for more than 30 days) were $620 million. Failures to deliver securities to retail and institutional customers were so common that they were not even recorded. Seventy-five brokerage firms were forced out of business by the financial problems associated with the losses of securities, and the operational problems caused by the unprecedented volume.

Prior to 1968, many of the brokerage firms were Dickensian in their back office operations. Elderly clerks worked at high walnut desks, meticulously recording each transaction in ink. If an error were made, the entire page had to be transcribed; no erasures were tolerated. Near the front of each back office was a small waiting room and a "cage," a cashier's office with a polished brass screen. Uniformed messengers sat on a bench, waiting to be called by the senior clerk to deliver securities to other firms on Wall Street. The securities and papers for each trade were held together with a pin, not with a paper clip or staple, since pins were traditional on the Street. Some of the more prestigious firms had pins with their initials engraved upon the head.

Into this gentle, Victorian world of elderly clerks, oiled walnut, polished brass, uniformed messengers, and engraved pins came trading days that simply swamped the system. Doubtless the people tried hard, but they were unable to keep up. A "fail to deliver" is a set of securities that is lost under the paperwork; an "aged fail to deliver" is a set of securities that is lost, period. Francis I. DuPont and Company, one of the firms that would have gone through bankruptcy if it had

not been purchased by private investors, tried to solve their back office problem by bringing in 700 new people and operating three shifts. But you don't solve problems by bringing in hundreds of untrained workers; you create them. DuPont had aged fails to deliver worth over $29.8 million, and their total equity was less than half of that amount. Theft became a problem for the first time, and it was not just with the new people. You have to realize that the registered reps (salespeople) were working just four hours a day (the trading hours on the New York Stock Exchange had been shortened) and were being paid at their old commission rates on the new volume; they were making a fortune. The clerks were working 12 to 15 hours a day, and were being paid at their old wage rates, without overtime. It was very inequitable, and very shortsighted. The result was a loss of morale, some theft, extensive errors, and eventual bankruptcy. (Statement of a brokerage industry executive)

Brokerage firms invested an estimated $200 million for computer equipment and data-processing systems to first supplement, and then replace, the earlier manual procedures. Automation, together with the technically proficient people required to run the new systems, and the improved physical facilities needed to house them, essentially changed the brokerage industry from a variable-cost to a fixed-cost basis.

The Street also began to spend hugely, and belatedly, on automation, with many firms undertaking crash programs to switch from manual to automated processing of their records. The Exchange later estimated that in both 1968 and 1969 its members spent $100 million on automation. Meanwhile, both growth in personnel and visions of the future were sending firms in search of new office space. It was available only on highly expensive long-term leases, but the firms signed.

While all this prodigious and often haphazard buildup of people, offices, and costs was going on, the industry had become engulfed in its now-celebrated "back-office" crisis. The exchanges shortened trading hours and the Big Board began to impose "restrictions" on the firms whose problems were deepest (e.g., forbidding them to hire new salesmen or to advertise). Later some of these same firms, among them Hayden, Stone and McDonnel, were to turn up as casualties.

Into this picture of spirited expansion and back-office disintegration came 1969, the beginning of the bear market and the first year of declining volume. The decline was not large; on the Big Board, for example, trading was eventually down only 3% for the year. But the Street had by this time stopped dreaming, much less thinking, of cycles, and it was no longer prepared for declines of any kind. . . .

At Hayden, Stone, which went from a pre-tax profit of over $7 million in 1967 to a loss of nearly $11 million in 1969, a former officer says there was only one executive who, at a relatively early date, sensed the real peril of the situation. That was the treasurer, Walter Isaacson, and in mid-1969 he would spread out his charts at every directors' meeting and make, with variations, the same speech: "Look, fellows, revenues are going down like this and costs are going up like this, and we have got to cut back now or be in real trouble." Nobody wanted to believe him. Finally, Isaacson got to be such a nuisance that Hayden, Stone did what any red-blooded management would do: it fired him.

When 1970 arrived, costs therefore had not really been chopped down to any substantial degree, and in certain major particulars were still rising. Notably, some of the new office space that had been contracted for was becoming available, and many firms were forced to absorb much higher occupancy costs. . . .

To these still severe cost problems were then added major declines in both revenues and capital. Revenues went down because trading volume fell sharply on the American Stock Exchange (down 32% for the first 10 months of 1970) and in the over-the-counter market (down an estimated 40%). Lower stock prices also reduced revenues; more commission money comes in on a 100-share trade of a $40 stock than on a comparable trade of a $30 stock, and this year (1970) there were simply more $30 stocks around. (*Fortune,* December 1970, p. 64)

3. *Institutionalization of the brokerage industry.* Prior to the early 1950s, trustees for charitable foundations and educational endowments, and managers of insurance companies, trust funds, and savings banks, invested primarily in bonds due to the security of the principal in these fixed income securities. The "prudent man" concept of investment management essentially held that a person could not be faulted, or sued, if that person acted in a fiduciary capacity to maintain the principal of the entrusted funds and the income of the endowed individuals or institutions. Maintenance of principal and income meant bonds and preferred stocks, and generally only a small percentage of the monies were invested in common stocks. However, the very great increase in common stock prices during the 1950s and 1960s brought much greater interest in equity investments. The New York Stock Exchange Index (a composite of all stock prices on the Exchange that measures changes relative to the starting date of December 31, 1965, when the Index was set equal to 50.00) grew from 12.01 in 1950 to 23.71 in 1955, to 30.94 in 1960, and finally to 50.00 in 1965. This fourfold increase in common stock prices convinced many fiduciary managers and trustees to switch larger and larger portions of the funds under their control to common stocks. The holdings of New York Stock Exchange listed stocks by financial institutions grew from $11.1 billion in 1950 to $230.5 billion in 1975 (Exhibit 5).

Financial institutions in 1975 held 33.6% of the total number of shares for all companies listed on the New York Stock Exchange. In addition, since professional investors tend to change stock positions, selling one issue and purchasing another,

Exhibit 5 *Estimated holdings of NYSE-listed stocks by institutional investors, 1950–1975 (000,000's omitted)*

	1950	1955	1960	1965	1970	1975
Life insurance companies	$ 1,100	$ 2,300	$ 3,600	$ 6,300	$ 10,900	$ 21,900
Property and casualty insurance	1,700	4,500	6,000	10,100	12,200	11,300
Open-end mutual funds	1,400	7,100	12,400	29,100	39,400	35,200
Closed-end mutual funds	1,600	4,000	4,200	5,600	5,900	5,400
Corporate pension funds	500	5,300	12,600	35,900	54,700	82,200
Government pension funds	—	—	—	1,400	5,000	22,800
Charitable foundations	2,500	4,100	5,300	16,400	14,100	22,100
Educational endowments	1,100	2,400	2,900	5,900	7,100	7,200
Nonprofit institutions	1,000	3,100	4,400	7,700	9,000	8,700
Common trust funds	—	1,000	1,400	3,200	4,200	6,100
Mutual savings banks	200	200	200	500	900	2,300
Foreign institutions	—	—	—	—	—	5,100
Total holdings	11,100	34,000	53,000	122,100	161,900	230,500
Institutional holdings as percentage of value of all listed common stocks	14.5%	15.5%	17.3%	22.7%	25.4%	33.6%

Source: New York Stock Exchange Fact Book, for 1963, 1971, and 1978.

more frequently than do private individuals, those same financial institutions accounted for 44.5% of all trading on the Exchange. Finally, the institutions have large portfolios, with numerous shares in each holding, and consequently they normally trade in blocks (over 10,000 shares). In 1965 only 9 blocks were traded daily on the Exchange; in 1975 the average was 188 blocks per day, and in 1978 the average had grown to 298 (Exhibit 6).

The dominance of financial institutions in common stock holdings was well known, and well documented; less well known, however, was the impact of those holdings upon trading procedures, brokerage operations, and security prices. Each of those factors was expected to have a direct influence on the development of the brokerage industry in the 1980s.

Of all the areas of growth, however, the most significant for the future structure, operations, and regulation of the (brokerage) industry has

Exhibit 6 *Sources of New York Stock Exchange volume in shares (percent) and the number of block (over-10,000-share) trades on the Exchange*

	1960	1965	1970	1975	1978
NYSE members	23.1	24.3	24.2	22.3	n.a.
Private investors	52.6	43.2	34.4	33.2	n.a.
Financial institutions	24.3	32.5	42.4	44.5	n.a.
Total trading	100.0	100.0	100.0	100.0	
Block trades per day	n.a.	9	68	188	298

Source: New York Stock Exchange Fact Book, for 1971 and 1978.

undoubtedly been the increase in the absolute and relative importance of investment in common stocks by financial institutions. (Securities Industry Study, Report of the Committee on Banking, Housing and Urban Affairs, United States Senate, February 4, 1972, p. 37)

One of the primary impacts of the financial institutions upon the brokerage industry has been the tendency for large block trades (a block is defined as over 10,000 shares; a large block is more than 50,000 shares) to be made on the "third market," off the floor of the exchange. Specialists on the exchange normally operate by matching purchase and sale orders, using their own capital, when needed, to purchase unwanted shares, and their own holdings to supply unavailable equities. The alleged function of the specialist is to smooth price changes, but large blocks create a "bumpy" market since no specialist has adequate capital to absorb a large block offering of an expensive stock.

The specialist who could buy 1,000 or even 10,000 shares is simply unable to cope with the capital required to digest block transactions of 100,000 or 500,000 shares—nor can such volume be absorbed readily by the classic auction market still conducted on the exchange floor for investors who want to buy or sell 100 or less shares.

Today, the market for large transactions between institutions is *not* an auction, is *not* conducted on or even very near the exchange floor, and is *not* made public until after the transactions are fully settled as to amount and price. (Charles D. Ellis, *Institutional Investing*, Dow Jones–Irwin, 1971, p. 228)

The second major impact of the financial institutions upon the brokerage industry was the development of firms that specialized in serving the institutions. Block trading on the exchanges was exceedingly profitable for the trader since, until 1972, no volume discount was permitted on the commission rates. A block of 10,000 shares traded at a commission that was exactly 100 times greater than the commission on 100 shares, although the costs of the transaction were essentially fixed. It was claimed that trades on the third market were made at the same rates, so that members of the New York Stock Exchange could not be penalized for failure to observe the rule that all trading of listed stocks be conducted on the floor of the Exchange; maintenance of the existing commission rates was said to show that nonfloor trading was to ensure an "orderly" market, not to permit price competition. The fixed commission rates were obviously very beneficial to the firms that could secure the trading orders of the large financial institutions, and nonprice competition developed to obtain those orders, primarily through offering "research" studies on the prospects of growth industries and the evaluation of selected companies. These studies, generally of a historical, econometric nature, were provided to the financial institutions, not to the general public.

The research studies became very good at identifying the factors in any industry or company that would attract the attention of the financial institutions: steady growth, high return on capital, technological advantage, and a market position. This certainly wasn't the intent of the researchers, but they were much better at predicting the future investments of the large institutions than they were at forecasting the future profitability of studied industries. That was good enough for a certain period of time, however, since large investments by a number of institutions would automatically raise the price of the selected stocks. The public was excluded from this cozy relationship, and gradually became very disillusioned with the securities business. (Statement of a brokerage industry executive)

The last impact of the financial institutions upon the brokerage industry came from the tendency of the institutions to

Exhibit 7 *Ten companies with price/earnings ratios above 40:1, together with five-year average growth in sales and earnings per share, and five-year average return on capital and equity, as of January 1, 1974*

	Average 5-yr growth in:		Average 5-yr return on:		Recent P/E ratio
	Sales (%)	Earnings/share (%)	Capital (%)	Equity (%)	
Schlumberger Ltd.	14.1	14.3	13.7	15.4	57:1
Baxter Laboratories	23.1	19.9	9.3	15.5	55:1
Polaroid	12.6	4.7	13.2	13.3	50:1
Johnson & Johnson	12.6	19.1	18.0	18.6	47:1
Fairchild Industries	7.1	105.0	8.0	12.4	43:1
McDonald's	30.5	34.9	16.3	31.5	41:1
Black and Decker	16.1	11.7	15.4	18.6	41:1
Hewlett-Packard	16.7	12.9	15.3	15.2	41:1
Kerr-McGee	9.8	5.9	8.0	11.4	40:1
Burroughs	14.8	10.4	9.7	29.1	40:1

Source: Moody's Handbook of Common Stocks, Spring 1974.

concentrate their investments amongst a relatively few equity issues. This institutional concentration produced the effect commonly referred to as the "two-tier market," with the stocks of some companies, recommended by brokerage researchers and purchased by investment managers, selling at price/earnings ratios far above the median for the total market. The selected stocks in the two-tier market were also known as the "nifty fifty" or the "favorite forty." Ten of these companies, with a price/earnings ratio of 40:1 or higher, together with the probable reasons for their selection, are shown in Exhibit 7.

4. *Consolidation in the brokerage industry.* The combined impact of the expansion, automation, and institutionalization of the brokerage industry brought about a consolidation of the brokerage firms. Increased costs of operation, caused by the need to add data processing equipment, physical facilities and support personnel, and decreased revenues, resulting from declines in the trading volume in 1969 and 1970, produced the first wave of bankruptcies and forced mergers.

In Mr. Welles' account (Christopher Welles, author of *Last Days of the Club,* a book under review by the *Wall Street Journal*) the trouble that the NYSE did have, and is still having, surfaced when the nature of its buyers and sellers began changing drastically after World War II. The banks, mutual funds, pension trusts, and other institutions became larger and larger and took over more and more of market trading.

The Exchange's tight little structure, set up to handle a flow of small buy and sell orders, began showing cracks. When the institutions began buying in blocks of 10,000 and more shares at a time, says Mr. Welles, their orders "produced on the Exchange floor the equivalent of a blown fuse."

Large blocks couldn't be handled by the usual procedures so member firms began handling them in much the same way that over-the-counter firms transact business. A "third market," over-the-counter houses dealing in NYSE listed stocks, arose and expanded. Institutions found ways to get around fixed commissions with "give-ups" and other devices. . . .

Through most of the 1960s, the shortcomings of most firms were blurred by a bull market. But the trading generated such a flood of paperwork that the system began drowning.

When the market sagged in 1969, many firms began to collapse. Mr. Welles describes a couple of the collapses in agonizing detail. (*Wall Street Journal,* December 19, 1975, p. 14)

The reduction in the number of brokerage firms continued in 1973 and 1974, when the New York Stock Exchange Index, which had been at 64.48 in the previous year, fell first to 51.82, and then collapsed to 36.13. Waves of selling, from both retail and institutional customers, produced greater trading volume, but the falling stock prices resulted in lower commissions, continued losses, and further mergers and bankruptcies.

If New York Stock Exchange figures may be taken as a guide, it all began way back in the early 1960s, when the number of Exchange member firms peaked at 681. For a while after that, the Exchange population fell slowly and then, with the arrival of Wall Street's "back-office" problems in the late 1960s, began to drop with a rush as the more inefficient firms were forced to liquidate or merge. Two recessions, ever-rising costs, and a declining stock market subsequently clobbered the Street's profits and accelerated the trend. Still more amalgamations resulted from the efforts of many larger firms to go "full-service" by means of acquiring smaller operations with complementary product lines. Between the end of 1968 and Mayday (the end of fixed commissions through order of the S.E.C. on May 1st) in 1975, the number of member firms declined from 646 to 505, an average loss of more than twenty firms a year. (*Fortune,* May 22, 1978, p. 59)

The end of fixed commission rates, ordered by the Securities and Exchange Commission in Washington to take effect as of May 1, 1975, brought further price competition, and increased the pressures toward consolidation. The 505 firms left in 1975 became 465 in April 1978.

The action since "Mayday" raises images of the old gasoline price wars that used to deci-

mate the ranks of service stations. The securities industry has been engaging in "commission-rate wars" on institutional trades, and these, too, have led to battlefield casualties. The new price competition has all but wiped out one class of firm, the small institutional broker whose main selling point is the research it does on stocks. It has helped extinguish some fine old names—White, Weld, for example, which has just been bought by Merrill Lynch. It has encouraged large firms to merge with their own kind and to acquire smaller firms, on the assumption that size will help them deal with this rugged new environment. (*Fortune,* May 22, 1978, p. 59)

The intent of the continued consolidations was to reduce costs, by combining the back-office operations and eliminating the surplus capacity, particularly in the expensive data processing equipment and personnel, and to increase revenues by joining the sales efforts of two or more firms. The consolidations brought economies of scale and concentrations of capital to the brokerage industry, both increasingly valid in the newly competitive environment, and it was feared in 1978 that the number of brokerage firms would continue to shrink, with eventual adverse effects upon both the retail and institutional customers and the corporate and municipal clients.

It is obvious that the consolidation trend among the nation's securities firms has hurt many of the people directly involved. The trend has cut employment in the industry generally and, as competitive commission rates have reduced the number of firms serving institutional customers, has taken a heavy toll among the highly paid analysts, traders, and salesmen covering that market.

It is less obvious how the consolidation trend is affecting the industry's customers—individual investors, institutional investors, and corporate clients who rely on the industry to raise capital. They are naturally wondering what the upheaval might mean for them. What will happen to the services they get as the number of securities firms continues to shrink? How will the customers fare if the industry ends up, as some believe it could, with a structure resembling the accountants' Big Eight?

A good many people, including some only recently roused to concern, regard the situation as ominous. The general fear appears to be the rise of an "oligopoly"—a condition in which the market is in the hands of a few sellers. An oligopoly might cripple the nation's capital-raising mechanism; reduce the availability of research, particularly research that attracts investors to small companies; eliminate regional brokerage firms that may help small companies to go public and make over-the-counter markets in their stocks; impair liquidity for large institutional blocks of stock; and leave individual investors in the grip of a few powerful firms that could raise commission rates at will. (*Fortune*, June 19, 1978, p. 141)

5. *Diversification of the brokerage industry.* Many firms in the brokerage industry, concerned by the decline in institutional commissions, the slowdown in retail sales, and the increase in operating costs began, in the mid-1970s, to search for new sources of revenue through diversification into new products and services. One immediately available, and apparently attractive new product was trading in futures contracts. A futures contract is a commitment to purchase or to sell a given good, often a commodity such as corn, cotton, wheat, etc., at a guaranteed price at some specified time, usually six months, in the future. Trading in futures has existed on commodity exchanges in the Midwest since the middle of the nineteenth century; it was originally developed as a means of protecting companies using the commodities from wide price gyrations caused by changes in crop plantings, growing conditions, and harvest yields. A company concerned about the future price of a commodity might contract to purchase ap-

proximately half of their needs six months in advance; they would obviously make some money if the price went up, and lose some if the price went down, but overall they were ensured that they could continue operations despite major price changes. Other companies, with more sophistication, began using futures contracts as a means of hedging. "Hedging" involves forecasting the price trends in the market, and then acting in a manner opposed to that forecast to provide protection against a judgmental error by the management or an unlikely event in the future. For example, the buyer for a large grain miller might forecast an abundant harvest of winter wheat, with falling prices, yet the company might still contract to purchase a portion of their needs at the existing price so that in the event of drought or disease they would have partial protection. Hedging provides partial protection against price changes, not complete protection.

Individual investors have been attracted to commodity futures trading for speculation, not for supply. An investor who correctly forecasts price movements can make very substantial profits, particularly since the regulations of the commodity exchanges are much more liberal than those of the stock exchanges, and only a 10% cash payment is required on the contracts. The customer in essence is allowed to borrow 90% of the cost of the contract from the brokerage firm; this leverage multiplies greatly the potential for profit, and loss.

If you buy a futures contract from a brokerage firm for $10,000, you need only invest $1,000. If the contract goes up by 10%, you have doubled your money. If the contract keeps on going up, you can make spectacular profits. But if the contract goes down 10%, you are wiped out, and if it goes down more than 10% you are more than wiped out; you have to repay the brokerage firm your losses. That is the reason I will not accept customer orders to trade in futures contracts; I don't like to hear that awful gasp on the other end of the telephone line. (Statement of a brokerage industry executive)

Despite the problems, and inherent dangers, many brokerage firms are now offering trades in futures contracts to their customers, and many more plan to offer this service as soon as the sales representatives can be trained and the trading procedures can be installed. The number of futures contracts traded on the commodity exchanges has increased 520% since 1971, with a major portion of that increase coming after brokerage firms became actively involved in 1975.

Individual investors also are in a mood to play the futures game, and the brokerage industry is only too eager to pave the way. Many Wall Street firms have been hurt badly since the May 1, 1975, end of fixed commissions, and in searching for alternative sources of revenues, they have discovered that futures brokerage can generate a lucrative stream of commissions. Last year futures commissions of New York Stock Exchange member firms totaled $351 million, or 8.5% of total industry commissions. . . . (*Business Week,* June 11, 1979, p. 68)

In addition to trading futures contracts on commodities, members of the brokerage industry have devised futures contracts on financial instruments such as stocks, bonds, and monetary units. It was possible, in the summer of 1979, to buy futures contracts on gold bullion, Japanese yen, and U.S. Treasury bills. Some individuals in the brokerage industry, and some observers of that industry, were concerned about the implications of trading in futures contracts on financial instruments.

Swarms of U.S. and foreign investors, both institutional and individual, are rushing into futures because of the small margin required

and because of the variety of contracts being traded. By doing so, they are shifting their dollars away from the traditional capital-formation mainstream—out of investment and into something close to out-and-out gambling. Yet, as the economies of the world gyrate madly, the futures market, with its speculative and hedging properties, increasingly becomes the only game in town. "The more uncertainty, the more business," says one futures industry official. "As human beings and citizens, we deplore the state of the economy. But that state is good for our business." (*Business Week,* June 11, 1979, p. 63)

Even when gold goes up, and I happened to have picked the right contract at the right moment, I ask myself what it really means. Gold is not really a valuable asset. And if I am buying it, I am admitting that the system is failing. (Statement by Mr. Leo Melamed, Chairman of the Chicago Mercantile Exchange, quoted in *Business Week,* June 11, 1979, p. 68)

In a further move toward diversification, many of the large brokerage firms in 1979 were offering complete financial planning services, including life insurance and savings accounts, to their retail customers. The intent was to be able to offer a wide range of financial services through the existing distribution network of the national brokerage firms.

A few years ago most (registered representatives of brokerage firms) could only talk stocks; today, both because the customer's interests have broadened and the salesman has needed alternative products to push, he can also talk bonds, options, deferred annuities, and tax shelters. The latest rage is to upgrade the salesman still further and turn him into a "financial planner." About 20% of Shearson Hayden Stone's salesmen, for example, have recently been taking an extensive course that teaches them about such heavy stuff as wills, estates, and trusts. At E. F. Hutton, a number of offices now being opened in smaller cities are not even considered regular brokerage offices; instead, they are "financial services" offices, whose staffs stand ready to do a complete financial-planning job for the customer. (*Fortune,* June 19, 1978, p. 144)

6. *Regulation of the brokerage industry.* Brokerage firms, for years, operated subject to the regulations of the Securities and Exchange Commission on disclosure and promotion, but without review of their competitive practices. A specific content and format had been developed for advising customers on the risks and potential of newly issued securities (Prospectus), and for informing investors on the position and performance of publicly owned companies (Form 10K), and restrictions existed on the advertising of investment alternatives. However, until 1975 there had been very limited government impact on the circumscribed structure of the brokerage industry, or the noncompetitive pricing policies. In May 1975, as described previously, the SEC required negotiated commissions (price competition) on trading of listed securities, and later that year, following the intent of Congress expressed in the Security Act Amendment of June 1975, began to push for the formation of a National Market System. The National Market System, depending upon the eventual interpretation of the new law, could be an electronic communication system linking the two national and four regional stock exchanges so that a customer could obtain the best price existing at any time; it was felt that this system would decrease the power of the specialist brokers on the New York Stock Exchange to essentially set trading prices. The National Market System could also be an electronic exchange system, listing all bids for the purchase or sale of securities, both listed and over-the-counter; it was alleged that this form would destroy the auction market conducted by the specialists, and eventually would eliminate the stock exchanges.

The SEC's clearest mandate still is to regulate the securities market, and it is here that its new activism will be felt first. In fact, the commission has been quite active trying to wean Wall Street away from a system of securities trading that has remained essentially unchanged for almost 200 years. At the same time, it has been pushing it toward a highly sophisticated method that will enable all investors, regardless of their broker's location, to buy and sell securities at the best price available anywhere in the country. The commission already has given its blessing to a pilot electronic trading system ... that is being called everything from the wave of the future to the death of the free enterprise system. (*Business Week,* November 27, 1978, p. 88)

In 1979, the Securities and Exchange Commission was considering the abolition of the New York Stock Exchange's Rule 390, which requires that all transactions of listed stocks be conducted on the floor of the Exchange and reported by the communication system of the Exchange. Advocates of abolition of Rule 390 believe that this would lead to more competitive pricing and easier access to the market; opponents allege that it would permit "in-house" trading by the large brokerage firms to the exclusion of the smaller companies, and would lead inexorably to the bankruptcy of those smaller firms. In-house trading refers to the execution of both buy and sell transactions within a single firm, not between firms, and not reported publicly. In 1979, the SEC was also writing new rules on financial disclosures by corporations, and requiring new interpretations of accounting conventions by auditors. Future actions by the SEC cannot be forecasted accurately at the date of this case (October 1979), but it can be acknowledged that the Chairman of the SEC, Dr. Harold E. Williams, seems determined to pursue an active role in the reform of the brokerage industry.

The best clues to his [Dr. Williams'] philosophy often are found in his speeches, which show a deep concern about the conflict between a traditional free market economy and the growing demands for individual equality. What is needed, he says, "is an equilibrium between the enormous energies of the free market and the compassion, equal opportunity, and social justice ... of democracy in such a way that we do not fetter the market." But Williams worries that the U.S. is becoming a society dominated by special interests. "Too many lobbyists and interest groups today either care absolutely nothing about the national interest as long as they get theirs, or blithely assume that getting theirs is in the national interest." (Interview with Dr. Harold E. Williams, Chairman of the SEC, published in *Business Week*, November 27, 1978, p. 87)

Class Assignment. Forecast the future conditions of the brokerage industry in 1990 to 1995. Be specific about the membership of that industry, and their probable products, operations, etc. Then consider the following questions:

1. What advice would you give to the presi-dent of one of the large, national brokerage firms, such as Merrill Lynch or E. F. Hutton? What should that company do now to prepare for the changed conditions of the 1990s?
2. What advice would you give to the managing partner of a small, regional brokerage firm? Envisage a retail-oriented firm, with perhaps 10 offices in the Midwest or South, and with a history of profitable operations, but with currently declining margins.

Alternative Assignment. In groups of three to four persons, study the existing conditions and current trends of other industries, such as public accounting, commercial banking, automotive manufacturing, fast-food franchising, etc. Follow the format generally of this study of the brokerage industry: identify five to six major characteristics or trends, and then be able to describe the current conditions, expected changes, and remaining uncertainties in each. Forecast conditions in that industry in 1990–1995.

First Citizens Bank of Santa Clara County

Susan McKettrick was appointed president of the First Citizens Bank of Santa Clara County in January 1978. She replaced her father, who had been president of the bank for slightly more than 50 years, and she was intent on changing the strategy of the family-owned firm.

Dad was president of the bank through the depression of the 1930s, and he kept the bank open and operating during that period, when most of the other local banks within California failed. That experience, however, influenced all of his later actions and decisions. He was absolutely certain that another depression would start 10 years after the end of World War II (the Great Depression had started in 1929, 10 years after the conclusion of World War I), so all of the policies of the bank for the past 25 years have emphasized conservatism, and the maintenance of a substantial cash and treasury bill position, much in excess of the regulatory requirements. The result is that we missed the immense growth that occurred in the Santa Clara area. We are larger than we were in 1950, but only about three times larger as measured by deposits. The First National Bank of San Jose, which was our size in 1950, is 10 times bigger today. (Statement of Ms. McKettrick)

Santa Clara County, which is located at the base of the San Francisco peninsula, between the Santa Cruz (coastal range) Mountains and the Diablo Hills, was settled in 1777 by Spanish explorers who were anxious to farm the very rich agricultural lands of the valley. A village was established at San Jose to supply food for the Spanish garrisons at San Francisco and Monterey, and a mission, named for St. Clare of Assisi, was established just slightly to the north. With the American occupation of California, following the Mexican-American War of 1844, the name of the mission was adopted as the name of the county. Santa Clara County remained primarily agricultural until the 1950s, when substantial changes occurred in population growth and industrial activity (Exhibit 1).

Ms. McKettrick, the new president and chief executive officer of the First Citizens Bank, was a graduate of the Harvard–Radcliffe program (a two-year curriculum in business education that was administered by Radcliffe College and staffed by Harvard University; it was considered to be a substitute for the M.B.A. during the period when women were denied admission to the Harvard Business School). She had worked at the bank as teller, cashier, branch manager, and vice president of personnel and planning from 1958 to 1972. She was promoted to executive vice president and treasurer in 1972, following the death of her brother in a boating accident on San Francisco Bay, and appointed president in 1978. As described previously, she was determined to change the overall strategy of the bank.

We are now a very small bank surrounded by very large financial institutions. When I was a girl, growing up in this area, if you went to a bank in Santa Clara County, you went either to the First National or to the First Citizens. Now, there are branches of the Bank of America ($3,038.7 million equity), Security Pacific ($920.0 million equity), Wells Fargo ($844.9 million equity), Crocker National ($632.7 million equity), and Bank of California ($149.3 million equity) in the county, along with offices of the regional banks, and representatives of foreign banks, from England, France and Japan. There is plenty of competition.

Despite the competition, we have remained a full-service bank, without specialization. We offer consumer loans, industrial loans, equipment leases, trust services, and municipal financing. The result is that we don't do a really good job in any of those areas, and therefore many

Exhibit 1 *Changes in population, employment, income, and property in Santa Clara County, 1950–1978*

	Total population	Agricultural employment	Manufacturing employment	Median household income	Real estate value (000's)
1950	291,000	22,310	15,819	$ 3,103	$ 376,400
1955	416,000	21,446	27,551	5,278	676,400
1960	642,315	21,012	46,361	6,712	1,371,600
1965	919,653	19,965	79,031	8,663	2,136,500
1970	1,064,714	12,792	113,250	11,559	3,256,200
1975	1,168,986	7,728	147,385	14,566	5,171,500
1978	1,219,800	5,994	161,848	n.a.	7,056,400

Source: County of Santa Clara "Info," June 1978; see Exhibits 3 to 21 for specific page and table references.

of our customers are those that the other banks don't really want. Let me give you an example. The Bank of America opened a "Science Center" office in Sunnyvale two years ago to centralize all their transactions with the high-technology firms in this area, and they staffed that branch with young, bright M.B.A.'s who had technical undergraduate training. We can't compete with them for new accounts since our commercial lending officers are older, not as aggressive, and don't understand the technology.

My thought is that we have to specialize. We have to segment the market, identify a group with growing needs for financial services, and then design our services and facilities and select our people to serve that group. We have to develop, to use a term that may be obsolete now but that still makes a lot of sense to me, a "distinctive competence."

My problem is that I'm not certain what group we should serve, or what services we should offer to develop that distinctive competence. We could concentrate on small technologically oriented companies, and provide some venture capital, receivable financing, inventory loans, etc., but the Bank of America is already doing exactly that. We could emphasize the service businesses in this area, but they don't need receivable or inventory financing, so that we would be limited to mortgages on their real estate. Numerous people have suggested, for the obvious reason, that we orient the bank toward women customers, but I'm not certain that is a viable concept; banks aren't like hair dressing salons.

The most obvious alternative is to direct our services toward older people, and provide trust services, tax preparation, real estate management, etc., but no bank that I know of, outside of New York City, has been successful following that strategy; there just aren't enough older people with money. We will have to study all of the alternatives before we make a move to commit the bank to a new direction, and we will certainly have to study the future economic and social conditions in this area. We missed all of our opportunities in the past; we don't want to miss any of them in the future. (Statement of Ms. McKettrick)

Class Assignment. Ms. McKettick hired a first-year M.B.A. student from Stanford to work as her assistant over the summer of 1978, with the primary assignment to prepare a forecast of demographic and economic conditions in Santa Clara County for the period 1990–1995. The student gathered the statistics on population, employment, income, housing, land, and motor vehicles shown in Exhibits 3 to 21, and elicited opinions on potential changes in the housing market, the microelectronic industry, and consumer financial services given in Appendices A, B, and C. Assume that you are the assistant to Ms. McKettrick; prepare a forecast of demographic and economic conditions in Santa Clara County for the period 1985–1990, and then recommend a strategy for the First Citizens Bank of Santa Clara to meet those conditions. (Exhibit 22 shows the bank's income statement and balance sheet for 1978.)

Exhibit 2 *Major population centers in Santa Clara County*

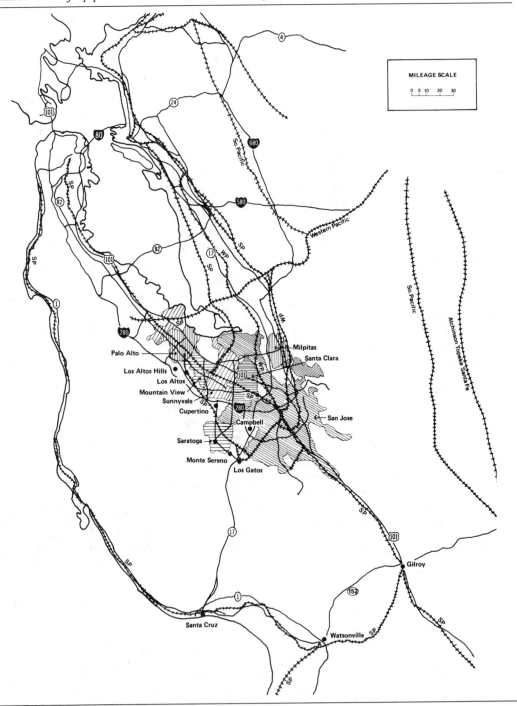

Exhibit 3 *Population by 10-year age groups by city within Santa Clara County, 1975*

	Total population	0–9 years	10–19 years	20–29 years	30–39 years	40–49 years	50–59 years	60+ years
Campbell	25,108	3,670	4,458	5,835	3,834	2,734	2,210	2,367
Cupertino	22,023	2,953	4,710	3,353	4,040	3,308	2,185	1,474
Gilroy	15,589	3,549	3,147	2,499	1,854	1,503	1,293	1,744
Los Altos	26,260	3,144	5,304	2,301	3,581	3,947	4,336	3,647
Los Altos Hills	6,993	776	1,909	566	830	1,266	1,096	550
Los Gatos	23,882	3,008	4,800	3,304	3,357	3,340	2,450	3,623
Milpitas	31,666	7,196	7,305	5,185	5,446	3,293	1,816	1,425
Monte Sereno	3,111	362	841	257	432	550	354	315
Mountain View	55,095	6,397	6,930	14,652	8,836	5,994	5,943	6,343
Morgan Hill	8,852	1,768	2,089	1,230	1,168	911	753	933
Palo Alto	52,633	5,615	9,061	9,571	7,538	6,352	6,470	8,026
San Jose	551,224	104,414	116,611	101,432	86,998	58,315	41,306	42,148
Santa Clara	82,978	11,774	16,055	17,053	11,618	9,854	8,751	7,873
Saratoga	29,150	3,855	7,835	15,697	12,882	4,028	5,159	3,511
Sunnyvale	102,154	14,794	18,815	19,228	15,697	12,887	11,427	9,306
Unincorporated	132,268	20,758	25,378	25,655	16,235	14,451	14,499	15,292
	1,168,986	194,033	235,248	214,295	175,492	133,864	108,400	107,654

Source: County of Santa Clara "Info," June 1978, Table 609, adjusted for consistency.

Exhibit 4 *Trends in population by 10-year age groups within Santa Clara County, 1950–1978*

	Total population	0–9 years	10–19 years	20–29 years	30–39 years	40–49 years	50–59 years	60+ years
1950	291,000	45,200	50,900	56,700	52,400	40,700	26,200	18,900
1955	416,000	69,100	74,600	79,400	77,200	57,400	34,100	24,200
1960	642,315	113,047	122,682	120,112	111,193	84,146	52,027	39,108
1965	919,653	166,457	184,850	168,296	150,823	115,876	73,574	59,777
1970	1,064,714	186,324	218,266	196,972	168,227	121,377	90,501	83,047
1975	1,168,986	194,033	235,248	214,295	175,492	133,864	108,400	107,654
1976 (est.)	1,184,200	193,029	232,469	219,892	183,551	139,735	106,578	108,946
1977 (est.)	1,205,000	194,006	236,180	220,518	189,183	147,011	106,040	112,062
1978 (est.)	1,219,800	195,168	236,641	222,003	193,948	150,035	107,342	114,663

Source: Company records, adjusted for consistency.

Exhibit 5 *Population by racial or ethnic grouping by city within Santa Clara County in 1975*

	Total population	Caucasian	Mexican	Black	Japanese	Chinese	Other	Unknown race
Campbell	25,108	22,299	1,033	167	380	157	430	642
Cupertino	22,023	19,817	315	139	405	265	351	731
Gilroy	15,589	7,961	5,413	40	207	88	536	1,344
Los Altos	26,260	23,276	242	37	350	246	356	1,755
Los Altos Hills	6,993	6,190	50	27	44	66	76	540
Los Gatos	23,882	21,294	431	29	163	79	150	1,736
Milpitas	31,666	22,330	3,435	1,841	276	286	1,903	1,596
Monte Sereno	3,111	2,946	58	7	35	19	19	27
Mountain View	55,095	40,021	3,896	1,628	1,243	824	2,816	4,667
Morgan Hill	8,852	5,847	1,989	43	157	22	258	536
Palo Alto	52,633	45,006	1,058	1,254	892	1,222	1,269	1,932
San Jose	551,224	392,197	82,267	19,143	7,969	4,569	22,290	22,789
Sunnyvale	102,154	84,015	7,050	1,958	1,785	1,927	4,077	1,342
Unincorporated	132,268	94,327	17,715	1,467	2,316	935	4,601	10,907
	1,168,986	879,227	133,125	28,809	17,627	11,650	43,768	54,780

Note: The term "Mexican" included both persons of Mexican descent (Chicano) and of Spanish heritage (Latino); the classification "other" includes persons of Filipino, Indian, and general Southeastern Asian origin.

Source: County of Santa Clara "Info," June 1978, Table 613, adjusted for consistency.

Exhibit 6 *Trends in population by racial or ethnic grouping within Santa Clara County, 1950–1978*

	Total population	Caucasian	Mexican	Black	Japanese	Chinese	Other	Unknown race
1950	291,000	265,000	n.a.	n.a.	n.a.	n.a.	n.a.	26,000
1955	416,000	366,000	n.a.	n.a.	n.a.	n.a.	n.a.	50,000
1960	642,315	543,870	77,755	4,187	10,432	2,394	3,038	639
1965	919,653	792,583	88,246	10,081	n.a.	n.a.	n.a.	28,743
1970	1,064,714	874,888	129,010	18,090	16,644	7,817	10,776	7,489
1975	1,168,986	879,227	133,125	28,809	16,627	11,650	43,768	54,780
1976	1,184,200	—	—	—	—	—	—	—
1977	1,205,000	—	—	—	—	—	—	—
1978	1,219,800	—	—	—	—	—	—	—

Note: Definition of the classification "unknown" has changed over time. In 1950 and 1955 it included all non-Caucasians; in 1970 it included all persons whom the census taker was unable or unwilling to classify by race or ethnic origin; in 1975 it included all persons who were unable or unwilling to classify themselves by race or ethnic origin.

Source: County of Santa Clara "Info," February 1979, Table 626, adjusted for consistency.

Exhibit 7 *Work force (persons over 20 years of age) and employment status by city within Santa Clara County in 1975*

	Work force	Employed full-time	Employed part-time	Unemployed	Retired person	Homemaker	Student (est.)	Other
Campbell	16,980	9,954	1,452	1,203	1,440	3,709	624	212
Cupertino	14,360	8,421	1,448	605	692	3,397	723	172
Gilroy	8,893	3,852	920	839	1,105	2,114	389	150
Los Altos	17,812	8,191	1,941	476	1,847	4,672	847	341
Los Altos Hills	4,308	2,000	455	107	259	1,199	302	85
Los Gatos	16,074	8,138	1,777	528	1,778	4,459	722	179
Milpitas	17,165	9,367	1,227	1,490	1,031	4,332	823	570
Monte Sereno	1,908	945	239	40	168	665	134	17
Mountain View	41,768	22,757	3,057	2,174	3,771	5,865	1,060	1,094
Morgan Hill	4,995	2,371	384	481	562	1,233	207	99
Palo Alto	37,957	18,557	4,325	1,737	4,791	6,591	4,091	734
San Jose	330,199	173,666	30,021	22,870	26,299	81,156	18,297	6,510
Santa Clara	55,149	30,061	4,406	3,388	5,163	10,485	2,705	900
Saratoga	17,460	8,798	1,977	680	1,364	5,182	1,221	195
Sunnyvale	68,545	39,251	5,764	3,890	5,860	13,419	2,686	1,687
Unincorporated	86,132	40,775	8,392	5,244	9,422	19,237	3,980	3,528
	739,705	387,104	67,785	45,752	65,552	168,345	38,811	16,473

Note: Work force is defined as persons over 20 years of age. The total of the various occupations does not equal the work force since respondents were permitted more than one answer (e.g., student or homemaker and employed part-time). The classification "other" includes persons who were unable or unwilling to classify themselves by employment status.
Source: County of Santa Clara "Info," June 1978, Table 612, adjusted for consistency.

Exhibit 8 *Trends in work force and employment status within Santa Clara County, 1950–1975*

	Work force	Employed full-time	Employed part-time	Unemployed	Retired person	Homemaker	Student (est.)	Other
1950	185,900	79,100	inc.	4,640	12,850	82,510	3,900	—
1955	272,300	119,800	inc.	6,810	17,180	119,800	8,710	—
1960	406,586	181,140	inc.	15,040	25,420	170,760	14,230	—
1965	568,356	253,270	28,985	30,120	40,050	221,650	23,300	—
1970	660,124	329,380	46,870	38,390	52,320	224,440	31,680	18,690
1975	739,705	387,104	67,785	45,752	65,552	168,345	38,811	16,473
1976 (est.)	758,702	402,870	69,800	41,720	75,370	171,990	40,210	16,840
1977 (est.)	744,814	415,300	72,050	38,740	67,230	173,560	39,520	17,200
1978 (est.)	787,900	425,470	74,060	35,450	68,790	175,700	39,390	17,490

Source: Company records.

Exhibit 9 *Occupation of employed persons (full-time and part-time combined) by city within Santa Clara County in 1975*

	Total employ.	Agri-culture	Durable goods mfg.	Non-durable	Constr. and trans.	Sales and dis.	Consumer service	Govt. service
Campbell	7,784	—	2,117	423	57	1,222	2,652	1,313
Cupertino	5,824	22	1,174	239	43	960	2,211	1,175
Gilroy	4,104	37	270	751	104	527	1,658	760
Los Altos	6,275	—	411	83	63	1,310	3,095	1,313
Los Altos Hills	913	—	—	—	21	174	442	276
Los Gatos	5,294	13	244	49	67	1,135	2,542	1,244
Milpitas	11,219	84	3,303	706	483	1,572	3,205	1,866
Monte Sereno	542	—	—	—	26	157	221	138
Mountain View	31,684	—	13,460	1,495	3,688	4,804	5,195	3,042
Morgan Hill	2,316	74	428	86	384	262	663	419
Palo Alto	29,969	—	11,013	1,226	1,028	7,954	5,637	3,111
San Jose	192,754	284	47,794	11,558	11,994	39,821	49,527	31,776
Santa Clara	53,473	—	17,253	1,947	5,538	11,423	8,290	9,022
Saratoga	6,212	17	211	40	84	1,397	2,873	1,590
Sunnyvale	53,658	—	20,680	1,964	5,796	9,773	9,837	5,608
Unincorporated	42,868	6,747	4,009	4,451	3,830	4,851	12,490	5,490
	454,889	7,278	122,367	25,018	33,206	87,339	110,538	69,143

Source: Company records; some figures have been disguised for confidentiality.

Exhibit 10 *Trends in occupation of employed persons (full-time and part-time combined) within Santa Clara County, 1950–1975*

	Total employ.	Agri-culture	Durable goods mfg.	Non-durable	Constr. and trans.	Sales and dis.	Consumer service	Govt. service
1950	79,100	22,310	6,407	9,412	6,961	11,623	12,184	10,203
1955	119,800	21,446	12,219	15,332	11,381	19,407	23,480	16,535
1960	181,140	21,012	24,997	21,374	19,563	30,794	36,952	26,448
1965	281,255	19,969	52,594	26,437	31,501	48,938	58,732	43,034
1970	376,250	12,792	83,903	29,347	37,248	69,606	83,151	60,203
1975	454,889	7,278	122,367	25,018	33,206	87,339	110,538	69,143
1976 (est.)	472,670	7,090	128,566	25,051	33,560	90,753	117,222	70,428
1977 (est.)	487,350	6,822	134,023	23,880	34,114	94,058	123,300	71,153
1978 (est.)	499,530	5,994	138,370	23,478	34,468	96,409	129,378	71,433

Notes: Durable-goods manufacturing within Santa Clara County includes fabricated metal products, office equipment and computers, light machinery, communication systems, electronic components, microelectronic supplies, aerospace units, and scientific instruments. Non-durable-goods manufacturing includes canned food products, frozen food products, printing, and publishing.

Construction and transportation includes employees engaged in those trades, plus electric power distribution and telephone communications. Sales and distribution includes employees in retail sales and wholesale distribution. Consumer services are both financial (banks, insurance companies, and savings institutions) and personal (automotive repair, medical assistance, etc.). Government services include federal, state, county, and city employees.

Source: Company records; some figures have been disguised for confidentiality.

Exhibit 11 *Households by income classification by city within Santa Clara County in 1975*

	Total households	Under $6,000	$6,000– 12,000	$12,000– 18,000	$18,000– 24,000	$24,000– 30,000	Over $30,000
Campbell	9,735	1,574	2,812	2,808	1,599	558	384
Cupertino	9,395	350	1,018	1,656	1,856	1,327	1,218
Gilroy	4,800	1,176	1,378	1,303	570	215	158
Los Altos	8,706	470	978	1,422	1,796	1,618	2,417
Los Altos Hills	2,035	71	115	158	291	342	1,058
Los Gatos	8,469	1,167	1,545	1,748	1,629	1,010	1,370
Milpitas	8,856	874	1,899	3,298	1,878	655	252
Monte Sereno	919	73	83	125	156	143	339
Mountain View	24,863	4,123	7,277	6,576	3,791	1,779	1,317
Morgan Hill	2,666	632	586	705	394	183	166
Palo Alto	20,929	3,373	4,464	4,333	3,474	2,347	2,938
San Jose	174,520	25,856	35,428	46,156	45,119	13,357	8,604
Santa Clara	29,574	4,804	7,627	8,580	5,159	2,172	1,232
Saratoga	8,270	338	683	993	1,430	1,669	3,157
Sunnyvale	37,911	4,600	9,222	9,747	7,648	3,953	2,691
Unincorporated	42,753	8,423	10,473	10,548	6,414	3,228	3,667
	392,401	57,904	85,588	100,161	83,224	34,556	30,968

Source: County of Santa Clara "Info," June 1978, Table 608, adjusted for consistency and supplemented by estimates.

Exhibit 12 *Trends in households by income classification within Santa Clara County, 1950–1978*

	Total households	Under $6,000	$6,000– 12,000	$12,000– 18,000	$18,000– 24,000	$24,000– 30,000	Over $30,000	Consumer Price Index
1950 (est.)	79,250	52,384	22,190	3,727	634	231	84	72.2
1955 (est.)	117,850	62,578	41,248	11,196	2,003	589	236	80.4
1960	188,235	79,653	75,640	26,918	3,953	1,505	564	88.7
1965	269,294	108,799	94,238	51,435	8,341	4,578	1,885	94.5
1970	321,022	96,949	105,937	70,625	29,534	11,236	6,471	116.3
1975	392,401	57,904	85,588	100,161	83,224	34,556	30,958	161.2
1976 (est.)	407,250	54,164	85,929	104,663	89,595	38,690	34,209	170.5
1977 (est.)	423,400	38,953	73,248	104,580	105,850	49,961	50,808	181.5
1978 (est.)	435,700	17,863	46,184	100,646	124,567	72,793	73,647	193.2

Source: Company records adjusted by consistency and supplemented by estimates. 1967 = 100 on consumer price index.

Exhibit 13 *Population, households, and housing by city within Santa Clara County, 1975*

	Total population	Household population	Group quarters population	Total housing units	Occupied housing units	Vacant housing units	Persons per household
Campbell	25,108	24,941	167	10,226	9,735	491	2.56
Cupertino	22,023	21,561	426	7,953	7,395	558	2.92
Gilroy	15,589	15,385	204	5,125	4,800	325	3.21
Los Altos	26,260	25,862	398	8,955	8,706	249	2.97
Los Altos Hills	6,993	6,947	46	2,087	2,035	52	3.41
Los Gatos	23,882	22,883	999	8,851	8,469	382	2.70
Milpitas	31,666	31,029	637	9,163	8,856	307	3.50
Monte Sereno	3,111	3,111	—	973	919	54	3.39
Mountain View	55,095	54,532	563	26,531	24,863	1,668	2.19
Morgan Hill	8,852	8,597	255	2,958	2,666	292	3.22
Palo Alto	52,633	51,541	1,092	21,882	20,929	953	2.46
San Jose	551,224	541,658	9,566	184,784	174,520	10,264	3.10
Santa Clara	82,978	80,534	2,444	31,341	29,574	1,767	2.72
Saratoga	29,150	28,755	395	8,515	8,270	245	3.48
Sunnyvale	102,154	101,731	423	40,344	37,911	2,433	2.68
Unincorporated	132,268	125,257	7,011	45,066	42,753	2,313	2.93
	1,168,986	1,144,324	24,662	414,754	392,401	22,353	2.92

Note: Group quarters population refers to persons living in accommodations provided by nonhousing organizations, as in military barracks, college dormitories, or nursing homes.
Source: County of Santa Clara "Info," June 1978, Table 602, adjusted for consistency.

Exhibit 14 *Trends in population, households, and housing within Santa Clara County, 1950–1978*

	Total population	Household population	Group quarters population	Total housing units	Occupied housing units	Vacant housing units	Persons per household
1950	291,000	291,000	n.a.	82,700	79,290	3,410	3.67
1955	416,000	416,000	n.a.	123,070	117,850	5,220	3.53
1960	642,315	632,472	9,843	194,647	188,235	6,412	3.36
1965	919,653	902,135	17,518	277,050	269,294	7,756	3.35
1970	1,064,714	1,036,904	27,810	340,740	321,022	19,718	3.23
1975	1,168,986	1,144,423	24,662	414,754	392,401	22,353	2.92
1976 (est.)	1,184,200	1,160,520	23,680	422,910	407,200	15,700	2.85
1977 (est.)	1,205,000	1,182,100	22,900	436,100	423,400	12,400	2.79
1978 (est.)	1,219,800	1,198,100	21,700	446,800	435,700	11,100	2.75

Note: Household population refers to persons living in standard housing units. A "household" is defined as an individual or a group of individuals, who may or may not be related, living within one housing unit. The number of households and the number of occupied housing units is therefore exactly equal.
Source: County of Santa Clara "Info," June 1978, Table 620, adjusted for consistency.

Exhibit 15 *Types of housing units by city within Santa Clara County, 1975*

	Total housing	Single units	2–4 units	5–20 units	20–40 units	Over 50 units	Mobile homes
Campbell	10,266	5,149	2,197	1,155	903	522	300
Cupertino	7,953	4,925	1,526	1,486	—	—	16
Gilroy	5,125	3,332	648	678	99	54	314
Los Altos	8,955	8,091	433	295	136	—	—
Los Altos Hills	2,087	2,016	62	5	—	—	4
Los Gatos	8,851	6,021	1,018	1,239	305	126	142
Milpitas	9,163	6,726	1,357	411	121	—	548
Monte Sereno	973	965	5	—	—	—	3
Mountain View	26,531	8,530	3,596	7,705	4,065	1,378	1,257
Morgan Hill	2,958	1,916	416	181	27	—	418
Palo Alto	21,882	14,289	1,938	2,772	1,607	1,213	63
San Jose	184,784	123,652	21,063	20,470	9,954	3,549	6,096
Santa Clara	31,341	16,707	4,228	7,108	2,102	754	442
Saratoga	8,515	8,280	132	79	24	—	—
Sunnyvale	40,344	20,602	4,737	6,038	2,926	2,452	3,589
Unincorporated	45,066	35,053	2,918	2,218	1,148	1,010	1,819
	414,754	267,144	46,274	51,840	23,417	11,058	15,011

Source: County of Santa Clara "Info," June 1978, Table 603, adjusted for consistency.

Exhibit 16 *Trends in types of housing units within Santa Clara County, 1950–1978*

	Total housing	Single units	2–4 units	5 or more units	Units* constr.	Units* demol.	Net units
1950	82,700	65,725	7,045	9,930	—	—	—
1955	123,070	100,965	9,760	12,345	41,280	910	40,370
1960	194,647	154,298	15,221	25,128	72,417	840	71,577
1965	277,050	193,337	31,553	52,185	82,963	560	82,403
1970	340,743	229,023	39,091	72,619	64,903	1,210	63,693
1975	414,744	267,144	46,274	101,326	77,491	3,480	74,011
1976 (est.)	422,900	272,840	46,730	103,330	9,096	940	8,156
1977 (est.)	432,120	278,230	47,340	108,550	10,100	900	9,200
1978 (est.)	441,620	283,290	48,290	110,040	10,620	1,120	9,500

Source: County of Santa Clara "Info," June 1978, Tables 620 and 621, adjusted for consistency and supplemented by estimates (*).

Exhibit 17 *Land available (acres) for residential development within Santa Clara County, 1975*

	Zoned single units	Zoned multiple units	Constraints on development
Campbell	50	60	No constraints
Cupertino	680	110	⅓ acre per unit for single-unit housing
Gilroy	560	310	No constraints
Los Altos	1,560	—	½ acre per unit for single-unit housing
Los Altos Hills	1,520	—	½ acre per unit for single-unit housing
Los Gatos	1,480	140	⅓ acre per unit for single-unit housing
Milpitas	2,010	260	No constraints
Monte Sereno	140	—	½ acre per unit for single-unit housing
Mountain View	30	110	No constraints
Morgan Hill	2,660	540	Limited to 80 acres development per year
Palo Alto	200	70	⅓ acre per unit for single-unit housing
San Jose	7,730	3,100	⅓ acre per unit for single-unit housing
Santa Clara	70	240	⅓ acre per unit for single-unit housing
Saratoga	2,320	20	⅓ acre per unit for single-unit housing
Sunnyvale	60	200	No constraints
Unincorporated	20,693	inc.	Limited by land conservation act; see note
	41,403	5,160	to Exhibit 19.

Source: County of Santa Clara "Technical Appendix," December 1978, p. 28.

Exhibit 18 *Trends in land available (acres) for residential development within Santa Clara County, 1950–1975*

	1950	1955	1960	1965	1970	1975
Incorporated (city) land						
Industrial and commercial	21,850	34,034	52,960	86,010	119,084	143,965
Residential land	24,909	37,638	58,421	78,855	95,123	113,281
Public land	72,863	77,087	92,471	112,227	125,165	128,140
Waste land	74,840	74,840	74,840	71,972	68,715	68,715
Total occupied land	194,462	223,599	278,692	349,064	408,087	454,101
Total incorporated land	272,947	285,023	345,575	416,659	468,870	479,971
Available for development	48,485	61,424	66,883	67,595	60,783	25,870
Unincorporated (rural) land						
Cropland harvested	152,980	148,056	115,030	96,596	74,364	72,133
Cropland fallow	59,741	57,451	56,166	39,480	34,146	30,387
Orchards	83,170	82,157	64,577	59,011	42,396	39,870
Woodlots	56,715	56,330	51,588	36,489	31,280	30,060
Pasture	249,511	246,047	242,128	226,829	224,008	222,643
Total unincorporated	602,117	590,041	529,489	458,405	406,194	395,093
Conservation Act land	—	—	82,600	149,900	246,100	374,400
Available for development	602,117	590,041	442,889	308,505	160,094	20,693

Source: County of Santa Clara "Info," undated, Table 632, adjusted for consistency and supplemented by estimates.

Exhibit 19 *Trends in land available (acres) for residential development within Santa Clara County,*
1975–1978

	1975	1976	1977	1978
Incorporated (city) land				
Industrial and commercial zone	143,965	144,132	144,640	146,720
Residential area	113,281	115,670	117,977	120,289
Public land	128,140	128,140	128,140	128,763
Waste land	68,715	68,008	67,500	65,420
Total occupied land	454,101	455,950	458,257	461,192
Total incorporated land	479,971	479,971	479,971	482,212
Available for development	25,870	24,021	21,714	21,020
Unincorporated (rural) land				
Cropland harvested	72,133	69,969	69,969	67,883
Cropland fallow	30,387	28,563	27,992	27,153
Orchards	39,870	39,870	39,870	38,714
Woodlots	30,060	30,060	30,060	30,060
Pasture	222,643	226,631	227,902	229,042
Total unincorporated land	395,093	395,093	395,093	392,852
Conservation Act land	374,400	374,700	375,900	376,300
Available for development	20,693	20,393	19,193	16,552

Notes: Total acreage in Santa Clara County is 875,064; the 15 cities have expanded since 1950 by annexing rural property that has been purchased for development, and changing unincorporated to incorporated land (incorporated land refers merely to land within the boundaries of an incorporated city). Farm property may now be protected by the California Land Conservation Act (the Williamson Act of 1960); land placed under the terms of this act is assessed at approximately one-sixth of the market value, but cannot be developed at a population density greater than one housing unit per 10 acres for a period of 10 years. To maintain the low assessment, the land must be reentered in the program each year (e.g., in 1978, none of the 376,300 acres of the Conservation Act land in Santa Clara County could be developed for high-density housing until 1988, and then only if the owners decided in 1978 to remove the land from the protection of the Conservation Act and pay the increased taxes for those 10 years).

Public land within the cities refers to land used for streets, schools, parks, and public buildings, or plotted for that use. All land as it is incorporated is plotted for public use, and is zoned for industrial, commercial, or residential use. Land listed as available for development has been zoned for residential use.

Single-unit housing can be built at a density of four units per acre, but local restrictions often limit development to three or two units per acre. Multiple-unit housing is usually built at a density of five units per acre for developments containing two to four units per building, and at a density of eight units per acre for developments with five or more units per building. Developments with five or more units per building are generally "high rise."

Waste land is generally considered to be unsuitable for industrial, commercial, or residential development due to water conditions, soil characteristics, or topographical incline.

Source: County of Santa Clara "Info," undated, Table 632, adjusted for consistency and supplemented by estimates.

Exhibit 20 *Population, motor vehicles, and vehicles per person by city within Santa Clara County, 1975*

	Total population	Auto-mobiles	Trucks and trailers	Motor-cycles	Travel trailers	Total vehicles	Vehicles per person
Campbell	25,108	14,178	1,120	882	1,239	17,419	0,693
Cupertino	22,023	13,427	1,278	258	1,751	16,713	0.758
Gilroy	15,589	8,403	3,218	382	640	12,643	0.811
Los Altos	26,260	18,079	872	191	2,173	21,305	0.811
Los Altos Hills	6,993	4,458	124	61	396	5,039	0.720
Los Gatos	23,882	14,546	1,430	594	1,800	18,370	0.769
Milpitas	31,666	15,191	2,059	669	1,751	19,670	0.621
Monte Sereno	3,111	1,936	533	28	175	2,672	0.858
Mountain View	55,095	36,964	5,388	457	4,678	47,487	0.861
Morgan Hill	8,852	4,720	1,843	109	309	6,981	0.788
Palo Alto	52,663	34,730	2,239	759	3,681	41,409	0.786
San Jose	551,224	290,056	47,635	23,865	37,991	399,547	0.724
Santa Clara	82,978	47,152	9,411	3,834	5,847	66,244	0.798
Saratoga	29,150	15,975	803	349	1,606	18,733	0.642
Sunnyvale	102,154	60,662	10,972	1,700	7,844	81,178	0.794
Unincorporated	132,268	74,504	36,782	3,359	11,369	126,014	0.952
Totals:	1,168,986	654,980	125,707	37,497	83,250	901,424	0.771

Source: Company records adjusted for consistency.

Exhibit 21 *Trends in population, motor vehicles, and vehicles per person within Santa Clara County, 1950–1978*

	Total population	Auto-mobiles	Trucks and trailers	Motor-cycles	Travel trailers	Total vehicles	Vehicles per person
1950	291,000	115,532	15,063	1,562	10,265	142,422	0.489
1955	416,000	172,384	24,218	1,543	14,335	212,480	0.510
1960	642,315	277,690	36,077	3,220	26,399	343,656	0.535
1965	919,653	422,276	55,055	12,032	40,531	529,894	0.576
1970	1,064,714	542,650	79,020	28,185	57,667	707,522	0.664
1975	1,168,986	634,980	125,707	37,497	83,250	901,424	0.771
1976	1,184,200	663,419	130,354	36,241	85,801	915,815	0.773
1977	1,205,000	704,823	140,870	38,290	91,055	975,038	0.809
1978	1,219,800	732,155	148,024	36,242	92,703	1,009,124	0.827

Source: County of Santa Clara "Info," undated and unnumbered.

Exhibit 22 *Income statement and balance sheet for the First Citizens Bank of Santa Clara County, 1978*

Interest on loans	$4,903,000	Cash and due from banks	$13,015,600
Interest on securities	1,461,600	U.S. Treasury securities	11,113,300
Miscellaneous operating income	884,700	State and municipal securities	14,322,600
		Consumer loans	31,947,300
Total income	7,249,300	Commercial loans	23,934,200
Salaries and wages	1,896,300	Banking facilities	4,139,000
Interest on deposits	3,381,500	Total assets	98,472,000
Provision for losses	128,200		
Charges for facilities	1,530,600	Demand deposits	32,698,200
		Time deposits	57,760,500
Total expenses	6,936,600	Accrued expenses	994,200
Profits before taxes	312,700	Common stock and capital surplus	1,465,700
Federal and state taxes	115,700	Profits and earned surplus	5,553,400
Profits to earned surplus	197,000	Total liability and equity	98,472,000

Source: Company records.

APPENDIX A: ANTICIPATED CHANGES IN THE REAL ESTATE INDUSTRY OF NORTHERN CALIFORNIA

Proposition 13, a constitutional amendment to limit local property assessments and to reduce local property taxes, was passed by California voters in June 1978. This amendment provided a basic formula for property assessments at the 1975 valuation level, permitted no more than a 2% annual increase until the property was sold or transferred, and resulted in an average reduction of 57% in property taxes. The legislation had been designed allegedly for the benefit of individual home owners, particularly in the growth areas of the state where property assessments and the resultant taxes had increased at over 40% annually since 1975, but it produced a number of unplanned and unpopular results. The Southern Pacific Railroad, the largest landowner in California, benefited from a tax savings of $17 million, while the Bank of America and the Atlantic-Richfield Oil Company received rebates of nearly $14 million each. Governmental units at both the county and local levels had been expected to be

forced to adjust to the decreased funding; however, the existence of a $5.5 billion surplus in the state treasury permitted supplemental allocations, and resulted in expanded rather than reduced services in some areas. In short, many of the long-term impacts of Proposition 13 were very uncertain in the fall of 1978 (the date of the case describing the strategic problems at the First County Bank of Santa Clara), but in general the new amendment was expected to influence housing patterns in five different, and somewhat contradictory, ways:

1. Increased single-unit housing would be built on plotted or developed (with streets, sewers, and water systems laid out and either committed or constructed) land. Prices for single-family homes had more than doubled in California from 1975 to 1978, and it was felt that the price rise was due to the pent-up demand of an expanding and affluent population. Increased construction was expected to satisfy that demand, financed by the much larger home mortgages permitted by the substantial tax savings of Proposition 13.

2. Decreased multiple-unit housing would be

215

built on plotted or developed land. Public outcry over the large savings passed on to railroads, banks, oil companies, and landlords had led to a demand that these savings be returned to customers and tenants in the form of rebates or price reductions. Numerous proposals for rent control were on local ballots in the fall of 1978, and Proposition 6 (in California, amendments to the state constitution are termed "propositions" and are numbered in sequence at each election) was to be submitted to the electorate in 1980. Proposition 6 would limit property tax relief to individuals, and would specifically exclude corporations and large (over-four-unit) developers. The belief was that very limited multiple-unit housing would be built until the uncertainty over the tax status of that property had been resolved.

3. Increased multiple-unit housing might be built in existing neighborhoods. Under Proposition 13, the assessment of property was to be raised at the time of sale to the sales price, adjusted for needed repairs, etc. It was expected that some developers might purchase single-family homes in existing neighborhoods, demolish the building (which would reduce the assessment to zero), and then build two- to four-unit housing, which would be assessed only at the cost of construction.

4. Decreased development of plotted or raw land. Cities, with substantially reduced budgets and limited taxing authority, were expected to be hesitant to invest funds in the construction of streets, sewers, water systems, and schools to develop land for additional housing. A substantial "construction tax" or fee for each new unit was under consideration in some areas, while other cities were acting to rezone residential areas for commercial or industrial use.

5. Decreased availability of unincorporated (rural) land. Farmland, placed under the protection of the Williamson Land Conservation Act of 1960, could be taxed at only one-sixth of the assessed value. Proposition 13 reduced that assessed value to 1975 levels; the result was expected to be substantially reduced financial pressure on the owners to sell the land for commercial development rather than maintaining it for agricultural use and personal investment.

APPENDIX B: ANTICIPATED CHANGES IN THE MICROELECTRONICS INDUSTRY OF NORTHERN CALIFORNIA

The economy of Santa Clara County is based upon the research, engineering, and production of microelectronic components and systems. It is estimated that 80% of the persons engaged in durable goods manufacturing within the county are involved, either directly or indirectly, with integrated semiconductor circuitry; these circuits are photoengraved, with exceedingly high precision, on silicon chips, and the central part of the county, particularly the cities of Palo Alto, Mountain View, Sunnyvale, and Santa Clara, is termed "Silicon Valley." Four major semiconductor firms, Fairchild Camera, National Semiconductor, Intel, and Hewlett-Packard, are located in that area. Historical market growth, since 1970, in silicon-based integrated circuitry has been 29% per year; future market growth has been estimated to slow to 18.7% annually (Exhibit B1).

There are four changes taking place within the microelectronics industry that are expected to affect future sales volume on a worldwide basis, and future employment needs in the local area:

1. *Decreased cost of components.* The continually decreasing cost of integrated circuitry has often been used as an example of the "learning-curve" theory, which states that the cost per unit of a specific product will decline by a fixed percentage for each doubling of the cumulative volume. Histori-

Exhibit B1 *Estimated sales (000,000's omitted) of silicon-based integrated circuitry, 1977–1980*

	1977	1978	1979	1980
MOS integrated circuits	$1,510	$1,967	$2,486	$3,093
Linear bipolar circuits	958	1,158	1,392	1,613
Digital bipolar circuits	1,056	1,201	1,275	1,413
Total silicon-based circuits	$3,524	$4,326	$5,153	$6,119
Annual increase	—	22.7%	19.1%	18.7%

Notes: MOS circuits are metal oxide semiconductors with very high density packing, and are used as memory chips and microprocessors. 16,000 bits of memory per chip were possible in 1977, up from 4,000 in 1974.

Linear bipolar circuits with very high speed but low density are used for switching and control in consumer electronics; digital bipolar circuits also with high speed and low density are used for switching and computation in data-processing units.

Source: Standard and Poor's Industrial Surveys, October 1978, p. E23.

cally, the cost of silicon-based microelectronic circuitry has declined 27.6% with each doubling in cumulative volume; the reduced prices have obviously increased the potential applications and the actual market size (Exhibit B2). It is anticipated that the cost per circuit will continue to decline in the future.

2. *Increased diversification of products.* The dividing line between a single microelectronic component and a full microprocessing system has become very unclear, owing to the greater circuit density that has enabled single chips to perform the functions of industrial control units, memory banks, data processors, and communication devices. Semiconductor manufacturing firms have entered consumer product markets, with digital watches, pocket calculators, and home radios, and they are expected to enter the industrial control and data processing industries before 1980.

3. *Increasing competition among manufacturers.* The nature of competition within the semiconductor industry, which had originally been on the basis of technical performance and sophisticated design, was becoming increasingly centered on component cost. This trend toward price competition was assisted by the industry practice

of "second sourcing," which meant that all silicon chips could be manufactured by at least two firms, and by the industry acceptance of the learning-curve theory, which resulted in deliberate price reductions to achieve volume. A third factor in the advent of price competition was just starting to become apparent in the fall of 1978; Japanese semiconductor manufacturing firms, which had previously produced only low-technology components for home consumption, and which currently represented only 7% of world wide capacity, were attempting to gain a market position in the high-technology end of the industry. The Japanese manufacturers were receiving financial assistance from the Japanese government, and marketing assistance from Japanese trading companies; they were able to provide quotations on both standard and specialized microelectronic components, at very attractive prices, to the producers of both consumer and industrial electronic products in 1978.

4. *Changing technology in product designs.* Metal-oxide-semiconductor (MOS) technology based upon the use of silicon had been standard in the microelectronic industry since 1968. In 1978, some firms were successfully experimenting with a "silicon-on-

217

Exhibit B2 *Production of integrated circuits, annual sales volume, and average selling prices, 1964–1975*

	Annual production (million units)	Cumulative production (million units)	Annual sales (millions)	Average price in current dollars	Average price in constant 1972 dollars
1964	2	2	$ 41	$18.50	$24.84
1965	10	12	79	8.33	11.21
1966	29	41	149	5.05	6.58
1967	69	110	228	3.32	4.20
1968	133	243	303	2.28	2.76
1969	253	496	413	1.63	1.88
1970	299	795	433	1.45	1.59
1971	362	1,156	443	1.23	1.28
1972	602	1,759	608	1.01	1.01
1973	1,060	2,819	1,049	0.99	0.94
1974	1,477	4,296	1,359	0.92	0.79
1975	1,375	5,671	1,100	0.80	0.63

Note: 1975 was regarded as a recession year, with reduced production that resulted from the stage of the economic cycle, and not from a change in the basic demand.
Source: Morgan Stanley, *Electronics Letter*, October 15, 1976, p. 3.

sapphire" technology (SOS), which greatly increased the packing density and the operating speed of the integrated circuits. General Electric Company and Hewlett-Packard were the developers of the new technology; neither produced the MOS circuits, although both used them in volume, and it was alleged that both firms were attempting to bypass the low-cost learning-curve positions of the other manufacturers by means of the new SOS procedures. Successful development of this new technology would have an immediate impact upon the existing semiconductor firms.

APPENDIX C: ANTICIPATED CHANGES IN THE FINANCIAL SERVICE INDUSTRY IN NORTHERN CALIFORNIA

The financial service industry includes all institutions providing facilities and procedures for the deposit and payment of funds to individual, commercial, and industrial ac-counts. The industry includes full-service banks, limited-service savings and loan associations, and specialty service credit unions, merchandise stores, mutual funds, and insurance companies. In California, the financial service industry has traditionally been dominated by large state-wide banks such as the Bank of America, Crocker National, Security Pacific, Western Bancorporation, and Wells Fargo, and large state-wide savings and loan associations such as First Charter, Gibraltar Financial, and Great Western Savings. The large banks and savings and loan associations draw deposits by means of extensive networks of branch offices; the five largest California banks average more than 250 offices each vs. an average of 18.1 offices for all banks within the state, vs. an average of 3.1 offices for all banks nationally. The competition between large state-wide banks and savings and loan associations for deposits has resulted in a wide dispersal and ready availability of financial services; in California there is a bank office for every 2,564 persons vs. 3,803 nationally. Some industry observers believe that the large number of bank offices represents excess capacity, and that many of the offices are uneconomic. They also believe that the much smaller regional and local banks may be unable to survive if the population growth slows within a given area, intensifying the competition, but they are uncertain of the effect that changes in banking technology, in banking participants, and in banking regulations will have upon that competition:

1. *Changes in banking technology.* Electronic fund transfer (EFT) systems essentially provide convenient on-line access to checking account services at remote locations. There are two types of electronic fund transfer systems. The automated teller machine (ATM) permits cash deposits or withdrawals outside normal banking hours and outside normal banking locations, while the point of sale (POS) terminal allows immediate noncash payments for purchases at retail stores. Both the ATM and the POS machines are connected, by the lines of the telephone system, to the data base of a bank's computer facility, and entries, both deposits and withdrawals, can be made with suitable safeguards in the customers' accounts. It has been estimated (David H. Pyle, *Changes in the Financial Services Industry in California,* University of California at Berkeley, 1978, p. 7) that the potential savings through the use of EFT technology within California are over $100 million annually.

2. *Changes in banking participants.* The limited service savings and loan associations and the specialty service credit unions, merchandise stores, mutual funds, and insurance companies have never been permitted to offer checking accounts for their customers; these financial institutions can issue negotiable instruments, but those instruments cannot be processed through the regional clearing houses, as can personal and corporate checks. However, the EFT systems bypass, obviously, the current check-clearing procedures, and the legal distinctions between checking accounts and other financial services for deposits and payments of funds become very blurred with the electronic transfer of money. The specialty financial service institutions may offer, or attempt to offer, EFT services in competition with the checking accounts provided by commercial banks.

3. *Changes in banking regulations.* National and state banking commissions will eventually be forced to recognize and regulate the changes imposed by EFT technology. Some of the policies that have been suggested have restricted the use of the electronic systems to ATM machines on the premises of a bank, or POS terminals within a store without telephone interconnections (for internal data records only). Other policies would permit the use of ATM and POS units for savings and loan associations (equivalent to the NOW or negotiated order of withdrawal accounts offered since 1972 by savings banks in New England), and would also allow the payment of interest on checking accounts. A policy change that was rejected by the legislature in California in 1978 would require mandatory sharing of all EFT machines at remote (nonbank) locations by all financial service institutions within the state. It was agreed by industry observers that the potential changes imposed by the new EFT technology on the financial service industry of California could be immense, and that the direction of those changes would be regulated by the California legislature.

George Spaulding

George Spaulding was a 1975 graduate of the M.B.A. program at the University of Michigan. He had majored in organizational behavior since he was interested in the general areas of industrial relations and labor negotiation, and had interviewed over the winter term for jobs in the personnel departments of large manufacturing companies. 1975, however, has not a good year for placement, and it was particularly not a good year for placement in the personnel function; the national economy was near the bottom of the post–Vietnam War recession, and personnel always seems to be one of the first areas to be cut back during periods of economic constraint.

George Spaulding, however, had an undergraduate degree in industrial engineering, which gave him a background in quantitative analysis and computer programming, so that he was offered a position in a consulting firm in New York City that specialized in the design of computer-based systems for the evaluation of employees of industrial companies, public utilities, financial institutions, governmental agencies, etc. The consulting firm had grown rapidly, and George was one of four new M.B.A.'s who were hired that spring; he got somewhat of a headstart on the others, however, since the academic year at Michigan ends in mid-April, and George was able to start work on June 1, three or four weeks before the others came.

> Consulting firms are somewhat like public accountants. There is no training program or formal sequence of assignments. Instead, you are given a desk in a large room, and are expected to be available when needed by the senior consultants or officers of the firm. The first few weeks are pretty dull, since everyone else is too busy to bring you up-to-date on their work, so you tend to get very short

assignments, such as proofreading a report or library research on a company. But, after about two weeks one of the senior consultants, a tall person from Texas who still maintained a southwestern accent and tan despite 10 years in New York City, came by and said, "I have a big project down in Georgia, and you're going to have to do." That was not a very nice introduction to professional consulting, but it was just his style. (Statement of George Spaulding)

The senior consultant, whose name was "Tex" Harris, and George Spaulding spent the next two weeks in Georgia and Alabama putting together a proposal to design an employee evaluation and compensation/motivation system for a big electrical utility holding company in the South. They met with company officials in Atlanta, to discuss requirements and potential problems in the system, and then visited division offices and field locations to talk to people there. The two men returned to New York to finish and submit the proposal, which was accepted very promptly. George was asked to return to the South to get further information about the payroll system and data-base structure, which differed for each of the operating divisions in the company.

> I spent four more weeks in Georgia, Florida, and Alabama, getting the data we needed to interface our system with the existing corporate records. I came back on weekends to see my wife, and to report to Tex, who always seemed pleased with my work, although he never said much that was complimentary. (Statement of George Spaulding)

George Spaulding finished the preliminary field work in the South on July 14, and returned to New York to help in the design of the system. He found that during his absence, two of the new M.B.A.'s had been assigned to the public utility project, together with another junior consultant who had been with the company for two to three years. One of the first problems faced by the group was the need for additional programming assistance, since the size of the utility project easily outstripped the firm's own resources.

The five of us—Tex, myself and the three new people—had a meeting to discuss our requirements, which were fairly standard: a good knowledge of COBOL, and some familiarity with IMS and CFMS, which are integrated data-base structures. We talked about this, and I found that I knew a lot more about the programming requirements than did any of the others, partially because of my work at Michigan, partially because of my work in the South, but primarily because I had spent the last six weeks reading every book I could find on file design and data-base management techniques. So, we agreed that I would interview most of the candidates. Then, just before we broke up, Tex said, "Look, let's agree that we don't want any women or blacks."

I was more surprised than shocked; it was so goddamn blatant. But I didn't want to make a big issue about this, so I just told him, "That's illegal in New York City, Tex." He told me that it was perfectly legal to pick the people we wanted. I told him that it was against corporate policy, and he did get upset then, and told me that he would take care of the corporate policy and I could take care of the interviewing. Then he calmed down and made some comment that I just wanted a woman to keep me company down in the South, and everybody laughed, and I thought that it had all been forgotten.

I did interview the candidates, and it was all so useless since we did not have a single woman or minority applicant for the jobs. But you know what it was like

to try to hire computer programmers and systems people on a part-time basis in 1975; the only people who were available were the hippies and the drifters. Some of them were damn competent, but they did not look like the typical occupants of Rockefeller Center; one of them who came in was barefoot, and many of them had hair down to their waists, or were wearing overalls. I picked the three best, but Tex did not like them, and he asked me, "Is that the best that you can do?" (Statement of George Spaulding)

Shortly afterward, George went down to the South for another extended trip, which lasted three weeks. When he returned, he found that he had been removed from the public utility project, and reassigned to the pool of junior consultants in the outer office.

I talked to Tex, of course, but he told me that the utility project had been slowed down by the client, and that they just had to cut the overhead until it started up again full-time. I sat around in the outer office for three months, doing the meaningless little jobs for other people, sometimes even for the other M.B.A.'s who had come in when I did. Finally, I saw the senior partner and told him about the lack of work. He told me that business had been slow that summer, and that maybe I had better start looking about for something else. I will always be able to remember that conversation; it was the first time, and I hope the only time, that I have ever been fired. He told me, "We can keep you on for 30 days, or maybe even for 60 days, but I think that you ought to start looking seriously for something else."

I asked him, "How can you say you don't have enough work, when everybody in the office is busy, except me?" He became angry then, and told me, "We assigned you to work with Tex Harris, one of our most competent and respected people, who is good at bringing young men into the firm. Here is his evaluation report on you: unsatisfactory attitude and uncooperative behavior. This is a small company, and we can't afford to keep people like that around. Now, I'm sorry, but I am busy this morning, even if you aren't."

I'm out, looking for another job, six months after I graduated from the M.B.A. program at the University of Michigan. And I want to tell you, it is a lot harder finding a good position when you don't have a placement office to help you, and when you know that everyone you talk with will call your prior employer and get those very negative, and completely undeserved, comments. I don't know where I went wrong. (Statement of George Spaulding)

Class Assignment. What mistakes were made by George Spaulding?

Wastewater Systems, Inc.

Wastewater Systems, Inc., was started in the spring of 1973, partially as a response to the Federal Water Pollution Control Act Amendment of 1972, which substantially increased the penalties for continued water pollution, the standards for permissible waste discharges, and the appropriations for improved treatment plants, and partially as a response to an exceedingly insightful forecast that energy costs were going to be much higher within the United States in the very near future. Robert Isherwood, the founder of the new company, had been the European sales manager for Environmental Engineering and Equipment Corporation, a large manufacturer of pollution control machinery based in Racine, Wisconsin. Mr. Isherwood had recognized very early in his overseas assignment that most of the air pollution equipment manufactured by his firm was salable in Europe, since it represented advanced design concepts and made use of innovative technologies, but that very little of the U.S. water pollution equipment could be used abroad since it was based upon the availability of inexpensive energy. Energy costs in Europe during the late 1960s and early 1970s were three to four times higher than they were in the United States, and European engineers

had developed pollution control processes for municipal sewage and waterborne industrial wastes that were considerably more capital-intensive but also much more energy-efficient. Mr. Isherwood had just accepted this difference in design concepts as a result of basic differences between the American and European Common Market economies, and had concentrated his efforts on the sale and installation of the air pollution control systems and solid waste collection and handling equipment manufactured by his firm, until the winter of 1972.

At a sales meeting and planning session held in November of that year by the Environmental Engineering and Equipment Corporation, Mr. Isherwood received the idea that led to the formation of his company. The sales meeting and planning session was an annual event, and executives from all the domestic and foreign divisions of Environmental Engineering were required to attend. Part of each meeting was spent in learning about new products and systems, either produced or proposed by the company, and part in updating the five-year marketing plan and agreeing upon sales objectives and expense budgets for the coming year. Prior to consideration of the five-year plan, it was traditional to listen to a long-range forecast of business conditions by the director of planning, a very bright and lively economist. At the 1972 meeting, that person concentrated on an expected change in energy costs. At that time, most governmental policy analysts and international trade managers expected the price of petroleum to continue to reflect the marginal cost of production; it was widely believed that substantial supplies of petroleum still existed, and that national demands were price sensitive, so that arbitrary changes by the producing countries could never be sustained. The director of planning presented some data which showed that the price–demand function had changed considerably over the past few years, and warned that pricing by the OPEC countries would become the result of political decisions, with religious overtones, rather than the derivation of economic equations. He finished with a five-year forecast of the consequences that, in retrospect, was exceedingly accurate.

Mr. Isherwood returned to Europe, visited the German manufacturer of water pollution equipment that was used extensively in the Common Market countries, and arranged an exclusive license to export that machinery to the United States. Water pollution control equipment, whether American or European in origin, is designed to filter or settle the nondissolved solids, to collect those solids as sludge, and then to burn the sludge, which is, of course, primarily organic matter. The dewatering process for the sludge is the key to the energy efficiency of the system. The American dewatering process consisted of a canvas belt that passed over a series of suction boxes; this method could achieve a 22% solid content. The German system, which had an international patent, used a colloidal membrane and a high-vacuum drum; it could achieve over 60% solid content, and the resulting combustion would be self-sustaining. That is, the energy developed in the combustion process provided enough heat to evaporate the remaining water.

Mr. Isherwood resigned from the Environmental Engineering and Equipment Corporation in the spring of 1973, and started Wastewater Systems, Inc., with $50,000 borrowed from his wife's parents and $10,000 of their own savings. The Arab oil embargo occurred in the fall of that year, and brought immediate energy consciousness to managers of municipal wastewater plants and governmental officials charged with implementing the recent pollution control legislation. Sales of Wastewater Systems, Inc., expanded from just slightly under $1.0 million in the first year of operations to well over $30.0 million in 1978, when the company was sold to one of the large conglomerates. Mr. Isherwood retired at the time of the sale, and now lives at Lake Tahoe, California.

Class Assignment. What are the ethical implications of the action by Robert Isherwood; specifically, how much do you owe your employer?

Chapter 5

STRATEGIC DESIGN IN LARGE SINGLE-INDUSTRY FIRMS

Strategy was defined in an earlier chapter as the long-term method of competition to be followed by a company. There are different methods of competition (alternative strategies) that are possible within each industry, and the function of the general manager of the company is to select the method (strategic design) with the greatest probability of success, given the specific opportunities and risks within the environment and the specific strengths and weaknesses within the corporation. This process of strategic management is shown in outline format at the top of the next page.

The process of strategic design differs, as was also explained in earlier chapters, both in the area of emphasis and in the level of complexity, between small single-product companies, medium-sized single-process divisions, and large single-industry firms. The decisive differences between these categories go beyond the size of the economic units, and concern the type of competitive advantage that can be gained by small companies, medium-sized divisions, or large firms, and the method of strategic planning that can be used by each to achieve the optimal competitive position.

Small companies, with a single product or a narrow product line, by definition have limited sales, and consequently they often search for a competitive advantage by combining product characteristics and market segments to find a high-margin "niche" with reduced competition. Smaller companies also often suffer from a shortage of financial and physical assets and technical and managerial skills, and therefore they are constrained in product development and market expansion. As a result, strategic planning for smaller firms is usually product–market oriented and resource based.

Product divisions of larger companies are also generally responsible for only a single product or product line, but their annual sales are often considerably larger than those of a small company, and consequently they are less able to find a market niche without competition. Product divisions usually must meet competition, not

Environmental characteristics
and trends

Economic

Technological

Social/political

Competitive

↓

Organizational mission or charter	Specific opportunities and risks within the industry	⎫
↓	↓	Selected strategy, or method of competition
Corporate performance and position	Range of strategic alternatives open to the firm	
↑	↑	
Managerial values and attitudes	Specific strengths and weaknesses within the company	⎭

↑

Money

Equipment

People

Market position

Organizational resources, or
assets and skills

---

avoid it, and they often search for a competitive advantage by combining capacity
expansions and technical improvements to find a low-cost production process. The
product divisions of large companies have access to the financial and physical assets
and the technical and managerial skills of the parent firm, so that they are not constrained by resources, but they are limited in sales growth and market expansion by
the competitive structure or environment of the industry. Strategic planning for
the product division of a larger company is, therefore, often product–process
oriented and environmentally based.

Large companies, operating within a single industry, generally have a range of
related products and product lines, that are sold to a variety of market segments
within that industry. The general managers within these firms have to consider
product–market positions for the specialty products that can provide higher margins, but they also have to take into account product–process positions for the volume products that require lower costs. General management in a large single-in-

dustry firm is a difficult task. Quite frankly, it is a task that seldom appears to be well done; the typical rates of return for large single-industry firms are considerably lower than the average returns on sales, assets, or equity of small single-product companies or large multiple-industry corporations. This reduced rate of return has often been ascribed to the maturity of the industry; it may be due to the complexity of the management task. In order to study this complexity, the process of strategic management in a single-industry firm has been divided into selection of the product–market position of the corporation and the consequent marketing policies, the selection of the product–process position of the company and the consequent investment plans, and the consideration of vertical integration and horizontal diversification.

Product–Market Position of the Corporation. It is common to think of large, single-industry firms as monoliths, with a generic product and a massive market. The view, while common, is inaccurate. Each of the basic single-product industries, such as steel, aluminum, petroleum, paper, or lumber, actually represents thousands of products and product lines that are sold to hundreds of markets and market segments. The steel industry, for example, offers products that vary by surface finish (hot-rolled and cold-rolled), by dimensional form (beams, plates, sheet, strip, bars, and tubing), and by alloy content, to major markets in transportation, construction, manufacturing, and packaging. The printed catalogue of one large steel company is 210 pages long, and lists approximately 340 different product lines, with an average of 18 size classifications or alloy variations per product.

Most companies operating within a single industry do not sell all products to all segments of that industry; there is a degree of product specialization and market orientation among even the largest of the single-industry firms. It is necessary, for meaningful strategic planning, to identify the major product lines and the relevant market segments of the industry, and the relative positions of the industry competitors within each product–market unit. A simple matrix can be used for this identification:

	Market segment 1	Market segment 2	Market segment 3	Market segment 4	Market segment 5
Product line 1	Company A Company B —	Company A — Company C	Company A Company B Company C	— — Company C	— Company B —
Product line 2	Company A Company B Company C	— Company B —	— — Company C	— Company B —	— Company B —

The competitive conditions of the industry within each product–market unit, or cell of the matrix, will differ by available margins, expected sales, potential entrants, etc., but a summary or surrogate statistic for many of these factors is the stage of the product life cycle. The competitive position of the company within each product–market unit will also differ by customer acceptance, product quality, brand reputation, promotional effectiveness, distribution availability, etc., but again a summary or surrogate statistic for many of these factors is the market share, if known, or a qualitative estimate of the corporate position relative to other competition. Each of the major product–market units of a single-industry firm can be positioned on this new matrix, with some estimate of the relative size of the unit in sales volume or assets employed:

Corporate market position (Company A)

		Dominant	Above average	Average	Below average	Weak
Product life cycle	Development					
	Growth				Unit 2-1	
	Maturity			Unit 1-1		
	Saturation		Unit 1-2	Unit 1-3		
	Decline					

The position of the product–market units of a single-industry firm on the matrix showing the product life cycle and the corporate competitive position, together with an understanding of the total market size, expected growth, and current margins of each of the units, provides a visual indication of the strategic alternatives open to the company. Some product–market units should receive more emphasis, and others less, and some product–market units should be added, and others eliminated, in order to improve the overall competitive performance of the firm. The corporate selection among these alternatives should be based upon an evaluation of the organizational strengths and weaknesses and the environmental opportunities and risks.

Marketing Policies of the Corporation. It might be expected that the marketing policies, on pricing, distribution, and promotion, would vary with the life cycle of the product and the competitive position of the company. The price level of a growth product with a dominant market position would normally reflect a considerably higher margin above direct costs than the price of a different product in the saturated stage of the life cycle and an average or below-average position in the market. Distribution and promotional policies also might be expected to differ for these two product–market units. However, single-industry firms have definite constraints on their marketing decisions. Price levels between different product–market units have to show a rational relationship or they will draw customers from one unit to another. Airlines, for example, almost eliminated first-class travel when they posted economy-class fares at a substantial discount below the existing tourist rates. Distribution for different product–market units often has to be through the same channel, or the costs may become excessive. Steel companies, for example, usually use the same sales force to market and the same warehouses to distribute both hot-rolled and cold-rolled steel, even though the applications and specifications differ markedly for the two products. The strategic planner in a large single-industry firm must consider the interdependencies of the product–market units in setting the marketing policies and designing the marketing programs and plans.

Product–Process Position of the Corporation. It is common to think of the manufacturing process of a large single-industry firm as a highly capital intensive production line that is capable of producing homogeneous products in massive numbers at low costs. That view, while common, again is essentially wrong. Most of the basic industries, such as steel, aluminum, paper, etc., have a degree of heterogeneity in their products and an amount of variation in their processing that is much greater than expected. The steel industry, again used as an example, requires very different machinery and equipment for the different finishes (hot-rolled or cold-rolled) and different dimensional forms (beams, plate, sheet, strip, bars, or tubing), even though the basic blast furnace (ore to iron) and conversion (iron to steel) processes are common for all the final products. A plant site of a large steel company may have 10 to 20 different processes to manufacture hundreds of different products.

Most companies operating within a single industry do not manufacture all products and have not invested in all processes; there is a degree of production specialization among even the largest of the single-industry firms, just as there is a degree of market orientation among those firms. It is necessary, for meaningful strategic planning, to identify the major product lines and the required productive processes of the industry, and the position of the competitors in each of these product–process units, or cells within the matrix:

	Manufacturing process 1	Manufacturing process 2	Manufacturing process 3	Manufacturing process 4	Manufacturing process 5
Product line 1	Company A Company B —	Company A Company B Company C	— —	—	—
Product line 2	—	—	Company A	—	—
Product line 3	— —	— —	— —	Company B Company C	— —

The competitive conditions of the industry within each product–process unit, or cell of the matrix, will differ by available margins, expected growth, potential entrants, etc., but a summary or surrogate statistic for many of these factors is, once again, the stage of the product life cycle. The competitive position of the company within each product–process unit will also differ by the technology employed, volume produced, and experience accumulated, but a summary or surrogate statistic for many of these factors is a qualitative estimate of the cost per unit relative to other competitors. Each of the major product–process units of a single-industry firm can be positioned on this new matrix relating product maturity to process cost, with some estimate of the relative size of the unit in terms of sales volume or assets employed:

Corporate manufacturing position (Company A)

	Dominant	Above average	Average	Below average	Weak
Development					
Growth				Unit 2-3	
Maturity			Unit 1-1		
Saturation				Unit 1-2	
Decline					

Product life cycle (bracket spanning Development, Growth, Maturity, Saturation, Decline)

   The position of the product–process units of a single-industry firm on this matrix showing the product life cycle and the corporate competitive position, especially when combined with the relative market position of the company, portray very graphically the strategic alternatives open to the firm. The strategic alternatives in manufacturing are primarily investment opportunities, to utilize new technologies, expand total capacities, or modernize existing facilities. Some product–process units should receive more capital, and some less, and some product–process units should be added, and others eliminated, in order to improve the overall competitive performance of the firm. The corporate selection among these investments should be based upon an understanding of the market position, an evaluation of the organizational strengths and weaknesses, and a forecast of environmental opportunities and risks.

Manufacturing Policies of the Corporation. The investment opportunities to improve the products, processes, or costs in manufacturing, and the managerial policies to plan, schedule, and control the manufacturing, are both constrained by the interrelationships among the product–process units. Many products have common raw materials, process facilities, or usable by-products so that expansion or contraction of capacity, or alteration of technology, at one product–process unit can have repercussions at other product–process units throughout the company. Manufacturing in a single-industry firm truly is a system, with a system defined as a "processing unit with interrelated components and known inputs and outputs." In many industries, the only practical way of understanding these interrelationships is to use mathematical models. The strategic planner in a single-industry firm must consider the constraints imposed by the interdependencies of the product–process units in evaluating manufacturing investments and establishing manufacturing policies, programs, and plans.

Vertical Integration by the Corporation. In addition to considering changes in the product–market and product–process positions of the company, the general manager of a single-industry firm should evaluate the strategic alternatives of vertical integration. Backward integration refers to the acquisition of supplier firms in order to utilize the value added and to ensure the supply of materials from this segment of the industry, while forward integration means the purchase of wholesaling and retailing companies, again to utilize the value added and to control the channels of distribution of that industry segment. These two concepts are shown graphically in the accompanying illustration.

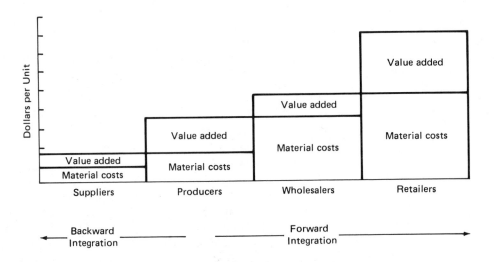

The supplier firms can range, of course, from the production and processing of raw materials to the manufacturing of needed components, while distributing companies can provide the shipping, storage, delivery, installation and repair of goods, the supervision of credit, and the generation of demand. Essentially, it is possible to think of the basic operations of an industry as a vertical continuum, ranging from raw material exploration to finished product sales, as shown at the top of page 231.

Supplying, producing, or distributing firms can be positioned over any portion of this vertical continuum. The strategic decision on the optimal position, or on the degree of vertical integration, either backward or forward, should include a calculation of the investment required and the return expected, and an evaluation of the organizational resources and skills and the environmental characteristics and trends relative to the planned expansion within the industry.

Examples from furniture industry	Basic operations of an industry	Examples from automobile industry
Retail store	Finished product sales	Auto dealership
	↑	
Wholesale firm	Finished product distribution	Auto transport
	↑	
Furniture manufacture	Finished product assembly	Auto assembly
	↑	
Drawer manufacture	Component assembly	Motor assembly
	↑	
Lumber cut to length	Part manufacture	Spark plug production
	↑	
Planing mill operation	Finished material processing	Steel forming (cold-rolled)
	↑	
Dry kiln operation	Semifinished processing	Iron refining (steel)
	↑	
Sawmill operation	Raw material processing	Ore smelting (iron)
	↑	
Timber harvesting	Raw material production	Ore mining
	↑	
Timberland ownership	Raw material supply	Ore exploration

Horizontal Diversification of the Corporation. The last of the major strategic alternatives open to a single-industry firm, after considering changes in the positions of the product–market units and the product–process units, and after evaluating movements, either forward or backward, in vertical integration, is the horizontal diversification of the product line. Essentially, horizontal diversification changes a single-industry firm into a multiple-industry firm. It is possible to think of all products of all industries on a continuum, with some overlapping between industries due to substitute products, and with each single-industry firm positioned along that continuum, as shown in the accompanying illustration.

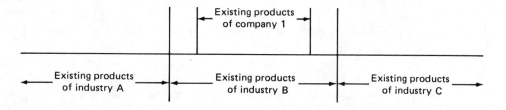

An industry has been defined in Chapter 3 as "the market for similar or substitute products or services, and the producing firms that supply those products or services." An industry basically delineates a group of competing firms that can affect the performance and position of one another by changes in product design, market segmentation, pricing level, distribution method, or advertising effort. The changes in product–market positioning that have been discussed earlier are primarily changes within a specific industry, since these movements would affect the performance and position of other companies within that group of competing firms. It is possible to consider changes in product–market positioning that would move a firm outside a given industry, along the continuum of horizontal diversification. These changes can be made with existing products, with new products, or with new technologies:

	Existing products	New products	New technologies
Existing markets within an industry	Industry concentration	Product development	Product research
New markets within an industry	Market development	Industry expansion	Industry exploration
New markets outside an industry	Related diversification	Conglomerate diversification	Technological diversification

It is often considered to be exceedingly difficult for a single-industry firm to move an existing product into a new industry, or to develop a new product or a new technology for another industry. This difficulty, it is felt, arises from the lack of transferability of resources, both physical assets and managerial and technological skills, from one industry to another. Functional and technical people who are accustomed to the competitive conditions and structure of one industry often find it nearly impossible to operate decisively in another industry, with very different competitive conditions and structure. It is all too easy to assume equivalent customer needs, buyer behaviors, distributor activities, and supplier loyalties, and then to find, in analyzing the causes of a spectacular failure, that the assumptions were incorrect.

Despite the difficulties, many single-industry firms have moved successfully into other industries, and have consequently been able to reduce their business risks through participating in markets with very different seasonal and cyclical trends, and have been able to utilize their resources more productively. The use of similar resources in two or more industries is termed "synergy," a word derived from a Greek expression that means "working together." An example of synergy would be the use of the same sales force to sell two very different products to the same customers, or to sell the same products to two very different markets. The problem is that synergistic benefits may be minimal. There is no question but that the concept is appealing; the problem is that the application often seems to be difficult and the returns disappointing. Horizontal diversification of a single-industry firm beyond the markets and processes of that industry does create problems, both in understanding the opportunities and risks within the new industry, and in utilizing the assets and skills of the existing company. The following cases illustrate these problems, and the special requirements of strategic design in a single-industry company.

Amdahl Corporation vs. IBM

Amdahl Corporation was formed in February 1971 to design, manufacture, and market a very large and technically advanced computer to compete directly with the central processing units produced by IBM. Mr. Eugene Amdahl, founder of the new company, was one of the pioneers in electronic data processing. During the late 1940s, while he was a Ph.D. student in physics at the University of Wisconsin, he was forced to spend 30 days using a mechanical calculator to disprove a statistical hypothesis; frustrated by the excessive time and hand calculations required, and assisted by two years of experience in radio electronics gained through wartime service in the navy, he volunteered to help in the design and construction of one of the first digital computers in the United States. Based upon vacuum-tube technology (each semiconductor in a modern computer was represented by one radio tube in the 1949 model), the machine at Wisconsin was difficult to program, awkward to use, and a tremendous advance over all other data-processing units available at that time. Mr. Amdahl was hired by IBM in 1951; he helped in the development of many of the early IBM computers, and was in charge of the design for the 360 series, which represented the third generation of central processing units, introduced in 1968.

In 1970, Mr. Amdahl was Director of Advanced Computer Design at IBM, and very dissatisfied. He and a group of other scientists and technicians had developed a very powerful computer based upon large-scale integrated (LSI) circuitry, which basically meant that more semiconductors and their associated interconnections (the "logic" of microelectronic design) could be packed upon each photoengraved chip, or 1/4 in. × 1/4 in. wafer of silicon oxide. The LSI circuitry reduced the labor cost for unit assembly, and shortened the time of data calculation, since there were fewer and shorter wires between elements in the computer design. Mr. Amdahl estimated that data processing could be performed 2.5 times faster on the new machine than on existing IBM computers, and that a unit could be built to handle 180% of the calculations and sell at 90% of the price of the 360 series. The senior management at IBM refused to fund further development or construction of the prototype; as a result, Mr. Amdahl was disappointed and discouraged.

> Brooding about why it was so difficult to push through a really superior machine for the top of IBM's line, Amdahl focused on some corporate policies he considered to be obstructionist. For one thing, very large machines had to bear the same 16% revenue allocation for marketing and support costs as smaller ones did, though their actual costs came to about 5% of revenue. At the same time, the design, development and tooling costs for large machines inevitably amounted to a higher percentage of revenue, because there were fewer units to carry those fixed expenses. "So," concludes Amdahl, remembered frustration evident in his voice, "there we were carrying an 11% burden of unincurred marketing costs and a higher than normal percentage of actually incurred development costs. Naturally, it was very difficult to justify a technically advanced computer." (*Fortune*, September 1977, p. 108)

In addition to the corporate policies of allocating marketing costs to all products at a fixed percentage, but charging developmental costs, with a high burden added for administration, to individual products at actual hours, Mr. Amdahl found that there was also a corporate rule against using different technologies on different products. One of the reasons for the continued financial success of IBM was the requirement that all models in

233

their line of computers make use of the same basic components, which provided enormous economies of scale, but which also discriminated against the larger, and more advanced machines. Mr. Amdahl made a special appeal to the senior management of the company to change these policies, which he felt to be prejudicial to technical advancement and design innovation, but his recommendations were again rejected.

When Amdahl confronted IBM's chairman and president with his request that the policies be changed, he received a respectful hearing but a very firm response: changing those policies would not be in the best interests of IBM. Perplexed, he started nosing around the company for an explanation.

The answer he pieced together turned out to lie in the relationships among the products in IBM's broad line. To maximize total revenues, Amdahl explained, IBM priced its machines so that the price/performance ratios would always be similar and the customer would always have to pay more for higher performance. If IBM had priced a high-performance computer low enough to get the volume needed for amortizing high development costs, its price/performance ratio would have been better than ratios for other parts of the line. Customers using middle-of-the-line computers would have migrated to the high end, either by replacing a number of smaller computers with one big one, banding together to share a big machine, or accepting over-capacity for a period of time.

With a markedly superior price/performance ratio available, in other words, lots of customers would spend less than they otherwise would; overall, IBM would forego more revenue than it would gain. And it would forego even more profit than revenue, since the margins on an advanced machine with a relatively low price would probably be thinner than on middle-of-the-line systems. So, for the sake of total corporate revenues and in-

come, Amdahl concluded, IBM would always have to burden advanced machines with inflated support costs and with component technology best suited for middle-sized machines. (*Fortune*, September 1977, p. 109)

Mr. Amdahl resigned from IBM in 1970 to form a new company dedicated to the construction of a powerful general-purpose computer that would be based upon advanced microelectronic technology, and that consequently could offer a much improved price/performance option to large data processors. He felt that he had discovered a structural weakness in the strategy of IBM which prevented them from competing effectively in this segment of the market, and that there were characteristics of the market segment and of the time period that would greatly help the smaller firm.

He picked the right product. RCA and General Electric had attempted to build middle-of-the-line computers, but they found that they could not compete due to the economies of scale that IBM realized in product design, component production, corporate marketing, and consumer service. Amdahl planned to build a top-of-the-line computer where IBM could not compete due to the very policies that had made them successful in the first place.

He picked the right market segment. Big computers are purchased by large companies that have established data processing departments with trained operators and sophisticated systems people. You don't have to spend much time selling to those companies since they understand the comparative features of available hardware, and you don't have to offer much help installing and servicing the equipment since they know the technical details. I hope that your students understand that I am attempting to be humorous when I say that all you have to do to sell large, expensive computers to big, experienced companies is to provide measurable performance improvements and absolute systems reliability. You don't even have to offer the short-term rentals and operating leases that can tie up so much of your money; the big customers can finance their own equipment at attractive rates. You just have to offer a better machine.

He also picked the right time. In 1969 IBM had been forced to "unbundle" the programming software from the computer hardware, and make the software available to any user. IBM had to place all their operating programs in the public domain. Amdahl had the idea of building a machine that would be compatible with IBM's software, so that he could avoid the expense of developing his own programming package, and so that his customers would not have to change their operating systems. IBM users had massive investments in their application programming and personnel training—I've heard estimates up to 100 billion dollars—that were dependent upon the IBM software, and they would never scrap an investment of that size to buy a new central processor and memory unit, no matter how cost-effective. Amdahl made his new computer compatible with the existing programming software, and compatible with the existing peripheral equipment, so that large companies could easily switch to his machine. 1970 was the first year that the unbundled programs were available, and Amdahl was the first company to take advantage of that opportunity. (Statement of an industry investor)

Mr. Amdahl started the new company in February 1971, to build a high-speed computer for large customers who needed additional capacity in their data-processing operations, and who could be expected to purchase a machine with a substantially improved price/performance ratio, provided that they could continue to use their existing applications programs and peripheral equipment. Assisted by the clarity of the stated strategy, by the attractiveness of the potential market, and by the reputation of his prior position, he was able to raise $15 million of startup capital, hire a group of scientists and technicians, build a research laboratory and prototype assembly plant in Sunnyvale, California, and begin the product development process. Few people expected him to succeed.

> Computer designer Gene M. Amdahl, architect of IBM's famous Series 360, is known for his original cast of mind, but when he quit IBM ... back in 1970 he seemed to have pushed originality to the point of eccentricity. In a bluntly worded letter of resignation, he declared his intention of competing with IBM by producing large-scale, general-purpose computers that would run on IBM software.
>
> Such audacity doubtless caused some indulgent smiles in Armonk (site of corporate headquarters for IBM, just north of New York City). With no wealthy backers, no experience in running a computer company, and a demonstrated distaste for administration, Amdahl was setting out to challenge the champion that was even then laying to waste General Electric and RCA. At most, it appears from an internal document, IBM thought of Amdahl as a vague threat to a few enormous computer installations used by customers with specialized needs. (*Fortune*, September 1977, p. 106)

The startup capital was raised, in approximately equal amounts, from E. F. Heizer, a venture capital firm in Chicago; from Fujitsu Ltd., a microelectronics company in Japan; and from Nixdorf Gmbh., a business equipment manufacturer in West Germany. $15 million was not expected to be sufficient for the full commercial introduction of the new computer, but it was expected to carry the company through the developmental stage to an operating prototype installed and accepted by a major customer. The installation and acceptance of an advanced data-processing unit would, of course, provide extensive publicity and an enviable reputation for the small company, and it was felt that a public stock issuance would be possible at that time, buoyed by the investor optimism that always surrounds technical advances, to bring in the funds required for full-scale manufacturing and marketing of the new product.

The company also started with approximately 70 employees, drawn equally from the design staff at IBM and from the electronic firms and data-processing companies in the Santa Clara region, termed "Silicon Valley," of northern California. The new employees were not entirely oriented toward high technology; persons with specific training and responsibilities in marketing, finance, and control were included in the management staff.

> Your students may feel, in the light of what happened, that this was just another example of a group of impractical scientists, with their heads in the clouds and their noses over a drawing board, ruining a perfectly good business plan. But it probably would not be too much of an exaggeration to say that there were as many MBA's as there were PhD's in that group, and they were there because Heizer and the other people who were supplying the money wanted them to be there. Venture capitalists learned a long time ago that pure technology does not sell many apples, and so they insisted that all of the management functions be represented in the forming group. I don't have to tell you that; I read the same thing in one of your books. (Statement of an industry investor)

> Most venture capital firms are interested primarily in the competence and character of the management since they feel that even mediocre products can be successfully manufactured, promoted, and distributed by an energetic and experienced management group that is able to work together easily and productively, even under the conditions of stress that will come from temporary reversals and competitive problems, while excellent products can be simply destroyed by poor management. Many venture capital firms state that basically they invest in management capability, not in product or market potential, but obviously this analysis of managerial capability is difficult. A partner or senior executive of a venture capital firm will normally spend at least a week at the offices of a company being considered for equity financing, talking with and observing the management, to form an estimate of their competence and character. In addition, the firm will usually insist that the company have a complete management group, with training, experience, and assigned responsibilities in all the functional areas of product design, marketing, production, finance, and control, and they will expect that each member of this management group have a thorough understanding of the industry and a high degree of commitment to the company. Most venture capital firms are definite that they will not consider a proposal from a company without a complete group of experienced, knowledgeable, and committed managers. (Hosmer, *Financial Management for the Smaller Business Firm*, p. 46)

Despite the preparation of an explicit business plan, the investment of substantial venture capital, the presence of experienced managerial personnel, and the efforts of proven computer scientists, the company encountered major problems in 1973 and 1974. These problems can be described under headings of technical, transitional, financial, and personnel:

1. *Technical problems.* One of the central features of the Amdahl computer design was to be the use of LSI (large-scale integrated) circuitry, with semiconductors and the related interconnections tightly packed on silicon chips. The use of LSI circuitry would, as described previously, shorten the time for data processing and reduce the

cost of frame assembly by eliminating much of the wiring, but current flow through the dense packing could produce temperatures high enough to destroy the circuit connections. The original intention was to solder the chips to a metal plate that would dissipate the heat, but the heat built up at the soldered points, which gradually loosened. The next solution was to bond the chips to ceramic plates, again for heat dissipation, but ceramic materials conduct heat more slowly than metallic parts, and the temperature imbalances caused warping. The ultimate answer to the problem, reached after extensive experimentation, was to bond a finned cooling stud, gold-plated to equalize heat transfer, to the back of each ceramic plate; these provided a means of heat dissipation, and gave a very distinctive appearance to the frame of the Amdahl computer.

2. *Transitional problems.* Heat buildup in the compacted circuitry was one of the major difficulties, but it was not the only technical problem faced by the design staff of the new company. The logic had to be developed and drawn, in very precise detail, for the standardized chips; the chips had to be combined and interconnected, without error, on the carrier boards; and the carrier boards had to be mounted and wired on the mainframe of the computer. To provide an indication of the complexity of the overall design task, there were 40,000 connections which had to be specified for each carrier board, and there were 51 carrier boards in the central processing unit, which meant slightly over 2 million connections to be indicated on the engineering drawings. The precise, complex nature of the design task took time, and there simply weren't enough people who had the ability to work concurrently on interrelated portions of a single, unified project. The development effort fell behind the time

schedule that had been established, and it fell far enough behind so that the prototype machine that had been expected in 1973 could not be completed until 1974. In 1974, IBM announced their new Model 168, which was an expected transition from the earlier Model 165, but it created extensive problems for the small Amdahl company since it was the first virtual machine.

The "virtual" feature of the new IBM computer greatly extended the power, although not the speed, of the central processing unit. All electronic data processors operate with a finite core memory, which is used to store the program, or operating instructions for the computer. The size of the core, obviously, limits the size of the program that can be run upon the machine. IBM developed hardware that permitted storage of part of the program on magnetic disks, and thereby greatly extended the virtual, although not the actual, size of the core. This feature increased the programming capability of the IBM machines, and Mr. Amdahl felt that he would have to offer the same feature, for the software to be fully compatible and for his computer to be truly superior. The sudden change in specifications brought extensive design modifications, which delayed the introduction of the Amdahl for an additional 15 months.

3. *Financial problems.* The technical difficulties encountered in design and the transitional requirements imposed by the actions of the major competitor brought very severe financial problems to the Amdahl Corporation. A public offering had been planned during 1974; it was necessary to delay that stock issuance since a prototype machine was not completed and installed. It became necessary for Mr. Amdahl to raise money for the continuation of the company from private, not public sources.

Gene Amdahl raised money from every organization that already had an investment in the computer company, and from many organizations that had no investment but wanted an opportunity to participate in the computer industry. The money was raised in the form of convertible debentures, or straight debt with an option to buy common shares later, and it came from nonstandard sources. Banks would not loan him money since his financial position was so poor, and venture capital firms would not buy his equity since they felt, now, that he could not succeed.

Gene Amdahl was good at raising money. He could explain, in a very calm and very logical way, why his company's eventual success was inevitable. And he became an excellent negotiator with financial people since he understood what they wanted, and could anticipate their demands. It took time, however. I've heard him give a talk in which he said that raising money took 90% of his time for more than two years, and that he covered all the major countries in the world. He is not a boastful person, but he said that the financial achievement of his company was greater than the technical achievement, and he may be right: 1974 was a recession year, and it is hard to convince people to invest in a failing designer of high-powered computers during a recession. (Statement of an industry investor)

Mr. Amdahl raised, reportedly, $11 million from E. F. Heizer, the venture capital firm in Chicago, and $23 million from Fujitsu, the electronics manufacturer in Japan, and approximately $15 million from miscellaneous sources, primarily insurance companies that provided long-term loans in exchange for liberal stock options. Heizer and Fujitsu now own, respectively, 23.4% and 28.7% of the company, after converting all of their debt to equity. Mr. Amdahl also arranged for Fujitsu to purchase all of the silicon chips for the early machines, assemble those chips on the carrier boards, and wire the boards into the mainframe of the computer. This subcontracting of assembly, with extended terms of payment, permitted the Amdahl company to expand production rapidly, once the final design was completed.

4. *Personnel problems.* While Mr. Amdahl was raising money, and fully occupied in traveling throughout the world and meeting with financial managers at insurance companies and investment firms, the managerial direction of the Amdahl Corporation seemed to simply fall apart. Technical development slowed, well behind the schedule, while overhead expenses soared, far beyond the budget, and employee morale rapidly declined. A new manager, Eugene White, was hired to act jointly with Mr. Amdahl in pushing the computer design through to completion, and in achieving the early sales and demonstrated performance that were needed to permit public financing of the firm.

Amdahl's first computer had to be scrapped on the eve of its planned introduction because IBM's new entries had rendered it obsolete. A public offering failed, and the company went deeply into debt with its backers. The development program fell far behind schedule. There was a nearly complete turnover of the management team. Under these stresses, board members who represented major investors in the company began, if not to panic, at least to lose so much confidence in Amdahl that they leaned on him almost enough to make him resign. In fact, Amdahl threatened to resign on several occasions, but he never followed through....

Tension in the boardroom reached a peak in early 1974, when Amdahl's enterprise almost went under. Chief among the problems was a collapse of management: some key officers proved simply unable to control the development process. Amdahl himself took over, but found it difficult to contend with Fujitsu's insistence that he fire hundreds of employees, Heizer's strong criticisms of the business plan ... and his own reluctance to become deeply embroiled in administration.

The solution was to bring in Eugene R. White, formerly a key manager of GE's computer operations. He first came aboard as a consultant and then, in August 1974, became president of Amdahl Corp. White, forty-six, is raspy-voiced and emphatic, and his practical talents are as impressive as Amdahl's conceptual abilities. He relishes precisely those administrative tasks that Amdahl loathes, and he was mainly responsible for reorganizing the company. Director John Connolly (not the political figure and former Secretary of the Treasury, but a separate individual with the same name and geographic location), a burly, outspoken businessman from Texas who has known Amdahl for decades, says, "Gene White has added as much to Amdahl Corp. as Gene Amdahl has. They are exact opposites and the best pair of men I have ever seen teamed up." (*Fortune*, September 1977, pp. 109–110)

Mr. White took immediate action to reduce expenses, particularly in the manufacturing area of the company, where the decision to postpone the introduction of the first computer model had left a large staff with very limited activities. Two hundred and fifty employees were laid off. Mr. White also felt that many of the marketing, finance, and control functions had not been performed as well nor developed as fully as might have been expected; there was an almost complete turnover of the management group that had been brought together at the start of the company. Finally, Mr. White insisted upon the establishment of explicit goals for each of the design groups; the scientists and technicians were forced to accept more direct supervision of the development process.

During the balance of 1974 and early 1975, the design of the Amdahl computer was changed to incorporate the new features of the IBM Model 168, and final testing of a prototype was completed. In late 1975, six Amdahl computers were sold, producing $14,400,000 in revenues, and in 1976 twenty-six

units were shipped, generating $92,800,000 in revenues and $22,700,000 in profits. As indicated by the rapid growth in sales, the new computer model was very enthusiastically received as a major technical advance, and the new computer company was very cheerfully welcomed as a viable competitor to IBM. (See Exhibits 1 and 2 for Amdahl's income statements and balance sheets for fiscal years 1971 to 1977.)

Everybody loves a David and Goliath story. But when the Goliath is IBM, they tend to yawn a bit: so many challengers have come along to test the computer giant and then faded quickly into oblivion. Nevertheless, a new contender seems to be succeeding where even such big competitors as RCA and General Electric failed. Last year, little Amdahl Corp. of Sunnyvale, California, took a noticeable bite out of the totally IBM-dominated market for top-of-the-line, general-purpose computers. In its first full year of marketing, Amdahl sold 27 of its new 470 V/6 computers to such prestigious customers as AT&T, American Airlines and the National Aeronautics and Space Administration, ringing up $92.8 million in sales....

Amdahl's marketing feat stunned the computer industry. As industry analyst L. Duance Kirkpatrick of Dean Witter & Co. says, "It was a coup to take any business away from IBM in that market and an impressive performance for a company that had its very first sale in late 1975...."

The high performance 470 V/6 is used by big companies for such varied operations as personnel and payroll and systems monitoring. Throughout the computer industry, it is considered a superior machine to the IBM 370-168, with which it directly competes. Incorporating unique "emitter-coupled" logic circuits, which are far faster than the integrated circuits used by IBM, the 470 can process 50% more data than the 370-168 in the same amount of time, costs 10% to 15%

Exhibit 1 *Income statements (000's omitted) for the Amdahl Corporation, 1971–1977*

	1971	1972	1973	1974	1975	1976	1977
Equipment sales	—	—	—	—	14,358	91,896	181,846
Equipment lease/maintenance	—	—	—	—	41	924	6,962
Total revenues	—	—	—	—	14,399	92,820	188,808
Cost sales	—	—	—	—	8,198	44,433	85,470
Cost lease/maintenance	—	—	—	—	287	4,135	13,580
Total costs	—	—	—	—	8,485	48,568	99,050
Gross margin	—	—	—	—	5,914	44,252	89,758
Engineer expenses	1,381*	3,985	11,527	9,085	8,711	9,333	16,669
S&A expenses	423*	1,481	3,024	2,660	3,319	8,569	20,260
Interest expenses	2	89	150	1,659	2,673	2,347	(1,420)
Total expenses	1,806	5,555	14,701	13,404	14,703	20,249	35,509
Income/(loss)	(1,806)	(5,555)	(14,701)	(13,404)	(8,789)	24,003	54,249
Income taxes	—	—	—	—	—	1,310	17,599
Net income	(1,806)	(5,555)	(14,701)	(13,404)	(8,789)	22,693	36,650

Source: Prospectus of the Amdahl Corporation, June 2, 1977, p. 9, and *Moody's Industrial Manual*, 1978, p. 1201, plus estimates (*) by industry investor.

less and is one-third smaller. It can be installed in less than a day, versus a week or more for the 370. "It's a superior system in price, performance and reliability," says Kirkpatrick flatly. (*Duns Review*, April 1977, pp. 23–24)

The 470 V/6 has proved to be 80% more cost effective than the 370-168. It provides 50% to 60% more throughput than the 168 ... and operates at 2½ times the internal processing speed. (Statement of an Amdahl computer user, quoted in *Datamation*, January 1977, p. 150)

Once a customer starts using a V/6, it appears, the machine sells itself. A sample of ten Amdahl users surveyed by Input, a computer marketing research firm, and nine more that Fortune queried, indicated at least satisfaction, and in many cases ardent support, for the V/6. Users were especially impressed by the machine's reliability. Carl Reynolds,

data processing director for Hughes Aircraft, exclaims that "our V/6 is unbelievably reliable. I've been in this racket for twenty years, and it's the most incredible engineering feat I've ever seen." Such endorsements are invaluable in the kind of reference selling that pervades the large-computer market. (*Fortune*, September 1977, p. 112)

The Amdahl Corporation was greatly helped in their rapid acceptance by customers in the high-performance computer market by the very rapid growth within that market. Sales of mainframe processing units within the United States and western Europe were expected to continue a pattern of growth at approximately 10% per year (see Exhibit 3) during the late 1970s, but the overall market for mainframe units could be divided into nine size classifications (see Exhibit 4), and it was reported that the growth would be con-

Exhibit 2 *Balance sheets (000's omitted) for the Amdahl Corporation, end of the fiscal years 1971–1977*

	1971	1972	1973	1974	1975	1976	1977
Cash/securities	658	17,421	1,926	55	84	32,131	71,932
Accounts receivable	—	—	—	—	4,230	1,327	12,778
Inventories	6*	417*	4,110*	9,090*	10,456*	33,948	35,088
Miscellaneous assets	59*	123*	35*	111	156	420	3,745
Current assets	723*	17,961*	6,071*	9,257*	14,926*	67,826	123,543
Plant and equipment	458*	1,142*	4,095	5,938	9,464	19,524	52,578
Depreciation	24*	96*	591	1,224	2,023	4,121	9,813
Fixed assets	434	1,046	3,504	4,615	7,441	15,403	42,765
Accounts payable	127*	779*	846	1,209	1,731	4,353	9,805
Due stockholder	—	—	1,025	2,498	15,832	19,240	16,876
Bank loans	31*	74*	—	—	—	—	6,250
Miscellaneous liabilities	43*	1,277*	1,487	601	2,650	8,730	18,444
Current liabilities	201*	2,130*	3,358	4,239	20,213	32,213	51,375
Bank loan	—	—	—	—	—	—	15,625
Convertible bonds	—	8,800*	12,800	29,500	30,912	—	—
Miscellaneous debt	—	—	—	215	—	—	6,844
Long-term debt	—	8,800*	12,800	29,715	30,912	—	22,469
Preferred	2,075	2,475	2,475	2,475	2,475	—	—
Common stock	687	12,953	13,004	13,008	13,022	72,468	77,694
Retained earnings	(1,806)	(7,361)	(22,062)	(35,466)	(44,255)	(21,562)	(14,770)
Total equity	956	8,067	(6,583)	(19,984)	(28,758)	50,906	92,464
Liabilities and equity	1,157	19,007	9,575	13,970	22,367	83,229	166,308

Source: Prospectus of the Amdahl Corporation, June 2, 1977, p. 9, and *Moody's Industrial Manual*, 1978, p. 1201, plus estimates (*) by industry investor.

centrated in the very small and the very large machines.

Percentage estimates of the probable growth in each of the size classifications for the mainframe computer market in the United States were not available, but numerous persons within the industry expected the growth to be concentrated in the very small and the very large units.

The place to be in the late 1970s and early 1980s in the computer industry will be in either of the two extremes on the product list. The other place to be, in a geographic sense, will be western Europe and, if you could get there, Japan. (Statement of an industry investor)

Amdahl has tied into one of the fastest growing segments of the computer industry. The market for high-performance computers is expanding at a 25 to 35% average annual rate and is expected to continue that pace for five years or longer. Amdahl has also sold three computers each in the Canadian and western

Exhibit 3 *Sales and estimates of sales (000,000's omitted) of mainframe computers manufactured by U.S. firms, 1976–1980*

	1976	1977	1978	1979	1980
Domestic sales	$ 5,300	$ 6,500	$ 7,500	$ 7,900	$ 8,400
International	5,300	5,800	6,600	7,000	7,400
Total sales	$10,600	$12,300	$14,100	$14,900	$15,800

European markets, which are growing even faster, and plans to expand its European business rapidly over the next several years. "The kind of customer that wants our system, both in the U.S. and abroad, is the very large company seeking another source of superior equipment besides IBM," says White (President of Amdahl Corp.). "And that's exactly what we're delivering." (*Duns Review*, April 1977, p. 25)

In order to take advantage of the rapidly expanding market for high-performance computers, and to solidify their competitive position within that market, the Amdahl Corporation acted in 1976 to strengthen their capital structure and to expand their productive capacity. First, $30,912,000 in convertible debentures and $2,475,000 in preferred stock were exchanged by the two firms that had provided the venture capital, E. F. Heizer and Fujitsu Ltd., for $33,387,000 of common stock, and then a public sale of equity, together with the exercise of some of the warrants owned by the large investors, netted $26,059,000 for the company. At the end of the fiscal year in 1977, Amdahl Corporation had a net worth of $92,400,000, a

Exhibit 4 *Size classifications (000,000's omitted) for mainframe computers, major manufacturers, and U.S. sales estimates by class*

No.	Classification	IBM	Honeywell	Other	1977 sales
—	Home computers	—	—	Apple, Pertec, Tandy, etc.	$ 400 (see note)
0	Minicomputers	—	—	DEC, H-P, Texas Instruments, etc.	4,500 (see note)
1	Small business	System/3–4	H–61/58	Burroughs 1710	300
2	Very small frame	System/3–8	H–61/60	Burroughs 1810	500
3	Small frame	360/20	H–62 level	DEC–2020	900
4	Small–medium frame	360/40	H–64 level	DEC–2040	1,000
5	Medium frame	370/145	H–66/10	DEC–2060	1,200
6	Medium–large frame	370/155	H–66/40	Itel AS/5	1,400
7	Large frame	370/168	H–68/80	Amdahl V/5	800
8	Very large frame	3033	—	Amdahl V/6	370
9	Not named	—	—	Amdahl V/7	30
Total U.S. mainframe computer sales in 1977 (millions)					$6,500

Note: Home computers and minicomputers are not included in the "mainframe" classification since core memory is based upon microprocessors (single LSI circuit chips) and not on a wired frame.
Source: Industry investor.

current ratio of 2.4:1, a debt/equity ratio of 0.79:1, a line of credit established at major U.S. banks of $50,000,000, and cash and marketable securities in the amount of $71,932,-000 (see Exhibit 2). The financial strength of 1977 marked a very dramatic change from the near bankruptcy of 1975.

The productive position of the company also changed, with assembly of the carrier boards and the wiring of the computer frames now performed in the Amdahl plant in California rather than in the Fujitsu factory in Japan. It was decided that computers for sale in Asia and in Australia would continue to be made in Japan, while units for delivery in Europe and South America would be manufactured in a new factory under construction in Ireland.

> Amdahl Corp. is expanding aggressively. For one thing, the company is making a major push into foreign markets; it already has six wholly owned subsidiaries. By 1978, it will have a plant in Ireland. According to Clifford Madden, vice president for finance and president of Amdahl International, tax concessions and labor rates are so favorable that, everything else being equal, it would make sense to supply the world from Ireland, and not just Europe and the Commonwealth countries. Madden all but rubs his hands in anticipation of gearing up abroad. "The animosity toward IBM," he gloats, "is broad, deep, and worldwide." (*Fortune*, September 1977, p. 120)

Throughout much of 1977, while changes were occurring rapidly in the customer base, financial position, and productive capacity of the Amdahl Corporation, industry observers and company executives were waiting for the competitive reaction by IBM.

> Gene Amdahl is spending around $9 million a year on R&D both to maintain the 470's edge and to broaden the company's product line as a buffer against the one

virtually inevitable problem it will face: a countermove by IBM. Industry analysts are certain that the giant will respond to Amdahl's encroachment, either this year or next. Of course, perennially close-mouthed IBM is disclosing nothing, but analysts figure the company will either boost the capacity and reduce the price of the 370-168 or convert some of its software into the mainframe hardware via a process known as microcoding, which would diminish Amdahl's ability to ride free on the software. (*Duns Review*, April 1977, p. 25)

The competitive reaction by IBM was delayed until late 1977, but finally took the form of an announcement of a new Model 3033 computer, which could operate at 1.6 to 1.8 times the capacity of their Model 168, and which could be sold at approximately 70% of the price of the earlier machine. The Amdahl Corporation responded by announcing a new V/7 processing unit that would operate at 1.3 times the capacity of the Model 3033 and yet sell at exactly the same price level. The stage was set for extended competition between the two firms in the high performance segment of the computer market.

> IBM has not been suffering Amdahl's inroads passively. It has sent flying squads of corporate brass to reason with the top executives of endangered accounts. According to some large-computer users, as well as Amdahl executives, IBM salesmen have hinted strongly that Amdahl won't survive and have even made veiled threats to reduce maintenance on IBM peripherals and software hooked up with Amdahl machines. Since 1976, moreover, IBM has slashed prices of central-processor memories and introduced variations on its large machines that seem to strike directly at Amdahl.
>
> None of those product announcements, however, involved a radical change in price/performance that might herald a new generation capable of destroying the V/6. That kind of response finally came

... when IBM announced its 3033 processor. With performance 1.6 to 1.8 times that of the Model 168 and a price about one-third lower, the 3033 represents a total price/performance improvement of some 140%, or even better. At the same time, IBM disclosed price cuts of about 30% on its current large machines. Within minutes of the news, journalists and security analysts were predicting a slackening in Amdahl's shipments and deep erosion of its margins.

Amdahl's return salvo came quickly. On Monday, after a weekend of "very little sleep and a lot of salami sandwiches," as one executive recalls it, the company announced a new computer it had been working on since late 1975: a V/7 machine that would be 1.3 to 1.5 times faster than IBM's 3033 but cost only 3% more.

To compensate for IBM's price reduction on the 168, Amdahl made a similar cut on the V/6. Almost as a gesture of defiant virtuosity, the company also announced a V/5, a smaller 168-class machine on the same superior price/performance curve as the other two models. In a report to its clients, Input [a market research firm specializing in the data-processing industry] called Amdahl's response "the fastest major business decision of 1977."

Since Amdahl had made very deep price cuts, margins seemed bound to wither. But when the second-quarter report emerged, nothing dire had happened. Shipments held up, and the squeeze on margins was quite mild. By negotiating a 20% price cut on Fujitsu's subassemblies, switching to new memory chips that cost less than one-fourth as much per byte as the old ones, and self-manufacturing more of its assemblies in higher volume, Amdahl managed to show a gross margin of 45.4%, only 2.2 points less than the figure for all of last year. And the results should improve as the lower costs of new parts work themselves through inventory.

Exactly what the 3033 means for the future is unclear, and IBM will say nothing about that. One thing the machine does *not* seem to portend is some radically new future system.... IBM's plan for such a system died quickly in 1975, victim of over-ambition and over-complication, and nothing of that kind is likely to come about, because IBM's customers have shown a growing resistance to change. As Frank Cary, IBM's chairman, puts it, "From now on, change will be evolutionary rather than revolutionary." Amdahl's designers feel quite capable of keeping up with evolution. (*Fortune*, September 1977, p. 112)

Class assignment

1. List the major strategic alternatives that were open to Mr. Amdahl in 1971, during the formation of the company. List five major resources (assets and skills) that were available to the firm, and five major environmental factors (characteristics and trends) that were present in the industry. Would you have selected the same strategic alternative of designing a high-performance computer for sale to very large users of data-processing equipment? What were the risks involved in that decision?

2. Define the product–market positions of IBM, Honeywell, Burroughs, Digital Equipment Company (DEC), and Amdahl Computer Corporation in 1977, at the date of the case. For comparative purposes, place the products of each company in a product line by market segment matrix, as described in the text. Limited information is provided in the case on market segments; estimate the probable usage of the different classes of computers. Which companies compete within the mainframe computer industry?

3. Amdahl and IBM compete on certain product lines within the mainframe computer industry. Consider the life cycles of the products and the relative positions of

the companies. What are the relative advantages/disadvantages for each company in marketing?

4. Define the product–process positions of IBM and Amdahl Computer Corporation. Limited information is provided in the case on production processes; estimate the probable advantages/disadvantages for each company in manufacturing.

5. Consider the possibility of expansion within the mainframe computer industry. What different products, markets, or processes should Mr. Amdahl consider as a strategic move for the Amdahl Computer Corporation?

6. Consider the possibility of vertical integration within the mainframe computer industry. What would be the advantages and disadvantages of this strategic move for the Amdahl Computer Corporation?

7. Consider the possibility of horizontal diversification outside the mainframe computer industry. What would be the advantages and disadvantages of this strategic move for the Amdahl Computer Corporation?

8. Consider the strategy of IBM in 1970. What response should the senior management of that company have made to Mr. Amdahl when he proposed that IBM build a large, high-performance mainframe computer based upon advanced technology?

Competition within the Steel Industry

The domestic steel industry in the United States is huge. 240 companies in 1977 shipped 91,147,000 tons of finished steel, with a market value of $39.7 billion ($436.5 per ton). The industry employed 337,396 production workers at an annual cost of $6.6 billion ($19,640 per worker), and 114,992 staff, supervisory, and managerial personnel at an annual charge of $2.6 billion ($22,800 per person). The companies reported total current assets of $12.3 billion, and total fixed assets, at original cost before the annual allowances for depreciation, of $41.3 billion. Stockholders' equity was $17.6 billion, and there were 815,000 shareholders. Profits for the year for the industry were $23.2 million, which represented a 0.13% return on owners' equity and a 0.056% return on assets employed.

The steel industry is not only big, it is central to the economic system of the United States. Forty percent of all manufacturing jobs are concerned with steel forming or machining, or the assembly of steel products. Seventy percent of all construction jobs are dependent upon steel beams or reinforcing rods. One hundred percent of all jobs in commercial transport require steel goods. The steel industry is big, critical, and in trouble. 1977 was a disastrous year, with permanent plant closings, increased foreign imports, rising production costs, regulated market prices, and heavy strike activity at the coal and iron ore mines. Hopefully, we won't see 1977 again, but we aren't going to see 1974 either (when the industry earned 17.1% on equity and 6.5% on sales); basically,

Exhibit 1 *Total U.S. steel shipments (thousands of tons), total U.S. steel production versus world steel production (percent), total U.S. profits after taxes (millions of dollars), and profits as percentage of sales revenues and owners' equity*

Year	U.S. total shipments	U.S. product vs. foreign (%)	U.S. profits after taxes	U.S. profits (% revenues)	U.S. profits (% equity)
1968	91,856	22.6	$ 992.2	5.3	8.2
1969	93,877	22.4	879.4	4.6	7.0
1970	90,798	20.1	531.6	2.8	4.1
1971	87,038	18.8	562.8	2.8	4.3
1972	91,805	19.2	774.8	3.4	5.8
1973	111,430	19.6	1,272.2	4.4	9.3
1974	109,472	18.6	2,475.2	6.5	17.1
1975	79,957	16.4	1,594.9	4.7	9.8
1976	89,447	17.2	1,337.4	3.7	7.8
1977	91,147	16.9	23.2	0.06	0.1

Source: A.I.S.I. Annual Statistical Report, 1977, p. 8.

the trends have been down for the past 10 years, and the industry has to recognize and deal with those trends. (Statement of an industry consultant)

Industry statistics from 1968 to 1977 show static growth, cyclical demand, a declining position versus foreign competitors, variable profits, and a disappointing return on both sales and equity. Exhibit 1 shows these trends; it should be understood that the low 1977 profits reflect a charge of $949.1 million for the sale or disposal of assets at discontinued operations. It is not expected that similar charges will be required in the immediate future in the industry.

The steel industry has numerous problems that have brought the return on capital far below the return generally available in other sectors of the economy. These problems include foreign competition, governmental regulation, obsolete equipment, inadequate financing, and cyclical demand. To understand these problems, and to recognize the strategic reactions of the individual companies within the industry to those problems, it is necessary first to comprehend the technology of steel manufacturing and the eco-

nomics of steel production. Exhibit 2 provides a basic graph of the process of steel manufacturing, and the following text describes the sequence of steps in this process.

Input Raw Materials. The input raw materials for steel manufacturing are iron ore, metallurgical coal or coke, and limestone; steel scrap, although not technically a raw material, is also used in the process at a later stage.

1. *Iron ore and benefication.* Iron is one of the most common elements on the earth, usually found in the form of iron oxides, but also as iron silicates and sulfides, and generally located in deposits of sedentary rock. A large deposit of nearly pure iron oxide was discovered in northern Minnesota during the 1870s, and this very high grade ore supplied the steel industry within the United States until the 1950s, when additional sources in Quebec, Labrador, and Venezuela were developed and additional processing of the lower-grade ores remaining in Minnesota was required. The additional processing serves to concentrate the iron compounds. The ore is ground to produce fine particles, and

Exhibit 2 *Sequence of processes in the manufacturing of finished steel products*

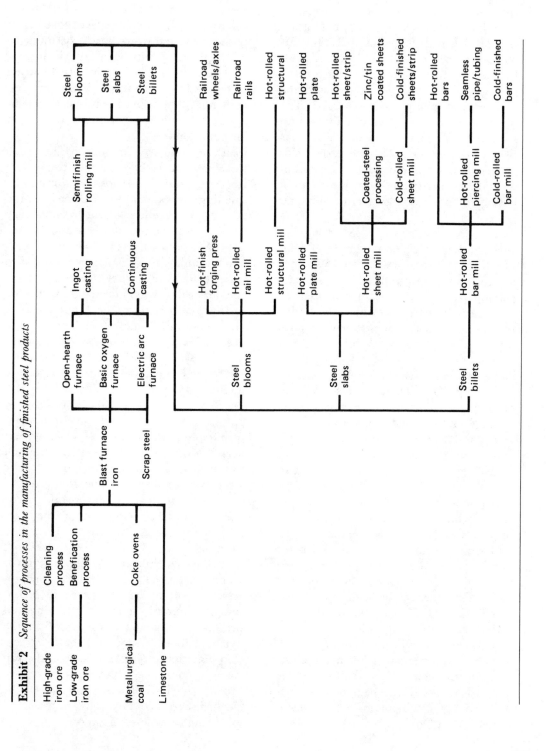

then the particles heavy with iron are separated from the rock and sand by both gravity flotation and magnetic attraction. Finally, the iron particles are sintered with heat or pelletized with clay to form small nodules of very high grade ore, and the rock or sand tailings are discharged. The discharge of iron benefication tailings into Lake Superior at the rate of 67,000 tons per day during the 1960s and early 1970s created one of the more famous environmental action suits, and led to the eventual passage of more stringent environmental protection laws.

2. *Metallurgical coal and coke.* Metallurgical coal is the most expensive grade of solid fuel; in 1978 it sold at $35.00 to $38.00 per ton, in comparison to the $12.00 to $16.00 per ton paid for the steam coal used at power generating plants and public utilities. Metallurgical coal is expensive since it has a low sulfur and ash content, and a medium amount of volatile hydrocarbons and water, and thus is particularly suitable for coking. The coking process involves heating the coal in the absence of oxygen to drive off the volatile gases and water vapor, and leave nearly pure carbon, with some sulfur (2% to 3%) and some traces of other elements. The nearly pure carbon in the coke is used in the blast furnace to reduce iron ore to the iron castings known as "pigs," which are the first refined form of the metal in the manufacture of steel.

Coking of metallurgical coal takes place in coke ovens, which are large, brick-lined structures that can hold 18 to 20 tons per loading, and that can be heated to approximately 2000 °F by gas burning in flues within the walls. The volatile hydrocarbons are driven off in the forms of phenol, ammonia, and methane while much of the sulfur is transformed into sulfur dioxide and hydrogen sulfide. The phenol, ammonia, and sulfur compounds are recovered by chemical processing while the methane is mixed with air and used as fuel in the coking process. Each charge of coke, when pushed from an oven, has to be immediately quenched with water sprays to prevent combustion, and then must be dried to be ready for use in the blast furnaces, with mixed iron and limestone. Quenching and drying cause extensive water and air pollution.

3. *Limestone and flux.* Limestone is added to the charge in the blast furnace to neutralize the sulfuric acids formed during the smelting process, and to combine with the silicates and sulfides of the ore. In very nontechnical terms, these chemicals cannot be separated from their iron compounds unless there is another substance present for which they have a greater chemical affinity than for the iron, and the calcium carbonate of the limestone provides this other substance. The neutralized acids and the calcium compounds, together with other fused impurities from the reduction process, float on top of the molten iron in the form of "slag."

4. *Sources of scrap steel.* Ferrous scrap is an important component in the steel manufacturing process, accounting for somewhat over 30% of the total production, although technically it is not a raw material. The scrap comes from three sources. "Home" or "revert" scrap is produced during the normal production process at the steel mill; it consists of defective ends clipped from billets, and irregular lengths sheared from bars and plates. "Prompt" scrap is made during the normal production process by the customers of a steel mill; it consists of trimmings from the stamping and pressing operations, and turnings from the machine tools. "Dormant" scrap is recycled material from junk dealers and scrap yards; it consists of obsolete, worn-out, or broken steel products, and must be cleaned, and sorted by alloy, to avoid introducing unwanted materials into the

steelmaking furnace. Sorting by alloy is difficult, except for automotive bodies, railroad parts, and demolition materials that have a known composition.

Smelting Iron in a Blast Furnace. The smelting process for any mineral involves separating the elemental metal from the oxides, sulfides, silicates, and carbonates with which it is normally compounded in the ore. Iron is smelted by mixing concentrated ore with the carbon of the coke and the calcium carbonate of the limestone, and blowing air heated to very high temperatures through the porous mixture to support gradual combustion and the chemical reactions of oxidation and reduction. Again using very nontechnical terms, oxidation involves an increase in the number of oxygen atoms in a compound (carbon oxidizes to carbon monoxide and then to carbon dioxide), while reduction involves a decrease in the number of oxygen atoms (iron oxide reduces to iron and oxygen). The basic chemical reaction in a blast furnace requires both oxidation and reduction, as the carbon in the coke first oxidizes with the heated air to form carbon monoxide, and then reduces the iron oxide of the ore to form carbon dioxide and iron. The sulfur becomes sulfur dioxide, and this combines with the calcium carbonate to produce calcium sulfide, while the silicon, phosphorus, and manganese impurities present in most ores are partially oxidized and float with the slag, and partially reduced and remain as impurities in the iron.

In operation, the blast furnace is loaded with alternate layers of coke, ore, and limestone. A typical blast furnace will hold 900 tons of input materials, and will produce, depending upon the quality and concentration of the ore, about 370 tons of molten iron per charge over a six-hour period. In actual practice, separate charges are not used; instead, input materials are continually added to the top of the furnace, and the mass sinks as combustion starts and the oxidation and

reduction processes occur, until the molten iron and slag drop to the bottom of the furnace, below the air input ports, where they are periodically drawn off. The slag is lighter, and floats on top of the molten iron, so that each can be tapped separately, into large ladles.

The blast furnace is shaped like a thick chimney, approximately 120 ft high and 30 ft in diameter, with the familiar skip-hoist running at an incline to the top of the furnace to carry raw materials for the charge, and with the complex gas collection and pollution control ductwork surrounding the outlet ports. Temperatures near the bottom of the furnace reach 2800 °F, so that the entire structure is lined with refractory brick, which is a ceramic material able to withstand the high temperatures and the concurrent physical abrasion and chemical impact of the smelting process. Huge ladles, either mounted on rail cars or carried by overhead cranes, complete the smelting process, dumping the slag in outside storage and carrying the iron to a steelmaking furnace.

Refining Iron in a Steelmaking Furnace. The blast furnace was designed to reduce iron oxides, sulfides, and silicates, and to separate the resulting iron from the large percentages of impurities in the mineral ores, while the steelmaking furnace was developed to remove the small traces of impurities remaining in the iron, and to lower the carbon content. Pig iron, from a blast furnace, contains 3 to 4% carbon; this high percentage makes the metal brittle, and difficult to either form or machine. A steelmaking furnace can lower the carbon content, and burn off some of the impurities, by exposing molten iron to high heat and oxygen. The original steelmaking furnace was the Bessemer converter, invented by Sir Henry Bessemer in 1856, which simply blew very high temperature air through molten iron in a pivoted retort. The chemical and physical reactions were violent, with carbonized particles and steel droplets being blown high above the open mouth of the retort, and the process was both wasteful and dangerous, but the result was a malleable, low-carbon steel, produced in large quantities and at low cost. Previously, steel had been made only by forging; striking a bar of hot iron with heavy and continual hammer blows will gradually bring the carbon to the surface, where it quickly burns off, and will eventually align the iron molecules to greatly increase strength and ductility. Wrought iron is a form of mild steel made by forging; prior to the invention of steam-driven hammers, it was exceedingly expensive, and used only for swords and armor. The invention of the converter, which made steel cheap enough for use on railroads, bridges, and shipping, was one of the major causes of the industrial expansion of the late nineteenth century.

The Bessemer* converter was both inefficient and dangerous, and three other steel-making furnaces were developed to replace the air-blown process; all three involve surface oxidation of the carbon and other impurities, and are consequently slower and less dramatic than the converter.

1. *Open-hearth furnace.* The open-hearth furnace was the earliest replacement for the converter; it consists of a large saucer-shaped vessel, made of refractory brick, that can hold 100 to 250 tons of molten iron and scrap steel. The vessel is heated both by combustion in flues within the

---

* Sir Henry Bessemer, who started as a manual worker casting lead type in a printing shop, was evidently an extremely ingenious, self-educated engineer. He developed a form of gold paint, for gilding, to replace the hammered gold leaf then in use, and used the profits from that enterprise for the construction of the first steel converting furnace. Following his technical and financial success with the converter, he was knighted (1879), and built a self-stabilizing steamer for channel crossings to eliminate seasickness among passengers on that traditionally stormy passage, a solar furnace to decrease the use of coal in an energy-short country, and a gigantic telescope to find God. None of his latter inventions were successful.

walls, and by open flames sweeping across the surface of the steel. Carbon and the traces of phosphorus, sulfur, and silica remaining in the iron are oxidized, and vaporized by the very high heat. Some of the iron is oxidized but not vaporized; as this material sinks into the molten metal, it is again reduced (iron oxide into iron and carbon monoxide), and the gas bubbles up through the steel, with the appearance of boiling. The shallow, saucer shape of the open-hearth furnace provides a large surface area, to maximize the exposure to air and the oxidation potential, but much of the atmospheric oxygen is consumed by the open flames used to heat the surface, and open-hearth refining is slow; approximately 10 hours are required per charge.

2. *Basic oxygen furnace.* The basic oxygen process is the second of the replacements for the Bessemer converter; it uses oxygen blown by high-pressure jets onto the surface of molten iron contained in a heated and pivoted retort. The oxygen jets have adequate physical force to agitate the liquid metal, and the chemical reaction quickly oxidizes the impurities and carbon as those substances come to the surface. The same "boiling" action occurs, as iron oxides are reduced to form carbon monoxide and dioxide gases, which bubble through the molten steel. The main advantage of the basic oxygen furnace is speed: a charge of 250 tons of pig iron and scrap steel can be refined in less than 1 hour.

3. *Electric arc furnace.* The electric furnace is the third of the replacements for the converter. The advantages of electrical processing are a very high temperature heat source, and the absence of combustion, which means that the amount of oxygen on the surface of the steel can be controlled, and consequently that the oxidation of the carbon and impurities in the steel can be regulated. The high heat and

oxygen control can be used to produce the most valuable grades of steel, with precise carbon content and specific alloy additives. In making alloy steels, it is important that the alloying metals, such as chrome, nickel, manganese, tungsten, and lead (for easier machining) not be oxidized, and this control is possible in an electric arc furnace. Most electric furnaces are built so that oxygen can be blown across the surface to speed the refining process; a charge of 200 tons can be refined in about four hours.

Casting and Semifinishing Steel. After the steel in an open-hearth, basic oxygen, or electric arc furnace has been refined to a specific carbon content (generally about 0.5%, down from the 3.5% in the iron from a blast furnace), and after the desired alloys have been added and thoroughly mixed by the boiling action of the carbon monoxide and dioxide gases, the liquid steel is tapped into a large ladle carried by an overhead crane, and then poured into molds to begin shaping the final products. There are two casting processes, ingot casting and continuous casting, that lead to semifinished products.

1. *Ingot casting.* An ingot is an individual mold, filled with molten steel. These molds differ in dimensions, depending upon the final product, but a common dimension would be 1½ ft × 3 ft × 8 ft, and a common weight would be 6 tons. When the surface of the casting has solidified, the mold is removed and the ingot is taken to a "soaking" pit, where the temperature is maintained at 2300 °F. The intent of the soaking process is to gradually achieve a completely even temperature throughout the steel prior to rolling into semifinished form; normally, when the ingot is first taken to the soaking pit furnace, the interior is considerably hotter than the solidified surface, and could not be put through the rolls of the semifinishing mill.

A semifinishing mill consists of a series of large, powered rolls that compress the ingot and shape the steel prior to the final finishing. If the steel cast in an ingot were allowed to cool totally, the interior would be honeycombed with small bubbles or even flawed with a large void due to gases such as oxygen and nitrogen that come out of solution as the steel solidifies, while the surface exposed to air would be brittle due to excessive oxidation while still hot. To prevent these defects, the top of each ingot casting, where the surface of the metal was not protected by the sides of the mold, is cropped by huge shears, and then the cast steel is rolled, while still hot enough to be very ductile, into semifinished forms termed blooms, slabs, and billets. There are no widely accepted definitions of these terms within the industry, and the dimensions of each differ depending upon the final usage of the steel, but in general a bloom is a large square, perhaps 12 in. × 12 in., or a large round 12 in. in diameter, used for making structural shapes or rails; a slab is usually rectangular, perhaps 4 in. × 36 in., used for making steel plates or sheets and strip; and a billet is a small square or round, used for making bar stock and wire rods. Obviously, an 18 in. × 36 in. × 8 ft ingot that has been rolled in a semifinishing mill into a 12 in.-round bloom would be much longer and, also obviously, the steel would have been strongly kneaded and compressed to make that transformation, eliminating any voids, bubbles, or cracks that might have formed during the cooling. Semifinishing mills that can transform ingots of steel into blooms, slabs, and billets are large and powerful machines; the usual procedure is to pass the steel back and forth between huge rolls that are screwed down 2 to 3 in. with each pass, until the final dimensions are achieved. The blooms, slabs, or billets are then sheared to standard lengths, and the semifinished shapes sent to a finishing mill, or to inventory.

2. *Continuous casting.* The use of continuous casting permits a steel manufacturing firm to bypass the casting of individual ingots and the rolling of semifinished products. Molten steel from a furnace is poured into a long vertical mold that is water-cooled and bottomless. The outer surface of the steel is chilled and solidified; the inner portion remains very ductile, nearly liquid, so that forming rolls, which pull the steel from the mold, can compress the metal and eliminate bubbles and cracks. The molds can be changed to form the dimensions of any standard bloom, slab, or billet, and shears can be adjusted to cut the semifinished shapes into the usual 20-ft lengths. It is not possible to continuously cast all alloys and all shapes of steel, but the process, where successfully applied, does reduce the labor cost, and does start to modernize steel manufacturing from the historical batch procedures.

Hot Rolling into Plate, Structural Shapes, and Bars. Blooms, slabs, and billets of the proper size, whether produced by continuous casting or by ingot casting and semifinish rolling, are shaped into finished products by a hot-rolling mill. Hot rolling involves, as might be expected, passing the steel, which has been heated to be ductile, between powered rolls. These rolls are normally in a series, with each set in that series more closely approximating the shape and dimensions of the finished product. Flat products such as plate (plate is usually considered to be 6 to ⅜ in. in thickness) and sheet (sheet is similar to plate, but less than ⅜ in. in thickness) are formed by plain rolls, without indentations. Bars, which may be round, square, or rectangular in cross section, are formed by rolls that have gradually narrowing indentations. Structural shapes such as I-beams, channel irons (which are "U"-shaped), and angle irons (which are "L"-shaped) are made on rolls that have a very complex series of in-

dentations. It is important that the steel bloom, slab, or billet completely fill the openings in each set of the series of rolls to produce finished products without voids or flaws, and yet not have excess steel that could either break the powered rolls or jam the feeding mechanism. Each hot-rolled product has a specific size and shape of bloom, slab, or billet to fit the rolls designed for that product.

The hot-rolling process forms the steel, and also provides much greater strength. Cast steel has a coarse crystalline structure that can easily fracture; rolling breaks down and elongates the crystals, which makes the steel more malleable and more resistant to breakage. A hot-rolling mill that can form finished steel products from semifinished blooms, slabs, or billets, and that forms these products by kneading the steel into shape with adequate force and pressure to rearrange the crystalline structure, is obviously a large and expensive machine. A series of rolls on a hot rolling mill may be 1200 ft long, and may be able to produce finished steel products, for the thinner cross sections, at speeds of 4000 ft per minute. Automated handling equipment is needed for both the blooms, slabs, and billets and for the finished products, together with heating furnaces for the input side and cooling racks for the output.

Hot rolling is the major hot-finishing process for steel products, but not the only one. Some steel products, particularly the wheels, axles, and couplers for railroad cars, are forged. Forging uses a hydraulic hammer to force heated steel into the shape of a machined mold, or die; forging also rearranges the crystalline structure of cast steel, increasing both strength and malleability. Railroad wheels and axles, etc., are forged; railroad rail is rolled in a hot-rolled mill similar to that used for structural steel shapes such as I-beams and channel irons.

Cold Finishing for Sheet, Strip, and Bars. Some of the sheet (⅜ in. and less in thickness, and 48, 60, or 72 in. wide), strip (the same thicknesses as sheet, but in narrower widths), and bars (round, square, or rectangular in shape, with a ⅛ to 4-in. cross section) produced in a hot-rolling mill will be cold-finished. Cold finishing involves annealing the hot-rolled product, by heating it evenly and cooling it slowly to relieve the stresses and reduce the hardness caused by hot rolling; pickling the steel, by passing it through a bath of sulfuric acid to remove the scale and rust; and then rolling it on a cold-finish mill. A cold-finish mill is a series of powered rolls that compress the surface of the steel to provide much more exact dimensions, a considerably smoother texture, and even greater strength. Cold-rolled products are used where improved appearance is important, as in automobiles and appliances, or where closer tolerances are needed, as in machinery assembly.

Plated Steel Products. Hot-rolled sheet steel may be plated with tin, to make containers such as food and beverage cans, or galvanized with zinc for building products such as barn roofs and siding, etc. The sheet steel prior to plating or galvanizing is termed "black plate"; it is usually cleaned of oxides and scale by pickling in sulfuric acid, annealed so that it may be more easily formed, and then the antirust coating of tin or zinc is applied by either electroplating or hot dipping.

Drawn Steel Products. Hot-rolled round bars, in small sizes termed "wire rods," are formed into steel wire by drawing the rods through heavy steel dies of the proper diameter. The wire is wound on a drum as it is pulled through the die, removed from the drum in coils, and then annealed prior to shipment.

Tubular Steel Products. Steel tubing and pipe for industrial use is made by two processes. The more common and less expensive process rolls a continuous strip of steel into a cylinder, and then automatically welds the seam; the less common process produces a seamless form by forcing a hot-rolled round bar, heated to be ductile, through an external die and over an internal mandrel. Both seamed and seamless pipe and tubing are used in machinery fabrication, and in industrial processing by chemical companies and oil refineries. Tubular steel products are not used for the familiar water and gas pipes in residential construction; those products are made by a continuous casting process that uses high-carbon iron, not steel.

The percentage distributions of these steel mill products manufactured by domestic firms during the period 1972–1977 are shown in Exhibit 3. Sheet and strip are the major product categories, accounting for 37.5% of total tonnage in 1977.

Many of the steel mill products are destined for a specific industrial market. Cold-finished sheet and strip, for example, is used primarily by the automotive and appliance manufacturers, while heavy structural beams are sold for building and bridge construction and tin-plated steel is designed for food and beverage containers. The percentage distribution of steel mill markets supplied by domestic firms during the period 1972–1977 are shown in Exhibit 4. Automotive manufacturing is the largest market category, using 23.6% of the total shipments in 1977 for hot-rolled sheet in frame components, cold-finished sheet in body panels and fenders, and bar stock for machined parts.

The previous sections of this case have described the technology, products, and markets of steel manufacturing firms; the following material explains the economics of the industry. The steel industry can be described as concentrated, with eight large firms accounting for 72% of industry shipments; as mature, with limited growth in real terms and cyclical in response to the level of economic activity; as price-competitive, with below-average returns on sales and assets; as capital-intensive, with large and expensive machinery and inadequate funds for replacement; as worker-influenced, with high labor costs and poten-

Exhibit 3 *Steel mill products (percent) shipped by the domestic steel industry, 1972–1977*

	1972	1973	1974	1975	1976	1977
Nonfinished cast ingots	0.5	0.6	0.6	0.7	0.6	0.5
Blooms, slabs, and billets	2.8	2.8	2.7	2.5	2.2	1.9
Semifinished wire rods	1.8	1.8	1.7	1.7	2.1	2.0
Total semifinished	5.1	5.2	5.0	4.9	4.9	4.4
Hot-rolled structural and piling	6.2	6.4	6.6	6.4	4.7	4.8
Hot-rolled plates	8.2	8.7	10.0	11.0	8.0	8.3
Hot-rolled railroad rails	1.0	0.8	0.9	1.6	1.5	1.3
Hot-rolled railroad products	0.7	0.6	0.7	0.8	0.8	0.8
Hot-rolled bar stock	15.1	14.3	14.8	14.9	14.1	15.0
Hot-rolled sheets	15.3	15.2	14.4	14.1	16.9	16.0
Hot-rolled strip	1.7	1.7	1.3	1.2	1.3	1.2
Total hot-rolled	48.2	47.7	48.7	50.0	47.3	47.4
Cold-finished bars	1.8	1.9	2.1	1.8	1.8	1.9
Cold-finished sheets	17.6	18.3	16.7	16.1	20.4	19.4
Cold-finished strip	1.4	1.4	1.4	1.1	1.3	1.3
Total cold-finished	20.8	21.6	20.2	19.0	23.5	22.6
Tin-plated sheet steel	6.7	6.5	6.9	7.1	7.2	7.0
Galvanized sheet steel	5.9	6.2	5.6	4.6	5.8	6.2
Total plated products	12.6	12.7	12.5	11.7	13.0	13.2
Drawn wire products	3.2	2.9	2.9	2.7	2.7	2.6
Tubular steel products	7.9	8.2	9.1	9.3	6.2	7.1
Specialty steel products	1.5	1.7	1.7	1.4	1.6	1.6
Total tonnage (millions)	91.8	111.4	109.4	79.9	89.4	91.4

Source: A.I.S.I. Annual Statistical Report, 1977, p. 31.

tially active unions; and as government-dominated, with mandated expenditures for pollution control and restrictive controls on pricing. These economic problems, which doubtless would be resolvable on a national basis, are exacerbated by international policies; 19.3 million tons of steel (21.0% of U.S. production) were imported into the United States and sold on a price basis in 1977. The economic characteristics of the steel industry, and international competition between steel-producing countries, have created strategic problems for U.S. steel companies. This case centers on those strategic problems.

Industry Concentration. There are 245 individual firms in the steel industry, but over 90% of these companies are not integrated steel producers that are able to transform the basic raw materials (metallurgical coal, iron ore, and limestone flux) into finished steel products. Fifteen percent are nonintegrated

Exhibit 4 *Steel mill markets (percent) supplied by the domestic steel industry, 1972–1977*

	1972	1973	1974	1975	1976	1977
Automotive manufacturing	19.8	20.8	17.3	19.0	23.9	23.6
Warehouse distribution	18.3	18.3	18.6	15.9	16.3	16.8
Building and highway construction	14.9	15.4	16.1	15.1	13.4	13.2
Food and beverage containers	7.2	7.0	7.5	7.6	7.7	7.4
Nonclassified shipments	6.6	6.4	6.3	6.9	6.6	7.3
Industrial machinery manufacturing	5.9	5.7	5.9	6.5	5.8	6.1
Steel products manufacturing	4.2	4.2	4.1	4.1	4.5	4.0
Oil and gas industry	3.0	3.1	3.9	5.2	3.0	4.0
Railroad equipment	2.9	2.9	3.1	3.9	3.4	3.6
Electrical equipment	3.1	3.0	3.0	2.7	3.0	2.9
Home appliance manufacturing	2.6	2.5	2.2	2.1	2.2	2.3
Commercial equipment manufacturing	2.0	1.8	1.8	1.7	2.0	2.0
Agricultural equipment manufacturing	1.6	1.6	1.7	1.8	2.0	1.8
Export shipments	2.8	2.8	3.6	2.2	2.1	1.2
Shipbuilding industry	1.0	0.9	1.2	1.8	1.1	1.0
Independent forging	1.1	1.1	1.2	1.4	1.1	1.0
Industrial fasteners	1.1	1.1	1.2	0.8	1.0	0.9
Mining industry	0.5	0.5	0.6	0.7	0.6	0.5
Ordnance and military	0.9	0.8	0.6	0.5	0.2	0.2
Aircraft and aerospace	0.1	0.1	0.1	0.1	0.1	0.1

Source: A.I.S.I. Annual Statistical Report, 1977, p. 32.

specialty firms that purchase pig iron and scrap steel, and operate refining furnaces, casting equipment, hot-rolling mills, and cold-finishing lines to produce specialty items, particularly tool steels and stainless. Sixty percent are nonintegrated regional firms that purchase steel scrap and operate melting furnaces, casting equipment, and hot-rolling mills to produce high-volume items such as reinforcing bars (for concrete construction) and merchant bar stock (for industrial machining) sold in a limited geographic area at a freight savings. These regional firms are the "mini mills" that have a lowered capital cost per ton, but also reduced productive flexibility and capacity. Finally, 15% are nonintegrated finishing mills that buy semifinished blooms, slabs, and billets, and produce cold-rolled sheet, strip, and bar stock, again for a regional market. The finishing mills operate on a freight advantage, since semifinished steel shapes can move at a lower rate than

completely finished steel products. All of the specialty and regional firms can provide quicker delivery and more personal service than can the large integrated mills.

The large integrated steel producers are the firms that dominate the steel industry; they manufacture an estimated 93% of the tonnage, and 85% of the dollar volume. This apparent discrepancy between productive tonnage and financial revenues is due to the low-volume and high-value nature of the products from the specialty firms and finishing mills. The integrated steel producers are dominated by eight large companies, listed in order of tonnage shipped in Exhibit 5.

In addition to the structural concentration, the steel industry has a marked geographic focus, with capacity located primarily in Pennsylvania, Indiana, Illinois, Michigan, and Ohio. The modern integrated mills are located on the Great Lakes, for inexpensive water transport of iron ore, either from the

Exhibit 5 *Sales, profits, and assets (000's omitted) of the eight largest integrated steel manufacturing firms within the United States, 1977*

	Sales	Profits	Assets	Profits (% sales)	Profits (% assets)
U.S. Steel	$9,691,100	$137,900	$9,914,000	1.4	1.3
Bethlehem	5,410,200	(448,200)	4,898,900	(8.2)	(9.1)
National	3,168,100	60,100	2,827,600	1.9	2.1
Republic	2,931,700	41,000	2,406,300	1.4	1.7
Inland	2,696,642	87,800	2,302,400	3.2	3.7
Armco	3,467,600	119,800	2,882,700	3.5	4.1
Jones & Laughlin	2,307,300	(2,981)	1,651,200	(0.1)	(0.2)
Lykes	1,786,500	(189,700)	1,697,200	(10.6)	(11.2)

Source: Annual Report for the respective companies.

Mesabi Range in Minnesota or from Labrador or Africa via the St. Lawrence Seaway, and for direct rail transport of metallurgical coal from mines in West Virginia, Ohio, and Pennsylvania. The midwestern states are also the center for the steel-using industries, in Chicago, Detroit, and Cleveland. Other integrated mills are located in Maryland (on the Atlantic coast, for economic receipt of foreign ore) and in Alabama (close to a regional source of both ore and coal). The nonintegrated mini mills, that operate solely on scrap, are geographically decentralized, close to customer locations to provide freight savings and delivery service.

Mature Conditions. The growth of the U.S. steel industry, whether measured by domestic steel shipments or total steel consumption, has been low; indices in Exhibit 6 show the increase in shipments at 15% over the 1967–1978 period, and the increase in consumption at 18% over the same time span, despite a 42% gain in overall industrial production.

Obviously, the rate of growth for the industry is related to the period of time selected, due to the cyclical nature of the industry. Many steel industry executives have assumed an annual 3% growth trend over time, but even that minimal figure is questioned now due to changes in the automotive and container markets.

The automotive market is shrinking, both literally and figuratively, and that has traditionally been the major market for steel in the United States. Automobiles are getting smaller, shorter, and lighter, and will take less steel. The container

Exhibit 6 *Indices of domestic U.S. steel shipments, of total U.S. steel consumption, and of total U.S. industrial production (1967 = 100)*

	1960	1965	1970	1972	1974	1976	1978
Index of industrial production	66	90	108	120	129	130	142
Index of domestic steel shipments	85	111	109	110	131	108	115
Index of total steel consumption	76	107	103	114	127	108	118

Source: A.I.S.I. Annual Statistical Report, 1978, for steel shipment and consumption data, and Statistical Abstract of the United States for industrial production figures.

market is also shrinking, although here the problem is the use of new packaging materials (aluminum and plastics) for beverages, and new preservation methods (freezing and drying) for foods. Some people are forecasting increased usage of steel for rail transportation and energy development, even leading to a steel shortage in the mid-1980s, but I look for a continuation of current trends, which basically means nearly stagnant growth. (Statement of an industry consultant)

Price Competition. Steel, in the common carbon grades and the usual shapes and sizes, is close to a commodity (although quality, as measured by the carbon content, alloy variances, and impurity traces, is important in the subsequent manufacturing process of forming, welding, and machining), and the steel producers sell on a price basis to large-volume users. The structure of the steel industry is an oligopoly, with a few very large sellers dominating the industry, and the theoretical response of an oligopoly is pricing at "administered" rather than at competitive levels. Administered prices are allegedly set by the largest firms at their full costs plus an expected return on their investments, and the smaller firms have to fit in, if possible, under that price structure. However, the steel in-

dustry, since the mid-1960s, has been a domestic oligopoly with surplus capacity caused by foreign imports, and prices now appear to be set at competitive rather than administered levels. The result has been reduced profits in comparison to other industrial firms (Exhibit 7).

Cost Structure. The steel industry is vertically integrated, with raw materials and semifinished products moving through a lengthy sequence of steps in the productive process. Steel mills are operationally complex, with numerous by-products such as the phenol, ammonia, and methane from the coke ovens, and with extensive reprocessing. Finally, the steel products are extremely diverse, ranging from heavy structural beams and hot-rolled plate to light cold-finished sheet and strip. These industry characteristics of vertical integration, operational complexity, and product diversification result in a complicated and imprecise cost structure, with transfer prices and allocated expenses that vary by product, process, and weight. An estimate of the basic cost structure, by process, for "average" weights and sizes of semifinished, hot-rolled, and cold-finished steel is given in Exhibit 8. In addition, an industry consultant described the cost problems of the industry in the following terms:

Exhibit 7 *Profits of domestic U.S. steel firms, as percentage of revenues and percentage of equities, as compared to U.S. manufacturers of durable and nondurable goods, 1960–1978*

	1960	1965	1970	1972	1974	1976	1978E
Profits/revenues							
Steel manufacturers	5.6	5.9	2.8	3.4	6.5	3.7	2.7
Durable-goods manufacturers	4.0	5.6	3.5	4.2	4.7	5.2	5.8
Non-durable-goods manufacturers	4.7	5.5	4.5	4.8	5.1	5.5	5.9
Profits/equity							
Steel manufacturers	8.6	8.8	4.1	5.8	17.1	7.8	5.4
Durable-goods manufacturers	8.5	13.7	8.3	10.8	12.6	13.7	14.5
Non-durable-goods manufacturers	9.8	12.2	10.3	10.5	17.1	14.2	15.2

Source: A.I.S.I. Annual Statistical Report, 1977, plus the *Statistical Abstract of the United States,* 1977, p. 579.

Exhibit 8 Estimated cost structure per ton of finished steel capacity, assuming no incremental costs for reprocessing scrap and no incremental revenues for by-product sales, at a modern (post-1960) integrated plant producing 3 million tons per year, 1976

	Ore beneficiation plant	Coke ovens	Blast furnace	Steel furnace	Continuous casting	Hot-roll mill	Cold-roll mill	Total costs
Iron ore	$12.15	—	—	—	—	—	—	$12.15
Metallurgical coal		$ 25.50	—	—	—	—	—	25.50
Limestone flux			$ 1.30	—	—	—	—	1.30
Processed ore			23.75*	—	—	—	—	—
Processed coke			40.10*	—	—	—	—	—
Pig iron				$ 82.35*	—	—	—	—
Steel scrap				46.00	—	—	—	46.00
Molten steel					$156.45*	—	—	—
Semifinished						$175.70*	—	—
Hot-rolled							$233.50*	—
Direct labor	2.70	2.50	7.50	10.50	8.30	25.00	27.00	83.50
Indirect labor	1.00	1.00	2.50	4.00	2.00	6.00	8.00	24.50
Energy	1.70	—	See Note	8.00	0.50	2.70	3.50	16.40
Maintenance	1.00	0.50	1.50	2.00	1.50	1.00	1.00	8.50
Depreciation	2.60	5.60	2.60	1.30	3.35	13.60	11.20	40.25
Interest	1.60	3.50	1.60	0.80	2.10	8.50	7.00	25.10
Site expenses	1.00	1.50	1.50	1.50	1.50	1.00	1.00	9.00
Total manufacturing cost	23.75	40.10	82.35	156.45	175.70	233.50	293.20	—
	per 1,400 lb	per 900 lb	per 1,000 lb	per ton				
Selling expenses					6.50	6.50	6.50	
Administrative expenses					9.20	9.20	9.20	
Market price	33.90	89.00			200.00	270.00	340.00	
	per ton	per ton						
Capital cost for facilities, per ton steel capacity	65.00	140.00	65.00	32.00	84.00	340.00	280.00	—

Notes: 1,400 lb of beneficiated ore and 900 lb of coked coal are needed to produce 1,000 lb of hot metal pig iron; 1,000 lb of hot metal pig iron and 1,000 lb of melting scrap are needed to produce 1 ton of steel. Costs for molten steel, cast steel, hot-rolled steel, and cold-finished products are expressed on a per ton basis.

Iron ore: 1,800 lb of raw ore is required at the beneficiation plant to yield 1,400 lb of pelletized ore at the blast furnace to yield 1,000 lb of pig iron. 0.9 ton of raw ore at $13.50/ton = $12.15.

Coal: 1,500 lb of metallurgical coal is required at the coke ovens to yield 900 lb of coke for use in the blast furnace to yield 1,000 lb of pig iron. 0.75 ton of metallurgical coal at $34.00/ton = $25.50.

Limestone: 400 lb of limestone flux is required in the blast furnace to yield 1,000 lb of pig iron. 0.20 ton of limestone at $6.50/ton = $1.30.

Scrap: 1,000 lb of steel scrap is used in the refining furnace together with 1,000 lb of molten iron to yield 2,000 lb of finished steel. 0.5 ton of scrap at $92.00/ton = $46.00.

Labor: Direct labor refers to workers assigned to a specific stage in the steelmaking process, including shift foremen. Indirect labor refers to workers assigned to a general area of the steelmaking plant, often for transport (crane operator, railway personnel, etc.).

Energy: Energy refers to purchased power and fuels and does not include by-product fuels from the coke oven, which is assumed to provide heat for blast furnaces and soaking pits.

Depreciation: Depreciation is based on 25-year useful life of the facility and is computed on a straight-line basis; actual depreciation in the industry is generally on allowable 18-year life, and is computed on an accelerated basis.

Interest: Interest charges assume 50% debt and 50% equity financing, and 10% interest rate (capital investment for the facility × 50% debt financing × 50% average amount outstanding over period of the loan × 10%).

Site: Site expenses are for support staff (engineering, personnel, and bookkeeping) and miscellaneous charges (local taxes, communication costs, etc.) that are part of the manufacturing overhead.

Selling: Corporate selling expenses are allocated at $6.50 per ton for both semifinished and finished products.

Administration: Corporate administrative expenses are allocated at $9.20 per ton for both semifinished and finished products.

Source: Costs are industry estimates, for class discussion only. (*) indicates transfer price from prior process.

It is common to say that the steel industry is capital-intensive, and that is certainly true: it would cost over $1,200 per ton of annual capacity to build an integrated steel mill today, and the economic size for a new mill is 4 million tons per year, so you're talking about a $4.8 billion investment. That is my definition of capital intensity.

But the steel industry is also material-intensive, labor-intensive, energy-intensive, and pollution-intensive; and the combination of those factors brings government interference. You can't understand the steel industry unless you realize that you have to combine capital, raw materials, and labor in large amounts, control the pollution, and deal with the government, in order to manufacture and market steel at a profit. (Statement of an industry consultant)

Raw Materials. The market prices of beneficiated iron ore, coked metallurgical coal, and heavy melting scrap (the best grade of prompt and obsolete scrap steel) have escalated since 1970. It is alleged that this is due to a growing shortage of premium-quality raw materials, and to the increasing severity of federal standards for coke ovens and beneficiation plants, both of which create problems in pollution control and waste disposal (Exhibit 9).

The cost of coke for the blast furnace increased 217% during the period 1970–1977; industry sources were certain that this dramatic growth was caused by the imposition of pollution controls on the coking process.

In the early 1970s, the United States was a heavy exporter of coke; we mined the coal, converted it to coke, used the coal gas here, and shipped the residue abroad. Now, we're an importer of coke, due to the new pollution standards. It is fairly easy to control air pollution from the ovens, since most of the gases are recovered as by-products, but you have to quench each charge of coke after it is pushed from the ovens, and that causes both air and water pollution under conditions where the pollution is very difficult and expensive to control. Many of the mills have shut down the coke ovens rather than make that expenditure on facilities that are obsolete, or nearly obsolete anyway. (Statement of an industry consultant)

Labor Charges. Labor charges in the steel industry are high, accounting for 36.8% of direct manufacturing costs. This percentage is partially caused by the labor-intensive nature of the steel process, and partially by the wage rates of the steel industry, which are higher than those in other manufacturing and service areas (Exhibit 10).

As might be expected, there are two antithetical responses to the substantial premium paid to steel industry employees, with a middle ground of understanding of the industry conditions:

It would also help a lot if the industry stopped giving away the store to the United Steelworkers Union. Steelworkers now get $13.56 an hour in pay and benefits, and their premium over the average compensation in manufacturing has widened astonishingly during the past twenty-five years from 18% to 65%. (*Fortune*, February 13, 1978, p. 127)

You have to visit a steel mill in July to understand the premium in pay. Steel mills are really an anachronism; they have not changed much in working conditions since the nineteenth century. They consist of old steel buildings, with dirt floors, and dust, dirt, and smoke everywhere, along with the fumes and the heat from the molten metal. When a furnace is tapped, or when an ingot is poured, someone has to walk up close with a ladle to get a sample; the ladle has a long handle, but the heat and the sparks are really unbearable. (Statement of an industry consultant)

Steel workers deserve every nickel they make. (Statement of a union official)

Exhibit 9 *Raw material prices (per ton) for the steel industry, 1970–1977*

	1970	1972	1974	1976	1977
Beneficiated iron ore	$18.94	$22.57	$ 28.90	$31.60	$33.90
Coked metallurgical coal	28.05	33.98	59.67	85.12	89.00
Heavy melting scrap	41.01	57.94	108.33	78.13	92.00

Source: Industry estimates.

Through the 1950s and 1960s, the normal cyclical performance of the steel industry was accentuated by a three-year strike sequence. Every three years the labor contract between the steel industry and the steel workers would come up for renewal, and every three years a strike would occur. Steel users would stockpile materials in anticipation of the strike, which forced the mills to operate near the limits of capacity before the strike, and far below capacity after the strike was settled, while the accumulated inventory was utilized. This boom-and-bust sequence was not profitable for the companies nor beneficial for the workers, and in 1973 it was agreed to submit unsettled issues to binding arbitration during all future contract negotiations. This "no strike" agreement has resulted in production stability for the industry and wage increases for the workers, but many of the current union leaders are not in favor of its continuation; they believe that it has constrained the bargaining power of the industry-wide union.

Capital Equipment. The original investment in currently used production facilities of the steel industry, before annual allowances for depreciation and amortization, was $41.3 billion (*A.I.S.I. Annual Statistical Report,* 1977, p. 16). It has been estimated that the replacement cost of these facilities would be over $100 billion. Because of the high replacement cost, some equipment is operated that is known to be inefficient in material, labor, and energy requirements.

William Kirwan, general superintendent of U.S. Steel Corp.'s two steel-making facilities here, thrusts a copy of *Iron Trade Review* towards a visitor. "Take a look at that," he says. "It gives you an idea of what we've got to work with here."

In the trade magazine is an article about the installation of a big steam engine that still drives one of the Youngstown Work's rolling mills. The article was published on March 19, 1908.

"My job is to convince the bosses that there's a future for us here in Youngstown," Mr. Kirwan says, "but you can't build a future on a steam engine that was installed in 1908." (*Wall Street Journal,* June 5, 1979, p. 1)

It is estimated that the older steel manufacturing facilities, built before the 1950s, op-

Exhibit 10 *Wage rates for the steel industry, and for all manufacturing and all nonagricultural (manufacturing, service, and clerical) employees, 1973–1977*

	1973	1974	1975	1976	1977
Steel industry employees	$6.31	$7.42	$8.31	$9.13	$10.25
All manufacturing employees	4.07	4.41	4.81	5.19	5.63
All nonagricultural employees	3.92	4.22	4.54	4.87	5.25

Source: Standard and Poor's Industry Survey, 1978, p. S–58, and the *Statistical Abstract of the United States,* 1978, p. 422.

erate at 20 to 25% above the costs outlined in Exhibit 8. These excess costs are in increased raw material and energy usage (an older blast furnace, operating at lower temperatures, requires about 5% more ore and 8% more coke per ton of finished pig iron) and in decreased labor productivity (the older blast furnace, with 1,350 tons capacity, requires the same size crew as a modern furnace, with 2,000 tons capacity). The older facilities are still operated since they are considered to be marginally profitable during periods of high demand.

So far this year, strong demand for steel across a broad range of markets has pushed domestic mills to the highest operating rates since 1974. Even the most marginal facilities—those that barely survived the 1977 closings—are profitable these days. But the threat of another recession soon puts into a kind of economic limbo these marginal facilities, which by various estimates may account for anything from 8% to 26% of steel making capacity. If the demand for steel should soften and operating rates fall, aging mills could be pushed first into the red and then into closing. . . .

In many ways, U.S. Steel's Youngstown Works is typical of American steel-making facilities that may soon be scrapped. Begun in 1892, it has become less and less competitive over recent years, and U.S. Steel clearly isn't going to spend a lot of money trying to fix it up. On the other hand, the plant is profitable, and can turn out about one million tons of steel a year, 3% of the company's capacity, so U.S. Steel executives in Pittsburgh don't seem ready to close it immediately, either. . . .

That the Youngstown Works isn't what it used to be is obvious from the most cursory inspection. Three blast furnaces are cold; only the fourth is melting raw iron out of iron ore with the aid of limestone and coke. In the open-hearth shop, where molten iron is turned into steel with intense heat and a stream of oxygen blown across it to remove excessive car-

bon, only five of the fifteen furnaces are operating on any given day; four are being renovated, and six have been abandoned. In the rolling mills, the steel ingots are squeezed into semi-finished shapes such as slabs, and then into finished products such as sheet steel, but only five of the nine rolling mills are running.

Moreover, only by severely cutting back operations here has the company managed to keep the Youngstown Works operating this long. The relatively small furnaces and the outdated rolling mills couldn't compete with much larger, more efficient mills in the Pittsburgh area and around the Great Lakes. And the Youngstown Works is even less able to compete with modern continuous casting facilities, which handle one operation after another without allowing the metal to cool, and without the need to reheat it. Thus, early last year, the company decided to consolidate many of the plant's operations and to run it like a mini-mill, with a limited number of products for a limited number of customers in a limited geographical area. (*Wall Street Journal*, June 5, 1979, p. 1)

Over the nine-year period 1970–1978, firms within the steel industry invested $19.7 billion in new or remodeled production facilities; these investments were financed partially by internal sources (earnings, depreciation, etc.) and partially by an increase in debt (Exhibit 11).

It has been estimated that over 20% of the capital expenditures since 1970 (*Standard & Poor's Industry Survey*, p. S-58) have been for pollution control equipment, and that more than $1 billion per year must be spent for the same purpose over the next five years.

The Industry's capital-spending options are extremely limited these days. Only a small fraction of their pinched cash flow is available for so-called "discretionary" projects, the rest being preempted for pollution control and the replacement of

Exhibit 11 *Capital investments, internal sources of funds, and changes in funded debt and working capital for the steel industry, 1970–1977*

	Retained earnings	Depreciation and miscellaneous	Total internal funds	Capital investments	In(decrease) debt	In(decrease) working capital
1970	$ 44.1	$ 1,127.9	$ 1,172.0	$ 1,736.2	$ 612.2	$ 48.0
1971	172.5	1,123.1	1,295.6	1,425.0	152.8	23.4
1972	372.5	1,215.5	1,588.0	1,174.3	105.8	519.5
1973	829.1	1,329.3	2,158.4	1,399.9	(256.8)	501.7
1974	1,800.8	1,533.0	3,353.8	2,144.7	(382.8)	826.3
1975	937.1	1,590.4	2,527.5	3,179.4	1,066.0	414.1
1976	700.3	1,614.3	2,314.6	3,252.9	1,396.0	457.7
1977	(532.7)	1,887.7	1,355.0	2,850.3	1,101.5	(393.8)
1978	759.0	2,009.8	2,768.8	2,538.3	(179.4)	51.1
	$5,082.7	$13,451.0	$18,533.7	$19,701.0	$3,615.3	$2,448.0

Source: *A.I.S.I. Annual Statistical Report,* 1978, p. 9.

essential facilities without which an entire steelworks might have to shut down. In this austere regime, the only discretionary projects that make any sense are those offering very handsome returns. (*Fortune,* February 13, 1978, p. 128)

It has also been estimated (*Wall Street Journal,* June 5, 1979, p. 1) that more than 25% of the steelmaking facilities within the United States are obsolete, and will have to be closed down within five years. The balance of the productive facilities in the steel industry have been at least partially modernized in recent years, although the extent of this modernization has necessarily been limited with a total replacement cost of $100 billion and annual investments averaging $2.2 billion, including the pollution control expenditures. Domestic U.S. steel plants are acknowledged to be old; they are not, except for the sites scheduled to be shut down, acknowledged to be inefficient.

The question of efficiency is still unclear because the books of European and Japanese producers are not open to audit by U.S. experts. U.S. plants, on the whole, are older than those of their competitors overseas. But U.S. steelmen are passionately proud of their technology. "The claim that we are archaic or aging offends me," says Stinson (George A. Stinson, Chairman of the National Steel Corporation). "Our sites are aging, but not our plants." (*Business Week,* September 19, 1977, p. 74)

Some critics say that the outmoded layouts of American steel plants put them at a disadvantage. But it ain't necessarily so. The largest and best-run steelworks in the U.S.—one that is also believed to have higher labor productivity than the average Japanese plant—is also one of the oldest and is fairly jumbled-looking. The Indiana Harbor works of Inland Steel Co., near Chicago, has grown in stages since 1902, and visitors on tour find themselves halted frequently at railroad grade crossings. Tom Katsahnias, the plant's general manager, admits there is a lot of crisscrossing of material—"jackassing" as it is called in the trade—compared with the relatively smooth flow at a more modern plant. But this probably adds "less than a dollar a ton" to production costs, he says. (*Fortune,* February 13, 1978, p. 126)

It is expected that gradual modernization of steel industry facilities will continue at the existing plants (termed "brownfield" sites), but that major expansion of capacity at a totally new location (termed a "greenfield" project) will not be attempted due to the cost of construction.

If the industry is too strapped to fully modernize its present capacity, expansion would appear to be out of the question. Because of soaring construction costs, the economics of grandiose greenfield projects look just as dubious now as they did when *Fortune* last examined the industry's needs for new capacity. According to a recent study by the President's Council on Wage and Price Stability, the heavy capital charges at a new greenfield facility would exceed whatever savings in production costs are possible.

The only company that strongly dissents from this view is U.S. Steel, which is going ahead and seeking environmental clearances for the big new plant it would like to build on land it already owns at Conneaut, Ohio, on the shores of Lake Erie. Designed for an initial raw-steel capacity of 3.8 million tons with room for further increments of capacity later on, Conneaut would feature large blast furnaces and 100% continuous casting. The price tag per annual ton of capacity would be about $1,000, four times what Bethlehem Steel spent when it put up its Burns Harbor plant near Chicago in the early 1960s; that was the last greenfield plant built in the U.S.

David Roderick, U.S. Steel's president, insists that the project will sooner or later make sense. Once the company got over what he calls the "capital punishment" of financing Conneaut, he says, it would have a plant producing steel with 35% less energy than the average plant currently in operation, and with 30 to 50% less labor, depending on the product. (*Fortune*, February 13, 1978, p. 128)

Governmental Impact. The steel industry and the federal government have traditionally operated on an adversary relationship; this was due at least partially to the early dominance of the national economy by steel,

coal, and railroad companies, and to an expressed lack of concern on public issues by the managers of those companies. In recent years, however, steel output has become less of a critical factor in the economy, with 1977 shipments of $39.7 billion compared to a $1.6 trillion gross national product, and steel executives have become either more publicly conscious or more tactfully spoken. Despite these changes, the adversary relationship has continued, with conflict and antagonism on three major issues:

1. *Pollution control.* Manufacturing steel is inherently a pollution-prone process, because of the need to refine large volumes of impure ore through the application of high heat; the eventual result is pure steel and waste products, which have to be recovered and processed for disposal. A decline in the quality of the available natural resources, both coal and ore, has been associated with an increase in the concern about environmental deterioration and public health, and these trends have resulted in extensive regulation by the Environmental Protection Agency. It is alleged that changes in the regulations, standards, and deadlines have a serious effect on the cost of operations and the financing of improvements.

One of the biggest problems is pollution. In 1971, U.S. Steel put expensive electrostatic precipitators on its open-hearth furnaces at Youngstown, but today the federal Environmental Protection Agency isn't satisfied, and is calling for new, more effective equipment to cleanse the air. U.S. Steel is disputing the EPA stand, but even if the company wins on this issue, it still will face other air pollution control investments over the next several years....

Consider, for instance, the sinter plant, a recycling operation in which waste particles from the steelmaking process are baked with other ingredients to make a material usable, like iron ore, in a blast furnace to manufacture more iron. A faint orange plume can be seen coming from the plant's stack, and one day Mr. Kirwan [general manager of the Youngstown Works of U.S. Steel Company] is going to have to stop even that faint haze.

"Watch this," he says, gunning his big Buick down a dirt road near the sinter plant. "I just kicked up more dust than that whole plant is turning out, but they're going to make me clean it up anyway. That's just environmental overkill. . . ."

Mr. Kirwan fears that his bosses in Pittsburgh may not think that the old plant is worth the expenditure of huge amounts of money to correct the remaining pollution problems. "When I started here 31 years ago," he says, "you couldn't see the sky for all the smoke coming from around here. All this blue sky you see now was bought with millions of dollars, and I just can't believe we're still fouling the atmosphere."

2. *Price regulation.* Price increases by the steel industry have been resisted since the end of World War II; this resistance has resulted in de facto price control. Governmental agencies charged with price and wage stability believed that rate increases in the basic materials, such as steel, that were used in numerous consumer and industrial products pushed the growh of inflation. A dramatic conflict occurred in 1962 between President John F. Kennedy and Roger Blough, Chairman of the U.S. Steel Company, over pricing. (President Kennedy commented in a press conference relative to the price increase announced that morning by Mr. Blough that "my father always told me that all businessmen were S.O.B.'s.") The same conflicts, although more muted, between the government and the industry on steel pricing have continued under Presidents Johnson, Nixon, Ford, and Carter.

You have to go back to the days of Teddy Roosevelt to understand the reason for this continual conflict, which started on economic control and now extends to pollution, pricing, mergers, and imports. The steel industry has always been portrayed as selfish and bad, while the government has always been described as good and interested in the public welfare. Steel industry people have generally been trained in production, while the agency personnel have an economics background. They just don't understand each other, even though they all have an inherent interest and stake in national problems.

Now, the government has developed econometric models that show the impact of steel pricing to be determinant in the rate of inflation, and they are determined to roll back steel prices, either by "jawboning" or by direct intervention. That is the reason the industry has been so unprofitable; the market would have accepted price increases of a reasonable magnitude, but the government would not. When you substitute governmental control for market action, you have eventual problems since the government action is bound to be short-term in orientation. They worry about what someone will say tomorrow; not about what will happen in 10 years. (Statement of an industry consultant)

3. *Merger restriction.* Mergers, even between the smaller companies within the steel industry, have been blocked by the Department of Justice, under the provisions of the Clayton Antitrust Act; it is apparently felt that further concentration within the industry would reduce competition very substantially due to the commodity nature of the steel products.

The structure of the U.S. steel industry is totally wrong, from a national-competitive rather than company-competitive point of view. To compete on a national basis against the government-supported steel producers in Japan, France, West Germany, or Great Britain, there should be just three U.S. steel firms, all with high production volumes for economies of scale and all with wide product lines for market coverage. U.S. Steel, to compete against Nippon Steel or British Steel, needs to be twice as big.

But you are not going to see that happen. Even mergers between the smaller firms such as Youngstown and Lykes have been strongly resisted by the Justice Department. They won't even let those companies build joint facilities, to spread the costs of pollution control, and to improve the costs of production (through higher volume). They still worry about maintaining competition between companies, not between countries. (Statement of an industry executive)

Joe Sims, deputy antitrust chief, says: "The first question you ask is why is it a joint venture? How come people can't do it by themselves?" Even sound economic reasons, he suggested, may be outweighed by the anticompetitive effects of a joint coke operation. The profit picture, he adds, "just isn't a major input" into a decision on what is legal and what is illegal under the Clayton Act. (*Business Week,* September 19, 1977, p. 88)

International Competition. Steel imports have increased from 1.2% of total U.S. steel consumption in 1955 to 17.8% in 1977 (and 20.8% of U.S. steel production in that year). The marketing appeal of the foreign steel producer has been the simple and convincing offer of a substantially reduced price per ton for the major types and grades of finished steel products. The result of this price competition has been substantial inroads in most of the steel product groups (Exhibit 12).

Steel imports into the United States have increased dramatically in recent years because world capacity now substantially exceeds world consumption, and the only large and unprotected market that is open to foreign steel manufacturing firms is the United States. The European and Japanese mills were rebuilt, after the destruction of World War II, with modern equipment and integrated sites during the 1950s and 1960s, and now steel mills in the developing countries (Mexico, Korea, Brazil, and India) are being rapidly expanded; the result is excess capacity, with the most advanced and lowest-cost facilities outside the United States (Exhibit 13).

Foreign steel production facilities are admittedly more modern than those in the United States, and wage rates, despite recent increases toward parity, are known to be lower abroad, but it is not clear that the overall costs of steel production are substantially less outside the United States. Comparative costs are important because they determine the "reference prices," which are the lowest figures at which imported steel products can be sold in the United States.

Exhibit 12 *Steel tonnage (000's omitted) imported into the United States by product group, 1960–1977, and 1977 imports as percentage of domestic production*

	1960 tons	1965 tons	1970 tons	1975 tons	1977 tons	1977 % U.S. production
Semifinished	68.4	282.6	170.6	242.8	297.7	13.5
Wire rods	408.2	1,283.6	1,055.5	1,112.7	1,341.5	73.3
Structural	317.3	938.8	1,186.0	876.1	1,817.1	41.4
Plates	211.7	733.8	968.7	1,403.3	2,116.4	15.5
Rails and products	10.4	23.9	72.2	175.4	207.2	10.8
Bars and tool steel	840.5	1,641.8	1,363.3	923.7	1,363.9	8.8
Pipe and tubing	480.0	929.8	1,926.9	1,684.7	2,473.7	38.1
Wire and products	547.2	866.3	886.1	647.1	977.2	41.1
Coated products	39.2	144.9	334.6	414.8	465.1	3.8
Sheets and strip	435.5	3,507.2	5,400.0	4,531.6	8,246.5	23.8
	3,358.7	10,383.0	13,364.5	12,012.4	19,306.6	20.8

Source: A.I.S.I. Annual Statistical Report for the respective years.

Exhibit 13 *Raw steel productive capacity (000's omitted) by sector of the world, 1950–1976*

	U.S.	Japan	Europe	Developing countries	Communist countries	Total
1950	96,800	5,300	53,200	13,300	39,200	207,800
1955	117,000	10,400	80,300	24,000	65,500	297,200
1960	99,300	24,400	107,900	34,100	115,900	381,600
1965	131,500	45,500	125,500	54,700	146,000	503,100
1970	131,500	102,900	151,700	76,200	192,900	654,200
1975	116,600	112,800	138,100	99,800	244,700	753,100

Note: "Raw steel" production refers to molten steel poured in ingots or formed by continuous casting; production of finished steel products is lower due to reprocessing.
Source: Putnam, Hayes & Bartlett, *Economics of International Steel Trade*, 1977, Table A–1.

The Administration plan gives official recognition to the fact that Japan and a few Third World countries really do have a comparative advantage in steel. The reference prices, put together with the help of new cost data supplied by Japanese steel companies, would appear, however, to demolish the notion that Japan is an invincible competitor. According to the Administration's figures, Japan's steelmaking costs are about 20% below this country's, but this advantage shrinks to an average of about 5% when freight costs and custom duties are taken into account. That is too small to win over customers who now buy domestic, except in coastal areas where Japanese freight costs are especially low.

These figures are hotly disputed, to be sure, by platoons of American economists, security analysts, and lawyers involved in dumping cases, who pore over Japanese-language statistical tables that have been photocopied and annotated nearly to the point of illegibility. A consulting firm that is helping to prosecute a dumping suit estimates that the Japanese advantage in production costs is only 10%, in which case the reference prices are too low. But two economists who have been carrying on research sponsored by the Japan Iron and Steel Exporters' Association give the Japanese a 30% edge.

There is plenty of empirical evidence that the Japanese must enjoy *some* sort of advantage. Two-thirds of Japan's productive capacity is in relatively new "greenfield" plants efficiently laid out alongside deep water, where superior ore from Australia is smelted in enormous, computerized blast furnaces.... (*Fortune,* February 13, 1978, p. 124)

It is generally accepted that Japan, although not western Europe, does have a competitive advantage in labor costs, because of their modern facilities and reduced wage rates, and that this advantage is increasing with the recent wage settlements in the United States and Europe (Exhibit 14).

It is not generally accepted that Japan is able to maintain the labor advantage throughout the steel-making process, because of the higher costs of raw materials and energy, all of which must be imported. Instead, it is suspected by many executives and consultants in the U.S. steel industry that the apparent competitive advantages of both Japan and Europe are based on government export subsidies, reduced capital costs, and inaccurately reported expense structures.

The Japanese exports of steel illustrate better than the exports of any other product, better even than the exports of small cars and television sets, the national structure that provides Japan with a definite competitive advantage. Steel is a commodity, yet they are able to nearly dominate world trade.

Exhibit 14 *Comparative labor productivity, wage rates, and labor costs in the steel industry within the United States, West Germany, and Japan*

	United States			West Germany			Japan		
	Hours/ ton	Dollars/ hour	Cost/ ton	Hours/ ton	Dollars/ hour	Cost/ ton	Hours/ ton	Dollars/ hour	Cost/ ton
1965	12.32	$ 4.70	$ 58.23	22.09	$1.84	$ 40.65	24.71	$0.81	$20.02
1970	12.39	6.05	74.96	14.99	3.13	46.92	13.25	1.67	22.13
1971	11.76	6.64	78.09	15.06	3.63	54.67	13.20	1.95	52.35
1972	10.87	7.46	81.09	13.42	4.36	58.51	11.69	2.46	28.76
1973	9.86	8.03	79.18	12.09	5.96	72.06	9.39	3.39	31.83
1974	9.78	9.36	91.54	11.43	7.12	81.38	9.18	4.19	38.46
1975	10.92	11.03	120.45	12.76	8.41	107.31	9.21	4.88	44.94

Source: Putnam, Hayes & Bartlett, *Economics of International Steel Trade*, 1977, pp. 31, 34.

Japan is the largest exporter of steel in the world. Last year they shipped 39 million tons of basic steel products abroad. In addition to those shipments of billets, bars, plates, and sheet, they are using much of their steel in ship building and auto manufacturing, and then exporting those products. Last year they produced 120 million tons of steel; over 50% of that was sent outside the country.

The economic structure of Japan is oriented toward that sort of competitive performance, on a world scale. The government provides funding to industries that it believes should expand, and that it believes can help other industries to expand. They make investment decisions based upon national economic benefits, not company cash flows.

Other institutions within the country are operated to support the "expandable" industries. The trading companies, which are a uniquely Japanese institution, provide input materials at prices that are based upon barter arrangements rather than purchase costs, and they sell the output products at prices that are based on capacity utilization rather than production costs. The entire structure of the Japanese economy is engineered to support the steel industry. (Statement of an industry executive)

French steelmakers enjoyed a 172% increase in exports to the U.S. during the first half of this year. Concedes a spokesman for France's largest company, Sacilor-Sollac, which last year produced 6.5 million of France's 23.2 million tons of steel: "We sell at levels which do not correspond to the level of our costs. This situation cannot last. To survive, we must put ourselves on Japan's level of productivity." By upgrading, the French hope to maintain exports at 40% of total production. (*Business Week*, February 19, 1977, p. 82)

Britain can be taken as the third example of a national steel industry programmed to achieve national economic goals. British Steel is the third largest producer in the world, after Nippon Steel and U.S. Steel. They are losing horrendous sums of money every year, but they won't cut employment and they won't cut production. Instead, they want to increase capacity.

The British government has committed $8.7 billion for capital improvements in the steel industry, to expand capacity and reduce costs. They can't use that steel at home, so again there will be subsidized exports to the United States. (Statement of an industry executive)

It is alleged that it is politically difficult for European governments to accept plant closings and high unemployment in the basic industries due to social welfare expectations, and that it is totally impossible for the Japanese government to even consider those alternatives, because of the lifetime employment policies of that country. Therefore, it is expected that subsidized exports to the United States will continue in the steel industry.

> European steel producers all have access to government support, either in financial terms, or in political terms. British Steel, for example, is nationalized, and is part of the governmental structure. In Japan, the steel industry is backed by an interlocking apparatus of banks and trading companies, all closely allied to the government. The U.S. steel industry does not compete against other steel companies; it competes against other sovereign governments, and their accepted policies are to transfer unemployment from the Ruhr, the Midlands, and Fukuyama to Pittsburgh, Youngstown, and Detroit. It sometimes seems that people in the U.S. government are not bright enough to understand that. (Statement of an industry consultant)

In order to prevent dumping (shipment by a foreign producer of substantial quantities of a product for sale either below "full cost," which is difficult to determine without full disclosure, or below "home market prices," which should be easier to determine but which can be disguised by the use of complex distribution channels) of steel on the U.S. market, the federal government in early 1978 established a set of "trigger prices" or "reference costs" for all steel mill products. The trigger prices are based on estimated production costs in Japan, which is assumed to be the low-cost producer under current conditions, and include ocean freight charges, U.S. import duties (7% of the sales price), and a standard profit margin (13% on the assets employed by the producer). Many executives

in the U.S. steel industry believe that the trigger prices are still too low, because of underestimation of the costs of production in Japan.

> The attitude of the government is that they don't want to protect "inefficient" U.S. producers from foreign competitors, and you often sense a feeling that the government economists believe that the dumping of foreign steel in this country gives U.S. consumers lower prices, and allows the United States to allocate our resources toward other industries, such as microelectronics and communication equipment, in which we have an inherent cost–volume advantage. This argument doesn't play very well in Youngstown, Ohio, or Tonawanda, New York, both of which are sites of closed steel mills; a billboard put up in the latter community by the United Steel Workers shows a caricature of an Asiatic worker with the slogan, "He doesn't want your job anymore; he already has it." That sign is particularly appropriate in Tonawanda; bridges on the interstate highway system in that area were totally built with Japanese steel. You cannot convince me that they can import coal from Korea, ore from Australia, and oil from Saudi Arabia, make steel in Yokahama, and then ship it to Buffalo, New York, and sell it cheaper than a mill 20 miles away that is using domestic coal and domestic ore. (Statement of an industry consultant)

Class assignment. The general assignment is to understand the productive process and the economic problems of the domestic steel industry, and the competitive strategies of the eight major steel producers. Specific questions are as follows:

1. Be able to describe the essential economic problems of the steel industry. If you were the president of U.S. Steel Corporation, and asked to testify before a congressional committee investigating unemployment in the older industrial areas, such as Youngs-

town, Ohio, and Tonawanda, New York, what points would you stress in your introductory comments? If you were a member of the congressional committee, what questions would you ask?

2. Be able to describe the relative competitive strategies of the eight largest steel producers. Exhibits 15 to 22 provide financial, marketing, and production information on those companies. Why have the differences developed between these companies in an assumedly homogeneous industry such as steel? Which company is in the best position to be financially successful over the next 10-year period?

3. Be able to understand the apparent optimism of industry executives in 1960. If you were president of Jones & Laughlin in 1960, prior to the purchase by LTV Corporation, what strategy would you recommend to the board of directors? In 1960, Jones & Laughlin earned $33.1 million after taxes and paid $19.1 million in dividends on sales of $778 million and equity

of $537 million. Three integrated steel mills were owned, in Pittsburgh, Alaquippa, and Cleveland, and the steel mill products were approximately the same as those currently produced.

4. Be able to understand the apparent position of members of the U.S. government. If you were Mr. Joseph Sims, Deputy Director of the Antitrust Section of the Justice Department (quoted on page 266), would you permit the merger proposed in 1977 of Jones & Laughlin (owned by LTV Corp.) and Youngstown Sheet and Tube (owned by Lykes Corp.)?

5. Be able to understand the maturing process of an industry. What happened to the domestic steel industry from 1960 to 1977, and why? What could happen to currently profitable industries, such as commercial banking and public accounting, from 1980 to 1997, and why? If you were the managing partner in Price Waterhouse, what strategy would you recommend to the other senior partners in 1980?

Exhibit 15 *Consolidated income statements (000's omitted) for the eight largest steel companies, 1977*

	U.S. Steel	Bethlehem	National	Republic	Inland	Armco	Jones & Laughlin	Lykes
Raw steel production (tons)	28,800,000	16,609,000	9,378,000	9,220,000	7,860,000	7,833,000	7,010,000	4,490,000
Finished steel shipment (tons)	19,700,000	12,405,000	7,621,000	6,657,000	5,586,000	5,483,000	5,430,000	3,476,000
Net sales	$9,609,900	$5,370,000	$3,138,861	$2,909,384	$2,681,604	$3,549,239	$2,229,019	$1,544,557
Other income	81,200	40,200	10,679	15,054	15,038	16,573	8,283	222,456
Equity in affiliates	—	—	18,569	7,265	—	22,926	—	19,823
Total income	9,691,100	5,410,200	3,168,109	2,931,703	2,696,642	3,588,738	2,307,302	1,786,453
Cost of goods sold	7,944,500	4,863,200	2,790,974	2,482,060	2,425,223	3,133,548	2,156,918	1,474,759
Selling and administration	349,500	284,600	115,945	95,505	included	274,559	79,080	105,449
Interest	154,800	82,500	56,091	33,798	47,468	56,087	32,782	68,947
Depreciation	372,000	300,100	136,874	94,417	99,219	included	60,161	52,414
Miscellaneous	768,400	—	—	88,177	31,632	3,449	—	175,796
	9,589,200	5,530,400	3,099,884	2,793,957	2,603,542	3,467,643	2,328,941	1,877,415
Income before charges	101,900	(120,200)	68,225	137,746	93,100	121,095	(21,639)	(90,962)
Plant closings	—	791,000	—	—	—	—	7,616	138,000
Minority interests	—	—	—	—	1,539	—	—	—
Income tax (credit)	(36,000)	(463,000)	8,100	96,715	3,760	1,263	(26,274)	(39,216)
Net income	137,900	(448,200)	60,125	41,031	87,801	119,832	(2,981)	(189,746)

Note: Other income is primarily interest on deposits and dividends from subsidiaries; for Lykes, other income is revenue from shipping company.

Miscellaneous expenses for U.S. Steel consist of $572,100 pensions and employee benefits and $196,300 local taxes; for Republic they consist of $86,064 pensions and $2,113 miscellaneous; for Inland they consist of $31,632 local taxes; and for Lykes they consist of $175,796 shipping expenses, net of operating subsidy.

Income taxes (credits) are net of investment tax credits.

Source: Annual Reports for the respective companies.

Exhibit 16 *Consolidated balance sheets (000's omitted) for the eight largest steel companies, 1977*

	U.S. Steel	Bethlehem	National	Republic	Inland	Armco	Jones & Laughlin	Lykes
Cash and securities	$ 698,900	$ 238,800	$ 102,776	$ 49,952	$ 58,845	$ 37,011	$ 21,203	$ 92,083
Accounts and notes receivable	1,086,600	496,700	320,412	255,173	274,669	373,440	255,182	217,604
Inventories	1,254,800	626,200	517,398	473,932	312,741	580,983	272,238	249,305
Refundable taxes	—	134,000	23,000	55,656	27,433	—	4,942	19,425
Miscellaneous	—	—	25,572	—	17,705	62,386	18,002	—
Total current	3,040,300	1,495,700	989,158	834,713	691,393	1,053,820	571,567	578,417
Fixed assets (net)	5,724,200	2,988,300	1,635,755	1,427,481	1,457,553	1,437,810	965,628	877,375
Investments	862,200	414,900	187,439	115,253	133,362	237,138	81,282	211,035
Prepaid expenses	287,700	—	15,294	28,883	—	143,462	32,732	30,399
Goodwill	—	—	—	—	20,044	10,524	—	—
Total long-term	6,874,100	3,403,200	1,838,488	1,571,617	1,610,959	1,828,934	1,079,642	1,118,809
Total assets	9,914,400	4,898,900	2,827,646	2,406,330	2,302,352	2,882,754	1,651,209	1,697,226
Accounts and notes payable	1,482,100	718,900	212,014	341,292	282,741	287,013	219,958	334,877
Accrued taxes	230,400	129,500	26,490	43,094	81,964	93,119	985	18,478
Miscellaneous	—	130,100	316,067	—	—	197,168	186,670	21,142
Total current liabilities	1,712,500	978,500	554,571	384,386	364,705	577,300	407,613	374,497
Long-term debt	2,364,400	1,305,600	736,292	481,945	651,041	673,546	687,714	—
Deferred taxes	445,800	—	244,523	205,970	135,937	83,043	73,487	30,352
Minority interest	250,000	—	11,242	—	3,980	85,831	12,974	—
Plant-closing residual	—	435,900	—	—	—	—	—	77,308
Total long-term	3,060,200	1,741,500	992,057	687,915	790,958	842,420	420,844	795,374
Preferred stock	—	—	—	—	1,688	14,458	11,419	76,277
Common stock	1,683,400	506,700	97,212	161,827	234,277	148,257	159,052	82,747
Capital surplus	61,600	—	121,484	157,617	—	122,293	88,518	3,512
Earned surplus	3,397,200	1,672,200	1,062,322	1,014,585	910,744	1,178,126	563,763	364,819
Total equity	5,142,200	2,178,900	1,281,018	1,334,029	1,146,709	1,463,134	822,752	527,355
Total debt and equity	9,914,400	4,898,900	2,827,646	2,406,330	2,302,352	2,882,754	1,651,209	1,697,226

Note: Jones & Laughlin is a wholly owned subsidiary of LTV Corp., a conglomerate with interests in steel, meat products (Wilson), and air-craft components (Vought). Corporate sales in 1977 were $4,703.2 million, and the loss for the year was $38.7 million. Current assets of the corporation were $865 million, fixed assets $1,200 million, current liabilities $1,086 million, long-term debt $596 million, and equity $383 million.

Source: Annual Report for the respective companies.

Exhibit 17 *General products (percent) for the eight largest steel companies, 1977*

	U.S. Steel	Bethlehem	National	Republic	Inland	Armco	Jones & Laughlin	Lykes
Steel mill products	76.5	72.2	95.0	80.0	78.3	67.5	90.0	69.1
Aluminum refining	—	—	2.0	—	—	—	—	—
Cement manufacturing	Yes	Yes	—	—	—	—	—	—
Chemical products	3.0	—	—	—	—	Yes	—	—
Core and ore sales	2.5	5.2	—	—	—	—	4.0	—
Fabricated heavy products	6.0	14.3	—	—	—	—	2.0	—
Fabricated buildings	4.5	—	5.0	15.0	11.2	9.7	—	—
Fabricated light products	2.0	—	—	5.0	7.5	6.5	4.0	—
Financial services	Yes	—	—	—	—	3.1	—	—
Forgings	Yes	Yes	—	Yes	—	—	Yes	—
Graphite and carbon	Yes	—	—	—	—	Yes	—	—
Industrial fasteners	Yes	Yes	—	—	—	Yes	—	—
Light aircraft	—	—	—	Yes	—	—	—	—
Metal-forming machinery	—	—	—	—	Yes	—	—	—
Mobile homes	—	—	—	—	3.0	—	—	—
Office equipment	—	—	—	Yes	—	—	—	—
Oil field machinery	—	—	—	—	—	13.2	—	16.4
Oil and gas exploration	—	—	—	—	—	Yes	—	—
Plastic industrial products	3.9	Yes	—	—	—	Yes	—	1.0
Plastic consumer products	—	Yes	—	—	—	—	—	—
Railroad equipment	Yes	Yes	—	Yes	—	—	Yes	—
Railroad operation	Yes	—	—	—	—	—	—	—
Real estate management	Yes	—	—	—	Yes	Yes	—	—
Ship building	—	8.3	—	—	—	—	—	—
Ship operation	1.4	—	—	—	—	—	—	12.4
Steel castings	Yes	Yes	—	Yes	—	—	Yes	—
Wire rope	Yes	Yes	—	—	—	Yes	—	—

Notes: "Yes" indicates the product is produced, yet represents less than 1% of annual sales volume, and the revenues are included in other categories in the published reports.

Chemical products are for agricultural and industrial use, and are based upon phenol, ammonia, and methane feedstock from coke-oven operation.

Fabricated heavy products are made from formed and welded plate and structural steel, and include bridges and culverts for highways, and pressure vessels, holding tanks, fractionating columns, and bulk storage facilities for petroleum and chemical industries.

Fabricated light products are made from formed and welded sheet and coated steel, and include steel doors and frames, steel racks and shelving, steel pails and drums, and other pressed steel products for general industrial use.

Exhibit 17 (*continued*)

Financial services include leases, mortgages, and general credit for commercial and industrial customers.

Light aircraft refers to the ownership of Mooney Aircraft Company of Kerrville, Texas, by Republic Steel Company.

Plastic industrial products include custom-molded items for the automotive, appliance, and furniture industries.

Plastic consumer products include proprietary items such as toys, games, and sporting equipment for retail sale; Republic Steel Company owns the Kusan Toy Company.

Railroad equipment includes cast steel frames and pressed steel parts for railcar manufacture; it does not include hot-rolled rails or forged wheels and axles, which are basic steel mill products.

Railroad operations refers to the ownership and management of railroads that transport general merchandise in addition to steel mill raw materials and finished products. U.S. Steel Company owns and operates four major railroads: Bessemer and Lake Erie; Birmingham Southern; Duluth, Missabe and Iron Range; and the Elgin, Joliet and Eastern.

Shipbuilding is primarily by Bethlehem Steel Company, which owns and operates marine construction and repair yards at Baltimore, Maryland; Beaumont, Texas; Boston, Massachusetts; San Francisco, California; and Singapore.

Ship operations refers to the ownership and management of both lake and ocean shipping lines that transport general merchandise in addition to steel mill materials and products. U.S. Steel Company owns and operates the Ohio Barge Line and Gulf Navigation Company. Lykes Corporation owns and operates a U.S. flag common carrier to and from major U.S. ports.

Source: Annual Reports for the respective companies, supplemented by industry estimates.

Exhibit 18 Average price per ton of steel mill products (000,000's omitted) for the eight largest steel companies, 1977

	U.S. Steel	Bethlehem	National	Republic	Inland	Armco	Jones & Laughlin	Lykes
Net corporate sales	$9,609.9	$5,370.0	$3,138.8	$2,909.3	$2,681.6	$3,549.2	$2,229.0	$1,766.9
Steel mill sales (%)	76.5	72.2	95.0	80.0	78.3	67.5	90.0	69.1
Steel mill sales	$7,352.0	$3,877.0	$2,981.0	$2,327.0	$2,099.0	$2,399.0	$2,006.0	$1,221.0
Steel shipped (tons)	19.70	12.40	7.62	6.66	5.58	5.48	5.43	3.47
Dollars per steel mill ton	$ 373.19	$ 312.67	$ 391.20	$ 349.49	$ 376.16	$ 426.59	$ 369.42	$ 351.87

Exhibit 19 *Steel mill products (percent) classified by product group for the eight largest steel companies, 1977*

	U.S. Steel	Bethlehem*	National	Republic	Inland	Armco*	Jones & Laughlin*	Lykes*
Semifinished steel	2.0	5.5	—	6.8	—	—	7.0	—
Hot-rolled structural and plate	22.0	39.0	—	—	15.0	4.0	20.0	20.0
Hot-rolled rails and rail products	3.0	5.5	—	4.7	—	—	6.0	—
Hot-rolled bars and rods	12.0	19.0	—	32.5	15.0	5.0	28.0	4.0
Hot-rolled sheet and strip	15.8	10.0	28.0	12.5	20.0	35.0	12.0	40.0
Cold-finished bar stock	2.0	Yes	—	Yes	2.0	Yes	Yes	—
Cold-finished sheet and strip	17.2	10.0	48.0	18.5	26.0	35.0	12.0	15.0
Plated products	13.8	8.0	21.0	13.2	22.0	—	10.0	25.0
Tubular products	10.2	3.0	8.0	8.9	—	16.0	—	6.0
Drawn products	2.0	Yes	—	0.9	—	—	5.0	—
Alloy and tool steels	Yes	—	—	—	—	8.0	—	—
Stainless steels	Yes	—	—	2.0	—	2.0	—	—

Source: Annual Reports for the respective companies, supplemented by industry estimates (*).

Exhibit 20 *Steel mill shipments (percent) classified by market segment for the eight largest steel companies, 1977*

	U.S. Steel*	Bethlehem*	National*	Republic*	Inland*	Armco*	Jones & Laughlin*	Lykes*
Agricultural machinery	3.0	3.0	—	Yes	7.0	Yes	—	Yes
Appliances	3.0	Yes	10.0	3.0	6.0	5.0	2.0	Yes
Automotive	24.0	7.0	40.0	20.0	18.0	5.0	10.0	25.0
Company export	2.0	1.0	yes	—	—	22.0	—	—
Company fabrication	7.0	11.0	3.0	12.0	11.0	10.0	3.0	—
Company warehouses	9.0	—	15.0	—	20.0	—	—	—
Construction	15.0	30.0	—	12.0	12.0	4.0	20.0	15.0
Containers	7.0	5.0	15.0	7.0	10.0	—	5.0	10.0
Industrial machinery	5.0	8.0	—	7.0	10.0			
Nonclassified	2.0	2.0	4.0	2.0	2.0	7.0	27.0	30.0
Oil and gas	4.0	Yes	7.0	4.0	—	12.0	—	5.0
Railroad	3.0	7.0	—	6.0	—	—	8.0	—
Ship building	5.0	8.0	—	—	—	—	—	—
Steel conversion	4.0	8.0	2.0	10.0	4.0	—	10.0	—
Warehouse distribution	7.0	10.0	4.0	18.0	—	20.0	15.0	15.0

Notes: Company export refers to steel shipments outside the United States; Armco has sales offices and warehouses in 33 countries.

Company fabrication refers to steel shipments to company-owned fabricating plants, for heavy, light, or building fabrication.

Company warehouse refers to steel shipments to company-owned "service centers" that store, process (cut to length, width, or shape and perform some bending/welding), and sell both manufactured steel products and purchased steel and nonferrous products. Inland Steel Company owns 28 warehouses that operate under the name Joseph Ryerson & Son; National Steel Company owns 24 warehouses that purchase a full line of steel products from other manufacturers, but specialize in hot-rolled and cold-finished sheet and strip; U.S. Steel Company owns 20 warehouses. Republic Steel Company owned 2 warehouses until 1975, when they were sold.

Steel conversion refers primarily to shipment of semifinished steel ingots, blooms, slabs, and billets to nonintegrated specialty mills and finishing mills; it also refers to the shipment of steel sheet and strip to large volume manufacturers of siding, shelving, etc.

Source: Form 10K reports for the respective companies, supplemented by industry estimates (*).

Exhibit 21 *Steel mill locations, by state, for the eight largest steel producing companies, 1977*

	U.S. Steel	Bethlehem	National	Republic	Inland	Armco	Jones & Laughlin	Lykes
Alabama	Fairfield	—	—	Birmingham	—	—	—	—
California	—	Los Angeles	—	—	—	—	—	—
Indiana	Gary	Burns Harbor	Portage	—	East Chicago	—	—	East Chicago
Illinois	Chicago	—	Granite City	South Chicago	—	—	—	—
Kentucky	—	—	—	—	—	Ashland	—	—
Maryland	—	Sparrows Point	—	—	—	Baltimore	—	—
Michigan	—	—	Ecorse	—	—	—	Warren	—
New York	—	Lackawanna	—	Buffalo	—	—	—	—
Ohio	Youngstown Lorain	—	—	Youngstown Cleveland	—	Marion Middletown	Cleveland	Youngstown
Oklahoma	—	—	—	—	—	Sand Springs	—	Sand Springs
Pennsylvania	Fairless Pittsburgh	Johnstown Bethlehem	—	—	—	Butler	Aliquippa Pittsburgh	—
Texas	Baytown	—	—	—	—	Houston	—	Houston
West Virginia	—	—	Weirton	—	—	—	—	—

Source: Annual Reports for the respective companies.

Exhibit 22 *Steel mill capacity (measured by shipment of finished steel products) and percent obsolete (operating at 10% or more above the industry cost structure)*

	U.S. Steel	Bethlehem	National	Republic	Inland	Armco	Jones & Laughlin	Lykes
Steel mill capacity (tons)	19,700,000	12,405,000	7,621,000	6,657,000	5,586,000	5,483,000	5,430,000	3,476,000
Percent obsolete	20.0	25.0	10.0	40.0	10.0	10.0	50.0	50.0

Source: Industry estimates.

Herman Miller, Inc.

Herman Miller, Inc., of Zeeland, Michigan, was formed in 1905 to manufacture traditional bedroom furniture, originally for sale through Sears Roebuck, but over the next 20 years the level of quality was gradually improved and the channels of distribution were slowly widened, so that in 1929 the company was also producing very high priced and very high quality furniture for sale through the large department stores in major cities. Mr. D. J. DePree, who had started work for the company as the office boy in 1909, became the president and one of the major stockholders by the early 1920s. Stories of his early work experiences and training are interesting, for they indicate some of the changes that have occurred in managerial education since that time.

> As a boy D. J. had read deeply. . . . While the King James Bible was his major literary influence, he also turned for advice to the columns of *American Boy* magazine. As an adult, he continued to read both and also the *Sunday School Times.* One day he read a *Sunday School Times* article called "How to Plan Your Day," and instantly began applying what he had learned. "That was simple enough," he explains, "because I had a clear knowledge of what needed to be done. After all, there was only the boss, a secretary, and me. I had to operate a typewriter, go into the factory to follow up orders, and so forth. I could control my time."

The time-saving tips worked so well that from then on DePree was able to finish his day's work at the furniture company by noon. The rest of the time he studied accounting, not out of any great love for numbers, but because the income tax had begun in 1913 and he could see that new skills would be called for. "I became extremely interested in cost accounting," DePree says. "It was fascinating to break the business down into a lot of little businesses. For example, we had a coal-fired burner and some generators, so we were a power business. Since we owned the property, we were a real estate business."

DePree also began reading books by efficiency experts, an activity interesting in the light of Herman Miller, Inc.'s later involvement in the management of office work. "The boss didn't like the idea of my spending all that time reading," DePree says. "However, he did pay my expenses to an efficiency convention in Milwaukee. My study of Frederick Taylor and the other time-management people began a lifetime of reading for me. . . ." (Ralph Caplan, *The Design of Herman Miller,* pp. 20–21)

The start of the depression, in 1929, brought Herman Miller close to bankruptcy. Consumer spending, of course, declined and industry competition substantially increased. Furniture manufacturing at that time was centered in three distinct areas in the United States: western New York, near Jamestown; western Michigan, near Grand Rapids; and western North Carolina, near High Point. The southern factories had lower wage rates and more modern machinery, and were better able to compete on a price basis. Many of the northern companies were closed by the early 1930s.

> The major problem at Herman Miller was that the company lacked direction. They made some furniture for Sears Roebuck in Chicago and some furniture for Wanamakers in Philadelphia, but there were no consistencies or economies between those product lines. My father felt that the solution was to get out of the traditional furniture industry, but there were very few alternatives that were both available and apparent at that time. (Statement of Mr. Hugh DePree)

In the spring of 1930, Mr. Gilbert Rhode, one of the first of the industrial designers who believed that form should reflect function, walked unannounced into the Herman Miller showroom. He had come to Grand Rapids to sell his designs for modern, undecorated furniture, but these designs had been rejected and even ridiculed by the larger manufacturers in that city, and the designer was now visiting the smaller companies in the surrounding area, attempting to interest someone in making and marketing his furniture.

I'm not certain that my father liked the appearance of modern furniture, but he did like the concept. At that time, furniture styles were dictated by the store buyers, who looked for novelties and minor changes to interest their customers, and the furniture market was dominated by four seasonal displays that were held each year in the Merchandise Mart (a large building, with open areas that were suitable for showing manufactured goods) in Chicago. Buyers made selections and placed orders on the basis of the seasonal styles, and marketing consisted of attempting to discover what arbitrary changes the buyers might like, or what style modifications the large manufacturers might make, prior to the show. The industry was totally reactionary; all furniture companies reacted to the whims of the buyers and the rumors of change, and none were able to achieve the economies of scale or the standardization of parts that could come with more suitable styles. The adoption of modern design meant that a company could avoid the continual style changes and the arbitrary buyer decisions, and could begin to be proactive in a segment of the market. This was a major change for the industry, and a major risk for the company for, of course, the modern segment of the market was still exceedingly small in the early 1930s. (Statement of Mr. Hugh DePree)

Herman Miller produced the Rhode designs, which consisted of very plain and unadorned beds, tables, chairs, desks, bookcases, shelves, and drawers, generally rectangular in shape and necessarily precise in manufacturing technique. Other manufacturers could use carvings and moldings to hide the workmanship in the joints and the edges; for Gilbert Rhode, the joints and edges were parts of the design, and should not be hidden. Mr. Rhode believed that people in the United States were going to live in smaller and simpler homes, as a result of the economic changes of the Depression and the social changes of the New Deal, and that they would want simpler and more useful furniture for their homes. His new designs were sold through department stores and furniture stores, primarily in the larger cities along the Eastern seaboard, but marketing was difficult due to a lack of understanding of design principles by the sales personnel and the retail customers; both felt that the lack of decoration should have resulted in a lower price, and did not recognize the level of skill and precision needed to manufacture undecorated modern furniture.

Our own salesmen were initially the broker type. They were 5%, 6%, 7% men with other lines to sell. They weren't interested in our Rhode line, because to sell it they would have to understand it. They were all highly intelligent men, but unaccustomed to bringing their intelligence into sales talk in the way the new line required. Their sales approach depended a great deal on friendship and entertaining and status, not on the real hard, intelligent selling of things that would help people. (Statement of Mr. D. J. DePree, quoted in Ralph Caplan, *The Design of Herman Miller*, p. 29)

For the next 15 years, Herman Miller produced both modern furniture designed by Gilbert Rhode and copies of Shaker furniture designed by a local woman, Frida Diamond. The Shaker styles were also simple, plain, and unadorned, based upon original work produced by the Shaker religious sects in New England and the Midwest. The company emphasized simple styling, excellent craftsmanship, and quality control.

> That [the combination of style, craftsmanship, and control] was the beginning of a design adventure that would carry the name and the products of this obscure little company across the world. In the United States only IBM, and in Europe only Olivetti and Braun, connoted design excellence in the way Herman Miller came to connote it. (Ralph Caplan, *The Design of Herman Miller,* p. 26)

Gilbert Rhode died in 1944, leaving the company with a commitment to modern design, but without a modern designer. Mr. DePree found another designer through the pages of the *Architectural Forum;* he was intrigued by an article in that journal proposing that walls be used for storage (a new concept in 1940, although widely accepted today). D. J. DePree called the author, George Nelson, arranged an interview, found that he had no experience in furniture design, and hired him. George Nelson continued the plain and undecorated designs of Gilbert Rhode, but with greater emphasis upon standardization of components (at that time, each of the 24 storage units in the lines of bedroom furniture designed by Gilbert Rhode and Frida Diamond had different drawer sizes) and modular sections (all the components of the wall storage system designed by George Nelson were modular, and interchangeable).

Charles Eames was the third designer hired by the company. Charles and Ray (Mrs.) Eames, working with Eero Saarinen, a well-known architect, had designed a line of molded plywood furniture that won the first prize in the Museum of Modern Art's design competition in 1946; they also developed the molding and bonding techniques to manufacture the furniture commercially, and the processing equipment and marketing rights were transferred to Herman Miller in 1948. Charles and Ray Eames followed up their success with molded plywood furniture by designing molded fiberglass seating for auditoriums, and suspended fabric seating for airports and other public areas.

> Systems implications are basic to Eames designs. For example, a molded fiberglass shell works equally well on its own four-leg pedestal base or on a tandem base. This systems effect was a key factor in our ability to move from residential to institutional design. In the sixties, an Eames-designed system of seat shells, castings and arm surfaces was used in lecture halls on all State University of New York campuses. (Statement of Mr. R. I. Blaich, vice president of Herman Miller, Inc., quoted in *The Design of Herman Miller,* p. 46)

In the early 1950s, Herman Miller could be described as a furniture company with a commitment to modern design, excellent taste, and high quality, with sales of approximately $4,000,000 per year in both the residential and institutional markets, and with after-tax profits of perhaps 2% on sales. The emphasis upon design, taste, and quality was expressed by George Nelson in an introduction to the 1948 Herman Miller catalog:

> The attitude that governs Herman Miller behavior, as far as I can make out, is compounded of the following set of principles.
> What you make is important. Herman Miller, like all other companies, is governed by the rules of the American economy, but I have yet to see quality of construction or finish skimped to meet a popular price bracket, or for any other reason.

Design is an integral part of the business. The designer's decisions are as important as those of the sales or production departments. If the design is changed, it is with the designer's participation and approval. There is no pressure on him to modify to meet the market.

You decide what you will make. Herman Miller has never done any market research or any pretesting of its products to determine what the market "will accept." If designer and management like a solution to a particular furniture problem, it is put into production. . . . (Statement of George Nelson, quoted in *The Design of Herman Miller,* p. 36)

The fourth designer for the company was Robert Propst, who in the 1950s had begun an architectural sculpture business in Boulder, Colorado, and who also lectured on engineering innovation at the University of Colorado, and contracted for design innovations with companies in the lumber, aviation, and concrete industries. Hugh DePree attended a design conference in Aspen, Colorado, in 1958, and hired him while there, originally for a set percentage of his time, but in 1960 this arrangement was changed to full time and Robert Propst moved to Ann Arbor, Michigan, 140 miles from Zeeland, to set up the Herman Miller Research Division.

We hired Robert Propst not as a furniture designer, but as an innovator. I felt that we had to diversify; I felt that we had to get out of the residential and institutional furniture industries because of the price constraints. We were innovators in design and leaders in quality, but other furniture companies quickly copied our designs in lower-quality materials and lower-cost processes, so that we were forced to compete on price with copies of our own innovations. Our strength was in design, but other companies had greater strengths in engineering, manufacturing, and marketing.

We tried to create a climate of freedom

for Bob Propst, with an assignment only to "explore problems for which a product, not necessarily furniture, might be the solution." Creative people are going to do what they want—they are going to follow up what they are interested in despite the barriers you put in their way. So you have to get an agreement that is mutually supportive. We thought that we had such an agreement, and we thought that we had a good working relationship between the parent firm and the research division in Ann Arbor, but Bob produced some exotic ideas for presentation to a furniture company that wanted to diversify. (Statement of Hugh DePree)

Mr. Propst presented 37 ideas for diversification to the parent company; these ranged from laser technologies to agricultural systems; some of the more interesting are described below:

1. *Sugar beet thinner.* Sugar beets are a major crop in Colorado; Robert Propst developed a farm implement to automatically thin the rows for greatly increased yields.
2. *Wooden roof structure.* The usual means of spanning large spaces during construction is with heavy steel beams or bar joists; Robert Propst developed a light wooden truss system with special steel connectors.
3. *Accurate survey transit.* Surveying is slow and occasionally inaccurate since it is subjective, based upon sighting a target through the telescope on a transit; Robert Propst developed the concept of projecting an amplified and phased light (an early version of the laser).
4. *Citrus fruit harvester.* Oranges and grapefruit are difficult to pick mechanically since each fruit has to be twisted on the stem to break off; they cannot be pulled off or shaken from the tree. Robert Propst prepared drawings of a mobile harvesting unit that would rotate the fruit.
5. *Home waste compactor.* Domestic rubbish is difficult to collect since it is loose and

stored in different-sized containers. Robert Propst built a prototype of a new appliance that would compact and package rubbish in a standard cube for automatic pickup.

6. *Ready-made dormitory bed.* With the end of maid service in college dormitories in the 1940s, beds were seldom made up during the day; Robert Propst invented a machine that would automatically make up a student's bed.

Hugh DePree, who had succeeded his father as president of Herman Miller in 1962, felt that it was necessary to narrow down this range of innovations since the company did not have the resources to continue with the simultaneous development of all 37 projects. A committee was established, consisting of himself, Robert Propst, Glenn Walters, the most successful sales executive in the company, and Vernon Poest, the chief financial officer, to evaluate the alternatives and select the most promising for further development and eventual manufacture and sale. The committee selected a project that had not been given much emphasis on the original list.

> Much of the time we spent discussing the various development projects, and attempting to find a future focus for the company, was in Bob's office in Ann Arbor. And his office was very special. He had designed the desks and files and bookcases and other display/storage units, and we had made them for him in the factory at Zeeland. They were designed to fit the way he worked, with material he was using immediately available and apparent, so that it could not be overlooked or forgotten, and with material he was not using stored and out of sight, so that it did not create the usual clutter of an office. The desks were smaller, really work areas designed for special purposes such as drafting, writing, typing, etc., and each was at the proper height and each had stands to hold the needed papers or books. All of the units

> were mounted on wall panels that were moveable to adjust to changes in personnel or activities. Bob thought of his office as a system—he termed it a "collection of reinforcing solutions," which is his definition of a system—and we thought that it was very efficient and enjoyable. The more we thought about it, the more we thought his concept of the office as a system made sense, and that was the start of the Action Office Project. (Statement of Mr. Hugh DePree)

The decision of the company, in 1963, was to build office furniture that could be attached to accoustical wall panels, with electrical and telephone wiring and connectors pre-installed in each panel, so that the work space could expand or contract, and the work components could be rearranged to meet changing task requirements. It was felt that this "open office" planning could save 15% to 20% in new construction costs since the interior walls and doorways were not needed, and could save up to 90% during remodeling since the work areas and components could be rearranged so easily. In addition, it was thought that the employee morale and productivity would increase markedly since the work spaces would be more personalized, the work components (desks, files, and display units) more adjustable, and the work materials more available. George Nelson, as the senior designer in the company, was assigned the task of finishing the concepts developed by the Research Division, and preparing them for production and sale, but the resulting designs were not commercially successful.

> Action Office I was beautiful, but very expensive. George had designed each of the components to be integral with the panel—a wall with shelves, for example, or a wall with a work surface and file drawers—and these huge parts were very difficult to manufacture and very awkward to ship. There were technical problems, inherent in the office systems concept, that were hard to overcome. Think

for a minute of three panels, each 62 in. high × 96 in. long, that have to interlock at a given point as part of two work spaces (a common wall, and two end walls, for example); the manufacturing tolerances have to be very precise for those panels to fit together. Or think about a desk or a work surface, 24 in. wide × 96 in. long, that has to be hung from a panel, and then support a 300-pound accountant resting his elbows on the surface of that desk or, even worse, sitting on the edge; the support structure has to be very strong for those components to last. George Nelson's solution for the precise tolerance and high-strength requirements of the system was to mold integral panels from reinforced plastics, which was the same technology we used for the fiberglass version of the Eames chair, but these parts were simply too difficult and too costly to make in the large sizes, and, of course, they lost much of the flexibility that was central to the original concept. We held a number of shows with the components of Action Office I, and they created a lot of industry interest, but they did not sell well. (Statement of Mr. Hugh DePree)

In 1965, the design of the components and the engineering of the connections and support structures was assigned to Robert Propst, but progress toward achievement of the Action Office concept remained slow and apparently fitful.

In 1965, we said "O.K., Propst, this is your concept and your system; you go ahead and design it." He was thinking of small, mass-produced parts that would fit together in modular form (the same end panels for a 2-ft file, a 4-ft file, and a 8-ft file, for example), and he began to think of better and better ways to connect and support these parts, but he was using machined steel and extruded plastics with which we have no experience, so that he was making headway on the designs, but nothing was happening to move the designs through the production and mar-

keting process. And Bob thinks in terms of a complete system; he feels that you either have X number of components, or you don't have anything. So, he was designing files and display units and typewriter stands, together with foot rests and pencil trays and curved panels, all of which do fit together but all of which also delay commercial introduction. (Statement of Mr. Hugh DePree)

In the fall of 1967, Hugh DePree went to an office planning conference in Chicago, and found that other companies, attracted by the surrounding displays of Action Office I, were thinking in similar terms, and designing similar components. Mr. DePree returned to Zeeland, and assigned Glenn Walters, then the sales vice president, the task of completing the design, organizing the production, and introducing the product to the market before June of 1968.

Just about this time I attended a seminar in Chicago on office design, and I came away shaken to my boots. There were other people talking about the same thing we had been talking about! I concluded we had to get it on the market, so we took the stuff away from Bob Propst and said, "This is no longer entirely your responsibility." I think that was the first time we recognized that some other people might have input into all this. It was also the first time the company was determined to take steps not to be knocked off. There was another first, too: the first time cost goals and price goals became design criteria. (Statement of Mr. Hugh DePree, quoted in *The Design of Herman Miller,* p. 92)

The assignment to Mr. Walters was very simple and direct: he was to "get Action Office II on the market by June of 1968," and he was authorized to do "anything necessary to accomplish this goal except sell the company." He hired additional draftsmen and engineers, forced the use of formed steel, cast aluminum, and laminated wood, materials that were known and processes that were used by the company, and brought the line to the market with only 67 components (five years later there were over 1,000 modular parts). Some of the major innovations occurred in marketing.

> We had been accustomed to selling to architects and to dealers, through our showrooms, and then the architects and dealers sold to our final customers. But that marketing process would not work for Action Office II since the customer had the problem—the architects and dealers didn't have the problem—and we had the solution, but no one in the distribution chain, neither our salespeople nor our dealers, understood that solution. Bob Schwartz [marketing manager of the company] developed a new distribution method. (Statement of Mr. Glenn Walters)

Mr. Schwartz developed the concept of using seminars, held in an abandoned supermarket in Grand Rapids, to demonstrate and explain the Action Office system. He believed that if the customers understood the system, they would want it, so he attempted to provide genuine information rather than sales propaganda.

> Herman Miller had no expertise in systems like this. What were we supposed to do with it? There was no known market for panel-hung accessories. If the salesmen couldn't sell the panel-hung concept, then the dealers certainly couldn't. We went directly to the business people. (Statement of Mr. Robert Schwartz, quoted in *The Design of Herman Miller,* p. 94)

The marketing plan worked (seats at the early seminars were at such a premium that Robert Schwartz even refused to admit D. J. DePree to one of them, saying, "you don't buy anything, D. J.") and customers were at first pleased with the Action Office II equipment, and then enthusiastic about the office

systems concept. Engineering continued to expand the number of the components, and the production process gradually became routine. The senior management had originally set a target, for the allocation of fixed costs, of $3,000,000 sales per year within three years from the date of the market introduction of the new product line; this sales goal was exceeded in 18 months.

From 1961 to 1968, Robert Propst had been working not only on the design concept and engineering implementation of the Action Office product line, but also on a totally new and totally different product line for hospitals. He had been interested in health care for a number of years, and at one time had designed a new hospital bed, and a new stretcher that could be used from the accident scene to the transport ambulance to the emergency ward to the x-ray department, and finally, to the hospital room without moving the patient, but his primary interest in health care came after spending a few months in a hospital.

> How did we get into the hospital business? Bob Propst slipped his disc. This is a providential company, haven't you heard? (Statement of Mr. Robert Schwartz, quoted in *The Design of Herman Miller,* p. 96)

Robert Propst felt that the furniture for health care facilities was improper since it had been designed for the hotel/motel market, and was very costly to sanitize, and he thought that the material management system in hospitals was obsolete since it involved continual handling and restocking, and was very costly to maintain. Mr. Propst suggested "discardable" structures and "disposable" materials to solve these two problems.

> Think of a simple bedside table in a hospital room. It is normally made of wood so that it can't be sterilized, and it is usually too large so that it won't fit in a dishwasher, and therefore it has to be

cleaned, by hand, using chemical disinfectants. These gradually destroy the finish, so that after a few years the appearance of the table and the other structures in the room has deteriorated so that the hospital room, instead of being bright and cheerful, has a gray and worn appearance. And you have incomplete sanitation. There ought to be a new surface on each of the structures each time a new patient is admitted.

Now, think of the drawer in that bedside table. It is normally empty. Each time a nurse comes in to see a patient for the first time, she has to bring in the hospital nightgown, towels, a thermometer, etc., that she has collected from the supply room on the floor. These standard items ought to be in the drawer of that table, and that drawer, fully stocked, ought to be replaced each time a new patient is admitted. (Statement of Mr. Robert Propst)

Mr. Propst suggested hospital furniture and equipment with a discardable surface layer that could be peeled away for complete sanitation and renewed appearance, and he recommended that this furniture and equipment be built as part of a system to store and use disposable sheets, towels, bandages, covers, etc. Kimberly-Clark Inc., a large consumer products firm (1962 sales of $515 million and profits of $31 million) was exceedingly interested in this concept due to the obvious relationship between their existing disposable tissues and the proposed medical products, and they established a new research division within their own company, and participated in a joint research effort with Herman Miller from 1961 to 1963.

The hospital industry in 1961 was big, clearly identifiable, rapidly growing, committed to improved patient care, but concerned with problems of labor cost and technical obsolescence. Professional administrators were becoming an important factor in hospitals—a number of universities were starting to offer degrees in

hospital administration—and this trend to professional administrators was leading toward product standardization, cost identification, contract purchasing, inventory control, and financial planning. Many companies wanted to enter the health care market, but they were trying to adapt their existing health care products to hospital conditions, rather than attempting to solve hospital problems. We concentrated on the problems, and developed entirely new products as part of a complete system. (Statement of Mr. Robert Propst)

In 1963, after a series of experiments with the new products at hospitals, it was proposed that a jointly owned distribution company be established by Kimberly-Clark and Herman Miller to market disposable products and discardable equipment to dispense those products in a complete logical system for health care institutions. It was felt that this system would create distinct cost savings for hospitals in patient rooms, laundry operations, central services, and nursing activities. The proposal, however, was rejected by the senior management at Kimberly-Clark in a brusquely worded report that was sent to Hugh DePree:

Background of Problem
This report contains a preliminary economic study of a new hospital supply system which is a joint project of the Herman Miller Company and the Kimberly-Clark Corporation. The details of the supply system are given in New Products Report No. 38, which concluded that the system is unique and feasible.

Objective
To estimate the potential profitability of the proposed Herman Miller and Kimberly-Clark hospital supply system.

Conclusions
1. The estimated return on investment before taxes for the project varied from 11% to 27% for the different situations studied.

2. This return does not meet the minimum requirement of 30% for this project. Therefore, under present conditions this project would not yield Kimberly-Clark a satisfactory return consistent with the risks involved.

Recommendation
In light of the estimated return on investment, further expansion of development work on this program does not appear to be justified. (Statement from Kimberly-Clark report, quoted in a Herman Miller document dated April 1965)

During 1963, Robert Propst began to think about using plastic rather than discardable structures for the health care logistical system. He believed that it should be possible to mold plastic components, such as drawers, slides, cabinets, and shelves, with a foam core for resiliency and light weight and a hard surface for sanitation and appearance. He designed these parts to have a thick cross-section so that indented detail would avoid the need for hardware (slides, stops, or handles on the drawers, for example) or assembly, and he wanted them to have a continuous outer layer, without seams or voids, that would withstand high temperatures and all common solvents so that they could be cleaned in a commercial dishwasher. He expected the molding process to produce close-tolerance components, with true interchangeability, and to generate a variety of colors, integral with the material. E. I duPont de Nemours, Incorporated, a very large chemical company (1964 sales of $2,254 million and profits of $472 million) had developed a product, Darvyl, that apparently could meet these specifications; it was a low-cost "self-skinning" plastic that formed a tough outer layer over a resilient inner foam (the resiliency of the foam made the finished parts quiet when set upon a table, etc., which was a further advantage for heath care use), and the tooling costs were substantially lower than the precisely matched steel dies needed for conventional injection molding (the expansion of the foam created the internal pressure needed to fill the mold cavity, unlike solid plastics which required very high hydraulic pressure). However, 30 days before the scheduled release of the first production parts, development of the Darvyl product was discontinued by DuPont.

Messrs. Bell, Ryan, Straw, and Rackus of the DuPont Company met in Zeeland with Vern Poest, Bob Propst, Bob Blaich, Glenn Walters, and Max DePree concerning the CHS project. (CHS was the acronym for "coherent hospital structures," the name that had been adopted for the health care system after the original term of "sanitary structures" had been dropped following the withdrawal of Kimberly-Clark, Inc.)

The meeting had been called at DuPont's request. They stated that after extensive market testing of Darvyl, a thorough research program, and the operation of a pilot production plant, they had come to the conclusion that the total potential of the program was insufficient to warrant continuing. Therefore, it was necessary for them to withdraw from their commitment to this material at this time.

There was, of course, discussion of a number of factors involved in the decision, and an effort was made to evaluate the consequences of the decision from various points of view. Following is a summary of points discussed and conclusions reached.

For the DuPont Company, this is a Corporation decision, not a Plastics Division decision. This implies a variety of factors entering into the decision, not just one or two.

We inquired as to the possibility of a later interest. There might be what was termed a "dim hope," but we do not assume a future potential from DuPont.

We asked about licensing. We had understood that if DuPont eventually decided not to product Darvyl, we would be assured of production by an acceptable licensee. DuPont apparently is not willing, at this time, to license their process.

The question was raised as to whether or not tools that were presently nearly complete could be used for other material. They felt that we should not plan on it. (Statement in Herman Miller internal report, November 1963)

Representatives of Herman Miller immediately contacted Dow Chemical, Allied Chemical, Polymer Corporation, and Union Carbide, but found a lack of interest by all four of those companies in developing a "self-skinning" foamed plastic to replace Darvyl. Cincinnati Milling Machine Company, a large machine tool manufacturer (1964 sales of $201 million and profits of $10.2 million) that also built injection molding equipment for the plastics industry, became interested in the Coherent Hospital Structures concept and offered to establish a joint R&D program, using foamed urethane. In a letter dated in June 1964, the Director of New Product Planning at Cincinnati Milling wrote to Mr. Hugh DePree to summarize the conditions and expectations of the proposed joint R&D program:

For many months we have been following with interest the progress of the CHS concept as it was being developed by Herman Miller Research. This stems from our interest in new products and new applications for plastic materials. The original parts, used by Herman Miller Research to test the feasibility of the system, were made of urethane foam in wooden molds. The production parts were planned to be molded from Darvyl. However, the Darvyl program was withdrawn by DuPont and it became necessary for an alternative method to be developed.

Working with the Research Division we proposed a mutual research and development project aimed at developing a resin system and manufacturing techniques to produce the CHS components. There were several discussions in Ann Arbor, Zeeland, and Cincinnati which led up to an agreement between Herman Miller, Inc., and the Cincinnati Milling Machine Company to mount such an experimental program. The program is essentially as follows:

1. The first phase is to produce the necessary parts for the test market program involving approximately 500 beds. These parts will be made using a urethane resin composition and aluminum molds. The principal reason for this is that urethane foam technology is more advanced than the technology for other foam compositions. This approach will allow us to produce parts which should be satisfactory for the test market program.

2. The cost of the molds for this original phase will be shared on a 50/50 basis by Herman Miller and CMMCo. It is estimated that the costs to be shared will be somewhere between $15,000 and $20,000.

3. CMMCo. will set up a development group under its Central Research Division (P. W. Crane) to do the development work. In addition to developing the techniques for producing the CHS components from urethane foam, this group will also investigate all other materials which appear to have the qualities necessary to make these parts. . . .

4. Because of the nature of the test marketing program, and the fact that delays have been experienced in getting this joint effort underway, the scheduling of parts is of particular concern. As of June 19, 1964, the following schedule appears feasible. [The schedule listed specific dates at which laboratory equipment and prototype molds were expected to be available.]

5. On the basis of the above work it appears to us at this time that complete units will not be available before September 15 and that it will probably be November 15 before we reasonably expect to be producing a sufficient quan-

tity of these parts to enable you to supply complete units to some of your prospective customers for evaluation. (Statement in letter from Cincinnati Milling Machine Company, June 24, 1964)

In late 1964, Herman Miller had contacted a number of hospitals that wanted to install the CHS system on an experimental basis. These included the Pekin Memorial Hospital and Monmouth Hospital in Illinois, the Ann Arbor Children's Hospital and the University of Michigan Burn Unit in Michigan, San Antonio Hospital in Redwood City, California, and a private hospital in Wilmington, Delaware. Hospital administrators and designers generally were enthusiastic about the concept of simplifying material handling through the use of modular structures that could easily be sanitized, as can be seen in the following unsolicited comment in a letter received from a hospital architect.

The CHS program aims the "systems" approach squarely at the heart of a number of hospital problems. It is the first nonmechanical system to hit the hospital market, and it is also the first comprehensive tool for the hospital industry, and its architects, to use in tackling hospital costs and services directly, all the way to bedside. It integrates into a system, for the first time, a myriad of previously differentiated pieces of equipment. (Statement in letter received by Herman Miller, Inc., March 1965)

Herman Miller, for obvious reasons, wanted to install a minimum of 500 experimental units, to test the operations of the system and to evaluate the reactions of the doctors, nurses, patients, and administrators. Despite the schedule proposed by Cincinnati Milling Machine Company, which anticipated delivery by November 1964, no parts had been received by February 1965, and a meeting between Dr. Willard Crane, director of the R&D project at Cincinnati Milling,

and representatives of Herman Miller revealed that the delays in delivery were likely to be extensive.

By this time they expected to assemble good information on costs, but instead they have occupied themselves with problems. It has turned out to be a larger and more time-consuming research project than originally thought. Because of these unexpected problems, it turns out that Cincinnati Milling has underestimated the technical obstacles and, consequently, the time which would be required to get into production on a pilot-plant scale.

The best equipment Cincinnati could buy was not suitable for making this type of molding and many alterations have been required. In addition, the best resins were not sufficiently uniform to give consistent results.

Dr. Crane states that Cincinnati has put more people on this project than originally intended and because of the time required, it is costing a good deal more than they originally anticipated.

Cincinnati is definitely planning on furnishing the parts for Pekin in early April and the others which have been scheduled so far for June and early fall. When they gain more experience with this initial phase, they will be in a far better shape to look beyond this point. (Statement in internal report prepared by Mr. Glenn Walters, April 2, 1965)

During 1965 and 1966, Mr. Robert Propst continued design work on the components for the CHS system under the assumption that foamed plastic units with either a "self-skin" or a sprayed outer layer would be available. With the completion of this design effort, the CHS system consisted basically of three standard drawers (3 in. × 21 in. × 15 in., 6 in. × 21 in. × 15 in., and 9 in. × 21 in. × 15 in.), with standard "organizers" that would fit into the drawers to hold the common items (medical instruments, medicine bottles, laboratory containers, etc.) used in hospitals. The drawers would fit into standard "holders" (three 3 in. drawers, one 3 in. and one 6 in., or a single 9 in. drawer could go into each holder), which were "C"-shaped, and which could be stacked vertically or combined horizontally in different patterns, with a tray, shelf, or work surface on the top. The "holders" were designed to attach to a rail bolted to a wall. The bedside table in a patient's room, which was described previously as an example of the ineffective and inefficient use of hotel/motel furniture for health care, could be replaced with a "holder" attached to a wall strip, with two drawers and a shelf top. The 3 in. drawer could have an "organizer" for the personal items—watch, money, rosary, etc.—brought by the patient and the special medicines— vials, bottles, or boxes—needed by the patient, while the 6 in. drawer could have an "organizer" for the common supplies. The entire unit could easily be taken off the wall and cleaned, in a commercial dishwasher, and the supply drawer could easily be replaced each time a new patient was admitted to the room.

There were two other standard components in the CHS system that were used primarily for central storage and distribution. The first was a "locker" that was 66 in. high, also "C"-shaped, that could hold 3 in., 6 in., or 9 in. drawers, in any sequence. The lockers also attached to wall rails, or to the rail on a "transporter" that was a four-wheel cart that could be moved about the hospital, either by hand or by motor for a train of carts. The drawers in the "locker" could be filled at a central supply area, such as the pharmacy, the laundry, or the supply room, and then the lockers could be transported by the carts to the nurses' stations, operating rooms, diagnostic laboratories, or doctors' offices, where the lockers could be mounted on the wall (the "transporter" had a foot-operated device to mount or remove lockers from the wall rail), or the drawers could be interchanged with

mounted drawer "holders." The intention of the system was that each supply item would be handled only once, from inventory to the drawer, and that each drawer would be handled only once, from the locker to the holder. The potential labor savings and inventory reductions were very substantial.

> Hospitals are "run and fetch" institutions. People, supplies, and equipment are constantly on the move and, in too many instances, this is a process of remarkable waste and inefficiency.
>
> Endless quantities of small items are transported by human carriers. Traffic congestion, particularly around elevators, is a routine frustration.
>
> The ordering, repackaging, transporting, dispensing, and accounting of supplies in the hospital is not supported presently by reasonable systems or equipment.
>
> Quota supply, delivered by lightweight transports to selected stock points during periods of low traffic density and dispensed by well human-factored devices, is a major CHS objective. (Statement in internal report prepared by Mr. Glenn Walters, April 12, 1967)

The CHS components, as designed by Robert Propst, were easily cleaned due to their molded plastic fabrication, and were bright and colorful. The drawers were available in three primary colors (red, yellow, and blue), while the "holders," "lockers," and "transporters" were a very light gray, or off-white shade. Waste disposal bins, which fitted into the same holders and lockers, were black. Any part that became marked or worn, such as the tray or shelf tops, could inexpensively be replaced, so that it was expected that the appearance of the components of the system would remain attractive.

The potential market for the CHS system was very substantial. In a report prepared in 1965, the market research personnel at Herman Miller estimated that 56,500 new beds would be added each year in general and

Exhibit 1 *Comparative prices for health care furniture and equipment estimated in 1966 by Herman Miller, Incorporated*

	Simmons Mfg. Co., conventional wood design	American Hospital Supply, fabricated steel design	Herman Miller, Inc., proposed CHS design
Bedside table with two drawers	$43.00	Not manufactured	$ 31.80
Wardrobe for patient's room	86.50	Not manufactured	59.00
Desk for patient's room with one drawer	38.50	Not manufactured	45.80
Intravenous solution cart, with three drawers	Not manufactured	$459.60	233.00
Housekeeping supply cart, with four shelves and four drawers	Not manufactured	532.00	256.00

Source: Company records.

long-term (chronic disease care and skilled nursing homes) hospitals. The estimated usage of CHS components was $174.00 per bed for the patient's room and $116.00 per bed for the supply system. The potential market for CHS components used in new construction was therefore believed to be in excess of $16,000,000 per year, with an equivalent amount invested each year for the modernization of existing hospitals. It was expected that the CHS products could take a substantial share of the market due to the inherent system qualities of simplified material handling, improved sanitation practices, and extended useful life, and because of the economical manufacturing methods which resulted in very competitive prices. Comparative prices for CHS units and commonly used health care structures produced by other manufacturers are given in Exhibit 1.

During 1967, American Sterilizer Company, a medium-sized hospital distributor (1966 sales of $54 million and profits of $2.7 million), approached Herman Miller to ask for marketing rights to the CHS system. They had heard of the development work on the components, were convinced of the benefits, and wanted to sell the system. American Sterilizer had sales offices throughout the country, sales personnel who were in daily contact with hospital administrators and purchasing agents, and an excellent reputation for product quality and marketing integrity. The executives at American Sterilizer suggested that it would be expensive and time-consuming for Herman Miller to duplicate their sales contacts and marketing experience in the health care industry, and they explained that the methods and conditions of sales were very different in this industry than in the residential or commercial furniture industries. The primary difference was felt to be in the diffusion of purchasing responsibility through the medical and professional hierarchy within a hospital, so that a company had to be well known and respected, with contacts throughout that hierarchy, to be included on the Requests for Bids which were distributed at the time that modernization of existing facilities or construction of new buildings was being considered. American Sterilizer required a discount of 20% from the list price for the marketing function, and insisted upon a five-year exclusive sales contract. Herman Miller tentatively agreed to accept these terms in October 1967, recognizing their very real lack of experience and contacts in the distribution of health care products.

In 1968, Herman Miller found themselves with a large and apparently receptive market for their proposed system and structures, a known and respected distribution organization (American Sterilizer Company) to reach that market, but no product. In four years, Cincinnati Milling Machine Company had been unable to complete the 500 sets of components needed for testing both the concept and the market. In a report prepared in August 1968, Mr. Robert Van Allsburg, who was in charge of the Co-Struc development ("Co-Struc" was also an abbreviation for "coherent structures," but was now used throughout the company in preference to the acronym CHS), expressed disappointment and discouragement with the performance of Cincinnati Milling.

> Cincinnati Milling Machine Company has delivered most of the Monmouth Hospital order, but is lethargic in completing delivery. CMMCo is supplying only two of the existing four orders and has stopped production molding. (We at Herman Miller have yet to receive a set of sample parts for quality standards approval.) CMMCo has advised that the month of August will be spent in changing their process and making proof runs. The month of September will be used to freeze both the product and the process. If CMMCo is satisfied with their progress during these two months, they expect to make a one- or two-shift economic run during the months of October and November at which time their objec-

tive is to isolate and identify their actual production costs. CMMCo will then reprice the product and consider the value of a corporate commitment to their continuation of the project. (Statement in internal report prepared by Mr. Robert Van Allsburg, August 9, 1969)

Mr. Van Allsburg recommended strongly that the foam-core urethane components produced with low-pressure forming molds be replaced with solid polypropylene made by high-pressure injection molds. He recognized that a number of the product advantages would disappear with the change in material and process, but he also felt that four years of experimentation had led to an untenable position for Herman Miller, and that it was necessary to change to a proven technology. In his report, Mr. Van Allsburg listed the differences between the two manufacturing methods as shown in Exhibit 2.

Injection-molded polypropylene was a proven technology; that is, a large number of plastic fabricating companies were prepared to bid upon the redesigned components, once the high-pressure steel dies were completed. No further delays in manufacturing were anticipated since parts of comparable size, precision, and finish were being produced by those fabricators. The problem was that the thick cross section, with the smooth outer surface and indented detail, and the resilient foam core, had to be sacrificed. As the redesign of the Co-Struc components for polypropylene injection molding continued during much of 1969, Mr. Robert Propst, the original designer, wrote a strong appeal to Mr. Hugh DePree, president of the company:

> Herman Miller, Inc., has by now made a large and significant research commitment to a necessary design innovation for hospitals. We have, at this point, substantial evidence pointing to the validity of the concept as it is presently expressed.
> In the last two years there has been an effort to commercialize the concept. Bob

Exhibit 2 *Differences between the foam-core and solid-core manufacturing processes*

	Foam-core urethane	Solid-core polypropylene
Continuous outer layer, with no seams or voids	Yes	Yes
Foam inner core, for lighter weight and resilience	Yes	No, but thinner cross sections will permit equal weight per part
Thick cross section, with smooth surface and indented detail	Yes	No, and thinner cross sections will require ribbing for strength
No need for hardware or hand assembly	Yes	Yes, if redesigned to avoid interference with required ribbing
Resistant to all known solvents	Yes	No, but polypropylene is resistant to all solvents used in hospitals
Resistant to temperatures in commercial dishwashers	Yes	Yes
Integral colors for all the components	No, requires sprayed latex colors	Yes
Close-tolerance parts for true interchangeability	Yes	Yes
Low-cost tooling	Yes	No, requires high-cost precision steel molds

Van Allsburg has been working on Co-Struc and the impression given is that his assignment is to bring this project to market without weakening the criteria and objectives of the system.

However, in the course of this activity, by chance or direction, there has been a manufacturing projection that modifies the essential character of the design and innovation so substantially that it could cancel out the validity of the system.

The responsibility for this work, I can understand, stems from the cost and delivery controversy that developed in the relationship with Cincinnati. This has developed into a rationale that says if we meet the criteria established by research we can go in any direction that is low cost and manufacturable.

This has emerged as a series of fractional arguments that injection molding is the answer to the problem with only minor erosion of the concept.

It is my conviction after looking at the projections made that this would be a huge setback for the concept and would provide a very inferior product.

The weaknesses in this direction of conventional injection molding are:

1. The single-surface, rib-backed structure is not a usable design concept mechanically or aesthetically. If this were a tenable design premise, there long ago would have been injection-molded case units on the market. . . .

2. This approach is a move backward in the face of a very strong thrust now to bring self-skinned foam structures to commercial application. It would be a huge irony to have Herman Miller adopt an older, less proficient approach after all this design effort while others capitalize on the foam structure potential.

3. Much of the unique mechanics and patentability we have designed into Co-Struc would be compromised or lost. The rigidity and stability of the foam structure allowed us to create a

whole new mechanical premise. The C-frame design, which allows hardwareless components and field separability, depends on the efficiency of stressed skinned behavior on the double-walled structures.

4. Because of the lessened efficiency of the single-walled structure, the weight of the whole system would increase significantly. This would weaken one of our best handling qualities.

5. There is a tremendous loss in simplicity of detail which nullifies much of our argument that we have a really new environmental capability. The cleanability and the simple, straightforward appearance would be gone. We would be back to looking like the underside of a Model T Ford. Bob Van Allsburg argues that we can hide this kind of detail. In Co-Struc there are no hidden details . . .

This all brings up the issue of where Herman Miller stands in terms of maintaining design standards that transcend all the compromises that mark the trail of the shortcut operators.

Hugh, in total I have the strongest sense of foreboding and loss if we continue to allow piecemeal logic disintegration of what was, at one time, a powerful and persuasive position. (Statement of Mr. Robert Propst in an internal memorandum, December 8, 1969)

In early 1970, Mr. Robert Van Allsburg, director of the Co-Struc program, submitted an investment request to Mr. Hugh DePree for $1,000,000 to support immediate production and marketing of the new health care system. There were five major elements in the request for funds:

1. Cincinnati Milling Machine Company was to be dropped as a supplier of Co-Struc components. Cincinnati Milling had finally produced three full sets of components for the Co-Struc health care system by using a two-stage foam-core technology (the foam core was cut from a foam slab, and then molded inside the finished component). This production technology, however, was still in the process of development, required considerable manual touch-up and repair, could produce parts to meet a color code only by spraying the final mold with latex paint, and was expensive.

In the four years that we have worked with CMMCo we find that instead of progressing from 20 to 25% lower than the original costs which they submitted to us, we are now 2½ times those original costs. There is even reason to believe that before CMMCo will be willing to move in the direction of the production commitment, we must be prepared to pay higher costs than the 2½ times our original goal. (Statement in report prepared by Mr. Robert Van Allsburg)

2. The Co-Struc components were to be accepted as a finished design. Complete sets of components had gradually and grudgingly been produced by Cincinnati Milling Machine Company, using both the one-stage and the two-stage foam technologies, and these complete sets had been installed at the Pekin Memorial and Monmouth Hospitals in Illinois and the University of Michigan Burn Unit in Ann Arbor. These systems had been enthusiastically accepted by the hospital personnel.

The Burn Unit is both an intensive care and an isolation unit. It has its own surgery, laboratory, central service storage, nurses' station, drug station, and linen room, in addition to the six patient beds. This test unit presents a miniature of a total hospital operation and has proven to be an excellent evaluation opportunity.

This installation has demonstrated:

1. A major gain in sanitation performance and efficiency
2. A customizing ability to meet a great variety of patient needs
3. An efficient and space-saving handling of linens and supplies
4. Long-term evidence of the easy and natu-

ral usage by nursing, housekeeping, and medical staff. (Statement in report prepared by Mr. Robert Van Allsburg)

3. The Co-Struc components were to be manufactured in solid polypropylene. No components made from solid polypropylene through injection molding had been tested in hospitals due to the high cost of the required tooling (large injection-molded parts cannot be made with temporary or makeshift tooling because of the high pressures involved in the production process), but Mr. Van Allsburg felt that the market reception would be equally enthusiastic since it was the function and not the composition of the parts that was critical to the success of the system. Mr. Van Allsburg recommended that Herman Miller totally drop the foam-core concept.

It seems significant at this point in this status report that we recognize to a great extent how we have been led down the garden path. The technology of foam urethane today does not seem as applicable to a part where a complete finished skin on all sides is required as we were led by CMMCo to believe. (Statement in report prepared by Mr. Robert Van Allsburg)

4. The injection-molding dies to manufacture Co-Struc components from solid polypropylene would require an investment of $500,000. This amount was the minimum required for complete tooling for all the components; it would pay for single-cavity molds (one part per cycle of the injection-molding machine), but since all the parts were large, this was not felt to be an uneconomic constraint (small plastic parts are usually made in multicavity molds, which can make from 2 to 24 parts per cycle to reduce fixed manufacturing costs). $500,-000 would purchase complete tooling for the 15-in. series of Co-Struc (all drawers were 15 in. long × 21 in. wide × 3 in., 6 in., or 9 in. deep, and the "organizers," "holders," "lockers," and "transporters"

were designed for that length). Many hospitals, however, had suggested an additional 9-in. series (all drawers to be 9 in. long × 21 in. wide × 3 in., 6 in., or 9 in. deep), both to save space and for the storage of small or seldom-used components. Molds for the 9-in. series would cost an additional $500,000; this investment could probably be delayed, but it probably could not be avoided.

This then is the situation today as regards the design and manufacturing of Co-Struc items as well as the satisfying of the criteria and specifications. We wish to continue a modest long-term development of foamed urethane, but go to market now with injection molding. . . . The timing is such that we should be on the market within about nine months from the date that we embark on full development of the alternate means of production. (Statement in report prepared by Mr. Robert Van Allsburg)

5. Direct marketing of the Co-Struc components would require a commitment of an additional $500,000. Mr. Van Allsburg was concerned by the five-year sales contract and the 20% sales commission demanded by the American Sterilizer Company, and he recommended hiring three experienced hospital supply sales people, with a salary of $20,000 to $25,000 per year and a minimum contract for three years, and then supporting those salespeople with additonal expenditures for travel, promotion, and instructional seminars.

As we move closer to finalizing arrangement both with Cincinnati Milling and Amsco (American Sterilizer Company), we realize even more that it is the intent of each of these companies to save for itself that "additional increment which the market will bear" which generally is the reward to the innovator. With both of these companies being considerably larger than Herman Miller, each has chosen to believe that HMI is not capable of going to the market alone, and that we have reasons other than those presented to them for asking them to share with us in this venture. Without going into extended details, each of these companies has used their own unique ways of trying to coerce us into contract conditions which are not in the best interest of Herman Miller. In short, the innovator is being squeezed out of a reasonable profit as well as the "rewarding increment." (Statement in report prepared by Mr. Robert Van Allsburg)

Following the receipt of the report from Robert Van Allsburg in the spring of 1970, Mr. Hugh DePree had to decide on the investment of $1,000,000 in a new product with an unproven market and a changed technology. The case writer asked Mr. DePree what he worried about as he approached that decision, and his reply is quoted as nearly verbatim as possible below:

I worried about the money. We could raise the money—any company with a record of 30 years of increasing sales and earnings can raise money—but I wondered if we ought to commit ourselves to an investment of that size. We had never come close to $500,000 in tooling previously; the complete tooling for the Action Office product line was only $50,000.

I worried about the market size. We knew that a market existed, but we were not certain of the size. There were no reference points—no existing sales to extrapolate—and we had no hard market research data. We had consultants and advocates—Sister Diane at St. Josephs Hospital believed in Co-Struc as an act of faith—and we had successful experiments—Monmouth Hospital in Illinois proved that our material handling concept did reduce costs and that our formed plastic components did increase sanitation—but successful experiments and faithful advocates do not, by themselves, create a market.

I worried about the timing. We knew a market of some size existed, but we also knew that there was a five-year time span from the start of planning for additional bed capacity at a hospital to the ordering of the needed equipment, and I wondered if we could hang on long enough, with a marketing commitment of just under $200,000 per year, to prove our point.

I worried about our pricing and margins. I don't particularly want to give your students information about our costs—variable costs always seem to understate the value of a product, particularly in high-precision plastics fabrication where the allocated fixed costs for tooling and design are such a large portion of the total—but I think that I could say that our break-even volume was at least $3,-000,000 per year.

I worried about our marketing. We had an innovative system that improved sanitation and reduced costs, but to get full systems advantage, it was necessary to cross departmental lines—the pharmacy, central supply, purchasing, and housekeeping services had to work closely with doctors, nurses, and administrators—and that is difficult to do in a hospital. The system had to be managed, and that is also difficult to do in a hospital; we would have to teach hospital personnel about systems management, delivery scheduling, and inventory control. Doctors are not interested in those managerial concepts; they want to provide medical services in a patient's room that looks like a "home away from home."

I worried about our innovative process. We had worked for eight years—erratically; with fits and starts of progress, but eight years is a long time—on a system that at the conclusion of the process had less than full commitment from both designers and management personnel. Many members of our management felt that we had no business in the hospital industry, and one critically important designer felt that we had no future in injection-molded plastics.

I worried about our company. An investment is never a single decision against single criteria; it is always a sequence of decisions against multiple criteria. At the time that we were considering Co-Struc, we had to recognize that Action Office had been introduced just two years previously, and that product line had already climbed to an annual sales rate just short of $5,000,000. We needed money there for inventory and accounts receivable, and we needed more money for improved tooling and expanded capacity—at that time we were buying panels from a manufacturer in Grand Rapids whom we knew was planning on copying our office systems concept. But, we didn't have the resources to change our strategy, which was to emphasize design and marketing and assembly, and let others invest in production.

I worried about our future. There was a very substantial risk in the Co-Struc investment, and that risk would affect our employees, and our community as well as ourselves. But decisions have to be made since delay, by itself, is also a decision. (Verbal statement of Mr. Hugh DePree)

Class Assignment. The assignment for the class is divided into four parts.

1. The case has described the processes of innovation that led to four new product lines at Herman Miller, Inc. (Gilbert Rhode's modern residential furniture, Charles and Ray Eames' modern institutional furniture, Robert Propst's office systems furniture, and Robert Propst's health care systems components). Develop a schematic drawing of the stages in the process of innovation that will indicate the progression of those stages.

2. Identify the major problems that can occur at each stage in the process of innovation; attempt to rank these problems by order of importance. Why is it difficult to diversify from a single-industry firm?

3. Consider the management of the process of innovation. What should be done to reduce or resolve the anticipated problems at each stage of the process? Had you been a consultant to Mr. Hugh DePree from the period of 1962–1970, what specific managerial recommendations would you have made to him?

4. Consider the investment decision that faced Mr. Hugh DePree in the spring of 1970. List five factors that would support making the investment, and five factors that would argue against making the investment. What action would you take? (Exhibits 3 and 4 show the consolidated balance sheet and income statement for 1969.)

Exhibit 3 *Consolidated balance sheet for Herman Miller, Inc., May 31, 1969*

Cash	$ 158,052	Accounts payable	$ 1,433,088
Marketable securities	750,000	Federal income tax	434,563
Accounts receivable	2,208,991	Other taxes accrued	125,990
Finished products inventory	240,515	Salaries and wages accrued	472,421
Work in process inventory	1,256,494	Miscellaneous accruals	132,944
Raw material and supplies	2,636,433	Current portion of debt	6,142
Prepaid expenses	62,020	Dividend payable	79,030
	7,312,505		2,684,893
Land and improvements	175,261	Long-term note payable	2,300,000
Buildings and equipment	1,525,818	Land contracts payable	12,450
Machinery and equipment	979,688	Miscellaneous payable	885
Office equipment	181,066		2,313,335
Construction in process	175,751		
Leasehold improvements	75,140	Deferred taxes on income	106,000
Accumulated depreciation	(865,821)	Minority interest	(18,330)
	2,246,903		87,670
Cash value of insurance	137,909	Common stock at $1.00/par	171,805
Miscellaneous	305,586	Additional paid-in capital	377,933
	443,495	Retained earnings	4,367,267
			4,917,005
Current and fixed assets	$10,002,903	Total debt and equity	$10,002,903

Source: Company records.

Exhibit 4 *Consolidated income statement for Herman Miller, Inc., for the fiscal year ending May 31, 1969*

Net sales for fiscal year 1969		$19,028,144
Materials consumed	$8,490,384	
Direct labor cost	1,460,323	
Manufacturing overhead	2,269,534	
Decrease (increase) in inventories	(435,027)	−11,785,214
Gross profit on sales		7,242,930
Selling and promotional expense	3,092,881	
Design and research expense	939,095	
Administrative and general expense	1,233,962	− 5,266,048
Operating income		1,976,882
Interest charges (income)	156,895	
Miscellaneous charges (income)	(37,252)	− 119,643
Net income before taxes and minority interest		1,857,239
Taxes based on income	990,000	
Minority interest	(4,189)	− 985,811
Net income after taxes		871,428

Source: Company records.

Edwin Judson

Edwin Judson was a 1972 graduate of Amherst College who had looked for jobs in both Boston and New York before coming back to Detroit, where his parents lived, to work for one of the large automotive firms, in purchasing.

> It was the typical job for the American Lit major from a liberal arts college. I had expected to go into publishing or advertising, but I wound up in purchasing. (Statement of Edwin Judson)

Mr. Judson joined the M.B.A. program at the University of Michigan in the fall of 1974, and just prior to graduation, in the spring of 1976, he approached the instructor of the Business Policy course to describe the ethical situation which he had encountered during his first week on the job at the automobile company.

> On the second or third day at work I was sent out to the plant to pick up some requisition slips from the foreman in one of the tool rooms. I don't know if you have ever been in an automobile plant, but they are big and confusing and you can get lost fairly easily. Well, I was lost, so I tried to get into an office where I could ask for directions—you can ask people in the plant, but it is so noisy that you can't hear them, and you're never certain that they'll give you the right directions. I went into what I thought would be an office, but it was a record storage area, with row after row of steel shelving, reaching close to the ceiling, and with thousands of cardboard files, each marked by number, on all the shelves. There was a door at one end, and I was heading in that direction, when I heard the voice of the person I worked for, the head of purchasing for the (name of a prominent automobile) motor division. He was from New York City and had an accent that you would remember easily. He was in the next aisle over, and I could hear him very clearly.
>
> My boss said, "I want five thousand dollars this time. That's a nice round figure, and it will help me to remember [name of a large automobile supply firm] for the rest of the year."
>
> The other person said, "George, you're getting too greedy. You've given us good business, and we appreciate it, but it's not worth five bills."
>
> My boss got upset and told the man, "Look, you'll be out on your tail if I give the word. We'll start running quality checks on your stuff until we find some that won't meet the specs, and then we'll reject everything you've sent us for a month."
>
> This didn't faze the other guy; he said, "George, we know the score; you don't have to tell us. But we can't go $5,000. We'll go $3,000 now, and $3,000 at the end of the year if everything goes right, and if your volume holds up, but that's the best that we can do."
>
> My boss agreed to that, after some grumbling, and they went out the door to the office without seeing me. I didn't know what to do then. (Statement of Edwin Judson)

Class Assignment. Make a specific recommendation to Edwin Judson regarding his future actions.

Firestone Tire and Rubber Company

The five major manufacturers of automobile tires and industrial rubber products within the United States have traditionally reported net income figures that, as a percentage of sales, were below the returns for other manufacturing firms, and that comparison has worsened during the 1970s. The average return on sales of the five tire producers was 2.54% in 1975, approximately half the return available for all domestic manufacturing companies (Exhibit 1).

A number of reasons have been ascribed for the low returns in the tire industry; one of the reasons is certainly the slow rate of growth. Total tire production in 1975 was just 12.5% higher than it had been in 1966, 10 years previously (Exhibit 2).

A second reason for the low rate of return in the tire industry is the existence of extreme price competition in the sales of "original equipment" tires to the automobile companies. General Motors, Ford, and Chrysler have enormous buying power, and they have historically not hesitated to utilize that power to extract price concessions from the five tire manufacturers. Goodyear is the largest supplier of tires for new cars, with 35% of the market, followed by Firestone with 25% and

Uniroyal with 20% shares. The balance is reputedly split evenly between General and Goodrich; none of the five firms report profit on their original equipment sales.

The auto companies buy five tires for every car they produce, so that in a typical year they are buying 40 to 50 million tires. The tire companies bid on those contracts not to get a low profit, but to get a low contribution to fixed costs. Their intent is to get enough volume to partially cover their overhead, and then to make up their profits on the replacement market. A tire sold to one of the Big Three auto companies for original equipment probably carries a price tag less than half that of the same tire sold for replacement. (Statement of a tire industry executive)

The replacement market, although larger in size and higher in list prices, has been only marginally profitable for the tire manufacturers since the early 1970s. Replacement tire sales have become dominated by large distributors, such as Sears Roebuck, Montgomery Ward, Atlas, J. C. Penney, K-Mart, and Western Auto Supply, who utilize their buying power and their brand names to gain

Exhibit 1 *Return on sales (percent) of the five major manufacturers of automobile tires within the United States, 1966–1977*

	Firestone	General	Goodrich	Goodyear	Uniroyal	Average tire company	Average mfg. company
1966	5.6	5.0	4.7	4.8	3.4	4.6	6.6
1968	6.0	4.6	3.8	5.1	4.0	4.8	6.1
1970	4.0	3.9	1.0	4.0	1.6	3.0	5.0
1972	5.0	6.0	3.4	4.7	2.6	4.1	5.3
1973	5.2	5.6	3.4	4.0	2.3	3.9	6.0
1974	4.2	4.5	2.8	2.7	1.9	3.0	5.3
1975	3.6	3.6	1.3	3.0	1.1	2.5	4.7

Source: Standard and Poor's Industry Surveys, 1977, p. R-209.

Exhibit 2 *Tire production (000's omitted) by type and segment, within the United States, 1966–1977*

	Automobile		Truck and bus		Tractor, etc.		Total all tires
	Original equip.	Replacement	Original equip.	Replacement	Original equip.	Replacement	
1966	47,388	101,946	7,401	14,613	2,331	2,974	179,077
1968	49,904	121,305	8,488	16,257	2,787	3,053	205,118
1970	37,575	129,795	8,560	16,713	1,372	2,597	198,608
1972	51,310	141,710	12,559	20,060	1,597	2,987	232,657
1973	56,059	142,313	13,541	22,869	1,908	3,575	246,508
1974	43,395	124,154	11,850	21,295	2,129	4,072	215,805
1975	39,395	122,956	8,077	19,751	1,929	3,189	201,571

Source: Standard and Poor's Industry Surveys, for 1977, p. R-203.

price concessions. Smaller tire manufacturers (Armstrong, Cooper, Dayco, Mansfield, and Mohawk) both bid on the contracts of the large distributors and supply tires under their own brand names to independent retailers. The large tire manufacturers have been reduced to operating their own stores in an attempt to retain adquate margins in the replacement market; Goodyear owned 1,750 retail outlets, while Firestone had slightly over 1,600 in 1975.

> The national chains have high sales volumes, while the independent retailers have low overhead expenses; consequently both are able to emphasize price in their consumer marketing, and squeeze the margins of the large tire companies. (Statement of a tire industry executive)

The high-quality, high-priced segment of the replacement tire market, which might have been expected to remain a stronghold of the larger manufacturers, was aggressively pursued by a foreign competitor after 1970. Michelin, which had established a market position and product reputation through supplying the original equipment tires for popular imported cars such as Volkswagen, Saab, and Renault, opened a factory in South Carolina specifically to produce replacement tires for the American market. In 1975, Michelin had a 5% share of the total market, but was concentrated in the high-quality segment.

> The large American companies had tried to avoid price competition by making so many different grades and types of tires that comparison between brands was difficult, if not impossible. Various consumer groups had asked the industry to employ product standards, such as sidewall thickness or tread wearability, but the manufacturers had always refused, saying that standards weren't applicable in tire sales. Then, along came a foreign competitor who sold high-quality radial tires, with exact specifications for comparability, and Michelin took over the high-priced segment of the market. The consumer groups were right; there was a demand for quality, independent of price. (Statement of a tire industry executive)

The large tire companies had attempted to diversify into nonrubber products, such as petrochemicals, plastics, aerospace, and electronics, but they found that it was difficult to achieve meaningful diversification in sales when their base businesses were so large. Goodyear had sales of $5.45 billion in

Exhibit 3 *Sales (percent) and income (percent) derived from tires and industrial rubber products for the major tire manufacturers, 1973–1975*

	1973		1974		1975	
	Sales	Income	Sales	Income	Sales	Income
Firestone	80.0	74.0	80.0	62.0	81.0	68.0
General	39.0	33.0	36.0	21.0	36.0	15.0
Goodrich	53.0	34.0	50.0	4.0	52.0	42.0
Goodyear	85.0	87.0	85.0	82.0	83.0	77.0
Uniroyal	58.0	45.0	55.0	38.0	58.0	53.0

Source: Standard and Poor's Industrial Surveys, 1977, p. R-201.

1975, but 83% remained in tires and industrial rubber products, while Firestone had sales of $3.72 billion and 81% in basic product lines; only General, the smallest of the Big Five, with sales of $1.75 billion, has been able to reduce their dependence on the tire industry below 50% (Exhibit 3).

> In summary, the tire industry is large, and marked by slow market growth, low-margin pricing, a concentrated structure, and a narrow product line; you really have to understand the competitive characteristics of the industry to understand the incredible situation at Firestone. (Statement of a tire industry executive)

Firestone had developed a steel-belted radial tire in 1972 to counter the market inroads of Michelin. The "radial" feature refers to reinforcing plies of fabric cords that are embedded at a 90° angle to the tread, while the "steel belt" is a protective layer of wire wound parallel to the tread. Radial tires have a more uniform cross section than the traditional bias-plied tires, that have the fabric cords at a 45° angle, and therefore they offer greater road adhesion, longer tread wear, and improved gas mileage, provided that the tires are properly inflated. If properly inflated, the tread remains flatter, and the road contact more even; if not properly inflated, the benefits of adhesion, durability, and mileage sub-

stantially disappear. The radial fabric plies are also somewhat more subject to damage from road hazards, curb impacts, etc., than the bias-plied tires, although again proper inflation tends to reduce the possibility of damage. The domestic tire manufacturers had resisted the radial design for a number of years, with the explanation that American drivers would not properly care for their tires, but the success of Michelin made a change necessary. Firestone was the second of the major firms to develop a radial tire for the American market, and the tire was sold for original equipment use on new cars under Ford and General Motor brand names, for replacement use on older cars under the Firestone "500" designation, and for replacement sales by many of the national retail chains under their own trade names. 23.5 million steel-belted radial tires were made as Firestone 500s; it is still unclear how many were made under other names.

In May 1978, the National Highway Traffic Safety Administration, a division of the Department of Transportation, stated that a 7-month investigation had discovered a safety defect in the Firestone 500 tire; the governmental agency was unable to define the exact nature of the defect, but they had looked at 14,000 separate instances of tire failures, and found that a disproportionate number of those failures had occurred on Firestone radial tires. This product-safety announcement received wide publicity.

> Firestone stands accused of selling defective tires—the 500 series of steel-belted radials. According to the federal authorities, these tires are prone to blowouts, tread separations, and other dangerous deformities, and have been the target of thousands of consumer complaints. Records supplied to congressional investigators by Firestone and other sources indicate that there have been hundreds of accidents involving 500-series radials, and that these accidents have caused at least thirty-four deaths. No other radial-tire line has been associated with nearly that number (*Fortune,* August 28, 1978, p. 45)

Firestone responded immediately. Company personnel explained that no fundamental defects existed in the tire, and that practically all the failures had been associated with customer neglect, and were the result of either improper inflation or excessive loading. They further stated that all defective tires had been replaced, and that their adjustment rate, which reflects the number of tires returned because of defects in material or workmanship, was no higher for the 500 than it was for any other line manufactured by Firestone, or for any other radial manufactured by General, Goodyear, Goodrich, etc.

> Firestone came out fighting, like a bear suddenly disturbed after a winter's hibernation. One of the reasons for the aggressive response was the fact that the original allegations were made by the Center for Auto Safety, a Washington-based consumer group founded by Ralph Nader; were investigated by the National Highway Traffic Safety Administration, headed by a former associate of Ralph Nader; and then were reported to the House Subcommittee on Product Safety, whose chief counsel was a former law partner of Ralph Nader. Firestone felt that they were going to be "Naderized"

and that the consumer advocates, governmental agencies, and legislative bodies had formed an alliance against them. Also, I understand that the first letter from the Center for Auto Safety, in Washington, to the president of Firestone was simply insolent; it claimed that Firestone was selling unsafe tires, although they had no evidence at the time to support that claim, and demanded that the corporation devote its entire marketing budget to improving the safety of its products. Firestone decided to fight. (Statement of a tire industry executive)

In an effort to obtain accurate data on the incidence and severity of failure of the Firestone radial tire, the National Highway Traffic Safety Administration mailed 87,000 survey cards to people who had bought new cars equipped with radial tires. The respondents were asked to identify tire brand; and to describe tire problems. Only 5,400 people replied, 6.2% of those surveyed, but it was said that, again, a disproportionate number of the failures seemed to be associated with the Firestone radials. Alarmed by the rumors of this finding and dismayed by the inadequacy of the sample, Firestone sued the Traffic Safety Administration, arguing that the survey was statistically unsound and claiming that the publicity would adversely affect the company; an injunction was granted, prohibiting the agency to publish the results of the survey.

The suit, which was alleged by the press to be an effort at censorship by Firestone, received wider publicity than had been expected by that company. In particular, the House Committee on Interstate and Foreign Commerce held hearings for 4 days, with full television coverage, on the need for complete disclosure, in the public interest, of information on product safety. The Firestone position was not helped when the Center for Auto Safety requested, under the Freedom of Information Act, the results of the original consumer survey from the National Highway Traffic Safety Administration, and then "inadvertently" released the data to the press. The survey did show a high incidence of failure on Firestone radial tires.

During the congressional hearings, Firestone claimed that the investigation centered on an obsolete tire, that had not been manufactured for 18 months; it was shown that some Firestone plants were still building 500 series radials, under a different name, at the time of the hearings. During the congressional hearings, Firestone claimed that sales of the tire had stopped; advertisements from current Miami and Birmingham newspapers, proclaiming special year-end sales of the 500 series radials, were shown to the committee. Firestone claimed that the apparent 12.4% failure rate from the NHTSA survey was statistically inaccurate and grossly inflated; company officials were eventually forced to admit that their adjustment rate for the 500 series averaged 17.5% during the six years in which the tires were produced. In the most damaging testimony, it was shown that the president of Firestone, Mr. Mario DiFederico, had been warned on November 2, 1972, while he was vice president for tire production, by Mr. Thomas Robertson, director of tire development, that the steel-belted radial tires were so poorly fabricated that the company would probably be unable to continue shipments to General Motors because of the separation failures. As a result of these, and other disclosures on the safety record of the 500 series radial tire, Firestone agreed on October 20, 1978, to recall and replace at no charge all of the radial tires manufactured during the past three years (the limit of liability under federal law); it was expected that this agreement would involve 13.5 million tires, cost $200 million, and irreparably damage the reputation of the firm.

There is a lesson to be learned from the recall of 13.5 million tires by the Firestone Company. That lesson is how not to react to a complaint on safety. The company took on the government regulators, the national press, the U.S. Congress, and the alleged representatives of consumer interests, and lost. They sued in federal courts; they complained to congressional committees; they attempted to tell their story on network television, but the result remained exactly the same. They lost.

Firestone lost in a big way. They are going to have to replace 7.5 million tires, and they are going to have to repurchase, at half price, 6 million more. The cost will be $200 million, and all consumer confidence in their company.

It did not have to work out this way. Firestone could have gotten a much less expensive, and much less publicized, settlement right at the start. If they had agreed to a recall then, only people who were dissatisfied with their tires would have brought them in for replacement. Now, everyone has heard about the safety controversy, and everyone wants replacement. Who wants to drive around on unsafe tires? The real problem is that no one has fully proven that the tires are unsafe; what has been proven is that you can't fight the government on a safety issue. (Statement of an industry executive)

Class Assignment. What, in your opinion, were the errors made by the senior management at the Firestone Tire and Rubber Company? Assume that you were president of one of the other major firms in the tire industry, perhaps Goodyear or Goodrich, and that you had just received a letter from the Center for Auto Safety in Washington, suggesting that one of your lines of tires was unsafe. What would be your response?

Chapter 6

STRATEGIC DESIGN IN LARGE MULTIPLE-INDUSTRY FIRMS

The earlier chapters of this text have described the process of strategic design for a single product–market unit (typified by smaller business firms), for a single product–process unit (represented by the medium-sized product divisions of large corporations), and for a single-industry unit (illustrated by large basic processing companies). In each instance, the intent of the strategic design was to select a long-term method of competition that would provide a competitive edge for the business unit. In each instance also, the process of strategic design was to evaluate a range of alternative patterns of competition through comparison with environmental characteristics and trends, organizational assets and skills, and managerial values and attitudes. This process of strategic design was represented by the simple schematic outline that is now doubtless very familiar, but we repeat it at the top of the next page.

Most large companies, however, are not single business units, and cannot use the strategic design process developed for those simpler situations. Most large companies, except for the firms in the basic processing industries, such as steel, aluminum, lumber, etc., have numerous products selling in various markets and manufactured by different processes. Most large companies, in short, are composed of a number of business units, each responsible for a specific product–market or product–process position, and each represented in the organizational structure by a product division. This is the familiar decentralized organizational structure of the diversified firm shown in the accompanying chart at the top of page 308.

Product divisions within a decentralized organizational structure can be grouped by technology, such as "high-voltage electronics" or "inorganic chemicals," or by industry, such as "electrical appliances" or "packaging materials," but despite these efforts to impose another level of supervision and control, the central characteristic of the decentralized organization remains the assignment of profit responsibility to managers of the product divisions. Each product division acts as an autonomous

Environmental characteristics
and trends

Economic

Technological

Social/political

Competitive

↓

Organizational mission or charter	Specific opportunities and risks within the industry	
↓	↓	Selected strategy, or method of competition
Corporate performance and position	Range of strategic alternatives open to the firm	
↑	↑	
Managerial values and attitudes	Specific strengths and weaknesses within the company	

↑

Money

Equipment

People

Market position

Organizational resources, or
assets and skills

---

profit center. This meant that, in the past, large diversified firms operated only as the sum of the strategies of each of the independent product divisions. It was possible, through transfer pricing, to arrange for the exchange of some materials and products between divisions, and through verbal encouragement, to achieve some degree of vertical integration and some portion of the economies of scale, but it was not possible to provide strategic direction to the overall firm. There were three major reasons, or inherent problems, that prevented centralized management of diversified firms:

1. *Problems in corporate evaluation of the proposed strategies of the product divisions.* Headquarters personnel in a diversified firm could require strategic statements from each of the product divisions, and could arrange an annual review of the proposed revenue and expense figures derived from each statement, in order to coordinate the plans and activities of the divisions. However, the corporate officers had only a limited knowledge of the numerous products, various markets, and

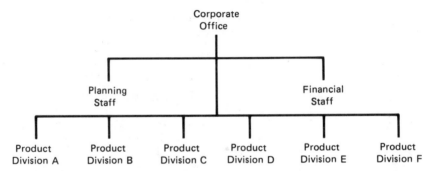

different processes represented within the firm, and were therefore vulnerable to the optimistic forecasts and persuasive abilities of the division managers. In a single-industry firm, the senior officers would normally have personal experience in, and intuitive understanding of, that industry; in a multiple-industry firm, this experience and understanding is often lacking. Consequently, it is difficult for the corporate management to critically review the proposed strategies of the various product divisions, or to recommend changes in those strategies to improve the overall competitive performance and position of the firm.

2. *Problems in corporate allocation of the constrained resources among the product divisions.* Headquarters personnel in a diversified firm could utilize capital budgeting techniques based either upon averaged cash flows such as payback period or return on investment, or upon discounted cash flows such as net present value or internal rate of return, to compare investment proposals from the divisions, and to select specific projects for funding. However, the traditional capital budgeting techniques assume equivalent risks for all projects, or equivalent adjustments for dissimilar risks. Projects in different industries have inherently different risks, and there is as yet no commonly accepted means of adjusting for those differences between industries. Consequently, it is difficult for the corporate management to critically review the investment proposals from the various product divisions, or to select proposals that would improve the overall competitive performance and position of the firm.

3. *Problems in corporate formulation of an overall strategy for the company.* The problems inherent in the annual strategic review and the investment project funding of the product divisions could be overcome in a diversified firm, through effort, training, and benevolence, but the senior management of that firm could not, using existing planning methods, design an overall strategy that would be more than the sum of the strategies of each of the product divisions. No formal planning method included the financial and technological interrelationships among the product divisions, or recognized the product–market or product–process strengths of the divisions, and no formal planning method permitted differentiated allocation of resources to the divisions to build upon these interrelationships and these strengths. Consequently, it was impossible for corporate officers to design an overall strategy for the total company that would relate to the environmental opportunities and risks, the organizational strengths and weak-

nesses, and the managerial values and attitudes. Portions of a diversified company might be very well directed by the division managers; there was no assurance, however, that this direction would be consistent throughout the firm, or that these portions would ever fit together into a successful pattern of competition.

The first of the formal planning methods for diversified firms that attempted to integrate the competitive position and performance of each of the product divisions into an overall corporate strategy was developed by the General Electric Company in the middle 1970s. General Electric, of course, is a diversified firm, with numerous products, various markets, and different processes, and in the early 1970s it was organized in a decentralized structure, with approximately 150 product divisions grouped by industry. The corporate managers were concerned, however, that despite continual sales increases and substantial technical developments, profits remained almost constant in absolute terms, and actually declined as a percentage of sales. The corporate managers were also concerned by the prior inability of one of the divisions to compete in the mainframe computer market, which had eventually resulted in the write-off of nearly $300,000,000 in developmental expenses and facility investments. It was felt that a strategic planning method should be developed to channel corporate resources to the divisions with the greatest probability of competitive success, and to deny those resources to the divisions with the lowest probability of success.

The strategic planning method developed by General Electric was termed a portfolio model since it evaluated each product–market unit in the company as an investment that could be increased, maintained, or decreased over time, similar to the portfolio or assortment of investments in stocks and bonds held by a mutual fund. The product–market units at General Electric were termed "strategic business units" (SBUs), each of which had a given product or product line, a specific market or market segment, an existing distribution channel, adequate productive capacity, and known competitors. The intent was to separate the company into business units that could act independently in the market through a clearly defined strategy, and then to control that action and direct that strategy through resource allocation by means of a corporate planning model rather than a capital budgeting process.

The central concept of the corporate planning model developed by General Electric was that each strategic business unit differed on two basic dimensions: the attractiveness of the industry, and the strength of the company within that industry. It was felt that each strategic business unit could be measured on those two dimensions, and then compared. As a result of the comparison, corporate resources could be channeled to the divisions that combined industry attractiveness and company strengths since these were the divisions with the greatest probability of competitive success.

The attractiveness of the industry was measured on a multiple factor scale that included such inputs as overall size of the market, annual growth, historical profitability, competitive structure, technological requirements, inflationary vulnerability, energy requirements, environmental impacts, and social, political, and legal considerations. These factors were weighted (by percentage) and then the business unit was measured (on a cardinal scale of 1 to 5) to obtain an approximate value that could be summarized and compared:

	Weight	Measurement	Value
Overall size	0.20	4.00	0.80
Annual growth	0.20	5.00	1.00
Historical margins	0.15	4.00	0.60
Competitive intensity	0.15	2.00	0.30
Technological requirements	0.15	3.00	0.45
Inflationary vulnerability	0.05	3.00	0.15
Energy requirements	0.05	2.00	0.10
Environmental impact	0.05	1.00	0.05
Social/political/legal	Must be acceptable		—
	1.00		3.45

The strength of the company within the industry was also measured on a multiple factor scale that included such elements as market share, share growth, product quality, brand reputation, price position, distribution network, promotional effectiveness, productive capacity, facility design, unit costs, material supplies, R&D abilities, and managerial personnel. Again, these factors could be weighted and the business unit could be measured along a comparative scale to obtain a summary figure:

	Weight	Measurement	Value
Market share	0.10	2.00	0.20
Share growth	0.15	4.00	0.60
Product quality	0.10	4.00	0.40
Brand reputation	0.10	5.00	0.50
Distribution network	0.05	3.00	0.15
Promotional effectiveness	0.05	2.00	0.10
Productive capacity	0.05	3.00	0.15
Productive efficiency	0.05	2.00	0.10
Unit costs	0.15	3.00	0.45
Material supplies	0.05	5.00	0.25
R&D performance	0.10	4.00	0.80
Managerial personnel	0.05	4.00	0.20
	1.00		3.90

Owing to the subjective nature of the weights that were applied to each of the factors, and to the inexact method of measurements along the comparative scales, the summary figures for the attractiveness of the industry and the strength of the company within that industry are not used directly to evaluate each business unit. That is, a business unit that measures 3.45 × 3.90, as in this example, is not automatically considered to be "better," or more likely to receive funding for further growth, than one that measures 3.35 × 3.80, or 3.35 × 4.00. Instead, all strategic business units are grouped along each dimension, with one-third above average, one-third average, and one-third below average, and are then visually displayed on a simple nine-cell matrix, as shown.

Company Strength within the Industry

	Above average	Average	Below average
Above average	Invest	Invest	Retain
Average	Invest	Retain	Divest
Below average	Retain	Divest	Divest

Industry Attractiveness (vertical axis label on left)

Business units that are above average on one of the dimensions of the General Electric planning model, and at least average on the other dimension, are considered to be optimal candidates for corporate investment and accelerated growth. Business units that are below average on one of the dimensions, and no better than average on the other, are felt to be prime candidates for disinvestment and eventual sale or liquidation. The balance of the business units are destined to be maintained, at approximately the current sales level and capital requirements, until either the attractiveness of the industry or the company's position within that industry changes, leading either to increased investment or to gradual disinvestment.

The General Electric corporate planning method is direct and explicit, but very subjective, depending upon comparative measures along multiple scales, and relative weighting of those measures. To avoid these problems, the Boston Consulting Group (BCG) developed a corporate planning model that is also direct and explicit, but considerably more objective. The BCG planning method permits precise measurements along individual scales that consequently do not require weighting, but this method does require acceptance of the assumption that a single statistic can serve as the surrogate for industry attractiveness, and that another statistic can serve as the surrogate for the competitive position of the company within that industry.

The Boston Consulting Group believes that the growth rate of the market, in percentage terms, can be used as a summary figure for the attractiveness of the industry, since high growth rates tend to be associated with high gross margins and low competitive pressures; high growth rates generally occur in the early stages of the product life cycle, before intensive competition affects industry prices, margins, and profits. The Boston Consulting Group also believes that the share of the market, again expressed in percentage terms, can be used as a summary figure for the competitive position of the company within that industry, since high market shares tend to be associated with low production and distribution costs. This relationship between high market share and low competitive cost is partially the result of the economies of scale that bring a constant decrease in average unit costs with each increase in annual production volume, but it is primarily the result of the experience curve that brings a continual decrease in average unit costs with each doubling of the cumulative production volume. The experience curve effect upon costs was described in Chapter 3; it results in an exponential-curve relationship since costs decrease by a continual percentage with each doubling of cumulative volume. The combination of the economies of scale (total annual volume) and the experience-curve effect (total cumulative volume) can have, it is alleged by members of the Boston Consulting Group, a dramatic impact upon the cost position of a firm, as indicated on the accompanying illustration.

Company productive cost relative to the largest competitor in a market segment

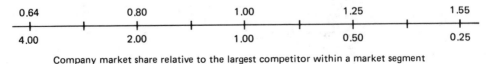

Company market share relative to the largest competitor within a market segment

Source: Boston Consulting Group, *BCG Perspectives, No. 152,* 1974.

The position of each business unit, or product division within the company, once it has been measured for market share and market growth, can be visually portrayed upon a simple four-cell matrix, such as the one shown here. The vertical axis represents market growth, in annual percentage, on an arithmetic scale; the horizontal axis represents market share, in percentage terms relative to the largest competitor, on a logarithmic scale to be consistent with the exponential nature of the experience curve.

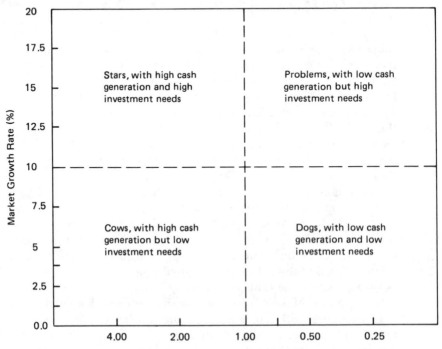

Market Share Relative to the Largest Competitor

The market growth rate is divided, arbitrarily, at 10% into "high"- and "low"-growth segments, and the market share relative to the largest competitor is divided, also arbitrarily, at 1.00 into "high"- and "low"-share segments. Obviously, a 1.00 market share relative to the largest competitor indicates that the company under consideration is one of the dominant firms within the industry. The position of each business unit can be marked on the matrix by a circle, with the radius representing the annual sales or assets employed in order to give some indication of the relative size of the units.

The central concept of the Boston Consulting Group planning model is that the cash flow characteristics of each cell in the matrix differ substantially. Business units in the upper left quadrant have a high market share and a high market growth; they require large amounts of cash for expansion of their working capital and productive facilities, but they also generate large amounts of cash due to their low-cost positions brought about by their economies of scale and cumulative production experience. Business units in the lower left quadrant have a high market share but low market growth; they generate large amounts of cash due to the low-cost positions, but they have few opportunities to invest these funds due to the low expected growth. Business units in the upper right quadrant have a directly opposite cash flow position; they generate small amounts of cash due to the higher-cost positions associated with a low market share, but they have high investment needs for product development and market expansion. Business units in the lower right quadrant generate a small amount of cash, but have only a limited need for that cash, due to their much slower growth. The names of these quadrants have become quite familiar, and have an obvious meaning: "star," "cash cow," "problem," and "dog."

There is a natural movement of business units over time within the quadrants of the strategic planning matrix, and this movement is associated with the product life cycle. "Stars" with high market growth and high market share tend to become "cows" as the growth phase of the life cycle slows, and then "cows" become "dogs" as the market matures and price competition increases to the extent that it is no longer profitable to maintain market share. "Problems" can become "stars" with adequate investment and successful management to increase market share; otherwise, they decline and become "dogs." At some point, every "dog" becomes a candidate for sale or liquidation.

The strategic planning method of the Boston Consulting Group centers upon the cash flow characteristics of the business units; the intent is that the corporate managers balance the cash investment needs of developing businesses with the cash-generating capabilities of the more mature units to optimize the long-term competitive position and performance of the firm. The consulting group recommends that equivalent portfolio displays be developed for 3 to 5 years in the future to show the projected positions of the business units given different investment decisions now and different managerial performance during the interim, and that these projected displays be evaluated in terms of an overall corporate strategy.

The last of the corporate planning models that will be described in this chapter was developed by McKinsey and Company, another large and successful consulting firm. The McKinsey method makes use of a nine-cell matrix, very similar to that originally proposed by General Electric. The dimension of industry attractiveness is based upon a multiple factor analysis that varies depending upon the industry involved, but that usually includes measures of market growth, industry structure, product usage, purchase behavior, customer motivation, distribution requirements, and promotional means. The dimension of company strengths within the industry is also a compendium of multiple factors that vary depending upon the company involved, but that usually include measures of market share, product advantages, relative prices, marketing expenses, production costs, capacity utilization, etc. As shown, each business unit is portrayed on the matrix in a "high," "medium," or "low" position on the two dimensions.

Company Strengths within the Industry

	High	Medium	Low
High	Invest	Invest	Maintain
Medium	Invest	Maintain	Divest
Low	Maintain	Divest	Divest

Industry Attractiveness

The McKinsey planning model is interesting and innovative since it assumes a relationship between the three major categories of "invest," "maintain," and "divest" on the portfolio matrix and the three major stages of "development and growth," "shakeout and maturity," and "saturation and decline" in the product life cycle. The McKinsey planning method also makes very explicit recommendations for the objectives and policies of business units in each of those portfolio categories, as shown in the table on page 315.

The three corporate planning models have obvious problems and subtle deficiencies, some of which may be discussed in class, but they do provide a means of relating the different product divisions within a diversified firm by either cash flow characteristics or life-cycle stages, and they do enable the corporate management to change investment policies, marketing policies, or production policies to improve the long-term competitive position and performance of the firm. The planning models do not, however, automatically include consideration of the overall environmental characteristics and trends, organizational assets and skills, or managerial values and attitudes. The senior management must, individually, evaluate the environmental opportunities and risks that will affect all the business units, regardless of industry, and consider the organizational strengths and weaknesses, beyond

	Invest and grow	Select and maintain	Divest and dispose
Primary objective	Build market position for long-term profit	Use market position for short-term profit	Use assets for short-term cash flow
Current investment	Maximum possible	Adequate amounts for high-return projects	Minimum necessary
Business risk	Accept and contain the risk	Limit the risk	Avoid all risk
Market share	Build share and diversify markets	Protect share and concentrate markets	Forgo share to increase cash flow
Pricing policy	Lead in pricing to build market share	Stabilize pricing to maximize profits	Lag in pricing to build cash flow
Product design	Vary the designs to diversify markets	Differentiate designs to maintain segments	Standardize designs to reduce costs
Production costs	Utilize economies of scale to reduce costs	Utilize experience curve to reduce costs	Utilize "ruthless" cost cutting
Marketing policies	Utilize creativity to extend coverage	Cut creativity but keep coverage	Forgo coverage to increase cash flow
Management type	Entrepreneurial, with high risk tolerance and growth orientation	Professional, with high adaptability and profit orientation	Dictatorial, with high experience and low-cost orientation

the financial resources, that will determine performance. Corporate management, in basic terms, is a continual process of relating organizational strengths and weaknesses to environmental opportunities and risks to design a long-term competitive position for the firm; corporate management is not the routine application of formal planning models.

Philip Morris, Inc.

In June 1969, Philip Morris, Inc., was a large and successful firm, with sales in the previous year of slightly over $1.0 billion and earnings after taxes of $47.9 million. Sales had increased by 59% over the prior five-year period, while profits were up 119% (Exhibit 1).

The company was in excellent financial condition, with a 2.18:1 current ratio, and a 0.60:1 debt/equity ratio (Exhibit 2).

Philip Morris was the fourth largest tobacco company within the United States, with a 15.1% share of the domestic market. The total market had remained relatively constant over the past five-year period (Exhibit 3).

The reasons for the slow growth (5.6% over five years) in the cigarette industry are well known. Consumer concerns about health and government regulations about advertising had together brought about a decrease in per

Exhibit 1 *Income statements (000's omitted) for Philip Morris, Inc., 1964–1968*

	1964	1965	1966	1967	1968
Sales revenues	$641,439	$704,544	$771,975	$904,841	$1,019,846
Cost of goods sold	277,522	292,588	311,784	363,115	409,912
Excise taxes on tobacco	216,774	241,908	265,032	310,731	337,744
Marketing and administrative expenses	93,413	107,069	115,919	132,219	149,354
Total costs and expenses	587,709	641,565	492,735	806,065	897,010
Operating income	53,730	62,979	79,240	98,776	122,836
Equity in income of subsidiaries	1,838	2,149	2,627	3,062	3,323
Total corporate income	55,568	65,128	81,867	101,838	126,159
Corporate expenses	4,830	5,395	7,637	8,443	11,386
Interest expenses	5,919	6,098	8,094	10,205	15,949
Other (income) expenses	353	1,212	992	1,873	(1,283)
Total corporate expenses	11,102	12,705	16,723	20,521	26,043
Profit before taxes	44,466	52,423	65,144	81,317	100,107
Federal income taxes	21,852	25,914	30,961	37,716	51,241
Profit after taxes	22,614	25,565	33,261	42,679	47,944

Source: Registration Statement of Philip Morris, Inc., August 29, 1969, p. 5.

capita consumption. The Surgeon General's report on Smoking and Health had been issued in January 1964, and had shown a statistical correlation between cigarette smoking and the incidence of lung cancer, emphysema, and heart disease, while the U.S. Congress had ruled that all cigarette packages had to carry a printed warning against smoking, and was considering a ban on the radio and TV advertising of cigarettes.

The domestic market for cigarettes was divided into three product segments: regular brands, king-size, and filter-tipped; such additional product types as the 100-mm lengths, low-tar or low-nicotine blends, and microfiltration filters had not been developed by 1969. The filter-tipped cigarettes were an obvious response to the public concerns over health, and were growing considerably more rapidly than the regular brands and king-size types (Exhibit 4).

Market shares of the leading cigarette brands change slowly, because of product loyalty among smokers. Changes that do occur can usually be ascribed to intensive advertising programs, innovative packaging concepts, or significant filter and blend improvements. Dramatic changes in market share during the five years prior to 1969 were primarily due to consumer concerns about health, and an obvious trend toward "milder" cigarettes (Exhibit 5).

Many of the popular brands of cigarettes were made in two or three product types; e.g., Pall Mall was sold in regular, king-size, and filtered form. The principal brands, and product types for each brand, by company are as follows:

R. J. Reynolds: Winston (filter-tipped), Camel (regular brand and filter-tipped), Salem (menthol filter), and Tempo (charcoal filter)

Exhibit 2 *Balance sheets (000's omitted) for Philip Morris, Inc., 1964–1968*

	1964	1965	1966	1967	1968
Cash and short-term securities	$ 18,714	$ 24,523	$ 27,043	$ 38,531	$ 36,533
Accounts receivable	41,123	41,158	46,454	58,692	70,427
Inventories	257,256	271,822	297,761	386,576	451,922
Prepaid expenses	2,082	1,755	1,636	2,108	2,803
Total current assets	319,181	339,259	372,895	485,908	561,685
Investment in unconsolidated subsidiaries	10,044	12,096	17,679	24,037	67,642
Plant and equipment, net	102,417	104,044	110,157	123,555	138,704
Goodwill and deferred charges	11,795	10,877	11,828	15,494	18,547
Total fixed assets	124,256	126,927	139,665	163,086	224,893
Total assets	443,438	466,277	512,549	648,994	786,578
Notes payable	56,700	57,300	27,200	82,600	153,800
Long-term debt (1 yr)	3,000	2,400	4,850	2,250	600
Accounts payable	19,266	17,426	22,159	33,094	76,227
Dividends payable	3,456	3,426	4,013	5,051	5,225
Excise taxes due	8,492	14,583	27,100	22,083	—
Income taxes due	14,199	16,447	16,360	15,453	13,427
Accrued expenses	11,055	13,838	17,956	20,206	—
Total current liabilities	116,168	125,455	119,638	179,736	249,279
Deferred income taxes	8,287	9,629	10,349	11,147	14,816
Deferred investment credits	1,901	2,114	2,522	2,915	3,389
Reserve for international	—	—	1,269	3,510	4,198
Long-term debt	99,300	98,400	128,959	171,500	200,400
Total long-term liabilities	109,488	110,143	143,099	189,072	222,803
4.0% preferred stock	16,187	15,987	15,787	15,587	15,387
3.9% preferred stock	11,231	11,100	10,970	10,840	10,708
Common stock	18,622	18,674	22,501	22,718	23,088
Capital surplus	47,921	48,619	45,987	48,722	53,544
Earned surplus	139,059	151,728	169,887	117,341	226,530
Total owners' equity	233,019	246,109	265,132	295,207	329,257

Source: Moody's Industrial Manual, 1970, p. 2262.

American Brands: Pall Mall (regular brand, king-size, and filter-tipped), Lucky Strike (regular brand and filter-tipped), Tareyton (charcoal filter), Half and Half (filter-tipped), Montclair (menthol filter), Carlton (charcoal filter), and Silva Thins (filter-tipped)

Brown & Williamson: Viceroy (filter-tipped), Kool (regular menthol and menthol filter), Raleigh (king-size and filter-tipped), Belair (menthol filter), and du Maurier (filter-tipped)

Philip Morris: Marlboro (regular filter and king-size filter), Parliament (filter-tipped),

Exhibit 3   *Percentage shares of the domestic cigarette market by the major tobacco companies, and total sales (billions of cigarettes), 1964–1968*

	1964	1965	1966	1967	1968
R. J. Reynolds	33.3	32.9	32.5	32.4	32.1
American Brands	25.4	25.2	24.4	22.2	21.9
Brown & Williamson	11.9	13.2	14.1	14.3	15.1
Philip Morris	9.8	10.3	10.9	12.7	13.6
Lorillard Company	9.4	9.1	9.3	10.1	10.0
Liggett & Myers	9.9	9.0	8.7	8.1	7.1
All others	0.3	0.3	0.1	0.2	0.2
Total percentage	100.0	100.0	100.0	100.0	100.0
Total sales	498.2	514.8	524.8	523.1	528.7

Source: Standard and Poor's Industry Surveys, 1970, p. T-104.

Philip Morris (regular brand, king-size, and filter-tipped), Alpine (menthol filter), and Benson & Hedges (extra-long filter)

Lorillard: Kent (filter-tipped), Newport (menthol filter), True (king filter), Old Gold (regular brand, king-size, and filter-tipped), and Spring (extra-long menthol filter)

Liggett & Myers: L&M (filter and extra-long filter), Chesterfield (regular brand, king-size, and filter-tipped), and Lark (charcoal filter)

All the major tobacco companies sell in international as well as domestic markets; the amount of information that is both available and reliable on international sales is not large, but it is generally reported that "free world" sales of cigarettes (i.e., outside Russia, Eastern Europe, and Red China) are approximately 1,500 billion units annually, or three times the size of the domestic U.S. market. Sales differ by region, of course, depending upon personal incomes, public restrictions, import duties, excise taxes, and cultural/religious traditions, but again it is reported that per capita consumption in western Europe and Japan averages 75% of that in the United States, while usage in Oceania, Central and South America, the Near East, Far East, and Africa trails down from 60% to less than 10%. Growth rates also differ by region, but are either not reported or not available.

The *Annual Report for 1970* of Philip Morris, Inc., which was published with the statement by the president, Mr. Joseph Cullman III, on recent performance and future goals printed in French, German, Spanish, and Italian as well as the more usual English, emphasized international sales, confirmed the size of the market (excluding the United States) at 1,500 billion cigarettes annually, and reported an average compound growth rate of 3.8% per year for regular brands and 13.8% for filtered brands. That report also compared the gross revenues and operating incomes for the domestic cigarette and international cigarette divisions (Exhibit 6).

In 1969, Philip Morris manufactured cigarettes abroad at 17 "affiliates" in Argentina, Australia, Belgium, Canada, Dominican Republic, Guatemala, Holland, India, Malaysia, Mexico, New Zealand, Nigeria, Puerto Rico, Sweden, Switzerland, the United Kingdom, and Venezuela. Fourteen "licenses" had been established in Austria, Bolivia, Colombia, Finland, France, Germany, Hong Kong, Italy, Morocco, Netherland Antilles, Panama, the Philippines, Turkey, and Yugoslavia.

Exhibit 4 *Sales by total and by company for the major product types within the domestic cigarette industry (billions of cigarettes), 1964–1968*

	1964	1965	1966	1967	1968
R. J. Reynolds					
Regular brands	52.7	50.1	45.4	40.4	37.2
King-size	0.2	0.1	—	—	—
Filter-tipped	113.2	119.1	124.9	129.3	132.3
Total sales	166.1	169.3	170.3	169.7	169.5
American Brands					
Regular brands	27.8	27.8	25.4	21.0	20.0
King-size	73.5	72.9	66.4	58.4	57.0
Filter-tipped	25.3	29.0	26.1	36.7	39.0
Total sales	126.6	129.7	127.9	116.1	116.0
Brown & Williamson					
Regular brands	2.9	2.4	2.5	1.9	2.1
King-size	5.5	4.5	4.3	3.7	3.1
Filter-tipped	50.7	61.1	67.3	69.2	74.4
Total sales	59.1	68.0	74.1	74.8	79.6
Philip Morris					
Regular brands	2.4	2.0	1.6	1.3	1.0
King-size	3.8	3.6	3.3	3.1	2.8
Filter-tipped	43.4	47.4	52.4	61.9	68.2
Total sales	48.6	53.0	57.3	66.3	72.0
Lorillard					
Regular brands	0.8	0.6	0.5	0.4	0.3
King-size	1.6	1.3	1.0	0.9	0.7
Filter-tipped	44.5	45.1	47.3	51.8	52.1
Total sales	46.9	47.0	48.8	53.1	53.1
Liggett & Myers					
Regular brands	7.1	6.0	5.3	4.2	3.3
King-size	10.6	9.6	9.0	8.2	7.1
Filter-tipped	31.7	30.5	31.3	29.9	27.3
Total sales	49.4	46.1	45.6	42.3	37.3
Other firms, not classified	1.5	1.7	0.8	0.8	0.8
Total industry					
Regular brands	94.2	89.4	80.9	69.6	64.1
King-size	95.7	92.5	84.2	74.3	70.9
Filter-tipped	308.3	332.9	359.7	379.2	393.7
Total sales	498.2	514.8	524.8	523.1	528.7

Source: Standard and Poor's Industry Surveys, 1970, p. T-105.

Exhibit 5 *Percentage shares of the domestic cigarette market for the 10 most popular brands, 1964–1968*

	1964	1965	1966	1967	1968
Winston (R. J. Reynolds)	13.7	14.0	14.2	15.6	15.9
Pall Mall (American)	14.4	14.1	14.0	13.1	12.7
Salem (R. J. Reynolds)	8.5	8.8	8.7	8.2	8.4
Camel (R. J. Reynolds)	10.7	9.7	9.3	8.4	7.7
Marlboro (Philip Morris)	5.0	5.3	6.0	6.6	7.4
Kool (Brown & Williamson)	3.8	4.5	5.0	5.4	6.1
Kent (Lorillard)	6.2	5.9	5.8	5.8	5.7
Lucky Strike (American)	6.4	6.4	5.7	4.6	4.2
Tareyton (American)	3.6	3.8	3.9	3.9	4.1
Viceroy (Brown & Williamson)	3.8	3.9	3.9	3.7	3.8

Source: Standard and Poor's Industry Surveys, 1970, p. T-105.

Most of the major tobacco companies, concerned by increasing restrictions and decreasing sales in the domestic cigarette market, have attempted to diversify through mergers and acquisitions. The acquired firms have been primarily in consumer products, with packaged foods and bottled liquors predominating:

R. J. Reynolds acquired McLean Industries, a containerized freight service that combines sea and land transport, and Archer Products, a manufacturer of aluminum foil and packaging materials, and operates a Food Division that produces and distributes My-T-Fine puddings, Vermont Maid syrups, Davis baking powder, Brer Rabbit molasses, College Inn canned soups, Hawaiian Punch canned juices, Chun King frozen oriental foods, and Patio frozen Mexican dinners.

The American Tobacco Company changed its name to American Brands, Inc., and now owns Sunshine Bisquits, Humpty Dumpty Foods, a Canadian manufacturer of potato chips, snacks and salad dressings, James Beam Distilling Company, and Duffy-Mott Foods, a large canner of fruits and vegetables.

Brown and Williamson is a wholly owned subsidiary of British American Tobacco Company Ltd., the largest cigarette manufacturer in the world, with headquarters in London, England. Divisions of Brown and Williamson in the United

Exhibit 6 *Operating revenues and incomes (000's omitted) for the Domestic Cigarette and International Cigarette Divisions of Philip Morris, Inc., 1967–1969*

	Domestic division		International division	
	Revenues	Income	Revenues	Income
1967	$652,341	$ 70,753	$181,043	$26,432
1968	724,570	87,954	211,702	31,391
1969	800,949	106,435	256,769	38,717

Source: Philip Morris, Inc., *Annual Report for 1970,* p. 18.

States include Vita Foods, a manufacturer of diet crackers, Lentheric, a producer of men's cologne, and Yardleys, a distributor of perfumes and soaps.

Lorillard merged with Loew's Theatres, Inc., a real estate firm that owns 121 motion picture theaters, numerous office buildings, and 17 hotels, including the Americana, Regency, Drake, and Warwick in New York City, the Americana in Bal Harbor, Florida, the Ambassador in Chicago, and the Mark Hopkins in San Francisco.

Liggett & Myers has a liquor division that distributes J&B scotch, Bombay gin, and Wild Turkey bourbon, and a pet-food division that produces Alpo canned dog food and Liv-A-Snaps dried dog snacks.

Philip Morris had started a diversification effort, but in 1969 their nontobacco products accounted for only 13% of sales revenues. Nontobacco consumer products included Clark's chewing gum, Personna razor blades, and Barbasol shaving creme; all were in markets dominated by larger firms, and all had relatively modest market shares (Exhibit 7).

Philip Morris had also expanded into industrial products such as packaging materials and printing services for consumer food products, printed labels for beer bottles, graphic arts and visual aids for educational programs, and chemical binders and adhesives for textiles. Market size, market share, and market growth information were not readily available on these products, but the *Annual Report for 1970* reported growth in revenues of approximately 8% annually for the Industrial Division(Exhibit 8).

In June 1969, the diversification program of Philip Morris, Inc., expanded very substantially, with the purchase of the Miller Brewing Company of Milwaukee, Wisconsin,

for $227 million. $130 million was paid to W. R. Grace and Company, a large conglomerate with interests in shipping, banking, chemicals, and food, and with operations in the United States, Europe, and South America, for 53% of the stock, and the balance of 47% was obtained in 1971 from the DeRance Foundation, a charitable trust, for $97 million.

The Miller Brewing Company was the eighth largest beer producer in the United States, with annual sales slightly over $135 million at the time of the purchase; sales had increased at a compound rate of 12% over the prior 5 years, while profits had risen at a compound rate of 19% (Exhibit 9).

Miller Brewing Company had, in 1969, an acknowledged reputation for a premium beer (Miller High Life—The Champagne of Bottled Beer), a nationwide distribution system (750 independent wholesalers in all 50 states), three geographically decentralized breweries in Wisconsin (4-million-barrel capacity), Texas (1.5-million-barrel capacity), and California (1.2-million-barrel capacity), and a bottle manufacturing plant in Milwaukee. Only the central brewery, in Wisconsin, was considered to be large enough to be operated economically. The company was financially stable, with a 2.26:1 current ratio, no long-term debt, and a book value of $71,700,000 (Exhibit 10).

In 1969, as stated previously, the Miller Brewing Company was the eighth largest beer producer and marketer in the United States. The beer industry was dominated by Anheuser-Busch, Schlitz, and Pabst; those three firms had grown very rapidly during the prior five-year period (Exhibit 11).

The annual increases in sales revenues and profits reported for most of the 10 largest breweries in the United States (the nine firms listed in Exhibit 3 plus Coors, which was privately owned and did not disclose revenues for beer sales, although reputedly fourth in

Exhibit 7 *Market size, market share, and market growth estimates for Philip Morris consumer products, 1969*

	Market size (millions)	Market share (%) (estimates)		Market growth (estimates)
Chewing gum	$400	Wrigleys	50.9	Static
		Dentyne	17.7	
		Beech-Nut	11.4	
		Trident	10.0	
		Chiclets	3.1	
		Life Savers	1.8	
		Clarks	0.8	
		Others	4.3	
			100.0	
Razor blades	$650	Gillette	64.7	10% annually
		Schick	21.5	
		Wilkinson	9.4	
		Personna	4.4	
			100.00	
Shaving cremes	$700	Gillette	25.5	10% annually
		Colgate	12.8	
		Noxzema	9.9	
		Rapid Shave	9.5	
		Barbasol	6.9	
		Old Spice	6.5	
		Edge	6.2	
		Rise	5.3	
		Schick	5.2	
		Mennen	4.8	
		Others	7.4	
			100.0	

Source: Market size from *Standard and Poor's Industry Surveys,* 1970; market share from the Target Group Index for 1975, adjusted for prior changes; and market growth from industry estimates.

Exhibit 8 *Operating revenue and income (000's omitted) for the Industrial Division of Philip Morris, Inc., 1967–1969*

	1967	1968	1969
Operating revenue of the Industrial Division	$71,457	$83,574	$84,659
Operating income of the Industrial Division	4,653	6,814	5,392

Source: Philip Morris, Inc., *Annual Report for 1970,* p. 23.

Exhibit 9 *Income statements (000's omitted) for the Miller Brewing Company, 1964–1968*

	1964	1965	1966	1967	1968
Net sales (see note)	$88,483	$99,023	$111,953	$126,047	$135,363
Interest and other income	217	520	863	1,155	1,359
Total revenues	88,700	99,543	112,816	127,202	136,722
Cost of goods sold	60,068	64,665	73,798	84,154	92,169
Marketing expenses	15,813	16,351	18,067	19,815	21,763
Administrative expenses	3,120	3,402	3,905	3,827	3,775
Total costs and expenses	79,001	84,418	95,770	107,796	117,707
Profit before taxes	9,699	15,125	17,046	19,406	19,015
Income taxes	5,120	7,910	8,700	9,820	9,980
Profit after taxes	4,579	7,215	8,346	9,586	9,035

Note: Sales revenues are reported net, after payment of federal and state beverage taxes. Gross sales in 1968 were $184,381,000 and beverage taxes were $49,018,000.
Source: Registration Statement of Philip Morris, Inc., August 29, 1969, p. 43.

overall size) were not entirely relevant, because of the impact of inflation. The wholesale price index for all commodities rose 8.1% during the period 1964–1968, while the price index for beer rose 4.7%. Industry growth rates and company market shares can be more accurately computed from data on sales in barrels (31 gallons, or 14 cases of twenty-four 12-oz bottles or cans) of beer. Beer is not as undifferentiated as is often assumed, and the industry data are commonly reported for premium, regional, and price (euphemistically termed "nonpremium" in industry publications) classifications. The following definitions are not technically accurate, but are accepted by industry personnel:

Exhibit 10 *Balance sheet (000's omitted) of the Miller Brewing Company at December 31, 1968*

Cash	$ 1,373	Accounts payable	$ 5,160
Marketable securities	19,537	Accrued taxes not on income	3,355
Accounts receivable	7,595	Accrued taxes on income	3,781
Inventories	7,165	Accrued salaries and wages	3,030
Prepaid expenses	1,082	Accrued miscellaneous	849
Total current assets	36,752	Total current liabilities	16,175
Investment in subsidiary	2,032	Deferred compensation	2,893
Property, plant, and equipment	91,787	Common stock	1,044
Less depreciation	39,805	Retained earnings	70,654
Total fixed assets	51,982	Total owners' equity	71,698

Source: Registration Statement of Philip Morris, Inc., August 29, 1969, p. 42.

Exhibit 11 *Sales and after-tax profits (000's omitted) of major breweries within the United States, 1964–1968*

	1964	1965	1966	1967	1968
Anheuser-Busch sales	$376,239	$421,858	$485,062	$554,879	$652,706
Anheuser-Busch profits	19,645	25,760	33,626	36,194	44,663
Schlitz sales	238,667	248,794	275,080	304,049	357,258
Schlitz profits	14,050	16,042	17,292	19,398	21,197
Pabst sales	227,610	253,585	282,015	320,456	355,306
Pabst profits	10,021	12,438	15,305	18,210	20,421
Carling (U.S. and Canada) sales	258,804	252,430	n.a.	246,899	237,739
Carling profits	16,571	11,320	n.a.	11,966	15,791
Falstaff sales	139,464	150,972	168,131	159,934	225,051
Falstaff profits	7,035	5,055	4,362	4,974	3,869
Schaeffer sales	n.a.	n.a.	n.a.	133,915	150,865
Schaeffer profits	n.a.	n.a.	n.a.	3,160	3,620
Hamms (Heublein) sales	125,808	128,575	135,396	151,936	149,413
Hamms profits	—	—	—	—	—
Miller (W. R. Grace) sales	88,483	99,023	111,953	126,047	135,363
Miller profits	4,579	7,215	8,346	9,586	9,035
Olympic sales	82,406	93,874	102,183	109,403	118,143
Olympic profits	5,306	6,144	6,416	7,008	6,307

Note: Hamms Brewery was a division of Heublein, Inc.; sales are from the Listing Application of Heublein Corporation, December 17, 1968, p. 17; profits were not reported. Miller Brewing Company was a subsidiary of W. R. Grace and Company; sales and profits are from Registration Statement of Philip Morris, Inc., August 29, 1969, p. 43.

Source: Moody's Industrial Manual, 1970, supplemented as noted.

Premium beers (Budweiser, Schlitz, Pabst, Carling, Miller, etc.) are normally brewed in large volume by a national company, and supported by extensive advertising, particularly on television.

Regional beers (Falstaff, Schaeffer, Hamms, Olympic, Strohs, and Blatz) are usually made from the same ingredients and by the same process as the premium beers, with equivalent aging and quality control, but they are not distributed nationally nor advertised equally, and consequently sell at a discount of 5 to 10% from the price of the premium beers.

Price beers (Goebel, Right Time, Buckeye, and Rolling Rock) are specifically designed to sell at a discounted price; materials are reduced in quality and the process in duration, and the result is often a beer that tastes "thin" to persons accustomed to the premium and regional brands since the alcoholic content may be at 3.0%, not at the generally accepted

Exhibit 12 *Beer industry sales (thousands of barrels) for the primary classifications and the Miller Brewing Company, 1964–1968*

	1964	1965	1966	1967	1968
Premium beer sales	18,300	20,400	23,200	25,600	28,000
Regional beer sales	64,300	65,500	67,600	69,400	71,400
Price beer sales	16,000*	14,500*	13,500*	12,000*	12,000*
Total beer industry sales	98,600	100,400	104,300	107,000	111,400
Miller company sales	3,290	3,670	4,150	4,580	4,850

Source: Registration Statement of Philip Morris, Inc., August 29, 1969, p. 12, plus Philip Morris, *Annual Report for 1974*, p. 32, supplemented by (*) industry estimates.

3.8%. Price beers have limited distribution and advertising, and sell at a discount of 20 to 25% from the premium beers.

Total beer sales within the United States grew at 3.1% annually during the five-year period 1964–1968, while premium beer sales grew at 10.8% annually (Exhibit 12).

The initial reaction of beer industry executives and cigarette company officials to the purchase of the Miller Brewing Company by Philip Morris, Inc., appeared to be a mixture of amused tolerance and light-hearted optimism:

> Tell Philip Morris to come right along (into the beer industry), but tell them to bring lots of money. (Statement of August Busch III, President of Anheuser-Busch Inc., quoted in *Business Week*, November 8, 1976, p. 58)

> Every Irishman dreams of going to heaven and running a brewery. (Statement of John Murphy, executive vice-president of Philip Morris assigned to manage Miller Brewing Company, quoted in *Business Week*, November 8, 1976, p. 58)

Class Assignment. Using the familiar means of portfolio analysis developed by the Boston Consulting Group, that classifies each product division by market growth and market share into "stars," "cows," "problems,"

and "dogs," evaluate each of the products of Philip Morris, Inc., as of the date of the case (after the acquisition of the Miller Brewing Company). That is, position each of the products of divisions of Philip Morris on the portfolio planning matrix (Exhibit 13).

1. The intent of the portfolio planning process is to develop a corporate-level strategy, or long-term method of competition, that is more than the sum of the strategies of each of the product divisions. Use the portfolio matrix you have developed to design an overall strategy for the Philip Morris corporation that will relate the total company to the environmental opportunities and risks, the organizational strengths and weaknesses, and the managerial values and attitudes.

2. Consider the portfolio planning method developed by General Electric that evaluates each product division not on the single dimensions of market growth and market share, but on multidimensional measures of industry attractiveness and company strengths (Exhibit 14). Position the Philip Morris products on this six-cell matrix; make assumptions from your own knowledge of the products to cover the input factors, such as competitive intensity and technological requirements, that have not been described in the case.

3. Which of the portfolio planning

Exhibit 13 *Portfolio planning matrix developed by the Boston Consulting Group*

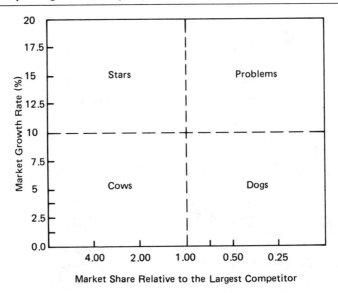

methods—that of the Boston Consulting Group or that of the General Electric Company—do you like best, and why?

4. Why did W. R. Grace and Company sell the Miller Brewing Company, and why did Philip Morris, Inc., enter the beer industry? Assume that both corporations had staffs trained in portfolio analysis.

Exhibit 14 *Portfolio planning matrix developed by the General Electric Company*

Company Strength within the Industry

		Above average	Average	Below average
Industry Attractiveness	Above average	Invest	Invest	Retain
	Average	Invest	Retain	Divest
	Below average	Retain	Divest	Divest

Standard Brands, Inc.

Standard Brands, Inc., is a large packaged food and liquor company that, despite the widespread reputation of many of its products, has remained relatively unrecognized by most American consumers. The company produces Blue Bonnet and Fleischmann's margarines, Egg Beaters egg substitutes, Royal gelatines and puddings, Chase & Sanborn coffee, Tender Leaf tea, Planter's peanuts, Baby Ruth and Butterfinger candy bars, Fleischmann's gin, vodka, and blended whiskey, and Souverain wines. In addition, the company has distribution rights for such imported products as Benedictine cordials, Delamin and Comandon cognacs, Bollinger champagnes, Antinori Italian wines, Deinhard German wines, Robertson's port, Dry Sack sherry, and Pernod liqueurs. Consumer products dominated sales (75% in 1976), but the company also produced high-fructose corn syrup (a low-calorie sweetener often used as a sugar substitute) for soft-drink bottlers, margarine, yeast and egg substitutes for commercial bakeries, and "service" brands of coffee, tea, gelatine, etc., for restaurants. Sales were concentrated in the United States (67% in 1976) and Canada (16%), with the balance (17%) primarily in Central and South America.

The product lines and brand names of Standard Brands, Inc., are well known, but the sales and profits of the firm have never reflected that brand recognition and market position. Sales over the period 1968–1976 grew at approximately the rate of inflation, while profits remained below industry averages (Exhibit 1).

In mid-1976, the directors of Standard Brands, Inc., apparently concerned by the below-average growth and returns and disturbed by the static stock price and dividends, elected Mr. Ross Johnson to be chairman of the board and Mr. Reuben Gutoff to be president. Both were young (Mr. Johnson was 44 and Mr. Gutoff was 47); both were former General Electric Company executives; and both had been directly involved with the process of strategic planning at that large, multiple-industry, divisionalized firm. Reuben Gutoff had been vice president for long-range planning, and was primarily credited with the development of the "strategic business unit" concept at G. E. Under the direction of Mr. Gutoff, that company had been divided into product-market units termed "SBUs," each of which had a given product or product line, a specific market or market segment, an existing distribution channel, adequate productive capacity, and known competitors. The intent, as described in the introductory text section of this chapter, was to separate the company into business units that could act independently in the market through a clearly defined strategy, and then to control that action and direct that strategy by means of a corporate planning model rather than a capital budgeting process.

The central concept of the corporate planning model developed by Mr. Gutoff for General Electric was that each strategic business unit differed on two basic dimensions: the attractiveness of the industry and the strength of the company within that industry. Each strategic business unit within the company was measured on those two dimensions, and then compared. Corporate resources were channeled to the divisions that combined industry attractiveness and company strengths since these were felt to be the units with the greatest probability of competitive success, while divisions that were low on both dimensions were either sold or used as sources of funds.

This "portfolio" planning process had been

Exhibit 1 *Sales revenues, expenses, and profits (000's omitted) of Standard Brands, Inc., 1968–1976*

	1968	1970	1972	1974	1976
Sales revenues	$953.4	$1,119.7	$1,168.9	$1,647.9	$1,809.9
Miscellaneous income	5.5	8.2	8.0	8.4	—
Total income	958.9	1,127.9	1,176.9	1,656.3	1,809.9
Cost of goods sold	664.2	793.1	784.9	1,183.4	1,265.1
Selling and administrative expenses	219.1	243.7	285.5	326.3	392.9
Interest expenses	8.4	14.9	15.7	25.0	18.3
Miscellaneous expenses	3.1	4.9	6.3	14.0	10.0
Total expenses	894.8	1,056.3	1,092.4	1,548.7	1,686.3
Profit before taxes	64.1	71.6	84.5	107.6	123.6
Federal and state taxes	31.1	34.2	40.5	51.7	56.0
Profit after taxes	33.0	37.4	44.0	55.9	67.6
Profit/sales revenues	3.4%	3.3%	3.7%	3.4%	3.7%
Profit/total assets	4.1%	4.1%	4.1%	3.7%	4.4%
Profit/owners' equity	12.9%	13.3%	13.4%	14.3%	14.5%
Median stock price during year	43.90	46.50	50.40	46.80	52.00
Price/earnings ratio during year	17.8×	16.6×	15.7×	11.6×	10.7×

Source: Moody's Industrial Manual for the respective years.

successful at General Electric Company, and it was obvious, since neither Mr. Johnson nor Mr. Gutoff had extensive experience with consumer products, and absolutely no experience with packaged foods and liquors, that it was the intent of the directors that the same planning process be employed at Standard Brands, Inc. The balance of this case describes the product lines of Standard Brands, together with relevant information on market shares, growth rates, competitive positions, etc., so that this method of strategic design for large, multiple-industry firms might be attempted by the student. All information is from published sources; independent estimates, when needed, are indicated with an asterisk (*).

1. *Margarines.* Margarine is a butter substitute used both for cooking and spreading, and made primarily from soybean oil, corn oil, and edible animal fats. Commodity prices for the oils and fats have increased with inflation since 1970, but have not evidenced sharp seasonal or cyclical swings, and the domestically produced materials have remained readily available. The total production of margarine has increased generally with the population since 1970, while per capita consumption has remained constant (Exhibit 2).

Standard Brands dominated the margarine industry, with a 31.2% market share in 1977 for their two popular brands: Blue Bonnet and Fleischmann's (Exhibit 3).

2. *Egg substitutes.* Egg substitutes are a recently developed soybean-based product for low-calorie and low-cholesterol diets. The product was introduced by Standard Brands in 1974, and sales have increased

Exhibit 2 *Domestic consumption, materials used, and average commodity costs for margarine, 1970–1977*

	Consumption		Materials used				Commodity average costs ($/lb)
	Total (MM lb)	Per capita (lb)	Soybean (MM lb)	Corn oil (MM lb)	Animal fat (MM lb)	Other oil (MM lb)	
1970	2,219	11.0	1,410	185	99	100	0.196
1971	2,268	11.1	1,385	186	169	91	0.212
1972	2,333	11.3	1,461	194	138	93	0.218
1973	2,351	11.3	1,491	213	80	107	0.302
1974	2,370	11.3	1,457	188	167	92	0.443
1975	2,368	11.2	1,568	188	52	112	0.379
1976	2,619	12.2	1,671	218	44	161	0.314
1977	2,510	11.6	1,584	243	80	120	0.391

Note: "Other" classification includes coconut, cottonseed, peanut, and safflower oil. The total of "material used" does not equal domestic consumption due to other additives, such as water, flavoring, sweeteners, stabilizing agents, etc. "Animal fats" are used only in lower-cost products, generally in combination with soybean or corn oil.

Source: Commodity Year Book, 1979, p. 218.

substantially since that time due to the public concern with heart disease. The total market was estimated at $35 million* in 1977, in terms of manufacturer's revenues. Standard Brands had a 70.5% share of that market, although their share was declining with the introduction of competitive products (Exhibit 4).

3. *Packaged desserts.* Packaged desserts include both flavored gelatines and instant puddings. The total market in 1977 was estimated at $425 million* in manufac-

Exhibit 3 *Market share percentages for the largest selling brands of margarine, 1975–1977*

	1975	1976	1977
Blue Bonnet (Standard Brands)	18.2	17.8	19.0
Parkay (Kraft Food Company)	13.5	13.1	13.5
Fleischmann's (Standard Brands)	10.3	11.7	12.2
Imperial (Lever Brothers)	10.8	10.4	9.9
Mrs. Filberts (J. H. Filbert, Inc.)	7.8	7.4	6.7
Mazola (Best Foods, div. of CPC International)	6.1	6.4	6.1
Chiffon (Anderson-Clayton, Inc.)	7.1	6.5	6.0
Miracle (Kraft Food Company)	3.1	2.9	2.7
NuMaid (Miami Margarine Company)	1.7	2.6	2.7
Nucoa (Best Foods, div. of CPC International)	2.8	2.4	2.3
A&P (Great Atlantic & Pacific Tea Company)	2.1	2.6	2.0
Promise (Lever Brothers)	2.5	2.4	1.9
All others	14.0	13.8	15.0
	100.0	100.0	100.0

Source: Industry estimates.

Exhibit 4 *Market share percentages for the largest selling brands of egg substitutes, 1975–1977*

	1975	1976	1977
Egg Beaters (Standard Brands)	91.3	83.8	79.5
Second Nature (Avoset Food Corp.)	8.7	11.0	13.2
All others	—	5.2	7.3
	100.0	100.0	100.0

Source: Industry estimates.

turer's revenues. The market was divided almost equally between the two product types, although the sales of flavored gelatine had remained almost static over the past three years, while the sales of instant puddings had been growing at 12% annually. Standard Brands maintained approximately a 25% share of each market (Exhibit 5).

4. *Coffee.* Coffee consumption within the United States has declined steadily since 1970, when 13.5 pounds per person were purchased annually; the equivalent figure for 1977 was 10.5 pounds (Exhibit 6). The reasons for this decline are felt to be a smaller number of people drinking coffee, increased competition from soft drinks, and a general resistance to recent price changes. World production of coffee is concentrated in the tropical areas of Central and South America and Africa, with over 50% grown in Colombia, Ecuador, and Brazil; it has been alleged that those three countries use export controls and tariff agreements to create shortages and maintain prices. Shortages were particularly severe in 1976 and 1977, because of adverse weather conditions during the growing season, and the commodity prices for green coffee beans increased 239%. Substantial exports were projected for 1978, however, and the increased sup-

Exhibit 5 *Market share percentages for the largest selling brands of packaged desserts, 1975–1977*

	1975	1976	1977
Jello gelatines (General Foods)	71.4	74.2	69.5
Royal gelatines (Standard Brands)	26.1	23.3	24.1
D-Zerta low-calorie (General Foods)	1.4	1.2	100.0
All others	1.1	1.3	1.6
	100.0	100.0	100.0
Jello puddings (General Foods)	51.8	54.8	56.5
Royal puddings (Standard Brands)	28.3	27.9	27.4
My-T-Fine puddings (R. J. Reynolds)	15.4	13.2	12.1
Ann Page (Great Atlantic & Pacific)	3.3	3.2	2.7
All others	1.2	0.9	1.3
	100.0	100.0	100.0

Source: Industry estimates.

Exhibit 6 *Domestic consumption, world surplus or shortage, and the resultant commodity prices for coffee, 1970–1977*

	Consumption		Persons drinking coffee (%)	Surplus or shortage (MM lb)	Commodity average costs ($/lb)
	Total (MM lb)	Per capita (lb)			
1970	2,803	13.9	n.a.	− 9,946	0.557
1971	2,798	13.7	n.a.	− 4,317	0.461
1972	2,803	13.6	n.a.	+ 3,317	0.544
1973	2.809	13.5	n.a.	−11,926	0.676
1974	2,747	13.1	n.a.	+ 9,933	0.702
1975	2,705	12.8	61.6	− 1,066	0.710
1976	2,511	11.7	59.1	−12,700*	1.420
1977	2,272	10.5	57.9	− 4,700*	2.410

Note: World "surplus or shortage" is the balance between annual consumption and annual exports (not annual production) of the coffee-growing countries.
Sources: Advertising Age, June 28, 1978, p. 44, for total and per capita consumption; *Standard and Poor's Industry Surveys,* 1979, p. F29, for world surplus/shortage; and *Commodity Year Book,* 1979, p. 113, for commodity prices.

plies were expected to bring prices back close to the 1975 levels.

Coffee within the United States is sold both in ground form, ready for brewing, and in powdered or freeze-dried form, ready for instant use. Instant coffee is estimated to have remained constant at approximately 28% of the market* over the past three years; market shares for the major brands of ground and instant coffee are given in Exhibits 7 and 8.

5. *Tea.* Tea consumption within the United States has risen since 1970, approximately 22.0% in total (Exhibits 9 and 10). It is believed that the increased consumption of tea is due partially to the higher cost of coffee as a warm beverage, and partially to the availability of an instant form of tea to make an iced beverage during the summer.

6. *Peanuts.* The peanut crop within the United States in 1977 was slightly over 4,000 million pounds. 1,180 million pounds were used for direct consumption, mixed in candy, roasted and salted for

snacks, or ground for peanut butter. 783 million pounds were pressed for oil, and nearly 1,000 million pounds were exported. The balance, mostly in nonedible grades, was used as a protein supplement in livestock feeds. The large supply, with the surplus sold for low-margin uses, has limited price increases to the rate of inflation (Exhibit 11).

Standard Brands, Inc., produced roasted and salted peanuts for snacks, and ground peanuts for peanut butter. The market shares of these two products were widely divergent (Exhibits 12 and 13).

7. *Candy.* Candy consumption has been declining within the United States since 1970; per capita purchases have dropped from 19.9 pounds in 1970 to 15.4 pounds in 1977 (Exhibit 14). The reasons for this decline are partially demographic, with fewer children in the 5- to 13-year age bracket, who consume much of the candy; partially economic, with substantial price increases that have made it dif-

Exhibit 7 *Market share percentages for largest selling brands of ground coffee, 1975–1977*

	1975	1976	1977
Maxwell House (General Foods)	24.9	24.1	24.9
Folgers (Procter & Gamble)	21.0	21.4	21.4
Hill Brothers (Hill Brothers Food Company)	7.6	7.5	7.0
MaxPax (General Foods)	4.1	4.5	4.0
Sanka (General Foods)	4.0	4.0	3.5
Chase & Sanborn (Standard Brands)	3.7	3.5	2.9
Butternut (Coca-Cola, Inc.)	2.7	2.8	2.7
Yuban (General Foods)	2.2	2.2	2.0
Chock Full O' Nuts (Chock Full O' Nuts, Inc.)	2.2	1.6	1.4
A&P Regular (Great Atlantic & Pacific Tea Co.)	1.8	1.7	1.3
All others	25.8	26.7	28.7
	100.0	100.0	100.0

Source: Industry estimates.

ficult for young children to buy candy; and partially social, with increased concern by parents on nutritional values and eating habits.

Commodity prices for sugar and cocoa beans, the source of milk chocolate, have always been subject to sharp cyclical swings. During periods of high commodity costs, some manufacturers have re-duced the size of their candy bars, while others have coated their bar and bulk candies with artificial chocolate, and sweetened them with corn syrup. For example, the Reggie candy bar, produced by Standard Brands and named for the N.Y. Yankee outfielder Reggie Jackson, contains no chocolate and no sugar.

Candy is distributed in packaged form

Exhibit 8 *Market share percentages for largest selling brands of instant coffee, 1975–1977*

	1975	1976	1977
Maxwell House (General Foods)	24.9	24.5	22.0
Sanka Brand (General Foods)	14.8	14.2	12.5
Taster's Choice Regular (Nestlé)	11.7	11.8	12.5
Nescafe (Nestlé)	11.0	12.6	12.0
Folgers (Procter & Gamble)	8.0	7.7	8.7
Taster's Choice Decaffeinated (Nestlé)	5.4	5.5	5.5
Maxim (General Foods)	5.5	5.3	4.5
Brim (General Foods)	3.5	3.5	3.0
Mellow Roast (General Foods)	—	—	2.5
Yuban (General Foods)	2.0	2.0	1.8
Kava (Bordens)	1.1	1.3	1.2
Decaf (Nestlé)	1.4	1.0	1.0
All others	10.7	10.6	12.8
	100.0	100.0	100.0

Source: Industry estimates.

Exhibit 9 *Domestic consumption, U.S. imports and stocks, and the resultant commodity prices for tea, 1970–1977*

	Consumption		Persons drinking tea (%)	Supplies		Commodity average costs ($/lb)
	Total (MM lb)	Per capita (lb)		Imports (MM lb)	Stocks (MM lb)	
1970	145.2	0.72	n.a.	137.2	56.0	0.458
1971	157.3	0.77	n.a.	175.4	74.1	0.487
1972	159.3	0.77	n.a.	151.5	66.3	0.507
1973	164.4	0.79	n.a.	173.2	75.1	0.483
1974	167.7	0.80	n.a.	160.1*	67.5*	0.620
1975	169.1	0.80	26.9	159.3*	57.5*	0.685
1976	173.9	0.81	27.3	168.6*	52.4*	0.742
1977	177.4	0.82	30.7	154.3*	29.3*	1.141

Sources: *Commodity Year Book,* 1979, p. 339, for consumption, imports, stocks, and commodity costs; and *Advertising Age,* June 26, 1978, p. 44, for persons drinking tea.

Exhibit 10 *Market share percentages for the largest selling brands of tea, 1975–1977*

	1975	1976	1977
Liptons (Thomas J. Lipton, Inc.)	51.0	50.1	50.6
Tetley (Beech-Nut, Inc.)	8.7	9.1	9.4
Tenderleaf (Standard Brands)	11.7	10.3	9.3
Salada (Salada Foods, Inc.)	7.1	8.0	7.7
Red Rose (Brooke-Bond Foods)	7.1	7.4	7.6
Constant Comment (R. C. Bigelow)	3.3	3.8	4.0
A&P (Great Atlantic & Pacific Tea Co.)	3.8	3.4	3.3
All others	7.3	7.9	8.1
	100.0	100.0	100.0

Source: Industry estimates.

Exhibit 11 *Domestic consumption, by type of consumer use, and commodity prices for peanuts*

	Consumption						Commodity average cost ($/lb)
	Candy (MM lb)	Salted (MM lb)	Butter (MM lb)	Other (MM lb)	Total (MM lb)	Per capita (lb)	
1970	243.2	238.8	540.4	42.9	1,065.3	5.28	0.128
1971	246.0	241.7	556.8	42.6	1,087.1	5.32	0.134
1972	259.8	254.4	578.1	43.2	1,135.5	5.49	0.144
1973	251.5	284.3	660.0	43.2	1,239.0	5.95	0.157
1974	217.0	278.3	651.0	34.8	1,181.1	5.63	0.176
1975	239.7	301.6	648.1	37.0	1,226.4	5.80	0.195
1976	235.0	253.8	617.9	42.0	1,148.7	5.35	0.197
1977	235.2	274.2	623.8	46.9	1,180.1	5.45	0.207

Source: *Commodity Year Book,* 1979, p. 255 for uses, and p. 254 for prices.

Exhibit 12 *Market share percentages for the largest selling brands of roasted peanuts, 1975–1977*

	1975	1976	1977
Planters (Standard Brands)	63.0	61.2	60.1
Diamond (Diamond Growers)	10.7	12.3	12.7
Skippy (Best Foods)	6.2	7.2	7.9
Fishers (Beatrice Foods)	5.2	5.4	5.3
A&P (Great Atlantic & Pacific Tea Co.)	4.3	3.7	3.9
Flavor House (Flavor House Products)	1.9	2.7	2.6
Guys (Guy's Foods, Inc.)	2.1	2.1	2.0
Franklin (American Home Foods)	1.9	1.5	1.4
All others	4.7	3.9	4.1
	100.0	100.0	100.0

Source: Industry estimates.

Exhibit 13 *Market share percentages for the largest selling brands of peanut butter, 1975–1977*

	1975	1976	1977
Skippy (Best Foods, Inc.)	29.2	31.7	32.8
Peter Pan (Swift & Company)	28.9	26.2	24.3
Jif (Procter and Gamble)	20.8	21.4	22.6
Planters (Standard Brands)	5.2	5.0	5.4
A&P (Great Atlantic & Pacific Tea Co.)	2.6	2.5	2.7
All others	13.3	13.2	12.2
	100.0	100.0	100.0

Source: Industry estimates.

Exhibit 14 *Domestic consumption, sales prices, and average commodity costs for candy, 1970–1977*

	Consumption		Mfgr's price ($/lb)	Average commodity costs			
	Total (MM lb)	Per capita (lb)		Sugar ($/lb)	Cocoa ($/lb)	Syrup ($/lb)	Peanuts ($/lb)
1970	4,013	19.9	0.485	0.177	0.342	0.068	0.128
1971	3,942	19.3	0.510	0.122	0.268	0.077	0.134
1972	3,882	18.8	0.521	0.127	0.321	0.106	0.144
1973	3,870	18.6	0.562	0.141	0.647	0.123	0.157
1974	3,732	17.8	0.759	0.344	0.985	0.163	0.176
1975	3,439	16.3	0.843	0.314	0.750	0.152	0.195
1976	3,585	16.7	0.840	0.192	1.090	0.104	0.197
1977	3,332	15.4	0.940	0.173	1.720	0.082	0.207

Source: Standard and Poor's Industry Survey, 1979, p. F32.

Exhibit 15 *Domestic sales of candy by product types, 1975–1977*

	1975		1976		1977	
	Weight (M lb)	Value (M $)	Weight (M lb)	Value (M $)	Weight (M lb)	Value (M $)
Package goods	1,429	1,211	1,548	1,338	1,408	1,337
Bar goods	932	895	1,077	990	996	1,122
Bulk goods	258	146	341	175	282	169
10 cent specialties	339	290	329	289	136	149
All others	479	286	286	117	508	279
	3,439	2,830	3,585	2,912	3,332	3,058

Source: Standard and Poor's Industry Survey, 1979, p. F32.

(1- or 2-pound boxes of chocolate-coated "bite-size" pieces, sold by the box), in bar form (the familiar chocolate-coated and paper-wrapped candy bars, sold individually), in bulk form (gum drops, sour balls, fudge, etc., sold by weight), and as 10-cent specialties (chewing gum, Life Savers, etc., sold in small packages). Relative percentages of these product groups have remained reasonably constant over the past three years (Exhibit 15).

Market share percentages for the major brands of candy bars have also remained reasonably constant over the past three years (Exhibit 16). Parents tend to buy the same brands for their children that they preferred while growing up, which provides an unexpected stability and continuity to the market. Many of the brands have been popular for years. For

Exhibit 16 *Market share percentages for the largest selling brands of bar candy, 1975–1977*

	1975	1976	1977
Snickers (Mars, Inc.)	6.0	6.2	6.5
Three Musketeers (Mars, Inc.)	5.7	5.9	6.3
Almond Joy (Cadbury–Schweppes)	6.4	6.1	5.9
Milky Way (Mars, Inc.)	5.3	5.4	5.7
Reese Peanut Butter Cups (Hershey)	5.8	5.7	5.5
Almond Chocolate Bar (Hershey)	5.4	5.6	5.4
Milk Chocolate Bar (Hershey)	5.5	5.5	5.4
M&M Plain (Mars, Inc.)	5.1	5.2	5.1
M&M Peanuts (Mars, Inc.)	4.6	4.2	4.1
Butterfinger (Standard Brands)	5.1	4.9	4.1
Crunchy Chocolate Bar (Nestlé)	4.6	4.3	4.0
Baby Ruth (Standard Brands)	4.0	3.8	3.6
All others	36.5	37.2	38.4
	100.0	100.0	100.0

Source: Industry estimates.

Exhibit 17 *Domestic sales of distilled whiskeys (gallons), by type, 1970–1977*

	American blends	American bourbon	Imported Scotch	Imported Canadian	Imported other	Consumption	
						Total	Per capita
1970	78,473	82,477	53,249	37,234	7,607	259,130	1.284
1971	70,739	76,210	54,324	38,691	6,253	246,217	1.205
1972	65,399	71,591	53,790	41,019	6,965	238,764	1.156
1973	57,498	65,547	54,431	43,698	5,749	226,923	1.090
1974	54,471	65,686	57,275	45,861	5,206	229,499	1.094
1975	52,315	66,960	56,916	49,801	5,440	231,432	1.094
1976	51,012	62,914	52,873	46,335	3,825	216,959	1.010
1977	50,193	61,876	51,058	47,164	3,461	213,752	0.988

Source: Industry estimates.

example, Baby Ruth, still one of the top 10 candy bars in sales volume, was introduced in 1894, and named for the baby daughter of President and Mrs. Grover Cleveland, not, as is usually assumed, for the former N.Y. Yankee outfielder who set a record for home runs in 1927.

8. *Liquor.* Sales of distilled liquors have been nearly static over the period 1970–1977, with consumption per person increasing less than 1.1% during that time span, but changes within the various categories of the whiskeys and nonwhiskeys have been substantial. It is expected that the consumption of whiskey will increase in the future, because of the traditional association of that alcoholic beverage with middle-aged and older persons, and that the use of the nonwhiskeys or white liquors, which are used in the mixed drinks favored by younger customers, will decline as the demographic age groups shift within the country, but no firm evidence of these trends has yet become apparent. Sales of rum, vodka, and other nonwhiskeys (primarily tequila, sake, and packaged cocktails) have grown rapidly since 1970, while the use of blended and bourbon whiskeys has declined (Exhibits 17 and 18).

Standard Brands, Inc., produced blended and bourbon whiskeys, gin, rum, cordials, and brandy, and imported Scotch and Canadian whiskeys, Mexican

Exhibit 18 *Domestic sales of distilled nonwhiskeys (gallons), by type, 1970–1977*

	Gin	Rum	Brandy and cordials	Vodka	Other nonwhiskeys	Consumption	
						Total	Per capita
1970	40,037	12,411	34,832	47,244	6,806	141,330	0.701
1971	39,082	13,288	34,783	49,634	7,816	144,603	0.708
1972	38,311	13,544	35,602	53,790	6,965	148,213	0.717
1973	37,565	14,566	37,564	57,881	8,816	156,394	0.752
1974	38,851	14,819	39,652	66,587	11,214	171,023	0.816
1975	41,013	16,321	42,687	73,237	13,810	187,068	0.884
1976	41,234	17,854	45,910	87,145	16,153	208,296	0.970
1977	42,837	22,500	47,164	89,136	16,875	218,512	1.009

Source: Industry estimates.

Exhibit 19 *Market share percentages for the largest selling brands of blended whiskey, 1975–1977*

	1975	1976	1977
Seagram's 7 Crown (J. Seagram & Sons)	56.2	55.6	55.4
Kesslers (Brown-Forman Distilling Co.)	8.5	8.3	8.3
Calvert Extra (J. Seagram & Sons)	9.7	8.2	7.8
Imperial (Hiram Walker, Inc.)	7.0	7.0	6.3
Fleischmann's Preferred (Standard Brands)	5.1	5.4	5.8
Schenley Reserve (Schenley Industries)	5.3	5.0	5.7
Corby's Reserve (Corby's Distilling, Ltd.)	2.2	2.7	3.5
Bellows Partners Choice (National Distilling Co.)	1.5	1.9	2.1
All others	4.5	5.9	5.1
	100.0	100.0	100.0

Source: Industry estimates.

tequila, French cognac, and Benedictine D.O.M. liqueurs (classified as brandy or cordials). Of this group of products, only the blended whiskey, gin, vodka, and Benedictine D.O.M. liqueurs had achieved significant (over 2%) market shares (Exhibits 19 to 22).

9. *Wines.* The consumption of U.S. produced wines increased by 39.7% from 1970 to 1977, while the sales of foreign produced wines in the United States grew by 128%. Foreign wines include the familiar names and expensive varieties from France, Germany, and Italy, and also inexpensive imports from Spain,

Portugal, and Hungary; most of the increase was represented by the latter types. For both domestic and imported wines, the major changes occurred in the table wines; not in the dessert (port or sherry), cooking (vermouth), or sparkling (champagne or cold duck) varieties (Exhibits 23 and 24).

Standard Brands, Inc., owned the Souverain vineyards in California, and imported Bollinger champagne, Antinori Italian wines, and Deinhard German wines; none of these products had achieved a significant (over 2.0%) market share (Exhibit 25).

Exhibit 20 *Market share percentages for the largest selling brands of gin, 1975–1977*

	1975	1976	1977
Gordon's (Renfield Importers, Ltd.)	21.7	22.2	23.3
Gilbey's (National Distilling Co.)	20.6	19.9	20.5
Beefeater's (Kobrand Corporation)	16.2	17.4	17.9
Seagram's (J. Seagram & Sons)	14.1	12.4	10.7
Tanqueray (Norton-Simon)	5.2	6.8	7.8
Fleischmann's Gin (Standard Brands)	7.6	8.2	7.6
Hiram Walker (Hiram Walker, Inc.)	5.4	4.8	4.0
Calvert's Gin (J. Seagram & Sons)	5.3	4.9	4.0
All others	3.9	3.4	4.2
	100.0	100.0	100.0

Source: Industry estimates.

Exhibit 21 *Market share percentages for the largest selling brands of vodka, 1975–1977*

	1975	1976	1977
Smirnoff (Heublein, Inc.)	41.6	40.4	39.0
Gordon's (Renfield Importers, Ltd.)	13.6	13.1	12.1
Gilbey's (National Distilling Co.)	9.1	8.9	8.7
Seagram's (J. Seagram & Son)	5.7	6.2	6.8
Wolfschmidt (J. Seagram & Sons)	4.9	5.4	6.2
Popov (Heublein, Inc.)	5.9	5.7	5.1
Fleischmann's Vodka (Standard Brands, Inc.)	4.9	5.2	4.9
Hiram Walker's Vodka (Hiram Walker, Inc.)	3.2	3.8	3.7
Mr. Boston (Mr. Boston Distilling, Inc.)	2.2	2.0	2.6
All others	8.9	9.3	10.9
	100.0	100.0	100.0

Source: Industry estimates.

10. *Corn syrup.* High-fructose corn syrup is used as a low-calorie commercial sweetener in the production of candy, baked goods, and some prepared sauces such as catsup, pickle relish, etc. Long-term market growth has been minimal, estimated at about 4% per year*, but cyclical swings in usage and price do occur, based upon the competitive costs and occasional shortages of sugar. Sales of corn syrup have recently been very substantial in Canada, where the use of saccharin has been banned in soft drinks; it is expected that an equivalent prohibition in the United States would result in annual growth rates here of 20 to 25%. Standard Brands, Inc., through the Clinton Corn Products Division, is one of the five major producers of high-fructose syrup; it is believed that all have approximately equal market shares, but that the reputation of Clinton Corn Products is above the others for quality control and product development.

Exhibit 22 *Market share percentages for the largest selling brands of liqueurs, 1975–1977*

	1975	1976	1977
Drambuie (W. A. Taylor & Co.)	12.2	11.8	11.3
Kahlua (J. Berman & Assoc.)	9.8	10.5	11.1
Galliano (McKesson Liquor Co.)	8.7	9.3	9.7
Benedictine D.O.M. (Standard Brands, Inc.)	9.5	8.7	8.0
Harvey's Bristol Cream (United Vintners, Inc.)	7.2	7.2	7.2
Southern Comfort (Southern Comfort Corp.)	5.8	5.8	5.6
Grand Marnier (Carillon Importers, Ltd.)	5.5	5.3	5.1
Cointreau (Renfield Importers, Ltd.)	5.0	4.8	4.9
Cherry Heering (W. A. Taylor & Co.)	3.2	3.4	3.5
Irish Mist (Heublein, Inc.)	2.3	2.7	3.3
All others	30.8	30.5	30.3
	100.0	100.0	100.0

Source: Industry estimates.

Exhibit 23 *Domestic consumption by type of U.S.-produced wines in gallons, 1970–1977*

| | Consumption by type of domestic wine | | | | | Consumption | |
	Table (M gal)	Dessert (M gal)	Vermouth (M gal)	Sparkling (M gal)	Flavored (M gal)	Total (M gal)	Per capita (gal)
1970	121,747	71,322	5,105	20,299	27,855	237,328	1.175
1971	130,127	71,028	4,892	22,005	41,014	269,065	1.317
1972	136,342	70,026	5,127	20,326	58,121	289,942	1.404
1973	145,877	66,382	5,311	18,935	55,536	292,041	1.403
1974	157,213	63,490	5,285	18,009	54,074	298,071	1.421
1975	173,511	64,640	5,282	18,435	56,842	318,710	1.507
1976	182,035	58,022	5,225	19,209	52,979	317,470	1.478
1977	205,135	54,487	5,203	21,334	45,467	331,626	1.532

Source: Standard and Poor's Industry Surveys, 1979, p. B75.

Class Assignment. The 10 major product groups of Standard Brands, Inc., have been described in terms of growth rates, market shares, competitive positions, etc. Develop a "portfolio" or "strategic business unit" planning procedure for the company. Specifically, identify the products that you believe should receive increased investments, and those that you suggest could be used as a source of funds. Then, consider the following three questions that add to the complexity of the portfolio planning model:

1. The Bakery Division sells "name" brands (advertised trade name products, such as Fleischmann's or Planter's) of margarine, egg substitutes, yeast (a by-product of the fermentation of grains, prior to distilling, in the production of liquor), and peanuts in bulk containers to commercial bakeries. How can these additional markets for existing brands of company products be included in the planning process?

2. The Food Service Division sells "service" brands (nonadvertised trade name products, generally sold at lower margins but usually of equivalent quality to the "name" brands) of margarine, egg substitutes, packaged desserts, coffee (the "service" brand of Standard Brand's coffee is

Exhibit 24 *Domestic consumption by type of U.S.-imported wines in gallons, 1970–1977*

| | Consumption by type of domestic wine | | | | | Consumption | |
	Table (M gal)	Dessert (M gal)	Vermouth (M gal)	Sparkling (M gal)	Flavored (M gal)	Total (M gal)	Per capita (gal)
1970	20,237	1,610	5,124	1,793	1,259	30,024	0.148
1971	24,703	1,929	5,367	1,877	2,280	36,156	0.177
1972	33,675	1,838	4,927	1,976	4,626	47,043	0.227
1973	39,371	2,129	5,026	2,021	6,893	55,440	0.266
1974	35,023	2,317	4,571	1,804	7,679	51,394	0.245
1975	35,525	2,120	4,278	1,928	5,467	49,319	0.233
1976	45,986	2,562	4,017	2,559	3,795	58,918	0.274
1977	56,065	2,553	3,743	2,934	3,427	68,722	0.317

Source: Standard and Poor's Industry Surveys, 1979, p. B75.

Exhibit 25 *Market share percentages for the largest selling brands of wine, 1975–1977*

	1975	1976	1977
Gallo (E. & J. Gallo, Inc.)	13.7	14.5	15.4
Almaden (div. of National Distillers)	10.2	11.2	11.3
Taylor (div. of Coca-Cola)	10.3	9.6	10.1
Paul Masson (Browne Vintners, Inc.)	9.0	9.3	9.3
Christian Brothers (Fromm & Sichel, Inc.)	8.4	8.5	8.1
Italian Swiss Colony (United Vintners, Inc.)	7.4	7.6	7.9
Mogen David (Mogen David Wine Corp.)	8.7	7.9	7.2
Manischewitz (Monarch Wine Corp.)	5.9	5.3	5.4
Inglenook (International Vintage Wines, Ltd.)	3.1	3.6	3.8
Charles Krug (Paterno Vintners, Inc.)	2.4	2.3	2.2
All others	20.9	20.2	19.3
	100.0	100.0	100.0

Source: Industry estimates.

called Famous Inn, not Chase & Sanborn), tea, liquor, and wines to restaurants. How can these additional markets for different brands of company products be included in the planning process?

3. The International Group sells "foreign" brands (special trade names, adapted to the language of the country, and usually a special formation, changed to fit the tastes of the population) of margarine, packaged desserts, and soft drinks based upon high-fructose corn syrup, in South America. How can this large and expanding market for new brands and changed products be included in the planning process?

Goodman Machine and Foundry Corporation

The Goodman Machine and Foundry Corporation had been formed in 1893 in Lansing, Michigan, to manufacture a side-dumping rail car. The car was designed with wooden sides that could be manually unlocked so that they would pivot from the top and permit loaded material to slide out underneath, and with a heavy steel floor that could be hydraulically raised to 40° for self-clearing. Sidney Goodman, the founder, was one of the first hydraulic engineers, and he patented a hydraulic accumulator that converted air pressure to hydraulic pressure and that could be charged from the brake line of the train, and he then designed the hydraulic valves and cylinders needed to tip the floor of the car high enough to dump the loaded material. The side-dumping feature was desirable both for spreading ballast beside the right-of-way for roadbed maintenance, and for dumping fill from the trestles and bridges for roadbed improvement. When the railroads had originally been built, during the 1850–1885 period, many gullies, streams, and swamps had been hastily bridged by wooden trestles which in later years often caught fire and burned from the ashes and hot coals dropped by steam locomotives. To avoid the fire hazard, and to create the more stable roadbed needed for heavier cars and engines, the trestles and short bridges were often filled in following 1885. Side-dumping cars were needed for both ballast and fill so that none of the material would land on the tracks and cause derailments. This feature also made the side-dumping cars very useful at mines to dispose of the tailings, waste rock, and overburden. Since all other side-dumping cars at that time operated off a steam line from the locomotive, with problems of condensation and loss of power as the steam cooled, and with dangers of leaks and burns in connecting the line between cars, the Goodman hydraulic design was quickly adopted as the standard for the major railroads in the Midwest and for the large mines in northern Michigan and Minnesota.

In 1910, the company expanded to manufacture the hydraulic rock crushers, screens, and conveyors needed to supply ballast to the railroads, and found that the same equipment could be used to process aggregate (sand and gravel) for road construction and concrete or asphalt preparation. Through association with road-building contractors, Goodman Machine and Foundry started in 1920 to build hydraulic dump-truck bodies which could be installed on the heavy-duty truck frames then being produced in Detroit, and also designed grading plows and snow plows that could be truck-mounted. In the 1940s and early 1950s the company added large dump trailers to haul aggregate to a construction site, and small motorized construction carts, with hydraulic drive, steering, and dump body, to spread aggregate and place concrete.

All of our products, until 1960, were used in construction or mining, and all consequently were built with heavy steel castings or weldments, and all had some association with hydraulics. We had a clear identity as a company; we limited what we did, we did it well, and we were certain that we knew where we were going. The 1960s were fabulous years, with growing expenditures for highway construction and even some spending for railroad improvements. We never used the term "strategy," but if we had, we would have said that our strategy was consistent with our external environment. Then, in the 1970s the midwestern railroads collapsed and the Interstate Highway System was completed, and our growth came to an end. Our sales have not collapsed, but our volume has been static since 1965, and now our most profitable products are commercial lawn mowers and estate tractors (off-shoots of the motorized construction carts). We're not certain where we are going anymore, but we've decided that we had better take a good look, now, before we get there. We're going to get active in strategic planning. (Statement of David Goodman, president of Goodman Machine and Foundry)

In 1977, Goodman Machine and Foundry was divided into four manufacturing divisions, each with a separate plant and product line, and three marketing divisions, each representing a separate distribution channel but with some overlap in the product lines (Exhibit 1). David Goodman, eldest son of the founder and 62 years of age, was the president and treasurer; Abraham Goodman, second son of the founder and 58 years old, was the vice president of marketing; Sidney Goodman II, grandson of the founder and 32 years old, was the director of dealer sales; and Doris Goodman-Bethea, granddaughter of the founder and approximately 30 years old, was the assistant treasurer. The vice president of manufacturing was Charles O'Connor, the only nonmember of the family to be an officer and director of the company. Both Sidney Goodman II and Doris Goodman-Bethea

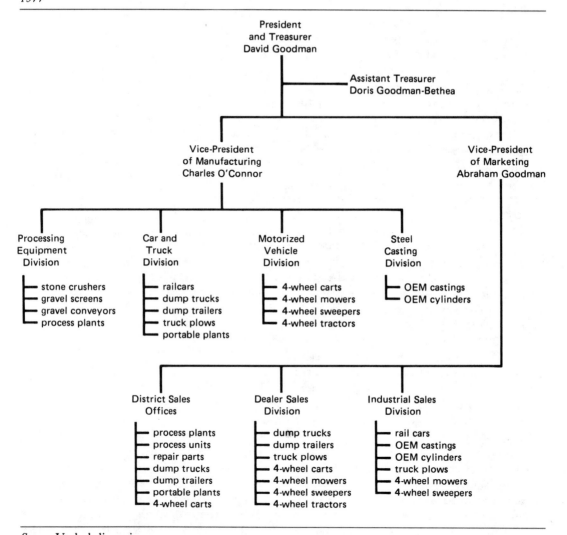

Source: Verbal discussions.

were graduates of the M.B.A. program at the University of Michigan.

Overall company sales of the four manufacturing divisions had been approximately static since 1970, while company profits after taxes had fallen nearly 50%. Despite the declining profits, the financial position of the firm remained exceedingly secure, as shown in Exhibits 2 and 3.

Doris Goodman-Bethea, the assistant treasurer of the company, explained the unusual balance sheet in the following terms:

> Our balance sheet is really an antiquarian's delight; it is typical of the old family companies that never paid much in dividends and never had much trouble in business. In our case, it is the result of my grandfather, who was active in the com-

Exhibit 2 *Income statements (000's omitted) for the Goodman Machine and Foundry Corporation, 1955–1976*

	1955	1960	1965	1970	1972	1974	1976
Processing Equipment Division	8,810	9,410	12,500	16,980	18,360	16,400	16,790
Car & Truck Division	5,900	10,080	9,910	9,440	9,460	9,330	10,310
Motor Division	3,650	6,190	9,240	9,920	9,170	9,660	10,660
Casting Division	2,040	2,810	3,110	5,700	5,940	5,160	7,360
Total sales revenues	20,400	28,490	34,760	42,040	42,930	40,550	45,120
Labor costs	5,350	7,600	9,110	10,920	11,430	11,120	12,420
Material costs	7,270	9,700	12,070	14,650	15,010	14,590	16,150
Mfg. overhead	3,060	4,170	4,980	6,190	6,430	6,590	7,030
Total direct costs	15,680	21,470	26,160	31,760	32,870	32,300	35,600
Contribution margin	4,720	7,020	8,600	10,280	10,060	8,250	9,520
Marketing expenses	1,220	1,760	2,220	2,530	2,840	3,110	3,210
Engineering expenses	470	650	870	1,070	1,130	1,210	1,260
General and administrative expenses	1,140	1,380	2,030	2,570	2,650	2,730	2,840
Total fixed expenses	2,830	3,790	5,120	6,170	6,620	7,050	7,310
Profit before taxes	1,890	3,230	3,480	4,110	3,440	1,200	2,210
Income taxes	290	1,590	1,710	2,050	1,710	590	1,100
Profit after taxes	970	1,650	1,770	2,060	1,730	610	1,110

Source: Company records; some figures have been disguised.

pany until 1971. Poor old gramps insisted that every bill be paid when received, whether it had discount terms or not, except for the taxes, and he would stretch those out every year, and pay penalties and interest, and get mad. Every time we earned a few dollars, he would set up a funded reserve; we had reserves for floods and depressions and fires, and every other disaster he could imagine. When I became treasurer last year—I'm really the assistant treasurer but Dad lets me make the financial decisions—I converted the money from funded reserves to use in the company. We have too much invested in the company, but there is no way to get it out without paying horrendous taxes. The problem is that the company is making money now as a financial institution, not as a manufacturing concern. If this company had a 1:1 debt/equity ratio last year, and paid interest on the debt, we would have been barely above break-even; and, if we had not had those huge inventories in a period of rising prices, we would have lost money. My father is right: we've got to start planning what we are going to do with $36 million in assets. (Statement of Doris Goodman-Bethea)

The balance of the case consists of descriptions of the product lines, market segments, and marketing policies for each of the divisions of the company, and discussions of the alternative product areas that were under consideration by the executives in the firm.

Processing Equipment Division. The major products of the Goodman Machine and Foundry Corporation were the conveyors, screens, and crushers used in aggregate processing plants throughout the Midwest, and manufactured by the Processing Equipment

Exhibit 3 *Balance sheet (000's omitted) for the Goodman Machine and Foundry Corporation, December 31, 1976*

Cash	$ 340	Accounts payable	$ 520
Accounts receivable	3,990	Accrued salaries and wages	340
Marketable securities	2,120	Federal income taxes due	830
Inventory—raw materials	8,420	State income taxes due	70
Inventory—in process	2,610	Property taxes due	440
Inventory—finished goods	3,780	Dividend payable	40
Prepaid expenses	410		
Cash value of life insurance	240	Total current liabilities	2,240
Total current assets	21,910	Deferred taxes, on income	110
Land, at cost	430	Preferred stock (first preference)	40
Buildings, less depreciation $3,470	1,650	Preferred stock (second preference)	45
Equipment, less depreciation $7,110	11,370	Common stock	130
Investments in other firms	1,420	Allocated reserves	12,000
Total fixed assets	14,870	Earned surplus	22,215
		Total equity	34,430
Total current and fixed assets	$36,780	Total liabilities and equity	$36,780

Source: Company records; some figures have been disguised.

Division. Aggregate processing refers to the mining, sizing, and cleaning of sand, gravel, and crushed rock for use in construction as mortar, cement, concrete, asphalt, and general foundation or drainage fill. Aggregate is the largest single commodity produced within the United States, at 2 billion tons each year. Despite this volume of national output, three times that of the coal industry and 11 times that of domestic iron ore, aggregate production remains a local industry, with 12,000 individual plants that are primarily small, family-owned concerns, because of the high transportation costs and low margins of the products.

Aggregate production is simple, and the processing equipment is not sophisticated. An alluvial fan of sand, washed down from nearby hills, or an esker or moraine of gravel, deposited by glacial action, is located and leased, and the topsoil is stripped away, exposing the bank of material. A power shovel or a heavy tractor with a front-end scoop is then used to load the sand, gravel, and rocks onto a conveyor belt running to a storage bin, from which the unsorted mixture is metered onto a bar screen. The bar screen is a vibrating unit with heavy steel bars spaced at 4 in. on the upper deck and at 2 in. on the middle deck, with a solid steel plate for the bottom deck. Rocks 4 in. and over in diameter are sent to a jaw crusher, which operates as the name implies, with hydraulically operated steel jaws that crush the larger pieces. Rocks between 2 in. and 4 in. in diameter are sent to a cone crusher, which is much faster, but limited in the overall size of the material it can handle. A cone crusher consists of a heavy steel cone turning slowly inside an equally heavy outer cone; the two cones are 5 in. apart at the inner periphery but only 1½ in. apart on the outer edge, so that medium-sized rocks, fed into the center opening, are pulled into the narrowing space between the rotating cones and fractured by the combined pressure and shearing forces.

The sand and gravel that falls through the 2 in. spaces on the middle deck of the bar screen, and the split and fractured material from the jaw crusher and the cone crusher, are carried on a second conveyor to another elevated storage bin, from which the mixture is metered onto a wire screen. The wire screen is also a vibrating unit; it has five decks with heavy wire coverings, each with successively smaller openings. Material 2 to 1¼ in. in diameter is sorted on the top screen for sale as crushed stone; material 1¼ to ¾ in. is sorted on the second deck for coarse gravel; material ¾ to ⅜ in. is sorted for fine gravel; ⅜ to ⅛ in. for coarse sand, and under ⅛ in. for fine sand. Each size of aggregate has a specific use in construction for mortar, cement, concrete, or fill. The sized aggregate is usually washed to remove dust and dirt, and is then carried by separate conveyors to open piles, where it is stored, ready for sale. The complete installation is the very familiar gravel pit, with sloping conveyors, elevated storage bins, and open storage.

Goodman Machine and Foundry made the belt conveyors, bar screens, jaw crushers, cone crushers, wire screens, and vibrating washers needed to process bank-run (random-sized) aggregate, and they sold this equipment both as replacements for individual units at a customer's plant, and as a complete processing system, ready for installation at a customer's location. Sales of the processing equipment, which had expanded rapidly after World War II, during the period of extensive highway

construction in the Midwest, reached a peak in 1972, and had declined about 10% since that time, despite the continually rising price level. The percentage of sales representing complete plants had fallen sharply, while replacement units and, especially, replacement parts were increasing (Exhibit 4).

Abraham Goodman, marketing vice president of Goodman Machine and Foundry, ascribed the changed pattern of processing equipment sales to changed conditions in the aggregate processing industry. He described this industry as mature, with limited growth potential on a national basis, depressed regionally by the completion of the Interstate Highway System in the Midwest, and confused by environmental regulations and requirements imposed by federal, state, and local governments (Exhibit 5).

Mr. Goodman explained verbally some of the changes occurring in the aggregate processing industry that were not apparent in the gross production figures:

> The major use of crushed rock is for the drainage fill and foundation layer of highways. For the Interstate System, crushed rock 24 in. thick by 15 ft wide had to be spread and compacted for each lane, and then the concrete or asphalt was laid on top of the stone, in a strip 12 in. thick. Eighty percent by weight of the portland concrete, and 94% by weight of the asphaltic concrete (black-top), was washed sand and gravel. Highway construction used a lot of aggregate.

Exhibit 4 *Sales of aggregate processing equipment (000's omitted) by the Goodman Machine and Foundry Corporation, 1955–1976*

	1955	1960	1965	1970	1972	1974	1976
Complete plants	$4,730	$4,690	$ 6,910	$ 9,310	$ 9,460	$ 7,140	$ 5,350
Replacement units	3,340	3,610	3,830	4,920	5,640	5,870	6,700
Replacement parts	740	1,110	1,760	2,750	3,290	3,390	4,740
Total sales	$8,810	$9,410	$12,500	$16,980	$18,360	$16,400	$16,790

Source: Company records.

Exhibit 5 *Production of sand, gravel, and crushed rock (tons, 000,000's omitted) within the United States, 1955–1976*

	1955	1960	1965	1970	1972	1974	1976
Processed sand	208	227	284	321	328	323	285
Processed gravel	382	415	517	484	462	404	384
Processed rock	577	683	911	1,102	1,030	875	777
Unprocessed material	50	72	118	277	349	494	523
	1,217	1,397	1,830	2,184	2,169	2,096	1,969

Source: Company records.

Highway construction is not coming to an end, but it will continue at a reduced level since the money just isn't available any longer. Costs of construction doubled over the past eight years, but the highway funds are down due to lower gas tax receipts, so there will be less construction. To a certain extent, large public works such as flood control dams and sewer projects, and big public utility contracts for nuclear and coal-fired generating plants, will supplant the highways, but they will not use as much crushed stone, sand, and gravel. We anticipate fairly steady sales of 2 billion tons of aggregate per year for the next 10 years; in essence, aggregate production has become a nongrowth industry. This is particularly true in the Midwest, where the large highway projects have been completed, and where few big public works are being planned.

Aggregate producers in this area are being troubled by environmental regulations, imposed by federal, state, and local governments. For years, sand and gravel plants did not accept their social responsibilities to be good neighbors in the communities in which they operated; they often had excessive dust, generally were eyesores, with rusty equipment and unpainted buildings, and seldom reclaimed the land. Now they need local permits to operate, must meet state standards on the discharged water from the washing operation, and have to get federal approval of reclamation plans. Regulation of rock quarries and gravel pits was changed in 1978 from the Department of Labor to the Bureau of Mines, and they are now subject to the same environmental controls as strip mining.

The result of the decreased aggregate production and the increased governmental controls has been lowered sales of new processing plants. Processors may invest in sheet metal shields to control the dust and settling basins to clean the water, but they won't buy many complete new plants. Fortunately, rock is an abrasive material, and our customers will continue to buy replacement units and replacement parts, but overall we expect our processing equipment sales to remain at about $16,000,000 per year, and perhaps tail off to about $14,000,000. (Statement of Abraham Goodman)

Goodman Machine and Foundry sold aggregate processing equipment through sales offices located in Lansing, Michigan; Columbus, Ohio; and Terre Haute, Indiana (Exhibit 6). Company officials felt that they dominated the three-state area, with approximately 60% market share; they also recognized that their sales volume and market share declined rapidly as they moved outside this central area. Total industry sales were not available from any reporting agency, but Abraham Goodman had been able to estimate processing equipment sales in each state by multiplying the aggregate production in that state, reported to the U.S. Department of

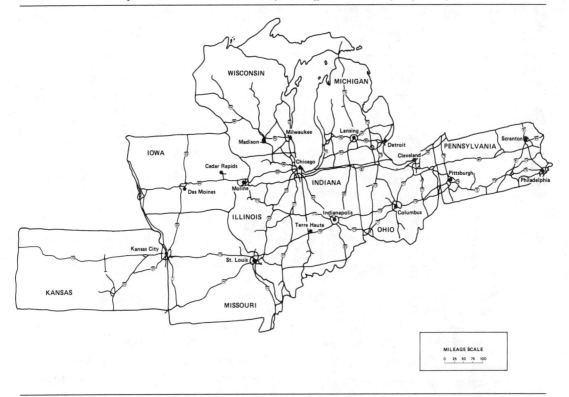

the Interior and published annually in an industry survey, by a constant factor for the machinery sales (Exhibit 7).

Abraham Goodman explained that the aggregate equipment industry did not attract the large manufacturers of construction machinery, such as Clark Equipment, Caterpillar Tractor, or Barber-Greene, and that most of the competitors in the industry were small to medium-sized firms that normally served a two- to three-state area, and that often produced processing equipment for other, related industries. He listed the following firms as the major competitors in the midwestern region:

Scranton Iron Works, Scranton, Pennsylvania, with a product line of aggregate processing machinery and anthracite coal mining equipment, and with total sales of approximately $30 million per year.

Ironi Brothers of Moline, Illinois, with estimated annual sales of $18 million primarily in aggregate processing equipment.

Missouri Shovel Company of Kansas City, Missouri, which made power shovels, cranes, and draglines in the smaller sizes that were used in commercial construction and aggregate mining, in addition to the aggregate processing equipment, with sales about $28 million per year.

Mathews Company of Cedar Rapids, Iowa, which manufactured specialized farm machinery and aggregate processing conveyors; they purchased the vibrating screens and rock crushers from the Ironi

347

Exhibit 7 *Estimates of aggregate processing equipment sales, per state in the midwestern region, sales of Goodman Machine and Foundry, and the resultant market share*

	Company sales (1976)	Industry sales (1976)	Market share (%) (1976)	Location of major competitor in area
New York	$ 647,000	$ 9,600,000	6.7	Scranton, Pa.
Pennsylvania	430,000	10,400,000	4.1	Scranton, Pa.
Ohio	3,778,000	6,300,000	59.9	Lansing, Michigan
Michigan	5,103,000	7,100,000	71.8	Lansing, Michigan
Indiana	2,472,000	4,900,000	50.4	Lansing, Michigan
Illinois	1,601,000	6,900,000	23.2	Moline, Illinois
Wisconsin	1,963,000	7,300,000	26.8	Moline, Illinois
Missouri	322,000	10,400,000	3.1	Kansas City, Mo.
Iowa	14,000	4,600,000	0.3	Cedar Rapids, Iowa
Minnesota	460,000	7,000,000	6.6	Kansas City, Mo.
Total, 10 states	$16,790,000	$74,500,000	22.5	

Source: Company records; figures by state for company sales and industry estimates have been disguised.

Brothers in Moline, Illinois, in order to be able to provide a complete plant. Sales of the Mathews Company were thought to be about $4 million per year.

The machine designs and operating specifications were approximately similar for the aggregate processing equipment produced by all the firms in the midwestern area, and so competition centered on personal relationships between the buyer and company personnel in the sales of new systems; on simplicity of installation in the sales of replacement units (a new Goodman cone crusher would fit into a system originally sold by Goodman without modification; a new Scranton or Ironi crusher would require some changes to the machine or some reworking of the system); and on prompt service in the sales of replacement parts (an inner cone casting for a Goodman crusher could be machined to fit on either the Scranton or Ironi units). Recently, some price competition had started, as the sales volume declined for all the manufacturers in the area, and the contribution margins, which had once been considered "excellent" by the

Goodmans, were now felt to be "disappointing" (Exhibit 8).

The conveyors, screens, crushers, and washers for aggregate processing were manufactured by Goodman Machine and Foundry in a modern (1965) 15,000-square-foot plant in Lansing, Michigan. Production of the aggregate processing equipment was basically a steel fabricating process, with sheet and plate steel cut, formed, and welded to make the frames for the conveyors, screens, and washers. Motors and power transmission units were mounted on the frames, and structural steel was cut and welded for the supports. Both the jaw crushers and the cone crushers were made from heavy steel castings, supplied at cost by the Casting Division. (All intercompany transfers in Goodman Machine and Foundry were at direct cost.) Machining requirements in the Process Equipment Division were limited, and generally with low tolerances, although the steel castings for the crushers were turned in a large boring mill for precision bearing mounts. Company executives felt that potential economies of scale

Exhibit 8 *Sales revenues, production costs, and contribution margins (000's omitted) for aggregate processing equipment manufactured by Goodman Machine and Foundry, 1955–1976*

	1955	1960	1965	1970	1972	1974	1976
Sales revenues	$8,810	$9,410	$12,500	$16,980	$18,360	$16,400	$16,790
Direct labor	2,260	2,480	3,240	4,460	4,900	4,540	4,890
Direct material	3,010	3,160	4,250	5,720	6,240	5,820	6,190
Manufacturing overhead	1,410	1,640	2,050	2,780	2,910	2,840	2,970
Total direct costs	6,680	7,280	9,540	12,960	14,050	13,200	14,050
Product margin	$2,130	$2,130	$2,960	$4,020	$4,310	$3,200	$3,740
Product margin (%)	0.241	0.226	0.236	0.237	0.234	0.195	0.163

Source: Company records.

were limited in job shop (1 to 5 units at a time) processing of this nature; they estimated that overall costs might decline by 6 to 8% if the volume doubled.

> Our material costs would not decline with increases in production since we buy direct from a mill now, or direct from an import broker, and these are the most economical ways to buy steel in volume. Our labor costs and manufacturing overhead might go down 15 to 20% with more repetitive work, and more jigs and fixtures to position the steel parts for forming and welding, but this is not production line type work, and we never would get production line type savings. (Statement of Gerald O'Connor)

Car and Truck Division. Company officials had considered changing the name of this division since it had become a misnomer, and did mislead some government regulators into thinking of automobiles and auto parts; the company had been required for four years to fill out EPA forms dealing with gasoline mileage and motor emissions. The cars, as described previously, were not automobiles; they were the hydraulically operated side-dumping rail units, while the trucks were not motorized, but were hydraulically operated rear-dumping road units. The road units

were produced in three models: a dump body without axles for mounting on the chassis of a heavy-duty truck; a dump trailer with dual axles on the rear and a "fifth wheel" on the front for mounting on a heavy-duty tractor; and a dump follower with single axles on the front and rear for attachment to a tractor–trailer combination. The dump trailers and followers were used primarily to haul aggregate from a processing plant to a construction site; the dump trucks were used for general construction work, often to haul excavated material from a construction site.

In addition to the rail cars and the dump trucks, trailers, and followers, the Car and Truck Division produced grading plows for mounting on a truck and for use in spreading aggregate in road construction, and snow plows. The grading plows were seldom used after 1965; most road contractors and many communities now owned special road graders that operated much faster, and provided more precise control, in spreading crushed stone and gravel. The sales of snow plows, which also were hydraulically operated and truck-mounted, varied with the severity of the winter weather in the Midwest.

The final product of the Car and Truck Division had been introduced in 1971, and had grown rapidly in sales volume. This new product was a portable aggregate processing plant that consisted of a loading conveyor, bar screen, cone crusher, wire screen, and separation conveyors, mounted on a low triple-axle trailer frame and powered by a 200-hp diesel engine. The advantage of the portable processor was that it could be brought to a small gravel pit, close to a construction site, and thus reduce the transportation costs for the sand, gravel, and crushed stone. The disadvantage of the unit was that it could not process rocks 4 in. and over in diameter since there was no room on the trailer for a jaw crusher, and that it produced excessive dust since there usually was not enough water for washing the sorted aggregate at a temporary site. The problem with the oversize rocks was not considered to be serious, since this material could often be sold as "field stone" for use in building decorative walls, fireplaces, etc. The problem with the dust was considered to be serious, since the process relied on air separation rather than water separation to remove the dirt, and the dust could therefore not be controlled by covering the screens and conveyors.

Despite the environmental problem of the portable processor, sales of this unit had expanded rapidly, and had overcome the sales declines since 1970 in dump bodies, dump trailers, and truck plows (Exhibit 9).

Abraham Goodman explained that ap-

proximately 70% of the dump bodies and dump trailers were sold directly to aggregate processors in the Midwest through the three district sales offices, and 30% were sold to general contractors through auto and truck sales agencies. The sales to aggregate processors had declined each year since 1970, affected by the slowdown in spending for highway construction (Exhibit 10).

I'm not certain that I gave you specific figures in discussing the impact of federal highway legislation on the sales of our aggregate processing equipment, and of course the same legislation affects the sales of our dump trucks and trailers. Spending in dollar terms was down 9.9% this year (1976) and 10.3% last year (1975), while highway construction costs went up about 20.0% over that same period, so that the overall result is that there is only about 60.0% as much actual construction now as there was in 1974. I wish that I could say that this situation was going to change in the near future, but I don't expect that it will. The Highway Fund is based on gasoline tax receipts, and the gradually increasing gas mileage requirements on new cars (18 mpg in 1978 to 27.5 mpg in 1985) will gradually decrease the gas tax receipts, despite more cars and more driving. Also, some of the Highway Fund will be spent on public transportation; there is growing contro-

Exhibit 9 *Sales (000's omitted) of the Car and Truck Division of the Goodman Machine and Foundry Corporation, 1955–1976*

	1955	1960	1965	1970	1972	1974	1976
Dump rail cars	$1,710	$ 1,050	$ 840	$ 370	$ 350	$ 510	$ 670
Dump bodies	3,770	4,180	5,970	4,860	3,660	2,980	2,170
Dump trailers	—	4,280	4,160	3,870	3,110	2,450	2,440
Truck plows	420	570	650	340	390	350	430
Portable processors	—	—	—	—	1,950	3,050	4,600
Total sales	$5,900	$10,080	$9,910	$9,440	$9,460	$9,330	$10,310

Source: Company records.

Exhibit 10 *New construction expenditures (000,000's omitted) within the United States, 1972–1982*

	1972	1974	1976	1978	1980	1982
Residential building	$59,727	$50,376	$60,520	$ 80,900	$ 85,000	$ 90,000
Industrial building	6,243	7,902	7,183	7,700	8,400	10,200
Commercial building	15,453	15,944	12,756	14,700	15,500	17,800
Religious and educational	1,651	1,573	1,616	1,700	1,800	1,800
Hospital and institutional	3,152	3,201	3,396	3,200	3,000	3,000
Farm nonresidential	2,003	2,529	2,502	2,700	3,100	3,600
Miscellaneous nonresidential	1,085	1,017	1,140	1,200	1,200	1,400
Total private construction	89,314	82,542	89,113	112,100	118,000	127,800
Telephone and telegraph	3,967	4,279	3,777	4,300	5,100	5,900
Railroad construction	422	575	555	700	1,200	1,900
Electric light and power	8,778	9,246	11,177	12,800	14,400	17,300
Gas and petroleum pipelines	2,018	2,524	3,887	3,100	3,400	3,700
Total utility construction	15,179	16,624	19,396	20,900	24,100	28,800
Public housing	1,547	1,772	1,709	2,100	2,800	3,700
Public health	1,002	1,238	1,786	1,700	1,500	1,200
Public education	6,647	7,310	7,760	6,300	6,300	5,400
Public highways	10,505	12,065	9,777	9,300	9,200	9,200
Military facilities	1,166	1,185	1,520	1,500	1,500	1,200
Conservation and flood containment	2,313	2,741	3,751	3,900	3,700	3,500
Sewer systems	1,954	2,681	5,286	5,400	6,100	6,700
Water systems	3,572	4,671	4,496	4,900	5,200	5,500
Total public construction	28,706	33,663	36,085	35,100	36,300	36,400

Source: Company records.

versy and debate in each session of Congress over that issue.

There will be plenty of other construction work—residential, commercial, and public—but these other projects don't use as much aggregate as the highways. We look, as I explained previously, for aggregate production to remain at about 2 billion tons per year, which hopefully will support our truck and trailer sales at current levels. (Statement of Abraham Goodman)

Precise figures for industry sales of dump truck bodies, dump trailers, and truck plows within the Midwestern area were not available, but Abraham Goodman was able to adjust national totals for these products by the

ratio of heavy truck sales in the 10-state area to heavy truck sales nationally (Exhibit 11). He recognized that this adjustment was inexact, but he felt that it provided an adequate figure to estimate market share. Industry sales of the side dumping rail car were reported both nationally and by the purchasing railroad; Mr. Goodman felt that the company competed on this product in the section of the United States that was east of the Missouri and Mississippi rivers, and computed industry sales on that basis.

Mr. Goodman said that two companies manufactured side-dumping rail cars in the eastern United States, while one firm had a dominant position, and apparently 100% market share, in the western section of the

Exhibit 11 *Estimates of rail car, dump body, dump trailer, and snow plow sales in the Midwest, sales of Goodman Machine and Foundry, and the resultant market share*

	Company sales (1976)	Industry sales (1976)	Market share (%) (1976)	Major competitor
Dump rail cars	$ 670,000	$ 1,900,000	35.2	Difco & Ortner
Dump bodies	2,170,000	17,000,000	12.7	Heil & Peabody
Dump trailers	2,440,000	9,000,000	27.1	Heil & Fruehauf
Snow plows	430,000	1,000,000	43.0	Heil Corp.
Portable processor	4,600,000	4,600,000	100.0	—
	$10,310,000	$33,500,000	30.7	—

Source: Company records; figures by product for company sales and industry estimates have been disguised.

country. All companies in the industry sold directly to the railroads, and competed on the basis of car specifications and bid prices.

Difco, Incorporated, of Findlay, Ohio, with annual sales of $10 million in side-dump rail cars, side-dump mine cars, and electric mine locomotives. Difco advertised their rail cars heavily in trade journals, hobby magazines (*Model Railroader* and *Trains*), and financial newspapers (*The Wall Street Journal*); many people in the industry felt that this advertising was ineffectual, but the company did have the largest market share, at 45%.

Ortner Car Company of Cincinnati, Ohio, with annual sales of $130 million in new and rebuilt box cars, gondola cars, hopper cars, and side-dump cars.

Pacific Car and Foundry of Bellevue, Washington, with annual sales of $1,420 million in logging trucks and equipment, rail cars, and mining machinery.

Mr. Goodman also explained that some dump bodies were made by small, local truck body shops, but that those firms generally specialized in building aluminum and wood delivery truck frames, and did not have the heavy steel-forming equipment or hydraulic expertise needed for dump trucks. Most dump bodies were made by two national concerns who sold the formed steel body, together with attachment castings and hydraulic equipment, to a truck dealer for mounting on the customer's chassis. Dump trailers and followers were made by the dump body manufacturers and by Fruehauf:

Heil Corporation of Milwaukee, Wisconsin, with annual sales of $101 million in dump bodies, dump trailers, snow plows, and refuse collection equipment.

Peabody International (formerly Peabody-Galion) of Stamford, Connecticut, with sales of $391 million in dump bodies, dump trailers, solid waste systems, construction equipment, steel castings, and forgings.

Fruehauf Incorporated of Detroit, Michigan, with sales of $1,801 million in freight trailers, flat trailers, dump trailers, cargo containers, and auto parts.

The steel thicknesses, welding joints, and hydraulic cylinders and valves were very nearly similar for the dump bodies, dump trailers, and dump followers produced by all the firms in the industry, and consequently competition centered on obtaining exclusive sales agreements with the truck dealers. Heil Corporation had a dominant position with midwestern dealers since they offered a standard 18% discount plus an additional discount depending on the quantity sold in a single year, plus a further discount for exceeding the prior year's sales. The total discount for very large Heil dealers could reach 28%. Goodman Machine and Foundry was able to compete for dealers only by offering a straight 24% discount, some of which was rebated to the final customer.

Snow plows were sold directly to the state and community highway departments, usually by a bidding procedure. A highway department would announce the number of plows they expected to buy, and invite bids. Price, of course, was important, but the mounting attachments for different-type trucks and installation assistance were also considered in awarding the contract. Goodman Machine and Foundry made only large truck-mounted "highway" plows with hydraulic controls, much larger and more complex than the smaller "driveway" units made by local welding shops and sold through auto supply stores to garages and service stations; competition for the large plows was primarily with the Heil Corporation. The Heil Corporation submitted bids through their local dealers, and thus offered installation assistance and gained community support when price was not the only consideration.

The portable processor for aggregate material was sold through the three district sales offices and, to a limited extent, through construction equipment dealers outside the Midwest. For the first 3 years, this unit encountered no competition. In late 1976, however, Allis Chalmers, a large company headquartered in West Allis, Wisconsin, with annual sales of $1,537 million in electrical motors and controls, diesel engines, construction equipment, mining machinery, and farm tractors, announced a similar unit with large full-color advertisements in the major construction and mining journals. For years, Allis Chalmers had manufactured crushing and screening equipment for coal and mineral mining operations, but they had not previously sold to the

aggregate processing industry, perhaps due to the small size and local nature of the 12,000 firms within this industry. Mr. Goodman was concerned that the entry of Allis Chalmers might herald a consolidation of the smaller companies, and a reorientation of the aggregate processing industry around large contractors.

> The aggregate processing industry has always been dominated by small, local operators, but there is no essential reason why this has to be true, and we may see some consolidation in the future. Before, any small-town businessman who could get a bank loan to buy the screens and crushers, and who had a friend with a few trucks, could build the conveyors and operate a gravel pit fairly inexpensively. Now the capital requirements are larger, and the reclamation laws are more stringent, and the days of easy growth are over. We may see a shakeout of the small operator, and the entry of the big construction firms. It makes sense for a big contractor to save money by leasing a site and processing aggregate locally, but this will be hard on the small companies. The problem is that we may have helped in that change by building the first portable processor which is ideal for a big construction firm that does not want to be tied down to a specific community or a single site. (Statement of Abraham Goodman)

Margins on the dump bodies and dump trailers had declined since 1970, pushed downward by price competition that had developed following the sales peaks that had been reached in 1965 (Exhibit 12). Margins on the portable processors were reported to be low due to the new nature of the product, and to the lack of established procedures and efficient methods in building the units, which did pack a complete system of conveying, crushing, and screening machinery and power transmission equipment in a very limited space. Company officials expected the mar-

Exhibit 12 *Sales revenues, production costs, and contribution margins (000's omitted) for the Car and Truck Division of Goodman Machine and Foundry, 1955–1976*

	1955	1960	1965	1970	1972	1974	1976
Sales revenues	$5,900	$10,080	$9,910	$9,440	$9,460	$9,330	$10,310
Direct labor	1,610	2,810	2,730	2,640	2,710	2,720	2,960
Direct material	2,180	3,180	3,170	3,480	3,560	3,540	3,940
Manufacturing overhead	800	1,230	1,140	1,220	1,270	1,320	1,140
Total direct costs	4,590	7,220	7,040	7,340	7,540	7,580	8,310
Product margin	$1,310	$ 2,860	$2,870	$2,100	$1,920	$1,750	$ 2,000
Product margin (%)	0.222	0.283	0.289	0.222	0.202	0.187	0.193

Source: Company records; some cost figures have been disguised.

gins on the portable processors to increase to 25% to 30% as the manufacturing process became more routine.

Manufacturing of the rail cars, dump bodies, dump trailers, snow plows, and portable processors was performed in a 30,000-square-foot plant, with an interior rail siding, heavy overhead cranes, exterior steel storage, and large assembly areas. The Car and Truck Division building was on the north side of the company's foundry, while the Processing Equipment Division's plant was on the south side; steel castings were used extensively by both divisions, and were moved inexpensively from the foundry to the machining or assembly areas by forklift trucks.

Manufacturing of the products of the Car and Truck Division was, as in the case of the aggregate processing equipment, basically a steel fabricating process, with steel plate cut, formed, welded, and combined with steel castings to make the dump bodies, dump trailers, rail cars, etc. Limited machining was required, except for drilling the trailer frames for mounting the road axles and hydraulic cylinders, and for boring and milling the two bolters (main cross members) on the car frames for mounting the rail trucks and axles. Unlike the aggregate processing equipment, however, company officials felt that

there were opportunities for economies of scale in producing the dump bodies and dump trailers.

> We make four models of the dump body, and three sizes in the trailer and follower, but the parts are essentially similar, and there is little variation in assembly. Cutting, forming, and welding these units are repetitive jobs, and you can keep your costs per unit down with volume, if you invest in automated equipment. I think that our problems in this division center on the loss of volume. Heil Corporation probably produces five times as many dump bodies as we do, and I'll wager that their costs are 20% less than ours. They give part of that 20% away in dealer discounts and customer rebates to keep their volume up and pay for the automated equipment. We have got to spend some money for faster welding equipment and automatic positioning fixtures to cut our costs, if we want to stay in this business. (Statement of Gerald O'Connor)

Motor Division. The Motor Division was started in 1950 to manufacture a motorized four-wheel construction cart. This cart was a small unit, with a 35-hp industrial gasoline engine, hydraulic drive to all four wheels, a hydraulic scraper blade on the front, and a hydraulic dump body on the rear; it was originally used to spread aggregate and place concrete at construction sites.

> Before World War II, all crushed stone, sand, and gravel used in the foundation and drainage fill for a building was spread by hand. A truck would dump the aggregate on the site, and laborers with shovels would load the material into wheelbarrows, wheel each load to the foundation, and spread it evenly, ready for compaction. Concrete was placed the same way: a transit-mix truck would back up to the site, and load wheelbarrows that would be pushed along scaffolding to the pouring forms. To speed up the process, and reduce the cost, numerous companies made motorized wheelbarrows, which were exactly what you would expect, about twice the size of the usual wheelbarrow and with a little motor on the front wheel. We made the construction cart, which was more a little dump truck than a big wheelbarrow, and it caught on almost immediately. (Statement of Abraham Goodman)

The company sold about $5,000,000 of construction carts annually from 1950 to 1965, but sales began to decline in that year as front-end loaders (large tractors with a hydraulically operated scoop or bucket on the front) were used to spread aggregate, and as concrete pumps (accordion pumps with no moving parts in contact with the abrasive materials) were used to place concrete. Fortunately, the four-wheel cart design had been adapted for use as a commercial lawn mower and commercial sweeper in the 1960s, and the sales of these units continued to expand throughout the 1970s. The commercial lawn mower had a 62-in. mowing "deck," with four staggered 20-in. rotary blades in a flat steel housing, and was used in mowing golf courses, city parks, and the verges of airports and highways. Since power to the rotary blades was transmitted hydraulically, with a high-speed hydraulic motor on each blade shaft, the mowing deck could be articulated

(hinged) to follow the contours of the land; this feature made the Goodman unit the only rotary mower available that could cut more than a 42-in. swathe, and the rotary design enabled the machine to pick up the grass clippings, dead leaves, and general lawn debris. Most commercial lawn mowers were small tractors that pulled a gang of reel mowers; the individual reel mowers could also follow the contours of the land, but they were unable to pick up the clippings or leaves, and they could not cut tall grass or stalky weeds.

The commercial sweepers had a 48-in. sweeping "deck," with four staggered 16-in. rotary brushes encased in a steel housing, and a vacuum attachment to pick up dust, dirt, papers, etc. The sweeping deck was also articulated, and the unit was used to sweep parking lots at shopping centers, commercial garages, and public areas. Both the sweeper and the mower had hydraulic steering, in addition to hydraulic power transmission, and the hydraulic steering gave very good control and a very small turning radius; those features were considered to be valuable in operation, for mowing or sweeping around obstacles.

> We have the reputation of making the Cadillac of commercial mowers and sweepers, and that is due to our hydraulic drive. We don't have a transmission and drive shaft, with universals and differentials for the wheels, and pulleys and V-belts for the accessories; instead, we have a gear box to give four speeds forward and one in reverse driving a hydraulic gear pump, with reversible hydraulic gear motors on each wheel. We have four-wheel drive, while the other commercial lawn mowers and sweepers have only two-wheel drive, so that they get stuck much more easily, and tear up the grass on the golf course or park much more readily. We have a hydraulic vane pump for the steering and the accessories, which gives us much greater flexibility in design, and much greater safety and reliability in

operation. There are no V-belts or open gears on our machines. Hydraulic power transmission is more expensive than belting and gearing, but some people seem willing to pay for the safety and reliability. (Statement of Abraham Goodman)

In 1970, Sidney Goodman II joined the company as a salesman in the dealer sales division; he convinced his father and uncle that winter to partially redesign the commercial mower with a 48-in. mowing deck for lawns and leaves, and a 48-in. hydraulic plow for snow. The new unit was called the Goodman Estate Tractor; it was advertised in *Better Homes and Gardens* and other consumer magazines, and was sold through garden supply houses in the affluent suburbs of large cities. Sales of the Estate Tractor were nearly $4 million in 1976; overall, sales gains in the commercial mowers and sweepers and the residential Estate Tractor had more than overcome sales declines in the construction carts (Exhibit 13).

Abraham Goodman felt that it was difficult to establish reliable market share information for many of the products in the Motor Division since these units appeared to compete against other products that performed essentially the same function, but in different ways. For example, there was only one other manufacturer of a four-wheel construction cart in the eastern United States, but there were numerous manufacturers of front-end loaders and concrete pumps which could either spread aggregate for foundations or place concrete in forms. Mr. Goodman estimated market shares of the company against closely similar products from reports of the field salesmen (Exhibit 14).

Mr. Goodman felt that the market for construction carts would probably continue to decline, and then stabilize at approximately $1,500,000 annually within the next 3 years due to the competition with other types of construction equipment that has been described previously. There was only one other competitor with a closely equivalent product:

Barber-Greene, Inc. of Aurora, Illinois, with annual sales of $160 million in asphalt paving machines, mixing plants, and general construction equipment.

The Goodman commercial lawn mowers competed against small farm-type (two-wheel) tractors with a sickle-bar mowing attachment, often used for airport and highway maintenance, and against large garden (four-wheel) tractors either pulling a gang of reel mowers that could cut up to an 84-in. swathe or using a rotary mower with a 42-in. swathe. Farm tractors were termed "two-wheel" since they had two large driving wheels 60 in. and larger in diameter to provide power and traction in plowing, harrowing, and cultivating; lawn and garden tractors were termed "four-wheel" since they had two small driving wheels 24 to 30 in. in diameter

Exhibit 13 *Sales (000's omitted) of the Motor Division of the Goodman Machine and Foundry Corporation, 1955–1976*

	1955	1960	1965	1970	1972	1974	1976
Construction carts	$3,650	$5,010	$4,840	$3,210	$2,640	$2,170	$ 1,680
Commercial lawn mowers	—	1,180	2,460	3,190	2,860	2,440	2,750
Commercial sweepers	—	—	1,940	2,770	2,150	2,180	2,480
Estate tractors	—	—	—	750	1,520	2,870	3,750
Total sales	$3,650	$6,190	$9,240	$9,920	$9,170	$9,660	$10,660

Source: Company records.

Exhibit 14 *Estimates of construction cart, commercial lawn mower, commercial sweep, and residential mower sales in the eastern United States, sales of Goodman Machine and Foundry, and the resultant market share*

	Company sales (1976)	Industry sales (1976)	Market share (%) (1976)	Major competitors
Construction carts	$ 1,680,000	$ 3,000,000	56.0	Barber-Greene
Commercial lawn mowers	2,750,000	18,000,000	15.3	Toro and Gravely
Commercial sweepers	2,480,000	10,000,000	24.8	Tennant and Elgin
Estate tractors	3,750,000	15,000,000	25.0	Deere and imports
	$10,660,000	$46,000,000	23.2	

Source: Company records; figures by product for company sales and industry estimates have been disguised.

and two small steering wheels of approximately equal size. Neither the small farm tractors or the large garden units (termed "park" tractors by their manufacturers) were directly equivalent to the Goodman commercial lawn mower with four-wheel hydraulic drive, 62-in. mowing deck, and grass/leaf pickup, but the "park" tractors were less expensive and were used extensively by city parks and private golf courses. There were two manufacturers of "park" tractors equipped for commercial mowing; both sold directly to cities and towns through a bidding procedure, and indirectly to private concerns through construction equipment dealers.

Toro Company of Minneapolis, Minnesota, with annual sales of $101 million in lawn mowers, lawn tractors, lawn watering systems, and commercial mowing machines.

Clark-Gravely of Clemmon, North Carolina, with sales of $86 million in lawn mowers, lawn tractors, garden tractors, and garden cultivators.

The Goodman commercial sweeper competed against three generally equivalent units. Commercial self-propelled sweepers could be divided into three types or sizes: small units, often powered by storage batteries, for use in factories and large public institutions; medium-sized machines for use primarily in

parking lots and shopping centers; and large road sweepers for city streets and airport runways. All three types had rotary brushes, vacuum pickup, and self-dumping storage. The Goodman sweeper was considered a medium-sized machine, for parking lots and shopping centers, and held a 24.8% market share against three other firms:

Tennant Company of Minneapolis, Minnesota, with annual sales of $69 million in small and medium-sized sweepers and machinery paints and lacquers.

Elgin Sweeper Company of Elgin, Illinois, with sales of $18 million in medium-sized and larger sweepers for parking lots and roadways.

Wayne Sweeper Division of FMC Corporation with sales estimated at $60 million in small, medium-size, and large sweepers.

The Estate Tractor manufactured by Goodman Machine and Foundry appeared to fit in a niche in the market not clearly dominated in 1976 by any firm. Lawn, garden, and small farm equipment could be divided into six size and price classes (Exhibit 15); all classes had extensive competition, except for the 30-hp units similar to those produced by Goodman. This segment did have an entry from John Deere, a large farm machinery manufacturer, and was attracting imports

357

Exhibit 15 *Size and price classifications of lawn, garden, and small farm machinery, 1976*

	Walking lawn mowers (4-wheel)	Riding lawn mowers (4-wheel)	Lawn tractors (4-wheel)	Garden tractors (4-wheel)	Estate tractors (4-wheel)	Small farm tractors (2-wheel)
	3–5 hp	5–8 hp	8–15 hp	15–25 hp	28–35 hp	35+ hp
	22-in. mower	30-in. mower	36-in. mower	42-in. mower	48-in. mower	60-in. sickle-bar
	—	—	30-in. snow plow	36-in. snow plow	48-in. snow plow	60-in. snow plow
	—	—	—	6-in. dirt plow	8-in. dirt plow	12-in. dirt plow
	$160 ea	$600 ea	$1,400 ea	$2,800 ea	$5,500 ea	$8,000 ea
	$208 mm/yr	$108 mm/yr	$127 mm/yr	$54 mm/yr	$15 mm/yr	$93 mm/yr
	Jacobsen	Jacobsen	Jacobsen	Deere	Deere	Deere
	Toro	Toro	Toro	Toro	Goodman	I-H
	Murray	WheelHorse	WheelHorse	WheelHorse	—	Ford
	AMF	AMF	Gravely	Gravely	—	Minneapolis
	Sears	Sears	Sears	Sears	—	Massey-Ferguson

Note: Costs per unit are median retail prices with applicable accessories; sales volume per year are disguised estimates. "Dirt" plows are for tilling.

Source: Conversations with company officials.

Exhibit 16 *Sales revenues of farm tractors and farm machinery in the United States, 1968–1976, and changes in the nature of American farms*

	1968	1970	1972	1974	1976
Sales of farm tractors (millions)	$1,391	$1,311	$1,766	$1,823	$2,451
Sales of farm machinery (millions)	$2,334	$2,888	$3,231	$4,960	$4,930
Acres per farm in the U.S.	330	343	361	396	392
Number of farmers (millions)	3.2	2.9	2.8	2.7	2.5

Source: Company records.

from Japan, where a four-wheel tractor of that size was often used in agriculture in preference to the larger and more powerful two-wheel American-style machines.

John Deere (28 hp) and Goodman Machine and Foundry (35 hp) produced the only lawn, garden, and small farm tractors manufactured within that size range in the United States. It was felt by company officials that John Deere (1976 sales of $3,604 million) might not emphasize lawn and garden equipment in their product promotion and sales planning due to the high growth rate of the American farm machinery market, and the changing patterns in American farming, which required larger and more powerful machinery (Exhibit 16).

Goodman Machine and Foundry was the only manufacturer of an "estate" tractor that sold through lawn and garden supply stores. John Deere, of course, distributed their lawn and garden equipment through their extensive system of franchised dealers, while the Japanese tractors of this size range were sold through independent farm machinery dealers and some import automobile agencies.

Margins on the products of the Motor Division had remained "adequate" in the opinion of company officials; they felt that these financial results were due to their quality position in the commercial lawn mower and sweeper markets, their product leadership in the estate tractor, and the lack of price competition in a growing industry (Exhibit 17).

Manufacturing of the construction carts,

Exhibit 17 *Sales revenues, production costs, and contribution margins (000's omitted) for the Motor Division of Goodman Machine and Foundry, 1955–1976*

	1955	1960	1965	1970	1972	1974	1976
Sales revenues	$3,650	$6,190	$9,240	$9,920	$9,170	$9,660	$10,660
Direct labor	870	1,470	2,070	2,150	2,010	2,140	2,310
Direct material	1,590	2,690	3,950	4,200	3,870	4,010	4,370
Manufacturing overhead	430	740	1,110	1,120	1,090	1,140	1,250
Total direct costs	2,890	4,900	7,130	7,470	6,970	7,290	7,930
Product margin	$ 760	$1,290	$2,110	$2,450	$2,200	$2,370	$ 2,730
Product margin (%)	0.208	0.208	0.228	0.246	0.239	0.245	0.256

Source: Company records; some cost figures have been disguised.

commercial lawn mowers, commercial sweepers, and estate tractors was basically an assembly operation, with purchased gasoline engines, gearbox transmissions, and hydraulic pumps, valves, motors, and cylinders mounted on a steel frame produced by the Car and Truck Division, and then completed with purchased axles, wheels, and tires and manufactured fiberglass body parts such as the hood and fenders. Assembly was performed in a modern (1970) 20,000-square-foot plant located in Jackson, Michigan, 38 miles south of Lansing. Company officials believed that there were few economies of scale in batch (100 to 250 units at a time) assembly of this nature; they estimated that overall costs might decline by 5 to 7% if the volume doubled.

> We have a semi-line assembly process now, and run each of the products down that line in fairly efficient batches. Our material costs won't go down since we are buying on an OEM [Original Equipment Manufacturer] discount now from the engine manufacturers and the hydraulic component firms, and they are larger than we are, and won't negotiate on price. We could save on labor with more specialization and more automated equipment, but labor is only 29% of our cost now. The real savings come when you can start to make your own motors and power transmission equipment on fully automated machines, but that would require 10 times our current volume. The problem is that the Japanese are well over that volume now; they could offer some very attractive prices on 35-hp four-wheel tractors, if they decide to go after that market. (Statement of Gerald O'Connor)

Steel Casting Division. The foundry, which had been a basic part of the operations of the company since 1895, was organized as a separate division since some steel castings, and some hydraulic cylinders made by the division, were sold to outside customers. Most of the products, however, were transferred within the company at cost. The foundry cast steel bolters (frame cross members), bearing plates (body pivot points), and mounting hardware (cylinder attachment points) for the side-dump rail cars; steel body parts, bearing plates, and mounting hardware for the dump trucks and dump trailers; mowing decks and sweeper decks for the motorized units; and end caps and pistons for the hydraulic cylinders. The foundry also included an extensive machine shop, to finish the steel castings, and to hone (grind the internal surface) the steel tubing used for the hydraulic cylinders.

> It may seem strange to you that a steel foundry is in the business of making hydraulic cylinders, but it was quite natural when the company started since it was impossible to buy heavy hydraulic equipment then. Now, we can make the cylinders cheaper than we can buy them. A big hydraulic cylinder is really a simple part to manufacture: we cast and machine the end caps and the piston, and we buy and hone the tubing, and then assemble the pieces. We only make heavy-duty "mill-type" cylinders 8 in. in diameter and over for our own use, and we sell these large cylinders to other machinery manufacturers. (Statement of Gerald O'Connor)

Sales of the Steel Casting Division had been growing at approximately 6% per year since 1965, primarily through sales of the large hydraulic cylinders; these were special-order items, not produced by many of the usual hydraulic component manufacturers, and were used on heavy construction equipment and some production machinery. Steel castings were also produced to order for machinery manufacturers in the Midwest (Exhibit 18).

Company officials were hesitant to provide definite figures regarding probable market shares for either the steel castings or the hy-

Exhibit 18 *Sales (000's omitted) of the Steel Casting Division of the Goodman Machine and Foundry Corporation, 1955–1976*

	1955	1960	1965	1970	1972	1974	1976
Steel castings	$1,860	$2,070	$2,090	$2,780	$2,920	$2,420	$3,210
Hydraulic cylinders	180	740	1,020	2,920	3,020	2,740	4,140
Total sales	$2,040	$2,810	$3,110	$5,700	$5,940	$5,160	$7,360

Source: Company records.

draulic cylinders since both were considered to be specialized products in poorly defined markets. Steel castings, for example, were described as ranging in size from small parts, weighing only a few ounces, made in the millions for the automobile industry, to huge units, weighing more than 10 tons, cast individually for steam turbine housings or nuclear pressure vessels. The castings sold by Goodman Machine and Foundry generally weighed 50 to 250 pounds, and were cast in multiple molds by a nonautomated process; it was felt that many other companies had equivalent capabilities, and that the Steel Casting Division probably produced fewer than 5% of the total steel castings sold within the midwestern region.

The hydraulic cylinders manufactured by Goodman Machine and Foundry were sold in a more clearly defined market segment. Numerous companies produced standard cylinders up to 6 in. in diameter, and special-order cylinders up to 8 in.; only three firms offered hydraulic cylinders over 8 in. in diameter, and it was felt that the Foundry Division was the largest of those three firms, manufacturing perhaps 40% of the large "mill-type" hydraulic cylinders in the Midwest.

> Almost every manufacturing company of any size in this area has a steel foundry, and many of them do contract work for outside firms. We are just one of 50 companies that could bid on providing steel castings in the medium size range. Our position in hydraulic cylinders is much better; most manufacturers of farm

equipment and construction machinery make their own cylinders, but few sell outside due to the need to supply engineering specifications and repair parts. If you want a hydraulic cylinder 12 in. in diameter and 8 ft long, we are one of the few places you can call to order one. (Statement of Abraham Goodman)

Both steel castings and hydraulic cylinders were sold directly to machinery manufacturing firms and truck assembly plants by the Industrial Sales Office, headquartered in Lansing, Michigan. Margins on these products varied with the economic cycle, owing to the occurrence of overcapacity and the start of price competition during the low portions of that cycle. 1974 had been a particularly poor year (Exhibit 19).

Summary. In the spring of 1977, members of the Board of Directors of Goodman Machine and Foundry were considering the adoption of portfolio planning methods in order to utilize the financial resources of the company in a more competitive manner. A consultant was invited to meet with the corporate executives, examine the four divisions, and assist in the start of strategic planning.

> You've had a hurried introduction to the family company, and to the members of our family, but I assume that you understand our operations fairly well because the businesses we are in are quite simple. Our problem is that the company has gotten two complex, our products have gotten too old, and our markets have gotten too crowded. We did not plan

Exhibit 19 *Sales revenues, production costs, and contribution margins (000's omitted) for the Steel Foundry Division of Goodman Machine and Foundry, 1955–1976*

	1955	1960	1965	1970	1972	1974	1976
Sales revenues	$2,040	$2,810	$3,110	$5,700	$5,940	$5,160	$7,360
Direct labor	610	840	1,070	1,670	1,810	1,720	2,260
Direct material	490	670	700	1,250	1,340	1,220	1,650
Manufacturing overhead	420	560	680	1,070	1,160	1,290	1,400
Total direct costs	1,520	2,070	2,450	3,990	4,280	4,230	5,310
Product margin	$ 520	$ 740	$ 660	$1,710	$1,660	$ 930	$2,050
Product margin (%)	0.225	0.263	0.212	0.298	0.279	0.180	0.278

Source: Company records; some cost figures have been disguised.

where we were going, and as a result we got into some low-growth, low-margin lines of business. We've got to plan where we're going much better in the future. (Statement of David Goodman, president of Goodman Machine and Foundry Corporation)

Class Assignment. Assume that you are the consultant employed by the board of directors of Goodman Machine and Foundry Corporation to help in the process of "planning where we're going," and that you have the information about the company contained in the case.

1. Divide the company into business units for strategic planning. Develop a number of alternative groupings, and be prepared to justify your recommendations on the proposed structure to the board of directors.
2. Evaluate each of the business units you have structured for strategic planning according to a set of criteria you believe to be

relevant. Be prepared to explain your evaluation with a matrix display showing the current positions of the business units.
3. Consider the range of strategic alternatives (product-market positions) that are open to the company. Be prepared to describe these alternatives in a logical fashion through the use of a decision diagram.
4. Evaluate each of the strategic alternatives (product-market positions) according to the set of criteria developed previously. It is impossible in a 20-page case to include complete information on all products and all markets that are open to the company. Where needed information is missing, indicate the form and probable source of the data.
5. Prepare an overall plan for the future of the company. Make assumptions about the missing data, and be prepared to explain your recommendations with a matrix display showing the proposed positions of the business units five years in the future.

Susan Shapiro

Susan Shapiro was a 1970 graduate of Smith College, where she had majored in chemistry, and a 1971 graduate of MIT with a Master of Science degree, also in chemistry, who came to the M.B.A. program at the University of Michigan after working for one year as a research chemist at Parke-Davis and Company in Ann Arbor.

> One of the reasons I came back to get an M.B.A. was that the scientists at Parke-Davis, which is a large drug company with an advanced research division in Ann Arbor, simply weren't ready for women in the laboratory. It got to the stage that there was going to be an armed confrontation the next time some male told me to get his coffee or write up his experiment. Chemistry labs aren't great places for confrontations; there's so much expensive equipment around that can get broken, so I decided that I ought to get either a Ph.D. or an M.B.A. I chose the M.B.A. because it only took two years, and because most companies seemed to accept women more fully in an administrative role than in a technical capacity. (Statement of Susan Shapiro)

Susan graduated from Michigan in the lower half of her M.B.A. class. This was partially because she felt that some of her courses, such as marketing, were exploitive; partially because she refused to work or study on Saturdays due to religious convictions, but primarily because she returned to the second year of the M.B.A. program seven weeks late.

> I spent the summer of 1973 in Israel, working on a kibbutz in the north, near the Lebanon border. The Yom Kippur War started that fall. I don't think that a good Jew ought to leave Israel just because a war starts, so I stayed, and worked as a volunteer in a military hospital until the need was past. Then I came back. Some of my professors understood, but most of them wanted me to make up the missed work, and there wasn't enough time in the rest of the term. I got three C's that term, and that really pulled my grade average down. (Statement of Susan Shapiro)

Susan enjoyed the quantitative aspects of finance and economics, and she interviewed with a number of firms for a position as a financial analyst. She found, however, that many of these companies evidently considered the grade-point average strongly in their selection procedures for positions in corporate finance, and she received very few invitations for plant visits. 1974 was a recession year which, of course, reduced the employment opportunities for all the members of her class, but she felt that her job search was more difficult than that of many of her friends, and she thought that this was due to her low class standing.

> By 1974, companies had gotten over hiring women despite their sex, and were beginning to hire women because of it. So, I don't think being a woman hurt me. And, I hope being a Jew didn't hurt me, but you never know. My grades were good, except for the third term, and for the marketing course. I explained the reason to all the interviewers, and they would nod their heads, but evidently thay did not understand. Two of the interviewers asked if I planned to take vacations in Israel after I started working; what business is that of theirs? (Statement of Susan Shapiro)

Representatives of two large chemical companies came to Michigan near the end of the interview period; both of them were interested in Susan because of her undergraduate and graduate work in chemistry, and because of her experience with Parke-Davis. Both companies invited her for plant visits; both extended job offers; and Susan accepted the offer from a company with corporate offices in New York City, close to her family and friends. She started the training program with that company in July 1974.

> We spent about three weeks in New York City, being told about the structure of the company and the uses of the products, and then they took us down to Baton Rouge, to look at a chemical plant. You realize that most of the M.B.A.'s who go to work for a chemical company have very little knowledge of chemistry. There were 20 of us who started in the training program, and the others generally had undergraduate degrees in engineering or economics. I don't know what you learn by looking at a chemical plant, but they flew us down South, put us up at a Holiday Inn, and took us on a tour of their plant the next day. (Statement of Susan Shapiro)

During the plant tour, the management trainees were taken into a drying room where an intermediate chemical product was being washed with benzene and then dried. The cake was dumped in a rotating screen and sprayed with benzene, which was then partially recovered by a vacuum box under the screen, but much of the solvent evaporated within the room, and the atmosphere was heavy with benzene fumes.

> Benzene is a known carcinogen; there is a direct, statistically valid correlation between benzene and leukemia and birth defects. The federal standard is 10 parts per million, and a lab director would get upset if you let the concentration get near 100 parts for more than a few minutes, but in that drying room it was over 1,-000. The air was humid with the vapor, and the eyes of the men who were working in the area were watering. I was glad to get out, and we were in the drying room only about 5 minutes.

> I told the foreman who was showing us around—he was a big, burly man with probably 30 years' experience—that the conditions in the room were dangerous to the health of the men working there, but he told me, "Lady, don't worry about it. That is a sign-on job [a job to which newly hired employees are assigned until they build up their seniority so that they can transfer to more desirable work]; we've all done it, and it hasn't hurt any of us."

> That night, back at the motel, I went up to the Director of Personnel, who was in charge of the training program, and told him about the situation. He was more polite than the foreman, but he said the same thing. "Susan, you can't change the company in the first month. Wait awhile; understand the problems, but don't be a troublemaker right at the start."

> I don't want to lose this job, but I don't want to keep it at the expense of those men getting leukemia, or their children having birth defects. What should I do? (Statement of Susan Shapiro)

Class Assignment. Make a specific recommendation to Susan Shapiro regarding her future course of action.

Industrial Ceramics PMPD at U.S. Chemical Industries

The Strategic Planning Committee at U.S. Chemical Industries consisted of seven persons: the president, three executive vice presidents (for domestic operations, foreign operations, and finance), two senior vice presidents (for engineering services and governmental relations), and the director of long-range planning. The committee met monthly for a detailed review of the strategy of at least one of the business units (termed "PMPDs" within the company, for product–market–process divisions) and annually for a comparative evaluation of all the units. None of the meetings were perfunctory: hard questions were asked and explicit answers were required even at the annual evaluation sessions, but the monthly reviews were considered to be inquisitions by the unit managers scheduled for appearance. John Sakowski, PMPD manager for industrial ceramics, was scheduled to make a presentation to the May 7 meeting of the Strategic Planning Committee.

The strategic planning process at U.S. Chemical Industries had been developed by the president, Dr. Richard Shortliffe, immediately after his appointment as the chief executive officer in 1976. U.S. Chemical Industries was an older firm, with a traditional orientation toward inorganic chemistry and with established products in the additive chemicals and processing equipment used by steel, glass, and paint manufacturers. Steel, glass, and paint are mature products, with limited growth and narrow margins, and U.S. Chemical had suffered for years by associa-

This case centers on an ethical problem; consequently, the names of all individuals, the characteristics of all products, and the locations and principal activities of all firms have been disguised.

tion with these basic industries. The previous president, who served from 1962 to 1975, had attempted to diversify out of the industrial markets into consumer goods and petrochemicals, but the oil embargo of 1973 and the economic recession of 1974 had resulted in moderate losses and a reduced dividend. Dr. Shortliffe, a very successful economic consultant and governmental administrator, had been appointed president in 1975 with the assignment from the board of directors to restore corporate profitability and the annual dividend. Dr. Shortliffe made a statement at the time of his appointment that was quoted extensively in the financial press, and distributed widely to company employees.

> Our mission is not to be a major supplier to the basic industries of the eastern United States and western Europe. Our mission is to be *the* major supplier. No one who is number 2 ever wins in sports, in business, or in life. Our mission is to be number 1, in market position, in economic return, and in social responsibility. We have an obligation to our stockholders, to our employees, to our customers, and to ourselves to become the dominant firm in industrial chemicals and processing equipment. (Statement of Dr. Richard Shortliffe)

Dr. Shortliffe spent the next two years working, with the assistance of a newly-recruited executive team and a corporate-level consulting firm, on the development of a strategic planning process for U.S. Chemicals. All the products were examined for market share, product quality, customer perception, and technological advantage; all of the markets were studied for annual growth, overall size, historical margins, and competi-

Exhibit 1

Market strength of Ceramics PMPD	Weight	Measure	Value
Annual growth	0.45	3.80	1.71
Overall size	0.15	1.70	0.25
Historical margins	0.20	3.10	0.62
Competitive intensity	0.20	2.90	0.58
			3.16

tive intensity; all the processes were evaluated for productive capacity, input efficiency, volume sensitivity, and improvement potential. The factors for each of these dimensions were weighted by a subjective percentage, measured on a cardinal scale, and then totaled to obtain an approximate value for product strength, market strength, and process strength (Exhibit 1).

Because of the subjective nature of the weights that were applied to each of the factors, and to the inexact method of measurements along the cardinal scales, the summary figures for the product strength, market strength, and process strength were not used directly to compare the various product–market–process divisions. That is, a PMPD that measured 3.16 on market strength, as in the illustration, was not automatically considered to be "better," or more likely to receive funding for further growth, than a PMPD that measured 3.00 or 3.15. Instead, all the 34 product–market–process divisions in the company were grouped along each dimension, with one-third above average, one-third average, and one-third below average, and then were visually displayed on a three-dimensional matrix, as shown.

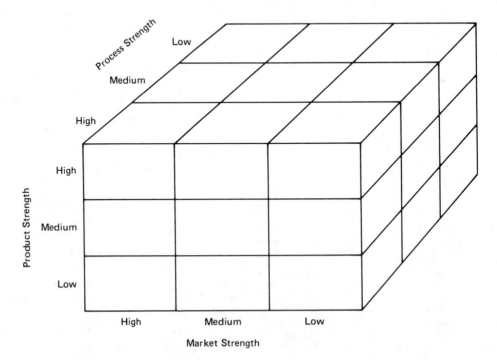

The U.S. Chemical "Planning Cube" was cast in translucent plastic, with shades of green (for high in each of the dimensions), yellow (medium), and blue (low) in a sculpture that was 8 ft high, mounted in the lobby of the U.S. Chemical Industries office building in Pittsburgh. Photographs of the sculpture were printed on the first page of the 1977 annual report of the company, and on the covers of the two most widely read business magazines. Models of the sculpture, 15 in. high, were displayed in the offices of all the senior executives. Colors of the sculpture became part of the jargon of the company; a manager scheduled for promotion might be praised as being "green all the way through," while a rejected marketing concept would be called a "triple blue."

The purpose of the strategic planning process, shorn of the colored sculpture and the corporate jargon, was to identify the present position and future potential of each of the 34 product groups within the company, and then to manage those groups to improve the long-term competitive position of the firm. Product groups that were low on two of the three dimensions, including market strength, were to be divested since it was felt that these divisions did not warrant further investment of corporate funds or management time. Product groups that had a medium ranking on two of the three dimensions, again including market strength, were to be harvested (used as sources of cash) either immediately by permitting high product strengths or process strengths to fall back to a medium position, or eventually by investing small amounts now to bring a low product or process position up to the medium ranking. A "harvested" PMPD would generate a positive cash flow since the medium position ensured adequate sales volume and profit margins, while only minimal investments were needed in product development, market promotion, or process expansion to maintain the volume and margins.

The funds generated by divesting the low-ranked PMPDs and harvesting the medium-ranked divisions were to be invested in the remaining product groups that had a high position on at least one dimension, generally market strength. Market strength was felt to be the predominant dimension, since this measure summarized values for annual growth, overall volume, competitive intensity, etc., and consequently was thought to be an external constraint, not a decision variable. The product and process positions could be adjusted, by internal decisions on investments, to match the external opportunity of the market.

We have developed a method of strategic planning that makes it possible for us to direct our product strengths and process strengths toward market opportunities. U.S. Chemical Industries is a diversified firm, yet we can now manage the individual divisions for the benefit of the corporation as a whole. This ability represents a major breakthrough in managerial economics and investment analysis, derived from the Boston Consulting Group and McKinsey two-dimensional matrices, yet extended into multidimensional management. Multidimensional management will be the management science of the future; with the computer we can go beyond the visual limitations of two dimensions and the conceptual limitations of three dimensions, and work with four, eight, or even 12 dimensions. We now have an ability to manage large, multiproduct, and multifunction organizations. (Statement of Dr. Richard Shortliffe)

The Industrial Ceramics PMPD at U.S. Chemical Industries produced molded and cast ceramic materials that were used in industrial applications for abrasion resistance, chemical durability, and thermal insulation. Ceramics are nonmetallic and inorganic materials that can be molded, pressed, or cast in a semifluid form, and then fired. The ultra-high temperatures in firing bring both chemical and physical changes that provide a tight "sintered" bond between grains in the microstructure of the material, and produce a smooth finish, a low coefficient of friction, extreme hardness, and high chemical and thermal resistance. Three divisions at U.S. Chemical Industries produced ceramic materials. The Thermal Ceramics PMPD manufactured standard silica firebricks for the lining of blast furnaces, Bessemer converters, and basic oxygen retorts in the steel industry; this was a high-volume, low-margin business that was scheduled for either disinvestment or harvest under the new planning procedures. The Electronic Ceramics PMPD produced semifinished silicon and germanium oxide parts for microelectronic components such as capacitors and transducers, while the Industrial Ceramics PMPD made very precise boron and silicon carbide castings for chemically inert catalyst carriers in petroleum refining and for abrasion and thermal resistant machine parts for the steel, paint, and paper industries. Nozzles and pipes for the sandblasting systems used to clean castings and remove scale from ingots, valves for the converting furnaces used to blow oxygen through molten steel, and bearings for the ladles that transported these very hot loads were examples of applications in the steel industry. The pressure rolls used to grind pigments and ores in the paint industry were fitted with sleeves of ceramic material, while all parts in contact with the Foudranier wire (high-speed screen upon which pulp fibers are formed and pressed) on a paper machine were made with ceramic castings. The number of applications for industrial ceramics was limited, and each new usage generally required special designs and experimentation, but the benefits could be substantial due to the extreme hardness and durability of the material.

The market for industrial ceramics within both the United States and western Europe was small, with a total volume of approximately $75 million in 1978. The growth, however, was steady at 15% per year and the margins historically had been excellent, with a pretax return on sales of 16% and a return on invested capital of 28%. The strategic planners in the company had ranked the market strength of the Industrial Ceramics PMPD fourth among all 34 divisions of the firm, due to the continued growth and high margins.

The product position of the Industrial Ceramics PMPD within the overall market was considered to be adequate, but certainly not dominant. U.S. Chemical Industries competed against Carborundum and Norton in the United States (both were manufacturers of aluminum carbide grinding wheels and silicon oxide abrasives, and both had expanded into industrial and electronic ceramics), and against Henkle and Hoechst in western Europe (both were very large companies with products and systems in inorganic as well as organic chemicals). It was felt that the Industrial Ceramics PMPD had approximately 25% of the market in the United States, after Carborundum with 40% and Norton with 35%, and that they held no more than a 10% share in Europe. John Sakowski, manager of the Industrial Ceramics division, had recommended investments of over $1,500,000 per year in laboratory development and institutional advertising to improve both the product quality and the customer's perception of that quality, and had expanded earlier marketing expenditures by an equivalent amount for direct sales engineers to discover new applications, prepare special designs, and supervise experimental trials, but the market share had not improved markedly since those investments and expenditures had started in 1976.

The process position of the Industrial Ceramics PMPD was recognized to be poor.

Production was divided between two plants, with few economies of scale and low experience-curve effects (the experience curve is a concept popularized by the Boston Consulting Group, and states that variable costs decline at a constant percentage with each doubling of the cumulative production volume; this results in an exponential curve of variable unit costs versus cumulative unit volume, and suggests that the leader in market share will eventually achieve a dominant cost position).

The oldest plant was located in Scranton, Pennsylvania, a depressed area in the northeastern section of the state that had originally been dependent upon anthracite coal mining and basic steel production, and that now suffered from underemployment and underinvestment. Production of industrial ceramics was a labor-intensive process, due to the need to carefully remove the pressed and molded parts from the dies while they were still friable, and accurately place them on trays for heat-treating, and the Scranton plant was one of the largest factories in the area, employing 175 women and 20 men. The workers were unionized, and militant; they received wage rates which were considered to be high by the personnel department at U.S. Chemical Industries, and they were not hesitant to strike for increased wages and benefits during contract negotiations. The buildings were old, although the equipment was modern; portions of the structure dated back to the start of firebrick production in the 1890s, and there was an abandoned pit on the property that had been the source of the silica clay. The high-temperature furnaces for heat treating had never been equipped for pollution control, and the operation of those furnaces had become the subject of continual disagreement and conflict between the Air Quality Control Board of the state and the Government Relations office in the company. Despite these problems, productivity at the plant remained satisfactory,

and total costs were not considered excessive by industry standards.

The more modern plant was located in Brownsville, Texas, on the southern Gulf Coast, close to the Mexican border. It had been built in 1968 to produce beads of ceramic material, for use as catalyst carriers in the petroleum refineries of the South Central states, but it was soon recognized that the other industrial ceramic parts were light in weight relative to their value, and consequently could be easily shipped considerable distances, so that the production of many of the ceramic nozzles, pipes, valves, and bearings had been transferred to this area. The work force was not unionized, consisting largely of Spanish-speaking immigrants, and air pollution regulations were not enforced, although the furnaces were equipped with partially effective control devices. Productivity at Brownsville was high, and the costs were lower than at Scranton; further, it was recognized that these costs could be even lower with increases in volume since the workers appeared willing to accept improved systems and better standards.

John Sakowski knew that the director of long-range planning, Myra Rossen, was going to recommend to the Strategic Planning Committee that all production of industrial ceramic materials be concentrated at Brownsville, and that the Scranton plant be closed.

> Her argument will be very simple. We haven't been able to gain market share, despite continual investments in product design and market development. So we should start to prepare the division for harvest, and the way you do that is to get a low-cost productive position, and then when you want to you can cut back on product investments and market expenditures and just sit there and watch the cash roll in. Right now we're ranked as a yellow–green–blue (medium on product strengths, high on market strengths, and

low on production strengths); she'll have 20 charts at the meeting to show that we ought to be a yellow–green–yellow, and ought to serve as a source of corporate cash.

I know that she's going to do this because one of her assistants told me. Myra is supposed to work with the PMPD managers in developing acceptable strategies, but all she does is to circulate assumptions about future economic and social–political conditions that we have to use in our planning, and then she develops alternative strategies for her committee. She wants to be the next president, and she's going to get there by walking up the back of every PMPD manager in the company.

I could sidetrack Myra, by recommending myself that we close Scranton. That is what the person in Long-Range Planning wants me to do; it would make Myra look bad since she would have no alternative to propose. But I would hate to do that. I'm from the Scranton area; I know those women in the Scranton plant. Their average age is 45,

and their average length of service is 18 years. I went to Confirmation Class at their church, and I graduated from high school with their children. Sure, we can offer them a chance to move to Brownsville, but these are Slavokian and Polish women who have never been out of eastern Pennsylvania in their lives; they have no knowledge of what Brownsville is like, and they wouldn't like it if they went there. We're talking about cash flow versus human lives, and I know where Myra stands on that equation. My problem is that I'm not really certain where I stand. What do you think I ought to do? The meeting comes up in another 10 days. (Statement of John Sakowski)

Class Assignment. It should be possible to use ethical analysis as well as financial analysis in solving business problems. Consider the ethical issues that are involved at U.S. Chemical Industries, and attempt to portray each issue on an ethical dimension, with a scale of values. Then estimate your position on each of those scales.

Chapter 7

STRATEGIC DESIGN
AND MERGERS
OR ACQUISITIONS

The first three chapters of the text described the process of strategic design for a single product–market unit (typified by small business firms), for a single product–process unit (represented by the medium-sized product divisions of large corporations), and for a single-industry unit (illustrated by large basic processing companies). In each instance, the intent of the strategic design process was to select a long-term method of competition that would provide a competitive edge for the business unit. In each instance, also, the process of strategic design was an evaluation of alternative patterns of competition through comparison with environmental characteristics and trends, organizational assets and skills, and managerial values and attitudes, as shown in our familiar chart at the top of the next page.

This method of strategy formulation, however, is not directly applicable to the large multiple-industry firms that are now dominant within the economy, both domestically and internationally. As described in Chapter 6, the product divisions of these diversified firms, each usually assigned a specific product–market–process position in a given industry, and each generally responsible for the development of a strategy to improve that competitive position over time, have often tended to act as autonomous profit centers, and it has been difficult for the corporate management to combine the separate strategies of these individual business units into a consistent and effective pattern of competition for the corporation as a whole. The headquarters staff at a diversified firm could not critically review the proposed strategies of the product divisions since they had only a partial knowledge of each of the multiple products, markets, and processes represented within the company, and consequently were vulnerable to the optimistic forecasts and persuasive abilities of the divisional managers. The financial analysts at a diversified firm could not optimally allocate the limited capital to the product divisions since they had no means of adjusting for the inherently different levels of risk between industries, and were ignorant of the current characteristics and changing trends within each industry

371

Environmental characteristics
and trends

Economic

Technological

Social/political

Competitive

↓

Organizational mission or charter	Specific opportunities and risks within the industry	
↓	↓	Selected strategy, or method of competition
Corporate performance and position	Range of strategic alternatives open to the firm	
↑	↑	
Managerial values and attitudes	Specific strengths and weaknesses within the company	

↑

Money

Equipment

People

Market position

Organizational resources, or
assets and skills

---

that determine those levels of risk. The information needed for corporate-level strategic planning was located in the product divisions, and was too complex and too amorphous, and perhaps too necessary for continued divisional control, to be easily transmitted to corporate headquarters. Until the advent of the portfolio planning procedures, described in Chapter 6, corporate managers in multiple-industry firms were unable to effectively combine the diverse strategies of the autonomous product divisions into a consistent and effective pattern of competition for the total corporation.

The new portfolio planning procedures, essentially, are a means of coalescing and codifying the large amounts of information from the product divisions that are needed for corporate-level strategic planning in multiple-industry firms. All the product divisions, defined as business units with a given product or product line, a specific market or market segment, an existing distribution channel, adequate productive capacity, known competitors, and an ability to act independently within an industry through a clearly defined strategy, are evaluated on two dimensions. These dimensions, as described previously, are the attractiveness of the industry and the strength of the division within that industry. For one planning method, the attractiveness of the industry is measured on a multiple-factor scale that includes such inputs as the overall size of the market, the annual growth, historical profitability, competitive intensity, technological requirements, etc., with each factor measured on a cardinal scale of 1 to 5, weighted by percentage, and totaled to obtain an approximate value that can be compared between divisions. The strength of the division within that industry is also measured on a multiple-factor scale, with inputs such as the market share, share growth, product quality, brand reputation, etc., again scaled, weighted, and totaled. Because of the inexact nature of the measures, and the subjective nature of the weights, the summary figures for the attractiveness of the industry and the strength of the division are not used directly to evaluate each business unit. Instead, all strategic business units are grouped along each dimension, with one-third above average, one-third average, and one-third below average, and then visually displayed on a simple nine-cell matrix, as shown in the accompanying table.

Company Strength within the Industry

	Above average	Average	Below average
Above average	Invest	Invest	Retain
Average	Invest	Retain	Divest
Below average	Retain	Divest	Divest

Industry Attractiveness

A second method of measurement of the attractiveness of an industry and the strength of a product division within that industry, designed for strategic planning in multiple-industry firms, is based upon single-factor rather than multiple-factor scales. This method does permit precise measurements and does omit subjective weighting, but it requires acceptance of the assumption that a single statistic can serve as the surrogate for industry attractiveness, and that another single statistic can serve as the surrogate for the competitive position of the company within that industry. Advocates of this method claim that the growth rate of the market, in percentage terms, can be used as a summary figure for the attractiveness of the industry since high growth rates tend to be associated with high gross margins and low competitive pressures. Advocates also state that the share of the market, again expressed in percentage terms, can be used as a summary figure for the competitive position of the company within that industry since high market shares tend to be associated with low production, distribution, and promotion costs. The position of each business unit or product division within the company, once it has been measured for market share and market growth, can be visually portrayed upon a simple four-cell matrix, as shown in the illustration.

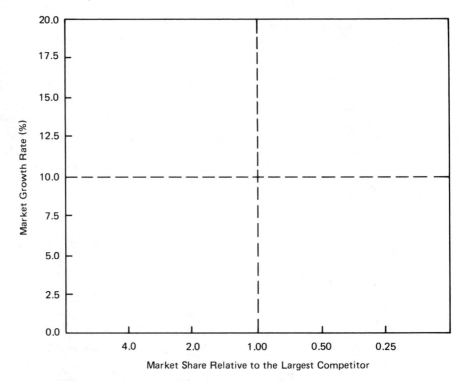

These corporate planning models do provide a means of evaluating the various product divisions within a multiple-industry firm by measuring competitive positions and cash flow characteristics, and they do enable the corporate managers of these companies to allocate resources among the divisions according to known policies, and to set objectives for the divisions using variable standards, but they do not permit the divisions to be tied together into an overall strategic posture that creates a competitive advantage for the firm. The detailed information on products, markets, processes, technologies, and competitors that is needed for meaningful strategic direction is still available only at the divisional level, and is not transmitted to the corporate executives in the summary figures and relative positions of the portfolio matrices. It may seem obvious at the corporate level that the company is concentrated in a number of mature industries with limited opportunities for future growth, or that the firm is active in a number of closely related industries without the joint efforts that are needed for reduced costs, but it is difficult to force major changes, rather than minor adjustments, in the strategies of the product divisions. The information needed to convince the product managers of the need for change is simply not available. Rather than attempting to force the managers of the existing product divisions into different competitive positions, it is organizationally simpler to propose completely new product–market units to fill these strategic gaps. These new units may result from internal development or external acquisition.

The internal development of a completely new competitive unit for a company, as opposed to simply designing a new product or service for an existing market, or locating a new market for an existing product or service, is outwardly attractive but financially expensive. It takes time, money, effort, and the assumption of risk to establish a new product–market unit that can be competitive within an industry. The internal development of new business units is termed, and probably correctly, "buying into" an industry since the process is so expensive. It often requires fewer resources to purchase an existing competitor within the industry than to establish a new competitive position; this has been particularly true over the past few years as high inflation rates have made the needed investments more costly, and as low capitalization ratios have made the proposed purchases less expensive. External acquisition, rather than internal development, has become the preferred method in adding new product–market units or new product–process units to the long-term competitive position of a firm.

External acquisition may be for the purpose of strengthening the competitive position of the acquiring company directly by adding a similar, related, or different product–market unit, or for the purpose of strengthening that competitive position indirectly by reducing the costs or expanding the operations of the acquired firm. There are numerous transfers between companies that can serve as the basis for an acquisition or merger:

Acquiring company		Acquired company
strengthen the competitive posture	←	similar product–market unit
expand the competitive posture	←	related product–market unit
reduce the competitive risk	←	different product–market unit
available distribution channels	→	reduce marketing costs
available manufacturing capacity	→	reduce manufacturing costs
available technological expertise	→	reduce developmental costs
available financial resources	→	expand marketing, manufacturing, or R&D
existing managerial systems	→	improve marketing, manufacturing, or R&D
ensure existing operations	←	surplus raw material supplies
integrate existing operations	←	usable transportations or distribution means

The intent of an external acquisition has to be to improve the financial performance and long-term competitive position of the joint organizations. There are, as shown above, numerous transfers that can accomplish that purpose, but for the analysis of a proposed acquisition, these various reasons can be summarized into two basic motives for merger:

1. *Improve the cash flow balance of the firm.* The cash flow balance of a multiple-industry firm, as measured by the portfolio matrices, serves as a surrogate for the potential growth and risk exposure of the company. A multiple-industry firm with the majority of its products in the low growth/high share quadrant of the matrix

is generating more cash than can effectively be reinvested, and is positioned in mature or maturing industries with limited opportunities for expansion and reduced potential for profits, but with relatively low market risks: the competitive positions of all firms within a mature industry change slowly, reducing the risk exposure. A multiple-industry firm with the majority of its products in the high growth/low share quadrant is using more cash than it can possibly generate, and is located in developing industries with extensive opportunities for growth, and increased potential for profit, but with high market risks: the competitive positions of firms within a developing industry change quickly, with new product designs, new promotional plans, or new production methods increasing the risk exposure. An acquisition to improve the cash flow balance of the firm will automatically improve the growth/support and risk/return ratios of the company.

2. *Improve the operating efficiencies of the firm.* The product–market–process position of a multiple-industry firm, as measured by competitive analysis, can normally be strengthened by expanding the product line, extending the market area, improving the distribution channels, or increasing the productive capacity, and an acquired company can help in one or all of those areas. Similarly, the product–market–process position of a single-industry division can be strengthened by the availability of greater financial resources, the application of improved managerial systems, or the use of established marketing methods and manufacturing facilities, and the acquiring company can help in one or all of those areas. An acquisition to improve the operating efficiencies of the firm does not automatically result in the combined use of the resources and capabilities of the two companies, but the potential for expanded operations, reduced costs, and improved performance is certainly present.

There are two basic reasons for considering an external acquisition, and there are two basic alternatives in making that acquisition: related or nonrelated diversification. A company can acquire another company with a related product–market–process position, generally for the purpose of improving the operating efficiencies of the joined firms, or it can acquire another company with a nonrelated product–market–process position, usually for the reason of improving the cash flow balance, growth potential, and risk exposure of the combined operations. A third possibility, that of acquiring another company with a similar product–market–process position, is normally prohibited by federal antitrust legislation due to the apparent decrease in competition within the industry, so that the basic alternatives remain related or nonrelated diversification:

1. *Nonrelated diversification.* Nonrelated acquisitions, or investments in new product divisions or business units without regard to the nature and degree of the relationships between those divisions and the units of the acquiring company, has often been recommended as a means of balancing business risks and evening corporate cash flows. Theoretically, this process can be shown to result in no lasting value to the stockholders, and to be impossible of accomplishment by the firm. For the stockholders, the argument is that it is as easy for an investor to arrange a diversified portfolio of the stocks of firms in many different industries as it is to purchase the stock of a diversified firm with investments in those differ-

ent industries. According to contemporary financial theory, which is based upon the concept of an efficient capital market with knowledgeable buyers and sellers acting to maximize their individual returns over time, the risk in any equity security is the sum of the systematic and unsystematic risks of the company. The systematic risk is the known level of risk associated with a given industry; all companies operating within that industry share that level of risk, weighted as to the degree of their participation in the industry, and then adjusted to their differences in capital structure. The systematic risk, since it is recognized by knowledgeable investors with rational expectations, is reflected in the prices of the securities. Unsystematic risk, which is not known by the investors and consequently not reflected in prices, is the level of risk associated with a single company. Stockholders can obviously reduce their exposure to unsystematic risk through diversification of their individual investments, so that diversification by the company adds no lasting value to the equity of the firm in an efficient capital market.

For the company, and particularly for the company whose management may not be totally committed to the efficient market hypothesis nor fully convinced of the rational expectations of their investors, the concept of locating and acquiring product divisions operating in countercyclical or counterseasonal industries, to balance the systematic risks and short-term cash flows, is outwardly attractive to consider, but actually difficult to accomplish. Truly countercyclical industries may not even exist; there are obviously some industries that tend to lead the business cycle (housing), and others that usually lag behind (machine tools), and there are some that are sensitive to interest rates (electrical utilities) and others that are nonsensitive (consumer electronics), but there are few that historically have had totally complementary business cycles. Even if products with complementary business cycles could be found, there would be no guarantee that the cycles observable in the past would be repeated in the future. Some products (lawn mowers and snow blowers) and some services (airline flights to Florida in the winter and to Europe in the summer) are obviously counterseasonal, but they tend to be related in other ways, often within the same industry. There are many reasons for a lawn mower manufacturer to make snow blowers (similar production processes, distribution channels, repair procedures, and financial needs) beyond the counterseasonal nature of the markets.

Stockholder returns in an efficient market and short-term cash flows on a cyclical or seasonal basis may not be valid reasons for nonrelated diversification, but the balancing of long-term cash movements, with the funds being transferred from static product–market positions in mature industries to dynamic situations in developing markets, does appear to provide a valid reason for these acquisitions. Nonrelating acquisitions, selected to balance the corporate cash flows, bring concurrent changes in growth potential and risk exposure that can improve the long-term competitive position of the firm.

2. *Related diversification.* Related acquisitions, or the investment in new product divisions or business units that are closely similar in product characteristics, market segments, distribution channels, production processes, etc., to the existing units of the parent company, can also improve the long-term competitive posi-

tion of a firm. This improvement is based upon the joint use of the combined resources of the acquiring company and the new division. The joint use of combined resources may be for the primary benefit of the existing firm through expansion of the product line, extension of the market area, assurance of the material supplies, or integration of the production and distribution processes, or it may be mainly for the benefit of the acquired company through use of the parent's engineering expertise, marketing ability, manufacturing capacity, financial resources, or managerial systems, but the benefits on both sides often remain more potential than actual due to the problems of achieving a synergistic relationship. Synergy, which is derived from a Greek term that means "working together," refers to the productive use of combined resources. An example of synergy would be using the same sales force to sell two different products to the same customers, or to sell the same product to two different markets. There is no question but that the concept of synergy is appealing; the problem is that the application often seems to be difficult, and the results disappointing. The difficulty probably comes from the fact that corporate resources, both physical assets and human capabilities, are not as transferable between business units as is commonly assumed. Production and distribution facilities, which were designed for one product, may require substantial change to add related products, or to serve related markets. Functional and technical managers, who are accustomed to the competitive conditions and economic structure of one industry, may find it awkward to operate efficiently in another industry, with totally different conditions and structure. It is very easy to assume, in acquisition analysis, that products or markets or industries are related, with similar customer needs, buyer behaviors, distributor activities, and supplier loyalties, but then to find, in diagnosing the causes of a subsequent failure, that the assumptions were incorrect.

Analysis of both related and nonrelated acquisitions requires projecting the cash flow balances, and the consequent risk/return and growth/stability ratios, of the combined companies, and understanding the potential for the joint use of the combined resources. The projection of cash flow balances, while not simple, is based on established procedures for the portfolio analysis of multiple-industry firms; each product division and possible acquisition is positioned on a four-cell matrix of market growth versus market share, or on a six-cell matrix of industry attractiveness versus company strengths. The construction of these matrices, and the methods of locating discrete business units upon them, have been described previously, and the description need not be repeated here. Understanding the potential for the joint use of combined assets and skills is not more complex, but it is less common, and the methods will be described. The critical decision, in looking at the opportunity to improve the operating efficiencies of a firm through the joint use of the combined resources resulting from a merger or acquisition, centers on the nature and degree of the relationships between the two companies. Companies with close relationships between the existing divisions and the proposed acquisitions, of course, have greater opportunities to improve their operating efficiencies. These relationships, as explained previously, are difficult to evaluate through casual or unstructured analysis, but they can be separated into a number of specific dimensions, such as product technologies or promotional policies, a scale can be established for the degree of relationship along each dimension, ranging from close to absent, and potential merger or acquisition candidates can be measured along each scale in a procedure similar to that used for the corporate planning models:

	Relationship					
	Close		Partial			Absent
	5	4	3	2	1	0
Product technologies						
Product characteristics						
Market segments						
Geographic areas						
Purchase patterns						
Customer motives						
Pricing levels						
Distribution channels						
Promotional means						
Process technologies						
Process characteristics						
Material requirements						
Material sources						
Job requirements						
Job standards						
Planning methods						
Scheduling methods						
Control methods						
Credit requirements						
Inventory requirements						
Capital requirements						

The scores for each of the business units considered for acquisition can be weighted by percentage, either for each of the dimensions or for each of the functional areas of marketing, production, and finance that have been used to group the dimensions. The total scores, weighted or unweighted, can then be visually displayed on a vector:

	Relationship of the business unit to the corporation					
	5.00	4.00	3.00	2.00	1.00	0.00
Business unit A						
Business unit B						

The relative positions of the business units of an acquisition candidate on the corporate planning matrix indicate the cash flow balance of the combined firms and the growth potential and risk exposure of the candidate. The positions of those same business units on an acquisition planning vector indicate the strength of the relationships between the candidate and the acquiring firm. Together, these comparisons provide a substantial portion of the information that is needed to evaluate the merger. Other factors that are important, however, include the comparative size of the investment, the competitive position of the candidate, and the need for increased funding or altered management. These factors, while important, are more sorting criteria that should be used to screen potential candidates before performing the extensive cash flow and relationship studies, not to rank those firms after investing the time and effort. A corporation seeking to expand through external acquisition should decide, in advance, if they wish to purchase the dominant company within an industry, or one of the secondary firms with a much smaller market share, and they should estimate, again in advance, the amount of money and the number of people that can be transferred to the acquired firm to improve performance and build market share. In short, the acquiring company should establish policies on the appropriate size, the expected position, and the availability of financial, functional, and technical resources, and then sort out candidates according to those policies or criteria, before doing detailed acquisition planning.

The same means used to measure and present the cash flow balance of the combined firms, the growth potential and risk exposure of the acquisition candidate, and the functional relationships between the business units of that candidate and the parent firm that are needed for acquisition planning can be used to consider divestitures. Divestitures result from unsuccessful acquisitions. Acquisitions have been a popular topic for at least 15 years, and the combination of depressed stock prices for many small and medium-size firms, together with the availability of substantial loan funds for many larger corporations, has made the purchase of new product divisions by external acquisition an easy financial decision and an attractive investment alternative. Not all of the acquired firms, however, were subject to detailed analysis before the purchase, and some have not been either financially or strategically successful after the merger. When the functional relationships between an unsuccessful division and the balance of the corporation are not strong, and where other opportunities exist for the use of corporate resources and the time of managerial personnel, the divestiture or sale of that business unit probably would improve the long-term competitive position of the parent corporation.

The decision to acquire or to divest a given product division or business unit after study of the cash flow balances between the industries and the functional relationships between the companies is only the first of two necessary actions. The second is the need to establish the price; there are four basic steps in setting the price for either acquisitions or divestitures:

1. *Estimate the current value of the assets.* The book value, appraised value, liquidation value, and replacement value of the assets of an acquisition candidate are all important, but not to establish the price to be paid for the firm. A business unit is a going concern, so the price for that concern has to be based upon the collective earning capability of its assets in future time periods, not on their recorded or estimated values at current price levels. Estimates of the current values of the

assets, however, are needed to consider sale of some of the surplus land, buildings, or equipment that may no longer be needed for operations, or to investigate liquidation of some of the accounts receivable, inventory, and investments that may be larger than needed. After these adjustments, the replacement value of the needed assets provides one indication of the worth of the acquisition.

2. *Estimate the future earnings of the company.* The historical operating results of an acquisition candidate are important, but not for simple extrapolation into the future. The revenue and expense figures both have to be adjusted for the expected benefits, through synergy, of the functional relationships between the new business units and the acquiring firm, for the anticipated modifications in the capital structure of the candidate, and for possible changes in the managerial expectations and performance. Finally, of course, the estimates of future earnings have to be adjusted for the opportunities and risks within the environment through an understanding of the competitive structure and economic conditions of the industry or industries involved in the merger. After these adjustments, the average of the expected future earnings multiplied by the capitalization rate, or price earnings ratio, that is typical for the industry, provides another indication of the worth of the acquisition.

3. *Estimate the future cash flows of the company.* The anticipated future earnings of an acquisition candidate are important, but not for direct conversion in the price to be paid for the firm. The earnings figures should be converted to cash flow estimates through recognition of the effects of fixed asset depreciation, working capital changes, and planned capital investments for either productive capacity expansion or product/market development. After these adjustments, the stream of expected cash flows discounted back to their net present value provides another indication of the worth of the acquisition. The discount rate selected for estimating the net present value of the acquisition can theoretically be either the cost of capital of the parent corporation or the risk-adjusted rate of return required by the market, but practically it can be any third figure selected by the management to reflect the uncertainties in the projected cash flows and the possibilities of alternative investments.

4. *Negotiate the purchase price.* For every acquisition, there are four figures that will be discussed in negotiations: the asset replacement values, the capitalized average earnings and the discounted cash flows that have been estimated for the candidate, and the price that will have to be paid to acquire the firm. If the preproposal studies have been well done, so that there is an understanding of the economic conditions of the industries, the opportunities for growth and exposure to risk of the business units, and the relationships between those business units and the parent corporation, then the four figures should be reasonably consistent and comparable, so that agreement can be reached in the negotiations.

The intent of mergers and acquisitions has to be to improve the financial performance and long-term competitive positions of both organizations. This can be accomplished if there is to be a strategic analysis of the industry characteristics and trends and the corporate resources and skills for both companies in order to understand the cash flow balances and consequent growth potential and risk exposure of the acquisition candidate, and to recognize the functional relationships and achieve the apparent economies of the combined operations. The following cases describe the problems in attempting to improve the long-term competitive position of a large corporation through external acquisitions.

Western Pacific Transport, Inc.

The Western Pacific Railroad was built between Oakland, California (directly across the bay from San Francisco), and Salt Lake City, Utah, in 1909. This was 40 years after the completion of the first transcontinental rail route, marked by the spectacular gold spike ceremonies joining the Union Pacific and the Central Pacific (now the Southern Pacific) at Promontory, Utah, in 1869. This "Overland Route" of the Union Pacific and Central Pacific dominated transportation between the Midwest and northern California for those 40 years, much to the concern of merchants in San Francisco and farmers in the Central Valley, near Sacramento, who felt that freight rates on that combined line were nearly confiscatory, due to the lack of rail competition and the absence of federal regulation. The Western Pacific was proposed as a competitive route, and financed by George Gould, who controlled the Denver and Rio Grande Western from Salt Lake City to Denver, the Missouri Pacific from Denver to Kansas City, the Wabash from Kansas City to Toledo, the Wheeling and Lake Erie from Toledo to Pittsburgh, and the Western Maryland from Pittsburgh to Baltimore. George Gould, a son of the more famous railroad financier Jay Gould, had dreamed of a transcontinental line completely under his own control, and he started construction of the last link, from Salt Lake City to Oakland,

in 1905. However, 1905 was too late for the construction of a major railroad extension. Land subsidies were no longer provided by the federal or state governments, and cheap labor was no longer available from Oriental or European emigrants; the new railroad, which had originally been estimated at $38 million, eventually cost $85 million, and caused the collapse of the Gould empire.

There are two stories about the building of the Western Pacific that should be interesting to your students since they show the roughshod nature of early railroad capitalism. The ideal route to cross the Sierras was through the Feather River Canyon, which is only 5,000 ft high as opposed to the 7,000-ft crossing of the Central Pacific at the Donner Pass. A 2,000-ft difference is a major advantage for a railroad because of the obvious savings in fuel costs, and through the Sierras there was an even greater advantage because of the more moderate winter conditions. Five thousand feet is below the major snow belt, and the Western Pacific doesn't get the severe storms that can dump 20 feet of snow and often block the other line. The Central Pacific had wanted to use the Feather River Route in 1869, but this was the site of the original gold rush, and the land along the river was owned by thousands of miners whose small claims were mostly abandoned, but still a legal problem to either purchase or confiscate. The Western Pacific formed a subsidiary mining company that filed claims for land above the river, and then they built the railroad by blasting rock and pushing fill down on the earlier claims, without worrying about purchase prices or compensation awards.

The other story has a happier ending. The city of Oakland, in 1909, was really a subsidiary of the Southern Pacific railroad, which had replaced the original Central Pacific in 1890. Ten thousand acres on the waterfront in Oakland were owned by Horace Carpentier, an attorney who was the first mayor of the city, and who had leased much of this land to the railroad for yards and docks. Both freight cars and passengers were carried by ferry across the Bay from Oakland to San Francisco. Horace Carpentier refused to lease any of his land to the Western Pacific, and so they were blocked from the Bay, and consequently from access to San Francisco. George Gould sued Carpentier, claiming that his land extended only to the high-water line at the time it was purchased, and that all new land, resulting from the filling of swamps and the construction of wharfs by the Southern Pacific, belonged to the city. George Gould won, and his victory resulted in the very large and modern port facilities in Oakland, owned by the city and shared by the Western Pacific. (Statement of a rail industry consultant)

The new railroad was not financially viable, due to very high service charges on the bonds issued for construction; the Western Pacific defaulted on interest payments in 1915, and was sold at auction, on the steps of the Oakland station, in 1916. The purchasers were the original bond holders, who converted much of their debt to equity. Traffic generated by World War I and the industrial expansion of the 1920s guaranteed the success of the line, until the depression of the 1930s, when a second bankruptcy occurred, followed

by a financial reorganization in 1942. The reorganized railroad operated successfully until the middle 1960s, when the huge investment required to change from steam to diesel locomotives, the substantial costs imposed by continued passenger services, and the large losses of freight to competing truck lines, all brought the Western Pacific close to a third bankruptcy. However, a new management group was appointed, headed by Mr. Al Perlman, the former president of the New York Central System, and the company's decline was halted, and then turned around. Passenger service was ended, unused branch lines were sold, portions of the debt were reduced, and marketing efforts were greatly increased. A loss of $11,767,000 in 1970 was changed to a profit of $7,014,000 in 1972. Income statements for the Western Pacific Railroad from 1970 to 1978 are given in Exhibit 1, and balance sheets for 1977 and 1978 in Exhibit 2.

> Railroads got into trouble for a number of reasons, many of which were a historical legacy from their extreme expansion and instant prosperity of the late nineteenth century. The systems became overly competitive: too many railroads were built, with seven alternative routes between Chicago and Kansas City, and three alternatives between Chicago and San Francisco, and then they competed on price and passenger service, not on the fast, efficient movement of freight. The labor unions became overly protective: featherbedding results in high variable costs in what should be a capital-intensive, high-fixed-cost industry, and then the variable costs block improved services. The regulations became overly restrictive: design of cars, operation of trains, and existence of tracks became matters of governmental concern, and prevented major changes. But probably the biggest problem was that the management became overly conservative: they did not think in terms of strategic change, but in terms of financial return. I have a

Exhibit 1 *Income statement (000's omitted) for the Western Pacific Railroad Company, 1970–1978*

	1970	1972	1974	1976	1978
Freight revenues	$66,283	$85,498	$103,540	$109,306	$143,158
Passenger revenues	261	—	—	—	—
Miscellaneous	1,297	2,537	3,864	1,798	1,070
Operating revenues	68,511	88,035	107,404	111,104	144,228
Transportation (operations)	29,510	34,136	38,768	41,859	52,927
Traffic (marketing)	3,689	3,598	4,761	5,322	7,740
Maintenance of way	9,932	11,614	14,970	15,652	19,700*
Maintenance of equipment	9,998	11,430	15,831	17,296	21,420*
Depreciation	5,109	4,780	7,915	5,233	7,900*
General and administrative	6,234	6,819	7,004	7,460	9,610
Property taxes	5,714	6,158	8,566	9,064	11,470
Equipment rental (net)	4,420	3,626	4,837	3,894	4,640*
Operating expenses	74,606	82,161	102,562	105,780	135,407
Operating income (loss)	(6,095)	5,874	4,842	5,324	8,821
Investment income (expense)	1,209	1,105	2,311	69	930
Property sale gain (loss)	(3,675)	5,491	—	710	1,908
Interest income (expense)	(3,277)	(2,640)	(2,159)	(4,192)	(5,648)
Nonoperating income (expense)	(5,743)	3,956	152	(3,413)	(2,810)
Income (loss) before taxes	(11,838)	9,830	4,994	1,911	6,011
Income credit or (tax)	71	(2,816)	(1,613)	(575)	(2,357)
Investment credit (tax)	—	—	—	639	1,803
Net income (loss)	(11,767)	7,014	3,381	1,975	5,457

Source: Moody's Transportation Manual for the respective years, supplemented by the *Prospectus* of the Western Pacific Railroad Company, June 15, 1977, and industry (*) estimates.

Exhibit 2 *Balance sheets (000's omitted) for the Western Pacific Railroad Company, December 31, 1977 and 1978*

	1977	1978
Cash and cash equivalents	$ 19,387	$ 15,602
Accounts receivable, less allowance for bad debts	24,121	28,845
Transportation materials and supplies	4,958	5,365
Corporate prepaid expenses	1,569	1,671
Total current assets	50,035	51,483

Exhibit 2 *(Cont.)*

	1977	1978
Transportation railway and rail equipment	261,692	277,355
Industrial real estate and commercial buildings	18,329	19,078
Accumulated depreciation and amortization	(91,556)	(94,758)
Total fixed assets	188,465	201,675
Notes and contracts receivable	1,026	1,229
Investments	3,242	2,846
Funds earmarked for property improvement	32	—
Deferred charges and other assets	3,952	5,781
Total miscellaneous assets	8,252	9,856
Total assets before allowance for loss	246,752	263,014
Allowance for loss on sale of the company	—	135,105
Total assets	$246,752	$127,090
Accounts payable and accrued expenses	$ 13,352	$ 14,012
Payroll and accrued wages	6,921	8,473
Amounts payable to other railroads	13,843	16,598
Current portion of long-term debt	3,558	4,542
Current portion of capital leases	2,149	2,055
Total current liabilities	39,823	45,680
Long-term debt due after 1 year	41,838	50,983
Capital leases due after 1 year	16,950	15,489
Casualty and other reserves	5,015	4,063
Deferred income taxes	18,928	—
Total long-term liabilities	82,731	70,535
Common stock—1,917,112 shares outstanding	36,211	36,211
Capital surplus	5,785	5,785
Retained earnings (deficit)	82,202	(30,302)
Total stockholders' equity	124,198	11,694
Current liabilities, long-term debt, and equity	$246,752	$127,909

Note: The Western Pacific Railway Company was sold in 1978 by Western Pacific Industries, a conglomerate with holdings in electronic manufacturing and metal products, as well as the railroad. The sales price was $14,000,000 plus the assumption of all debt; this represented a loss of $135,105,000 on the reported (book) value of the assets, which is reported both as an "allowance for loss" on the asset side of the balance sheet, and as a charge against retained earnings.
Source: Annual Report for 1978.

simple rule: when executives within an industry concentrate on financial returns, that industry is in trouble.

Railroads have gone through the product life cycle, but they remain the most cost-effective and energy-efficient means we have of moving heavy freight over long (more than 250-mile) distances. We are going to have to learn to manage mature products and services, for our entire economy is rapidly maturing. The management of mature industries requires operational improvement and cost control. My problem is that I don't think that business schools are doing that: they are teaching the analysis of financial returns, not the management of railroads. (Statement of a rail industry consultant)

An important element in the improved service and extended marketing effort by the Western Pacific railroad was the establishment of an intermodal, or "transport" division in 1973. Intermodal refers to the use of standardized containers that can be loaded with a variety of cargos, that can be moved by truck, train, or ship, and that can be easily interchanged between those modes of transport to obtain the maximum freight savings and customer convenience of each. Railroad intermodal traffic is commonly called "piggyback," and the concept of this service is as old as the railways: farm wagons going to market and stage coaches loaded with passengers were often carried on flat cars until approximately 1870, when considerations of personal safety and merchandise damage forced the transfer of both people and products to the regular cars. In 1955, some railroads turned back to the piggyback concept in order to regain traffic that had been lost to the truck lines.

Trucking companies, although inherently more expensive than railroads for the transportation of long-haul merchandise and bulk commodities, began to compete energetically for the balance of the rail traffic following the development of the highway system in the 1930s, and they enjoyed a number of competitive advantages. A trucking company could serve all customers, while the railroad was limited to the manufacturing and distributing firms that were located on a rail siding. A trucking company could accept small shipments from a number of customers to fill the vehicle, while the railroad was limited to a large shipment from a single customer, or to a combined shipment from a freight forwarder (a company that specialized in assembling small shipments from a number of shippers into a single carload moving to a specific destination). A trucking company could dispatch a vehicle from a terminal to the next destination as soon as it was loaded, while the railroad had to wait for a full train to be assembled. Overall, the convenience, flexibility, and speed of the trucking companies gradually took much of the noncommodity and non-long-haul traffic from the railroads, and the rail share of total freight ton-miles (1 ton of freight moved 1 mile) declined from 66.6% in 1946, at the end of World War II, to 36.1% in 1975.

Railroads were left with their traditional freight traffic, which consists of long-haul merchandise moving in box cars, and bulk commodities, such as coal, ore, cement, and cereal grains in gondolas, hoppers, and covered hoppers. They lost most of their short-haul traffic, and much of their express (high-speed) traffic, and unfortunately these were the classes of freight that carried the higher rates. The switch in dollar revenue from train to truck is even more dramatic than the change in ton-miles.

This was not totally the result of inexorable economic forces. Rail management can be criticized for clinging to traditional operating and marketing methods in the face of their eroding market share. Much more could have been done

Exhibit 3 *Operations of the Western Pacific Railroad Company, 1977 and 1978*

	Class I Railroads, 1977	Western Pacific, 1977	Western Pacific, 1978
Gross ton-miles (cars and contents) (thousands)	—	11,789,000	12,054,000
Net ton-miles (contents only) (thousands)	—	4,967,000	5,122,792
Percentage of net to gross ton-miles	41.2	43.3	42.4
Loaded car miles (thousands)	—	128,818	126,238
Empty car miles (thousands)	—	73,602	71,486
Percentage of loaded to total car miles	56.8	63.6	65.6
Net tons per loaded car (contents only)	42.3	39.7	38.4
Cars per train, loaded and empty	67.2	54.8	57.1
Gross tons per train (cars and contents)	4,210*	3,193	3,331
Train speed, miles per hour	19.7	31.2	30.1
Miles per freight car day	49.2	112.2	106.1
Miles per locomotive day	185.0*	343.2	298.9
Revenue per net ton mile (contents only), cents	2.11	2.52	2.76

Source: Annual Report for 1978 and *Standard and Poor's Railroad Industry Survey*, 1978, p. R33, and industry (*) estimates.

to provide competitive services, but the senior management at railroads frequently came from the legal or financial staff, and they had little experience in marketing and almost no recognition of operating problems. That inbred obsolescence is changing, and railroads now perform sophisticated market analysis to identify traffic opportunities, use automated information technology to improve freight service, and have installed centralized train controls to speed shipments. There is still a lot to be done—the average freight car is only moving 2½ hours per day—but rail management is starting to be innovative and aggressive. (Statement of a rail industry consultant)

In 1979, the Western Pacific was a profitable, aggressive railroad which served primarily as a "bridge" route, moving traffic between San Francisco and Salt Lake City, with only limited service of the industries and shippers along that route, except near the major yards and distribution points of Stockton, Sacramento, and Reno. Products carried were primarily processed foods (32.1% of revenues in 1976), auto parts (9.2% of revenues), steel (6.8%), lumber (6.6%), pulp and paper (6.2%), and chemicals (5.7%). Statistics reflecting the operations of the railroad, and comparisons with national averages for Class I roads (railroads with revenues over $50,000,-000), are given in Exhibit 3.

The Western Pacific in 1979 operated 1,719 miles of track that was reported to be in good condition, without the deferred maintenance that was a partial cause of the slower train speeds on other railroads. The company owned 139 locomotives, of which 63 were modern 3,000-hp units (Exhibit 4). The average age of the road locomotives was 12.2 years, and the age of the switching locomo-

Exhibit 4 *Equipment inventory of the Western Pacific Railroad Company, December 31, 1978*

	Acquired in 1978	Retired in 1978	Total equipment
1,500-hp road locomotives	—	—	18
1,750-hp road locomotives	—	—	6
2,000-hp road locomotives	—	—	9
2,250-hp road locomotives	—	—	15
2,500-hp road locomotives	—	1	18
3,000-hp road locomotives	—	—	63
1,200-hp switching locomotives	—	—	7
1,500-hp switching locomotives	—	—	3
Box cars for general service	243	218	3,612
Box cars for special service	—	1	171
Gondola cars for general service	1	17	388
Gondola cars for special service	—	3	287
Hopper cars (open-top) for general service	—	1	450
Hopper cars (covered) for special service	8	—	453
Tank cars for general service	—	15	14
Flat cars for general service	30	32	190
Flat cars for container (COFC) service	132	55	324
Flat cars for trailer (TOFC) service	26	32	81
Caboose cars	—	—	54
Business cars	—	—	1
Ballast and dump cars (track maintenance)	—	—	29
Derrick and snow removal cars	—	4	2
Boarding outfit cars (maintenance crews)	—	1	14
Miscellaneous service cars	21	7	183

Source: Annual Report for 1978.

tives was 19.9 years; the company estimated that the economic service life of a road locomotive was 18 years, followed by 7 years as a switching locomotive. The average age of the freight car fleet was 13.8 years, and the company estimated that the economic service life of a freight car was 25 years.

The primary rail competition for the Western Pacific came from the Southern Pacific, which ran along a roughly parallel route from Oakland, California to Ogden, Utah, where it connected with the main line of the Union Pacific (Exhibit 5). Ogden is 40 miles north of the Western Pacific terminal at Salt Lake City. Rail competition also came from the Santa Fe, whose route to the Midwest ran southwest to Los Angeles before crossing Arizona and New Mexico and then turning northeast to Kansas City and Chicago; this route was 600 miles longer than the combined rail mileage of the Western Pacific, Union Pacific, and Chicago and North Western, but it was a through route, under the control of a single company, and the Santa Fe was able to offer "third-night" delivery. Third-night delivery meant that a loaded trailer or container that was delivered to the railroad before 6:00 p.m. in the evening in Chicago would be delivered in Oakland during the night of the third subsequent day; this was considered to

Exhibit 5 *Trackage for Western Pacific and major competitors*

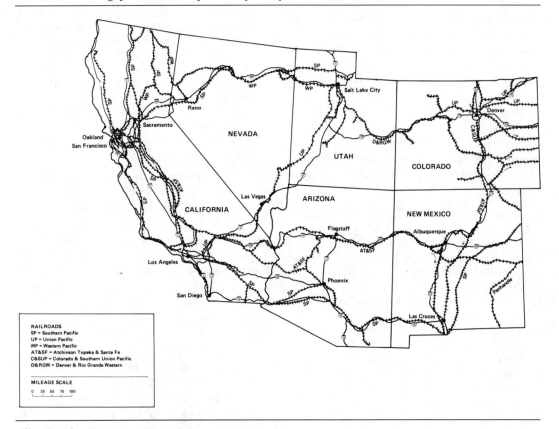

be exceedingly fast rail service. The Southern Pacific could offer fourth-morning delivery on the combined route; the difference was caused by the need to inspect and classify cars at the interchange yards between the three carriers. The Western Pacific offered fourth-evening delivery; this delay was caused by the need to switch cars from the Union Pacific terminal at Ogden down to Salt Lake City, and by additional sorting and classification at that yard. The Western Pacific did not have the volume of traffic of their main competitors, and consequently could not expect to have the cars "preblocked" (arranged in final destination order) on their arrival at Salt Lake City. The Western Pacific also had to wait for a full trainload of cars to be accumu-

lated, as they were delivered from the Union Pacific and the other connecting carrier, the Denver and Rio Grande Western.

To overcome the disadvantages of its slower routing and lower volume, the Western Pacific attempted to provide more thoughtful service and more widespread marketing. The railroad preblocked cars heading east from San Francisco, so that yard movements en route were expedited, and they did extensive selling, both in San Francisco and in Chicago, since shippers and receivers could specify the route to be followed. The Western Pacific also arranged with the Burlington Northern and the Rio Grande Western, and with the Chicago Northwestern and Union Pacific, to handle trains as a through movement between the Midwest and California, as if operated by a single carrier. The railroads pooled their locomotives to facilitate these interline movements, called "run-through trains," and it was possible (although not common) to see a Western Pacific engine pulling a train into the Chicago yards. The Overland Mail was an example of a very successful run-through train; it consisted of trailers, loaded with mail and other express cargo, carried on flat cars between Chicago and the West Coast. The "Falcon" was another example, that started on the Chicago and North Western:

> What do you do with a passenger railroad after the passenger trains are gone? On the always-surprising Chicago and North Western, the answer is simple: run freight trains, but run them as if they were passenger trains.
>
> Other railroads have seen the demise of passenger service as an opportunity to pull up the second track, rip out the automatic Train Control, and slash the maintenance budget, but C&NW—in recent years at least—has had another idea: Use the passenger track to revive, and improve, that nearly extinct railroad classic, the hot-shot merchandise train.
>
> Enter the "Falcon," the passenger train's freight train, the streamliner reincarnated and transfigured for the 1970s. Reenter, too, Union Pacific (and Western Pacific and Southern Pacific) with run-through agreements.... The cars behind the power units carry trailers, containers, and auto racks rather than bedrooms, roomettes, and drawing rooms ... but the rest of the resemblance is still there, including a passenger-style 90 pounds of air in the brake line rather than the 70 used in regular freight service. There's a speed limit of 70 miles per hour, and even that is winked at occasionally. Finally, the four "Falcons"— Nos. 241, 243, and 245 westbound and No. 242 eastbound—are labeled "First Class." Somebody at North Western is serious.

> To find out just how serious ... I rode No. 245 all the way from Chicago's Wood Street Yard to the edge of the UP line at Fremont. What I found was a railroad in transition, somewhere between the exhaustion and near extinction it faced a decade ago and the glorious future that beckons today, just maddeningly out of reach. Half dream, half reality, the "Falcon" is a microcosm of just about everything that's right—and wrong—in American railroading in 1978. (*Trains Magazine,* February 1979, p. 22)

To improve service and expand marketing, the Western Pacific was organized functionally, with vice presidents for finance, operations, marketing, and law, directors of management (computer) services, personnel, and public relations, and a president of Western Pacific Transport, which was the intermodal subsidiary of the railroad. The organizational structure is shown in Exhibit 6.

John Gray was president of Western Pacific Transport, Inc., the intermodal subsidiary of the Western Pacific Railroad Company. As described previously, intermodal sales had been started by the Western Railroad in 1973, and had become so successful, with an annual compound growth rate of over 30%, that the intermodal division was established as a separate subsidiary in 1978. Improved customer service, with an emphasis upon speed and convenience, and extensive market contacts, in both San Francisco and Chicago, had led to the intermodal sales increases, which can be illustrated with the gains in handling mail and express on the "Falcon" and the "Overland Mail" trains (Exhibit 7).

Western Pacific Transport, in common with other railroads, offered two types of intermodal service. The first was the familiar piggyback transport, in which a regular highway trailer was carried on a flat car between terminals. This was termed TOFC (trailer on a flat car) service; it provided the convenience of road pickup and delivery and the economy of rail transport, but there remained some

Exhibit 6 *Organizational structure of the Western Pacific Railroad Company, 1975*

President, Western Pacific Railroad Co.

- **Vice-President Finance**
  - Treasurer of the Corporation
  - Controller of the Corporation
  - Direct Economics and Cost Analysis
    - Manager Tax Analysis
- **Vice-President Operations**
  - Director of Engineering
  - Director of Mechanical Services
  - Director of Train Operations
  - Director of Transportation
    - East Division Superintendent
      - Train Masters
    - Western Division Superintendent
      - Train Masters
- **Vice-President Marketing**
  - Director of Market Development
    - Manager Equipment Planning
    - Manager Price Analysis
    - Manager Market Information
  - Director of Market Services
    - Eastern Sales Manager
    - Western Sales Manager
    - Manager Sales Administration
- **Vice-President Law**
  - General Counsel of Corporation
  - Secretary of the Corporation
  - General Claims Agent
- **President, Western Pacific Transport**
  - Director of Intermodal Sales
  - Director of Intermodal Operations
- **Director of Management Services**
  - Manager Computer Operations
  - Manager Transportation Programs
  - Manager Business Programs
- **Director of Personnel Management**
  - Manager Labor Relations

Source: Company records.

	1974	1975	1976	1977
Mail and express revenues	$205,000	$91,000	$1,604,000	$3,200,000

Source: Prospectus of the Western Pacific Railroad Company, June 15, 1977.

fairly severe problems. It was necessary to transport the running gear (wheels, axles, and brakes) of the trailer, which added to the nonrevenue weight, and the height of the trailer, above the wheels, created wind resistance and made a top-heavy load that was difficult to secure to the rail car. Finally, highway trailers have no standard length; they range from 24 ft for the double trailers (one tractor pulling two trailers) to 45 ft for the longest units that are legal only in some of the western states. The variable length complicates the loading on rail cars, which are either 40 or 50 ft long, and makes it very difficult to fit two trailers on one car.

The second type of intermodal service offered by Western Pacific Transport used standard containers rather than nonstandard trailers, and was called COFC (container on a flat car). The containers are 8 ft wide by 8 ft high (some of the early containers were 8 ft 6 in. high, but these are being replaced in the United States) and either 20 or 40 ft long. The shorter units are used for cargos with high densities, while the longer containers are restricted to lighter products with large space requirements, termed "high cube" cargos. The containers are built so that they may be stacked, one on top of another, in storage yards, and so that they may be lifted by either a crane or a forklift truck. Two 20-ft containers will fit onto a 40-ft rail car or highway trailer, and they are made with special clamps so that they may be easily secured to the car or the trailer. Both the rail car and the trailer can be specially built (skeletonized,

with reduced weight and investment) for dedicated container service.

Containers are almost ideal for transport, due to the simplified handling, reduced weight, and lowered center of gravity and wind resistance, but they can require special facilities for loading and unloading. A single 20-ft container on a truck can be loaded at a shipping dock as if it were a highway trailer; two 20-ft containers on the same truck, however, require a crane to pick off the second unit for loading or unloading. Many manufacturers and distributors do not have a crane available at the shipping dock, and do not have space to roll the containers off the truck and onto the factory or warehouse floor. It is anticipated, however, that container use will dramatically increase within the United States; there are already over 2,500,000 units in use worldwide.

Western Pacific Transport offered nine plans to establish the rates for intermodal service; these plans differed depending upon which companies owned the equipment, and which companies provided the pickup and delivery services (Exhibit 8).

Plan I was basically a contractual agreement between a trucking firm and the railroad in which the railroad carried the trailers on a line haul, between terminals. Plan II was the railroad's means of competing against those trucking firms, in which the railroad offered complete pickup and delivery service at all points along the main line of the railroad. Plans III and IV were for large shippers and ocean carriers who owned the containers and,

Exhibit 8 *Rating plans of Western Pacific Transport, Inc., for intermodal service*

	Pickup to terminal	Terminal to terminal	Terminal to delivery	Trailer/container owner	Railcar owner
Plan I	Trucking firm	Railroad	Trucking firm	Trucking firm	Railroad
Plan II	Railroad	Railroad	Railroad	Railroad or shipper	Railroad
Plan IIA	Shipper	Railroad	Shipper or consignee	Railroad	Railroad
Part III	Shipper	Railroad	Shipper or consignee	Shipper	Railroad
Plan IV	Shipper	Railroad	Shipper or consignee	Shipper	Shipper
Plan V	Trucking firm	Part rail and part highway	Trucking firm	Trucking firm	Railroad
Postal rate	Railroad	Railroad	Railroad	U.S. Postal Service	Railroad
Mini-Bridge	Sea carrier	Railroad	Railroad or trucking firm	Sea carrier	Railroad
Empty container	Railroad	Railroad	Sea carrier	Sea carrier	Railroad

Source: Company records.

in the case of Plan IV, also owned the rail cars. These large shippers were able to arrange for delivery from the rail terminal to the consignee, either with their own trucks or by a contract carrier.

Mini-Bridge service referred to transport between a port, such as Oakland, and a second port, such as Houston or New Orleans. The rate that applied was the ocean tariff as if the goods, generally packed in containers, had gone by sea. Full-bridge service was between Oakland and New York or Boston, for shipment to Europe, and again ocean tariffs applied. Nonbridge service was for containers brought to Oakland by a sea carrier but destined for a nonport area, such as Kansas City; here the rail rates of Plan III or IV applied.

Oakland is a major port, and most of the ships that dock there are now equipped to handle containers. In 1977, 75% of American export and import trade was unitized in con-

tainers since they save the high labor cost of cargo handling by longshoremen, and the port delays such handling often required. The containers also protect against the losses caused by port pilferage, and the environmental effects of seaborne transit. Many of the containers carried by Western Pacific Transport were brought to Oakland by containerized vessels and, since there is greater import than export trade, a special rate had to be established to return empty containers to the shipping companies.

In 1978, the full revenue for Western Pacific Transport under the nine intermodal rate plans described previously was $17,700,000 (Exhibit 9).

John Gray, president of Western Pacific Transport, was pleased with the past growth and current level of intermodal service, but he was also concerned with two major problems during the spring of 1979. The first problem was operational: the terminal yard at Oak-

Exhibit 9 *Revenue of the rating plans of Western Pacific Transport, Inc., for intermodal service*

Plan I	Trucking firm pickup and delivery, with railroad line haul	$ 592,000
Plan II	Railroad pickup and delivery, with railroad line haul	746,000
Plan IIA	Shipper pickup and delivery, with railroad line haul	570,000
Plan III	Shipper pickup and delivery, with railroad line haul but shipper ownership of container	117,000
Plan IV	Shipper pickup and delivery, with railroad line haul but shipper ownership of container and railcar	6,496,000
Plan V	Trucking firm pickup and delivery, with line haul split between railroad and highway	378,000
Postal	Railroad pickup and delivery, with railroad line haul, of U.S. Mail	3,092,000
Mini-Bridge	Containers delivered by sea carrier for railroad line haul to another port, under ocean tariffs	5,667,000
Empties	Containers returned to sea carrier, under special rate	55,000
Total revenues for intermodal service		$17,713,000

Source: Company records.

land was cramped, and capacity limitations in loading and unloading trailers and containers occasionally made it impractical to accept all of the intermodal business offered by customers. Loading and unloading was done by a giant forklift that could easily pick up a 25-ton trailer or container, but this machine was slow in positioning the unit on a flat car since the operator could see neither the container nor the car due to the massive size of the lifting mechanism, and had to rely on hand signals from an assistant on the ground. The forklift also required extensive space since it operated at right angles to the car, and had a wide turning radius. Mr. Gray had designed a special crane that moved parallel to the rail cars, and that could be controlled by an operator on the ground so that placement of the trailers or containers was much faster. Two of the new cranes had been ordered, and Mr. Gray planned to park trailers and store containers in a row, alongside a track, load a complete train, and then dispatch that train to the next terminal in order to provide quicker service to the customers and generate less congestion in the yards.

The second problem was institutional rather than operational. Intermodal traffic has not developed as rapidly in the United States as it has in the rest of the world; only 17% of rail revenues in the United States were from intermodal trailers and containers in 1979, versus more than 40% in Europe, and much of the existing intermodal traffic was imposed on the railroads by the large shipping companies and ocean carriers, many of whom owned their own containers and rail cars, and operated on the lowest possible rates of Plan IV and the Mini-Bridge.

Part of the reason for the delay in development of intermodal service is said to be technical. American freight cars are larger and heavier than comparable European equipment, and consequently less adaptable to containers and trailers. A U.S. flat car was designed to carry 55 to 70 tons in steel beams or process machinery, and loading such a car with a 20-ton highway trailer is considered by some in the industry to be energy-inefficient and capital-excessive. However, the existing intermodal equipment does work and, as described previously, some dedicated intermodal equipment is being developed that is lighter in weight and less capital intensive. The major cause of the delay seems to be institutional: railroads in the United States have always been separated from trucking firms, shipping companies, and freight forwarders by both federal laws and agency restrictions, and it is alleged that the cooperation and coordination essential for full intermodal service is missing.

> We don't have the right equipment. We're loading a flat car, designed in 1880 to carry steel rails, with a trailer designed in 1930 to run on the highway, by means of a hydraulic forklift which is just a bigger version of a machine designed in 1950 for the lumber industry. But, we're starting to get the right equipment. We have containers, and some of the railroads are starting to run light-weight, skeletonized cars (a "skeletonized" car is one built with minimal framing to support a single trailer or container).
>
> Our major problem is that the trucking companies don't trust the railroads, and the railroads don't understand the trucking companies. Many truckers simply refuse to try piggyback service, despite obvious savings on the longer hauls, and many railroads don't realize that a trucking company, when they finally do bring a trailer to the rail yard, want that trailer to move, and not to just sit there for three nights while a train is made up. Sometimes I wonder if we'll ever get true intermodal service in this country. (Statement of a rail industry consultant)

Mr. John Gray, who had worked for the Western Pacific railroad since graduation from the M.B.A. program at Stanford University in 1972, had a very direct response to the problem of combining rail and truck transportation for full intermodal service: he wanted to buy a trucking company. The proposed deregulation of the motor carrier industry under consideration by Congress in 1978 would permit Western Pacific Transport to serve shippers not on the WP rail system, and to move those shipments entirely over the highway. The legal requirement that rail-roads and trucking companies be separate was coming to an end; Mr. Gray wanted to end the traditional separation as well.

Many of the small and medium-sized trucking companies within the United States are family-owned, and are for sale only when they encounter a financial problem or the death of a family member. Mr. Gray, however, had located a company that was profitable, adequately financed, and yet the owners wished to retire. The company was Motor Cargo, Inc., with operating rights between Los Angeles, California, and Salt Lake City, and then on to Denver, Colorado, and back to Reno, Nevada. Revenues of the firm had been reasonably stable over the past few years, at $5,700,000, although the market share had been slipping, and the profits were steady, although largely dependent upon gains from the disposal of assets. The income statements for the company for 1975 to 1977 are given in Exhibit 10, while the balance sheets for the same years are in Exhibit 11.

A comparison of revenues and expenses of Motor Cargo, Inc., in percentage terms, with the industry averages for 28 trucking firms operating in the same Pacific Mountain (California, Nevada, and Utah) area is given in Exhibit 12. Drivers' and helpers' wages for Motor Cargo are considerably less than those for the industry since the company rented many of their trucks and tractors from owner–operators who did their own driving; this was considered to be an expensive method of operation for a line-haul company that operated primarily between large urban centers. Drivers' and helpers' wages together with truck and tractor rentals for Motor Cargo totalled 37.2% in 1976 versus 32.8% for the industry; the same totals, after Motor Cargo purchased additional tractors in 1977, were 35.9% vs. 31.4%. Terminal workers' wages were somewhat less than the industry averages due to the long line hauls, without the need for frequent freight transfer at the terminals, and employee benefits were re-

Exhibit 10 *Income statements (000's omitted) for Motor Cargo, Inc., 1975–1977*

	1975	1976	1977
Intercity truckload revenues	$1,601	$2,047	$2,103
Intercity less-than-truckload revenues	2,821	3,509	3,457
Intracity less-than-truckload revenues	170	157	152
Total revenues	4,592	5,713	5,712
Drivers' and helpers' wages	835	1,006	1,115
Terminal workers' wages	617	747	677
Employment benefits	323	349	496
Officers' and supervisors' salaries	503	651	642
Vehicle fuel and oil	167	233	264
Vehicle parts and repairs	190	272	293
Vehicle tires and tubes	56	81	116
General supplies	217	277	301
Operating taxes and licenses	167	204	225
Operating insurance	139	237	194
Communications and utilities	77	91	117
Depreciation and amortization	197	168	186
Truck and trailer rentals	715	1,119	935
Building and office equipment rentals	82	202	219
Miscellaneous expenses*	89	146	75
Loss or (gain) on disposal of assets	(39)	(124)	(789)
Interest expenses*	87	58	80
Total expenses	4,422	5,717	5,149
Corporate income (loss) before taxes	170	(4)	563
Federal and state income (taxes) or credit	(55)	46	(141)
Corporate income (loss) after taxes	115	42	424

Source: Trinc's Blue Book of the Trucking Industry for the respective years, supplemented by industry (*) estimates.

duced due to a labor contract, signed during a period of financial instability for the company, that was due to expire in 1981. Motor Cargo paid the fuel and oil expenses, and provided repair parts and service, tires and tubes, and operating taxes and insurance for the rented tractors, so that these vehicle expenses were approximately equal for the company and the industry.

Western Pacific Transport employed a transportation consultant to estimate future traffic over the routes traveled by Motor Cargo, and these estimates are given in Ex-

hibit 13. The traffic on many of these routes had expanded rapidly during the 1970s, with the population growth and the industrial development in the Southwest and Mountain states. Traffic on the Los Angeles to Salt Lake City route, for example, had grown at 23% per year. The consultant did not simply extrapolate past traffic trends, but instead worked from basic data on population changes and industrial needs; he provided projections assuming a "most likely" continuation of the current (1978) level of economic activity, a "worst possible" decline of the area

Exhibit 11 *Balance sheets (000's omitted) for Motor Cargo, Inc., 1975–1977*

	1975	1976	1977
Cash and cash equivalents	$ 612	$ 580	$ 508
Accounts and notes receivable	719	890	723
Parts and supplies inventory	69	184	130
Property equipment (net)	1,078	1,224	1,863
Total current and operating assets	2,478	2,878	3,224
Accounts and notes payable	379	659	491
Accrued expenses and wages	312	448	509
Long-term debt due within 1 year	86	67	32
Long-term debt due after 1 year	658	608	668
Common stock and retained earnings	1,043	1,096	1,524
Total debt and equity	2,478	2,878	3,224

Source: Trinc's Blue Book of the Trucking Industry for the respective years.

Exhibit 12 *Comparison of revenues and expenses (percent) of Motor Cargo, Inc., with industry averages for 28 carriers operating in the Pacific Mountain area, 1976 and 1977*

	1976		1977	
	Company	Industry	Company	Industry
Intercity revenues	97.2	91.1	97.3	91.3
Intracity revenues	2.8	8.9	2.7	8.7
Total revenues	100.0	100.0	100.0	100.0
Drivers' and helpers' wages	17.6	25.6	19.5	27.4
Terminal workers' wages	13.1	15.9	11.8	16.3
Employees' benefits	6.1	15.3	8.7	16.6
Officers' and supervisors' salaries	11.3	6.8	11.2	6.7
Vehicle fuel and oil	4.1	4.3	4.6	4.5
Vehicle parts and repairs	4.8	4.4	5.1	4.4
Vehicle tires and tubes	1.4	1.1	2.0	1.3
General supplies	4.8	3.5	5.2	3.5
Operating taxes and licenses	3.6	3.4	3.9	3.2
Operating insurance	4.1	2.3	3.4	2.4
Communications and utilities	1.6	1.4	2.0	1.3
Depreciation and amortization	2.9	2.8	3.3	2.6
Truck rental (with driver)	19.6	7.2	16.4	4.0
Building and office equipment rental	3.5	1.4	3.8	1.5
Miscellaneous expenses	2.6	1.6	1.3	0.6
Loss (gain) on disposal of assets	(2.2)	(0.2)	(13.7)	(0.4)
Interest expense	1.0	1.0	1.4	1.0
Total expenses	100.0	97.6	92.5	96.9

Source: Trinc's Blue Book of the Trucking Industry for the respective years.

Exhibit 13 *Projected truck traffic (millions of ton-miles) on the routes of Motor Cargo, Inc.*

	SLC to LA	LA to SLC	Den to LA	LA to Den	SLC to Den	Den to SLC	SLC to Reno	Reno to SLC	Den to Reno	Reno to Den	Total
1977	119.3	153.8	42.4	70.5	44.7	109.8	33.3	46.6	40.8	27.1	688.3
1978	119.6	150.8	42.4	70.7	44.8	110.2	33.4	45.9	40.1	26.7	684.6
	131.3	176.6	55.6	89.5	47.1	118.5	38.5	49.1	42.6	27.6	775.4
	142.4	199.0	68.0	102.2	49.3	126.2	43.4	52.9	45.9	26.8	856.1
1979	122.0	157.4	42.9	72.0	45.7	112.4	34.1	47.9	42.0	27.9	704.3
	152.5	230.0	78.6	112.6	53.8	139.0	39.5	59.1	47.8	31.6	944.5
	181.1	298.5	112.1	150.6	61.6	165.6	44.5	69.6	53.4	35.1	1,172.3
1980	125.3	160.3	43.9	73.4	46.7	118.1	34.6	48.8	42.9	28.6	722.6
	173.5	284.0	102.1	136.8	60.6	157.8	39.8	67.5	51.3	35.6	1,109.0
	218.7	399.8	156.7	196.1	73.8	195.1	44.6	85.0	59.3	42.2	1,471.3
1981	126.9	163.4	45.0	74.8	47.6	122.1	35.3	49.8	43.9	29.1	737.9
	187.6	341.3	127.6	159.6	64.8	171.8	41.2	74.5	54.0	38.8	1,261.2
	244.6	507.9	205.0	239.2	81.1	218.5	46.6	97.7	63.4	48.6	1,752.1

Source: Company records; some figures have been disguised for confidentiality.
Note: 1977 figures are actual ton-miles; 1978–1981 figures are "worst possible," "most likely," and "best possible" estimates.

economic activity to the level of the 1974 recession, and a "best possible" continuation of the current level of activity and the recent (1976–1978) changes in population and industry, which some observers felt could not continue indefinitely at their very rapid pace.

Motor Cargo, in 1977, had a 5.7% share of the truck traffic over their routes; this was down from a 5.9% market share in 1976 and 6.0% in 1975. Their 1977 revenue per ton-mile was $0.1417 ($5,560,000 revenues for intercity traffic divided by 39,233,000 ton-miles in 1977). Revenue per ton-mile was, of course, dependent upon the mix of freight handled, but it was assumed that the mix would remain approximately similar over the future years, with some gradual increase in the higher-rated items such as fresh produce and electronic parts from southern California.

One of the acknowledged reasons for the decline in market share of Motor Cargo was their use of older, and less efficient, equipment, particularly on the heavily traveled Salt Lake City and Los Angeles routes, where "triples" (one very large tractor pulling three 24-ft trailers, each with an average load of 6 tons) were legal. Motor Cargo had purchased, in 1977, a number of the new tractors and trailers, and had paid for their purchase by selling some of their older, depreciated vehicles that still had market value; this transaction resulted in the pretax gain reported on the 1977 income statement of $789,000, and the details are described in Exhibit 14.

Additional equipment, with a purchase price of $2,076,000, was needed over the next two years to provide modern equipment on all routes, and to eliminate the costly practice of renting tractors. Details are shown on Exhibit 14. Rules of thumb followed in the

		Number of units			
		Trucks	Tractors	Trailers	Book value
1977	Beginning of year	5	19	141	$1,224,000
	Purchases	1	12	11	887,000
	Retirements	2	8	62	(62,000)
	Depreciation	—	—	—	(186,000)
	Ending of year	4	22	91	1,863,000
1978	Beginning of year	4	22	91	1,863,000
	Purchases	4	10	24	1,112,000
	Retirements	—	2	—	(12,000)
	Depreciation	—	—	—	(242,000)
	Ending of year	8	30	115	2,721,000
1979	Beginning of year	8	30	115	2,721,000
	Purchases	2	8	25	964,000
	Retirements	1	3	—	(20,000)
	Depreciation	—	—	—	(320,000)
	Ending of year	9	35	140	3,345,000

Source: Company records; some figures have been disguised for confidentiality.
Note: Dollar figure for retirements is the undepreciated book value; retirements in 1978 and 1979 are expected to generate only minimal gains as the market value for that equipment is close to the recorded book value.

trucking industry are that one tractor is required for each 1,200,000 ton-miles of annual capacity, and that three trailers (for "triples" and "doubles," where legal, and for loading/unloading at the company's terminals and the customers' plants) are needed for each tractor. A delivery truck is also needed for each four tractors, to make some of the less-than-truckload deliveries, transferred at terminals from over-the-road trailers, and to provide intracity service. Large diesel tractors cost $54,000 in 1977, and had to be ordered one or two years in advance, while delivery trucks cost $35,000 and trailers averaged $18,000. All the vehicles were depreciated over 10 years on a straight-line rate, following a ruling of the Interstate Commerce Commission. If the equipment-replacement schedule of Exhibit 14 were followed, the company in 1973 would have modern, efficient equipment, adequate for the current (1977) level of traffic; expansion above 39,-233,000 ton-miles (688,300,000 ton-miles for the total market × 5.7% market share for the company) would require additional investments. A line of credit of $3,000,000 was available from the Western Pacific railroad for the purchase of equipment and the expansion of working capital by the transport subsidiary, at an interest rate of 12.75%. Net working capital in the trucking industry was generally considered to be approximately 7.2% of revenues.

Mr. Gray was certain that Motor Cargo, Inc., with the proper equipment, could run with an operating ratio of 92.0 to 94.0%; the operating ratio of a trucking company is the percentage of revenues required to cover all costs for employees, vehicles, and terminals, including insurance, depreciation, rentals, and miscellaneous expenses, but not including gains or losses on the disposal of assets or interest payments on the debt. He was not certain, however, whether he should continue negotiations for the purchase of the Motor Cargo trucking company.

Class Assignment. Assume that you are an executive assistant to Mr. Gray, working in his office as part of a training program in transportation immediately after your graduation from an M.B.A. program. Assume that he has asked you to report to him after considering the following questions:

1. List the advantages and disadvantages of the acquisition of Motor Cargo, Inc., by Western Pacific Transport. What course of action would you recommend?

2. Prepare an estimate of the value of Motor Cargo, Inc., to Western Pacific Transport. What price, in cash, would you suggest at the start of negotiations? What price would you recommend as a final offer?

3. Prepare an estimate of the value of Motor Cargo, Inc., to an owner of that company, 55 years old with an expressed intention to retire. What price will that person demand at the start of negotiations? What price will that person accept at the conclusion?

Natomas Company

The Natomas Company, a petroleum exploration, development, and production firm with headquarters in San Francisco, California, and operations in Sumatra, Java, Oklahoma, and the North Sea, experienced exceedingly rapid growth during the period 1971–1977 (Exhibit 1).

The Natomas Company had been founded in 1853 in Natoma, California, to construct a canal from the American River to a group of placer mines operating just to the west of the town of Folsom, in the Sacramento Valley. Placer mining requires a very large amount of water, flowing at a regulated speed through a "riffle" box built with low traverse ridges, to wash away the sand and light gravel and yet leave the nuggets and heavier gold specks trapped in the eddies before each ridge. Through control of the water supply, the company was able to control the mines, and

profits during the early years were substantial. The company also purchased 60,000 acres of farmland in the central valley of California, and supplied water for irrigation of that land, which it then rented to emigrants from the Midwest. Finally, the company operated dredges in the Sacramento River, both to mine the gold-bearing deposits and to prepare sand and gravel for use in construction.

By 1960, both mining and dredging were completed in the Sacramento area, and much of the land had been sold during the Depression of the 1930s. Natomas operated as a holding company, whose primary investment was a noncontrolling interest (48%) in American President Lines, a large shipping company based in Oakland that provided both passenger and freight service throughout the Pacific Ocean. In 1967, doubtless directed by

Exhibit 1 *Sales revenues, net income, and earnings per share for the Natomas Company, 1971–1977*

	1971	1972	1973	1974	1975	1976	1977
Sales (millions)	$45.1	$66.9	$112.5	$261.1	$200.4	$407.4	$577.7
Profits (millions)	1.0	4.0	11.2	65.9	17.9	57.1	72.5
Earnings per share	0.14	0.56	1.52	8.86	2.41	7.68	9.33

Source: Annual Report of the company for the respective years.

the Asiatic orientation of its major holding, Natomas purchased the Independent Indonesian-American Petroleum Company, which had exclusive rights for 30 years to explore, develop, and produce oil and natural gas from offshore sectors near Java and Sumatra. This was considered to be a very fortuitous purchase.

> Companies are like people: the successful ones are either very foresighted or very lucky, and many times you can't tell the difference. Natomas bought a little exploration company in Indonesia that had lots of prospects and no oil, for 135,000 shares of stock, worth about $2,700,-000. Then the wells started coming in. By 1972, their operating income from Indonesia, after all expenses, was $5,400,-000, exactly twice what they had paid for the company. They had another gold mine, bigger by far than the ones they had controlled on the American River in California.
>
> The really hilarious part about Natomas is their land. Most nineteenth-century mining companies, if they survived at all, wound up with land in the Nevada mountains or the Australian outback. Natomas still has 10,000 acres in the Sacramento suburbs. (Statement of an investment analyst)

The earnings of Natomas rose sharply in 1974, pushed upward by the price increase for petroleum instituted by the OPEC countries in the fall of 1973. Revenues increased from $2.86/barrel to $10.80/barrel during that period. Indonesian oil was considered to be high-quality and low-sulfur, and therefore

commanded a premium price from industrialized nations on the world market. In 1977, the price was $13.24/barrel, and company revenues from the Indonesian holdings were $354,100,000, up from $4,000,000 in 1971 (Exhibit 2).

Foreign petroleum sales, in 1977, were solely produced in Indonesia. Two offshore areas were licensed from the Indonesian government: northwest Java, which generated 21,600 barrels per day, and southeast Sumatra, which yielded 26,800 barrels per day. Natomas also held minority interests in the North Sea, the Gulf of Suez, and the Bay of Bengal, but none of these other areas were producing in 1977, and prospects for production appeared to be slim except for one sector of the North Sea.

> Progress continued toward scheduled first oil production in mid-1979 from the Buchan field (in the United Kingdom sector of the North Sea) in which Natomas has a 14% interest. . . . The field's first development well, spudded late in the year (1977), was completed at an initial test rate of 7,100 BOPD [barrels of petroleum equivalent per day]. . . .
>
> A wildcat well located some three-and-a-half miles southeast of the Buchan field failed to find commercial hydrocarbon and was abandoned. . . .
>
> During 1977 a third well was plugged and abandoned on a concession site in the German sector of the North Sea, where Natomas holds interests varying from 7% to 12% in various blocks. . . .
>
> Also during 1977, the Egyptian government agreed to an extension of contract

Exhibit 2 *Sales revenues, direct costs, and operating income (000,000's omitted) for the major divisions of the Natomas Company, 1971–1977*

	1971	1972	1973	1974	1975	1976	1977
Foreign petroleum sales	$ 4.0	$26.5	$55.2	$179.6	$150.1	$312.5	$354.1
less direct costs	3.7	21.0	44.6	121.0	110.1	258.4	300.1
Operating income (loss)	0.3	5.5	10.6	58.6	40.0	54.1	54.0
American petroleum sales	—	—	—	—	—	0.6	41.1
less direct costs	—	—	—	—	—	1.9	24.9
Operating income (loss)	—	—	—	—	—	(1.3)	16.2
Petroleum marketing revenue	23.2	22.8	27.5	28.6	41.1	81.4	166.0
less direct costs	21.9	21.2	23.9	26.5	38.6	79.6	162.7
Operating income (loss)	1.3	1.6	3.6	2.1	2.5	1.8	3.3
Petroleum refining revenue	15.2	15.7	28.0	51.4	—	—	—
less direct costs	16.7	18.2	24.1	49.6	18.5	—	—
Operating income (loss)	(1.5)	(2.5)	3.9	1.8	(18.5)	—	—
Geothermal sales revenue	—	—	—	—	6.8	10.7	13.0
less direct costs	—	—	—	—	3.7	4.3	4.8
Operating income (loss)	—	—	—	—	3.1	6.4	8.2
Real estate sales revenue	2.6	1.8	1.7	3.4	2.3	2.1	3.4
less direct costs	1.5	1.4	1.3	1.2	1.2	1.5	1.6
Operating income (loss)	1.1	0.4	0.4	2.2	1.1	0.6	1.8
Ocean Transport equity in APL earnings only	2.0	1.0	(5.5)	5.8	(1.4)	7.4	8.6
Total operating income	3.2	6.0	13.0	70.5	26.8	69.0	92.1
Corporate expenses	(2.5)	(2.6)	(2.0)	(4.6)	(8.9)	(11.9)	(19.7)
Changes in accounting	—	—	1.8	—	(2.0)	—	—
Total profit after tax	0.7	3.4	12.8	65.9	15.9	57.1	72.4

Source: Annual Reports of the company for the respective years.

terms for the (Gulf of Suez) area. Late in the third quarter, Ras Shukheir No. 3, a wildcat well, was plugged and abandoned. Additional seismic exploration is scheduled prior to any further drilling efforts.

Effective July 31, 1977, Natomas and its partners terminated their production sharing contract, awarded by the Indian Oil and Natural Gas Commission in 1974, after two exploratory wells in the Bay of Bengal contract area had been drilled and abandoned. (Natomas Company, *Annual Report for 1977*, p. 9)

The Indonesian area, while producing steadily, was not without problems. The national government of that country had forced policies of relinquishment and renegotiation upon Natomas. The southeast Sumatra contract area, which originally included 51,000 square miles, was reduced by 12,750 square miles in 1974, and an additional reduction, or relinquishment, was planned for 1978. The northwest Java area, originally 21,000 square miles, was reduced by 10,500 square miles in 1975. In addition, the percentage of petroleum production shared by Pertamina, the national oil agency of Indonesia, was revised sharply upward in 1976. These changes, of course, reduced both the opportunity and the incentive for additional investment in oil exploration and development in the region.

> A renegotiation of our Indonesian production sharing contracts, due essentially to Pertamina's financial crisis, severely reduced our per barrel profits and cash flow, and only sizable increases in production and sales helped to offset this change. These changes—if not modified for new investments—will reduce our incentive to do further exploration and development in that country. (Natomas Company, *Annual Report for 1976*, p. 4)

North American petroleum production started in 1976 with the formation of a Houston office of Natomas to explore and develop oil and natural gas fields in the United States and Canada. The domestic production expanded rapidly in 1977 with the acquisition of Apexco, a Tulsa-based exploration firm, for $127,000,000 in cash. Apexco, at the time of the acquisition, had daily production of 63,-700,000 cubic feet of natural gas, and 2,900 barrels of oil, concentrated in Oklahoma, Texas, and Louisiana. The company also had reserves of 22,000,000 equivalent barrels of oil (reserves of natural gas and petroleum distillates are often expressed in terms of energy-equivalent barrels of oil) in North America.

The petroleum marketing revenues listed in Exhibit 2 were a result of the brokerage and trading of crude oil and, to a limited extent, refined products. The brokerage and

trading operations were originally separate from the production of crude oil in Indonesia and North America; company officials at offices in New York and Los Angeles bought petroleum products on the open market, and resold those products in the United States and Canada. In Canada, purchased gasoline and fuel oil were landed at a company-owned terminal in Quebec City, and sold through company-owned retail outlets in the provinces of Quebec and Ontario. Brokerage operations had started in 1958, with the purchase of the American President Lines, as a means of increasing bulk shipments and freight revenues, and had an obvious impact on the later purchase of the Independent Indonesian-American Petroleum Company. In 1976, the Marketing Division was made responsible for the sale of Indonesian crude oil in the United States, in order to reduce the virtually complete dependence on the Japanese market, and the prior brokerage and trading on the open market was discontinued. The company office in New York was closed, and marketing operations were centralized in Los Angeles.

The petroleum refining revenues, also shown in Exhibit 2, were a result of the purchase, in 1969, of the West Indies Oil Company, a small refinery and oil terminal on the island of Antigua, in the Caribbean. The refinery was not financially successful, however, and the property was sold in 1976 at a substantial loss.

In 1974, Natomas purchased the Thermal Power Company of northern California for $34,600,000 in cash. The Thermal Power Company had been formed to generate electricity from geothermal steam, which occurs as the result of the intrusion of molten material from the earth's core into weak spots in the earth's crust. These weak spots occur on geologic fault lines, which are prevalent in northern California; surface manifestations of the intrusion of molten material into the fault lines are hot springs and geysers.

Dry steam can be produced from wells

drilled in areas with hot springs and geysers, and the drilling technique is essentially the same as that used for petroleum. The Thermal Power Company owned a series of wells in The Geysers, California, an area about 70 miles northeast of San Francisco, and sold the steam to the Pacific Gas and Electric Company at a price related to the cost of alternative fuels. Geothermal production at The Geysers in 1977 was 522 megawatts, and the total geothermal potential was estimated to be 1,800 megawatts (for comparative purposes, San Francisco requires 650 megawatts). Despite the shortage of domestic energy, permission to expand geothermal production at The Geysers had been delayed by the presence of small amounts of hydrogen sulfide in the steam.

> Exploration and development of The Geysers geothermal field in northern California is being pursued as rapidly as possible. With an estimated potential of 1,800 megawatts in our joint venture area, and only 522 megawatts developed to date, it still appears that without a major breakthrough in cutting red tape, it could take 10 years to reach full potential. More than two years are required to drill the necessary steam wells and construct a single 110-megawatt generating plant, and this cannot begin until the frustratingly slow process of obtaining the necessary permits from a multiplicity of state and local agencies is completed. (Natomas Company, *Annual Report for 1976*, p. 4)

Real estate revenues were partially derived from office rentals in the company's modern 22-story building in the financial district of San Francisco (Natomas' staff occupied less than 10% of the space in the building) and partially from continuing sales of land in the Sacramento Valley. In 1977, the company still owned 2,700 acres of land near Sacramento; the land was valued at $6,000 to $10,000 per acre.

In 1976, after several years of erratic and unsatisfactory earnings by the American President Lines, Natomas purchased additional stock adequate to obtain control (54%) and initiated a series of strategic changes. Round-the-world service was discontinued, and routes were restricted to the Pacific Ocean and Arabian Gulf, with sailings scheduled between Seattle, Oakland, and Los Angeles on the West Coast of the United States to Japan, Taiwan, the Philippines, Indonesia, Singapore, India, Pakistan, Saudi Arabia, and Kuwait. Twenty ships were operated, of which 15 were modern containerized cargo vessels, and 5 were bulk carriers. Scheduling efficiencies and operating economies were emphasized by the new management, and the results in profit levels were almost immediate. Profits as a percentage of sales changed from a deficit in 1975 to 2.8% in 1976 and 2.9% in 1977.

In March 1978, the Natomas Company agreed to acquire the Brown-Badgett Coal Company of western Kentucky for 850,000 shares of common stock, valued at $20,000,000, and $8,100,000 in cash. The Brown-Badgett Coal Company had produced nearly 2 million tons of steam coal (for electric power generation) in 1977 from one underground and four surface mines with proven reserves of 24 million tons, and had options on additional properties with reserves of over 100 million tons. The net worth of the Brown-Badgett Coal Company was approximately $14,000,000 at the time of the acquisition.

The cash flow of the Natomas Company was substantial, assisted by provisions for the depletion of the oil reserves and depreciation of the capital equipment. Cash sufficient to purchase the Thermal Power Company for $33,600,000 and Apexco for $127,400,000 had been generated during 1974, 1975, and 1976, and it was anticipated that cash surpluses of $50,000,000 to $80,000,000 above the amounts needed for reinvestment in existing

Exhibit 3 *Sources and applications of funds (000,000's omitted) for the Natomas Company, 1972–1977*

	1972	1973	1974	1975	1976	1977
Gain (loss) continued operations	$ 5.9	$ 8.9	$ 64.0	$ 34.4	$ 57.1	$ 72.5
Depletion and depreciation	3.8	16.3	37.2	40.3	86.1	95.4
Deferred revenues (see Notes)	1.5	7.7	33.5	23.7	45.2	(3.9)
Minority interests (see Notes)	0.8	1.6	2.7	—	—	—
Undistributed earnings from APL	(0.9)	—	(4.1)	—	(7.4)	(4.9)
Gain (loss) discontinued operations	(2.5)	3.9	1.8	(18.5)	—	—
Cash flow from operations	8.6	38.4	137.2	79.9	181.0	159.1
Funds provided by operations	8.6	38.4	137.2	79.9	181.0	159.1
Issuance of long-term debt	15.2	30.0	31.0	98.7	79.5	78.9
Issuance of corporate equity	18.4	—	—	—	—	59.6
Sale of subsidiary equity	8.2	—	—	—	—	—
Miscellaneous sources of funds	(0.5)	0.7	1.7	0.9	0.3	0.2
Total sources of funds	49.9	69.1	169.9	179.5	260.8	297.8
Capital expenditures	24.5	56.2	95.8	148.2	98.5	105.3
Purchase of Thermal Power Co.	—	—	26.3	7.3	—	—
Purchase of Apexco, Inc.	—	—	—	—	127.4	—
Loan to unconsolidated subsidiary	—	—	—	—	15.0	—
Reduction of long-term debt	7.3	13.5	47.8	—	32.1	156.0
Dividends paid to stockholders	1.0	1.0	3.6	7.4	8.7	14.1
Total applications of funds	32.8	70.7	173.5	162.9	281.7	275.4
Increase (decrease) working capital	17.1	(1.6)	(3.6)	16.6	(20.9)	22.4

Source: Annual Report of the company for the respective years.
Notes: Deferred revenues result from a provision of the Indonesian production sharing contract which, until 1976, permitted the company to recover costs of exploration and development by receiving a higher-than-expected percentage of current production. The company must accept a lower-than-expected percentage of future production in order to adhere to the contract.

operations would be produced in future years (Exhibit 3).

As might be expected, the financial position of the Natomas Company was secure, with a debt/equity ratio of 0.59 and a current ratio of 1.37. The return on stockholders' equity in 1977 was 18.6% (Exhibit 4).

The major problem facing the senior management of the Natomas Company in early 1978 was considered to be the overdependence upon foreign revenue sources. Indone-

sian petroleum sales in 1977 were 61.8% of total corporate sales, down from 81.9% in 1974, but the continued reliance on foreign operations appeared to expose the company to economic uncertainty and political unrest. Diversification within the United States was felt to be essential, both by company officials and investment analysts.

The challenge to management continues to be the need to reinvest our substantial

Exhibit 4 *Balance sheet of the Natomas Company, December 31, 1977*

Cash	$ 13,444,000	Accounts payable	$ 91,405,000
Short-term investments	56,750,000	Notes payable to banks	23,419,000
Accounts receivable	53,978,000	Current portion of debt	1,579,000
Inventories	30,699,000	Total current liabilities	116,403,000
Prepaid expenses	4,519,000		
Total current assets	159,390,000	Long-term debt	117,296,000
Investment in APL	71,842,000	Deferred revenues	99,694,000
Notes receivable from subsidiaries	19,316,000		
Total investments	91,158,000	Preferred stock at $1 par	2,500,000
		Common stock at $1 par	7,469,000
Petroleum producing equipment	658,943,000	Capital surplus	178,644,000
Petroleum marketing equipment	12,414,000	Earned surplus	200,611,000
Geothermal producing equipment	55,546,000	Total equity	389,224,000
Real estate and buildings	14,279,000		
Accumulated depreciation	(269,131,000)		
Total property and equipment	472,069,000		
Total assets	$722,617,000	Total liabilities and equity	$722,617,000

Source: Annual Report for 1977.

cash flow in profitable assets that broaden the company's earning base. (Natomas Company, *Annual Report for 1976*, p. 4)

We plan to continue this realignment of income sources (from a foreign to a domestic base) in 1978 and the following years by expanding domestic operations through internal growth and acquisition.... (Natomas Company, *Annual Report for 1977*, p. 1)

Summary: The company's large cash flow from the Indonesian contract producing operations, with exploration continuing, should provide funds for further expansion, with diversification being stressed. (*New York Stock Exchange Reports*, published by Standard & Poor's Corporation, September 12, 1978, p. 1638)

Natomas, in the barnyard lexicon of the consulting industry, has three cash cows and one dog. They need a couple of stars. (Statement of an investment analyst)

Class Assignment. Assume that you are a recent employee of a small but prestigious investment banking firm in San Francisco. Assume further that the senior partner of the firm has explained to you that he believes it to be important for the company to become much more active in the merger and acquisition area, both in order to develop new clients and to expand existing services; and assume finally that he has suggested that you start in this new area by studying the Natomas Company, with the intention of eventually making a specific proposal to that company for a potential acquisition candidate.

1. Establish five or more acquisition policies, or sorting criteria, that you believe are relevant to the current position, available resources, and management objectives of Natomas.

2. Locate at least one publicly owned company that meets your selection criteria. Remember that, if this were an actual assignment, you would be unable to contact potential candidates for acquisition due to the impact that knowledge of

an impending purchase has upon stock prices, and that you would have to work from published sources. It is suggested that you use the *American Stock Exchange Stock Reports,* the *Over-the-Counter Stock Reports* and the *Industry Surveys* published by Standard and Poor's Corporation, and available at most business libraries.

3. On the assumption that your proposed acquisition candidate has been approved by the board of directors of Natomas, prepare a firm price for the purchases of the common stock of the company, and establish a sequence of steps to complete the acquisition.

4. Consider changes in the organizational structure and systems of both Natomas and the acquired company that would be needed to successfully integrate the new acquisition into the older company.

Roger Worsham

Arnold Abramson and Company is a regional accounting firm, with offices in Michigan and northern Wisconsin. It was founded in 1934 to provide auditing and tax services in the Bay City, Saginaw, and Midland triangle in Michigan and, despite the depression, was immediately successful due to the economic growth of that area. Following World War II, the firm opened offices in Flint and Detroit, to the south, and in Traverse City, Petosky, and Alpena to the north. The northern offices were successful, as competition was very limited, so the company continued to expand across the Upper Peninsula, with new offices in Escanaba (1952), Marquette (1954), and Ironwood (1954) in Michigan, and in Rhinelander (1957), Ashland (1959), and Wausau (1961), Wisconsin.

The southern offices of Arnold Abramson and Company, in Flint and Detroit, competed directly with the large, national CPA firms, the so-called "Big Eight," but they were able to operate successfully until the mid-1960s by providing more personalized services and by charging somewhat lowered rates. However, competition sharply increased in the late 1960s and early 1970s as the tax laws became more complex, the auditing procedures more rigorous, and the bookkeeping more automated. The Big Eight firms were able, through their extensive training programs and their continual staff additions, to provide more extensive help and assistance to their clients on tax changes and data-processing procedures, and many of the small and medium-sized companies that had been customers of Arnold Abramson for years switched to one of the national firms. It was eventually necessary to close the Detroit office, and to reduce the size of the staff at Flint.

Some of the partners of Arnold Abramson and Company recommended the merger of their company with one of the national CPA firms, but the founder, Mr. Arnold Abramson, was not only still living but was still active, and he and his two sons were adamant in their opposition to any sale or merger. They believed that their past policies of personal attention, prompt response, and reduced billings would maintain the firm in the smaller cities and towns of northern Michigan and Wisconsin. Even when some of their clients in the northern areas of the two states felt it necessary to obtain the data-processing assistance and tax expertise of the national firms, Mr. Abramson and his two sons continued their resistance to the possibility of merger, and continued to emphasize their concept of personalized service.

> The old gentleman was 84 when I joined the firm, and he simply was not going to surrender to Arthur Andersen or Price Waterhouse. And you know, he had a point: there is room left in the world for the more personal approach, even in auditing. The old man was adamant about this. I understand that at the partners' dinner this year he laid it right on the line to the other members of the firm. "You are to keep the local banks, retail stores, and manufacturers as your clients; if you lose your clients to those people from Detroit, we'll shut down your office." He always referred to representatives of the Big Eight firms as "those people from Detroit" even though they might be from offices in Lansing, Grand Rapids, or Milwaukee. (Statement of Roger Worsham)

Roger Worsham was a 32-year-old graduate of the M.B.A. program at the University of Michigan; he had majored in accounting, but he had found it difficult to obtain employment at the large national CPA firms. He had interviewed eight of the largest companies, and had been rejected by all eight. The Director of Placement at the School of Business Administration had explained that this was due to his age, and that the Big Eight firms were exceedingly hesitant to hire anyone over 28 to 30 years of age since they felt that the older entrants were unlikely to stay with the firm over the first few years of auditing, which some people found to be dull and tedious. Roger Worsham, however, felt that perhaps his personality was more at fault than his age; he found it difficult to converse easily in the interviews, and he was afraid that he projected himself as a hesitant, uncertain individual. He had worked for six years as a science teacher in a primary grade school, after graduating from college, and interviewers always asked about his decision to change

professions, and always seemed to imply that he was not certain about his objectives in life nor his commitment to accounting.

At the suggestion of the faculty member who taught the small business management course at the Business School, Mr. Worsham applied to some of the smaller CPA firms in the state, and was almost immediately accepted by Arnold Abramson and Company.

> I met Mr. Abramson, Jr., and he talked about what I wanted to do in accounting, not what I had done in teaching, and that interview went really well, and I knew when he asked me if my wife and I would mind living in a small town that he was going to offer me a job. It does not pay as much as working for some of the other firms, but I can get my CPA (in Michigan, two years of auditing experience is required after passing the written examinations to obtain a CPA) and then I assume they'll pay me more, or I can move into industry. (Statement of Roger Worsham)

Roger Worsham was assigned to one of the northern offices, and he moved his family (wife and two small children) to the area and started work immediately after graduation. Within the first six months he participated in the audit of a savings and loan association, a farm equipment dealership, a large retail hardware store, and a nearly bankrupt machinery manufacturing firm. His family enjoyed the area in which they were living, and he enjoyed the work that he was doing, and he felt that his life was beginning to take on a direction and purpose. But then he found clear evidence of fraud, and encountered a situation that threatened his newly found security and employment:

> We were doing the annual audit for the machinery manufacturer. This company had not been doing well; sales had been declining for four or five years, losses had been reported for each of those years, and the financial position of the company had steadily deteriorated. I was going

through the notes payable, and found that they had a loan, and a large one, from the savings and loan association in [name of the city in which Mr. Worsham and his family lived].

Now, first, it is illegal for a savings and loan association to make a loan to a manufacturing firm; they are restricted by law to mortgages based upon residential real estate. But, even more, I knew this loan was not on the books of the savings and loan since I had been the one to audit the loan portfolio there. I had looked at every loan in the file—I had not statistically sampled from the file, which is the way you would usually do it—and had checked each loan to see that it was supported by a properly assigned mortgage and a currently valid appraisal. The only thing I had not done was to add up the total for the file to check with the reported total, since the usual way is to sample, and you don't get a total when you sample. I still had my working papers back at our office, of course, so I went back and ran the total and, sure enough, it was off by the amount of the loan to the manufacturing company.

It was obvious what had happened: someone had taken the folder covering the illegal loan out of the file prior to our audit. It became obvious who had done it: the president of the savings and loan association was a lawyer in the town who, I found by checking the stockholder lists, was the largest owner of the manufacturing company. He was also on the board of directors of the local bank, and reputedly was a wealthy, powerful person in the community.

I took my working papers and a Xerox copy of the ledger showing the loan, and went to see the partner in charge of our office the next morning. He listened to me, without saying a word, and when I finished he told me: "I will take care of this privately. We simply cannot afford to lose a client of the status of [name of the lawyer]. You put the papers you have through the shredder."

I was astonished. The AICPA code of ethics and the generally accepted auditing standards both require that you either resign from the engagement or issue an adverse opinion when you find irregularities. This was not a small amount. The loan was not only illegal, it was in default, and would adversely affect the savings and loan association.

I hesitated, because I was surprised and shocked, and he told me: "I will not tell you again. You put those papers through the shredder or I'll guarantee that you'll never get a CPA in Michigan, or work in an accounting office in this state for the rest of your life."

I didn't know what to do. (Statement of Roger Worsham)

Class Assignment. Make a specific recommendation to Roger Worsham regarding his future actions.

First Arizona Corporation

The First Arizona Corporation is a major brokerage firm and investment banking house with offices throughout the six southwestern states, and with memberships on the two large national and many of the smaller regional exchanges. In addition to conducting a substantial retail business with investors in the rapidly growing "Sun Belt" region, members of the firm were active in raising venture capital for small companies, underwriting new issues for medium-sized firms, and assisting in mergers and acquisitions for the larger corporations in the area.

> Venture capital, public issues, and corporate mergers may seem very different, but they are all related. We are continually on the lookout for companies within our region that need more capital for growth, for we feel that we can assist those firms and provide that capital through a private placement, a public issuance, or a merger with a much larger and better financed parent. The form may differ, but the intent remains the same: raising the funds needed to sustain growth. (Statement of a senior partner of First Arizona Corporation)

In early 1979, First Arizona Corporation arranged the acquisition of the Taylor Machinery Company, a small producer of oil-well drilling equipment in McCamey, Texas, by Hatcher Oil Tools, Inc., the third-largest firm in the industry. Taylor Machinery had sales in 1978 of $23.8 million; Hatcher Oil Tools had sales the same year of $1.7 billion. The Hatcher management was interested in acquiring Taylor Machinery Company since the smaller firm had developed a number of patented drilling devices, including a blow-out valve that was acknowledged to be the best in the industry, and a drilling bit that was considered to be ideal for the very hard and brittle rock found in the overthrust region of the Rockies, where major explorations for oil and gas were just beginning. Representatives of Hatcher had approached Taylor Machinery asking for a license to manufacture both products on a worldwide basis, but Mr. Taylor had refused, saying that he planned to expand his company to become an international producer in the near future. The president of Hatcher, whose corporate offices were located in Los Angeles, then contacted the local partner in First Arizona, and suggested the possibility of a tender offer to acquire a majority of the stock in Taylor

Machinery. The management of the Taylor company and members of the Taylor family owned less than 24% of the outstanding stock; the balance was widely spread throughout Texas as a result of two in-state stock sales during the 1960s (shares of stock that are offered for sale in a single state avoid the registration requirements of the Federal Securities and Exchange Commission, and need only be registered with the Secretary of State in the state where the shares are sold). Normally, 24% of the equity is considered to be adequate for control, but the Taylor company had paid no dividends since 1974, and Mr. Taylor had been brusque and occasionally tactless in responding to stockholder comments on the dividend policy. It was felt that the Taylor company would be vulnerable to a tender offer; in such an offer, the price which an acquiring company is willing to pay for shares in the stock of the acquisition candidate is widely advertised, and the shareholders submit firm agreements, or tenders, to sell at that price within a limited period of time, often 60 days. If a majority of the shares are offered, the tenders are accepted, and the stock is purchased. In this instance, First Arizona advised on the price to be proposed for the shares, arranged for the registration and publication of the offer, and managed the receipt of the tenders and the eventual payment for the stock. Fifty-eight percent of the shares were tendered, and purchased, so that First Arizona Corporation was able to turn over majority control of the Taylor Machinery Company to Hatcher Oil Tools, Inc., in March 1979. The acquiring company immediately shut down the Taylor factory in McCamey, a very small town with approximately 1,800 inhabitants, and transferred all engineering and manufacturing operations to their main plant in Burbank, California. Most of the employees were given an opportunity to transfer to the new location, but few accepted; the differences between West Texas and east Los Angeles (Burbank is part of the

Los Angeles metropolitan area, to the east of the central city) were considered to be too great.

For $19.6 million, Hatcher bought the designs for new drilling equipment that will boost their sales on the world market by at least $100 million per year, a very good sales force and distribution network in West Texas, New Mexico, and southern Colorado, an old and poorly equipped plant, and the economic collapse of a nice little town. Everybody who lived in McCamey worked for Mr. Taylor; when the new owners closed the plant and pulled out, there just wasn't anything left. Sure, the people had an opportunity to move to Burbank, but who wants to live in Smog City? (Statement of an individual concerned by the acquisition)

Mr. Taylor had obviously not accepted the terms of the tender offer, and had energetically resisted the acquisition attempt, but the offer remained open even after Hatcher Oil Tools had purchased the majority of the stock, so that he and the other members of management staff received slightly more than $4.7 million. Mr. Taylor was offered the position of general manager of the Taylor Division of Hatcher, but he refused angrily, and resigned from the company, a bitter and defeated man.

The really lousy part of the acquisition, and I think that this really smells, is that First Arizona took a company away from its founder, deprived about 400 people in a West Texas town of their employment, and got very well paid for doing so. The usual rule in an acquisition is that the investment banker receives 5 to 7% of the purchase price. First, Arizona got $1.4 million. My father, who worked for the company for 23 years, got a check for $700, for two weeks' severance pay. The partner in Los Angeles, who did nothing except meet with Hatcher and set up the deal, probably got 100 times as much for a bonus. (Statement of an individual concerned by the acquisition)

Members of First Arizona Corporation who were contacted by the casewriter felt that their firm had acted legitimately in structuring the financial exchange that brought managerial control of the Taylor Machinery Company to Hatcher Oil Tools, Inc., and that the payments for their services were both earned and deserved.

I don't believe that there is an ethical issue involved here; it is an economic issue. Mr. Taylor was an exceedingly capable engineer, but a short-sighted business person. He felt that he could sit on his products, and neglect his stockholders. Those stockholders had a right to a return on their investments, just as you and I have a right to a return on our investments, or a right to dispose of those investments in their own way. We offered the stockholders a very fair price for their shares, far above the net asset value, and they accepted that offer. I see nothing ethically or morally wrong with an open market transaction, and I feel that academic people often attempt to substitute their own standards for those of the marketplace. (Statement of a senior partner of First Arizona Corporation)

Class Assignment. Are ethical issues involved in the acquisition of the Taylor Machinery Company by Hatcher Oil Tools, Inc., and what standards should be used to judge that transaction?

Chapter 8

STRATEGIC DESIGN IN PUBLIC (NONPROFIT) INSTITUTIONS

Strategic design has been defined, in earlier chapters, as the process of developing a long-term method of competition for a business unit that would provide a competitive edge or advantage for that unit. The process of strategic design was further defined as the evaluation of alternative patterns of competition through comparison with environmental characteristics and trends, organizational assets and skills, and managerial values and attitudes. This process was represented by the simple schematic outline that has been used to integrate the various sections of the book, repeated at the top of the next page.

The emphasis or orientation of this process of strategic design varies, depending upon the type of the business unit:

1. Small companies, with a single product or a narrow product line, by definition have limited sales, and consequently they often search for a competitive advantage by combining product characteristics and market segments to define a high-margin market "niche" with reduced competition. Smaller companies also often suffer from a shortage of financial and physical assets and technical and managerial skills, and therefore they are constrained in product development and market expansion. As a result, strategic planning for smaller firms is usually product–market oriented and resource based.

2. Product divisions of larger companies, also generally responsible for only a single product or product line, usually have annual sales considerably larger than those of smaller firms, and consequently they are less able to find a market niche without competition. Product divisions usually must meet competition, not avoid it, and they often search for a competitive advantage by combining capacity expansions and technical improvements to develop a low-cost production process. The product divisions of large companies have access to the financial and

Environmental characteristics
and trends

Economic

Technological

Social/political

Competitive

↓

Organizational mission or charter	Specific opportunities and risks within the industry	Selected strategy, or method of competition
↓	↓	
Corporate performance and position	Range of strategic alternatives open to the firm	
↑	↑	
Managerial values and attitudes	Specific strengths and weaknesses within the company	

↑

Money

Equipment

People

Market position

Organizational resources, or
assets and skills

physical assets and the technical and managerial skills of the parent firm, so that they are not constrained by resources, but they are limited in sales growth and market expansion by the competitive structure or environment of the industry. Strategic planning for the product division of a larger company is, therefore, often product–process oriented, and environmentally based.

3. Single-industry firms generally have a range of related products and product lines that are sold to a variety of market segments, and produced by a number of manufacturing processes, within one industry. These firms search for a competitive advantage by considering both product–market positions for specialty items that can provide higher margins, and product–process postures for volume products that require lower costs, and then by integrating the marketing and production policies to exploit the interrelationships between the products and processes. Strategic management within a single-industry firm is a difficult task; these are often the basic processing companies, in mature industries, with limited

growth and narrow margins. Strategic planning for these single-industry firms, therefore, has to be both product–market and product–process oriented, and both resource and environmentally based.

4. Multiple-industry firms generally have a number of divisions, each with an assigned product line, a specific market segment, and an independent production process, operating in different industries. These companies search for a competitive advantage by using the cash flow from divisions in low-growth industries or low-share markets to invest in higher-growth industries or higher-share markets, and by exploiting functional and technical relationships between the divisions to improve the efficiency of the firm through joint use of resources and skills. The balancing of cash flows between divisions enables the corporate management to set growth/stability and risk/return ratios for the firm, while the combining of functional and technical operations permits the management to establish a focus for the company. Strategic planning for multiple-industry firms is relationship oriented, and both resource and environmentally based.

These four groups of economic units—small companies, product divisions, single-industry firms, and multiple-industry corporations—include all possible business operations, but they do not include the nonbusiness organizations, such as government agencies, academic institutions, health care centers, etc., that are generally classified under the term "nonprofit." Nonprofit is an accepted though inaccurate description: many business firms operate, inadvertently, on a nonprofit basis, while some public agencies and charitable organizations transfer a substantial surplus to their equivalent of an equity account at the end of each fiscal year. Nonbusiness would seem to be a more accurate classification than nonprofit. These nonbusiness institutions vary tremendously in size and activity, but overall they form a large and growing sector of the American economy. In 1978, nonbusiness organizations employed 23.3 million persons, out of the total national workforce of 94.3 million, and this number was growing at a compound rate of 3.5% while manufacturing, for example, was remaining basically stable. Exhibit 1 details the composition of the national work force over the period 1970–1978 for comparison of employment and growth among the various sectors.

Employers in the nonbusiness sector of the economy can be divided into federal, state, local, and private classifications. Exhibit 2 estimates the number of employees in each class of organization, by major service category such as education, health care, welfare, etc. Education and health care are the largest nonbusiness functions, with 7.2 million and 6.5 million persons employed in each. The miscellaneous function is truly varied, including sewers, law courts, and zoos.

Nonbusiness organizations perform a wide range of functions, from governmental to charitable, but they cannot be clearly divided into public versus private institutions on the basis of either funding or ownership. Obviously, some of the functions, such as military defense or judicial decisions, are completely public, and supported by tax revenues, while others, such as religious instruction or civic associations, are primarily private, and dependent upon donated monies, but there is a shading between public and private funding for many of the nonbusiness institutions. Educational services are provided by both public and private colleges and

Exhibit 1 *Employment (000's omitted) in the major sectors of the U.S. economy, 1970–1978*

	1970	1976	1977	1978
Agriculture, forestry and fishing	3,566	3,417	3,383	3,501
Mining and petroleum exploration	515	770	814	828
Construction trades	4,814	5,162	5,504	6,043
Manufacturing and miscellaneous industrial	20,758	20,002	20,638	21,448
Transportation and communication	5,317	5,652	5,833	6,192
Total industrial employment	34,970	35,003	36,172	38,012
Wholesale distribution	2,670	3,462	3,597	3,616
Retail distribution	12,327	14,562	15,109	15,636
Total distribution employment	14,997	18,024	18,706	19,252
Banking and brokerage, etc.	1,695	1,954	2,061	2,153
Insurance and real estate	2,246	2,840	4,977	3,254
Total financial services	3,941	4,794	5,038	5,407
Business services	1,402	1,763	1,924	2,128
Automotive services	599	749	794	872
Household services	1,781	1,382	1,406	1,396
Hotel and lodging	978	1,015	1,068	1,075
Entertainment and recreation	716	922	968	1,018
Miscellaneous commercial services	1,896	1,845	1,854	1,846
Total commercial services	7,373	7,673	8,014	8,355
Health care services	4,467	6,122	6,328	6,535
Educational services	6,123	7,115	7,122	7,176
Welfare services	827	1,321	1,429	1,525
Miscellaneous professional services	1,477	2,600	2,765	3,091
Miscellaneous public administration	4,473	4,793	4,972	5,020
Total noncommercial services	17,367	21,991	22,616	23,347
Total national work force	78,627	87,485	90,546	94,373

Source: Statistical Abstract of the United States, 1980, Table 668.

universities; the differences between those groups are certainly muted as almost all private colleges and universities receive public funds, in varying amounts, and as most public institutions have some private donations. Health care is also provided by both public and private hospitals, with the same mixture of public and private funding. The differences between public and private funding, and ownership, are not clear, except for the nonbusiness institutions at each end of a spectrum of functions. Exhibit 3, which lists this spectrum of functions, is meant to be illustrative more than complete, and to display the shading of public versus private distinctions in the major areas of social, educational, health care, and cultural services.

The nonbusiness, nonprofit organizations which perform the functions listed in

Exhibit 2 *Employment (000's omitted) in the professional and public service sector of the U.S. economy, by type of organization and by type of service, 1978*

	Federal	State	Local	Private	Total
Educational services	27	1,508	5,051	590*	7,176
Health care services	254	638	678	4,925*	6,495
Public welfare	285*	457*	496*	287*	1,525
National defense (civilian)	987	—	—	—	987
Police protection	58	72	559	—	689
Postal service	650	—	—	—	650
Highway maintenance/design	5	263	320	—	588
Natural resources	297	183	34	—	514
Financial administration	108	124	192	—	424
Miscellaneous	217*	294*	1,874*	1,914*	4,299
	2,888	3,539	9,204	7,716*	23,347

Source: Statistical Abstract of the United States, 1980, Table 510, with estimates (*) for private employment to be consistent with Table 668 totals shown in Exhibit 1.

Exhibit 3 can be divided generally into governmental agencies, at the federal, state, and local levels, and into health care facilities, educational institutions, and private service organizations. As discussed previously, the public versus private nature of many of these organizations may not be clearly delineated, and their activities often overlap, but these six categories do differ on such dimensions as overall size, funding flexibility, external constraints, and internal tasks, and these differences do create special requirements for managerial direction. Despite these differences, there are also a number of similarities that affect managerial practices and policies at almost all nonbusiness organizations:

1. *Service orientation.* Most nonbusiness organizations produce services rather than products. These services range, as shown in Exhibit 3, from legislative representation to religious instruction, but they all tend to be intangible in nature and variable in design. The intangible nature means that the services are not physical products that can be counted, measured, or stored in inventory, and the variable design refers to the need to change the specifications of the service to meet the requirements of a client. These intangible and variable characteristics make social services difficult to produce, and the production processes awkward to control. The production problem comes from the need to schedule operations to meet a varying level of demand. The services cannot be stored, and the result is that either the clients wait for attention or the employees wait for work; neither situation is desirable, but both are unavoidable. The control problems come from the lack of standards to evaluate either service quality or employee performance. Services cannot be measured, except by very imprecise means. A physical product can be designed with explicit tolerances about the critical dimensions, and the output parts can be measured, and rejected if the measurements fall outside the tolerances. Services lack these definite dimensions and tolerances, and the result is that it is difficult to ensure quality, and hard to

Exhibit 3 *Range of functions performed by public (supported primarily by tax revenues) and private (supported primarily by donated funds) nonbusiness organizations*

	Legislative services	Area representation Political compromise Legal enactment
	Judicial services	Legal interpretation Judicial decisions Penalty assessment
	Fiscal services	Revenue collection Resource allocation Fiscal/monetary management
	Regulatory services	Restrictive policies Protective policies Promotional policies
	Military services	Strategic forces Tactical forces Domestic forces
	External services	Foreign relations Foreign trade Foreign aid
	Internal services	Communication system Transportation system Financial system
Public nonprofit organizations	Community services	Police protection Fire protection Sanitation
	Social services	Child care Family welfare Old age assistance
	Educational services	Schools Colleges and universities Job training
	Health care services	Physicians Clinics Hospitals
	Cultural services	Orchestras Libraries Museums
	Charitable services	Donations Assistance Activities
	Religious services	Worship Instruction Activities
	Civic services	Discussion Promotion Activities

evaluate performance. An individual who services 20 clients per day in a welfare agency or health care center may be shortcutting quality, and performing much worse, than another worker who serves only 10 to 12 persons on a daily basis, but with much more complete and thoughtful attention. Many nonprofit organizations now have a reputation for slow and indifferent services, but that reputation may be more a natural consequence of the intangible and varied nature of the services provided than an adverse reflection on the intentions of the managers or the efforts of the employees. Strategic design in a nonbusiness organization has to consider the special problems imposed by the imprecise and individualized nature of the services.

2. *Nonmarket pricing.* Imprecise and individualized services are also produced by many business firms, as in auditing, consulting, and banking, but these firms have an advantage in that their services have a monetary value, or price, in a competitive market, and that market price can be used as a surrogate for quality and as a measure of performance. An individual performing $400 of audit services during a day, or arranging loans with equivalent interest income, can be thought of as performing better than another person providing services or arranging loans with much lower daily revenues. There are problems with this reasoning, which will be discussed in Chapter 12, but competitive prices do provide one indication of service quality and individual performance. In most nonprofit or nonbusiness situations, however, the daily revenues have very little relationship with the quality of the service or the effort of the individual since these revenues are usually not determined by either market pricing or full costing. Instead, the revenues are often determined by the client's ability to pay, and the services are provided because they are felt to be needed, not because they are thought to be either cost-effective or price-elastic. Strategic design at a nonbusiness organization has to recognize that revenues offer very little assistance in ensuring quality or improving performance.

3. *External funding.* The lack of a relationship between revenues and services imposed by the nonbusiness nature of these public and private institutions, with prices determined more by the client's ability to pay than by the organization's need for income, brings a reliance upon external sources of funding. These external sources may be public, with tax revenues allocated by the federal, state, and local governments, or private, with gifts and donations provided by either foundations or individuals, but both bring the resource contributors to a nearly dominant position in the managerial process. Certainly, the maintenance of congressional relations is a major task of most public administrators at the federal level, and the same attention must be paid to legislative committees within the states, and within local units and private organizations that receive a portion of their funding from federal or state agencies. The function of the administrator is to justify the proposed expenditures by describing the service benefits and the need for their continuance. This same justification is needed by private institutions in contacting potential donors or arranging future fund drives. Strategic design at a nonbusiness organization has to recognize the direct and pervasive influence of the external funding sources.

4. *Professional personnel.* The staff at many nonbusiness organizations can be divided

between professional and managerial/operational personnel. The professionals at health care centers are the physicians, nurses, and medical technicians; the professionals at educational institutions are the faculty members who represent, particularly at major colleges and universities, multiple academic disciplines; the professionals at welfare agencies are the social workers, who often disagree with the managerial personnel on the direction of those agencies; and the professionals in federal, state, and local governments range from foreign service officers to police and fire department personnel. Each member of a profession has a divided allegiance, partially to the profession and partially to the organization, and each profession has standards of conduct and measures of performance that may have little relationship to the output services of the organization. Strategic design at a nonbusiness organization has to recognize the differing norms and values of the professional personnel.

5. *Multiple constituency.* The major difference between nonbusiness and business organizations is not the lack of a profit motive—profit maximization is not the central mission at most business firms—but the presence of multiple and varied constituency groups. These groups certainly include the recipients of the services, who tend to be varied among themselves due to the range of services commonly provided, and it also includes representatives from the funding agencies, members of the professional associations, people from public interest societies, and the managerial and operational personnel. Each of these groups, typically, has a separate concept of the proper mission or set of activities for the organization. Nonprofit organizations, both public and private, exist for a number of reasons, some of which have very little relationship to the services actually provided for specific groups of people within the community or nation. In actual fact, the recipients of the services may be the least important and least influential members of the total constituency; the service recipients tend to lack power due to the nonmarket pricing of the services, and the nonprofessional nature of their membership. Students at most colleges and universities do not need to be told that they are considered to be less important and less influential than some other groups in the overall direction and daily operations of those institutions, and an equivalent statement could be made about service recipients at many other nonprofit organizations. Strategic design at a nonbusiness organization has to recognize the differing interests and objectives of the various constituency groups.

The service orientation, nonmarket pricing, external funding, professional personnel, and multiple constituency groups combine to bring uncertain direction and ambiguous programs to many nonbusiness organizations. The planning focus shifts in these organizations from the outputs, which cannot be measured due to the intangible and varied nature of the services, to the inputs, which can be measured in financial terms, but which can also be influenced by the funding sources, professional associations, external interest groups, internal employee divisions, and the public media. These multiple influences on the budgetary process bring a political dimension to the management of nonprofit institutions, with "political" referring to the method of achieving an acceptable compromise between the conflicting groups, each with varying degrees of power, or ability to obstruct the final performance of the organization. This same political dimension is present in many business firms. Both business and nonbusiness organizations tend to be large, complex associations of professional and nonprofessional employees, with multiple functions, processes, and clients, and, to some extent, with an output of unmeasurable products and services, but the nonbusiness organization adds the problems of nonmarket pricing and external funding. The external funding provides the opportunity for the various pressure groups to influence the operations of nonbusiness organizations, and the differing interests and objectives of these constituency groups ensure that conflict and compromise will be part of that influence process. Strategic design in nonbusiness organizations, therefore, has to be political as well as analytical.

The influence of both internal and external constituency groups upon the operations and programs of nonbusiness organizations, and the need for political compromise between these groups, is particularly apparent in governmental units at both the federal and state levels. This is due partially to the large size of many of these organizations, with their complex services and varied clientele, but also to some special problems associated with public management:

1. *Assigned personnel.* In most governmental organizations it is difficult to select or change the personnel. The employees are governed by civil service regulations which were originally designed to prevent the use of federal or state payrolls for political patronage, but which have come to provide nearly total tenure, and to encourage some lack of incentive and effort. Public managers have a very limited ability to change or improve the personnel.

2. *Existing structure.* In most governmental organizations it is difficult to alter the managerial structure, or the assignment of tasks to groups and subgroups. The existing structure is partially determined by legislation, partially by tradition, and partially by resistance to change. Public managers have a very limited ability to change or improve the formal structure.

3. *Legislated systems.* In most governmental organizations it is difficult to modernize the managerial systems, or the formal methods for planning, control, and motivation. Planning in governmental units necessarily centers on the annual budget, and on the multiple influences and uncertain outcomes of the budgetary process; long-term planning is particularly difficult due to the lack of long-term funding. Control procedures are primarily oriented toward assigning responsibility for input spending, since the output services are so variable, and usually unmeasurable. Motivation methods, including job assignments, employee promotions, and individual pay rates, are generally determined by Civil Service regulations, and reward longevity more than effort or attention. Public managers have an extremely limited ability to change or improve the systems.

4. *Potential publicity.* In most governmental organizations it is difficult to avoid public discussion of policy decisions, public influence on budgetary processes, and public questions about personal motives. The existence of multiple constituency groups, both within and without the government, almost ensures that at least one will use the public media in an attempt to influence funding levels or service definitions. To counter the influence of these groups, public managers

need an understanding of the information gathering and publishing process of the news media, and an ability to supply public statements and private comments that fit into that process. Pressure groups and public managers together often try to use the media to communicate indirectly with various persons in the decision hierarchy or the budgetary system who cannot be contacted directly. These persons would include preoccupied members of the legislature and high-ranking administrators in the executive branch. It is difficult not to be cynical in any discussion of the use of private media organizations to influence public policy decisions, but the ability to supply public statements and private comments that fit into the media process certainly requires consistency, so that the manager cannot be accused of changeability; clarity, so that the manager cannot be misquoted or distorted; and a certain element of the dramatic, so that the manager cannot be ignored. Public managers have to develop an ability to relate to the public media.

5. *Elected officials.* In most governmental organizations it is difficult to avoid conflict or at least dissension between elected officials and senior administrators. This conflict is due partially to the temporary position of the elected official, or those appointed by an elected official, in comparison to the permanent tenure of the administrative staff; members of the staff always have the option of delaying the introduction of new policies or the implementation of new procedures with which they disagree in the hope that the policies and procedures will change with a change in elected personnel. The conflict or dissension is also caused by the need for reelection on a regular basis. Reelection takes time that might otherwise be spent in overseeing the performance of the permanent staff, and it also forces a short-term orientation on the elected or appointed personnel. The need to seek reelection in two, three, or four years means not only that changes must be initiated within that time period, but that the results of those changes must be apparent, and hopefully be appreciated; there is consequently a natural tendency for elected officials to select programs with short response times, and to neglect the longer-term plans which may be of primary interest to members of the staff. Public managers have to develop an ability to resolve potential conflicts between elected officials and administrative personnel.

Management in nonprofit, nonbusiness organizations, whether private service agencies or public governmental units, is difficult because the factors that have been described in the text combine to prevent the development of a clearly stated, generally accepted mission or purpose for the organization. The service orientation and nonmarket pricing result in imprecise outputs, with few standards of performance and no quality controls, while the professional personnel and multiple constituencies bring numerous inputs, with dual personal allegiencies and variable individual motives. Both the imprecise outputs and the multiple inputs affect the short-term plans in the annual budgetary process, imposed by the external funding requirements of all nonprofit organizations. Public or governmental organizations add the complexities of assigned administrative personnel, existing managerial structures, and legislated planning, control, and motivation systems, which together bring a resistance to change in policies and procedures, while the special needs of the elected officials and the public nature of the news media create a demand for change in performance. The result of these conflicting pressures on public managers is a natural tendency to avoid precision in defining the mission or purpose or "strategy" for the organization. The interrelationships among these factors that result in an indefinite strategy can be shown in graphic form as follows:

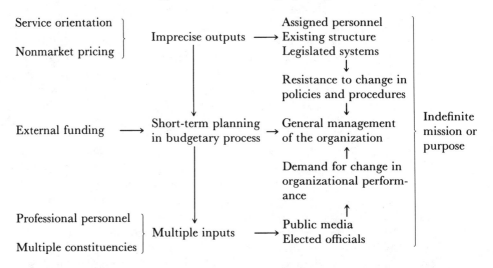

There are numerous factors in nonprofit, nonbusiness organizations that tend to result in the lack of a clearly defined and widely accepted statement of a mission or purpose for those organizations, but there is no inherent reason why this situation must continue. The characteristics of these organizations, which have been described in the text and then depicted graphically, result in pressures upon the executives serving in general management or directive positions that cause these people to resolve short-term financial and operational problems while neglecting longer-term objectives, to negotiate immediate compromises between conflicting groups while ignoring more universal interests, and to attend to external relationships, particularly with the funding agencies, while disregarding internal control and motivational needs. The time pressures for an immediate response are greater in the nonprofit and public organizations than they are in business due to the existence of the competitive groups in the multiple constituency, and these pressures result in a managerial orientation toward the short-term and the particular, rather than the long-term and the universal. Public managers tend to look at immediate problems rather than long-term directions, and they often work with a part of the organization rather than the complete whole. Public management, in summary, tends to be compressed and fragmented.

Unfortunately, the compressed and fragmented nature of public management creates many of the problems it faces, and continues most of the time pressures it endures. Public managers have to spend time justifying service programs to the funding sources, and resolving jurisdictional disputes with other agencies, because the precise benefits of the services to be provided to different groups within the nation, region, or community, and the exact limitations of those services and service areas, have never been clearly defined. Public managers also have to be engaged in negotiating with professional groups and motivating operational employees because the specific methods of providing the services have never been fully designed. Public managers are continually concerned with short-term and particular problems because the long-term and universal mission or purpose of the organization has never been completely resolved. Each nonprofit organization needs a statement that describes the service types, defines the service recipients, and designs the service methods, so that members of the organization can identify the nature of its operations and the reasons for its existence. This statement, of course, must be sensitive to economic, social, and political changes within the environment, responsive to financial, physical, and personnel resources in the organization, and integrative of professional, managerial, and operational values and attitudes of the employees. The statement, in short, must be strategic, and define a long-term concept of performance that can win support from all members of the constituency groups, and that can be achieved within the constraints imposed by the environmental trends and the organizational resources.

Strategy, for a nonprofit, nonbusiness organization, involves a long-term concept of services that will be provided, not a long-term method of competition that will be followed. The long-term method of competition for a business firm defines a competitive position or posture that, hopefully, will result in an operational edge or advantage for that company within its industry or industries. The long-term concept of service for a public agency or nonprofit organization defines a comparative position or posture, relative to other agencies and organizations, that will result, again hopefully, not in an operational edge or advantage, but in a wider understanding and fuller support for the operations of that organization. Nonprofit, nonbusiness organizations do not exist in a vacuum, independent of other organizations. Instead, they exist as part of a spectrum of organizations providing nearly equivalent services to approximately similar groups by closely parallel methods. The essential element in strategic design for nonprofit organizations is to recognize the existence of this spectrum, and to define the services, clients, and methods in comparison to those of the other organizations. Strategic design, properly done, provides a rationale for the continued existence and further support of a nonprofit organization, not a competitive advantage.

Nonprofit organizations do not compete in economic terms for clients or consumers, but they certainly do contend for financial support and public approval. A clear statement of the various services, client groups, and process methods, in comparison to those of other organizations, is essential for this external support and approval, and for the internal effort and even enthusiasm by members of the organization. Employees in a nonprofit organization or public agency, whether at the professional, managerial, or operational levels, need to know the comparative position and overall direction of their institutions in order to contribute their efforts in an effective and efficient manner. A clear statement of the strategy of a nonprofit organization is needed both for external information and internal motivation.

A clear statement of the strategy of a nonprofit organization is difficult to prepare since it normally needs to be expressed on four levels, as with large, multiple-industry firms. These levels, for the mutiple-industry firm, are the product–market positions and the product–process positions of the various divisions, the marketing and production relationships among those divisions within a single industry, and the financial relationships, which serve as surrogates for the growth and margin opportunities of the divisions, between different industries. An industry has been defined (in Chapter 3) as the market for similar or substitute products and services, and the producing firms that supply those products or services, together with the supplying and distributing companies. In less precise terms, an industry basically includes a group of competing firms that can affect the performance and position of one another by changes in product design, market demarcation, pricing level, distribution methods, advertising effort, etc. The level or degree of competition and the pattern or method of competition within each industry determines the opportunities and risks for each of the participating firms.

This economic concept of an industry as a group of competing firms is not completely applicable to most nonprofit institutions. Nonprofit organizations do not compete directly, but they do exist, as was expressed previously, as part of a spectrum of organizations providing nearly equivalent services to approximately similar groups by closely parallel methods, and they do contend, among those organizations, for financial support and public approval. It is an oversimplification to speak of a health care industry, or a higher education industry, or a community service industry, due to the total absence of price competition, but it is legitimate to think of these groups of nonprofit organizations as associations, each with known participants and an identifiable pattern of service revenues, external funds, fixed costs, and variable costs that is typical for each of the participants within the association. "Association" is not a good term, but it does express a worthwhile concept. The concept is that of closely similar organizations with identifiable patterns of revenues and expenses contending for financial support and public approval. Just as strategic design for a business firm culminates in the positioning of that firm within an industry or industries, strategic design for a nonprofit institution can be viewed as the positioning of that organization within an association or associations. This positioning, as stated previously, has to be on four levels:

1. *Service characteristics and recipient groups.* The primary element in strategic design for a business firm is the definition of the product–market position, or the selection of the product characteristics, both tangible and intangible, that relate to the consuming needs and purchasing patterns of customer groups within a market segment. Product–market positioning is particularly important for a smaller company, which must normally attempt to find a niche with few other participants to obtain a competitive advantage. This same product–market positioning is important for nonprofit organizations, although it is considerably more complex. Nonprofit organizations provide services, not products, and these services tend to be, as was described earlier, intangible and varied, and consequently their characteristics are more difficult to define. The recipient groups, also, tend to be more varied and more vague than the customer groups in a market segment, with fewer explicit demographic characteristics, consumer needs, and request patterns, so that the clients for the services are also difficult to

describe. To assist in the definition of the service characteristics and the identification of the recipient groups, it is useful to think of the range of possible services and the spectrum of potential recipients, and then to select both current and proposed positions along each of those vectors. This selection, of course, should be made in comparison to the service–recipient positions of other organizations within the association of contending institutions, and this comparison requires an understanding of those positions, and the various trends that affect the overall demand and the individual segments. Market analysis is useful in strategic design for nonprofit institutions, even though a relative advantage cannot be established due to the lack of direct competition.

2. *Service characteristics and processing methods.* The second step in strategic design for a business firm is the definition of the product–process position, or the selection of the production technology and plant capacity that relate to the product characteristics and market demand, and establish the output costs. Product–process positioning is particularly important for the product division of a large firm, which must usually attempt to develop a "low-cost" position to compete against other large firms in a national market. The same product–process positioning is important for nonprofit organizations, although again it is considerably more complex. The production processes for services are less defined, the technological methods are less advanced, and the scheduling and control problems are more complicated. Finally, few managers in public organizations think in terms of production processes as a means of distinguishing between institutions; instead, they tend to think of the operating processes necessary to produce the various services as something that must be done, with reasonable efficiency, but not as something that is central to the mission of the organization. However, there are economies of scale in public organizations, there are benefits to experience, and there is a pattern of fixed versus variable costs that can be changed by investment. A "low-cost" position may not be a meaningful concept for nonprofit organizations, but the possibility of expanded or improved services based upon reduced processing costs certainly is meaningful. To assist in the selection of the process technology and site capacity that will result in reduced costs for given service characteristics and demand levels, it is useful to think in terms of a range of capacities, and the alternative technologies for each capacity stage. The selection should be made in comparison to the cost positions of other organizations producing nearly equivalent services for closely similar client groups. This comparison requires an understanding of the current and potential members of the industry or association of contending institutions, and an understanding of the current and potential economics (pattern of service revenues, fixed costs, and variable costs that is typical of the members) of that association. Industry analysis is also useful in strategic design for nonprofit institutions, even though an economic equilibrium cannot be established due to the lack of price competition.

3. *Organizational focus within an association.* The third stage in strategic design for a business firm is the definition of a focus for the firm between alternative product–market and product–process positions in the same industry. The products, markets, and processes within an industry are usually interrelated. Some prod-

ucts are linked by their market segments, distribution channels, or promotional means, and others are connected by their raw materials, processing methods, or basic technologies. Even the largest of single-industry firms cannot afford to produce all products for all markets by all processes, and must select those that are most logically related to obtain a competitive advantage; that is, the large firms must emphasize products that are distributed by the same channels, or produced by the same methods, or made of the same materials, etc., to reduce overall costs. This emphasis or focus is particularly important for firms that operate within a mature industry, with limited growth, extensive competition, and narrow margins, and that need a competitive advantage against both domestic and foreign producers. This emphasis or focus is also important for nonprofit organizations, although the method of selection is considerably more complex. The relationships between the services, recipients, and processes in public organizations are not as clearly defined as in most business firms, and the benefits of joint efforts cannot be as precisely estimated. Also, most managers in public organizations do not think in terms of a focus for that organization; instead, the tendency is to offer multiple combinations of services, recipients, and processes, which results in the familiar problem of "being all things to all people." To achieve a focus, it is useful to consider all possible relationships by constructing a simple matrix based upon the recipient groups and the operating processes for each of the services:

	Recipient group 1	Recipient group 2	Recipient group 3	Recipient group 4
Operating process 1	Service A	—	—	—
Operating process 2	Service B	Service C	—	—
Operating process 3	—	—	Service D	—

It is usually difficult to quantify the benefits of a particular focus, or concentration upon similar recipient groups or operating process for the selected services, but estimates of the cost benefits can be prepared, with the expectation that reduced costs can be translated into improved or expanded services. The term "synergy" is often used within business firms to describe the potential benefits of closely related activities; the problem, as discussed earlier, is that the concept is attractive, but the benefits may be minimal, owing to the need for coordinated efforts by different groups within the organization to achieve those benefits. The same implementation problem certainly exists within nonprofit institutions, but it can be overcome with attention to the organizational structure, which assigns definite responsibilities for the performance of the needed tasks, and the managerial systems, which provide formal procedures for the planning, control, and motivation of those tasks. Overall, a study of the functional relationships between alternative services in order to create a centralized focus in activities and a potential savings in costs is certainly useful at nonprofit organizations, even though it is difficult to quantify and then realize the benefits of this focused orientation.

4. *Organizational balance between associations.* The last stage in strategic design for a business firm is the definition of the balance of that firm between industries. Many companies operate in more than one industry, in order to avoid the risks of concentration, and to receive the benefits of diversification. The problem in a diversified firm comes in determining the proper balance, or relative level of activities, between industries. Most diversified firms are organized with a product division in each industry, or a strategic business unit (SBU), which has been defined in a prior chapter as a portion of the company with a given product or product line, a specific market or market segment, an existing distribution channel, adequate productive capacity, and known competitors. The intent is to divide the company into business units that can act independently in each industry through a clearly defined strategy, and then to control that action and direct that strategy through resource allocations by means of a corporate planning model rather than a capital budgeting process. This corporate planning model is the familiar matrix that compares each strategic business unit within a diversified firm on two basic dimensions: the attractiveness of the industry, and the strengths of the company within that industry. Multiple-industry firms search for a competitive advantage by channeling resources to the divisions that combine industry attractiveness and corporate strengths since these are considered to be the divisions with the greatest probabilities of growth and return.

It is not as common for nonprofit organizations to participate in multiple associations as it is for companies to operate in multiple industries, and often the participation outside the major area of activity is on a reduced scale. However, it does occur. Colleges and universities, for example, are active primarily in higher education, and normally accept the development and transmission of knowledge as their primary functions, but universities with a medical school also offer health care, and colleges with a football team can be said to provide entertainment. It is essential to recognize the existence of these noncentral activities, and to determine the relative emphasis that should be placed upon them, in order to decide upon the proper balance for the organization. The corporate planning matrix, based upon a comparison of industry attractiveness and company strengths, would seem to be of limited value for nonprofit organizations since it identifies opportunities for further growth and profit, not needs for additional assistance and service. However, some understanding of an expected expansion of demand for the services, and some recognition of the current capability in performance by the organization, should be included in establishing a balance between activities for nonprofit organizations. A modified version of the corporate planning model can be used, with the services divided into those that show above-average, average, and below-average need expectations, and those that have above-average, average, and below-average organizational capabilities; see the table at the top of the next page.

Organizational Capabilities

	Above average	Average	Below average
Above average		Service C	
Average	Service A	Service B	
Below average			Service D

(left axis label, rotated: Service Growth Expectations)

Combined use of the organizational focus matrix, which indicates the similarities in recipient groups and processing methods among the various services, and of the organizational balance matrix, which illustrates the differences in future needs and current capabilities for those services, would appear to be of definite assistance in strategic planning at nonprofit institutions. The intent of strategic planning, once again, is to develop a long-term concept of the services that are to be provided that will be sensitive to economic, social, and political changes within the environment, responsive to financial, physical, and personnel constraints among the resources, and integrative of the professional, managerial, and operational values and attitudes of the employees. The intent, in short, is to define a long-term concept of organizational performance that can win support from all members of the constituency groups, and that can be achieved despite problems caused by environmental changes and organizational limitations.

The analytical process needed to define this long-term concept of organizational performance for nonprofit or nonbusiness institutions follows the same sequence that has been recommended for business firms, although with some difference in content. The following topics have to be examined:

1. *Charter or mission of the organization.* Many nonprofit institutions have a written charter, which usually dates from the time of the founding of the organization, and which generally is based upon the enabling legislation. Despite the written format and legalistic basis, the charter often remains a general statement of the philosophy of the institution and the direction of its efforts rather than an explicit listing of the organizational goals and an exact description of the proposed services. The charters at many private nonprofit agencies, providing social, educational, health care, cultural, and charitable services, are obsolete, having remained unchanged despite obviously changing organizational activities and recipient needs; while the legislation at most governmental service units, at the federal, state, and local levels, is imprecise, being subject to continual interpretation and gradual change. The charters at all nonprofit organizations provide

only limited guidance in developing a long-term concept of performance for those organizations, and the mission statements, which are general understandings by the members of each organization of the basic purpose for that organization, and the reasons for its existence, are of limited use because of the range of opinion usually represented in the various groups of the constituency. Statements from the charter are much less precise, and opinions about the mission are much less unanimous, at nonprofit institutions than at business firms. The mission and the charter should provide a starting place for the process of strategic design, but at nonprofit institutions this point of departure is usually indefinite, and often unsatisfactory.

2. *Values and attitudes of the personnel.* Most nonprofit institutions have a wide range of constituency groups, including employees from the professional, managerial, and operational units within the organization, and representatives from the service recipients, funding sources, elected officials, regulatory agencies, public associations, and news media outside the organization. Each individual within one of these constituency groups has a set of attitudes, beliefs, and performance standards that is partially unique to the individual, and partially typical of the group. Since a strategy for a nonprofit institution, to be effective, has to achieve some level of support from each of these groups, it is important to recognize the personal values and group goals of the members, and include them in the strategic design process. The problem, however, is that the recognition of attitudes, beliefs, values, and goals is not an exact science, with established methods for quantitative measurement; instead, it is an indefinite area where reliance has to be placed upon a considerable degree of managerial empathy and personal understanding. A second problem is that the reconciliation of conflicting attitudes, beliefs, values, and goals is not a simple task, with all individuals and groups acting on the basis of economic rationality; instead, it is an illogical area where reliance has to again be placed upon a considerable degree of managerial patience and personal effort. The number of constituency groups is much larger, and the personal values and performance standards of the members of those groups are more diverse, at nonprofit institutions than at business firms. Personal values and group goals have to be included in the strategic design process at all organizations, but at nonprofit institutions this inclusion is particularly important, and unusually difficult.

3. *Performance and position of the organization.* Directive managers at all nonprofit institutions find it difficult to evaluate the past performance and current position of their organizations. There are no objective measures of performance, such as growth in sales revenue or return on owners' equity, and there are few precise measures of position, such as comparative market shares or relative production costs. This lack of objective measures and precise indicators is partially due to the intangible nature of the services that are provided, partially to the nonmarket system of pricing that is followed, and partially to the multiple groups of constituents that are serviced; it is difficult to evaluate the performance of organizations that are providing intangible services to diverse clients at prices that have a very limited relationship to the needs of the market or to the costs of the process. Because of the lack of objective measures, it is common to turn to subjec-

tive opinions, and to compare the prestige, not the performance, of organizations providing equivalent services to similar constituencies by parallel methods. The intent is to look at the reputation and standing of an organization within the association of contending organizations. The problem is that the opinions on this relative standing may be both subjective and biased; persons asked to evaluate institutions may have a point of view that is either consciously or unconsciously oriented by professional associations, social values, or personal ambitions. Measuring the past performance and current position of a nonprofit organization is difficult, but it remains important since a comparison of this performance and position with the organizational charter or mission and with the individual values and group goals plays a major role in defining the need for strategic change within the institution. These comparisons are simpler, and the need for change more obvious, at business firms because of the ease of using financial ratios as surrogate measures for the performance of the marketing, production, and development functions. No surrogate measures exist for nonprofit institutions, which increases the complexity of the strategic design process at those institutions.

4. *Characteristics and trends of the environment.* All nonprofit institutions have to fit within an association of other organizations providing nearly equivalent services to approximately similar constituencies by closely parallel methods; this adjustment to an association is required for a nonprofit institution to contend for financial support and public approval. Accurate environmental analysis is needed to identify the characteristics of the association, and to anticipate the economic, social, political, and technological trends that may change those characteristics in the future. Identification of association characteristics and anticipation of association trends is a complex analytical task, but it is approximately equal in difficulty at either business firms or nonprofit organizations. A general manager at a business firm has to examine forecasts based upon different methodologies, select the most probable set of future conditions derived from those forecasts, and then state those future conditions as assumptions, or premises, for strategic planning. The assumptions may be on economic, social, political, or technological dimensions, but together they define the specific opportunities and risks for a firm within a given industry. Exactly the same process is needed for strategic planning at a nonbusiness institution; it is difficult but not impossible.

5. *Assets and skills of the organization.* All nonprofit institutions have to utilize their available resources in order to perform successfully within an association of other organizations providing nearly equivalent services to approximately similar constituencies by closely parallel methods; this performance within an association is necessary for a nonprofit institution to contend for financial support and public approval. Accurate resource analysis is needed to specify the capabilities of an organization, and to match those capabilities to the opportunities and risks for that organization within the association. Specifying the capabilities of an organization, and matching those capabilities against the requirements of an association, is a complex task but again not more difficult for a nonprofit institution than for a business firm. The general manager at a business firm has to examine the financial, physical, and positional assets of the firm, and the functional and

technical skills of the personnel, and then translate these general resources into the specific strengths and weaknesses that match the opportunities and risks for the firm within a given industry. Exactly the same process is needed for strategic planning at a nonbusiness institution; again, it is difficult but not impossible.

6. *Range of alternative strategies.* All nonprofit institutions have available to them a large number of possible combinations of service characteristics, recipient groups, and process methods. These possible combinations are constrained by the examination of the environment, which produces a series of specific opportunities and risks in the future of the association, and by the analysis of the resources, which defines a set of specific strengths and weaknesses in the capability of the organization. Together, the future opportunities and risks and the current strengths and weaknesses serve as boundaries for the selection of the proper strategy. Within those boundaries, however, there exists a range of strategic alternatives, or different concepts of service, and that range extends beyond the usual traditions of the association of contending organizations, and goes past the accepted conventions of the professional, managerial, and operational employees of the institution. The identification of these alternatives is a creative task that requires imagination, innovation, and perception. These characteristics, unfortunately, are often missing at both business firms and nonbusiness institutions; this lack is particularly apparent at many nonprofit organizations, which tend to accept existing strategies.

The process of strategic design at nonprofit organizations requires a comparison of the performance and position of the organization with the mission or charter of the institution and the values and attitudes of the personnel, an examination of the characteristics and trends of the environment and the assets and skills of the organization, and an identification of the full range of alternative strategies, or different concepts of the service to be provided, that are open to the institution. Part of this process requires logical thought and analytical effort, part of the process requires managerial empathy and political reconciliation, and part of the process requires individual innovation and personal creativity. The process of strategic design is not well done at most nonprofit organizations, because of the complexity involved in combining all these elements, and because of the ease of accepting existing concepts of service. It is a process, however, that will become increasingly important with greater constraints upon the funding sources, and greater demands by the recipient groups. The following cases illustrate the need for strategic design in public (nonprofit) institutions.

G.S.B.A. at the University of Michigan

The first college or university outside the original 13 states was chartered by the Legislature of the Territory of Michigan (which included the area now covered by the states of Michigan, Wisconsin, and Minnesota, and parts of northern Ohio and Indiana) in 1817. The university had been proposed by Augustus B. Woodward, who was then the federal judge for the territory, was named the Catholepistemiad Michigania, a Greek term for "universal institution," and was located in Detroit, which was then a frontier village on the edge of a very sparsely populated and largely unexplored wilderness.

> The entire population of the Territory of Michigan in 1817 was probably less than 5,000 persons. There were a few small settlements along the lakes, but the interior was known only to the fur trappers and to a few government surveyors, who described the area as a vast swamp, filled with bears, wolves, and hostile Indians, and largely uninhabitable. It was an audacious effort to found a university under those conditions.
>
> Judge Woodward was an audacious individual, and evidently a thinking one. He was the person responsible for bringing Pierre L'Enfant, the designer of Washington, D.C., to Detroit. The judge had proposed avenues ½ mile wide to limit the spread of fire and to permit the easy movement of troops for defense. Since the town had burned totally in 1805, and had been occupied by the British from 1812 to 1815, you might have thought that his recommendations would have been seen to have some merit. But, as usually happens in urban planning, the new ideas were rejected in favor of the old, and the only results of L'Enfant's work are much narrower avenues that radiate from the downtown section of the city. (Statement of a local historian)

In 1837, the "universal institution" was moved to Ann Arbor, and renamed the University of Michigan. Ann Arbor was selected since a local farmer had donated 40 acres of land; the legislature authorized two buildings, which were constructed, and the first class of 17 students was admitted in 1841.

> Ann Arbor got its name, as you probably already know, since the wives of the first two settlers were both named Ann, and since the area was forested with huge oak trees in groves, which were then termed arbours. The official post office address, until about 1900, was Ann's Arbour. Even in 1841, the character of the area was decidedly rural; the first janitor for the college received no pay, but was given half of the 40 acres, which now form the central campus, to farm. There were just two buildings: Mason Hall, which burned in 1955, and the President's House, which still remains. The President's House was designed by a New York architect, who never visited Ann Arbor, and consequently did not realize the availability of open space. He sent the design of a town house, much more suited for the crowded conditions and "row" construction traditions of the eastern cities, with no windows on the sides. Windows were not added until the 1870s. (Statement of a local historian)

In 1977, 140 years after the move to Ann Arbor, the University of Michigan had expanded to more than 45,000 students, enrolled in 17 schools or colleges, on three campuses, as shown at the top of the next page.

The University of Michigan has grown in reputation as well as in size. An American Council on Education survey in 1974 of nonprofessional graduate program faculties, which at Michigan are grouped in the School of Literature, Science and the Arts, ranked 12

School or college	Number of students
School of Architecture and Urban Planning	459
School of Art	446
School of Business Administration	1,719
School of Dentistry	874
School of Education	3,327
School of Engineering	4,299
School of Law	1,093
School of Library Science	379
School of Literature, Science and the Arts	16,167
School of Medicine	1,830
School of Music	923
School of Natural Resources	980
School of Nursing	1,017
School of Pharmacy	543
School of Public Health	777
School of Social Work	780
Total at the Ann Arbor campus	36,355
Total at the Dearborn campus	4,839
Total at the Flint campus	3,474
Total of credit extension students	1,189
Total attending the University of Michigan	45,837

of these departments in the top five nationally, and 23 in the top ten. A 1975 survey conducted by Columbia University on professional graduate programs described Michigan as one of the nation's leading universities; 13 of the 15 professional schools on the Ann Arbor campus were ranked among the top ten, in competition with other prestigious universities. The full listing of these professional schools is given in Exhibit 9.

Many of the students who come to Michigan never fully recognize the academic tradition of excellence that is represented here. Somehow, you always seem to hear more about Harvard, Stanford, and Berkeley in newspapers and the public press, but in academic journals and reputation, Michigan is certainly on a par with those other schools. This has always been true in the past; it is not certain that it can continue to be true in the future, due to the financial problems faced by the university. (Statement of a university faculty member)

The cause of the concern felt by many faculty members and administrative personnel on the continued quality of the instructional programs and research was primarily financial. Revenues at the university simply had not kept pace with inflation (Exhibit 1).

Over the six years from 1970 to 1976, the revenues of the university per full-year equivalent student had increased 47.5%, but inflation, as measured by the Index of State and Local Government Purchases, had risen 50.5%.

I suppose that your students will not fully recognize the impact of that difference between our 47.5% increase in revenues and the 50.5% increase in inflation, but I feel that it will result in a steady and discernible decline in the very quality of the university if continued over time. And, I

Exhibit 1 *Comparison for the General Fund budget (000's omitted) of the University of Michigan for the academic years 1969–1970 and 1975–1976*

	1969–1970	1975–1976	Increase in amount	Increase in percent	Increase in percent per FYES
State appropriations	$ 63,829	$ 99,831	$36,002	56.4	49.6
Student fees	28,586	50,400	21,813	76.3	68.5
Indirect costs	10,500	11,336	836	8.0	3.0
Other revenue	1,907	2,900	992	52.0	46.3
Deficiency from working capital	1,755	—	1,755	—	—
	$106,580	$164,468	$57,888	54.3	47.5

Source: University Record, September 22, 1975, p. 3.
Note: FYES means "full-year equivalent student."

see no reason why this situation will not continue over time. We have to start planning now for a somewhat parsimonious future. (Statement of university administrator)

The financial shortfall caused by the inability of the university to maintain revenue increases equal to the pace of inflation was primarily absorbed through reductions in expenditures for library books, technical equipment, organized research, and property maintenance and improvement (Exhibits 2 and 3).

Social Security costs up 125%, health insurance up 19.6%, utility costs up 133%,

Exhibit 2 *Comparison of expenditures (000's omitted) by object for the General Fund budget of the University of Michigan for the academic years 1969–1970 and 1975–1976*

	1969–1970	1975–1976	Increase in amount	Increase in percent
Faculty and staff salaries	$ 72,420	$110,314	$37,893	52.3
Retirement contributions	5,264	7,380	2,116	40.2
Social Security	2,294	5,167	2,873	125.2
Health insurance	1,162	3,445	2,283	196.5
Other staff benefits	1,492	2,018	525	35.2
Total compensation	$ 82,634	$128,326	$45,692	55.3
Student aid	$ 2,584	$ 11,513	$ 8,928	345.5
Equipment purchases	1,008	575	(434)	(43.0)
Book purchases	1,195	1,573	378	31.7
Utility costs	2,468	5,764	3,295	133.5
Other noncompensation	17,703	17,672	(30)	(0.2)
Total noncompensation	$ 24,960	$ 37,099	$12,138	48.6
Budget cuts during year	(1,015)	(958)	57	—
Total expenditures	$106,580	$164,468	$57,888	54.3

Source: University Record, September 22, 1975, p. 3.

Exhibit 3 *Comparison of expenditures (000's omitted) by program for the General Fund budget of the University of Michigan for the academic years 1969–1970 and 1975–1976*

	1969–1970	1975–1976	Increase in amount	Increase in percent
Departmental instruction	$ 59,003	$ 89,936	$30,932	52.4
Other educational services	2,476	3,905	1,428	57.7
Library services	5,401	7,924	2,523	46.7
Organized research	7,161	8,529	1,368	19.1
Extension instruction	1,824	2,167	342	18.8
Student services	3,702	5,643	1,941	52.4
Student fees allocated	1,085	1,691	605	55.8
Student aid	2,584	11,513	8,928	345.5
State and public services	1,981	2,477	496	25.0
General administration	1,377	2,149	766	55.2
Business operations	5,299	7,671	2,372	44.8
Utility costs	2,468	5,764	3,295	133.5
Plant operations and maintenance	11,621	15,242	3,620	31.2
Plant improvements	1,605	809	(795)	(49.5)
Total budget	$107,594	$165,425	$57,830	53.7
Budget cuts during year	(1,015)	(958)	57	—
Total expenditures	$106,580	$164,468	$57,888	54.3

Source: University Record, September 22, 1975, p. 4.
Note: Budget cuts during the year refer to enforced savings in expenditures brought about by reductions in state appropriations after the start of the fiscal year.

and we expect another 30% to 40% increase here next year. Equipment purchases for research down 43%, organized research up only 19%—organized research is the term we use for internal funding of departmental and individual faculty research projects, and includes only data gathering, computer time, student assistants, and experiment materials, and not faculty salaries, which are in the departmental instruction budget, but our faculty certainly are not going to be very productive in research and writing without more funds here—and library book purchases up only 31%. We are being forced to spend money in the wrong places, and we are neglecting the research and learning that made the University of Michigan a very special place. We are spending money on liability insurance, which went up from $104,000 in 1969 to somewhat over $3,000,000 in 1976 for an increase of 2,875%, and we are reducing the amounts allocated for research. We have major problems, and we have got to establish a new set of priorities for funding. (Statement of a university administrator)

A confusing element in university financing is that many of the available funds are restricted, and can be used only for certain designated purposes, or paid only to certain designated units. The total operating budget of the University of Michigan in the 1975–1976 academic year was $269,451,000, but $104,983,000 of this amount was restricted, and allocated by different budgets. There were four major budgets which made up the total operating budget of the university:

1. *General Fund budget,* which includes expenditures for general teaching, research, library service, student aid, administrative costs, and physical property maintenance. In 1975–1976, the General Fund ex-

penditures were, as listed previously, $164,-468,000.

2. *Designated Fund budget,* which includes gifts and grants from alumni and foundations that are restricted to certain departments or units within the university. Funds donated to the Rackham Graduate School, which primarily supervises Ph.D. students working in the academic departments, cannot, for example, be allocated to other units on the campus. In 1975–1976, the Designated Fund budget was $8,638,000.

3. *Restricted Fund budget,* which includes gifts and grants from alumni, foundations, industry, and the federal government that are restricted by their donors to certain uses within the university. Funds donated for research in wastewater treatment, for example, cannot be used on other projects. The Restricted Fund budget is primarily for funded research; in 1975–1976 this budget amounted to $86,150,000, of which $68,179,000 was contributed by various agencies of the federal government for research in both the physical and social sciences.

4. *Auxiliary Activities budget,* which includes revenues from activities within the university that are expected to maintain themselves by these revenues; these operations include the residential halls, dining facilities, the Michigan League, the Michigan Union, and the University Hospital. Revenues in 1975–1976 from these auxiliary activities were $10,195,000.

The budgetary situation became especially severe in the 1975–1976 academic year. After approving an initial state appropriation, Governor Milliken ordered substantial cuts in state funding for higher education. The University of Michigan responded by announcing a freeze on all faculty hiring, by raising student tuition, and by initiating substantial "belt-tightening" measures. Tuition increases were substantial, yet they covered only a portion of the allocated costs of instruction (Exhibit 4).

Exhibit 4 *Comparison of tuition charges at the University of Michigan for the academic years 1969–1970 and 1975–1976*

	1969–1970	1975–1976	Increase in amount	Increase in percent
Resident fees				
Lower division	$ 480	$ 848	$ 368	76.7
Upper division	480	960	480	100.0
Graduate school	540	1,160	620	114.8
Law school	680	1,316	636	93.5
Public health	960	1,600	640	66.7
Dentistry and medicine	960	1,680	720	75.0
Nonresident fees				
Lower division	1,540	2,756	1,216	79.0
Upper division	1,540	2,968	1,428	92.7
Graduate school	1,648	3,008	1,360	82.5
Law school	1,740	3,000	1,260	72.4
Public health	2,140	3,240	1,100	51.4
Dentistry and medicine	2,140	3,360	1,220	57.0
Cost of instruction				
Undergraduate	1,966	2,903	937	47.5
Graduate and professional	3,892	5,864	1,972	50.5

Source: University Record, September 22, 1975, p. 4.

In addition to the current financial problems, which have been described, administrative personnel at the University of Michigan were concerned about three other trends which they felt would have a distinct impact upon the university:

1. *Decreased demand for undergraduate education.* The college-age population, which had expanded rapidly throughout the 1960s as a result of the "baby boom" following World War II, had begun to grow much more modestly in the late 1970s; it was expected to reach a plateau in the 1977–1981 period, and then begin to decline sharply, about 25% in total, until 1995. These demographic trends were certain, and not estimates; that is, an 18-year-old college student in 1995 was born and recorded on the census figures in 1977. In addition to the decreased numbers of college-age persons, there seemed to be a decreased demand for a college education:

   Among the significant trends is the current disillusionment as to whether going to college contributes to finding a job.... Despite the views of those of us who reside in universities about the value of an education, we must recognize that we are perceived as prejudiced observers, and the steady drumfire of articles and books questioning the need for a college education have raised doubts in the minds of many potential students, their parents, and the taxpayers. (Statement of President Fleming, State of the University Address, reprinted in the *University Record,* October 13, 1975, p. 3)

2. *Decreased opportunities for graduate (nonprofessional) education.* The University of Michigan, in company with many other graduate-oriented universities, staffed many of the undergraduate courses with Ph.D. students who served as teaching fellows, and also completed many of the research projects with Ph.D. students who served as research assistants. This apprenticeship system helped both the university finances and the faculty productivity. However, it was felt that the number of Ph.D. students would decline in the future, due to the lack of opportunity for the graduates in most of the academic fields:

   The haunting problem in graduate education today in many fields is the number of doctoral candidates that are being turned out. The problem arises because a heavy proportion of Ph.D. recipients has always gone into academic institutions, and the great growth era which caused them to be absorbed is over. (Statement of President Fleming, State of the University Address, reprinted in the *University Record,* October 13, 1975, p. 3)

3. *Decreased funding due to alternative social needs.* Universities expanded rapidly during the 1950s and 1960s, which was a period that combined increased demand for higher education with available funding. The University of Michigan, for example, grew from 14,800 students in 1951 to 45,000 in 1976, and from a $40,000,000 operating budget to over $269,000,000 in 1976. Higher education was given a definite priority by the legislature for state funds, for the political process recognized the social benefits of expanded knowledge and trained personnel in the physical and social sciences, the humanities, and the professions. However, by 1977, other social needs, particularly welfare and urban problems, had supplanted higher education in the political competition for funding:

   The apparent promise of higher education has never been achieved. In the 1950s there was the Salk vaccine and the space program and other very dramatic developments, and state funding increases were almost automatic. No legislator wanted to be on record as voting against scientific advances. But that era came to an end with the riots and disruptions of the 1970s, and it came to be very easy to vote against increased funding for the universities. Plus, there were now other, much more pressing social needs such as unemployment compensation, welfare payments, health care assistance, and inner city programs. The unemployment rate in Michigan exceeds the national average, and in the city of Detroit it is a human tragedy. It is a poignant commentary on our society that welfare and law enforcement have become the two largest items in the budget of the state. (Statement of a university administrator)

In response to the financial, demographic, and political pressures, the University of Michigan began a long-range planning effort in the fall of 1975. It was decided that each of the 17 schools and colleges on the campus, together with the various centers and institutes and programs that crossed the boundaries of the traditional schools and colleges, would prepare a document stating the goals and objectives of the unit, and describing the instructional programs, research projects, staffing requirements, and enrollment levels needed to achieve those goals and objectives. It was expected that these documents would be reviewed by the academic vice president, evaluated by a university-wide committee, and then used to "delineate the directions and alternative courses of action for the University of Michigan."

On a number of occasions it has become clear that we need to improve the procedures by which we establish University priorities and allocate resources. In the Spring of 1974 the Executive Officers of the University agreed that each Vice President should launch an evaluation effort within his own area of responsibility. At my request the University's Program Evaluation Committee and the Office of Academic Planning and Analysis have developed a three-phase evaluation and planning project in which all instructional and instruction-related units under the jurisdiction of the Office of Academic Affairs will participate.

Results of this project will have a growing impact upon decision-making and budgeting as successive phases are completed. There are indications that the Michigan economy will regain some of its momentum by 1978. Whether or not that occurs, the Office of Academic Affairs plans to develop a discretionary General Fund account which can be employed to allocate monies to high priority needs. Your own evaluation and planning reports and subsequent advice by the University's Program Evaluation, Budget Priorities, and Long Range Planning Committees will all influence the allocation of those discretionary funds. (Memorandum to All Deans and Directors from Academic Vice President Rhodes, October 27, 1975)

The Evaluation and Planning Project initiated by the academic vice president had three distinct phases:

Phase I   Activation of each unit's objectives and their major operational implications (to be completed by May 15, 1976, and reviewed by the Program Evaluation Committee by August 15)

Phase II   Evaluation of operations for each unit in light of the objectives stated in Phase I

Phase III Delineation of directions and alternative courses of action based upon the statements of Phase I and the evaluations of Phase II

The Evaluation and Planning Project was felt both by members of the faculty and by persons in the community to be a major change from prior resource allocation methods:

An ambitious new planning and evaluation program begins this month for instructional and instruction-related units at the University. One of its primary objectives is to help the University establish priorities for the future and decide how best to allocate its resources to conform to those priorities.

Included are all 17 schools and colleges,

the University libraries, and more than 20 centers, institutes, and other academic units which report to the vice president for academic affairs.

The very bedrock of academic programming is outlined for review: curriculum and degree programs, faculty research and service obligations, and staffing and enrollment levels, to name a few. (*University Record,* November 10, 1975, p. 3)

An unusually clear example of what a large university can do when under pressure to spread its resources thinner is provided by a document the U-M Office of Academic Affairs sent out a few days ago to deans of the 17 schools and colleges and directors of other academic units on the Ann Arbor campus.

The document doesn't look dramatic. It is simply 10 typewritten pages blandly titled "Evaluation and Planning Project—Phase I. Objectives of Academic Units."

Inside, it isn't bland. The 10 pages call for the nearest approach to centralized, long-range planning ever tried on this campus where relations between academic units and the central administration have traditionally been described as "decentralized" and "autonomous."

The plan doesn't come close to calling for centralization in the sense that anyone will attempt to pass down orders through a one-way chain of command. It does, however, outline a process that will lead to written agreements, signed by U-M deans and center directors and by Vice President for Academic Affairs Frank H. P. Rhodes, containing five-year plans for each academic unit. (*Ann Arbor News,* November 12, 1975, p. 5)

The School of Business Administration at the University of Michigan was, of course, one of the instructional units required by the academic vice president to participate in Phase I of the Evaluation and Planning Project, and consequently had to prepare a document stating the goals and objectives of the School and describing the instructional programs, research projects, staffing requirements, and enrollment levels needed to achieve those goals and objectives.

At the date of the case, the School of Business Administration offered four instructional programs:

1. *B.B.A. program,* which provides a two-year full-time course of study leading either to immediate employment in business, or to further graduate study. The option of further graduate study was important, and both faculty members and administrative personnel often referred to the B.B.A. as a "preprofessional" degree.

   In addition to providing a sound background for professional success in management of business, government, and other organizations, the program can serve as a rigorous preparation for graduate study in business administration, law, or other fields. (Statement in the *1977–1978 Bulletin of the School of Business Administration, University of Michigan,* p. 11)

2. *M.B.A. program,* which provides a two-year full-time course of study leading to entry-level employment in a number of functional or technical specialties, and eventual general management responsibility. The "general management" character of the program was stressed by many of the faculty members and administrative personnel.

   The achievement of managerial competence requires a broad range of skills to identify problems, seek out relevant information, exercise practiced judgment, and implement solutions within the context of a rapidly changing environment. (Statement in the *1977–1978 Bulletin of the Graduate School of Business Administration, University of Michigan,* p. 10)

3. *M.B.A. evening program,* which provides a four- to five-year part-time course of study

for persons currently employed in the southeastern Michigan area.

Persons employed full-time have an opportunity to earn the Master of Administration degree through an evening program. Admission procedures and standards, degree requirements, and course content are precisely the same for Evening Program students as for other M.B.A. degree candidates. (Statement in the *1977–1978 Bulletin of the Graduate School of Business Administration, University of Michigan,* p. 15)

4. *Ph.D. program,* which provides a three- to five-year full-time course of study leading toward research and teaching in the various functional and technical areas of business administration.

Whatever the student's previous education, he or she is expected to possess the individual capacity to exceed it; to become a creative contributor to his or her special field of teaching and research. The Ph.D. candidate should realize that he or she is aspiring to enter a profession of scholarship in which his or her initiative must provide the main impetus to improvement. Emphasis in the program is placed on thorough training in economic analysis and policy, in one or more of the functional fields of business, and in the application of accounting, mathematics, statistics,

behavioral science, and the computer to the solution of business problems. (Statement in the *1977–1978 Bulletin of the Graduate School of Business Administration, University of Michigan,* p. 40)

Enrollment in the School of Business Administration in 1976 totaled 1840 students, divided among the four instructional programs as shown in Exhibit 5.

Students were accepted in the B.B.A. program after completing their sophomore year in the College of Literature, Science and the Arts or the Engineering School; these students had a 3.4 grade-point average (A = 4.0), and were at the median or above in their L.S.&A. class.

Students accepted in the M.B.A. program had an average test score of 610 on the G.M.A.T. examination, which placed Michigan in the top five of the Graduate Schools of Business Administration nationally. Forty-five percent of the entering class generally have undergraduate degrees in engineering or the physical sciences; 35% have degrees in the social sciences or humanities; and 15% have degrees in business administration. A wide geographic dispersion is represented, with 20% attending undergraduate colleges in the Northeast, 10% in the Southeast, 54% in the Midwest, 9% in the Far West, and 7% in Eu-

Exhibit 5 *Enrollment in the degree programs of the School of Business Administration at the University of Michigan*

	Fall entrance	Winter entrance	Total first year	Total all years
B.B.A. program	240	50	290	550
M.B.A. (day) program	275	75	350	650
M.B.A. (evening) program	100	50	150	580
Ph.D. program	15	5	20	60
				1,840

Note: Enrollment in the M.B.A. (evening) program is expressed as "full-time equivalent" students; that is, each student is assumed to be taking full-time coursework, or five courses per semester. Evening program M.B.A. students actually take two courses per semester, so that the number of individuals enrolled in the evening program is 250% of the full-time equivalents shown in the exhibit.

Exhibit 6   *Required courses in the undergraduate B.B.A. program at the University of Michigan*

		Fall term		Winter term
First year	SMS-300	Data Processing	SMS-301	Introductory Probability
	OB-300	Behavioral Theory	PC-311	Production Management
	FIN-300	Money and Banking	FIN-301	Business Finance
	MAR-300	Marketing Management	MAR-301	Marketing Management
	ACC-271	Accounting (or elective)	ACC-272	Accounting (or elective)
Second year	BE-300	Economics of Enterprise	BE-310	Business Conditions
	LHC-305	Business Law		Elective
	PC-490	Corporate Management		Elective
		Elective		Elective
		Elective		Elective

rope, Africa, or Asia. The average age is 24, and the majority of the students have either military or work experience. In 1976, 20% of the entering class were women.

The undergraduate program was heavily structured, with 14 of the 20 courses required; however, many of the students had taken accounting during their sophomore year, which gave them some additional flexibility in selecting electives (Exhibit 6).

Adequate electives to permit undergraduates to major in the area were offered only by the accounting and marketing departments.

The graduate M.B.A. program was also structured, with 9 of the 18 courses required (Exhibit 7). Placement examinations could be taken for the first-year required courses; passing the exam satisfied the degree requirement for the course, and made it possible to

substitute an elective course. 60 hours were required for graduation.

Adequate elective courses were offered to permit graduate students to major in Accounting, Business Economics, Finance, Insurance and Actuarial Mathematics, International Business, Marketing, Organizational Behavior and Industrial Relations, Policy and Control, and Management Science. The functional fields of the entry-level jobs accepted indicates generally the division of the class among these departments: 30% in Finance, 19% in Computer-Based Systems Consulting, 17% in Accounting, 11% in Marketing, 9% in Operations Research and Management Science, 4% in Production, 2% in Human Resources Management, and 8% in miscellaneous areas. Seventy percent of the class of 1976 accepted jobs with large or-

Exhibit 7   *Required courses in the graduate M.B.A. program at the University of Michigan*

		Fall term		Winter term
First year	ACC-501	Accounting (4 crs)	FIN-551	Financial Management (4 crs)
	OB-501	Human Behavior (4 crs)	MAR-551	Marketing Management (4 crs)
	SMS-501	Probability (4 crs)	PC-551	Analytical Methods (4 crs)
	SMS-500	Information Systems (3 crs)		Elective (3 crs)
Second year	BE-601	Business Economics (3 crs)	PC-659	Business Policy (3 crs)
	Four	Electives	One	Seminar in major field
			Three	Electives

Exhibit 8 *Industries selected by 1976 graduates of the M.B.A. program at the University of Michigan*

Nonmanufacturing	60%	Manufacturing	40%
Advertising	1%	Automotive	12%
Commercial banking	12%	Chemical and pharmaceutical	4%
Consulting (general)	5%	Consumer goods	4%
Consulting (systems)	7%	Electrical and electronic	9%
Financial services	6%	Food and beverage	1%
Investment banking	5%	Mechanical equipment	2%
Public accounting	15%	Paper and forest products	1%
Retailing	3%	Petroleum and gas	2%
Utilities	1%	Miscellaneous manufacturing	5%
Miscellaneous nonmanufacturing	5%		

ganizations, with the remaining 30% equally divided between medium-sized and smaller firms. The type of industry selected for the first employment is given in Exhibit 8.

There were 63 faculty members who maintained a full teaching schedule (two courses in the B.B.A. or M.B.A. program per term, plus additional work with the Ph.D. students in reading and research seminars and thesis supervision), divided among the major functional and technical areas of administration as shown in Exhibit 9.

Phase I of the Evaluation and Planning Project required a statement of the goals and objectives of each instructional unit, and a description of the educational programs, research projects, staffing requirements, and enrollment levels needed to achieve those goals and objectives. In short, the academic vice president had requested a detailed report on the proposed strategy of each of the 17 schools and colleges on the campus. Dr. Floyd A. Bond, Dean of the School of Business Administration, recognized that these reports would

Exhibit 9 *Faculty numbers and discipline orientations at the School of Business Administration at the University of Michigan*

Accounting		12	Law, history, and communication		5
Auditing	6		Law	3	
Tax	4		Business history	1	
Managerial accounting	2		Business communication	1	
Business economics		4	Marketing		8
Finance		8	Organizational behavior		6
Money and banking	2				
Investments	3		Policy and control		6
Corporate finance	3		Strategic management	3	
			Management systems	1	
International business		3	Operations management	2	
			Statistics and management science		8
			Statistics	5	
			Computer systems	3	

be utilized for resource allocation over the coming years, and that it was essential that the statement submitted by the School of Business Administration be thoughtfully and convincingly prepared.

Class Assignment. Prepare a statement of the proposed strategy for the School of Business Administration at the University of Michigan; the statement should include both a definition of the goals and objectives for the School, and a description of the instructional programs and research projects, faculty numbers and disciplines, and enrollment projections and admission requirements needed to achieve those goals and objectives, all bearing a logical relationship to the current resources of the School and the apparent trends in management education. Major changes in the level of expenses (e.g., increased faculty numbers) should be accompanied by proposed programs (e.g., executive education) to generate the required resources.

Maria Hansen Health Center

In mid-1979, Mercy Hospital, an acute medical care facility, and Maplewood Neuropsychiatric Hospital, a midterm psychiatric care facility, were combined to form the Maria Hansen Health Center. Both institutions had originally been started by the Sisters of the Holy Spirit, a Roman Catholic religious order; both institutions were located in Madison, Wisconsin, although on opposite sides of the city; both institutions had a commitment to improved health care in Madison and the surrounding area of Dane County; and both institutions had some overlap among board members and administrative personnel. After the merger, there was a single governing board and management structure for the Health Center, and it was planned eventually there would be a common medical staff to serve both facilities. On November 9, 1979, the merger was solidified when the governing board approved the issuance of a formal statement of the Health Center's philosophy, mission, role, and goals. This document, which is reproduced in Appendix A, was designed to guide the daily operations and future planning of the Health Center, and re-flected the benevolent spirit and desire to serve of the namesake of that center: Maria Hansen. Maria Hansen had been born into a wealthy family in Liège, Belgium, in 1782, but had experienced hardship and poverty during her early life when her parents were forced into exile by the French Revolution. Based upon her personal experience, and her observations of the needs of others, she founded the Sisters of the Holy Spirit in 1833. The order's vow was one of service—to educate the children, nurse the sick, help the destitute, and particularly, to assist women who were in hospitals or prisons—and it was the stated objective of the Maria Hansen Health Center to continue that tradition of service in providing health care to the community in Dane County.

The Maria Hansen Health Center was part of a larger organization: the Sisters of the Holy Spirit Health Corporation, which was headquartered in West Allis, Wisconsin, just outside Milwaukee. The Sisters of the Holy Spirit had been active in the ownership, management, and staffing of hospitals in the

United States for over 100 years, and in 1980 the order was the largest nonprofit religious provider of health care services in the country, with 17 hospitals in the tristate area of Wisconsin, Iowa, and Illinois. These hospitals had originally been organized in five geographic divisions, with an independent governing board for each division, but the larger Sisters of the Holy Spirit Health Corporation had been formed in 1976 to provide a central focus for corporate planning and a secure source for hospital financing, while leaving operating decisions and service planning decentralized to meet local conditions. Each individual hospital or area health center now had a governing board that recognized and responded to the local conditions. Strategic decisions and debt approval fell under the authority of the corporate "Big Board." Both religious and lay personnel were involved in management at the corporate and local levels.

The Sisters of the Holy Spirit Health Corporation was a large and well-respected health care organization. The 17 hospitals provided 4,952 beds within the service area that included over 3 million people. During 1979, 187,154 patients were admitted, for a total of 1,516,730 patient-days (number of occupied beds × number of days occupied during the year). The hospitals treated 437,189 emergency patients during the year, and had 686,271 outpatient visits (an outpatient visit is an appointment at a clinic in one of the hospitals for medical services of a nonemergency nature). Operating revenues of the Health Corporation in 1979 were $419 million, up 13% from 1978, and operating expenses were $402 million, also up 13%. Simplified income statements for the Sisters of the Holy Spirit Health Corporation are given in Exhibit 1, and balance sheets in Exhibit 2.

The Maria Hansen Health Center was one of the 17 local hospitals or area health centers of the Sisters of the Holy Spirit Health Corporation. It provided, as described previously, both medical and psychiatric services

Exhibit 1 *Consolidated income statements (000's omitted) for the Sisters of the Holy Spirit Health Corporation, 1978 and 1979*

	1978	1979
Patient service revenues	$427,759	$490,907
Less contractual allowances	(66,829)	(82,696)
Net patient service revenues	360,930	408,211
Other operating revenues	9,261	10,789
Total operating revenues	370,191	419,000
Operating expenses	327,313	367,922
Interest expenses	12,557	14,462
Depreciation and amortization	17,209	19,433
Total operating expenses	357,079	401,817
Income from operations	13,112	17,183
Nonoperating revenues	4,676	5,991
Income available for reinvestment	17,788	23,174

Source: Corporation records; some figures have been disguised for confidentiality.

Exhibit 2 *Consolidated balance sheets (000's omitted) for the Sisters of the Holy Spirit Health Corporation, 1978 and 1979*

	1978	1979
Cash and investments in short-term securities	$ 15,814	$ 21,721
Accounts receivable for patient services	52,401	48,083
Inventories of medical and service supplies	5,597	5,755
Assets held in trust—noncurrent	5,699	4,422
Miscellaneous current assets	3,561	3,370
Total current assets	83,072	83,351
Designated assets	27,255	48,872
Assets held in trust	26,906	27,728
Investments in physical plant and equipment	399,631	428,439
Less accumulated depreciation	(110,199)	(128,342)
Deferred financial costs	5,628	5,063
Miscellaneous long-term assets	3,963	1,684
Total long-term assets	353,184	383,444
Total unrestricted assets	436,256	466,795
Current portion of long-term debt	3,676	9,800
Accounts payable	18,401	19,980
Overpayment by third-party compensation	8,804	6,601
Accrued liabilities	19,844	22,246
Total current liabilities	50,725	58,627
Deferred reimbursement of third-party payors	1,841	1,941
Deferred compensation	2,322	2,792
Accumulated income for reinvestment	2,323	8,241
Long-term debt	207,021	198,336
Total long-term liabilities	213,507	211,287
Unrestricted funds balances	172,027	196,881
Total liabilities and unrestricted funds balances	436,256	466,795

Source: Corporation records; some figures have been disguised for confidentiality.

to the Madison and Dane County communities, and these services were evidently needed for there was a high occupancy rate and an increasing number of admissions (Exhibit 3).

The largest facility in the Maria Hansen Health Center was Mercy Hospital, which was a 558-bed, nonprofit, voluntary acute-care hospital; it was described as the "flagship of the Sisters of the Holy Spirit fleet" because it was modern, successful, and generated operating margins for reinvestment considerably above the industry average of 3.5% quoted for similar-sized units. (The operating margin for a health care institution is defined as the income from operations divided

Exhibit 3 *Facility utilization statistics for the Maria Hansen Health Center, 1977–1979*

	1977	1978	1979
Available beds at Mercy and Maplewood hospitals	683	683	683
Admissions to Mercy and Maplewood hospitals	22,029	23,035	24,056
Patient days at Mercy and Maplewood hospitals	207,502	211,854	205,035
Average length of patient stay (number of days)	9.42	9.20	8.52
Average daily census (number of patients)	569	580	562
Occupancy rate (daily census/available beds)	83.24%	84.98%	82.25%

Source: Corporation records.

by the total operating expenses.) Both revenues and expenses for Mercy Hospital had increased rapidly during the period 1973–1978, following the pattern of medical costs established nationwide (Exhibit 4).

Mercy Hospital had been founded in 1911 by members of the Sisters of the Holy Spirit congregation from Dubuque, Iowa; they responded to an appeal expressed by the pastor at one of the large parish churches in Madison for a tuberculosis sanitarium. Tuberculosis is an infectious disease that was very common in the late nineteenth and early twentieth centuries due to crowded living conditions and poor sanitation practices; it was the leading cause of death in the United States from 1884 to 1909, but declined in occurrence and severity with improved housing and better care, and has now been nearly eliminated through the use of antibiotics. Mercy Sanitarium was originally located in a large private home that had been donated to the church, but in 1917 the medical needs of the community and the financial support of the parish led the Sisters to build a new 110-bed hospital on 11 acres of land close to the church. The hospital was expanded during the 1940s, bringing the total bed capacity to 558, and crowding the available land. In 1977, the hospital was moved to 240

Exhibit 4 *Income statements (000's omitted) for Mercy Hospital, 1973–1978*

	1973	1974	1975	1976	1977	1978
Gross patient service revenues	$32,394	$34,042	$39,321	$45,298	$53,026	$69,965
Less contractual allowances	(6,004)	(4,775)	(6,115)	(7,412)	(9,478)	(10,991)
Net patient service revenues	26,390	29,267	33,206	37,886	43,548	58,974
Other operating revenues	109	180	139	764	830	1,118
Total operating revenues	26,499	29,447	33,345	38,650	44,378	60,092
Operating expenses and depreciation	25,149	27,622	31,690	36,363	42,005	53,285
Interest expenses	124	13	109	109	906	4,797
Total operating expenses	25,273	27,735	31,799	36,472	42,911	58,082
Income from operations	1,226	1,712	1,546	2,178	1,466	2,010

Source: Corporation records; some figures have been disguised for confidentiality.
Note: Neither "other operating revenues" nor "income from operations" includes interest from the endowment or contributions from supporters of Mercy Hospital.

acres on the eastern edge of Madison, with new buildings and adequate room for expansion. The same bed capacity, 558, was maintained to avoid the need to obtain expansion approval from state and federal licensing boards.

The new buildings were designed to minimize the mechanical, electrical, and structural obsolescence that would normally occur during the next 50 years of occupancy. The site was planned around the concept of a "health care campus" which was expected to include the hospital, an office building for the practicing physicians (completed in 1978), an ambulatory surgery facility (construction of this $2 million addition had begun in 1979), and eventually other buildings for mental health (to transfer the patients from Maplewood and to integrate the psychiatric and medical care of those patients), and for physical rehabilitation, extended care, and geriatric service. It was believed to be important that the services offered by the Maria Hansen Health Center be both integrated and diversified to serve the total health needs of the community.

The replacement hospital and the new office building were financed through operating income, financial donations, and two public bond issues totaling $54,000,000 (Exhibit 5).

The 558 beds at Mercy Hospital were primarily for medical and surgical use, although many were reserved for obstetrics, pediatrics, and intensive care (Exhibit 6).

The total utilization of the beds at Mercy Hospital had been over 80% for years, and no decline in demand was expected as the Madison City and Dane County areas were believed to be in the beginning, rather than the later, stages of growth. Patient admissions were increasing, reflecting the growing demand, although the average length of stay for each patient was decreasing as part of an effort to reduce health care costs (Exhibit 7).

Mercy Hospital was staffed by 2,500 employees, which included 400 physicians and 75 house officers (interns and residents, completing their medical training). The hospital played a major teaching role, as nearly one-third of the medical students at the University of Wisconsin were assigned to assist the physicians for practical training in the various specialties. Physician reimbursement was on a fee-for-service basis (as opposed to a contract salary), and each physician billed patients directly for his/her services.

Mercy Hospital provided both primary and secondary medical care within the Dane County service area, but attempted to avoid tertiary care unless it were unavailable at other health care institutions within the area. Primary, secondary, and tertiary care classifications are somewhat ambiguous, but they refer basically to the degree of specialization of the attending physician. Primary care is provided by a general practitioner or "family" doctor; for more complex medical conditions, the patient is referred to a specialist for secondary care, and for the most complex conditions, the patient may be referred to an advanced specialist for tertiary care. The degree of specialization of the physician often correlates with the sophistication of the technology and the size of the service area, as shown in Exhibit 8.

Maplewood Neuropsychiatric Hospital was established in the mid-1920s by the Sisters of the Holy Spirit to provide midterm psychiatric treatment, with the average patient stay ranging from 4 to 9 months. Maplewood had 155 beds, was served by 25 psychiatrists, had an occupancy rate of 67% in 1979, and was described by one vice president at the Maria Hansen Health Center as an "institution in distress." The low-occupancy figure was caused partially by the availability of public facilities for the treatment of mental illness, or at least for the separation of those who were mentally ill from their families and other members of the community, and partially by the obsolete nature of the facilities and the changing patterns in psychiatric care. Also,

Exhibit 5 *Balance sheets (000's omitted) for unrestricted funds of Mercy Hospital, 1973–1978*

	1973	1974	1975	1976	1977	1978
Cash and short-term securities	$ 6,974	$ 6,253	$ 580	$ 1,880	$ 1,437	$ 2,152
Accounts receivable	1,243	1,842	2,780	3,402	6,184	8,747
Inventories and supplies	376	444	480	532	779	843
Assets held in trust (short-term)	—	—	—	—	2,030	641
Miscellaneous current assets	31	88	47	512	811	226
Total current assets	8,624	8,627	3,887	6,326	11,241	12,609
Designated assets	—	—	—	—	908	6,619
Assets held in trust (long-term)	—	—	—	—	8,097	6,826
Physical plant and equipment (net)	12,081	14,042	33,356	69,614	68,237	68,186
Miscellaneous long-term assets	—	—	—	—	8,745	2,863
Total long-term assets	12,081	14,042	33,356	69,614	85,987	84,494
Total unrestricted assets	20,705	25,858	37,243	75,940	97,228	97,103
Notes or loans payable	—	—	—	—	1,432	—
Current portion of long-term debt	92	92	102	92	102	29
Accounts payable	567	3,483	4,322	5,630	4,579	3,231
Accrued liabilities	1,815	2,333	2,925	2,700	1,912	2,214
Miscellaneous current liabilities	1,429	137	1,756	913	1,508	370
Total current liabilities	3,903	6,045	9,105	7,335	9,537	5,844
Long-term debt	3,952	3,560	8,517	46,484	60,524	57,932
Unrestricted funds balance	12,850	16,243	19,621	23,542	27,168	33,327
Total liabilities and funds	20,705	25,848	37,243	75,940	97,228	97,103

Source: Corporation records; some figures have been disguised for confidentiality.
Note: In addition to the unrestricted funds, the Maria Hansen Health Center had restricted funds that averaged $4 million over this period. Restricted funds are donations restricted by the donor for a specific purpose, such as nursing scholarships, and the corresponding assets are usually investments in securities for income.

Maplewood was 10 miles from the new site of Mercy Hospital, and it was difficult to provide medical, as opposed to psychiatric treatment, over that distance.

The last facility added to the Maria Hansen Health Center was the Oak Medical Clinic, which had been started in 1979 as a satellite unit to provide primary medical care for a neighborhood community. The Oak Medical Clinic had no inpatient beds, but offered outpatient diagnosis and treatment only; persons requiring hospitalization were sent to Mercy Hospital for medical reasons or to Maplewood for mental illness. It was felt that Mercy Hospital had an obligation to continue primary care treatment for the residents in the immediate geographic area it had vacated, after the move to the new location, and the Oak Medical Clinic was considered an experiment in an effort to meet that obligation. In 1979 somewhat over 5,000 patients visited the Clinic, but the anticipated utiliza-

Exhibit 6 *Bed distribution and usage at Mercy Hospital, 1979*

	Number of beds	Percentage	Usage (%)
Medical and surgical use	434	77.8	88.0
Obstetrics	48	8.6	81.0
Pediatrics	32	5.7	61.0
Surgical intensive care	18	3.2	n.a.
Medical intensive care	10	1.8	n.a.
Coronary intensive care	10	1.8	n.a.
Burn unit intensive care	6	1.1	n.a.
Totals	558	100.0	81.7

Source: Discussions with hospital personnel.

tion was 14,000 visits per year. In 1979, it was a deficit operation, with funding coming from a four-year "seed" grant from a federal agency, and from MHHC capital reserves and institutional subsidies.

Mercy Hospital, the Maria Hansen Health Center, and the Sisters of the Holy Spirit Health Corporation were all part of the national system of health care within the United States. This system had expanded rapidly during the period 1960–1980, with overall expenditures for health care rising from $23.2 billion in 1960 to $118.5 billion in 1975, and an estimated $210 billion in 1980. This massive growth was partially due to inflation in the general price level, but was primarily caused by increased demand for health care, and increased costs in meeting that demand. The demand rose because of the in-

creased age distribution in the United States, which resulted in more older people in need of health care, and increased insurance coverage, which brought the ability to pay for health care to a larger proportion of the population. The costs rose because of the advanced technologies that were used for diagnostic and therapeutic services, and the additional personnel and higher salaries that were required to operate the more complex equipment and provide the new services.

Growth in the expenditures for health care and advances in the technologies of health care, however, failed to solve such problems as equal access and assured quality of that care, and even created additional problems in excess bed capacities and duplication of services. These problems, and the rapidly rising costs, caused the federal government to take

Exhibit 7 *Facility utilization statistics for Mercy Hospital, 1974–1979*

	1974	1975	1976	1977	1978	1979
Available beds	558	558	558	558	558	558
Admissions	20,851	20,409	20,843	20,337	21,513	22,446
Patient-days	168,721	168,149	168,517	165,441	173,242	166,486
Average length stay (days)	8.6	8.3	8.1	8.2	8.1	7.4
Average daily census (persons)	464	461	460	453	475	456
Occupancy rate (census/beds)	82.8%	82.6%	82.5%	81.2%	85.1%	81.7%

Source: Corporation records.

Exhibit 8 *Definitions of the levels of medical care provided within the United States, 1979*

	Physician contact	Frequency of occurrence	Level of technology	Amount of investment	Size of service area
Primary	First	High	Moderate	Low	County
Secondary	Referral	Moderate	High	Moderate	State
Tertiary	Re-referral	Low	Very high	High	Region

Source: Conversations with hospital personnel.

an active role in regulating health care, both through the passage of control legislation and through the proposal of National Health Insurance. Health care became known as "the most regulated, unregulated industry in the country." Cost containment, improved access, quality control, and more explicit planning to avoid duplicate facilities and excess capacities were all required by new federal and state agencies, created by legislation during the late 1960s and early 1970s:

1966   Comprehensive Health Planning and Public Health Service Act (federal): Created state and area planning agencies (Comprehensive Health Planning Commissions, or CHPCs) that were given responsibility for all aspects of the health care system within a geographic region, including facilities design and service approval.

1967   Amendment to the Comprehensive Health Planning and Public Health Service Act (federal): Required the state planning agencies to assist local hospitals in developing capital expenditures programs, and provided local governmental units with representatives on each CHPC.

1972   Amendment to the Social Security Act (federal): Prohibited reimbursement through Medicare, Medicaid, etc., to a health care institu-

tion if prior capital expenditures by that institution had not been approved by the state CHPC. Review and approval were needed if capital spending exceeded $100,000, or if changes in capacity or service were planned.

1974   National Health Planning and Resource Development Act (federal): (1) Created local Health Systems Agencies (HSAs) in areas of 500,000 to 3,000,000 population, to collect and analyze data on health care services and facilities within the area, and to prepare a Health Systems Plan (HSP) and Annual Implementation Plan (AIP) for that area. (2) Created State Health Planning and Development Agencies (SHPDAs) to integrate local Health Systems Plans (HSPs) into a preliminary state-wide health plan. (3) Created State Health Coordinating Councils (SHCCs) to review and approve preliminary state-wide health plans, and to review and approve Health Systems Agencies' (HSAs) budgets and Annual Implementation Plans.

1978   Wisconsin Public Health Code Act (state): Defined the role of the local HSAs and state SHPDAs in granting a Certificate of Need (CON) for capital expenditures at a health care institution. Certificate of Need approval was required for any new health care facility, for any change in bed capacity or health service, for any purchase of a CAT scanner (complex and costly x-ray device), or for any capital expenditure in excess of $150,000.

The Certificate of Need requirement obviously affected the expansion plans of every health center or hospital within the state of Wisconsin. Certificate of Need approval was granted only after a review of the proposed plans by several agencies, including the local HSA, the area CHPC, the state SHPDA, and the Wisconsin Department of Health. Approval of the plans was based on several criteria, including community need for the proposed facilities or additional services, the quality of care to be provided, the physical design of the facility, and the potential for cost containment or reduction. A failure to receive CON approval prior to starting construction meant that reimbursement from Blue Cross or governmental funds would be withheld for all health care services provided in the new facility.

The Certificate of Need legislation in the Wisconsin Public Health Code was passed in early 1978; by the middle of that year, the Maria Hansen Health Center was engaged in a "bloody battle" for approval of the capital expenditures for an ambulatory surgery facility to be constructed on the Mercy Hospital site. Ambulatory surgery refers to surgical services and procedures that require anesthesia and a period of postoperative observation, but not overnight admission to a hospital or extended care by professional nurses. Ambulatory surgery was obviously designed to reduce the cost of simple surgical procedures. The Maria Hansen Health Center applied to the area CHPC for approval of the new facility, but was told that the plans did not meet the criteria adopted by the State Health Planning and Development Agency.

These criteria were designed to ensure that the population of an area had access to good-quality surgery services, while avoiding unnecessary duplication of facilities. The area CHPC suggested that approval would be granted only if Mercy Hospital would trade four of its present inpatient operating rooms for the proposed outpatient unit, thus maintaining the same area capacity for surgical services. The CHPC viewed ambulatory surgery as a substitute for inpatient surgery, not as an extension of inpatient surgery, and argued that there was a surplus of operating rooms in the Madison area. Planners at the Maria Hansen Health Center responded that there were some limitations in the methodology that the Comprehensive Health Planning Commission had used to reach that conclusion; specifically, that the CHPC had used outdated population figures for the area to establish the need for surgical services, and then had counted operating rooms at a federal hospital that served only veterans from southern Wisconsin, and also counted operating rooms at the university hospital that served primarily re-referral patients from throughout Wisconsin, in estimating the available supply. Approval was granted only after executives at the Maria Hansen Health Center gathered data from Mercy Hospital that showed a trend approaching the CHPC's desired 25% outpatient/inpatient surgical ratio, and then were able to demonstrate that the 1980 projection of 25.6% could not be realized without the new facility because of constraints on the existing surgical resources (Exhibit 9).

In addition to the efforts by federal and state agencies to restrict expansion and prevent duplication of health care facilities, there were direct efforts at cost control initiated by the "third-party" groups that paid for health care. These groups, including Blue Cross, Medicaid, and Medicare, paid for 79.0% of hospital charges in 1976, and their portion of the total was constantly increasing; private

Exhibit 9 *Trends in outpatient/inpatient surgical procedures at Mercy Hospital, 1974–1980 (1979–1980 estimated for outpatient surgical facility)*

	1974	1975	1976	1977	1978	1979*	1980*
Outpatient surgery	1,233	1,706	1,687	1,729	2,426	3,200	3,950
Inpatient surgery	11,099	10,481	10,363	9,797	10,662	11,060	11,460
Total procedures	12,332	12,187	12,050	11,526	13,088	14,260	15,410
Outpatient percent	10.0	14.0	14.0	15.0	18.5	22.4	25.6

Source: Corporation records.

individuals paid for less than 3.0%, as shown in Exhibit 10.

The Blue Cross organization was particularly active in efforts to enforce cost containment within hospitals. A system called Prospective Reimbursement had been designed by Blue Cross, and then adopted "voluntarily" by all hospitals in Wisconsin that treated patients who were Blue Cross subscribers. This plan was adopted defensively by the hospitals as an alternative to the rate-setting procedures already used by Blue Cross in some other states. Rate setting limited hospital revenues through establishing, at the start of each year, fixed rates for the various hospital services and the diagnostic and therapeutic procedures based upon existing costs; the effect was that the hospitals had to absorb any cost increases. The Prospective Reimbursement plan set an annual ceiling on inpatient cost increases; the effect here was that hospi-

tals had to absorb any increases above the established limit. Periodic checks were required during the year to monitor cost increases. In the event of a cost overrun, some cost-cutting measures such as a reduction in staff were required to stay within the ceiling and to ensure full reimbursement from Blue Cross. Cost increases at Mercy Hospital had traditionally been close to those reported nationally for all community-type hospitals (Exhibit 11).

The Maria Hansen Health Center, through its major unit, Mercy Hospital, was the dominant factor in the provision of primary (first physician) and secondary (referral physician) health care to the residents of Dane County. Mercy Hospital was the largest health care facility in the county, with the exception of the University of Wisconsin Hospital, which emphasized tertiary (re-referral physicians) care for the much larger population throughout the

Exhibit 10 *Trends in third-party reimbursement for hospital services (percent) at Mercy hospital, 1972–1976 (data not available for 1977 and 1978)*

	1972	1973	1974	1975	1976
Blue Cross	45.5	46.2	44.4	42.1	40.4
Medicare	22.7	22.5	25.2	27.9	32.8
Medicaid	5.1	7.1	5.0	4.6	5.7
Commercial insurance	22.1	20.0	21.8	22.0	18.1
Private individuals	4.6	4.2	3.6	3.4	3.0
	100.0	100.0	100.0	100.0	100.0

Source: Corporation records.

Exhibit 11 *Trends in annual cost increases for hospital services (percent) at Mercy Hospital compared to national average for all hospitals, 1972–1976 (data not available for 1977 and 1978)*

	1972	1973	1974	1975	1976
Annual cost increase at Mercy Hospital	13.5	8.2	10.1	15.1	11.7
Annual cost increase nationally	11.4	7.0	10.8	15.2	13.7

Source: Corporation records.

state and the midwestern region. Mercy Hospital also had the highest utilization ratio of the five hospitals within Dane County (a sixth hospital, Federal, served only veterans, and has been omitted from this analysis); see Exhibit 12.

The Maria Hansen Health Center also provided some health care services to residents of Columbia, Dodge, Jefferson, Janesville, Green, and Iowa counties; these areas are adjacent to Dane County, and the services provided were generally for secondary or referral care that was not available at the smaller hospitals in the adjacent coun-

Exhibit 12 *Bed capacity, occupancy rate, and average length of stay for five hospitals in Dane County, 1973–1979*

	1973	1974	1975	1976	1977	1978	1979
Mercy Hospital							
Number of beds	558	558	558	558	558	558	558
Occupancy rate (%)	82.8	82.8	82.6	82.6	81.2	86.1	81.7
Average stay (days)	8.1	8.2	8.3	8.1	8.0	8.0	7.3
Mount Horeb Hospital							
Number of beds	169	169	169	169	169	169	169
Occupancy rate (%)	82.4	82.8	80.5	77.6	76.0	73.8	75.9
Average stay (days)	6.8	6.4	6.1	6.2	6.1	6.5	6.3
Oregon Hospital							
Number of beds	26	68	82	82	82	78	74
Occupancy rate (%)	105.5	42.4	68.2	62.6	60.5	65.7	71.1
Average stay (days)	7.0	6.6	7.2	6.9	6.5	6.9	7.5
University of Wisconsin							
Number of beds	850	893	873	949	893	900	891
Occupancy rate (%)	n.a.	75.8	77.2	74.8	75.8	80.9	80.3
Average stay (days)	n.a.	10.6	11.5	11.1	10.8	10.9	10.7
Verona Hospital							
Number of beds	81	81	110	91	108	108	108
Occupancy rate (%)	65.9	85.6	70.4	79.8	80.5	69.2	75.7
Average stay	9.9	10.5	9.8	9.5	9.6	8.6	8.3
Total beds	1,684	1,769	1,792	1,849	1,810	1,813	1,800

Source: Corporation records.

Exhibit 13 *Patient discharge date by service area for Mercy Hospital and for all hospitals within area, 1975–1977*

	Number of hospitals in area	Total area discharges			Mercy Hospital discharges		
		1975	1976	1977	1975	1976	1977
Dane County	5	26,221	26,653	27,053	10,071	10,410	10,155
Adjacent counties	11	44,555	46,916	47,906	6,069	6,043	5,961
State and Midwest	—	—	—	—	4,357	4,524	4,454

Source: Corporation records.

ties. Finally, some services were provided to people living outside the adjacent counties; these services tended to be for tertiary, or re-referral care, by members of the University of Wisconsin Medical School faculty who brought some of their patients to Mercy Hospital. In 1977, patients discharged from Mercy Hospital were 49% from Dane County, 29% from the adjacent counties, and 22% from other areas in Wisconsin or the midwestern states (Exhibit 13).

Planners at the Maria Hansen Health Center thought that Mercy Hospital would continue to dominate health care services in Dane County, and remain an important provider of those services in the adjacent counties, in the future (Exhibit 14). They also recognized that the hospital could substantially expand the advanced tertiary care provided to residents of Wisconsin, and other states in the midwest. These opportunities were available because Mercy Hospital offered a wide spectrum of diagnostic and therapeutic services, and because the medical staff providing those services was young and well qualified. Eighty-five percent of the physicians who held admitting privileges (a term used to describe doctors who are registered to practice at a hospital) were less than 54 years of age. Seventy percent of the physicians were board-certified (a term used to describe doctors who have passed qualifying exams in their medical specialties, and who continue to take advanced courses in those specialties an-

nually), and 50% held faculty teaching positions at the University of Wisconsin. Finally, the nursing staff, medical technicians, and support personnel delivered a very special kind of health care: quality medical attention that was graciously and compassionately extended. This latter characteristic, which was very obvious in the attitudes and efforts of persons throughout the hospital, was partially due to the religious orientation of the Health Center, partially to the service traditions of the founding Congregation, and partially to the continued presence of members of the Sisters of the Holy Spirit on the nursing staff and in the administrative structure of the hospital. Planners at the Maria Hansen Health Center felt that they had a very special institution, which had to be preserved, and extended.

Formal planning at the Maria Hansen Health Center had been instituted by the president of that organization, Mr. James Michelsen. Mr. Michelsen had previously been the Executive Director of Mercy Hospital, and after the move to the new location was completed in the summer of 1977, and after the problems associated with that move were resolved, he began to work on planning procedures that would go beyond the normal personnel schedules, annual budgets, capital allocations, and facility designs. The intent was to study the future health care needs of Dane County, and the referral areas of the adjacent counties, and then to consider alternative means of meeting those needs, with

Exhibit 14 *Comparison of facilities and services available at hospitals in Dane County and the adjacent counties' service areas, 1978*

	Dane County					Adjacent counties										
	Mercy Hospital	Mount Horab	Oregon Hospital	University of Wisconsin	Verona Hospital	Dodge County	Arlington	Cottage Grove	Brookville	St. Francis	Evansville	Osteopathic	Brownstown	Hudson	Milton	Green County
Type of approval																
JCAH accreditation	X	X	X	X	X	X	X	X		X	X		X	X	X	X
Residency program	X			X		X										
Medical school affiliation	X			X		X										
Professional nursing	X			X		X										
Type of facility																
Coronary care unit	X			X		X	X	X			X					
Intensive care unit	X	X	X	X	X	X	X	X	X	X	X	X	X	X	X	X
Open heart surgery	X			X												
Diagnostic radioisotope	X	X	X	X	X	X	X	X	X	X	X	X	X	X	X	X
Therapeutic radioisotope	X			X												
Self-care unit		X			X							X				
Extended care unit			X				X	X								
Burn care unit	X			X												
Rehabilitation unit	X			X		X			X				X	X	X	X
Psychiatric unit	X			X		X									X	
Outpatient unit	X	X		X	X	X		X		X	X		X			X
Alcoholism unit	X	X		X					X				X	X		
Types of services																
X-ray therapy	X			X		X		X		X				X		
Cobalt therapy				X		X										
Radium therapy				X		X										
Blood bank	X	X	X	X	X	X	X	X	X	X	X	X	X	X	X	X
Electroencephalography	X	X		X		X		X		X			X	X	X	
Respiratory therapy	X	X	X	X	X	X	X	X	X	X	X		X	X	X	X
Hemodialysis	X			X		X							X			
Psychiatric service	X			X									X	X	X	
Social work service	X	X	X	X	X	X	X	X	X	X	X	X	X	X	X	X
Family planning service	X					X										
Abortion service			X	X		X		X	X		X			X		
Home care service							X						X			
Dental service		X		X		X										
Obstetrical service	X	X		X	X	X		X			X					
Pediatric service	X		X	X		X	X	X	X	X			X	X	X	

Source: Corporation records.

easier individual access, greater facility utilization, improved medical effectiveness, and lower overall costs. Mr. Michelsen established Condition Review Teams to evaluate improved methods of treating clinical conditions (diseases), Community Need Panels to examine alternative means of responding to health problems, and a Central Planning Committee to select and then fund the new programs. The objective of the planning process was to be proactive, rather than reactive, in health care management.

> Most health care planning in the United States is focused on the supply side of the equation, not on the demand side. It is oriented toward "This is what we can do," not toward "This is what needs doing," and the result is professional shortsightedness and, occasionally, medical arrogance. Michelsen is trying to change that approach. (Statement of a health care consultant)

The Condition Review Teams (CRTs) were small groups of representatives from the various medical specialties, nursing and technical staffs, administrative personnel, and funding organizations, such as the Heart Association or the March of Dimes, that studied specific clinical conditions such as arthritis, diabetes, substance abuse (alcoholism or drug addiction), or coronary/artery disease, evaluated the medical programs used by the Health Center for diagnosis and treatment, and then considered alternative diagnostic and therapeutic programs. Each illness or "clinical condition" was studied by a separate team, and at the end of the study, the group reported its findings and proposed actions needed to improve or expand the current programs to the Central Planning Committee. One Condition Review Team found that the treatment of diabetic patients could be improved by better identification of diabetes among pregnant women, a more thorough educational program on diabetes, and an expanded foot care service (diabetes particu-

larly affects the lower extremities, and makes walking painful). The findings of each CRT were summarized in one-page documents that outlined the proposed actions, the underlying assumptions, the expected results, the required resources, and the consequences of approval or disapproval. The reports were submitted to the Central Planning Committee before the beginning of the annual budgetary process so that, if approved, funding could be started in the subsequent year. Since the start of formal planning at the Maria Hansen Health Center, 10 illnesses or conditions had been studied; these were chosen because of the high incidence of mortality (coronary/artery disease), the severity of the illness (obstructive lung disease), or the pervasiveness of the problem (substance abuse). It was expected that, over time, most of the major clinical conditions would be studied.

The Community Need Panels (CNPs) quickly became known as "Think Tanks"; these were temporary committees formed to study medical services needed by the community, rather than clinical conditions treated by the hospital, and included such topics as special needs of the elderly, or rehabilitation services for the handicapped. The Community Need Panels consisted of representatives from the professional and administrative staffs at Mercy Hospital, from the corporate headquarters of the Sisters of the Holy Spirit Health Corporation, and from local health agencies, community organizations, and consulting firms. Each CNP was assigned a specific issue, and then was expected to review current literature, identify local trends, visit successful examples, and "brainstorm" for innovative responses, which resulted in the "Think Tank" pseudonym. Each CNP had to formulate a consensus on a proposed direction for the Health Center, but that direction did not include program costs or facility investments; the intent was to consider community needs, and alternative means of meeting those needs, and not, at this stage, the financial, professional, and governmental constraints. Estimates of program revenues and costs, and preliminary designs of facility requirements, were developed by the planning staff after review and approval by the Central Planning Committee.

The Central Planning Committee (CPC) was a permanent group composed of the president, the executive vice president, all vice presidents, two appointed members from the board of directors, and several elected representatives of the physicians. The committee met once a month to review reports from the Condition Review Teams and the Community Need Panels, and to consider changes in the service area demands. New programs recommended by the Condition Review Teams, if approved, were submitted to the Resources Committee, where additional funds were budgeted for the proposed alteration or expansion of existing services. New directions suggested by the Community Need Panels, if approved, were sent to the planning staff, assisted by outside consultants, for feasibility study and expense calculations before being submitted in final form to the board of directors. In order to shorten the time between the first consideration of a new direction or program to serve a community need and the final consideration by the board of directors, and to obtain some experience in the operations of the program on an experimental basis, the Central Planning Committee had control of a $500,000 annual budget called the New Program Fund. Portions of this fund could be allocated to the operating expenses (not capital expenditures) of new programs approved by the CPC. New programs, as defined by the planning staff, were those that would expand the scope, depth, or volume of service in a clinical area, place new or added demands on the Health Center, require the acquisition of new technology, result in an organizational change, contribute to a collaborative arrangement with another health care provider in the service area, or (probably) involve an appli-

cation for a Certificate of Need to state and federal agencies.

Mr. Michelsen, president of the Maria Hansen Health Center, believed that the Central Planning Committee should be used to "fine-tune" the organization, and keep it closely aligned to advances in medical care and treatment (study of clinical conditions) and to changes in service area patterns (study of community needs). The decisions facing the Central Planning Committee in the summer of 1980, however, were concerned with major diversifications outside the current programs of medical care at Mercy Hospital, not with minor adjustments to those programs. In a very real sense, this problem arose from the success of the planning process: numerous proposals had been generated for new efforts and extended services in such areas as geriatric care, alternative financing, physical rehabilitation, mental health, and personal wellness. All the proposals were important for different groups within the service areas, and all the proposals met the guidelines in the Statement of Philosophy, Mission Role, and Goals adopted for the Health Center, but there were no standards for selection among them. In addition, there was a definite concern that diversification away from the accepted medical services of Mercy Hospital might imperil the special qualities of that institution. Five major alternatives were under consideration by the Central Planning Committee, and each had numerous subchoices in the scope and level of the proposed care.

Geriatric Service. Geriatrics is a term used to describe the elderly, and usually refers to persons who are 65 years of age and over. The topic of care for the elderly had been assigned to a Community Needs Panel, and an extended meeting had been held during the week of September 5, 1979, to study the reports of external consultants and to consider the demographic trends, economic problems, and medical requirements of the aged. Physicians explained the process of aging, and members of the committee described alternative health care facilities for the aged in terms of residential care, intermediate care, extended care, and acute care (hospitalization). The consultants' reports and the CNP's discussions were only the beginning of the analysis and planning that would be needed before specific programs could be undertaken, but it was felt that the needs of the elderly would become critically important in Dane County and the referral service area, and would affect the existing operations of Mercy Hospital if special provisions were not made for their care in other facilities.

Several characteristics of the geriatric population were identified. As a group, the elderly were increasing rapidly in numbers: the twentieth century had seen a sevenfold increase in the 65+ age bracket, and in 1980 one of every nine Americans was in that bracket. A large portion were widowed, and there were many more females than males within the group. The elderly had seen many significant changes in their lifetimes (i.e., horse transportation replaced by automobiles, and kerosene lanterns replaced by electric lighting), but they tended to be resistant to changes in their own lives, having set patterns of daily life. With advancing years, the aged were increasingly being institutionalized in nursing homes, but their desire for independence remained strong, and few were content to give up their homes or apartments.

Problems of the aged were related to income, health, and isolation. Federal figures for 1980 showed that those persons 65 and over who lived alone or with nonrelatives had a median income of $3,495, a figure below the poverty level. Employment was seldom possible, due to age discrimination and physical disability, and inflation had reduced the value of their individual savings or private pensions. For most older Americans, Social Security checks provided at least 90% of their total income, and substantial increases in Social Security payments were not expected, beyond annual adjustments for inflation, due to funding problems.

The low income affected the living conditions of the elderly, and their health. Housing with inadequate heat or ventilation for comfort, neighborhoods with inadequate protection for exercise, and diets with inadequate vitamins and minerals for sustenance, brought health problems. The elderly received health care services reimbursed by Medicare/Medicaid, but these payments were barely adequate and provided them with minimal care, usually of the type that was geared to institutionalization for short illnesses. The elderly used hospital facilities five times as often as the younger population, and stayed nearly twice as long, even though in many instances the acute care hospital was inappropriate to their needs, which really required a lower level of care over a longer time period. Some of the health problems of the elderly were chronic degenerative diseases, which required acute care; most were not, but few other facilities were available, except outpatient clinics or private office visits, and these were not reimbursed with federal funds.

Isolation was another problem in providing medical care for the aged, except through institutionalization. Many older persons had to relinquish their drivers' licenses because of physical infirmities, such as failing eyesight, and others had to abandon their cars due to high operating costs. Public transportation was often unavailable, or unsuitable due to schedules, etc. Family members or younger friends occasionally could help the elderly to reach health care facilities, but their assistance could not be relied upon completely. Once a family unit had consisted of three generations living together, but it was more common in the 1970s for families to be geographically and emotionally distant. Transportation remained a major problem for the elderly.

The Maria Hansen Health Center felt that

Exhibit 15 *Trends in patient age distribution (percent) at Mercy Hospital, 1974–1978*

	1974	1975	1976	1977	1978
0–14 years old	10.7	8.2	7.1	6.0	4.7
15–64 years old	72.2	78.9	74.7	75.7	76.2
Over 64 years old	17.1	17.9	18.2	18.3	19.1

Source: Corporation records, based upon discharge data by age group.

it had to respond in some way to the special health care needs of the elderly. The percentage of patients in the 65+ age group was steadily increasing at Mercy Hospital, and it was expected to reach 25% by the mid-1980s (Exhibit 15).

Population projections for Dane County predicted a 66% increase in persons 65 years of age and older during the decade of the 1980s, and planners at the Maria Hansen Health Center recognized that this would create a substantial demand for the existing inpatient services at Mercy Hospital if other levels of care were not available. Members of the Community Needs Panel assigned to the topic of geriatric service had compiled a list of 40 ways in which the Health Center might be able to help the elderly meet their health care needs, and it was hoped that many of these ideas, which included continued independence, health maintenance, self-actualization, spiritual advice, available comradeship, and improved mobility, could be combined with different levels of medical service to provide meaningful care for the elderly. Ultimately, a package that would postpone permanent institutionalization of older persons and yet improve the quality of life of those individuals with health care problems was the goal of the Health Center. It was recognized, however, that this package would have to be designed within definite cost constraints and concerns for reimbursement.

The elderly have, on average, very limited private funds to pay for health care services, so that the type of reimbursement available from local, state, or federal sources becomes critical in the design of geriatric care facilities. The federal government is dominant in this area, having supplanted prior local and state funding, but the amount of federal assistance, through Medicare and Medicaid, increases with the severity of the health condition and the need for hospitalization, which makes it very difficult to fund the more supportive, and less expensive, levels of care (Exhibit 16).

At the date of the case, no final recommendation on geriatric service had been forwarded by the Community Needs Panel to the Central Planning Committee. Instead, further study of the alternatives was planned. It was decided, however, that as an interim step the Health Center should recognize the current role of Mercy Hospital as a provider of acute medical care, and organize a special group of professionals to consult with elderly patients during their hospital stays and to assist those patients in the transition between the hospital and the next level of care. These professionals, working in "Continuity of Care Teams," each consisting of a nurse and a social worker, would assess the patient's need for continued health care after discharge from the hospital, discuss alternative means of providing that care, and then help in the movement of the patient to the next facility, which might be for extended care, intermediate care, or residential care. Once the patient had been transferred, the team would make followup visits to ensure successful adjustments to the new surroundings. It was expected that the Continuity of Care Teams would function as the

Exhibit 16 *Levels of health care services and sources of reimbursement within Wisconsin, 1979*

1. Residential care (visiting nurse)
   - Personal residence — Private payment/some local support
   - Family residence — Private payment/some local support
   - Senior citizens' housing — Private payment/some local support
2. Residential care community (no nursing)
   - Life Care Center (private endowment) — Private payment/some local support
   - Home for Aged (community support) — Private payment/some local support
3. Intermediate care (limited nursing)
   - Free-standing — Medicaid/some state support
   - Hospital-related — Medicaid/some state support
4. Extended care (skilled nursing)
   - Free-standing — Medicaid/some state support
   - Hospital-related — Medicaid/some state support
5. Acute care (skilled nursing and medical services)
   - Hospital — Medicare/Medicaid/other insurance

Source: Corporation records.

liaison between Mercy Hospital and the Dane County community, and would be the first step in providing a more complete range of geriatric services, but it was also recognized that these teams were only a first step, and that a much greater effort would be needed both to serve the elderly at the Health Center, and to reduce the demands upon Mercy Hospital.

Alternative Financing. One of the newer trends in health care delivery systems within the United States has been the emergence of the "HMO" or Health Maintenance Organization as an alternative financing and delivery mechanism for health care. An HMO is defined as "an organization designed to deliver a set of comprehensive services to a voluntarily enrolled population at a predetermined and prepaid price." The important concept in this definition is the delivery of comprehensive health care services. Medical insurance normally has a voluntarily enrolled population and predetermined and prepaid prices, but the services are not comprehensive (physicians' fees are omitted, for example, together with some diagnostic and therapeutic procedures) and the services are not delivered

(patients have to find a hospital or other health care facility that is able to provide the medical care at preset prices). HMOs typically offer a full range of physician's services, inpatient and outpatient hospital visits, emergency room treatments, diagnostic laboratory testing, therapeutic procedures, and some home health care at a single health care facility. There are differences among HMOs, but in the two major types the physicians practice in a central office building or clinic, attend primarily to patients who are members of the HMO, and are paid on a contract per member or salary per year basis, not on the usual fee-for-service basis (Exhibit 17).

The Group and Staff types were most typical of the HMO operations in existence in 1980, and most exemplified the spirit of the HMO concept. In these, the physicians practiced in a central facility, usually adjacent to a hospital so that diagnostic and therapeutic services were readily available, and they spent either all or a majority of their professional time delivering health care to HMO members. These types of HMOs were endorsed by the federal government as being consistent with national health care goals, and were widely used in several states, including Cali-

Exhibit 17 *Differences among three types of Health Maintenance Organizations*

Type of HMO	Physician location	Physician commitment	Physician payment
Group Health Maintenance Organization	Central office	100% to members	Amount per member
Staff Health Maintenance Organization	Central office	Over 50% to members	Fixed salary
Independent Practice Association	Private offices	Under 50% to members	Fee-for-service

Source: Conversations with planners at the Maria Hansen Health Center.

fornia and New York, to provide local health care services.

The Independent Practice Association type of HMO was a more recent development; it consisted of a group of private physicians who agreed to treat HMO members as part of their regular practice, while the diagnostic and therapeutic aspects of care were provided by a participating hospital. Most of the Independent Practice Associations were formed as a competitive reaction to the more formal Group or Staff HMOs; they gave much greater flexibility to the physicians since fewer than 50% of their patients, and often only 5 to 10%, would be members of the prepaid organization.

No HMO of any type existed in Dane County in 1980. In 1973, a group of doctors in the area had organized the Dane County Physicians Medical Care Organization, which was designed to look into the feasibility of an Independent Practice Association type of prepaid health plan. That plan was never implemented because of the high cost of the medical malpractice insurance that was required for the organization. The group was still in existence in 1980, but it remained largely inactive. In addition, there was a Milwaukee-based Group HMO, the Independence Health Plan, and a state-wide Staff HMO, the Wisconsin Master Health Plan, and both had approached physicians within the community in an attempt to expand geo-

graphically, but only limited interest had been evidenced by the doctors.

The amount of interest among potential patients was unclear. The University of Wisconsin Hospital had begun a market feasibility study for a Group HMO, but had not compiled the results at the date of the case. Staff members at the Maria Hansen Health Center felt that there was a demand for some type of HMO within the Madison area; many members of the community were well educated, and allegedly receptive to new and innovative approaches to health care. The Chamber of Commerce had indicated to members of the management at the Health Center that they favored an HMO since employers within the area traditionally paid the health insurance costs of their employees, and were obviously interested in reduced costs and more comprehensive services. It was not clear, however, that the local firms and private individuals fully understood the restrictive provisions of the HMO concept (clinic-type operations, with no assurance that a patient would see the same physician on subsequent visits, and no choice among health care facilities); it is easy to favor reduced costs and expanded services, if these are the only characteristics of an improved plan that have been described. Planners at the Maria Hansen Health Center felt that it would be necessary to describe more fully the operations of an HMO, and

461

then conduct a detailed survey to determine the market demand for a Health Maintenance Organization within the Dane County area.

An Organizational Action Group, which was basically a study team similar to the Community Needs Panel but with responsibility for implementation as well as investigation, had been assigned the task of considering alternative methods for the delivery and financing of health care services, and the job of establishing guidelines for a possible HMO. It was decided first that an Independent Practice Association would be the type that would be proposed, since this would be the one most likely to gain acceptance and participation by the area physicians, which would in turn bring membership applications from local firms and other employers. Next it was decided that, at the start, services would be limited to standard medical treatments, inpatient and outpatient hospital care, emergency room services, short-term mental health counseling, and substance-abuse assistance; this would exclude intermediate and extended care in nursing homes, dental work, eye examinations, drug prescriptions, rehabilitation treatments, chiropractic services, and long-term psychiatric help, although these might be added later as experience was gained in market needs and cost controls. Finally, it was decided that these services would be offered only to employed persons; this would exclude the poor and the elderly, two groups most in need of improved health care at predetermined costs, but again it was thought that these groups could be added later as experience was gained in obtaining reimbursement from Medicare and Medicaid. Insurance risks would be assumed equally by the Health Center and the Independent Practice Association. Quality assurance would be the responsibility of the provider physicians. All groups, including the Health Center, the provider physicians, and the subscribing members, would have to co-operate to restrict excess demand and control rising costs.

Without the results of the proposed market research study, it was not possible to predict the viability of an HMO in Dane County, but it was certain that the development of an alternative financing and delivery system for comprehensive health care would fit within the stated philosophy, mission, and role of the Maria Hansen Health Center. The facilities at Mercy Hospital could be utilized for the diagnostic and therapeutic procedures and the acute medical care required by the Independent Practice Association plan, and there was a large pool of physicians to draw upon within the area, but the successful introduction of this new type of health care delivery system would be dependent upon the Health Center acquiring additional skills. The service, an unknown quantity in the area, would have to be marketed to the community, and a significant amount of time and creativity would have to be used in assuring the public that the HMO was indeed as good as having a family physician, and perhaps even better. The medical facilities at the hospital and the provider physicians at their separate offices would have to be coordinated with the rising customer base to ensure complete and timely services. Finally, the physicians would have to be convinced of the value and need for this alternative to traditional care; resistance could be expected, and the plan would have to be presented to the physicians in a rational and nonthreatening manner. At the date of the case, no decision had been reached on forming a Health Maintenance Organization in the Dane County area; it was recognized that this new financing and delivery system for health care services would take a very considerable investment in planning effort to bring to a successful completion.

Rehabilitative Programs. Rehabilitation refers, in very general terms, to the "treatment or training of the ill or disabled to allow each individual to obtain the maximum potential for life." Physical therapy is the most common form of this treatment or training, with special exercises to restore damaged muscles and with prosthetic devices to replace missing limbs, etc., but recent developments have stressed a more complete approach to rehabilitation, with personal instruction (termed "aid to daily living," or ADL), vocational training, and social education combined with the physical treatments. The intent now is to provide a range of remedial services in order to correct speech, hearing, and visual problems, to improve bodily movements and emotional adjustments, and to teach employable skills and encourage social interactions. Rehabilitation is now seen as a process that begins with the diagnosis of an injury or disease that may impair human performance. After the condition is treated medically, and the condition is stabilized partially, rehabilitation begins with an evaluation of the potential for improvement, and then continues with the prescription of treatments for physical therapy, prosthetic restoration, speech, visual, and audio assistance, and ADL and vocational training, all emphasizing self-assurance, self-reliance, and the ability to return to a meaningful life. Each patient receives continual reevaluations of progress versus potential, and renewals of the prescriptions for treatment and training. Since each condition differs, in degree if not in diagnosis, and since each patient responds differently to the treatments and reacts differently to the training, rehabilitative programs have to be highly individualized, and tend to be very costly. However, marked success has been achieved in a number of instances with the new, integrated treatment for disabling diseases and accidents, and many individuals have been enabled to lead satisfactory lives. Rehabilitative programs are a major, although substantially unrecognized, success of medical science in the 1970s.

Mercy Hospital had provided a small reha-

bilitative program for years, with six inpatient beds and a number of outpatient clinics. It was felt, however, that the program was not integrated, with personal, vocational, and social training supplementing the physical therapy, and that the size was not adequate for the area. A Community Needs Panel had been set up to examine rehabilitative services, and they concluded that the projected increase in the elderly population over the next decade, and the growing prevalance of disabling conditions among all age groups, meant that the Maria Hansen Health Center should make a much greater effort in rehabilitative programs. In 1978, over 1,400 patients had been discharged from Mercy Hospital with one of the 12 medical conditions (hemiplegia or paralysis of one side of the body, paraplegia or paralysis of the lower limbs, quadraplegia or paralysis of both upper and lower limbs, lower limb amputation, upper limb amputation, cervical pain, multiple sclerosis, hip fracture, chronic arthritis, cerebral palsy, and obstructive lung disease) that normally required rehabilitative treatments. Based upon averages for the length of stay, extent of therapy, ratio of success, etc., for each of these conditions, consultants working for the CNP estimated that these patients would require 30 to 36 inpatient beds, and the related outpatient facilities.

Inpatient physical therapy was available within Dane County at Mercy Hospital (6 beds) and at the University of Wisconsin Hospital (27 beds for adults only), but the occupancy rate at both of these facilities was 95%. (An occupancy rate over 80% at a health care facility essentially means that there is a waiting list for admission, since it is impossible to balance need and supply that closely, with the need occurring on a stochastic basis over the full year.) The University of Wisconsin Hospital primarily served referral patients from throughout the state, so that most of the disabled persons discharged from Mercy Hospital had to be sent to the Rehabilitation Institute, a state-run therapeutic and training facility in Milwaukee, 68 miles to the east. The distance posed a hardship for many of the patients and their families, and was a particular problem for the younger children, who felt isolated from their parents in the large (240-bed) institution. Six other hospitals in Dane and the surrounding counties offered physical therapy (see Exhibit 14), but only on an outpatient basis, and only in a nonintegrated program, without ADL, vocational training, or social education. Patients had to be sent to other institutions for those services so that their treatments, which medically should be concurrent, usually were scheduled sequentially because of the distance between the institutions; this often created morale problems, and a feeling of helplessness in some of the patients. A feeling of helplessness, once it has been incurred in a disabled person, usually blocks further progress in treatment and training.

Members of the Community Needs Panel had recommended the construction of a new 50-bed rehabilitation clinic, adjacent to Mercy Hospital, so that the physician's services and laboratory facilities could be shared, but separate so that an integrated program with physical therapy, personal instruction, vocational training, and social adjustment could be provided. Vocational training could be offered through collaboration with the state Department of Education, which had a Bureau of Rehabilitative Training, and psychological and social services could be extended through cooperation with the state Department of Public Health and the county Human Services Board. The joint use of the facilities with governmental units would, of course, reduce costs and increase income, but it would also generate administrative problems since no one assumed that the state and county agencies would provide funding without seeking control of their por-

tions of the program. Collaborative efforts, however, were an explicit element in the philosophy, mission, and goals of the Maria Hansen Health Center, and success in collaboration could provide a national example to other health care institutions. The national importance of the proposed multidisciplinary (combining many medical specialties), integrated (combining therapy and training on physical, personal, vocational, and social levels), and collaborative (combining medical treatment and governmental training) rehabilitative service was underscored by a suggestion from the Community Needs Panel that special programs be developed for stroke, arthritis, and rheumatism. The incidence and severity of those disease conditions are increasing rapidly as the national population becomes older.

At the date of the case, no decision had been reached by the Central Planning Committee on the Rehabilitation Clinic proposed by the Community Needs Panel.

Mental Health. Members of the administrative staff and medical personnel at the Maria Hansen Health Center were in agreement that the mental health services of the Center were inadequate. Maplewood Neuro-Psychiatric Hospital was located in an obsolete building, constructed in 1926, on the western edge of Madison, 12 miles from the new site of Mercy Hospital, with limited medical care (patients in a mental hospital often have medical problems that remain undiagnosed and untreated for a variety of reasons, primarily because of the inability of the individuals to describe clearly a set of symptoms) and without the facilities for the more advanced, noninstitutionalized alternatives in psychiatric care. The occupancy rate in 1979 was 67%, which is considered low for a midterm or extended care hospital in which admissions and discharges can be scheduled to balance the usage of the available beds and treatment facilities. Maplewood was, as described by a vice president of the Health center, "an institution in distress."

The Community Needs Panel assigned to investigate the topic of mental health met in June 1980 to receive a report from a professional consulting firm on recent developments and current trends in that field. The consultant reported, and most of the members of the CNP already understood, that the treatment of mental health problems had changed dramatically during the 1960s and 1970s. The emphasis was now on the maintenance of mental health rather than the treatment of mental illness, and the treatment was now arranged in a series of steps or stages that included long-term hospitalization only as the last resort (Exhibit 18).

The increased emphasis upon promotional effort and primary and secondary treatments, and the increased use of day care and resident care for tertiary treatments, brought a decreased number of patients in psychiatric hospitals. Also, recent advances in psychopharmacology (treatment of mental illnesses by drug therapy) shortened the average stays of the patients in those hospitals. The result was a surplus of beds, and low occupancy rates. It was not expected that hospitalization would be eliminated completely as a method of psychiatric care, but it was felt that hospitals would become more centers for the delivery of a range of psychiatric services.

Members of the Community Needs Panel felt that the Maria Hansen Health Center had not moved in a meaningful fashion to-

Exhibit 18 *Steps in mental health maintenance and mental illness treatment, 1980*

Promotional effort (community education)	Develop community awareness of the types of mental health problems, stressing early recognition of the symptoms before illness develops.
Primary treatment (crisis prevention)	Provide professional consulting (education) by clinical nurses and social workers to instruct individuals and their families on mental health problems, and the means of resolving those problems. Offer professional assistance (outreach), also by clinical nurses and social workers, to persons with mental health problems before the mental problems become mental illnesses.
Secondary treatment (crisis information)	Provide psychotherapeutic counseling by clinical personnel, both on an immediate (emergency) and on a continuing (outpatient) basis, for persons with mental illnesses.
Tertiary treatment (patient rehabilitation)	Provide psychiatric services, medical attention, and some degree of residential care to guarantee an environment conducive to the therapeutic regimen. Residential care or hospitalization may be on a day basis, with the patient returning to his/her home each night; on a resident basis, with the patient returning to an institutional home each night; on an inpatient basis, with the patient remaining in the hospital each night, but for only one or two weeks; or on a long-term basis. Long-term hospitalization is considered, as described previously, the last resort of mental health treatment, and is viewed as a failure of the system.

Source: Conversations with hospital personnel.

ward the concept of a psychiatric hospital as the center for the delivery of a range of mental health services. Few of these services were available through either Maplewood or Mercy Hospitals (Exhibit 19).

The other medical institutions in Dane County also placed much greater emphasis on mental illness than on mental health. The University of Wisconsin Hospital and the Wisconsin Psychiatric Hospital both provided only inpatient care for tertiary treatments, and the state facility was basically for long-term patients only. The other levels of treatment were available from private practitioners, but there was no coordinated program for mental health within the community.

Members of the Community Needs Panel recommended that the Maria Hansen Health Center approach the development of a coordinated program for mental health in Dane County on an incremental basis. Inpatient hospitalization would remain at Maplewood over the short term, with improved medical services for the patients, while primary and secondary treatments would be started at Mercy Hospital. Day and resident care would be added informally at the Maplewood

site, although with limited capital expenditures, for eventually all mental health services would be concentrated at the Health Center. It was expected that the Maplewood Hospital services and staff could be moved to Mercy Hospital in five to six years, but that the full development of a coordinated mental health program would take eight to ten years, and encounter two problems.

The first problem was financial. Traditionally, reimbursements from third-party payors (insurance companies and governmental agencies) for mental health care have lagged behind payments for physical health services. Further, many of these benefits were limited to hospitalization, which imposed the tertiary level of care upon patients who might be much better served at the primary or secondary levels. Some liberalization in these constraints on reimbursement was apparent in 1980 as inpatient hospital costs increased rapidly, and as outpatient care was seen to be a less expensive alternative, but planners at the Health Center felt that it would be difficult to fund the entire program. One funding possibility was to contract with the state government to provide mental health services in Dane County, with the expectation that the

Exhibit 19 *Availability of mental health maintenance and mental illness treatments from the Maria Hansen Health Center, 1980*

	Mercy Hospital	Maplewood Hospital
Promotional effort	n.a.	n.a.
Primary treatments		
Education	Limited	Limited
Outpatient	n.a.	n.a.
Secondary treatments		
Emergency	Limited	n.a.
Outpatient	n.a.	n.a.
Tertiary treatments		
Day care	n.a.	n.a.
Resident care	n.a.	n.a.
Inpatient care	n.a.	n.a.
Long-term care	n.a.	155 beds

Source: Corporation records.

coordinated program would reduce the need for hospitalization, and therefore become, in essence, self-funding, but discussions on such a contract were only at the exploratory stage at the date of the case.

The second problem stemmed from people, not money. The professional staff at Maplewood was accustomed to working in the traditional manner, with an individual relationship between the psychiatrist and each patient, and with all aspects of care directed by the psychiatrist. The coordinated program would require a team approach, with psychiatrists, physicians, psychologists, clinical nurses, and social workers interacting with numerous patients at different levels of treatment. Some resistance to a change of this magnitude could be expected.

Personal Wellness. Wellness refers to the health of an individual, particularly to the positive actions that can be taken by individuals to maintain or even improve their health. The concept of wellness was developed in response to the increasing prevalence of life-style-related diseases such as heart attacks, strokes, cancer, cirrhosis, and hypertension. Habitual smoking, excess alcohol, improper nutrition, and sedentary behavior have all been linked to a deterioration in health and to the onset of these diseases. For many physicians and health care planners, the recent emphasis on the diagnosis and treatment of the life-style-related diseases, and the lack of attention paid to their prevention, has appeared to be a reversal of a more logical approach. This reversal is illustrated in a fable that is well known in the health care field:

> It has been many years since the first body was spotted in the river. Some old-timers remember how spartan were the facilities and procedures for managing that sort of thing. Sometimes, they say, it would take hours to pull 10 people from the river, and even then only a few would survive.

> Though the number of victims in the river has increased greatly in recent years, the good folks of Downstream have responded admirably to the challenge. Their rescue system is clearly second to none: most people discovered in the swirling waters are reached within 20 minutes, many in less than 10. Only a small number drown each day before help arrives; a big improvement from the way it used to be.

> Talk to the people of Downstream and they'll speak with pride about the new hospital at the edge of the waters, the flotilla of rescue boats ready for service at a moment's notice, the comprehensive plans for coordinating all the manpower involved, and the large number of highly trained and dedicated swimmers always ready to risk their lives to save victims from the raging currents. Sure it costs a lot, but, say the Downstreamers, what else can decent people do except to provide whatever it takes when human lives are at stake.

> Oh, a few people in Downstream have raised the question now and again, but most folks show little interest about what's happening Upstream. It seems there's so much to do to help those in the river, that nobody's got time to check on how all those bodies are getting there in the first place. That's the way things are, sometimes. (Donald Ardell, *High Level Wellness*, Bantam Press, New York, 1979, p. 4)

Wellness programs view disease prevention as the responsibility of the individual, for often a change in personal habits or life-style is required. These programs, however, extend far beyond health education. Most hospitals offer health care classes, on such topics as prenatal nutrition and the benefits of regular exercise, but the success rate of these sessions in altering behavior considered to be detrimental to health, such as tobacco smoking or alcohol abuse, tends to be very low. A continuing program is needed, not disjointed classes.

Wellness programs usually consist of a

four-part sequence of activities: health assessment, individual counseling, class instruction, and periodic reevaluation. The health assessment is an evaluation of the individual's current health status, and usually includes a medical history, laboratory tests, physical examination, and a life-style profile. Because achieving and maintaining a state of personal wellness is often dependent on the individual's life-style, the profile is a very important part of the health assessment. Questionnaires, ranging in complexity from simple hand-scored forms to computer-analyzed booklets, are used to "measure" life-style characteristics. Counseling between a staff person and the individual follows, and includes a review of the health assessment and an identification of personal goals to achieve wellness. It is at this stage in the four-part sequence that the individual's responsibility for his/her own wellness becomes clear. Counselors are instructed to guide and suggest goals, but never to substitute their judgment for that of the individual. The instructional classes are designed to help the individual attain his/her health goals. Based on the premise that changes in life-style positively affect an individual's health status, and that these changes require continual reinforcement, ongoing classes are offered in a variety of topics, such as stress management, physical fitness, proper nutrition, weight control, dental care, and emotional well-being. After a period of time, each individual is reevaluated and his/her goals are restructured based on the degree of progress and the desire for improvement. Some wellness centers have gone beyond this basic concept of the program, and have offered physical fitness facilities, nutritional meals, and mobile health vans, but the four-part sequence remains the basis of all wellness programs.

In 1980, wellness programs were offered at 15 hospitals and medical centers within the United States. Four of the hospitals had wellness centers with separate facilities and permanent staffs, and five more had permanent staffs which were housed in a portion of the regular facilities; the balance of the wellness programs were organized and run by an existing department within a hospital, such as Personnel. Startup expenses most often came from the hospital's operating budget, but some institutions provided grants to cover these costs. Ongoing expenses could be covered by individual fees, but this tended to restrict the program to the affluent members of the community.

Planners at the Maria Hansen Health Center felt that people within the Dane County service area would benefit from a wellness program, since the major causes of death at Mercy Hospital were heart disease (27.06% in 1977), cancer (26.51%), and stroke (6.35%), and were at least partially related to life-style. The planners also felt that people within the service area would be receptive to the program; many residents had expressed concerns about personal health, and bikers, joggers, etc., were very evident in the area. Problems in the program were expected to come from staffing. No one at the Health Center had experience with wellness, although a director for the program might be recruited from one of the existing programs, and a staff might be assembled, for class instruction and personal counseling, on a voluntary basis from the University of Wisconsin. Also, the program would have to be marketed, to generate enthusiasm for wellness and to encourage commitment to the program among people who were not currently engaged in health maintenance activities, and no one at the Health Center had any experience in marketing (hospitals normally do not market their services, for patients rarely have a choice about the need to enter a hospital). Finally, there was some concern that a wellness program might be seen to be in conflict with the normal activities of the Health

Center; it was intended that the program be a supplement to traditional medical care, not a substitute for that care. However, some patients might mistake the health assessment for the annual physical exam, and decrease their involvement with a family physician. And if operating fund allocations had to be made, and funds were diverted into the wellness program and away from existing medical programs, then some resistance from physicians might be encountered. The Community Needs Panel suggested that a wellness program was an attractive possibility, but made no firm recommendation to the Central Planning Committee.

The Central Planning Committee at the Maria Hansen Health Center, during the summer of 1980, was considering five specific proposals for diversification outside the current programs of medical care at Mercy Hospital: geriatric service, alternative financing and delivery (HMOs), physical rehabilitation, mental health, and personal wellness. The Health Center was not limited to chosing one alternative, but all could not be implemented, and certainly all could not be implemented at the same time. Some difficult choices had to be made.

> Diversification may seem to be a strange problem for a hospital, but separate programs to supplement the existing medical care are needed to reduce the cost, improve the effectiveness, and extend the availability of that care. The problem is one of decision among the alternatives.
>
> We feel that we are leading in health care diversification because of our system of planning, but leaders can't look to others for help in choosing among diversification programs. Our choice of programs must be made within financial, regulatory, and philosophical considerations. We can forecast the financial needs and negotiate the regulatory requirements, but how do we deal realistically with the major philosophical issues, such

as who gets what level of care. And that brings up another question—are we getting away from what we have done well in the past? In the past we offered good quality, *concerned* medical care. In the future, we propose to offer a variety of health care services, some of which will compete with others. Can we manage that complexity, and that competition, and still maintain our concern for the individual? (Statement of the Director of Planning at the Maria Hansen Health Center)

Class Assignment. Consider the medical care system within the United States, which is only partially described within this case; what are the major trends within medical care, and what are the reasons for these trends? Then, answer the following questions against the background of your understanding of the future of the medical care system:

1. Assume that you are Mr. Michael Corvo, Director of Planning at the Maria Hansen Health Center. What alternative would you prefer, and why?
2. Assume that, as Mr. Michael Corvo, you have asked to present your recommendations to the board of directors of the Sisters of the Holy Spirit Health Corporation (the "parent" organization for the Maria Hansen Health Center). Develop a set of measures to assist the members of the board in comparing the diversification alternatives.
3. Assume that you are Mr. James Michelsen, President of the Maria Hansen Health Center; what other groups (constituencies) would you wish to bring into the decision process on the diversification of health care services at the Health Center?
4. As a student in a class on strategic management, list five to seven important differences between public institutions such as the Maria Hansen Health Center, and private organizations such as business firms of approximately equal size.

APPENDIX A: STATEMENT OF THE PHILOSOPHY, MISSION, ROLE, AND GOALS OF THE MARIA HANSEN HEALTH CENTER*

Statement of Philosophy. We are called forth as an extension of Jesus Christ in the healing mission of the Church. Historically we began our work in keeping with the teaching of Mother Maria Hansen in bringing mercy and compassion to those in need. Faithful to the teachings of the foundress, and as an extension of Christ's healing mission to those in need of health care, the Maria Hansen Health Center is dedicated to value the dignity of each person. The Maria Hansen Health Center is committed to provide health care services which reverence human life, render public witness to Christ's active love for all persons, and reach out to those suffering from illness.

Based on this philosophy, the staff of Maria Hansen Health Center believes that each person is a unique individual with a physical, social, psychological, and spiritual reality. All of us are brothers and sisters, one to another, loved into existence by our Creator. As we provide service to persons we recognize that their physical, social, psychological and spiritual needs stem from a relationship to God as our Loving Father. Since the whole person as a unique being suffers from pain, from loss, from broken relationships, we will strive to bring relief by alleviating suffering and by providing an environment of hope, peace and therapeutic relationships.

All available resources and personal energies will be directed toward promoting the health of the whole person whose social, emotional, mental and physical needs affect relationship to himself as a being of dignity and worth, relationship to others as brothers and sisters of a loving Creator, and relationship to

* From corporation records, distributed as a pamphlet to all employees upon joining the Health Center and available to all patients.

his environment in the lifestyle that promotes peace, justice and compassion.

Statement of Mission. The mission of the Maria Hansen Health Center is to improve, both independently and through collaborative efforts, the physical and mental health of people within the service area. This effort will be extended to meet the needs of people in other communities as our resources permit. As part of this mission, the Maria Hansen Health Center will seek to enhance the spiritual well-being of the people it serves and of the Center's staff.

The mission will be carried out in a way that promotes reverence for life, love, justice, compassion and service to others, especially to those in need. The services provided by the Center will be directed toward enabling each person receiving care to realize his or her optimal fullness of being.

Statement of Role. The Community Service Area shall be Dane County. The Referral Service Area shall be contiguous portions of Columbia, Dodge, Jefferson, Janesville, Green, and Iowa Counties.

Responsibility to the Community Service Area. Either through direct provision or through collaboration with others, we shall assume a leadership role in assuring that the primary and secondary level mental and physical health care needs of the Community Service Area are met. First priority in all decisions relating to programs, patient admissions, allocation of beds and other resources, and granting of medical staff privileges shall be given to serving residents of the Community Service Area.

Responsibility to the Referral Service Area. Either through direct provision or through collaboration with others, we shall assume a leadership role in assuring that secondary level mental and physical health care needs of the Referral Service Area are met. Every effort shall be made to encourage the provision of primary level care services by other providers in the Referral Service Area. Primary level care services shall be provided by the Maria Hansen Health Center to the extent such services are not or will not be provided by others.

Responsibility to Other Service Areas. In order to meet the secondary level care needs of the Community and Referral Service Areas, programs will be made available to other communities only to the extent necessary to provide the volume of services necessary to ensure an appropriate level of quality and economic viability for such programs; and to the extent there is unused program capacity after meeting the needs of the Community Service Area and Referral Service Area, as delineated previously.

Responsibility for Tertiary Care Services. We shall be a provider of tertiary level care services if the following conditions are met:

a. There is a demonstrated need for such services in the Community Service Area; and
b. Residents of the Community Service Area do not have access to such services because such services are not or will not be provided elsewhere in Dane County or an adjacent community; or because there is unreasonable waiting time, travel time, lack of community acceptance or some other barrier to access to the residents of the Community Service Area; and
c. Such provision shall not jeopardize meeting the needs of the Community and Referral Service Areas, as described previously.

Emphasis will be placed on diversification in order to develop alternatives to inpatient acute mental and physical health care for improving the effectiveness and the efficiency of care. Such diversification may include: the settings in which care is delivered, such as home care or ambulatory care. The types of care delivered, such as rehabilitation or extended care. The substitution of less costly resources within the current patterns of care. The allocation of resources to inpatient

acute mental and health care programs shall remain essentially stable (as adjusted for inflation), with consequent growth in commitment to programs which provide alternatives to inpatient acute care.

We shall support programs aimed at keeping people mentally and physically healthy and preventing illnesses and injury.

We shall be a direct provider of primary mental and physical health care services when access to such services is found to be inadequate and alternatives provision of such services cannot be established.

We shall provide a major share of the diagnostic, therapeutic and rehabilitative services to the Community Service Area within the context of primary and secondary care levels of service.

Secondary level care programs shall be aimed at the diagnostic and treatment of major causes of morbidity and mortality as identified for the Community and Referral Service Areas.

Emphasis shall be given to improving the quality of care, as measured by outcome and patient satisfaction, and to improving productivity as measured by reducing the total cost of care and the cost per unit of service.

Emphasis will be placed on the contribution of education to the role of the Center. The Maria Hansen Health Center will sponsor patient, community and professional education in order to improve the health status of the community it serves.

Statement of Goals. The fourteen goals of the Maria Hansen Health Center are divided into goals for planning and development (3), for program implementation (4), and for service characteristics (7):

Plan cooperatively to identify the unmet physical and mental health care needs of the people within the service area.
Plan cooperatively to develop programs for health maintenance, diagnosis, treat-

ment and rehabilitation, as required by the people within the service area.

Provide opportunities for and encourage community involvement and direction in the delivery of health care.

Implement independent and/or collaborative programs for the delivery of diagnostic and therapeutic physical health services.

Implement independent and/or collaborative programs for the delivery of diagnostic and therapeutic mental health services.

Implement independent and/or collaborative programs for the delivery of rehabilitative and chronic health services.

Implement independent and/or collaborative programs for the delivery of preventive health services.

In implementing the provision of health services, promote community, governance and staff awareness of the philosophy, mission, role and goals of the Center.

Provide services in ways that enhance the spiritual well-being of each of those giving and receiving care.

Provide services so that they are fully accessible to all of those in the community who require them.

Provide services that are of uniform high quality.

Provide services that are effective and cost efficient.

Develop comprehensive programs of education for the promotion and maintenance of good health directed at community and staff.

Recognize the Center's social responsibilities to the community and make resources available to fulfill those obligations.

Chapter 9

STRATEGIC DESIGN
AND IMPLEMENTATION

Strategic management is concerned with the definition of the major goals and objectives for an organization, and the design of the functional policies and plans and the organizational structure and managerial systems to achieve those goals and objectives, all in response to changing environmental conditions, institutional resources, and individual motives and values. Strategic management can be defined generally as leadership in purposeful organizations, and specifically as the functions and responsibilities of the general manager of a business firm or nonprofit institution whose task is to combine and direct the efforts and activities of the other members of the organization toward the successful completion of a stated mission or purpose.

Strategic design is a portion of that task. The first six chapters of the text described the process of strategic design for a single product–market unit (typified by small business firms), for a single product–process unit (represented by the medium-sized product divisions of large corporations), for a single-industry firm (illustrated by large basic processing companies), for multiple-industry firms, with either related or nonrelated products, and for nonprofit institutions. In each instance, the intent of the strategic design process was to select a long-term method of competition for the business firm, or a long-term concept of service for the nonprofit institution that would differentiate and clearly identify the organization. In each instance also, the process of strategic design was an evaluation of alternative patterns of competition or service through comparison with environmental characteristics and trends, organizational assets and skills, and managerial values and attitudes, as shown on the top of the next page.

Strategic design, however, does not complete the functions and responsibilities of the general manager. The selected strategy, which is the method of competition chosen for a business firm or the concept of service identified for a nonprofit institution, has to be clearly expressed through explicit statements about the goals, poli-

Environmental characteristics
and trends

Economic

Technological

Social/political

Competitive

↓

Organizational mission or charter	Specific opportunities and risks within the industry
↓	↓
Corporate perform-ance and position	Range of strategic alternatives open to the firm
↑	↑
Managerial values and attitudes	Specific strengths and weak-nesses within the company

Selected strategy, or method of com-petition

↑

Money

Equipment

People

Market position

Organizational resources, or
assets and skills

---

cies, programs, and actions for each of the organizational units. These functional objectives, policies, programs, and actions define the tasks or jobs that are essential for strategic success, and the organizational structure and managerial systems are then designed to coordinate and integrate the performance of those tasks. This view of strategic implementation can also be expressed in outline format as shown at the top of the next page.

Strategic management cannot, in practice, be separated into the twin halves of formulation and implementation since the selected method of competition or con-cept of service can only be expressed in terms of the implementing objectives, poli-cies, programs, and actions, and since the strategic alternatives can only be consid-ered in terms of the information provided and performance recorded by the existing structure, systems, and people. Strategic management is not a divided process; it is the simultaneous consideration of the formulation and implementation of strategy, and this consideration is essential for the success of the organization due to the con-tinual process of change in the environmental characteristics and in the or-

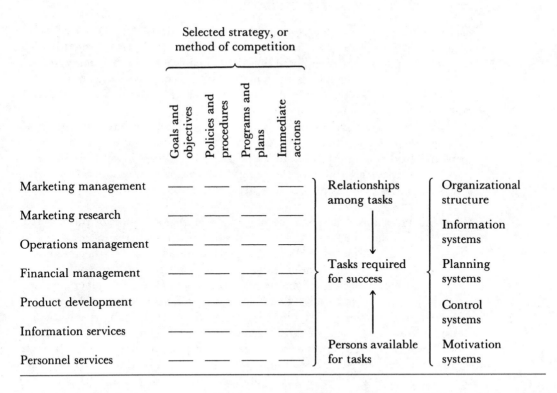

ganizational resources which must be reflected in the method of competition for a firm, or the concept of service of a nonprofit institution.

Strategic management, then, consists of the simultaneous and continual formulation and implementation of the method of competition for a business firm or the concept of service for a nonprofit institution. The implementation portion requires a translation of this method of competition or concept of service into a precise series of statements on objectives, policies, programs, and actions for each major division, functional area, and technical department within the organization, or the selected strategy will remain an unachieved expression of intentions and hopes. The content and intention of the objectives, policies, programs, and actions need to be defined:

Goals and Objectives. The first step in the implementation of strategy is to express clear and realistic objectives for each of the units within the organization. These objectives are the results that are expected in marketing, production, finance, product development, and the various staff units; they are statements of where the functional and technical units are expected to be at a specific time in the future. These goals give members of the units the sense of direction and purpose that is necessary to coordinate the efforts of the functional and technical specialists, and they permit evaluation of the performance of the departments. Functional objectives, in short, serve as targets for achievement and standards for control:

1. Goals and objectives are usually expressed in quantitative terms. The primary areas of responsibility for each organizational unit have to be defined, a scale of

measurement for each area of responsibility has to be devised, and then a goal or target can be established on each scale. Quantitative objectives are clear and precise, but it must be remembered that they are limited, and that many important activities cannot be measured in quantitative terms. When qualitative objectives are used, they have to be carefully expressed to avoid misunderstanding and confusion.

2. Goals and objectives are often the subject of negotiations between the general manager of the organization and the head of the functional or technical department involved since the achievement of the objectives is dependent not only upon the activity and ability of the department, but also upon the policies prescribed and the resources allocated by the central administration.

Policies and Procedures. The second step in the implementation of the selected strategy is to develop corporate policies and standard procedures for each of the units within the organization. Policies and procedures serve as parameters for the decisions and actions of organizational members; they are the guides to be followed to achieve the stated objectives in marketing, production, finance, product development, and the various staff units. The objective specifies the target or results that are expected; the policies specify the manner by which these results are to be accomplished. (Objective: achieve 20% market share for product A. Policies: price is to be 1.8 times the direct variable costs of product A; distribution is to be through exclusive company representatives, and promotion is to be by industry trade journals.) Policies may be either positive (allow company representatives 22.5% discount off the list price) or negative (do not cut the list price to increase market share; do not engage in price fixing or market allocation with competitors). Policies and procedures are general statements which convey the intentions and instructions of the corporate management, and serve as guidelines so that the individual decisions and actions throughout the organization can be consistent with the selected strategy. If a meaningful difference exists, functional policies serve as guidelines for decision and standard procedures serve as guidelines for action, but both are intended to describe the customary or accepted method of reacting to certain recurring, similar situations. In short, policies and procedures together state the expected guidelines for both decisions and actions within an organization, and consequently they serve to coordinate the efforts of the functional and technical specialists within that organization.

1. Policies and procedures may be expressed with either quantitative or qualitative terms. Obviously, the quantitative terms are more clear, but they also tend to become fairly rigid rules and regulations, and they cannot then permit a range of discretionary actions on the part of the functional or technical personnel involved with a situation. "Sell at 1.8 times the direct variable cost" is a clear quantitative policy, but it precludes the marketing flexibility and prompt reaction to competitive pressure of "Don't sell below full cost."

2. Policies and procedures probably should be expressed in written form, since copies of the documents can then be made available to everyone concerned with the operations of a functional or technical unit, and this availability tends to

eliminate misunderstandings and confusion. However, written policies and procedures can become codified into a quasi-legal system for the firm, and not kept current. Published policies and procedures should be reviewed periodically, and changed to remain consistent with changes in the corporate strategy.

Programs and Plans. The third step in the implementation of the selected strategy is the design of the functional programs and the development of the budgetary plans. Functional programs involve the description of the specific activities proposed by each organizational unit to achieve the stated objectives within the policy guidelines, while the budgetary plans concern the estimated expenditures for these activities, expressed on a monthly or quarterly pro forma accounting statement. To give an example, an advertising program might be established as part of the marketing department's effort to achieve an objective of 20% market share for a specific product, and this advertising program might operate under the twin policies, or directions from the corporate management, to concentrate on the stimulation of secondary demand through trade journals rather than primary demand through consumer magazines, and to limit expenditures to an annual rate approximating 5% of the projected sales of the product. The advertising program would then detail the magazines and the issues selected, and the message and format of the ads. The advertising budget would report the cost of these ads, together with the managerial and clerical expenses and the allocated overhead of the program, on a pro forma accounting statement.

1. Functional and technical programs often tend to continue unaltered despite modifications or outright changes in the selected strategy of the corporation; this resistance to change is caused by the loyalty and adherence to established activities that can build up within organizational units. Functional and technical programs should be reviewed periodically, and redirected to remain consistent with changes in the corporate strategy.
2. Functional and technical budgets can be expressed in fixed terms (the amounts to be spent during an accounting period), in variable terms (the amounts to be spent at various levels of sales or production), or in discretionary terms (the amounts to be spent, if needed in the opinion of the executive in charge of a program). Budgetary plans also tend to continue unaltered despite modifications or changes in the selected strategy of the corporation; this is due to the natural inclination to start the planning process at the current expense level. The functional and technical budgets should be reviewed periodically, and revised to remain consistent with changes in the corporate strategy.

Immediate Actions. The last step in the implementation of the selected strategy by preparing a series of statements on the objectives, policies, programs, and actions for each of the functional and technical departments within the organization is the decision to take appropriate actions to start on the new strategy. Functional and technical activities can be described as the first step in the sequence of tasks required by a plan or program to achieve specific goals and objectives within given policies and procedures; they are what has to be done now to start to implement the corporate strategy.

The translation of the selected strategy, or long-term method of competition for a firm, into a series of statements on the goals and objectives, policies and procedures, programs and plans, and immediate actions for each of the units within an organization defines the tasks that are required for the success of that strategy, and those tasks and the relationships among the tasks in turn determine the organizational structure and managerial systems. The following case illustrates the need for explicit consideration of the process and problems of strategy implementation.

Hamlin Machinery Company, Inc.

During the summer of 1975, one of the faculty members in the Policy and Control Department at the University of Michigan was asked to visit a small company in the northern part of the state that was having financial problems. This company, which had been founded in 1967 by a professor in the Engineering School, was located in Kalkaska, a small town in the northwestern portion of the lower peninsula, and specialized in the production of thermoplastic forming, molding, coating, laminating, mixing, and recycling equipment for very low volume applications.

The strategy of our company, in very simple terms, is to supply low-volume forming machinery for the small plastic fabricators. Most of the blow molding, injection molding, and plastic extruding equipment that is available is very expensive, in the $250,000 and up price range, requires very costly dies, and is useful only in large-volume applications. A blow molder to turn out plastic milk bottles, for example, will cost $600,000, will require a $120,000 die set, and will make 180 bottles per minute. For large companies, that system is ideal. We don't sell to the large companies; we sell to the small local firms. There are 6,700 plastic fabricators in the United States, and only 500 of them are large; we sell to the other 6,200. We don't make a blow molder for

large items, such as milk bottles, so that was probably a poor example for me to use, but if we did, we would design a much smaller machine, that would cost about $60,000 and require a $10,000 die set, and turn out maybe 10 bottles per minute. For large-volume applications, our equipment is simply not economical; but there are a lot of small-volume needs in formed plastics. The large-volume applications are mostly in packaging, for food products, detergents, and health-care items. The low-volume needs are in special parts for the automotive, appliance, office machinery, and furniture industries, and for toys, hardware, and household items. If you wanted to make a toy plastic firetruck, you probably wouldn't want 180 of them per minute, and you certainly wouldn't want to spend $120,000 for the die. Our equipment would give you 10 per minute, which after all will add up to 6,000 in 10 hours, and since there is only one cavity in the die, rather than multiple cavities for the big machines, the tooling will be much less expensive. Our equipment fits a very specific niche in the market. (Statement of Professor Hamlin)

Professor Hamlin started the company in 1966 when he recognized that the new thermoplastic resins, such as polyethylene, polystyrene, and polyvinyl, which became available in the 1960s, would gradually replace the older thermosetting resins, such as epoxy and phenolic compounds, since they were much less brittle and consequently much easier to form and to mold. He thought that the improved properties of the thermoplastic materials, which could be engineered for specific applications through the addition of reinforcing fibers or modifying chemicals, and the simpler fabrication methods would result in a very considerable expansion in the use of plastic resins and in the number of plastic fabricators, who would need new machinery. Professor Hamlin was correct in both forecasts (Exhibit 1).

The company grew rapidly during the first seven years, with sales reaching the million dollar mark in 1968, and slightly over $4 million in 1972. However, profits did not keep pace with the increased sales, and the company was financed with factored accounts receivable, short-term bank loans, equipment leasing, and personal loans from Professor Hamlin. The accounts receivable factoring and the equipment leasing were arranged through a commercial finance company at interest rates that averaged 12.5%. At the insistence of the bank, which of course charged considerably lower rates, Professor Hamlin in 1970 combined all but $25,000 of his short-term advances to the company in the form of subordinated 10-year debentures, which improved the equity position since the debentures were subordinated to all debt, and thus considered part of the equity. In 1971, the company sold common stock equal to 10% of

the total outstanding to the sales manager, the production manager, and the chief engineer for $10,000. In the same year, Professor Hamlin gave stock equal to 15% of the total to his son, Lawrence, who served as president of the company, and he also gave stock equal to 5% of the total to each of the other executives. The result of these transactions was that Professor Hamlin owned 40% of the equity, while each of the four others owned 15%. As a result of these transactions, and as a result of the growth in retained earnings, the debt/equity ratio of the firm improved substantially (Exhibit 2).

In 1973, the petrochemical plants became unable to produce adequate thermoplastic resins due to the Arab oil embargo, which cut sharply the supply of petroleum feedstocks. This resulted in an informal rationing of thermoplastic materials, which many of the smaller companies claimed was unfairly biased in favor of the larger users. With distinctly limited raw material supplies, the small fabricators did not wish to add additional capacity, and many of their orders for new machinery and equipment were cancelled. The sales of the Hamlin Machinery Company declined for the first year since its founding, and the company suffered a loss of $182,200 before giving effect to income tax credits for prior years. The unsettled machinery market continued through 1974, and resulted in another year of reduced sales for Hamlin, although the operating loss was cut to $49,200 due to budget cutbacks (Exhibit 3).

Exhibit 1 *Plastic resin shipments (millions of pounds) and plastic fabricators operating within the United States, 1960–1972*

	1960	1962	1964	1966	1968	1970	1972
Thermosetting	1,404	1,595	1,877	2,314	2,778	3,004	3,481
Thermoplastic	846	1,843	4,797	9,050	13,373	17,322	20,686
Fabricators	1,107	1,780	3,470	4,250	4,860	5,440	6,710

Source: Company records.

Exhibit 2 *Income statements and balance sheets for the Hamlin Machinery Company, Inc., 1968-1972*

	1968	1970	1972
Sales	$1,112,400	$1,978,700	$4,004,100
Material cost	355,300	675,600	1,481,500
Labor cost	311,500	573,800	1,201,200
Manufacturing overhead	104,600	158,900	354,300
Total manufacturing costs	771,400	1,408,300	3,037,000
Gross margin	341,000	570,400	967,100
Marketing expenses	58,400	153,600	310,500
Engineering expenses	43,900	113,200	284,800
General and administrative expenses	51,200	82,700	87,200
Interest expenses	29,100	63,900	79,300
Total overhead expenses	182,600	413,400	761,800
Profit before taxes	158,400	157,000	205,300
Federal and state income taxes	69,100	67,400	91,500
Profit after taxes	89,300	89,600	113,800
Cash	5,260	8,040	21,820
Accounts receivable	142,050	318,650	600,580
Inventory	159,420	237,510	297,440
Total current assets	306,730	564,200	919,840
Machinery and equipment (net)	143,780	282,800	423,240
Total current and fixed assets	450,510	847,000	1,343,080
Accounts payable	107,250	57,950	123,450
Factor's loan on accounts receivable	113,420	243,710	278,970
Short-term bank loan	37,000	28,000	104,000
Short-term stockholder's loan	46,700	25,000	—
Total current liabilities	304,370	354,660	506,420
Equipment financing contracts	114,440	206,240	308,960
Subordinated debentures	—	85,400	85,400
Total long-term debt	114,440	29,640	394,360
Common stock	39,400	39,400	69,400
Retained earnings	(7,700)	161,300	372,900
Total equity	31,700	200,700	442,300
Total liabilities, debt, and equity	$ 450,510	$ 847,000	$1,343,080

Source: Company records.

Exhibit 3 *Income statements and balance sheets for the Hamlin Machinery Company, Inc., 1973 and 1974*

	1973	1974
Sales	$2,978,600	$3,370,600
Material cost	1,140,600	1,290,300
Labor cost	924,800	1,069,900
Manufacturing overhead	325,300	363,600
Total manufacturing costs	2,390,700	2,723,800
Gross margin	587,900	646,800
Marketing expenses	308,400	354,300
Engineering expenses	254,600	148,200
General and administrative expenses	94,200	89,700
Interest expenses	112,900	103,800
Total overhead expenses	770,100	696,000
Profit (loss) before taxes	(182,200)	(49,200)
Credit on federal and state income taxes	85,200	16,300
Profit (loss) after taxes	(97,000)	(32,900)
Cash	13,180	7,040
Accounts receivable	579,180	580,510
Inventory	345,510	315,740
Total current assets	937,870	903,290
Machinery and equipment (net)	384,480	346,870
Total current and fixed assets	1,322,350	1,250,100
Accounts payable	110,640	121,450
Factor's loan on accounts receivable	353,430	360,940
Short-term bank loan	105,000	105,000
Short-term stockholder's loan (Prof. Hamlin)	32,000	32,000
Total current liabilities	601,070	619,390
Equipment financing contracts	290,480	232,810
Subordinated debentures (Prof. Hamlin)	85,400	85,400
Total long term debt	375,880	318,210
Common stock	69,400	69,400
Retained earnings	276,000	243,100
Total equity	345,400	312,500
Total liabilities, debt, and equity	$1,322,350	$1,250,100

Source: Company records.

The financial position of the company, which had improved steadily until 1972, as evidenced by the current ratios and the total debt/total equity ratios, began to deteriorate substantially in 1973 and 1974 (Exhibit 4).

The faculty member from the Policy and Control Department at the University of Michigan was asked to consult on the financial problems of the company, with particular reference toward preparing a financial proposal for submission to a venture capital firm to obtain additional equity. This type of proposal requires definite information on a company's product lines, market segments, marketing plans, production facilities, financial needs, etc., and in the process of gathering this information, it soon became apparent that the problems of the company were interpersonal and organizational rather than financial. Each of the four executives within the company appeared to follow a different path, and each disagreed strongly with the suggestions and recommendations of others for the improvement of the overall company situation.

Francis Blackman, Chief Engineer. Mr. Blackman was approximately 55 years old and a graduate of the state teachers' college at Mount Pleasant, Michigan. He had worked as an instructor in the manual training course at a local high school, and as a draftsman for a package machinery manufacturer in a small town close to Kalkaska, before coming to work for Prof. Hamlin as an engineering assistant at the start of the company. He had been promoted to Chief Engineer in 1969, when Prof. Hamlin felt unable to continue both teaching and writing at the University of Michigan and active participation in the management of the Hamlin Machinery Company. Much of Mr. Blackman's engineering training was self-taught, but he certainly gave the outward appearance of a competent and resourceful designer who kept current through study of mechanical engineering and popular scientific journals at his home. At the time of the interviews, Mr. Blackman was very upset about recent budgetary cuts in the engineering staff, and about recent requests for improved planning and control of the engineering activities:

I have some ideas for a new recycling machine (scrap thermoplastics could be recycled provided they were thoroughly ground and then mixed in proper proportions with fresh materials; the size of the particles in grinding and the proportion of the materials in mixing differed for each of the major types of thermoplastics, which made the design of recycling equipment difficult), but I won't give them to the Hamlins.

They made me buy stock in the company, just before it all came apart. Fortunately, we have a stock repurchase agreement (all four of the younger executives had a formal, written agreement that if they left the company for any reason, they would sell their stock back to the corporation at a price that would be 10 times a weighted average of the three most recent years per share earnings), and I may make them take my stock back, even though I will lose some money.

Exhibit 4 *Financial ratios of the Hamlin Machinery Company, Inc., 1968–1974*

	1968	1970	1972	1973	1974
Current ratio	1.01:1	1.59:1	1.82:1	1.56:1	1.46:1
Debt/equity ratio (assuming debentures = equity)	13.2:1	1.96:1	1.54:1	2.05:1	2.14:1

Source: Company records.

The thing that really bothers me is that I've had to get rid of some of my people. The engineering budget has been cut nearly in half. It's not very nice to have to tell some of your best people that you don't want them anymore, but I had to do it. They were local people, too, whom I had known for years, which made it even worse. O.K. But, now Larry (Lawrence Hamlin, son of the founder and president of the firm) wants me to continue to design new equipment. He says that new machinery is necessary to broaden our sales base. He doesn't understand that you can't cut back on engineering personnel and still come out with new designs.

Also, Larry wants me to plan just when we'll finish the various projects we have under way in the engineering department. He doesn't understand that you can't forecast when you'll finish a design project since you never know what problems you'll run into. Larry just doesn't understand engineering. His father understood engineering, of course, but he is not here much anymore (Professor Hamlin had suffered a heart attack in 1973, partially brought on by the strains and disappointments of the company's performance that year; in 1975 he limited his participation to attendance at the monthly directors' meetings).

Now, Larry wants to charge us for the cost of parts that need to be replaced under our warrantee. That's ridiculous. Why am I supposed to be responsible just because something broke. Why not charge it back to the shop; they're the ones who made it. John (John Hegenaeur, the production manager) is always talking about the fact that he has to use shop labor and ship parts to fix our experimental designs. Well, that is the way you design new machinery; you build a prototype, and you run it, and you find out what's wrong, and then you fix what's wrong. Both Larry and John complain because our drawings and bills of material [a bill of material lists the parts and

subassemblies needed for the completion of each machine; it represents a summary outline of the engineering drawings, and of the parts listed on each drawing] have some errors. Well, that is just the way things are in new machinery design; you cannot catch all the errors before they get out to the shop.

I liked working for Prof. Hamlin; he was an engineer, and he understood these things. But he is older now, and he is not here much, so he just doesn't control Larry. I don't like working here anymore, but if I leave, they're going to have to buy my stock back. I don't see why I should lose money on account of Larry and Prof. Hamlin. (Statement of Mr. Blackman)

John Hegenaeur, Production Manager. Mr. Hegeneaur was 34 years old, and a graduate of Purdue University, in electrical engineering. He had worked for Reliance Electric, in the Detroit sales office, for six years, and had received an M.B.A. in the evening program at the Dearborn campus of the University of Michigan before coming to work for Hamlin in 1969. At the time of the interviews, Mr. Hegenaeur was concerned by the size of the customer discounts offered by the sales department, and by the errors in the shop drawings provided by the engineering department:

Everyone says that we're losing money. I don't think that we're losing money; I think that we're giving it away. We actually made about $290,000 last year, but Tom Walsh gave it away in sales discounts. [Following the business downturn in the middle of fiscal 1973, the sales manager, Mr. Thomas Walsh, had felt that it was essential to offer special discounts and allowances off the list prices as an inducement to the customers to purchase new machinery. These discounts and allowances had averaged 3½% off the list price in 1973, and 7% in 1974.]

We also lose a lot of money because every time one of the new machines breaks down, one of Francis's people comes out in the shop, grabs a part off the shelf, and just disappears with it. I don't know how much this costs us; I just know we never have the parts around when we need them.

Tom [Thomas Walsh, sales manager] keeps saying that we have to speed up production; he keeps telling Larry that we could sell a lot more equipment if he could just get quick delivery. We don't have the money to carry an inventory of finished machines, so what we have to try to do is to carry an inventory of the parts, and then put the machines together to order. We can build a machine in about two weeks if we have all the parts on hand when we start construction, but there are always a couple of purchased parts we have to order, and it takes three to four weeks to get those parts here from the manufacturer. I don't think that five- to six-week delivery on special machinery is very bad; Tom ought to tell the customers that five- to six-week delivery is just the way life is.

Sometimes, and unfortunately it is not just sometimes, parts are left off the bill of material, and then we don't know that they are missing until we start assembly. When we find that something is missing, we have to order the part, but unless it is a standard item we have to wait to get delivery. I can understand why the customers get mad under this situation, since it means that we will be three to four weeks late, past our promised delivery. What I don't understand is why we keep getting these sloppy bills of material. [During one of the interviews with Mr. Hegenaeur, the conference in his office was interrupted by the shop foreman who said in a very disgusted tone, "Those people [the engineers] have done it again; they left the hydraulic cylinder controls off the parts list for the sheet-former. I asked Ed [Edward Mathews, the purchasing agent for the company] to call the distributor in Detroit, but they don't have the valves in stock. What do you want me to do now?" Mr. Hegenaeur suggested a rush order to the manufacturer in San Diego, with a request for air freight shipment, but admitted that there would be a minimum delay of two weeks.]

I'm proud of our inventory control system for standard parts [parts that were interchangeable between two or more machines, or that were used on popular models of machines, were considered to be "standard," and were stocked in labeled bins and checked weekly for minimum and reorder quantities]. It's a manual system but it works. Larry and I have talked about automating it, if we ever get the money. (Statement of Mr. Hegenaeur)

Thomas Walsh, Sales Manager. Mr. Walsh was 35 years old, and was a large, substantial person with a friendly, candid manner. Although he had grown up within the city of Detroit, people were often surprised to find that he had studied animal husbandry at Michigan State University, and people were often even more surprised to find that he also had a Ph.D. in agricultural economics from Purdue. He had come to work for the Hamlin Machinery Company in 1968 because he had known Lawrence Hamlin in the Army, but he explained that he was interested in the job opportunity because he had been certain that he could buy relatively inexpensive farmland in the area near Kalkaska, and experiment on a part-time basis with sheep raising. At the date of the case, Mr. Walsh was concerned by the slowness of delivery on customer orders for new equipment, and by a delay on the part of Lawrence Hamlin in seeking new sources of financing:

I understand the problems that John [John Hegenaeur, production manager] faces. I would not take his job for twice the salary that he is paid. He has to get out the production without enough money to buy the parts that he needs, and certainly without the money to stock machines for quick delivery. I feel that

Larry ought to go out and find the money; you know that it's available. I'll bet that I could find the money in a week. Larry has never approached the big banks in Detroit, or the big insurance companies in Chicago or New York. Instead, he keeps on dealing with a little bank down in Lansing. To get money, you have to go to the people who have it, and then you have to sell yourself and your company. Larry won't do that; he just says that the money isn't available as long as we keep having losses. Well, I think that it's pretty obvious that we're going to keep on having losses as long as we don't have the money. It's a vicious circle, but Larry isn't doing enough to break out of it.

I think that the real problem we face is not the money. As I say, we can always get that. Our real problem is that the president of the company, and the production manager, don't understand the basic reasons we need the money. Look at it from my point of view. We employ seven salesmen, and they work hard, and they build up a rapport with the potential customers in their area by calling on them and providing service to them. Finally, the customer will get an order for additional volume of existing parts or a contract for completely new parts, and he'll call up our salesman and say that he needs a new machine. Well, our person will drive up to see him, and together they'll work out the specifications on the equipment, and they'll agree on a price, and then they'll call here and I have to tell them six-week delivery. The customer will say "forget it" since he can get delivery much quicker someplace else. Our customers, who are small plastic fabricators making parts for other companies, need the equipment today, not six weeks from today, since they have to start making deliveries of their products tomorrow, not six weeks from tomorrow. That is what Larry and John don't understand, and it is a basic fact in the operation of our company.

I expect that John has complained to you that I cut prices on our machines. I sure do. We'd be dead if I didn't cut prices and make deals. This is another thing that Larry and John don't understand. We sell to the small plastic fabricator, not the big boys, and the person we deal with is usually the owner, not just an employee. It's his money that he's spending, and he wants to bargain on the price. When the market is up, I can be hard-nosed and only give 1 or 2%, but when the market is down, as it is right now, I'm lucky to be able to hold it to 5%.

Plastics Systems [the major competitor for Hamlin in the low-volume and low-cost segment of the plastics machinery industry] will bargain on price right down to their costs, and they'll throw in quick delivery too. They're tough people to compete against since their president understands the industry. But, we're going to run an ad campaign that will shake him up. [Mr. Walsh displayed a sample full-page ad that was to run in a number of trade journals in the next month; the picture showed a pair of hands sharpening a pencil with a penknife, while the copy stated, in large type, that "we have the sharpest pencil in the plastics machinery industry."]

One problem that we haven't talked about is that no one has ever defined the objectives for the company. I think that we all want capital gains, but the way the stock ownership is split up now, the Hamlins will make four times as much in capital gains as I will. I think that that arrangement makes it obvious that the rest of us will put in just exactly one quarter as much effort. The present situation just isn't fair, and it generates the conflict that must be apparent to you. I think that we would work together much better if we all had equal ownership; it would be like a law firm, with all the partners equal. You don't see conflicts and arguments in a law firm, and I think that we would be unbeatable if we could work together that well. I'm going to suggest to

Prof. Hamlin, the next time that he's here, that the real and lasting cure for this company would be for all of us—Francis, John, me, Larry, and Prof. Hamlin—to share equally in the ownership, with each of us having 20% of the stock. If we don't do something drastic, like that, to cure this situation, I'm going to start my own company because I know that I can get the money and, with the money, I know that I can get the sales. I don't want to do that, because it just isn't fair to the others, but I'm going to be forced to do it if we keep on the way we're going now. I just don't want to waste any more of my life, and I certainly don't want to keep on working for peanuts. But if Prof. Hamlin will give each of us an additional 5% of his stock, then I'll guarantee not to quit, and it'll be an easy guarantee to keep since I know that the sales and profits will just start rolling in once we start working together, and not at cross purposes. (Statement of Thomas Walsh)

Lawrence Hamlin, President. Mr. Hamlin, son of the founder, was 36 years old. He had grown up in Ann Arbor, Michigan, and had then studied history at Yale University before serving in the army and obtaining an M.B.A. from the Thunderbird School of Management in Arizona. He returned to Michigan in 1966 to help his father start the company, and had served as president since 1971. At the time of the interviews, he was concerned about the lack of organization and cooperation within the company:

Tom [Thomas Walsh, sales manager] is certainly right when he says that we are working at cross purposes. I'm discouraged since I don't know what to do about it. People keep saying that we've just got to get organized. I agree, but in a company with just four executives, there are a limited number of ways in which you can draw an organization chart. And I think that we've tried them all, and they haven't really helped.

Right now, I think that our major problem is in engineering. We've spent a lot of money there, but except for the injection molders and the sheet formers which were designed by my father, our designs always seem to be just a little worse than our competitors. Our designs never seem to look as clean and functional, and our machines don't seem to cycle quite as rapidly as some of the others. However, this is something that is hard to hit too hard on since the maintenance experience on our equipment is quite a bit better than it is on some of the others.

Our major problem with engineering is with the parts lists. John [John Hegenaeur, production manager] is right: there may be up to 10% of the parts left off the bill of material on a new machine. I think that this is just inexcusable since you can follow the power transmission, the hydraulic system, the electrical system, and the electronic controls through in a logical sequence in your mind, and the missing parts just jump right out at you. That is, if you have an electric motor in the parts list, then you have to have something on the shaft of that motor to transmit the power. If it is a V-belt pulley, then you have to have a V-belt and a companion V-belt pulley on the drive shaft, and that drive shaft has to have two bearings, and some further means of transmitting the power. The problem is that following through the sequences in this fashion takes time, and Francis [Francis Blackman, chief engineer] isn't willing to spend the time. I've talked to him a hundred times about this, but he doesn't recognize that it is a problem, so he puts his lowest-paid draftsman on tracing the parts sequences, and the result is that the errors keep appearing. If Francis would spend 20 hours himself doing this, and checking the prints, it would probably save John Hegenaeur 200 hours out in the shop, and we could deliver some of these new models on time. But I can't get him to understand that the time he saves costs us money in the long run.

We've tried to standardize our equipment, of course, but it seems that at least half of our customers want something a little bit different, and the result is that half of our orders have to cycle from sales to engineering to production to shipment. Of course, the obvious delays come in the shop, but you can't blame John for things that aren't really his fault. Just the other week, we had a large customer from the West Coast order one of our K-40 extruders. We promised eight-week delivery, and looking at the machine you would think that there was no way we could miss on that time schedule, especially since our shop is not that busy right now. But, the drawings were three weeks in engineering, and then it took two weeks to get delivery on the special parts, and one week in assembly before we found that some of the parts were missing, so now we're late, and the customer is upset and Tom is disgusted. Tom waits until the promised delivery date, and then looks to see where the machine is; by that time, of course, the unit is in the shop, so Tom thinks that John Hegenaeur is responsible, and yells at him. John isn't solely responsible; the fault extends completely through the company. In this particular case, the drawings sat in the engineering department since some of the provisions on the sales order were not clear. I explained that to Tom, but he said, "Five minutes; that's all it takes. Call me up and in five minutes I'll explain what the customer needs, so don't tell me that we can't build a machine in eight weeks just because I left five minutes worth of information off the sales order."

I hate to keep coming back to jump on poor Francis [Francis Blackman, chief engineer], but another problem we have in his area is interchangeable parts. We make seven different models on the K series extruders, and I think that many of the parts ought to be interchangeable. Francis says that we have to use different-sized parts because of the different capacities and pressures involved. I understand that, but I still don't think that we need seven different sizes of hydraulic cylinders, for example. Maybe we ought to use a 3-in. diameter cylinder on all of the three smaller models of the machine, instead of a 2-in. diameter cylinder on the smallest unit and a 2½-in. cylinder on the next one up, and a 3-in. cylinder on the next in line. Francis says that would make the machines too expensive, since we would be putting in extra capability, but that's looking just at the purchased cost of the cylinders. If we could standardize, and get interchangeable cylinders, then we could reduce the number of items in our inventory, and stock a lot more of each item. This would help production fully as much as getting more money.

I know that Tom [Thomas Walsh, sales manager] has talked to you about our need for more money. I agree that we need more money, but let's face it, we had just under one-half million in equity in 1972, and it wasn't enough. Our bank, which Tom calls that little branch down in Lansing, is part of a state-wide system with capital of $180,000,000. I like the people there, and I believe them when they tell me that we won't get much, given our present circumstances, if we try going to Chicago or New York looking for long-term debt. And they're not willing to advance us much more money, given our losses in the past two years and our present poor debt/equity ratio.

They tell me that we have to do more planning; that we have to plan for profits. I agree, but it's difficult to get this started. I asked Tom to give me a forecast of sales, by months, for the next year, but he says that it is impossible to forecast sales of individual machines, due to our wide product line, so he gave me total sales for the full year, on a pessimistic, most likely, and optimistic basis, and then said to divide those figures by 12 to get monthly forecasts. Well, you can't plan on those figures, particularly when you don't know the discounts and allowances that are going to be given off the list prices. It's the same sort of thing in engineering. Francis says that he can't plan the engineering work schedule since he doesn't know how long some of the projects are going to take. John is working on the problems of more accurate production scheduling, but he says that it's all dependent upon having accurate bills of material, or a much bigger inventory to avoid the inherent delays.

I think that the only thing to do is to get some venture capital: if we could get about $250,000 of new equity, we could leverage that money with additional bank debt, and begin to stock both finished machines and purchased parts in adequate quantity to guarantee quick delivery. That's why we asked you to come over; you know venture capital, and you can prepare a financial proposal that we can submit to the various venture capital firms.

We ought to be able to make profits. We have two major competitors, both of whom started about the same time that we did, and they are both profitable, so that the market is there. One of them, Plastic Systems, was just a small machine shop in Brooklyn when they started to build low volume/low cost injection molders. They don't have any special engineering talent, although they do have some very aggressive salesmen, and they have sales of about $15,000,000 now, and a net worth well over $1,000,000. Another is a division of a chemical equipment manufacturer in Houston; you can't get a report on the sales of that division, but I would estimate that they're doing about $15,000,000 also. And there are some small, local shops in most of the major fabricating areas that take quite a bit of the business, but I would believe that we are about number 3 in size. Despite the setback in 1973 (the thermoplastic feedstock shortage resulting from the Arab oil embargo), the market is growing. You can't get figures on market share in a small industry like this, of course, but I am afraid that our market share is slipping. I think that we have to do something fairly drastic right now. (Statement of Mr. Lawrence Hamlin)

Class Assignment. The assignment for members of the class is to prepare specific, detailed plans and recommendations to help this company recover from its present unfavorable situation.

Exhibit 5 *Income and expense accounts for the Hamlin Machinery Company, Inc., 1974*

Sales revenues, at catalog list prices	$3,622,414	
less special allowances on sales	240,752	
less cash discounts on invoice payments	11,041	$3,370,621
Labor cost of sales		
Machine shop workers	347,553	
Assembly shop workers	708,707	
Indirect workers	13,612	1,069,872
Material cost of sales		
Beginning inventory—add	345,510	
Purchases and transfers—add	1,260,501	
Ending inventory—deduct	− 315,750	1,290,271
Manufacturing cost of sales		
Payroll taxes—Social Security	44,893	
Payroll taxes—Michigan Unemployment	24,587	
Payroll taxes—Federal Unemployment	4,276	
Insurance—Workman's Compensation	25,656	
Insurance—Blue Cross and Blue Shield	24,587	
Shop supplies and small tools	11,190	
Fuel oil purchases	4,072	
Electrical power and light	7,869	
Water and sewage payments	203	
Building lease payments	23,840	
Property taxes on equipment	14,915	
Depreciation on equipment	38,155	
Fire insurance on equipment	12,834	
Fire insurance on inventory	17,910	
Fire insurance on mechanic's tools	342	255,329
Supervision cost of sales		
Vice president of production	24,000	
Scheduling clerk—production	12,620	
Secretary—production	8,934	
Purchasing agent	14,322	
Inventory and shipping clerk	10,714	
Secretary—purchasing	8,047	
Shop foreman	17,100	
Payroll taxes on supervisory staff	6,606	
Insurance on supervisory staff	2,584	104,927
General expenses of supervision		
Production telephone expense	2,932	
Production travel expense	412	3,344
Total cost of goods sold		$2,723,743
Gross margin on sales		$646,878

Exhibit 5   *(continued)*

	Salary	Commission	Travel	
Marketing expenses				
Vice president of sales	$ 24,000	$ 7,631	$ 6,916	
Secretaries (2)	17,922	—	—	
West Coast sales manager	18,000	5,341	5,956	
West Coast salesman	14,400	3,066	7,403	
East Coast sales manager	18,000	4,860	3,813	
East Coast salesman	14,400	1,113	8,311	
Southern sales manager	18,000	4,197	5,086	
Southern salesman	14,400	830	6,903	
Midwest salesman	18,000	6,410	8,444	
Service manager	14,400	—	4,014	
Servicemen (see Note)	4,818	—	12,773	
	$176,340	$33,448	$69,619	$279,407
Payroll taxes on sales staff			12,167	
Insurance on sales staff			4,761	
Sales telephone expenses			14,947	
Sales car rental expenses			4,082	
Sales airline ticket expenses			11,472	
Sales trade show fees			3,000	
Sales trade magazine advertising			20,031	
Sales printing expenses			4,464	74,924
Engineering expenses				
Vice president of engineering			24,000	
Assistant chief engineer			20,000	
Mechanical engineer			18,000	
Electrical engineer			18,000	
Draftsmen (4)			39,393	119,393
Payroll taxes on engineering staff			8,265	
Insurance on engineering staff			3,233	
Engineering supplies			3,084	
Engineering telephone expense			1,682	
Engineering travel expense			4,549	
Engineering guarantee expense (see note)			7,977	28,790
General and administrative expenses				
General manager			24,000	
Accountant			15,600	
Secretaries (2)			16,041	55,640
Payroll taxes on administrative staff			3,839	
Insurance on administrative staff			1,502	
Office supplies			2,871	
Postage			3,004	
Legal expenses			2,359	

Exhibit 5   *(continued)*

Auditing expenses	3,840	
Data-processing expenses	1,740	
Depreciation on office equipment	860	
Administrative travel expenses	2,730	
Administrative telephone expenses	1,077	23,822
Allowance for bad debts	3,200	
Product liability insurance	3,117	
Business continuation insurance	2,447	
Officers' life insurance	1,014	
Corporate registration fee	75	
Corporate contributions	380	$10,233
Interest expenses		
Equipment financing at 12.0%	29,799	
Factors loan at 13.4%	57,314	
Bank loan at 9.2%	9,660	
Stockholder's loan at 6.0%	1,920	
Stockholder's debentures at 6.0%	5,100	$103,793
Total marketing, engineering, administrative, and interest expenses		$696,002
Profit (loss) for 1974, before income tax adjustment		(49,124)

Note on servicemen's salaries: The servicemen used to install and repair equipment at the customers' plants were the company's regular assembly shop workers who volunteered for this assignment because of the opportunity to travel, and because of a $3.00 per hour bonus in pay. The salary figure ($4,818) for servicemen represents this total bonus.

Note on engineering guarantee expense: The cost of purchased and machined parts used to repair the company's equipment during the 90-day guarantee period was charged back to the engineering department, since the majority of these parts were used on new designs. The cost figure ($7,977) includes material and direct labor only; no manufacturing overhead was included.

Source: Company records.

Chapter 10

STRATEGIC IMPLEMENTATION AND STRUCTURAL DESIGN

Chapter 1 defined the method of selecting the optimal strategy, or long-term method of competition for a firm, through a consideration of the environmental characteristics and trends, the organizational assets and skills, and the managerial values and attitudes, and the subsequent chapters described variations in this process of strategic design that are required for small businesses, product divisions of larger companies, single-industry firms, multiple-industry corporations, and public institutions. However, the selection of the optimal strategy does not complete the responsibilities of the general manager. It is necessary to inform the other members of the organization about the selected strategy, and then to design the organizational structure and systems to implement that strategy. Information about the selected strategy can be transmitted by the preparation of explicit statements about the goals and objectives, policies and procedures, programs and plans, and immediate actions for each of the major functional and technical areas within the firm. In turn, these departmental objectives, policies, programs, and actions define the individual tasks or jobs that are essential for strategic success, and the organizational structure and systems should then be designed to coordinate and integrate the performance of those tasks. This view of strategic implementation can be expressed graphically as shown on the top of the next page.

Strategic implementation combines the definition of tasks within an organization with the development of an organizational structure to coordinate the actions and decisions of persons responsible for those tasks, and the design of the organizational systems to plan, control, and motivate the performance of each of those persons. This chapter describes the design of the organizational structure.

Definition of the Organizational Structure. An organization has been defined (Barnard) as a system of the consciously coordinated activities of two or more per-

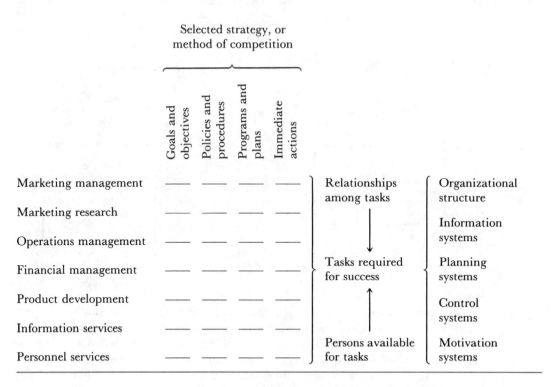

Selected strategy, or
method of competition

	Goals and objectives	Policies and procedures	Programs and plans	Immediate actions				
Marketing management	—	—	—	—	}	Relationships among tasks	{	Organizational structure
Marketing research	—	—	—	—				Information systems
Operations management	—	—	—	—		↓		
Financial management	—	—	—	—	}	Tasks required for success	}	Planning systems
Product development	—	—	—	—		↑		Control systems
Information services	—	—	—	—				
Personnel services	—	—	—	—	}	Persons available for tasks	{	Motivation systems

sons who are able to communicate with each other, and willing to contribute their actions to accomplish a common purpose. The common purpose is the key to the concept of an organization; members have to be able to communicate to agree upon the common purpose, and they have to be able to coordinate their activities to achieve it. The organizational structure is one of the means used to promote this communication and this coordination. In all except the simplest organizations, there is a division of labor: members tend to specialize in certain tasks which, due to experience, ability, or training, they can do more effectively or efficiently than others. The organizational structure refers to the formal pattern of relationships among these specialized tasks, and promotes communication by channeling the information flow and encourages coordination by allocating individual responsibility and establishing relative authority.

The structure of a business organization is generally portrayed in the familiar two-dimensional format, with the horizontal axis showing the assigned tasks, often grouped by the basic functional or technical specialties and occasionally arranged in more primary classifications by product line, market segment, geographic area, or technological process. The vertical axis shows the relative authority of the various positions, and the interconnections represent the formal or expected flows of information. The typical organizational chart illustrates these horizontal and vertical relationships and this network of information flows, as shown at the top of the next page.

The structures of all business organizations are not similar, since the tasks within

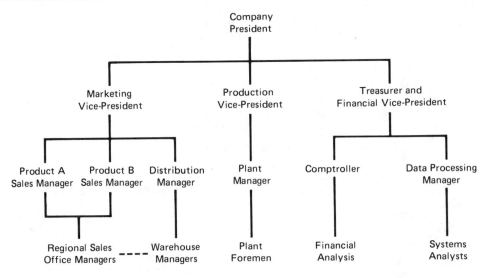

each firm will differ, depending upon the strategy or long-term method of competition selected, and consequently the pattern of relationships and the flow of information among those tasks, or the structure of the organization, will also differ. As an example, the structure of a steel company, integrated from ore and coal mining through to refining, conversion, finishing, and distribution, will differ markedly from that of an electronics firm manufacturing consumer products from purchased components for sale through normal retail channels. In that instance, the industries are obviously different, but even within the same industry there can, and often will be unique structures employed. A chain of retail stores, selling high-fashion and high-margin clothing, will emphasize the tasks of anticipating style trends and selecting merchandise lines, and will organize the structure around the buyer, while another chain of stores, selling lower-styled and lower-priced clothing, will stress the tasks of cost control and facility management, and will organize the structure around the position of the store manager. The structure of an organization will differ, depending upon the strategy selected, and the purpose of this chapter is to explain the process of designing the structure for a business organization following a specific strategy.

Design of the Organizational Structure. The design of the organizational structure, which as described previously involves the assignment of individual responsibility for certain tasks, the allocation of relative authority to various positions, and the restriction of information flows to established channels, is a sequential process that moves logically from definition of the tasks required by the strategy and understanding of the relationships between these tasks to grouping the related activities in a first approximation of the structure, considering measures of performance for these grouped activities, recognizing the differences that exist between the groups, designing integrative methods to coordinate the differentiated groups, and then drafting the total organizational structure. This process will be described in that series of steps:

1. *Definition of the critical tasks.* The first step in structural design is the definition of the tasks imposed by the strategy of the firm. These tasks or activities are primarily described by the functional and technical goals and objectives, policies and procedures, programs and plans, and immediate actions contained in the statement of the strategy of the firm, and it is only necessary at this stage to allocate responsibility for the achievement of those objectives, within those policies and programs. As a very simple example, assume that a manufacturer of small kitchen appliances has decided to expand their market area from eastern and midwestern regions to the Far West. Assume as part of this strategic change that the objective of a 25% market share after five years has been set for the marketing department, with a 5% straight-line increment per year over that time period. Assume further that the distribution policy is to use both large retail chains, such as Sears, K-Mart, Penney's, etc., to be sold through their regional offices, and local gift stores, hardware stores, appliance stores, etc., to be sold directly. Assume that the advertising policy is to use ads in Sunday newspapers and daytime television stressing local themes. Finally, assume that a sales program has been adopted with a budget for one sales person to work with the large chains, three people to call on the local stores, and adequate advertising expenditures. The resultant tasks are shown in the organizational structure in the accompanying chart.

The definition of the routine tasks is not difficult; they are, as explained previously, primarily described by the statement of the corporate strategy. The problem comes in identifying the critical tasks, the key activities that have to be exceedingly well done for the strategy to be successful. Not all activities are equally critical in every company. Consider cost control, for example. Almost all companies employ comptrollers, and prepare reports on production costs, yet this position, which is critical for a high-volume manufacturer of low-margin industrial components, is not as important for the low-volume manufacturer of specially designed industrial machinery; here, product engineering and production scheduling are more central to the strategy, since they will determine the final costs.

The critical tasks specified by each strategy are the building blocks of the organizational structure; they are the activities that have to be well done for the company to succeed, and they are the areas where poor performance would endanger the financial results, or even the long-term survival of the firm. These key tasks can be in the functional management areas (marketing, production, finance, design engineering, or product development), the technical support services (cost control, information processing, market research, etc.), or in the strategic directive decisions. It is necessary to identify them clearly and explicitly.

2. *Understanding the relationships among the tasks.* Once the tasks or activities imposed by the strategy have been identified, and particularly once the critical tasks required by the dominant competitive issues in the strategy have been clearly specified, it is necessary to consider the relationships among these tasks. Most activities within an organization are related either by the flow of material through the productive process or by the flow of information through the managerial process. As the second step in organizational design, it is necessary to consider these material and information flows between tasks, and to reduce them schematically to an understandable format. The material flow for an integrated steel company is shown in the accompanying very simplified format.

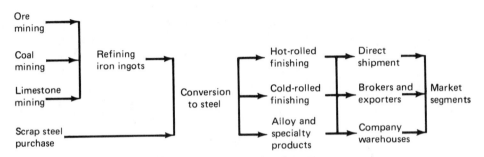

The routine tasks in steel production are raw material procurement or purchasing, and management of the distinct stages in the productive process of refining (blast furnaces to produce iron ingots), conversion (open hearth, electric, or basic oxygen furnaces to produce steel ingots), finishing (hot-rolled mills to produce structural shapes and steel plates, cold-rolled mills to produce sheets and bars, and specialty mills to produce tubes, wire, alloys, etc.), distribution (by direct shipments, independent brokers, or company warehouses), and sales. The critical tasks, due to the very mature nature of the industry, are to (1) match production to demand by product line through scheduling to maximize facility utilization in a capital-intensive industry; (2) establish price lists by product line through comparison of supply and demand to maximize revenues in a price-competitive industry; (3) allocate resources for capacity expansion and modernization in a low-growth industry; (4) plan geographic locations to minimize distance from raw materials and shipments to customers in a high freight-cost industry; (5) evaluate technological improvements to maintain the competitive position in a basic industry; and (6) record costs to provide control of the productive process in an integrated industry. The information flow for an integrated steel company, also in very simplified format, is shown.

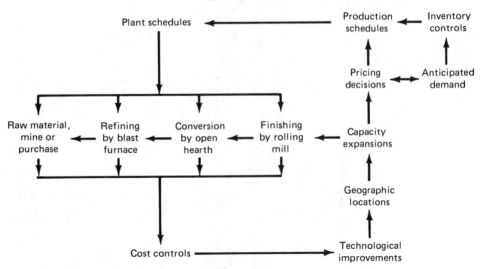

Another, and simpler illustration of the need to understand the relationships among the tasks within an organization prior to the design of the organizational structure can be seen in a small chain of retail stores selling high-fashion and high-margin clothing. The material flow in this instance is exceedingly simple:

$$\text{supplier shipment} \longrightarrow \text{corporate warehouse} \longrightarrow \text{store inventory} \longrightarrow \text{customer purchase}$$

The information flow, however, is much more complex within the chain of high-fashion clothing stores. Both industry sales trends and company sales trends, by store, must be monitored, and the future demands by style, color, and size must be anticipated. Then the selected merchandise lines have to be ordered from clothing manufacturers who, due to the style-competitive nature of the industry, often have an excess of orders for the current fashions that are selling well, so that both delivery dates and product prices must be individually negotiated. The information flow of a chain of high-fashion clothing stores is as shown at the top of the next page.

The dominant competitive issue in the high-fashion clothing industry is the selection of styles, colors, and sizes; at a retail chain, this is the task of the buyer, and consequently the position of the buyer is often central in the organizational structure. The tasks of the buyer are not related to the other activities of warehouse storage and store management by the material flow, but they are central in the information flow. An understanding of both the material flow in the production process and the information flow in the managerial process is essential in organizational design.

3. *Classification of the related tasks.* The definition of the tasks imposed by the strategy of the firm and the examination of the relationships among these tasks re-

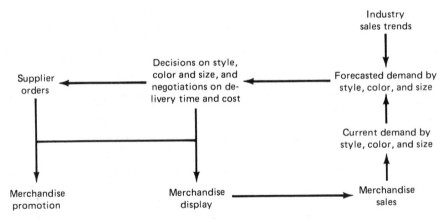

sults in the identification of operational stages in the production process or material flow through the organization and of decision points in the managerial process or information flow of the organization. These operational stages and decision points often differ by managerial function, geographic location, product line, market segment, or technical content. The process stages and decision points should be classified according to these dimensions, as shown in Exhibit 1 for the integrated steel mill.

4. *Measures of performance.* For each of the operational stages in the production process or material flow, and for each of the decision points in the managerial process or information flow, measures of performance must be established. Chapter 11, on the design of planning, control, and motivation systems, discusses the problems involved in establishing measures of organizational performance in considerably greater detail, but it is necessary to consider the number and type of these measures during this stage of structural design.

Performance measures for the operational stages in the material flow are more commonly encountered and more easily established than performance measures for the decision points in the information flow. Operational measures are generally on a cost basis for the production function, and on a revenue basis for marketing. It is necessary to understand the impact of allocated costs and the extent of transfer prices, both of which are discussed in Chapter 11, upon the precision of the performance measures, and it is also necessary to evaluate the legitimacy of the single measure versus multiple measures, but in general the performance of operational stages can be evaluated by cost or revenue measures.

Performance measures for the decision points in the information flow through an organization are often much more difficult to establish on a legitimate and accepted basis. The influence of these decisions may spread over numerous organizational units and may project forward over extensive time periods, which makes cost or revenue measures on a single unit and for a single time period essentially irrelevant. Instead, perception and innovation are needed to establish relevant performance measures. For example, production scheduling

Exhibit 1 *Classification of tasks for the integrated steel mill*

Process stage or decision point	Managerial function	Geographic area	Product line	Market segment	Technical content
Ore mining	Operations	Hibbing, Minn.	Ore	Internal	Extraction
Ore transport					
By rail	Operations	Duluth, Minn.	Ore	Internal	Logistics
By ship	Operations	Erie, Pa.	Ore	Internal	Logistics
Iron refining	Operations	Pittsburgh, Pa.	Iron ingots	Internal	Metallurgy
Steel conversion	Operations	Pittsburgh, Pa.	Steel ingots	Internal	Metallurgy
Hot-rolled finishing	Operations	Pittsburgh, Pa.	Hot-rolled steel	Internal	Manufacture
Cold-rolled finishing	Operations	Pittsburgh, Pa.	Cold-rolled steel	Internal	Manufacture
Distribution	Marketing	Boston, Mass. Newark, N.J. Pittsburgh, Pa. Cleveland, Ohio Chicago, Ill.	Hot rolled and cold rolled	Regional	Customer requirements
Cost analysis	Information systems	Headquarters and at mills	—	—	Cost accounting
Technological improvements	R&D	Headquarters	—	—	Engineering design
Geographic location	Finance or operations	Headquarters	—	—	Operations research
Capacity expansion	Finance or operations	Headquarters	—	—	Investment analysis
Demand forecasts	Marketing	Headquarters	—	—	Market analysis
Inventory controls	Finance or operations	Headquarters	—	—	Operation research
Production schedules	Finance or operations	Headquarters	—	—	Operation research

is critical at an integrated steel mill to maximize utilization of the capital-intensive facilities and to minimize delays between receipt and shipment of large customer orders. The performance of the scheduling staff could, therefore, be evaluated on a balance between the setup time as a percentage of the total operating time, and mean time for delivery, all within the constraints of a given inventory investment policy. Suggested performance measures for both the operational stages and the decision points in an integrated steel mill are shown below in Exhibit 2.

    5. *Grouping of activities.* The various operational stages in the production process or

Exhibit 2 *Measures of performance for the integrated steel mill*

Process stage or decision point	Managerial function	Proposed measure of organizational performance
Ore mining	Operations	Cost per ton
Ore transport	Operations	Cost per ton
Iron refining	Operations	Cost per ton for given inputs
Steel conversion	Operations	Cost per ton for given inputs
Steel finishing	Operations	Cost per ton for given products
Steel distribution	Marketing	Sales revenues by product line
Cost analysis	Finance or accounting	Accuracy of estimates by products
Technological improvements	R&D or engineering	Cost improvements by project
Geographic locations	Finance or operations	Cost improvements by project
Capacity expansions	Finance or operations	Revenue improvements by project
Demand forecasts	Marketing	Accuracy of estimates by products
Inventory controls	Finance or operations	Balance between inventory cost and customer service
Production schedules	Finance or operations	Balance between facility utilization and customer service

material flow and the decision points in the managerial process or information flow can be grouped into organizational units, after they have been classified for differences in managerial function, geographic location, market segment, and technical content, and after the measures of performance have been proposed. These units form the first approximation of the organizational structure. The intent of this preliminary grouping should be to represent the natural material flows and information flows of the organization while recognizing the differences in managerial function, geographic location, product line, market segment, and technical content, and while combining the measures of performance in a rational pattern. This is obviously not a simple task, nor is it a problem with a single solution. Many arrangements of the operational stages and decision points are possible, depending upon the relative weighting of the differences and the subjective merging of the measures of performance. Of course, some of the operational stages where the differences in managerial function, geographic location, etc., are minimal, and where the measures of performance are identical, can be quickly linked in a graphic representation of the material flow, as shown for the steel industry.

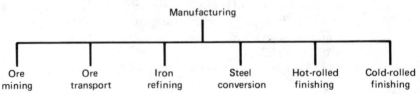

Others of the operational stages, where the differences in managerial function, geographic location, product line, etc., are more definite, can be arranged in two or three alternative patterns, still following the product flow, but varying with a subjective evaluation of the importance of the differences; see the accompanying illustration.

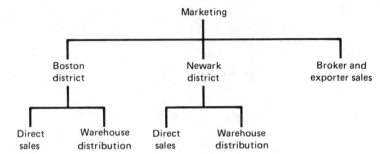

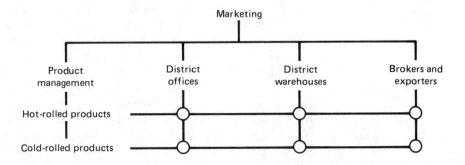

The three alternative organizational units proposed for the marketing function within the selected example of an integrated steel firm vary with the relative importance placed on the differences in market segment, geographic location, or product type. All of the three units probably are workable, provided that they are supported by a carefully designed information system and specific proposals for organizational planning, managerial control, and individual motivation. One of the three units proposed is doubtless best, depending upon the relative importance assigned to market segment, geographic area, or product type by the strategy of the firm. That is, a steel company that emphasized direct shipment of standard hot-rolled and cold-rolled products to large industrial users, automotive firms, and appliance manufacturers would select the first alternative; a steel company that competed by supplying precut and preformed structural members for construction projects and truck-load shipments to small and medium-sized users would select the second alternative; and a steel company that supplied a range of alloys and nonstandard shapes for special applications might be expected to select the third. These differences in strategy cannot be quantified, but they can be recognized and reflected in the preliminary groupings of the functional activities of the firm into organizational units.

The groupings of the functional activities usually show a common measure of performance, despite the differences that exist in the geographic area, the product line, the market segment, or the technology involved. The decision points in the information flow, however, generally have more varying and less precise measures of performance; consequently, they are more difficult to arrange in the preliminary groupings. The structure shown for the information-processing activities in an integrated steel mill is only one of the many alternatives that are possible.

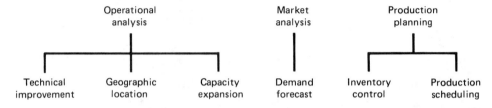

6. *Coordination of the organizational units.* After the tasks have been defined, classified for differences in managerial function, geographic area, product line, market segment, and technical content, designed for performance measurement, and grouped into organizational units, it is necessary to arrange for the coordination of those units. Many means of coordination are possible, such as casual dialogues, informal meetings, formal committees, project teams, corporate policies, and established procedures, all of which will be discussed in a latter section of this note on organizational unit differentiation and integration, but the primary means for the coordination of individual units within an organization is the hierarchy of authority. Authority refers to the ability of one individual within an organization to influence the behavior and actions of others within that organization, while the hierarchy is the vertical scale of authority within the organizational structure. Authority, of course, is never absolute, even in apparently dictatorial situations; it always involves the acceptance by the subordinate of the decisions and instructions of the superior. But the hierarchy of authority does establish the relative ability of individuals within the organization to influence the behavior and actions of others, and is required for the coordination of the various organizational units.

It is necessary to position the organizational units within the hierarchy of authority in order to provide for the coordination of the activities of those units, but it is also necessary to recognize the potential for organizational conflict that may arise between the units. The potential for conflict comes from basic differences between the units, and these differences are not so much in the classifications of managerial function, geographic function, product type, market segment, or technical requirements as they are in the measures of performance. Differences in measures of unit performance result in differences in orientation of unit members, and the differences in orientation can result in covert disagreements and overt arguments. To avoid these disagreements and arguments it is necessary to establish a firm center of authority over the dissimilar units and a definite channel of communication between the units. Occasionally, it is useful to position one of the information-processing units between the functional units to assist in the process of communication. The accompanying examples from the organizational structure of an integrated steel mill show both alternative means of avoiding conflict.

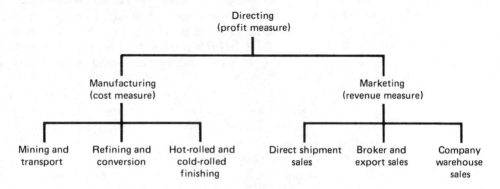

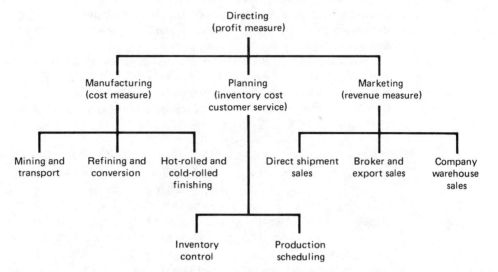

7. *Organizational differentiation.* Coordination between organizational units can be imposed by an authoritative position set above the units in the hierarchical scale, and coordination may be improved by an information-processing unit

positioned between the functional units in the organizational structure, but coordination may not be enough for effective (achieve unit objectives) and efficient (conserve unit resources) performance. Members of an organization tend to work most effectively and efficiently not when their tasks are coordinated (bring the parts of an organization together into a balanced relationship) by a superior authority, but when their activities are integrated (bring the parts of an organization together into a complete entity) by voluntary cooperation. One of the few generalizations that can legitimately be made about human behavior is that people do prefer to cooperate voluntarily rather than to be forced to act as the result of authoritative direction. Authority is often resisted, and while the use of authority can result in coordinated actions, it can also result in circumvented orders and ignored instructions. The use of authority has limits since it always depends upon the acceptance by the subordinate of the orders and instructions of the superior; the use of cooperation has no limits beyond the full capacity of the system of which the organization is a part. Voluntary cooperation or integration of the various functional, technical, and directive units is best, but this is difficult to achieve because of the differences that exist between the organizational units and the organizational members.

Some of the major differences between organizational units have already been described along the dimensions of managerial function, geographic area, product line, market segment, and technological content of the required tasks. These are the obvious differences, imposed by the selected strategy of the firm. There are also more subtle differences, not as immediately apparent, that make communication and cooperation between organizational units very difficult. These secondary differences can be described in terms of the types of problems encountered by members of the various units, the quality of the information available for the problem solution, the process of decision, and the impact of the output:

a. *Problem definition.* Problems encountered for decision can be highly structured, with all the variables and the relationships among those variables known, or they can be unstructured and amorphous, with neither the variables nor the relationships known or even imagined. Problems involving production schedules tend to be structured: problems involving managerial personnel tend to be unstructured.

b. *Problem continuity.* Problems encountered for decision can be routine, with most of the variables and relationships repetitive and familiar, or they can be uncommon, with the need to define the variables and relationships anew on each occasion. Routine decisions permit the establishment of standard policies and procedures, or the use of existing mathematical models, for decision; uncommon and infrequent decisions require managerial thought and imagination.

c. *Problem level.* Problems encountered for decision can be specialized, and involved with only one managerial function, product type, market segment, or technical area, or they can be integrated, and involve numerous functions, products, markets, and technologies. Problems limited to one functional or technical area are generally considered to be "operating," while problems that cross the boundaries between numerous functions, areas, etc., are defined as "strategic."

d. *Information stability.* The information available for decisions can be highly stable and fixed, or it can be subject to change as the environmental conditions and organizational resources change. The rate of change is not constant across all economic, technological, social, political, and competitive aspects of the environment, nor across all financial, physical, technical, and personnel resources of the firm; consequently, different organizational units within the firm are forced to adjust to different rates of change.

e. *Information certainty.* The information available for decision can be classified under conditions of certainty (a single outcome with known consequences for each decision or action), risk (a distribution of outcomes for the decision or action with known probabilities of occurrence), or uncertainty (a distribution of outcomes with unknown probabilities of occurrence). The degree of certainty is not constant across all aspects of the environment or all resources of the firm; consequently, different organizational units within the firm are forced to adjust to different conditions of risk and uncertainty.

f. *Information precision.* The information available for decision may be expressed in either quantitative or qualitative terms. The precision of quantitative data can vary, as between units sold and overhead cost per unit. Qualitative information would include such essential but nonnumeric data as managerial values, social obligations, and employee morale. Organizational units vary in the precision of the information they receive.

g. *Process terms.* Language used in the decision process often varies between organizational units. Each unit can develop special terms, such as "cash flow stream" for financial analysis or "on stream" for production management, and differences in terms can make communication and cooperation difficult between units.

h. *Process structure.* Participation in the decision process often varies between organizational units. Each unit can develop different degrees of specialization in the individual job definitions, and different relationships among these specialists, depending upon the homogeneity or the heterogeneity of these jobs; these factors can affect the extent of participation by the various members of the organizational unit in the decision process, and differences in participation can make communication and cooperation between units difficult.

i. *Process behavior.* Individual behavior during the decision process often varies between organizational units. Each unit can develop special roles (expected behavior of persons occupying hierarchical or technical positions in the unit) or special norms (expected behavior of persons acting as members of formal or informal groups), and differences in roles and norms can make communication and cooperation between units difficult.

j. *Decision extent.* Decisions made by different units within the organization can vary on the dimension of the future extent of the consequences of that decision. The question is how far into the future will the decision extend. For example, a decision on overhead cost allocations can be readily changed, so the future extent of that decision is limited, but a decision on a major capital-expansion program cannot be reversed, once constructed, and the consequences will extend for the economic life of the facility. Differences in the future extent of decisions can make cooperation between units difficult, particularly when those differences are not explicitly recognized.

k. *Decision impact.* Decisions made by different units within the organization can also vary on the dimension of the organizational impact of the consequences of that decision. The question here is how far across the organization the decision will impact. A decision on the salary of a market research analyst will probably affect only the market research unit, but a decision on variable commission rates for different products for the sales force will probably affect the entire firm. Differences in the organizational impact of decisions can make cooperation between units difficult, again if those differences are not explicitly recognized.

l. *Decision feedback.* Decisions made by different units within the organization will vary on the dimension of the time span required for feedback. The question here is how long will it be before accurate information is available to assess the validity of the original decision. A decision to change the production schedule at a job shop can probably be assessed at the end of the week; a decision to change the capacity of a major capital expansion program may not be assessed accurately at the end of a decade. Differences in decision feedback can affect the interaction and cooperation of organizational units.

A classical research study (Lawrence and Lorsch, 1967) determined that the differences between organizational units in terms of problem types, information characteristics, decision processes, and output influences often resulted in different cognitive and emotional orientations among the members of those units. That is, members of functional, technical, and directive units within the same organization tend to think in different terms about organizational objectives, policies, programs, and activities. The authors of the study measured these differences in thought patterns along the dimensions of (1) orientation toward unit goals, as in sales revenues vs. new products; (2) orientation toward time horizons, as in immediate sales vs. longer-term product development; and (3) orientation toward interpersonal behavior, as in informal sales exchanges vs. formal and more precise engineering conversations. The authors also hypothesized that these attitudinal and behavioral differences developed partially as a result of preselection (persons with a given pattern of thinking and acting tend to join groups that have the same patterns of thought and action) and partially as a result of socialization (persons who join a group with a given pattern of thinking and acting tend to adopt those same patterns of thought and action). Regardless of the measures employed or the causes proposed, these attitudinal differences have an obvious impact upon communication and cooperation between organizational units.

An analysis of the differences between the major functional, technical, and directive units within an integrated steel firm in terms of problem types, information characteristics, decision processes, and output influences is given in Exhibit 3. Major differences may be noted between manufacturing, which in-

Exhibit 3 *Differentiation of the major functional, technical, and directive units within an integrated steel mill*

Differentiation	Manufacturing	Marketing	Operational analysis	Market analysis	Production planning	Corporate direction
Problem definition structured to unstructured form	Structured	Structured	Unstructured	Structured	Structured	Unstructured
Problem continuity routine to rare occurrence	Routine	Routine	Rare	Routine	Routine	Rare
Problem level operating to strategic type	Operating	Operating	Strategic	Strategic	Operating	Strategic
Information stability slow to rapid change	Slow	Medium	Rapid	Medium	Medium	Rapid
Information certainty certain–risk–uncertain	Certain	Risk	Uncertain	Uncertain	Certain	Uncertain
Information precision quantitative to qualitative	Mixed	Mixed	Quantitative	Quantitative	Quantitative	Qualitative
Process language special to general terms	Special	General	Special	Special	Special	General
Process structure low to high participation	Low	Medium	High	High	High	Medium
Process behavior low to high roles and norms	High	Medium	Low	Low	Low	Medium
Decision extent low to high future extent	Low	Low	High	Medium	Medium	High
Decision impact low to high organizational impact	Low	Low	High	Medium	Medium	Low
Decision feedback slow to fast decision evaluation	Fast	Fast	Slow	Medium	Medium	Slow

cludes ore mining, ore transport, iron refining, steel conversion, and both hot-rolled and cold-rolled finishing, and operational analysis of technological improvements, geographic locations, and capacity expansions. These differences might be expected to cause communication and cooperation problems between the two organizational units. Market analysis seems much closer along these 12 dimensions to the marketing activity, and those units might be able to work well together. Substantial differences exist between the corporate directive function (general management) and both the manufacturing and marketing activities, which may explain many of the problems in communications and the lack of rapport that are often claimed to exist between the general management and the operating personnel.

Differences do exist between the various organizational units within a firm that go far beyond the obvious features of managerial function, geographic area, product line, etc. These more subtle distinctions are in such areas as the problem types, information characteristics, decision processes, and output influences of the units and the cognitive and emotional orientations of the members; together they make communication and cooperation between organizational units very difficult. We now describe specific means of integrating these units for improved communication and cooperation.

8. *Organizational integration.* Integration refers to the voluntary spirit of cooperation between members of different organizational units that helps to achieve a unity of individual effort and an improvement in organizational performance. Members of organizations who work together easily and freely, with a minimum of authoritative directions and constraints, appear to accomplish more individually and, more important, to achieve more organizationally. To attain this unity of effort, it is necessry to adjust for the differences that do exist between organizational units; this adjustment can be performed through collaborative plans, structural integrators, interdepartmental projects teams, formal committee meetings, or informal group meetings and interpersonal dialogue:

a. *Collaborative plans.* There are very distinct differences between the directive personnel (general managers, and other from corporate headquarters) and the various functional and technical units within an organization. These differences are along the dimensions of the problem types, information characteristics, decision processes, and output influences of the units and the cognitive and emotional orientations of the members, and were enumerated for the selected example of an integrated steel mill in Exhibit 1; they can also be illustrated by the activities and attitudes of the members of most organizations. Collaborative planning can be used to overcome the problems caused by these differences. Formal planning systems are described in much greater detail in Chapter 11, but in essence collaborative planning refers to the joint agreement between personnel from the general management area and members of the various functional and technical units on the goals and objectives, policies and procedures, programs and plans, and immediate actions for each of the units. The relationships amongst these planning components has been expressed graphically earlier in the text:

	Goals and objectives	Policies and procedures	Programs and plans	Immediate actions
Marketing management	——	——	——	——
Marketing research	——	——	——	——
Operations management	——	——	——	——
Financial management	——	——	——	——
Product development	——	——	——	——

Agreement on the goals, policies, programs, and actions is needed for integration between the directive unit and the functional and technical activities within an organization. Chapter 11 describes the means of achieving this agreement through formal planning systems.

b. *Structural integrators.* Differences in problem types, information characteristics, decision processes, etc., also exist between many of the functional and technical units within an organization. In the instances where these differences are extreme, as they appear to be between the operational analysis and manufacturing units described in Exhibit 3, it is possible to improve cooperation by positioning a formal integrator between the departments in the organizational structure. The integrator, which may be a single individual or a small group, should have knowledge and competence in both areas (i.e., in both manufacturing and operational analysis), respect by the members of both units, and influence upon the final decisions. The purpose of the integrator is to reduce conflict and improve the potential for collaboration by ensuring that the analysis and recommendations of each group are understood by members of the other group. The integrator does not necessarily work for a compromise, but more for communication and understanding. It is, of course, a very awkward position to evaluate and reward, but it can be very effective in improving organizational performance where substantial differentiation exists between units.

c. *Project teams.* A project team is a group of individuals drawn from different functional and technical units within the organization to work full-time on a specific task. A team can be thought of as an informal matrix organization; it helps to promote communication and cooperation between the individual members from the differentiated units because of the common task and the close associations. Objectives, policies, and programs have to be established for the team as with any other organizational unit, but the temporary nature of the project oftens makes agreement and understanding of these objectives, policies, and programs difficult. Despite this problem, project teams can be used to integrate two or more differentiated units within an organization.

d. *Formal committees.* A committee is a group of individuals drawn from different functional and technical units within an organization to work part-time on a given task; the committee differs from the project team in the part-time nature of the assignment, which results in less clear understanding of the purpose and less close association of the members. Committees and meetings are used extensively for communication and coordination between organizational units, but the differences among those units in problem types, information characteristics, decision processes, etc., often make complete cooperation and integration difficult.

e. *Informal meetings.* Informal meetings and interpersonal dialogues among individuals from different functional and technical units within an organization are the last of the processes that may be used for integration. Here, the lack of a specific and defined objective, and the existing organizational differences, often make communication difficult.

In summary, collaborative plans, structural integrators, project teams, formal committees, and informal meetings can all be used to improve communication and cooperation between the different directive, functional, and technical units within an organization. The integrators would be the only integrative method to appear on the organizational chart since they represent permanent personnel.

9. *Design of the organizational chart.* Preparing the organizational chart is the next-to-last step in organizational design. This chart graphically represents the directive, functional, and technical tasks required by the strategy of the firm, and the relationships among those tasks. The tasks are complicated by multiple locations, products, markets, and technologies, and the relationships are complex, being based upon the material flow of the productive process, the information flow of the managerial process, and the assigned authority of the hierarchical scale. As a result of this complexity, the organizational chart is necessarily an oversimplification of the complete structure, but the two-dimensional graph does enable members of the firm to recognize and discuss their assigned positions and intended relationships.

There are numerous alternatives in the design of the organizational chart. The definitions of the critical tasks, the identification of the relationships among those tasks, the classification of the tasks for differences in managerial responsibilities, geographic areas, product lines, market segments, and technological contents, the preparation of measures of performance for each of the activities, the association of similar activities in organizational units, the coordination of these units by levels of authority, the recognition of the differences between these units, and finally the integration of the units can all be combined in an almost infinite variety of patterns. It is probably impossible to achieve a perfect pattern of positions and relationships, but it is possible to prepare a logical pattern through consideration, in sequence, of the factors described in this chapter. Exhibits 4 and 5 show completed charts for two of the many alterna-

Exhibit 4 *Alternative design for the organizational structure of an integrated steel company*

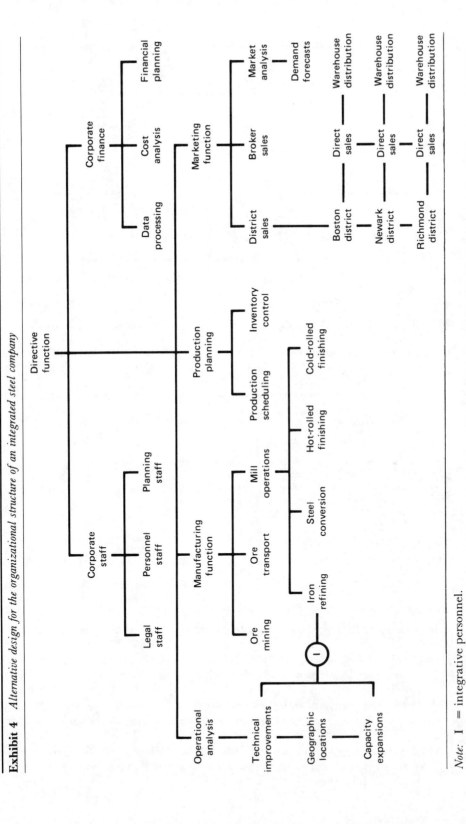

Note: I = integrative personnel.

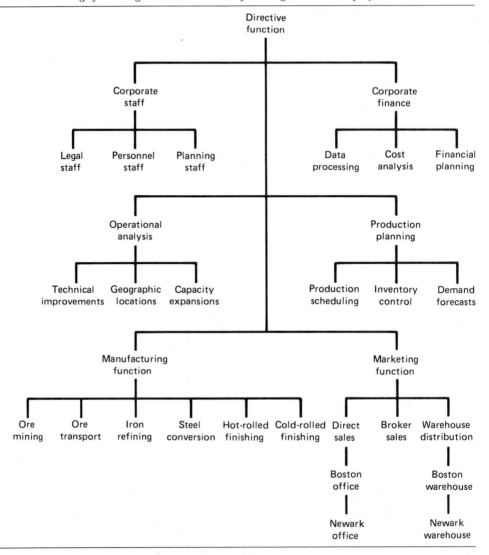

tive structures that would be possible for the selected example of an integrated steel company.

10. *Evaluation of the organizational chart.* The last step in the design of the organizational structure is the evaluation of the completed pattern of positions and responsibilities. This evaluation should be on two levels: the logical consistency of the structure design and the behavioral impact upon the organizational members. There are eight major factors to be considered in the logic of the design:

a. Clear definitions of the tasks imposed by the strategy of the firm, and particularly of the critical tasks required for strategic success. The critical tasks should be identified clearly and explicitly.

b. Clear delineations of the relationships among the tasks brought about by the material flow of the productive process and the information flow of the managerial process.

c. Accurate classifications of the tasks by managerial responsibility, geographic area, product line, market segment, and technical content. These differences are crucial for the preliminary grouping of the tasks.

d. Definite measures of performance for each of the tasks. These measures may be financial (revenues, costs, or profits), quantitative (units produced or products introduced), or qualitative (customer satisfaction, etc.). Measures of performance are discussed at considerably greater length in Chapter 11.

e. Logical grouping of the tasks to combine related managerial responsibilities, geographic locations, product lines, market segments, technological processes, or measures of performance. The grouping of related tasks into organizational units represents the first approximation of the final structure.

f. Established levels of authority to coordinate the organizational units and to combine the measures of performance. Authority alone cannot be relied upon to integrate the various tasks required by the material flow and the information flow within the organization; authority needs to be supplemented with systematic planning, control and motivation procedures, and other integrative processes.

g. Clear understanding of the problems of communication and cooperation between organizational units caused by differences in problem types, information characteristics, decision processes, and output impacts.

h. Specific procedures to overcome the problems of communication and cooperation between organizational units through the design of planning and control systems, the positioning of integrators within the structure, the use of project teams, or the reliance upon committees and formal meetings.

The most valid evaluation of the organizational structure designed for a business firm, of course, is the performance of that firm relative to the cost of the structure. However, it is difficult to sort out the impact of environmental factors and the influence of corporate strategy, structure, and systems upon performance. Therefore, it is necessary to rely upon an examination of the logical consistency of the structure, as described above, or upon an analysis of the behavioral influences of the design. There are two major dimensions to these behavioral influences:

a. *Individual clarity.* Individuals within the organization should understand their assigned tasks, and the relationships of those tasks with others throughout the organization. Ideally, each individual should be able to reproduce the organizational chart, indicating an understanding of the critical tasks, relationships among those tasks, classifications of the tasks, etc.

b. *Organizational flexibility.* Individuals within an organization should understand the need for gradual change in their assigned tasks and in their relationships with other tasks within the organization, as the corporate strategy changes to adjust to trends and events within the environment. Individuals have a desire for stability and continuity; organizations have a need for change. Ideally, each individual should recognize the relationship between the corporate strategy and the structural design.

Full understanding of the corporate strategy and the organizational structure, however, depends upon the design of the planning, control, and motivation systems, which are described in Chapter 11. The balance of this note on structural design will be devoted to describing some of the standard forms, such as the functional, divisional, or matrix organizations, some of the common terms, such as "unity of command" or "span of control," and other influences upon organizational behavior such as informal roles and norms and cultural values and attitudes.

Standard Types of Organizational Structures. There are six common forms of organizational structures used for business firms. None of these six types should be selected indiscriminately; that is, it is necessary to examine the tasks imposed by the strategy, the relationships among these tasks, the differences between them, etc., before deciding upon the optimal organizational structure. However, these standard forms are used in discussing the alternative structures that are possible for business firms, and the terms should be recognized and understood:

1. *Functional organization.* The functional organization is the simplest form available, with a directive position (general manager) and separate functional and technical units for such activities as marketing, production, finance, product development, and data processing; see the accompanying illustration.

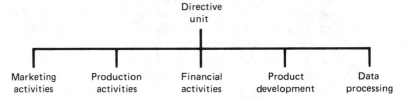

The functional form of organization is commonly used for smaller firms and for the product divisions of larger corporations. Functional structures are alleged to be ineffective in very large companies since members tend to believe that their basic allegiances are to the functional or technical units, not to the performance of the complete organization.

2. *Extended functional organization.* The extended functional organization, with one of the functional activities divided into numerous separate units due to the importance of that activity in the strategy of the firm, is most commonly used by vertically integrated firms. The example shown is from a firm that has integrated the production function backward to basic raw materials, but other examples could have been selected from companies that integrated forward into direct distribution and retail sales with, as a result, an extended marketing function.

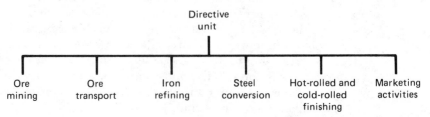

Large integrated companies with an extended functional form of organization often have limited provisions for coordination beyond authoritative direction; this omission can result in problems of communication and cooperation between the unbalanced functional and technical units.

3. *Divisional organization.* The divisional organization is often used by medium-sized firms with multiple product lines, geographic locations, or market segments. As shown, each division should contain identifiable products, a specific market area or market segment, separate marketing methods (price levels, distribution channels, and promotional means), and independent production processes (facilities and personnel). Financial management and data processing, along with the legal, personnel, and planning activities, are usually considered to be corporate responsibilities in a divisional organization, and are not assigned to the divisions.

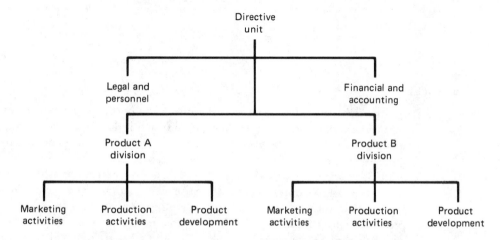

In companies where the marketing methods or the production processes are not completely separate, it is necessary to establish transfer prices or allocate joint costs between divisions; this can easily lead to disagreements between the division managers, and can also confuse the measures of division performance. Further, it is necessary to recognize that in companies with dissimilar products or markets, the key tasks may differ between divisions, so that the organizational format of the divisions should also differ, with a resulting lack of similarity and apparently desirable uniformity.

4. *Grouped divisional organization.* In large corporations, with numerous product–market divisions that operate almost autonomously, each on an independent profit-center basis, it has been found difficult to evaluate the performance of the various divisions and to allocate the limited resources among them. That is, the corporate management of multidivisional firms could never be certain whether the performance of a given division was the result of market conditions or management effort (i.e., a division could return 12% on the investment in an industry where the mean return on investment was 18%, and be ranked above a division that returned 11% in an industry where the average was only 8%). Further, resources were often provided to divisions with a past history of growth, but perhaps without a future potential. To avoid these problems in the central di-

rection of the whole organization, it is possible to group various divisions by industry into "strategic business units," each of which can compete with a range of products within a specific industry (see the accompanying illustration). This enables the corporate management to study the industries, to evaluate divisional performance, and to allocate scarce resources relative to the growth rates, profit margins, and market shares of each industry.

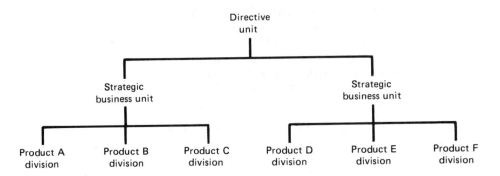

The problems of the grouped divisional form of organizational structure center on the difficulties of clearly identifying each industry, and each market segment within the industry, so that the conclusions on growth rates, profit margins, and market shares are valid, and accepted by all levels of management.

5. *Matrix organization.* As shown, the matrix form of organizational structure represents an effort to improve coordination of the functional and technical activities for various products or projects by assigning responsibility for coordination to product or project managers. The intent is that the product or project manager can utilize resources from each of the functional and technical units to accomplish given objectives.

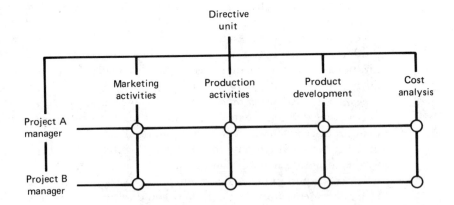

The problems inherent in the matrix form of organization concern the dual allegiance imposed on each functional and technical employee, and the divided authority and responsibility of functional, technical, and project managers. This ambiguity can result in interpersonal conflicts, and in planning, scheduling, and control problems for the functional and the technical activities. To avoid these problems, it is necessary to have absolute clarity of objectives, policies, and programs for each of the units, and to have explicit agreement on these objectives, policies, and programs by all the personnel.

6. *Mixed organization.* The last common form of organizational structure shown is mixed, or a combination of the other forms. A company with a strategy that emphasized different products or different markets, with different marketing tasks but universal production facilities and common financial resources, would be an example of a mixed organization.

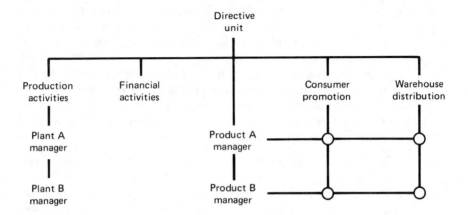

Common Terms in Organizational Design. In addition to the standard types of organizational structures that have been described, there are a number of terms in common use in structural design that should be recognized and understood:

1. *Span of control.* The span of control refers to the number of subordinate units or individuals that can be supervised by a single manager within a hierarchy. It is probably not possible to accept the principle of an optimal number for all situations, for the supervisory effort will necessarily vary with the similarity of the activities, the complexity of the interrelations, the ability of the workers, and the problems of communication.

2. *Unity of command.* The unity of command is the reverse of the span of control; the principle is that each member of an organization should have only one supervisor. It is probably not possible to accept this principle completely since in situations with the need to coordinate highly complex functional and technical activities, as in the matrix organizational structure, one worker will necessarily have two or more supervisors.

3. *Duality of line and staff.* Line refers to positions in the direct hierarchical structure, or chain of command, with authority to direct the activities of others within that structure; these are primarily functional positions. Staff refers to positions outside the hierarchy that do not have authority over others in the organization;

they serve to inform or advise rather than to direct, and are primarily technical activities. The earlier rigid distinctions between line and staff have blurred with the recent expansion of importance of the technical activities and tasks within organizations.

4. *Parity of responsibility and authority.* It is often stated that responsibility and authority should be combined equally for each position in the hierarchical structure; the principle is that a person who is responsible for the performance of a given organizational unit should have the authority to make decisions and direct operations within that unit. This principle has become partially obsolete with the expanded functional and technical interrelationships within organizations that have diffused responsibility and blurred authority.

5. *Comparison of centralization and decentralization.* Centralization refers to the retention of authority and responsibility for both strategic and operating decisions at the level of the corporate management. Centralization is alleged to be effective only in a stable environment, with repetitive work processes. Decentralization refers to the delegation of authority and responsibility to the lower levels of the organization, providing functional and technical managers with the authority to make decisions within their area of responsibility. Decentralization is said to be more effective in a rapidly changing environment, and to result in more prompt decisions and greater job satisfaction. This principle, however, probably depends more on the strategy of the firm than on the characteristics of the environment.

This chapter has described the design of the organizational structure for a firm based upon the strategy of that firm through sequential steps of defining the critical tasks, identifying the relationships among those tasks, classifying the tasks for differences in managerial responsibilities, geographic areas, product lines, market segments, and technical processes, preparing the measures of performance for each of the activities, grouping similar activities in organizational units, coordinating these units by levels of authority, recognizing the behavioral and attitudinal differences between these units, and arranging for integrative processes to overcome those differences and encourage communication and cooperation. The organizational structure, however, is only a portion of the total process for strategic implementation. Planning, control, and motivation systems are needed to supplement the structure; the design of these systems is described in Chapter 11.

Environmental Research Associates, Inc.

Stuart Isleton was a 1965 graduate of the MBA program at Columbia University who had worked as a financial analyst and strategic planner at a very large insurance company in New York City since graduation. The wave of social and environmental legislation of the late 1960s (Occupational Safety and Health Act of 1967, Federal Water Pollution Control Act of 1968, and the Federal Clean Air Act of 1970) had sharply increased the legal responsibilities and financial liabilities of many of the industrial clients of the insurance company, and the senior management had decided, in 1976, to acquire an environmental consulting firm in order to assist their clients in meeting the statutory requirements of the new regulations and to help their personnel in understanding the actuarial impact of those regulations. It was also felt that by offering this additional service it would be possible to sell expanded insurance to existing customers, and to attract new customers. One of the major corporate-level consulting firms was retained to search for possible acquisitions in the air and water pollution and the occupational safety and health areas, and they submitted a report recommending Environmental Research Associates, Inc., a company with experience in both pollution control and workplace improvement, and with offices in Lake Forest and Addison, Illinois. This company was believed to be available for purchase since the founders, Dr. and Mrs. Wilson, were close to retirement age, and he had recently suffered a severe heart attack. The vice president for administration of the insurance company contacted the Wilsons, investigated the reputation of their company and the competence of their employees, and negotiated the terms of purchase. Stuart Isleton was sent to Illinois to be the current liaison between the two companies, and the eventual manager of the new subsidiary.

I was selected, I suppose, since my original home was in Illinois so that I know the Chicago area, and since my undergraduate degree was in chemistry so that I understood what the consultants were doing. Finally, I was one of the few people in the insurance company with an M.B.A., so that everyone assumed that I was trained in line management. I'm not certain of that assumption: it seems to me that the M.B.A. is more oriented toward analysis than action, but I'm here now, and I'm supposed to run this company. The plan is that the Wilsons are going to retire in another month, and I will be appointed president at that time. (Statement of Stuart Isleton)

Environmental Research Associates had been formed in 1954 by Dr. and Mrs. T. R. Wilson, while he was a member of the chemical engineering department at Northwestern University and she was teaching in the Evanston school system. Dr. Wilson had been named Theodore Roosevelt Wilson by his father, an enthusiastic supporter of the former president, and the son was known as "Teddy" by his friends and "Teddy Bear" by his detractors. Mrs. Wilson had been active in the company since the formation; she had an undergraduate degree in chemistry from the California Institute of Technology, and had completed all of the course work and the advanced research for a Ph.D. but had never received the doctorate since at that time the university refused to grant advanced degrees to women. Mrs. Wilson had been named Henrietta, but was known as "Heddy" or "Heddy Bear." These nicknames were important since Dr. and Mrs. Wilson had been among the first to express active concern over the deterioration of the biological environment brought about by the widespread use and cumulative effect of the complex chemical pesticides and herbicides. They had often testified before congressional committees on environmental problems, and had been interviewed so frequently on network television that they became known as the "Heddy and Teddy Show." He was pleasantly absent-minded and she was brilliantly acerbic; together they did much to popularize the need for environmental protection and pollution control.

The media publicity and political activity, however, did little to improve the sales revenues and financial position of the Wilson's consulting firm, and it remained quartered in the living room of their home in Evanston, Illinois, until 1962, when it was moved to an abandoned drugstore. During this early period, many corporations were not concerned with environmental pollution, and governmental grants for environmental research were largely directed toward universities. By 1965, however, many manufacturing companies and public utilities were beginning to recognize environmental responsibilities, in advance of the legislation that would force both recognition and action upon them, and they started to employ Environmental Research Associates, due to the acknowledged scientific expertise of the Wilsons, despite the reputation of the owners as belonging to the "other" side. The combined reputation, for technical competence and environmental action, was of definite help in obtaining the institutional research contracts to develop sampling procedures and analytical techniques for detecting trace elements in pollution control, and in hiring the young chemists and systems analysts needed to complete the contracts. By 1976, at the time of the acquisition by the insurance company, the consulting firm had grown to 84 employees, had revenues just slightly under $3,000,000, and had moved partially into a new building, designed by Dr. and Mrs. Wilson, in Lake Forest, and partially into a large office complex in Addison. Lake Forest and Addison are both suburbs of Chicago, but approximately 20 miles apart; Lake Forest is to the north of the city, on the shore of Lake Michigan, while Addison is to the west, near the O'Hare Airport.

In 1975, after eight months spent working formally as the Treasurer of Environmental Research Associates, and informally as the administrative assistant to the two former owners, Stuart Isleton felt that he had a good understanding of the operations of the consulting firm. He expressed this understanding in a diagram (Exhibit 1) that showed the process flow of the work at the Lake Forest office, which handled air pollution analysis and control, occupational safety and health, and biological research. The process flow at the Addison office, which concentrated upon industrial and municipal water pollution, is shown later in Exhibit 2.

Forty-five percent of the revenues of the company were derived from air pollution studies. Source sampling, the start of those studies, was described by Stuart Isleton as a highly technical, challenging, and occasionally dangerous occupation. The source samples were obtained either by stack climbing or by field placement. Stack climbing meant exactly what it appeared to mean: a worker climbed the outside of a smoke stack or other discharge duct, inserted a probe through an inspection port, obtained temperature, pressure, and velocity readings, and collected a timed sample of the gases on specially designed filters and condensation plates. It was necessary to carry 35 pounds of equipment to obtain the readings and the samples, and some of the stacks, particularly at public utilities and chemical companies, were over 120 feet high. The ports for sampling were generally near the top of the stack, since it was essential that the gases be mixed and the samples representative; nearer the ground the gases were often still separated and turbulent, and accurate readings and specimens could not be obtained. Climbing to the inspection ports was by means of steel rungs set into the masonry of the smokestack, or by catwalks and ladders to the discharge ducts. Safety hoops, which were half-round bars of steel, often surrounded the catwalk ladders and chimney rungs, but stack climbing was not a favorite assignment at Environmental Research Associates. All climbing on the tall smokestacks was done by three specially designated employees, but the other members of the firm were expected to be willing to climb 50 to 60 feet above the ground to obtain samples from ductwork and low chimneys.

The stack climbers for the tall chimneys were not steeple-jacks or construction workers; they were college kids—one of them was a graduate of Yale in art history, and another was a dropout from the

Exhibit 1 *Schematic work flow in the Lake Forest office of Environmental Research Associates*

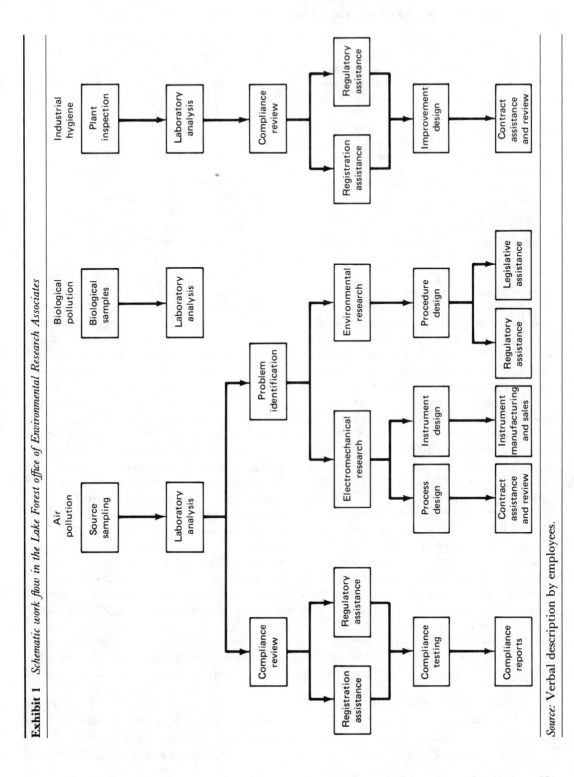

Source: Verbal description by employees.

University of Arkansas in civil engineering—and they seemed to be totally without fear. They were also in very good physical condition; you have to be in good shape to climb 12 to 15 stories on a ladder, carrying testing instruments and sampling equipment. The Wilsons never paid these three men any extra money, and they didn't assign them exclusively to source sampling; they would have one of them working inside on a computer model, and send some poor economist from Wellesley out to get source samples from the cupola (highest portion) of a blast furnace, way up in the air on a narrow catwalk. (Statement of Stuart Isleton)

Field placement was a much simpler and safer means of source sampling for air pollution than stack climbing, and was used for ambient air quality studies. "Ambient" refers to the air surrounding a source or potential source of air pollution, and stack sampling and field placement were often used together to determine the impact of a specific source upon air quality in a given area. Field placement sampling was done by means of high-volume air filters, termed "hi-vols," which used a battery-powered fan to draw air through a series of fabric filters and carbon absorbers; particles were trapped in the fabric while gases and vapors were bonded to the surface of the carbon which was subsequently cleaned with a reagent such as alcohol. Instruments in the "hi-vols" also continuously recorded information on air temperature, relative humidity, barometric pressure, wind speed, wind direction, and solar radiation. The combined stack samples, field samples, and meteorological data could be used to prepare air quality dispersion models, which were mathematical predictions of the effect of changes in the type and level of source emissions upon ambient air quality within a given area.

The location of the air filter units, which look like large beehives, is important to get nondistorted samples. Field placement, of course, conjures images of meadows and hayfields, but the more common siting is in parking lots and on apartment roofs; you try not to get close to gas stations or busy highways. Overall, the locations are determined by a computer program that shows the expected distribution in the results of a series of tests under identical conditions for varying numbers and sitings of the filters. You want identical results for sequential tests, which is the scientific principle of a reproducible experiment, but there is always some variation. (Statement of Stuart Isleton)

The laboratory at Lake Forest was modern, and equipped for inorganic analysis of every element in the periodic table to the low-ppb (parts per billion) level through electrochemical and radiochemical separation and identification equipment. Organic analysis could identify traces of pesticides, herbicides, and industrial solvents and polymers also to the low-ppb level by means of mass spectroscopy, gas chromatography, x-ray diffraction, and electron spectrophotometry. It is not necessary to explain the operations of these very precise analytical instruments except to state that the physical properties of each pure substance are a manifestation of the structure, mass, and spatial orientation of the atoms within the molecules or ions. Consequently, each pure substance has a different atomic weight (which can be measured on a mass spectroscope), a different rate of absorption in a specific medium (which can be measured on a gas chromatograph), and a different refractive index when exposed to electromagnetic radiation (which can be measured on x-ray diffraction instruments or electron spectroscopes). Impure organic substances can be separated by the gas chromatograph, while impure inorganic materials, even in traces too low for the electron spectroscope, can be identified by their atomic absorption or neutron activation rates. Eight persons worked within the lab, assisted on almost a full-time basis by Dr. Wilson.

> You can generally find Teddy in the lab; he knows what he is doing there, and he is good at it. Usually, he is trying to improve an analytical method for some obscure compound, but he will run the standard tests and procedures when the regular workers fall behind. I'm glad to see him in the lab since that means he is not issuing contradictory instructions and work assignments to the other employees. (Statement of Stuart Isleton)

The results of the laboratory identification of the chemical compounds present in the stack samples and field samples, and an estimate of their volumes based upon the sampling procedures, were occasionally sent directly to the customer; this occurred when companies wanted to conduct an "emissions inventory" at a site to understand their problems prior to regulation. A more common sequence was to send a report detailing the laboratory identifications and the sampling procedures to a group of five persons working on compliance review to determine if a given plant or process was in compliance with the current emission standards set by governmental agencies. On the federal level, air pollution standards were set by the Environmental Protection Agency (EPA), the National Institute of Health (NIH), the Occupational Safety and Health Administration (OSHA), the Department of Transportation (DOT), and the Department of Energy (DOE). Most of the states and many of the larger cities and metropolitan counties also had regulatory agencies concerned with air pollution. A company operating in Chicago, for example, was subject to air pollution standards set by the five federal commissions and by the Illinois Department of Natural Resources, the Cook County Board of Health, and the City of Chicago Smoke Control Board. The employees in the compliance review section maintained records of air pollution regulations on the federal, state, and local levels.

When the sampling procedures and laboratory analysis indicated that a company was in compliance with the existing air pollution regulations at all levels, the Environmental Research Associates staff would often complete the required forms and provide registration assistance to obtain the permits and approvals needed to continue operations. When a client was generally in compliance with existing regulations, but did have some noninjurious discharges that were contrary to regulations, or when there were technical questions regarding the interpretation of the regulations, the Environmental Research Associates employees could offer regulatory assistance, and negotiate with the agencies for the issuance of the permits and approvals.

> You might think that a plant or process would either meet standards or not, and that we should help to enforce the rules, not to abrogate them. And many of our people feel exactly that way. But some of the regulations are unclear, and others are obsolete, and a few are directly contradictory. For example, many of the municipal rules on air pollution date from the days of the steam locomotive, for smoke abatement, and discharges are measured by color and not by content or volume; if it's black, you can't release it into the atmosphere. That rule makes more sense than the situation in Boston, where the test is visibility; if you can see a discharge 2 miles away, it is unlawful. They have a smoke control inspector with a telescope on the top of the Custom House Tower. He has a stack of postcards, and when he sees a discharge he locates the site on a map of the city, assigns the responsibility, fills out a postcard to that company, and mails it. You are in trouble if you ignore the postcard. The problem is that the most visible discharge is steam condensing in the air, which is also the most harmless. (Statement of Stuart Isleton)

Once the required permits and approvals are obtained, either through registration or negotiation, periodic testing and reporting was generally required to ensure continued compliance. Environmental Research Associates provided this periodic service, generally on a quarterly or semiannual basis.

> Your students probably would like examples of the work that we do; this is a complex company, providing a variety of services, and the examples should clarify those services. Most sewage treatment plants now burn the sludge, after it has been dewatered and dried; each contract for a new incinerator has to include the provision that the equipment will meet certain emission specifications. We do the original testing for compliance, so that the incinerator can be accepted and the contractor can be paid. Then that incinerator has to be licensed by a local, state, or regional air pollution control board in order to operate, and we do the testing for the original license, and on a periodic basis, for the renewal of the license. (Statement of Stuart Isleton)

When company tests showed that the emission level of a specific plant or process did not meet existing regulations, or proposed regulations that were known to be close to adoption, or when the stack samples and field samples from a given site did not appear to be logically related, the report describing the sampling procedures and the laboratory identifications was sent to a group specializing in problem identification. Governmental contracts for technical assistance in developing pollution standards and measurement methods were also directed to this group, which consisted of a systems analyst, a mechanical engineer, and a chemistry Ph.D. These people specified the parameters of the problem, in both chemical and economic terms, and then suggested resolution of the problem through either electromechanical development and design, or environmental research.

Problems in air pollution can be exceedingly complex, with interrelated inputs that can create unexpected results. The example that is often cited here is the impact of sunlight on the nitrous oxides and assorted hydrocarbons of automotive emissions to form smog in southern California. But that problem was not difficult to understand; it is just difficult to resolve. A better example of the complex nature of air pollution problems would be discharges from two neighboring plants, both relatively harmless by themselves, that combine to form a new and very noxious substance. Chemical reactions don't stop just because the inputs involved are outside the limits of a chemical plant. We do extensive environmental studies, using dispersion models from various plants and processes in an area, attempting to establish responsibility for a given condition.

I have an unusual illustration of the problems you can encounter in attempting to establish responsibility. A large bakery in St. Louis made chocolate cupcakes one day each week; chocolate, baking in large volume, has a very distinctive aroma, and this aroma spread throughout the neighborhood. People in the area complained, not because of the smell, but because they claimed that the odor was eating holes in their laundry. This was an ethnic neighborhood in which the women hung laundry out to dry instead of using automatic driers. They also said that the odor created breathing difficulties for infants and older persons. People in the area encountered, as you might expect, company indifference and bureaucratic inaction; bakery officials said that cupcake aroma did not damage textiles, and government agencies said that baking chocolate was not on the list of proscribed contaminants. It was not until the wife of the local state senator washed his two monogrammed silk bowling shirts and left them out to dry that the possibility of pollution was considered; he displayed the tatters on the floor of the senate and demanded action. We received calls from the bakery, from the conglomerate that owned the bakery, from the city government, and from the state pollution control board, all on the same day.

We set up hi-vol air filters in the area, and found that on days when they baked vanilla cupcakes there was no problem, but on the chocolate cupcake days there were measurable amounts, and not just traces, either, of hydrochloric acid in the air. We traced the source to a textile bleaching mill that discharged waste chlorine only when the smell of the chlorine would be disguised by the aroma of the chocolate. The chlorine combined with water vapor to form hydrochloric acid; the impact on the wet laundry was obvious. The bleachery was fined, and the bakery was absolved of blame. (Statement of Stuart Isleton)

The environmental research group consisted of three systems analysts and economists, assisted by other members of the firm when needed, who studied the impact of industrial emissions through the use of large-scale computer-based models, and then designed procedures, either changes in measurement methods or enforcement standards, to correct the problem. The suggested changes were sent either to the regulatory agencies or legislative committees, on the state or federal level, that had contracted for the original study, or to companies that were considering new industrial processes and had paid for an analysis of potential pollution problems and probable regulatory responses.

Not all of our environmental studies are sponsored by regulatory agencies or legislative committees; often it is a company with socially conscious management that is responsible. Owens-Corning Fiberglass, for example, paid for an extensive study of the environmental impact of their high-temperature furnaces to melt the glass and their phenolic resins to bind the glass fibers. They have over 20 plants, in the United States and abroad, and they wanted to know the probable regulatory standards so that they could act in advance of legislation. (Statement of Stuart Isleton)

The electromechanical research group consisted of four design engineers, also assisted by other members of the firm occasionally assigned to work with them, who developed new processes to control air pollution, or new instruments to measure air emissions. Most of the means of controlling air pollution are standard, commercially available pieces of equipment such as gravity separators, fabric filters, water sprayers, electrostatic precipitators, or combustion incinerators. Normally, the design engineers would recommend the proper size and type of this equipment, and estimate the cost of installation and operation for a client. Environmental Research Associates did not build, sell, or install air pollution control equipment, but they would design special pieces of equipment when needed, and they would, of course, test and assist in the approval and registration of equipment built and installed by other firms.

We don't do much special design of pollution control equipment, primarily since there are so many other large firms active in supplying both standard and special systems. We do get the occasional odd or unusual job, however. A good example would be an iron mine in northern Minnesota that concentrated the ore prior to shipment. They had installed a complete system of gravity separators and water sprayers to control the dust and fumes, but the fumes were so acidic that the ductwork corroded and the system deteriorated. The bark of birch trees downwind from the plant turned reddish orange in color. There was no one living in that area, and surprisingly the orange birch trees were much healthier than the white ones; the emissions seemed to kill the leaf-eating insects. But the mine was subject to state-wide air pollution standards, and had to stop operations. We designed a wooden scrubber (water spray with impingement baffles) that trapped most of the dust and almost all of the acid fumes. (Statement of Stuart Isleton)

In many instances, problems in air pollution abatement centered more on the process controls than on the equipment designs; the process had to react to change in input conditions, and this required automated instrumentation. For example, changes in the particle size of solid contaminants required changes in air speed for effective gravity separation; an instrument to measure particle size could be wired to the controls of a variable-speed motor on the fan driving the air stream. Or, the presence of excess sulfur dioxide, above the regulatory limit, in the emissions of a power plant required changes in the fuel mixture at the boiler and in the spray pressure at the scrubbers. Particle-size counters and sulfur dioxide detectors were common, commercially available instruments. Engineers at Environmental Research Associates would design special instruments, that were not commercially available, to monitor and control the operations of a client's air pollution equipment. Many of these instruments, because of their need to detect trace amounts of known substances, were adaptations and simplifications of the laboratory spectrographs and chromatographs.

One of our more unusual instruments was an x-ray diffractor that we made to detect minute amounts of silver, copper, and gold in the fumes from the smelting furnace of a junk dealer in San Francisco. The owner of the junk yard, which was a large one that dealt only in nonferrous metals, was a man with absolutely no social conscience or environmental concern; he did not care if he polluted the entire Bay Area, but he did not want to waste any of his silver, copper, or gold in that polluting. Lead and zinc were O.K., since they were cheaper; he would not pay an extra penny to detect and stop the loss of those two metals. Many of our instruments are used for loss control, although usually not for such a narrow range of elements in the periodic table. (Statement of Stuart Isleton)

A small machine shop, with precision tooling and experienced workers, made the instruments, following the designs of the engineers. Electronic and microelectronic parts were purchased and modified, while mechanical components were machined and assembled, and the completed instrument was tested over a range of conditions, and then mounted in an airtight container that was capable of withstanding the harsh environment of an air pollution system. The foreman of the machine shop was in charge of purchasing needed parts and supplies, and of selling and shipping the completed units. A small catalog, listing over 70 available designs for the detection of specific substances ranging from amyl acetate to vinyl chloride, had been mimeographed and distributed to the manufacturers of air pollution control equipment.

Biological pollution, shown as a separate department on the schematic work flow of Exhibit 1, accounted for less than 5% of the revenues of Environmental Research Associates. Two biologists were employed, and they were concerned with the presence of injurious substances such as pesticides, herbicides, lead, mercury, or the phenolics and biphenyls in living organisms; they received samples from dead or diseased plants and animals, and conducted laboratory tests, with the assistance of the lab technicians, to identify the responsible substances. Analysis of these biological specimens was both difficult and time-consuming, and few other environmental consulting firms attempted to perform laboratory work in this area.

In air pollution, you start with a given process at a specific site, and you know the precise inputs and the probable outputs of that process, and the meteorological conditions at that site, so that your laboratory analysis, while complex, is at least straightforward. In biological pollution, you don't know the source or the site, so you have to guess at the substances, and laboratory work is as much logical deduction as scientific analysis. Sherlock Holmes was a prime advocate of logical deduction, and the determination of causes in biological pollution is really detective work. The people in the lab like to do it, but I know that we're losing money, even though we don't have a good cost system in place as yet. I think we ought to stop working on biological pollution problems.

In addition to the lack of profit opportunities, biological studies can be very disruptive of the normal work patterns. Someone is always sending us a cat with a mysterious ailment; after they become better, they wander around the office, sleeping on top of the computer terminals (due to the warmth of the CRT display units). We even had two Canadian geese, in cages, that created a continual uproar with their honking; they were here so long they became pets, known, of course, as "Heddy" and "Teddy." (Statement of Stuart Isleton)

Industrial hygiene, also shown as a separate department in the schematic work flow of Exhibit 1, was responsible for somewhat over 20% of the revenues of the consulting firm. Industrial hygiene can be defined as the protection of the health and well-being of industrial employees through design of the work environment. Toxic chemicals, dangerous machinery, harmful radiation, and extremes of heat, humidity, and noise are found in many manufacturing processes; consultants in industrial hygiene believe that safe and healthful working conditions can be established through recognition and control of those environmental hazards. Environmental Research Associates employed five industrial hygienists, certified by the American Industrial Hygiene Association, who visited the plant of a client to evaluate physical prob-

lems, and used the laboratory of the consulting firm to identify chemical toxicants. Plant or process conditions were reviewed against the provisions of the Occupational Safety and Health Act of 1967 for safety compliance, and against the standards of the American Industrial Hygiene Association for legal liability. After review, assistance was provided in registration procedures and regulatory approval with federal, state, and local agencies. Problems in compliance or liability were assigned to design engineers, who did not have to be certified by the AIHA but who worked with the industrial hygiene consultants to eliminate exposure to chemical and physical irritants, and to reduce levels of noise, heat, and humidity. Noise reduction was particularly difficult, due to the inherent functions of such process machinery as impact hammers, hydraulic pumps, and air compressors, but the consultants from Environmental Research Associates used octave-band analyzers to locate the exact noise sources, and then to study the effect of speed changes, enclosure methods, or absorption materials upon those sources. In addition to the evaluation and improvement of working conditions, the industrial hygiene consultants were often called upon for expert testimony in court cases and regulatory actions, and for professional assistance in machinery design.

Our work in industrial hygiene brings us into court almost continually since we are called as expert witnesses in personal lawsuits, compensation claims, and defect citations. An industrial company has to be able to show, in a court battle or agency hearing, that they were aware of, and took steps to eliminate, potential hazards. For example, we do continual analyses for lead in the blood of employees in battery manufacturing plants, along with surveys for lead exposure in the plants themselves. We make the same tests and surveys for the presence of cyanide in chrome-plating operations. If one of our companies is sued for negligence in the illness or disability of an employee, we have to be able to provide records to show that the levels of chemical toxicants or physical irritants (airborne dust or fibers) or heat, humidity, and noise were below those considered safe by regulatory agencies, and these records are given much greater weight if presented by a certified AIHA professional.

Industrial hygiene is an obsolete term that dates from the 1920s, but in a very real sense it involves "applied" air pollution control since the professionals in this field work primarily with airborne substances (toxicants and irritants) and airborne conditions (heat, humidity, and noise). Industrial engineers look after most of the other workplace conditions, such as mechanical hazards and dangerous tools. Let me give you an example of the "applied" nature of consulting in this area. Our industrial hygienists worked with a farm machinery manufacturer in the South to improve the air-conditioning system on the cab of a tractor to be used to spray chemical herbicides on cotton fields. A condition that is termed air pollution outside the cab is considered to be industrial hygiene inside the cab since that is where the worker is located, and you need AIHA certified personnel to design proper working conditions. We took comparative samples, inside and outside the cab, and analyzed those samples in the lab to show the effect of different type filters on the workplace conditions. We finally found a combination of filters that would meet regulatory standards, and then prepared a maintenance manual setting forth replacement schedules and repair procedures; the result is that now it is the tractor owner, not the tractor manufacturer, who is responsible for unsafe conditions in the cab. (Statement of Stuart Isleton)

In addition to serving clients in manufacturing firms and public utilities, employees from the air pollution and industrial hygiene departments often cooperated in contract research studies for professional groups, governmental agencies, and industrial associations. These research studies involved development of better sampling procedures, advanced analytical techniques, or modified regulatory standards for the improvement of working conditions. Stuart Isleton described three contracts that were in various stages of completion at the date of the case as examples of these joint air pollution and industrial hygiene research projects:

The American Society of Testing and Material Engineers (ASTME) often contracts with Environmental Research Associates to design procedures for the measurement of specific process emissions and workplace contaminants. The intent is to develop sampling procedures that will guarantee the reproducibility of experiments, and consequently the reliability of reports. Right now we are working on a more accurate means of sampling for gypsum dust dispersion at building sites. Gypsum is the basic component of wallboard, a common construction material, and ASTME engineers will be responsible for evaluating the level of this airborne health hazard as part of their regular work in testing the strength and quality of the on-site building materials.

The Environmental Protection Agency generally has three or four contracts in process with Environmental Research Associates at any given time for the development of analytical methods that can be automated for workplace surveillance. For example, we have one group that has spent eight months on the design of a process instrument, based on the principle of a laboratory chromatograph, to continually monitor polybrominated biphenyls (PBB) and polychlorinated biphenyls (PCB) emissions at a chemical plant. Our chemists and engineers like sponsored research of this nature, since it means that they can work with scientists from the local universities on challenging problems, but it is not very profitable. We have to submit a firm proposal for each contract, at a set price, and we wind up with cost overruns and no proprietary rights to the instrument designs.

I much prefer research contracts with industry associations such as the Iron and Steel Institute, which has a contract with Environmental Research Associates right now for a special study of the operating changes and financial impacts of the OSHA standards applied to open-hearth furnaces. Cost overruns are no problem with industry associations, as long as your study is producing meaningful results, since they will negotiate a final settlement, and a successful industry study often leads to consulting engagements with most of the industry members. (Statement of Stuart Isleton)

The water pollution activities of Environmental Research Associates were located in an office building in Addison, Illinois, approximately 20 miles to the southwest of the main office in Lake Forest. The two sections of the company were allegedly separated, since there was not enough room in the Lake Forest building for the complete staff, but Stuart Isleton felt that the reasons were more historical than spatial:

Dr. and Mrs. Wilson have never been particularly interested in the problems of water pollution; they believe that the sampling procedures are less difficult, the laboratory analysis less rigorous, and the remedial actions less innovative. To a certain extent they are right; over 50% of water pollution consulting is concerned with municipal sewage, which is not a very attractive topic, and the sampling procedures, analytical techniques, and treatment methods are all known. Industrial water pollution, however, is another matter; this area of consulting has the same toxic substances and the same technical problems as industrial air pollution. The only difference is that in industrial water pollution, the chemical substances are dissolved or suspended in water, and not carried by air cur-

rents. Our problem is that the people in Addison concentrate on municipal water pollution since there is so much federal and state money available for funding in that area. (Statement of Stuart Isleton)

The work flow of the water pollution activities of Environmental Research Associates, divided into the municipal and industrial areas, is shown in schematic form in Exhibit 2.

Water pollution consulting had been started by Environmental Research Associates in 1974 when many of the industrial and utility clients of the firm, satisfied with their past assistance in solving air pollution and industrial hygiene problems, asked for future help in meeting water pollution regulations. Dr. and Mrs. Wilson had interviewed a number of candidates to direct this new area, including some of the young scientists and engineers working for them in the Lake Forest office, but they had decided that they needed an older manager with specific experience in waterborne pollution, and they had hired Mr. Albert Lakey, who was then Chicago District Director of the Office of Water Programs in the U.S. Environmental Protection Agency. Mr. Lakey was a large, friendly man, with an undergraduate degree in economics from the University of Illinois and 25 years of experience in various programs in the federal government, ranging from the Office of Price Stabilization during the Korean War to the Bureau of Wildlife Management in the 1960s. He had numerous friends throughout the Midwest who were active in water pollution control, either as officials in the municipal organizations that were responsible for sewage disposal, or as managers of the engineering firms that provided design and construction services for sewage plants.

Mr. Lakey, in his first actions as the director of the Water Pollution Department at Environmental Research Associates, had rented the offices in Addison, explaining that it was necessary to be close to the Chicago airport

Exhibit 2 *Schematic work flow in the Addison office of Environmental Research Associates*

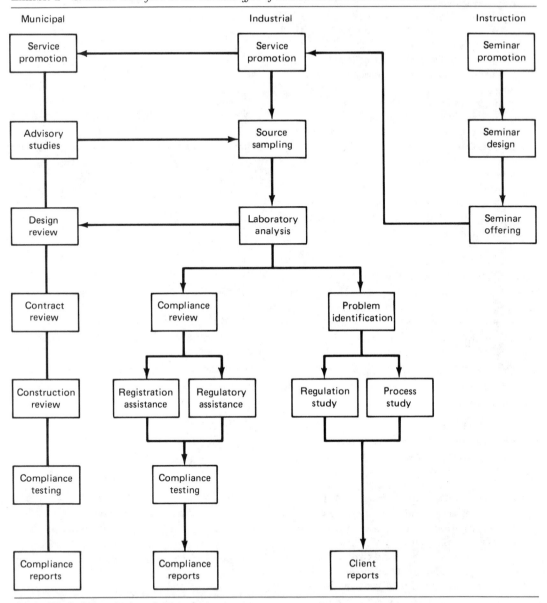

Municipal   Industrial   Instruction

Source: Verbal descriptions by employees.

for easy access to clients, and had hired a friend, George Rivers (the name and location of the consulting firm, and the names and backgrounds of the two founders have been disguised; the names of the two specialists in water pollution, Lakey and Rivers, have not been disguised, despite the apparently unusual word associations, and are used with their permission) to be marketing coordinator. Mr. Rivers was an even larger and friendlier man than Mr. Lakey; he also was from the Chicago District of the Office of

Water Programs, and also had an undergraduate degree from the University of Illinois 25 years previously, although in marketing. Mr. Lakey had been hired on a profit-sharing basis, with instructions to rapidly develop the water pollution services of Environmental Research Associates, and he believed that aggressive promotion was necessary to accomplish that goal.

> Al Lakey and George Rivers are not well liked out here [at the Lake Forest office]; they are called "Webfoot" and "Waddles," and when you meet them, you'll understand why. I suppose people here feel that they don't have a professional approach to pollution control, but you can't deny that they have been very successful in building sales. In just two years, they have been able to develop enough business so that the Addison office now represents 30% of our revenues, and that percentage is growing rapidly. It was originally thought that we would refer water pollution clients to them, but now they are referring air pollution clients to us. (Statement of Stuart Isleton)

Mr. Lakey and Mr. Rivers strongly emphasized service promotion, as shown on the schematic work flow of the water pollution department in Exhibit 2. One of their magazine advertisements had won a national award: a full-page photograph showed a man's arm, clothed in a business suit with a white cuff and gold cufflink, projecting from a pool of obviously polluted water, with dark scum and floating debris, holding the business card of Environmental Research Associates. The caption read, "If pollution problems are getting you down, reach for help fast." The business card gave the address and telephone number of the Addison office only. Line-drawing reproductions of the ad had been run in the business section of the *New York Times,* and in the Sunday editions of many midwestern and far western newspapers. The two senior consultants also attended every convention that dealt with pollution problems, rented a suite of rooms at the major hotel, and provided "hospitality" services. Mr. Lakey was a featured speaker at many of these conventions; where Dr. Wilson might also attend and discuss technical problems in a small seminar, Mr. Lakey would address the full session on economic problems, federal funding, and future progress.

> Al Lakey is an effective speaker, and a very effective salesman, but he has got to start paying attention to expenses. He has the typical governmental bureaucrat's approach to money, which is that there is always plenty more down in the treasury someplace. He flies first-class to those conventions, stays at the best hotels, takes customers and competitors alike to dinner, and then expects me to approve his travel vouchers. He has to start working within a budget. (Statement of Stuart Isleton)

Municipal clients for water pollution services, who contacted Environmental Research Associates either as a result of the advertisements in magazines and newspapers or as a result of the personal contacts at conventions, usually wanted advisory studies, not plant designs. Most sewage plants are designed by local civil engineering firms using the known technology of settling tanks and filtering screens for the suspended solids and bacteriological action for the dissolved nutrients. Mechanical components for the sewage plants, such as pumps, screens, and clarifiers, are made by a number of national manufacturers, while the actual construction of the concrete tanks and the installation of the heavy pipes and manufactured components is performed by large contractors. Sewage plant design and construction is a disjointed industry, with different participants at each of the major stages, and many of the municipal officials responsible for the operation of sewage systems like to employ an overall consultant to help in defining requirements, reviewing plans, observing construction, approving operations, and preparing final reports. Mr. Lakey had hired 12 persons, some with a background in civil engineering and others with experience in municipal government, to provide this assistance.

Advisory studies, shown as the first step in the schematic of municipal water pollution consulting on Exhibit 2, involved reviewing the forecasts of population change within an area, considering regional patterns in transportation, employment, and housing that might influence the degree and speed of that change, and then recommending capacity parameters to meet the needs of the expected population. Historical weather patterns were also studied, to forecast the probable occurrence of severe storms that could overload the capacity of the sewage treatment plant; in many communities, the storm sewers and the sanitary sewers are interconnected, and the sewage plant must be designed to handle sudden surges from heavy rains. Finally, industries and utilities in the area were surveyed to estimate the amount of water used in processing and to anticipate the discharge of physical or chemical wastes that could clog the mechanical equipment or affect the bacteriological treatment at the sewage plant. Samples were often taken from sewer pipes near the larger industrial firms to check the reliability of the survey data; these samples were sent both to the Environmental Research Associates laboratory at Lake Forest, and to commercial laboratories in Chicago for analysis.

> I've talked with Al about this [sending water pollution samples to commercial laboratories for analysis], and he says that we don't give fast enough service. It's fast enough for everybody out here; he is just going to have to change. (Statement of Stuart Isleton)

The specialists in municipal water pollution also reviewed the designs prepared by the civil engineering firms, advised on the terms of contracts negotiated with the local construction companies, appraised the progress of the actual construction, and took samples at the completion of the project to ensure that the treatment plant was able to meet the performance specifications of the construction contract, and the pollution standards of the regulatory agencies. Members of the staff also provided assistance in registering the completed plant, and obtaining the proper permits and approvals, from regional, state, and federal agencies.

Industrial water pollution studies were not emphasized in the Addison office; only two members of the staff were permanently assigned to this area, although additional personnel could be requested from the municipal consulting area, when needed. The industrial water pollution studies were very similar, in both the sequence of steps and the nature of the activities at each step, to industrial air pollution consulting. Samples were taken, both from discharge pipes at the manufacturing plant and from bodies of water in the drainage system surrounding the plant site, and information was recorded on water temperature, oxygen content, and flow rate. The samples were analyzed, and a report was generated on the type and volume of physical and chemical pollutants, and the impact of those pollutants upon ambient water quality. The report was reviewed to determine if the plant or process was in compliance with the water pollution standards set by the federal government; few state and almost no local governmental units had enacted industrial water pollution regulations, nor enforced the few regulations that were in effect. Registration assistance with the relevant federal agency was provided when the discharges clearly met existing standards; when the discharges did not meet those standards, negotiations were often started with the agency to modify the standards, citing the minimal impact of the physical or chemical material upon the ambient water quality. The Addison office included no systems analysts or design engineers, so that very little assistance could be offered to clients to develop new processes to eliminate specific pollutants, or new instruments to improve the performance of existing processes.

Instructional clinics were the third consulting service provided by the Addison office of Environmental Research Associates. Mr. Lakey, in 1976, had started to offer a series of three-day seminars in water pollution; participants were charged $400 apiece to attend lectures on legal interpretations of pollution standards, demonstrations of technological developments in pollution processes, and discussions of federal sources for pollution funding. Ten seminars were held each year, primarily oriented toward municipal water pollution, but substantial numbers of people from industry had asked for permission to attend, and Mr. Lakey and Mr. Rivers at the date of the case were developing a new series directed specifically towards industrial problems. Speakers were invited from university faculties and equipment manufacturers to describe new technical processes, and from the federal agencies to explain new regulatory standards, while Mr. Lakey specialized in leading discussions on expected levels of funding in the federal budget. The seminars were often held in rapidly growing resort areas, such as Palm Springs, California, or Hilton Head, South Carolina, so that the participants could, in the words of the advertising brochure announcing the series of seminars for 1979, "inspect modern sewage plants, built with the most advanced equipment and most innovative systems."

I'm not certain of exactly what goes on at those seminars; they make a lot of money and probably lead to some new business, but I'm afraid that the scientific content may be minimal. I've heard that George Rivers will challenge anyone on the golf course; when you first meet him you might think that he couldn't even see a golf ball down at his feet [Mr. Rivers de-

scribed himself to the casewriter as being "portly" and "somewhat stout" in physical appearance], but he was a professional baseball player when he was younger, and he is very well coordinated and very strong. I don't know whether we ought to expand the seminars, to include air pollution and industrial hygiene, or to eliminate them altogether. (Statement of Stuart Isleton)

Mr. Isleton, as described previously in the case, expected to be appointed the president of Environmental Research Associates in the spring of 1979, upon the retirement of Dr. and Mrs. Wilson. He felt that a number of problems needed to be resolved quickly, after his appointment, and he discussed these problems openly and frankly with the casewriter:

We have to do something about our two offices in Addison and Lake Forest. The dual locations are wasteful, since people spend a lot of time driving back and forth, and sending written reports and laboratory samples between the two places. Also, the split responsibilities between water pollution at Addison and air pollution and industrial hygiene at Lake Forest are artificial, and reduce our opportunity to participate in the most rapidly growing sector of pollution control consulting: environmental impact studies. The Environmental Policy Act of 1973 was intended to force consideration of environmental impact along with technological feasibility and financial return in the planning of all large construction projects. Impact studies require a knowledge of the existing environmental systems, air, water, and biological, and a precise identification and a quantitative assessment of the effect of the project upon the interrelationships of those systems. The bottom line of environmental impact studies is an evaluation of project benefits versus environmental costs. We have to become active in this area, but we need to have closer cooperation and coordination between the air, water, and biological areas.

We have to do something about our lack of organization. At any given time, a biochemist who graduated from Notre Dame three months previously can be in Washington testifying before a congressional committee, while a public policy and government affairs person will be here in Lake Forest, building a computer model, and a systems analyst with 10 years experience will be in some marsh in Wisconsin trying to trap ducks that have been exposed to PCB emissions. There are no formal job assignments. Teddy will wander out of the lab every now and again, look around for someone who doesn't appear to be busy, and ask that person to help him write a project report or visit a client to get stack samples. Heddy will come out of the office five minutes later, and tell that same person to do something else. You have to do what Heddy asks, because she has a very good memory, and you want to do what Teddy asks, because he is such a nice guy, so that somehow the work gets done. But there is no formal hierarchy of authority to direct activities.

We have to do something about our lack of systems. Heddy serves tea every afternoon, and people stop by and tell her what they're doing. Teddy sits there, and nods his head, and asks technical questions. Then the two of them stay late at night, in the back office that has been furnished like a living room, and read all the reports before they are sent out to industrial clients or government agencies. That's a poor way to run a company; we have to have better systems for planning, scheduling, and reviewing the completion of the various projects.

We have to do something about our lack of information. We have two bookkeepers working for an accountant, Mrs. Armstrong, but they just make out the payroll, approve the travel vouchers, and record the invoices. I've started monthly statements, which show that we're losing about $5,000 each month, but we have no revenue information by service or cost information by activity to take effective actions. We really have to set up a formal structure, allocate revenues and costs by department, and make people responsible for profitable operations.

We have to do something about the lack of morale. This place is a zoo. I don't mean the animals, although there are always four or five cats wandering around, named Heddy I, Heddy II, etc., and a sad-looking mongrel they call Stuart. I mean the people. Last month we had the Great Paper Airplane Contest; *Scientific American* published a study on the aerodynamic properties of paper airplanes and challenged readers to improve on existing designs; we had people throwing paper gliders from one end to the other of this old barn. This month they're doing imitations of Dr. and Mrs. Wilson. Fun is fun, but we're losing money. [The casewriter would have to admit that Dr. and Mrs. Wilson were both easy to mimic. Dr. Wilson was a renowned scientist and kindly man, but very absentminded; he continually patted his pockets, attempting to locate glasses, pencils, calculators, pipes, matches, and tobacco. He still climbed smokestacks for new clients, despite his age and heart condition, to ensure the safety of ladder rungs and catwalks, and he did this climbing in a business suit, with his pockets bulging with instruments and filters; it was alleged that he stopped every 10 rungs to pat at least one pocket. Mrs. Wilson was an exceedingly intelligent and gracious woman who assumed that everyone understood scientific terms and concepts; she was quite capable of saying to a young assistant who had just come back from testifying before a congressional committee, "My dear, did you not tell the senator that differential thermal analysis can be employed reliably only on polymeric samples?"]

We have to do something about this building. [Dr. and Mrs. Wilson, in 1976, had built an attractive office building on a landscaped lot in Lake Forest, but had run out of money before it was completed. The internal space had never been subdivided, and desks for the air pollution specialists and industrial hygienists were scattered about, apparently at random, in a large empty room.] The noise level is too high, and we've got to provide more privacy and better working conditions. (Statement of Stuart Isleton)

Class Assignment. Develop an organizational structure for Environmental Research Associates, assuming that Dr. and Mrs. Wilson do retire in another month and that Stuart Isleton is appointed to be the president of the firm. Consider each of the following steps in your design of the organizational structure.

1. Define the tasks imposed by the strategy of Environmental Research Associates, understand the relationships among those tasks, and be able to identify operational stages in the productive process, or flow of the consulting reports through the organization, and to specify decision points in the managerial process, or flow of information. The production process, or work flow, has been largely diagrammed in Exhibits 1 and 2; think about the problems in defining the work flow of the organization if these schematics had not been provided. Develop an equivalent diagram for the information flow.

2. Establish a measure of performance for each of the operational stages in the productive process, and each of the decision points in the managerial process. Environmental Research Associates is providing consulting service; think about the differences between measures of performance for a service firm and a manufacturing company.

3. Group the operational stages in the productive process and the decision points in the managerial process in organizational units, following your analysis of the differences among those operational stages and

decision points in managerial function, geographic location, market segment, or technical content. Think about the alternative groupings that are possible.

4. Arrange for the coordination of the organizational units by establishing a hierarchy of authority. Authority refers to the ability of one individual within an organization to influence the behavior and actions of others within the organization, and the hierarchy is the vertical scale of that authority.

5. Consider the differentiation of the organizational units. Differentiation refers to the secondary differences between members of organizational units that may make communication and cooperation between the units very difficult; these secondary differences can be described in terms of the types of problems encountered by members of the various units, the quality of the information available for the problem solution, the process of decision, and the impact of the output.

6. Arrange for the integration of the organizational units. Integration refers to a voluntary spirit of cooperation between members of different organizational units; integration can be achieved through collaborative plans, structural integrators, interdepartmental project teams, or formal committee meetings.

7. Develop an organizational structure for Environmental Research Associates, following the design process outlined in the text and suggested by the previous questions. Be prepared to explain the logic of your proposed structure.

8. Design an internal arrangement for the Lake Forest office building of Environmental Research Associates, following the plan given in Exhibit 3. Office modules, using movable partitions and panel-hung furniture of the type developed by Herman Miller, Inc. (see that case for a description of "Action Office" furniture) are

Exhibit 3 *Diagram of the office building in Lake Forest, Illinois, occupied by Environmental Research Associates*

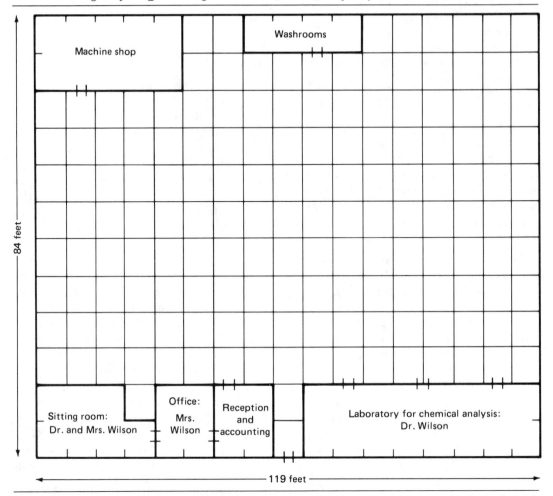

Note: Plan is crosshatched at equal intervals to show that office modules are normally built with panel-hung furniture in multiples of 7 ft.

usually built in multiples of 7 ft, with the following modular recommendations:

7′ = corridor width
7′ × 7′ = secretarial area, with one desk and typing stand
7′ × 14′ = junior executive/engineer with one desk and small (3-person) conference area

14′ × 14′ = middle executive/engineer with one desk and large (5-person) conference table
14′ × 21′ = senior executive with one desk, small (3-person) conference area, and a very large (12-person) conference table

At the date of the case (spring 1977), Environmental Research Associates had 87 employees, assigned generally as follows, although there was very considerable movement and flexibility between these assignments:

3 source sampling
8 laboratory analysis
5 compliance review
3 problem identification
3 environmental research
4 electromechanical research

1 machine shop foreman
4 machine shop workers
2 biological pollution
5 industrial hygiene
2 water pollution managers
12 municipal water pollution
2 industrial water pollution
7 draftsmen/engineering help
23 secretaries/office help
3 accounting/bookkeeping
—
87 total personnel

Champion International, Inc.

Champion International, Inc., is an integrated forest products firm that is the result of a merger in 1967 of U.S. Plywood Corporation, a major building materials supplier with sawmills and plywood plants on the West Coast and distribution warehouses throughout the country, and Champion Papers Incorporated, a large manufacturer of printing papers and business stationery, with pulp and paper mills in Ohio, North Carolina, and Texas. The original name of the merged firm was U.S. Plywood–Champion Papers, Inc., but that title was felt to be overly long and cumbersome, so that it was changed to its present form in 1972. The two companies, which were approximately equal in size at the time of the merger (Champion's 1966 sales were $428,235,000, and after-tax profits were $18,314,000: U.S. Plywood's 1966 sales were $444,678,000, and after-tax profits were $18,756,000), were combined in order to realize greater returns from the joint use of their timber resources, and to smooth out the cyclical swings in their annual sales.

The two companies seem made for each other. Their products, though derived from a single raw material, were not competitive and served radically different markets; thus there was no problem with the Justice Department.

Equally important, the existing resources of either company promised to strengthen the position of the other. Champion, for instance, had had ambitions of establishing itself in the West for decades, but could never find the timber base to support itself. U.S. Plywood's timberlands, concentrated in the western U.S. and Canada, seemed ready-made to do the job. . . . U.S. Plywood, on the other hand, has been moving rapidly into southern pine plywood, largely on other people's timber, and Champion's timberlands in North and South Carolina, Georgia, and east Texas should provide a base for still further expansion.

Then too, paper and building materials respond to somewhat different cycles, with the result that in a year like 1967 when Plywood's earnings would certainly have been down, Champion's would almost certainly have been up. "We'll be less dependent on any single market," President Gene Brewer adds, "than either company has ever been before."

Most important of all, the new company will be vastly more efficient in utilizing its timber resources than either company had been before. "While each company uses the tree," Chairman Bendetsen points out, "they use different parts of the tree." Champion, for instance, has been pulping trees in which the base log could have gone into higher value-added sawmill processing. If it sold a sawlog to a sawmill, it lost the chips which it could use for pulp, and had to buy them back at market prices. U.S. Plywood, on the other hand, had been selling such chips to the Japanese, and it had been leaving tree tops behind in the woods, both of which could have gone into making pulp. In the merged company, each tree will ideally go into its highest-value end use. "This I believe to be by far the most profound of the benefits to be derived from the merger," Karl Bendetsen (Chairman) says. And Gene Brewer (President) adds, "It promises a bigger and brighter future for both of us." (*Forbes,* March 15, 1967, p. 48)

Some explanation of the utilization of timber in the forest products industry may be useful here, to explain the comments made in the previous quotation. Plywood and veneers are cut from the largest, straightest, and most valuable logs; lumber is manufactured from the medium-grade logs; and pulp chips (a chip is a wood flake approximately ⅜ in. x 1 in. x 1 in.) are produced from the smallest and most crooked logs, the tops of trees, and the waste wood generated in a sawmill (when a round log is cut into rectangular lumber, there is very considerable waste which can be chipped for use in pulp and paper manufacture). Plywood and lumber have higher margins in their final sales prices than an equivalent volume of wood in the form of pulp chips, so the economic advantage of an integrated forest products firm, producing plywood, lumber, and pulp, is the ability to sort logs by quality standards into specific groups

or classes, and then use each class for the highest-value end product.

The merger made us into a single entity with both parts stronger in every way. We really expect to make our two plus two equal five. (Statement of Mr. Gene C. Brewer, President of Champion International, Inc., quoted in *Business Week,* March 1, 1976, p. 66)

Investment analysts in the major brokerage firms and trust officers in the large banks evidently understood the economic advantages of the integrated forest products firm, and apparently agreed with the hopeful forecasts made by the Chairman and the President of the newly integrated company; the price of Champion International's stock, which had been $22.00 per share immediately following the merger in February 1967, rose steadily throughout the year, and closed on December 31 at $42.00 per share.

There was no question but that U.S. Plywood–Champion Papers [the original name of Champion International] was an interesting equity situation. It was a merger that made sense, in an era of illogical acquisition and senseless purchase by many of the big conglomerates. It was a synergistic merger, in which each partner could help the other, for the benefit of both. In a good market, the stock was bound to increase in price. (Statement of an investment analyst)

Following the merger, the company expanded productive capacity and modernized production facilities, in an effort to utilize more effectively and profitably their very substantial timber resources, while continuing to acquire additional timberlands and to eliminate, through investment increases, the minority positions in various subsidiaries of the prior U.S. Plywood Corporation (Exhibit 1).

In addition to the capacity expansion and

Exhibit 1 *Capital expenditures, timber acquisitions, and investment increases (000,000's omitted) of Champion International, Inc., 1968–1974*

	1968	1969	1970	1971	1972	1973	1974
Capital expenditures	$97.7	$99.5	$80.2	$49.2	$ 83.4	$137.2	$229.8
Timber acquisitions	49.8	16.7	30.6	8.6	121.4	14.3	24.7
Investment increases	7.4	1.7	9.0	12.3	13.5	0.9	1.9

Source: Moody's Industrial Manual for the respective years.

timberland acquisition programs, the company purchased, either by an exchange of stock or by the payment of cash, a number of companies in the furniture and home furnishings industry (Exhibit 2).

The diversification into furniture and home furnishings was pushed by Mr. Karl Bendetsen, chairman of Champion International from 1967 to 1972, and by Mr. Thomas Willers, chairman and chief executive officer from 1972 to 1975, in order to make more ef-fective use of the company's timber resources and channels of distribution.

There is a very logical rationale for diversification into furniture and home furnishings. Lumber, plywood, and rugs are not as different as you might expect, and hardwood lumber, veneer, and composition board (made from wood chips and adhesive, pressed together) are directly related to furniture; they are the raw material input for furniture manufacturing.

Exhibit 2 *Mergers and acquisitions of Champion International, Inc., 1968–1974*

July 1968	Acquired Drexel Enterprises, a large manufacturer of high-quality living room, dining room, and bedroom furniture for residential use, and institutional furniture and equipment for laboratory, library, church, classroom, and dormitory use, through an exchange of 1,137,800 shares of $1.20 convertible preferred stock and 1,280,000 shares of common, with an approximate value of $120 million.
Dec. 1969	Acquired Trend Industries, a large manufacturer of wall-to-wall carpeting for residential and commercial installation, and area rugs for retail sale, through an exchange of 3,122,280 shares of common stock, with an approximate value of $96 million.
Dec. 1969	Acquired Birmingham Ornamental Iron Company, a medium-sized manufacturer of wrought iron and aluminum patio furniture for outdoor use, and ornamental wrought iron railings for residential construction, through an exchange of 121,580 shares of common stock, with an approximate value of $3.8 million.
Dec. 1970	Acquired Roberts Consolidated, a large manufacturer of carpet installation materials, including plywood and metal tackless strips for carpet attachment, aluminum molding for carpet edging, and special equipment for carpet cleaning.
Dec. 1970	Acquired Path Forks Coal Company, a coal mine in Harlan County, Kentucky, that was purchased to provide an assured supply of low-sulfur coal for the company's plants, through an exchange of 182,476 shares of common stock, with an approximate value of $4.7 million.
Jan. 1974	Acquired A. W. (Securities) Ltd., a holding company for Associated Weavers, a large British manufacturer of printed carpeting and upholstery fabrics, for $93,000,000 in cash.

Source: Moody's Industrial Manual for the respective years.

Champion International, through their Canadian subdivision (Weldwood of Canada, a 73.6% owned subsidiary) produces lumber and veneer of birch, maple, and beech; these are the northern hardwoods that are used in the manufacture of top-quality furniture, and they are not available in the South. Champion International was able to integrate vertically from hardwood lumber and veneer production in the North through to high-quality furniture manufacture in the South, and increase substantially the value-added of their products.

The carpeting acquisitions were also sensible. I don't know if you have thought about it, but no one uses hardwood flooring in residential construction any more; instead, wall-to-wall carpeting is laid directly onto sanded plywood subflooring. They bought two high-volume, low-cost carpet weaving firms, in the United States and in England, and they bought the company that manufactures the carpet installation materials and tools. This is horizontal integration; they planned to sell plywood subflooring, installation materials, and wall-to-wall carpeting through their own distribution network. The church, library, classroom, and dormitory furniture would also fit directly into their national distribution system for building materials; a contractor building a church would naturally come to the building material supply center for the wooden church pews and chancel. The strategic concept of vertical and horizontal integration in the forest products industry was inspired. (Statement of an investment analyst)

In 1974, following seven years of continuous capital expansion and product diversification, Champion International was a company with very substantial sales ($2.5 billion), extensive timber holdings (2.4 million acres within the United States), three related product lines (lumber and plywood, paper and packaging, and furniture and home furnishings), 143 manufacturing plants (ranging from plywood mills in British Columbia to coal mines in Kentucky), a declining return on equity (8.0% at the start of 1975 vs. International Paper Company's 14.7% and Weyerhaeuser Company's 14.4%), and very real organizational problems (fighting between the divisions over timber utilization, capital allocation, and product distribution). In September 1974, Mr. Andrew Sigler, 43 years old, with an A.B. from Dartmouth College, an M.B.A. from Amos Tuck, two years' service as a line officer in the U.S. Marine Corps, and 18 years' experience at Champion Paper Company and Champion International, was appointed president and chief executive officer, with the obvious assignment to "straighten out the situation and restore the profitability." The balance of the case describes the situation faced by Mr. Sigler at the start of 1975, and is divided into sections on sales revenues, timber resources, product lines, production facilities, distribution channels, financial position, organizational structure, and apparent problems.

Sales Revenues. Sales had increased substantially during the period 1968–1974, but profits as a percentage of sales had never risen above the relatively low figure of 1968 (Exhibit 3).

Timber Resources. In 1974, Champion International owned 2,400,000 acres and managed an additional 250,000 acres of timberland in the United States, and had long-term contracts to harvest sawlogs or pulpwood on an additional 4,400,000 acres in Canada. The domestic timberlands were concentrated in five major areas or blocks, with 524,000 acres in east Texas, 348,000 acres in northern Alabama, 395,000 acres along the North Carolina–South Carolina border, 668,000 acres in central Montana, and 460,000 acres in Oregon and northern California. Weldwood of Canada, a 73.6% owned subsidiary of Champion International, owned 59,000 acres and had exclusive cutting rights

Exhibit 3 *Revenues by division, expenses, and profits (000,000's omitted) of Champion International, Inc., 1968–1974*

	1968	1969	1970	1971	1972	1973	1974
Building material	$ 679.6	$ 730.3	$ 676.3	$ 808.8	$ 983.3	$1,163.6	$1,119.4
Paper and packaging	510.9	539.1	600.3	600.4	668.7	785.6	1,059.5
Home furnishings	169.0	180.5	162.7	183.7	211.8	251.0	346.1
Other revenues	3.4	5.6	6.6	6.9	7.9	7.8	7.3
	1,283.4	1,492.5	1,445.9	1,599.8	1,871.7	2,208.0	2,532.3
Cost of goods	993.8	1,157.2	1,169.4	1,293.1	1,510.7	1,747.1	2,008.8
Marketing and administration	183.3	210.1	210.2	217.4	236.8	272.5	315.0
Expense or (income)	(8.4)	(10.4)	(10.6)	(10.4)	(8.0)	7.5	1.2
Interest expense	13.3	16.4	18.2	27.7	25.3	30.7	51.8
	1,182.1	1,373.4	1,392.6	1,527.8	1,764.8	2,057.8	2,376.8
Income before taxes	101.3	119.1	53.2	71.9	106.8	149.8	155.2
Income taxes	46.7	50.9	20.9	26.5	47.3	61.1	54.3
Income after taxes	54.6	68.1	32.3	45.4	59.5	86.7	100.8
Income as % sales	4.2	4.5	2.2	2.8	3.2	3.9	4.0

Source: Moody's Industrial Manual for the respective years.

on 580,000 acres in Ontario, while the Caribou Pulp and Paper Company, a joint venture with a Japanese firm, had pulpwood harvesting rights on 3,900,000 acres in central British Columbia. Much of the timberland in Canada is owned by the national or provincial governments, and long-term cutting contracts, or "rights" to the saw timber or pulpwood on this land, are sold by a bidding procedure similar to that used in the United States for offshore oil leases.

The timberland within the United States is managed intensively. Selective cutting and planned rotation is practiced on the high-value timber, primarily southern pine, Douglas fir, and northern hardwoods, while the low-value trees, such as red alder, aspen, or poplar, are harvested by clear cutting and whole-tree chipping, and the land is then replanted with coniferous seedlings. Five company-owned nurseries genetically breed trees that are faster growing and more resistant to disease, insects, and drought, and raise seedlings for reforestation. In 1974, 26 million seedlings were planted on company lands. Company foresters believe that these genetically developed seedlings, growing in scientifically managed forests, protected against fire and overcrowding, can produce as much wood fiber in 25 years as a natural seedling growing in an unmanaged environment can equal in 75 years.

Slightly more than 55% of the wood fiber needs for the company are produced on company lands; the balance is purchased from local farmers, independent loggers, tree plantations, and national forests. The state and national forests are important sources of sawlogs and pulpwood; approximately 65% of the merchantable softwood saw timber within the United States is located on public lands, and perhaps 25% of the softwood pulpwood. This publicly owned timber is sold to sawmills and pulpmills within a given area by a sealed-bidding procedure. Champion International purchased 15 to 20% of their timber requirements from public lands through sealed bids.

Product Lines. The products of Champion International can be grouped into the primary classifications of basic wood products (lumber, veneer, and plywood), paper products (printing papers, business stationery, and paperboard cartons), manufactured wood products (kitchen cabinets, household furniture, institutional furniture, and carpeting), purchased products (miscellaneous building materials and office supplies purchased for resale), and corporate products (land development sales and coal production). The individual products, and 1974 sales revenues for each product, are given in Exhibits 4 to 8; total sales for each product group may not agree with those reported in Exhibit 3 due to reclassifications.

The softwoods listed in Exhibit 4 include pine, spruce, and fir. Softwood veneer is rotary-cut, or peeled from a log turning against a sharp knife so that a thin sheet, ⅛ in. thick, unwinds much like a roll of paper. Softwood plywood is made by laminating an odd number of veneers with the grain of alternate sheets at right angles to the sheets immediately above and below. The result is a lightweight panel, usually 4 ft x 8 ft in size, that is extremely strong, and that is used in place of lumber for the sheathing (exterior covering of a house, underneath the finished siding), roofing, or subflooring in residential or commercial construction. Softwood plywood used for sheathing or roofing is generally unsanded, and fairly rough in appearance, while that used for flooring is sanded and smooth so that the floor covering, linoleum, tile, or carpeting can be laid directly on the surface. Softwood specialty plywood is sanded, and has patterns cut into the surface, either in a geometric decoration or to resemble finished lumber siding for residential construction.

The hardwoods listed in Exhibit 4 include birch, maple, and beech in the north, and

---

Exhibit 4 *Basic wood products and 1974 sales estimates by product of Champion International, Inc.*

Softwood plywood, primarily used for sheathing, subflooring, and roofing in residential and commercial construction	$312,007,000
Softwood veneer and specialty plywood, used as decorative paneling and exterior siding for residential and commercial construction	75,862,000
Softwood lumber, primarily used for framing and trim on residential and commercial construction	150,000,000*
Hardwood plywood and laminated paneling, sold to kitchen cabinet, store fixture, and lower-quality household furniture manufacturers	150,166,000
Hardwood veneer, sold to high-quality household and institutional furniture manufacturers, and some laminated specialties (handles)	8,752,000
Hardwood lumber, sold in higher grades to furniture manufacturers, and in lower grades for industrial uses (pallets, crating, etc.)	24,915,000*
Particleboard, manufactured from wood chips and adhesive pressed to medium density (¾ in.) and sold to furniture manufacturers	67,576,000
Hardboard, manufactured from wood flakes and adhesive pressed to high density (⅛ in.) and sold to cabinet and store fixture manufacturers	50,000,000*
Logs, primarily sold from West Coast surplus for export to Japan	39,495,000
Total sales of basic wood products	$878,773,000

Source: Annual Report and Form 10-K for 1974, supplemented by independent estimates (*).

oak, gum, and tupelo in the south. Hardwood veneer is straight-sliced, or cut by a knife moving across the log, to produce a sheet similar to a very thin piece of lumber. It is cut in this manner since hardwood veneer is used in place of lumber in furniture manufacturing; the intent is to produce a grain and an appearance indistinguishable from sawn lumber. The hardwood veneer is then glued to a "core stock" of ¾ in. particleboard or laminated lower-grade lumber, and used for veneered furniture; most higher-grade hardwood logs are so expensive that it is not economical to saw them into lumber, and use the lumber for solid wooden furniture. Some hardwood veneers are glued to softwood plywood, or ⅛ in. hardboard, and used for the sides and fronts of kitchen cabinets, store fixtures, or lower-quality household furniture.

Particleboard and hardboard are "reconstituted" wood products. Particleboard is made by mixing wood fibers, produced from pulpwood chips, with adhesives and the natural lignin of the wood, and then pressing the material to a medium density; particleboard is generally manufactured in sheets ¾ in. x 4 ft. x 8 ft., and is primarily used for furniture

core stock. Hardboard is a less expensive product. It is composed of wood flakes and some sawdust, mixed with adhesives, and pressed to a hard density in sheets ⅛ in. x 4 ft. x 8 ft.; hardboard is used in kitchen cabinets, store fixtures, etc.

The paper products manufactured by Champion International are listed in Exhibit 5; they include coated and uncoated fine papers, and paperboard. The coating on printing papers is a fine clay that produces a hard and nearly impervious surface so that the ink does not run or blotch, and very fine impressions can be reproduced, particularly with colored photographs. Coated printing papers are used for limited circulation magazines, such as the *New Yorker* or the *National Geographic,* and for advertising brochures and annual reports. The annual reports of Champion International are printed on their best grade of coated paper, and the color reproductions are superb.

Noncoated fine papers produced by Champion International are used for printing nonillustrated books and general circulation magazines, and for conversion to business stationery and envelopes, computer printouts,

Exhibit 5 *Paper products and 1974 sales estimates by product of Champion International, Inc.*

Coated fine papers, for printing illustrated books, limited-circulation magazines, advertising brochures, and annual reports	$216,311,000
Uncoated fine papers, for printing books and general circulation magazines, and for business use as stationery, envelopes, etc.	300,000,000*
Paperboard and bleached packaging papers, used for milk cartons, folded cartons, and specialty printed packaging	222,885,000
Milk cartons, produced from polyethylene-coated paperboard, and sold under the PurePak and DairyPak labels	100,401,000
Folded cartons, produced from waxed paperboard for frozen-food packaging, and from uncoated paperboard for printed boxes	49,687,000
Envelopes, manufactured from uncoated fine papers and bleached packaging papers, in both standard and clasp styles	38,587,000
Rolled paper sticks, produced from bleached packaging papers, for lollipops and medical products	5,000,000*
Total sales of paper products	$932,871,000

Source: Annual Report and Form 10-K for 1974, supplemented by independent estimates (*).

and copier supplies. Conversion is the paper industry term for cutting the large rolls of paper produced by the paper machine into standard sizes (8½ in. x 11 in., for example), and then packaging and preparing these standard sizes for retail sale. Champion International specializes in fine papers for printing and general business use; the company does not produce the manila kraft used for paper bags or wrapping purposes, nor the cellulose fibers used for paper towels, toilet paper, or personal tissues.

The paperboard produced by Champion International is basically a stiff and heavy grade of paper, approximately $\frac{1}{32}$ in. thick. It is used, when coated with polyethylene, for milk cartons and orange juice cartons, and when coated with wax, for frozen-food cartons. In uncoated form, or when coated with clay for printing, it is used for small folded cartons for various drug and cosmetic products. The company does not produce the corrugated board used for industrial packaging and shipping boxes.

The manufactured products produced by Champion International, Inc., include finished building materials, chemical adhesives and stains, high-quality wooden and upholstered furniture, wrought-iron outdoor furniture, carpeting, and carpet installation tools, and are listed in Exhibit 6. As explained earlier, these manufactured products are either vertically integrated with the basic wood products of the company, or horizontally integrated with the various channels of distribution used by the company.

Champion International distributes their softwood and hardwood lumber, plywood, and veneer and their manufactured flush doors, kitchen cabinets, and construction ad-

---

Exhibit 6 *Manufactured products and 1974 sales estimates by product of Champion International, Inc.*

Flush doors, manufactured from particleboard or honeycomb core, with lumber banding (along edges) and hardwood or softwood veneer facing, and sold for residential or commercial construction	$ 33,089,000
Kitchen cabinets, manufactured from hardwood plywood, softwood framing, and hardboard paneling, and sold for residential or commercial construction	16,621,000
Chemical adhesives, sealants, and stains, sold for industrial (plywood and furniture manufacturing) uses, and for construction (interior panels and exterior siding are now often glued to the lumber framing)	23,359,000
Wooden furniture, manufactured from high-grade hardwood veneer, lumber, and particleboard, and sold under the Drexel and Heritage brands for both household and institutional (office, hotel, church, and school) use	100,220,000*
Upholstered furniture, manufactured from lower-grade hardwood lumber and woven fabrics, and sold under the Drexel and Heritage brands for household use	20,000,000*
Iron furniture and decorative railings, manufactured from wrought iron and sold under the Birmingham brand for outdoor patio use	2,000,000*
Woven carpeting, of tufted broadloom, shag, and printed axminster styles, manufactured in integrated (both spinning and weaving) mills and sold under the Trend and Roxbury brands for both household and institutional use	223,834,000
Carpet installation materials, including plywood and metal tackless strips for carpet attachment, aluminum molding for carpet edges, and special equipment for carpet cleaning	46,328,000
Total sales of manufactured products	$465,451,000

Source: Annual Report and Form 10-K for 1974, supplemented by independent estimates (*).

Exhibit 7 *Purchased products and 1974 sales estimates by product group of Champion International, Inc.*

Purchased building materials, including roofing products, building paper, insulation materials, metal doors and shutters, and general hardware items, purchased from other manufacturers for resale	$121,254,000
Purchased office supplies, including pens, pencils, typewriter ribbons, notebooks, etc., purchased from other manufacturers for resale	64,551,000
Purchased industrial supplies, including paper wipes, towels, and cleaning items, purchased from other manufacturers for resale	66,786,000
Total sales of purchased items	$252,591,000

Source: Annual Report and Form 10-K, supplemented by individual estimates (*).

hesives, sealants, and stains through a chain of 120 combination sales offices and warehouses in the United States, and 20 sales offices and warehouses in Canada. To expand the available product line, and to provide full service to the current customers, the company purchases for resale other building supplies, such as roofing, insulation, and hardware items. Champion International distributes their paper and paperboard products through 24 other combined sales offices and warehouses, and again to provide increased sales volume and greater customer service, they purchase office supplies, such as pens, pencils, and pads, and industrial items such as towels and wiping cloths, for resale. These purchased products are listed in Exhibit 7.

Champion International has two products that do not fit into the company's normal patterns of vertical integration from the forest to the building contractor or furniture manufacturer, or of horizontal integration across all

building materials, home furnishing, and office supplies. These products are the development and sale of company land for residential and commercial construction, and the production of company coal for the energy requirements of the southeastern pulp and paper mills; they are described in Exhibit 8.

Production Facilities. Champion International operated 143 major factories or manufacturing plants, in the United States, Canada, and abroad; these plants are identified for each of the major product groups and major geographic areas in Exhibit 9.

The softwood studmills listed in Exhibit 9 are very high volume sawmills designed to cut only 2 in. x 4 in. x 8 ft dimension lumber from small-diameter logs, and from the small-diameter cores that are left after the veneer is peeled from a large plywood log.

The pulpmills in the United States are located at Pasadena, Texas; Courtland, Ala-

Exhibit 8 *Corporate products and 1974 sales estimates by product group of Champion International, Inc.*

Coal, produced by a company-owned mine in Harlan County, Kentucky, for use by the company's pulp and paper mills and furniture plants in the Southeast. 420,000 tons mined in 1974, but revenues were not reported due to intercompany transfer only. Additional coal deposits are located beneath company landholdings in Alabama, Kentucky, and Montana	n. a.
Real estate development and sales, to make use of the higher-value lands owned by the company, including 70,000 acres within 50 miles of Houston, and in vacation areas in the mountains of North Carolina, South Carolina, and Georgia	$7,300,000*

Source: Annual Report and Form 10-K, supplemented by individual estimates (*).

Exhibit 9 *Manufacturing plants of Champion International, Inc.*

	U.S.	Canada	Int'l
Softwood plywood and veneer mills	13	5	—
Softwood sawmills	9	4	—
Softwood stud (2 in. x 4 in. x 8 ft) mills	3	1	—
Hardwood plywood and veneer mills	4	2	1
Hardwood mills	1	2	—
Particleboard mills	4	3	1
Hardboard mills	3	—	—
Pulpmills	4	1	2
Papermills, for fine papers and paperboard	4	1	2
Milk carton converting plants	5	—	—
Folded carton converting plants	4	—	—
Envelope manufacturing plants	6	1	2
Rolled paper stick plants	2	1	—
Flush door manufacturing plants	2	—	—
Kitchen cabinet manufacturing plants	3	—	—
Chemical adhesives and sealants	3	—	—
Chemical preservatives and stains	2	—	—
Wooden bedroom furniture	3	—	—
Wooden dining room furniture	5	—	—
Wooden living room furniture	2	—	—
Upholstered living room furniture	4	—	—
Wooden church furniture	1	—	—
Wooden laboratory furniture	1	—	—
Wooden office furniture	1	—	—
Wooden subassembly (panels, etc.) plants	6	—	—
Iron outdoor furniture and railings	2	—	—
Woven carpeting mills	5	—	3
Carpet installation material plants	7	1	2
Coal mines	1	—	—

Source: Annual Report for 1974, supplemented by Moody's Industrial Manual, 1974.

bama; and Canton, North Carolina; integrated paper mills are located on the same sites, and at Hamilton, Ohio. The Hamilton paper mill runs on pulp shipped from Canton, North Carolina. The Canadian pulp and paper mills are located in Quesnel, British Columbia, and are a joint venture between Weldwood of Canada (73.6% owned subsidiary of Champion International) and Daishowa-Marubenie International of Japan. The foreign pulpmill is in Brazil, where the company owns 74,000 acres of Brazilian timberlands, and the foreign papermills are in Belgium, where printing paper and business stationery is produced for the European market.

The foreign operations are not extensive, particularly for a company that calls itself "International," but they are bound to grow, especially in Brazil. There will be a worldwide shortage of pulp in about 10 years; already the Scandinavian mills are buying pulp from the southern United States, and after the present surplus of wood fiber in that area runs out, there will be only two more possible areas with large supplies of timber: Brazil and Siberia. Siberia is out, because of the climatic and political problems, which leaves Brazil. Champion is running a small pulp and paper mill there now, learning to make high-grade printing papers from low-grade pulp produced from eucalyptus trees; if they are able to do that, they will be in the forefront of the expansion in that area. (Statement of an investment analyst)

The manufacturing plants for the basic wood products are grouped near the pulp-mills in the southern United States, both so that they can draw upon the timber from company-owned lands, and so that the waste products from the plywood plants and saw-mills can be chipped (reduced to wood flakes approximately ⅜ in. x 1 in. x 1 in.) and used as the raw material input for the pulp mills. There are five major geographic areas where the company combines timberland ownership and basic wood products manufacturing facilities; three of these areas have integrated pulp mills, but it is anticipated by industry observers that eventually pulp mills will be built in Montana and on the West Coast (Exhibit 10).

The grouping of the basic wood products production facilities near the timberlands and the pulp mills was the result of deliberate strategic decisions and capital appropriations.

During 1974, U.S. Plywood (original name for the basic wood products division of Champion International) added significant amounts of manufacturing capacity.

In Bonner, Montana, a plywood mill was completed, and it began scheduled operations. Built on Champion International's 668,000 acre holding, Bonner will be one of North America's largest plywood plants when it reaches full capacity operations. The $27 million plywood complex has annual capacities of 300 million square feet of ⅜ in. plywood and 126 million board feet of lumber.

The first stage in the Newberry, South Carolina project was completed in 1974. One example of Champion International's strategy of making maximum use of its forest resources, the $17 million Newberry mill burns bark to operate steam veneer dryers, peels logs for plywood veneer, cuts studs from leftover log cores, and ships the residual chips to Champion Papers' Canton, N.C., pulp

Exhibit 10 *Major geographic areas that combine timberlands and manufacturing facilities owned by Champion International, Inc., 1974*

Geographic area	Timberland owned (acres)	Pulp mill	Softwood		Hardwood	
			Plywood	Sawmill	Veneer	Sawmill
Texas	524,000	1	2	2	1	—
Alabama	348,000	1	1	1	1	—
Carolinas	395,000	1	2	1	2	1
Montana	668,000	—	2	2	—	—
West Coast	460,000	—	6	3	—	—

Source: Annual Report for 1974, supplemented by *Moody's Industrial Manual,* 1974, and industry estimates.

and paper mill. Current annual capacity amounts to 90 million square feet of ⅜-in. plywood, 11.7 million board feet of studs, and 200,000 tons of chips annually.

The present Newberry mill is the keystone in U.S. Plywood's plan for a major Southeast forest products complex. Additions to the Newberry mill, and construction of a veneer mill at Elberton, Georgia, 80 miles to the west, are currently planned for the future. Supported by more than 300,000 acres of Champion International woodlands, the Newberry–Elberton complex will combine to produce 230 million square feet of ⅜-in. plywood, 117 million board feet of lumber, and 700,000 tons of chips each year.

[An] acquisition furthers the company's goal of maximum utilization of wood. The Corrigan, Texas, mill, purchased from Louisiana Pacific Corporation, has an annual manufacturing capacity of 170 million square feet of ⅜-in. plywood, and will ship 120,000 tons of residual chips to Champion Papers' Pasadena, Texas, pulp and paper mill. (Champion International, Inc., *Annual Report for 1974*, p. 19)

Distribution Channels. Champion International uses separate distribution channels for building materials, paper products, office supplies, household furniture, institutional furniture, and carpeting.

The basic wood products (softwood plywood and lumber, hardwood veneer and lumber, particleboard, and hardboard) and some of the manufactured products (flush doors, kitchen cabinets, and the chemical adhesives, sealants, and stains) are marketed in the United States through a national distribution system of 120 combined sales offices and warehouses, termed building supply centers. These centers do cover most of the major markets within the country; for example, there are four centers in Michigan, located in Detroit, Saginaw, Midland, and Battle Creek. Thirty-four percent of the sales of the centers are to construction customers, such as

builders of single family and multiunit residences, commercial contractors, mobile home manufacturers, and housing component makers; 24% of the sales of the centers are to industrial customers, such as kitchen cabinet makers, store fixture manufacturers, furniture companies, boat building firms, or toy–game–novelty producers; 35% of sales are to retail firms, including 19,000 independent lumber dealers, a number of multiyard chains, and some mass merchandisers such as discount stores; and 7% of sales are to miscellaneous accounts, primarily governmental units and the military. Sales personnel at each of the building supply centers specialize in one of the three major markets.

U.S. Plywood's program of sales force specialization was completed [during the year]. Sales force specialization means staffing each warehouse with sales experts specially trained in serving one of our three major markets. Construction market salespeople know the needs of residential builders, for example. Industrial customers are served by people who know that area intimately. And retail customers, such as lumber dealers, have their own sales and service force. This strategy has many advantages: better two-way communication between company and customer; better market penetration; and customer confidence. (Champion International, Inc., *Annual Report for 1974*, p. 23)

The same distribution system of building supply centers is used in Canada, where Weldwood of Canada operates 25 combined sales offices and warehouses, and in Hawaii, where Lewers and Cooke, a wholly owned subsidiary, has three warehouses, and is active in real estate development and residential construction.

Fine papers, both coated and uncoated, and paperboard are sold directly to printers, converters, and other large users by a printing paper sales force, with offices in 12 cities across the United States. Milk cartons, folded cartons, and rolled paper sticks are sold by a packaging paper sales force, with offices in 11 cities. In addition, there is a wholesale paper warehouse chain, with 24 different locations, that stocks both company paper products and the purchased office supplies and industrial supplies. Federal Office Products, a 100% owned subsidiary, markets the company's business stationery, envelopes, and the purchased office supplies to retail stores, while Nationwide Papers, another 100% owned subsidiary, sells the company's printing papers, stationery, envelopes, and the purchased industrial supplies to small printers and packagers and general industrial and institutional users.

> Champion's two [paper] distribution businesses performed at record levels during 1974. Nationwide, which distributes Champion's and other manufacturers' papers (75%) and industrial products, such as towels and wipes (25%) from 24 warehouse sales centers, took advantage of strong demand to increase market share. . . .
>
> Federal Office Products is the country's largest wholesaler of office equipment and business supplies. Federal stocks some 15,000 products, and distributes them exclusively to stationers and office products retailers out of 16 locations across the country. (Champion International, Inc., *Annual Report for 1974*)

Household furniture is distributed through 3,000 selected retailers, primarily the higher-quality and higher-priced furniture stores and department stores in each area. In addition, the company has established 26 Drexel/Heritage outlets in major metropolitan markets that display and sell, on an exclusive basis, the wooden and upholstered furniture manufactured by Champion International. Institutional furniture, 20% of the total furniture sales, is marketed by company salespeople directly to churches, schools, offices, motels,

and architects, with some assistance from the building supply centers.

Carpeting produced by the company is distributed through 10,000 independent retailers, including department stores, furniture stores, discount chains, and a few building supply firms.

Financial Position. The financial strength of the company, as measured by the current ratio and the debt/equity ratio, had declined from 1968 to 1974; this may be seen in Exhibit 11. All figures in Exhibit 11 are net; that is, the depreciation, depletion, or amortization charges have been subtracted from the original asset value.

Organizational Structure. In September 1974, just prior to the appointment of Mr. Andrew Sigler as president and chief executive officer of the company, Champion International was organized into three basic product groups (Building Materials, Paper and Allied Products, and Home Furnishings), with a corporate financial staff and legal staff, and a few miscellaneous corporate divisions, such as Employee Relations, Realty Sales, Timberland Management, etc. This structure is shown graphically in Exhibit 12.

The Building Materials Group included four divisions: U.S. Plywood, Weldwood of Canada, Lewers and Cooke (distributors of building supplies and builders of residential developments in Hawaii), and Diversified Products. The Diversified Products Division contained a number of miscellaneous acquisitions, such as Roberts Consolidated Industries (manufacturers of the carpeting installation materials and tools), Chemware (manufacturers of chemical adhesives, sealants, and stains), Del-Mar (manufacturers of kitchen and bathroom cabinets), and Flexible Materials (manufacturers of flexible hardwood veneer for TV cabinets, hi-fi consoles, and automotive dashboards). All of the divisions in the Building Materials Group operated under their own names; e.g., the signs on the sides of

Exhibit 11 *Balance sheets (000,000's omitted) of Champion International, Inc., and the primary financial ratios, 1968–1974*

	1968	1969	1970	1971	1972	1973	1974
Cash	$ 18	$ 15	$ 20	$ 13	$ 29	$ 30	$ 33
Market securities	14	3	4	101	72	21	17
Receivables	150	162	165	190	207	247	283
Inventories	231	263	260	293	318	367	354
Advances to subsidiaries	52	42	—	—	—	—	—
	477	485	450	597	626	665	687
Plant and equipment	386	449	502	499	532	617	795
Timber and land	142	147	165	162	262	295	271
Investments in subs.	79	81	79	96	116	112	176
Construction funds	123	85	50	42	43	47	6
	730	762	796	799	953	1,071	1,248
Total current and fixed assets	1,207	1,247	1,246	1,396	1,579	1,700	1,935
Current liabilities	178	182	181	194	257	298	327
Long-term debt	406	397	378	487	569	592	717
Deferred taxes	27	20	31	46	61	60	77
Minority in subsidiaries	29	25	26	20	17	9	8
	640	624	616	747	904	959	1,129
Preferred stock	48	51	52	54	55	55	55
Common stock	159	174	182	188	188	188	188
Retained earnings	340	395	393	403	427	479	542
Reacquired stock	2	3	3	4	5	19	21
	567	623	630	649	675	741	806
Total debt and equity	1,207	1,247	1,246	1,396	1,579	1,700	1,935
Current ratio	2.7	2.7	2.5	3.1	2.4	2.2	2.1
Debt/equity ratio (%)	69.1	60.4	56.3	71.4	80.9	81.7	90.7
Profit/equity ratio (%)	11.4	12.0	5.2	7.3	9.3	13.0	14.3

Source: Annual Report for 1974, supplemented by Moody's Industrial Manual for the respective years.

the 120 building supply centers and the lettering on the doors of the thousands of trucks delivering the building supplies all read "U.S. Plywood," not "Champion International."

The Paper and Allied Products Group included five divisions: Champion Papers (manufacturers of paper and paperboard, and marketers to large users), Champion Packaging (manufacturers and marketers of the milk cartons, juice cartons, frozen food cartons, and the drug/cosmetic boxes), Distribution Division (Nation-Wide Paper Company and Federal Office Supplies, Inc., which sold paper and paper products to small indus-

Exhibit 12 *Organizational structure of Champion International, Inc., 1973–1974*

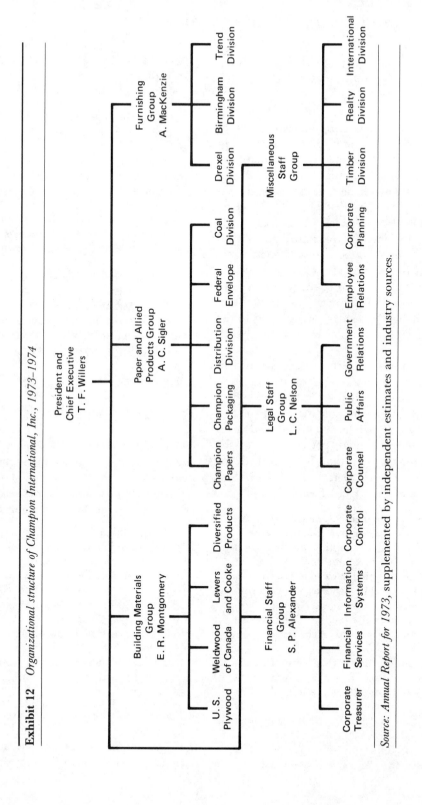

Source: Annual Report for 1973, supplemented by independent estimates and industry sources.

trial users and retail stores), Federal Envelope Division (manufacturer of envelopes in nine dispersed plants), and the Coal Division (the coal mine in Kentucky). Again, all divisions in the Paper and Allied Products Group operated under their own names; the sign at the entrance to the pulp and paper mill in Canton, North Carolina, read "Champion Paper Company," and the lettering on the office doors of any of the nine envelope manufacturing plants was "Federal Envelope Corp." The Path Fork Harlan Coal Company was included in the Paper and Allied Products Group, where it might seem to be somewhat of an anomaly, since most of the coal produced was used in the paper mills in Canton, North Carolina, and Hamilton, Ohio, although some was also shipped to the Drexel furniture plants in High Point, North Carolina.

The maintenance of the independent identities and the original corporate names seven years after the merger was felt by some industry observers to be an indication that the two companies, although legally joined, had never been totally integrated, perhaps due to the "dual management" that had marked the first few years of operations of U.S. Plywood–Champion Papers, Inc.

In the average merger, one company unquestionably takes over another, and so there isn't much question about who is going to be boss. But matters weren't anything like that clear-cut last month when Karl Robin Bendetsen moved into the handsome oak-paneled chairman's office in the U.S. Plywood's stylish, modern skyscraper on Third Avenue in New York.

Bendetsen, until then president of Champion Papers, was taking over as chairman of the newly merged U.S. Plywood–Champion Papers, Inc. Rarely have two so nearly equal companies merged: last year's $1 billion in pro forma sales, for instance, were split 54%–46% between the companies. Even the new

board of directors reflects this equality: each of the component companies have contributed 10 members to the 20-man board. And there is nothing like a dominant block of stock: the largest individual holding, running around 1% of the total voting strength, is held by a former Champion director.

Since Sol V. (Tony) Antonville retired last year, U.S. Plywood itself has had no chairman. But it has had a president, a highly effective one: Gene Brewer. Brewer, still in his old office, became president of the merged companies at the same time that Bendetsen became chairman.

Who is the new chief executive officer? Nobody. The official name for this delicate arrangement is "dual management." Brewer, in addition to being president, is chairman of the executive committee. Bendetsen, in addition to being chairman, is chairman of the finance committee. Says Gene Brewer: "This is about as close to a 50–50 merger as you can get in corporate life." (*Forbes Magazine*, March 15, 1967, p. 46)

Despite the lack of clear-cut authority inherent in the dual management compromise, organizational problems were not anticipated in the new company, doubtless because of the separate nature of the two businesses.

The old Champion and Plywood operations will function as divisions of the new company, each maintaining its own brand and product identity, but with central corporate control and coordination coming from the top corporate staff in New York. Except at the corporate level, there is little duplication of personnel, so that the internecine warfare so common in newly merged companies should be kept to a minimum. (*Forbes Magazine*, March 15, 1967, p. 49)

The cooperation and easy working relations that had been so confidently expected at the time of the merger, due to the separate natures and locations of the two businesses with their shared needs for timber, capital, and steady (noncyclical) growth, did not materialize; instead, there were reported to be personal animosities and departmental jealousies almost from the start of the joint effort.

A dozen executives and 20 or 30 other members of Champion corporate staff are moving from Hamilton and elsewhere to New York, and as they align themselves with their counterparts at U.S. Plywood, the infighting that is normal to the situation is almost certain to begin. Even before the merger became effective on Feb. 28th, at least one Champion vice president was wondering whether his new Plywood subordinate was quite the man he wanted for the job: "I get the feeling he doesn't respect me. I can't work with someone like that." Similar conflicts would seem to extend all the way to the top. Certainly Brewer and Bendetsen could not even settle upon a new name for the company, much less which of the two should become chief executive. (*Forbes Magazine,* March 15, 1967, p. 49)

It is not necessary to report in detail the organizational problems and the personnel changes which occurred between the time of the merger (1967) and the appointment of Mr. Andrew Sigler as president and chief executive officer (1974), except to indicate to some extent the situation that faced Mr. Sigler at the time of his appointment. Mr. Gene Brewer, president of U.S. Plywood from 1958 to 1967, and then president and co-manager of the merged company, resigned in 1969, allegedly due to the continuous conflict, and the lack of progress toward the resolution of that conflict.

Top executives learn to talk softly at the time of a merger since they never know what office they'll be sitting in when things shake down—reality seldom matches expectations. At U.S. Plywood–Champion Papers, Inc., the reality last week was that Gene C. Brewer, president, who had confidently welcomed

merger two years ago, was out. (*Business Week,* March 29, 1969, p. 60)

Gene Brewer was an insightful executive; in U.S. Plywood he adopted the unpopular position that Plywood, a sales-oriented company, had to move into manufacturing on a large scale to control costs. He was right, and he was elected president at age 40. Then he pushed for the merger with Champion Paper to get more efficient use of their combined timberlands, and to smooth out the countercyclical swings of the housing and paper industries by their combined sales. Again he was right, but he could not bring about the full integration that was needed. This was not for want of trying. Gene was an outgoing, friendly man of great personal charm; at Plywood he could rely on personal relationships to direct and motivate people, but this did not work in the much larger, more impersonal combined company. (Statement of an industry observer)

Despite the end of the "dual management" concept in 1969, Mr. Karl Bendetsen, chairman and chief executive officer of Champion International from 1967 to 1972, appeared to be frustrated in his effort to bring about the full integration.

Champion International, one of the largest forest-products companies in the world, has had a very tough time putting its house in order.... Karl Bendetsen, head of Champion Papers at the time of the merger, stamped his corporate style on the firm. While Bendetsen ran Champion International with an iron hand, he did not quite succeed in forming a consolidated forest products company. (*Financial World,* April 30, 1975, p. 18)

Karl Bendetsen was one tough cookie. When he became president of Champion Paper Company in 1960, it was a paternalistic, lethargic firm with shrinking profit margins. During the first week on the job, he got rid of 27 executive Cadillacs, 7 company airplanes, and a 37-man public relations staff. Things shaped up at Champion Papers when Bendetsen was in charge; you either shaped up or you shipped out. But, I think that he found in the larger and more complex company that sometimes when you pound the table, all you get is a very sore hand. (Statement of an industry observer)

In 1972, Mr. Bendetsen reached the mandatory retirement age of 65, and was replaced as chairman and chief executive officer by Mr. Thomas F. Willers.

Karl Bendetsen really didn't want to retire. He had built Champion Paper from a little paper company down in North Carolina to a large industry leader, and he had arranged the merger with U.S. Plywood in an attempt to make it into a stock market performer. I'm certain that he felt that in another month or two the pieces would start to fall into place, and he would be recognized as an industrial statesman.

But the pieces had not fallen into place, and he was being forced to retire by company policies (at age 65) and, quite frankly, by dissatisfied directors. I'm certain he looked around for a similar person, with similar characteristics, and found Thomas Willers. Willers had been president of Hooker Chemical from 1966 to 1968, had managed the aftermath of acquisitions there, and had a reputation as a strong, demanding executive.

Willers had no experience in making paper or selling lumber. His appointment was a victory for the "generic" theory of management, which is that the practice of management is similar in all industries, and that all a manager needs is a strong will, a vigorous personality, and extreme self-confidence. (Statement of a retired industry executive)

Mr. Willers recognized the problem of integrating the two halves of the company, but he appeared to be confident that this problem could be quickly resolved.

At Champion International, Willers faces the task of melding the forest products and paper businesses, where he concedes "there was a slow start, and a failure to get some people together." Now, he feels "whatever might have been errors are behind us," and management can "get on with the job with no animosity."

Willers' financial background could be a plus, since Champion's profits are only beginning to recover from the plunge they took in 1970 to $32.5 million on sales of $1.4 billion.... (*Business Week*, October 28, 1972, p. 37)

In late 1974, after three years of strong economic expansion within the United States, most indices of business activity began to turn down (see Exhibit 13), and the sales, profits, and return on investment of Champion International were in a discernible decline. Mr. Willers was replaced as Chief Executive Officer of the company in September of that year by Mr. Andrew Sigler. Mr. Sigler, as reported earlier, was 43 years old, with an A.B. from Dartmouth College, an M.B.A. from the Amos Tuck Graduate School of Business Administration at Dartmouth, two years' service in the Marine Corps, and 18 years' experience at Champion Paper Company; his most recent position was Executive Vice President of the Paper and Related Products Group of Champion International, Inc.

It was reported at the time of Mr. Sigler's appointment that the conflict and dissention that had marked the company since the merger in 1967 still existed.

When U.S. Plywood Corp. and Champion Paper, Inc., merged in 1967, creating one of the largest forest products companies in the world, it looked like a perfect marriage. By using a common resource base—timber—to manufacture both building products and paper, the new company expected to flatten out the volatile business cycles of each industry. Instead, internecine warfare between the plywood and paper factions over

Exhibit 13 *Indices of national economic activity and the sales, profits, and return on investment of Champion International, Inc., 1971–1975*

	1971	1972	1973	1974	1975
Gross national product (constant 1972 $ in billions)	$1,107	$1,171	$1,235	$1,214	$1,191
New housing starts (thousands of units)	2,085	2,379	2,057	1,352	1,171
Total paper production (10,000 tons)	5,508	5,945	6,130	5,934	5,226
Printing and fine paper prod. (10,000 tons)	1,120	1,200	1,310	1,270	1,080
Champion International sales (millions of dollars)	1,600	1,872	2,208	2,532	2,399
Champion International profits (millions of dollars)	45	60	85	100	61
Champion International r.o.e. (at beginning of year)	7.3%	9.3%	12.7%	14.2%	8.0%

Source: Statistical Abstract of the United States for 1976, pp. 393, 737; Standard and Poor's Industrial Survey for 1977, p. P-12; and Champion International, Annual Report for 1976.

everything from the corporate name to allocation of assets and priority of timber use created turmoil. (*Business Week,* March 1, 1976, p. 66)

This organizational turmoil, which was apparent both to writers for national business publications and to analysts for large financial institutions, was explained in the following terms by a retired paper industry executive:

The conflict in the company got totally out of hand. A person I know, who has since left Champion, was sent out from the paper division to the West Coast to begin a survey of wood resources as part of the preliminary planning for a new pulp mill to integrate the company's operations in that area. He was kept waiting for three days to see the senior person in the plywood division, and was then called into that person's office and told, "I don't like you. I don't like your company. You can do your survey out here, but you are to stay off our property. You are not to interfere with the plywood and lumber operations, and you are not to contact anyone in U.S. Plywood. Now, get out." That was typical of the overt fighting within the company, and there was plenty of covert fighting going on too.

I think that your students ought to understand something about the causes of this conflict, which continued despite the efforts of one very nice guy and two very tough executives. Champion International did not just have far more than its share of quarrelsome people, ready to disagree as a matter of principle, and prepared to push their own divisions and their own careers at the expense of the corporation; they certainly had some of those people—all companies do—but more important, there were two major issues that were never resolved: capital and timber.

You take a guy, and put him into a management position, and tell him that his quarterly bonus and his next promotion both depend on how well he does, and he's going to try to double the profits or the shipments or the computer services or whatever it was you put him in charge of. Now that women are joining the management level in considerable numbers, I'm going to be interested to see what happens; I think that they'll react exactly the same way. It's just human nature, or it's just human nature within our competitive society.

Now, you take that same person in a capital-intensive industry undergoing rapid technological change—and your students may think that both paper and lumber production are stodgy, unchanging technologies, but that is not true; microprocessors are used all through sawmills now, to maximize recovery and minimize waste—and you're going to have people arguing and politicking for the capital they need to double their profits or sales or services.

The capital budgeting concepts—net present value and internal rate of return—are great, but they are designed for leisurely, dispassionate analysis, under reasonably stable market conditions, and reasonably gradual technological change. With rapid technological change, externally imposed governmental regulations on pollution control, worker safety and energy usage, uncertain markets, and, particularly, personal involvement by the managers in the outcome of the capital allocation process, the quantitative analysis of alternative investments breaks down. If I set the hurdle rate at 15%, and if the investment is critical to the growth of your unit or division or group, then you'll prepare an appropriation request at 16.3%, and I won't be able to dispute you because of the new technology that I don't understand and the changing market that I can't forecast. If I set the hurdle rate at 20.0%, you'll show the same project at 20.7% return, and if I set the rate at 30.0%, you'll show why this project has to be done, regardless of return, in order to stay in the business. Quantitative investment analysis relies on forecasts of revenues and expenses, and these forecasts, under conditions of change and uncertainty, have to be subjective, not objective. When a person's career is involved, these capital budgeting decisions become political, not economic, in nature.

This problem of subjective capital appropriation requests and a political capital budgeting process is present in every company where they have a changing technology and an unstable market, but it is present in spades in Champion International because they have two technologies, both complex, and two markets, both cyclical. The people who put the company together back in 1967 understood the countercyclical nature of the paper and lumber industries, but they did not recognize the behavioral implications of these swings. One year paper will make all the money, and the next year building supplies [see Exhibit 14 for confirmation of this statement], and it is always "their" money that ought to stay in "their" division.

Then all the divisions of Champion International are vertically integrated from the forest to the retailer, and in the case of the home furnishings group, even to the final retail customer. This vertical integration creates further problems, for in a vertically integrated firm, with transfer prices and shared costs, the profit shows up wherever you want it to appear. This extends the politicking and the arguing, for now the distribution warehouses can fight with the plywood mills and the sawmills within the building material division over expansion and modernization plans. Transfer prices and shared costs are a real problem for Champion International, because so many materials are transferred between product groups. Think of a furniture plant in this company that can get hardwood lumber and veneer from the Canadian division, particleboard from the wood products division, and adhesives from a company-owned chemical plant, and then can sell its production through a company-owned retailer. Or, an even simpler illustration: the pulpmills get 30% of their wood re-

Exhibit 14 *Net sales and income from operations (000,000's omitted) of the major product groups of Champion International, Inc., 1971–1975*

	1971	1972	1973	1974	1975
Net sales of:					
Building material group	$ 809	$ 983	$1,164	$1,119	$1,106
Paper and paper products	600	669	786	1,060	976
Home furnishings	184	212	251	346	311
Other (assume real estate)	7	8	8	7	7
	1,600	1,827	2,209	2,532	2,400
Income from operations					
Building material group	62	100	142	62	44
Paper and paper products	38	34	63	171	103
Home furnishings	10	11	14	9	15
General corporate expense	(20)	(21)	(30)	(33)	(23)
Preinterest and pretax income	90	124	188	208	139

Note: Total sales by product group may not agree with Exhibits 4 to 7 due to changes in product classifications.
Source: Annual Report for 1975.

quirements in the form of wastewood chips from the plywood mills and the sawmills.

Wood supply is a real problem for this company. When you stop to think about it, most companies buy their input components from someone else (automotive assembly, for example) or they have reasonably homogeneous raw materials (as in petrochemicals or the steel industry). But timber is a replenishable natural resource with differing species and varying grades. The people who put this company together wanted integrated use of the timber, with the good logs going to the plywood mills, the medium logs to the sawmills, and the poor logs, waste materials, and logging residues to the pulpmills. But the small logs and, particularly, the logging residues cost a lot more to harvest and process (remove the bark and reduce to chip form), so that every pulpmill manager understands that he can boost his return on investment by using the larger logs. And in a paper company with 2,700,000 acres of timberland, he can find those larger logs.

Champion International is a sleeping giant. They have good timberland, modern production facilities, and an integrated product line. But they also have 150 manufacturing plants scattered all over the United States and Canada, generally located in rural areas because the timber is back there, but with poor communications and consequently with managers that are accustomed to being autonomous. They have eight—count 'em, eight—distribution channels, and 10 separate sales forces, so that they don't have the economies of scale that you might expect. And finally, they have organizational problems, so that the company has never had everyone working together to advance the interests of the corporation rather than their own interests, or the interests of their own special group. I do not envy Andrew Sigler; he has a hard job ahead of him trying to pull that company together. (Statement of a retired industry executive)

Class Assignment. Assume that you were a staff assistant to Mr. Sigler in 1974, and that soon after he became president and chief executive officer of Champion International he called you into his office and, after a discussion of the problems and potential of the company, he gave you the following assignments:

1. Develop three different organizational designs for Champion International, each combining the various elements of the company in a logical structure. Then be prepared to recommend one of your designs for immediate implementation, and be prepared to defend your recommendation. Assume that Mr. Sigler has told you, "This company has frustrated and defeated three good people; it is not going to frustrate and defeat a fourth. I want three logical alternatives, and your recommendations as to which is best, and why."

2. Start to think about control systems. How would you evaluate the performance of the managers of each of the divisions shown on your organizational chart? What do you think will be the natural reactions of these managers under your proposed measurement system; could there be any dysfunctional reactions, not in the long-term interests of the company?

3. Start to think about capital budgeting and timber allocations. How would you improve each of these decision processes, to avoid the organizational problems described in the case?

Chapter 11

STRATEGIC IMPLEMENTATION AND SYSTEMS DESIGN

Chapter 10, on the design of the organizational structure, described the need to detail the selected strategy through a series of statements about the goals and objectives, policies and procedures, programs and plans, and immediate actions for each of the product divisions within a firm, and then for each of the functional and technical units within those divisions. These statements, properly prepared, inform the members of an organization about the selected strategy, and define the individual tasks or jobs that are critical for strategic success. The organizational structure and managerial systems can then be designed to coordinate and integrate the performance of those tasks. Strategy implementation, or the achievement of the long-term competitive position selected for the firm, requires a sequence of detail → define → design. This sequence is expressed graphically as shown at the top of the next page.

Definition of the tasks required for strategic success is central to the design of the organizational structure and managerial systems. These tasks are the activities and decisions imposed by the series of detailed statements about goals and objectives, policies and procedures, programs and plans, and immediate actions. These tasks are what has to be done, and done well, for the selected strategy to succeed. A very simple example was given in Chapter 10. Readers were asked to assume that a manufacturer of small kitchen appliances had decided to expand their market coverage from the eastern and midwestern states to the West Coast. As part of this strategic change, the objective of a 25% market share after five years had been set for the marketing department, with a 5% straight-line increment per year over that time period. The distribution policy of the company was to use both large retail chains such as Sears, K-Mart, Penney's, etc., which were sold through regional offices, and local gift stores, hardware stores, appliance stores, etc., which were sold directly. The advertising policy was to use ads in Sunday newspapers and daytime television stressing local themes. A marketing program had been developed, with a budget for one salesperson to work with the large chains, three people to call on the

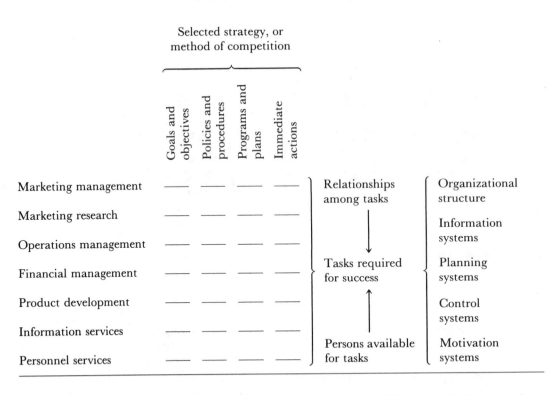

Selected strategy, or
method of competition

	Goals and objectives	Policies and procedures	Programs and plans	Immediate actions		
Marketing management	—	—	—	—	Relationships among tasks	Organizational structure
Marketing research	—	—	—	—		Information systems
Operations management	—	—	—	—		
Financial management	—	—	—	—	Tasks required for success	Planning systems
Product development	—	—	—	—		Control systems
Information services	—	—	—	—		
Personnel services	—	—	—	—	Persons available for tasks	Motivation systems

local stores, and adequate advertising expenditures. The tasks defined by these statements were set up in an organizational structure, as shown here.

It is important that these tasks required for strategic success are defined in "do-able" terms; that is, in terms that can be explained clearly and logically to an individual, with the expectation that that person will be able to perform the activities and make the decisions involved in the assignment. Tasks in many organizations are defined in general or even wistful terms, without the detail needed for understanding or the realism necessary for accomplishment. "Improve profits" is not a do-able task; it is a pious hope. But the assignment to "Establish a new sales territory on the West Coast, with the goal of obtaining 25% market share in five years following given policies on pricing, distribution, and promotion, and drawing on an explicit schedule for financial and human resources" is do-able. The tasks have to be defined by the earlier strategic statements, the definitions have to be understandable, the assignment has to be realistic, and the overall job has to be capable of performance by qualified members of the organization.

It is also important that the tasks required for strategic success be divided into the routine tasks that have to be performed for nearly every company following almost any strategy, and the key or critical tasks that must be performed exceedingly well for a specific method of competition to be successful. Cost control, for example, is critical for a manufacturer of low-margin industrial components, but it is not as important for a marketer of high-margin luxury goods. The development of a distinctive promotional appeal, and the publication of that appeal through memorable magazine and television advertising, on the other hand, is much more important for the marketer of luxury goods than the manufacturer of industrial components. Critical tasks differ for each strategy.

The critical tasks specified by a competitive strategy are the building blocks of the organizational structure; they are the activities that have to be well done for the company to succeed, and they are the areas where poor performance would endanger the financial results, or even the long-term survival of the firm. These key tasks can be in the functional management areas (marketing, production, finance, or engineering), the technical support services (cost control, information processing, market research, etc.) or in the strategic directive decisions. It is necessary to identify them, clearly and explicitly, before attempting to design the organizational structure and managerial systems to implement the strategy of a firm.

The organizational structure of a firm should be based upon an identification of the critical tasks, and upon an understanding of the relationships among those tasks. These relationships are caused by the flow of material through the productive process, and by the flow of information through the managerial process, of a company. Tasks related by the production flow can be viewed as operational stages in the production process, while the tasks related by information flow can be thought of as decision points in the managerial process. As described in Chapter 10, these operational stages and decision points within an organization often differ by managerial function, geographic location, product line, market segment, or technical content. Similarities within these classifications can be used to group the operational stages and the decision points into a first approximation of the organizational structure. The intent of this preliminary grouping should be to represent the natural material flows and information flows of the organization, to recognize similarities in the classifications of managerial function, geographic location, product line, market segment, and technical content, and to form the operational stages and decision points into a rational pattern. This is obviously not a simple task, nor is it a problem with a single solution. Many arrangements of the operational stages and decision points are possible, depending upon subjective evaluations of the relationships in material flow and information flow, and upon relative weightings of the similarities in managerial function, etc. Any arrangement, doubtless, is workable, given a logical evaluation of the relationships and a rational understanding of the similarities, but alternative forms should be studied in an attempt to select an optimal grouping of the functional and technical activities of the firm into organizational units.

These organizational units, which are groupings of the functional and technical activities of the firm, have to be coordinated. Coordination refers to the effective and efficient ordering of individual or group activities; it involves people working together for a single output rather than separately for multiple outputs. Many means of coordination are possible, such as casual dialogues, informal meetings, formal committees, project teams, corporate policies, and established procedures, but the primary means for the coordination of individuals and units within an organization is the hierarchy of authority. Authority refers to the ability of one individual within an organization to influence the actions and decisions of others within that organizational structure. Authority, of course, is never absolute, even in apparently dictatorial situations; it always involves an acceptance by the subordinate. And the hierarchy is not a precise, nor even a proportional scale. But the hierarchy of authority does establish the relative ability of individuals within an organization to influence the behavior and actions of others, and is required for the coordination of the various organizational units.

The hierarchy of authority, and the organization of units representing selected groupings of the firm, can be graphically represented by an organization chart. The organization chart is necessarily an oversimplification of the complete structure of the firm, given the complex relationships that are based on the material flow and information flow, and recognizing the multiple locations, products, markets, and technologies that are imposed by the strategy, but the two-dimensional graph does enable members of a firm to recognize and discuss their assigned positions and intended relationships.

There are numerous alternatives in the design of the organizational chart. The definitions of the critical tasks, the identification of the relationships among those tasks, the classification of the tasks for differences in managerial responsibilities, geographic areas, product lines, market segments, and technological contents, the association of tasks with similar classifications in organizational units, and the coordination of those units by a hierarchy of authority can all be combined in an almost infinite variety of patterns. It is probably impossible to achieve a perfect pattern of positions and relationships, but it is possible to prepare a logical pattern through consideration, in sequence, of the factors and concepts summarized in this chapter. There are six standard patterns—functional, extended functional, divisional, grouped divisional, matrix, and mix; see Chapter 10 for definitions and illustrations—but the most common pattern is probably the mixed, shown here at the top of the next page.

The mixed organizational chart is probably the most common, because of the flexibility of that form in meeting the requirements of complex corporate strategies. Each organizational structure, however, should be evaluated prior to adoption, and that evaluation should be on two levels: the logical consistency of the structural design and the behavioral impact on the organizational members. There are five major factors to be considered in the logic of the design:

1. Clear definitions of the tasks imposed by the strategy of the firm, particularly of the critical tasks required for strategic success. The critical tasks should be identified clearly and explicitly.
2. Distinct delineations of the relationships among the tasks brought about by the material flow of the productive process and the information flow of the manage-

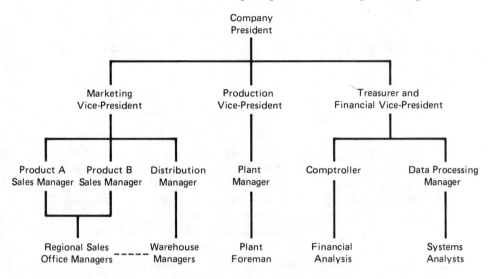

rial process. All tasks within an organization are related; the important relationships should be clear.

3. Accurate classifications of the tasks by managerial responsibility, geographic area, product line, market segment, and technical content. These differences are crucial for the preliminary grouping of the tasks.

4. Logical grouping of the tasks to combine related managerial responsibilities, geographic locations, product lines, market segments, and technological processes. The grouping of related tasks into organizational units represents the first approximation of the final structure.

5. Definite hierarchy of authority to coordinate the activities of the organizational units. Authority alone cannot be relied upon to integrate the various tasks required by the strategy of the firm; authority needs to be supplemented with systematic planning, control, and motivation procedures. Much of the balance of this chapter is concerned with the design of those systematic procedures.

The most valid evaluation of the organizational structure designed for a business firm, of course, is the performance of that firm relative to the cost of the structure. However, it is difficult to sort out the impact of environmental trends, the effect of organizational resources, and the influence of corporate strategy, structure, and systems upon performance. Therefore, it is necessary to rely upon an examination of the logical consistency of the structure, as described previously, or upon an analysis of the behavioral influences of the design. There are two major dimensions to these behavioral influences:

1. *Individual clarity.* Individuals within the organization should understand their assigned tasks, and the relationships of those tasks with others throughout the organization. Ideally, each individual should be able to reproduce the organizational chart, indicating an understanding of the critical tasks, relationships among those tasks, classifications of the tasks, etc.

2. *Organizational flexibility.* Individuals within an organization should understand the need for gradual change in their assigned tasks and in their relationships with other tasks within the organization, as the corporate strategy changes to adjust to trends and events within the environment. Individuals have a desire for stability and continuity; organizations have a need for change. Ideally, each individual should recognize the relationship between the corporate strategy and the structural design, and the consequent need for continual change.

This summary of the process of structural design has omitted the twin concepts of differentiation (problems of communication and cooperation between organizational units caused by differences in problem types, information characteristics, decision processes, etc.) and integration (specific procedures to overcome the problems of communication and cooperation between organizational units through the use of structural integrators, project teams, formal committees, etc.). These concepts were omitted not because they are unimportant, but because they are difficult to explain in summary terms. It is important to recognize the problems of differentiation, and to understand the procedures for integration, and readers are referred to Chapter 10 for that recognition and understanding.

The final organization chart depicts a number of positions, each representing certain tasks that are imposed by the strategy of the firm, related by the production processes and information flow, and grouped by similarities in managerial function, geographic area, product characteristics, etc. These tasks have to be coordinated for the complete organization to function effectively and efficiently. This coordination is accomplished partially by the hierarchy of authority within the structure, partially by the methods of integration between the units, but primarily by the procedures for planning, control, and motivation in the systems. The balance of this chapter is concerned with the design of the managerial systems for planning, control, and motivation.

Planning, control, and motivation are critical activities in the management of productive organizations, but the concepts behind these activities have been defined in very general and imprecise terms. These definitions are usually accurate, and often insightful, but not exact enough to be truly helpful in designing the managerial systems needed to routinize and assist the three activities.

1. Planning has been defined as the process of anticipating the future consequences of current actions and decisions. Planning involves consideration of the future, but it is not limited to forecasting approaching events or coming opportunities and problems; instead, it requires estimating the eventual outcome of a cause-and-effect chain stretching into the future, with interrelated causes and probabilistic effects, where the relationships and probabilities are highly uncertain and sometimes even unknown. Planning of this nature is a complex innovative process that is directed toward producing a desirable future state for an organization. Planning is not waiting for something, good or bad, to happen; instead, it is a much more active process of deciding what should be done now to adjust to apparent changes and uncertainties in the environment, and then forecasting the outcomes of these current decisions and actions in measurable terms at definite times in the future. In summary, managerial planning sets standards for in-

dividual or divisional performance in the short term that should lead to an improved organizational position over the long term.

2. Control is the complement of planning; it is the process of comparing actual results with the expected outcomes of the planning process, analyzing the variances, and instituting changes if needed. Control implies a set of standards, a comparison of performance against those standards on a repetitive or continual basis, and the possibility of corrective action when a deviation occurs. Feedback and correction are central to the concept of control; these elements are present in a physical system, such as the thermostat controlling a furnace, and should be present in a managerial system, as in the budget controlling expenditures. Managerial control is a complex comparative process that is directed toward initiating operational changes to achieve the desired future state of the organization. Control of this nature is not primarily repressive, setting boundaries to action, or generally censorious, allocating blame for shortfalls, although both of these aspects are present in any system; instead, it is a more positive process for deciding what should be changed now to achieve the future outcomes of the planning process. Managerial control, in summary, corrects individual and divisional performance in the short term to lead to an improved organizational position over the long term.

3. Motivation is the complement of control; it is the process of rewarding the individual or division whose performance has brought actual results close to the planned outcomes. Motivation attempts to create conditions so that members of an organization can fulfill their own needs, which often differ on numerous dimensions, by meeting the organizational standards. Goal congruity is central to the motivational concept; each individual has needs which should be recognized and expectations which should be understood, and each organization has standards which must be met. Motivation of this nature can be either positive or negative, with both rewards and sanctions, but the incentives have to be tied to the anticipated outcomes of the planning process, to the comparative evaluations of the control system, and to the needs and expectations of the organizational members. Managerial motivation, in summary, rewards or punishes individual and divisional performance over the short term in order to lead toward an improved organizational position in the long term.

Planning, control, and motivation are obviously related, both conceptually and pragmatically, and are obviously needed to direct and coordinate the activities of an organization, both vertically between the levels of the hierarchy and horizontally across the functional and technical units of the division. Coordination and direction are the outcomes of the planning → control → motivation sequence, but it is difficult to develop formal procedures, or systems, to implement this sequence because of the range of activities represented by each of the segments or stages. The activities involved in planning, for example, can differ depending upon the time horizon (long term, midterm, or short term), the managerial level (upper, middle, or operating management), the organizational perspective (corporate, divisional, or functional) and the investment requirements (large, medium, or small) of the project. Obviously, planning for a major acquisition at the corporate level is conducted differently than planning for a capital expenditure at one of the product divisions, or planning for monthly expenses at one of the functional units; the depth of the study, the reliability of the information, and the extent of the commitment all differ. The differences in process and content, however, can be understood by separating the general concept of planning into three specific applications of strategic planning for the method of competition, program planning for the allocation of resources, and budgetary planning for the projection of results. The concept of control can also be divided into the establishment of standards, the recording of performances, and the analysis of variances, while motivation can be expressed as the evaluation of contributions, the design of incentives, and the responses of individuals. These stages in the planning → control → motivation sequence, their relationships, and some of the managerial techniques or methods associated with them, can be shown graphically:

Planning system	Strategic planning (method of competition)	Environmental assumptions Organizational resources Managerial intentions Strategic alternatives
	Program planning (allocation of resources)	Net present value Internal rate of return Cost–benefit analysis Competitive position analysis
	Budgetary planning (projection of results)	Revenue forecasts Expense estimations Numerical measures Descriptive standards
Control system	Operational accounting (recording of performance)	Cost accumulation systems Cost allocation systems Responsibility centers Transfer prices and shared costs
	Comparative evaluation (analysis of variances)	Organizational control Program control Management control Operational control
Motivation system	Organizational response (design of incentives)	Perceptual response Financial response Positional response Personal response
	Individual response (actions and decisions)	Personal influence Interpersonal influence Social influence Cultural influence

Strategic Planning. Strategic planning, of course, refers to the design of the long-term method of competition for a business firm, or the long-term concept of service for a governmental, educational, or medical organization. The inputs into the strategic planning process are the organizational performance and position which should be compared to the corporate mission and charter and to the managerial values and attitudes, the environmental characteristics and trends which result in specific opportunities and risks, the organizational assets and skills which provide explicit strengths and weaknesses, and the range of strategic alternatives open to the firm or service organization. These inputs, and the outputs in terms of product–market positioning, product–process positioning, portfolio balancing, and acquisition analysis, were the topics of the first six chapters. The relationship decision, or the selection of the method of competition or concept of service to be followed by the organization appeared, in those chapters, to be static; that is, to be made once, and then implemented by the structure and systems design. In reality, all of the input factors—the corporate performance, managerial intentions, environmental characteristics, and organizational resources—are continually changing, and the strategic decision must be continually reviewed and corrected. This continual review and, when needed, correction, requires a formal procedure, or system, to focus attention on these changes, and on the future opportunities and risks. In most organizations, managerial attention is focused on immediate problems, not future possibilities. The essential purpose of strategic planning should be to consider the future, and prepare for it; numerous examples can be cited of business firms and service organizations that have failed to do this.

The formal procedures for strategic planning differ depending upon the size and diversity of the firm. A small company, with a single product or product line, needs only to establish a regular time for meetings of the president and functional managers, and a reporting system for economic conditions and industry trends. This group of executives, aided by common interests and complementary activities, can examine assumptions about the future, evaluate alternatives for the company, and establish plans for the products and services.

Strategic planning in a large company, with multiple product–market positions and product–process postures within a single industry, or across multiple industries, is much more complex than in a smaller firm, and has to be iterative, with continual recycling between the hierarchical levels of corporate executives, divisional managers, and functional personnel. The planning process usually starts with environmental assumptions about the future, prepared by the corporate staff; all divisions should use the same base of economic, social, and political data in their planning. The economic assumptions may be limited to business activity and price-level forecasts, or may range much wider to include fiscal and monetary policies, regulatory and legislative actions, tax changes, wage rates, material costs, etc. Each division then provides a study of its current position and past performance within the industry, generally with data on industry sales, market percentages, company revenues, manufacturing costs, expected margins, divisional expenses, corporate allocations, capital charges, and pretax profits. These figures are usually stated for the past five years, estimated for the current year, and anticipated for the next five years. The nine-year span makes trends and changes very obvious. Information is also normally provided on the market shares of the major competitors in the industry, and the strengths/weaknesses of the division versus these leaders on such dimensions as product design, brand reputation, distribution coverage, promotional effectiveness, productive capacity, manufacturing costs, etc.; the intent is to support the sales forecasts and show the reasons for the profit trends. Ideally, different forecasts should be prepared comparing the expected results of alternative strategies, and the market assumptions and financial requirements of these other methods of competition. In a meeting between corporate executives and divisional managers, the alternatives are examined, a strategy is selected, the forecasts are considered, and the projections are eventually accepted or revised.

Strategic planning in large companies was earlier thought to start with a statement of corporate objectives, usually in financial terms, and the divisional plans were expected to add up to meet those objectives. This directive planning forced the divisional managers to prepare forecasts based on corporate expectations, not industry conditions, and resulted in errors, mistakes, and revisions. Directive planning can be successful in an expanding market since it creates a challenge which may be achievable; in a static or stagnant industry, it merely creates an illusion which may be fatal.

Ideally, strategic planning should be innovative and imaginative, based upon a good understanding of the industry and upon insightful recognition of possible changes in the method of competition. In actual practice, planning is often routine, with straight-line projections of revenues, costs, and profits. The routine nature and linear projections are often a result of the formalized planning process that requires equivalent figures from each division for consideration at the corporate level. A "fill in the blanks and get back to work" attitude can easily develop from the use of standardized forms and repetitive estimates. Chapter 12, on the design of the planning system, will consider means of increasing the innovative content of strategic planning, and avoiding the routinized performance.

Program Planning. Program planning is the second step or stage in the planning → control → motivation sequence. A program can be thought of as a set of coordinated activities designed to improve the competitive position of a business firm, or to expand the beneficial services of a nonprofit organization. The introduction of a new product, the modernization of an existing plant, or the addition of a complementary service are all examples of programs. Programs tend to have a lengthy time span, three to five or more years, multiple activities, and extensive assets; they are large projects derived from the strategic plan of the organization, and they specify the personnel required and the resources needed to reach the competitive position or service level defined by the selected strategy.

Program planning is used to specify the activities and to allocate the resources needed to achieve a given strategic position. The activities are usually described in very general terms, almost on the level of the number of people required to perform each of the functional and technical tasks; more specific definitions of these tasks are left to the budgetary planning stage where measures of performance are established and targets for achievement are negotiated on a short-term basis. Changes in the program and changes in the personnel permit short-term planning, often on a one-year cycle, for the activity specifications, but capital allocations have to be on a longer-term basis. The financial inflows and outflows for each program or project, and the relative timing of those cash movements, must fit the overall capital sources and uses of the organization. Most active organizations have many more beneficial uses for capital than available sources, and are consequently continually short of cash, so the flow of funds has to be accurately estimated, and the use of those funds carefully planned. Program planning estimates the flow of funds over the life of each program or project, and then evaluates the relative desirability of these programs or projects. There are three formal methods for this evaluation:

1. *Financial return.* The financial return models are based on the relative size and timing of the cash inflows and outflows. Payback period and the accounting rate of return are the simplest of three comparative financial models; the payback period uses the total of the annual profits after tax plus the depreciation from the project over the period of time needed to equal the initial investment as the ranking criteria, while the accounting rate of return uses the ratio of the average annual profits after tax plus the depreciation of the project to the initial investment. Both of these methods neglect the time value of money, and attach no importance to the timing of the cash flows.

   The net present value method of investment analysis uses the difference between the sum of the present value of the expected cash outflows and the sum of the present value of the expected cash inflows, both at a given discount rate, as the ranking criteria for programs. Each future cash flow is discounted at the rate of $1/(1 + i)^n$, where i equals the interest rate or cost of capital, and n equals the number of years. The internal rate of return method of investment analysis uses the discount rate that equates the present value of the expected cash outflows (investments) with the present value of the cash inflows (after-tax profits plus depreciation charges); in essence, the internal rate of return of a project is the discount rate at which the net present value is zero. Both of these methods neglect the uncertainties inherent in the estimation of future cash flows.

   Computer simulation is the most complex method of investment analysis. The risk in each projected cash flow is represented by a distribution of the likely events in that cash flow, and a probability estimate for each event. The simulation program generates a probability distribution of the net present value of the project, given probability distributions of the positive and negative cash flows. The mean value and standard deviation of the net present value distribution can be used as the ranking criteria for the program. This method neglects the problem of interdependence of cash flows from one period to another. Most simulation programs assume independence; if, instead, correlation between periods is assumed (earlier failure of an investment project probably correlates with later failure), the mean value of the distribution will remain the same, but the standard deviation will expand. It is difficult to use an expanded distribution as a ranking criteria for investment projects.

2. *Cost–benefit analysis.* Cost–benefit analysis is often used in nonprofit institutions as a substitute for the capital budgeting procedures, or financial return models,

used in business organizations. The financial return models for investment analysis assume that the positive cash flows are the benefits of the project, or can be used as surrogates for those benefits. In most nonprofit or nonbusiness situations, the cash inflows may have very little relationship with the benefits of the project since the revenues are often not determined by either market pricing or full costing. Instead, revenues may be determined by the recipient's ability to pay, and the services are provided because they are felt to be needed, not because they are thought to be either cost-effective or price-elastic. The costs of a nonprofit program can be measured by the cash outflows, or use of resources, but the benefits have to be gauged on some other measure than the cash inflows, and a financial equivalent for the services is often used. This financial equivalent is usually based on an estimate of social and individual benefits as, for example, in the incremental tax payments and income potential of a high school graduate versus a nongraduate over the person's lifetime, discounted back to present value, that are often used as the economic rationale for public education. The financial equivalents are subjective, and can be arbitrary, but cost–benefit analysis does provide a ranking criterion for the investment analysis of programs in the public sector.

3. *Competitive position analysis.* Both financial return models and cost–benefit techniques concentrate on the size and timing of cash flows, or on the cash equivalents for social and individual benefits, as the ranking criteria for programs developed to implement a selected strategy. A third ranking method, although much more difficult to quantify, centers on the competitive position or service level likely to be achieved by the program. The competitive position of a firm is difficult to measure, except in terms of market share, share growth, or productive efficiency, and the attainment of a service level for a nonprofit organization is even more troublesome to evaluate, but these are the primary determinants of long-term success for the respective organizations, and should be recognized in program or project evaluations. Discounted cash flow models, whether with actual or equivalent inflows, give primary emphasis to short-term results, because of the compounding of the discount rate over time, and ignore such essential results as pollution control, safety improvement, or support service expansion because of their lack of positive cash flows. Competitive position analysis will become more important, over time, than financial return models in the comparative evaluation of programs to implement a selected strategy.

The usual procedure for the generation and approval of the program plans requires development of alternative programs at the divisional level, following the selected strategy or method of competition of the corporation. Program planning, in essence, computes the capital cost of the strategy, and considers alternative means of achieving a given competitive position or service level, not whether that position or level is desirable or attainable, which is the province of strategic planning. Most program planning is done by financial analysts; one or two alternatives are chosen by the divisional managers, and then submitted to the corporate executives for final selection, approval, and allocation of the constrained capital.

Budgetary Planning. Budgetary planning is the third step or stage in the planning → control → motivation sequence. Budgets are estimates of the revenues and expenses associated with each program or project developed to achieve the competitive position or service level envisaged in the selected strategy. Budgets really are programs expressed in terms of income and expenses; they detail and "fine tune" the programs. A budget also assigns responsibility for the activities contained in the program. This assignment of responsibility is probably the most important element in the definition of the concept: a budget is not so much a forecast of results as it is a commitment by members of a unit within an organization to achieve those results. The distinction between a forecast and a commitment is essential in understanding the planning process, from strategy selection to resource allocation to budgetary responsibility. The budget brings members of the functional and technical units within each division of an organization to agree, in essence, to move partway toward reaching the competitive position proposed by the selected strategy. The overall planning process, and the differences between the three steps or stages, can be summarized in terms of the organizational level, the time horizon, and the conceptual output:

Planning stage	Organizational level	Time horizon	Major output of the planning stage
Strategic planning	Corporate	5–10 years	Selection of the method of competition leading to a competitive advantage for the firm
Program planning	Divisional	3–5 years	Allocation of the resources and plan of activities needed to achieve the competitive position
Budgetary planning	Unit	12 months	Commitment by members of the organization to achieve goals leading towards the competitive position

The time horizon for each stage is, obviously, an average or typical range, and is not meant to be an absolute requirement. The time horizon usually varies with the industry. Public utilities, with long time spans needed for regulatory approval and plant construction, generally perform strategic planning over 12 to 15 years, and program planning over 5 to 8 years. Consumer goods manufacturers often are on a 5-year and 3-year sequence, but program planning for consumer products with a high style content would be closer to 1 year, or even less. Almost all budgetary planning, however, is on a 12-month cycle since the intent is to forecast revenues and expenses with reasonable accuracy, and to have the forecasts comparable to the financial records of the standard fiscal year for control purposes.

Budgetary planning, usually over a 12-month period, results in a commitment by members of the functional and technical units within a division to perform program activities that lead toward the competitive posture or service level of the organizational strategy. Most of the units within a division are responsible for activities in more than one program; their activities, in essence, cut across the programs. As shown, the overall corporate strategy can thus be viewed as a matrix, with numerous programs for allocating resources and various units for performing activities. This conceptual view of the planning process is critical in establishing the control procedures, for it is necessary to evaluate separately the performance, and when needed revise the content, of the corporate strategy, the divisional programs, and the functional and technical budgets. Many of the problems in both planning and control come from confusion among these separate managerial functions.

	Research Unit	Marketing Unit	Engineering Unit	Production Unit	Distribution Unit
Program A Existing Business					
Program B Product Development					
Program C Market Expansion			Overall Strategy of the Firm		
Program D Cost Improvement					
Program E Capacity Increase					

Budgetary planning combines forecasting the revenues and expenses associated with the various programs of a division, and setting goals and objectives for the functional and technical units involved in those programs. The goals and objectives are the results that are expected in research, marketing, engineering, production, distribution, and the various staff units; they are statements of where the functional and technical units are expected to be at specific times in the future. These goals give members of the units the sense of direction and purpose that is necessary to coordinate their efforts, and they permit evaluation of the performance of the departments. They serve, in short, as targets for achievement and as standards for control.

These "targets for achievement and standards for control" can be financial, nonfinancial, or nonquantitative measures of performance. The financial measures are based upon anticipated revenues, or expenses over a 12-month period, and give the appearance of precision and detail, but in reality revenues, costs, and profits are summary figures for many diverse activities in the functional or technical units, and are subject, of course, to the accounting conventions. Financial standards define areas of responsibility, provide constraints on spending, and permit forecasts of cash flow, but they do not accurately reflect short-term performance. Nonfinancial measures are needed to supplement the budgeted revenues, expenses, and profits; many of the nonfinancial measures are also quantitative, and are based upon unit measures such as total output, ratio measures such as output per worker, or percentage measures such as reject rate or labor utilization. These nonfinancial numerical standards can provide detailed and precise measures of performance, but only for the organizational units where the output is clearly measurable on a single scale, as in the line production of standardized products. The output from job shop processing of nonstandardized products, or the delivery of different services on a demand basis, cannot be measured on a single scale, and the performance of these organizational units must be evaluated by surrogate measures such as the number of satisfied customers, by process measures such as the waiting time for service, by input measures such as the number of persons employed, or by nonquantitative measures such as a subjective impression of efficiency. None of these measures of performance is fully satisfactory; the input and process standards do not accurately reflect outputs, but they are less liable to manipulation and intentional error than are the surrogate and subjective measures.

Input and process standards of performance are often used for budgetary planning since the outputs of many organizational units are difficult to measure in either financial or nonfinancial terms. Most organizational activities can be conceptualized in an input → process → output framework. The complete firm, obviously, takes the input factors of materials, labor, and capital, and processes them to produce goods and services and, properly managed, profits for a return on the capital. Each of the divisions within a firm, and each of the functional and technical units within the divisions, even market research departments and bookkeeping offices, use known inputs to process specific outputs. This simple conceptual framework of the input → process → output relationships is important for an understanding of planning and control systems since measurement and evaluation must be directed at one or more of those stages.

Ideally, outputs should be measured. Most organizational units exist to produce a good or service as part of a program within the overall strategy of the corporation, so that measurement and evaluation of that good or service should be the most valid means of determining how well each unit is performing. However, many services, such as market research or bookkeeping, and some goods, such as nonstandardized products, cannot easily be measured in either financial or numerical terms, so that budgetary planning must be based upon either the process or the inputs, not the outputs.

The process within an organizational unit may be structured, with a known relationship between inputs and outputs, or it may be unstructured, without that known relationship. Structured processes tend to be repetitive, stable activities, often in the production area. The manufacture of garden rakes would be an example of a structured process with known inputs of material and labor. Standard cost systems can be used for structured processes since valid direct and indirect costs can be computed at various levels of production. Unstructured processes require judgment and a sequence of managerial decisions for completion; they tend to be unique, nonrepetitive tasks, often in the engineering or marketing area, without a known relationship between inputs and outputs. The design of a new garden rake, with reinforced plastic substituting for the usual spring steel, would be an example of an unstructured process since it is impossible to estimate accurately the engineering time needed to complete the design. Discretionary cost systems are usually used for nonstructured processes since valid direct and indirect costs cannot be computed, and the actual expense level rests with the decisions of the unit manager. Creative tasks, by definition, have no prior performances upon which to base standard costs, so that neither the input requirements nor the output quality can be predicted with assurance, and process standards have to be used. These process standards are often expressed in the form of stages in the creative process that are to be reached at given times and costs; the time and cost relationships among the stages can be estimated in a formal project review method such as PERT or CPM. These relationships, however, are estimates, based upon managerial judgment, not known times and costs based upon prior performance. The planning and control of unstructured, creative processes is difficult, yet will become more common as economic, technical, and governmental changes bring greater uncertainties, and more unique tasks, to organizational management.

Measures of performance for the planning and control of organizational units, whether based on input requirements, process stages, or output results, and also whether concerned with structured or unstructured processes, can be single, multiple, or composite in nature. Single measures are estimates along one dimension only, such as input costs, output revenues, or process efficiency. The assumption of a single measure is that all managerial activities in a functional or technical unit can be summarized on one scale, and the consequence is that all managerial attention tends to be focused on that scale, perhaps to the exclusion of other important criteria. Multiple measures avoid the problems of concentrating upon a single factor, but they impose other problems in selecting the more important versus less important measures, and may even prevent agreement on what constitutes "good" or "poor" performance. Composite measures combine multiple scales with explicit weighting for each; the weights are on the basis of percentages, and may change over time or between organizational units. Composite measures are theoretically most satisfactory, but actually least understood by the managers of the organizational units they are designed to control, and most liable to manipulation by those managers through trade-offs between the long term and the short term, and between risks and returns.

In summary, budgetary planning refers to the estimation of the revenues and expenses associated with each program or project developed to achieve the competitive position or service level envisaged in the selected strategy, and to the establishment of the goals and objectives for the functional and technical units involved in those programs. In many instances, the goals and objectives for the organizational units and the revenues and expenses of the program plans are identical; the functional and technical units are simply held responsible for meeting the financial forecasts for each program. Often, however, these financial standards must be supplemented with nonfinancial measures, expressed in numerical rather than monetary terms, or with nonquantitative measures that are subjective rather than objective. The intent, in every instance, is to develop measures of organizational performance that will serve as targets for achievement and as standards for control. These measures of organizational performance may be based upon the outputs, the process, or the inputs of the individual units, and the processes may be structured, with repetitive and routine activities that have a known input-output relationship, or unstructured, with unique and creative managerial tasks that have unknown or uncertain input-output relationships. The development of valid measures of organizational performance through budgetary planning is difficult, but there are three generalizations that should be remembered:

1. Budgetary plans should tie back to the strategic plans for the long-term method of competition selected for the firm, and to the program plans for the allocation of resources and the definition of activities needed to achieve that competitive position. Following the three-level concept of organizational planning, the annual budget should be seen as a consequence of the prior planning, not an independent exercise.

2. Budgetary plans should reflect the expected revenues and expenses of the programs, and should provide standards of performance for the organizational units that are responsible for the various activities within each program. Following the matrix concept of budgetary planning, the annual budget should be seen as a commitment to organizational performance, not as a forecast of financial results.

3. Budgetary plans should be understood by the manager and other members of each organizational unit, and should be based upon known cost relationships or discretionary expense amounts. Following the input → process → output concept of organizational performance, the annual budget should be seen as a realistic and measurable level of achievement, not as an arbitrary assignment.

The process of establishing an annual budget that leads directly from the prior strategic plans and program plans of the organization, that reflects the expected revenues and expenses of the programs and provides valid standards of performance for the units, and that is understood and accepted by the managers and members of those organizational units is difficult. It is particularly difficult to achieve these objectives of budgetary planning for the unstructured processes within an organization, which probably constitute, depending upon the industry, at least 50% of all managerial activities in organizations. The problem is that the manager and members of an organizational unit responsible for an unstructured managerial process can usually meet arbitrary or unilateral standards of performance by either cutting costs or reducing quality. To avoid the appearance of unilateral or arbitrary decisions on performance standards, it is usually recommended that greater participation in the budgetary process be achieved, and that less incrementalization and formalization of the budgets be attempted. There are problems with all three recommendations:

1. *Problems of increased participation.* Budgetary planning is the annual process of forecasting revenues and expenses for the programs, and setting standards of performance for the organizational units, generally over a 12-month period. In forecasting these revenues and expenses, and setting these standards, it is often recommended that the managers of the organizational units responsible for the performance of program activities participate in the process to increase organizational commitment and individual motivation. Participation does generate commitment, and the recommended means of achieving participation is to develop the revenue and expense forecasts and the organizational performance standards through superior/subordinate negotiations. This process is termed management by objectives; the intent is that the subordinate responsible for the performance and the superior responsible for the review of that performance

should together establish the scales of measurement and the expected levels of performance on those scales, prior to evaluation. It is believed that the process of negotiation, with a sequence of proposal, counterproposal, compromise, and eventual agreement, will result in challenging but achievable organizational standards and control criteria. The concept is appealing, but the problem is that the annual budget is developed from the strategic plans setting the long-term competitive posture of the firm, and the program plans allocating the resources and defining the activities needed to achieve that competitive posture, and consequently many of the standards of performance for the organizational units cannot be changed in participatory discussions, but have been assumed in the prior planning. It is, of course, possible to request changes in those prior plans, but that is often organizationally difficult. Participatory discussions on setting budgetary standards can easily lead to feelings of frustration and cynical distrust on the part of the subordinate, and to an apprehension of interpersonal incompetence on the part of the superior. Participative discussions for the purposes of mutual understanding of the prior plans, not for the purpose of establishing independent standards, probably are more productive in complex organizations.

2. *Problems of reduced incrementalism.* Incrementalism refers to the very common tendency, in preparing an annual budget, to adjust the prior year's figures to meet the current conditions, and not to base the budget on the corporate strategy and the program plans. Incrementalism starts with the concept that each organizational unit is "entitled to" an amount which, at the minimum, is the same as last year's, and which probably would be increased by an organization-wide percentage to reflect growing costs and greater inflation. Incremental budgets rely on the prior period as the frame of reference, rather than on the prior plans. Zero-based budgeting was developed to avoid incrementalism; this budgetary process identifies the activities within each organizational unit, and prepares alternatives for the activities. These alternatives may be different ways of performing the given activity, through a new technology, for example, or a more centralized department, or different levels of performance. Each alternative is then costed so that the superior, in the superior/subordinate discussions, can select an improved method of performance or a changed level of effort. The intent of zero-based budgeting is to force examination of the annual expense levels, and to analyze and justify each activity; the result is actually to place greater emphasis upon the participative discussions, because of the wide range of possible expenditures, and upon the interpersonal aspects of those discussions. Annual budgets in complex organizations should be based upon the strategic plans of an organization, and upon the program plans allocating the resources and defining the activities needed to implement the selected strategy, and not upon interpersonal negotiations.

3. *Problems of reduced formalization.* Formalization refers to the common tendency for the managers and members of organizational units, once an annual budget has been approved, with expected revenues and expenses and accepted standards of performance, to adhere to that budget regardless of changing conditions. A formalized budget tends to freeze organizational activities for a year, despite obvious environmental changes. This tendency is particularly apparent during peri-

ods of economic expansion; the normal reaction of a divisional or functional manager is to adhere to the budget over the short term, and neglect the long-term consequences. Supplemental budgets, which provide additional amounts above the original allocation, and variable budgets, which offer different amounts depending upon the level of production, can be used, but both suffer from time delays, and both are reactive rather than proactive. Functional and technical managers should be able to follow events; instead, they tend to follow the budget, and no budgetary process seems to be able to provide the flexibility that is needed.

Budgetary planning is needed to estimate the revenues and expenses associated with each program in the organizational strategy, and to establish standards of performance for the functional and technical units involved in those programs. The development of valid budgetary plans that accurately measure unit performance and that are understood and accepted by unit managers is difficult. This difficulty is increased by the problems involved in the participation, incrementalization, and formalization of the budgetary process. Despite the problems, it is necessary to estimate revenues and expenses, and set standards of performance, to provide for the coordination of efforts and integration of activities that are needed for successful organizational direction. Strategic management truly is an art and not a science, and the budgetary planning process is one of the primary examples of that distinction.

Operational Accounting. Operational accounting is the fourth stage in the planning → control → motivation sequence. It follows budgetary planning, which in essence is the projection of results, and involves the recording of those results. The results may be financial, numerical, or qualitative; the accounting process normally records only the financial results, but operational accounting is an expanded form to record both the financial and numerical outcomes of managerial activities.

The financial results of managerial activities include revenues, expenses, assets, and liabilities. Financial accounting centers on the recording and proper valuation of the assets and liabilities; managerial accounting is involved with the accumulation and proper allocation of revenues and expenses, both to organizational programs and to organizational units, with primary emphasis upon expenses and costs. This note will discuss, in very summary form, types of costs, and types of cost accumulation systems and allocation systems, before describing responsibility centers for the control of costs and revenues.

1. *Types of costs.* Costs are generally divided between direct versus indirect and between fixed versus variable for allocation to products, processes, or services.
   a. *Direct costs* can be identified with specific departments, products, or processes. Indirect costs cannot be easily identified for allocation, and have a general applicability. In a small machine shop, direct costs would include labor and material; indirect costs would include the owner's salary.
   b. *Fixed costs* remain constant over a range of production rates; semifixed costs vary in a discontinuous fashion or step function with production, and variable costs vary directly with the production rate. Again using the example of

a small machine shop, a fixed cost would be the foreman's wages, a semifixed cost would be the electric bill for both power and light, and a variable cost would be the material used in production.

2. *Types of cost accumulation systems.* Costs may be accumulated for allocation to products, processes, or services by the job, by the product, by the process, or by the area:

a. *Job costing* collects expenses for each individual product as it moves through the production process; it is used where products are individually produced and heterogeneous. An example of job costing would include a company making nonstandardized machinery for customers' orders.

b. *Product costing* collects expenses for each group of similar products as they move through the production process; it is used where products are mass-produced, but still heterogeneous. An example of product costing would include a company making standardized machines for inventory.

c. *Process costing* collects expenses for a time period, with no attempt to separate those costs by individual products or groups of products; it is used when products are mass produced and homogeneous. An example of process costing would include a refinery producing one grade of gasoline.

d. *Area costing* collects expenses for a physical space, with no attempt to separate these costs by individual products or groups of products; it is used for overhead expenses that are recorded by each area, or center, responsible for the incurrence of the cost. An example of area costing would be an engineering department within a machine shop or oil refinery.

3. *Types of cost allocation systems.* Costs may be allocated to products, processes, or services through direct costing, standard costing, or full-costing systems:

a. *Direct costing* charges the variable product costs of direct labor, direct material, and direct overhead, with no allocation of fixed expenses or indirect overhead to the product, process, or service. Direct costs are those that vary directly with the rate of production; at the close of each accounting period, the actual indirect costs are charged to the period as general overhead expenses.

b. *Standard costing* charges the estimated production costs of standard labor, standard material, and standard overhead, with an allocation of fixed expenses and indirect costs at a predetermined level of production, to the product, process, or service. Standard costs are those that should have been incurred at a given level of production; at the close of each accounting period, the actual indirect costs are reconciled with the standard overhead costs through variance analysis.

c. *Full costing* charges the actual production costs of direct labor, direct material, and a "fair" share of the overhead, with an allocation of fixed expenses and indirect costs at a predetermined charge per labor hour, square footage, or service usage. Full costs are those that were incurred at a given level of production; at the close of each accounting period, the actual indirect costs should have been completely allocated to the specific units of production.

4. *Cost-decision analysis.* Many financial decisions involve alternative courses of ac-

tion, with different costs attached to each alternative. This is differential costing, and while it is not directly applicable in program costing (determining the direct and indirect costs associated with a specific program) or responsibility costing (determining the direct and indirect costs associated with an organizational unit), the cost terms are familiar, and should be explained to avoid confusion.

a. *Out-of-pocket costs* are relevant to a financial decision since they require an allocation of current resources to the alternative under study, while sunk costs represent a resource previously allocated, and thus should be irrelevant to the decision.

b. *Marginal costs* are those expenses added by producing one extra unit of the good or service, while incremental costs are those added by producing a predetermined number of additional units; both marginal and incremental costs are usually relevant to a financial decision.

5. *Cost-process analysis.* Costs within an organizational process may be engineered or discretionary, depending upon the nature of the input → process → output relationships. Again these concepts are only indirectly applicable in program costing and responsibility costing, and the structured versus unstructured nature of organizational processes has been explained previously, but the cost terms are familiar, and should be defined to avoid confusion:

a. *Engineered costs* are the expenses associated with a structured organizational process in which there is a known relationship between inputs and outputs. The term "engineered" is used since it is possible to make valid engineering-type estimates of the costs of all the input components.

b. *Discretionary costs* are the expenses associated with an unstructured organizational process in which there is no known relationship between the inputs and the outputs. The term "discretionary" is used since it is not possible to make valid estimates of the costs of the input components, and the expense level must be set by individual judgment and managerial discretion. As discussed previously, at least 50% of all managerial processes are unstructured, and involve discretionary costs, and that percentage will increase as economic, technical, and regulatory changes bring greater uncertainty and unpredictability to managerial tasks.

Program costing and responsibility costing allocate the direct costs and an equitable share of the indirect costs to organizational programs designed to achieve a competitive position envisaged in the corporate strategy, or to an organizational unit responsible for performing some of the activities required by the program. These costs may be accumulated by job costing, product costing, process costing, or area costing, and may be allocated by direct costing, standard costing, or full costing; the essential element is that both revenues and costs be accumulated accurately and allocated "fairly." Fairness is not an objective standard, it is a subjective belief by the manager and members of an organizational unit that these summary financial measures have been carefully prepared, can be partially controlled, and will eventually be used. Accurate accumulation, equitable allocation, and eventual use of financial measures of performance is termed responsibility accounting. There are four types of responsibility centers, depending upon the type of financial measure used for comparative evaluation.

1. *Cost center.* A cost center is an organizational unit in which the manager is assumed to have control over expenses but not revenues, and in which the performance of the unit is evaluated by a comparison of actual versus budgeted costs. For a cost center with engineered costs, the budget can be prepared with accurate estimates of the input components, often through the use of a standard costing system, and the comparison of actual versus budgeted performance is meaningful, after analysis of the variances caused by changes in the input costs or in the output volume. For a cost center with discretionary costs, in which the budget is prepared with managerial judgments on the level of input components, the comparison of actual versus budgeted performance is not meaningful, except as a means of balancing planned and actual expenditures.

2. *Revenue center.* A revenue center is an organizational unit in which the manager is assumed to have control over income but not expenses, although the unit is often constrained by a fixed-amount budget. Marketing departments and sales offices are often evaluated as revenue centers; some technical units such as internal consulting and personnel development staffs can also be considered as revenue centers through the use of a pricing system in which other organizational units using these services, on an elective basis, have to pay for them, and thus provide a partial measure of the performance of the staff groups.

3. *Profit center.* A profit center is an organizational unit in which the manager is assumed to have control over both revenues and expenses, and in which the performance of the organizational unit can be evaluated through a comparison of actual versus budgeted profits. Profit, of course, summarizes a number of widely different managerial activities in a single financial measure, and is an easily understood term, but there are problems. First, profit for an organizational unit is the result of accounting conventions, based on current revenues and historical costs, with some arbitrary allocations for asset depreciation and corporate overhead, but more important, profit does not include noneconomic considerations such as the social costs of pollution or the individual costs of layoffs, and emphasizes very short-term monetary results rather than a long-term competitive position. Profit centers have been a widely used concept in responsibility accounting, particularly for the product divisions of a diversified and decentralized firm. The concept is not applicable, however, for product divisions managed by portfolio theories of market share and market growth, or company strengths and industry attractiveness, and does not recognize the organizational interdependencies of many product divisions using similar distribution channels or related product technologies. The reliance on profit centers for the evaluation of the performance of organizational units probably will decrease in the future, because of these shortcomings of the profit concept.

4. *Investment center.* An investment center is an organizational unit in which the manager is assumed to have control over revenues, expenses, and investments, and in which the performance of the organizational unit can be evaluated

through the use of financial ratios such as the return on investment (pretax profits divided by the capital employed) or financial summaries such as residual income (pretax profits less a charge for the capital employed). Assets, both current and fixed, are normally required to generate profits, and it is felt that these investment ratios and summaries provide the most comprehensive measures of organizational performance since both profits and assets are included in the evaluation standard. The problems, of course, come from the short-term orientation of the profit concept, and from the difficulties in measuring the employed capital. Assets have to be defined, and then valued at original price, depreciated value, replacement cost, or estimated worth. Even cash, the most easily valued of all the assets, can be troublesome in measuring the capital employed by a product division since the level of cash can be the amount actually recorded in the division accounts, or the amount actually used by drawing on corporate accounts. After measuring the employed capital, and after establishing the return on investment or the residual income of a division, the use of these investment criteria as performance standards can result in dysfunctional decisions, such as a hesitancy to invest in needed facilities because of the increase in the capital employed, or an eagerness to dispose of backup equipment due to the decrease in assets. The use of investment centers for performance evaluation will probably also decrease in the future, because of these behavioral problems.

All responsibility centers, whether measured on costs, revenues, profits, or investment ratios, are subject to transfer pricing and overhead allocation problems. Both transfer prices and shared costs represent financial transactions between decentralized responsibility centers, and both create administrative problems because these intercompany transfers obviously affect the measures of performance for the organizational units.

1. *Transfer prices.* A transfer price is simply the amount recorded for an exchange of goods or services between units in the same organization. Transfer prices may be based on equivalent market prices, actual production costs, or arbitrary executive decisions. Equivalent market prices are ideal, when available; for many products and most services, however, no independent market exists, and the prices for closely similar or substitute products may be constrained by the use of integrated production facilities or separate distribution channels. Actual production costs change with volume, due to the variable absorption of overhead per unit, and marginal production costs, which theoretically should be used for optimal corporate performance, change with capacity; at less than full capacity, marginal charges are the variable costs of material and labor only, while at full capacity, marginal charges are the opportunity costs of not selling to outside customers. Transfer prices can be set by a two-step system, charging variable costs per unit plus fixed costs per period, with the fixed costs transferred at the percentage of capacity which the purchasing division has either reserved or utilized. The two-step pricing system is applicable only when large volumes are purchased, because of the complexities in recording costs and estimating percentages. Most transfer prices are set by negotiation between divisions, or by arbitrary decisions by corporate executives; neither provides the incentives toward

cost reductions, internal sourcing, and cooperative effort that are desirable in large decentralized firms.

2. *Shared costs.* A shared cost is an allocation of corporate overhead between units in the same organization. This allocation may be set as a percentage of sales revenues, division salaries, service usage, square footage, capital investment, etc. No overhead allocation method, except relative use of the available services, is completely logical and, as in transfer pricing, no method provides the incentives toward cost reduction and cooperative effort that are desirable. It should be noted, however, that the existence of severe cost allocation and transfer pricing problems may indicate the existence of an improper organizational structure, with the organizational units divided needlessly, and evaluated poorly by related cost, revenue, or profit standards.

Responsibility accounting totals the revenues, expenses, profits, and investments associated with specific organizational units, ready for comparison with the budgeted financial standards of performance. Operational accounting expands this service, to include numerical and qualitative measures of performance, both of which are needed to supplement the more common but more limited financial evaluations. In the very human search for certainty and precision that characterizes much of management, the quantitative measures tend to replace the qualitative, the financial scales tend to dominate the numerical, and single standards tend to supplant the multiple and composite forms. The function of operational accounting is to ensure that this does not happen, and that financial, numerical, and descriptive measures are all used in the comparative evaluation of budgetary plans with actual operations to improve the performance of organizational units and to reward the efforts of individual managers.

Comparative Evaluation. Comparative evaluation is the fifth step or stage in the planning → control → motivation sequence. It involves a comparison of planned versus actual results, through an analysis of the variances, and provides information to the managers and members of the organizational units for the improvement of performance. Information for the improvement of managerial performance in the various programs leading toward the competitive position or service level of the selected strategy is central to the concept of control. Control is effective only when it helps the managers and members of organizational units; managerial assistance, not repressive standards or continual complaints, is the essence of control.

This assistance to the managers and members of the organizational units should be on three levels, corresponding to the three stages of planning. Planning, as described previously, can be divided into the three sequential steps of strategic planning to select the long-term competitive position or service level of the organization; program planning to allocate the resources and define the activities needed to achieve that competitive position or service level; and budgetary planning to estimate the revenues and expenses associated with each program, and to establish standards of performance for the functional and technical units responsible for performing the activities. These three stages of planning were depicted as a matrix; see the accompanying illustration.

	Research Unit	Marketing Unit	Engineering Unit	Production Unit	Distribution Unit
Program A Existing Business					
Program B Product Development					
Program C Market Expansion		Overall Strategy of the Firm			
Program D Cost Improvement					
Program E Capacity Increase					

Control is needed at all three stages of planning, or dimensions on the matrix, to compare actual results with expected outcomes so that, when necessary, the current operations may be corrected or the existing plans may be changed. It is common to concentrate this control effort on the activities of the functional and technical managers since these organizational units generally have financial performance standards that make comparative evaluations easy, a short time frame that makes changed results apparent, and a low hierarchical position that makes corrective action possible. This emphasis upon the operating units, however, neglects the long-term viability of the selected strategy and the midterm completion of the funded programs; control is needed at all three levels of organizational strategy, program efficiency, and managerial activities to improve the total performance of the firm.

1. *Organizational control.* Organizational control measures the execution of the selected strategy of the firm. The strategic plans, of course, define a long-term method of competition or concept of service for an organization, and the organizational controls should evaluate progress toward achieving that competitive position or service level. It is certainly difficult both to identify the desired position and to measure progress toward achieving that position in financial or quantitative terms, but some of the dimensions should be industry figures on growth rates and market shares, company forecasts on sales revenues and overhead costs, and competitive comparisons on product designs, brand reputations, distribution channels, manufacturing efficiencies, etc. The senior management of a company is responsible for positioning the company within an industry or industries, with the intent of achieving a long-term competitive advantage over other firms within those industries; organizational control should evaluate that strategic decision by comparing expected results with actual outcomes on numerous financial, numerical, and descriptive dimensions. Important variances should result in changes in the strategic plans, in the resource allocations and managerial activities that were designed to implement those plans, or in the senior management. It is necessary to create an atmosphere of accepting environmental and organizational changes, and of recognizing the need to plan for those changes, within the senior management of most organizations; a control system that revealed inattention to those requirements, and a motivation system that

penalized that inattention, would help greatly in developing the needed attitudes and abilities.

2. *Program control.* Program control measures the execution of the program designed to achieve the long-term competitive position of the organizational strategy. Program planning, as described previously, estimates the flow of funds over the life of each program or project, and specifies the activities needed to complete that program or project. Program control compares the estimated usage of funds with the actual expenditures, and particularly compares the planned activities with the actual achievements. Most programs consist of a number of activities or tasks that are interrelated by time; many of the tasks cannot be started until others are completed, so that delay in one activity creates additional delays, and additional costs, in others. Program control systems usually recognize these interrelationships, either through simple comparisons of the estimated versus actual completion dates for each activity, or with formal network models such as PERT and CPM that explain changes in the time and cost requirements. Major variances in resource usage or completion dates should be analyzed for the causes, and could result in program changes, activity changes, or managerial changes. Again, it is necessary to develop a tradition of completing programs and projects on time and to cost estimates among the middle management of most organizations; a control system that not only shows the deficiencies but helps to correct those deficiencies would assist in developing the needed attitudes and abilities.

3. *Managerial control.* Managerial control measures the performance of the organizational units that are responsible for the functional and technical activities within each program. Budgetary planning, as described previously, estimates the revenues and expenses associated with each program or project, usually on an annual basis, and sets the goals and objectives for the functional and technical units involved in those programs. These goals and objectives are the results that are expected in research, marketing, engineering, production, distribution, and the various staff units; they are statements of where the functional and technical units are expected to be at specific times in the future, and they serve as targets for achievement and standards for control. The goals and objectives for the functional and technical units may be financial, reflecting the anticipated revenues and expenses, or numerical, showing unitary or percentage measures of performance, or descriptive, with qualitative and subjective standards. The managerial process within each functional and technical unit may be structured, with a known relationship between the inputs and outputs, or unstructured, without that known relationship. Managerial control, as used here, refers to the comparison of planned results with actual outcomes for unstructured managerial processes, such as product engineering or market planning, where the proper level of inputs cannot be determined with accuracy. Operational control, also as used here, refers to the comparison of planned versus actual results for structured managerial processes, mainly in the production or operations area, where the proper level of inputs can be determined accurately.

Managerial control involves comparison of planned versus actual results for unstructured functional and technical activities. Major variances in performance are analyzed, and may result in changes in the budgetary plans, in the managerial activities, or in the unit personnel. It should be remembered, however, that the purpose of the control system is to provide information for the managers and members of the organizational units that will eventually lead to improvements in their performance; assistance to the managers, not evidence of incompetence or inability, is the objective of control, and that assistance should lead to changes in the plans or in the activities more readily than to changes in the personnel.

4. *Operational control.* Operational control measures the performance of the functional and technical units within an organization that have a structured managerial process, with known input-to-output relationships. The inputs to a structured managerial process are termed "engineered costs," and since the relationships are known, the variances can be analyzed precisely into categories that explain the causes of differences between planned and actual expenditures. These categories, in engineered cost analysis, include volume variances for changes in the unit numbers of the output, price variances for changes in the unit costs of the input, and efficiency variances for the residual element, not explained by changes in output volume or input costs. Variance analysis has come, through repetitive explanation of the techniques used in engineering cost categorization, to refer primarily to the identification of the volume, price, and efficiency components in the operational control of manufacturing processes; it should refer to understanding the reasons for the differences between planned outcomes and actual results at all levels of control.

Comparative evaluation of planned versus actual results, through an analysis of the variances, with the intent of providing information to the managers and members of organizational units for the improvement of performance, is the essence of control. This analysis, and this assistance, should be provided at the organizational level to measure the achievement of the selected strategy of the firm; at the program level to evaluate the usage of allocated resources and the completion of specified activities to implement that strategy; at the managerial level to gauge the performance of the unstructured functional and technical units working on those programs; and at the operational level to judge the efficiency of the structured manufacturing processes. At each level of control, it is important to separate the evaluation of the organizational unit, as an economic entity, from the evaluation of the manager of that unit as an individual person. Primarily, it is necessary in the analysis of variances at all levels of control to understand that some of the factors in the performance of an organizational unit are subject to the direction of the manager, and some are not. The factors not subject to the direction of the manager of an organizational unit usually include problems outside the organization, and problems outside the unit. Changes in the economic cycle or in the competitive situation are examples of the first group of noncontrollable problems; changes in the allocated overhead, shared costs, or transfer prices are examples of the second group. For the evaluation of managerial performance, rather than the measurement of organizational achievements, it is important to recognize that some factors can be foreseen in the planning stage, that some can be managed in the control stage, and that some can be neither foreseen nor managed. Accurate identification of these classes of problems is essential for the development of organizational incentives to reward managerial performance. The development of these incentives is the province of the next step in the design of the managerial systems.

Organizational Response. The organizational response is the sixth stage in the planning → control → motivation sequence. Organizational response refers generally to the reaction of an organization to managerial performance, as measured by the comparative evaluations of the control system, and specifically to the design of incentives to reward that performance. A planning system becomes a control system when organizational units and individual managers are evaluated on the variances between planned results and actual outcomes, and a control system becomes a motivation system when the performance levels of both organizational units and individual managers are recognized and rewarded. Recognition is fully as important as reward; both are included in the concept of an organizational response, which may be of four types:

1. *Perceptual.* A perceptual response is the recognition of achievement of either an organizational unit or individual manager by the balance of the organization. Recognition of achievement, with that achievement measured by the comparative evaluation of planned versus actual performance, is apparently the simplest, certainly the least expensive, but unfortunately one of the least common of all organizational responses. Members of an organization like to believe that their contributions to the organization are perceived and acknowledged by others; this acknowledgment, however, has to be more informal than formal, and more unforced than directed. Company newsletters and congratulatory meetings do not work; the respect of coworkers and comments of peer managers do, but it is impossible to design the latter as part of a motivation system. The perceptual response of an organization is complex, and largely unmanageable, but critical in the motivation of the managers and members of the organization.

2. *Financial.* A financial response is the payment of a monetary reward for managerial achievement, again with that achievement measured by the comparative evaluation of planned versus actual performance. The monetary rewards are normally tied to the budgetary measures of performance, with a commission paid on sales or a bonus awarded for profits. It is essential that the measures of performance used to compute the monetary rewards be considered carefully, for most of the single financial standards can be manipulated; sales may be recorded in the wrong period, or profits can be increased by a cut in developmental expenses. Monetary incentives should be tied to multiple or composite measures, and to financial, numerical, and descriptive dimensions of performance. With proper measures and dimensions, financial rewards can be effective since they provide both increased income for the individual, and a form of perceptual re-

sponse: comparative incomes represent one means of acknowledging the relative contributions of managers and members to an organization.

3. *Positional.* A positional response is the promotion of a person for managerial achievement. The positional response is only partially effective, since normally there is considerable time delay between the recording and evaluation of performance and the announcement of the promotion, but, as with the monetary reward, a positional change is a form of perceptual response, and indicates recognition of the contributions of that person to the organization.

4. *Personal.* Personal responses are the nonfinancial and nonpositional responses by an organization; they include the office locations, decor distinctions, parking provisions, and club memberships that indicate status within the organization. Status, of course, is also part of the perceptual response.

The financial, positional, and personal incentives of an organization should, obviously, be designed to reinforce the performance measures and comparative evaluations of the control system, and to supplement the perceptual response that is crucial in motivation. The effort and commitment of various managers within an organization will differ, however, even if evaluated with similar standards and rewarded with the same incentives. This variety of response is due to personal differences between individuals, and even within the same individual at different times, and results in an individualized reaction to the planning, control, and motivation systems.

Individual Response. The individual response is the seventh, and last, stage in the planning → control → motivation sequence. Individuals react differently to formal incentives, even in closely similar situations with nearly identical organizational influences; this is because individuals are truly different. People differ in physical abilities, mental capacities, interpersonal skills, social expectations, cultural beliefs, educational levels, past experiences, current conditions, and future needs. The large number of dimensions that can be used to describe personal differences makes it nearly impossible to forecast individual reactions to the motivational systems within an organization, but it is possible to identify many of the forces that influence individual decisions and actions, and it is possible to predict typical or average behavior. These forces, and the relationships among them, are shown in the accompanying illustration at the top of the next page.

The organizational forces which influence individual decisions and actions are the hierarchical structure, information system, assigned tasks, planning system, control system, and motivation system. The hierarchical structure creates a position for the individual relative to others within the organization, the information system provides a portion of the data needed to perform the assigned tasks, and the planning, control, and motivation systems together generate the performance measure, the comparative evaluations, and the financial, positional, and personal incentives. These organizational forces, however, do not determine behavior; they merely influence it, and their influence may be minor in comparison to the per-

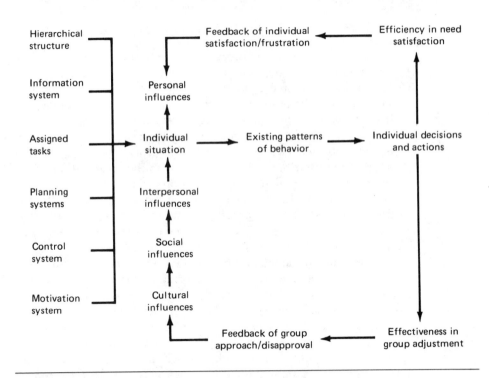

sonal, interpersonal, social, and cultural factors. These factors need to be briefly defined for greater clarity in understanding individual decisions and actions in an organizational context.

1. *Personal influences* upon behavior refer basically to the personality of the individual. Personality is the combined result of perception, learning, and memory which lead to cognition, and the personal needs and drives which lead to motivation. Cognition is the ability to think objectively about alternative courses of action, and motives are the subjective scales used to compare the alternatives. Together, the cognition and motivation of an individual result in a distinctive pattern of responses to stimuli, which is termed learned behavior. Learned behavior is an important influence upon individual decisions and actions in an organizational context since these personal factors are basic to need satisfaction and group adjustment.

2. *Interpersonal influences* upon behavior come from interactions among individuals in informal groups. People do not exist as isolated patterns of learned behavior, separate from others; instead, they exist as participants in dual interactions, small groups, formal organizations, and national or ethnic societies, and each type of association results in a socialization process that modifies the individual personality. People learn what is expected of them within the different associations, and act at least partially to obtain assistance and approval from the other members. Socialization in dual interactions and small groups results in attitudes, which are beliefs about others, and traits, which are ways of reacting to others. Both attitudes and traits are learned patterns of behavior that come

from experience with others, communication from others, or emulation of others. Attitudes and traits are important influences upon behavior in an organizational context since these interpersonal factors set the patterns of need satisfaction and group adjustment.

3. *Social influences* upon behavior come from interactions among individuals in formal organizations. People are usually members of multiple organizations, for economic, political, religious, social, educational, and medical reasons, and each organization has a separate structure and ideology. The structure results in positions, roles, and status for members; a position is the expected tasks, a role is the expected method of performing those tasks, and status is the expected esteem. The ideology provides norms and values; norms are shared attitudes about the expected behavior of people in each position, and values are shared attitudes about important activities of each position. Roles, status, norms, and values are all important influences upon behavior in an organizational context, particularly since these differ between organizations, and may result in conflicting standards of behavior for individuals who are members of more than one organization.

4. *Cultural influences* upon behavior come from interactions among individuals in national or ethnic societies. People are usually members of one national and one ethnic society, which may or may not overlap, and each society has a structure and an ideology. The social structure results in norms, or expected patterns of behavior, and status, or accepted levels of esteem, while the social ideology provides norms and values. An informal recording of the social norms and values is the ethnic or national tradition; a formal recording of social norms and values is the legal system. Social roles, status, norms, and values are all important influences upon behavior in an organizational context, particularly since these social factors may conflict with the personal, interpersonal, and organizational standards of behavior.

Each individual within an organization has an existing pattern of behavior that is based upon personal cognition and motivation, interpersonal attitudes and traits, social roles and status, and cultural norms and values. That pattern of behavior is influenced partially by individual needs for personal (food, shelter, and clothing), interpersonal (friendship), social (esteem), and cultural (self-development) benefits, and partially by organizational forces that come from the hierarchical structure and managerial systems. Behavior in organizations is complex, not simple; for the manager concerned with the design of a motivational system, the essential concept is the recognition that formal incentives may have a very limited influence on individual performance.

Individual decisions and actions within an organization are guided, not directed, by the combined impact of the organizational structure and the managerial systems for planning, control, and motivation. These systems, to be effective, must be consistent. Consistency is essential, and it is emphasized by repeating here the graphic display of the relationships between the stages of the planning—control—motivational sequence that must be understood for the consistent design of the managerial systems:

		Environmental assumptions
	Strategic planning (method of competition)	Organizational resources
		Managerial intentions
		Strategic alternatives
		Net present value
Planning system	Program planning (allocation of resources)	Internal rate of return
		Cost–benefit analysis
		Competitive position analysis
		Revenue forecasts
	Budgetary planning (projection of results)	Expense estimations
		Numerical measures
		Descriptive standards
		Cost accumulation systems
Control system	Operational accounting (recording of performance)	Cost allocation systems
		Responsibility centers
		Transfer prices and shared costs
		Organizational control
	Comparative evaluation (analysis of variances)	Program control
		Managerial control
		Operational control
		Perceptual response
Motivation system	Organizational response (design of incentives)	Financial response
		Positional response
		Personal response
		Personal influence
	Individual reaction (decisions and actions)	Interpersonal influence
		Social influence
		Cultural influence

The following cases illustrate the need for consistency in the design of the organizational structure and managerial systems in order to guide individual decisions and actions toward the successful achievement of the selected strategy.

Great Lakes Discount Sales, Inc.

In March 1978, Mr. Joseph Innocenti, president and recent founder of Great Lakes Discount Sales, Inc., was attempting to arrange interviews with graduating M.B.A. students at various eastern and midwestern universities. Mr. Innocenti wanted to hire two new executives for his chain of health and personal-product stores, and he had contacted 10 of the major schools of business administration in the area, but had been completely unsuccessful in his search.

> The placement people keep telling me that I'm too late in trying to set up interviews, and that I should have made arrangements early last fall. The company didn't exist last fall, so how could I have made arrangements then? It's fairly obvious that placement offices at business schools are oriented only toward the large companies, all of which have personnel departments to look after the details of recruiting, and that no one pays much attention to the needs of the smaller firms.
>
> At the schools where I have been able to set up interviews, the students don't seem very interested. I think that students are oriented toward large companies, too, with the job security and employment benefits that are part of the big company package. M.B.A.'s always seem to go to work for big, successful companies that are just past the maturity stage in the product life cycle. I think that decision is certainly shortsighted, but it is just part of the placement process that systematically excludes smaller firms in the growth stage of that cycle. Maybe I ought to look for people with four or five years of experience who recognize these problems, and stop trying to hire M.B.A.'s who don't, but I hate to take someone else's rejects.
>
> I want to hire a person to be treasurer, and I want to hire a person to be operations manager, and I may want to hire a third person for financial analysis and corporate planning. We can do without these people this year, but it will slow our growth substantially. It will mean that I'll have to look after all the detail of day-to-day operations. I want to delegate that detail to others, so that I can spend my time on long-term plans and policies. That's where the money is. (Statement of Mr. Innocenti)

Mr. Innocenti was a 1972 graduate of North Carolina State University, where he had played basketball and majored in marketing, merchandising, and product promotion. He had planned on getting a job with an advertising agency in Raleigh or Charlotte after graduation, but there were few opportunities in advertising for B.B.A. candidates that year, so he had accepted a position as a salesman with a large proprietary drug products firm. He selected this company partially because his parents had owned a drugstore in New Jersey for years, so that he was acquainted with the products, but primarily because he felt that the executive development program, as it was described to him, meant that he could be promoted rapidly. Mr. Innocenti was tall, energetic, and personable, and managed to increase sales in the central Michigan territory to which he was assigned, after a very short training program, by nearly 50% in the first year, and by considerably more than 100% after three years. He felt that this sales record deserved recognition and promotion, but the district manager for the firm, a much older man, just cautioned him not to work so hard since the head office might come to expect equivalent performance from everyone in the district. Mr. Innocenti was discouraged by this response, and by the apparent lack of real opportunity within the company, and so resigned his position to enter the M.B.A. program at the University of Michigan.

> That company was typical of large corporations, where the only way to get ahead was to go along with the system. If I had stayed, I could have replaced that old guy as district manager in another 10 years, and 5 years later I could have been regional manager, provided I didn't rock the boat. Well, I decided to get an M.B.A. and try to get into corporate headquarters, where I could accomplish something, and make some money. I want to rock a few boats. (Statement of Mr. Innocenti)

While attending the University of Michigan, Mr. Innocenti worked part-time as a consultant for a wholesale distributor in Jackson (approximately 25 miles west of Ann Arbor, the site of the university) that had been one of his customers while he was with the proprietary drug firm. This company distributed ethical (requiring a prescription from an M.D.) and proprietary (no prescription required) drugs, and also the familiar beauty aid products such as toothpaste, shaving cream, hair shampoo, deodorant spray, etc. The company had been very successful during the 1950s and early 1960s since it served all of the central and western portions of the lower peninsula of Michigan, and major growth had occurred in this area as auto parts manufacturers and their employees moved out of the Detroit metropolitan region to escape the congestion and deterioration of that city. However, in the late 1960s, sales had started a gradual decline as drugstore chains spread into the area, and the decline had accelerated as first rack jobbers set up displays of proprietary drugs and personal care products in grocery stores and convenience outlets, and then mass merchandisers added the same items at their locations in shopping centers. The drug chains, rack jobbers, and mass merchandisers bought directly from the manufacturer since their volume was high, and thus cut directly into the sales of the wholesale distributors such as the one in Jackson. Reliable figures were not available to show the changes in the distribution pattern of health care and beauty aid (HBA) products in the service area of the Jackson wholesaler, but Mr. Innocenti estimated the trends as shown in Exhibit 1.

Chain drugstores were defined as companies with three or more retail locations that generated adequate volume to buy directly from manufacturers. There were 173 chain locations in the service area of the Jackson wholesaler in 1977, owned and operated by nine different companies, whereas in 1960 there had been 14 locations owned by a single firm. The independent drugstores were defined as individual proprietorships with three or fewer retail locations that remained customers of the wholesale distributors. More than 100 independent drugstores had gone out of business in Michigan during the period 1960–1977.

Exhibit 1 *Trends in the retail sales (percent) of health care and beauty aid products in central and western Michigan, 1960–1977*

	1960	1965	1970	1975	1977
Independent drugstores	97.5	90.0	75.0	60.0	50.0
Chain drugstores	2.5	5.0	10.0	15.0	15.0
Rack sales at grocery stores	—	—	5.0	10.0	15.0
Mass merchandising stores	—	5.0	10.0	15.0	20.0

Source: Joseph Innocenti.

Independent drugstores aren't finished; some will remain very successful, particularly when they are associated with a medical clinic, or located close to a health care facility. The sales in those stores will be primarily ethical drugs, at the prescription counter. That is dandy for the drugstore, since the margins are much higher for ethical drugs than for proprietary drugs and personal products, but it is not good for the distributor. A wholesaler makes money on the front-end products (sales at a drugstore are divided into "back-end," or prescription drugs and medical supplies, and "front-end," or proprietary drugs such as headache remedies and sinus tablets and personal care items such as oral antiseptics and hair preparations; the terms "front-end" and "back-end" are obviously derived from the location of the prescription counter, at the rear of most stores), while the retailer makes money on the back-end items. A retail drugstore that concentrates on back-end items is usually thought of as a pharmacy; they can be very profitable with the right location.

Independent drugstores that are not associated with a medical practice or health care facility are going to have a hard time. For years, the local drugstore relied on convenience purchases—people needed a tube of toothpaste of a bottle of shampoo, and they would stop in while they were shopping in the area—but now it is more convenient to get these products from the rack jobber at the grocery store, and much cheaper to get them from the mass merchandiser at the shopping center. (Statement of Mr. Innocenti)

Rack jobbers are wholesale distributors that purchase HBA products, generally the faster-moving, heavily promoted items for personal care such as toothpastes, shaving creams, hair conditioners, and deodorant sprays, directly from various manufacturers and then, instead of selling through the normal retail drug outlets, set up small racks or displays of the products in grocery stores, chain stores, and convenience stores. The rack jobber services each store at least once a week, bringing the products in a panel truck, physically stocking the shelves, and then computing a bill for the items sold from the display. Retailers accept this service, even though it provides less of a discount than is available from normal trade channels, since it involves no handling of the goods, no problem with slow-moving items, and no investment in inventory. In essence, the retailer just allocates the space to the rack jobber, collects the money from the customers, and retains a percentage for overhead and profit. Mr. Innocenti felt that rack-jobbing companies were successful since they offered commonly used products at convenient points of purchase, but he was also certain that no further opportunity remained in that market channel for the Jackson drug distributor.

> The advantage of rack-jobbing is that it puts products that the customer wants in a place where it is very convenient for the customer to buy; everybody walks through a grocery store or supermarket two or three times a week, and has to go right past the HBA display. The problem in rack-jobbing is that it is too easy; you just bring the products to the store each week, stock the shelves, compute the bill, and collect the money. Now there are too many people in that business. We [the Jackson distributor] could not get into the business since the best stores already have a contract with another jobber. The other problem with rack-jobbing is that it is impossible to offer discount prices; you have to split the commission with the retailer, and that does not leave much left over for price cutting. You get the convenience business, but you don't get the volume business. (Statement of Mr. Innocenti)

Some of the rack jobbers, in an effort to substantially increase their sales volume, had opened health and beauty aid stores in small shopping centers, along retail streets, or near downtown areas. These HBA stores were usually small, under 1,500 square feet, with one or two employees, and carried the usual proprietary drugs and personal items, together with some cosmetics and toiletries, all of which were generally sold at 10 to 15% off the suggested list price. Some of these shops were successful on a local basis, where they had happened to select a very convenient location or had happened to find a very noncompetitive environment, but none had been successful enough to develop into regional chains. Mr. Innocenti felt that this was due to a lack of a strong marketing appeal.

> I don't believe that a 10 to 15% savings is enough of a customer appeal to bring people to shop at an HBA store. People will go in, if they are in the area and need a HBA product, but they won't drive and park to get there. The rack jobber can't lower consumer prices, since the discount from the manufacturer is only 30 to 35%, depending on the overall volume. Also, there is no excitement about shopping in a HBA store; they tend to be dull and uninteresting. You go in, select your toothpaste or mouthwash, and leave; that's part of everyday living, but that's not the way to build customer loyalty or store volume. (Statement of Mr. Innocenti)

The chain drugstores, which had expanded rapidly in the East and the Far West from 1955 to 1965, and in the South and the Midwest from 1965 to 1975, could be divided into two types: the variety chain, which relied upon a wide product mix, ranging from ethical drugs to housewares, cosmetics, and liquor, to bring customers to the store, and the discount chain, which relied upon reduced prices and increased advertising. The product mix at a variety drugstore can be very extensive; the percentage of sales for each class of products sold at this type of store, on a national basis during 1977, was as follows: prescription drugs and medical supplies, 17.4%; proprietary drugs and health aids, 5.9%; personal products and beauty aids, 12.4%; toiletries and perfumes, 11.0%; cosmetics, 6.4%; stationery, 3.1%; school supplies, 2.1%; tobacco, 9.8%; candy, 3.9%; kitchen items, 4.5%; household goods, 3.0%; toys and games, 3.8%; photo supplies, 4.1%; liquor, beer, and wine, 4.8%; newspapers and magazines, 2.5%; food products and convenience items, 2.0%; food service and coffee/tea/soft-drink sales, 1.1%; clothing, 0.9%; luggage, 0.4%; hardware, 0.4%; electronic supplies, 0.3%; and furniture, 0.2%. The variety drugstores tend to be large, with 12,000 to 15,000 square feet, to provide self-service displays and sales counters for the range of merchandise, and they also tend to be located in the larger shopping centers, although not the regional malls, to offer convenient parking and "one-stop" customer shopping. The discount drug chains generally have a more limited selection of merchandise and smaller stores, with 8,000 to 10,000 square feet, and sell at prices that vary between 15 and 20% off the list prices "suggested" by the manufacturers, with larger discounts occasionally advertised on promotional products on a weekly, monthly, or seasonal basis. The discount stores tend to be located in a free-standing building along a major retail street, or in part of an older shopping center, in order to reduce the rental expenses. Mr. Innocenti believed that the expansion of both the variety and the discount drugchains was past because they no longer appeared to provide a focused marketing appeal to the consumer.

> Sales are slipping at the variety drug stores, and the natural reaction is to bring in more products. They put in 24 ft [shelf space] of automotive goods, 24 ft of athletic equipment, 12 ft of luggage, and start to sell television sets, small appliances, and garden chemicals. That is unfocused marketing, and they can't compete on variety or price with the stores that specialize in those products; all they can offer is the one-stop shopping. The

discount drug chains have much the same problem; they don't really focus on low prices because they don't have the margin. They get 35 to 38% off from the manufacturer, again depending upon the overall chain volume, and they often get an additional 5% for the special promotions, but they have high advertising expenses and large store costs.

Both the variety drug chains and the discount drug chains are stuck with the size and nature of their physical plant; those large stores are expensive to rent, heat, and maintain, and the big inventory is difficult to supervise and reorder. Both types now have a hodge-podge strategy, and I think that their days are past. (Statement of Mr. Innocenti)

The mass merchandisers, such as K-Mart, Kresge's, Korvette's, and Meijer's, have often added health and beauty aid products to their existing lines of clothing, furniture, hardware, etc., and in some instances they have also added a pharmaceutical counter to sell prescription drugs and an optical center to sell eyeglasses. Most of the health and beauty aid products are sold at 10 to 15% off the suggested list prices, but Mr. Innocenti felt that HBA sales had expanded at the mass merchandising stores due to convenient shopping more than to price appeal.

> The mass merchandisers get the customer in the store with their huge range of everyday products, and then they give each person a shopping cart and expect them to pick up weekly needs at slightly reduced prices. The customer appeal is convenience, not price. (Statement of Mr. Innocenti)

Joseph Innocenti, while working for the drug wholesaler in Jackson as a part-time consultant, prepared a comparative matrix that displayed in very simplistic terms the differences between the seven existing channels for the retail sale of health and beauty aid products (Exhibit 2).

Joseph Innocenti believed that a gap existed in the marketing structure for HBA products. All the retail outlets appeared to rely upon the appeals of convenience, price, and product mix in different combinations to

---

Exhibit 2 *Comparison of the major retail sales outlets for HBA products, 1977*

	Prescription store revenue (%)	HBA items store revenue (%)	HBA items convenience	HBA items price discount (%)	HBA item range	Non-HBA range
Independent drug apothecary	60	40	In store	List	Limited	None
Independent drug community	35	50	In area	0–5	Medium	Limited
Rack jobber at grocery store	—	5	In store	List	Limited	Large
Rack jobber at HBA store	—	100	In area	10–15	Medium	None
Chain drugstore, variety type	17	18	In center	5–10	Large	Large
Chain drugstore, discount type	23	37	In center	15–20	Large	Medium
Mass merchandising chain	—	2	In store	10–15	Medium	Huge

Source: Joseph Innocenti.

attract customers to the store, but none emphasized price to the exclusion of the other factors, and none added an attractive or interesting shopping environment.

Personal care products constitute a huge market, with somewhere between $13 and $17 billion in annual sales, depending upon where you draw the line between beauty aids, cosmetics, and toiletries. In every other market of that size, you will find a "price" segment, and a "price" channel of distribution. In the HBA products, you don't, yet. All the HBA products are branded, and most of them are advertised; therefore, the manufacturers won't give discounts large enough to permit a retailer or retail chain to sell on a total price basis. What is needed are unbranded products, or privately branded products, without advertising, but with exclusive distribution rights to bring customers to the store for substantial price savings. (Statement of Mr. Innocenti)

Joseph Innocenti had proposed to the owners and managers of the wholesale distributing firm in Jackson that they consider opening discount HBA stores, similar in concept to those now run by the rack jobbers, but with either generic (unbranded) or company (privately branded) products to attract customers to the store. Each store would also carry the full line of personal products stocked by the distributor, so that the individual buyers would have a choice, and so that the overall company sales would increase, but the primary marketing appeal would be an exceedingly low price on the unbranded and unadvertised merchandise. The stores would be placed in "strip" shopping centers along streets with low retail traffic counts, and consequently low rental fees, and they would be expected to draw customers rather than rely on an existing clientele.

All the other retailers selling HBA products rely on the customer being in the store, or in the shopping center, or in the neighborhood, and therefore the rents and other store expenses tend to be high. A medical clinic or health care facility is going to have only one pharmacy in the building, and they charge a suitable rent. A shopping center is going to have only one drugstore, and they charge for the traffic at the center. We will be away from the high-traffic areas, so that our rent will be low, and we will bring customers to the store with our very low priced generic products. (Statement of Mr. Innocenti)

The managers of the wholesale drug firm in Jackson were interested in the concept of the discount HBA stores, with the customer appeal based upon very low priced generic products, and they made an offer to Joseph Innocenti to join their company after graduation, and to continue work on his proposal. Mr. Innocenti accepted the offer, with the understanding that he would be appointed president and made a partial (15%) owner of the retail subsidiary, if the stores were opened. During his last term at the University of Michigan, he was a member of a seminar on small business formation, and as a part of the assignment for that class he prepared a report on the availability and cost of the generic products. He visited small contract fillers and packagers (companies that would fill aerosol cans, glass bottles, or plastic tubes, or that would box loose items and attach them to cards with transparent film; most large consumer-products firms such as Gillette or Mennen do not have adequate capacity for their full demand, and rely on contract fillers and packagers for the excess) in Chicago, Indianapolis, and Cincinnati, and found that packaging services would be readily available, provided that he gave his orders far enough in advance so that these firms could "work in" his requirements. He also visited local pharmaceutical and specialty chemical companies in the East and Midwest and found, as he had expected, that the formulations of most popular personal care products were well known, and could easily be duplicated. He also found, again as he had suspected, that many of the health care products could be purchased in bulk. Prices were very low, approximately one-tenth of the retail price for equivalent branded health care and personal care products; the difference, of course, accounted for the advertising expenses, distribution costs, administrative overhead, and profit of the consumer-product companies. The proposed quality was equal to the existing products of those companies, and Mr. Innocenti planned to institute strict quality control at the receiving warehouse in Jackson.

After graduation, Mr. Innocenti took a trip to eastern and southern Europe with his wife, partially as a vacation after two years in a very rigorous M.B.A. program and partially as a business trip to look for additional products. He found that he could buy razor blades in Czechoslovakia, medical items in Austria, and cosmetics in Italy. All of these products could be purchased in bulk, shipped by air, and then packaged in the United States. He felt that the existing packaging in eastern Europe often made their products look a little "cheap," but that problem would be overcome with contract packaging in the United States.

Mr. Innocenti conducted extensive market research, during the winter while completing the last year of the M.B.A. program and during the summer, after returning from Europe. He observed, while comparison shopping, the quantities and brands of HBA products purchased and the average purchase amount per customer at each of the different types of retail outlets, and he conducted interviews with customers leaving those outlets. He found that the respondents were often reticent regarding the reasons for the selection of a particular product, but remarkably forthright regarding the reasons for shopping at a specific store. Cross-tabulation

of the interview data, by income level, home location, and occupational group, was attempted against store type, product brand, and purchase volume, but little information was developed beyond the fairly obvious conclusion that middle-income families tend to buy in quantity in stores which offered some discount from the suggested list prices. Over 5,000 interviews were completed, and the results are summarized in Exhibit 3.

Mr. Innocenti was particularly pleased with one result of the market research interviews: the high percentages of shoppers who suggested the need for a clean and attractive store interior. This output reinforced one of his prejudices, which was that many discount stores followed old-fashioned promotional methods, with too much merchandise crowded into too small a space resulting in narrow aisles and disorderly displays, and too many price signs and posters covering the windows, walls, and racks, leading to hurried and confused shopping for personal products.

> Most people hear of a new store that is outside of their normal pattern of shopping from friends and relatives and neighbors, and you won't get that word-of-mouth advertising unless the store is clean and attractive. This is particularly true for personal products. People want pleasant surroundings, with wide aisles and clear signs for easy shopping and selection, and they want a brighter, cleaner appearance, with fresh, clean products for personal care. Most cut-rate stores are a little dusty or dirty—after all, you can't really clean the windows or the racks with all those signs on them—and who wants to buy dirty toothpaste or cosmetics. (Statement of Mr. Innocenti)

Mr. Innocenti planned to remodel each store with large clear windows and freshly painted white walls, and to design the interior with neatly stocked shelves, uncluttered aisles, and modern light fixtures. He envisaged putting a stylized map of the store on

Exhibit 3 *Customer survey questions and responses (percent) at discount HBA sales locations in central and western Michigan*

	Jobber discount HBA store	Chain discount drugstore	Mass merchant HBA department
Why did you shop at this store?			
Lower prices on products	70	68	64
Better selection of products	8	10	13
More convenient location	22	22	23
	100	100	100
Do any other stores in the city offer the same savings as this store?			
Yes, some supermarkets	5	7	11
Yes, some drugstores	3	25	8
Yes, some merchandise stores	8	4	22
No, don't know of others	46	38	35
Don't know	38	26	24
	100	100	100
How did you first learn of this store?			
Told by relatives or friends	40	28	47
Passed by store while in area	18	54	41
Read newspaper advertisement	28	5	3
Don't remember	14	13	9
	100	100	100
Would you shop at another store that offered 10% lower prices on HBA products, but was less convenient?			
Definitely yes	11	8	3
Probably yes	14	12	8
Probably no	46	32	27
Definitely no	12	24	35
Don't want to decide now	17	22	27
	100	100	100
Would you shop at another store that offered 25% lower prices on HBA products of equivalent quality?			
Definitely yes	37	31	24
Probably yes	33	27	22
Probably no	19	21	27
Definitely no	2	5	6
Don't want to decide now	9	16	21
	100	100	100

Exhibit 3   (*continued*)

	Jobber discount HBA store	Chain discount drugstore	Mass merchant HBA department
What would be important to you at the other store, with 25% lower prices?			
Convenient parking	19	29	31
Clean, attractive interior	32	38	26
Wide range of products	15	19	22
Available public transportation	5	4	4
Don't want to decide now	29	10	26
	100	100	100

Source: Joseph Innocenti.

the side walls in clear, bright colors to show the location of the various products and to eliminate the usual aisle signs, which he thought were unattractive and confusing, and he wanted to use small plastic price signs, again in clear, bright colors, on the shelves instead of the usual dull and distracting paper posters.

> It ought to be possible to have a bright, cheerful store, where people would enjoy buying personal care products at discount prices, and where they would probably buy more, because of the atmosphere and the prices. I want a store where people would take time, and stock up for future needs, instead of hurriedly buying one product for immediate use. (Statement of Mr. Innocenti)

Each store was planned to be approximately 2,000 square feet in size, with two wide aisles running from the checkout counters back to the rear of the store. These aisles would be lined with racks for the branded health care and personal care products that were to be purchased directly from the wholesale distributing firm. Shelves along the back wall were to be for the unbranded products, so that customers would have to walk to the back, past the other products, to find the lowest-price merchandise; it was anticipated that many of the customers would select some

of the branded products as they moved through the store. The shelves along the back wall were specially designed so that they could be replenished from the stockroom, at the rear of the store, to reduce congestion and confusion in the aisles.

Annual sales were estimated for each store at $382,500; this had been computed by multiplying an expected average purchase amount times the anticipated daily customer count times 300 shopping days per year. The market research program had determined that the average purchase amount of those who came specifically to a discount drugstore or mass merchandising chain to buy HBA products for family use was $13.48. The average purchase amount of those who came to the shopping center for other errands, and then bought HBA products on an impulse basis, was much lower at $2.93, but Mr. Innocenti believed that the proposed stores, because of their less convenient locations, would attract much less impulse shopping. He expected that the average purchase in the new stores would be slightly higher, at $15.00, because of the effort required to shop there and because of the availability of the very low priced unbranded products, both of which would tend to encourage customers to "stock up." The market research program had also shown that for each 50,000 population within a market area, 340 persons per day visited one of the discount drug stores or mass merchandising chains to buy HBA products for family use. Mr. Innocenti believed that 25%, or 85 persons per day, could be attracted to the new retail outlets, because of the much lower prices. He planned to keep the stores open 12 hours per day, from 9:00 in the morning to 9:00 at night, and six days per week, or 300 days per year. The result of these computations was the annual sales estimate per store of $382,500 ($15.00 average purchase × 85 customers per day × 300 days per year).

Mr. Innocenti believed that the average purchase would be split two-thirds for the unbranded products and one-third for the branded merchandise. The margin on the unbranded products was to be 25%, and they were to sell at 40% off the list prices for equivalent items. The margin on the branded products would be 20%, since they were to sell at 10 to 15% off list prices, or approximately equivalent to the discount prices offered by the rack jobbers at their HBA stores or by the mass merchandisers in their drug departments. The typical margin on purchases, then, would be 23.3% (25.0% × ⅔ + 20.0% × ⅓), and the gross margin on annual sales at each store would be $89,100. The annual expenses for each store were estimated, conservatively, at $69,800, as shown in Exhibit 4.

The managers of the wholesale drug firm in Jackson were impressed with the market research, product procurement, and financial projections of Mr. Innocenti, and they approved his plans for the discount sales of both generic and branded HBA products by a formal vote of the board of directors. It was decided to open five stores: one in Jackson (population 43,000), two in Lansing (population 126,000), and two in Grand Rapids (population 187,000). (Lansing is 30 miles to the north of Jackson, while Grand Rapids is 80 miles to the northwest; all three cities were on the normal distribution routes of the drug wholesaler.) Five stores were to be opened in order to achieve adequate volume to purchase the unbranded products; minimum orders were required by the contract fillers and packagers for each product, and these minimum levels were approximately five times the expected sales per store for those products. The five stores would also cover the expected administrative overhead, and provide a reasonable return on the planned investment. The investment per store was only $35,000, including the inventory; this was 1/10 of the investment in a chain drugstore since the proposed outlets were much smaller, and more plainly, although still attractively, furnished. The board of directors of the wholesale distributing firm gave permission to

Exhibit 4 *Annual expenses estimated for discount HBA stores, as proposed by Great Lakes Discount Sales, Inc.*

$16,800	store manager's salary, at $1,400/month
18,700	three cashiers, working 40-hour week at $3.00/hour
2,900	payroll taxes and unemployment insurance, at 8.1% of wages
6,000	rental payments, at $3.00/square foot
2,400	utilities, for heat, light, and air conditioning
2,400	maintenance and cleaning service
1,800	insurance for fire and theft
800	telephone and communications
18,000	local advertising
$69,800	estimated annual expenses

Source: Joseph Innocenti.

Mr. Innocenti in the fall of 1977 to locate and rent the stores, arrange for the remodeling and stocking, and hire the necessary personnel. The name "Great Lakes" was selected since it was planned, if this first effort was successful, to expand into the other midwestern states bordering the lakes. An attractive logo was selected, in blue and white, showing stylized sailboats and the company name in block letters; this logo was to be used on the corporate letterhead, newspaper ads, store signs, and generic products.

Mr. Innocenti immediately began searching for possible store locations, and found a number of sites of the proper size, with good parking and an attractive neighborhood. He signed the leases, and gave orders to a local contractor for the necessary rebuilding, painting, and cleaning. He also found that he could hire store managers more easily than he had expected; he advertised in the Sunday papers in Lansing, Jackson, and Grand Rapids, and had a sizable number of good applicants. He chose the best five, none of whom had extensive retail experience, but all of whom appeared to be intelligent, hard-working, and willing to learn. Mr. Listrak was a lineman for the Central Michigan Power Company who wanted a less strenuous, indoor occupation; Mrs. Tigue was a teacher who had recently been laid off by a rural school system due to a decline in enrollment; Mr. Micalone was a barber whose business had fallen off with the new, much longer hair styles; Ms. Starr had been discharged after four years as a supply clerk in the Marine Corps; and Mrs. Boersma was a housewife whose children had left for college and she wanted to find additional income and outside employment. Mr. Innocenti assigned each of these people full responsibility for the rebuilding, painting, and cleaning of the store area, the stocking of the inventory, and the hiring of the hourly-paid employees at the respective store locations. He explained that he would visit each store weekly during the con-

struction phase, but that he wanted these people to make decisions locally, and not to expect continual assistance or directives from the central office.

Mr. Innocenti rented office space in a building in downtown Jackson, hired a secretary and a bookkeeper, purchased office equipment, and arranged for the incorporation of the company as a partially owned subsidiary of the drug wholesaling firm. The table of organization (Exhibit 5) which he gave to the attorney handling the details of the incorporation and registration listed a number of positions which he did not expect to fill until the spring. As described previously, he expected to recruit graduating M.B.A.'s, whom he believed would have the youth and flexibility needed to adapt to totally new methods of personal product merchandising, but he also wondered if he did not need executives with more experience in these higher-level jobs.

In January 1978, after all the stores had been opened, and had survived the hectic conditions brought on by the extensive remodeling and the Christmas rush, Mr. Innocenti called the five store managers together for the first formal company meeting; he congratulated them on their past accomplishments, and explained to them their future responsibilities. He repeated that he wanted each of them to accept full responsibility for the operations of their stores; that he wanted each of them to feel that they were running a business of their own. He said that the corporate office would allocate shelf space among the various product groups, following a standardized store layout, but that they could select individual brands of products from the lines carried by the Jackson Wholesale Drug Company. That company would deliver the merchandise, maintain records of the inventory, and recommend special prices and promotions on the branded products, but that the store managers were free to accept or reject those recommendations. He suggested

Exhibit 5 *Organizational structure for management of discount HBA stores, as proposed by Great Lakes Discount Sales, Inc.*

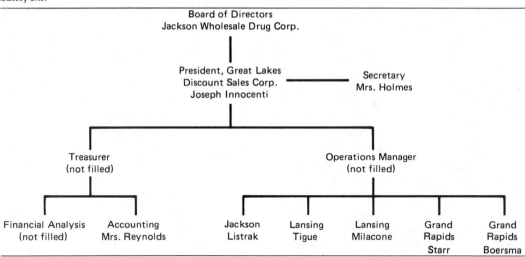

Source: Joseph Innocenti.

that the five managers meet once a week to coordinate their advertising, and he said that he was afraid that he was going to insist upon continual cleaning and spic-and-span maintenance, but that except in those two areas they were free to make their own decisions in store operations and product promotions. He concluded by saying that he wanted the store managers to have "bottom-line" responsibility for store profits; that each store would be run as a profit center, and that an equitable way would be found to share those profits with the managers. Later, Mr. Innocenti explained that this decentralized form of management, with individual responsibility for profits joined to the delegated authority to make the decisions that would affect those profits, was not only in keeping with the most modern theories of business organization, but also met his own personal beliefs about management.

> I want to treat those people the way I always wanted to be treated, but never was. I want to give them autonomy. I want to let them set up their own stores,

and get them started in their own ways. I want to let them work hard, and receive the benefits of their work. Those men and women will benefit, and the company will benefit, since combining clearcut responsibility and delegated authority in this fashion unlocks a tremendous reservoir of individual effort and goodwill.

> I don't like to talk about it too much, but I really do believe in the concept of organizational integration, which means that you join the individual's goals to those of the organization, since this means that the individual manager will find a source of satisfaction in work, beyond just the salary and the commissions, and will work much harder to succeed. The store managers now have the responsibility for store profits, and they have the authority to manage the day-to-day operations of the stores that will affect those profits, and they have the motivation to use that authority. Responsibility, authority, and personal motivation go hand-in-hand, and lead to successful operations. If the store managers look after the short-term operations and sales, and if I look after the long-term policies and plans, then to-

gether we can make this company very, very successful. (Statement of Mr. Innocenti)

Class Assignment. Members of the class should evaluate the organizational structure and systems of Great Lakes Discount Sales, Inc., and make specific recommendations, if they are felt to be needed, in the planning system, the control system, and the motivation system of the company.

Hampfel-McFarland Company

The Hampfel-McFarland Company was founded in Grand Rapids, Michigan, in 1933 by George Hampfel and Joseph McFarland. Both were sheet-metal workers who had been laid off during the Depression; they formed the new company so that they might bid directly on jobs that involved the repair or replacement of the sheet-metal ducts and piping that were used for fume or dust control in industrial plants. Grand Rapids at this time was the center of the furniture industry within the United States. The production of furniture requires various cutting, shaping, sanding, and finishing operations; these operations create dust and exhaust fumes which must be removed from the plant both for worker health and to prevent the possibility of explosion and fire. (Fine sawdust particles suspended in the air can explode, particularly when mixed with the alcohol and lacquer vapors from the finishing operations.) The company specialized in the manufacture and installation of components for the dust and fume control systems needed by the furniture industry, and was quickly successful through offering day-and-night repair service at reasonable charges.

Since there were two of us in the company, one of us could work during the day making the parts, and the other could work at night putting them up. The furniture companies liked that service since it meant that they could get their machines back in production quickly, and save some money. During the Depression, it was important to save some money for your customers. (Statement of Mr. George Hampfel)

By 1938, the two partners had been so successful that they were asked by a local bank to purchase the assets of their previous employer at a bankruptcy sale; as part of this arrangement, which enabled the bank to close out a loan which was totally in default, the two partners were granted additional working capital. With the new machinery, the larger building, and the expanded financing, they were able to start to sell complete new emission control systems; as the long depression of the 1930s came gradually to an end, the new installation service, as opposed to the previous replacement and repair, came to be the major portion of their business.

Over the next 35 years, from 1940 to 1975, the changing industrial base of the region, coupled with the increased prosperity of the country and the growing concern over working conditions and environmental pollution, led to a continual expansion in the breadth of the company's product line and the dollar volume of the company's sales. By 1975, the company produced and installed emission control systems for the metal casting, metal plating, wood working, electronics manufacturing, and spray painting industries. Major applications included smoke control from industrial furnaces and ovens, fume ventilation from spraying and plating operations, dust collection from cutting, buffing, and sanding machines, and pollution abatement from cement plants, iron foundries, and steam boilers. The company operated throughout southern Michigan, northern Indiana and Illinois, and eastern Wisconsin, and the company sales approached $6,000,000 annually.

Company profits, however, had not kept pace with the increase in sales revenues. Mr. Hampfel felt that this was at least partially due to the fact that his partner, Mr. McFarland, had retired from the day-to-day marketing, production, and installation functions of the firm, and was in complete control of the financial records. Mr. McFarland, who had taken a few evening courses in accounting during the 1950s in an effort to improve the cost control and financial forecasting performance of the firm, had gradually become increasingly concerned with the details of bookkeeping and journal entry. By 1970, he had hired five bookkeepers and three secretaries who were segregated in a second-floor office at the main plant, and who kept very meticulous records of the company's revenues and expenses. At the conclusion of each fiscal year, on December 31, Mr. McFarland would send to his partner a written slip of paper with an estimate of the annual profit or loss; approximately three months later, at the conclusion of the yearly audit, Mr. McFarland would meet his partner in the office of the bank which had provided the original financing for the firm, confirm his earlier estimate of the financial results (profit or loss) for the prior year, announce the line of credit (maximum amount of short-term loans) desired by the company for the coming year, ask if there

were any questions, and return to his office. No other financial reports, either written or verbal, were distributed during the year.

I didn't want to fight with him [Mr. McFarland] because of the old days. Many a time, he and I worked right straight through the night to finish a job and keep a customer happy. He was a very skilled worker, a very hard worker, and a daredevil. In the old days, we didn't have much safety equipment, and it was dangerous to climb 50 or 60 ft high on an iron smelter cupolo to put in a new section of blower pipe. But he was always the one to say, "Let me do it." I'm not going to be the one now to tell him that he can't do the accounting. (Statement of Mr. George Hampfel)

In the middle of June 1975, Mr. McFarland died suddenly, of a heart attack. Mr. Hampfel immediately asked his son, George Hampfel, Jr., who was a recent graduate of the M.B.A. program at the University of Michigan and an employee of a major accounting firm in Chicago, to come back to Grand Rapids and assume the position of treasurer. The older Mr. Hampfel told his son that he had concluded an arrangement with the widow of his ex-partner to purchase her interests in the company, and he explained that he would be willing to give this ownership position to his son provided that George, Jr. was willing to provide the sort of operating and financial information that the company needed. George Hampfel, Jr., understood the problem that the company faced, and the need that his father had for more current and detailed management information, since he had known Mr. McFarland.

Accounting became an obsession to the old man [Mr. McFarland]. He would talk to me, when he would not talk to my father or anyone else in the company, because I was taking the accounting courses at the University of Michigan, so he felt that I was one of the elect. He didn't understand much accounting, but he was fascinated by the concept that the books must balance. He had an almost mystical belief that if, at the end of a full year, after tens of thousands of individual journal entries, the total debits equaled the total credits, then everything was all right.

They kept the original books of entry in incredible detail. They recorded the receipt of each box of capscrews, and then they deducted the use of those capscrews through shop requisition slips, but they never allocated the costs against any job; instead, they just wanted to keep track of the number of capscrews they had at any given time. They would not even tell the purchasing agent how many capscrews of a given size there were in inventory; they would let him figure it out for himself. It was totally financial accounting, with no element of managerial accounting whatever.

My father wants managerial accounting reports, but of course he doesn't call them that. If I accept his offer, and I think that I shall, we will have to start from scratch to develop an information system and a control system. It will be an awful job, but I think that it could be an immeasurable help to the company also. The primary problem is that my father thinks that I can just sit down and write out the reports that he needs from the existing records, and the secondary problem is that he really doesn't have any idea what reports he does need.

I would have to develop, totally, the information system and the control system, and tie the reports in to the structure of the company and the needs of the business. I think that I would like some help on that. (Statement of Mr. George Hampfel, Jr.)

In order that students may be able to offer meaningful consulting assistance to Mr. George Hampfel, Jr., in his new position as treasurer and partial owner of the Hampfel-McFarland Company, and help in the design of the new planning and control systems, the balance of this case provides information on the product descriptions, marketing plans, production methods, installation requirements, organizational structure, and current problems of the company.

Product Descriptions of the Hampfel-McFarland Company. The Hampfel-McFarland Company manufactures, sells, and installs complete emission control systems, repairs and modifies existing systems, and produces unrelated sheet-metal products. Company sales in 1974 were just slightly under $6,000,000, with complete systems accounting for 54% of that total, repairs and modifications 37%, and miscellaneous unrelated products 9%.

The complete systems for dust and/or fume control vary, of course, by size and complexity, depending upon the requirements of the productive process they are designed to serve, but generally each system consists of a number of roughly similar components. These similar components are the collector hoods, the collector pipes, the header pipes, blower pipes, separator units, blower fans, and special units.

1. *Collector hoods.* The collector hoods are sheet-metal forms that cover the grinding machines, heating furnaces, plating tanks, spraying booths, and other pieces of equipment that produce the dust, fumes, waste products, or pollutants that are to be removed by air. The collector hoods are generally designed individually for each application, but some new pieces of equipment are now delivered with the collector hood as an integral part of the unit, while other commonly used machines have stan-

dard collector hoods that have been built many times in the past, and do not require redesign.

2. *Collector pipes.* The collector pipes are sheet-metal sections of piping that convey the dust, fumes, waste materials, or pollutants from the collector hoods on the individual machines, furnaces, etc., to the header pipes. The collector pipes are generally made in smaller diameters, due to the limited air required, and are usually produced from lighter-gauge steel, due to the limited amount of wear. Common diameters for collector pipes are 4, 5, 6, 7, 8, 10, 12, and 14 in.; they are made in both straight sections and elbows of 30, 45, and 90°.

3. *Header pipes.* The header pipes are sheet-metal sections of piping that join the collector pipes from the individual machines, furnaces, tanks, etc., to the main blower pipes that carry the dust, fumes, waste materials, or pollutants to the central separator units. The header pipes are generally designed individually for each application, since the number and the location and the diameter of the collector pipes and the size of the main blower pipe will usually differ for each system; however, some of the more common units, such as a header pipe that will accommodate four 6-in. collector pipes and connect to a 12-in. blower pipe, have been built many times in the past and can be made from existing drawings.

4. *Blower pipes.* The blower pipes are sheet-metal sections of piping that carry dust, fumes, waste materials, or other pollutants suspended in air from the collection point at the header pipe to the processing point at the separator unit. Blower pipes tend to be in the larger diameter, due to the volume of air required, and they often are made of heavier-gauge steel, due to the

wear involved. Common diameters for blower pipes are 16, 18, 24, 30, 36, 42, 48, 60, 72, and 84 in.; the larger pipes are obviously for very large systems. Blower pipes are also made in straight sections and elbows.

5. *Separator units.* The separator units are sheet-metal units that are used to separate dust, fumes, waste materials, or other pollutants from the air that is used to transport the materials, and then to discharge the clear air at the top and the pollutants at the bottom. There are four major types of air separator devices:

a. *Cyclone air separators* are the familiar cylinder and cone-shaped units that are seen on factory roofs. They operate on the principle that, since they are very much larger in diameter than the incoming blower pipe, the air will slow down as it enters the cyclone, and suspended particle matter such as sawdust or planer shavings will settle out of the air stream at the slower speeds. Cyclone collectors vary between 5 and 12 ft in diameter; they are generally used for coarse or heavy particle matter, but do not work well on fine dust, and do not work at all for smoke or fumes.

b. *Bag filter separators* are simple enlargements of the common vacuum cleaner. Industrial bags are made of different materials, depending upon the particle matter to be collected, and may be 16 to 48 in. wide and 10 to 30 ft long. They are usually hung from the top, with the exhaust air forced into them from the bottom. Several bags are used in parallel; periodically, the air stream to a single bag is cut off, and the bag deflates, depositing the particle matter in a hopper. Bag filter separators are often used for fine dust, but they do not work at all for smoke or fumes. The bag filters are not 100% effective for very fine dust, and consequently they are seldom used where clear air laws are stringent.

c. *Wet scrubber separators* are thought to be more efficient collectors of the smaller pollutant particles, such as very fine cement dust or coal dust, than either of the first two units, and they will even separate some of the vapor pollutants. The dirty air stream comes into the collector, where its speed is greatly increased, either by reducing sharply the diameter of the pipe, or by installing a powered fan. The air, now moving at 135 to 175 miles per hour, is sprayed with water, producing an atomized mist. The dust particles adhere to the water droplets, and some of the vaporized chemicals are dissolved by the water; the air stream then enters a cyclone, which separates the slurry (watery mixture) by gravity. The slurry falls to the bottom of the cyclone, where it collects in a hopper, and then may be either taken or piped to a settling pond where the water evaporates, leaving the dust and chemicals behind.

d. *Electrostatic precipitator separators* are the most technically advanced collectors of the smaller pollutant particles. The precipitator is a large unit, often 20 ft high x 10 ft wide x 5 ft thick, so that the air stream slows down as it enters the separator. The dirty air first passes through a series of copper plates, where the dust particles are given a positive electrical charge. The air then passes through another series of negatively charged copper plates and, like iron filings attracted to a magnet, the dust particles adhere to the electrostatic plates. Periodically, the air flow and the electrical currents are shut off and the plates are shaken, dropping their builtup layers of dust into a hopper below.

6. The *blower fan* or power unit consists of a purchased fan, mounted on a steel shaft with low-friction bearings, encased by a sheet-metal housing, and driven by an electric motor. The air flow within the emission control system is determined by the size and speed of the blower fan. Blower fans are available in sizes from 24 to 84 in. in diameter, and are driven by motors that range from 5 to 75 hp.

7. *Special units* are occasionally required due to the corrosive nature of the fumes or the high temperatures of the air to be carried within the system. These special units are usually made of stainless or alloy steel, and are designed to neutralize the corrosive fumes by chemical action or to cool the heated air by a heat exchanger or water spray. The smoke and fumes from a smelting furnace, for example, would be at a temperature of 600 °F; this would melt the usual galvanized steel used for collector hoods and blower pipes. A heat exchanger is used, made of a high-temperature alloy steel with an inner and outer sleeve; the furnace smoke and fumes are in the outer sleeve, with cool air in the inner sleeve. The cool air is heated to about 400 °F, which of course reduces the temperature of the furnace emissions, and the heated air is then blown into the furnace to support combustion and to conserve fuel.

An example of a simple system is shown in Exhibit 1. This particular system has been designed for sawdust collection within a furniture factory, and it operates like a giant vacuum cleaner, drawing the sawdust and wood shavings in from the various machines within the factory (saws, planers, jointers, sanders, etc.) via the collector hoods and the collector pipes to the header pipes, and then transporting the waste material through the blower pipe to the cyclone separator. The

Exhibit 1 *Example of an emission control system for sawdust collection and separation at a furniture manufacturing company*

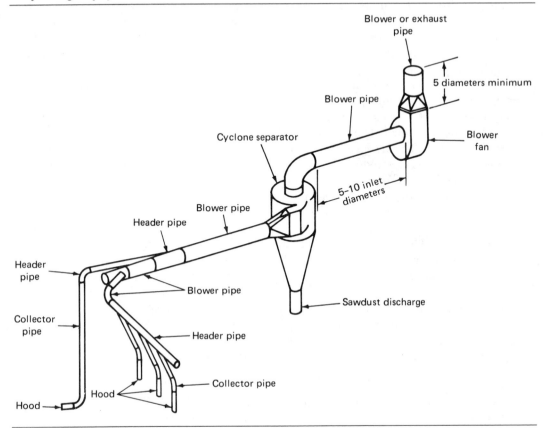

Source: Company records.

collection, transportation, and separation of sawdust in this manner requires an air speed of 4,000 feet per minute. This velocity must remain constant throughout the system, since insufficient speed causes clogging, and excessive speed produces wear. (The means of calculating the air speed for all parts of a system are described in the marketing and customer engineering section of this case.)

The material composition of the various components within each system is determined by the abrasive nature of the material or the corrosive nature of the fumes the system is designed to handle, and by the temperature at which the system is designed to oper-

ate. Components may be fabricated from galvanized steel, alloy steel, stainless steel, and glass- or ceramic-coated steel, although 85% of the work is with galvanized (zinc-coated) steel. Material thicknesses range from 22-gauge to 3/8 in. plate, although again 85% of the work is with standard weights of sheet metal for each size components: e.g., 36-in. blower pipes are normally made from 3/16-in. sheet steel.

Marketing and Engineering Services of the Hampfel-McFarland Company. The initial customer contact usually originates through a letter or telephone call requesting either a price estimate or engineering assistance on the fabrication and installation of a new emission control system or the modification and repair of an existing system. The Hampfel-McFarland company has never advertised or performed missionary sales work, but Mr. Hampfel feels that the company is well enough known so that it is asked to bid or assist on "a goodly portion" of the available emission control business within their area. After receiving the request, a salesman is sent to interview the customer. The company has five salesmen who are termed "sales engineers," but none have extensive engineering training; instead, all are long-term employees who have worked in the shop on sheet-metal fabrication and in the field on air system installation, so that they have extensive practical knowledge. On approximately 30% of the calls, the salesman is told that the proposed or modified system has been entirely designed by the customer's engineering department or by an engineering consultant, and Hampfel-McFarland is asked only to submit a formal bid on the fabrication and installation, as described in the drawings and specifications which are given to the salesman. Most of the larger systems, with a value from $250,000 to over $1,000,000, are sold in this manner. For the smaller systems, which represent perhaps 70% of the calls, the company is asked to recommend the design and then bid on the fabrication and installation. In these cases, the salesman will estimate the volume and weight of the dust or waste materials to be moved,

will establish the location of the sources generating these materials, will sketch the dimensions of the collector hoods covering these sources, will measure the distance the material is to be transported, and will recommend the type of separator and the size of the blower fan to be used.

The drawings and specifications, if available, or the information on the requirements of the system, are then brought back to the Grand Rapids office and given to the engineering staff. Again, the formal engineering training of the designers and estimators is limited, but all members of the department have had extensive drafting and practical experience. The designers convert the information recorded by the salesmen to the specific components needed for the system. Exhibit 2 gives an illustration of this conversion for a dust control system being designed for a foundry using sand shakers to form the moulds for casting; for brevity, only the first few components of this system are listed.

The designer generally selects the components so as to roughly balance the total duct area throughout the systems; that is, the four 7-in. collector pipes, each with an area of 0.267 square foot, or 1.068 square feet total (4 x 0.267), connect to a 14-in. header pipe with an area of 1.069 square feet. If two 14″ header pipes came together, representing 2.136 square feet total, the designer would connect them to a 20-in. blower pipe, with an area of 2.1817 square feet.

After selecting and sizing the components,

Exhibit 2 *Components for dust control system for foundry sand shakers in molding department*

No.	Component name	Duct area (sq ft)	Pipe straight (ft)	Pipe elbow	Pipe entrance	Total length (ft)
4	Shaker hoods pattern #8713	1.355	—	—	—	—
4	7-in. collector pipes	0.267	12.6	90° × 2.0 ft	30° × 2.6 ft	17.2
1	14-in. header pipe with four 7 in. × 30° junctions	1.069	26.0	—	—	26.0

Source: Company records.

Exhibit 3 *Air volume and air speed calculations for dust control system for foundry sand shakers*

No.	Component name	Duct area (sq ft)	Resistance factor	Resistance component	Air volume	Air speed
4	Shaker hoods pattern 8713	1.335	—	—	929	718
4	7-in. collector pipes	0.267	0.0841	0.001447	929	3,590
1	14-in. header pipe with four 7 in. × 30° junctions	1.067	0.0337	0.000875	3,717	3,478

Source: Company records.

the designer looks up within published tables the resistance factor, or friction that the air and the conveyed material will encounter against the sides of the piping. The resistance factor is a function of the weight and nature of the material to be carried, and the number and angle of the bends in the pipe; it is expressed as a resistance per 1,000 ft of the component. The air volume is then computed, based upon the size and speed of the blower fan and the number and size of the divisions within the piping leading back to each component. Finally, the air speed is computed, based upon the formula: air velocity = air volume/duct area × resistance (Exhibit 3).

The resultant air velocity and hood suction at each dust or waste material source is compared to a standard needed to pick up the material. If the air velocity at the pickup points is not great enough, the designer increases either the size or speed of the blower fan, and calculates the air velocities once again.

After the air velocities have been determined, and the size of each component has been definitely set, the list is given to an estimator for bidding. Technically, the estimator is to compute the material and labor needed both to fabricate and install each piece. (The material used at installation consists of supports and braces for the piping and other components.) Actually, since many of the pieces have been made many times in the past, standard costs have become accepted for these units. All collector pipes and blower pipes in standard sizes, and all other components that have a pattern number (the pattern number refers to the template that is used to layout the cutting and forming dimensions on the sheet metal) indicating previous manufacture, now have standard costs that are used in bidding, and no calculations on labor or material are performed. The estimator computes the labor and material costs only for those components within the system which are nonstandard; these are often the header pipes (Exhibit 4).

The estimator totals the costs for all of the components required within the system, and then multiplies by 1.5 to allow for both the

Exhibit 4 *Labor and material cost estimates for dust control system for foundry sand shakers*

No.	Component name	Fabricate material	Fabricate labor	Install material	Install labor	Total costs
4	Shaker hoods pattern 8713	$26.87 each		$14.00 each		$163.48
4	7-in. collector pipes with 90° elbows × 17.2 ft	$41.17 each		$10.00 each		$204.68
1	14-in. header pipe with four 7 in. × 30° junctions	$21.41	$117.43	$4.17	$20.00	$163.01

Source: Company records.

manufacturing and administrative overhead. The full report for each system, consisting of both engineering calculations and cost estimates, is then given to Mr. George Hampfel, Sr., who studies it for a short period of time, and adjusts the total price upward or downward depending upon his "feel" for the situation. All seven members of the engineering department were in agreement that Mr. Hampfel had an uncanny ability to accurately estimate costs. One member of the department stated that, "When a bid goes out of here it is right; Mr. Hampfel won't be off more than a $5.00 bill on a $250,000 job." Only the final price for the system, as adjusted by Mr. Hampfel, is sent to the customer; no supporting details are included in the bid.

Bids are sent to customers at fairly regular intervals throughout the year, but a majority of the orders are received in the late spring for shipment over the summer. Approximately 60% of the dollar volume of annual billings usually falls in the four-month period from June to September. This seasonality is partially due to the weather, since outside installation is simpler during the summer, but it is primarily due to the model years associated with the automobile and home appliance industries. The installation, modification, or repair of an emission control system often requires the shutdown of the productive equipment, and this work is usually scheduled for the annual plant shutdown for the model changes.

Production and Installation Functions of the Hampfel-McFarland Company. When an order is received for the fabrication and installation of a new emission control system, or for the modification or repair of an existing system, a job order is prepared by the engineering department listing the customer, delivery date, and required components. Engineering drawings are completed for the new items, particularly header pipes, for which no existing patterns are available. The job order

and the related prints are then sent to the shop foreman.

The production of the sheet-metal components for an emission control system within the shop can be broken into three major operations:

1. *Layout.* Sheet metal layout involves descriptive geometry. This is the process of unfolding and drawing the three-dimensional shape of the finished component onto the one-dimensional surface of the sheet metal, prior to cutting, bending, and rolling. A straight section of pipe is a fairly simple example, since it requires only a rectangular sheet of metal of the proper dimensions, but an elbow or entrance section requires a triangular piece with two curvilinear edges, and some of the more intricate components, such as collector hoods or header pipes, involve very complex geometric analysis. Patterns, which represent this analysis as performed for prior jobs, are used when available. In 1975, the company had 1,105 patterns; each pattern can be visualized as a template which is laid over the sheet metal to assist in marking out the required shape for cutting and bending. Almost every job sent to the shop, however, involved one or two components which had never been made by the company previously, and consequently had to be laid out by a skilled worker from the blueprints.
2. *Fabrication.* After layout, either by pattern or by hand, the sheet metal is cut to the required shape and dimensions by powered shears. The flat piece is then formed into the three-dimensional shape through the use of both hand tools and powered machinery; a brake is a machine that will bend sheet metal at a sharp angle, while the rolls refer to a different machine that will produce a gradual curvature.
3. *Assembly.* Assembly is the process of joining the fabricated shapes into finished units through welding or riveting, and

then combining the units into a complete component. Collector pipe or blower pipe, for example, is usually assembled in 4-ft lengths (the standard width of galvanized sheet metal), and then the 4-ft sections are welded or riveted, with elbows or entrances as required, into the desired lengths, up to 20 ft.

The miscellaneous products, such as machine guards, motor covers, part baskets, and hydraulic tanks, which together represent 9% of the total company revenues, are manufactured by the same process of layout, fabrication, and assembly that are used for the emission control systems.

The installation of the completed components for a new or remodeled emission control system outside the shop requires delivery and placement:

1. *Delivery.* The company operates a fleet of seven trucks of different sizes to carry the system components to the job site; some of the trucks are equipped with a light crane to make installation easier.
2. *Placement.* The company normally sends a crew of workers to set the components in place, and to erect the supporting structural steel. Electrical components (motors and control switches) are mounted, but not wired. Placement requires the use of hand tools, portable welders, and, occasionally, light cranes.

The production shop of Hampfel-McFarland occupies the entire ground floor of an older brick building in the industrial section of Grand Rapids. The work flow is from an extensive sheet metal inventory to 7 layout benches, then to 4 shears, 5 brakes, and 2 sets of rolls for fabrication, and finally to 11 welding benches for assembly. Finished units are stored near the loading dock, ready for shipment to the customer's location.

The work force of Hempfel-McFarland is entirely unionized; all employees are members of the United Brotherhood of Sheetmetal Workers. Wage rates are the major component of production costs; Mr. Hampfel estimated that the total cost structure of the company could probably be broken down into 60% wages, 15% material, 15% shop overhead, and 10% general overhead and profit. Wage rates in 1975 averaged $9.76 per hour.

The wage rates in sheet-metal fabrication and installation are high since the workers are considered to be skilled tradesmen, and receive four years of training through a union-run apprenticeship program. The apprenticeship program combines on-the-job training with classroom instruction; particular emphasis is placed on the descriptive geometry needed for sheet-metal layout. The program, however, concentrates on the layout, fabrication, and assembly of heating and air-conditioning duct systems, a type of work that involves much lighter metals and much simpler components than those used by Hampfel-McFarland. For this reason, recent employees tend to be of a much lower skill level than the older workers.

The work force fluctuates in response to demand. There are approximately 70 full-time employees, who work straight through the year, and there are an additional 50 part-time employees who are hired for the peak demand period during the summer months. Seasonal employees are available through the union hiring hall.

The employees can be separated into four major classifications, although there is considerable movement back and forth between the assignments, depending upon the order volume and the level of skill required.

1. *Layout men.* Layout is considered to require the highest degree of skill in sheet-metal work. Even though 90 to 95% of all layout work uses patterns, the balance involves very complicated analysis, calculations, and projections. The layout men tend to be the oldest employees in the company, who have worked both inside on fabrication and assembly and outside on delivery

and installation, and have selected this job as the most desirable. The layout men, however, often work on other tasks, such as the fabrication and assembly of nonstandard and complex components.

2. Leadsmen. Leadsmen are considered to be the second-highest skilled group in the company; they are the foremen of the installation crews. Each crew, which may vary between two and seven men, usually takes one of the company trucks, which is equipped with portable welders, hand tools, and other field equipment, and drives to the job site. For small jobs, the components are usually loaded on the company truck; for larger systems, the components are shipped by either contract or common carriers. The leadsman on each job is responsible for the entire installation phase; he communicates with the shop foreman requesting additional material shipment, required design changes, or closer adherence to tolerances. During slack periods, the leadsmen also work on tasks inside the shop, such as fabrication and assembly.

3. *Fabrication and assembly.* The workers assigned specifically to fabrication and assembly are usually older men who wish to avoid the travel required for field installation, and yet lack the skill or seniority required for full-time layout work. They fabricate and assemble the components, and do some of the simpler layout tasks.

4. *General.* The largest group of workers includes all the seasonal employees and perhaps 25 to 30 additional full-time men. They both work inside on fabrication and assembly, and outside on the installation crews, as assigned by the shop foreman.

All job assignments and production scheduling is set by the foreman; he starts the various components into production based upon his perception of the time required for completion, the delivery date for the completed system, and the present loading on the shears, brakes, and rolls from other jobs. Individual work assignments are made on an availability basis. When an employee completes an assigned task, he reports to the shop foreman to receive another job. The foreman attempts to match individuals and their particular skills with specific tasks, again in light of the work load on the available facilities. Tasks assigned to layout men often include both layout and fabrication operations, but no assembly. Other individuals are assigned to complete the assembly of components begun by the layout men, or to initiate and complete components from start to finish. In addition to job assignment and production scheduling, the shop foreman is responsible for sheet-metal ordering and inventory control, design modifications, component tolerances, and quality control, final shipment of the completed systems, and supervision of the installation crews.

Problems in the shop production include bottlenecks which continually develop around the shears and brakes. There is a considerable setup time required for each new operation on these machines, and workers with an assigned job are often idle waiting to utilize the units. Component orders for large systems can monopolize the available machine time, and the smaller jobs and emergency repair orders are either forced to wait, or to break into an established sequence of operations, which substantially increases the setup costs and machine downtime. The machines are expensive (a new shear capable of cutting ⅜-in. steel plate would cost $28,000 installed), so that while the company has room for additional equipment, Mr. Hampfel has been reluctant to make the investment. However, the foreman estimates that 5% of shop time is wasted, due to bottlenecks, and he has repeatedly asked for additional machines.

Problems in field installation revolve about the coordination between marketing, engineering, and production. Often, additional collector pipe or blower pipe is needed, above that estimated by the engineering department, and occasionally new elbows or pipe bends are required, to avoid an obstruction in the customer's plant which was not recorded by the salesmen. Finally, errors often occur in sheet-metal fabrication and assembly, and it is not uncommon for the components to require extensive reworking in the field in order to be joined together. All of these problems are magnified when the installation crew is a considerable distance (up to 300 miles) from the shop, and has to wait for additional materials or return to rebuild a single component. Some of the leadsmen estimated that the total hours lost were in the range of 7 to 8%.

Mr. George Hampfel, Jr., recognized the problems and opportunities that were inher-

ent in the Hampfel-McFarland Company since he had worked in the shop and on installation crews during summer vacations while he was in college and the M.B.A. program, but he was not exactly certain how he should set up the management information and control systems for the company.

Class Assignment. The existing management information and control system for the Hampfel-McFarland Company consists of a single figure (annual profit or loss) written on a 3 in. x 5 in. piece of note paper. In addition, you are given the organizational chart shown in Exhibit 5. What improvements would you recommend?

Exhibit 5 *Organizational structure of the Hampfel-McFarland Company, 1975, prior to the death of McFarland*

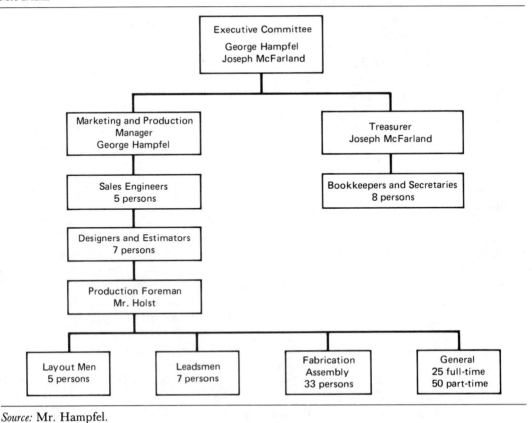

Source: Mr. Hampfel.

Black Hills Bottling Company "B"

George Freidenrich was asked by his grandfather to return to Rapid City, South Dakota, and assist in the management of the Black Hills Bottling Company. He spent eight months studying the cost structure and market segments of the soft-drink bottling industry in the Western Plains states, and then recommended to his grandfather that the company open a "pop shop" or factory outlet in Pierre, South Dakota, 172 miles northeast of Rapid City. The new store, which was built in the parking lot of a large shopping center to provide easy access, sold Royal Crown, Diet Rite, and Nehi national brands at regular prices and Black Hills, a new company brand at discount prices. They even offered a new product, Black Hills "Blackstrap," which was a very dark cola with a somewhat stronger flavor; it became one of the best-selling soft drinks in the area. Surprisingly, the national brands also sold well despite the lack of any price appeal; the higher margins here provided funds for local advertising, which in turn created a demand in local chain stores. Overall, the pop shop was felt to be very successful.

> I thought that our marketing concept would work because we had the national brands to assure quality, the company brands to offer savings, and the location to provide convenience. I did not expect Blackstrap to sell so well, and I certainly never expected chain stores in the area to start placing orders since I always thought of Royal Crown as the third person in a two-man race (Coca-Cola and Pepsi), but our advertising created the demand, and the chain stores were willing to buy from us even though we were competing with them at the pop shop since we were not cutting price on the national brands. The chain stores even want to buy Blackstrap from us, although we

have explained that we can't offer the usual discounts. (Statement of George Freidenrich)

During the summer and fall of 1978, the bottling line at Rapid City was operating two shifts to keep up with demand, and the company was buying cans of Royal Crown and Diet Rite from the franchised bottler in Minneapolis.

> The trucking costs were ridiculous, but we wanted to get some experience operating heavy trucks for bulk shipment, and we wanted to see how cans would sell in our area. Everything we've done this year has really been market research; we wanted to find out what would work and what wouldn't. Now we know, and now we're ready to make some fairly major investments. (Statement of George Freidenrich)

On the basis of sales estimates provided by the test marketing, it was decided to open two pop shops in Sioux Falls (population 265,000) and one in Aberdeen (population 177,000), and to set up a canning line in Pierre (near the center of the state) and a bottling line in Aberdeen (near the eastern border). The intent was to establish a solid base in South Dakota and then move westward to Casper, Wyoming (population 135,000) and southward to Scotts Bluffs, Nebraska (population 82,000); in both of these cities there were existing Royal Crown bottling franchises that were thought to be for sale.

> This is a planning situation where you can look either at the problems or at the opportunities. We decided to be aggressive, and pursue the opportunities, but we want to get established quickly, before the bottler in Denver, Colorado, begins to move northward. The problem, however, is that we're going to become a much big-

ger company, geographically dispersed over three states, and much more difficult to run. (Statement of George Freidenrich)

Class Assignment. Design the organizational structure and managerial systems for the Black Hills Bottling Company, given that the planned expansion will occur. Be specific on the measures of performance you propose for each of the positions shown on your organizational chart, and on the incentives that will be offered to persons assigned to those positions.

First Citizens Bank of Santa Clara County "B"

Assume that Ms. Susan McKettrick, president of the First Citizens Bank of Santa Clara, has decided that the bank will remain a "full-service" institution, and not attempt to orient its services toward any specific market segment. Assume also that the revenues of the bank, in 1978, came from the sources shown in Exhibit 1, and that this relative balance is expected to continue in the future, following the full-service strategy.

It was not possible, owing to a lack of cost accounting information, to accurately identify the sources of the pretax income of $312,-700. The bank, in 1978, had a central office in downtown Santa Clara, and branches in Sunnyvale and Mountain View, and the organizational structure was based upon the three locations. All offices offered consumer, real estate, and commercial loans and, of course, teller service; the Santa Clara office

Exhibit 1 *Revenues of the First Citizens Bank of Santa Clara County in 1978*

Interest on consumer loans, primarily secured	$2,481,700	34.2%
Interest on real estate loans, primarily commercial property	509,100	10.4%
Interest on commercial loans, both secured and unsecured	1,919,200	26.5%
	4,903,000	67.7%
Interest on U.S. Treasury securities	935,400	12.9%
Interest on state and municipal securities	526,200	7.3%
	1,461,600	20.2%
Trust department income	504,200	6.9%
Service charges on demand deposit accounts	284,000	3.9%
Miscellaneous income, primarily safe deposit rentals	96,500	1.3%
	884,700	12.1%
Total of interest and income	$7,249,300	100.0%

Source: **Company records.**

Exhibit 2 *Organizational structure of the First Citizens Bank of Santa Clara County*

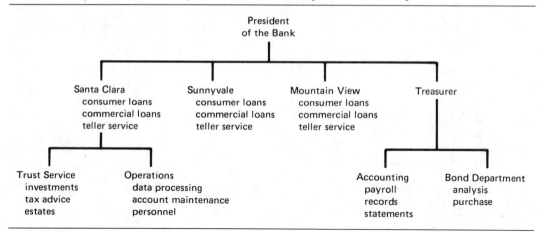

Source: Conversations with senior officers.

provided trust services for the customers of all the branches, and check clearing, deposit recording, and data processing for the accounts at all the branches (Exhibit 2).

Class Assignment. Develop proposals for change, if needed, in the organizational structure and design new managerial systems for the First Citizens Bank of Santa Clara County. Assume that you are a recent graduate of an M.B.A. program and an assistant vice president of the bank, and that Ms. McKettrick has asked you, as a person

trained in management, to assist her in the reorganization. Finally, assume that Ms. McKettrick has told you that since apparently there are no opportunities for specialization in providing financial services in the area, the bank will have to operate more effectively and efficiently than its competition in order to survive. What are the important tasks in banking? How would you structure those tasks? How would you plan, control, and motivate the performance of those tasks?

Western Pacific Transport, Inc., "B"

Western Pacific Transport, the intermodal freight subsidiary of Western Pacific Railroad, purchased Motor Cargo, Inc., in the spring of 1979. Motor Cargo, Inc., operated four large truck terminals in Los Angeles, Salt

Lake City, Denver, and Reno, and their primary revenues came from intercity shipments between those points (Exhibit 1).

Western Pacific Transport operated rail-yards with either straddle cranes or forklift

Exhibit 1 *Income statements (000's omitted) for Motor Cargo, Inc., 1975–1977*

	1975	1976	1977
Intercity truckload revenues	$1,601	$2,047	$2,103
Intercity less-than-truckload revenues	2,821	3,509	3,457
Intracity less-than-truckload revenues	170	157	152
Total revenues	4,592	5,713	5,712
Drivers' and helpers' wages	835	1,006	1,115
Terminal workers' wages	617	747	677
Employment benefits	323	349	496
Officers' and supervisors' salaries	503	651	642
Vehicle fuel and oil	167	233	264
Vehicle parts and repairs	190	272	293
Vehicle tires and tubes	56	81	116
General supplies	217	277	301
Operating taxes and licenses	167	204	225
Operating insurance	139	237	194
Communications and utilities	77	91	117
Depreciation and amortization	197	168	186
Truck and trailer rentals	715	1,119	935
Building and office equipment rentals	82	202	219
Miscellaneous expenses*	89	146	75
Loss or (gain) on disposal of assets	(39)	(124)	(789)
Interest expenses*	87	58	80
Total expenses	4,422	5,717	5,149
Corporate income (loss before taxes)	170	(4)	563
Federal and state income (taxes) or credit	(55)	46	(141)
Corporate income (loss) after taxes	115	42	424

Source: Trinc's Blue Book of the Trucking Industry for the respective years, supplemented by industry (*) estimates.

trucks to load and unload trailers and containers at Oakland, Sacramento, Reno, and Denver, and they maintained a very small fleet of trucks (two or three tractors and flatbed trailers) at each of those points to deliver the Plan II and Postal Rate intermodal freight, both of which required pickup and delivery at the customer's location by the railroad. In addition, Western Pacific Transport had sales offices to provide marketing services and delivery information to intermodal customers in Oakland, Salt Lake City, Denver, Kansas City, Chicago, Houston, and New York City. The last two offices specialized in the Mini-Bridge service, in which rail transport of the intermodal containers substituted for ocean shipping; Mini-Bridge services accounted for 33% of Western Pacific Transport's revenues in 1978.

Class Assignment. Develop an organizational structure and managerial systems for Western Pacific Transport to combine the trucking and intermodal freight businesses. Assume that the Transport Division will be responsible for sales and operations, but that finance, data processing, personnel, and legal services will continue to be provided by the railroad, as shown in Exhibit 5 of the original case. Assume that the "operations" for the Transport Division includes loading and unloading the trailers or containers on rail cars, but not dispatching or running the trains.

Dow Chemical Company "B"

The Dow Chemical Company is a large and historically successful chemical company, with corporate headquarters in Midland, Michigan, major production sites in Michigan, Texas, Louisiana, Canada, Germany, France, Italy, Yugoslavia, Brazil, Australia, and Japan, and sales throughout the world. The company is divided into five geographic divisions: United States, Europe/Africa, Latin America, Canada, and Pacific. Each of the divisions was organized somewhat differently, to reflect national and cultural variances, but all had a semi-matrix structure, as shown in Exhibit 1 for the U.S. division.

The basic corporate structure of the U.S. Division of Dow Chemical is functional, with separate departments for sales, manufacturing, and R&D (basic research, product development, and process engineering or "technical services"). Cutting across these functional chains of command are nine department managers, 31 business managers, and 65 product managers. The nine departments are grouped according to the chemical nature or market orientation of their products, and follow a classification of inorganic chemicals, organic chemicals, metal products, functional products, plastic coating materials, plastic molding materials, health care products, agricultural products, and consumer products. The groupings are not entirely logical, and tend to have a historical rather than a chemical derivation (e.g., magnesium, which is a metal, is currently grouped with the organic chemicals since it was originally a by-product of brine processing to make caustic soda and chlorine).

The 31 business managers are each responsible for a group of products within one of the departments. Each business manager works with representatives from Customer Sales, Product Manufacturing, and R&D/Technical Services, each is assisted by a Marketing Manager, and each has profit responsibility for the assigned products but lacks formal authority over the functional representatives.

> We call each product group a "business" since it is our intent that they all act like small businesses; they should set objectives and then work to achieve those objectives with the support of the corporation but independent of the hierarchy of the organization. We want flexibility and profit responsibility. But the business manager has no authority over the other members of the business group. The manager has to convince the functional people to accept or modify objectives, and then the functional people set the policies and plan the programs to achieve those objectives. The functional people have to communicate both upward and down-

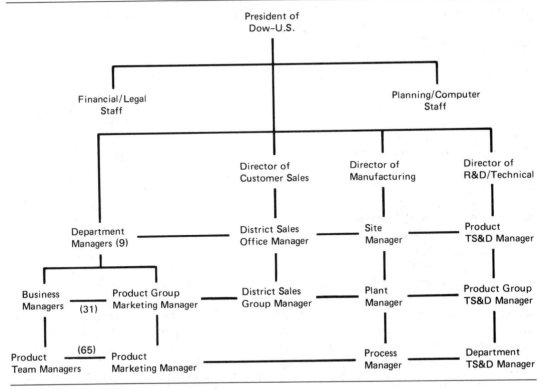

Source: Discussion with company executives.

ward in their own departments. Capital allocations have to be approved by senior management, and policies and plans have to be approved by the functional directors, so that we do get integration. (Statement of a senior Dow executive)

The 65 product managers are each responsible for a single product or product line within one of the business units. They also work with representatives from Product Manufacturing and R&D/Technical Services, although not directly with people from Customer Sales; information and requests to the district sales offices are transmitted by the product group marketing manager. Each product manager has profit responsibility, but no formal authority.

The 65 product managers have responsibility for 51 end products (sold for non-chemical processing by other industries, or for consumer use) and 14 intermediate products (sold for chemical processing by other companies). The product management teams are our primary planning units. These 65 products account for 70% of our sales and, probably, 100% of our profits. These are our established, major products. One way to look at it is that the business manager looks after new products on the way up or old products on the way down, and delegates responsibility for the reliable products to the product manager. (Statement of a senior Dow executive)

Class Assignment. Design the managerial systems for the current organizational structure of the Dow Chemical Company. Be specific, and include suggestions for planning, control, and motivation according to the outline shown above.

1. Where are the problems likely to surface; in short, what portions of your design do you find less than totally satisfactory?
2. The Dow Chemical Company operates in five geographic divisions and 87 countries. Not all products are made in all divisions, and many are transferred between divisions. The transfer price at Dow for all products is the sum of the variable production costs (material, labor, power, maintenance, and disposal) plus the allocated production costs (space and depreciation) at full capacity. What impact does this transfer price have upon planning, control, and motivation? What impact does international operations have upon planning, control, and motivation?

Goodman Machine and Foundry Corporation "B"

In the spring of 1978, Mr. David Goodman, the president and treasurer of Goodman Machine and Foundry Corporation and the eldest son of the founder, retired due to poor health. He was succeeded as president by his son, Sidney Goodman II, and as treasurer by his daughter, Doris Goodman-Bethea. The new general managers of the company were both in their early 30s, were both graduates of the M.B.A. program at the University of Michigan, and were both determined to expand sales and profits rapidly. The reason for the decision to expand, and to follow a much more aggressive strategy, was a desire by all members of the Goodman family to be in a position to pay the estate taxes, when necessary, and to maintain the existing control of the company. Mr. David Goodman owned 90% of the common stock and had suffered a series of debilitating heart attacks.

> When our grandfather died in 1972, Dad was able to pay the inheritance taxes personally, although he had to sell most of his other property and borrow heavily to do so. Now, just six years later, we are faced with the same problem. Hopefully, Dad will live for many more years, but we can't count on that, and the doctors are not optimistic. When he dies, we will have to sell 35 to 40% of his stock to pay the taxes, or use corporate funds for redemption (a closely held corporation was permitted to use corporate funds to purchase stock from an estate to maintain family control of the company), but that would destroy our liquidity. If we sell the stock on the open market, we will get a very low multiple of earnings since there has been no growth since 1970. Our plan is to boost the sales and earnings, and then arrange a public issuance, with registration on the American Stock Exchange, when needed. We know how to increase sales and earnings, but we are going to need a little help in managing the larger company. (Statement of Doris Goodman-Bethea)

The new managers of the company felt that the existing strategy was too diffused, with too many products in too many markets. To provide a sharper focus, and greater concentration of the available resources, Sidney Goodman and Doris Goodman-Bethea proposed that the Motor Division (construction carts, commercial lawn mowers, commercial sweepers, and estate tractors) be sold to a manufacturer of residential lawn mowers and garden tractors who wanted a larger product line,

with the higher horsepowers and wider profit margins of commercial machines. They also proposed to purchase the Missouri Shovel Company of Kansas City, Missouri, which made heavy equipment (belt conveyors, bar screens, jaw crushers, cone crushers, wire screens, and vibrating washers) for the aggregate processing equipment, and power shovels, cranes, and draglines in the smaller sizes that were used in commercial construction and aggregate mining. Lastly, they planned to open sales offices in Decatur, Illinois; Stevens Point, Wisconsin; Minneapolis, Minnesota; Kansas City, Missouri; and Erie, Pennsylvania. The intent was to dominate the aggregate processing equipment industry in the Midwest.

> We are going against the usual rules for strategic planning. We are giving up our products in the upper right-hand quadrant (high growth/low share) of the planning matrix, in order to reinforce our position in the lower left-hand sector (low growth/high share). This strategy can be successful, however, since we can use our volume to reduce costs, and maintain our margins in a price-competitive industry. (Statement of Doris Goodman-Bethea)

In June 1978, the two managers had negotiated tentative agreements for the sale of the Motor Division and the purchase of the Missouri Shovel Company. Ms. Goodman-Bethea had been in charge of the negotiations; she had a frank and open approach that seemed to disarm her opponents, many of whom apparently did not expect a young and attractive woman to be so adept at financial bargaining. The prices that were negotiated were said to be "very fair, very equitable"; essentially, adequate funds would be obtained from the sale of the growing Motor Division to pay for the nearly stagnant Missouri Shovel Company. David Goodman and Doris Goodman-Bethea, however, hesitated to confirm the final arrangements, despite the balanced prices of the proposed change and the firm approval by other members of the Goodman family.

> Financial haggling is fun; that is the reason so many M.B.A.'s go into investment banking. But managing a large industrial company in a mature, price-competitive industry is hard work, and I'm not certain that the M.B.A. training prepares a person to do that. Our company, if we go through with the divestment and acquisition, will have $63,000,000 in sales, two plants and a foundry in Lansing, a big plant in Kansas City that lost money four out of the last five years, eight district sales offices in remote locations, a large product line, and a big market. We may need some help in running a company of that size. You are the expert in management; what can you tell us that will help us to manage this company successfully? (Statement of Doris Goodman-Bethea)

Class Assignment. Prepare specific recommendations for the Goodman family members on the management of the Goodman Machine and Foundry, Inc., under the assumption that the Motor Division will be sold and the Missouri Shovel Company will be acquired.

Standard Brands, Inc., "B"

Assume that in 1980, three years after the date of the Standard Brands case described earlier, and after very substantial expenditures for both product development and brand promotion to improve the competitive position of many of the divisions, the portfolio planning matrix showed a better balance among the products (Exhibit 1).

Assume that the senior management of the company has sold the candy division (Baby Ruth and Butterfingers), and plans to sell the liquor division (Fleischmann's gin, vodka, whiskey, etc.) and the wine division (both domestic and imported) to obtain funds for investment in the more rapidly growing Food Service and International divisions. The food Service Division sells "service" brands (non-advertised trade products, generally sold at lower margins but usually of equivalent quality to the "name" brands) of margarine, egg substitutes, packaged desserts, coffee, and tea to restaurants. The International Division sells "foreign" brands (special trade names, adapted to the language of the country, and usually a special formulation, changed to fit the tastes of the population) of margarines, packaged desserts, and soft drinks based upon the high-fructose corn syrup, in South America. Assume that both have been growing rapidly since 1977. Finally, assume that the company plans to establish a New Products Division to develop new food products for distribution through the established channels, and a Planning Department to consider acquisitions of smaller companies with new food products.

Class Assignment. Develop an organizational structure, and design the managerial systems for Standard Brands, given the assumed situation in 1980. Be specific on the measures of performance you propose for each of the divisions, and on the incentives that will be offered to the heads of those divisions.

Exhibit 1 *Assumed portfolio planning matrix, with sales revenues, market growth rates, and market share figures by product line, for Standard Brands, Inc., 1980*

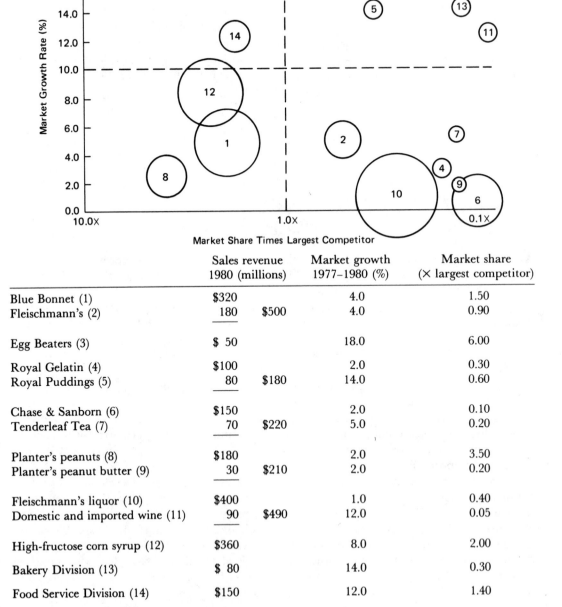

	Sales revenue 1980 (millions)		Market growth 1977–1980 (%)	Market share (× largest competitor)
Blue Bonnet (1)	$320		4.0	1.50
Fleischmann's (2)	180	$500	4.0	0.90
Egg Beaters (3)	$ 50		18.0	6.00
Royal Gelatin (4)	$100		2.0	0.30
Royal Puddings (5)	80	$180	14.0	0.60
Chase & Sanborn (6)	$150		2.0	0.10
Tenderleaf Tea (7)	70	$220	5.0	0.20
Planter's peanuts (8)	$180		2.0	3.50
Planter's peanut butter (9)	30	$210	2.0	0.20
Fleischmann's liquor (10)	$400		1.0	0.40
Domestic and imported wine (11)	90	$490	12.0	0.05
High-fructose corn syrup (12)	$360		8.0	2.00
Bakery Division (13)	$ 80		14.0	0.30
Food Service Division (14)	$150		12.0	1.40
International Division (15)	$120		16.0	1.10

Source: Extrapolations from prior case, supplemented with estimates.

Western Plywood and Lumber Corporation "A"

The corporate offices of the Western Plywood and Lumber Corporation were located in the financial district of San Francisco. Approximately 75 people worked there in positions ranging from the chairman of the board to the mailroom clerk, but the majority were engaged in the staff functions of financial planning, corporate accounting, public relations, and personnel services. Most of these employees were typical of the headquarters staff of other large corporations, and were indistinguishable from the persons going in and coming out of the other office buildings in San Francisco, but George Madders stood out. He drove either a Bentley or a Rolls-Royce to work—he owned both, but used the Rolls, which was a convertible, only when the weather was suitable—and he dressed the way one would expect the owner of a Rolls-Royce to dress, with expensive good taste but somewhat "flashy" clothing. He was a tall person, with a very athletic appearance, and a very outgoing, friendly personality.

> Everyone in the financial district knew George, and he knew them, by name. It was amazing to go to lunch with him; he would stop to talk with 20 to 30 people on the street, and another 10 in the restaurant. This wasn't forced at all; he just knew and remembered people, and people remembered and liked him.
>
> George was a corporate attorney for Western Plywood, but I don't think he worked very hard at it. He also owned an antique store, and was a partner in an art gallery, and spent a lot of time playing tennis or squash, and sailing on the Bay.
>
> He owned a very old house, on the coast above Sausalito, that he had rebuilt

This case centers on an ethical problem; consequently, the names of all individuals, the characteristics of all products, and the locations and principal activities of all firms have been disguised.

> when he first came to California, in 1960. It was filled with early American furniture and oil paintings, and had a view that looked out over the ocean. During the summer he would have garden parties there, and it was impossible to come away without feeling envious. Particularly since he was not married, but would always have a stunning woman with him, and it was always a different one at every party. (Statement of a corporate officer)

It was assumed by his friends in San Francisco that George Madders had inherited wealth. He was from the East Coast, a graduate of Princeton and the Yale Law School, and he occasionally spoke of problems with a trust fund. However, the assumptions were wrong, and the trust fund was nonexistent. George Madders was a thief, and had systematically stolen $100,000 each year for 14 years.

> His method was very simple. One of his jobs was to process claims against the company for defective merchandise or poor service. In any firm with sales over $1 billion annually, you will get some material that is not up to grade, and in any company with over 9,000 employees, you will get some late deliveries and misdirected shipments and injurious behavior. These claims could come from the wholesalers and large distribution yards that had purchased lumber or plywood from Western, or from the builders and contractors who had used the material, or from the companies, hospitals, or government units that owned the buildings. There aren't many claims of this nature; George probably handled only about 15 legitimate cases each year.
>
> When he wanted some money, he would put through a completely fraudu-

625

lent claim. He would open up a bank account in the name of a fictitious lumberyard or contractor or company in some eastern city, and then submit a claim, negotiate a "settlement," have a check issued, and then hand deliver the check for a "final and binding agreement." He would come back with all the papers signed, and no indication that the company, the claim, and the settlement were all imaginary, and the signatures all forged.

His theft was discovered purely by accident. He happened to pick the name of a company in Cleveland that actually existed, and when he deposited the check in a Cleveland bank it was accidentally credited to the account of the real company. The internal auditors at that com-

pany, of course, picked up the unexpected payment and wrote to the treasurer at Western Plywood, asking for the reason. It did not take long then to track down what was happening, and George was arrested. You can imagine the newspaper reports; this embezzlement gave us some bad publicity, just when we didn't need any bad publicity. We have got to set up some controls, for I'm certain that George may have been the most engaging thief, and the most audacious one, but he's not the only one in this company. (Statement of a corporate officer)

Class Assignment. Design a control system to prevent corporate embezzlement of the type described in the case.

Western Plywood and Lumber Corporation "B"

The Western Plywood and Lumber Corporation, a large forest products company operating in Washington and Oregon, was convicted in 1975 of conspiring with other sawmills, veneer mills, and paper mills in the area to restrict the prices paid for timber purchased from the federal government.

Five timber companies and two individuals were convicted in Federal Court in Portland, Oregon of collusion in bidding on federal timber on auction in the Willamette National Forest. Convicted were.... (*Wall Street Journal*, July 17, 1975, p. 20)

Timber on federal land is usually purchased by a sealed bidding process. The U.S.

This case centers on an ethical problem; consequently, the names of all individuals, the characteristics of all products, and the locations and principal activities of all firms have been disguised.

Forest Service clearly identifies the timber to be sold, either by a bright spray of paint on the trunk of each tree marked for selective cutting, or by paint on the trunks of the trees on the perimeter of a block proposed for clear cutting, and then foresters from interested companies are invited to inspect the tract, compute the volume and quality of the logs, estimate the costs and time for logging, and submit a sealed bid. All bids are opened on a given day, and the timber is awarded to the highest bidder.

Many sawmills and plywood mills on the West Coast are highly dependent upon timber sales from federal lands due to the large acreage in national forests in that area. Eighty-five percent of the wood supply on the West Coast is on land owned either by the very large pulp and paper companies, such as Crown Zellerbach and Weyerhaeuser, or by the federal government. The limits on cutting,

Exhibit 1 *Average prices paid for Douglas fir stumpage per 1,000 board feet, on the West Coast, 1960–1974*

	1960	1970	1971	1972	1973	1974
Stumpage prices	$32.00	$41.90	$49.10	$71.70	$138.10	$202.40

Source: Statistical Abstract of the United States, 1977, p. 725.

brought about by increased environmental concerns and conservationist pressures on the government, and the expansion in demand caused by growth in single-family housing, resulted in dramatic price increases in the bids submitted for stumpage (standing timber, ready for cutting) during the 1970s (Exhibit 1).

The very substantial increase in stumpage prices from 1970 to 1974 resulted in the eventual collusion of many of the forest product companies in the area to restrict further price increments.

The stumpage prices in 1974 simply got out of hand, and the pressures on the foresters preparing the bids became immense. Foresters basically are nice people; they go into forestry because they like the outdoors, and they drive around in pickup trucks and hike through the woods and measure timber and have a good time. But they were not having a good time in 1974. The managers in their companies were blaming them for the price increases, and saying "you've got to do something; we're losing money." You see, there was no equivalent stumpage increase in the South since most of the land there is privately owned, with very few national forests except in the mountains of West Virginia and Tennessee, so that the market prices for southern pine plywood and lumber, which compete directly with Douglas fir, remained fairly steady. The West Coast mills could not just increase the prices of their products. They were all stuck, and they were losing money.

Now, remember that each of the mills on the West Coast is a profit center, and the mill managers, the shift foremen, and the log buyers all receive a bonus based upon profits, and all are evaluated for promotion based upon profits. The foresters, in charge of log procurement, were the ones who really felt the pressure. They would see each other, back in the woods, inspecting the tracts of timber, and they would eat together, in those small diners and lunchrooms up in the mountain towns, and it was just natural for them to agree on how to solve their problems. You could imagine one of them saying, "You bid $195.00 per thousand board feet on this tract, and I'll come in at $193.00, but next week I'll put in our bid at $187.00 and you be certain to come in under that." They did it just that way, and they brought the average cost of timber sold on the West Coast in 1975 down to $169.50.

The government sued them, won the case in the Federal District Court in Portland, and fined each of the companies very substantially. No one went to jail as a result of this conviction since the government was unable to prove that the mill managers and the area managers knew what was happening. But if it happens again, I will guarantee you that some of those people will go to jail, since the government will claim that they were forewarned by the previous case and should have established safeguards against rigging the bids. And forest products companies generally have done a good job in pollution control, land reclamation, timber replanting, etc., but they really don't need any more bad publicity on collusion and price fixing. They simply have to set up some controls.

Class Assignment. Design a control system to prevent collusion and the fixing of prices for the purchase of timber from the federal government and private landowners.

Western Plywood and Lumber Corporation "C"

The Western Plywood and Lumber Corporation, a large forest products company operating in Washington and Oregon, built a large pulp and paper mill in southern Oregon in 1958 to manufacture the liner board and corrugating medium used in corrugated boxes. The company then built three box plants in central and southern California in 1964 to utilize the output of this mill in making boxes for packaging and shipping fresh produce.

> The idea was to use our low-grade timber, and the scrap wood from our sawmills and plywood plants, in making pulp and kraft paper, and then to integrate forward into corrugated boxes. The idea was good, and our r.o.i. was excellent, but we didn't know a thing about marketing boxes, and we got hit with an antitrust suit on price fixing. Corrugated shipping boxes are close to a commodity item, and they are sold on price. We didn't know it, but our sales manager was making deals on price with every other box manufacturer in California. (Statement of a company official)

The Western Plywood and Lumber Corporation was not alone in the indictment, and price fixing on corrugated board and boxes was not limited to California. Twenty-three paper companies were indicted in 1976, and 22 of them eventually pleaded "no contest."

> Eight more corporate defendants, all paperboard concerns, appeared in federal court here (Chicago) yesterday to change their pleas to no contest from innocent in the government's biggest price-fixing case in more than 10 years.

This case centers on an ethical problem; consequently, the names of all individuals, the characteristics of all products, and the locations and principal activities of all firms have been disguised.

Judge James B. Parson accepted each plea change. The previous day, he accepted identical plea changes from 12 other defendants in the case. On both days, he adjudged each corporation guilty and fined each the maximum penalty of $50,000. This brought the total fines thus far to $1 million.

Two more concerns will seek such plea changes today. They are among the 23 paperboard makers indicted last February on federal antitrust charges of conspiring to fix prices and rig bids on folding cartons. One company is pleading innocent. Also included in the criminal action were 50 individuals, mostly sales managers and regional managers, employed by the companies. All but two of these wish to plead no contest to the charges; hearings also began today on their pleas.

A no contest conviction is the same as a guilty finding, but can't be used as evidence in any resulting civil action.

The government alleges that all defendants participated in a conspiracy from 1960 through most of 1974 to maintain noncompetitive prices for folding cartons, in violation of the Sherman Antitrust Act.

No-contest pleas were accepted yesterday from. . . . (*Wall Street Journal,* July 21, 1976, p. 7)

In addition to the fine of $50,000 on the corporation, which has been criticized as being far too low in view of the extensive nature of the alleged conspiracy, and in addition to the fines and suspended jail sentences imposed on the general manager and marketing manager of the California Box Division, the Western Plywood and Lumber Corporation was subject to an unusual provision in the settlement. Each year a senior officer of the corporation was required to appear before a judge, prepared to demonstrate that the company was not continuing to fix prices on corrugated shipping cartons in violation of the Sherman Antitrust Act.

A unique antitrust settlement was imposed on ... in a Justice Department antitrust prosecution. In addition to the standard agreement not to fix prices in the future, U.S. District Court Judge Charles B. Renfrew insisted that once a year for 10 years each company send an officer to appear before him in court to answer questions under oath about how well it is living up to the order. (*Business Week*, September 29, 1976, p. 36)

Class Assignment. Design a control system that will enable the Western Plywood and Lumber Corporation to satisfy the judge in a U.S. District Court that no price fixing or illegal sales agreements have occurred in violation of the Sherman Antitrust Act.

Chapter *12*

STRATEGIC MANAGEMENT AND PLANNING

Chapter 11, on the design of the managerial systems, described the need to define the tasks required for strategic success, and then to design the organizational structure and managerial systems to coordinate the performance of those tasks. Each strategy, or long-term method of competition, imposes certain tasks, or managerial activities, that have to be done well for the strategy to be successful. These tasks are the building blocks of the organizational structure and managerial systems. The tasks can be in the functional management areas (marketing, production, finance, or engineering), the technical support services (cost control, information processing, market research, etc.) or in the strategic directive decisions, and they may be routine (required for nearly every company under almost any strategy) or critical (essential for a specific company under a selected strategy) in nature. As shown in the accompanying chart at the top of the next page, it is necessary to identify these tasks, clearly and explicitly, before attempting to design the organizational structure and managerial systems to implement the strategy of the firm.

The organizational structure, of course, is based upon an identification of the critical and routine tasks, and of the relationships among those tasks caused by the flow of material through the productive process, and by the flow of information through the managerial procedures, of a company. Tasks related by the production flow are the operational stages in the production process, while the tasks related by the information flow are the decision points in the managerial process. These operational stages and decision points within an organization often differ by managerial function, geographic location, product line, market segment, or technical content. Similarities within these classifications can be used to group the operational stages and the decision points into a first approximation of the organizational structure. The intent of this preliminary grouping should be to represent the natural material flows and information transfers of the organization, to recognize similarities among the managerial functions, geographic locations, product lines, etc.,

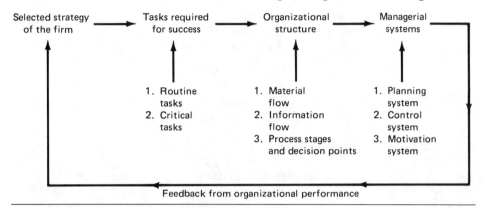

and to form the operational stages and decision points into a rational pattern. A hierarchy of authority is then superimposed on the preliminary groups, to indicate which organizational units should be able to influence the decisions and actions of other units within the organization, and which organizational units should be added to coordinate the decisions and actions of the entire company. The result of this design process is the organizational chart, which is an oversimplification of the complete structure of the firm, given the complex relationships that are based on the material flow and information flow, recognizing the possible alternatives that come from the multiple locations, products, markets, and technologies, and understanding the real ambiguities that are present in any scale of authority, but the two-dimensional graph does enable members of a firm of recognize and discuss their assigned positions and intended relationships, and is needed for the development of the managerial systems.

The design of the managerial systems is based upon the organizational structure of the firm. Each position on the final organizational chart represents certain tasks that are imposed by the strategy of the firm, related by the production processes and information flow, grouped by similarities in managerial function, geographic area, product characteristics, etc., and ranked by levels of relative authority. The tasks have to be coordinated for the complete organization to function effectively and efficiently. This coordination is accomplished partially by the formal hierarchy of authority within the structure, partially by the informal methods of integration by the units, but primarily by the procedures for planning, control, and motivation in the managerial systems. These systems are interrelated, in an explicit sequence, as shown at the top of the next page.

The function of the planning system is to produce an improved future state for an organization, but the procedures to accomplish this objective are complex since they must anticipate the future consequences of the plans, must integrate the different levels of the process, and must regulate the personal interactions of the planners. These requirements are critical in the design of the overall planning system, and should be described more fully:

1. *Need to anticipate the future consequences of planning.* Planning, when directed toward producing an improved future state for an organization, obviously involves fore-

	Strategic planning (method of competition)	Environmental assumptions Organizational resources Managerial intentions Strategic alternatives
Planning system	Program planning (allocation of resources)	Net present value Internal rate of return Cost benefit analysis Competitive position analysis
	Budgetary planning (projection of results)	Revenue forecasts Expense estimations Numerical measures Descriptive standards
Control system	Operational accounting (recording of performance)	Cost accumulation systems Cost allocation systems Responsibility centers Transfer prices and shared costs
	Comparative evaluation (analysis of variances)	Organizational control Program control Managerial control Operational control
Motivation system	Organizational response (design of incentives)	Perceptual response Financial response Positional response Personal response
	Individual reaction (decisions and actions)	Personal influence Interpersonal influence Social influence Cultural influence

casting, but this forecasting is not limited to predicting environmental opportunities and risks or estimating organizational revenues and expenses. Instead, planning requires anticipating the eventual outcome of a cause-and-effect chain stretching 5 to 10 years into the future, where the causes are managerial decisions, environmental events, and organizational actions, and the effects are highly uncertain and sometimes totally unknown. Planning of this nature is a complex intellectual process that requires imagination and innovation, not just extrapolation; it is the joint process of deciding what should be done now to adjust to apparent trends and expected changes in the environment, and then forecasting the outcomes of those decisions in measurable terms at definite times in the future. In short, the planning process is difficult since it requires predicting the future consequences of current actions over a lengthy time span.

2. *Need to integrate the different levels of planning.* Planning, when centered on deciding what should be done now to adjust to apparent trends and expected changes in the environment, has to cycle through the three stages or levels of strategic planning, program planning, and budget planning. It is necessary firstly to select a long-term method of competition or concept of service for the organization, and then to develop middle-term programs to allocate the resources and specify the activities needed to achieve the proposed competitive position or level of service, and finally to estimate the short-term revenues and expenses and establish the standards of performance for each of the functional and technical units associated with the various programs. Planning of this nature is a complex developmental process; the plans have to sequence from one to another, without inconsistencies, despite different time horizons, managerial levels, and topical contents. Here the planning process is difficult since it requires integrating different conceptual levels.

3. *Need to regulate the personal interactions of planning.* Planning, when focused on combining the three conceptual levels of strategy selection, resource allocation, and budget preparation, has to involve repetitive interactions by many members of management. Repetitive interactions are necessary since decisions at each conceptual level are, in essence, compromises between the desirable and the possible. A dominant strategic position is desirable, but generally not possible due to economic and competitive factors in most industries; well-funded programs are desirable, but usually not possible due to financial constraints in most companies; high performance standards are desirable, but often not possible due to knowledge and ability limitations among most employees. Plans at each stage are a compromise, and these compromises are reached by interactions among managers at different organizational levels who have different viewpoints and information bases. Here the planning process is difficult since it requires regulating repetitive interactions across different managerial levels.

A planning system that is often used to adjust to the triple problems of predicting the uncertain consequences of the plans, integrating the different stages of the process, and regulating the continual interactions of the planners, is based on an annual cycle, with established times for the completion of each phase, and iterative patterns of design and approval for each stage. The set times are needed because of the interrelationships between the different conceptual levels of planning—one phase cannot start until the others are finished—and the iterative patterns are required to formalize the interactions of the different managerial levels in planning. The plans become more definite, and more explicit about future projections, as the cycle of eight basic steps is completed:

1. *Statement of the planning objectives.* The annual planning cycle starts with a statement by the president or senior administrator on the general direction of the corporate strategy, and the desired competitive position or service level in the foreseeable future. This is a difficult statement to prepare; it is hard to express specific objectives without prejudging the subsequent plans, and it is awkward to propose desirable outcomes without generating obvious conflicts. Objectives, if they are too specific, determine the plans more than they guide them. Divisional

managers often feel forced to prepare plans based more on corporate expectations than on industry conditions, and these plans can easily result in shortfalls and errors, not in improved performance. As mentioned in Chapter 11, directive planning of this nature can only be successful in an expanding economy since it then creates a challenge which may be achievable; in a static or declining industry it merely creates an illusion that may be fatal. Conflicts, the other half of the dilemma in any statement of planning objectives, comes from excessive optimism bringing together divergent goals, such as a higher return on investment and greater expenditures for product development and market expansion. Senior executives should attempt to describe the direction of the organization and the expectations of the management in verbal terms that will depict a desirable and achievable position for the business firm or service agency, and avoid the financial and numerical goals that can bring undue pressure and apparent discrepancies.

2. *Forecast of the economic conditions.* The second step in the planning cycle is a forecast of economic conditions over the first portion of the planning period, perhaps five to six years. Strategic plans are usually developed for a much longer time span, 10 to 12 years, but it is difficult to prepare forecasts that far into the future that will be accepted by all members of management, so the shorter period is often used. The forecasts generally include a prediction of the level of business activity for each year, and an explanation of the influence of fiscal and monetary policies, legislative actions, tax changes, interest rates, and trade balances upon that level of activity. The economic forecasts are usually prepared by the corporate staff, and often include social and political prophecies as well as economic predictions; after approval by the president or senior executive they are distributed to the divisions. The intent is that all division managers should use the same economic, social, and political assumptions in preparing industry forecasts and strategic plans.

3. *Preparation of the divisional plans.* Strategic planning at the divisional level, for related product lines in specific market segments with known production processes and costs, should be a time for study and reflection. The purpose of the planning process, of course, is to understand the structure of the industry and to forecast changes in the environment, and then to develop a long-term method of competition that will fit that structure, adjust to those changes, and eventually achieve a market advantage or competitive edge for the company. The purpose of planning at the division level, however, often conflicts with the process. The process usually starts with an examination of the division's past performance within the industry, looking at data on industry sales, market percentages, company revenues, manufacturing costs, gross margins, divisional expenses, corporate allocations, capital charges, and pretax profits. These figures are usually examined for the past five years, estimated for the current year, and predicted for the next five years. The nine-year span makes trends and changes very obvious, but it also makes extrapolation very natural. There is a tendency at the divisional level to simply project past figures into the future. To support the predictions, it is common to ask that the divisions supply data on the market shares of the major competitors in the industry, and the strengths/weaknesses of the divi-

sions versus those other firms on such dimensions as product design, brand reputation, distribution coverage, productive capacity, manufacturing costs, etc. These are difficult dimensions to measure, however, and difficult comparisons to make. The process of strategic planning at the divisional level tends to emphasize format over content, and to enforce the continuation of existing strategies rather than the development of new methods of competition.

4. *Consolidation of the divisional plans.* Strategic planning at the corporate level should be a process of selection among the divisional plans to provide a sustainable balance in the financial sources and application of funds, and a desirable balance in the risk, return, and growth rates for the corporation. The intent here, of course, is to combine the various product–market and product–process positions of the divisions to generate a distinctive strategic position and a long-term competitive advantage for the complete firm. Once again, however, the purpose of planning often conflicts with the process. The strategic plans from the divisions, after review by the corporate staff for logical consistency and a common format, are submitted to the corporate executives for selection and approval. Selection should be the critical corporate function; it should be possible for corporate executives to identify some divisional plans for expansion, some for rejection, and others for revision and eventual approval. The problem, however, is that the knowledge of the products, markets, processes, technologies, and competitors is concentrated at the divisional level, and it is difficult to transmit this knowledge to the corporate level accurately and fully. To avoid problems in transmission, the data are usually summarized in financial ratios such as return on sales or return on assets, or in portfolio matrices such as market growth versus market share, or industry attractiveness versus company strengths. It is difficult to generate an overall competitive position for an organization with information on the divisions limited to the summary data of financial ratios and portfolio matrices, and with plans from the divisions prepared by extrapolation of past conditions rather than anticipation of future trends. The process of strategic planning at the corporate level tends to emphasize choice among plans rather than integration of divisions, and to reinforce the continuation of an existing strategy rather than the development of a new method of competition.

5. *Preparation of the divisional programs.* After approval of the competitive strategies proposed by each of the divisions, the next step in the planning cycle is the development of detailed programs to allocate the resources and specify the personnel required to achieve the competitive position or service level defined by each strategy. These programs are usually prepared by the divisional staff, with predicted cash inflows and outflows for each time period, and with expected activities by the functional and technical units over a specific time schedule. The problem with planning at this stage is that programs are, to a large extent, determined by the approved strategy of each division, and yet constrained by the financial resources of the organization. Changes in the allocated resources should bring changes in the divisional strategies, yet it is organizationally difficult to propose strategic change at this time in the cycle since the new plans cannot be compared to the proposed plans of the other divisions, in a selection process, but have to be accepted or rejected unilaterally. The preparation of

detailed programs after the approval of the divisional strategies tends to lead toward a restriction in the number of alternatives presented, and toward an assumption that only differences in the size and timing of the projects, not in the methods of competition, need to be considered.

6. *Coordination of the divisional program.* The investment programs from each division, after review by the corporate staff for computational accuracy and a common format, are submitted to the corporate executives for selection and approval. Again, selection should be the critical corporate function, and it should be possible to identify some divisional programs for expansion, some for rejection, and some for revision. The problem, as in the consolidation of the divisional plans, is that the knowledge needed to critically evaluate investment programs is concentrated at the divisional level, and therefore selection becomes a comparative rather than an evaluative process, with the comparisons based upon financial return calculations, such as the discounted cash flow models, or on economic value estimations, such as cost–benefit analysis, not on expected competitive positions. The coordination of investment programs after the selection of the divisional strategies tends to lead toward nearly automatic funding of the programs to the limit of the corporate resources.

7. *Preparation of the divisional budgets.* After the approval of the competitive strategies proposed by each of the divisions, and the funding of the programs required to implement those strategies, the seventh step in the planning cycle is the preparation of revenue and expense budgets, and the setting of performance standards, for each of the functional and technical units involved in the programs. Each budget, in essence, is a commitment by members of the various organizational units to achieve goals leading toward the competitive position of the approved strategy, and to complete activities required by the cost and time schedules of the programs, and therefore the budgets usually include financial, numerical, and descriptive measures of performance. The budgets are normally prepared by the members of the functional and technical units, with assistance from the divisional staff and approval by the divisional manager, and express the financial, numerical, and descriptive results expected over the first year of each program, on a quarterly or monthly basis. The problem at this level of planning is that the functional and technical activities have been, to a large extent, predetermined by the funded programs and selected strategies. Changes in the expected activities should bring changes in both strategies and programs, yet again it is organizationally difficult to propose changes at this stage of the cycle. The preparation of divisional budgets, after the approval of divisional strategies and the funding of divisional programs, tends to lead toward forcing the functional and technical units to accept imposed standards of performance rather than negotiating those standards with the divisional manager, or developing those standards through logical analysis.

8. *Integration of the divisional budgets.* The approval of the divisional budgets, with financial, numerical, and descriptive standards of performance for each of the functional and technical units within a division, is nearly automatic. Corporate executives do not have the detailed knowledge of products, markets, processes, and technologies necessary to question the estimated revenues, expenses, and

other measures of activity, and they don't have the time: the integration of the divisional budgets is the last stage in the planning cycle, and major changes in the budgets would require equally major changes in the previously approved strategies and programs. The budgets, in monthly or quarterly segments for the first year of the divisional programs, are almost automatically accepted, and the planning cycle is completed.

The annual planning cycle, as described and as shown in Exhibit 1, is an iterative process of preparation and then approval for the divisional strategies, programs, and budgets. The preparation for each stage of the cycle is assigned to different levels of management, due to the increasingly detailed knowledge of products, markets, processes, and technologies that is required, while approval remains theoretically with the corporate executives though actually the divisional strategy predetermines to a very considerable extent the investment programs and the organizational activities. Set times are usually established for the completion of each stage. This cycle, with iterative procedures to formalize the interactions of the different managerial positions, and with set times to maintain the interrelationships of the different conceptual levels, is shown in graphic format on the following page.

The problems with the annual planning cycle have been described. Primarily they come from the tendency, at the divisional level, to extrapolate past results and not anticipate future conditions, and from the absence, at the corporate level, of the detailed information on products, markets, processes, technologies, and competitors that is needed to evaluate rather than merely compare the divisional plans. Many of the formal planning procedures that have been developed over the past few years, such as portfolio matrices and investment models, are means of summarizing data for corporate executives. These procedures have not been fully successful, however, since they provide adequate information to compare divisions, but not to direct them. Organizational planning should involve direction of all organizational units (divisions and the functional/technical staff) toward a long-term competitive position that offers some market advantage or process economies to the firm.

Organizational planning has been systematized over the past few years, with iterative procedures and precise schedules for the approval of divisional strategies, programs, and budgets, and organizational planning has been decentralized, with different structural levels responsible for the preparation of the strategies, programs, and budgets, but the planning has remained basically extrapolative rather than conceptual, and static rather than dynamic. To avoid these problems, it is suggested that divisional managers prepare alternative strategies, and convey arguments for and against each alternative to the corporate executives. There are different methods of competition that are possible within each industry, and the proper strategy should be selected based upon consideration of the organizational assets and skills relative to the competition, the environmental changes and trends relative to current conditions, and the divisional performance and position relative to managerial expectations. These alternatives should not be "optimistic," "most likely," and "pessimistic" projections of the existing operations, but meaningful methods of competition ranging from "innovative" to "conservative." Joint selec-

Exhibit 1 *Graphic display of the annual planning cycle for a business firm or service institution*

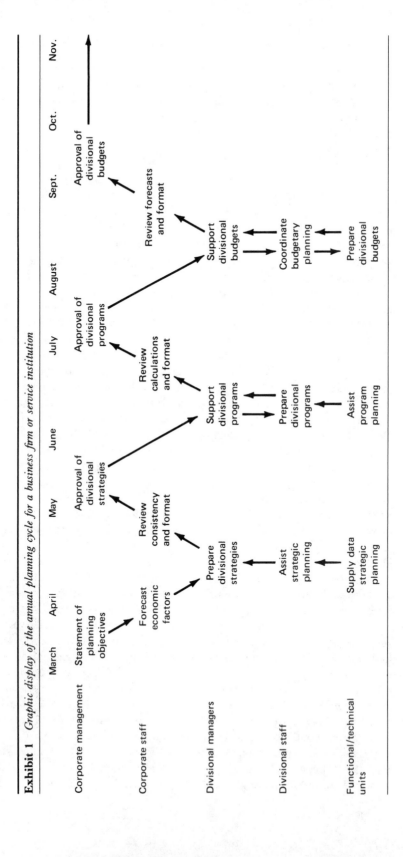

	March	April	May	June	July	August	Sept.	Oct.	Nov.
Corporate management	Statement of planning objectives		Approval of divisional strategies		Approval of divisional programs		Approval of divisional budgets		
Corporate staff		Forecast economic factors	Review consistency and format		Review calculations and format		Review forecasts and format		
Divisional managers			Prepare divisional strategies		Support divisional programs	Support divisional budgets			
Divisional staff			Assist strategic planning		Prepare divisional programs				
Functional/technical units			Supply data strategic planning	Assist program planning		Coordinate budgetary planning			
						Prepare divisional budgets			

tion of the optimal strategy, by corporate executives and divisional managers, would eliminate the present onus for failure which falls mainly on the divisional personnel, and which seems to prevent imagination and change in strategic planning. Evaluation of major strategic alternatives on a regular basis, rather than comparison of existing strategic units, would assist in integrating the conceptual stages of planning, coordinating the hierarchical levels of management, and projecting the future consequences of current decisions which, as explained at the start of this chapter, are the major problems in planning.

This chapter has concentrated on the problems, and not the process of planning. In the conclusion it might be well to summarize, very briefly, the basic steps that are needed first to start, and then to continue, organizational planning. The first approach to formal planning is the most difficult, since it normally requires changes in both the organizational structure and in the control and motivational systems. There are five steps:

1. Define strategic planning units within the organization as product–market–process divisions that can operate within a single industry following a specific strategy against known competitors.
2. Evaluate the position and performance of each planning unit or division within the industry through extensive analysis, concentrating on the economics of the industry and expected changes, and on the strengths/weaknesses of the division relative to existing competitors.
3. Obtain agreement from the planning unit managers on both the definition and the position/performance of each unit, and then consider alternative strategies for each division as basic methods of competition within the industry.
4. Assign a strategic role (market growth, product development, cash generation, etc.) to each planning unit, and balance these assignments to obtain an overall risk–return position and cash flow posture for the firm.
5. Change the organizational structure and managerial systems for planning, control, and motivation to reflect the division of the company into planning units, and the assigned strategic role for each unit.

The annual iterations of formal planning procedures are simpler, since they are more routine, but the routine nature can easily lead to simple extrapolation of current conditions rather than the more complex anticipation of future changes. Again, there are five steps:

1. Prepare a statement of corporate expectations for the firm, and a forecast of economic conditions for the society. Both are difficult to prepare, and require thought and attention; both should be distributed to the planning unit managers.
2. Require the manager of each planning unit to update the existing five-year strategic plan, and prepare alternative "innovative" and "conservative" plans with reasons for their adoption. Obtain agreement between corporate executives and divisional managers on the optimal strategy for a long-term competitive advantage.
3. Require the staff of each planning unit to convert the selected strategy into in-

vestment requirements, for both fixed and working capital, and into personal needs for the functional and technical units. Obtain agreement between corporate executives and divisional managers on the allocated resources.

4. Require the functional and technical members of each planning unit to convert the selected strategy into a 12-month budget, with revenues by product line, expenses by classification, and standards of performance by position. Obtain agreement between corporate executives and divisional managers on the assigned revenues, expenses, and measures of performance.

5. Think of what can go wrong, and establish contingency plans.

The last requirement of formal planning, to anticipate possible problems and prepare contingency plans, is not unimportant, and should be considered in the discussion of the following cases.

The Farmers and Merchants National Bank of Sacramento

The Farmers and Merchants National Bank of Sacramento was founded in 1874 to provide banking services in Sacramento, the capital city of California, and, after passage of a branch banking act in the 1920s, in the immediately adjacent counties of the central portion of the state and the foothills of the Sierras. The bank had always been profitable, even through the depression of the 1930s, due to the secure nature of its loans and the conservative philosophy of its management, and in 1978 the senior executives looked back upon a 104-year history of gradually increasing revenues and earnings (see Exhibit 1 for income statements for the period 1973–1977) and a superb financial position (see Exhibit 2 for the equivalent balance sheets and Exhibit 3 for the yields on loans and securities, interest rates paid, and financial ratios).

The senior management and members of the board of directors of the Farmers and Merchants National Bank were pleased with

the steady growth and secure financial position of the bank, but they were concerned that the annual increases in earnings were not comparable either to those of the large statewide banks and bank holding companies, or to those of the smaller, regional financial institutions. Increases in after-tax earnings for the state-wide banking systems with offices in the Sacramento area over the five-year period 1973–1977 ranged from 237% for the Bank of California (owned by BanCal Tri-State Corporation) to 43.1% for the United Bank of California (owned by the Western Bancorporation), and averaged nearly 80%. Increases in the after-tax earnings of the two regional banks, neither of which had branches outside the three-county Sacramento area, averaged over 100%. The increase in earnings for the Farmers and Merchants National Bank, as shown previously, were 31% over the same 1973–1977 period (Exhibit 4).

Members of the senior management at the Farmers and Merchants National Bank be-

Exhibit 1 *Income statements (000's omitted) for the Farmers and Merchants National Bank of Sacramento*

	1973	1974	1975	1976	1977
Commercial loan interest	$ 1,967	$ 2,697	$ 2,732	$ 3,801	$ 5,399
Construction loan interest	—	—	322	478	551
Real estate loan interest	4,466	5,085	5,598	6,229	6,060
Consumer loan interest	5,413	5,870	7,672	9,521	11,473
Direct lease financing	2,224	2,729	2,962	4,098	5,530
Credit card loan interest	1,857	1,854	2,028	2,260	2,690
U.S. Treasury securities	1,819	1,646	1,527	1,627	1,684
Obligations of U.S. government	375	375	355	355	420
State and municipal securities	1,294	1,674	1,653	2,108	2,235
Trust department income	187	269	329	379	470
Service charge on deposits	1,404	1,437	1,437	1,478	1,700
Miscellaneous income	2,107	1,506	1,339	983	1,044
Total operating income	23,113	24,692	27,954	33,317	39,256
Salaries and benefits	2,268	7,736	7,646	8,746	10,329
Interest on time deposits	7,612	8,852	9,831	12,000	13,842
Interest on borrowed funds	39	42	62	122	541
Net occupancy expense	1,234	1,496	1,693	1,781	2,148
Net equipment expense	813	835	887	998	1,108
Provisions for loan losses	472	543	659	750	1,140
Miscellaneous expenses	2,128	2,427	2,701	3,916	4,361
Total operating expenses	18,566	20,958	23,479	28,313	33,469
Gross income before taxes	4,547	3,734	4,475	5,004	5,787
Federal and state income taxes	1,696	1,208	1,637	1,782	2,027
Net income after taxes	2,851	2,526	2,838	3,222	3,760

Source: Annual statements for the respective years; some figures have been altered for confidentiality.

lieved that the growth of the large state-wide banks and bank holding companies was due to their ability to shift financial resources and managerial personnel to areas of high demand such as Orange County (south of Los Angeles, midway to San Diego) and Santa Clara County (south of San Francisco, near the base of the Bay area peninsula), where industrial expansion and population migration created rapid regional development. The senior executives also thought that the growth of the two other local banks, the First National Bank of Sacramento and the Yolo County National Bank, was due to the same factors operating in the Sacramento market area, although here it seemed to be caused more by commercial than by industrial expansion. Orange County and Santa Clara County were known for high-technology firms producing microelectronic components, data-processing equipment, and communication systems. The Sacramento market area had limited manufacturing growth, except in the San Joachim valley which seemed to be receiving the "spillover" from Santa Clara, across the Bay, but this market area was becoming the center for distribution, retail sales, and customer service for the Central Valley of California. Growth in the Central Valley had been "steady" in the 1960s, "accelerating" in

Exhibit 2 *Balance sheets (000's omitted) for the Farmers and Merchants National Bank of Sacramento*

	1973	1974	1975	1976	1977
Cash and due from banks	$ 39,279	$ 35,057	$ 35,902	$ 50,914	$ 50,793
U.S. Treasury securities	28,906	26,402	22,964	26,818	24,775
Obligations of U.S. government	5,660	5,453	4,951	4,660	13,130
State and municipal securities	30,705	34,978	39,107	49,121	49,121
Total securities	65,181	66,833	67,022	80,599	87,026
Commercial loans	26,253	29,812	38,152	51,100	67,383
Construction loans	—	—	1,873	4,105	3,246
Real estate loans	62,100	71,688	72,395	75,772	69,325
Installment loans	52,417	59,993	77,856	96,537	109,414
Direct lease amounts	20,737	22,429	28,184	37,454	49,622
Credit card amounts	9,522	11,248	13,292	14,976	18,775
Miscellaneous loans	618	718	659	1,107	1,369
Total loans and leases	171,647	195,828	232,411	281,051	319,134
Less reserve for losses	1,238	1,180	1,225	1,422	2,000
Net loans and leases	170,409	194,648	231,186	279,629	317,134
Miscellaneous assets	10,019	10,151	16,931	9,951	12,386
Cash and securities, loans and leases, and miscellaneous assets	284,888	306,689	351,041	421,093	467,339
Demand deposits	106,183	110,773	119,179	132,176	156,115
Savings deposits	100,275	107,207	123,420	151,520	162,057
Other time deposits	52,363	61,524	79,623	96,353	109,992
Total customer deposits	258,821	279,504	322,222	380,049	428,164
Federal funds purchased	—	—	—	10,000	—
Other liabilities	6,208	6,359	6,776	7,497	8,614
Notes payable	579	553	538	522	5,484
Stockholders' equity	19,280	20,273	21,505	23,025	25,077
Total corporate funds	26,067	27,185	28,819	41,044	39,175
Customer deposits, corporate funds, and owners' equity	284,888	306,689	351,041	421,093	467,339

Source: Annual statements for the respective years.

the early 1970s, and it was felt that it might be "explosive" in the late 1970s and early 1980s. Exhibit 5 shows the changes in population and in bank deposits in Sacramento, Yolo and Placer counties (the area normally included in any discussion of the Sacramento "three-county" market), in Napa and Solano counties to the west, in San Joachim County to the south, and in Sutter and Yuba counties to the north.

Despite the growth in the revenues of the bank, from $23.1 million in 1973 to $39.2

Exhibit 3 *Yields on loans and securities, interest rates paid, and financial ratios (percent) for the Farmers and Merchants National Bank of Sacramento*

	1973	1974	1975	1976	1977
Yield on commercial loans	8.14	10.35	9.17	8.47	8.44
Yield on construction loans	—	—	10.21	9.73	9.75
Yield on real estate loans	7.00	7.57	7.95	8.01	8.25
Yield on consumer loans	10.15	10.86	11.42	11.51	11.56
Yield on lease financing	10.72	11.12	11.57	11.69	11.78
Yield on credit card financing	18.88	18.78	17.80	16.99	18.36
Average yield on all loans	9.21	9.97	10.21	10.44	10.52
Yield on treasury securities	5.77	5.95	6.29	6.46	6.49
Yield on state and municipal securities	4.36	4.53	4.52	4.38	4.57
Yield on other securities	5.53	6.76	6.57	6.62	7.10
Average yield on all securities	5.14	5.30	5.35	5.22	5.38
Net income as percent of total income	12.33	10.23	10.15	9.67	9.57
Net income as percent of total equity	14.78	13.61	14.25	14.47	15.81
Net income as percent of total assets	0.99	0.85	0.86	0.84	0.85
Loan losses as percent of total loans	0.31	0.34	0.29	0.22	0.19
Interest paid on savings deposits	4.67	4.93	4.96	4.97	4.98
Interest paid on certificates of deposit	5.50	7.65	6.67	6.41	6.51
Interest paid on public deposits	5.71	8.73	7.16	6.07	5.95
Interest paid on all deposits	4.96	5.55	5.47	5.36	5.38
Loans and leases as percent of total deposits	66.31	70.14	72.17	70.01	74.55
Securities as percent of total deposits	25.24	23.91	20.83	21.24	20.29
Demand deposits as percent of total deposits	41.00	39.63	37.04	34.87	36.55

Source: Annual statements for the respective years.

million in 1977, supported by equivalent growth in loans outstanding and customer deposits, the market share of the Farmers and Merchants National Bank within the three-county Sacramento area had declined. The market shares for all banks with offices in this area, as measured by the total for demand deposits (checking accounts) and time deposits (saving accounts and certificates), are shown in Exhibit 6.

The decline in market share for the Farmers and Merchants National Bank was not substantial, from 12.0% in 1970 to 9.9% in 1975, and members of the management felt that their share in consumer loans and auto leasing was growing, but it was difficult to measure market share in area borrowings because many of the state-wide banks processed large loans through industry specialists in their central offices. The board of directors, wishing to increase the growth rate and regain the market share, voted in early 1977 to start formal planning procedures, with emphasis upon improving the competitive position of the bank, and authorized the employment of a strategic planner. George Mikkelsen, who had an M.B.A. from the Harvard Business School and three years' ex-

Exhibit 4 *After-tax earnings (000's omitted) for commercial banks and bank holding companies with offices in the Sacramento area, 1973–1977*

	1973	1974	1975	1976	1977	5-year growth (%)
Bank of California (division of Ban-Cal Tri-State)	$ 6,579	$ 6,647	$ 3,292	$ 2,677	$ 22,248	237.2
Bank of America, N.A.	221,074	256,606	302,800	336,771	396,276	79.2
California First Bank	4,922	5,820	6,412	10,782	12,302	147.4
Crocker National Bank	32,078	24,612	40,072	46,272	53,839	67.8
Farmers and Merchants National Bank	2,851	2,526	2,838	3,222	3,760	31.8
First National Bank of Sacramento	2,027	2,635	3,241	3,638	4,195	106.9
Security Pacific Bank	60,925	56,632	66,093	76,328	100,319	64.6
Sumitomo Bank of California	3,183	4,784	5,186	5,486	5,815	82.6
United California Bank (division of Western Bancorp.)	32,206	35,224	27,014	32,529	46,092	43.1
Wells Fargo Bank and Trust, Inc.	43,459	47,369	56,791	63,500	86,289	98.5
Yolo County National Bank of Sacramento	1,043	1,241	1,433	1,789	2,029	94.5

Source: Company records.

perience at one of the corporate-level consulting firms, was one of four persons interviewed for the position, and was hired by the president and appointed vice president for planning in June 1977. He worked with other officers of the bank throughout the balance of the year and in February 1978 presented the following long-range business plan to members of the board of directors.

Long-Range Strategic Business Plan

The Long-Range Strategic Business Plan for the Farmers and Merchants National Bank addresses the period 1978–1982, during which time the total assets of the bank are projected to increase 75% in real terms (disregarding the expected rate of inflation). This rapid growth compares to 28.1% in real terms from 1972 to 1977, and 10.3% from 1967 to 1972 (64.1% and 33.4%, respectively, including the rate of inflation). In 1983, revenues in real terms for the Farmers and Merchants National Bank will total $68.0 million, and profits

after taxes will be $7.2 million. It is anticipated that the dividend rate will be doubled in 1983, as a direct consequence of the expanded profitability.

Most large banks and corporations have acknowledged the need for strategic planning in order to survive and prosper in an increasingly competitive business environment. Faced with the prospect of more intensive competition from *all* types of financial institutions, as well as the problem of accelerating operating costs, the officers of the Farmers and Merchants National Bank have devoted considerable time and effort to preparing the Long-Range Strategic Business Plan. The following summarizes the major objectives and strategies of this plan.

Over the next five years, the major business objective of Farmers and Merchants National Bank will be to maximize the growth of income and assets by developing a full complement of commercial banking services and a stronger corporate bank image, while at the same time

Exhibit 5 *Population in 1975 and population changes since 1960, and bank deposits in 1975 and bank deposit changes since 1960, for the eight-county region surrounding Sacramento, California*

	Population, 1975	Population change, 1970–1975 (%)	Population change, 1969–1970 (%)	Bank deposits, 1975 (millions)	Bank deposit change, 1970–1975 (%)	Bank deposit change, 1960–1970 (%)
Sacramento	678,888	8.5	26.2	$2,636.9	103.6	41.2
Yolo	101,201	10.1	39.7	336.7	83.4	57.9
Placer	90,912	17.2	36.2	270.3	74.2	47.2
	871,001			3,243.9		
Napa (west)	90,272	14.2	20.1	260.3	89.5	41.3
Solano (west)	187,179	8.9	27.8	426.7	73.1	52.7
	277,245			687.0		
San Joachim	299,576	2.9	16.4	1,099.0	69.4	43.7
Sutter (north)	46,048	9.9	25.6	125.3	64.3	48.6
Yuba (north)	44,955	0.5	32.1	122.1	43.7	51.3
	91,003			247.4		
U.S. total (for comparison)	—	4.8	13.4	—	56.6	45.3

Source: Company records.

Exhibit 6 *Total deposits (000's omitted) and market shares (percent) for banks operating within the Sacramento market area for 1970 and 1975*

	1970		1975	
	Deposits	Share	Deposits	Share
Bank of California	$ 106,200	6.5	$ 266,000	8.2
Bank of America	428,000	26.2	759,100	23.4
California First Bank	96,400	5.9	133,000	4.1
Crocker National Bank	119,300	7.3	249,500	7.7
Farmers and Merchants National Bank	196,000	12.0	322,300	9.9
First National Bank of Sacramento	143,700	8.8	361,500	11.2
Security Pacific Bank	116,000	7.1	171,700	5.3
Sumitomo Bank of California	—	—	84,100	2.6
United California Bank	109,500	6.7	165,200	5.1
Wells Fargo Bank and Trust	240,200	14.7	548,000	16.9
Yolo County National Bank	78,400	4.8	183,700	5.6
	$1,633,800	100.0	$3,243,900	100.0

Source: Company records.

maintaining Farmers and Merchants' position as a leading consumer bank. Thus, a major, long-term goal will be to place additional emphasis on corporate banking without reducing the other components of the bank's portfolio. Farmers and Merchants will continue to provide highest-quality banking services for individual as well as corporate customers. To minimize the need for alternative sources of funds to support portfolio growth, a major emphasis will be placed on developing and increasing demand and time deposits.

Introduction

The management of the Farmers and Merchants National Bank has committed itself to systematic planning for the growth of the corporation. This Long-Range Strategic Business Plan is the culmination of eight months of planning effort by senior executives and their staffs, and has three main purposes:

1. To establish the long-range business objectives of the Farmers and Merchants National Bank.
2. Given these long-range business objectives, to define explicit courses of action.
3. Given those courses of action, to utilize the formal planning process within the corporate organization for modification and improvement of financial performance.

While the Long-Range Strategic Business Plan presents a framework of specific objectives and policies, it is also a "living" document which will evolve and change as the corporation grows. Rather than restrict creative thought, the plan attempts to organize and coordinate the decision-making process in the most flexible manner, allowing management to anticipate and plan for change instead of merely reacting to it.

Definition of Our Business and Business Philosophy

For the past 104 years, Farmers and Merchants National Bank has served Sacramento and the surrounding communities. It has grown with and assisted the growth of this prosperous Central Valley region. Management recognizes the value of the bank's regional identity as well as its vast potential for future growth. Therefore, Farmers and Merchants will continue to foster its relationships with business, individuals, and municipalities in Sacramento and nearby Central Valley counties. For the next five years, the bank will concentrate its business and growth efforts in an area bounded by Solano County to the west, San Joachim County to the south, and Yuba County to the north.

Farmers and Merchants National Bank adheres to sound, conservative banking principles and professional management responsibilities. The bank's primary concern is to fulfill its obligations to shareholders, customers, employees, and the public, and bases its business activities on a commitment to:

1. Safeguard the assets and deposits of the bank.
2. Provide quality services to the customers of the bank at a rate of return that will ensure stable growth and a sufficient profit for the shareholders.
3. Create a meaningful work environment for the employees of the bank.
4. Contribute significantly to the welfare and prosperity of the communities served by the bank.

These same commitments that have allowed the bank to grow in the past will provide the foundation for growth in the next five years.

Situational Analysis

Strategic planning begins with an assessment of current operating strengths and weaknesses, environmental characteristics and trends, and the resulting opportunities for growth and profit improvement. Before planning objectives are established, management must know what it has to work with, what problems need to be resolved, and what alternative courses of action are available.

The situational analysis recognizes the following competitive strengths of the Farmers and Merchants National Bank:

1. An excellent reputation for high quality consumer banking services
2. A group of customers who are "heavy users" of consumer banking services
3. An excellent profit performance based upon key financial ratios
4. An extensive and well-coordinated branch office system
5. A high-quality loan portfolio
6. A profitable credit-card progam
7. An extensive base of knowledge in bank data processing
8. An experienced group of managers and staff in many operating areas
9. A secure financial position, with low leverage and high liquidity
10. A conservative banking philosophy that has allowed growth without endangering assets

The situational analysis also recognizes the following characteristics, which seem to represent competitive weaknesses:

1. A low awareness of the bank's commercial banking services
2. A low awareness of the bank outside the three-county area
3. A low utilization of the bank's EDP capabilities in performance measurement and internal management
4. A high turnover in nonmanagerial personnel of the bank
5. The lack of a cost accounting system to accurately price the services of the bank
6. The lack of market research capabilities to introduce new products or services and to plan new promotions and advertisements
7. The low market value and minimal trading activity of the bank's stock

The situational analysis further recognizes six strategic alternatives to increase the assets and income of the bank:

1. Expand the commercial banking services, and improve the commercial market share.
2. Expand the consumer banking services, and maintain the retail market share.
3. Expand the geographic base of the bank, to offer both commercial and consumer banking services beyond the current three-county boundaries.
4. Market the business management services (computerized payroll and bookkeeping services for smaller business firms).
5. Market the personal trust services (computerized record keeping and investment counseling services for individuals and pension funds, etc.).
6. Improve the profit margins by reducing operating expenses and increasing fees and service charges.

To achieve the objectives of the bank, management exercises control over a number of "critical variables" or factors that affect substantially the bank's performance. These critical factors represent the major focal points for strategic planning, and include staffing levels, budgetary allocations, product/service decisions, marketing policies, expansion plans, and credit policies.

Obviously, there are limits on the change of the critical variables without impairing either the annual earnings or the financial stability of the bank. These limits are the constraints on strategic planning, and include the profit objectives set by management, the banking regulations established by federal and state agencies, the availability and cost of capital, and the availability and cost of qualified employees.

The use of critical variables under known constraints in strategic planning is dependent upon assumptions about the future. Although it is impossible to predict unknown events accurately, the situational analysis recognizes the following economic assumptions:

1. Market interest rates will gradually rise, with average commercial prime reaching 9½% in 1980.
2. Real value of the dollar will gradually decline, with average annual inflation reaching 7% in 1980.
3. Economic conditions in the Sacramento three-county area will continue to improve more rapidly than the projected 4% to 5% national GNP growth.
4. The Federal Reserve Board will respond to executive and congressional pressures by easing monetary controls, but will remain basically committed to a conservative monetary policy.
5. Operating expenses, led by personnel and money costs, will continue to erode earnings, so that budgetary planning and operating efficiency will become primary strategic concerns.
6. Electronic equipment and systems will be integrated into commercial banking in California in the form of ATMs (automatic teller machines), EFTs (electronic funds transfer systems), and POSs (point-of-sale cash registers capable of transferring funds from individual bank accounts).
7. Interest-bearing deposits with checking account services will be introduced into commercial banking in California in the form of NOW (negotiated order for withdrawal) accounts.
8. Consumer credit approval and supervision will be gradually removed from commercial banking in Califor-

nia, and become a function of the retailing and merchandising institutions.
9. State-wide banks and bank holding companies will continue to expand in the Sacramento three-county area to exploit the potential for growth.
10. State-wide and national nonbank financial institutions, such as brokerage firms and insurance companies, will begin to offer quasi-banking services in the Sacramento three-county area to participate in the potential for growth.

Long-Range Business Objectives

Overall corporate objectives for the Farmers and Merchants National Bank may be classified into three groups: growth rate, market orientation, and profit improvement. Although there is some overlapping, each category represents a distinct area of emphasis, as outlined below:

Growth-rate objectives. The Farmers and Merchants National Bank will undertake a controlled, well-planned program of growth over the next five years. Objectives of this program will be:

1. Increase the total assets of the bank by 75% in real terms during the period 1977–1982.
2. Increase the market share of the bank (as measured by deposits) to 12.0% in the three-county Sacramento market area over the period 1977–1982.
3. Establish branches of the bank in the counties to the north, west, and south of the Sacramento market area prior to 1982.
4. Increase the earnings per share of the bank in real terms by 15% compounded annually over the period 1977–1982.
5. Double the equity of the bank, in real terms, through retention of earnings and not through dilution of shareholders' value during the period 1977–1982.

Market orientation objectives. An awareness of the needs of customers and the variety of products and services offered by competitors is essential for strategic planning. In order to achieve its growth objectives, the Farmers and Merchants National Bank must become a more "market-conscious" organization. The bank should increase its responsiveness to its target audiences of individual and corporate customers, shareholders, and investors, and continue to work to meet their needs. Specific objectives of this program will be:

1. Organizational change in the structure of the bank to emphasize marketing and customer service prior to 1982.
2. Market research capabilities and staff added to the personnel of the bank prior to 1979.
3. Public relations program and staff added to the personnel of the bank prior to 1979.
4. Investor relations program and staff added to the personnel of the bank prior to 1979.
5. Increase the price/earnings ratio of the common stock of the bank from the current 7.0 to a minimum of 10.0 prior to 1982.

Profit improvement objectives. Several factors will pose a threat to the bank's profitability over the next five years. Increasing personnel costs and the general inefficiencies resulting from our increased size and growth will require a concerted effort to reduce operating expenses and improve efficiency. The key to the profit improvement of the Farmers and Merchants National Bank will be the development of cost accounting capability and a cost control system so that we may concentrate efforts on our most profitable services, and increase the productivity of our personnel. Objectives of this program will be:

1. Develop a manual cost accounting program in 1978, and an automated

system for cost reporting and control by 1980.
2. Computerize all lending programs of the bank by 1978.
3. Reduce operating expenses of the bank to 82.0% of operating income from the current 85.0% of income, by 1982.
4. Increase the deposits of the bank to $50.00 per dollar of employee expense, from the current $41.54 per dollar of expense, by 1982.
5. Fill 70% of management positions through internal promotion by 1982.

Summary of the Long-Range Strategy

Management makes strategic decisions regarding certain critical variables, within existing constraints, in order to achieve the growth rate, market orientation, and profit improvement objectives, given the assumptions of the economic conditions and the competitive strengths and weaknesses of the corporation. This section describes the decisions that have been made (i.e., the "how to" plan) for accomplishing those objectives.

Farmers and Merchants National Bank will emphasize deposit growth. In order to support loan growth, deposits of the bank must increase proportionately to avoid the need to borrow funds. Branch-site planning will concentrate on increasing the bank's deposit base; new branches will be established where deposit growth will be maximized. In addition to branch office expansion, deposits will be generated through loan and leasing agreements, especially when compensating balances can be utilized. Marketing programs designed to increase both the total number of deposit accounts and the size of each account will also be developed.

Farmers and Merchants National Bank will upgrade staff through hiring and in-house training. Between 1977 and 1982, the total projected employment will increase 36%, through the addition of 10 new branches and three new departments; the cost of this employment will increase 44% (in real terms), reflecting the hiring and training of highly qualified personnel.

The bank will improve the sophistication of its lending staff in order to expand its commercial and wholesale banking services by hiring experienced loan officers, and by developing comprehensive on-the-job training programs. Greater emphasis will be placed on sales training for all bank employees.

The bank will improve the areas of data-processing and operations administration by hiring specialists for systems development, operational analysis, and computer programming. Cross-training will be emphasized in the operational areas to increase the flexibility and mobility of the staff.

The bank will add to the professional account and investment analysis staff in the Trust Department through external hiring. Trust personnel will attend educational courses outside the bank to broaden their legal/financial background.

The bank will expand the accounting department to include functional divisions for cost accounting, tax accounting, and funds control through external hiring and in-house training of accounting/systems analysts.

The bank will establish a marketing department, with staff for market research, public relations, and investor relations through external hiring and in-house training.

The bank will promote managerial personnel from existing staff in the consumer loan, commercial loan, data-processing, accounting, and trust departments, with minimal external hiring.

The Farmers and Merchants National Bank will begin to emphasize commercial banking services. Commercial loans will be augmented with new, broader-image services that will support the evolution of wholesale banking. Cash management services will be automated, beginning with lock-box service in 1978, and will ex-

pand into other areas of financial management and consulting.

The Farmers and Merchants National Bank will continue to emphasize consumer banking services. Outstanding loans will be increased by approximately 18% per year, and new banking services will be developed in response to market demand. Auto leasing will expand dealer and fleet contacts, and consider new geographic areas, such as Santa Clara and San Francisco counties. Credit cards will improve their cardholder and merchant accounting systems.

The bank will require that each income-generating department evaluate current fee schedules, and revise those schedules as needed to improve the profitability of the bank's services.

The bank will direct its marketing programs toward specific customer segments. Retail banking services will be designed and sold to the target "heavy-user" audience identified in the 1975 Market Research Institute study: adults, 25 to 59 years old, professional or white-collar employment, married, with incomes above $15,000 per year. Commercial loans and wholesale banking services will be directed toward well-managed, profitable small and medium-sized accounts with sales between $2 million and $50 million. Business management services (computerized payroll and bookkeeping) will be offered to small businesses with at least five full-time employees.

The bank will continue to follow fundamental operating and loan policies that have been successful in the past. Although management must remain responsive to a changing environment— and even anticipate and plan for change—there is sufficient confidence in current guidelines to maintain them for the future. In brief, strategic long-range business policies will be to:

1. Continue current lending policies based on conservative banking principles, as well as growth objectives.

2. Continue loan volume policies based on the "balanced portfolio" concept.
3. Continue geographic area policies based on the Central Valley orientation.
4. Continue technological improvements in electronic data processing to reduce labor and space requirements; data processing will remain centralized.
5. Continue operational improvements in work productivity and staff training and assignments; projected savings are substantial.

Results of the Long-Range Strategy

Pro forma financial statements have been prepared for the five-year period 1978–1982, with actual results for 1977 for comparison, to indicate the probable outcome of the improved long-range strategy of the Farmers and Merchants National Bank. These pro forma statements are based upon the following assumptions and conventions, listed in the order of the lines upon the projected balance sheets and income statements:

1. Cash will be the "plug figure" in the balance sheet, and will represent total assets minus governmental securities, net loans, and miscellaneous assets [see Exhibit 7].
2. Governmental securities (federal, state, and municipal) will be 21% of deposits.
3. Net loans (commercial, construction, real estate, and consumer loans plus auto lease and credit-card financing, less provision for loan losses) will be 75% of deposits.
4. Miscellaneous assets (primarily banking office buildings and equipment) will increase as follows for the 1977 actual and 1978–1982 projected years, with expansion at $125,000 per branch, and with current improvements expected to equal annual depreciation:

    12,386   12,775   13,150
    13,400   13,650   13,900

5. Total bank deposits in the Sacramento three-county area are $4,339,-000,000 at the end of fiscal 1977, and can be expected to grow at a minimum of 5% annually in real terms, ignoring the anticipated 7% inflation factor. Market share of the Farmers and Merchants National Bank is expected to improve 0.5% per year over the five-year period through expansion of the marketing effort and reorientation of the banking philosophy. Twelve new branches are to be established in the northern, western, and southern counties; each new branch can be expected to gain $2 million in deposits each year for the first five years of operations [see Exhibit 8].
6. Demand deposits will decrease as a percentage of the total deposits at the FMNB bank, reflecting the expected introduction of interest-bearing accounts with checking account services:

    36.4%   35.0%   34.0%
    31.0%   32.0%   33.0%

7. Time deposits will be 100% minus the demand deposits, reflecting the expected increase in interest-bearing accounts.
8. Miscellaneous liabilities (accrued salaries and wages, accounts payable, and notes payable) will increase over time with the personnel and operating costs of the bank:

    14,098   15,500   17,000
    18,500   20,000   21,500

9. Stockholders' equity will increase with after-tax earnings each year less expected dividends of $1,170,000; dividends will be increased in 1983 reflecting the improved competitive and financial position of the bank.
10. Investment income will be 5.4% of federal, state, and municipal securities, reflecting continued demand for governmental financing.

Exhibit 7 *Pro forma financial statements for Farmers and Merchants National Bank 1977–1982*

	1977	1978	1979	1980	1981	1982
Cash	$ 50,793	$ 49,952	$ 57,798	$ 66,727	$ 76,909	$ 88,394
Securities	87,026	96,900	109,200	123,200	138,700	155,900
Net loans	317,124	346,200	390,200	439,900	495,400	556,900
Miscellaneous assets	12,386	12,800	13,200	13,400	13,700	13,900
Total assets	467,339	505,852	570,398	643,227	724,709	815,094
Demand deposits	156,115	161,600	176,900	193,500	211,400	230,200
Time deposits	272,049	300,000	343,400	393,000	449,100	512,300
Miscellaneous liabilities	14,098	15,500	17,000	18,500	20,000	21,500
Owners' equity	25,077	28,752	33,098	38,227	44,209	51,094
Total	467,339	505,852	570,398	643,227	724,709	815,094
Investment income	4,339	5,232	5,896	6,652	7,490	8,418
Loan income	31,703	35,658	39,410	43,550	48,053	52,905
Miscellaneous	3,214	3,700	4,300	5,000	5,800	6,700
Total income	39,256	44,590	49,606	55,202	61,343	68,023
Interest expenses	13,842	16,200	18,543	21,222	24,251	27,664
Personnel expenses	10,329	11,593	12,401	13,248	14,108	14,965
Occupancy expenses	3,256	3,400	3,550	3,650	3,750	3,850
Loss provision	1,140	1,040	1,170	1,320	1,485	1,670
Miscellaneous expenses	4,902	4,094	5,456	6,072	7,747	7,482
Total expenses	33,469	37,137	41,120	45,512	50,341	55,631
Gross income	5,787	7,453	8,486	9,690	11,002	12,392
Income taxes	2,027	2,608	2,970	3,391	3,850	4,337
Net income	3,760	4,845	5,551	6,299	7,152	8,055

11. Interest income on total outstanding loans will decrease reflecting expected increased commercial demand for financing and decreased consumer activity:

    10.5% 10.3% 10.1%
    9.5%   9.7%   9.5%

12. Other income (trust department fees, checking account charges, and business management services revenues) will increase over the five-year period with the expanded services and altered philosophy of the bank:

    3,214 3,700 4,300
    5,000 5,800 6,700

13. Interest expenses on time deposits will be 5.4%; interest on any borrowed funds will be included in miscellaneous expenses.

14. Personnel expenses will decrease as a percentage of revenues, reflecting economies of scale and improved control procedures:

    26.3% 26.0% 25.0%
    24.0% 23.0% 22.0%

15. Occupancy and equipment expenses will increase with the number of branches, at $50,000 per branch per year.

16. Loan-loss provisions will be constant

Exhibit 8 *Market share for the Farmers and Merchants National Bank, 1977–1982*

	1977	1978	1979	1980	1981	1982
Deposits in area	$4,339,000	$4,556,000	$4,784,000	$5,023,900	$5,274,000	$5,538,000
FMNB market share	0.986	0.100	0.105	0.110	0.115	0.120
FMNB deposits	428,168	455,600	502,300	552,500	606,500	664,500
FMNB new branches	—	3	3	2	2	2
Prior-year deposits	—	—	6,000	18,000	34,000	54,000
Current-year deposits	—	6,000	12,000	16,000	20,000	24,000
Total FMNB deposits	428,168	461,600	520,000	586,500	660,500	742,500

at 0.003% of net loans, reflecting increased stability of commercial loans and decreased volume of consumer loans.

17. Miscellaneous expenses will be constant at 11.0% of revenues.
18. Income taxes will be constant at 35.0% of gross profits.

Class Assignment. Evaluate the long-range planning procedures of the Farmers and Merchants National Bank of Sacramento.

1. As a member of the board of directors of the bank, would you accept the plan?
2. As Mr. George Mikkelsen, vice president for planning, what changes would you recommend in the planning procedures for subsequent years? Assume that the five-year strategic business plan will be updated each year; be specific in your recommended changes.

Planning in the Steel Industry

The National Steel Corporation is the third-largest steel producer in the United States, with sales in 1978 of $3,788 million and after-tax profits of $112 million. Earnings in that year were 2.9% on sales, 3.5% on assets, and 8.3% on equity (comparable industry figures for the same year were 2.8, 3.4, and 7.3%). Revenues over the past five years have grown with inflation, whereas earnings have been cyclical, generally following the economy (Exhibit 1).

The company was reasonably well financed, with a 1.71:1 current ratio and a 0.76:1 debt/equity ratio in 1978, despite the recent history of low earnings and the recent investment of nearly $1 billion in new plant and equipment (Exhibit 2).

The National Steel Corporation has not di-

Exhibit 1 *Simplified income statements (000's omitted) for the National Steel Corporation, 1974–1978*

	1974	1975	1976	1977	1978
Sales revenues	$2,780,408	$2,293,582	$2,898,384	$3,192,561	$3,788,681
Operating expenses	2,302,233	2,062,485	2,600,772	2,914,550	3,375,214
Depreciation expenses	111,849	114,414	128,704	138,402	148,139
Interest expenses	22,978	29,854	48,047	56,091	54,076
Total expenses	2,437,060	2,206,753	2,777,523	3,109,043	3,577,429
Pretax income	343,348	86,829	120,861	83,518	211,252
Income taxes	−163,804	−18,861	−26,309	−18,270	−94,700
Minority claims	− 3,780	− 9,927	− 8,815	− 5,123	− 4,178
Total income	175,764	58,041	85,737	60,125	112,374

Source: Annual Reports for respective years.

Exhibit 2 *Simplified balance sheets (000's omitted) for the National Steel Corporation, 1974–1978*

	1974	1975	1976	1977	1978
Cash and securities	$ 326,698	$ 60,108	$ 79,920	$ 110,200	$ 257,841
Accounts receivable	251,614	226,469	244,622	321,620	452,406
Inventories	278,628	444,875	615,848	517,398	576,322
Miscellaneous current assets	—	31,671	55,011	50,271	22,293
Total current assets	856,940	762,623	995,440	999,489	1,308,862
Plant and equipment	2,662,137	2,975,034	3,211,949	3,382,086	3,451,254
Reserve for depreciation	−1,411,013	−1,501,803	−1,596,707	−1,728,108	−1,835,206
Investments in subsidiaries	152,028	145,209	155,413	156,897	154,835
Deferred charges, etc.	28,381	29,416	31,945	41,784	50,296
Total fixed assets	1,431,532	1,647,856	1,802,599	1,852,659	1,821,179
Total assets	2,288,473	2,410,478	2,798,039	2,852,148	3,130,041
Account payable	215,153	196,034	219,897	194,778	308,162
Taxes and current debt	122,695	30,450	50,506	45,837	94,378
Payroll and accruals	252,702	276,446	304,364	317,248	363,151
Total current liabilities	580,552	502,929	574,767	557,862	765,711
Long-term debt	496,613	698,856	960,150	1,013,266	1,021,521
Capital stock	95,974	96,319	96,775	97,212	98,100
Capital surplus	95,407	100,313	115,919	121,484	117,999
Retained earnings	1,000,921	1,012,061	1,050,489	1,062,322	1,126,710
Total equity	1,192,303	1,208,693	1,263,122	1,281,018	1,342,809

Source: Annual Reports for respective years.

versified out of the steel industry. 95.0% of the revenues of the company come from steel mill products, 2.0% from aluminum and magnesium refining, and 3.0% from metal building fabrication. The steel mill products are primarily hot-rolled sheet and strip (28.0%), cold-finished sheet and strip (48.0%), plated products (21.0%), and tubular products (8.0%). These steel products are supplied to appliance manufacturers (10.0%), automotive firms (40.0%), company warehouses (15.0%), can producers (15.0%), the oil and gas industry (7.0%), steel converters (2.0%), and wholesale distributors (4.0%), with the balance unclassified. Readers are referred to the case "Competition within the Steel Industry" for definitions of steel products, markets, and processes.

The National Steel Corporation operated three integrated steel mills in Weirton, West Virginia; Granite City, Illinois; and Ecorse, Michigan. Major plants for the production of finished steel products, but without integrated facilities for smelting iron or refining steel, were located at Portage, Indiana (tin plate and galvanized sheet), at Steubenville, Ohio (chrome-coated sheet and bars), at Houston, Texas, Terre Haute, Indiana, La-Grange, Georgia, Delanco, New Jersey, and Monroe, Louisiana (metal building construction), at Liberty, Texas (pipe and oil country products), and at Gerald, Missouri (welded steel tubing). Ore mining subsidiaries were located in Minnesota, coal mines in Pennsylvania and West Virginia, and limestone quarries in Ohio. The company was reputed to be self-sufficient in raw materials (adequate ore, coal, and limestone for 25 to 40 years), reasonably advanced in technology (70% of the steel was produced with continuous casters), and notably aggressive in management (Mr. George Stinson, the chairman, was head of the American Iron and Steel Institute, and a vocal advocate of the industry).

Class Assignment. Assume that you have recently been promoted to the position of vice president for planning at the headquarters office (in Pittsburgh) of the National Steel Corporation. Assume further that the company has not had a planning system previously, and that your assignment from Mr. Stinson, the chief executive officer, is to recommend, and then install formal planning procedures. Assume, finally, that you have a good knowledge of industry products, markets, processes, and problems, as summarized in "Competition within the Steel Industry." How would you fulfill the assignment?

Planning in the Brokerage Industry

Paine Webber, Inc., is one of the largest retail brokerage firms in the United States, with revenues in 1978 of $384.1 million and after-tax profits of $12.7 million. The present corporation was formed in 1974 as a reorganization of Paine Webber, Jackson and Curtis, which was the successor to the privately held partnerships of Paine Webber and Company, founded in Boston in 1880, and Jackson and Curtis, started in Chicago in 1889. Revenues have expanded rapidly since the reorganization of the company, which was arranged to permit public ownership, greater capital, and increased growth, but profits, except for 1974 when returns were minimal due to a national recession, have remained nearly constant, and have sharply declined when expressed as a percentage of revenues, assets, or equity (Exhibits 1 to 3).

In 1978, Paine Webber, Inc., was one of the

Exhibit 1 *Summary income statements (000's omitted) for Paine Webber, Inc., 1974–1978*

	1974	1975	1976	1977	1978
Commissions earned trading	$ 77,561	$ 98,457	$113,656	$122,604	$166,453
Capital gains from trading	17,871	29,035	37,319	38,243	42,142
Interest on customers' debt	30,202	33,911	39,551	62,543	133,125
Fees from underwriting	13,369	27,016	30,128	38,455	36,622
Miscellaneous income	3,657	3,185	4,570	5,274	5,768
Total income	142,662	191,604	225,224	267,119	384,110
Employment expenses	76,895	97,690	116,489	130,346	160,880
Promotion expenses	8,173	8,764	11,009	13,824	15,840
Communication expenses	13,216	14,254	18,247	21,766	25,412
Occupancy expenses	10,112	10,484	11,391	13,625	15,080
Floor brokerage commissions	5,696	7,657	8,234	9,035	12,570
Miscellaneous expenses	11,866	11,283	13,673	14,882	18,724
Total expenses	141,203	167,883	202,613	248,893	359,581
Pretax income	1,459	23,721	22,611	18,226	24,529
Income taxes	8	11,521	10,676	7,791	11,777
Total income	1,451	12,200	11,935	10,435	12,752

Source: Moody's Bank & Financial Manual for the respective years.

Exhibit 2 *Summary balance sheets (000's omitted) for Paine Webber, Inc., 1974–1978*

	1974	1975	1976	1977	1978
Cash and equivalents	$ 19,866	$ 15,384	$ 22,535	$ 34,711	$ 47,446
Accounts receivable from brokers	26,957	35,605	59,136	98,209	220,988
Accounts receivable from customers	204,304	270,853	413,551	618,193	789,715
Securities owned by firm	71,911*	89,385*	155,645*	254,640	229,524
Securities held w/resale	12,000*	100,000*	350,000*	553,353	1,240,745
Exchange memberships	1,036	1,229	1,291	2,362	1,999
Offices and equipment, net	7,333	7,451	9,096	11,268	12,686
Miscellaneous assets	5,548	5,946	8,959	17,125	26,861
Total assets	$348,955	$525,853	$1,020,213	$1,589,860	$2,569,964
Loans due to banks	$121,291	$133,587	$ 337,863	$ 534,250	$ 525,495
Accounts receivable due to brokers	38,675	44,609	75,045	101,757	222,448
Accounts receivable due to customers	80,228	83,776	103,365	128,437	218,264
Securities sold w/repurchase	7,000	115,350	331,773	540,111	1,169,826
Securities sold undelivered	3,244	20,116	32,450	129,257	238,920
Dividends and interest payable	3,202	4,060	4,336	4,503	6,177
Accrued wages and expenses	11,028	21,004	21,389	28,650	53,547
Income taxes due	1,915	12,726	6,523	5,334	9,968
Total current liabilities	$266,583	$435,228	$ 912,744	$1,472,299	$2,444,645

Exhibit 2 *(continued)*

	1974	1975	1976	1977	1978
Subordinated debentures	$ 23,800	$ 22,100	$ 30,400	$ 34,700	$ 33,500
Preferred stock $1.30/share	27,436	27,436	27,436	27,436	27,436
Common stock	5,339	5,339	5,339	5,341	5,361
Capital surplus	19,368	19,368	19,368	19,383	19,491
Earned surplus	6,429	16,382	24,926	30,701	39,531
Total equity	31,136	41,089	49,633	55,425	64,383
Total liabilities and equity	$348,955	$525,853	$1,020,213	$1,589,860	$2,569,964

Note: "Securities held w/resale" represents securities, primarily government bonds, held in inventory but under a contract for resale at a fixed price; "securities sold w/repurchase" represents the reverse. These are "long" and "short" positions for speculation against market price movements or interest-rate changes.
Source: Moody's Bank and Financial Manual for the respective years.

larger firms in the brokerage industry, with 157 offices in the United States, Europe, and Japan, 2,511 registered sales representatives, an orientation toward retail rather than institutional trading, an increasing emphasis upon underwriting, and a concern about profits:

> Our top priority for 1979, as it has been for some time, is to improve profitability. Although Paine Webber's revenues have grown more rapidly than many competitors, and our return on equity has been good by industry standards, overall profitability has not been satisfactory. (Statement by Mr. Donald B. Marron, President of Paine Webber, Inc., in the *1978 Annual Report*)

Class Assignment. Assume that you have been appointed director of planning for Paine Webber, Inc. Assume further that the company has not used formal planning procedures previously, and that the president, Mr. Marron, has asked you to develop a planning system to improve profitability over the long term. Assume finally, that you have a good knowledge of the sources of revenue, classes of expenses, and major trends and changes in the industry, as summarized in the case "The Future of the Brokerage Industry." How would you fulfill the assignment?

Exhibit 3 *Profits as a percent of sales, assets, and equity for Paine Webber, Inc., 1974–1978*

	1974	1975	1976	1977	1978
Profits as percent of sales	1.02	6.37	5.29	3.91	3.32
Profits as percent of assets	0.41	2.30	1.17	0.65	0.49
Profits as percent of equity	4.66	29.69	24.04	18.82	19.80

Source: Computed from the prior exhibits.

Chapter 13

STRATEGIC MANAGEMENT AND LEADERSHIP

Strategic management has been defined previously as the simultaneous and continual formulation and implementation of a long-term method of competition for a business firm, or a long-term concept of service for a nonprofit institution. The formulation of strategy was the topic of the first six chapters of the book; it is a process of evaluating alternative methods of competition or patterns of service through comparison with environmental characteristics and trends, organizational assets and skills, and managerial values and attitudes, as shown graphically at the top of the next page.

The emphasis or orientation of this process of strategic design varies, depending upon the type of organization:

1. *Small companies,* with a single product or a narrow product line, by definition have limited sales, and consequently they often search for a competitive advantage by combining product characteristics and market segments to define a high-margin market "niche" with reduced competition. Smaller companies also often suffer from a shortage of financial and physical assets and technical and managerial skills, and therefore they are constrained in product development and market expansion. As a result, strategic planning for smaller firms is usually product–market oriented and resource based.

2. *Product divisions of larger companies,* also generally responsible for only a single product or product line, usually have annual sales considerably larger than those of smaller firms, and consequently they are less able to find a market niche without competition. Product divisions usually must meet competition, not avoid it, and they often search for a competitive advantage by combining capacity expansions and technical improvements to develop a low-cost production process. The product divisions of large companies have access to the financial and physical assets and the technical and managerial skills of the parent firm, so that

Environmental charac-
teristics and trends

Economic

Technological

Social/political

Competitive

↓

Organizational mission or charter	Specific opportunities and risks open to the organization	

↓

| Past performance and position of the firm or institution | Range of strategic alternatives open to the firm or institution | Selected strategy, the method of competition or concept of service |

↑

| Managerial and professional values | Specific strengths and weaknesses within the organization | |

↑

Money

Equipment

People

Market position

Organizational re-
sources, or assets and
skills

they are not constrained by resources, but they are limited in sales growth and market expansion by the competitive structure or environment of the industry. Strategic planning for the product division of a larger company is, therefore, often product–process oriented and environmentally based.

3. *Single-industry firms* generally have a range of related products and product lines that are sold to a variety of market segments, and produced by a number of production processes, within one industry. These firms must search for a competitive advantage both by considering product–market positions for specialty items that can provide high margins, and product–process postures for volume products that require low costs, and then by integrating the marketing and production policies to recognize the interdependencies between the products and processes. Strategic management within a single-industry firm is a difficult task; these are often the basic processing companies, in mature industries, with limited growth and narrow margins. Strategic planning for these single-industry firms,

therefore, has to be both product–market and product–process oriented, and both resource and environmentally based.

4. *Multiple-product firms,* with product–market and product–process positions in different industries, search for a competitive advantage by balancing the corporate cash flows among the various divisions, and by understanding the nature and degree of relationships between the individual products. The balancing of cash flows between divisions provides an opportunity for the corporate management to set growth/stability and risk/return ratios for the firm; while understanding the functional and technical relationships between products brings a potential to improve the operating efficiency of the firm through joint use of resources and skills. Strategic planning for multiple-industry firms is relationships oriented, and both resource and environmentally based.

5. *Nonprofit institutions* have an apparent similarity to single-industry firms; they provide a range of related services to a variety of population segments, and the services are produced by a number of operational methods. Competitive advantage is not an issue in nonprofit institutions, but comparative positioning is important, and strategic management is a difficult task due to the very large number of alternative positions that are both possible and desirable. Strategic planning for nonprofit institutions is both service-segment and service–process oriented, and both resource and environmentally based.

The selection of the optimal method of competition or concept of service, however, does not complete the process of strategic management. It is necessary to inform other members of the organization about the selected strategy, and then to design the organizational structure and managerial systems to implement that strategy. Information about the selected strategy can be transmitted by the preparation of explicit statements about the goals and objectives, policies and procedures, programs and plans, and immediate actions for each of the major functional and technical areas within the organization. In turn, these departmental objectives, policies, programs, and actions define the individual tasks that are essential for strategic success, and the organizational structure and managerial systems can then be designed to coordinate and integrate the performance of those tasks. Strategy implementation, the other half of strategic management, is shown graphically at the top of the next page.

Strategy implementation, basically, is the achievement of a long-term competitive position for a business firm, or a comparative position for a service agency, and requires a sequence of task definition, structural design, and systems design:

1. *Definition of the critical tasks.* The critical tasks within an organization are defined by the series of statements on the goals and objectives, policies and procedures, programs and plans, and immediate actions for each of the functional and technical units. The critical tasks are the activities and decisions imposed by the strategy of the organization; they are what has to be done, and done well, for that strategy to succeed. It is important that these tasks be defined in "do-able" terms, that is, in terms that can be explained clearly and logically to an individual, with the expectation that a qualified person will be able to perform the activities and make the decisions involved in the assignment.

Selected strategy, or
method of competition

	Goals and objectives	Policies and procedures	Programs and plans	Immediate actions		
Marketing management	—	—	—	—	Relationships among tasks	Organizational structure
Marketing research	—	—	—	—		Information systems
Operations management	—	—	—	—		
Financial management	—	—	—	—	Tasks required for success	Planning systems
Product development	—	—	—	—		Control systems
Information services	—	—	—	—		
Personnel services	—	—	—	—	Persons available for tasks	Motivation systems

2. *Design of the organizational structure.* The structure of an organization is based upon an identification of the critical tasks, and upon an understanding of the relationships between those tasks. These relationships are caused by the flow of material through the productive process, and by the flow of information through the management process, of the organization. Tasks related by the production flow can be viewed as operational stages in the production process, while the tasks related by the information flow can be thought of as decision points in the managerial process. These operational stages and decision points often differ by managerial function, geographic location, product line, market segment, or technical content; similarities within these classifications can be used to group the operational stages and decision points into a first approximation of the organizational structure. These groupings, which form organizational units, need to be coordinated by a hierarchy of authority. The related operational stages and decision points, and the relative levels of authority, together form the organizational structure needed for strategy implementation.

3. *Design of the managerial systems.* The organizational structure consists of a number of positions, each representing certain tasks that are imposed by the strategy of the firm, related by the production processes and information flow, grouped by similarities in managerial function, geographic area, product characteristics, etc., and ranked on a hierarchical scale. These tasks have to be coordinated for the complete organization to function effectively and efficiently. This coordination is accomplished partially by the hierarchy of authority within the structure, but primarily by formal procedures for planning, control, and motivation within

the systems. These systems form a sequence that can be depicted graphically as follows:

Planning system	Strategic planning (method of competition)	Environmental assumptions Organizational resources Managerial intentions Strategic alternatives
	Program planning (allocation of resources)	Net present value Internal rate of return Cost–benefit analysis Competitive position analysis
Control system	Budgetary planning (projection of results)	Revenue forecasts Expense estimations Numerical measures Descriptive standards
	Operational accounting (recording of performance)	Cost accumulation systems Cost allocation systems Responsibility centers Transfer prices and shared costs
Motivation system	Comparative evaluation (analysis of variances)	Organizational control Program control Management control Operational control
	Organizational response (design of incentives)	Perceptual response Financial response Positional response Personal response
	Individual reaction (actions and decisions)	Personal influence Interpersonal influence Social influence Cultural influence

Strategy formulation and implementation, when considered simultaneously so that there is a single process and not two separate halves, and continually so that this process can adapt to the ongoing course of changes in environmental conditions, organizational resources, and managerial attitudes, define the methods of strategic management. Strategic management is the responsibility of the general manager, whose function is to combine and direct the efforts and activities of the other members of the organization toward the successful achievement of an improved competitive position or service level. The simultaneous and continual process of strategic management will be the last to be depicted graphically, as follows:

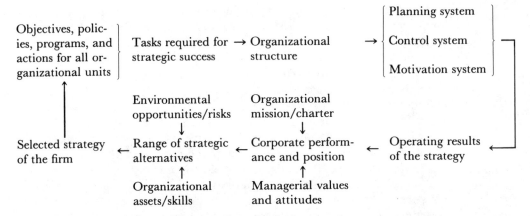

Strategic management is the responsibility of the general manager of the organization, but the task cannot be accomplished by a single person. The amount of information needed to evaluate each alternative, the number of alternatives to be considered, the detail in the statements on objectives, policies, programs, and actions, the definition of the critical tasks, and the design of the organizational structure and managerial systems are simply too great. Strategic management has to be an organizational task, not an individual effort.

Strategic management is an organizational task, and requires an integrated effort by all members of the organization for successful completion, yet there are behavioral barriers to this integration. These barriers were discussed briefly in Chapter 12:

1. *Future uncertainties.* Planning, when directed toward producing an improved or desired future state for an organization, involves anticipating the eventual outcome of a cause-and-effect chain stretching 5 to 10 years into the future, where the causes are managerial decisions, environmental events, and organizational actions, and the effects are highly uncertain and sometimes totally unknown. Planning requires the ability to visualize an uncertain and unknown future. Many members of an organization are accustomed to thinking in terms of certainty or risk, where either the outcome of an event is known, or the probabilities of a range of possible outcomes are known, and they may find it impossible to consider future conditions that are not simple extrapolations of past trends. The uncertain outcomes and unknown quantities of the future often present a barrier to organizational communication, and integrated effort, in planning.

2. *Conceptual interdependencies.* Planning, when centered on deciding what should be done now to adjust to uncertain trends and unknown outcomes in the future, involves cycling through the three conceptual stages of strategic planning, program planning, and period or budgetary planning. It is necessary firstly to select a long-term method of competition or concept of service that is related to changing managerial values, organizational resources, and environmental trends, and then to develop midterm programs that will allocate the resources

and specify the activities needed to achieve the proposed competitive position or service level, and finally to estimate the short-term revenues and expenses, and set the nonfinancial standards, that will provide measures of performance for all the functional and technical units associated with the various programs. Planning requires the ability to comprehend an entire organization. Many members of an organization are accustomed to thinking in terms of immediate operations, and find it impossible to recognize the impact of short-term functional or technical changes upon the long-term competitive position or service level of the organization. The interdependencies of the three conceptual stages often present a barrier to organizational communication, and integrated effort, in planning.

3. *Managerial interactions.* Planning, when focused on combining the three conceptual stages of strategy selection, resource allocation, and budget preparation, involves repetitive interactions by many members of management. Repetitive interactions are needed since decisions at each conceptual level are, in essence, compromises between the desirable and the possible. A dominant strategic position is desirable, but generally not possible because of the economic and competitive factors in most industries; well-funded programs are desirable, but usually not possible because of the financial constraints in most companies; high performance standards are desirable, but often not possible because of the ability and commitment limitations of many employees. Plans at each stage are a compromise, and planning requires the ability to be satisfied with compromises. Many members of an organization are accustomed to deciding and acting authoritatively, based upon their position within a hierarchical structure, and find it impossible to accept compromises based upon discussions within an iterative system. The interactions of the different managerial levels often present a barrier to organizational communication, and integrated effort, in planning.

The function of the general manager of an organization is to ensure that the strategic management process is completed, from formulation to implementation to performance and then back to formulation, despite the future uncertainties, the conceptual interdependencies, and the managerial interactions of the formal planning procedures. This, however, is the role of a leader, not a manager. A leader is an individual within an organization who is able to influence the attitudes and opinions of others within the organization; a manager is merely able to influence their actions and decisions. Leadership is not a synonym for management; it is a higher order of capability. Leadership brings a member of the organization to say, "I'll do it because I think you're right"; management may bring the same person just to say, "I'll do it even though I know you're wrong." The difference between the enthusiasm and the reluctance of those two statements is often the difference between the success and failure of an organization.

Leadership is an amorphous quality. The results can be seen: leadership brings cooperation among members of an organization, while management, which can also bring cooperation, occasionally leads to policy circumvention, personal conflict, and individual withdrawal. The process of leadership is not obvious, although there are four theories to account for the impact upon other individuals:

1. *Personal theory of leadership.* There are distinguishing characteristics or traits of personality that usually accompany a leadership role; these traits are personal intelligence, self-assurance, physical size, technical knowledge, emotional stability, etc. These traits may combine in a personal style that is anticipative (foresee changes and act in advance to prepare the organization) or reactive (observe changes and act afterward to adjust the organization), and they may be measured as personal drives for power, for achievement, or for affiliation.

2. *Interpersonal theory of leadership.* There are distinguishing characteristics in the patterns of interactions with others that usually accompany a leadership role; these patterns range from outward friendliness and respect to rigid neutrality to inward suspicion and distrust. The interpersonal styles that result from these patterns may be exploitive (direct others without regard to their individual needs or values), benevolent (direct others with regard to their alleged needs and values), consultative (direct others after consideration of their opinion and needs), or participative (direct oneself and others after joint consideration of the group's opinions and needs).

3. *Positional theory of leadership.* There are distinguishing characteristics in the ability to use the structure and systems of an organization that usually accompany a leadership role; the structure and systems, of course, provide the relative positions in the authority hierarchy, and the sanctions/rewards of the motivational processes. Organization styles of leadership range from coercive (using the sanctions, such as discharge or demotion), to authoritative (using the position, and the common acceptance of that position), to incentive (using the rewards, such as salary increases or promotion).

4. *Social theory of leadership.* There are distinguishing characteristics in the ability to use the power relationships among the subgroups of an organization; the subgroups form coalitions that can exercise power due to their possible refusal to continue contributing their effort or expertise to the organization, which would bring a lowering of the competitive position or service level, and might cause a breakup of the organization. Social styles of leadership range from political (using the subgroups) to apolitical (ignoring the subgroups).

Leadership is a complex phenomenon. Most of the traits of individual personality, patterns of interpersonal competence, uses of organizational processes, and manipulation of political subgroups seem to be present, in varying degrees, in all leadership roles, and leadership styles seem to be a composite of these personal, interpersonal, positional, and social alternatives:

	Exploitive		
		Coercive	
Anticipative	Benevolent		Political
		Authoritative	
Reactive	Consultative		Apolitical
		Incentive	
	Participative		

There is an inherent preference among university researchers for the participative/incentive/apolitical style of leadership—an academic hope that nice guys, both male and female, truly will finish first—but unfortunately there are numerous examples of the success of the exploitive/coercive/political mode of behavior. This apparent contradiction is due to the reduced importance of the leadership style as compared to the organizational strategy, structure, and systems in a changing, competitive environment. The critical element in organizational success is not the outward behavior of the general manager, but the comparative strategy selected for the organization, the structure and systems designed to implement that strategy, and the enthusiastic participation of the membership.

A general manager has a limited number of choices in attempting to improve the long-term competitive position or service level of an organization. That person can change a product/market posture attempting to find a high-margin market niche, or the product/process position seeking to locate a low-cost production method. The various product or service positions can be concentrated in a single industry, or diversified among related or nonrelated industries, and the process postures can be integrated backward toward raw material supplies or forward toward retail distribution. The organizational influences that can be changed are the goals and objectives, policies and procedures, programs and plans, and immediate actions expressed for each of the functional and technical units, and the organizational mechanisms that can be changed are the organizational structure, and the planning, control, and motivational systems. The general manager has a choice in the timing of actions, the sequencing of decisions, and the selection of personnel, and he or she can concentrate on informing others, showing others, or pushing others. These methods to improve corporate performance are shown graphically in Exhibit 1, but the essential element is that the choices are limited, and none deal directly with the enthusiastic participation and commitment of the members of the organization. This participation and this commitment are needed since the choices on the strategy, structure, and systems, although limited, are too complex to be formulated and implemented by a single individual. An integrated and coordinated organizational effort is needed.

Organizations are composed of individuals, and these individuals differ on a number of behavioral characteristics, or dimensions. These characteristics include interpersonal relationships (formal to informal), individual orientations (tasks vs. people), risk preferences (low to high), time orientation (short to long), uncertainty tolerance (minimal to complete), goal orientation (corporate to individual), and problem-solving style (intuitive to analytical). These individuals also differ in memberships of the functional and technical subgroups, or organizational units, and in levels on the authority hierarchy. Each of these personal characteristics, group memberships, and hierarchical levels creates a slightly different view of the position, performance, and problems of the organization, and therefore a slightly different view of the need for change in the strategy, structure, and systems. The selection of the strategy, and the design of the structure and systems, must be the result of an integrated and coordinated organizational effort, despite the diverse personal interests, behavioral characteristics, group memberships, and positional levels of the members, and to bring about this integrated and coordinated effort, it is necessary to create a *sense of direction and purpose.*

A sense of direction and purpose is needed to ensure that all members of the orga-

Exhibit 1 *Decision elements in the managerial process to improve organizational performance*

Strategic changes	Strategic patterns	Organizational influences	Organizational mechanisms	Managerial choices	Managerial roles	Organizational response
		Goals and objectives	Organizational structure			
	Vertical integration			Timing of actions	Informing others	
Product–market		Policies and procedures	Planning system			Complex, due to individual traits and group memberships
	Related diversification			Sequencing of actions	Showing others	
Product–process		Programs and plans	Control system			
	Nonrelated diversification			Selection of personnel	Pushing others	
		Immediate actions	Motivation system			

667

nization, including the senior executives, the functional and technical specialists, the supervisory personnel, production workers, office employees, and maintenance staff are able to work together productively and, hopefully, enthusiastically, with coordinated decisions and integrated actions to improve the long-term competitive position or service level of the organization.

It is not easy to create this sense of direction and purpose, and the consequent integration and coordination of the decisions and actions of the members of the organization. All the members must understand the current strategy, and guide their decisions and actions in line with that strategy, while recognizing the need for change, and accepting the compromise nature of changes reached through the planning process. Each member of an organization can have three views or impressions of the strategy of that organization. The first view can be termed the "proper" strategy for the organization. Each member, depending upon his or her position within that organization, is able to gauge the current performance and position of the business firm or service agency, and has some understanding of the environmental opportunities and risks and the organizational strengths and weaknesses. Each member, therefore, has a concept of what the organization *ought* to be doing.

The second view of the corporate strategy by the individual members of the organization can be termed the "present" strategy. Each member, again depending upon his or her position within the firm or agency, has some contact with the goals and objectives, policies and procedures, programs and plans, and current actions of the functional and technical departments, all of which are, or should be, based upon the selected strategy of the company. Each member, therefore, has a concept of what the organization presently is doing.

The last view of the corporate strategy by the individual members of the organization can be termed the "personal" strategy. Each member within the organization is affected by the organizational structure and by the managerial systems for planning, control, and motivation. The relationships imposed by the structure and the behavior encouraged by the systems give each person a concept of what he or she *should be* doing for organizational improvement and personal self-interest. The sources of these three individual concepts or perceptions of the organizational strategy are shown in schematic form at the top of the next page.

The three perceptions of the organizational strategy by the individual members of that organization must be consistent for improved corporate performance and a strengthened competitive position or service level. Members of an organization who believe that what the organization ought to be doing, what the organization is doing, and what it is in their best interest to do are not only approximate or parallel but identical will base their decisions and actions in line with that strategy. Coordinated decisions and cooperative actions in line with a rationally selected strategy will result, over time, in improved organizational performance and a more secure competitive position or a more beneficial service level.

Identical perception of the strategy of an organization by all the members of the organization is an impossibility, but an impossibility that can be approached. The approach requires a consistent selection of the strategy from the current performance and position of the firm relative to the environmental opportunities and risks,

Organizational mission or charter

Corporate performance and position

Managerial values and attitudes
} Individual perception of the "proper" organizational strategy

Opportunities and risks within the industry

Range of strategic alternatives open to the firm

Strengths and weaknesses within the company

Departmental goals and objectives

Departmental policies and procedures
} Individual perception of the "present" organizational strategy

Departmental programs and plans

Departmental immediate actions

Individual sense of direction and purpose, resulting in improved corporate performance and competitive position

Corporate organizational structure

Corporate planning system
} Individual perception of the "personal" organizational strategy

Corporate control system

Corporate motivational system

---

the organizational strengths and weaknesses, and the managerial values and attitudes; a consistent statement of the selected strategy in the functional and technical goals and objectives, policies and procedures, programs and plans, and immediate actions; and a consistent design of the organizational structure and the planning, control, and motivational systems. This strategy selection, translation, and structure/systems design cannot be performed by one person, but one person can monitor the process and inspire consistency. A consistent analytical and developmental approach to the strategy, structure, and systems of an organization is the true responsibility of the general manager of that organization, and the definition in this text of organizational leadership and strategic management. The following cases illustrate the need for this leadership and management.

Lonestar Electronics Corporation

The Lonestar Electronics Corporation was founded as the Lonestar Chemical Coatings Company in 1964 by Dr. Jimmy Garcia, who, at the time, was a Ph.D. student in chemical engineering at the University of Houston. Dr. Garcia had developed a totally inert epoxy chemical compound that could be used to encapsulate sensitive electronic instruments for protection against shocks and moisture. He had developed the material under a grant from the National Aeronautics and Space Administration to protect the navigational instruments and avionic systems used in the space program, but the epoxy coatings, although very strong and shock absorbent, were too heavy for use in space vehicles and were superseded by a foamed polyurethane plastic which was also both chemically and electrically inert so that it did not affect the operations of the electronic systems, but which was much lighter in weight. Dr. Garcia was disappointed, but not dismayed. He turned to the oil industry, which was also centered in Houston, coated a number of the instruments used for petroleum exploration with the new material, and found a ready

This case was prepared from an earlier version written by Professor Steven R. Brandt of the Graduate School of Business Administration at Stanford University, and is used with his permission, and with the permission of the Board of Trustees of Leland Stanford Junior University.

market. Sales of the coatings over the first year were only slightly more than $50,000, but the margins were large enough to support Dr. Garcia and his family, and to start a product development program in electronic instrumentation.

Over the next three years Dr. Garcia, with the help of other doctoral students from the University of Houston, designed a series of simple electronic instruments and the related data-processing systems used in petroleum exploration. These instruments included gravimeters to measure variations in the gravitational forces produced by different densities of rock beneath the surface, magnetometers to measure variations in the magnetic forces produced by different types of rock, and seismometers to measure the refraction of shock waves from different strata of rock. The instruments were, of course, coated with the epoxy resin, which made them very durable and suitable for field exploration. The company's products were widely advertised in petroleum newsletters and geological journals under the slogan "Tough as a Texan," and they rapidly achieved a respected market position for field instrumentation in the petroleum industry.

In 1967, the company was incorporated under the Lonestar name, and additional electronic instruments were designed for process controls in the petroleum refining and petrochemical manufacturing industries. These new instruments converted temperature, pressure, and flow measurements to digital equivalents for use in automated processing systems; the instruments were technologically very simple but operationally very reliable, and they were widely used, particularly for the harsh conditions of catalytic refining. In 1968, the first technological breakthrough occurred in the company's research program with the development of an ion electrode analyzer that could measure the concentration of electrically charged particles in a liquid, and eventually identify the chemical nature of the substance in the solution. The ion electrode had an immediate application in the petrochemical production of feedstocks, the chemical polymerization of plastics, and the cryogenic processing of industrial gases. Sales of the company expanded from $1.5 million in 1967 to over $5.0 million in 1970.

Assembly of the instruments was originally concentrated in a factory in Baytown, on Galveston Bay, 30 miles to the east of Houston. The factory building had been an abandoned warehouse, which Dr. Garcia purchased at a tax sale and repaired; it was located in a heavily industrialized and unattractive section of the city, with storage tanks, railroad yards, and trucking terminals, but it was close to a residential area with high unemployment so that the company was easily able to hire assembly personnel.

Most of the workers were unskilled or semiskilled when hired, but Dr. Garcia had established an extensive training program, and a stepped series of promotions to the more difficult tasks, so that the output quality on the basic instruments was considered to be the equal of the more modern plants and more skilled workers in the electronic centers on Route 128 west of Boston and in the Bay area south of San Francisco. Output costs, however, were much lower due to reduced wage rates, high productivity standards, and a no-

ticeable enthusiasm and effort among the workers. At least part of the reason for that enthusiasm and effort was a direct appeal to ethnic pride; a large framed notice in Spanish, signed by Dr. Jimmy Garcia, was posted on the employee entrance door:

> Estamos aquí para trabajar unidos. Tenemos que demonstrarles a los demás que nuestra raza es productiva y triunfadora. El que no desee tomar esa responsabilidad, no tendrá trabajo conmigo. (Signed statement of Dr. Jimmy Garcia, posted at the Lonestar Electronics plant in Baytown, Texas)

No English version was posted anywhere in the building; however a literal translation would read as follows:

> We are here to work together. We have to demonstrate to the rest of the world that our race is productive and competent. Those who are not willing to take on that responsibility, will not have a job with me. (Translation of the signed statement of Dr. Jimmy Garcia)

All line supervisors and staff personnel who worked at the Baytown factory were fluent in Spanish. All production documents, including job orders, time cards, and inspection reports, were written in Spanish. Originally, all design engineers, marketing personnel, and the accounting and financial staff who worked at the corporate offices in Houston were expected to learn and be able to use Spanish while visiting the factory, but that requirement had been dropped in the mid-1970s as the company became much larger, with additional plants in other sections of the United States, and in Japan. By 1978 the only remnant of this founding policy that was still evident was the color of the identification badges that had to be worn while visiting company engineering offices or production facilities; the badges of employees able to speak Spanish were red, while those of others were blue, yellow, or white, depending upon the length of service. Some of the employees in Europe and Japan had learned Spanish in order to qualify for a red badge, and a letter of congratulations from Dr. Garcia.

Sales in 1970 were $5.2 million; in 1978 they were $47.8 million. This extremely rapid growth had been brought about by a series of acquisitions that had expanded the product line, the market area, and the productive capacity of the firm. Mr. Lawrence "Quid" Jones, a successful attorney in Houston and an early investor in Lonestar, had arranged the mergers as a means of increasing the sales revenues of the company to the level that would permit eventual registration on the New York Stock Exchange. Mr. Jones was certain that he could obtain the necessary financial resources, and that Dr. Garcia could provide the needed management expertise, to make the larger company a very profitable vehicle for personal investment.

> Jimmy Garcia had an unusual combination of talents; he understands the technology of solid-state physics, and he understands the application of that technology to industrial processes and communication systems. The world is filled with complex processes and large-scale systems in which the quality of the outputs can be improved, or the costs of the inputs can be reduced, by the application of solid-state physics. Lots of people understand the technology—that can be taught at a university—but very few people combine that understanding with an ability to envisage the applications. Jimmy has the ability, and he also has the ability to motivate people. We bought these other companies in order to give him a larger base for his managerial and technological talents. (Statement of Mr. "Quid" Jones)

The acquired companies, located in Atlanta, Boston, San Diego, and Great Britain, were purchased relatively inexpensively since 1970–1974 was a period of economic depression in the electronics industry; government funding for advanced research decreased sharply with the completion of the Apollo space program and the termination of the Vietnam War, and many electronics firms found it difficult to make the transition from government contracts to industrial products. Jimmy Garcia and Quid Jones together investigated a number of companies that were experiencing problems of that nature, selected five or six that had obvious technological capabilities but that needed help in applications engineering, market planning, or production cost control, and Mr. Jones then negotiated the terms of acquisition or merger. Four companies, with overall sales of $14.7 million, were purchased for just slightly more than $3.5 million in equity and $1.2 million in cash during the period 1972–1974. The two executives considered the acquisition program to be a success: internal product development, geographic area expansion, and aggressive market promotion brought the sales revenues of the original company in Houston and the four acquired firms to $29.0 million in 1975, and to $47.8 million in 1978 (Exhibit 1).

The acquisition program from 1972 to 1974 had been financed primarily by the issuance of common stock in exchange for the assets of the merged firms; the sales expansion from 1975 to 1978 was financed by the use of bank loans and long-term debt (see Exhibit 2). The large amount of this debt, $17.9 million, had become worrisome to Lonestar executives in 1978, and the expressed concerns of the Board of Directors had started the process of strategic reexamination that is described in the balance of this case.

The products of the combined companies consisted of electronic instruments, systems, and components. Instruments comprised 52% of company sales in 1978, and were grouped into four basic lines:

1. *Geological exploration instruments* included the gravimeters, magnetometers, and seis-

Exhibit 1 *Income statements (000's omitted) for Lonestar Electronics Corporation, 1975–1978*

	1975	1976	1977	1978
U.S. domestic sales	$25,533	$28,880	$30,337	$33,866
U.S. export and foreign sales	3,477	6,502	9,576	13,919
Total corporate sales	29,010	35,382	39,913	47,785
Direct labor costs	4,568	5,407	5,878	7,013
Direct material costs	8,256	9,986	10,256	10,862
Direct manufacturing overhead	1,866	2,368	2,584	2,935
Total direct costs	14,690	17,671	18,718	20,810
Contribution to corporate expenses	14,320	17,711	21,195	26,975
Selling expenses	3,071	3,327	4,274	5,325
Administrative expenses	7,279	9,308	11,842	14,133
Research expenses	1,995	2,301	2,980	4,131
Interest expenses	575	772	1,370	2,148
Total corporate expenses	12,840	15,708	20,466	25,737
Profit before taxes	1,500	2,003	729	1,238
Federal and state taxes	778	1,032	350	633
Total corporate profit	722	971	379	605

Source: Company records.

mometers that were the original products of the firm. Sales in 1978 were $7.8 million, and customers were primarily petroleum exploration companies and oil-well service agencies, both in the United States and abroad. Demand by these customers had remained nearly constant for a number of years, despite the large increases in exploration expenditures, since the simple hand-held instruments produced by Lonestar were being supplanted by much more accurate and much more expensive instrument systems, often mounted in a truck or helicopter. Sales of the basic instruments continued, however, because of their convenience and durability in field exploration, and because of their use as a check on the larger and more complex systems. Lonestar had approximately 50% of the hand-held market, but less than 8% of the total market for geological exploration instrumentation.

2. *Chemical analysis instruments* produced by Lonestar were based on the ionization principle; a dual electrode, immersed in a liquid, was able to measure the charged particles (ions) within the liquid, and to identify, by characteristics of the transmitted current, some of the chemical substances in the solution. Very sensitive ion electrodes are used in medical electronics to measure sodium, potassium, and calcium in blood or urine; less sensitive ion electrodes are used in industrial processes to monitor calcium and chloride in petrochemical production, and carbon dioxide and nitrogen in cryogenic (supercooled) gas operations. Lonestar concentrated on the industrial processing market, which it dominated, with sales of $7.4 million; the

Exhibit 2 *Balance sheets (000's omitted) for Lonestar Electronics Corporation, 1975–1978*

	1975	1976	1977	1978
Cash and cash equivalents	$ 644	$ 972	$ 1,044	$ 1,551
Accounts receivable	3,384	4,619	5,876	8,229
Inventories	5,223	6,332	7,643	9,422
Miscellaneous current assets	413	527	642	547
Total current assets	9,664	12,450	15,205	19,749
Land, buildings, and equipment	19,064	21,179	25,913	29,969
less accumulated depreciation	6,253	8,540	10,236	11,109
Total fixed assets	12,811	12,639	15,677	18,860
Total corporate assets	$22,475	$25,089	$30,882	$38,609
Accounts payable	$ 2,063	$ 1,844	$ 2,489	$ 4,062
Short-term bank loans	2,500	3,840	8,263	7,300
Income taxes due	599	763	248	463
Miscellaneous current liabilities	324	471	583	1,419
Total current liabilities	5,486	6,918	11,583	13,244
Long-term debt	4,691	4,691	5,440	10,600
Common stock	6,758	6,969	6,969	7,270
Capital and earned surplus	5,540	6,511	6,890	7,495
Total equity	12,298	13,480	13,859	14,765
Total liabilities and equity	$22,475	$25,089	$30,882	$38,609

Source: Company records.

market was thought to be growing at 15% annually.

3. *Microwave analytical instruments* are used in the design, manufacture, and repair of microwave equipment. Microwaves are a form of electromagnetic energy with wavelengths that fall midway on the spectrum between the long waves of radio broadcasts and the shorter lengths of visible light; electromagnetic transmission in this frequency range can be used for military and commercial radar, long-distance communications, industrial heating, and residential cooking. Lonestar did not make the familiar oscilloscopes used to depict and measure waveforms, but they did manufacture analog and digital units to convert microwave measurements for use with automated equipment, and produced a line of amplifiers to magnify the waves, and a line of signal sources to reproduce them. The microwave instruments were assembled at the Boston and Atlanta plants, and the company sales in 1978 were $5.3 million annually. The microwave instrument market was growing at 30 to 35% per year, and was dominated by such well-known companies as Hewlett-Packard,

Varian Associates, and Texas Instruments. Lonestar was believed to have about 12% of the market for microwave converters, amplifiers, and signal sources.

4. *Process control instruments* manufactured by Lonestar were used to measure temperature, pressure, and flow in the petroleum, petrochemical, and chemical industries; these instruments were usually part of a cybernetic (feedback) system, with the controls wired to a microcomputer or microprocessor that could adjust input materials, pump speeds, temperature settings, etc. The Lonestar instruments were known more for durability than for sensitivity, and they were purchased for use in very harsh environments, particularly catalytic refining. Sales in 1978 were $4.3 million; this was less than 3% of the total process control instrument market for the petroleum and chemical industries, but nearly 30% of the market for instruments that were exposed to harsh conditions and rapid deterioration. Sales growth in this market segment was expected to increase to 25% annually, although in the past it had averaged only 10%, because many refineries were now attempting to improve their output efficiency through more automated processing.

Electronic systems produced by Lonestar were complete units, each designed to perform a specific function. Five different systems were marketed by the company in 1978:

1. *Radio-telephone systems,* based on microwave technology, were used for medium-distance communications to supplement the telephone networks in developing countries. The Lonestar systems were standardized, in three basic sizes, to reduce the manufacturing costs and repair problems, and they were designed to interface easily with existing telephone equipment, and to avoid interference with prevailing radio and radio-telephone traffic. Each unit consisted of a transmitter, receiver, and aerial that could be placed at a manual telephone exchange to communicate with other exchanges within the country, and within adjoining countries. Messages were automatically relayed by each exchange in the system. Sales in 1978 were $8.7 million, and growth was expected to average 25% annually for at least the next 10 years. Competitive systems were manufactured by General Electric Ltd., a British firm totally separate from the American company with the same name, and by Siemens, a German manufacturer of heavy electrical and electronic equipment. Market share information was not available, due to the global nature of the sales efforts by the three companies, but Lonestar executives felt that they maintained an approximately equal percentage of the rapidly growing market.

2. *Radar analysis systems,* also based on microwave technology, were used to test the complex communication, navigation, and fire control systems mounted about carrier-based aircraft, to analyze problems with those systems, and to identify possible causes. The radar analyzer was the most complex electronic system produced by Lonestar; it was sold to the Navy for slightly under $1.0 million per unit, and three units had been sold in 1978. Sales of six to eight units per year were possible to the Air Force, after additional design work estimated at $1.5 million to adjust to the different systems used on land-based planes, and a further sales potential of 20 or 30 units per year existed among commercial airlines, if FAA and CAB approval could be obtained. Competitive units were manufactured by the Raytheon Corporation, a large electronics firm headquartered outside Boston, but those radar analyzers were not as technically advanced, nor as precise in identifying the probable causes of system failures.

3. *Telephone encoders,* with integrated circuitry, could digitize a human voice, encode the digital equivalents for efficient telephone transmission, decode the message, and re-create the voice at the receiving end with individual characteristics intact. The encoder was used primarily for confidential business conversations between the office locations of large corporations. Conversations could be decoded only by telephone equipment with the same digital analyzer for the voices and the same encoder circuitry for the transmissions; changes in the encoder chips were made at regular intervals to maintain confidentiality and system integrity. The encoder was the civilian outgrowth of a military research program; civilian sales were $1.6 million per year to manufacturing companies, law firms, and financial institutions both in the United States and abroad. No military or governmental units were produced since the design, with the completion of the contract research program sponsored by the U.S. government, had become public property, and government purchases were made by a competitive bidding process. Lonestar had lost the competitive bid for $11.0 million in telephone encoder equipment in 1978, but planned to submit a bid for 1979 at a "considerably lower margin" to regain the contract that year. Growth in the civilian market was expected to be 40% per year; growth in the government market had begun to slow down, and was forecast at 18 to 20% annually over the next few years, followed by a period of decline after all embassies, legations, and military posts were equipped with the encoders.

4. *Language instructors* used essentially the same circuitry contained in the telephone encoder, but with "read-only" memory chips that could be programmed at the factory with digital equivalents to recreate a voice speaking in French, Russian, Chinese, etc. Unlike language records, which could be used only for passive listening, this teaching machine required active participation: the student read a sentence from the programmed instruction booklet, and the machine digitized the voice, compared the digital equivalents with the correct form stored in memory, reproduced individual words that had been mispronounced, and again compared the student's pronunciations of those words with the correct form. To go on to the next lesson, it was necessary for the student to say correctly each word that had originally been mispronounced, and then to pronounce correctly the entire sentence. Sales of the language instructor were only $0.8 million in 1978, but they were expected to grow rapidly as usage spread at both schools and colleges. No competitive units were produced.

5. *Talking toys* were a very simplified form of the language instructor that had been made for installation in stuffed animals. The unit responded to a human voice with simple innocuous messages such as "If the weather is nice, let's go out and play" or "I'm tired, now, and I want to take my nap"; the messages were selected at random from a memory bank with 20 alternatives. Parents, if dissatisfied with the standard messages, could order read-only memory chips with their own statements up to 12 words long. The talking toy unit had been introduced in 1978, almost too late for the Christmas season, and sales had been $0.5 million to a toy manufacturer who had hurriedly produced a stuffed animal named "Larry, the Loquacious Bear." Sales were expected to be four to five times higher in 1979.

The components produced by Lonestar Electronics consisted of contract research, cable connectors, and magnet wire. Contract research, of course, was not technically a component or part, but company executives grouped research revenues and expenses under this classification for convenience.

1. *Contract research* in advanced electronic design was performed for two large companies in the petroleum industry, and for governmental agencies in the United States and abroad. Contract research for the U.S. military had been deemphasized in recent years by the company because instruments or systems developed under these contracts became public property, as in the case of the telephone encoders, and did not remain proprietary products. Contract payments to Lonestar in 1978 were $3.8 million, with $2.4 million from the U.S. government. It was felt that the total of government contracts for which Lonestar was qualified to bid would remain relatively stable over the coming years, at approximately $200 million, while contract research from corporations would grow at 10 to 15% annually from the currently relatively small base of $25 million.

2. *Cable connectors* were used to join coaxial cables and waveguides for the transmission of microwave signals between operating units within a system. Wires and connectors of the type used to transmit electricity cannot be used for microwaves because the electromagnetic impulses radiate energy, with resultant loss of power and precision. To reduce the power loss and maintain the precision, coaxial cables and tubular waveguides have to be used. The coaxial cable consists of two concentric conductors separated by a winding or extrusion of an inert plastic, generally polyethylene. The microwave signals travel on the inner conductor, which is a solid wire, while the outer conductor, made of metal tubing, acts as a shield to keep the energy from escaping. Wave guides operate on the same principle, but consist of hollow metal tubing with the signals traveling inside, reflected from the inner walls. Connectors for the coaxial cables and waveguides have to be precisely machined and completely insulated to prevent distortion of the signals and loss of energy. Lonestar had purchased a company in San Diego that had the reputation of making the high-quality connectors (to join two cables or tubes), couplers (to join a measurement instrument to a cable or tube), and terminals (to join an operating unit to a cable or tube), and then had changed the insulating material to the inert epoxy compound originally developed by Dr. Garcia; this raised the quality level and component performance even higher. Sales were $3.3 million in 1978, and growing at 18% annually. Lonestar dominated the high-performance segment of the microwave connector market, with an estimated 65% share, but they represented only 15% of the total market.

3. *Magnet wire* was very precisely drawn copper or aluminum wire, with cross sections measured in thousandths of an inch, that was used to wind the magnetic cores needed for many electronic and electromagnetic instruments. During the 1960s and early 1970s magnet wire had been continually in short supply, but the integrated circuitry developed in the mid-1970s supplanted many of the magnetic cores. Lonestar had purchased the major European producer of magnet wire in 1974, partially for the product line which still sold well abroad, but primarily for an entrance into the European Common Market. The acquired firm, which was located in Great Britain, had wire sales of $1.7 million in 1978, and served as a distributor for many of the instruments and systems produced in the United States.

Members of the planning staff at Lonestar Electronics, as part of the process of strategic reexamination, had identified the major market segments for each of the product lines and allocated 1978 sales revenues by segment (Exhibit 3), and had evaluated the competitive strengths of the company by product line (Exhibit 4). Staff members had asked corporate executives to rate each of the products, using a five-point scale, for design strengths, marketing strengths, manufacturing strengths, and R&D strengths. "Design strength" referred to the reputation of the product line for quality and performance; "marketing strength" considered the contacts of the sales force and the impact of the advertising upon customers; "manufacturing strength" measured the cost efficiencies of the production process; and "R&D strength" meant the tech-

Exhibit 3 *Sales revenues (000's omitted) of Lonestar Electronics Corporation by product line and by market segment for 1978*

	Petroleum industry	Chemical industry	Electronic industry	Miscellaneous industry	Military and government	Schools and colleges	International
Geological exploration	$ 5,013	—	—	—	$ 98	$ 277	$ 2,370
Chemical analysis	1,769	$3,948	$ 234	—	—	109	1,311
Microwave analysis	—	—	3,140	$ 422	922	197	693
Process controls	2,440	1,362	—	—	—	—	514
Instruments	9,222	5,310	3,374	422	1,020	573	4,888
Radio telephone	2,303	—	—	—	—	—	6,383
Radar analyzer	—	—	—	—	2,591	—	—
Telephone encoder	426	—	—	1,015	—	—	178
Language instructor	—	—	—	—	—	785	—
Talking toys	—	—	—	517	—	—	—
Systems	2,729	—	—	1,532	2,591	785	6,561
Contract research	727	—	—	—	2,362	—	739
Microwave connectors	—	—	2,590	—	—	—	618
Magnetic wires	—	—	629	—	—	—	1,113
Components	727	—	3,219	—	2,362	—	2,470
Totals	$12,678	$5,310	$6,593	$1,954	$5,973	$1,358	$13,919

Source: Company records.

Exhibit 4 *Competitive strengths and gross margins of Lonestar Electronics Corporation by product line, 1978*

	Total sales (thousands)	Gross margin (thousands)	Gross margin (%)	Design strength	Market strength	Manufacturing strength	R&D strength
Geological exploration	$ 7,758	$ 4,290	55.3	Med +	High	High	Med −
Chemical analysis	7,371	4,810	65.2	High	Med +	High	Med
Microwave analysis	5,364	2,490	46.4	Med	Med	Med	Med +
Process controls	4,316	2,920	67.6	Med +	Med	High	Med −
Radio telephone	8,686	5,130	59.0	Med	Low	Med	Med +
Radar analyzer	2,591	2,020	77.9	Med +	Med −	Med −	High
Telephone encoder	1,619	1,100	67.9	High	Med −	Low	Med +
Language instructor	785	560	71.3	High	Med −	Med	Med +
Talking toys	517	270	52.2	High	Med	Med	Med +
Contract research	3,828	760	19.8	Med	Med −	n.a.	Med
Microwave connectors	3,208	1,450	45.2	High	Med	Med	Med +
Magnetic wire	1,742	1,150	66.0	Med	Med −	Med +	n.a.
	$47,785	$26,970	56.4				

Source: Company records.

nical capability of the design staff. All ratings were made relative to the strongest competitor. The results were summed, and then were translated to "high," "medium plus," "medium," "medium minus," and "low." "High" meant, of course, that company executives considered the design characteristics, marketing capabilities, production efficiencies, or engineering abilities represented by a particular product line to be very much better than those of the major competitor.

Manufacturing of instruments and systems was concentrated at Houston, Atlanta, and Boston; the plant in San Diego was small, and produced only the microwave cable connectors, while the factory in Britain was even smaller, and made only magnet wire. Both of the smaller plants served as sales offices for the larger divisions. The Houston plant, which was actually located in Baytown, 30 miles east of Houston, manufactured the instruments for geological exploration, chemical analysis, and process controls; the Atlanta factory made the microwave analysis instruments and the radar analyzer system; and

Boston produced the radio telephone, the telephone encoder, the language instructor, and the talking toys. All three of the major plants did some contract research. In addition to the company-owned factories, a joint venture had been started in Japan to manufacture some of the instruments for sale in the Far East and South Pacific areas.

Lonestar Electronics was organized in a simple matrix, with four decentralized factories that served as profit centers, responsible for engineering design and product sales as well as manufacturing, and an International Division that supervised the magnet wire plant in Britain, the joint venture in Japan, and export sales to all countries except the United States and Canada. It was the intent of Dr. Garcia that the five units, all led by division vice presidents, operate autonomously as small business ventures, but cooperatively, assisted in policy decisions and planning by corporate vice presidents for R&D, Marketing, Personnel, and Finance (Exhibit 5).

Exhibit 5 *Organizational structure of Lonestar Electronics Corporation, 1978*

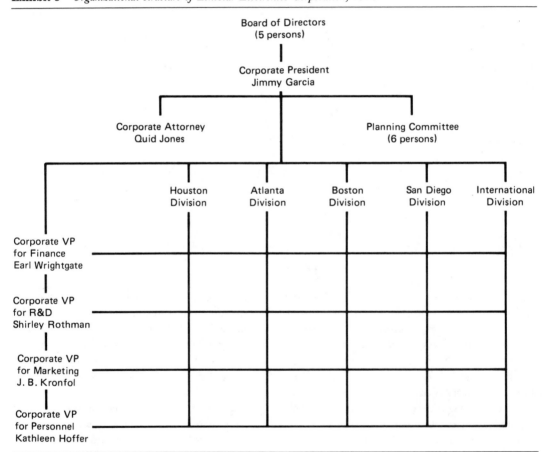

Source: Company records.

Management in high technology is very different from management in basic industries. In petroleum, for example, you know the market, which will be straightforward extrapolation from prior years; you know the price, which will be a stepwise function set by the oil-producing countries; and you know the technology, which will be proven by Exxon, Texaco, and Gulf. Management in the petroleum industry is similar to a linear programming model that is too large to solve, but you can estimate solutions from the model on a response surface since you know the major input variables and process contraints. In advanced electronics, the market, price, and technology are interrelated, and you never know one until the others are pinned down. Home computers didn't exist three years ago, and they couldn't exist until the very large scale integrated circuitry was developed, which brought the price down and increased the market so that Apple Computing and Tandy Radio Shack could invest in the development of standardized units for home and hobby use. In advanced electronics, you have to plan for possibilities. That is why we have the two sides to our company. The divisional vice presidents are responsible for sales growth, the corporate vice presidents are responsible for profits. It's the ideal division of managerial responsibilities, and will be the management style of the future, not only in high technology, but in the basic industries as material supplies and economic conditions become more uncertain. (Statement of Dr. Jimmy Garcia)

The Planning Committee at Lonestar Electronics was central to the management of the company. It consisted of six people: Jimmy Garcia, corporate president; Quid Jones, corporate vice president for legal affairs (Mr. Jones spent approximately 30% of his time at Lonestar, now that the acquisition program was completed, devoting the balance to his private legal practice); Earl Wrightgate, corporate vice president for finance; Shirley Rothman, corporate vice president for R&D; J. B. Kronfol, corporate vice president for marketing; and Kathleen Hoffer, corporate vice president for personnel. The Planning Committee met monthly to review the operations of one of the four major divisions (San Diego was considered to be too small for regular review), and to structure the annual planning process. This process required a series of interactions between members of the committees and the divisional vice presidents. In January of each year, Shirley Rothman and J. B. Kronfol prepared forecasts of technological developments and market conditions over the next five years; these forecasts were sent to the divisional vice presidents, who prepared annual estimates of sales revenues, manufacturing costs, gross margins, overhead expenses, and pretax profits for that five-year period. These estimates were adjusted in negotiations between the divisional vice presidents and members of the Planning Committee at the next regularly scheduled review of each division, which occurred on three-month intervals. The adjustments were generally upward since it was felt that most of the divisional vice presidents did not fully recognize the potentials of the advancing technology or the opportunities in the expanding economy.

After agreement was reached on a five-year plan, the divisional vice presidents prepared estimates of capital investments and personnel needs over a three-year period; these figures were also adjusted in negotiations with the Planning Committee, generally downward since it was felt that the divisional vice presidents tended to overestimate their needs for money and people. Finally, the divisional vice presidents prepared detailed monthly budgets of revenues and expenses over the coming year; these were approved without alterations by the members of the Planning Committee if they reflected properly the results of the earlier decisions on expected sales, margins and profits, and allocated capital and personnel.

> We have a five year–three year–one year planning cycle, and that planning cycle drives the company. The divisional vice presidents don't understand the need for planning; they would much rather just sit there (at their respective plants) and make things, but soon they would find that their products were obsolete and their sales were declining. Our sales aren't declining; they are increasing at a compound rate of 18%.
>
> I know that there is some animosity between the two sides of the company; there is bound to be animosity if you push hard enough. There is going to be more animosity, since we are going to keep on pushing. (Statement of Dr. Jimmy Garcia)

The operations of each of the divisions were reviewed every four months. At these meetings, which were held at the plant sites in Baytown, Atlanta, and Boston or at the international offices in Houston so that supporting data and divisional personnel would be readily available, the actual performance figures were compared with the budgeted expectations, variances were analyzed, and changes were discussed. These meetings were occasionally vituperative, particularly since profits had been below the planned level for the past two years.

> When we leave these meetings we know what was wrong, who was responsible, and how it is going to be fixed. The divisional vice-presidents put up with that inquisition because, under our bonus plan, they are getting paid much more than the corporate vice presidents. (Statement of Dr. Jimmy Garcia)

The bonus plan was simple, and bonus payments could be substantial. The plants were profit centers, but the divisional vice president at each plant was paid a bonus based upon the increase in sales revenues for the preceding three-month period over the equivalent three-month period in the prior year, after an adjustment for inflation. An increase in sales of 35%, as had occurred at the Boston plant in 1979, was translated into a bonus payment of 35% of the vice president's salary for the period. Marketing personnel at each of the plants received bonus payments based upon revenue increases, while the engineering and production staff were evaluated and paid on cost reductions, also after an adjustment for inflation. The corporate vice presidents were paid a commission based upon profit increases above the budgeted amounts; no corporate vice president had received a bonus since the second quarter of 1976.

The Board of Directors consisted of Jimmy Garcia, Quid Jones, and representatives from the two venture capital firms and one insurance company that had made substantial investments in the common stock and long-term debentures of Lonestar. The board had not been active, traditionally meeting only twice a year to approve the plans and, during the period 1970–1974, acquisitions of the firm. However, in 1978, the three outside directors began to suggest quarterly meetings, and to push for a more active role in the management of the company. Jimmy Garcia, however, still held 38% of the stock, Quid Jones 8%, and 15% was spread among seven wealthy families in the Houston area, so that Dr. Garcia was easily able to resist the requests for greater control by representatives of the three financial institutions.

> If push comes to shove, it will be nine people in Houston against an insurance company in New Jersey and two venture capital firms in Chicago; they have the money but we have the votes. But the situation is not going to be allowed to deteriorate to that extent. We are going to give those people what they want: listing

on the New York Stock Exchange. (Statement of Dr. Jimmy Garcia)

Listing on the New York Stock Exchange was the overriding objective of the Lonestar Electronics Corporation. This listing, which would permit easier trading of the company's common stock and provide greater visibility to the company's rapid growth, was expected to result in an improved price–earnings ratio, and would enable the large investors to sell their shares for very considerable capital gains. Listing requirements in 1978, set by the Board of Governors of the Exchange, were for pretax earnings of $2.5 million, tangible assets of $16 million, and a market value of $8.0 million in publicly held shares, spread among at least 2,000 holders. A public issuance was planned, as soon as the pretax earnings reached $2.5 million, and it was thought that the insurance company and one of the venture capital firms would participate with a secondary offering (sell some of their shares at the same time) so that the 2,000-shareholder requirement could easily be met. The shares of Dr. Garcia, Quid Jones, and the nine families in Houston were considered to be "publicly" held, even though they were not actively traded, so that no problem was anticipated in meeting the $8.0 million market value requirement.

The five-year plan for the company prepared in 1978 anticipated pretax profits of $2.9 million in 1979; it was felt that a listing application could be submitted to the New York Stock Exchange and a new issue registration could be sent to the Securities and Exchange Commission that year, and that the formal listing and actual issuance could be accomplished in 1980. The public stock issuance would provide adequate funds for further growth during the next five-year planning period (Exhibit 6).

The members of the Planning Committee, although in agreement that the company now had the base of established product lines and qualified technical and functional people needed for growth in both revenues and prof-

Exhibit 6 *Pro forma income statements (000's omitted) for Lonestar Electronics Corporation over the five-year planning period 1979–1983*

	1979	1980	1981	1982	1983
Sales revenues	$57,500	$68,800	$80,000	$95,100	$110,000
Direct costs	24,100	28,200	32,000	38,000	44,000
Contribution	33,100	40,600	48,000	57,100	66,000
Selling expenses	6,300	6,900	7,200	8,100	8,800
Administrative expenses	16,900	18,600	20,800	23,800	26,400
Research expenses	4,200	5,000	7,200	8,000	9,000
Interest expenses	2,800	3,400	2,400	2,400	1,200
Total corporate expenses	30,200	33,900	37,600	42,300	45,500
Profits before taxes	2,900	6,700	10,400	14,800	20,600
Federal and state taxes	1,500	3,500	5,400	7,700	10,700
Total corporate profits	1,400	3,200	5,000	7,100	9,900

Source: Company records.

its, disagreed somewhat on the policy emphasis required to sustain that growth. These disagreements were revealed in conversations between the case writer and individual members of the committee. The opinions, and the educational/employment backgrounds of the persons involved, are given below.

Dr. Jimmy Garcia, President of Lonestar Electronics. B.S.E.E. University of Texas, Rhodes Scholar at Oxford University, M.S. and Ph.D. in chemical engineering, University of Houston. Founder of Lonestar Electronics. 43 years old.

> Productivity is the key to profits. If you can make anything—bicycles, TV sets, or radar analyzers—cheaper than someone else, you can make money. By cheaper, of course, I mean less expensively; anyone can cheapen a product. Making a product less expensively than your competitors requires standardized designs, volume sales, process improvements, and committed workers. People in this company, and in U.S. industry generally, don't understand the need for productivity gains on an annual basis. All of our plants are falling behind on productivity, even Baytown. We have to develop an incentive system for the production personnel and the hourly workers that will focus their attention squarely on more output at less cost.
>
> We are getting complaints now from our outside directors, and even from Quid Jones, that our corporate overhead is too high; building this central staff is part of a conscious effort to develop a Lonestar "culture" within the company. All the great companies, such as Texas Instruments, Kodak, IBM, Hewlett-Packard, and Matsushita, have that culture. As we grow, we have to learn from companies that have grown. And one thing we can learn is that their employees identify closely with the company. There is a tie that goes beyond simply "having a job"; there is a willingness to give an extra effort, to cut costs, and improve productiv-

ity. If we are going to compete with the Japanese in industrial electronics, I think that we have to instill a Lonestar spirit into people, and that takes money. You don't develop commitment by cutting back. We have that commitment now in our corporate executives, and among some of the older employees at Baytown. We will have that commitment in the divisions, or we'll get some new people out there. We won't go dragging along, as we have in the past, with minimal profits and continual problems. (Statement of Dr. Jimmy Garcia)

Mr. Lawrence "Quid" Jones, Corporate Vice President for Legal Affairs and Acquisitions/Mergers. B.A., University of California at Los Angeles, four years in the U.S. Air Force, and J.D., University of Houston. Private law practice in Houston for 23 years. 56 years old.

> I'm not worried. We sacrificed profits for growth in the past, but now we have the size—the critical mass that you just have to have in business to be successful—so that we can begin to get both profits and growth.
>
> I think that we're going to have to watch expenses at all levels. Jimmy wants to totally control costs out at the divisions, but then he has to hire a large corporate staff to help him do it. We disagree on the size of the staff, but this is not a major disagreement; over time, he'll come to see that the autonomous profit-center concept is best. You hire a good manager, and give that person money, people, and responsibility, and then you sit back and watch the performance. Good managers have an entrepreneurial drive that is locked up inside themselves by corporate rules and regulations; you have to release that spirit and that drive, and let people work for you. (Statement of Mr. Quid Jones)

Mr. Earl Wrightgate, Corporate Vice President for Finance. A.A., B.Sc. (engineering), B.B.A. (finance), M.S.E.E., University of

Florida. Sixteen years with Stewart-Warner Corp. as financial analyst and comptroller, and four years as a private consultant. 47 years old.

> Our planning is becoming more and more sophisticated. We've had the present planning system in place for three years now, and each time we cycle through the system we become more adept at using it.
>
> Planning is critical in a dynamic industry such as industrial electronics, subject to rapid technological and competitive change. The 1960s and early 1970s in this industry were a period of easy opportunity; the 1980s are going to be a period of intense competition. That competition is going to be both domestic and foreign, particularly from Japan. Centralized planning and low-cost production are the strengths of this company, and will enable us to meet that competition. (Statement of Mr. Earl Wrightgate)

Dr. Shirley Rothman, Corporate Vice President for Research and Development, B.A. and Ph.D. (physics), Illinois Institute of Technology, and M.B.A., University of Chicago. Three years in electronic research for Hewlett-Packard; three years as divisional R&D manager for Fairchild Semiconductor; and five years as scientific advisor to Chicago Capital Corp. 39 years old.

> A continual problem in all high-technology firms is the degree of the split between theoretical research on scientific principles and applied development of commercial products. Most of our work now is in product development, and our R&D budget is being spent primarily for product engineering and process improvement. We have to build up our corporate research staff since scientific innovation gives a three- to five-year edge to the firm that develops it. We have a good basis in microwave technology now; as our R&D budget increases, I think that we should concentrate in this area since there are opportunities for meaningful innovation here. (Statement of Dr. Shirley Rothman)

Mr. Joseph Kronfol, Corporate Vice President for Marketing. B.S. University of North Carolina, and M.B.A., Georgia State University. Nine years as market planner and marketing manager at Merriman Microwave Corp. (acquired by Lonestar in 1973). 34 years old.

> I think that we ought to emphasize international sales. Our instruments are selling well to industrial users in Europe and Japan, and our radio-telephone system was designed for the underdeveloped countries in Africa, Asia, and Latin America. There really is a global economy, and I feel that we have to participate in that economy. Fortunately, we have a good start; nearly 30% of our sales volume now comes from overseas. As our budget expands, I plan to open corporate sales offices abroad. We will have divisional sales offices in the United States, where the demand is large enough to support independent marketing programs, and corporate sales offices abroad. (Statement of Mr. Joseph Kronfol)

Ms. Kathleen Hoffer, Corporate Vice President for Personnel. B.A., University of Connecticut and M.B.A., University of Houston. Twelve years in human resource management for Exxon Corporation. 38 years old.

> It is a pleasure to work for a company that emphasizes planning as strongly as does Lonestar. And it is a particular pleasure for me to work for a company that equates financial planning and manpower planning. I really think that we are on the brink of achieving the new style of management proposed by Dr. Garcia. (Statement of Ms. Kathleen Hoffer)

Class Assignment. Evaluate the past performance and present position of Lonestar Electronics, and, as an independent consultant retained by the board of directors, make specific recommendations to Dr. Garcia on the strategy, structure, and systems of the company.

Sherwin-Williams Company

In 1977, Sherwin-Williams, the largest household paint and industrial coatings manufacturer in the world, experienced its first loss in the 111-year history of the firm. Starting in the late 1960s, the company had begun a major shift in emphasis: from a conservatively managed and vertically integrated paint manufacturer to an aggressively directed and horizontally diversified paint marketer. This strategic shift was precipitated by technological and competitive changes within the paint industry, and resulted in substantial sales gains. Profits, however, did not keep pace, registering a decline each year after 1974, and resulting in the eventual $8,200,000 loss (Exhibit 1).

As a result of the loss, which had not been anticipated by management, the company was forced to suspend dividend payments for the first time since 1885, the stock price dropped to approximately one-half of the book value, and a new board of directors was elected with seven outside members and only two representatives of the corporate management. The balance of the case describes the formation and early history of the Sherwin-Williams company, changes in the paint industry during the 1960s which led to the change in corporate strategy, details of that change, and the eventual consequences. The assignment for students is to examine this process of strategic change within a basic industry, determine what went wrong at each stage, and identify the alternatives that should have been considered.

Sherwin-Williams was founded in 1866 by two veterans from the Civil War to produce the first ready-mixed paint made in the United States. During the period of early growth, vertical integration was stressed, and by 1900 the company was producing pigments, resins, and oils for the paints, brushes and ladders for the application, and metal containers for the packaging. The firm also integrated forward, and by the 1930s had a chain of branch stores that served both retail customers and contract painters. In 1945, the company introduced "Kem-Tone," the first water-based wall covering with a latex base for roller application; this "do-it-yourself" paint opened a huge market for home decoration and house maintenance. Company sales and profits grew at a compound rate of over 12% through the 1950s and early 1960s. By 1964, sales were $313 million, profits after taxes were $17 million, and the return on stockholders' equity was over 10%. Sherwin-Williams was considered to be a growth company.

The paint industry changed, however, in the 1960s. Growth, which had been averaging over 8% per year in both the domestic and the industrial segments of the market, slowed to less than 3% overall, while industry competition increased, distribution methods changed, and technical advances accelerated (Exhibit 2).

The paint industry is divided into two major product categories: trade paints and industrial finishes. Trade paints are primarily water-based, and are used for the interior decoration and exterior protection of both new and used buildings. Trade paints is a somewhat obsolete term referring to sale through wholesale and retail trade outlets to contractors, builders, and the general public. Industrial finishes are generally solvent-based (for faster drying) and are sold directly to manufacturers for factory application on industrial machinery, motor vehicles, home appliances, farm implements, outdoor and casual furniture, etc. Not all of the trade sales are water-based latex paints; some are solvent-based for automotive refinishing, roadway marking, or marine use, and some are aerosol-packaged for consumer convenience. A schematic of

Exhibit 1 *Income statements (000's omitted) for Sherwin-Williams Company, 1968–1977*

	1968	1970	1972	1974	1976	1977
Net sales	$452,526	$559,924	$658,285	$802,266	$969,205	$1,035,989
Other income	2,103	1,217	1,444	1,993	382	2,416
Total income	454,629	561,141	659,729	804,259	969,587	1,038,405
Cost of goods	280,002	354,474	418,492	513,713	659,223	732,049
S&A expenses	136,206	170,121	196,254	226,884	270,288	283,847
Interest expenses	3,212	7,005	6,238	8,084	13,154	17,965
Total expenses	419,420	531,600	620,984	748,681	942,665	1,033,861
Profit before tax	35,209	29,541	38,745	55,578	26,922	4,544
Excluding (loss) gain	—	1,745	(2,260)	—	(2,778)	(16,434)
Including (tax) credit	(16,220)	(14,689)	(18,248)	(26,299)	(11,463)	3,683
Profit after tax	$ 18,989	$ 16,597	$ 18,237	$ 29,279	$ 12,681	$ (8,207)
Return on sales (%)	4.2	2.9	2.7	3.6	1.3	neg.
Return on assets (%)	5.1	4.3	4.3	5.7	2.1	neg.
Return on equity (%)	9.6	7.2	7.3	10.4	4.3	neg.

Source: Annual Reports for the respective years.
Note: Excluding (loss) gain refers to exceptional losses or gains realized on the sale or disposal of assets.

the paint industry markets is shown in Exhibit 3.

Of all paint industry sales (80% of trade paint sales), 40.8% are architectural coatings, for internal and external usage; 10% of the sales of architectural coatings are for new buildings, and 90% for the protection and decoration of existing structures. Consequently, trade sale paints are not as directly tied to new housing construction as might seem intuitively apparent (Exhibit 4).

Trade paints are sold through local hardware stores, large chain stores such as Sears, Ward's, and Penney's, national discount stores such as K-Mart and Korvette, regional variety stores such as Meijers and Pay-Less, and specialty paint stores. The specialty paint stores may be either locally or company-owned. In 1976, there were 15,000 retail stores specializing in paint sales in the United States, of which 5,700 were owned, operated, or franchised by paint manufacturers. In addition, paint sales in some of the

Exhibit 2 *Paint industry sales (millions of gallons), 1968–1976*

	1968	1970	1972	1974	1976
Trade sales	434	444	452	458	495
Industrial	395	366	434	463	477
	829	810	886	921	972

Source: Standard & Poor's Industry Surveys, 1977, p. B-130.

Exhibit 3 *Paint industry markets (percent), 1976*

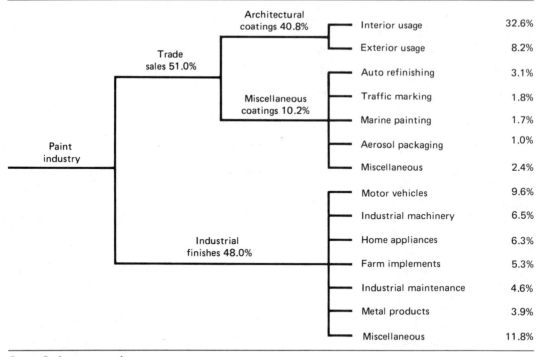

		Architectural coatings 40.8%	Interior usage — 32.6%
			Exterior usage — 8.2%
	Trade sales 51.0%		Auto refinishing — 3.1%
		Miscellaneous coatings 10.2%	Traffic marking — 1.8%
Paint industry			Marine painting — 1.7%
			Aerosol packaging — 1.0%
			Miscellaneous — 2.4%
			Motor vehicles — 9.6%
			Industrial machinery — 6.5%
			Home appliances — 6.3%
	Industrial finishes 48.0%		Farm implements — 5.3%
			Industrial maintenance — 4.6%
			Metal products — 3.9%
			Miscellaneous — 11.8%

Source: Industry consultant.

smaller discount and variety stores were made through leased departments operated or franchised by paint manufacturers.

The percentages of paint sold through the various channels of distribution changed during the period 1950–1975, with the dominant trend showing a movement away from hardware stores to large chains, and then to the discount houses (Exhibit 5).

The percentage of paint sold by the specialty paint stores appears to be reasonably stable; this is caused by the sales to residential builders and painting contractors, who purchase 35% of the trade sales paint. Members of the general public purchase 46%, while commercial and industrial firms buy 11% (for building maintenance, etc., by both large and small firms, and for production finishing by the smaller companies who cannot buy directly from the paint manufacturers; some industrial finishes are sold through the trade sales channels), while governmental units,

Exhibit 4 *New housing construction and trade paint sales, described by index, with 1970 = 100*

	1970	1971	1972	1973	1974	1975	1976
New housing	100	140	158	144	92	76	96
Trade paints	100	104	111	106	114	106	115

Source: Industrial Outlook for 1978, U. S. Domestic and International Business Administration, February 1978, p. 119.

Exhibit 5 *Paint industry distribution channels (percent), 1950–1975*

	1950	1960	1970	1975
Local hardware stores	28	19	12	7
Paint specialty stores	53	55	50	48
Building supply stores	14	10	8	6
National chain stores	5	14	23	18
Discount chain stores	—	2	7	21
	100	100	100	100

Source: Industry consultant.

both state and federal, buy 6%, and 2% is exported. Neither imports (less than 1% of sales) nor exports are important in the paint industry; it is felt that the heavy weight and relatively low value of the product preclude lengthy shipments.

Statistics are not available to show relative changes in the percentage of trade paint sales by company-owned and independent specialty stores; it is felt that these percentages have been reasonably constant, although for different reasons. Company-owned stores have a much greater share of their business with builders, contractors, and commercial/industrial accounts; about 65% of their sales go to this group, and 35% to the general public. Builders and contractors receive a substantial discount for volume purchases; they have no reason to move to the discount stores, while the commercial and industrial firms often require products not carried by the national or discount chains. Independently owned paint stores have tended to diversify into other home decorating products, such as wallpaper, floor coverings, window draperies, sofa and armchair slipcovers, and unpainted furniture. These products appeal to consumers who can make all decorating purchases at one location and thus match colors and textures; 70% of the sales of the independent paint stores are to the general public, and only 30% to builders, contractors, and the commercial/industrial accounts.

Of the specialty paint stores, 5,700 are company-owned, and 9,300 are independently owned. Sherwin-Williams dominates distribution through company-owned paint stores, with 1,786 locations in 1976, over twice as many as the next largest retail-oriented paint manufacturer (Exhibit 6).

Retail margins on paint are theoretically 35 to 40%. In practice, however, margins have been reduced to 30 to 33%, due to the discounts offered to residential builders and painting contractors by the specialty paint stores, and to the strong price competition that has developed at the consumer level, with national chains, discount chains, and some specialty stores using newspaper ads to promote both interior and exterior coatings at "special, low, low prices." Discount stores and national chains are using standard colors of paint as "price leaders" to bring customers to the stores; with high volume and little or no customer service, they can operate at a significantly lower gross margin than can the specialty shops that must provide decorating advice and color matching.

The larger paint manufacturers and retailers support their distribution and pricing efforts with extensive consumer advertising. $16,070,000 was spent in 1976 on advertisements on television and radio, and in magazines and newspapers (Exhibit 7).

Industrial finishes represent, as described previously, 48% of the total sales of the paint industry. Industrial finishes are chemical coatings sold directly to manufacturers for

Exhibit 6 *Paint industry distribution through company-owned stores: the 10 largest chains, 1975*

	Number of stores
Sherwin-Williams Paint Company (national chain)	1,785
Mary Carter Paint Company (national chain)	820
Porter Paint Company (southern states)	455
PPG Industries (national chain)	290
M. A. Bruder Paint Company (Pennsylvania and Ohio)	275
SCM (Glidden-Durkee), Inc. (national chain)	210
Yenkin Majestic Paint Company (north-central states)	150
Cook Paint and Varnish Company (south-central states)	145
Martin Paint & Chemical (New York, Connecticut, and New Jersey)	130
Davis Paint Company (south-central states)	130

Source: Industry consultant.

factory application on motor vehicles, process machinery, home appliances, and farm machinery, and for factory maintenance on steel structures, oil tanks, refinery equipment, and utility stations. Industrial finishes are usually formulated for specific applications, and often for individual customers, so that technical competence is important in marketing, together with personal sales, prompt delivery, and quality control.

The major trend in industrial finishes over the past five years has been in the direction of major technological changes, spurred by government requirements and customer demands for energy-efficient and environment-protective coatings. Industrial finishes were originally based on light petroleum solvents that evaporated rapidly for fast drying and a smooth finish. One change that is occurring is that many of the chemical coatings are now water-based, to reduce the use of scarce feedstocks and to facilitate compliance with environmental restrictions. Other technological developments in the paint industry are coil coating, electrodeposition, electrostatic spray, radiation curing, and powder painting.

Exhibit 7 *Paint industry promotion: expenditures (000's omitted) by 10 largest advertisers, 1975*

	National TV and radio	Local TV and radio	National magazines	Local newspapers	Total amount
Sears Roebuck	$3,275	—	—	$1,180	$ 4,455
SCM (Glidden-Durkee)	1,150	$1,165	$465	—	2,780
DuPont	2,165	250	—	—	2,415
Sherwin-Williams	305	10	750	110	1,175
PPG Industries	760	45	190	—	995
Benjamin Moore	685	205	10	80	985
NL Industries	—	415	485	—	900
Cook Paint and Varnish	—	470	—	430	900
Mary Carter	—	350	15	400	765
Martin Paint & Chemical	—	—	—	700	700
					$16,070

Source: Industry consultant.

Generally speaking, the industrial market divides itself into two parts: the large manufacturers who almost invariably require custom-made finishes for specific applications, and the small and medium-sized manufacturers who can frequently use standardized products from factory stocks. The large manufacturers, particularly in the automotive, appliance, furniture, and metal products industries, are the ones who are insisting upon high-technology coatings, and those coatings have to be engineered to meet very specific performance requirements and very sophisticated application techniques.

Coil coating is one of the new application techniques that requires a totally different formulation for the paint. A coil of steel or aluminum is uncoiled, painted with a spray at speeds of 350 ft per minute, and then either recoiled or formed into finished products. This process is used in the mobile home industry to keep costs down, and in the metal siding industry to maintain volume; it's even being used now for metal containers such as beer and soft-drink cans. Obviously, a coating that can stand the stresses involved in coiling and then forming the steel or aluminum has to be formulated very differently from a coating that would be applied in the more conventional way after the metal parts have been made.

Another new technology is an application process known as electrodeposition. Formed metal parts are dipped into a tank holding an aqueous-based coating material. In a manner not unlike electroplating, the paint is deposited on the surface in a completely uniform film. Sharp edges and corners are as uniformly covered as are the flat surfaces; no brush or spray-applied coating could ever achieve such uniformity.

Electrostatic spray is a means of reducing the waste and achieving a more uniform coating on flat surfaces. The metal part to be painted is given a negative charge, and the paint droplets are given a positive charge; the result is that the part attracts the paint, just like two magnets. Then the paint can be dried with radiation curing. Infrared ovens have been used for years, but now the emphasis is switching to ultraviolet energy, or a beam of electrons. Coatings can be cured by exposure to ultraviolet radiation or electron beams in 1 to 10 seconds that would take 30 minutes in the more common gas-fired oven.

Powder painting is just getting started, but it is certain to increase in usage over time. Powder is really paint in solid rather than liquid form. You apply the powder to the part by electrostatic spray, and then you heat the part, often in an ultraviolet oven, and the powder is converted to a continuous and uniform film. The powder coatings contain no solvents, so that there are no contaminating emissions into the atmosphere. Also, powder coatings are economical since the overspray can be reused.

The enactment of air pollution and environmental protection laws, and the increases in the costs of petroleum products, has forced the paint industry to reformulate its products and change its application technology. The result has not been a poorer product; instead, we have been able to improve such properties as adhesion, flexibility, and resistance to wear and weather. These developments, however, have not been devised by the smaller companies or the weaker-hearted. A lot of money has been spent by DuPont, PPG, SCM, and Sherwin-Williams; they may reap a good return on their investments. (Statement of a paint industry consultant)

Despite the existence of both price and technological competition, the paint industry was not concentrated. There were 1,560 separate paint manufacturers in 1976, up slightly from 1430 in 1965. The larger firms produced both trade paints and industrial finishes, while the smaller companies generally specialized either in trade sales within a given geographic area, or in chemical coatings for a specific industrial market. There were a number of these smaller companies: the 10 largest firms in the industry produced an estimated $3,190,000,000 worth of paint and coatings, or 52% of the total $6,075,000,000 industry sales (Exhibit 8).

Two of the firms among the top 10 producers in the paint industry, PPG Industries and Standard Brands, reported exceptionally successful operations in 1976.

> PPG Industries reports that its coatings and resins lines contributed 21% of its peak volume and 15% of its pretax operating earnings in 1976. This year (1977), the division posted the highest first-quarter sales and profits in history. Officials add that PPG's emphasis on such sophisticated techniques as electrocoating, ultraviolet and electron-beam curing, and high-solids painting has enabled it to achieve greater market penetration and strengthen its competitive position. PPG says that it produces the majority of the paints used in the electrodeposition process in this country. As a result, it has obtained a greater share of the automotive, appliance, and metal-fabricating markets.

Nor has PPG neglected trade paints, which are among the few products this industrial giant sells directly to the public. Pittsburgh "Hide-A-Spray" paint for use with airless spraying equipment makes it possible to paint a two-bedroom apartment in 40 minutes, which significantly reduces labor costs. . . .

> PPG Industries' claim that it has grown at a faster pace than the industry appears to be borne out by the record. Its sales of coatings and resins in 1976 amounted to $484,000,000, up 8.1% from 1975 and 62.2% above 1970. By contrast, the industry's sales in 1976 were up 3.4% from 1975, and 14.8% from 1970. (*Chemical Industry Newsletter,* not dated, p. 7)

Standard Brands Paint Company, which manufactures paint and distributes it and related products through more than 70 stores in California and Arizona, has enjoyed an outstanding record of growth. In fact, it is on Herold's list of America's Fastest-Growing Companies. Since going public in 1961, sales have risen at a compounded annual rate of 15.1%, and earnings at a compounded rate of 20.0%. For the year ended September 30, 1976, sales reached a peak of $134,700,000, and earnings $0.87 per

Exhibit 8 *Paint industry sales (000's omitted): shipments by the 10 largest producers, 1976*

	Trade sales	Industrial finishes	Paint revenues	Total corporate revenue	Paint as percent of corporate revenue
Sherwin-Williams	$ 458,200	$ 224,000	$ 682,200	$ 951,900	71.6
DuPont	284,700	325,300	610,000	8,412,400	7.2
PPG Industries	198,400	285,600	484,000	2,254,800	21.4
SCM (Glidden)	265,400	97,500	362,900	1,331,900	27.2
DeSoto (Sears)	246,000	—	246,000	246,000	100.0
Inmont Corp.	36,500	166,500	203,000	534,265	38.0
Mobil Chemical	—	195,000	195,000	23,122,900	0.8
Cook Paint and Varnish	114,000	38,000	152,300	152,300	100.0
Standard Brands	134,700	—	134,700	134,700	100.0
Benjamin Moore	95,000	25,000	120,000	120,000	100.0
	$1,832,900	$1,356,900	$3,189,800		

Source: Annual Reports for the respective firms, supplemented by estimates by an industry consultant.

share. This year will show more new records. . . . One clue to Standard Brands' success: management says that, thanks to a continued program of automating, expanding, and improving, it costs less to produce a gallon of paint in 1976 than it did in 1970. (*Chemical Industry Newsletter,* not dated, p. 11)

In summary, there were two major changes in the paint industry that became apparent in the late 1960s, when growth slowed to less than 3% per year. Trade sales changed as the water-based latex paints made "do-it-yourself" much easier and more popular; the customer base for home maintenance and decoration became individual homeowners, more than professional painters and contractors, and these new consumers bought paint from national and discount chains, not from local hardware and specialty paint stores. Industrial sales changed with the new technologies, and with government-imposed energy restrictions and pollution requirements. Some companies apparently adjusted successfully to these industry shifts; Sherwin-Williams did not, although the senior management claimed that they recognized the problem as early as 1961.

The Sherwin-Williams Company is 110 years old. It has been known for its skill and success in formulating and manufacturing a wide variety of paints. It has also been known for its conservative management and strong finances that have allowed us to pay a dividend every year since 1885. We are proud of our record, and have no intention of abandoning those hard-won skills that can still serve us. . . . However, the world has been changing rapidly and we have been changing with it and adding new skills and new dimensions to Sherwin-Williams to better fit today's and tomorrow's realities.

In 1971 we were 105 years old and a troubled company. Over the previous five years, sales had increased by $150,-

000,000 or 37%. However, net income had dropped $7,400,000 or 33%. Return on stockholders' equity had dropped from 12.9% to 6.9%. The return on total assets had dropped from 9.1% to 3.9%. . . . While the ship was not totally dead in the water, it had lost an awful lot of headway. (Statement of Mr. Walter Spencer, President of Sherwin-Williams Company, quoted in the *Wall Street Transcript,* June 28, 1976, p. 44,078)

Starting in 1971, the management at Sherwin-Williams made four basic changes in the strategy of the company. They increased the marketing emphasis in trade sale paints, aiming at the expanding market segment of do-it-yourself consumers. They expanded the research and development effort in industrial finishes, hoping to maintain their existing dominance. They emphasized diversification in the vertically integrated divisions of the company, which previously had supplied only raw materials and metal containers for paint manufacturing, and they altered the management processes of the firm from a centralized, functional structure to a decentralized, divisional organization, with profit responsibility at the operating level. The balance of the case describes these changes in detail.

1. *Increased marketing emphasis in trade sale paints.* Sherwin-Williams in 1970 had 1,885 company-owned stores, 310 leased departments in discount chains, and approximately 8,000 independent dealers in small hardware stores, building supply yards, and local paint retailers. However, the leased departments were being taken over by the discount chains as the leases expired, and sales by the independent dealers were declining as retail customers moved to the lower-priced chains.

Sherwin-Williams in 1970 did not have all that much choice in trade sales marketing. The very success of their sales effort in the discount chains ensured their eventual takeover by the chains themselves, and that takeover, with increased price promotion, accelerated the movement of retail customers from the independent dealers. They had to fall back on their own stores. (Statement of an industry consultant)

The typical Sherwin-Williams store in 1970 had 5,000 square feet of floor space, stocked only paint and painting supplies, and primarily sold to area painting contractors, local manufacturing firms, industrial and commercial maintenance accounts, and members of the general public. The stores were located in commercial areas, with other wholesalers and industrial suppliers, not in shopping centers, and neither the location nor the merchandise attracted the "do-it-yourself" customer.

Our research indicated that the typical Sherwin-Williams customer was a male, over 45 years old. Our reputation was for top quality, reliability, and a top price. We were not attracting the younger buyers, or the women who have traditionally made the purchasing decisions on redecoration. They wanted bigger, better-looking stores and a wider choice of redecorating items, and a wider price and quality range in paint products. (Statement of Mr. Walter Spencer, president of Sherwin-Williams Company, quoted in the *Wall Street Transcript,* June 28, 1976, p. 44,078)

The company first divided their retail outlets into four store types, depending upon their location and their product/market orientation:

a. *Commercial service stores,* which carried a large inventory of trade sale paints and some industrial finishes, had very limited display space, and sold primarily to large painting contractors and small to medium-sized manufacturing firms and commercial accounts. These stores were located in metropolitan areas, and remained in the commercial section of each city, with easy access and loading facilities for delivery trucks and contractor vehicles.

b. *Automotive service stores,* which stocked paints and lacquers for auto refinishing, and sold to wholesale jobbers, automotive dealers, paint and body shops, and fleet maintenance firms. The automotive service stores also carried spraying equipment and supplies, and provided a color-mixing service to match the original finish on any foreign or domestic vehicle. These stores were also located in metropolitan areas, and also emphasized product distribution and service more than personal selling and display.

c. *Combined commercial/retail stores,* which were the traditional Sherwin-Williams branches, with a substantial inventory of standard paint products and some decorating and color displays. The combined stores were located in smaller towns and semirural areas, and sold to small building contractors, automotive repair shops, local manufacturing firms, and area residents.

d. *Decorating service stores,* which were the newer and much larger branches that were primarily located in the suburbs of large metropolitan areas, and that sold home decorating products and provided home decorating advice to retail customers. In 1971, the company had no decorating service stores in operation, but they knew what they wanted: 10,000 to 14,000 square feet of space, primarily devoted to display, with 25% paint, 25% floor coverings, 15% draperies, 15% wall coverings, and 20% accessories. The only inventory was to be in paint and paint products, while the other items would be stocked in a central warehouse in each city. The rugs, draperies, and wallpapers were represented by large (2 ft x 3 ft) samples on display racks that could be compared to select and match colors. In addition to the samples, a Color Harmony Guide was developed, which used microfiche and a large display screen to combine paint colors (900 hues), wallpapers (600 patterns), and carpets (300 selections) in a photographic vignette.

Customers coming into our stores are not really coming after our product, paint. They could find that product at any number of other places. They are coming to buy our know-how in applying and matching and complementing colors and shades into a planning whole. (Statement of the group vice president for coatings, quoted in *Chemical Week,* January 29, 1975, p. 35)

In 1974, the company adopted a colorful new logo, with the Sherwin-Williams name in block letters against a band of yellow, orange, red, and blue hues; this new logo was used on all stores, trucks, brochures, advertisements, and the company letterhead. It replaced the 1895 trademark, which showed a bucket of paint pouring over the globe, with the slogan, "we cover the earth." The company also introduced new lines of paint.

To appeal to all segments of the retail market, and particularly to the mobile younger group, we introduced a year ago two new lower-priced lines. . . . We now cover the entire price range and believe that you can buy the best

value in paints at any price in a Sherwin-Williams store. While this approach is only a year old, it has been a tremendous success and we are tapping an entirely new market. (Statement of Mr. Walter Spencer, president of Sherwin-Williams Company, quoted in the *Wall Street Transcript,* May 27, 1973, p. 33,120)

Over the five-year period 1971–1975, Sherwin-Williams opened 117 new stores, relocated and remodeled 390 others, and expanded and remodeled 453 more (Exhibit 9).

The expansion of the retail sales effort by Sherwin-Williams Company obviously required market research, location planning, merchandise selection, and personnel training. Mr. Walter Spencer, President of Sherwin-Williams, described this effort in a talk to the New York Security Analysts in 1976:

This (expansion of retail sales) meant a total reorganization, new people, new jobs, new priorities, and much training and retraining. I now want to introduce Ron Curley, our group vice president of coatings, to give you a brief summary of the results we have had in meeting the problems we identified in the early seventies.

Mr. Curley: Our desire to use to advantage our then current position in the market with over 1,800 store locations, to further penetrate the decorative products business, obviously required careful planning.

We believed that the potential limitations

Exhibit 9 *Retail outlets of Sherwin-Williams Company, 1971–1975*

	1971	1972	1973	1974	1975	Total
Total stores at end of the year	1,847	1,838	1,778	1,786	1,702	—
Stores opened	11	24	35	32	15	117
Stores closed	39	33	95	24	99	290
Stores relocated and remodeled	75	105	73	80	57	390
Stores expanded and remodeled	25	76	88	242	22	453

Source: Annual Reports for the respective years.

or problems generally fell into three categories: (1) merchandise, (2) store locations, and (3) people.

In 1973–1974 we created our own marketing research department, which, with the aid of consultants, began a work project to discover, among much other information, two basic things:

1. What merchandise did people think of when they thought of a complete supply of decorative products?
2. What kind of physical store did people think of when they imagined such a complete offering?

This resulted in merchandise such as floor coverings, draperies, bedroom and bath accessories, etc. being used in limited degrees (due to space) in about 100 of our regular small stores as an initial test.

While this merchandise test was taking place, a new type of store was being built in Charlotte, North Carolina. We called it Decorating World. This was our merchandise and display laboratory.... The results have been very rewarding, not just because it did, from the outset, more retail business in more lines than we had ever done in a store, but because it highlighted areas of merchandise that were wrong and many that were right. It also highlighted fixturing and displays that were extremely good, and some that were not.

We feel secure now in our merchandise selection and our new stores now incorporate the design changes, both in fixturing and floor plan, which we learned in Charlotte were required.

Our research department was also busy defining what an ideal store location for our type of merchandise would be. A model was created and tested in markets where we had "in-house" knowledge for comparison purposes. Our model scored extremely high.

We have to date "strategized" every city in which we intend to create a new store or where we intend to move an old store to a new location within the next three years. We know where we want to be, and we do not intend to accept any compromise locations.

During this time of research, design, and

testing, a new training program was created for selected managers from our large chain. The objective: to provide a cadre of well-balanced managers for the new-type store. This program starts with a special analysis of personal characteristics, and provides additional "in-store" training in one of 55 selected training stores. Those successful candidates then attend seminars designed to improve their skills in problem solving, performance and productivity evaluation, and special seminars on product knowledge and selling techniques.

Our manager needs are identified through 1980, and we have the capability of satisfying those needs. (Statement of the group vice president of coatings, quoted in the *Wall Street Transcript,* June 28, 1976, p. 44,078)

The "Decorating World" mentioned by the group vice president of coatings was a 27,000-square-foot retail store, located in Charlotte, North Carolina, that was used to test merchandise selections and selling/display methods. Based upon the experience at Charlotte, 37 "New Dimension" stores, with 20,000 square feet of floor space, were built in the suburbs of major cities, offering unpainted furniture, lamps, mirrors, and other accessories in addition to the floor coverings, draperies, wallpapers, and multiple lines of paint.

It is important to note that our Coatings Group is rapidly changing from a manufacturer that operates stores to a merchandiser that produces many of its own products. (Statement in the *Annual Report for 1973,* p. 2)

Sales of the Coatings Group, which was responsible for the manufacture and marketing of both trade paints and industrial finishes, more than doubled during the period 1968–1977, with a substantial portion of that expansion taking place in the resale (floor coverings, window draperies, wallpapers, and decorating accessories) products (Exhibit 10).

Exhibit 10 *Sales (000's omitted) of the Coatings Group of Sherwin-Williams Company, 1968–1977*

	1968	1970	1972	1974	1976	1977
Trade sale paints	$190,600	$224,400	$267,400	$284,100	$332,700	$327,900
Resale products	4,200	28,700	43,600	87,400	124,500	178,300
Industrial finishes	121,900	148,500	167,700	191,400	239,900	251,500
Coatings Group sales	$316,700	$401,400	$478,700	$562,900	$697,100	$757,700

Source: Annual Report for 1977, p. 27, supplemented with industry estimates.

2. *Increased R&D effort in industrial finishes.* Concurrent with the increased marketing emphasis in trade sales paints, Sherwin-Williams began, in 1970, an expanded research and development effort in industrial finishes. Research and development was required due to a governmental regulation that manufacturers of industrial finishes eliminate the light petroleum solvents that caused extensive air pollution, and due to customer demands that the finishes be longer lasting and more protective. Sherwin-Williams deliberately selected the automotive and appliance industries to concentrate their R&D effort, and invested substantial amounts in the development of new chemical coatings for factory application, and new application systems for less energy dependent and less environmentally destructive operations.

The other part of the Coatings Group sales is industrial or product finishes. Part of these sales to small and medium-sized accounts is sold through our branches with standard stocked industrial items. The large industrial users are serviced out of five zone offices by a highly experienced direct sales force. We have deliberately decided to go after the high-volume, high-technology industrial coatings business with this sales force. In this way we feel we can take maximum advantage of our large manufacturing facilities and our highly sophisticated R&D laboratories. Therefore, we are concentrating in the areas of high-speed, high-technology factory-applied finishes. With our engineering expertise in coatings and coating applications, we are also prepared to specify and engineer complete finishing systems in such diverse areas as coil coatings, electrodeposition lines, and powder coatings. As customers' requirements become more stringent and environmental standards stricter, we feel this will become more necessary along with highly sophisticated high-solids and water-dispersible coatings, and coatings applied in the dry powder form. (Statement of Mr. Walter Spencer, president of Sherwin-Williams Company, quoted in the *Wall Street Transcript*, May 27, 1973, p. 33,120)

3. *Increased diversification in the vertically integrated divisions.* The third of the major strategic changes initiated by the senior management of Sherwin-Williams in the early 1970s was the diversification of the supply divisions of the firm. These supply divisions, termed the Chemical Group and the Auxiliary Group, had originally produced solvents, both petroleum derivates and turpentine, pigments for color additives, and binders such as linseed oil and the synthetic resins, for the Coatings Group, together with metal containers, brushes, rollers, and painting trays. During the 1960s these two supply divisions had begun to sell commodity chemicals and standard painting supplies to other companies, so that in 1970 only 25% of their products were transferred internally, and 75% were sold externally, generally in price-competitive markets. The result was a series of losses for the Chemical Group.

Our Chemical Group last year (1971) accounted for $49 million of external sales and a loss of $3.6 million before tax adjustments. Of this, discontinued operations accounted for $2.3 million of the loss. In Chemicals, we are moving away from the commodity chemicals to more specialized products to solve customer problems. We have also moved more into consumer items, such as our Flavor and Fragrance Division. With new plants coming on stream, such as isophthalonitrile, zinc oxide, and plastic concentrates, and this strategic change in emphasis, we feel we can reverse the losses of the last few years in the Chemicals Group. We are the largest producers in the nation in some important specialty chemicals, such as paracresol, saccharin, and isatoic anhydride. (Statement of Mr. E. C. Baldwin, chairman of Sherwin-Williams Company, quoted in the *Wall Street Transcript,* February 14, 1972, p. 27,204)

In 1971, the Chemical Group began to emphasize R&D, particularly in applications related to color, and started groups to market textile dyes and treatments, plastic color additives, printing inks and paints, and food flavors and fragrances. The manufacture of both lead-based and arsenic-based chemicals, both of which had been used in paints at one time, was discontinued.

The Auxiliary Group had purchased an aerosol packaging firm, Sprayon Products, in 1966 to supply aerosol paints to the Coatings Group; this division had expanded, and in the early 1970s was one of the largest aerosol contract packagers in the United States. The Auxiliary Group, in 1969, had acquired the Osborn Manufacturing Company to supply power-driven wire brushes for paint removal; this division also had expanded, and in the early 1970s was the largest producer of wire brushes for foundry equipment (to remove sand and slag from the castings) in the United States. The Auxiliary Group seemed to be exceptionally profitable.

The second largest part of our business is the Auxiliary Group. Last fiscal year (1971) it accounted for 9.2% of the sales and 24.6% of the before-tax profit. These are essentially mechanical operations consisting of metal containers, brushes, roller coaters, painting trays, grinding wheels, foundry equipment, and a printing plant.

Containers is the largest part of this, accounting for more than 50% of the group's sales. We originally went into container manufacturing to supply the needs of the paint plants. We now have four factories and 65% of the sales are outside the Sherwin-Williams Company. We do not make food or beverage containers, but general-line metal cans for the paint industry, coffee, oil, solvents, charcoal lighter, and aerosol. Aerosol containers are growing very rapidly and with the installation of our newest line in our Elgin, Illinois, plant, we now have about 10% of the industry capacity.

A high percentage of our paint brush and roller coater production is sold through our branch store outlets.

With the capital goods industry picking up rapidly, the backlog of Osborn Manufacturing Company in foundry machinery and power-driven wire brushes is very high, and we are looking for a very good year. (Statement of Mr. E. C. Baldwin, chairman of Sherwin-Williams Company, quoted in the *Wall Street Transcript,* February 14, 1972, p. 27,204)

International Operations, the last of the vertically integrated divisions of the company, was not emphasized during the 1970s. Small paint manufacturing plants were owned in Mexico, Brazil, and the Netherlands, and licensing agreements had been signed with paint industry firms in 19 other countries, but little had been done to develop branch stores or retail sales except in Canada, where a subsidiary operated 130 Sherwin-Williams stores.

Sherwin-Williams of Canada is a 74.2% owned subsidiary that sells the products of the Coatings Group through 130 Canadian branch stores. Canada is just now beginning to follow the trends that have appeared in the U.S.; i.e., a growing do-it-yourself market that is becoming increasingly price conscious.

On other international fronts, the company's activity has been slowed because of unsettled political and economic conditions overseas. We're not going ahead as rapidly as projected a year ago. But I still believe if you want to be any kind of sizable factor in business today, you're going to be an international company. (Statement of Mr. Walter Spencer, president of Sherwin-Williams Company, quoted in *Chemical Week,* January 29, 1975, p. 35)

4. *Decentralized managerial processes.* Sherwin-Williams changed, during the early 1970s, from a functionally organized, centralized firm to a decentralized, divisional structure. The formal result of this change is shown in the organizational chart of the company in Exhibit 11.

In the last several years we have had a number of important organizational changes which, I believe, better orient us to specific businesses. In other words, we are moving from a functional to a divisional operation. We now have group vice presidents for Coatings, for Chemicals, and for Auxiliaries. These vice presidents have complete responsibility for research and development, for manufacturing, and for marketing products, within those areas. This means, I believe, that we have gone a long way in decentralization of specific decision making and in recognizing the differences in the different

Exhibit 11   *Organizational structure of Sherwin-Williams Company, 1974*

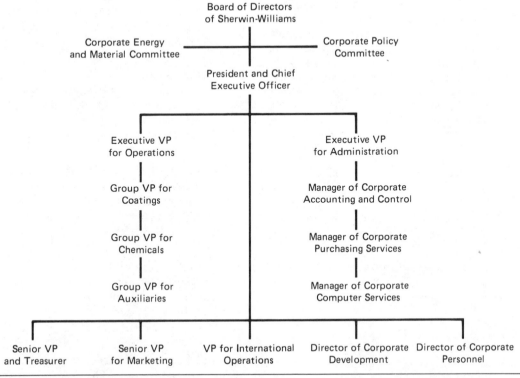

Source: Verbal descriptions in the *Wall Street Transcript,* June 24, 1974, p. 37,360.

businesses in which we are engaged. Each of these major parts of our business is of course a profit center and each of these parts is broken down into smaller parts which in themselves are profit centers. We are making every effort to get a good fix on the return on the assets employed in each segment of our business. We believe that the changes give us a greater flexibility and permit us to respond more quickly to changes in the market-place. (Statement of Mr. E. C. Baldwin, chairman of Sherwin-Williams Company, quoted in the *Wall Street Transcript,* June 21, 1971, p. 24,559)

As part of the change in the managerial processes at Sherwin-Williams, a formal system for strategic planning was initiated in 1971.

We are embarked on significantly more for-malized planning. We are trying to strike a balance between short-range profit and long-range profit. We are trying to make better use of these resources that we have. We are trying to be aware of new technologies and the changes in life-style. Our planning activities center is in the office of our director of corporate development, and I am pleased to tell you that we have significant participation of our outside directors in long-range planning through a planning committee of our board of directors. (Statement of Mr. E. C. Baldwin, chairman of Sherwin-Williams Company, quoted in the *Wall Street Transcript,* June 21, 1971, p. 24,559)

The group vice presidents for Coatings, Chemicals, and Auxiliaries, and the division managers within each of those groups, were evaluated for performance on the basis of pretax returns on the gross assets employed.

I do not think you can look just at the pretax margins (on sales). I am much more concerned about the kind of return we get on assets employed. That is why I talk about market management and asset management.

I do not know whether we are ever going to return to the good old days in terms of margins on sales. That means if you are going to

do a job as far as getting an acceptable return on assets, then you have to do a much better job of asset management. The coating business is particularly raw material intensive (with unscheduled cost increases), and very competitive. And, of course, as you go more and more into retail sales it gets ever more competitive. There are not very many retailers who make 10% on their sales. You have to turn over those assets. (Statement of Mr. Walter Spencer, president of Sherwin-Williams Company, quoted in the *Wall Street Transcript,* June 28, 1976, p. 44,078)

A statement on the sources and uses of funds during the period 1971–1977 to support the strategic changes described previously in the operations of the Sherwin-Williams Company is given in Exhibit 12, with the following explanations of some of the entries:

a. Cash from sale of assets of $4,653,000 in 1972 was due to disposal of commodity chemical plants, including a linseed oil factory in Cleveland and an insecticide processing facility in New Jersey.

b. Cash from sale of assets of $16,283,000 in 1975 was due to disposal of Osburn Manufacturing Company (power-driven brushes and foundry equipment), with the explanation that the division "did not meet the ongoing strategy of the firm."

c. Cash from sale of assets of $5,313,000 in 1976 was due to disposal of the titanium dioxide factory in Ohio, and the textile printing dye laboratory and plant in North Carolina, with the explanation that "very large capital investments would have been required just to remain the No. 7 supplier in titanium dioxide, and the No. 12 supplier in textile dyes."

d. Cash from sale of assets of $2,037,000 in 1977 was due to disposal of the flavors and fragrance laboratory and plant in Connecticut, and of the powder coating factory in Chicago.

e. Equity sales from 1971 to 1976 were

Exhibit 12 *Source and application of funds (000's omitted) statement for Sherwin-Williams Company, 1971–1977*

	1971	1972	1973	1974	1975	1976	1977
Income from operations	15,175	20,497	24,502	29,279	28,588	18,435	(8,207)
Sale of assets	—	4,636	—	—	16,283	5,313	2,037
Depreciation	11,920	12,519	12,869	13,555	12,750	12,839	16,924
Deferred taxes	1,432	1,782	2,335	2,724	536	1,751	211
Bank loans	—	—	—	—	4,842	—	6,560
Debenture sales	—	—	—	—	50,000	—	—
Capital leases	—	—	—	—	—	—	10,175
Equity sales	253	957	1,218	—	211	142	—
Work capital decrease	—	—	—	—	—	17,655	26,951
	27,780	40,391	40,924	45,558	113,210	56,135	54,651
Cash dividends	11,741	11,766	11,838	11,848	12,924	12,935	9,975
Additions to assets	11,402	16,178	15,669	19,242	27,582	41,073	28,977
Additions to leases	—	—	—	—	—	—	12,917
Repurchased debentures	1,303	2,462	4,465	1,955	2,000	500	2,000
Miscellaneous	194	992	359	1,736	4,219	1,627	782
Work capital increase	4,140	6,733	8,593	10,777	66,485	—	—
	28,780	40,391	40,924	45,558	113,210	56,135	54,651

Source: Annual Reports for the respective years.

due to stock purchases by members of management under an executive incentive program.

f. Repurchases of debentures from 1971 to 1977 were due to the sinking-fund provisions of the 5.45% debentures due 1995.

g. Miscellaneous applications of funds from 1972 to 1977 are assumed to be cash expenses associated with the disposal of assets.

Sales and profits by division for the period 1971–1977, the results of the strategic changes described previously in the operations of Sherwin-Williams, are shown in Exhibits 13 and 14, with the following explanation of some of the entries:

a. Losses in the Chemical Group of $3,-

Exhibit 13 *Net sales (000's omitted) by division of Sherwin-Williams Company, 1971–1977*

	1971	1972	1973	1974	1975	1976	1977
Coatings	425,791	479,883	511,048	562,943	597,502	697,137	757,672
Chemicals	52,064	48,172	47,901	62,673	69,301	73,206	82,380
Auxiliaries	50,417	60,057	70,695	87,697	97,936	87,244	86,343
Canada Division	36,969	40,969	42,647	50,714	54,148	61,878	56,647
Sprayon Division	14,281	16,923	18,428	19,948	23,498	25,055	27,927
International	11,447	12,281	14,010	18,291	24,468	24,685	25,020
	590,969	658,285	704,729	802,266	866,853	969,205	1,035,989

Source: Annual Reports for the respective years.

Exhibit 14 *Pretax income (000's omitted) by division of Sherwin-Williams Company, 1971–1977*

	1971	1972	1973	1974	1975	1976	1977
Coatings	28,083	35,084	38,094	39,638	18,436	25,610	16,148
Chemicals	(3,421)	(2,121)	(89)	8,396	8,728	1,709	969
Auxiliaries	7,714	10,515	10,907	16,526	19,471	18,438	10,645
Canada Division	518	898	482	1,597	1,169	1,825	(1,362)
Sprayon Division	1,432	1,899	2,037	1,097	976	1,083	1,462
International	1,498	1,235	1,815	2,345	1,439	(2,473)	1,930
Total preallocation	35,824	47,510	53,246	69,599	50,219	46,182	29,792
Corporate allocation	(6,420)	(8,765)	(9,357)	(14,021)	(12,714)	(19,260)	(25,248)
Gain or (loss)	—	(2,260)	—	—	12,728	(2,778)	(16,434)
Total pretax	29,404	36,485	43,889	55,578	50,233	24,144	(11,890)
Income (tax) credit	(14,063)	(18,248)	(19,387)	(26,299)	(21,645)	(11,463)	3,683
Total income	15,341	18,237	24,502	29,279	28,588	12,681	(8,207)

Source: Annual Reports for the respective years.

421,000 in 1971, $2,121,000 in 1972, and $89,000 in 1973 are alleged to have been due to price competition and undercapacity utilization in commodity chemicals.

b. Loss in the Canadian Division of $1,362,000 in 1977 is alleged to have been due to inventory buildup at the retail stores, resulting in an eventual price markdown on obsolete materials.

c. Loss in the International Division of $2,473,000 in 1976 is alleged to have been due to revaluation of Mexican currency.

d. Increase in the allocations for corporate general and administrative expenses from 1971 to 1977 is alleged to have been caused by rising interest costs. Interest expense in 1971 was $6,599,000; in 1977, interest expense was $17,965,000.

e. Gain of $12,728,000 in 1975 was due to sale of the Osburn Manufacturing Company. Losses in 1972, 1976, and 1977 were due to disposal of operating divisions, as described in the text.

As a result of the loss of $8,207,000 in 1977 ($11,890,000 before credit for income taxes paid in prior years), Sherwin-Williams was forced to suspend dividend payments for the first time since 1885, the stock price dropped to less than half of the book value, the stockholders elected a new board of directors, and the chairman of the board and chief executive officer, Mr. Walter Spencer, resigned.

Mr. Walter O. Spencer, 51, chairman and chief executive of Sherwin-Williams Company, resigned after overseeing the paint maker's worst performance in history last year. The company lost more than $8 million on sales of $1 billion in 1977 and later announced that it would restructure its board with a new majority of outside directors.... Spencer wrapped up his 29-year career at Sherwin-Williams by citing "tremendous problems in totally restructuring the company," and he added, "The job is no longer any fun." (*Business Week*, April 3, 1978, p. 34)

Mr. Walter Spencer was replaced as chairman and chief executive officer of the

Sherwin-Williams Company in April 1978 by Mr. William Fine, who had previously been president of the firm. Operations, however, remained marginal; the company reported sales of $1,132.3 million for the year ending December 1978, but profits were only $5.2 million, and these followed a reported gain of $5.3 million from sale of assets. In June 1979, Mr. John Breen, 45 years old and formerly executive vice president of Gould, Inc. (a large manufacturer of electrical and electromechanical products), was appointed chairman and chief executive officer of the company.

Class Assignment. Put yourself in the position of Mr. Breen. What would you do as chief executive officer of the Sherwin-Williams Company?

Problems at the SBA

The Small Business Administration was created by the U.S. Congress in 1953 to help smaller business firms throughout the country overcome the twin problems of limited resources and extensive competition by providing financial assistance and managerial counsel. The federal government first gave financial aid to business organizations during the depression era of the 1930s through an agency known as the Reconstruction Finance Corporation, although this assistance was primarily directed toward larger firms, to expand employment. During World War II (1941–1945), Congress appropriated special funds for the expansion of smaller companies in defense-related industries through the Smaller War Plants Administration, and this program was continued during the Korean War (1950–1953) by the Small Defense Plants Act. The Small Business Development Act of 1953 was intended to continue the concept of governmental assistance, but to expand that concept from military production to the full range of both industrial and consumer products and services, and to help all small companies compete in an economy that was believed to be increasingly dominated by much larger firms. The declaration of policy that introduced the new law read as follows:

The essence of the American Economic System of private enterprise is free competition. Only through full and free competition can expanded markets, new entries into business, and open opportunities for the expression and growth of personal initiative and individual judgment be assured. The preservation and expansion of such competition is basic not only to the economic well-being but to the security of this Nation. Such security and well-being cannot be realized unless the actual and potential capacity of small business is encouraged and developed. It is the declared policy of the Congress that the Government should aid, counsel, assist, and protect insofar as is possible the interests of small business concerns in order to preserve free competitive enterprise, to insure that a fair proportion of the total purchases and contracts for supplies and services for the Government be placed with small business enterprises, and to maintain and strengthen the overall economy of the Nation. (Title II, Section 202 of Public Law 163, the Small

Business Development Act of 1953, dated July 30, 1953, p. ii)

Congress left the definition of small business to the agency it had created, except to state that a small business was to be considered one that was "independently owned and operated, not dominant in its field." The SBA expanded this very general definition of small businesses, and established standards that vary with the type of activity (manufacturing, distributing, retailing, etc.) and with the capital and employment needs of the industry (job shop machining vs. electronic design, for example), but in current terms a manufacturing company is considered to be small if it employs fewer than 1,500 persons, a wholesale firm meets the standard if it sells less than $22.0 million annually, a retail store or chain less than $7.5 million, a service company less than $6.0 million, a construction firm less than $6.0 million averaged over the past three years, and a farm or farm-related business under $1.0 million. By these standards, the constituency of the SBA is enormous: 97.6% of the 10,750,000 business operations within the United States are classified as small, and 99.2% of the 3,300,000 farms join that group. By these standards also, the activities of the SBA are essential: 43% of the gross national product, 48% of the total business revenues, and 58% of the nonfarm employment are derived from small business firms, and these levels would be increased if more of the 250,000 new businesses started each year were able to survive. The agency estimates that slightly more than 60% fail during the first three years of operations, usually due to a lack of adequate financing or training. It was felt that the mission of the SBA was to reduce that failure rate by providing small business financing, when unavailable from the private sector, and professional counseling for the entrepreneurs.

The idea of the SBA is inherently attractive, both economically and politi-

cally. Small business firms do have a much harder time raising money than do the large corporations, and small business managers often lack the sophistication of their counterparts in larger organizations. The one advantage small companies do have is a general sentiment in their favor among most members of our society; the government should be able to provide small businesses with money and advice, and reap a political reward for doing so. (Statement of a small business consultant)

The government has provided substantial amounts of money. The enabling legislation of 1953 established a revolving fund of $275 million to be used for making credit and capital available to smaller business firms. This amount has been increased by the Congress each year in the annual appropriation bills, usually with no controversy and very limited dissent, so that in 1978 the SBA was able to approve 164,417 loans for a total of $5.8 billion. During the first 24 years of operations, from 1953 to 1977, the agency approved 1,053,360 loans with a cumulative value of $30.3 billion.

The loan programs of the SBA are of three general types: ordinary business loans, economic disaster loans, and physical disaster loans. Economic disaster loans are designed to help small businesses cope with the financial problems caused by governmental regulations, such as air pollution controls or consumer protection measures, while the physical disaster loans, which can now be made to small businesses, homeowners, farmers, and nonprofit organizations, are obviously designed to help repair the damages caused by floods, hurricanes, and tornadoes. The ordinary business loans represent a major activity of the SBA; during the late 1970s, the number of these "nondisaster" loans to small businesses approved annually has remained approximately constant at 32,000, with a rise in the dollar volume reflecting the rate of inflation, from $2.6 billion in 1976 to $3.2 billion in 1978.

> Half of the dollar volume of loans in 1978 was for ordinary business purposes ($3.2 billion/$5.8 billion), but this group represented only 19% of the total number of loans (32,000/164,400). This apparent imbalance was caused by numerous farmers and homeowners applying that year for small disaster loans to cover the losses caused by flooding. The applications for physical disaster loans increased 600% between 1977 and 1978. This was due not so much to an Act of God as it was to an Act of Congress; the legislators made farmers and homeowners eligible for flooding loans for the first time in 1978. (Statement of a small business consultant)

Ordinary business (nondisaster) loans from the SBA are subject to that agency's lending objectives and security policies. The Small Business Administration has described its lending objectives, in various publications, to be (1) to stimulate small business in deprived areas, (2) to encourage minority enterprise and opportunity, and (3) to promote small business contributions to general economic growth. The SBA has stated that it is not in competition with private lenders, and that it is authorized to make loans only when funds are not available from other sources on "reasonable terms." The agency insists that the borrower must be of "good character," and must be able to demonstrate that she or he will be able to manage the business effectively. The loan must be "of such sound value or so secured as reasonably to assure repayment." With certain exceptions to be noted below, loans under the various programs are available for both new and established businesses, and can be used to finance construction, conversion, or expansion of physical facilities, to purchase equipment, machinery, or supplies, or to supply working capital. Ninety-eight percent of the business

loans are for more than one year; they have an average maturity of nearly eight years.

Under all of the ordinary business loan programs, the SBA makes funds available in three ways: guaranteed loans, participation loans, and direct loans. Guaranteed loans are made by private lending institutions, such as commercial banks, under a guarantee by the Small Business Administration that the agency will purchase 90% of the unpaid balance up to $500,000 in the event of borrower default; in essence the SBA provides collateral (the guarantee) that makes the loan commercially possible. A participation loan is made by both a private lending institution and the SBA; the bank and the agency agree upon a percentage share of the loan, often 75% for the agency. A direct loan is made wholly by the agency itself. By law, the SBA may not make a participation loan if a guaranteed loan is available, nor a direct loan if a participation loan is possible; for a direct loan, the prospective borrower must present letters of refusal from at least two private lending institutions. Interest rates for direct loans, and for the government's share of participation loans, are by statute tied to the cost of money to the federal government. The interest rates for guaranteed loans, and for the bank's share of a participation loan, are set by the bank involved, within limits laid down by the agency.

Most SBA loans are of the guaranteed type: 86% in 1978. Although reputedly wary at first of doing business with a government agency, 10,000 of the country's 15,000 banks were making loans to small businesses under the terms of the Small Business Administration's guaranteed loan program in 1978, with a total amount invested (which is not included in the SBA loan amounts until the 90% repurchase is required) of $23.0 billion. The cumulative loss rate on guaranteed business loans, in dollar volume, was stated to be 4.18% at the end of fiscal year 1977, while the delinquency rate for the complete portfolio of SBA loans, again in dollar volume, was said to be 6.4%.

Ordinary business (nondisaster) loans provided by the Small Business Administration were classified into eight programs, as listed below:

1. *Regular business loans.* Regular business loans were the first and remain by far the largest of the SBA's business loan programs; 88% of the agency's 31,727 business loans in 1978 were made under the 7(a) program, so called because it was provided for in Section 7(a) of the Small Business Development Act of 1953. During 1978 the agency approved 27,942 loans under this program for $3.1 billion; in 1977, 27,-305 loans were approved for $2.9 billion.

2. *Economic opportunity loans.* The "EOL" program is the result of legislative and executive intent during the late 1960s and early 1970s to bring into the economic mainstream members of minority groups that had traditionally been left on the edges. Under EOL, the second largest of the business loan programs, loans are made to low-income owners of small businesses, or to owners denied the opportunity to obtain adequate financing through private channels because of "social or economic disadvantage." The agency usually regards membership in a racial or ethnic minority group as presumptive evidence of social or economic disadvantage, a practice that Congress had confirmed with legislation. Other applicants are eligible, of course, but it is expected that those persons be able to demonstrate their economic or social disadvantages. In 1978, EOL loans were granted to 3,300 applicants for a total of $103.5 million, down about 10% in number and 8% in dollars from 1977, continuing a downward trend in the program since 1975.

3. *Displaced business loans.* In 1968, Congress amended the original Small Business Development Act to include a program to help small businesses damaged by federal urban renewal projects. Displaced Business Loans declined significantly both in the number of loans and the dollar volume during the late 1970s, from 132 loans for $25.0 million in 1976 to 77 loans for $9.2 million in 1978. Legislation in 1978, however, authorized the SBA to include firms adversely affected by state or local renewal projects, so that this program was expected to increase in importance in the future.

4. *Local development company loans.* The intent of the Development Company loan program is to help "public-spirited" citizens, organized in a corporation and interested in planned economic growth, to promote the growth and well-being of small businesses in their own communities. Under the program these corporations, which may be either nonprofit or profit-making, may obtain long-term SBA funding to buy land, build a factory, purchase machinery and equipment, or acquire and convert an existing building in order to help a specific small business. SBA funds in this program may not be used for working capital. The development company may borrow up to $500,000 for each small business firm it helps, but it is required to bear a reasonable share of the cost of the project, generally at least 10%. Moreover, the development company must have at least 25 stockholders, of whom 75% have to live within the community. During 1977, 353 loans to local development companies were approved for $46.6 million, and four loans to state development companies, included in the program for the first time that year, were funded for $3.8 million. In 1978, 408 local and state development company loans were approved for a total of $65.0 million.

5. *Small business investment company loans.* The

"SBIC" loan program was established by the Small Business Investment Act of 1958, and is administered by the central office of the SBA. Under the Act, the SBA licenses, regulates, and helps to fund investment companies that specialize in providing long-term loans, equity financing, and venture capital to small business firms, particularly those with advanced technologies, innovative products, or expanded markets. The agency is authorized to advance $4 for every $1 of private capital invested in an SBIC, up to a limit of $35.0 million per firm. SBICs organized under section 301(d) of the Small Business Investment Act are an important aspect of this program; these companies, known as MESBICs, invest only in firms "owned at least 50% by individuals from groups underrepresented in the free enterprise system." For the purposes of the program, such groups are defined as racial and ethnic minorities, but, as in the Economic Opportunity Loans, other groups remain eligible, but must demonstrate "underrepresentation." MESBICs, whose initials stand for Minority Enterprise Small Business Investment Companies, can borrow from the SBA at a subsidized interest rate, 3% below the current cost of money to the federal government. In September 1977, there were 273 SBICs and 84 MESBICs, with total capital resources of almost $1.1 billion; of this capital, 56% has been provided by the SBA and the balance was private investment. Since the beginning of the program in 1958, more than 40,000 small firms have received $2.8 billion in financing from small business investment companies; in 1977 there were 2,056 financings for $196.8 million from SBICs, and 418 financings for $21.8 million from MESBICs.

6. *Seasonal line of credit loans.* This program was installed in 1977 to provide a short-term line of credit to small companies needing funds on a seasonal basis; under this program, the SBA approved 366 loans for $44.0 million in 1978.

7. *Assignable contract loans.* This program was also installed in 1977 to provide a short-term line of credit to small companies needing funds to meet contract obligations. During 1978, the SBA approved loans under this program for $21.0 million.

8. *Handicapped assistance loans.* This program is not strictly oriented toward small business, since it includes nonprofit organizations employing handicapped workers, as well as business firms owned or operated by handicapped individuals. During 1978, the SBA approved 316 loans for $24.3 million to assist handicapped persons.

The second general category of loan programs provided by the SBA are the nonphysical or economic disaster loans to small business firms. Although there were 11 programs in this category in 1978, their total volume was a small fraction of the ordinary business loans approved by the SBA in that year, being less than 10% in loan numbers and 6% in dollar volume. These loan programs have for the most part been specifically legislated, at least in their intent, which is to help small businesses cope with the financial problems posed by such governmental requirements as air pollution controls, consumer protection measures, product safety standards, and occupational safety and health requirements. Reasons for the granting of economic disaster loans have in the past also included such unforeseen events as international agreements to limit nuclear arms, national decisions to abandon restrictive tariffs, congressional permits to close military bases, and executive orders to discontinue industrial subsidies, in addition to the normal regulatory requirements. Because the need for many of these loans is sporadic by nature, the activity in individual programs is highly variable. During 1978, 3,509 economic disaster loans were approved under the 11 programs, for a total disbursement of $206.2 million.

Physical disaster loans are the third category of loan programs provided by the SBA; these loans can be made to small businesses, homeowners, farmers, and nonprofit organizations to repair damages caused by floods, hurricanes, or tornadoes. After each severe storm, state and local officials pressure representatives of the federal government to have the affected area declared a "disaster area"; this designation makes the area residents eligible for low-interest loans under the physical disaster loan program conducted by the SBA. From its first year of operations through 1978, the agency has approved 697,722 disaster loans, for a total of $6.8 billion. The number and dollar value of the loans vary by year, of course, depending upon meteorological events. In 1977, there were 19,051 disaster loans for $359.8 million, while in 1978 there were 114,960 disaster loans for $2.6 billion; the increase, as explained previously, was due to Congress having directed the SBA to extend the program to cover flooding damage suffered by homeowners and farmers.

In addition to the three loan programs (ordinary business, economic disaster, and physical disaster loans), the SBA conducts a Procurement Program, inherited from the Small Defense Plants Act of the Korean War, to ensure that small businesses receive a "fair share" of federal contracts and purchases. Smaller business firms were estimated to have supplied $34.5 billion in products and services to the government during 1978; most of this large amount was purchased directly by federal departments and agencies, without the intervention of the SBA, but approximately $5.0 billion was in the form of "set-asides," or contracts for the purchase of needed goods and services that the SBA had insisted be reserved for competitive bidding by small businesses only. The SBA, under the Procurement Program, identifies small businesses eligible to bid upon each contract, and certifies, with a "Certificate of Competency," that the small business which won the contract through the low bid has the needed equipment, machinery, and personnel to perform the work.

Since the late 1960s, the SBA has particularly emphasized procurement assistance for minority-owned small business firms. This program, called 8(a) since it was organized under Section 208(a) of the Small Business Opportunity Act of 1968, has grown from 28 contracts worth $9.0 million in 1969 to more than 18,000 contracts valued at nearly $3.0 billion in 1978. The SBA provides technical and managerial assistance to those selected firms, and also arranges assignable-contract loans, if needed.

Technical assistance and managerial training is offered to the owners and managers of all small business firms under the terms of the Management Development program. The SBA conducts classes, workshops, and clinics for management education, publishes pamphlets and booklets on management methods, and arranges individual conferences on management problems. Counseling on small business problems is provided by a staff of agency professionals and by a pool of agency volunteers, organized in SCORE (the Service Corps of Retired Executives) and ACE (the Active Corps of Executives). In 1978, over 12,000 executives had offered to share their experience and knowledge with small business owners and managers throughout the country, and the SBA estimated that these volunteers had helped nearly 157,000 small businesses. The Small Business Administration also had joined forces with colleges and universities to form Small Business Institutes, in which faculty and students combine to offer free personal counseling to small business owners as part of a course in applied management practices, and had further funded University Business Development Centers, in which the faculty and staff are paid to provide both technical and managerial assistance at the formation stage to small business ventures. Finally, the Management Development Program sponsored a "call contract" plan under which the agency would pay a private consultant for up to three days of consulting work when requested by an SBA borrower; these consultants were selected by competitive bidding for the right to respond to these calls within a state or regional area.

The last function of the Small Business Administration is advocacy, or representation of the interests of small business firms before other units of government, at the federal, state, and local levels, and with various industry and trade associations. Under this heading, the structure of the agency contains a number of offices dealing with such issues as congressional relations, public information, interagency affairs, etc.

The three SBA programs of Financial Assistance, Procurement Assistance, and Management Development, and the other agency activities of advocacy and representation, are performed by 4,500 federal workers, most of whom are employed under the rules of the Civil Service System, and specifically under the provisions of the Civil Service Reform Act of 1978. The intent of the Reform Act was to speed the firing process, simplify the hiring procedures, and improve the motivational methods for federal employees. Dismissals for incompetence had been rare in the civil service prior to 1978, for it was necessary to show that the mission of an agency or department had been damaged by the performance of an employee before that person could be discharged. Under the new system, it is necessary only to demonstrate to a "reasonable" person that the employee's performance has been "inadequate." It is still possible to delay a dismissal or other disciplinary action for months through the process of appeals provided in the Reform Act, so that a rash of firings was not expected at the time of passage of the act, but it was expected that a sense of individual responsibility and accountability for performance would increase, and independent observers have reported that this has occurred.

For hiring, all jobs in the Civil Service System after 1978 were to be filled by open competition, based upon the education, experience, and, when required for some of the lower-level positions, examination scores of the applicants. Job openings now have to be listed at federal job centers scattered throughout the country, and hiring departments or agencies can consider only the top three applicants for each position, as ranked by the Civil Service Commission; potential employers within the government cannot consider such extraneous matters as the sex, age, racial/ethnic groupings, or, more important in governmental service, the political affiliation or personal friendships and influence of the applicant.

Finally, the Civil Service Reform Act of 1978 attempted to reward merit rather than longevity with salary increases and career promotions. Specifically, middle managers in the civil service, in the salary grades GS-13 to GS-15 (roughly at the 1978 pay levels of $23,000 per year to $38,000 per year) were to be given merit increases in salary at the discretion of their superiors, rather than automatic annual increases as had occurred in the past; while the higher-level federal managers and policy analysts, above the GS-15 rating, were termed members of the Senior Executive Service, and these 8,000 or so individuals were to sacrifice some of their security in return for merit increases and annual bonuses based upon excellent performance. The Reform Act required that all employees above GS-5 be regularly evaluated, and that each agency develop a set of performance standards for each position.

The central office of the Small Business Administration, in Washington, D.C., was organized with an administrator, a deputy administrator, associate administrators in charge of financial assistance (the three loan programs), of operations (the 10 regional offices and 63 district offices), of procurement assistance, and of management development. In addition, there were assistant administrators in charge of administration (budget and computer services), of congressional and public affairs, of minority small business, of advocacy, and a general counsel. An organizational chart of this central office is shown in Exhibit 1. In very general terms, the central office conducts relations with Congress, studies the needs and problems of small business, promotes the interests of small business within government, distributes public information, provides technical assistance to the field offices, and reviews and evaluates the work of the regional and district offices. The main activities of the SBA, which are processing loan applications, servicing existing loans, arranging procurement contracts, and providing managerial assistance, are conducted at the district and branch levels, except for the SBIC and Local Development Company loans, which are processed at the Washington office. Organizational charts for the regional and district offices are shown in Exhibits 2 and 3. The administrator, deputy administrator, associate administrators, and regional directors shown on these charts are all outside the Civil Service System; the administrator is appointed by the president and, after being confirmed by Congress, can make the other senior appointments without review by the Civil Service Commission.

The Small Business Administration was formed to "aid, counsel, assist and protect insofar as possible the interests of small business concerns in order to preserve free competitive enterprise..." (Small Business Development Act of 1953, p. ii), and has received over $30.0 billion funding for loans, in addition to substantial annual budgets for operations. Un-

fortunately, during much of its history the SBA has been not so much famous for its good works as it has been notorious for its alleged corruption and mismanagement.

When it set up the Small Business Administration in 1953, Congress instructed the new agency to promote "free competitive enterprise" by helping out the smallest and weakest competitors. And to begin with, that is what the SBA tried to do. It lent money to financially strapped small businesses whose applications for credit had been rejected by banks, procured government contracts for them, and counseled their managers. The agency also came to the aid of businessmen and homeowners hit by natural disasters.

But over the years ... Congress has saddled the SBA with a dizzying array of additional programs, and an agency that started out smelling like a rose has ended up as an overgrown, pest-plagued, bureaucratic weed. Today, it seems, there is hardly anything the SBA doesn't do. It lends money to small businessmen who are uprooted by the construction of new highways, who suffer losses because of unfavorable weather, or who need help to comply with government regulations. It guarantees surety bonds for contractors and offers them seasonal lines of credit. When the 1972 SALT agreement limited the number of antiballistic missiles and caused some small businessmen in Montana to lose money, the SBA came to the rescue with a loan program designed especially for them.

In all, the agency provided more than $4 billion worth of loans under twenty separate programs during the last fiscal year. It also set aside for small businessmen some $19 billion worth of government contracts, or nearly a third of the total let by the federal government. The SBA accomplished all this on a budget of $935 million and with a staff of nearly 4,300.

What the agency is best known for,

Exhibit 1 *Organizational chart of the central office of the U.S. Small Business Administration, 1976*

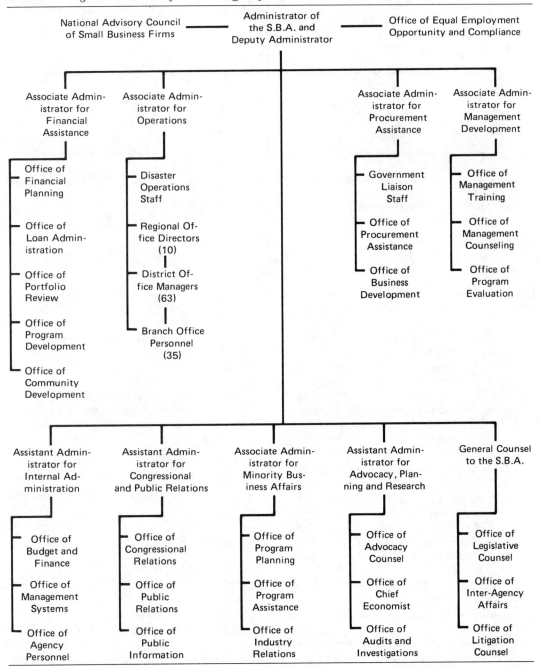

National Advisory Council of Small Business Firms ——— Administrator of the S.B.A. and Deputy Administrator ——— Office of Equal Employment Opportunity and Compliance

Associate Administrator for Financial Assistance
- Office of Financial Planning
- Office of Loan Administration
- Office of Portfolio Review
- Office of Program Development
- Office of Community Development

Associate Administrator for Operations
- Disaster Operations Staff
- Regional Office Directors (10)
- District Office Managers (63)
- Branch Office Personnel (35)

Associate Administrator for Procurement Assistance
- Government Liaison Staff
- Office of Procurement Assistance
- Office of Business Development

Associate Administrator for Management Development
- Office of Management Training
- Office of Management Counseling
- Office of Program Evaluation

Assistant Administrator for Internal Administration
- Office of Budget and Finance
- Office of Management Systems
- Office of Agency Personnel

Assistant Administrator for Congressional and Public Relations
- Office of Congressional Relations
- Office of Public Relations
- Office of Public Information

Associate Administrator for Minority Business Affairs
- Office of Program Planning
- Office of Program Assistance
- Office of Industry Relations

Assistant Administrator for Advocacy, Planning and Research
- Office of Advocacy Counsel
- Office of Chief Economist
- Office of Audits and Investigations

General Counsel to the S.B.A.
- Office of Legislative Counsel
- Office of Inter-Agency Affairs
- Office of Litigation Counsel

Source: Conversation with agency personnel.

Exhibit 2 *Organizational chart of the regional offices of the U.S. Small Business Administration, 1976*

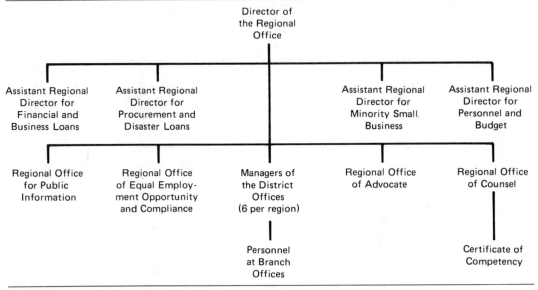

Source: Conversation with agency personnel.

though, isn't its largess, but its problems—one of which is that it has been repeatedly rocked by scandal. During a 1973 investigation, for example, Congress turned up evidence of, among other things, kickbacks to lending officers, bribery, and loans to bankrupt companies.... (*Fortune,* November 1977, p. 204f)

There have been so many instances of SBA corruption that they must be qualified by year. In the last ten years, it turns out, over a hundred stories have been printed in major newspapers chronicling several dozen major cases of corruption and fraud at the Small Business Administration....

One major story reported that $3.5 million in SBA money was discovered missing in a quick check of the files in New York City, while in Chicago, SBA officials were caught steering government contracts to friends. And on the local scene [San Francisco], there was the ongoing trial of [name of the political figure]

accused of accepting bribes in connection with an SBA loan he got for his now defunct travel agency.

This prodigious output of scandal is impressive for a relatively small (4,500 employees) and obscure agency.... (*San Francisco Examiner and Chronicle,* June 24, 1979, p. 26)

The scandals that have been revealed, and the mismanagement and theft that allegedly still continue (1978) at the Small Business Administration, can be grouped into eight classes based on the use and misuse of SBA programs:

1. Use of SBA Regular Business Loans for the personal benefit of an official in the SBA.

A lot of testimony focused on the dealings of [name of an individual], the director of the SBA's district office in Richmond, Virginia. He had approved nearly $11 million in loans, lease guarantees, and government contracts for companies, including mere shells, in which he or his future brother-in-law had an

Exhibit 3 *Organizational chart of the district offices of the U.S. Small Business Administration, 1976*

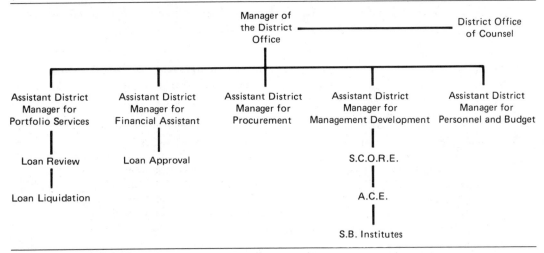

Source: Conversation with agency personnel.

interest.... (*Fortune,* November 1977, p. 205) SBA officials reported today that the agency's own review of financial portfolios had uncovered "serious problems ... though not so serious as at Richmond" in one quarter of the SBA field offices: Cincinnati, Detroit, Helena, Jacksonville, Marquette (Wisconsin), Milwaukee, New Orleans, Oklahoma City, San Antonio, San Diego, St. Louis, and the District of Columbia. (*New York Times,* March 27, 1974, p. 5)

2. Use of SBA Regular Business Loans to obtain kickbacks for the personal benefit of an official in the SBA.

The U.S. Attorney's office here [Chicago] is investigating charges that some Small Business Administration loan officers have solicited kickbacks ... to approve loans, sources said.

Loan officers reportedly have demanded bribes of $500 to $800 from applicants. Earlier this month, one loan officer [name of an individual] was arrested in the office of a loan applicant who had recently received a $35,000 loan. The Federal Bureau of Investigation said that he was found with $500 in marked bills that had been given to the businessman by the FBI. (*Wall Street Journal,* March 31, 1978, p. 23)

3. Use of SBA Regular Business Loans for the benefit of persons believed to be associated with organized crime.

Known underworld figures in this area [New Orleans] have for years enjoyed a cozy relationship with the local office of the Small Business Administration and have been able to obtain loans easily, an investigation by the *New York Times* has found.

The relationship has resulted in millions of dollars in federal funds going to persons with known Mafia backgrounds and their associates, to the consternation of law enforcement authorities, concerned about underworld figures using legitimate businesses as fronts.... (*New York Times,* February 28, 1974, p. 2)

4. Use of SBA Economic Opportunity Loans for the benefit of persons not members of racial minority groups.

The application for a $345,000 federal loan guarantee to help buy a South Dakota radio station came from Tom Tom Communications, Inc.

"When I saw the company name, I thought it might be an Indian enterprise," one Small Business Administration official said yesterday.

But Evelyn Cherry, chief of the special projects division of SBA's office of finance, soon learned otherwise.

More than 90 percent of the company's stock is owned by Tom Brokaw, the well-paid host of NBC's "Today" show.

And Brokaw also has an explanation for how the company got its name.

"My partner in the venture, John Thomas Kearns, is also known as 'Tom,' " Brokaw said, "so we named it Tom Tom."

The loan guarantee has come under fire because it was approved under a program that . . . was intended chiefly to help minorities buy broadcasting stations.

SBA officials defended the loan guarantee to Brokaw.

It would not take anything away from minorities, they said, and in any event, the program under which it was approved was not intended for minorities alone. (*San Francisco Chronicle,* November 16, 1978, p. 14)

5. Misuse of SBA Economic Opportunity and Ordinary Business Loans by the recipients.

The road to scandal, like the one leading to other damnable regions, is often paved with good intentions. The latest example, disclosed last week, is a federal investigation into an ambitious program to help minority entrepreneurs.

Justice Department investigators began looking into the apparent squandering of millions of dollars advanced to minority businessmen over the last 10 years by the Small Business Administration. The agency may have $26 million in outstanding payments that it expects never to see again. Much of it was misspent, as in the case of a New York contractor who used $200,000 to buy a racehorse. (*New York Times,* November 12, 1978, Sec. IV, p. 4)

Blacks do not have a monopoly on misspending federal funds; it just happens that the current investigation is centering on the Eco-nomic Opportunity Loan Program. I could name a white Detroiter who did not buy a race horse with an SBA loan; he bought an entire racing stable. (Statement of a small business consultant)

6. Mismanagement of SBA Economic Opportunity and Ordinary Business Loans by SBA officials.

The [SBA] agency's investigation of the New York–New Jersey region also reached the following conclusions: Its employees often violate their own regulations regarding advance payments; there is scant follow-up on the use of advance payments, and records are so inadequate that the names and addresses of the recipients of the advance payments are often lost.

In addition, the investigators found that the minority-owned businesses frequently took the advance payment funds, converted them to certificates of deposit in a bank, then pocketed the interest after repayment.

Employees of the small business agency have also been implicated in the investigation, officials said, and may be subject to Justice Department action. There have been allegations of kickbacks and instances of favoritism, in which the agency's employees in the New York office altered repayment dates so that the companies appear up to date when they are in fact more than a year overdue. (*New York Times,* November 9, 1978, p. 1)

7. Misuse of the SBA Loan Guarantee Program by banks and other private financial institutions.

The quality of SBA's loans deteriorated further [in the early 1970s] when the agency shifted its emphasis from making loans directly to businessmen to guaranteeing up to 90% of loans made by private banks. SBA officials were proud of the new program—it allowed the agency to make more loans with less funds, and the size of the basic loan program doubled in the space of two years.

Unfortunately, as the SBA relied more and more on the banks' analysis in evaluating loan applications, the banks, with practically all of their investment guaranteed, had little incentive to do the job well. In many cases, they didn't even bother to notify the SBA when a borrower stopped paying—except, of course, when it came time to collect their 90% guarantee.

Not surprisingly, as the number of loans mounted under the guarantee program, so did the agency's losses.

The SBA has already had to make good on its guarantee for a horrendous 15.3% of the loans extended in 1973, but this figure represents only a fraction of the potential expense.

Since the guarantee program has expanded so rapidly in recent years, most of the loans haven't yet had time to go bad. And the SBA has effectively postponed many of its losses by refinancing, even though there is little hope that even these second loans will ever be paid off. (*San Francisco Examiner and Chronicle*, June 24, 1979, p. 26)

8. Misuse of the SBA Small Business Investment Company Loan Program by venture capital firms and other private financial institutions.

There has been no formal investigation of SBICs, except to find that the entire concept of the program is wrong since the SBA loans money to venture capital firms theoretically to make equity investments, but the SBA charges interest on those loans, so the venture capital firms don't make equity investments. Instead, they make investments in convertible bonds, and charge their clients with heavy interest payments; the result is that they are draining money out of the small companies they are supposedly helping, and mailing that money to the federal government on a quarterly basis, to service the SBA debt.

There are some ugly situations in the SBIC area. It is possible to borrow money from the SBA at a low interest rate, and then, instead of buying equity in small or starting firms, to invest it in the second mortgage of a shopping center, motel, or apartment house at a much higher interest rate, and pocket the difference. Second mortgages on real estate projects, with some ownership provisions, are particularly popular at many SBICs since, along

with the difference in interest, you get the depreciation benefits so that you don't even have to pay income taxes on the money you are, in essence, stealing from the government. (Statement of a small business consultant)

As a result of these and other newspaper reports of mismanagement and scandal in the Small Business Administration, Congress directed the General Accounting Office, headed by the Comptroller General, to make an intensive audit of SBA programs. The GAO selected at random 980 of the 80,582 business loans outstanding as of June 1975 in the "7(a)" Ordinary Business Loan Program, and concluded from a study of those loans [The Small Business Administration Needs to Improve Its 7(a) Loan Program, Report to the Congress by the Comptroller General of the United States, GGD-76-24, not dated, cover page] that "Problems exist in the Small Business Administration's 7(a) loan program which need correction."

Specifically, the General Accounting Office found that 53% of the loans studied were for the purpose of repaying debts to participating banks and other private lenders and to the SBA itself for previous loans, purposes explicitly prohibited by SBA rules. Loans under the terms of the 7(a) program were intended to be used only for improving or expanding facilities and equipment, purchasing supplies and materials, or providing working capital. The GAO also found that six of the 24 district offices involved in the study had approved loans to companies with substantial assets that could easily have obtained credit from private lenders, again contrary to SBA policies. The investigators found numerous instances of questionable loans being approved simply because SBA loan specialists had failed to evaluate the borrowers' prospect and projections adequately; 19% of the evaluations were judged to be inadequate since they failed to use such techniques as cash flow analysis. Although the agency had obtained the required financial statements from most applicants (in 84.5% of the cases studied), loan specialists had failed in over 90% of the sample to obtain the required documentation showing that the applicants had been refused credit by private lenders. In addition, although SBA rules require that collateral be assessed, the GAO found that in 34.5% of the cases the collateral had not been either identified or appraised. The GAO next found that once 7(a) loans were approved, the Portfolio Management Division did not service the loans well enough to foresee company problems, and assist the company management. Field service visits, required by agency rules, were not made since portfolio management personnel were so occupied with delinquent firms and liquidations that they had no time left for current loans. Portfolio managers did not usually know a firm was in trouble until it missed a series of repayments. Even on bank loans guaranteed by the SBA, it took an average of 113 days before a portfolio manager received a notice of default; some banks reported only quarterly, others semiannually.

Finally, the GAO concluded that the management assistance received by 7(a) borrowers was of minimal value. The efforts of the Portfolio Management and Management Development personnel were often not coordinated at the district level, so that only 18% of the firms in the GAO sample had received management assistance. Among companies that had been helped, some borrowers felt that the counselors from the SCORE program were too elderly, that the faculty and students from the university programs were too inexperienced, and that professionals from the SBA staff were too concerned with agency policies and record keeping.

The publication of the reports by the General Accounting Office on the 7(a) Loan Program and 8(a) Procurement Program [Questionable Effectiveness of the 8(a) Procurement Program of the Small Business Administration, Report to the Congress by the Comptroller General of the United States, GGD-75-57, not dated] led to a further series of magazine and newspaper articles, some of which questioned the basic mission or concept of service of the organization.

The agency's problems start with its vague conception of its financial mission. The SBA was designed to be a "lender of last resort"—the idea is that after a small businessman is turned down by a bank, he can take the rejection letter to the SBA, and if the agency decides it is "reasonably assured" of getting its money back, it will lend him the money—usually at a very attractive rate of interest. It all sounds great if you're one of the loan recipients, but the grander purpose is less clear. The agency perennially has been split between those who saw it as a hardnosed lender and those who saw it as a social service agency. But neither role fits the loan program very well.

After all, the banks could be expected to skim off the best small business prospects for themselves, leaving the SBA with the rejects. Of those denied conventional financing, the SBA could fund only a tiny fraction. Why concentrate assistance—and a low-interest subsidy—on the bad prospects rather than the good ones? And, given its limited budget, which of the rejects was the SBA supposed to help?

These are questions the SBA has never gotten around to answering, although a number of answers are possible. The agency, for example, could have seen its mission as the promotion of new enterprises in areas the banks regard as too risky, or where technical and productive breakthroughs might have broad benefits that the banks don't care about. Or it might have tried to promote competition by funding new entrants in local industries dominated by a few firms.

Instead, the SBA has muddled along, serving what one agency official called "the upper-middle class of the turned-down firms," seeking only its "reasonable assurance" of repayment. Most of the loans go to businesses in sectors of the economy already overpopulated with small firms, and already well served by local banks: restaurants, grocery stores, wholesale and retail merchandisers. Nor are these the kinds of industries where new businesses are likely to pioneer technical innovations. (*San Francisco Examiner and Chronicle,* June 24, 1979, p. 27)

Disturbed by the newspaper and magazine reports of continuing problems at the SBA, and dismayed by the audit reports of the General Accounting Office, some members of the legislative and executive branches of the federal government began to consider the possibility of abolishing the Small Business Administration.

Congress ought to seriously consider abolishing the Small Business Administration if the agency can't be straightened out,

the head of the Senate's Small Business Committee said.

Sen. Gaylord Nelson (D., Wis.) said recent disclosures of serious problems in the SBA's minority contracting program show that the agency needs "a very substantial reorganization and tightening up." If the SBA can't be administered efficiently and effectively, he added, he favors folding the agency and firing "all 4,500 employees and getting rid of every single office in the U.S." (*Wall Street Journal,* November 22, 1978, p. 14)

Class Assignment. Assume that you have been appointed by the president to be the administrator of the Small Business Administration. Assume further that you have been told by the president that he is committed to a program to aid small business and minority business within the United States, but that the agency must be "efficiently and effectively" run. What would you do?

Chapter 14

STRATEGIC MANAGEMENT AND COMMUNICATION

Chapter 13 defined strategic management as the simultaneous and continual formulation and implementation of a long-term method of competition for a business firm, or a long-term concept of service for a nonprofit institution. Simultaneous consideration of the formulation and implementation of strategy is needed since strategic management is truly a single process, not two separate halves, and continual consideration is necessary so that this process can adapt to the ongoing series of changes in environmental conditions, organizational resources, and managerial attitudes. This complete process of strategic management is outlined graphically as shown at the top of the next page.

Strategic management is too complex to be accomplished by a single person. The amount of information needed to evaluate each alternative, the number of alternatives to be considered, the detail in the statements on objectives, policies, programs, and actions, the time required to define the critical tasks, and the expertise needed to design the organizational structure and managerial systems are simply too great. Strategic management has to be an organizational process, not an individual effort.

Strategic management is an organizational process, and requires an integrated performance by all members of the organization for successful completion, yet there are behavioral barriers to this integration, caused by the future uncertainties, conceptual interdependencies, and managerial interactions of planning, and there are communication problems. Members of an organization have to be able to report quickly, clearly, and concisely to other members on the portion of the strategic management process assigned to them, or to their organizational units. The following two notes, on the presentation of written and oral reports, provide explicit suggestions for report language and format to improve the brevity, clarity, and precision of organizational communications.

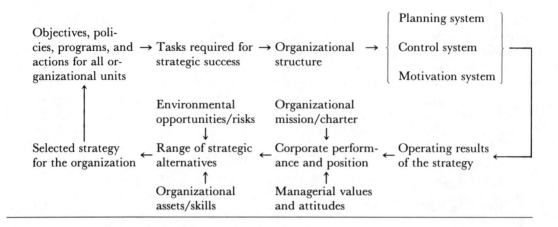

Note on the Presentation of Written Reports

Written reports are required in the management of most large organizations, to convey recommendations or instructions, and to convince members of the organization to accept and implement these recommendations or instructions. In a sense, written reports can be viewed as an end product of the managerial process: defining organizational problems, identifying probable causes, evaluating alternative solutions, and proposing specific actions, all for the improvement of the organization's effectiveness and efficiency. Ideally, each report should be complete, accurate, and convincing, leading to immediate improvement in organizational performance. However, many reports prepared for actual situations are not well done: the alternatives considered may not be complete, the analysis performed may not be accurate, or the language and format used may not be convincing. A short instructional note distributed in the fourth term of the M.B.A. program cannot improve either the analytical methods or the functional concepts used by the students in report preparation—after all, the first three terms of the program deal almost exclusively with methods and concepts—but the note may be able to help students in the language and format of report presentation. Graduates of an M.B.A. program should recognize that they are going to spend much of their time over the first few years of their employment in writing reports, and that they are going to be evaluated at least partially on the preparation and presentation of those reports. Consequently, the reports ought to be well written; it takes very little extra time to do so, and it does not require any inherent natural ability. All that is required is consideration for the reader.

This note lists 10 major recommendations for the language and format of written reports

719

in order to convey information with consideration for the reader. Students should recognize that no reader, whether in a university course or a business organization, will spend as much time studying a report as the author might wish or expect. Therefore, the important concepts within the report have to be conveyed quickly, clearly, and concisely. These 10 suggestions for report language and format are intended to improve the brevity, clarity, and precision of written presentations:

1. Need for an executive summary
2. Need for a table of contents
3. Suggestions for the report structure
4. Suggestions for the section structure
5. Suggestions for the paragraph structure
6. Suggestions for the sentence structure
7. Problems of exhibits and appendices
8. Advantages of comparative charts and matrices
9. Need for definite recommendations
10. Need for detailed pro forma statements

Each of these recommendations is illustrated with both good and poor examples from prior student reports on the problems of a small local company that specialized in the custom remodeling of cars and motorcycles. Hopefully, some of the examples selected will make the company problems, basic causes, and alternative solutions clear, so that it will not be necessary for students to first read the original case that was the subject for these assigned reports.

Need for an Executive Summary. Executives in many organizations require that the major conclusions and recommendations of a report be clearly stated in a single paragraph on the title page. The executive summary serves three functions:

1. *The summary permits a reader to very quickly judge the relevance of the material to his or her assigned tasks and need for information.* Each member of an organization does not need

to read all the reports that are prepared within that organization. Indeed, in many large firms it would be personally impossible to read all the material written by staff personnel, reproduced in large numbers on electrostatic copying machines, and then distributed to a mass audience. Prior to the advent of the xerographic process, copies were limited to the three or four carbons that could be made on a manual typewriter, unless a special stencil was prepared for a mimeograph or multilith printer, and consequently copies of reports, memos, and letters were sent only to those members of the organization who had either a direct need for the information, or had directly requested to be kept informed. Now, most managers receive many more reports than they can read attentively. Consequently, one of the most direct ways to offer assistance and show consideration to the reader is to provide a title-page summary which gives a short review of the report content, since this enables the recipients to gauge the relevance of the material to their own responsibilities and activities.

2. *The summary enables a reader to more easily follow the logic of the presentation.* Some degree of suspense may be desirable in mystery fiction, and some discussion of the background before reaching the conclusion is common in philosophical discourse, but almost all administrative studies are helped by an early statement of the major conclusions concerning the dimensions and causes of the problem, and the primary recommendations for improvement. Reports are very much easier to follow when the logical outcome is known in advance. Therefore, a title-page summary that provides a clear and concise statement of the recommendations, and the reasons for those recommendations, shows consideration for the readers since it permits each of them to read and understand the con-

tents of the report much more quickly and readily.

3. *The summary forces the author to reach definite recommendations and to select the essential supporting arguments.* The need to provide explicit organizational recommendations and to state the important analytical conclusions is not a commonly acknowledged function of an executive summary, but it should be recognized that it is relatively easy to disguise a lack of content in a lengthy report by looking at all the alternatives, without recommendations, or by investigating all the problems, without conclusions. It is very difficult, however, to camouflage these omissions in a short summary. The title-page summary ensures that the report has been written with consideration for the reader since it forces a clear statement of the conclusions and recommendations, and compels an orderly ranking of the reasons for these conclusions and recommendations from the supporting analysis.

A properly prepared summary should list the major conclusions and recommendations of the report. In short, the summary should truly summarize. This may appear to be hopelessly obvious, and trite, but many summaries are written as outlines of the content, and others are prepared as explanations of the assignment, or apologies for the result. The outline should be part of the table of contents, and the explanation of the assignment or the apology for the result should be placed in a letter of transmittal, if either is truly required. Remember that the function of most reports is to define a problem, identify the causes of that problem, and then recommend definite actions for improvement, and the function of the summary is to condense this content into a single readily understandable paragraph. Therefore, a reasonable rule to follow is that an executive summary that includes three sentences beginning with the

phrases "The major problems are . . . ," "The causes of these problems are . . . ," and "Consequently, I recommend that . . . " may seem very standardized and routine, but this format will convey quickly and understandably the conclusions and recommendations of the author. Consider the following three examples, and select the one that you feel most closely fills the three functions stated for an introductory summary:

The most immediate problems faced by the Detroit Automotive Corporation are a low level of sales that is much below the break-even point, and a negative cash flow that will lead to complete bankruptcy in six months. The cause of these problems is a lack of attention to the central issues facing the company, a continual preoccupation with peripheral details, and a continual experimentation with new products and services. I recommend that the company immediately discontinue used-car reconditioning (requires mechanical expertise), collision repair (requires price estimating and cost control), and standard customizing (requires production scheduling), and concentrate on the replicar manufacture of the MG-TD with a fiberglass body on an American Motors chassis and drive system. Through aggressive advertising and direct sales, this strategy can provide the cash flow needed to rebuild the company.

We have examined with care the accounting records, order backlog, and production documents of the Detroit Automotive Corporation, and we have conducted extensive library research and field interviews in the automobile industry. We have reviewed the strengths and weaknesses of the organization, the characteristics and trends of the environment, the values and attitudes toward risk of the management, and the major functional policies and plans to achieve the objectives, and we have prepared the following strategy for your consideration. As part of our analysis, we have prepared pro forma income statements and balance sheets showing the results of this strategy. The resultant report follows, which we trust you will read with interest and attention. If you have further questions, please contact us.

This report looks at the functional problems of marketing, production, finance, and engineering, at the organizational problems of unclear assignments and changing directions, and at the strategic problem of the lack of a defined method of competition. Then environmental factors and organizational resources are evaluated, to determine a new strategy for the firm. The value of the new strategy will be directly related to the vigor with which changes in operating and organizational procedures are implemented.

Need for a Table of Contents. Executives in many organizations often require that a one- or two-page outline be included as part of the introductory material for written reports. This outline, or table of contents, also serves three functions:

1. *The table of contents permits faster reading with much clearer comprehension.* Almost all written material is easier to understand—and remember that material is written for understanding, not just for reading—if it is preceded by an outline that graphically displays the logical structure of the content. The executive summary, as described previously, gives the logical outcome of a report, with the problem definition, the analytical conclusions concerning the causes of the problem, and the recommended actions for improvement. To some extent, the table of contents repeats this information, but it amplifies and itemizes each section to show the logical structure, or sequence of concepts, within the report. That is, the executive summary condenses the opinions of the author ("This is the problem as I defined it, these are my conclusions, and this

is what I recommend"), whereas the table of contents explains the thought processes followed by the author in reaching these opinions ("These are the major factors I looked at in defining the problem, these are the analytical methods I used in reaching my conclusions, these are the alternative courses of action I considered in searching for improvement, and this is the series of reasons I would like to be certain to convey to you to support my recommendations"). An outline of the logical sequence of concepts within a report certainly makes reading much easier and comprehension much more certain; consequently, the inclusion of a table of contents, or logical sequence of concepts, as part of the introductory material is one of the most important means of providing assistance to the reader.

2. *The table of contents permits selective reading, with very considerable time savings.* Just as every administrator within an organization does not need to read every report that is prepared within that organization, so each executive interested or concerned with a general problem area does not need to read every page of the reports dealing with that problem. In many instances, only the sections of a report dealing with the functional or technical aspects of a problem, or the recommended changes for improvement, are directly relevant to the interest and activities of a manager. An outline of the conceptual content of a report certainly encourages selective reading; again, the inclusion of a table of contents, or page location of the sections, as part of the introductory material is an important means of providing assistance to the reader.

3. *The table of contents forces the author consciously to design a logical structure, or sequence of concepts, before writing the report.* This logical structure is probably the most essential element in the presentation of written ma-

terial, and it is probably also the most neglected. There have certainly been many allegations by employers, in both business firms and nonprofit organizations, over the past few years that graduates of university programs in administration do not know how to write administrative reports, and there have also been many excuses by the graduates themselves that they were never trained in writing. These excuses are unfortunately true, because of the high costs of correcting individual reports on a detailed and helpful basis, and the excessive time demands for advising individual students on definite yet sympathetic terms. However, these excuses, although true, are probably not valid. Graduates of administrative programs have admittedly not been trained in writing, but they have been trained in logical thought processes—as a matter of interest, this training might serve as the definition of a good university, and the function of a conscientious faculty member—and this logical thought process should be apparent in both the preparation and presentation of written reports. If the logical structure is clear, a report cannot be poorly written since it can easily be understood. If the logical structure is unclear, the report probably cannot be considered to be well written since it will be difficult to read and to understand. Therefore, graduates of administrative programs may lack training in such essentials as spelling and grammar, and they may lack experience in such refinements as word choice and personal style, but they can still write a convincing report by concentrating upon their strengths: a logical process of thought in preparation and a logical sequence of concepts in presentation. The inclusion of a table of contents, which shows explicitly the logical structure and conceptual sequence of the study, ensures that the report has been prepared with consideration for the reader.

A properly prepared table of contents should list the major concepts of the report, arranged in a logical sequence, and displayed on at least two levels. The levels refer to the sections and subsections that are used to structure and format the content. Each section and subsection should include both a title and a short descriptive sentence. Time should be spent in deciding upon the report structure, the section and subsection titles, and the descriptive phrases. Among other reasons for this recommended effort, it should be recognized that if the executive summary and the table of contents are both clearly and concisely written, the text of the report may be read hurriedly, if at all, and the recommendations of the report may be accepted readily, without hesitance. The function of a written report, of course, is to convince other members of an organization to accept and then implement changes necessary to improve the performance of that organization; often, the table of contents, provided that it is carefully prepared, can convey an understanding of the situation necessary to convince other members, and the text of the report is used only as backup or support, to describe the analysis, alternatives, and recommendations in greater detail. To a very real extent, the best written report is the one that will never be completely read.

The table of contents should certainly be prepared prior to writing the text of the report. It should be admitted, however, that a fairly common experience is to feel that time is simply not available to spend on the luxury of an outline, and that in order to meet a deadline it is necessary to start immediately on the text. This may be a common feeling, but it is also a common failing. First, it is usually exceedingly obvious, and very disappointing, to a reader that a report has been written without a well-developed logical structure; second, it is usually not true that much time can be saved by omitting the structural outline. It may seem at the start that the rate of progress toward completion is sluggish and slow, but once the sections and subsections are blocked out, each with a title and a short descriptive sentence, the balance of the text can be filled in very rapidly. Read the following well-written table of contents, and consider how rapidly the report could be finished by adding descriptive text and prepared exhibits, charts, and matrices:

Operating Problems of the Company. Detroit Automotive Corporation has major operating problems in all the functional areas:

1. *Marketing problems.* A consistent marketing plan does not exist in the company; pricing is at a variable multiple of direct costs, and promotional expenditures are spread too widely to be effective.
2. *Production problems.* An organized productive system does not exist in the company; scheduling is on a personalized basis, and control is lenient at best.
3. *Financial problems.* The financial position of the company has deteriorated substantially since 1973; current operations are below break-even, and a continuation will lead to a negative cash position in March 1975.
4. *Personnel problems.* Continuing losses, and the resultant stresses and disorganized efforts to reach a solution, have brought problems of managerial conflict and employee morale.

Strategic Problems of the Company. The executives of the Detroit Automobile Corporation ascribe the operating problems to the economic downturn of 1974–1975; it is the conclusion of this report that the cause of the problem is not external, but primarily internal:

1. *Lack of a defined strategy.* The company has no defined product–market position; at present the owners are continuing their past efforts at new car customizing and custom part sales,

and have added used-car reconditioning, collision repairs, sun roof installations, fiberglass fabrications, and classic car reproduction.
2. *Lack of definite management.* The company has no general manager; Mr. Glass attends to details such as answering the telephone, talking to parts customers, purchasing minor supplies, etc. No individual in the management group is attending to the long-term central issues facing the company.

Strategic Alternatives Open to the Company. It would appear that there are five basic alternatives open to the Detroit Automotive Corporation at this time:

1. *Sell the company.* This alternative is rejected since neither Mr. Glass nor the other owners would agree, and since the assets of the company have no ready cash value beyond the secured debt.
2. *Reduce the size of the company to achieve a lower break-even.* This alternative is rejected since the 1972 investment in new plant and equipment makes a return to the earlier size and cost structure very difficult.
3. *Continue the present diversification strategy of the company.* This alternative is rejected since it is anticipated that the diversification strategy will lead to complete bankruptcy unless there is a dramatic increase in the level of economic activity in the Detroit area within the next few months; this increase is not anticipated.
4. *Emphasize services for which there is an existing market* (used-car reconditioning and collision repair) but which require capabilities which the company does not have (price estimating, production scheduling and cost control expertise, and mechanical repair labor). This alternative may be viable.
5. *Emphasize services for which a market must be developed* (new-car customizing and replicar manufacture) but which utilizes resources the company now has (style and design engineering, chassis

alterations, fiberglass forming, and spray painting). This alternative may also be viable.

Selection of the Strategy for the Company.

The strategy of market development (new-car customizing and replicar manufacture) to increase revenues above the break-even is recommended, despite the very obvious risk:

1. *Major resources* of the firm are the style and design engineering, and worker competence at chassis alterations, fiberglass forming, and spray painting; the skills needed for production development probably cannot be obtained quickly.
2. *Major environmental conditions* are the depressed state of the automotive industry and the consequent lack of discretionary income for luxury purchases in the Detroit area. It is felt, however, that a market exists for luxury cars in other sections of the country.
3. *Major managerial influences* are a high tolerance of risk and a high degree of commitment to customized (individually styled) automobiles.
4. *Major time consideration* is that a national marketing plan for customized automobiles may be started immediately.

Implementation of the Strategy for the Company.

It is suggested that the market development strategy be started immediately with the following functional changes:

1. *Marketing plans.* Advertising for customized car services and the reproduced classic cars should be started in the major financial papers (*Wall Street Journal, Barron's, Business Week,* etc).
2. *Production plans.* Manufacture of 10 MG-TD (1947) fiberglass replicars on an American Motors chassis and drive train, and 10 Rolls-Royce (1932) convertibles on an Oldsmobile chassis and drive train, should be started.
3. *Financial plans.* Complete sale of the used-car inventory and reduction of

the custom parts inventory to furnish immediate funds for promotion and production. A $50,000 increase in the bank loan will be required.

4. *Personnel plans.* Wage reductions to all workers, coupled with an explanation of the crisis facing the company; salary discontinuance to all managers, together with the start of a profit-sharing bonus.

The preparation of a structural outline of this nature is, as explained previously, the most important step in the presentation of a written report. The following portions of this instructional note discuss language and format suggestions to fill in the outline for the final written report.

Suggestions for the Report Structure. The structure of the final report should, of course, follow the structure of the outline presented in the table of contents; it is necessary only to fill in the sections and subsections of this outline with some additional descriptive text and with selected supportive data from the various steps of the analysis, and then utilize typography to indicate the sequence of sections, subsections, and supporting detail. This note has three suggestions to ensure that this sequence will be clear in the mind of the reader:

1. *Primary sections.* The title of each primary sections should be underlined, and the text should be double-spaced, without indentations. These typing instructions, unfortunately, cannot be illustrated in a printed text.
2. *Subsections.* The title of each subsection should be enumerated (1, 2, 3, etc.) and the text should be indented, and might be single-spaced for contrast.
3. *Supporting detail.* It always seems to be a temptation to pack supporting data into the single-spaced text of a subsection, but this merely makes the information difficult to read and to comprehend quickly, and detracts from the general appearance and persuasion of the report. Instead, most

supporting detail should be formatted beneath the subsection as a chart, graph, or matrix, without either a title or alphabetic numeration.

The following example was selected to show the use of typography to separate the sections, subsections, and supporting detail in a written report for the purpose of making comprehension much quicker and easier for the reader. In order to save space and reading time in this instructional note, the entire section is not reproduced:

Strategic Alternatives Open to the Company. Despite the dismal sales performance of the past year, and the deteriorating financial position of the firm, there are five basic alternatives that remain open to the Detroit Automotive Corporation. The strategic decision must be made quickly, however, for continued losses will soon block the more attractive options:

1. *Sell the company.* Mr. Glass and the other owners are not in favor of a sale, but a more important reason against this alternative is that it is felt that the company cannot be sold as a going concern under the existing economic conditions in the area, and it is estimated that the liquidation value is below the current liabilities and secured debt [see Exhibit 1].

Suggestions for the Section Structure. Each section of an administrative report should deal primarily with one topic (past problems, current problems, anticipated problems, alternative solutions, etc.) and the coverage of that topic should be complete; that is, a single topic should not be described in two or more sections. Further, it is strongly suggested that each section follow the semioutline format that has been described previously, with an introductory paragraph or paragraphs followed by a series of subsections that amplify and explain the primary topic of the sec-

Exhibit 1

Account	Book value Sept. 30	Cash value liquidation	Basis of estimation
Cash	$ (1,442)	$ (1,500)	Additional bank charges for negative balance
Accounts receivable	29,746	22,300	25% discount due to 16-day accts. rec. in cash business
Raw material inventory	13,240	10,600	20% discount on steel, fiberglass, and paint
Sun roof inventory	6,427	3,200	50% discount, since difficult to sell
Used car inventory	12,270	11,000	10% discount, since sold at auction
Custom parts inventory	28,320	19,800	30% discount, since sold to dealers
Advances to employees	4,927	000	100% discount, since hard to collect
Building, less depreciation	103,909	77,200	25% discount, since building is in poor location
Equipment, less depreciation	49,793	32,300	35% discount, since equipment is special purpose
	$247,190	$174,900	Current liabilities and secured debt = $209,700.

tion. It may seem standardized and dull to write, "There are five major environmental trends that will affect the long-term validity of the firm, and should be reflected in the competitive posture selected for the company," or "There are six sequential steps required for the implementation of the recommended changes," but these phrases, together with the subsequent listings, do convey the meaning of an author quickly and accurately to a reader and, quite frankly, the phrases and listings are simple and easy to write. It doubtless will seem a mockery to use an equivalent phrase in this instructional note, but there are two major suggestions for the listings:

1. The *content of each subsection* should be limited to one concept (short-range financial problems, intermediate financial problems, etc.), and should generally be supported with only one exhibit, graph, chart, or matrix.
2. The *title of each subsection* should clearly identify the concept, and should be selected to contrast or compare with other titles in the listing. The parallel construction of subsection titles (pricing problems, promotional problems, etc.) provides very considerable assistance to a reader.

The following two examples were selected to show the desirability of limiting each section of a report to the discussion of a single topic, and then structuring the discussion of that topic in the form of an introductory paragraph followed by a list of clearly identified specifics. Both writers have discovered two marketing problems in the course of their analysis; consider which of them more clearly describes these problems to the reader.

> Promotional literature on Detroit Automotive products might tip the scales in the company's favor. A direct-mail campaign should be started to those customers who have visited the dealership but have not yet made up their minds. De-

troit Auto's prices are lower than the industry average, which means that the dealers can sell more strongly the price benefit, which may be important to push dealer selection. Prices are not tied to material or labor cost, and vary all over the map. A cost control system should be established quickly by Mr. Glass or Mr. Verolk to record costs more accurately. No company can be successful if costs are not known. Material costs should be recorded when delivered. Magazine advertising should be changed since people with money don't read *Hot Rodder* magazine. It is interesting that the decision process for car customizing takes three weeks, so promotional literature is best.

Operating Problems of the Company. Detroit Automotive Corporation has major operating problems in all the functional areas; these will be described briefly under the headings of marketing, production, finance, and personnel:

1. *Marketing problems in pricing.* No firm pricing policy apparently exists; prices as a percentage of direct material and labor vary widely:

Job	Material and labor cost	Sales price	
#23	$2,138	$ 2,086	0.98×
#46	$1,777	$ 3,400	1.94×
#11	$3,788	$10,900	2.90×

2. *Marketing problems in promotion.* No definite promotional policy apparently exists; the company last year spent more than $28,000 advertising in magazines that probably reached the wrong market segment:

Custom Hot Rodder	$22,304
Dirt Track	6,344
	$28,648

Readership of both is assumed to be young, without money for new-car customizing.

Obviously, in the prior example, the supporting detail could have been included as part of the paragraph describing the problem. However, formatting the supporting evidence, when possible, greatly assists the reader since the spatial relationships make comparison of the data simple and the significance of the data obvious. Consider the following example, which contains exactly the same information as was given previously, but is considerably more difficult to read and comprehend quickly:

> The direct material and labor cost of job 23 was $3,138, while the sales price was $2,086, for a 0.98 price/cost ratio. Job 46 was sold for $3,400, but cost only $1,777, which is 1.94%. The most profitable job was number 11, at 2.90 times the direct cost of $3,788, which is $10,900. Prices are not set at a constant percentage of fixed and variable costs; improvements in bidding procedures are needed.

Suggestions for Paragraph Structure. Each paragraph of an administrative report should focus on a single concept, fact, or point of view (price levels, production schedules, or interpretation of financial ratios), and the coverage of that thought or opinion should be complete; that is, the same concept or fact should not be discussed from the same point of view in two or more paragraphs. Beyond this very definite subject-matter limitation, this instructional note has only three major suggestions for the paragraph structure in written reports:

1. Paragraphs within an administrative report should start with a topic sentence that clearly delineates the subject matter of the paragraph, and the sentences that follow should support, explain, or elaborate that topic. As described previously, no other topic should be permitted within the paragraph. This topical sentence is particularly important in administrative reports since one of the more common forms of speed reading is the obvious shortcut of reading for comprehension only the first sentence in each paragraph. It may seem contradictory to prepare a detailed written document for speed reading, but to be effective in a large organization, an administrative report must be read and understood by a wide range of people, with varying degrees of interest in and need for the information, analysis, and recommendations contained in the report. Topical sentences to introduce each paragraph are needed to provide brevity and clarity for this range of readers, and to ensure that each person, depite the time invested and the reading style employed, understands the major recommendations and the reasons for those recommendations.

2. Paragraphs within an administrative report should be of varying length, reflecting the variable need of each topic for support or explanation. Paragraphs within a properly prepared administrative report often tend to be short since much of the supporting data or explanatory detail will be formatted or enumerated for rapid comprehension. It is well to remember that lengthy paragraphs, with unformatted data or unenumerated detail, often appear to be disorganized, and it is difficult for a reader to either comprehend quickly or follow easily the logical structure of the author. It is important that detail support, not obscure, the major points in the analysis and recommendations of the report.

3. Successive paragraphs within an administrative report should have an obvious sequence that may be chronological (ordered by time), functional (ordered by activity), or consequential (ordered by importance). This sequence should be established when the outline or table of contents is prepared, and should be carried through to the text by the use of topical sentences that provide a natural transition from one paragraph to the next. If this natural

transition and obvious sequence is omitted, it is very easy for a reader to fail to follow the logical argument of the author, and consequently to lose interest in the content of the report. To provide this natural transition, it is strongly suggested that each section start with a topical paragraph that describes the content of that section, and that each subsection, or paragraph, start with a topical sentence that both summarizes the content and identifies the place of that paragraph within the section.

The first example that follows is a paragraph that manages to ignore all four suggestions given in this instructional note for paragraph construction; the second example provides the same information structured in single-subject paragraphs, introduced by topical sentences, supported by variable detail, and organized with a natural sequence or transition:

Detroit Automotive Corporation was started in 1970 by Buford Glass. After a few years' work in a gas station in Ypsilanti, the company bought a former De-Soto sales agency and garage in Lincoln Park. Mr. Glass may have made a mistake when he moved to Lincoln Park since it is not a good suburb of Detroit. The median income per household in Lincoln Park is only $10,250, and only 15% of the families there make over $15,000 per year. The median income per household in Southfield is $19,690, and 68% of the families make over $15,000 per year. He also keeps on making a mistake since the shop is not kept organized and clean. He should hire a person to clean the shop, meet the customers, and look after the sale of the custom auto parts. Theft is said to be a problem since the neighborhood has deteriorated. The financial position of the company is so poor (1.4:1 debt/equity ratio and 0.9:1 current ratio) that they can't afford to move, but they should at least paint the outside of the building, and have better

security. They also should rearrange the production, which won't cost much either, to keep the grinding operation out of the showroom. Southfield would be a better location, if they can get a bank loan to move there.

The company, very simply, is not properly situated, organized, or staffed to successfully market the custom rebuilding of expensive automobiles to higher-income clients.

1. The location of the D.A.C. showroom and shop is poor. Lincoln Park is a southwestern suburb in Wayne County, with a low median income per household. The more affluent northern suburbs, such as Southfield, are 20 to 25 miles away in Oakland County, and the only major highway, Route 75, does not come close to the company's neighborhood. The result is that it is difficult to attract customers to the company.

2. The organization of the D.A.C. showroom and shop is poor. The grinding of fiberglass parts, a very noisy and dusty operation, is being done in the showroom part of the building in order to keep the dust from the paint area in the shop. The result is that it is difficult to show customers the products of the company.

3. The staff of the D.A.C. showroom is poor. The grinding of fiberglass parts is the only unskilled operation in the company, yet these are the employees the customer first encounters. They are described in the case as surly and uncommunicative. The result is that it is difficult to impress customers with the competence of the company.

Suggestions for Sentence Structure. It is not the intention of this note to provide detailed instructions on syntax (arrangement of words in phrases and sentences) or grammar (forms of words in phrases and sentences). Syntax and grammar are important, but the rules are complex, and probably never will be completely clear to a person who has not studied a foreign language, and learned the grammatical principles of that language thoroughly enough to be able to understand and apply the equivalent principles in English composition. And quite frankly, adherence to accepted standards of syntax and grammar should not be the major objective of English composition, except perhaps in legal briefs or scientific articles, where precision of meaning is essential. In most administrative situations, the reader is probably more accustomed to verbal communication, with its inherent inaccuracies and omissions, and will generally read written reports with the same understanding and allowances. Obviously, an effort should be made to be correct, and to include a noun or pronoun of the proper person and a verb of the proper tense in each sentence, but the essential considerations are clarity and interest. The writer of an administrative report should develop a style in word choice and sentence structure that conveys the concepts, facts, and point of view of the author clearly and concisely, and that holds the attention of the reader. This note has five suggestions for developing a style that provides this clarity, conciseness, and interest:

1. *The tenor of sentences does not need to be formal.* Many people feel that a repressed style of the "Yours of the 16th received and contents duly noted" is required in management. It should be considered, however, that this conventional phrasing may seem merely dull in a short letter but intolerable in a lengthy report. The tone of an administrative report probably should reflect the personality of the writer, and a "breezy," informal style can be both concise and informative, in proper situations and in proper amounts. The two examples that follow have exactly the same conceptual content; they differ only in the formality of the style:

Buford Glass has got to get his act in gear; he has got to decide what he wants to do with his own life before making plans where his company is to go.

It is essential that Mr. Glass examine his personal ambitions, values, attitudes, and beliefs, and then define the overall objectives of the Detroit Automotive Corporation to be consistent with these ambitions and values. The relative risk and return of each potential strategy must be examined with care before the strategic decision can be formulated properly.

2. *The words used in sentences do not need to be specialized.* The specialized vocabulary of persons working in the same profession or living in the same social group is termed jargon. Jargon also has the secondary, and much more derogatory meaning of unintelligibility. To maintain interest and ensure clarity to a range of readers, some of whom may not be acquainted with the specialized terms and others of whom may be so well acquainted with them that they appear to be tedious and dull, it is necessary to avoid both types of jargon. This can be done not by using only short and simple words, which tend to be unexpressive and uninteresting, but by using only terms that can be easily defined in a standard dictionary or technical reference book, and by being absolutely certain that the author understands these definitions. It is doubtful that the author of the following example understood all of the terms employed:

Market segmentation studies should be undertaken, to the extent possible under the severe time constraints and adverse financial factors, to determine the parameters of the corporate sales environment and to synthesize the demand analysis.

3. *The precise meaning of sentences should be clear.* Clarity is critical in an administrative report; nothing is more irritating to a reader than to be forced to repeatedly study a single sentence to comprehend the intended meaning. Fortunately, it is not difficult to select a sentence structure and

phrasing that will promote clarity and help understanding. There are three simple rules. Each sentence should be complete, including an identifiable subject and verb; each sentence should be direct, restricting the number of modifying terms and phrases; and each sentence should be unified, expressing a single concept, opinion, or recommendation. Unfortunately, it is possible for the writer of an administrative report to neglect all three of these prescriptions.

The volume which the large auto part retailers utilize and its importance to the producers allows them to command wholesale prices which are below its manufacturing cost for all but the most efficient firms whose sales take place in automotive accessories that are highly saturated markets which are themselves susceptible to the economic cycle that in 1974 appears to be headed downward.

4. *The phrasing of sentences should be parallel.* Parallelism refers to the use of terms and phrases that are similar in structure and form. In a series of nouns, all should be either singular or plural. In a series of verbs, all should be of the same tense. In a series of terms, all should have the same number of modifying adjectives. In a series of phrases, all should have similar verbs and similar structures. Parallel structure and form assists greatly in speed reading; it is particularly important in the titles of sections and subsections, and in the composition of topical sentences.

Marketing plans. Immediate change of the marketing plans for the MG-TD (1947 roadster) and the Rolls-Royce (1932 convertible) fiberglass replicars is essential for the projected recovery of the firm:

a. *Pricing policies.* Prices should be set at 2.5× direct costs; replicars are a luxury product, and increased prices will help to gain customer acceptance. Prices should be approximately 60% of the collector's cost of buying an original vehicle.

b. *Distribution policies.* Dealers should be established at 25% sales commission; replicars are a novel product, and local demonstrations and service will help to overcome customer resistance. Dealers should be reputable garages with an available showroom and interested personnel.

c. *Promotional policies.* Advertisements should be scheduled at $25,000 annual rate; replicars are an unknown product, and illustrated ads will help to increase customer contacts. Advertising should be in financial journals with readers who can afford to buy the car.

5. *The length of sentences should be variable.* A series of lengthy sentences can easily seem difficult and dull to the reader; some variety in sentence length is needed both to increase reader interest and to add topic emphasis. A short sentence, such as "Start now" is much more memorable, and much more likely to incite the desired response from the reader, than the longer example given below that has exactly the same informational content.

It is critical, in the context of the long-range planning methods proposed for the Detroit Automobile Corporation, that the changes in the functional activities consistent with the newly developed strategy be instituted quickly.

Problems of Exhibits and Appendices. It is a common practice to put quantitative detail, such as comparative financial ratios, expected revenue projections, or investment return calculations in exhibits and attach them to the back of the text, referenced only by a short note such as "See Exhibit 5." It is also common to organize background information on such topics as company history, industry trends, or organizational resources in appendices, and attach them to the back of the report with an equally short reference in the text. There is one problem that is somewhat basic with both of these methods of including supporting information: the exhibits and appendices are very seldom read. Undoubtedly, a conscientious reader should follow the instructions in the reference statements or footnotes, and should switch from the text to the proper exhibit or appendix and then back to the text, but this normally does not happen. The world is not filled with conscientious readers; instead, it is filled with people who want to finish a given task quickly so that they may go on to other tasks that are either more pressing or more interesting. Executives in large organizations read reports for content, and they expect a logical presentation of that content in an orderly page-by-page sequence. Interruptions in that orderly sequence tend to be ignored, and consequently supportive information segregated in exhibits and appendices tends to be unread.

Since the author of an administrative report cannot rely upon the recipients studying supportive data that are placed, out of sequence, in exhibits and appendices, how can a knowledge of this material be conveyed to the reader? It's very simple. The essential information has to be summarized within the text, and the reader is then referenced back to

an exhibit or appendix only for additional detail or explanatory calculations. Example 1 shows the summary of pro forma financial statements within the text, with references to supporting exhibits. In particular, note the introductory sentence, or topical sentence, that clearly states the meaning of the figures.

Advantages of Matrices, Graphs, and Diagrams. Solid text in a lengthy report can seem dull to the reader, even though properly structured in sections, properly organized in paragraphs, and properly expressed in sentences, unless the author has an unusually interesting and expressive writing style. For most of us who do not have the inherent ability or the previous training to develop such a style, it is advantageous to use matrices, graphs, and diagrams; they do serve to break up the text, and to convey large amounts of information concisely.

1. *Comparative matrices.* It is difficult to transmit numerical information in the text of an administrative report, since a paragraph containing numerous dates, ratios,

Example 1 *Replicar operations for the first year are expected to show a loss, despite severe reductions in existing administrative and engineering expense levels; however, substantial profits should be reached in both 1976 and 1977. (See Exhibit 6 for comparison with current revenues and expenses and supportive details for the forecasts.)*

	1975	1976	1977
MG–TD (1947) replicars at $5,900 each	$ 88,500	$179,000	$267,500
Rolls (1932) replicars at $14,650 each	43,900	102,500	219,700
Custom parts sales at cost + 25%	20,000	5,000	2,000
Used-car sales at cost − 20%	5,200	—	—
Total sales revenue	$158,600	$286,500	$489,200
MG–TD direct costs at $2,200 each	$ 33,000	$ 66,000	$ 99,000
Rolls direct costs at $6,400 each	19,200	44,800	96,000
Custom parts cost	16,000	4,000	1,500
Used-car cost	6,500	—	—
Shop overhead	21,900	35,000	48,000
Total direct costs	$ 96,600	$149,800	$241,500
Gross margin	$ 61,000	$136,700	$247,700

Example 2 *Financial problems.* The financial position of the company has deteriorated substantially in the past two years; this has been caused partially by the operating losses, and partially by the continual growth in inventory.

	1972	1973	1974
Current ratio	2.4	1.8	1.3
Acid-test ratio	1.6	0.9	0.6
Return on sales (%)	4.3	1.0	Deficit
Return on assets (%)	8.3	1.4	Deficit
Return on equity (%)	22.3	6.4	Deficit
Accounts receivable (days)	9.0	8.0	16.0
Inventory (days)	44.0	93.0	112.0
Accounts payable (days)	12.0	28.0	47.0

percentages, units, and dollars simply looks uninteresting and difficult. Most readers will either skip or skim the material, which means that they will not understand the trends and relationships. The following paragraph describes in detail the deteriorating financial condition of the company, and indicates some of the causes of that deterioration, but few readers will take the time to fully understand the meaning of these jumbled and uninteresting figures.

The current ratio has gone from 2.4 to 1 in 1972 to 1.8 to 1 in 1973 to 1.3 to 1 in 1974. The acid-test ratio has declined from 1.6 to 1 in 1972 to 0.9 to 1 in 1973 to 0.6 to 1.8 in 1974. Working capital is $29,943 now, but was $79,331 in 1972. Return on sales was 4.3% in 1972, 1.0% in 1973, and -8.6% now. Return on equity was 22.3% in 1972, 6.4% in 1973, and a deficit now. Accounts receivable are now 16, but they were 9 days, and inventory has gone from 44 in 1972 to 93 in 1973 to 112 in 1974, while accounts payable have also increased from 12 in 1972 to 28 in 1973 to 47 in 1974.

The same quantitative information can be displayed in a comparative matrix, much more concisely and much more convincingly. For the more obvious trends

and relationships, no explanation is needed beyond an introductory statement, or topical sentence, providing the reader with the major conclusions to be drawn from the figures; see Example 2.

There are two final suggestions for comparative matrices that may seem to be of minor importance, but which do help in conveying quantitative information quickly. The figures should be selected for inclusion, so that irrelevant data do not obscure the trends and relationships in the matrix, and the figures should be formatted in orderly rows and columns so that the visual comparisons are simple and obvious.

2. *Interpretative graphs.* A graph, or visual presentation of quantitative data, is obviously less precise than the actual figures displayed in a matrix, but the trends and relationships are more clearly shown, and much more easily understood. It is suggested that a graph be used when precision is not critical, and when the trends and relationships are not obvious. Charts are particularly useful to show changes in trends, and nonlinear relationships. Unfortunately, the very simple company that has provided all the previous examples for the various suggestions to improve the

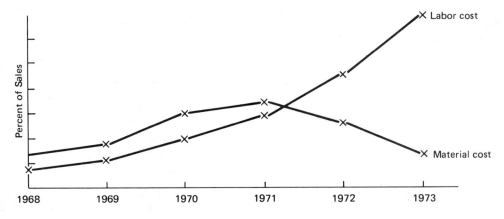

preparation of written reports cannot be used here to show either a change in trends or a nonlinear relationship; all the financial ratios declined at a steady pace over the entire history of the firm. But it is not hard to envisage and then display a more complex situation, as shown in the illustration at the top of the page.

3. *Analytical diagrams.* A diagram is a visual presentation that is intended to explain relationships rather than display information. A particularly useful form in administrative reports is the decision diagram, which can be used to show strategic alternatives and the probable consequences of each alternative, or a sequence of decisions and events. The alternatives currently available to the very simple company that has been used for illustrative purposes in this note are not particularly complex, and probably do not need to be visually displayed, but in many reports a diagram of the decision process would provide very definite assistance to the reader in understanding the range of alternatives, as shown in the accompanying diagram at the top of the next page.

Need for Definite Recommendations. Recommendations are central to an administrative report. A properly prepared report will normally consist of separate sections on prob-

lems, causes of the problems, recommendations, and consequences of the recommendations. However, many writers attempt to hedge on their recommendations, either by discussing each of the alternatives at length without reaching a conclusion, or by expressing their conclusion in conditional terms, dependent upon other actions or events. Do remember that it is difficult to hedge on recommendations without seeming exceedingly obvious; basically, you either support a given list of improvements or you do not. You might as well state your recommendations firmly, so that they can be easily understood and readily followed. If the recommended changes work out poorly, the author is likely to be blamed anyway, despite the qualifications and hesitations, and the changes are much more likely to be successful if they are stated forcefully and convincingly. Consider which of the following recommendations, which have nearly identical content, will probably result in improved performance by the firm.

The proposal to build fiberglass copies of classic cars, using purchased frames, motors, and drive train components, seems attractive due to the greatly increased margins, if the market develops as expected. If not, then probably the best action would be to recondition used cars

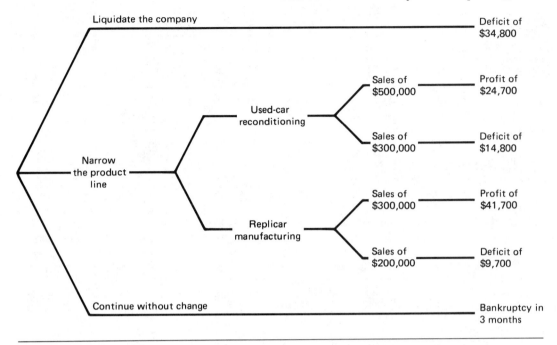

and rebuild damaged cars, even though this does not fit the only real skill the company has.

I recommend that the Detroit Automotive Corporation concentrate solely on the production and sale of fiberglass replicars. This is the high-risk strategy, but it does make use of existing skills and does provide an adequate margin. The probability of success for this strategy may seem low, at 70%, but it is much higher than for all the other alternatives:

	Estimated probability of success (%)
Continue company on existing strategy	0
Reduce fixed expenses to 1972 level	20
Concentrate on reconditioning used cars	45
Concentrate on manufacturing replicars	70

Buford Glass can substantially increase the probabilities of success by energetically and enthusiastically implementing the marketing, production, financial, and personnel policies listed in the next section.

Need for Detailed Pro Forma Statements. One of the better definitions of an M.B.A. is "a person who is able to forecast the financial consequences of administrative actions." Financial forecasting involves the preparation of pro forma balance sheets, income statements, and cash budgets; these should be prepared in adequate detail to permit the reader to understand the derivations of the various figures, with notes on the ratios and assumptions used, and should be placed in an exhibit or appendix attached to the end of the report. As suggested previously, the major conclusions from each exhibit or appendix should be summarized within the report, and the reader should be referenced back to the exhibit or appendix only for addi-

Exhibit 2 *Pro forma income statements for the Detroit Automotive Corporation, 1975–1977*

	1975	1976	1977
MG–TD (1947) replicar sales at $5,900 each	$ 88,500	$179,000	$267,500
Rolls (1932) replicar sales at $14,650 each	43,900	102,500	219,700
Custom parts sales at cost + 25%	20,000	5,000	2,000
Used car sales at cost − 20%	5,200	—	—
Total sales revenue	157,600	286,500	489,200
MG–TD direct costs at $2,200 each	33,000	66,000	99,000
Rolls direct costs at $6,400 each	19,200	44,800	96,000
Custom parts at purchased costs	16,000	4,000	1,500
Used cars at purchased costs	6,500	—	—
Shop overhead (see Notes for details)	21,900	35,000	52,000
Total direct costs	96,600	149,800	248,500
Gross margin	61,000	136,700	240,700
Selling expenses (see Notes for details)	52,000	60,000	105,000
Administrative expenses (see Notes for details)	19,600	25,000	25,000
Interest cost at 8% on bank loan	7,400	5,000	3,000
Depreciation on building and equipment	4,100	4,000	3,800
Total corporate expenses	83,100	94,100	136,800
Profit or (loss) before taxes	(22,300)	42,700	103,900
Income taxes (−) or credit (+)	+2,600	−8,800	−41,500
Profit or (loss) after taxes	(19,700)	33,900	62,400

Notes: Sales of replicars in units are estimated to be as follows:

MG–TD (1947) roadster	15 cars	30 cars	45 cars
Rolls (1932) convertible	3 cars	7 cars	15 cars

Custom parts and used cars are to be liquidated, with discounts from the normal selling price, to obtain cash.

Direct costs of replicars are for material and labor, and have been estimated by Mr. Glass, with the material cost confirmed by suppliers.

Shop overhead is estimates by years as follows:

Payroll taxes at 17% of wages	$ 3,540	$ 7,530	$13,260
Employment insurance at 8% of wages	1,670	3,540	6,240
Shop supervision at annual rate	9,600	12,000	14,400
Shop supplies at 15% of labor	3,130	6,650	10,700
Electrical power at 5% of labor	1,250	2,220	3,900
Oil heat at current level + 10%/yr	1,190	1,310	1,440
Fire insurance at 11% shop assets	1,520	1,750	2,120
Total shop overhead	$21,900	$35,000	$52,000

tional detail or explanatory calculations. It is suggested strongly that the financial forecast be rounded off to four significant figures (i.e., that the forecasts be reported in hundreds, thousands, or millions, as required by the size of the firm), and that the explanations be complete, and be provided for each major section of the financial statement (see Exhibit 2).

This note has offered 10 suggestions to improve the language and format of written reports, and to increase the brevity, clarity, and interest of those reports. It is often difficult, however, to convert very general suggestions into very specific words, sentences, and paragraphs. Potential authors should not be discouraged. There is substantial help available for people who may have limited prior experience or inherent ability in writing, but who also have an assignment to prepare a written document. The books I should recommend for help are as follows:

1. Roget's *Thesaurus in Dictionary Form* (published by Berkeley Medallion in paperback). If you have already used the term "environment" twice in a single paragraph, and want to find a synonym to avoid using it for a third time, Roget's will give you a minimum of 20 choices.
2. Allen's *Synonyms and Antonyms* (published by Everyday Handbooks in paperback). This handbook is also alphabetized, in dictionary form, so that it is easy to locate the entries, but you will find that Allen's is slightly more selective, and considerably more precise, in providing alternative word choices.
3. Webster's *New World Dictionary* (published by World Printing Company). If you are not certain whether a fundamental truth or law is a "principle" or a "principal," you can look it up in any good dictionary. Dictionaries are useful for the meaning of words, but not for the spellings, since they do not usually give the various verb tenses or the noun plurals, where most of us have trouble.
4. Webster's *New World 33,000 Word Book* (published by World Printing Company). The *Word Book* does not give definitions, but it does give spellings in a very concise and very complete form. If you don't know whether the past tense of the verb "to plan" is "planed" or "planned," you can look it up quickly here.
5. Kierzek and Gibson's *Handbook for Writing and Revision* (published by Macmillan). The *Handbook* provides very explicit rules for punctuation and grammar.
6. Bromage's *Writing for Business* (published by the University of Michigan Press). Professor Bromage does not offer a reference text, but an engaging description of the various linguistic errors we all commit, and very helpful suggestions for improvement. This is a book to be read and enjoyed, not to be referred to hurriedly.

Note on the Presentation of Oral Reports

Oral reports are required in the management of most large organizations, and their use is often very similar to the use of written reports, which were described in the preceding note. Both oral and written reports may be used to convey recommendations or instructions, and to convince members of the organization to accept and implement those recommendations and instructions, or they may be employed to convey information on the status of a project or conclusions on the causes of a problem, and to achieve agreement on the validity of that information or the accuracy of that analysis. Oral and written reports can both be used to communicate information, analysis, and recommendations, but they differ markedly, not in the purpose or the content, but in the form and structure of the communication. A written report should be a complete document, defining organizational problems, identifying probable causes, evaluating alternative solutions, and proposing specific actions, whereas the oral report must be a concise statement, summarizing the conclusions and recommendations, and providing an opportunity for discussion and consensus. A written report is available to be studied; an oral report is presented to be understood. These differences are major, and they are not recognized by both students and managers, many of whom often seem to believe that an oral report is just a verbal presentation of the written material.

Oral reports are a specialized form of the more general oral communications, which can range from interpersonal dialogues to massive monologues and national speeches. The essential element of all oral communication, however, is interest; once the interest of the audience is lost, further communication either stops completely or becomes very sporadic. Interest is essential; it is much more important to be interesting than to be exhaustive, detailed, and dull. Very few of us, faculty, students, or managers, have the natural abilities and personal characteristics that make our verbal statements inherently interesting, but all of us can present interesting oral reports; all that is required is careful definition of the audience, complete preparation of the material, and a determination to be brief. This note offers 10 suggestions to improve the interest of oral reports, and to detail the means of audience evaluation, material preparation, and concise presentation:

1. Need for defined audience
2. Need for explicit objectives
3. Need for complete outline
4. Need for supportive detail
5. Need for clear visual aids
6. Suggestions for the introduction
7. Suggestions for the presentation
8. Suggestions for the conclusion
9. Suggestions for answering questions
10. Suggestions for overcoming nervousness

Each of the 10 recommendations will be illustrated with both good and poor examples from earlier student group reports on the problems of the same, sad company that was used to illustrate the preceding note on the presentation of written reports. Again, it is hoped that the examples selected will make the company problems, basic causes, and alternative solutions adequately clear, so that it will not be necessary to first read the original case that was the subject for these assigned oral reports.

Need for Audience Definition. Thoughtful preparation is essential for a successful oral report, and although this prescription may seem obvious and trite, it is surprising that the primary aspects of this preparation, a definition of the nature of the audience and a consideration of the objectives of the report, are often neglected. The audience includes both the people within the room who will listen to the presentation and others, within the organization, who may later hear about portions of the report, perhaps in distorted or incomplete form. It is not possible to avoid all the problems in second- and third-stage communications, as each participant in the chain adds his or her preconceptions and personal attitudes to the message, but it is possible to recognize the possible impact of ambiguous or imprecise statements upon people who believe themselves to be affected by the decisions and actions arising from the report, and to ensure that those statements are clear and verifiable.

The audience within the room, the people involved in the first stage of communication, usually differ along dimensions of technical sophistication, managerial level, and project involvement, and an oral report must recognize these differences. The ideal audience, of course, would be homogeneous, and all reports could be designed to fit a single level of comprehension and information about the topic. The ideal, however, is seldom achieved in managerial situations, and a more typical audience will represent a range of knowledge, understanding, and involvement. The temptation is either to aim for the median, or to appeal to the senior management, but it is better to recognize that differences do exist, and to specifically adapt to them, while not delaying the presentation with technical explanations or background information. Consider which of the following statements should be used for a management group with a good understanding of analytical techniques, which would best hold the interest of an audience with a wide range of financial sophistication, and which probably should never be used since it cannot be understood verbally by persons with no prior training in financial analysis, and would irritate all others.

The debt/equity ratio is currently 3.6:1, up from 2.4 last year. The current ratio is 0.9:1, down from 1.4 in 1972.

The deterioration in the financial position of the company can be shown by changes in the debt/equity and current ratios. For those of you who have not previously been exposed to financial analysis, or been bored by financial analysts, let me just explain that the debt/equity ratio measures the ability of a company to raise debt financing, and the current ratio measures the ability of the company to repay debt obligations. A current ratio of 2.0 to 1 is good, 1.5 to 1 is O.K., and 1.0 to 1 is shakey; the current ratio of the Detroit Automobile Corporation is 0.9:1, and the debt/equity ratio is equally poor.

The current ratio, which is computed by adding together the cash, accounts receivable, inventory, and prepaid expenses, and then dividing by the accounts payable, short-term bank loans, and other payables due within one year, is 0.9:1. The debt/equity ratio, which is computed by dividing the total debt, including current liabilities, deferred taxes, bank loans, and corporate bonds, by the total equity, including preferred and common stock at par, the capital, surplus, earned surplus, and an adjustment for convertible debentures, is 3.6:1.

Audience evaluation is important, to recognize the range of involvement and information that usually exists within a group assembled to listen to an oral report, and audience definition simply carries this recognition through to an identification of the specific categories within the group. Most audiences in an administrative setting can be divided into three or four categories, or subgroups, based upon the managerial level and functional area of the members. Material included in the report should be expressed in a form that is understandable to all the subgroups, but not in such detail that it is boring or uninteresting to others. There is a narrow line between explanation and tedium, and the first requirement for a successful oral presentation is to recognize and define that line.

Need for Explicit Objectives. The second requirement for a successful oral presentation is a very explicit definition of the objectives of the report. Oral reports can be prepared to inform an audience, to resolve a problem, to agree upon a recommendation, or to start a course of action, and the content and structure of the report will differ, depending upon the reasons that have been determined for the meeting. The person presenting the report should be certain that those reasons are very clear. A clear objective can be stated succinctly, almost on the level of "as a result of this presentation, my audience will . . . ," or "the purpose of the meeting this morning is to. . . ." The second form of the objective statement, of course, can be used in the presentation to ensure that members of the audience understand the reasons for their attendance.

The objectives of oral reports often vary with the stage of completion of a project or study. A final report will center on conclusions and recommendations, but interim reports usually describe problems and progress, or discuss directions and scope. The length of time to completion of many projects and studies necessitate these progress reports, partially to communicate to other members of the organization the data accumulated and the conclusions reached so far—in other words, to provide a "snapshot" of the findings—and partially to ensure that the project is proceeding in the direction and method anticipated by the other members. It is important that people within an organization who are involved or will be affected by a project or study periodically be brought to the same level of understanding as the group performing the study, to eliminate any surprises upon completion of the project, and to achieve agreement on the accuracy and meaning of the accumulated data. If the facts are questioned at the time of the final report, the statements of opinion which follow—the conclusion and recommendations—will almost automatically be rejected. To avoid that problem, interim reports can be used to discuss the data and the preliminary conclusions, and to provide an opportunity for factual questions and eventual agreement.

Interim reports also serve as a useful means of reviewing the direction and scope of the study. A major project rarely moves from initiation to completion as originally planned;

new facts are discovered, new problems are encountered, and new alternatives are developed. The group working on the project usually needs the approval of other members of the organization to change the scope or timing of the study to include these new issues. The discussion that follows an interim report provides an opportunity for the management of the company to comment on the work that has been formed, and to plan for the work that remains to be done, with additional tasks or extended investigations, if needed.

Need for Complete Outline. A logical structure, or a clearly apparent sequence of the background facts, analytical conclusions, and final recommendations, is important for written reports, and essential for oral presentations. The readers of a written report can always turn back a few pages if the logical structure is not clear, or if they fail to follow the connection between the stated conclusions and the final recommendations; the listeners to an oral report don't have that luxury. Members of an audience who don't understand the sequence of concepts, or the relationships between facts, conclusions, and recommendations in a report, have only two choices: they can verbally interrupt the presentation or they can stop listening. It is always awkward to verbally interrupt, particularly in a meeting where different levels of managerial reponsibility and different degrees of technical sophistication are represented; the younger persons tend to feel that if the senior people don't object, why should they, and the older members of the audience may think that the material is clear to the younger personnel, more recently trained in analytical techniques, and hesitate to reveal their own lack of understanding. The result is that there are very few interruptions of poorly structured presentations, but there also is very little communication. Communication stops when people don't understand the logical structure of the presentation.

The logical structure of an oral report should be prepared in outline format, with the major topics arranged in a clearly apparent sequence, and displayed on at least two levels. The levels refer to the sections and subsections that are used to organize and format the content. Each section and subsection should include both a title and a brief descriptive sentence or sentences, and care should be taken in selecting the titles and phrasing the sentences. This note offers four suggestions for the content of the sections and subsections, and the format of titles and sentences.

1. The content of the sections should be integrative, and should introduce the topics to be discussed in the subsections, and show their relationships to the other sections of the report. In essence, each section of an oral report should say to the audience: "This is why this material is important, so keep listening, and these are the topics we are going to discuss now, in this order."

2. The content of the subsections should be descriptive, and should explain one topic or concept that is clearly related to the other topics or concepts in the section, yet is clearly identified as a separate topic or concept that may be completely described in one subsection. "Unity" is one of the most important principles in administrative communication, both oral and written, and unity refers to the discussion of one topic, at one time, in one subsection or paragraph of a report. In essence, each subsection of an oral report says to the audience: "Here is everything you need to know about this topic or concept for all of us to achieve the objectives of this presentation and this meeting."

3. The meaning of each sentence in the integrative section and descriptive subsections

should be clear. "Clarity" is another of the important principles in administrative communication, and it is more important in oral than in written reports since members of an audience cannot study a spoken sentence to comprehend the intended meaning as they can in a written document. It is not difficult to select a sentence structure and phrasing that promotes clarity and helps understanding. There are three simple rules. Each sentence should be complete, including an identifiable subject and verb; each sentence should be direct, restricting the number of modifying terms and phrases; and each sentence should be conclusive, expressing either facts or opinions forcefully and forthrightly. There is a tendency in administrative reports, both written and oral, to attempt to avoid responsibility by expressing conclusions or recommendations in hesitant terms and subjunctive tenses, as in "It might be well to consider the possibility of. . . ." Unfortunately, the hesitancy does not avoid responsibility, but the indefinite recommendations often confuse the audience, so that the organizational actions are much less likely to be effective, and consequently the desire to avoid responsibility may be much more necessary.

4. The title of each integrative section and descriptive subsection should be short, and parallel. "Parallelism" is the third of the important principles in administrative communication; it refers to the use of terms and phrases that are similar in structure and form. In a parallel series of nouns, all should be either singular or plural. In a parallel series of verbs, all should be of the same tense. In a parallel series of terms, all should have the same number and form of modifying adjectives or adverbs, and in a parallel series of phrases, all should have a similar number and sequence of nouns and verbs. Parallel struc-

ture and form assists greatly in speed reading; it is particularly important in the titles of the sections and subsections of an oral report for the titles will often be used in the visual aids, where rapid reading and quick comprehension are essential.

The intent of the outline, with integrative sections, descriptive subsections, clear sentences, and short, parallel titles, should be to prepare a concise document (no more than two pages) that summarizes both the content and the phraseology of the complete report; if the material can be expressed clearly in this concise form, it can be presented clearly in an expanded form, and the oral report will be structured to hold the interest of the audience. The following example is intended to illustrate the advantages of a clear and concise outline in the preparation of an interesting oral report.

Operating Problems of the Company. Detroit Automotive Corporation has major operating problems in all the functional areas:

1. *Marketing problems.* A consistent marketing plan does not exist in the company; pricing is at a variable multiple of direct costs, and promotional expenditures are spread too widely to be effective.
2. *Production problems.* An organized productive system does not exist in the company; scheduling is on a personalized basis, and control is lenient at best.
3. *Financial problems.* The financial position of the company has deteriorated substantially since 1973; current operations are below break-even, and a continuation will lead to a negative cash position in March 1975.
4. *Personnel problems.* The continuing losses, and the resulting stresses and disorganized efforts to reach a solution, have brought problems of managerial conflict and employee morale.

Strategic Problems of the Company. The executives of the Detroit Automobile Corporation ascribe the operating problems to the economic downturn of 1974–1975; it is the conclusion of this report that the cause of the problems is not external, but primarily internal:

1. *Lack of a defined strategy.* The company has no defined product–market position; at present the owners are continuing their past efforts at new-car customizing and custom part sales, and have added used-car reconditioning, collision repairs, sun roof installations, fiberglass fabrications, and classic car reproductions.
2. *Lack of a definite management.* The company has no general manager; Mr. Glass attends to details such as answering the telephone, talking to parts customers, purchasing minor supplies, etc. No individual in the management group is attending to the long-term central issues facing the company.

Strategic Alternatives Open to the Company. It would appear that there are five basic alternatives open to the Detroit Automotive Corporation at this time:

1. *Sell the company.* This alternative is rejected since neither Mr. Glass nor the other owners would agree, and since the assets of the company have no ready cash value beyond the secured debt.
2. *Reduce the size of the company to achieve a lower break-even.* This alternative is rejected since the 1972 investment in new plant and equipment makes a return to the earlier size and cost structure very difficult.
3. *Continue the present diversification strategy of the company.* This alternative is rejected since it is anticipated that the diversification strategy will lead to complete bankruptcy unless there is a dramatic increase in the level of economic activity in the Detroit area

within the next few months; this increase is not anticipated.

4. *Emphasize services for which there is an existing market* (used-car reconditioning and collision repair) but which require capabilities which the company does not now have (price estimating, production scheduling and cost control expertise, and mechanical repair labor). This alternative may be viable.
5. *Emphasize services for which a market must be developed* (new-car customizing and replicar manufacturing) but which utilizes resources the company now has (style and design engineering, chassis alterations, fiberglass forming, and spray painting). This alternative may also be viable.

Selection of the Strategy of the Company. The strategy of market development (new-car customizing and replicar manufacturing) to increase revenues above the break-even is recommended, despite the very obvious risk:

1. *Major resources* of the firm are the style and design engineering, and worker competence at chassis alterations, fiberglass forming, and spray painting; the skills needed for production development probably cannot be obtained quickly.
2. *Major environmental conditions* are the depressed state of the automotive industry and the consequent lack of discretionary income for luxury purchases in the Detroit area. It is felt, however, that a market exists for luxury cars in other sections of the country.
3. *Major managerial influences* are a high tolerance of risk and a high degree of commitment to customized (individually styled) automobiles.
4. *Major time consideration* is that a national marketing plan for customized automobiles may be started immediately.

Implementation of the Strategy for the Company. It is suggested that the market

development strategy be started immediately with the following functional changes:

1. *Marketing plans.* Advertising for customized car services and the reproduced classic cars should be started in the major financial papers (*Wall Street Journal, Barron's, Business Week,* etc.).
2. *Production plans.* Manufacturer of 10 MG-TD (1947) fiberglass replicars on an American Motors chassis and drive train, and 10 Rolls-Royce (1931) convertibles on an Oldsmobile chassis and drive train should be started.
3. *Financial plans.* Complete sale of the used-car inventory and reduction of the custom parts inventory to furnish immediate funds for promotion and production. A $50,000 increase in the bank loan will be required.
4. *Personnel plans.* Wage reductions to all workers, coupled with an explanation of the crisis facing the company; salary discontinuance to all managers, together with the start of a profit-sharing basis.

Need for Supportive Detail. In describing the differences between written and oral reports earlier in this note, it was stated that a written report should be a complete document, defining organizational problems, identifying probable causes, evaluating alternative solutions, and proposing specific actions, whereas the oral report should be a concise statement, summarizing the conclusions and recommendations, and providing an opportunity for discussion and consensus. Nowhere are these differences in the structure and format of the two forms of administrative communication more apparent than in the decision to include or exclude supportive detail. Detail is inherently dull, and the extensive discussion of detail will eventually lead to loss of interest, and lack of communication. However, detail is also frequently needed for understanding, and a complete absence of supportive facts and figures will just as surely bring questions about the validity of the conclusions and the worth of the recommendations. This dichotomy can be resolved in a written report by summarizing the essential information within the text, and by referring the reader back to an exhibit or appendix for the supporting data and explanatory calculations. This procedure works in a written report since the person reading the document can decide individually whether or not to follow his or her interests or questions back to the referenced exhibit. This procedure does not work as well in an oral presentation since people listening to the report do not have the same freedom of choice; they are constrained by the interests and actions of the group.

The person presenting an oral report has to recognize this problem of individual questions and group constraints, and attempt to adjust the content and format of the report to resolve the problem. There are four possible solutions:

1. *Ignore the supportive detail completely.* Complete absence of the background data is usually not successful in oral presentations since it leaves the impression of a superficial study, without analytical depth, and easily leads to rejection of the major conclusions and recommendations, or at least to questions about their validity. If the purpose of an oral report is to inform an audience and arrive at an eventual consensus, it is probably wrong to start the discussion following the report with questions of background fact and analytical value.

2. *Discuss the supportive detail hurriedly.* A common approach to the problem of individual questions and group constraints is to attempt to show that the background data are available, if needed, and to display the information briefly on a vue-graph, and describe it quickly. It is impossible to understand data that are briefly displayed and quickly described, so that this method

usually irritates some members of the audience, who tend to feel that if the material is not important it should not be mentioned, and that if it is important it should be discussed at greater length. Again, if the purpose of the oral report is to convince the audience and arrive at a consensus, it is probably not advisable to start by irritating various individuals or groups who are present at the meeting.

3. *Distribute the supportive detail previously.* Another common approach to the problem is to imitate the recommended structure of written reports, summarizing the data in the presentation, and referring members of the audience to printed exhibits or appendices that were distributed at the start of the meeting for the supportive data and explanatory calculations. This is an apparently logical approach which should work, but doesn't. People handed a set of exhibits at the start of the meeting tend to leaf through the material, following their curiosity, and ignoring the introduction and early stages of the presentation. Further, referencing the material during the presentation again starts people looking at the exhibits and not paying attention to the talk. The printed data and the verbal materials cannot really be integrated, and therefore cannot fully be convincing. It does not even work well to hand out the exhibits at the end of the presentation; by that time people's questions about the sources of the data and the validity of the conclusions have hardened, almost as if the supportive material had been completely omitted.

4. *Describe the supportive detail selectively.* The approach to resolving individual questions about data sources and analytical methods without boring, irritating, or ignoring other members of the audience that seems to be most successful is to provide supportive detail selectively, for the major points in the presentation. Select the two or three

most important analytical conclusions in the report, and support those conclusions with an explicit description of the accumulated data and necessary calculations. Members of an audience tend to believe, by inference, that equivalent material is available to support the other, less important conclusions in the report, and consequently they tend to accept those conclusions. Obviously, a well-prepared oral presentation will have the material ready, to respond to questions if they arise, and will not rely completely upon convincing by inference. Since only selected conclusions will be supported, it is suggested that this be explained during the report, as in the following example.

Strategic Alternatives Open to the Company. Despite the dismal sales performance of the past year, and the deteriorating financial position of the firm, there are five basic alternatives that remain open to the Detroit Automotive Corporation. The strategic decision must be made quickly, however, for continued losses will soon block the more attractive options:

1. *Sell the company.* Mr. Glass and the other owners are not in favor of a sale, but a more important reason against this alternative is that we believe that the company cannot be sold as a going concern under the existing economic conditions in the area—we have approached three potential purchasers informally, but were rebuffed each time—and we estimate that the liquidation value is far below the current liabilities and secured debt. *This is an important part of our final recommendation, and we feel that it would be worthwhile to take some time, and describe exactly how we reached this conclusion* [see Exhibit 1].

Exhibit 1

Account	Book value Sept. 30	Cash value liquidation	Basis of estimation
Cash	$ (1,442)	$ (1,500)	Additional bank charges for negative balance
Accounts receivable	29,746	22,300	25% discount due to 16-day accts. rec. in cash business
Raw material inventory	13,240	10,600	20% discount on steel, fiberglass, and paint
Sun roof inventory	6,427	3,200	50% discount, since difficult to sell
Used-car inventory	12,270	11,000	10% discount, since sold at auction
Custom parts inventory	28,320	19,800	30% discount, since sold to dealers
Advances to employees	4,927	000	100% discount, since hard to collect
Building, less depreciation	103,909	77,200	25% discount, since building is in poor location
Equipment, less depreciation	49,793	32,300	35% discount, since equipment is special purpose
	$247,190	$174,900	Current liabilities and secured debt = $209,700

Need for Clear Visual Aids. Clear visual aids are essential for oral reports; well done, they can turn an ordinary oral presentation into an effective administrative meeting, with the conclusions of the speaker accepted, and the recommendations adopted. Visual aids help in the process of oral communication, and in the achievement of meeting objectives, by ensuring that the content of a report is understood, and that the interest of an audience is maintained. Members of an audience can think at a rate of 400 words per minute, but most speakers can clearly pronounce only 100 words per minute; the result is that the attention of an audience tends to waiver, and many members of the audience start to daydream, unless the words can be supplemented with other impressions. Visual aids provide those other impressions. The ideal in oral communication is to encourage people to think about what is being said, not merely to listen to the words that are being spoken, and the combined oral and visual impressions help to start and sustain this thinking process.

Visual aids can, of course, include blackboards, flip-charts, scale models, etc., but the simplest form both to prepare and to use is the slide transparency. Slide transparencies are easy to prepare since they can be reproduced from material that has been typed, drawn, or written on a standard 8½ in. x 11 in. sheet of paper, and they are convenient to use since they can be enlarged upon a screen with an overhead projector. The other alternatives, such as flip-charts and blackboards, are difficult to prepare, awkward to carry, and cannot be enlarged so they may be difficult to view in a large room. Slide transparencies are best for oral presentations (except where professional assistance is available to prepare 35-mm photographic slides, in color, for the visual aids) and this note has seven suggestions for the preparation and use of these transparencies:

1. *The wording on each slide should be short.* The material on visual aids should be easy to comprehend, and easy to remember, and therefore the wording should be short and direct, with only three to seven words per statement, and three to seven statements per slide. For the integrative slides, similar to the integrative sections of the outline, the section and subsection titles can be used, with only slight modification.

   OPERATING PROBLEMS OF THE COMPANY

   1. MARKETING PROBLEMS

   2. PRODUCTION PROBLEMS

   3. FINANCIAL PROBLEMS

   4. PERSONNEL PROBLEMS

   The full outline should never be placed on a slide, both because too many words make it difficult for the audience to comprehend the meaning quickly, and because too many speakers have a tendency to simply read the material verbatim, which will bore half the audience and irritate the other half—the implication is that they are incapable of reading the slide themselves. Instead, short and simple phrases should be used on the visual aids, to help the speaker in discussing the topics and to help the audience in understanding the structure and remembering the content of the report. Think of each integrative slide as an outline; if members of the audience started to take notes, they would use the phrases from the visual aids to organize their written comments.

2. *The statements on each slide should be formatted.* As stated previously, the material on visual aids should be simple to comprehend, and easy to remember, and therefore the wording should be short and direct, with only three to seven words per statement, and those statements should be formatted, or placed either sequentially or

Example 1

EMPHASIZE USED CAR RECONDITIONING AND COLLISION REPAIR	
HAVE LOCAL MARKET	LACK ESTIMATING ABILITY
HAVE INSURANCE CONTACTS	LACK SCHEDULING EXPERIENCE
HAVE SUITABLE EQUIPMENT	LACK COST CONTROLS
EMPHASIZE NEW CAR CUSTOMIZING AND REPLICAR MANUFACTURE	
HAVE STYLE/DESIGN SKILLS	LACK LOCAL MARKET
HAVE FIBERGLASS COMPETENCE	LACK PROMOTIONAL EXPERIENCE
HAVE GROWING REPUTATION	LACK SOME EQUIPMENT ($22,000)

comparatively upon the slide. Information can be conveyed both by the wording of the statements, and by their placement, and formatting determines the placement. For many of the descriptive slides, corresponding to the descriptive subsections of the outline, comparative statements of the advantages and disadvantages of specific actions can be very effective, particularly with those statements formatted to emphasize the comparison, as shown in Example 1.

In discussing a comparative slide of this nature, the speaker should never just read the written statements, but should elaborate and explain the major concepts. That is, a speaker might say, in reference to the first half of this slide, that "There is a large local market, estimated at $5 million dollars annually for used-car reconditioning and collision repair in the southeastern Michigan area, and we have the contacts with the insurance adjustors and the equipment within the shop to sell and serve that market, but we lack the management ability to estimate the prices, schedule the jobs, and control the costs in order to *profitably* sell and serve that market."

3. *The letters on each slide should be legible.* Short and direct statements, formatted to improve comprehension, are needed on each slide, and the lettering should be large enough to be clearly visible in all parts of the room. The combined oral and visual impressions that should encourage the audience to think about the topics being discussed lose their power rapidly when they can't be read, or when they can be read only with difficulty, by squinting. Large letters are needed; these large letters are termed "kindergarten" type in educational circles, and "executive" type in the business world. Regardless of the name, they are available on the IBM Selectric typewriter, and should be used, or the letters should be reprinted with a dark pencil in a size that can easily be read when enlarged upon the screen.

4. *The numbers on each slide should be rounded.* It is difficult to communicate numerical data in an oral presentation. A simple statement such as "the 1975 pro forma revenues of $157,600 are composed of $88,500 in sales of 15 MG-TD replicars at $5,900 each, $43,900 in sales of 3 Rolls replicars at $14,650 each, $20,000 in sales of custom parts at cost plus 25%, and $5,200 in sales of used cars at cost minus 20%" is comprehensible in a written document, but unintelligible in an oral report. A reader can see the figures as a group, with the relationships between the figures explained by their placement; a listener can only hear

the figures as a series, with no knowledge of the spatial relationships. Never read numerical data in an oral report; the figures will not be understood.

Numerical data in an oral presentation should be formatted on a slide to show the relationships, and all estimated figures should be rounded, for easy comprehension. Remember that you will be discussing, not reading, this material, so that the slide does not have to contain the supportive detail and explanatory calculations that would be required in the exhibit of a written report. Numerical data that have been formatted in a comparative matrix

can be discussed interestingly and convincingly by concentrating on the obvious trends, not on the minute details, as shown in the pro forma statement [see Exhibit 2].

5. *The graphics on each slide should be clear.* Charts and graphs can be very effective in conveying trends and relationships, and decision diagrams can be very efficient in summarizing alternatives, but these graphic displays have to be simplified in an oral presentation so that the major conclusions and recommendations from each slide are immediately obvious. A complex graphic display forces the audience either to study the slide and ignore the discus-

Exhibit 2

	1975	1976	1977
MG–TD (1947) REPLICARS	15 CARS	30 CARS	45 CARS
ROLLS (1932) REPLICARS	3 CARS	7 CARS	15 CARS
MG–TD (1947) REPLICARS	$ 88,500	$179,000	$267,500
ROLLS (1932) REPLICARS	43,900	102,500	219,700
CUSTOM PARTS SALES	20,000	5,000	2,000
USED-CAR SALES	5,200	—	—
TOTAL SALES REVENUES	157,600	286,500	489,200
MG–TD DIRECT COSTS	33,000	66,000	99,000
ROLLS DIRECT COSTS	19,200	44,800	96,000
CUSTOM PARTS COST	16,000	4,000	1,500
USED-CAR COST	6,500	—	—
SHOP OVERHEAD	21,900	35,000	48,000
TOTAL DIRECT COSTS	96,600	149,800	241,500
SELLING EXPENSES	52,000	60,000	105,000
ADMINISTRATIVE EXPENSES	19,600	25,000	25,000
INTEREST COSTS	7,400	5,000	3,000
DEPRECIATION	4,100	4,000	3,800
TOTAL FIXED COSTS	83,100	94,100	136,800
PROFIT (LOSS) PRETAX	(22,300)	42,700	103,900
TAX (−) OR CREDIT (+)	+2,600	−8,800	−41,500
PROFIT (LOSS) AFTER TAX	(19,700)	33,900	62,400

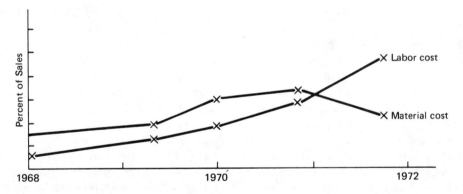

sion, or to ignore the slide and listen to the words. Neither alternative is desirable for the speaker. A simple rule for the use of graphic visual aids in oral presentations is that each slide should be understood by everyone in the room within 30 seconds—members of an audience will not spend more time attempting to decipher visual material while a talk is continuing—and therefore the concepts within the display have to be limited, the drawings in the graphic have to be simplified, and the scales of measurement have to be obvious; see the illustration at the top of the page.

Overlay graphics, or slides that have been designed to be superimposed one upon another, can be very effective in showing changes over time, or the expected results of alternative actions. Different colors can be used for the future years, or the various actions, to increase the visual impact. The attention of an audience will not waiver when a speaker says: "This is the base situation, which we have described to you, and these are our future projections [placing on the colored overlay] provided that we decide now to. . . ."

6. *The discussion of each slide should last about two minutes.* It is important that an audience have a sense that an oral report is progressing at a steady pace toward a known conclusion. Pace is probably the most important element in a presentation to hold the attention and interest of the audience. The changing of slides in a regular and orderly time sequence helps immeasurably to start and maintain that sense of pace. Therefore, it is suggested strongly that the material on each slide, both statements and graphics, be either expanded or contracted to require approximately two minutes for discussion or explanation. A 20-minute oral report, which is an optimal length since the attention of any audience will waiver after 20 minutes, probably should include 10 slides. The changing of these slides in an orderly time sequence will not only give a sense of pace to the audience, but a sense of timing to the speaker, and help to prevent dawdling over some topics, racing through others, and running over the alloted time span. Never run over the alloted time; your audience will be wondering when you are going to stop, not thinking about what you are going to say.

7. *The display of each slide should follow four rules.* Visual aids, which have been prepared with short and direct wording, in formatted statements, using large type, rounded numbers, and clear graphics, can lose much of their effectiveness through errors in display. This note has four rules for the display of slides:

a. Never display a slide, but discuss a different topic, not depicted on that slide; the attention of the audience is certain to be divided, and the process of communication is certain to be slowed, or stopped.

b. Never display a slide, and explain that slide in detail; the combined verbal and visual impact upon the audience will be lost. Visual aids should structure and reinforce the words, not require explanation. Therefore, discuss the important concepts on each slide; don't just read the statements or explain the figures.

c. Never display a slide, but cover a portion so that it cannot be read; the interest of at least half the audience will be on the covered portion, wondering what it contains or resenting that method of restriction. Use emphasis in the discussion, and occasionally a pointer, to direct attention to the various topics on the slide, not an artificial restraint.

d. Never display a slide, and then switch back to the slide a second time; the sense of pace among the audience will be lost if slides are reshown, and the slides are very likely to get out of order. This lack of order may not be troublesome during the talk, but it can be a major problem after the presentation. In responding clearly and concisely to questions, it is helpful to be able to go directly to the relevant slide, and that search is much easier if all the visual aids are maintained in their original order.

Suggestions for the Introduction. The first two to three minutes of an oral report are critical for the success of the presentation. During that short time period, it is necessary to reassure the audience that they are present for a worthwhile purpose, to explain to them the structure and topics of the report, and to summarize for them the conclusions and recommendations of the study. The need for explicit introductory comments is another indication of the very real differences between oral and written reports. A person picking up a written report understands why he or she is going to read that report, and is mentally prepared to read it, with some degree of concentration. There may be procrastination and delay, and there may even be resignation or dislike, but a person responsible for reviewing or acting upon a written report understands the reasons for the assignment, can select a convenient time for the task, and can stop reading as soon as the material appears to lack personal relevance, analytical depth, or logical conclusions. People at a meeting may not understand the reasons for their attendance; they may or may not find the time convenient for their schedules; and they cannot leave the meeting if they find the report to be personally irrelevant, poorly prepared, or downright dull. They have to sit there, but they don't have to appreciate the efforts of the group, approve the contents of the report, or even listen to the words of the speaker. In short, there may be some hostility, and there may be some lethargy, among the audience, and it is necessary to explicitly recognize those feelings, and attempt to reduce them in the introductory statements.

In the design of the introductory statements, it is essential to remember that not everyone attending an oral presentation really wants to be there; many members of the audience have other organizational problems or personal concerns that they consider to be either more interesting or more pressing. It is also essential to remember that not everyone listening to the oral presentation is in full agreement with the methodology of the study or the conclusions of the report, particularly since the recommendations that will follow from the methodologies and the conclusions may affect different managerial levels and functional groups in different, and perhaps unanticipated ways. In order to overcome that lethargy, and reduce that hostility, it is necessary to inform every person in the room about the purpose, format, content, and conclusions of the meeting, and this can be done in a series of *brief* statements.

1. *Brief statement of the purpose of the meeting.* It is necessary to explain why people have been asked to attend, and what results are expected from the meeting. These statements should provide reassurance. If the intent of the meeting is to distribute information about a project, then the opposition will be automatically muted, particularly if a preliminary draft of the findings has been circulated to managers who may be affected by the eventual recommendations, and some agreement has been reached on the relevant facts. If the intent is to reach a decision, then the opposition has been notified, and again if a preliminary draft of the conclusions and recommendations has been circulated, followed by individual meetings with the affected managers and acceptable revisions to address their concerns, then some compromise may be reached on the final recommendations. Opposition and resentment build upon surprise; it is suggested that you notify people at the start of each meeting on the purpose and expected results of that meeting, and avoid those surprises.

2. *Brief statement of the agenda of the meeting.* It is also necessary to describe the sequence of activities in the meeting, with an estimate of the time required for each activity. These statements should also provide reassurance, both by limiting the probable extent of the meeting, and by providing an explicit opportunity for discussion before

reaching any conclusion or accepting any recommendation. The agenda for a typical meeting will include report presentation, general discussion, and eventual decision. Opposition and resentment also build upon constraint; it is suggested that you notify people at the start of each meeting on the opportunity for discussion, and for the presentation of opposing views, and avoid any charges of censorship.

3. *Brief statement of the methodology of the study.* It is useful to describe the sources of the data and the methods of analysis that were used by the study group, or by the person presenting the report. These statements should provide legitimacy, by showing that the sources of data were reasonably complete, and that the methods of analysis were truly suitable. A word of warning here: It is essential not to boast about the width and depth of the study, or even appear to be boastful. Never say: "We examined 167 separate articles in scholarly journals, interviewed 57 line managers in business organizations, and contacted 683 retail customers in detailed field studies." Instead, say: "We gathered our data by library research, management interviews, and retail studies" in a straightforward statement, and provide additional information on the numbers and times involved only if asked.

4. *Brief statement of the outline of the report.* It is also useful to describe the sequence of topics in the report. The intent is to explain the logical structure and to summarize the intellectual content, so that members of the audience can more easily follow the presentation of the material. Again a word of warning: Don't be detailed in the overview of the structure and content of the material or it will appear that you are giving the report twice. A visual aid with the titles of the major sections from the outline will help

the comprehension of the audience, and ensure the brevity of the speaker.

> OPERATING PROBLEMS OF THE COMPANY
>
> STRATEGIC PROBLEMS OF THE COMPANY
>
> STRATEGIC ALTERNATIVES OPEN TO THE FIRM
>
> SELECTION OF THE STRATEGY FOR THE COMPANY
>
> SUGGESTIONS FOR IMPLEMENTATION OF THE STRATEGY

5. *Brief statement of the recommendations of the report.* Finally, it is useful to summarize the major conclusions or recommendations of the study. The intent here is to advise the audience of the outcome of the presentation. The "Note on the Presentation of Written Reports" explained that "some degree of suspense may be desirable in mystery fiction, and an extended discussion of the background before reaching a conclusion is common in philosophical discourse, but almost all administrative reports are helped by an early statement of the major conclusions concerning the dimensions and causes of the problem, and the primary recommendations for improvement." This is an instance in which oral and written communications are nearly identical; an early statement of the major conclusions and recommendations is helpful in both. However, there is one last word of warning: don't be detailed in the summary of the recommendations or it may appear that you are inviting questions or objections at that point. A visual aid with the recommendations in very simple form will provide a "reference point" for the audience to use in understanding the presentation to follow, and will help the speaker to maintain control of the meeting since the slide can be removed as soon as the summary is completed. It is suggested

that both the brief statement of the outline and the brief statement of the recommendations be formatted on the same slide, to adhere to the "two-minute" rule. The following is an example of this combined visual aid:

> OPERATING PROBLEMS OF THE COMPANY
>
> STRATEGIC PROBLEMS OF THE COMPANY
>
> STRATEGIC ALTERNATIVES OPEN TO THE COMPANY
>
> SELECTION OF THE STRATEGY FOR THE COMPANY
>   1. EMPHASIZE NEW-CAR CUSTOMIZING AND REPLICAR MANUFACTURE
>   2. DEEMPHASIZE USED-CAR RECONDITIONING AND COLLISION REPAIR
>   3. ELIMINATE CUSTOM PART AND USED-CAR SALES
>
> SUGGESTIONS FOR IMPLEMENTATION OF THE STRATEGY
>   1. MARKETING PLANS
>   2. PRODUCTION PLANS
>   3. FINANCIAL NEEDS

Often, the person presenting an oral report to a corporate audience will not know the final objective or complete agenda of the meeting, and may not have the authority to set those objectives or determine that agenda. In this instance, the speaker should stress the subject matter and time requirements of the report in his or her introductory statements, rather than the objectives and agenda of the meeting, and then continue as before. The essential characteristics in the introductory portion of an oral report remain brevity and neutrality, regardless of the content. It is essential to inform everyone in the room about the subject matter, time requirements, data sources, logical structure, and final recommendations of the report in order to improve the process of communication during the balance of the presentation, yet this has to be done without arousing inappropriate questions or hostile comments from members of the audience, who may have little interest in the topic or little liking for the conclusions. Brief neutral statements about the subject, timing, methodology, structure, and recommendation can accomplish that goal. Consider the following comments by a partner in a consulting firm as one possible way to introduce an oral report addressed to the corporate managers and financial backers of the Detroit Automotive Corporation.

Thank you. We were asked two months ago to analyze the current problems and make recommendations for the long-term competitive success of the Detroit Automotive Corporation. We expect this report on the results of our study to be brief—no more than 20 minutes—so that there will be ample time for questions and discussion.

Much of our data is from company officials and the financial records of the corporation, but we have conducted two market research projects—one in the Chicago area and one here in Detroit—and we have found some very useful information in published form on the new-car customizing and replicar manufacturing industries. The published data on these two industries are much better, more complete, than I had thought that they would be when we started.

To keep within our time constraints, we plan to cover [here the speaker put on the vuegraph the slide previously described] the operating problems of the company, the strategic problems, the strategic alternatives that are open to the firm, our recommendations for the future, and our suggestions for implementation.

Our recommendations, very briefly, are that the Detroit Automotive Corporation should emphasize the new-car customizing and replicar manufacturing portions of its current business, should deemphasize the used-car reconditioning and collision repair, and should completely eliminate the custom part and used-car sales.

This is, of course, a major change in the direction of the company. We feel that this change can be made successfully with more direct sales promotion and advertising, more formal shop procedures and equipment, and a larger bank loan. We believe that between $35,000 minimum and $50,000 maximum in additional funds are needed, beyond the amounts that will be recovered from the sale of the custom part and used-car inventories.

Now, unless there are some questions on the content and procedures of our report [here the speaker did not look up to see if there were any questions as he removed the transparency from the projector], I would like to introduce my associate, Donald James, who was primarily responsible for the analytical portion of the study, to describe the current problems of the company, and the causes of these problems. We found those causes to be much more complex, and much more outside the range of control of the current management, than we had expected. But, Donald, you explain those problems, and our conclusions regarding them.

Suggestions for the Presentation. The actual presentation of an oral report, including the introductory statements, the central portion, and the concluding summary, should be simple and relatively easy, almost anticlimactic, after the nature of the audience has been fully defined, the objectives explicitly stated, the outline carefully prepared, the supportive detail completely organized, and the visual aids thoughtfully designed. All that is needed, then, is a speaker who can present the material with a clear voice and an unhurried, self-confident style. This note, however, has five suggestions that should help in this presentation, and ensure that style:

1. *Stand for the presentation.* Some meetings are small enough to be held around a conference table, and others, although larger, will have a chair and desk set out for the speaker, but the temptation to sit down should be avoided. Standing tends to focus attention on the speaker, and offers

some measure of authority to the person addressing the audience, most of whom will be seated. Stand naturally, but relaxed, and don't fidget. If you can't think what to do with your hands, put them in your pockets, or waistband. If you feel that your posture is stilted or awkward, lean against a desk or walk about the room, but walk slowly, without quick movements. Speak quietly but deliberately, without excessive gestures or distracting mannerisms. The intent is to create the impression that you are in complete control of the meeting, and rather enjoying the situation; that attitude of good-humored self-confidence is infectious.

2. *Look at the audience.* Try to maintain some eye contact with members of the audience by looking at them, not at the projector or the screen or the floor or the wall at the rear of the room. You should know the material well enough so that you can discuss each slide easily, with only occasional glances at the visual aids. Also, try to maintain some verbal contact with the audience; it may seem pretentious and mechanical to say "there are four points here that I want *you* to remember," but referring to the audience directly is another way of maintaining contact. The intent here is to create the impression that you and the audience, together, are participating in the oral report, and that you could not do it without them; that, of course, is literally true.

3. *Maintain a set pace.* As mentioned previously, the pace or sense of progression of a presentation is critical for holding the interest and attention of an audience. Change the slides on a regular and orderly time sequence. Never describe the material on one slide in excessive detail; you will lose the attention of the audience. All speakers, at some time in an oral presentation, have an instinctive feeling that members of the audience do not understand a

specific point, or have no interest in the material on a given slide; the temptation is to repeat the material, in much greater detail, attempting to convince the doubters, but that temptation should be resisted for the effort seldom is successful. Instead, ask "Is that clear?" and then repeat only the most important topics, usually prefaced with a statement such as "All that I want to convey here is . . ." and rely on questions after the conclusion to clarify that section, if necessary. Remember the two-minute rule, and keep the presentation moving. The intent is to create the impression that the report is progressing at a steady pace toward a known, and close, conclusion.

4. *Rehearse the oral presentation.* Many speakers feel self-conscious and amateurish practicing an oral report, particularly if two or three people are involved, so that some must listen while others address a nonexistent audience. The temptation is to feel that "we don't have to do this; we don't need to go through this childish routine to do a good job at the meeting." Unfortunately, you do. Practice is needed to gauge the timing, set the pace, and learn the material. Practice is also needed to develop experience with the visual aids, and with the display equipment such as projectors and screens; make certain you know where the on/off switch is located, and the focus knobs and replacement bulbs. The intent of serious rehearsals is to create the impression of a solid, professional performance.

5. *Start without any delay.* The person or group presenting an oral report will normally be introduced by an executive of the company or a member of the audience. Usually, the person or group presenting the report will not know exactly what the person performing the introduction will include in his or her remarks. That person may cover some, or all, of the introductory statements on the

purpose and agenda of the meeting, the content or timing of the report, or even the methodology, outline, or conclusions of the project. You should be prepared to start at any stage, without excessive repetition. Also, you should be prepared to start immediately, without excessive delay. Don't wait after the introduction, getting slides in order, arranging chairs, looking about for the light switch, or whispering last-minute instructions, changes, or condolences. Instead, after the introduction, say, "Thank you. As [name of the person] explained, we are here to. . . ," or "Our report today will cover. . . ." The intent here is to create an impression of complete and total preparation.

Suggestions for the Conclusion. The three major portions of an oral report are the introductory statements, the central presentation, and the concluding summary. The functions of these three segments, in colloquial terms, are to "tell 'em what you're going to tell 'em, tell 'em what you know, and then tell 'em what you've told 'em." This last function, to "tell 'em what you've told 'em," is important, for it is essential that a speaker not just slowly run down, and lamely ask for questions. Instead, it is necessary to have a definite ending to an oral report, both to let the audience know that the time has come for questions and discussion, and to ensure that those questions and that discussion start from the basic premises and conclusions of the report. If the report does not come to a natural ending, and most do not, this note has three suggestions to form the conclusion:

1. *Restate briefly the outline of the report.* It is useful, in the concluding summary, to restate briefly the sequence of topics in the presentation. The intent is to explain again the logical structure of the content, so that members of the audience can more easily accept the conclusions and recommendations that come from the con-

tent. It is important not to be detailed in this summary of the structure, for the audience can very easily become bored with repetition. A copy of the same visual aid used for the introductory statements, with just the titles of the major sections of the outline, will help the acceptance of the audience, and ensure the brevity of the speaker. This slide is shown below, with the final recommendations and suggestions for implementation added.

2. *Restate briefly the recommendations of the report.* It is also useful in the concluding summary to restate briefly the major recommendations of the presentation. The intent here is to make certain that all members of the audience understand these recommendations, and their logical derivation from the material covered in the presentation. Again, it is important not to be detailed, but to describe only the two or three major recommendations that you wish the audience to remember, and discuss. The visual aid shown below does limit the number of recommendations, and does show the derivation of these recommendations from the prior analysis.

OPERATING PROBLEMS OF THE COMPANY

STRATEGIC PROBLEMS OF THE COMPANY

STRATEGIC ALTERNATIVES OPEN TO THE COMPANY

SELECTION OF THE STRATEGY FOR THE COMPANY

1. EMPHASIZE NEW CAR CUSTOMIZING AND REPLICAR MANUFACTURE

2. DEEMPHASIZE USED CAR RECONDITIONING & COLLISION REPAIR

3. ELIMINATE CUSTOM PART AND USED-CAR SALES

SUGGESTIONS FOR IMPLEMENTATION OF THE STRATEGY

1. MARKETING PLANS AND PROGRAMS

2. PRODUCTION PLANS AND PROGRAMS

3. FINANCIAL NEEDS AND SOURCES

3. *Finish with a single direct sentence.* Ending oral reports is much more difficult than starting; most reports have a natural beginning, after the introduction of the speaker, but few have a natural ending. It is necessary to create that natural ending with one short and very direct sentence, generally forecasting the results if the recommendations are adopted. A word of warning: Never oversell those results. Never say, "If the Detroit Automotive Corporation will follow these recommendations, I am certain that their financial problems are past and that their future profitability is ensured." An overly optimistic final sentence will not convince any person in the audience. Members of an audience are convinced to accept conclusions and adopt recommendations by the logical structure and supportive detail of the report, and by the combined verbal and visual impressions of the presentation, not by any excessive claims in that conclusion. A suggested final sentence for the oral report described in this note might be: "We feel that these recommendations make greatest use of the strengths of the company, and have the greatest probability of success, given the present operating and strategic problems of the firm." After the final sentence, say "Thank you" and look up for questions. If the report was well done, there will be questions asking for clarification of peripheral issues; if the report was not well done, there will be questions attacking the justification of the major recommendations.

Suggestions for Answering Questions. Questions are inevitable at the end of an oral report. Given the different managerial levels and functional areas represented in most meetings, and given the various degrees of involvement with the project and agreement with the conclusions located in most audiences, it is almost impossible to expect that everyone in the room will quietly accept the recommendations and file out, without some questions and discussion. As stated previously, if the report has been well prepared, with explicit objectives, a logical structure, and supportive data, and well presented with clear visual aids and a relaxed speaking style, the early questions will very likely be friendly, and will often be requests for further information on peripheral issues. Here the display of supportive detail that was not included in the central portion of the presentation can be very useful. To the question, "Have you looked at the market for customized cars outside the Midwest?", there should be only one response: "Yes, and here is what we found" as the speaker displays a slide with market data by state. As an aside, it is useful to keep the visual aids that were not used in the central part of the presentation in a ring binder, with an index sheet, so that they cannot get out of order, and can be immediately located to display supportive data in response to questions.

For reports that were not well prepared and presented, the early questions often will be aggressive attacks on the validity of the data or the legitimacy of the conclusions. Even if a report has been well done, eventually some aggressive or hostile questions may be asked since the recommendations of most studies or projects cannot find universal acceptance amongst all members of an audience. The ability to respond effectively to these questions will in the end have a direct effect upon the adoption of the recommendations; therefore, aggressive or hostile questions should not be viewed entirely in a negative sense. Effective responses to aggressive questions is an art that requires extensive practice and rapid thinking; this note has five suggestions to help the thinking process:

1. *Don't hurry in responding.* It is useful to rephrase most questions, partially to defuse the loaded ones and soften the hostile ones, and partially to ensure that everyone

in the room understands the question. Remember that a person in the second row, addressing a question to the speaker, probably cannot be heard at the back of the room, and if the question cannot be heard, your answer cannot be understood. Take time in responding; it is not necessary or useful to blurt out a quick response to an aggressive or hostile question. Finally, do not be afraid to be complimentary, if deserved. The simple statement, "That's a good question," followed by a direct and relevant answer will often overcome personal opposition.

2. *Don't ramble in responding.* Answers to aggressive or hostile questions should be direct, relevant, and brief. Remember that it is possible to back yourself into an illogical position by continuing to expand or elaborate in response to a question from the audience. When possible, refer to a visual aid. The use of a slide accomplishes three purposes: the question is related to the structure and content of the presentation, the response is given clarity and focus, and the speaker is constrained by the material on the slide.

3. *Don't bluff in responding.* Despite lengthy preparation for an oral report, and the development of extensive supporting data carefully formatted on slides, it is always possible for a question to be asked that cannot be answered factually. Never attempt to bluff; remember that the person asking the question may have the "missing" data. Instead, simply say: "I don't know about that particular point. I'll check on it after the meeting and get back to you." Often, the information requested, within a realistic range, will have only a minimal effect upon the conclusion and recommendations of the report; finish your comments by saying, "I think that you'll agree that this would not have a major impact unless. . . ."

4. *Don't ignore major issues in responding.* Some hostile questions are asked on peripheral issues, in an attempt to delay the eventual decisions of a meetings. Extensive debate over the background facts and analytical methods of these minor points can easily lose the interest of the majority of the audience, and lead the discussion away from the major conclusions and recommendations of the report. If an issue cannot be resolved quickly or clarified rapidly during the meeting, and if that issue is not central to the presentation, further discussion should probably be postponed, for a smaller meeting or individual conference. Simply say: "This issue doesn't appear to be of much interest to most of the other people in the room. Could we agree to disagree for now, and meet later to resolve it?"

5. *Don't avoid direct confrontations in responding.* Some hostile questions are asked and reasked in an attempt to engage the speaker in a personal debate. Repetitive statements on these issues, particularly if expressed in argumentative terms or a quarrelsome tone, can also easily lose the interest of the majority of the audience, and lead the discussion away from the major conclusions and recommendations of the report. Direct confrontation is suggested. Respond clearly and concisely to the issues expressed in the question, and then deal with the hostility. A direct question, "Does this resolve your problem?" forces the individual either to express his or her concerns more fully, or to accept the response. Direct confrontation permits a speaker to more easily control the course of a meeting, and to more fully avoid the buildup of animosity in the discussion. Remember that after confrontation, a conciliatory attitude is not unwelcomed by others in the room; a statement such as "I understand your concerns, and I appreciate your willingness to express them clearly and openly" often helps in main-

taining communication, and provides an opportunity for meaningful discussions later, and even eventual agreement and cooperation.

Suggestions for Overcoming Nervousness. Everyone is nervous the first few times they have to address a large audience. Professional actors are nervous before the opening of a play. Professional athletes are nervous before the start of a contest. To overcome nervousness in presenting oral reports, be prepared and be confident in your preparation. The majority of this note has provided instructions for your preparation; there are two suggestions for your confidence:

1. *Have complete notes for the first two minutes of the presentation.* On one sheet of paper, list the names of everyone associated with the project; it is very easy, and very awkward, to forget names when you are standing at the front of the room. On this same sheet of paper, list the topics, and a few comments about each topic, in your introductory statements; it is very easy to forget the sequence and to omit some of the topics when you are starting the presentation. Use large type that is easy to read, but don't read your notes; you should hold them only for confidence and reassurance.
2. *Have a prepared slide for the second two minutes*

of the presentation. After the first few introductory statements, about the content and timing of the report and the methodology of the study, you can easily switch to the visual aid that displays the structure and recommendations. The slide, of course, lists the headings so that you cannot forget the sequence or content of this portion of your talk. Halfway through the discussion of the slide, you will look up and find that your audience is interested, and that your nervousness has disappeared.

This note on the presentation of oral reports has explained the need to define the audience, set the objectives, outline the structure, select the data, and prepare the slides for a successful report, and then has suggested standard forms and procedures for the introduction, discussion, conclusion, and question phases of that report. The intent has been to enable the speaker to talk *with* an audience, not *at* an audience. "Talking with" an audience means involving those people in the presentation through a steady pace and an interesting combination of the verbal and visual presentation, so that they are thinking about the content of the report, rather than listening to the words of the speaker. Pace and interest are critical; if you can bring both to the presentation of your report, the audience will be involved, and the meeting will be successful.